THE RIGHT TO LIFE UNDER INTERNATIONAL LAW

The Right to Life under International Law offers the first-ever comprehensive treatment under international law of the foundational human right to life. It describes the history, content, and status of the right, considers jurisdictional issues, and discusses the application of the right to a wide range of groups, such as women, children, persons with disabilities, members of minorities, LGBTI persons, refugees, and journalists. It defines the responsibility of not only governments but also the private sector, armed groups, and non-governmental organisations to respect the prohibition on arbitrary deprivation of life. It also explains the nature and substance of the duty to investigate potentially unlawful death as well as the mechanisms at global and regional level to promote respect for the right to life.

Stuart Casey-Maslen is an international lawyer specialising in the use of force and the protection of civilians. He is an honorary Professor at the Centre for Human Rights at the University of Pretoria. He has written widely on international human rights and humanitarian law, arms control and disarmament law, and *jus ad bellum*.

The late Christof Heyns was a member of the UN Human Rights Committee (2017–2020), the former UN Special Rapporteur on extrajudicial, summary or arbitrary executions, and Director of the Institute for International and Comparative Law in Africa (ICLA) at the University of Pretoria. He was recognised internationally as a leading expert in the field of international human rights law, including right to life issues and regional human rights mechanisms, and published widely on these matters.

The Right to Life under International Law

AN INTERPRETATIVE MANUAL

STUART CASEY-MASLEN
University of Pretoria

WITH A FOREWORD BY CHRISTOF HEYNS

CAMBRIDGE
UNIVERSITY PRESS

University Printing House, Cambridge CB2 8BS, United Kingdom

One Liberty Plaza, 20th Floor, New York, NY 10006, USA

477 Williamstown Road, Port Melbourne, VIC 3207, Australia

314–321, 3rd Floor, Plot 3, Splendor Forum, Jasola District Centre,
New Delhi – 110025, India

103 Penang Road, #05–06/07, Visioncrest Commercial, Singapore 238467

Cambridge University Press is part of the University of Cambridge.

It furthers the University's mission by disseminating knowledge in the pursuit of education, learning, and research at the highest international levels of excellence.

www.cambridge.org
Information on this title: www.cambridge.org/9781108494786
DOI: 10.1017/9781108859868

© Stuart Casey-Maslen and Christof Heyns 2021

This publication is in copyright. Subject to statutory exception and to the provisions of relevant collective licensing agreements, no reproduction of any part may take place without the written permission of Cambridge University Press.

First published 2021

A catalogue record for this publication is available from the British Library.

ISBN 978-1-108-49478-6 Hardback

Cambridge University Press has no responsibility for the persistence or accuracy of URLs for external or third-party internet websites referred to in this publication and does not guarantee that any content on such websites is, or will remain, accurate or appropriate.

Contents

Foreword by Christof Heyns		page ix
Acknowledgements		xi
Table of Cases		xii
	An Historical Introduction to the Right to Life	1
	PART I OVERVIEW OF THE RIGHT TO LIFE UNDER INTERNATIONAL LAW	7
1	The Status of the Right to Life	9
2	The Content of the Right to Life	21
3	Jurisdiction and the Right to Life	65
4	The Relationship between the Right to Life and Other Human Rights	85
	PART II MAJOR THEMES	101
5	Deaths as a Result of Armed Conflict	103
6	Jus ad Bellum, Aggression, and the Right to Life	122
7	The Use of Force in Law Enforcement	141
8	Counterterrorism	180
9	The Death Penalty	207
10	Deaths in Custody	233
11	Abortion	254
12	Euthanasia and Suicide	269

13	Poverty and Starvation	291
14	Assemblies, Demonstrations, and Protests	308
15	Arms Control and Disarmament	334
16	Enforced Disappearance	357
17	Accidents, Disease, and Natural Disasters	374
18	Pollution and Climate Change	390
19	Autonomous Use of Force	400
20	Slavery	415
	PART III THE PROTECTION OF AT-RISK GROUPS AND INDIVIDUALS	427
21	Women	429
22	Children	454
23	Racially Motivated Killings	493
24	LGBTI Persons	515
25	Persons with Disabilities	525
26	Older Persons	555
27	Journalists	565
28	Human Rights Defenders	577
29	International Migrants	586
30	Internally Displaced Persons	594
31	Refugees	601
	PART IV ACCOUNTABILITY	609
32	The Right to Life and State Responsibility	611
33	The Right to Life and the Responsibility of International Organisations	629
34	Corporate Responsibility and the Right to Life	647
35	The Right to Life and the Responsibility of Non-State Armed Groups	659

36	The Right to Life and Non-governmental Organisations	672
37	The Right to Life and the Responsibility of Individuals	680
	PART V HUMAN RIGHTS MACHINERY PROTECTING THE RIGHT TO LIFE	689
38	The UN Human Rights Machinery and the Right to Life	691
39	Regional Human Rights Machinery and the Right to Life	712
	PART VI OUTLOOK	733
40	Customary Rules Pertaining to the Right to Life	735
41	The Future of the Right to Life	739
Index		742

Foreword

The realisation of the right to life is a precondition for the protection of all other human rights. Violations of the right to life are total and irreversible. Deadly violence, even more so than other forms of violence, destroys individuals and communities. The United Nations Human Rights Committee, in its 2018 General Comment on the right to life, reiterated the position it had taken in its 1982 General Comment – that the right to life is 'the supreme right'.

Over the millennia, in communities around the world, religious, ethical, and legal rules have developed aimed at protecting the value of life, and at restoring the value of life if this norm is or has been breached. The very existence of international human rights law can be seen as a global response to the carnage that took place in the middle of the last century. The local, regional, and global expressions of the human preoccupation with personal and collective security, and the elimination of arbitrary deprivations of life, have shaped the development of many branches of international law. In its purest form, this aspiration to ensure the security of the individual finds its expression in the protection provided to the right to life.

The modern focus on the individual has led to an emphasis on the recognition of the equal value of each individual life, and resistance against the idea that the life of any person can be sacrificed in the pursuit of any other social objectives. The guiding star of international law has indeed been called, by myself and others, the 'protect life' principle, namely the ideal – still far too often breached – that the only possible justification for the intentional deprivation of one person's life lies in the protection of the life of another.

While the core values underlying the right to life as part of international law have deep roots in cultures around the world, the applicable standards became much more coherent, nuanced, and expressly stated during the decades since the Second World War. Nevertheless, in spite of great strides made at the outset, much uncertainty remains. Developments in technology and shifting social values require constant expansion, adjustment, and further development of the substantive as well as the procedural content of the right. And, given the political sensitivity of all matters perceived as affecting State security, while the outline of the right is widely accepted, the exact contours of the right are subject to constant contestation by States and other parties. As a result, countless developments, small and large, in the way in which the right to life is perceived today have occurred during the last couple of decades.

Yet, surprisingly, in an era when there are general treaties available on most human rights, no up-to-date, comprehensive textbook is available on this most fundamental of rights. Someone trying to come to grips with the nuances of this core area of human rights will seek fruitlessly for the benefit of a comprehensive textbook which can serve as a first port of call.

A comprehensive treatment of the right, which is general enough to provide the 'big picture' between its two covers but specialised enough to cover the details of the most important elements of the right, is necessary for a range of reasons. It provides a proposed conceptual framework within which scientific engagement with the topic can take place, and a starting point for the development of alternative frameworks in the future. Such a book can allow researchers who work on aspects of the right or related themes to get a sense of where their works fit in. It can give newcomers – including those from other disciplines – an entry point. And it will allow everyone who works in the field to take stock of where things are. It can never claim to be the final word, but it provides a framework within which a much more meaningful discussion can take place.

This is the void that Stuart Casey-Maslen's new book so admirably fills. The book provides a comprehensive yet tightly constructed framework that identifies the main issues and arranges them in a logical structure. Then, one by one, in economical yet elegant prose, the author provides an in-depth discussion of each issue, which could stand on its own feet but also builds on what was said before. This is the beauty of this single-author treatise, as opposed to say an edited collection – a single, deft, and reassuring voice guides one through the vast and contested terrain where the realisation of the right to life is pursued.

Stuart is singularly well placed to be the one who writes the first comprehensive treatise on the right to life. He has a rich background and deep expertise not only in human rights law but also in the other areas of law which affect our understanding of the right: the laws of war, disarmament, international criminal law, and international law in general. In addition, he is highly qualified in the areas of ballistics and forensics. His expertise is on the one hand academic, and he is one of the most prolific authors on issues related to the right to life. On the other hand, he also had a deep involvement as a practitioner and has played a leading role in the development of many of the international standards concerning the right to life that have emerged during the last decade.

Anyone whose work relates to the protection of the right to life – as an academic or as a practitioner – will benefit greatly from reading and using this book. Its publication is a major contribution towards our understanding of the right to life, and the protection of the 'supreme right'.

Christof Heyns
Professor of Human Rights Law and Director, Institute for International and Comparative Law in Africa (ICLA), University of Pretoria
Member of the UN Human Rights Committee (2017–2020)
UN Special Rapporteur on extrajudicial, summary or arbitrary executions (2010–2016)
In Loving Memory, 10 January 1959 to 28 March 2021

Acknowledgements

My thanks go to Dr Abi Dymond for her great contribution on less-lethal weapons in Chapter 7, 'The Use of Force in Law Enforcement'. My thanks also to the students who contributed background research, especially Sanskriti Sanghi for her work on the right to life of children and Elizabeth Vincento for her work on violence against women. It has been a great pleasure to work with Dr Thomas Probert on the Freedom from Violence in Africa Project at the University of Pretoria over the last four years. I have drawn on that experience in this work. I am most grateful to the professionals at Cambridge University Press for their unstinting support of this work: to Laura Blake, Marianne Nield, and especially Finola O'Sullivan, with whom it was a great privilege to collaborate over the past two decades. Her departure from the press is a great loss. My thanks go also to Vigneswaran Viswanathan and his team, in particular to Rachel Paul for her excellent copy-editing. I greatly miss Jack Glattbach, a hugely talented editor, mentor, and good friend who passed away just as this manuscript was being completed.

This book could not have been written without the generous and insightful guidance and inspirational leadership of Professor Christof Heyns. Personally, I owe so much to Christof. He contributed the Foreword to this book in January 2021. His death in March 2021 was a devastating loss to the family he adored. The human rights community lost a deeply respected member, as the testimonies that came privately and publicly in the days following his passing so clearly demonstrated. Rare are those who have both vision and attention to detail. Rarest of all are those who combine intellectual brilliance with humility, kindness, and selflessness. Christof was such a man. The obituary on the website of the Law Faculty at the University of Pretoria justly referred to a legal giant who would be sorely missed by all. While I rage at the iniquity of someone who gave so much to others being taken so young, he would not have. Always the better man, Christof. Always the better man.

Table of Cases

INTERNATIONAL AND REGIONAL BODIES

African Commission on Human and Peoples' Rights

Interights & Ditshwanelo v. Botswana, Decision (Comm No 319/06), adopted in Banjul, during the fifty-seventh Ordinary Session of the African Commission, 4–18 November 2015, 226

International PEN, Constitutional Rights Project, Civil Liberties Organisation and Interights (on behalf of Ken Saro-Wiwa Jnr) v. Nigeria, Decision (Comm Nos 137/94, 139/94, 154/96 and 161/97), 31 October 1998, 227

Kobedi v. Botswana, Decision, 2011, 226, 230

Noah Kazingachire, John Chitsenga, Elias Chemvura, and Batanai Hadzisi (represented by Zimbabwe Human Rights NGO Forum) v. Zimbabwe, Decision, 2012, 152

Purohit and Moore v. The Gambia, Views (Comm No 241/2001), May 2003, 535

African Committee of Experts on the Rights and Welfare of the Child

Michelo Hunsungule and others (on Behalf of Children in Northern Uganda) v. The Government of Uganda, Decision (Comm 1/2005), 15–19 April 2013, 469

Social and Economic Rights Action Centre and Centre for Economic and Social Rights v. Nigeria, Decision (Comm No 155/96 (2001)), 27 May 2002, 109, 390

African Court of Human and Peoples' Rights

African Commission on Human and Peoples' Rights v. Libya, Order for Provisional Measures (App No 004/2011), 25 March 2011, 587, 323, 730

Ally Rajabu and others v. Tanzania, Decision (App No 007/2015), 28 November 2019, 226, 729

Caribbean Court of Justice

Jabari Sensimania Nervais v. The Queen and Dwayne Omar Severin v. The Queen, Judgment, 27 June 2018 [2018] CCJ 19 (AJ), 211, 726

Table of Cases

Committee against Torture

Aemei v. Switzerland, UN doc CAT/C/18/D/34/1995, 29 May 1997, 53
Avedes Hamayak Korban v. Sweden, UN doc CAT/C/21/D/88/1997, 16 November 1998, 54
Z T v. Australia, UN doc CAT/C/31/D/142/2000, 19 November 2003, 54

Committee on the Elimination of Discrimination against Women

A T v. Hungary, Comm No 2/2003, 26 January 2005, 434
Alyne da Silva Pimentel v. Brazil, Views (Comm No 17/2008), 27 September 2011, 451, 452
Vienna Intervention Centre against Domestic Violence and the Association for Women's Access to Justice on behalf of Banu Akbak, Gülen Khan, and Melissa Özdemir v. Turkey (Fatma Yildirim v. Austria), Views (Comm No 6/2005), UN doc CEDAW/C/39/D/6/2005, 1 October 2007, 434

Committee on the Rights of Persons with Disabilities

Mr X v. Argentina, Views, UN doc CRPD/C/11/D/8/2012, 18 June 2014, 533

Committee on the Rights of the Child

W M C v. Denmark, Views (adopted on 28 September 2020), UN doc CRC/C/85/D/31/2017, 3 November 2020, 700

Eastern Caribbean Court of Appeal

Spence and Hughes v. The Queen, Crim App Nos 20 of 1998 and 14 of 1997, Judgment, 2 April 2001, 211

ECOWAS Court of Justice

Dorothy Chioma Njemanze and three others v. Federal Republic of Nigeria, Judgment (Case No ECW/CCJ/APP/17/14), 12 October 2017, 435

Eritrea-Ethiopia Claims Commission

Partial Award: Jus Ad Bellum – Ethiopia's Claims 1-8, 19 December 2005, 127

European Commission on Human Rights

Kathleen Stewart v. United Kingdom, Decision on Admissibility, 10 July 1984, 177
M D v. Turkey, Decision, 30 June 1997, 160
Stewart v. United Kingdom, Report of the Commission, 2 July 1985, 317
Tugar v. Italy (App No 22869/93), 18 October 1995, 353, 354, 355
Y v. the Netherlands, Appl No 16531/90, 605

European Court of Human Rights

A, B, and C v. Ireland, Judgment (Grand Chamber), 16 December 2010, 263, 264

Abdu v. Bulgaria, Judgment (Merits and Just Satisfaction) (Fourth Section), 11 March 2014, 501

Abdulaziz, Cabales and Balkandali v. United Kingdom, Judgment (Plenary of the Court), 28 May 1985, 439

Abdulkhadzhiyeva and Abdulkhadzhiyev v. Russia Judgment (Third Section), 4 October 2016, 27, 90

Abdullah Yaşa and others v. Turkey Judgment (Second Section), 16 July 2013, 145, 178, 319

Acar and others v. Turkey, Judgment (Fourth Section), 24 May 2005 (as rendered final on 12 October 2005), 27, 89, 91, 164, 723

Aghdgomelashvili and Japaridze v. Georgia, Judgment (Fifth Section), 8 October 2020, 522

Ahmet Özkan v. Turkey, Judgment (Second Section), 6 April 2004, 510

Akkum and others v. Turkey, Judgment (First Section), 24 March 2005, 511

AL (XW) v. Russia Judgment (First Section), 29 October 2015 (rendered final on 29 January 2016), 605

Al Nashiri v. Poland, Judgment (Fourth Section), 24 July 2014, 718

Albekov and others v. Russia Judgment (Third Section), 9 October 2008 (as rendered final on 6 April 2009), 356

Al-Jedda v. United Kingdom, Judgment (Grand Chamber), 7 July 2011, 79

Alkin v. Turkey, Judgment (Second Section), 13 October 2009, 162

Al-Saadoon and Mufdhi v. United Kingdom, Decision on admissibility (Chamber), 30 June 2009, 79

Al-Saadoon and Mufdhi v. United Kingdom, Judgment (Fourth Section), 2 March 2010, 224, 432, 605, 717

al-Skeini and others v. United Kingdom, Judgment (Grand Chamber), 7 July 2011, 119, 252

Andreea-Marusia Dumitru v. Romania, Judgment (Fourth Section), 31 March 2020, 34, 177

Andronicou and Constantinou v. Cyprus, Judgment (Chamber), 9 October 1997, 163

Anzhelo Georgiev and others v. Bulgaria, Judgment (Fourth Section), 30 September 2014, 148

Armani da Silva v. United Kingdom (App No 5878/08), application lodged on 21 January 2008, 164

Armani da Silva v. United Kingdom, Judgment (Grand Chamber), 30 March 2016, 150, 164, 192–93, 716

Aslakhanova and others v. Russian Federation, Judgment (First Section), 18 December 2012, 368

Association for European Integration and Human Rights and Ekimdzhiev v. Bulgaria, Judgment (Fifth Section), 28 June 2007 (as rendered final on 30 January 2008), 583

Ataykaya v. Turkey, Judgment (Second Section), 22 July 2014, 318–19

Table of Cases

Austin and others *v.* United Kingdom, Judgment (Grand Chamber), 15 March 2012, 327

B S *v.* Spain, Judgment, 24 July 2012, 496

Bakan *v.* Turkey, Judgment (Second Section), 12 June 2007, 169

Banković and others *v.* Belgium and others, Decision on Admissibility (Grand Chamber), 12 December 2001, 77, 78, 82

Bazorkina *v.* Russian Federation, Judgment (First Section), 27 July 2006, 367

Behrami and Behrami *v.* France, and Saramati *v.* France, Germany and Norway, Decision on Admissibility (Grand Chamber), 2 May 2007, 632, 637

Benzer *v.* Turkey, Judgment (Former Second Section), 12 November 2013 (as rendered final on 24 March 2014), 116, 120, 156, 202, 238, 511

Bouyid *v.* Belgium, Judgment (Grand Chamber), 28 September 2015, 148, 504

Buturugă *v.* Romania, Judgment (Fourth Section), 11 February 2020 (rendered final on 11 June 2020), 94

Cangöz and others *v.* Turkey, Judgment (Second Section), 26 April 2016, 191

Cantaragiu *v.* Moldova, Judgment (Second Section), 24 March 2020, 241

Case of Centre for Legal Resources on Behalf of Valentin Câmpeanu *v.* Romania, Judgment (Grand Chamber), 17 July 2014, 544

Catan and others *v.* Moldova and Russian Federation, Judgment (Grand Chamber), 19 October 2012, 66, 77, 622

Ciorcan and others *v.* Romania, Judgment (Third Section), 27 January 2015 (rendered final on 27 April 2015), 144

Çoşelav *v.* Turkey, Judgment (Second Section), 9 October 2012 (as rendered final on 18 March 2013), 242

Crăiniceanu and Frumuşanu *v.* Romania, Judgment (Third Section), 24 April 2012 (rendered final on 24 July 2012), 84

D H and others *v.* Czech Republic, Judgment (Grand Chamber), 13 November 2007, 507

Dink *v.* Turkey, Judgment (Second Section), 14 September 2010 (rendered final on 14 December 2010), 569

Djavit An *v.* Turkey, Judgment (Third Section), 20 February 2003 (as rendered final on 9 July 2003), 308

Dodov *v.* Bulgaria (App No 59548/00) 47 EHRR 41 (2008), 561

Douet *v.* France, Judgment (Fifth Section), 3 October 2013 (rendered final on 3 January 2014), 33, 143

Dudchenko *v.* Russian Federation, Judgment (Third Section), 7 November 2017 (as rendered final on 5 March 2018), 300, 301

Er *v.* Turkey, Judgment (Second Section), 31 July 2012, 372

Esmukhambetov and others *v.* Russian Federation, Judgment (First Section), 29 March 2011, 201

Esref Yaşa *v.* Turkey, Report, adopted on 8 April 1997, 88

Evans *v.* United Kingdom, Judgment (Grand Chamber), 10 April 2007, 262

Fabris and Parziale *v.* Italy, Judgment (First Section), 19 March 2020 (rendered final on 12 October 2020), 37, 242, 281

Fernandes de Oliveira *v.* Portugal, Judgment (Grand Chamber), 31 January 2019, 41

Table of Cases

Finogenov and others v. Russian Federation, Judgment (First Section), 20 December 2011, 147, 191, 204, 205, 639
Gagiu v. Romania, Judgment (Third Section), 24 February 2009 (rendered final on 24 May 2009), 243
Georgia v. Russia (II), Judgment (Grand Chamber), 21 January 2021, 79
Giuliani and Gaggio v. Italy, Judgment (Grand Chamber), 24 March 2011, 156, 169, 315–16, 317
Gongadze v. Ukraine, Judgment (Second Section), 8 November 2005 (rendered final on 8 February 2006), 369, 569–70
Guerdner v. France, Judgment (Fifth Section), 17 April 2014, 508
Güleç v. Turkey, Judgment, 27 July 1998, 171, 316, 317, 512
Güzelyurtlu and others v. Cyprus and Turkey, Judgment (Grand Chamber), 29 January 2019, 623
Haas v. Switzerland, Judgment (First Section), 20 January 2011, 280
Hassan v. United Kingdom, Judgment (Grand Chamber), 16 September 2014, 80, 82
Heinisch v. Germany, Judgment (Fifth Section), 21 July 2011, 561
Herrmann v. Germany, Judgment (Grand Chamber), 26 June 2012, 714
Ilaşcu and others v. Moldova and Russian Federation, Judgment (Grand Chamber), 8 July 2004, 354
Ilhan v. Turkey, Judgment (Grand Chamber), 27 June 2000, 27, 87, 717
Iordachi and others v. Moldova, Judgment (Fourth Section), 10 February 2009 (as rendered final on 14 September 2009), 583
Isayeva v. Russian Federation, Judgment (App No 57950/00) (First Section), 24 February 2005, 200, 202
Issa and others v. Turkey, Judgment (Second Section), 30 March 2005, 513–14
Jabari v. Turkey, Judgment (Fourth Section), 11 July 2000, 229
Jaloud v. The Netherlands, Judgment (Grand Chamber), 20 November 2014, 69, 120, 252–53
Janowiec and others v. Russian Federation, Judgment (Grand Chamber), 21 October 2013, 57, 58, 248
Jasinskis v. Latvia, Judgment (Third Section), 21 December 2010 (rendered final on 21 March 2011), 542, 544
Jeanty v. Belgium, Judgment (Third Section), 31 March 2020, 242, 281
Kadiķis v. Latvia (No 2), Judgment (Third Section), 4 May 2006, 301
Kakoulli v. Turkey, Judgment (Fourth Section), 22 November 2005, 160
Kalashnikov v. Russian Federation, Judgment (Third Section), 15 July 2002 (rendered final on 15 October 2002), 242–43
Kallis and Androulla Panayi v. Turkey, Judgment (Fourth Section), 27 October 2009, 169
Karataş and others v. Turkey, Judgment (Second Section), 12 September 2017, 153
Keller v. Russian Federation, Judgment (First Section), 17 October 2013 (rendered final on 17 February 2014), 236
Kılıcı v. Turkey, Judgment (Second Section), 27 November 2018, 318
Kitanovski v. North Macedonia, Judgment (First Section), 22 January 2015, 27, 89, 90, 166
Koch v. Germany, Judgment (Fifth Section), 19 July 2012, 279–80
Koku v. Turkey, Judgment (Second Section), 31 May 2005, 369

Table of Cases

Kontrová v. Slovakia, Judgment (Fourth Section), 31 May 2007, 440, 441
Kotilainen and others v. Finland, Judgment (First Section), 17 September 2020, 716
Ksenz and others v. Russian Federation, Judgment (Third Section), 12 December 2017, 150
Kudrevičius and others v. Lithuania, Judgment (Grand Chamber), 15 October 2015, 308
Kukhalashvili v. Georgia, Judgment (Fifth Section), 2 April 2020, 150, 166
Kurt v. Austria, Judgment (Fifth Section), 4 July 2019, 440, 441, 442, 463, 464, 486
Kurt v. Turkey, Judgment (Chamber), 25 May 1998, 367–68
Lăcătuş and others v. Romania, Judgment (Third Section), 13 November 2012, 507
Lapunov v. Russian Federation (Appl no 28834/19), Communicated on 14 November 2019, 523–24
Loizidou v. Turkey, Judgment (Preliminary Objections) (Grand Chamber), 23 March 1995, 77
M C and C A v. Romania, Judgment (Fourth Section), 12 April 2016 (as rendered final on 12 July 2016), 522
Makaratzis v. Greece, Judgment (Grand Chamber), 20 December 2004, 14, 88, 164
Mammadov and others v. Azerbaijan, Judgment (Fifth Section), 21 February 2019 (rendered final on 21 May 2019), 241
Marius Alexandru and Marinela Ștefan v. Romania, Judgment (Fourth Section), 24 March 2020 (rendered final on 24 July 2020), 44, 383, 384
Mastromatteo v. Italy, Judgment (Grand Chamber), 24 October 2002, 57, 247
Mazepa and others v. Russian Federation, Judgment (Third Section), 17 July 2018, 569
McCann and others v. United Kingdom, Judgment (Grand Chamber), 27 September 1995, 57, 146, 149, 163, 190–91, 191, 192, 247, 316, 714, 715, 716, 722
Menteş v. Turkey, Judgment (Grand Chamber), 28 November 1997, 510
Mižigárová v. Slovakia, Judgment (Merits and Just Satisfaction) (Fourth Section), 14 December 2010 (rendered final on 14 March 2011), 236, 500
Mocanu and others v. Romania, Judgment (Grand Chamber), 17 September 2014, 83, 84
Moldovan and others v. Romania, Judgment No 2 (Former Second Section), 12 July 2005, 507
Molla Sali v. Greece, Judgment (Merits) (Grand Chamber), 19 December 2018, 500
Mortier v. Belgium, Judgment (Second Section), 3 December 2018, 280–81
Mozer v. Moldova and Russian Federation, Judgment (Grand Chamber), 23 February 2016, 77, 622
Murdalovy v. Russian Federation, Judgment (Third Section), 31 March 2020, 29
Mustafayev v. Azerbaijan, Judgment (Fifth Section), 4 May 2017 (rendered final on 4 August 2017), 241
Nachova v. Bulgaria, Judgment (Grand Chamber), 6 July 2005, 34, 145, 166, 238, 240, 496, 500, 716, 717
Nagmetov v. Russian Federation, Judgment (First Section), 5 November 2015, 25
Nagmetov v. Russian Federation, Judgment (Grand Chamber), 30 March 2017, 26
Navalnyy and Gunko v. Russian Federation, Judgment (First Section), 10 November 2020, 148
Nencheva and others v. Bulgaria, Judgment (Fourth Section), 18 June 2013 (as rendered final on 16 December 2013), 300, 543, 544

Table of Cases

Nicolae Virgiliu Tănase *v.* Romania, Judgment (Grand Chamber), 25 June 2019, 27, 87, 94

O'Keeffe *v.* Ireland, Judgment (Grand Chamber), 28 January 2014, 463

Öcalan *v.* Turkey, Judgment (Grand Chamber), 12 May 2005, 79, 224

Öneryildiz *v.* Turkey, Judgment (Grand Chamber), 30 November 2004, 43, 135, 393

Opuz *v.* Turkey, Judgment (Third Section), rendered final on 9 September 2009, 439, 440, 441

Osman *v.* United Kingdom, Judgment (Grand Chamber), 28 October 1998, 88, 178–79, 440, 441, 442, 464

Pad and others *v.* Turkey, Judgment (Decision on admissibility) (Third Section), 28 June 2007, 78

Paposhvili *v.* Belgium, Judgment (Grand Chamber), 13 December 2016, 54

Paşa and Erkan Erol *v.* Turkey, Judgment (Second Section), 12 December 2006 (as rendered final on 23 May 2007), 355

Perişan and others *v.* Turkey, Judgment (Second Section), 20 May 2010, 173

Petyo Popov *v.* Bulgaria, Judgment (Fifth Section), 22 January 2009, 33

Pocasovschi and Mihaila *v.* Moldova and Russia Judgment (Second Section), 29 May 2018 (rendered final on 29 August 2018), 243

Poede *v.* Romania, Judgment (Fifth Section), 15 September 2015, 522

Pretty *v.* United Kingdom, Judgment (Fourth Section), 29 April 2002, 279

Rachwalski and Ferenc *v.* Poland, Judgment (Fourth Section), 28 July 2009, 149

Sabanchiyeva *v.* Russian Federation, Judgment (First Section), 6 June 2013, 61–62

Satybalova *v.* Russian Federation, Judgment (Third Section), 30 June 2020, 194–95

Shavadze *v.* Georgia, Judgment (Fifth Section), 19 November 2020, 717

Shchebetov *v.* Russian Federation, Judgment (First Section), 10 April 2012, 717

Shchiborshch and Kuzmina *v.* Russian Federation, Judgment (First Section), 16 January 2014 (as rendered final on 2 June 2014), 147, 541–42

Shuriyya Zeynalov *v.* Azerbaijan, Judgment (Fifth Section), 10 September 2020, 90, 717

Šilih *v.* Slovenia, Judgment (Grand Chamber), 9 April 2009, 58, 248

Soering *v.* United Kingdom, Judgment (Plenary of the Court), 7 July 1989, 54, 353, 604

Solomou and others *v.* Turkey, Judgment (Fourth Section), 24 June 2008, 160

Streletz, Kessler, and Krenz *v.* Germany, Judgment (Grand Chamber), 22 March 2001, 14

Süleyman Çelebi and others *v.* Turkey, Judgment (Second Section), 24 May 2016, 320

Tagayeva and others *v.* Russian Federation, Judgment (First Section), 13 April 2017, 179, 186, 193–94, 316, 716

Talpis *v.* Italy, Judgment (First Section), 2 March 2017, 442, 464

Tanış and others *v.* Turkey, Judgment (Fourth Section), 2 August 2005, 369

Tërshana *v.* Albania, Judgment (Second Section), 4 August 2020, 440, 716

Timurtas *v.* Turkey, Judgment (First Section), 13 June 2000, 368

Toğcu *v.* Turkey, Judgment (Second Section), 31 May 2005, 368

Tsechoyev *v.* Russian Federation, Judgment (First Section), 15 March 2011, 717

Ukraine *v.* Russian Federation (App No 20958/14) (Grand Chamber hearing), 11 September 2019, 137

Table of Cases xix

Varnava and others *v.* Turkey, Judgment (Grand Chamber), 18 September 2009, 203, 369, 372, 623
Vasil Sashov Petrov *v.* Bulgaria, Judgment (Fifth Section), 10 June 2010, 509
Vo *v.* France, Judgment (Grand Chamber), 8 July 2004, 262
Volintiru *v.* Italy, Communicated Case (Appl No 8530/08), 19 March 2013, 562
Volodina *v.* Russian Federation, Judgment, 9 July 2019, 442, 464
Yaşa *v.* Turkey, Judgment (Chamber), 2 September 1998, 88, 512
Yuriy Illarionovich Shchokin *v.* Ukraine, Judgment (Fifth Section), 3 October 2013 (rendered final on 3 January 2014), 241–42
Z and others *v.* United Kingdom, Judgment (Grand Chamber), 10 May 2001, 301

Human Rights Committee

Abduali Ismatovich Kurbanov *v.* Tajikistan, Views (UN doc CCPR/C/79/D/1096/2002), 6 November 2003, 114
Baboeram Adhin *v.* Suriname (Comm No 146/1983), 4 April 1985, 13
Bousroual *v.* Algeria, Views (UN doc CCPR/C/86/992/2001), 30 March 2006, 358–59
Brown *v.* Jamaica, Views, 11 May 1999, 31
Chisanga *v.* Zambia, Communication No 1132/2002, Views adopted on 18 October 2005, 32
Chitat Ng *v.* Canada, Views (Comm No 469/1991), UN doc CCPR/C/49/D/469/1991, 7 January 1994, 214, 229
Chongwe *v.* Zambia, Views, UN doc CCPR/C/70/D/821/1998, 9 November 2000, 26, 28, 86
El Boathi *v.* Algeria, Views (UN doc CCPR/C/119/D/2259/2013), 17 March 2017, 362–64
Eversley Thompson *v.* St Vincent, Views, UN Doc CCPR/C/70/D/806/1998, 18 October 2000, 211
Florentina Olmedo *v.* Paraguay, Views (Comm No 1828/2008), UN doc CCPR/C/104/D/1828/2008, 26 April 2012, 96–97, 312–13
Gorji-Dinka *v.* Cameron, Views (Comm No 1134/2002), adopted on 14 March 2005, 25
Ioane Teitiota *v.* New Zealand, Views (Comm No 2728/2016), UN doc CCPR/C/127/D/2728/2016, 7 January 2020, 396, 397, 398, 603
Joaquín David Herrera Rubio and others *v.* Colombia, Views (UN doc CCPR/C/OP/2), 2 November 1987, 362
Johnson *v.* Ghana, Views, 27 March 2014, 32
Judge *v.* Canada, Views, 2003, 55–56
Katwal *v.* Nepal, Views (UN doc CCPR/C/113/D/2000/2010), 1 April 2015, 358
Khadzhiyev *v.* Turkmenistan, Views (UN doc CCPR/C/122/D/2252/2013), 6 April 2018, 236
Kindler *v.* Canada, Views, 30 July 1993, 31, 32
Kovaleva and Kozyar *v.* Belarus, Views, UN doc CCPR/C/106/D/2120/2011, 27 November 2012, 63
Lovelace *v.* Canada, Views, 30 July 1981, 69–70

Luboto v. Zambia, Views, 31 October 1995, 32

Marcellana and Gumanoy v. The Philippines, Views (UN doc CCPR/C/94/D/1560/2007), 30 October 2008, 93

Mellet v. Ireland, Views (UN doc CCPR/C/116/D/2324/2013), 17 November 2016, 40, 258, 259, 462

Mojica v. Dominican Republic, Views (UN doc CCPR/C/51/D/449/1991), 15 July 1994, 94

Norma Portillo Cáceres and others v. Paraguay, Views (UN doc CCPR/C/126/D/2751/2016), 25 July 2019, 95, 135, 136, 392

Patrick Coleman v. Australia, Views (Comm No 1157/2003), UN doc CCPR/C/87/D/1157/2003, 10 August 2006, 309

Prutina and others v. Bosnia and Herzegovina, Views (UN docs CCPR/C/107/D/1917/2009, 1918/2009, 1925/2009, and 1953/2010), 358, 457

R S v. Trinidad and Tobago, Views (UN doc CCPR/C/74/D/684/1996), 2 April 2002, 220

Sanjeevan v. Sri Lanka, Views (Communication No 1436/05), 8 July 2008, 38, 729

Suarez de Guerrero v. Colombia (Comm No R11/45), 31 March 1982, 13

Turdukan Zhumbaeva v. Kyrgyzstan, Views (UN doc CCPR/C/102/D/1756/2008), 19 July 2011, 250, 277

Van Alphen v. The Netherlands, Views (Comm No 305/1988), adopted on 23 July 1990, 25

Yassin and others v. Canada, Views, 26 July 2017, 67

Yekaterina Pavlovna Lantsova v. Russian Federation, Views (UN doc CCPR/C/74/D/763/1997), 26 March 2002, 99, 295

Inter-American Commission on Human Rights

Beatriz v. El Salvador, Report on Admissibility (Petition 2003-13), Report No 120/17, OAS doc OEA/SerL/V/II164 Doc 141, 7 September 2017, 265

Case of Disabled Peoples' International and others v. United States, Report on Admissibility (Case No 9,213), 75

Clarence Allen Lackey and others v. United States, Merits (Case Nos 11,575, 12,333, and 12,341), Report No 52/13, 15 July 2013, 546

Coard and others v. United States, Report No 109/99 (Case 10,951), 29 September 1999, 80, 81

Community of Rio Negro of the Maya Indigenous People and Its Members v. Guatemala, Report No 13/2008 of 5 March 2008, 80, 83

Eduardo Nicolas Cruz Sanchez and Herma Luz Melendez Cueva v. Peru, Report No 13/04 (Case 136/03), OAS doc OEA/SerL/V/II122 Doc 5 rev 1 (2004), 197

Eduardo Nicolas Cruz Sanchez and others v. Peru, Report No 66/10 (Case 12,444) (Merits), 31 March 2011, 197

Family Members of Anastasio Hernández-Rojas, Petitioners v. United States, Complaint, March 2016, 175

Table of Cases xxi

Franklin Guillermo Aisalla Molina (Ecuador v. Colombia), Admissibility Report No 112/10, 21 October 2011, 75

Matter of Julio César Cano Molina Concerning Cuba, Resolution 24/2014 (Precautionary Measure No 307-14), 10 September 2014, 539–40

Michael Domingues v. United States, Decision (Case 12,285), Report 62/02, 308, 468, 472

Napoleon Beazley v. United States, Decision (Case 12,412), Report No 101/03, 29 December 2003, 208, 467, 468, 472

Paola del Rosario Guzmán Albarracín and Relatives v. Ecuador, Report No 110/18 (Case 12,678), Merits, 5 October 2018, 281

Patients at the Neuropsychiatric Hospital v. Paraguay, Decision on Precautionary Measures (Case No PM 277-07), 29 July 2008, 539

Richmond Hill v. United States, Case No 9213, Report No 3/96, OAS doc OEA/SerL/V/II91 Doc 7, 1996, 75, 82

Víctor Rosario Congo v. Ecuador, Report 63/99 (Case No 11,427), 13 April 1999, 537–38

Inter-American Court of Human Rights

Almonacid-Arellano and others v. Chile, Judgment (Preliminary Objections, Merits, Reparations and Costs), 26 September 2006, 668, 681, 682

Aloeboetoe and others case, Judgment (Reparations), 10 September 1993, 502

Artavia Murillo and others ('In Vitro Fertilization') v. Costa Rica, Judgment (Preliminary objections, merits, reparations and costs), 28 November 2012, 264, 465, 721

Atala Riffo and Daughters v. Chile, Judgment (Merits, Reparations and Costs), 24 February 2012, 521

Blake v. Guatemala, Judgment (Merits), 24 January 1998, 83

Case of Furlan and Family v. Argentina, Judgment (Preliminary Objections, Merits, Reparations and Costs), 31 August 2012, 465

Case of Goiburú et al v. Paraguay, Judgment (Merits, Reparations and Costs), 22 September 2006, 361

Case of the Indigenous Community Xákmok Kásek v. Paraguay, Judgment (Merits, Reparations and Costs Judgment) 24 August 2010 Series C No 214, 298, 724

Case of the Ituango Massacres v. Colombia, Judgment (Preliminary Objections, Merits, Reparations and Costs), 1 July 2006, 203, 723

Case of the Massacres of El Mozote and Nearby Places v. El Salvador, Judgment (Merits, Reparations, and Costs), 25 October 2012, 430, 465, 467

Cruz Sánchez and others v. Peru, Judgment (Preliminary Objections, Merits, Reparation, and Costs), 17 April 2015, 15, 153, 156, 196, 238, 722

García Lucero and others v. Chile, Judgment, 28 August 2013, 83

Godínez Cruz v. Honduras, Judgment (Merits), 20 January 1989, 58, 722

González Lluy and others v. Ecuador, Judgment (Preliminary Objections, Merits, Reparations and Costs), 1 September 2015, 297, 298, 723–24

Hacienda Brasil Verde Workers v. Brazil, Judgment (Preliminary Objections, Merits, Reparations and Costs), 20 October 2016, 418

Huilca Tecse v. Peru, Judgment (Merits, Reparations and Costs), 3 March 2005, 581

Juridical Condition and Human Rights of the Child, Advisory Opinion OC-17/2002, 28 August 2002, 465, 466

Kawas-Fernández v. Honduras, Judgment (Merits, Reparations and Costs), 3 April 2009, 581

López Soto and others v. Venezuela, Judgment (Merits, Reparation, and Costs), 26 September 2018, 420

Moiwana Village v. Suriname, Judgment (Preliminary Objections, Merits, Reparations and Costs), 15 June 2005, 59, 61, 91

Montero-Aranguren and others (Detention Centre of Catia) v. Venezuela, Judgment (Preliminary Objection, Merits, Reparations, and Costs), 5 July 2006, 58, 133, 141, 146, 153, 162, 244, 245, 248, 722

Myrna Mack-Chang v. Guatemala, Judgment (Merits, Reparations, and Costs), Separate Opinion of Judge García Ramirezo, 25 November 2003, 18

Nadege Dorzema and others v. Dominican Republic, Judgment (Merits, Reparations, and Costs), 24 October 2012, 153, 159, 722

Neira Alegría v. Peru, Judgment (Merits), 19 January 1995, 196–97

Osorio Rivera and Family Members v. Peru, Judgment (Preliminary Objections, Merits, Reparations and Costs), 26 November 2013, 29, 366–67, 372

Rochela Massacre v. Colombia, Judgment (Merits, Reparations, and Costs), 11 May 2007, 27, 89, 91, 164, 723

Santo Domingo massacre v. Colombia, Judgment (Preliminary Objections, Merits and Reparations), 30 November 2012, 118, 203, 722

Sawhoyamaxa Indigenous Community v. Paraguay, Judgment (Merits, Reparations and Costs), 29 March 2006, 298, 299, 724

The Environment and Human Rights (State Obligations in Relation to the Environment in the Context of the Protection and Guarantee of the Rights to Life and to Personal Integrity: Interpretation and Scope of Articles 4(1) and 5(1) in Relation to Articles 1(1) and 2 of the American Convention on Human Rights), Advisory Opinion OC-23/17, 15 November 2017, Requested by the Republic of Colombia, 74

Velásquez Rodríguez v. Honduras, Judgment (Merits), 29 July 1988, 58, 618, 721

Vélez Restrepo and Family v. Colombia, Judgment (Preliminary Objections, Merits, Reparations and Costs), 3 September 2012, 571

Veliz Franco and others v. Guatemala, Judgment (Preliminary Objections, Merits, Reparations and Costs), 19 May 2014, 59

Ximenes-Lopes v. Brazil, Judgment (Merits, Reparations and Costs), 4 July 2006, 540

Yakye Axa Indigenous Community v. Paraguay, Judgment (Merits, Reparations and Costs), 17 June 2005, 298, 299, 560, 724

International Court of Justice

Ahmadou Sadio Diallo (Guinea v. Democratic Republic of Congo), Judgment (Admissibility), 24 May 2007, 615, 707

Application of the Convention on the Prevention and Punishment of the Crime of Genocide (The Gambia v. Myanmar), Order, 23 January 2020, 450, 495

Barcelona Traction, Light and Power Company Ltd (Belgium v. Spain), Judgment, 5 February 1970, 311, 617, 635, 661, 706

Case Concerning Armed Activities on the Territory of the Congo (Democratic Republic of the Congo v. Uganda), Judgment, 19 December 2005, 70, 74, 76, 106, 706

Case Concerning Military and Paramilitary Activities in and against Nicaragua (Nicaragua v. United States of America) Judgment (Merits), 27 June 1986, 10, 39, 110, 124, 306, 550, 639, 664

Case Concerning Oil Platforms (Islamic Republic of Iran v. United States of America), Judgment (Merits), 6 November 2003, 125

Case Concerning the Application of the Convention on the Prevention and Punishment of the Crime of Genocide (Bosnia and Herzegovina v. Serbia and Montenegro), Judgment, 26 February 2007, 354, 494, 625

Case Concerning the Arbitral Award of 31 July 1989 (Guinea-Bissau v. Senegal), Judgment, 12 November 1991, 24

Case Concerning the Arrest Warrant of 11 April 2000 (Democratic Republic of the Congo v. Belgium), Judgment, 14 February 2002, 68

Corfu Channel Case (United Kingdom v. Albania), Judgment (Merits), 9 April 1949, 1089

Difference Relating to Immunity from Legal Process of a Special Rapporteur of the Commission on Human Rights, Advisory Opinion, 29 April 1999, 636

Fisheries Case (United Kingdom v. Norway), Judgment, 18 December 1951, 17

Interpretation of the Agreement of 25 March 1951 between the WHO and Egypt, Advisory Opinion, 20 December 1980, 634

Legal Consequences for States of the Continued Presence of South Africa in Namibia (South West Africa) Notwithstanding Security Council Resolution 276 (1970), Advisory Opinion, 21 June 1971, 706

Legal Consequences of the Construction of a Wall in the Occupied Palestinian Territory, Advisory Opinion, 9 July 2004, 67, 70, 71, 74, 106, 706

Legality of the Threat or Use of Nuclear Weapons, Advisory Opinion, 8 July 1996, 12, 14, 36, 70, 81, 104, 115, 134, 135, 206, 394, 707

North Sea Continental Shelf Cases (Germany v. Denmark; Germany v. The Netherlands), Judgment, 20 February 1969, 16

Nuclear Tests (Australia v. France; New Zealand v. France), Judgments of 20 December 1974, ICJ Reports 1974, pp 267-68, 641

United States Diplomatic and Consular Staff in Tehran Case (United States v. Iran), Judgment, 24 May 1980, 614

Western Sahara, Advisory Opinion, 16 October 1975, 129

International Criminal Court

Prosecutor v. Alfred Yekatom, 490

Prosecutor v. Bosco Ntaganda, Judgment (Case No ICC-01/04-02/06) (Trial Chamber VI), 8 July 2019, 423, 499

Prosecutor v. Germain Katanga, Decision on the Confirmation of Charges (Pre-Trial Chamber I) (Case No ICC 01/04 01/07), 30 September 2008, 667

Prosecutor v. Germain Katanga, Decision on Sentence (Case No ICC-01/04-01/07) (Trial Chamber II), 23 May 2014, 499–500

Prosecutor v. Patrice-Edouard Ngaïssona, 490

Prosecutor v. Ruto, Decision on the Confirmation of Charges (Pre-Trial Chamber II) (Case No ICC 01/09 01/11), 23 January 2012, 668

Prosecutor v. Thomas Lubanga Dyilo, Judgment (Trial Chamber I), 14 March 2012, 110

International Criminal Tribunal for Rwanda

Prosecutor v. Athanase Seromba, Judgment (Case No ICTR-2001-66-A), 12 March 2008, 448

International Criminal Tribunal for the former Yugoslavia

Prosecutor v. Ante Gotovina and Mladen Markač, Judgment (Trial Chamber I) (Case No IT-06-90-T), 15 April 2011, 410

Prosecutor v. Ante Gotovina and Mladen Markač, Judgment (Appeals Chamber) (Case No IT-06-90-A), 20 November 2012, 410

Prosecutor v. Anto Furundžija, Judgment (Case No IT-95-17/1-T) (Trial Chamber), 10 December 1998, 124, 735

Prosecutor v. Boškoski and Tarčulovski, Judgment (Trial Chamber II) (Case No IT-04-82-T), 10 July 2008, 112

Prosecutor v. Dragomir Milošević, Judgment (Trial Chamber III) (Case No IT-98-29/1-T), 12 December 2007, 339

Prosecutor v. Galić, Judgment (Trial Chamber) (Case No IT-98-29-T), 5 December 2003, 409

Prosecutor v. Krstić, Judgment (Case No IT-98-33-T) (Trial Chamber), 2 August 2001, 494, 499, 708

Prosecutor v. Kunarac, Judgment (Trial Chamber) (Case No IT-96-23-T & IT-96-23/1-T), 22 February 2001, 422

Prosecutor v. Milorad Krnojelac, Judgment (Trial Chamber) (Case No IT-97-25-T), 15 March 2002, 422

Prosecutor v. Prlić, Judgment (Trial Chamber) (Case No IT-04-74-T), Vol 4, 29 May 2013, 305

Prosecutor v. Tadić, Decision on the Defence Motion for Interlocutory Appeal on Jurisdiction (Appeals Chamber) (Case No IT-94-1), 2 October 1995, 111, 306

Prosecutor v. Tadić, Judgment (Trial Chamber) (Case No IT-94-1-T), 7 May 1997, 111

Prosecutor v. Zoran Kupreškić and others, Judgment (Case No IT-95-16-T) (Trial Chamber), 14 January 2000, 333

Permanent Court of International Justice

Factory at Chorzów, Judgment (Jurisdiction), No 8, 1927, PCIJ, Series A, No 9, 616
German Settlers in Poland, Advisory Opinion, 1923, PCIJ, Series B, No 6, p 22, 617
Phosphates in Morocco Case, 1937, PCIJ, Series C, No 84, p 494, 612, 613
Rights of Minorities in Upper Silesia (Minority Schools), Germany v. Poland, Judgment (No 12), 26 April 1928, 4

Special Court for Sierra Leone

Prosecutor v. Morris Kallon and Brima Buzzy Kamara, Decision on Challenge to Jurisdiction: Lomé Accord Amnesty (Appeals Chamber) (Case Nos SCSL-2004-15-AR72(E) and SCSL-2004-16-AR72(E)), 13 March 2004, 664, 665
Prosecutor v. Sam Hinga Norman, Decision on Preliminary Motion Based on Lack of Jurisdiction (Appeals Chamber) (Case No SCSL-2004-14-AR72(E)), 31 May 2004, 649, 661

Special Tribunal for Lebanon

Interlocutory Decision on the Applicable Law: Terrorism, Conspiracy, Homicide, Perpetration, Cumulative Charging (Case No STL-11-01/I), 16 February 2011, 184
Prosecutor v. Salim Jamil Ayyash and others, Judgment (Case No STL-11-01/T/TC), 18 August 2020, 184

NATIONAL COURTS

Australia

R v. Tang, [2008] HCA 418, 419

Belize

Lauriano v. Attorney General of Belize (1995) 3 Bz LR 77 (Court of Appeal), 211

Botswana

Makwati v. State 1996 BLR 682 (Court of Appeal), 166

Canada

Carter v. Canada (Attorney General), 2015 SCC 5, decided 6 February 2015, 288
Lamb v. Canada (Attorney General), 2018 BCCA 266, decided 6 February 2019, 290
Nevsun Resources Ltd v. Araya, 2020 SCC 5, Judgment rendered on 28 February 2020 (Supreme Court of Canada), 655, 678

India

Mithu v. State of Punjab, Judgment (Criminal Appeal No 745 of 1980), 7 April 1983 (Supreme Court), 210

Ireland

Attorney General v. X [1992] 1 IR 1 (Supreme Court), 40, 462

Malawi

Kafantayeni v. Attorney General, Constitutional Case No 12 of 2005 [2007] MWHC 1 (High Court), 210

Netherlands

Mothers of Srebrenica Association and others v. The Netherlands, Judgment (Case No ECLI:NL:HR:2019:1223), 19 July 2019, 639, 640

Nuhanović v. The Netherlands, Judgment (Case ECLI:NL:HR:2013:BZ9225), 6 September 2013 (Supreme Court of the Netherlands), 639

Rwanda

Igohozo v. Prosecution [2016] 3 RLR (High Court), 266, 470

South Africa

State v. T Makwanyane and M Mchunu, [1995] CCT/3/94, ZACC3 (Constitutional Court), 209

Switzerland

Nada v. State Secretariat for Economic Affairs and Federal Department of Economic Affairs, Federal Supreme Court, No 1A 45/2007, ILDC 461, 18

Uganda

Absolom Omolo Owiny v. Uganda, Criminal Appeal No 321 of 2003, [2008] UGCA 2, Judgment of 7 April 2008, 173

Attorney General v. Susan Kigula and 417 others (Constitutional Appeal No 3 of 2006) [2009] UGSC 6 (21 January 2009) (Supreme Court), 212, 230

United Kingdom

Adan v. Secretary of State for the Home Department, Judgment, 6 April 1998, [1999] 1 AC 293 (HL), 603

Airedale NHS Trust v. Bland [1993] AC 789 (House of Lords), 272

Table of Cases xxvii

Attorney-General's Reference (No 3, 1994), 262
R v. Miller [1983] 2 AC 161, [1993] 1 All ER 821 (House of Lords), 273

United States

Altony Brooks v. Lieutenant Johnson and others, Judgment (Case No 17-7448), 10 May 2019 (US Court of Appeals, Fourth Circuit), 150
Anthony Piazza and other v. Jefferson County, Alabama, and Mike Hale and others, Judgment (No 18-10487), 9 May 2019 (US Court of Appeals, Eleventh Circuit), 152
Armstrong v. Village of Pinehurst, Judgment (Case No 15-1191), 11 January 2016 (US Court of Appeals, Fourth Circuit), 153, 174
Arnold v. Buck, Judgment (Case No 3:11-cv-1343 (VLB)), 2 August 2013 (US District Court for Connecticut), 175
Atkins v. Virginia, 536 US 304 (2002), Certiorari to the Supreme Court of Virginia, Case No 00-8452, 20 June 2002 (US Supreme Court), 547
Bailey v. United States, 516 US 137 (1995) (US Supreme Court), 155
Baxter v. Montana, Opinion of the Court (Case DA 09-0051), decided 31 December 2009 (Supreme Court of Montana), 286–87
Betty Lou Heston and others v. City of Salinas and others, Judgment (Case No C 05-03658 JW), 30 January 2009 (US District Court for the Northern District of California, San Jose Division), 175
Bobby James Moore v. Texas, Petition for Writ of Certiorari to the Court of Criminal Appeals of Texas, Case No 18-443, 586 US ___ (2019) 1, 19 February 2019 (US Supreme Court), 548
Buck v. Bell, 274 US 200 (1927), decided 2 May 1927 (US Supreme Court), 274
Bucklew v. Precythe, 587 US ___ (2019) (US Supreme Court), 230
Graham v. Connor, 490 US 386 (1989), 15 May 1989 (US Supreme Court), 149
Hall v. Florida, 572 US 701 (2014), Case No 12-10882, 27 May 2014 (US Supreme Court), 548
Jane Roe and others v. Henry Wade, District Attorney of Dallas County, 410 US 113, Decided 22 January 1973 (US Supreme Court), 267
Joseph Jesner and others v. Arab Bank PLC, No 16-499, 584 US ___ (2018) (US Supreme Court), 656, 657
Kiobel and others v. Royal Dutch Petroleum Co and others, Amicus Curiae of the United States supporting the Petitioners, December 2011 (US Supreme Court), 656, 685
Madison v. Alabama, Judgment (Docket No 17-7505), 27 February 2019 (US Supreme Court), 227, 563
Nestle v. John Doe I and others, Amicus Curiae of the United States, May 2020 (US Supreme Court), 657
Planned Parenthood of Southeastern Pennsylvania and others v. Robert P Casey and others, 505 US 833, Decided 29 June 1992 (US Supreme Court), 267
Presbyterian Church of Sudan and others v. Talisman Energy, Inc, 582 F3d 244 (2009) (US Court of Appeals, Second Circuit), 656

Roper v. Simmons, No 03-633, 1 March 2005 (US Supreme Court), 213, 472
Sherman v. Sherman, 330 NJ Super 638 (Ch Div, 1999) (New Jersey Superior Court), 60
Siderman de Blake v. Argentina, Judgment, 965 F2d 699 (1992), Decided 22 May 1992 (US Court of Appeal, Ninth Circuit), 361
Sosa v. Alvarez-Machain, 542 US 692 (2004) (US Supreme Court), 656, 685
Sumner v. Shuman, Judgment (Case No 86-246), 22 June 1987 (US Supreme Court), 210
Tel-Oren v. Libyan Arab Republic, 726 F2d 774 (1984) (US Court of Appeals, District of Colombia), 657
Thomas D Arthur v. Jefferson S Dunn, Commissioner, Alabama Department of Corrections, and others, Petition for Writ of Certiorari to the US Court of Appeals for the Eleventh Circuit (Case No 16-602), 580 US ___ (2017), 21 February 2017 (US Supreme Court), 230
United States v. Matthew Dean Moore and Melvin Williams, Government Brief (Case No 11-30877) (US Court of Appeals, Fifth Circuit), 173
United States v. Otto Ohlendorf and others, Trial of the Major War Criminals, Vol IV (1947), 681, 682
Verizon Communications v. Law Offices of Curtis V Trinko, 540 US 398, 408 (2004) (US Supreme Court), 652
Washington v. Glucksberg, 521 US 702 (1997), decided 26 June 1997, 272
West v. Atkins, 487 US 42 (1988) (US Supreme Court), 686
Wilkerson v. Utah, 99 US 130 (1879) (US Supreme Court), 231
Wolf v. Rose Hill Cemetery Association, 832 P2d 1007 (1991) (Colorado Court of Appeal), 60
Woodson v. North Carolina (1976) 426 US 280 (US Supreme Court), 210

An Historical Introduction to the Right to Life

0.01 It has been said that the struggle for human rights 'is as old as history itself, because it concerns the need to protect the individual against the abuse of power by the monarch, the tyrant, or the state'.[1] Speaking in 1978 on the occasion of the thirtieth anniversary of the Universal Declaration of Human Rights, US President Jimmy Carter declared that, of all human rights, 'the most basic is to be free of arbitrary violence – whether that violence comes from governments, from terrorists, from criminals, or from self-appointed messiahs operating under cover of politics or religion'.[2] Those fundamental realities notwithstanding, the right to life, per se, is a relatively recent addition to the law of nations. 'To say that each person ought not to be killed is an easily comprehensible moral statement, however much it may in practice be violated.' In 'contrast', Kenneth Minogue suggested, 'the idea that each person has a "right" to life is, on the face of it much more puzzling'.[3]

0.02 In the ancient world, the Code of Hammurabi is the oldest set of complete laws known to exist. Promulgated by King Hammurabi, who ruled Babylon in the first half of the eighteenth century BCE, the text speaks of his desire 'to further the well-being of mankind' by creating protections 'so that the strong should not harm the weak'.[4] In fourth-century BCE China, Meng Zi, a disciple of Confucian thought, declared that 'all human beings' by nature share a common humanity, moral worth, inherent dignity, and goodness.[5] In the same century, the philosopher Xunzi affirmed that in order to eliminate

---

[1] A. H. Robertson and J. G. Merrills, *Human Rights in the World: An Introduction to the Study of the International Protection of Human Rights*, Manchester University Press, Manchester, 1996, p. 9.
[2] Reproduced in W. Laqueur and B. Rubin (eds.), *The Human Rights Reader*, Meridien, New York, 1979, p. 326.
[3] K. Minogue, 'The History of the Idea of Human Rights', in Laqueur and Rubin (eds.), *The Human Rights Reader*, p. 3.
[4] P. G. Lauren, 'The Foundations of Justice and Human Rights in Early Legal Texts and Thought', chap. 7 in D. Shelton (ed.), *The Oxford Handbook of International Human Rights Law*, Oxford University Press, Oxford, October 2013, pp. 163–93, at 164–5.
[5] I. Bloom, 'Fundamental Institutions and Consensus Statements: Mencius Confucianism and Human Rights', in W. T. deBary and T. Weiming (eds.), *Confucianism and Human Rights*, Columbia University Press, New York, 1998, pp. 101–2.

conflict, 'nothing is as effective as the institution of corporate life based on a clear recognition of individual rights'.[6]

0.03 Elsewhere in Asia, between the end of the fourth and the opening of the third century BCE, Kautilya (also known as Chanakya), an Indian philosopher, economist, prime minister, and royal counsellor contributed largely to the Sanskrit treatise, *The Arthashastra*, in which he argued that the rule of law alone 'can guarantee security of life and the welfare of the people'.[7] Asoka the Great, the third king of the Mauryan dynasty who ruled a 'vast, powerful, and multi-ethnic Indian subcontinent' for nearly forty years in the third century BCE, issued the far-sighted Edicts of Asoka. These stipulated 'equal protection under the law regardless of political belief or caste, respect for all life, environmental protection, humanitarian assistance for those who suffer, humane treatment of employees and servants, the hearing of petitions and the administration of justice; the banning of slavery, the right to be free from "harsh or cruel" punishment, and the possibility of amnesty from the death penalty'.[8]

0.04 In contrast, for centuries Europe was less prominent in articulating a notion of rights or some form of protection of the weak. In the late third century and early second century BCE, Stoic philosophers argued that the laws of nature dictated ethical rules to all human beings. Zeno of Citium, one of the founders of Stoicism, insisted on the worth and dignity of each human life.[9] In Rome, the jus gentium – the law of peoples – recognised certain rights as pertaining to all human beings.[10] But this early concept of a law of nations[11] explicitly authorised slavery[12] and allowed appalling brutality to be perpetrated against individuals – especially, but not only, non-Romans.[13] In the fifth century CE, however, Justinian's *Institutes* foresaw justice as 'an unswerving and perpetual determination to acknowledge all men's rights'.[14] The Qur'an refers to the sanctity of life and respect for all human beings, rooted in the obligations that believers owe to Allah.[15]

[6] Cited in the United Nations Educational, Scientific and Cultural Organization (UNESCO), *The Birthright of Man*, Paris, 1969, p. 303.
[7] Lauren, 'The Foundations of Justice and Human Rights in Early Legal Texts and Thought', p. 171, citing Kautilya, *The Arthashastra*, transl. L. N. Rangarajan, Penguin, London, 1987, p. 119.
[8] Lauren, 'The Foundations of Justice and Human Rights in Early Legal Texts and Thought', p. 171.
[9] Ibid., pp. 173–4.
[10] See, e.g., D. M. Jackson, 'Jus Gentium', in D. K. Chatterjee (ed.), *Encyclopedia of Global Justice*, Springer, 2011, available at http://bit.ly/3m3GwJC.
[11] On the relationship between jus gentium and the law of nations, see, e.g., G. E. Sherman, 'Jus Gentium and International Law', *American Journal of International Law*, vol. 12, no. 1 (January 1918), pp. 56–63.
[12] Gaius's *Institutes of Roman Law*, Book I: Status or Unequal Rights (De Personis), text at http://bit.ly/33dYQbu, §52; see also J. Allain, 'On Slavery and the Law of Nations – from Slavery in International Law', chap. 1 in *Slavery in International Law: Of Human Exploitation and Trafficking*, Martinus Nijhoff, January 2013, pp. 9–56, available on ResearchGate at http://bit.ly/3fwijZY.
[13] See, e.g., V. V. Palmer, 'Empires as Engines of Mixed Legal Systems', Working Paper No. 17-13, Public Law and Legal Theory Working Paper Series, Tulane University School of Law, August 2017, available on SSRN at http://bit.ly/3nYsc5A.
[14] Lauren, 'The Foundations of Justice and Human Rights in Early Legal Texts and Thought', p. 175, citing P. Birks and G. McLeod's translation of Justinian's Institutes, published by Cornell University Press, Ithaca, 1987, p. 37.
[15] Lauren, 'The Foundations of Justice and Human Rights in Early Legal Texts and Thought', p. 168.

0.05 The right to life, as such, did not find its way into the *Magna Carta* in thirteenth-century England. That said, recognised therein were the right to trial by jury and the prohibition of the use of force without judicial writ, clearly means by which the right to life may be safeguarded.[16] Likewise, the 1689 Bill of Rights in England did not refer to the right to life, though it did outlaw the infliction of 'cruel and unusual punishments'.[17] At the same moment in history, however, helping to spur the natural law that typified the Age of Enlightenment,[18] philosopher John Locke published his two treatises of government in which he asserted that every individual, irrespective of his circumstances, possesses

> a title to perfect freedom and uncontrolled enjoyment of all the rights and privileges of the law of nature equally with every other man or number of men in the world and has by nature a power not only to preserve his property – that is his life, liberty, and estate – against the injuries and attempts of other men, but to judge and punish the breaches of that law in others.[19]

In this regard, in his *Philosophical Dictionary* of 1764, Voltaire – who did much to spread the philosophy of Locke in France[20] – praised the British Constitution for having 'arrived at that point of excellence' wherein man was 'restored' to his natural rights, which comprised 'entire liberty of person and property'.[21]

0.06 The first legal document in which the right to life was explicitly enunciated, however, was the 1776 Virginia Declaration of Rights in the United States.[22] The Declaration of Rights was largely drafted by George Mason, a Virginian planter and politician (and slave owner), who introduced it at the Fifth Virginia Convention in Williamsburg.[23] The Declaration, which was adopted by unanimous vote on 12 June 1776, affirmed that 'all men are by nature equally free and independent, and have certain inherent rights, of which, when they enter into a state of society, they cannot, by any compact, deprive or divest their posterity; namely, the enjoyment of life and liberty'.

0.07 The Virginia Declaration of Rights served as the basis for Thomas Jefferson's draft text for the Declaration of Independence, which referred to 'rights inherent & inalienable, among which are the preservation of life'. Following revisions by the four other members of the 'Committee of Five' (John Adams, Benjamin Franklin, Robert Livingston, and Roger Sherman), the second paragraph of the first article in the 1776 Declaration of Independence famously stated, 'We hold these truths to be self-evident, that all men are

---

[16] Art. 39, *Magna Carta*; concluded at Runnymede, England, 15 June 1215, text available at http://bit.ly/2z5qYyB.
[17] An Act Declaring the Rights and Liberties of the Subject and Settling the Succession of the Crown; received royal assent, 16 December 1689, available at http://bit.ly/2PlgeGw.
[18] A. Gottlieb, *The Dream of Enlightenment*, Penguin, London, 2017, pp. 133–4.
[19] J. Locke, *Two Treatises of Government*, Hafner Library of Classics, New York, 1947, p. 163.
[20] B. Russell, *History of Western Philosophy*, Routledge (Republication), London, 2004, pp. 552, 584.
[21] Reproduced in 'The Philosophical Background', in Laqueur and Rubin (eds.), *The Human Rights Reader*, p. 79.
[22] Text available at http://bit.ly/2OCbG9k.
[23] See, e.g., P. Wallenstein, 'Flawed Keepers of the Flame: The Interpreters of George Mason', *Virginia Magazine of History and Biography*, vol. 102 (April 1994), pp. 229–60, at 253.

created equal, that they are endowed by their Creator with certain unalienable Rights, that among these are Life, Liberty and the pursuit of Happiness.'

Surprisingly, the 1789 Declaration of the Rights of Man promulgated in France did not explicitly protect the right to life, though it did refer to the right to security as one of the 'natural and imprescriptible rights'.[24]

0.08 In 1790, Mary Wollstonecraft published *A Vindication of the Rights of Woman: with Strictures on Political and Moral Subjects*. Therein, she asserted that women were human beings who deserved the same fundamental rights as men, declaring: 'I shall first consider women in the grand light of human creatures, who, in common with men, are placed on this earth to unfold their faculties.'[25] She went on to advocate that 'if the abstract rights of man will bear discussion and explanation, those of woman, by a parity of reasoning, will not shrink from the same test'.[26] Issued over the following two years, in Parts I and II of *Rights of Man*, Thomas Paine delivered an explicit rebuttal to Edmund Burke's attack on the French Revolution, arguing that human rights depend on nature and asserting that the role of an elected government is to protect the family and their inherent rights.[27]

0.09 In the aftermath of the First World War, the protection of minority rights became an issue of concern in the League of Nations. Eloquently described by Julius Stone in his 1932 tome, *International Guarantees of Minority Rights*, published by Oxford University Press,[28] the League protected the lives of members of minorities in both general and dedicated treaties. Thus, for example, under Article 63 of the Treaty of Saint-Germain-en-Laye of 10 September 1919, Austria undertook 'to assure full and complete protection of life and liberty to all inhabitants of Austria without distinction of birth, nationality, language, race or religion'. Under the Minorities Treaty of 28 June 1919, both Germany and Poland made similar undertakings with respect to minorities in Upper Silesia.[29]

0.10 But outside the protection of minorities and even then only in 'extreme cases in which a government treated a racial or religious minority with such cruelty that it repulsed the conscience of the rest of the world',[30] States were loath to see international law intervene into domestic matters of concern. Thus Colon-Collazo recalled a proposal by Chile in the 1936 Inter-American Conference for the Maintenance of Peace that each American republic agree to recognise 'the right of every individual to life, liberty, and the free exercise of his religion'. The proposal was rejected on the basis that it was 'too

---

[24] Art. 2, Declaration of the Rights of Man; approved by the National Assembly of France, 26 August 1789, text available at http://bit.ly/2RL9ZZ8.
[25] British Library, 'Mary Wollstonecraft, A Vindication of the Rights of Woman', at http://bit.ly/2ITsrj7.
[26] M. Wollstonecraft, *The Rights of Woman*, Everyman edition, Dents, London, 1929, p. 11.
[27] British Library, 'Rights of Man by Thomas Paine', at http://bit.ly/3lJHs5K.
[28] J. Stone, *International Guarantees of Minority Rights: Procedure of the Council of the League of Nations in Theory and Practice*, Oxford University Press, London, 1932. See also H. Rosting, 'Protection of Minorities by the League of Nations', *American Journal of International Law*, vol. 17, no. 4 (October 1923), pp. 641–60.
[29] See also Permanent Court of International Justice, *Rights of Minorities in Upper Silesia (Minority Schools)*, Germany v. Poland, Judgment (No. 12), 26 April 1928, available at http://bit.ly/32WWhdX.
[30] J. Colon-Collazo, 'II. The Drafting History of Treaty Provisions on the Right to Life', in B. G. Ramcharan (ed.), *The Right to Life under International Law*, Martinus Nijhoff, Dordrecht, 1985, pp. 33–4.

revolutionary'.[31] It was the barbaric actions of Nazi Germany that would instigate acceptance of the need for such a revolution.

0.11 As the descriptor indicates, however, human rights continue to inhere only in human beings. For the sake of clarity, the American Convention on Human Rights even confirms in its text that '"person" means every human being'.[32] Maurice Cranston postulates:

> No one wants to die a violent death or be injured or bound. These aversions are so naturally felt that we speak of them as natural. ... Unlike lobsters or porcupines, *homo sapiens* has no physical defenses in his own body. The strongest man on earth can, while he is asleep, easily be killed or be injured or captured. This vulnerability gives a special urgency to his desire to avoid such fates.[33]

Animal rights – the notion that animals are also entitled to respect for their own existence and that their cruel treatment is prohibited[34] – are not recognised by contemporary international law.

0.12 The human right to life ordinarily begins at birth, although the American Convention on Human Rights explicitly protects it 'in general, from the moment of conception'.[35] The right is also, in effect, extinguished at death, although nowhere is that made explicit nor indeed is the notion itself defined. In the Minnesota Protocol on the Investigation of Potentially Unlawful Death (2016), death is defined as 'the irreversible cessation of all vital functions, including brain activity'.[36] Janus was the god of beginnings and ends in Roman mythology: the 'god who looked both ways'.[37] Like the Roman God, Janus, on the cover of the book, the right to life looks both forward and back in time. When it is suspected that death has been caused unlawfully, consideration of the right to life assesses whether the deprivation of life has been arbitrary. During life, the right needs protection, demanding all reasonable effort to prevent avoidable death.

---

[31] Ibid., p. 33.
[32] Art. 1(2), American Convention on Human Rights; adopted at San José 22 November 1969; entered into force 18 July 1978.
[33] M. Cranston, 'What Are Human Rights?', in Laqueur and Rubin (eds.), *The Human Rights Reader*, pp. 21–2.
[34] See, e.g., A. Taylor, *Animals and Ethics: An Overview of the Philosophical Debate*, 3rd ed., Broadview Press, Toronto.
[35] Art. 4(1), American Convention on Human Rights.
[36] Minnesota Protocol on the Investigation of Potentially Unlawful Death (2016), Office of the UN High Commissioner for Human Rights, New York/Geneva, 2017, Glossary. 'Death is "natural" when it is caused solely by disease and/or the ageing process. It is "unnatural" when its causes are external, such as intentional injury (homicide, suicide), negligence, or unintentional injury (death by accident).'
[37] World History Encyclopedia, 'Janus', at https://bit.ly/39dc4Z3.

PART I

Overview of the Right to Life under International Law

1

The Status of the Right to Life

INTRODUCTION

1.01 This chapter describes the international legal status of the right to life and both its substantive and procedural elements. It was in 1945 that fundamental human rights, such as the right to life, were first reflected in international law. The Charter of the United Nations (UN Charter)[1] was adopted following, and predominantly in response to, the ravages of the Second World War and the Holocaust. The preamble to the Charter noted the determination of the peoples of the United Nations 'to reaffirm faith in fundamental human rights . . . [and] in the dignity and worth of the human person'.[2]

1.02 One of the declared purposes of the global body is to achieve international cooperation in 'promoting and encouraging respect for human rights and for fundamental freedoms for all without distinction as to race, sex, language, or religion'.[3] UN member States further undertake 'to take joint and separate action' in cooperation with the United Nations, with a view to achieve 'universal respect for, and observance of, human rights and fundamental freedoms for all without distinction as to race, sex, language, or religion'.[4] Aside from this evocation of the prohibition of discrimination, however, the Charter does not identify which human rights and fundamental freedoms are to be respected.

1.03 In 1948, the Universal Declaration of Human Rights[5] addressed this obvious lacuna. Article 3 of the Declaration affirms that 'everyone has the right to life, liberty and security of person'. The Universal Declaration of Human Rights is ostensibly a soft-law instrument, without direct legally binding force, although many, if not all, of the Declaration's articles

---

[1] Charter of the United Nations; adopted at San Francisco 26 June 1945; entered into force 24 October 1945 (hereinafter, UN Charter). As of 1 May 2021, there were 193 UN member States: 49 States were formally party to the UN Charter and a further 144 were admitted to the United Nations on the basis of Article 4 of the UN Charter, having declared their acceptance of the obligations contained in the Charter.
[2] UN Charter, second preambular para.
[3] Art. 1(3), UN Charter.
[4] Arts. 56 and 55(c), UN Charter.
[5] Universal Declaration of Human Rights; adopted at Paris, by UN General Assembly Resolution 217, 10 December 1948. Resolution 217 was adopted by forty-eight votes to zero with eight abstentions (Byelorussian SSR, Czechoslovakia, Poland, Saudi Arabia, South Africa, Soviet Union, Ukrainian SSR, and Yugoslavia). Honduras and Yemen did not take part in the vote.

are reflective of customary law.[6] The Convention on the Prevention and Punishment of the Crime of Genocide (the Genocide Convention),[7] adopted by the UN General Assembly the same year as the Universal Declaration, is a treaty with explicit legal obligations to prevent and repress widespread violations of the right to life when committed with the requisite intent to destroy, in whole or in part, a minority.[8] This is so, even though the text of the Convention does not specifically refer to the right to life.

1.04 Adopted a year later, the four 1949 Geneva Conventions prohibit the wilful killing of 'protected persons' in situations of international armed conflict, including sick, wounded, or shipwrecked combatants and civilians in occupied territory, making such killing a crime of compulsory universal jurisdiction.[9] In non-international armed conflict, Article 3 common to the 1949 Geneva Conventions[10] provides that in such situations, 'violence to life and person, in particular murder of all kinds' against anyone 'taking no active part in the hostilities' is 'and shall remain prohibited at any time and in any place whatsoever'.[11] Further, the 'carrying out of executions without previous judgment pronounced by a regularly constituted court, affording all the judicial guarantees which are recognized as indispensable by civilized peoples',[12] is also prohibited (and is a war crime under the jurisdiction of the International Criminal Court).[13] Although, of course, the Geneva Conventions are instruments of international humanitarian law and not human rights treaties, the effect of these common provisions is to protect the life of all those who are not directly participating in hostilities in connection with an armed conflict.

---

[6] See, for example, H. Charlesworth, 'Universal Declaration of Human Rights (1948)', *Max Planck Encyclopedia of Public International Law*, February 2008, paras. 13–18, at http://bit.ly/2zKA9nC; and H. Hannum, 'The Status of the Universal Declaration of Human Rights in National and International Law', *Georgia Journal of International and Comparative Law*, vol. 25 (1995–96), pp. 287–397, available at http://bit.ly/2DgGyKw.

[7] Convention on the Prevention and Punishment of the Crime of Genocide; adopted at New York, by UN General Assembly Resolution, 9 December 1948; entered into force 12 January 1951. As of 1 May 2021, 152 States were party to the Convention, the latest to adhere being Mauritius, on 8 July 2019. One further State, the Dominican Republic, is a signatory.

[8] The Convention specifies that genocide is any of a series of acts committed with the *dolus specialis* of 'intent to destroy, in whole or in part, a national, ethnical, racial or religious group, as such'. Art. 2, 1948 Genocide Convention.

[9] For example, Arts. 146 and 147, Convention (IV) relative to the Protection of Civilian Persons in Time of War; adopted at Geneva 12 August 1949; entered into force 21 October 1950.

[10] Common Article 3 applies to non-international armed conflicts, but in its judgment in the *Nicaragua* case, the International Court of Justice (ICJ) affirmed that there 'is no doubt that', in the event of international armed conflicts, the rules contained therein 'also constitute a minimum yardstick, in addition to the more elaborate rules which are also to apply to international conflicts'. ICJ, *Case Concerning Military and Paramilitary Activities in and against Nicaragua (Nicaragua v. United States of America)* Judgment (Merits), 27 June 1986 (hereinafter, ICJ, *Nicaragua* judgment), para. 218.

[11] For example, Art. 3, Convention (I) for the Amelioration of the Condition of the Wounded and Sick in Armed Forces in the Field; adopted at Geneva 12 August 1949; entered into force 21 October 1950.

[12] Ibid.

[13] Art. 8(2)(c)(iv), Rome Statute of the International Criminal Court; adopted at Rome 17 July 1998; entered into force 1 July 2002. As of 1 May 2021, 123 States were party to the Convention and a further 31 States were signatories (although four – Israel, Russia, Sudan, and the United States – had declared that they would not be ratifying the Rome Statute).

1.05 The American Declaration on the Rights and Duties of Man, also known as the Bogota Declaration, was adopted on 2 May 1948, preceding by seven months the promulgation of the Universal Declaration of Human Rights. Article I of the Bogota Declaration stipulates that 'every human being has the right to life'. In 1950, the Convention for the Protection of Human Rights and Fundamental Freedoms (better known as the European Convention on Human Rights),[14] a regional human rights treaty adopted by the Council of Europe, explicitly recognised the right to life, stipulating that 'everyone's right to life shall be protected by law. No one shall be deprived of his life intentionally save in the execution of a sentence of a court following his conviction of a crime for which this penalty is provided by law.'[15] As of 1 May 2021, forty-seven States were party to the Convention.[16] But it would not be until 1966, with the adoption by the UN General Assembly of the International Covenant on Civil and Political Rights, that the right to life would be instituted as a global treaty norm in the modern era.

THE RIGHT TO LIFE AS A TREATY NORM

1.06 A treaty is the first of three primary sources of international law listed by the Statute of the International Court of Justice that the Court is obligated to apply with a view to resolving disputes as to the tenets of international law.[17] Treaties – 'international conventions, whether general or particular', in the words of the Statute – are defined in the 1969 Vienna Convention on the Law of Treaties as an 'international agreement concluded between States in written form and governed by international law, whether embodied in a single instrument or in two or more related instruments and whatever its particular designation'.[18]

1.07 First and foremost in global treaty law with respect to the right to life is the International Covenant on Civil and Political Rights (ICCPR). The ICCPR was adopted by the UN General Assembly in New York on 16 December 1966,[19] entering into force a decade later on 23 March 1976. As of 1 May 2021, it had a total of 173 States Parties.[20] The

---

[14] Convention for the Protection of Human Rights and Fundamental Freedoms; adopted at Rome, by the Council of Europe, 4 November 1950; entered into force 3 September 1953.

[15] Art. 2(1), 1950 European Convention on Human Rights.

[16] Albania, Andorra, Armenia, Austria, Azerbaijan, Belgium, Bosnia and Herzegovina, Bulgaria, Croatia, Cyprus, Czechia, Denmark, Estonia, Finland, France, Georgia, Germany, Greece, Hungary, Iceland, Ireland, Italy, Latvia, Liechtenstein, Lithuania, Luxembourg, Malta, Moldova, Monaco, Montenegro, the Netherlands, North Macedonia, Norway, Poland, Portugal, Romania, Russian Federation, San Marino, Serbia, Slovak Republic, Slovenia, Spain, Sweden, Switzerland, Turkey, Ukraine, and the United Kingdom. On the European continent, only Belarus and the Holy See are not party to the Convention.

[17] Art. 38(1), Statute of the International Court of Justice, adopted at San Francisco 24 October 1945.

[18] Art. 2(1)(a), Vienna Convention on the Law of Treaties; adopted at Vienna 23 May 1969; entered into force 27 January 1980 (VCLT). As of 1 May 2021, 116 States were party to the VCLT. A further 15 States were signatories. The VCLT largely codifies customary international law on treaties.

[19] UN General Assembly Resolution 2200A (XXI), adopted on 16 December 1966 by 104 votes to 0.

[20] Afghanistan, Albania, Algeria, Andorra, Angola, Antigua and Barbuda, Argentina, Armenia, Australia, Austria, Azerbaijan, Bahamas, Bahrain, Bangladesh, Barbados, Belarus, Belgium, Belize, Benin, Bolivia, Bosnia and Herzegovina, Botswana, Brazil, Bulgaria, Burkina Faso, Burundi, Cambodia, Cameroon, Canada, Cape Verde, Central African Republic, Chad, Chile, Colombia, Democratic Republic of Congo, Republic of Congo, Costa Rica, Côte d'Ivoire, Croatia, Cyprus, the Czech Republic, Denmark, Djibouti,

following States were not party to the Covenant as of writing: Bhutan, Brunei, China (a signatory),[21] Comoros (a signatory), Cook Islands, Cuba (a signatory), Holy See, Kiribati, Malaysia, Micronesia, Myanmar, Nauru (a signatory), Niue, Oman, Palau (a signatory), Saint Kitts and Nevis, Saint Lucia (a signatory), Saudi Arabia, Singapore, the Solomon Islands, South Sudan, Tonga, Tuvalu, and the United Arab Emirates.[22]

1.08 Article 6(1) of the ICCPR stipulates that 'every human being has the inherent right to life. This right shall be protected by law. No one shall be arbitrarily deprived of his life.' No derogation from these provisions is possible, even in a 'time of public emergency which threatens the life of the nation and the existence of which is officially proclaimed'.[23] The central importance of this provision under international law can be seen in the fact that, when assessing the legality of the threat or use of nuclear weapons under international human rights law for the purpose of an Advisory Opinion, the International Court of Justice specifically considered and applied Article 6 of the Covenant.[24]

1.09 The Human Rights Committee, tasked with oversight of the implementation of the ICCPR by the Covenant's States Parties,[25] has issued three General Comments on the right to life. In its first General Comment on the right to life (No. 6), issued in 1982, the

---

Dominica, the Dominican Republic, East Timor, Ecuador, Egypt, El Salvador, Equatorial Guinea, Eritrea, Estonia, Eswatini, Ethiopia, Fiji, Finland, France, Gabon, The Gambia, Georgia, Germany, Ghana, Greece, Grenada, Guatemala, Guinea, Guinea-Bissau, Guyana, Haiti, Hungary, Iceland, India, Indonesia, Iran, Iraq, Ireland, Israel, Italy, Jamaica, Japan, Jordan, Kazakhstan, Kenya, the Democratic People's Republic of Korea, the Republic of Korea, Kuwait, Kyrgyzstan, the Lao People's Democratic Republic, Latvia, Lebanon, Lesotho, Liberia, Libya, Liechtenstein, Lithuania, Luxembourg, the former Yugoslav Republic of Macedonia, Madagascar, Malawi, Maldives, Mali, Malta, Marshall Islands, Mauritania, Mauritius, Mexico, the Republic of Moldova, Monaco, Mongolia, Montenegro, Morocco, Mozambique, Namibia, Nepal, the Netherlands, New Zealand, Nicaragua, Niger, Nigeria, Norway, Pakistan, Palestine, Panama, Papua New Guinea, Paraguay, Peru, Philippines, Poland, Portugal, Qatar, Romania, Russian Federation, Rwanda, Saint Vincent and the Grenadines, Samoa, San Marino, São Tomé and Príncipe, Senegal, Serbia, Seychelles, Sierra Leone, Slovakia, Slovenia, Somalia, South Africa, Spain, Sri Lanka, Sudan, Suriname, Sweden, Switzerland, Syria, Tajikistan, Tanzania, Thailand, Togo, Trinidad and Tobago, Tunisia, Turkey, Turkmenistan, Uganda, Ukraine, United Kingdom, United States of America, Uruguay, Uzbekistan, Vanuatu, Venezuela, Vietnam (also written Viet Nam), Yemen, Zambia, and Zimbabwe.

[21] The Secretary-General of the United Nations, as the depositary of the ICCPR, notes that 'upon resuming the exercise of sovereignty over Hong Kong [in 1997], China notified the Secretary-General that the Covenant will also apply to the Hong Kong Special Administrative Region'. The Covenant had been applied to Hong Kong by the United Kingdom while Hong Kong was under its jurisdiction. Hong Kong is a partial subject of international law, with authority to conclude treaties under the name 'Hong Kong, China'. Given Article 48 of the ICCPR, however, which limits adherence to States, it is unclear by which means under international law the region is a party to the Covenant.

[22] Article 48(1) provides that the Covenant is open for signature by any UN 'member state *or the member of any of the specialised agencies*', by any State Party to the Statute of the ICJ, 'and by any other State which has been invited by the General Assembly of the United Nations' to become a party to the Covenant (emphasis added). Thus, while the ICCPR does not apply the 'all States' formula employed in many other global human rights treaties, its provision on adherence is tantamount to an embrace of those 197 States that the UN Secretary-General believes are encompassed by the formula (193 UN member States, 2 observer States, and 2 other States: Cook Islands and Niue).

[23] Art. 4(1) and (2), ICCPR.

[24] International Court of Justice, *Legality of the Threat or Use of Nuclear Weapons*, Advisory Opinion, 8 July 1996, paras. 24 and 25.

[25] See Arts. 28–45, ICCPR, for details on the operation of the Committee.

Committee described the right to life as 'the supreme right from which no derogation is permitted even in time of public emergency which threatens the life of the nation'.[26] Two years later, the Committee adopted a second General Comment on the right to life (No. 14), reiterating this description.[27] At the end of October 2018, the Committee issued its third – and by far the most elaborate – General Comment on Article 6. General Comment No. 36 explicitly replaces the two earlier General Comments (Nos. 6 and 14).[28]

1.10 In its General Comment No. 36, the Committee again describes the right to life as the 'supreme right from which no derogation is permitted', noting that this is so 'even in situations of armed conflict and other public emergencies which threaten the life of the nation'.[29] The right to life, the Committee observes,

> has crucial importance both for individuals and for society as a whole. It is most precious for its own sake as a right that inheres in every human being, but it also constitutes a fundamental right whose effective protection is the prerequisite for the enjoyment of all other human rights and whose content can be informed by other human rights.[30]

In its views, expressed in 1985 in relation to the case of *Baboeram Adhin v. Suriname*, the Committee stated that the right enshrined in Article 6 'is the supreme right of the human being' and that, therefore, 'the deprivation of life by the authorities of the State is a matter of the utmost gravity'.[31] Given its view that the victims in the case had been arbitrarily deprived of their lives contrary to paragraph 1 of Article 6, the Committee did 'not find it necessary to consider assertions that other provisions of the Covenant were violated'.[32]

1.11 The notion of a hierarchy of rights might be open to question, but the portrayal of the right to life, at least under the Covenant, as a 'supreme right' gainsays such a stance. Theo van Boven, for instance, has asserted that while the 'interdependence and indivisibility of all human rights has become axiomatic and largely uncontested', there is 'little doubt' that the rights to life and to freedom from torture 'are more fundamental or basic than the right to rest and leisure'.[33] Judge Weeramantry, in his dissenting opinion in the International

---

[26] Human Rights Committee, General Comment No. 6: Article 6 (Right to life), adopted at the Committee's sixteenth session, 1982, para. 1.

[27] Human Rights Committee, General Comment No. 14: Article 6 (Right to life), adopted at the Committee's twenty-third session, 1984, para. 1.

[28] Human Rights Committee, 'General comment No. 36 (2018) on article 6 of the International Covenant on Civil and Political Rights, on the right to life', UN doc. CCPR/C/GC/36, 30 October 2018, para. 1. General Comment No. 36 was subsequently edited and published as UN doc. CCPR/C/GC/36 of 3 September 2019 (hereinafter, Human Rights Committee, General Comment 36 on the right to life).

[29] Ibid., para. 2, citing its Views in *Suarez de Guerrero v. Colombia* (Comm. No. R.11/45), 31 March 1982, para. 13.1; and in *Baboeram Adhin v. Suriname* (Comm. No. 146/1983), 4 April 1985, para. 14.3.

[30] Human Rights Committee, General Comment 36 on the right to life, para. 2.

[31] Human Rights Committee, *Baboeram Adhin v. Suriname*, Views adopted on 4 April 1985, para. 14.3.

[32] Ibid., para. 15.

[33] T. van Boven, 'Categories of Rights', in D. Moeckli, S. Shah, and S. Sivakumaran (eds.), *International Human Rights Law*, Oxford University Press, Oxford, 2010, p. 181.

Court of Justice's 1996 Advisory Opinion on the legality of the threat or use of nuclear weapons, categorised the right to life as 'one of the rights which constitute the irreducible core of human rights'.[34]

1.12 The primacy of the right to life is also reflected by judgments issued by the regional human rights courts. This is in relation not only to the respective human rights treaties but also, on occasion, to the status of the right in global instruments. In 2001, for instance, the Grand Chamber of the European Court of Human Rights referred in its judgment in the *Streletz* case to the 'the pre-eminence of the right to life in all international instruments on the protection of human rights'.[35] Its convergence in those instruments is 'significant', indicating that the right to life 'is an inalienable attribute of human beings and forms the supreme value in the hierarchy of human rights'.[36] Three years later, the Grand Chamber affirmed in its judgment in the *Makaratzis* case that Article 2 of the 1950 European Convention on Human Rights,[37] which 'safeguards the right to life and sets out the circumstances when deprivation of life may be justified, ranks as one of the most fundamental provisions in the Convention, from which no derogation is permitted'.[38]

1.13 The Inter-American Court of Human Rights has taken a similar position on the status of the right to life under the 1969 Inter-American Convention on Human Rights[39] (also known informally as the Pact of San José).[40] In 1999, in its judgment in the *Villagrán-Morales* case, the Court declared: 'The right to life is a fundamental human right, and the exercise of this right is essential for the exercise of all other human rights. If it is not respected, all rights lack meaning. Owing to the fundamental nature of the right to

---

[34] ICJ, *Legality of the Threat or Use of Nuclear Weapons*, Advisory Opinion, 8 July 1996, Dissenting Opinion of Judge Weeramantry, at http://bit.ly/2z1ga3V, p. 506, and cf. also p. 507.

[35] European Court of Human Rights, *Streletz, Kessler, and Krenz v. Germany*, Judgment (Grand Chamber), 22 March 2001, para. 85.

[36] Ibid., para. 94.

[37] As noted above, as of 1 May 2021, forty-seven States were party to the Convention, while only European States Belarus and Holy See were not party.

[38] European Court of Human Rights, *Makaratzis v. Greece*, Judgment (Grand Chamber), 20 December 2004, para. 56.

[39] Article 4(1) of the Convention provides that 'every person has the right to have his life respected. This right shall be protected by law and, in general, from the moment of conception. No one shall be arbitrarily deprived of his life.' American Convention on Human Rights; adopted at San José, 22 November 1969; entered into force, 18 July 1978. Article 1 of the (non-binding) 1948 American Declaration of the Rights and Duties of Man, adopted at Bogotá by the Ninth International Conference of American States, also protected the rights to life, liberty, and the security of person.

[40] As of 1 May 2021, twenty-four member States of the Organization of American States (OAS) were party to the Pact, while the remaining eleven were not. States Parties are the following: Argentina, Barbados, Bolivia, Brazil, Chile, Colombia, Costa Rica, Dominica, Dominican Republic, Ecuador, El Salvador, Grenada, Guatemala, Haiti, Honduras, Jamaica, Mexico, Nicaragua, Panama, Paraguay, Peru, Suriname, Uruguay, and Venezuela. The United States is a signatory to the Pact. Antigua and Barbuda, Bahamas, Belize, Canada, Cuba, Guyana, St. Kitts & Nevis, St. Lucia, and St. Vincent and Grenadines are States not party. Trinidad and Tobago denounced the Convention in 1998, while Venezuela denounced it in 2012. In 2019, however, Venezuela deposited its instrument of ratification. For the updated list of adherence to the Inter-American Convention on Human Rights, see http://bit.ly/2EraKCa.

life, restrictive approaches to it are inadmissible.'[41] In its judgment in the *Cruz Sánchez* case, the Court recalled that it has 'repeatedly observed that the right to life occupies a fundamental place in the American Convention, since it is the essential basis for the exercise of other rights'.[42]

1.14 In its interpretation of Article 4 of the 1981 African Charter on Human and Peoples' Rights,[43] the African Commission on Human and Peoples' Rights notes that the right to life is 'universally recognised as a foundational human right'.[44] The Commission thereafter stresses the inter-relationship with the other rights recognised in the Charter: 'In order to secure a dignified life for all, the right to life requires the realisation of all human rights recognised in the Charter, including civil, political, economic, social and cultural rights and peoples' rights, particularly the right to peace.'[45]

1.15 Article 5(1) of the 2004 Arab Charter on Human Rights[46] specifies that 'every human being has an inherent right to life'. It is further specified that 'this right shall be protected by law. No one shall be arbitrarily deprived of his life.'[47] The Arab Human Rights Committee, established under the 2004 Charter, has not elucidated its understanding of the normative status of the right to life under general international law.

1.16 The 2012 Association of South-East Asian Nations (ASEAN) Declaration on Human Rights,[48] an instrument that is not legally binding, stipulates in its Article 11 that 'every person has an inherent right to life which shall be protected by law. No person shall be deprived of life save in accordance with law.'

THE RIGHT TO LIFE AS A CUSTOMARY NORM

1.17 Custom is the second of the three primary sources of international law dictated by the Statute of the International Court of Justice for use in international legal disputes submitted to it. A norm of customary international law ordinarily binds every State. This is irrespective of whether the norm in question has been codified in a treaty and – if it has – whether any given State has adhered to that treaty.

---

[41] Inter-American Court of Human Rights, *Case of the 'Street Children' (Villagrán-Morales) v. Guatemala*, Judgment (Merits), 19 November 1999, para. 144.
[42] Inter-American Court of Human Rights, *Cruz Sánchez and others v. Peru*, Judgment (Merits, Reparation, and Costs), 17 April 2015, para. 257 (unofficial translation). In the original Spanish: 'La Corte ha indicado en reiteradas ocasiones que el derecho a la vida ocupa un lugar fundamental en la Convención Americana, por ser el presupuesto esencial para el ejercicio de los demás derechos.'
[43] African Charter on Human and Peoples' Rights ('Banjul Charter'); adopted at Nairobi, 28 June 1981; entered into force, 21 October 1986.
[44] African Commission on Human and Peoples' Rights, 'General Comment No. 3 on the African Charter on Human and Peoples' Rights: The Right to Life (Article 4)', adopted at Banjul (fifty-seventh Ordinary Session), November 2015 (hereinafter, African Commission General Comment on the right to life), para. 5.
[45] Ibid., para. 6.
[46] Arab Charter on Human Rights; adopted at Tunis, 22 May 2004; entered into force, 15 March 2008.
[47] Art. 5(2), 2004 Arab Charter on Human Rights.
[48] ASEAN Declaration on Human Rights, adopted by the Heads of State/Government of ASEAN Member States at Phnom Penh, 18 November 2012.

1.18 To qualify as a customary rule, a norm must reflect State practice and associated opinion that the norm is binding under international law.[49] State practice – occasionally known by its Latin moniker, *usus* – describes both what States do (or do not do) and, especially, how they say they act.[50] Treaty-making may constitute relevant practice.[51] The wording in the Statute of the International Court of Justice makes it clear that the requisite practice must be general among States, but does not necessarily need to be universal or 'perfect'. Thus, in its judgment on the merits in the *Nicaragua* case, the Court stated that it

> does not consider that, for a rule to be established as customary, the corresponding practice must be in absolutely rigorous conformity with the rule. In order to deduce the existence of customary rules, the Court deems it sufficient that the conduct of States should, in general, be consistent with such rules, and that instances of State conduct inconsistent with a given rule should generally have been treated as breaches of that rule, not as indications of the recognition of a new rule.[52]

1.19 The second of the two elements in the formation of custom is that the relevant State practice must be 'accepted as law'. The 'frequency, or even habitual character' of the acts (or omission) 'is not in itself enough'.[53] The requirement, described by the Latin phrase *opinio juris sive necessitatis*, is usually shortened to *opinio juris*. Thus, in its judgment in the *North Sea Continental Shelf* cases, the Court delineated the element of *opinio juris* in the following terms:

> Not only must the acts concerned amount to a settled practice, but they must also be such, or be carried out in such a way, as to be evidence of a belief that this practice is rendered obligatory by the existence of a rule of law requiring it. ... The States concerned must therefore feel that they are conforming to what amounts to a legal obligation.[54]

As the Court further recalled, many international acts, such as in the field of ceremonial and protocol, 'are performed almost invariably, but which are motivated only by considerations of courtesy, convenience or tradition, and not by any sense of legal duty'.[55] As is the case with State practice, however, *opinio juris* does not need to be universally consistent, though it must be general and settled.

---

[49] In fact, as Rosalyn Higgins (a former President of the International Court of Justice) has observed, despite the particular articulation of custom in the Statute of the International Court of Justice, its formation is not 'evidence of a general practice accepted as law', but rather depends on the existence of those two elements (State practice and *opinio juris*). R. Higgins, *Problems and Process: International Law and How We Use It*, Clarendon Press, Oxford, 1994, p. 18, citing P. Van Hoof, *Rethinking the Sources of International Law*, Deventer, the Netherlands, 1983, p. 87. Thus, as Higgins suggests, customary international law is better defined as being 'evidenced by' a general practice accepted as law.

[50] H. Thirlway, *The Sources of International Law*, Oxford University Press, Oxford, 2014, p. 66.

[51] M. N. Shaw, *International Law*, 8th ed., Cambridge University Press, Cambridge, 2017, p. 60.

[52] International Court of Justice, *Nicaragua* judgment, para. 186.

[53] International Court of Justice, *North Sea Continental Shelf Cases (Germany v. Denmark; Germany v. The Netherlands)*, Judgment, 20 February 1969, para. 77. See also ICJ, *Nicaragua* case, para. 188.

[54] International Court of Justice, *North Sea Continental Shelf Cases*, Judgment, para. 77.

[55] Ibid.

1.20 That every person without distinction has the right to life is certain. It is termed an 'inherent' right in Article 6 of the ICCPR, indicating that the provision was codifying a pre-existing customary rule. As noted above, the right to life has been recognised by regional human rights courts as 'foundational' and 'fundamental'. The African Commission on Human and Peoples' Rights has declared that the 'right not to be arbitrarily deprived of one's life is recognised as part of customary international law'.[56] The right has been termed 'supreme' by the Human Rights Committee. That it is a customary norm has also been endorsed by the world's leading international lawyers.[57] Thus, for instance, Nigel Rodley affirmed in 2010 that 'there can be little doubt that the right to life is a norm of customary international law'.[58] No State has gainsaid this affirmation. Moreover, there is no evidence that any State may lay claim to the status of persistent objector to the customary rule.[59]

THE RIGHT TO LIFE AS A PEREMPTORY NORM

1.21 While the status of the right to life's substantive prohibition on arbitrary deprivation of life under customary law is clear, its status as a peremptory norm of international law has been less certain.[60] In 2019, Dire Tladi, the International Law Commission (ILC) Special Rapporteur on peremptory norms of general international law (jus cogens) noted that there was 'some support for the peremptory character of the right to life, or at least the prohibition on the arbitrary deprivation of life'.[61] A norm of jus cogens is a customary norm that cannot be overridden by treaty and from which no derogation is possible. It is a norm accepted and recognised 'by the international community of States as a whole', which can be modified only by a subsequent norm of general international law having the same character.[62]

1.22 Chapter III of the ILC's 2001 draft articles on the responsibility of States for internationally wrongful acts is entitled 'Serious breaches of obligations under peremptory norms of general international law'.[63] The Commentary by the ILC's Special Rapporteur, James Crawford, declares that 'those peremptory norms that are clearly accepted and

---

[56] African Commission General Comment on the right to life, para. 5.
[57] As the Statute of the International Court of Justice stipulates, 'the teachings of the most highly qualified publicists of the various nations' are a 'subsidiary means for the determination of rules of law'. Art. 38(1)(d), Statute of the International Court of Justice.
[58] N. S. Rodley, 'Integrity of the Person', in D. Moeckli, S. Shah, and S. Sivakumaran (eds.), *International Human Rights Law*, Oxford University Press, Oxford, 2010, p. 221.
[59] If the breadth of *opinio juris* is such as to result in the formation of a customary rule, a State that objects to the rule may still potentially hold the status of persistent objector. ICJ, *Fisheries Case (United Kingdom v. Norway)*, Judgment, 18 December 1951, p. 19; and see, e.g., Thirlway, *The Sources of International Law*, pp. 86–88.
[60] Rodley, 'Integrity of the Person', pp. 221–2.
[61] 'Fourth report on peremptory norms of general international law (jus cogens) by Dire Tladi, Special Rapporteur', UN doc. A/CN.4/727, 31 January 2019, para. 128.
[62] Art. 53, 1969 Vienna Convention on the Law of Treaties. See also 'Second report on jus cogens by Dire Tladi, Special Rapporteur', International Law Commission, UN doc. A/CN.4/706, 16 March 2017, para. 74.
[63] Draft Articles on Responsibility of States for Internationally Wrongful Acts, Text adopted by the ILC at its fifty-third session, in 2001, and submitted to the UN General Assembly in UN doc. A/56/10.

recognized include the prohibitions of aggression, genocide, slavery, racial discrimination, crimes against humanity and torture, and the right to self-determination'.[64] While the list is not exhaustive, the absence of a reference to the right to life, or at least to summary or extrajudicial executions, is striking. In 2010, Christian Tomuschat considered the peremptory nature of the right as a whole is 'a somewhat doubtful classification' on the basis that the right to life 'is never guaranteed in an absolute manner, but is subject to restrictions established by law'.[65]

1.23 Leading global and regional human rights bodies do not share such doubts. In the *Villagrán-Morales* case, the Inter-American Court of Human Rights 'underscored' the jus cogens nature of the right to life.[66] In their separate opinions to the Inter-American Court's judgment in the same case, Judges Cançado Trindade and Abreu-Burelli agreed.[67] In 2001, the Human Rights Committee indicated that Article 6 of the ICCPR in its entirety was a peremptory norm.[68] Other authorities generally concord with this assessment, believing that the right to life is a norm of jus cogens.[69] The ILC Special Rapporteur on jus cogens has acknowledged that 'the permissibility of the death penalty is not an obstacle to the emergence of the right not to be arbitrarily deprived of life as a norm of jus cogens'.[70]

1.24 The better view is that it is indeed necessary to distinguish the normative status of the right to life *in toto* and the core, substantive prohibition of arbitrary deprivation of life. Indeed, in its latest General Comment on the right to life, the Human Rights Committee affirmed: 'Reservations with respect to the peremptory and non-derogable obligations set out in article 6 are incompatible with the object and purpose of the Covenant. In particular, no reservation to the prohibition against arbitrary deprivation of life of persons ... is permitted.'[71] In 1987 in Section 702(c) of the Restatement of the Law,

---

[64] Commentary to Article 40(3)–(5), 'Report of the ILC', GAOR, Supp. No. 10 (UN doc. A/56/10), 2001, pp. 283–4.

[65] C. Tomuschat, 'The Right to Life – Legal and Political Foundations', in C. Tomuschat, E. Lagrange, and S. Oeter (eds.), *The Right to Life*, Martinus Nijhoff, Leiden, 2010, pp. 5–6.

[66] Inter-American Court of Human Rights, *Case of the 'Street Children' (Villagrán-Morales) v. Guatemala*, Judgment (Merits), 19 November 1999, para. 139.

[67] Ibid., Separate Opinion of Judges Cançado Trindade and Abreu-Burelli, para. 2.

[68] Human Rights Committee, 'General Comment No. 29: Article 4: Derogations during a State of Emergency', adopted at its seventy-second session, UN doc. CCPR/C/21/Rev.1/Add.11, 31 August 2001, para. 11.

[69] See, e.g., Inter-American Court of Human Rights, *Myrna Mack-Chang v. Guatemala*, Judgment (Merits, Reparations, and Costs), Separate Opinion of Judge García Ramírez, 25 November 2003, para. 49; M. Nowak, *UN Covenant on Civil and Political Rights. CCPR Commentary*, Engel, Kehl am Rhein, 2005, p. 122; Federal Supreme Court (Switzerland), *Nada v. State Secretariat for Economic Affairs and Federal Department of Economic Affairs*, No. 1A 45/2007, ILDC 461, para. 7.3; A. Clapham, 'Weapons and Armed Non-State Actors', chap. 6 in S. Casey-Maslen (ed.), *Weapons under International Human Rights Law*, Cambridge University Press, Cambridge, 2014, p. 182; and Report by Angelo Vidal d'Almeida Ribero, UN Special Rapporteur on Religious Intolerance, on the Implementation of the Declaration on the Elimination of All Forms of Intolerance and of Discrimination Based on Religion or Belief, UN Commission on Human Rights, UN doc. E/CN.4/1987/35, 24 December 1986, para. 73.

[70] 'Fourth report on peremptory norms of general international law (jus cogens) by Dire Tladi, Special Rapporteur', UN doc. A/CN.4/727, 31 January 2019, para. 130.

[71] Human Rights Committee, General comment 36 on the right to life, para. 68.

Third, Foreign Relations Law of the United States, published by the American Law Institute, the prohibition of 'murder' as a customary human rights rule was described as a norm of jus cogens.[72]

1.25 No State has sought to 'derogate' by treaty from the international legal rule. When acts of arbitrary deprivation of life have been overtly committed by State authorities, they have been treated by other States as unlawful, and even as possible international crimes.[73] As Nigel Rodley opined in 2010, the 'core content of the right cannot seriously be contested as jus cogens, as must the prohibition of the death penalty without basic fair trial standards'.[74]

1.26 There is thus no possibility of entering a lawful reservation to the prohibition on arbitrary deprivation of life. The only human rights instrument that allows derogation from the right to life is the 1950 European Convention on Human Rights, and then only in a situation of international armed conflict. Thus, under Article 15(2), no derogation may be made from Article 2 on the right to life 'except in respect of deaths resulting from lawful acts of war'. Article 2 of the Convention does not use the term 'arbitrary' to define the circumstances in which the taking of life will be unlawful, which are set out in paragraph 2 of the article.[75] Thus, the 'reservation' is a procedural means to allow 'acts of war' that would not violate the prohibition on arbitrary deprivation of life.[76]

1.27 In sum, as the African Commission on Human and Peoples' Rights has stated: 'The right not to be arbitrarily deprived of one's life' is 'recognised as a jus cogens norm, universally binding at all times'.[77] This is an accurate statement of international law.[78]

---

[72] In 1990, Daniel Murphy termed the jus cogens norms delineated in Section 702 of the Third Restatement as 'certainly a safe list'. D. T. Murphy, 'The Restatement (Third)'s Human Rights Provisions: Nothing New, but Very Welcome', *International Lawyer*, vol. 24 (1990), p. 917, at 922.

[73] For instance, in February 2018, the Prosecutor of the International Criminal Court, Ms Fatou Bensouda, announced that she was opening a preliminary examination into the situation in the Philippines. She stated that 'it has been alleged that since 1 July 2016, thousands of persons have been killed for reasons related to their alleged involvement in illegal drug use or dealing. While some of such killings have reportedly occurred in the context of clashes between or within gangs, it is alleged that many of the reported incidents involved extra-judicial killings in the course of police anti-drug operations.' ICC, 'Statement of the Prosecutor of the International Criminal Court, Mrs Fatou Bensouda, on opening Preliminary Examinations into the situations in the Philippines and in Venezuela', 8 February 2018, at http://bit.ly/2PpEt6o.

[74] N. S. Rodley, 'Integrity of the Person', p. 222.

[75] 'Deprivation of life shall not be regarded as inflicted in contravention of this Article when it results from the use of force which is no more than absolutely necessary:

(a) in defence of any person from unlawful violence;
(b) in order to effect a lawful arrest or to prevent the escape of a person lawfully detained;
(c) in action lawfully taken for the purpose of quelling a riot or insurrection.'

[76] W. Schabas, *The European Convention on Human Rights: A Commentary*, Oxford University Press, Oxford, 2017, pp. 601–2.

[77] African Commission General Comment on the Right to Life, para. 5.

[78] See, also, 'Fourth Report on Peremptory Norms of General International Law (Jus Cogens) by Dire Tladi, Special Rapporteur', International Law Commission, UN doc. A/CN.4/727, 31 January 2019, para. 130.

THE RIGHT TO LIFE AS A GENERAL PRINCIPLE OF LAW

1.28 General principles of law serve as the third primary source of international law identified by the Statute of the International Court of Justice. They are generally understood to offer an opportunity to the Court to identify rules common to domestic regimes in the absence of a treaty or customary rule on a particular issue.[79] As such, therefore, the notion is potentially less relevant to an assessment of the international legal status of the right to life.

1.29 That said, the right to life is certainly a general principle of law. Three-quarters of the world's States have written Constitutions that explicitly recognise or guarantee the right to life (or at least its protection).[80] Moreover, murder (and other forms of homicide) is universally prohibited in domestic legal systems.[81] Thus, Tomuschat, despite his doubts as to the peremptory nature of the right, argues that the 'most plausible' argument is that the right 'constitutes today a general principle of international law'.[82] In its General Comment on the right to life under the African Charter, the African Commission on Human and Peoples' Rights duly stated that the right not to be arbitrarily deprived of one's life is *also* recognised as part of the general principles of law.[83]

---

[79] R. Jennings and A. Watts (eds.), *Oppenheim's International Law*, 9th ed., Longman, London, 1992, vol. 1, p. 40.

[80] This is the case with the constitutions of 158 of 197 States: Afghanistan, Albania, Andorra, Angola, Antigua and Barbuda, Armenia, Azerbaijan, Bahamas, Bangladesh, Barbados, Belarus, Belize, Benin, Bhutan, Bolivia, Bosnia and Herzegovina, Botswana, Brazil, Bulgaria, Burkina Faso, Burundi, Cabo Verde, Cambodia, Cameroon, Canada, Central African Republic, Chad, Chile, Colombia, Congo, Cook Islands, Costa Rica, Côte d'Ivoire, Croatia, Cuba, Cyprus, Czechia, Democratic Republic of the Congo, Djibouti, Dominica, Dominican Republic, Ecuador, Egypt, El Salvador, Equatorial Guinea, Eritrea, Estonia, Eswatini, Ethiopia, Fiji, Finland, The Gambia, Georgia, Germany, Ghana, Greece, Grenada, Guatemala, Guinea, Guyana, Haiti, Honduras, Hungary, India, Indonesia, Iran, Iraq, Ireland, Israel, Jamaica, Japan, Kazakhstan, Kenya, Kiribati, Kyrgyzstan, Latvia, Lesotho, Liberia, Liechtenstein, Lithuania, Madagascar, Malawi, Malaysia, Maldives, Mali, Malta, Marshall Islands, Mauritius, Mexico, Micronesia, Moldova, Mongolia, Montenegro, Morocco, Mozambique, Myanmar, Namibia, Nauru, Nepal, New Zealand, Nicaragua, Niger, Nigeria, North Macedonia, Norway, Pakistan, Palau, Panama, Papua New Guinea, Paraguay, Peru, Philippines, Poland, Portugal, Romania, Russian Federation, Rwanda, Saint Kitts and Nevis, Saint Lucia, Saint Vincent and the Grenadines, Samoa, Sao Tome and Principe, Senegal, Serbia, Seychelles, Sierra Leone, Singapore, Slovakia, Slovenia, Solomon Islands, Somalia, South Africa, South Sudan, Spain, Sudan, Suriname, Switzerland, Tajikistan, Tanzania, Thailand, Timor-Leste, Togo, Tonga, Trinidad and Tobago, Tunisia, Turkey, Turkmenistan, Tuvalu, Uganda, Ukraine, United States, Uruguay, Uzbekistan, Vanuatu, Venezuela, Vietnam, Zambia, and Zimbabwe. Analysis of information on the Law on Police Use of Force Worldwide website, https://policinglaw.info.

[81] See, e.g., with respect to the prohibition of murder in Argentina, Australia, Canada, China, Egypt, France, Germany, India, Iran, Israel, Japan, Russia, South Africa, Spain, the United Kingdom, and the United States: K. J. Heller and M. D. Dubber (eds.), *The Handbook of Comparative Criminal Law*, Stanford Law Books, Stanford, 2011, pp. 38–9, 78–9, 123–4, 165–6, 196–7, 229–30, 277, 308–9, 339–41, 380–1, 408, 435–8, 473–5, 547, 588, 589.

[82] Tomuschat, 'The Right to Life – Legal and Political Foundations', p. 16.

[83] African Commission General Comment on the right to life, para. 5.

2

The Content of the Right to Life

INTRODUCTION

2.01 This chapter outlines the content of the right to life in both its substantive and procedural elements. The 1948 Universal Declaration of Human Rights states simply that 'everyone has the right to life, liberty and security of person'.[1] The Declaration, a soft-law instrument, did not delineate the contours of the right to life; as Chapter 1 observed, the first global treaty to do so was the International Covenant on Civil and Political Rights[2] (ICCPR), in its Article 6. Paragraph 1 of Article 6 stipulates that 'every human being has the inherent right to life. This right shall be protected by law. No one shall be arbitrarily deprived of his life.'[3] The prohibition on arbitrary deprivation of life, which is at the heart of the substantive protections of the right to life under customary law, is the primary focus of this chapter. This is complemented by the duty to protect the right 'by law', which encompasses a duty to investigate alleged or suspected violations of the right.

2.02 The formulation of the right to life in the ICCPR is closely mirrored by the corresponding wording in the three regional human rights treaties that followed the Covenant's adoption in 1966. According to the 1969 Inter-American Convention on Human Rights, 'every person has the right to have his life respected. This right shall be protected by law and, in general, from the moment of conception. No one shall be arbitrarily deprived of his life.'[4] The 1981 African Charter on Human and Peoples' Rights provides that 'every human being shall be entitled to respect for his life and the

---

[1] Art. 3, Universal Declaration of Human Rights; adopted at Paris by UN General Assembly Resolution 217, resolution adopted on 10 December 1948 by forty-eight votes to zero, with eight abstentions (Byelorussian SSR, Czechoslovakia, Poland, Saudi Arabia, Ukrainian SSR, Union of South Africa, USSR, and Yugoslavia).
[2] International Covenant on Civil and Political Rights; adopted at New York 16 December 1966; entered into force 23 March 1976. The General Assembly resolution that adopted the Covenant – Resolution 2200A (XXI) – was passed by 104 votes to 0 and without abstention.
[3] As of 1 May 2021, the ICCPR had 173 States Parties. The following States are not party to the ICCPR: Bhutan, Brunei, China (a signatory), Comoros (a signatory), Cook Islands, Cuba (a signatory), Holy See, Kiribati, Malaysia, Micronesia, Myanmar, Nauru (a signatory), Niue, Oman, Palau (a signatory), Saint Kitts and Nevis, Saint Lucia (a signatory), Saudi Arabia, Singapore, the Solomon Islands, South Sudan, Tonga, Tuvalu, and the United Arab Emirates.
[4] Art. 4(1), American Convention on Human Rights; adopted at San José 22 November 1969; entered into force 18 July 1978.

integrity of his person. No one may be arbitrarily deprived of this right.'[5] The 2004 Arab Charter on Human Rights provides that 'every human being has an inherent right to life'.[6] It is further specified that 'this right shall be protected by law. No one shall be arbitrarily deprived of his life'.[7]

2.03 In contrast, the European Convention on Human Rights,[8] whose adoption in 1950 preceded the elaboration of Article 6 of the ICCPR, takes a different approach. Article 2 of the Convention provides, in part, as follows:

1. Everyone's right to life shall be protected by law. . . .
2. Deprivation of life shall not be regarded as inflicted in contravention of this Article when it results from the use of force which is no more than absolutely necessary:
   (a) in defence of any person from unlawful violence;
   (b) in order to effect a lawful arrest or to prevent the escape of a person lawfully detained;
   (c) in action lawfully taken for the purpose of quelling a riot or insurrection.

Thus the European Convention on Human Rights does not preclude 'arbitrary' deprivation of life, but rather describes conditions according to which a deprivation of life may be lawful. The contours of the protection of life have subsequently been clarified by the jurisprudence of the European Court of Human Rights.

2.04 A distinct approach with respect to the right to life of children is employed in the 1989 Convention on the Rights of the Child (CRC).[9] The CRC is the most widely ratified human rights treaty, with 196 States Parties as of writing.[10] Article 6(1) of the Convention provides that its contracting States 'recognize that every child has the inherent right to life'.[11] There was an obvious reluctance among negotiating States to refer in the Convention to the possibility for States Parties to kill children, even in a non-arbitrary and lawful manner, so there is no corresponding prohibition on arbitrary deprivation of life. Instead, States Parties are positively obligated to 'ensure to the maximum extent possible the survival and development of the child'.[12]

2.05 The States Parties to the Convention on the Right of Persons with Disabilities – 181 as of writing – 'reaffirm' that 'every human being has the inherent right to life and shall take all necessary measures to ensure its effective enjoyment by persons with disabilities on an

---

[5] Art. 4, African Charter on Human and Peoples' Rights; adopted at Nairobi 27 June 1981; entered into force 21 October 1986.
[6] Art. 5(1), Arab Charter on Human Rights; adopted at Tunis 22 May 2004; entered into force 15 March 2008.
[7] Art. 5(2), 2004 Arab Charter on Human Rights.
[8] Convention for the Protection of Human Rights and Fundamental Freedoms; adopted at Rome 4 November 1950; entered into force 3 September 1953.
[9] Convention on the Rights of the Child; adopted at New York 20 November 1989; entered into force 2 September 1990.
[10] Only the United States of America, a signatory, is not a State Party to the Convention.
[11] The description of the right as 'inherent', repeating the language of Article 6(1) of the ICCPR, attests to its customary nature under international law.
[12] Art. 6(2), CRC.

equal basis with others'.[13] The International Convention on the Protection of the Rights of All Migrant Workers and Members of Their Families provides that 'the right to life of migrant workers and members of their families shall be protected by law'.[14]

2.06 As noted above, the duty to protect by law the right to life is the underlying basis for the procedural element of the right. This duty, the Human Rights Committee stipulates in its General Comment 36 on the right to life, 'entails that any substantive ground for deprivation of life must be prescribed by law'.[15] In addition, it obligates States Parties to the ICCPR to

> organize all State organs and governance structures through which public authority is exercised in a manner consistent with the need to respect and ensure the right to life, ... including establishing by law adequate institutions and procedures for preventing deprivation of life, investigating and prosecuting potential cases of unlawful deprivation of life, meting out punishment and providing full reparation.[16]

The duties upon States to both base their forcible actions on a legal basis and to investigate any alleged violations are thus central to the protection 'by law' of the right to life, as this chapter describes.

2.07 Also of note is the fact that the right to life has come to be generally understood in terms of the 'respect, protect, fulfil' tripartite typology. This categorisation emanated from the field of economic, social, and cultural rights,[17] but has been transported into doctrinal understanding of, at least, fundamental civil and political rights.[18] Thus States not only have an obligation to respect and protect the right to life; they must also fulfil (i.e., promote and facilitate) its enjoyment. Fulfilment of the right to life comprises actions such as enabling social and economic development, including social inclusion; combating poverty and inequality; and other actions that promote human dignity and reduce vulnerability to harm. As Manfred Nowak has affirmed, the duty to 'ensure' human rights set out in Article 2(1) of the ICCPR comprises a duty both to protect and to fulfil human rights.[19]

---

[13] Art. 10, Convention on the Rights of Persons with Disabilities; adopted at New York 13 December 2006; entered into force 3 May 2008. As of 1 May 2021, 181 States and the European Union were party to the Convention and a further 9 States were signatories.

[14] Art. 9, International Convention on the Protection of the Rights of All Migrant Workers and Members of their Families; adopted at New York 18 December 1990; entered into force 1 July 2003. As of 1 May 2021, fifty-six States were party to the Convention and a further twelve States were signatories.

[15] Human Rights Committee, General Comment No. 36: Article 6: right to life, UN doc. CCPR/C/GC/36, 3 September 2019 (hereinafter, Human Rights Committee, General Comment 36 on the right to life), para. 19.

[16] Ibid.

[17] See, e.g., G. Giacca, *Economic, Social and Cultural Rights in Armed Conflict*, Oxford University Press, Oxford, 2014, pp. 51–2.

[18] M. Craven, *The International Covenant on Economic, Social, and Cultural Rights*, Oxford University Press, Oxford, 2002, pp. 109–10.

[19] M. Nowak, *UN Covenant on Civil and Political Rights. Commentary*, 2nd rev. ed., Engel, Kehl am Rhein, 2005, p. 37.

THE PROHIBITION OF ARBITRARY DEPRIVATION OF LIFE

2.08 Since it is only *arbitrary* deprivation of life that is prohibited by international law[20] – not deprivation of life per se – it is axiomatic that not all taking of life is unlawful. For instance, in exceptional circumstances, it is legally permissible for the State through its agents to kill a national (or the national of another State) or to act in such a manner that a person under its jurisdiction foreseeably dies. A narrowly construed possibility to deprive someone of their life is potentially open to other actors, including private individuals, most obviously where life is taken when acting in lawful self-defence or the defence of others. Private individuals may also lawfully give consent for medical assistance to be denied or withdrawn from a terminally ill relative (or another person for whom they are legally responsible), leading proximately to the patient's death. It may further not contravene international law for a person to take his or her own life (see below and Chapter 12), although this is controversial, and in any event the exercise of such a 'right', if indeed it exists, is very strictly circumscribed.

2.09 At the heart of the challenge in articulating the content of the prohibition on arbitrary deprivation of life is of course the notion of 'arbitrariness'. Under international law, a treaty term is to be 'interpreted in good faith in accordance with the ordinary meaning to be given to the terms of the treaty in their context and in light of its object and purpose'.[21] In addition, a 'special meaning shall be given to a term if it is established that the parties so intended'.[22] These are not only conventional provisions on treaty interpretation but also reflective of customary law.[23] Ordinary dictionary definitions of the word 'arbitrary' include 'unrestrained and autocratic in the use of authority'[24] or 'based on chance rather than ... on reason' and 'using unlimited personal power without considering other people's wishes'.[25]

2.10 The employment of the term 'arbitrary' in the ICCPR was not achieved without opposition. Its potential inclusion was criticised prior to the adoption of the Covenant for being 'ambiguous and open to several interpretations'.[26] The Netherlands, for example,

---

[20] See Chapter 1 with regard to the customary nature of this rule.
[21] Art. 31(1), Vienna Convention on the Law of Treaties; adopted at Vienna 23 May 1969; entered into force 27 January 1980 (hereinafter, VCLT).
[22] Art. 31(4), VCLT.
[23] In 1991, the International Court of Justice declared in its *Judgment on the Arbitral Award of 31 July 1989* that Articles 31 and 32 of the Convention 'may in many respects be considered as a codification of existing customary international law'. International Court of Justice, *Case Concerning the Arbitral Award of 31 July 1989* (*Guinea-Bissau v. Senegal*), Judgment, 12 November 1991, para. 48. In 2018, the International Law Commission (ILC) submitted its Draft conclusions on subsequent agreements and subsequent practice in relation to the interpretation of treaties, in which it declared that 'Articles 31 and 32 of the Vienna Convention on the Law of Treaties set forth, respectively, the general rule of interpretation and the recourse to supplementary means of interpretation. These rules also apply as customary international law'. Conclusion 2 in ILC, *Draft conclusions on subsequent agreements and subsequent practice in relation to the interpretation of treaties*, adopted by the Commission at its seventieth session, in 2018, and submitted to the UN General Assembly in UN doc. A/73/10, para. 51.
[24] *Oxford English Dictionary* definition, at http://bit.ly/2DO7sYT.
[25] *Cambridge English Dictionary* definition, at http://bit.ly/2GLfvce.
[26] See 'Draft International Covenants on Human Rights', Annotation prepared by the UN Secretary-General, UN doc. A/2929, 1 July 1955, p. 83, para. 3; see also Y. Dinstein, 'The Right to Life, Physical Integrity and

had called for the approach to the scope of the right to life to follow that in the European Convention on Human Rights.[27] Nonetheless, the term 'arbitrary' was ultimately incorporated in the text of the ICCPR that was adopted.

2.11 In 1955, it was clarified during the negotiation of the Covenant that the term '"arbitrarily" meant both "illegally" and "unjustly"'.[28] Subsequently, the 'Committee of Experts', who had been tasked by the Committee of Ministers of the Council of Europe with interpreting the prohibition as a whole, asserted that arbitrary deprivation of life 'contained elements of unlawfulness and injustice, as well as those of capriciousness and unreasonableness'.[29] In broadly similar terms, in its General Comment 36, the Human Rights Committee stated that the notion of 'arbitrariness' is not to be equated simply with 'against the law', but more broadly understood 'to include elements of inappropriateness, injustice, lack of predictability, and due process of law'[30] as well as 'elements of reasonableness, necessity, and proportionality'.[31]

2.12 That said, the central notion of the term is still one of consistency with the law. As the Human Rights Committee itself declares in its 2018 General Comment on the right to life, 'Deprivation of life is, *as a rule*, arbitrary if it is inconsistent with international law or domestic law.'[32] Were the notion of arbitrariness only a reflection of the tenets of domestic law and not also the requirements of international law, this would serve to divest the right to life of effective protection at the national level. In such a circumstance, it would theoretically be open to a domestic regime to explicitly allow the security forces to engage in, for example, summary or extrajudicial executions.

2.13 In the context of the 1981 African Charter, the African Commission on Human and Peoples' Rights similarly considers that a deprivation of life is arbitrary 'if it is impermissible under international law, or under more protective domestic law provisions. Arbitrariness should be interpreted with reference to considerations such as appropriateness, justice, predictability, reasonableness, necessity and proportionality.'[33] In its 2015 judgment in the case of *Nagmetov v. Russia*, a Chamber of the European Court of Human Rights held that Russia had violated the right to life on the basis that Russian domestic law explicitly prohibited the firing of tear-gas canisters at the head or face.[34] This finding was approved by the Grand Chamber of the Court in its judgment on

---

Liberty' in L. Henkin (ed.), *The International Bill of Rights: The Covenant on Civil and Political Rights*, 1st ed., Columbia University Press, New York, 1981, p. 116 note 13.

[27] Nowak, *UN Covenant on Civil and Political Rights. Commentary*, 2nd rev. ed., p. 111.
[28] 'Draft International Covenants on Human Rights', UN doc. A/2929, 1 July 1955, p. 83, para. 3.
[29] Nowak, *UN Covenant on Civil and Political Rights. Commentary*, 2nd rev. ed., p. 111.
[30] Human Rights Committee, *Gorji-Dinka v. Cameron*, Views (Comm. No. 1134/2002), adopted on 14 March 2005, para. 5.1; *Van Alphen v. The Netherlands*, Views (Comm. No. 305/1988), adopted on 23 July 1990, para. 5.8.
[31] Human Rights Committee, General Comment 36 on the right to life, para. 12.
[32] Ibid. (added emphasis).
[33] African Commission on Human and Peoples' Rights, 'General Comment No. 3 on the African Charter on Human and Peoples' Rights: The Right to Life (Article 4)', adopted at Banjul (57th Ordinary Session) November 2015 (hereinafter, African Commission General Comment on the right to life), para. 12.
[34] European Court of Human Rights, *Nagmetov v. Russia*, Judgment (First Section), 5 November 2015, para. 40.

Russia's appeal in 2017.[35] The African Commission further affirms that any deprivation of life that results from a violation of 'the procedural or substantive safeguards in the African Charter, including on the basis of discriminatory grounds or practices, is arbitrary and as a result unlawful'.[36]

2.14 In sum, an arbitrary deprivation of life will occur when the deprivation occurs in violation of international law or, where it is more protective of life, domestic law.[37] First and foremost, this encompasses situations where a person dies during or as a consequence of a substantive violation by a State of fundamental human rights, such as through inhumane treatment, discriminatory action, or the failure to ensure a fair trial, as well as in case of material violations of economic, social, or cultural rights. Arbitrary deprivation of life will also occur when other bodies of international law have been substantively violated, such as the law of armed conflict (LOAC)/international humanitarian law (IHL),[38] disarmament law, environmental law, or jus ad bellum. An arbitrary deprivation of life may also occur when the State has acted recklessly or unjustly or if it fails to act with due diligence to protect life. This may, for example, involve negligent action (or wilful inaction) from a public health perspective to tackle pollution or to prevent suicides, fatal accidents, or serious disease. Most obviously, as of writing, the States were still struggling to contain and suppress the global COVID-19 pandemic.

VIOLATION OF THE RIGHT TO LIFE WHERE THE VICTIM SURVIVES

2.15 As a general rule, death must have resulted for the right to life to be violated. But in addition to situations where a person dies, deliberate or reckless action that was either intended to, or was likely to, deprive a person of their life in an unlawful manner, but which did not in fact do so, may violate the right to life.

2.16 In the *Chongwe* case,[39] on which the Human Rights Committee rendered its views in November 2000, the Committee observed that Article 6(1) of the ICCPR 'entails an obligation of a State party to protect the right to life of all persons within its territory and subject to its jurisdiction'. Roger Chongwe had claimed, and Zambia as respondent State Party did not contest, that the authorities had 'authorised the use of lethal force without lawful reasons, which could have led to the killing of the author'. In the circumstances, the Committee found, Zambia had not acted in accordance with its obligation to protect Mr Chongwe's right to life under Article 6(1) of the Covenant.[40]

---

[35] European Court of Human Rights, *Nagmetov v. Russia*, Judgment (Grand Chamber), 30 March 2017, para. 47.
[36] Ibid.
[37] This means that, potentially, the protection of the right to life will be more expansive in certain States than in others. This will be so, where their domestic legal framework is especially protective of life, going beyond the dictates of international law.
[38] For the purpose of this work, these terms are to be considered synonyms.
[39] Human Rights Committee, *Rodger Chongwe v. Zambia*, UN doc. CCPR/C/70/D/821/1998, 9 November 2000.
[40] Ibid., para. 5.2.

The Content of the Right to Life

2.17 In its judgment in the *Ilhan* case, rendered earlier in 2000, the European Court of Human Rights' Grand Chamber had understood the protective nature of the right in similarly broad terms. Therein, the Court had declared that 'the degree and type of force used and the unequivocal intention or aim behind the use of force may, among other factors, be relevant in assessing whether in a particular case the State agents' actions in inflicting injury short of death must be regarded as incompatible with the object and purpose of Article 2 of the Convention'.[41]

2.18 In its later judgment in the *Acar* case, the European Court found a violation of the right to life of two applicants who 'were wounded in the course of a sustained and lethal attack with firearms which resulted in the death of eight of their fellow villagers'. The Court concluded that the applicants 'were the victims of conduct which, by its very nature, put their lives at grave risk, even though, in the event, they survived'.[42] In its subsequent judgment in the *Rochela Massacre* case, the Inter-American Court of Human Rights cited the *Acar* judgment in support of its findings of 'extraordinary circumstances that lay a foundation' for a violation of the right to life under the Inter-American Convention with respect to the three survivors of the massacre. The Court reached its decision 'taking into account the force employed, the intent and objective of the use of this force, and the situation in which the victims found themselves'.[43]

2.19 In 2015, a chamber of the European Court addressed the use of firearms against one of the applicants which did not turn out to be lethal. The Court's First Section affirmed that the text of Article 2 of the European Convention, 'read as a whole, demonstrates that it covers not only intentional killing, but also situations where it is permitted to use force which may result, as an unintended outcome, in the deprivation of life'.[44] In 2019, the Court's Grand Chamber held in the *Nicolae Virgiliu Tănase* case that it

> emerges from the Court's case-law that, where the victim was not killed but survived and where he or she does not allege any intent to kill, the criteria for a complaint to be examined under this aspect of Article 2 are, firstly, whether the person was the victim of an activity, whether public or private, which by its very nature put his or her life at real and imminent risk and, secondly, whether he or she has suffered injuries that appear life-threatening as they occur. Other factors, such as whether escaping death was purely fortuitous ... or whether the victim was infected with a potentially fatal disease ... may also come into play. The Court's assessment depends on the circumstances.

The Grand Chamber concluded that, while there was 'no general rule', it 'appears' that 'if the activity involved by its very nature is dangerous and puts a person's life at real and

---

[41] European Court of Human Rights, *Ilhan v. Turkey*, Judgment (Grand Chamber), 27 June 2000, para. 76.
[42] European Court of Human Rights, *Acar and others v. Turkey*, Judgment (Fourth Section), 24 May 2005 (as rendered final on 12 October 2005), para. 77.
[43] Inter-American Court of Human Rights, *Rochela Massacre v. Colombia*, Judgment (Merits, Reparations, and Costs), 11 May 2007, paras. 123–5.
[44] European Court of Human Rights, *Kitanovski v. North Macedonia*, Judgment (First Section), 22 January 2015, para. 53. See further *Abdulkhadzhiyeva and Abdulkhadzhiyev v. Russia*, Judgment (Third Section), 4 October 2016, paras. 70, 71.

imminent risk, like the use of life-threatening violence, the level of injuries sustained may not be decisive and, in the absence of injuries, a complaint in such cases may still fall to be examined under Article 2'.[45]

2.20 In similar terms, the African Commission on Human and Peoples' Rights has stated:

> Where a State or its agent has attempted unlawfully to kill a person, but that person survives, where it has unlawfully threatened the life of a person, or where it has forcibly caused a person to disappear and that person's fate remains unknown, in addition to the violation of other rights, a violation of the right to life has occurred.[46]

To date – and its views in the *Chongwe* case notwithstanding – the Human Rights Committee has, in practice, largely preferred to consider cases where unlawful force is used but the victim or victims survive not under Article 6 but rather under Article 7. Unlawful use of force by State agents thus generally falls to violate the Covenant within the scope of the prohibition of torture and other forms of cruel, inhuman, or degrading treatment or punishment. That said, in its General Comment 36, the Committee states that during a situation of armed conflict, 'practices inconsistent with international humanitarian law, *entailing a risk* to the lives of civilians and other persons protected by international humanitarian law, . . . would also violate article 6 of the Covenant'.[47]

VIOLATION OF THE RIGHT TO LIFE IN CASE OF ENFORCED DISAPPEARANCE

2.21 As the African Commission has declared, a violation of the right to life may occur in the event of an enforced disappearance – that is to say, where a person is deprived of liberty by agents of the State (or those acting with its support or acquiescence), where this is followed by a refusal to acknowledge the deprivation of liberty, or by concealing the fate or whereabouts of the disappeared person.[48] The disappeared person may have been summarily executed or he or she may still be alive, detained incommunicado. The 2006 International Convention for the Protection of All Persons from Enforced Disappearance does not itself refer to the right to life. But the earlier Declaration on the Protection of all Persons from Enforced Disappearance, adopted by UN General Assembly in 1992, stipulated that any act of enforced disappearance 'violates or constitutes a grave threat to the right to life'.[49]

---

[45] European Court of Human Rights, *Nicolae Virgiliu Tănase v. Romania*, Judgment (Grand Chamber), 25 June 2019, para. 140.
[46] African Commission General Comment on the right to life, para. 8.
[47] Human Rights Committee, General Comment 36 on the right to life, para. 64 (added emphasis).
[48] Art. 2, International Convention for the Protection of All Persons from Enforced Disappearance; adopted at New York, 20 December 2006; entered into force 23 December 2010. As of 1 May 2021, 63 States were party to the Convention and a further 48 States were signatories.
[49] Art. 1(2), Declaration on the Protection of all Persons from Enforced Disappearance, adopted by UN General Assembly Resolution 47/133 without a vote on 18 December 1992.

2.22 In its General Comment No. 6 on the right to life, issued in 1982, the Human Rights Committee had declared:

> States parties should also take specific and effective measures to prevent the disappearance of individuals, something which unfortunately has become all too frequent and leads too often to arbitrary deprivation of life. Furthermore, States should establish effective facilities and procedures to investigate thoroughly cases of missing and disappeared persons in circumstances which may involve a violation of the right to life.[50]

In its General Comment 36 on the right to life, however, issued in 2018, the Committee was considerably more progressive in its interpretation of Article 6 of the Covenant. Therein, the Committee stated that enforced disappearance 'in effect removes that person from the protection of the law and places his or her life at serious and constant risk', which 'thus results in a violation of the right to life as well as other rights recognized in the Covenant'.[51]

2.23 In its 2020 judgment in the *Murdalovy* case, the European Court of Human Rights noted that it has made 'findings of the presumption of death in the absence of any reliable news about disappeared persons' for periods ranging from four years to ten years and that therefore 'where a person is detained by State agents and then remains missing for more than eighteen years, that situation can be regarded as life-threatening'. The court held that the victim must be presumed dead and that a violation of the right to life by the respondent state – Russia – had occurred.[52] In the case of Article 4 of the American Convention on Human Rights, the Court considers that 'owing to the nature of enforced disappearance, the victim is in an aggravated situation of vulnerability, which gives rise to the risk that several different rights may be violated, including the right to life'.[53]

EXAMPLES OF POTENTIALLY ARBITRARY DEPRIVATION OF LIFE

The Duty to Protect the Right to Life by Law

2.24 Article 6(1) of the ICCPR provides that the right to life 'shall be protected by law'. The term *law* here refers to domestic law. Thus each of the States Parties to the Covenant is obligated to adopt new legislation or amend existing laws to guarantee the right to life. In most cases, the right to life is explicitly protected in the nation's Constitution;[54] in others, a human

---

[50] Human Rights Committee, General Comment No. 6: Article 6 (Right to life), adopted at the Committee's sixteenth session, 1982, para. 4.
[51] Human Rights Committee, General Comment 36 on the right to life, para. 58.
[52] European Court of Human Rights, *Murdalovy v. Russia*, Judgment (Third Section), 31 March 2020, paras. 44–45 and 54.
[53] Inter-American Court of Human Rights, *Osorio Rivera and Family Members v. Peru*, Judgment (Preliminary objections, merits, reparations and costs), 26 November 2013, para. 169.
[54] This is the case in the following 158 States (of a total of 197, as recognised by the UN Secretary-General and which could adhere to the ICCPR): Afghanistan, Albania, Andorra, Angola, Antigua and Barbuda, Armenia, Azerbaijan, Bahamas, Bangladesh, Barbados, Belarus, Belize, Benin, Bhutan, Bolivia, Bosnia and Herzegovina, Botswana, Brazil, Bulgaria, Burkina Faso, Burundi, Cabo Verde, Cambodia, Cameroon, Canada, Central African Republic, Chad, Chile, Colombia, Congo, Cook Islands, Costa Rica, Côte d'Ivoire, Croatia, Cuba, Cyprus, Czechia, Democratic Republic of Congo, Djibouti, Dominica,

rights act may be employed to give effect to this international legal obligation. In all, murder must be a criminal offence subject to penal sanction. Failure to do so may, in and of itself, amount to a violation. In its General Comment 36, the Human Rights Committee affirms that 'a deprivation of life that lacks a legal basis ... is, as a rule, arbitrary in nature'.[55]

2.25 In one respect, the inclusion of a specific legislative obligation in Article 6 of the Covenant may appear surprising. This is due to the fact that, under paragraph 1 of Article 2, each State Party is already obligated 'to respect and to ensure' all of the rights set out in the Covenant, while in paragraph 2 of the same article:

> Where not already provided for by existing legislative or other measures, each State Party to the present Covenant undertakes to take the necessary steps, in accordance with its constitutional processes and with the provisions of the present Covenant, to adopt such laws or other measures as may be necessary to give effect to the rights recognized in the present Covenant.

What appears at first sight to be a redundant insertion in Article 6(1) may be understood as a reiteration of the fundamental importance of the foundational and customary right to life, and of the requirement that its effective protection be grounded in domestic law.

2.26 As noted above, similar obligations are also set out in certain of the regional human rights treaties. Article 2(1) of the 1950 European Convention on Human Rights stipulates that 'everyone's right to life shall be protected by law'. Article 4(1) of the 1969 Inter-American Convention on Human Rights provides that 'every person has the right to have his life respected. This right shall be protected by law.' Article 5(2) of the 2004 Arab Charter on Human Rights similarly requires that the 'inherent' right to life 'shall be protected by law'. In contrast, no specific obligation for its legislative protection is incorporated in Article 4 of the 1981 African Charter on Human and Peoples' Rights.[56]

Dominican Republic, Ecuador, Egypt, El Salvador, Equatorial Guinea, Eritrea, Estonia, Eswatini, Ethiopia, Fiji, Finland, The Gambia, Georgia, Germany, Ghana, Greece, Grenada, Guatemala, Guinea, Guyana, Haiti, Honduras, Hungary, India, Indonesia, Iran, Iraq, Ireland, Israel, Jamaica, Japan, Kazakhstan, Kenya, Kiribati, Kyrgyzstan, Latvia, Lesotho, Liberia, Liechtenstein, Lithuania, Madagascar, Malawi, Malaysia, Maldives, Mali, Malta, Marshall Islands, Mauritius, Mexico, Micronesia, Moldova, Mongolia, Montenegro, Morocco, Mozambique, Myanmar, Namibia, Nauru, Nepal, New Zealand, Nicaragua, Niger, Nigeria, North Macedonia, Norway, Pakistan, Palau, Panama, Papua New Guinea, Paraguay, Peru, Philippines, Poland, Portugal, Romania, Russian Federation, Rwanda, Saint Kitts and Nevis, Saint Lucia, St Vincent & the Grenadines, Samoa, Sao Tome and Principe, Senegal, Serbia, Seychelles, Sierra Leone, Singapore, Slovakia, Slovenia, Solomon Islands, Somalia, South Africa, South Sudan, Spain, Sudan, Suriname, Switzerland, Tajikistan, Tanzania, Thailand, Timor-Leste, Togo, Tonga, Trinidad and Tobago, Tunisia, Turkey, Turkmenistan, Tuvalu, Uganda, Ukraine, United States, Uruguay, Uzbekistan, Vanuatu, Venezuela, Vietnam, Zambia, and Zimbabwe.

55 Human Rights Committee, General Comment 36 on the right to life, para. 11.
56 Although the African Commission's General Comment on the provision recalls that 'building blocks of a proper State system for the protection of the right to life will include the enactment of appropriate domestic laws that protect the right to life and define any limitations on the right in accordance with international standards'. African Commission General Comment on the right to life, para. 10.

The Death Penalty

2.27 A sentence of death that is executed following an unfair trial, on the basis that it either contravenes domestic law[57] or applicable international standards,[58] will automatically be arbitrary in nature. As Nigel Rodley affirmed, this norm is also a peremptory norm of international law.[59] A death sentence imposed after an unfair trial is similarly prohibited under regional human rights law. According to the African Commission, for example, any State Party to the African Charter whose criminal justice system does not 'at the time of trial or conviction' fulfil the criteria laid down in Article 7 of the African Charter[60] or where the proceedings 'have not stringently met the highest standards of fairness' will violate the right to life in any case in which the death penalty is subsequently applied.[61]

2.28 The Human Rights Committee also observes that States that have not abolished the death penalty and which are not party to the Second Optional Protocol to the ICCPR 'or other treaties providing for the abolition of the death penalty' may 'only apply the death penalty in a non-arbitrary manner, with regard to the most serious crimes and subject to a number of strict conditions'.[62] Such conditions exclude the possibility of compliance with the right to life where there are extreme delays in the execution of a death sentence, 'especially when the long time on death row exposes sentenced persons to harsh[63] or stressful conditions, including, solitary confinement,[64] and when they are particularly vulnerable due to factors such as age, health or mental state'.[65]

2.29 Also arbitrary, in the view of the Committee, would be a method of execution that itself constitutes inhumane treatment, such as stoning, injection of untested lethal drugs, the use of gas chambers, burning or burying alive, or public executions.[66] In asserting that a failure to respect Article 7 of the Covenant in the execution of the death penalty 'would inevitably render the execution arbitrary in nature and thus also in violation of article 6',[67]

---

[57] The Human Rights Committee observes in its General Comment 36 that a death sentence which is issued at the end of legal proceedings 'conducted in violation of domestic laws of criminal procedure or evidence will generally be both unlawful and arbitrary'. Human Rights Committee, General Comment 36 on the right to life, para. 11.

[58] See further Chapter 9 of this work for a detailed exposition of these standards.

[59] N. S. Rodley, 'Integrity of the Person', in D. Moeckli, S. Shah, and S. Sivakumaran (eds.), *International Human Rights Law*, Oxford University Press, Oxford, 2010, p. 222.

[60] Article 7 lays down the right to appeal; the right to be presumed innocent until proven guilty by a competent court or tribunal; the right to a defence, including the right to be defended by counsel of the defendant's choice; the right to be tried within a reasonable time by an impartial court or tribunal; and conviction only for an act or omission that constituted a legally punishable offence at the time it was committed (respecting the principle of *nullum crimen, nulla poena sine lege*).

[61] African Commission General Comment on the right to life, para. 10.

[62] Human Rights Committee, General Comment 36 on the right to life, para. 10.

[63] Human Rights Committee, *Brown v. Jamaica*, Views, 11 May 1999, paras. 6.13, 6.15.

[64] Human Rights Committee, Concluding Observations on the sixth periodic report of Japan, UN doc. CCPR/C/JPN/CO/6, 20 August 2014, para. 13.

[65] Human Rights Committee, *Kindler v. Canada*, Views, 30 July 1993, para. 15.3.

[66] Human Rights Committee, General Comment 36 on the right to life, para. 40.

[67] Ibid. See also on this issue Human Rights Committee, General Comment No. 20 on Article 7 of the ICCPR, UN doc. CCPR/C/21/Add.3, 10 March 1992, para. 6.

the Committee's interpretation of the right to life is, to some extent, a progressive development of international law.

2.30 According to Article 6(2) of the ICCPR, the death penalty may only be imposed upon conviction for a crime that is considered 'most serious'. That notion is defined strictly by the Human Rights Committee as one involving intentional killing.[68] Consequently, crimes 'not resulting directly and intentionally in death,[69] such as attempted murder,[70] corruption and other economic and political crimes,[71] armed robbery,[72] piracy,[73] abduction,[74] drug[75] and sexual offences, although serious in nature, can never serve as the basis, within the framework of article 6, for the imposition of the death penalty'.[76] Moreover, the Committee affirms that 'a limited degree of involvement or of complicity in the commission of even the most serious crimes, such as providing the physical means for the commission of murder, cannot justify the imposition of the death penalty'.[77]

USE OF FORCE IN LAW ENFORCEMENT OR COUNTERTERRORISM

2.31 As described in Chapter 7, detailed international standards govern the use of force in law enforcement. These rules apply not only to ordinary policing but also to counterterrorism operations (where these fall outside the conduct of hostilities during a situation of armed conflict; see Chapter 8 on this issue). General principles of necessity and proportionality apply to all use of force by law enforcement officials, including military or other security personnel performing law enforcement duties.[78]

2.32 The principle of necessity as it applies to law enforcement holds that any force used must be only the minimum necessary in the circumstances to achieve a legitimate law

---

[68] Human Rights Committee, General Comment 36 on the right to life, para. 35, citing its views in *Kindler* v. *Canada*, 30 July 1993, para. 14.3; and the Report of the Special Rapporteur on extrajudicial, summary, or arbitrary executions, 9 August 2012, UN doc. A/67/275, 9 August 2012, para. 35.

[69] Human Rights Committee, Concluding Observations on Iran, UN doc. CCPR/C/79/Add.25, 3 August 1993, para. 8.

[70] Human Rights Committee, *Chisanga* v. *Zambia*, Communication No. 1132/2002, views adopted on 18 October 2005, para. 7.4.

[71] Human Rights Committee, Concluding Observations on Libya (1998), para. 8; Concluding Observations on Iran (1993), para. 8; Concluding Observations on Sudan (1997), para. 8.

[72] Human Rights Committee, *Chisanga* v. *Zambia*, Views, 18 October 2005, para. 7.4; *Luboto* v. *Zambia*, Views, 31 October 1995, para. 7.2; and *Johnson* v. *Ghana*, Views, 27 March 2014, para. 7.3.

[73] Human Rights Committee, Concluding Observations on the United Kingdom, UN doc. UN doc. CCPR/CO/73/UK, 6 December 2001, para. 37.

[74] Human Rights Committee, Concluding Observations on Guatemala (2001), para. 17.

[75] Human Rights Committee, Concluding Observations on Thailand, UN doc. CCPR/CO/84/THA, 8 July 2005, para. 14.

[76] Human Rights Committee, General Comment 36 on the right to life, para. 35.

[77] Ibid.

[78] As the 1979 UN Code of Conduct for Law Enforcement Officials stipulates: 'In countries where police powers are exercised by military authorities, whether uniformed or not, or by State security forces, the definition of law enforcement officials shall be regarded as including officers of such services.' Commentary (b) on Article 1, Code of Conduct for Law Enforcement Officials; adopted at New York by UN General Assembly Resolution 34/169 (resolution adopted without a vote on 17 December 1979; hereinafter, 1979 UN Code of Conduct).

enforcement purpose.[79] The principle of proportionality dictates that the force used must be proportionate to the threat posed by an individual or group of individuals or the harm to be avoided by that use of force.[80] In the words of the UN Special Rapporteur on extrajudicial, summary, or arbitrary executions: 'If necessity can be visualized as a ladder, proportionality is a scale that determines how high up the ladder of force one is allowed to go. The force used may not go above that ceiling, even if it might otherwise be deemed "necessary" to achieve the legitimate aim.'[81]

2.33 Law enforcement officials must comply with both principles: failure to respect the tenets of either necessity or proportionality will usually mean that the victim's human rights have been violated.[82] In the words of the Office of the UN High Commissioner for Human Rights (OHCHR): 'Each use of force must be justified and justifiable.'[83] The burden of proof that the law was complied with by any given law enforcement operation ordinarily falls upon the State. As a chamber of the European Court of Human Rights reaffirmed in its 2013 judgment in *Douet v. France*, 'it is normally for the Government to provide relevant evidence that the use of force was both proportionate and necessary'.[84]

2.34 As is generally the case, the principle of legality will also determine whether a human rights violation has occurred when a law enforcement official kills a person in the course of his or her duties. Thus Principle 1 of the 1990 UN Basic Principles on the Use of Force and Firearms by Law Enforcement Officials (hereinafter, 1990 UN Basic Principles) requires governments and law enforcement agencies to 'adopt and implement rules and regulations on the use of force and firearms against persons by law enforcement officials'. As explained by a guide to police use of force and firearms published by the OHCHR and the UN Office on Drugs and Crime (UNODC):

---

[79] According to Article 3 of the UN Code of Conduct for Law Enforcement Officials, 'Law enforcement officials may use force only when strictly necessary and to the extent required for the performance of their duty.'

[80] In the official commentary on Article 3 of the 1979 UN Code of Conduct, it is stipulated: 'National law ordinarily restricts the use of force by law enforcement officials in accordance with a principle of proportionality. It is to be understood that such national principles of proportionality are to be respected in the interpretation of this provision. In no case should this provision be interpreted to authorize the use of force which is disproportionate to the legitimate objective to be achieved.' Similarly, Principle 5 of the 1990 UN Basic Principles on the Use of Force and Firearms by Law Enforcement Officials (hereinafter, 1990 UN Basic Principles) provides: 'Whenever the lawful use of force and firearms is unavoidable, law enforcement officials shall exercise restraint in such use and act in proportion to the seriousness of the offence and the legitimate objective to be achieved.'

[81] Report of the Special Rapporteur on extrajudicial, summary or arbitrary executions, UN doc. A/HRC/26/36, 1 April 2014, para. 66.

[82] S. Casey-Maslen and S. Connolly, *Police Use of Force under International Law*, Cambridge University Press, Cambridge, 2017, p. 82.

[83] OHCHR, *United Nations Human Rights Guidance on Less-Lethal Weapons in Law Enforcement*, Geneva, 2020, para. 3.7 and associated footnote.

[84] Author's translation from French original: 'De plus, il incombe normalement au Gouvernement d'apporter des preuves pertinentes démontrant que le recours à la force était à la fois proportionné et necessaire.' European Court of Human Rights, *Douet v. France*, Judgment (Fifth Section), 3 October 2013 (rendered final on 3 January 2014), para. 30, citing *Petyo Popov v. Bulgaria*, Judgment (Fifth Section), 22 January 2009, para. 54.

To prevent abuse, domestic law needs to define when law enforcement officials may use force and for what purpose. In order to safeguard against arbitrary interpretation and abuse, the provisions must be clear and unambiguous, so that they are foreseeable both to those applying them and to those that will be affected by their application, i.e. both to law enforcement officials and the public.[85]

In its 2020 judgment in the *Andreea-Marusia Dumitru* case, the European Court of Human Rights concluded that at the time of the facts in question, 'the national legislation [in Romania] did not contain . . . any provision regulating the use of firearms in the context of policing operations, apart from a duty to provide a warning, and that the law did not offer any guidance concerning the preparation and control of such operations'.[86]

2.35 Indeed, specific international legal rules reflecting the principles of necessity and proportionality apply where firearms are used. These are set out in Basic Principle 9 of the 1990 UN Basic Principles, the default rule being as follows: 'Law enforcement officials shall not use firearms against persons except in self-defence or defence of others against an imminent threat of death or serious injury . . . and only when less extreme measures are insufficient to achieve these objectives.' An imminent threat is one that is reasonably expected to materialise in, at most, a matter of seconds.[87] Exceptionally, it may be lawful to use firearms when a threat is temporally proximate but not necessarily imminent. In such as case, the threat must be both 'grave' and one that pertains to life alone. If this is not the case, an escaping suspect – or a convicted criminal – may not lawfully be shot with a view to preventing his or her flight.[88]

2.36 A heightened standard applies when any law enforcement official opens fire with intent to kill: 'In any event, intentional lethal use of firearms may only be made when strictly unavoidable in order to protect life.'[89] Imminence is integral to the notion of any action that is strictly unavoidable, and in this case, an imminent threat of serious injury will not suffice. Thus the rare examples where such intentional lethal use of force may be lawful concerns a situation where a hostage taker is about to shoot his or her hostage or a bomber is about to detonate an explosive device, whether remotely or where the bomb is body-borne. To be lawful, no reasonable alternatives to prevent those outcomes must exist to killing the hostage taker or bomber.

Use of Illegal Weapons and Unlawful Use of Weapons

2.37 Where an agent of a State uses a weapon, whether for the purpose of law enforcement or in the conduct of hostilities during an armed conflict, that weapon must be

---

[85] A. Osse, *Resource Book on the Use of Force and Firearms in Law Enforcement*, OHCHR/UNODC, New York, 2017, p. 16.
[86] European Court of Human Rights, *Andreea-Marusia Dumitru v. Romania*, Judgment (Fourth Section), 31 March 2020, para. 99 (author's translation from French original) and cf. also paras. 96–8.
[87] Report of the Special Rapporteur on extrajudicial, summary or arbitrary executions, 1 April 2014, para. 59.
[88] See, e.g., European Court of Human Rights, *Nachova v. Bulgaria*, Judgment (Grand Chamber), 6 July 2005, para. 95; and see also for possible examples of where the grave threat to life exception may apply: Casey-Maslen and Connolly, *Police Use of Force under International Law*, pp. 98–9.
[89] Basic Principle 9, 1990 UN Basic Principles.

lawful per se and, if it is, its use must also be in a lawful manner. Typically, a weapon that is outlawed by a disarmament treaty to which any given State is party may never be used. Indeed, the ordinary undertaking is expressed in terms that a State Party will 'never under any circumstances' use the weapon that the treaty prohibits. This is the case for anti-personnel mines,[90] cluster munitions,[91] and – hopefully a purely theoretical example – nuclear weapons.[92] This blanket undertaking 'applies to each State Party at all times, not merely during a situation of armed conflict. It further applies under all circumstances, even in self-defence or as a belligerent reprisal against nuclear [or other] aggression.'[93]

2.38 In contrast, the 1992 Chemical Weapons Convention,[94] which contains a similar general prohibition on use of chemical weapons,[95] nonetheless explicitly allows use of certain chemical agents, such as riot-control agents (e.g., tear gas), in law enforcement operations. This is so 'as long as the types and quantities are consistent with such purposes'.[96] Of course, in order to be used in a lawful manner, such agents must be employed in accordance with the law enforcement rules set out above.

2.39 The 1971 Biological Weapons Convention[97] does not explicitly prohibit the use of biological weapons. Under Article I of the Convention, however, its States Parties undertake 'never in any circumstances' to 'develop, produce, stockpile or otherwise acquire or retain' biological weapons.[98] In 1996, States Parties included in the Final Declaration of the Convention's fourth review conference the affirmation that use is 'effectively prohibited under Article I of the Convention'.[99]

---

[90] Art. 1(1)(a), Convention on the Prohibition of the Use, Stockpiling, Production and Transfer of Anti-Personnel Mines and on Their Destruction; adopted at Oslo 18 September 1997; entered into force 1 March 1999.

[91] Art. 1(1)(a), Convention on Cluster Munitions; adopted at Dublin 30 May 2008; entered into force 1 August 2010.

[92] Art. 1(1)(d), Treaty on the Prohibition of Nuclear Weapons; adopted at New York 7 July 2017; entered into force 22 January 2021.

[93] S. Casey-Maslen, *The Treaty on the Prohibition of Nuclear Weapons: A Commentary*, Oxford University Press, Oxford, 2019, para. 1.71.

[94] Convention on the Prohibition of the Development, Production, Stockpiling and Use of Chemical Weapons and on Their Destruction; adopted at Geneva, 3 September 1992; entered into force 29 April 1997.

[95] According to Article I(1)(b) of the Convention, each State Party 'undertakes never under any circumstances' to 'use chemical weapons'.

[96] Art. II(1)(a) and (9), 1992 Chemical Weapons Convention.

[97] Convention on the Prohibition of the Development, Production and Stockpiling of Bacteriological (Biological) and Toxin Weapons and on Their Destruction; opened for signature, 10 April 1972; entered into force 25 March 1975.

[98] Use is mentioned in a number of instances in the preamble to the Convention, among others by reference to the 1925 Geneva Protocol. In that protocol, States Parties agreed to extend an existing prohibition on the use of chemical warfare to 'the use of bacteriological methods of warfare'. Protocol for the Prohibition of the Use of Asphyxiating, Poisonous or Other Gases, and of Bacteriological Methods of Warfare; adopted at Geneva, 17 June 1925; entered into force 8 February 1928 (1925 Geneva Protocol).

[99] Fourth Review Conference of the Parties to the 1971 Biological Weapons Convention, Geneva, 25 November–6 December 1996, UN doc. BWC/CONF.4/9, Final Declaration, Commentary on Article I, para. 3.

2.40 Particular concerns have been expressed in many quarters about the remote use of force, such as through remotely piloted aircraft, more popularly known as drones.[100] These weapons platforms are used both in the conduct of hostilities in situations of armed conflict and for law enforcement, almost invariably with a view to the intentional killing of the target or targets. Such weapons platforms are not unlawful per se. The legality of their employment will depend on compliance with the applicable bodies of law. This will be, in addition to human rights law, the principles and rules governing law enforcement or the conduct of hostilities, as the case may be, and potentially also jus ad bellum: the law on inter-State use of force.

2.41 More problematic legally is where force is employed autonomously, that is to say, when decision-making on targeting and firing of weapons is effectively taken out of the hands of a human.[101] Again, this may occur within or outside the conduct of hostilities during an armed conflict. In a 2014 report to the UN Human Rights Council, the Special Rapporteur on extrajudicial, summary, or arbitrary executions observed that the autonomous use of force 'has far-reaching potential implications for human rights, notably the rights to life and human dignity, and as such it is also a human rights issue. Based on the experience with armed drones, there is also a danger that such weapons will be used outside the geographical scope of established armed conflicts'.[102] The Special Rapporteur recommended that autonomous weapons systems should remain on the agenda of the Council as well as in disarmament or humanitarian law fora.[103] It is not possible to determine with certainty, however, that an autonomous use of lethal force would always be unlawful per se.

2.42 Use of weapons in the conduct of hostilities is explicitly regulated under IHL. The inter-relationship between human rights law and IHL is explored further in Chapter 5 of the present work, but for present purposes, it is relevant to recall the general principle that if a violation of IHL has occurred by the use of a weapon (considered under that body of law to be a 'means of warfare') and a person is killed, ordinarily a violation of the right to life will also have occurred.[104] Thus, for example, if a civilian is killed by the use of an unlawful weapon (such as one that is inherently indiscriminate) or is intentionally targeted and killed by a generally lawful weapon, this will not only violate the principle of distinction under LOAC/IHL, it will also violate the right to life. Likewise, if a combatant is killed by the use of ammunition whose employment is unlawful (for instance, on the basis that it is of a nature to cause unnecessary suffering, such as is the case with an exploding bullet), or is killed unlawfully while seeking to surrender, ordinarily a violation of the right to life will also have occurred.

---

[100] See generally, e.g., S. Casey-Maslen, M. Homayounnejad, H. Stauffer, and N. Weizmann, *Drones and other Unmanned Weapons Systems under International Law*, Brill, Leiden, 2018.

[101] See generally, e.g., M. Homayounnejad, 'Lethal Autonomous Weapon Systems Under the Law of Armed Conflict', PhD thesis, King's College London, 2019.

[102] Report of the Special Rapporteur on extrajudicial, summary or arbitrary executions, 1 April 2014, para. 144.

[103] Ibid.

[104] International Court of Justice, *Legality of the Threat or Use of Nuclear Weapons*, Advisory Opinion, 8 July 1996, para. 25. Means of warfare include offensive cyber operations ('cyberattacks').

The Content of the Right to Life

2.43 In most cases, a weapon whose use is outlawed during armed conflict is outlawed also in peacetime. In exceptional cases, though, this symmetry does not exist. As noted above, this is the case with certain less-lethal toxic chemicals used in riot control. Likewise, the use of expanding ammunition, such as hollow-point or soft-point bullets, is prohibited as a means of warfare under IHL[105] (and is generally considered to be a war crime).[106] In a situation of law enforcement, however, such ammunition is lawful. Thus perhaps surprising to some, it is prohibited to use a particular form of ammunition against an enemy soldier in time of war but not against one's own citizens in peacetime.[107] Of course, such peacetime use is still subject to the rules of law enforcement, and particularly those governing the use of firearms, as discussed above.

Deaths in Custody

2.44 The risk of a death occurring in custody is especially acute. Detainees may, of course, die of natural causes and the State may not be held responsible,[108] but the risk of death as a result of violence, whether suicide or homicide, is commonly heightened compared to the outside world. A violation of the right to life may occur either because the State or its agents have failed in their duty to respect the life of a detainee – whereunder the State is held to a standard close to strict liability under tort law[109] – or because they have taken insufficient steps to protect that person's life, not only from attack by other detainees but also from suicide (or acts of self-harm that might lead to death).[110] This duty of protection is one of 'due diligence'.[111]

---

[105] Declaration (IV,3) concerning the Use of Expanding Bullets, adopted at The Hague 29 July 1899; entered into force 4 September 1900. The Declaration prohibited use between States Parties of bullets that 'expand or flatten easily in the human body, such as bullets with a hard envelope which does not entirely cover the core or is pierced with incisions'.

[106] See Art. 8(2)(b)(xix) and (e)(xv), Statute of the International Criminal Court, adopted at Rome 17 July 1998; entered into force 1 July 2002 (ICC Statute).

[107] The reason for this distinction is that expanding ammunition is less likely to pass through the body of the target ('overpenetrate') than is a full-metal-jacket round and hit an innocent bystander, a particular concern during a law enforcement operation.

[108] Unless there was a wilful or negligent failure to ensure the provision of necessary medication or medical treatment.

[109] See generally on this body of law: J. C. P. Goldberg and B. C. Zipursky, 'The Strict Liability in Fault and the Fault in Strict Liability', *Fordham Law Review*, vol. 85 no. 2 (2016), pp. 743–88, at http://bit.ly/3obHbtp.

[110] In its judgment in the *Fabris* case, the European Court of Human Rights recalled that with respect to acts of self-harming by a detainee, the authorities have a positive obligation to act where they knew or should have known that a real and immediate risk existed of suicide. European Court of Human Rights, *Fabris and Parziale v. Italy*, Judgment (First Section), 19 March 2020 (rendered final on 12 October 2020), para. 76. The case concerned the voluntary inhalation of kitchen cooking gas by a drug addict with mental health issues. On the basis of the facts of the case, the Court did not find either a substantive or procedural violation of the right to life under the European Convention on Human Rights.

[111] The standard of due diligence, which is often considered akin to all reasonable effort, is breached by negligent action on the part of a state. See, e.g., T. Koivurova, 'Due Diligence', last updated February 2010, *Max Planck Encyclopedia of Public International Law (MPEPIL)*, at http://bit.ly/2tdO179 (subscription required). See also J. Kulesza, *The Principle of Due Diligence in International Law*, Brill, The Netherlands, 2016. The most detailed work on the contours of due diligence to date was published at the beginning of December 2020: H. Krieger, A. Peters, and L. Kreuzer (eds.), *Due Diligence in the International Legal Order*, Oxford University Press, Oxford, 2020. See http://bit.ly/39IQCZj.

2.45 Indeed, owing to the level of control the State exercises over a detainee, it will normally be deemed to hold the burden of responsibility to demonstrate that it is not responsible for any death in a custodial setting. In the view of the African Commission on Human and Peoples' Rights:

> Where a person dies in State custody, there is a presumption of State responsibility and the burden of proof rests upon the State to prove otherwise through a prompt, impartial, thorough and transparent investigation carried out by an independent body. This heightened responsibility extends to persons detained in prisons, in other places of detention (official and otherwise), and to persons in other facilities where the State exercises heightened control over their lives.[112]

According to the soft-law instrument, the Minnesota Protocol on the Investigation of Potentially Unlawful Death, published by the OHCHR in 2017, particular circumstances in which the State will be held responsible for a death, unless it is proven to the contrary, include 'cases where the person suffered injury while in custody or where the deceased was, prior to his or her death, a political opponent of the government or a human rights defender; was known to be suffering from mental health issues; or committed suicide in unexplained circumstances'.[113] A failure, and especially a refusal, by a State to furnish evidence to support its contention that any given death in custody was in fact lawful is likely to result in a determination that the State was responsible under international law for either causing or failing to prevent an unlawful death.[114]

Poverty and Starvation

2.46 A famine, that is to say a situation of widespread starvation that is provoked or aggravated by human action, amounts to a serious violation of the right to life.[115] In other instances, however, individuals may starve to death or die of thirst and the State will not be held responsible unless it has failed, at the very least, to discharge its core minimum duties to respect, protect, and fulfil the rights to food and to water.[116] The nature

---

[112] African Commission General Comment on the right to life, para. 37. See similarly Human Rights Committee, *Sanjeevan v. Sri Lanka*, Views, 8 July 2008, para. 6.2.

[113] *Minnesota Protocol on the Investigation of Potentially Unlawful Death (2016)*, OHCHR, New York/Geneva, 2017, para. 17.

[114] See, e.g., Human Rights Committee, *Barbato v. Uruguay*, Views, 21 October 1982, para. 9.2.

[115] The famine in Ethiopia in 1984–6 was due to a number of factors, but significant among them was the refusal of the Ethiopian government to allow food to be delivered to civilians in areas where rebel forces were operating. Alex de Waal argued that in northern Ethiopia the famine led to more than 400,000 deaths, more than half of which were ascribed to human rights violations 'causing the famine to come earlier, strike harder and extend further than would otherwise have been the case'. A. de Waal, *Evil Days: Thirty Years of War and Famine in Ethiopia*, Human Rights Watch, New York/London, 1991, p. 5.

[116] Committee on Economic, Social and Cultural Rights (CESCR), 'General Comment No. 3: The Nature of States Parties' Obligations (Art. 2, Para. 1, of the Covenant)', UN doc. E/1991/23, 14 December 1990, para. 10: 'a State party in which any significant number of individuals is deprived of essential foodstuffs, of essential primary health care, of basic shelter and housing, or of the most basic forms of education is, prima facie, failing to discharge its obligations under the Covenant. . . . In order for a State party to be able to attribute its failure to meet at least its minimum core obligations to a lack of available resources it must demonstrate that

of these duties may also change in exceptional circumstances, such as during a situation of active armed conflict, but the prohibition of intentional starvation exists also under IHL[117] (and is a war crime under the jurisdiction of the International Criminal Court where it occurs in an international armed conflict).[118]

2.47 The duty to protect life obligates States to take 'appropriate measures to address the general conditions in society that may give rise to direct threats to life or prevent individuals from enjoying their right to life with dignity'.[119] Such measures include 'where necessary, measures designed to ensure access without delay by individuals to essential goods and services such as food [and] water'.[120] Widespread hunger and malnutrition and extreme poverty and homelessness[121] may thus give rise to a violation of the right to life, depending on the action and reaction of the government in question. An arbitrary refusal to countenance offers of food and/or water aid from other States where that refusal foreseeably leads to widespread death of individuals under the State's jurisdiction will also constitute a violation of the right to life.[122]

Abortion

2.48 Abortion, the possibility for a pregnant woman to voluntarily terminate her pregnancy before it comes to term, is a highly charged issue in many States. This is especially the case in the Americas, where the 1969 Inter-American Convention on Human Rights

---

every effort has been made to use all resources that are at its disposition in an effort to satisfy, as a matter of priority, those minimum obligations.'

[117] Art. 54(1), Protocol Additional to the Geneva Conventions of 12 August 1949, and relating to the Protection of Victims of International Armed Conflicts (Protocol I); adopted at Geneva, 8 June 1977; entered into force 7 December 1978; Art. 14, Protocol Additional to the Geneva Conventions of 12 August 1949, and relating to the protection of victims of non-international armed conflicts (Protocol II); adopted at Geneva, 8 June 1977; entered into force 7 December 1978; International Committee of the Red Cross (ICRC) Study of Customary IHL, Rule 53 (Starvation as a Method of Warfare), at http://bit.ly/2BNHBAi; see also, e.g., G. Giacca, *Economic, Social and Cultural Rights in Armed Conflict*, Oxford University Press, Oxford, 2014, p. 32.

[118] Art. 8(2)(b)(xxv), Rome Statute of the International Criminal Court.

[119] Human Rights Committee, General Comment 36 on the right to life, para. 26.

[120] Ibid., citing the Committee's Concluding Observations on the Democratic People's Republic of Korea (2001), para. 12.

[121] Human Rights Committee, General Comment 36 on the right to life, para. 26, citing the Committee's General Comment No. 6 on the Right to Life, adopted at the sixteenth session of the Committee, 1982, para. 5; and the Committee's Concluding Observations on Canada (1999), para. 12.

[122] In early 2019, for instance, the President of Venezuela, Nicolas Maduro, ordered that main roads should be blocked to prevent aid from the United States being delivered to a country where hunger and even starvation had become acute in many areas. See, e.g., S. Schulman, 'Hunger and Survival in Venezuela. Malnutrition Is the Mother of the Whole Problem', Special Report, *IRIN*, 21 November 2018, at http://bit.ly/2WU6F1u. In its 1986 judgment in the *Nicaragua* case, the International Court of Justice (ICJ) had affirmed, controversially, that 'there can be no doubt that the provision of strictly humanitarian aid to persons or forces in another country, whatever their political affiliations or objectives, cannot be regarded as unlawful intervention, or as in any other way contrary to international law'. ICJ, *Case Concerning Military and Paramilitary Activities in and against Nicaragua (Nicaragua v. United States of America)*, Merits, Judgment, 27 June 1986, para. 242.

explicitly requires that the right to life 'shall be protected by law and, in general, from the moment of conception'.[123] The prohibition can be traced back to many of the world's major religions whose tenets typically regard abortion as sinful because a child is deemed to be a gift from God.[124]

2.49 The Human Rights Committee dedicates considerable space in its 2018 General Comment on the right to life to the issue of abortion. In general, the Committee affirms, although it is open to States Parties to the ICCPR to 'adopt measures designed to regulate voluntary terminations of pregnancy, such measures must not result in violation of the right to life of a pregnant woman or girl, or her other rights under the Covenant'.[125] Thus the Committee argues, 'restrictions on the ability of women or girls to seek abortion must not, inter alia, jeopardize their lives, subject them to physical or mental pain or suffering which violates [the prohibition on inhumane treatment in] article 7, discriminate against them or arbitrarily interfere with their privacy'.[126]

2.50 Accordingly, citing its Views in the case of *Mellet v. Ireland*, the Committee declares that States must 'provide safe, legal and effective access to abortion where the life and health of the pregnant woman or girl is at risk, and where carrying a pregnancy to term would cause the pregnant woman or girl substantial pain or suffering, most notably where the pregnancy is the result of rape or incest or is not viable'.[127] The *Mellet* case concerned a complaint by a pregnant woman in Ireland that she was forced to travel to the United Kingdom to abort a foetus that had abnormalities that were likely to be fatal. Abortion in Ireland was criminalised in almost all circumstances until a legislative change in 2013 and constitutional and legal changes adopted in 2018.[128]

2.51 More controversially, the Committee argues that States Parties to the ICCPR 'may not regulate pregnancy or abortion in all other cases in a manner that runs contrary to their duty to ensure that women and girls do not have to undertake unsafe abortions,

---

[123] Art. 4(1), American Convention on Human Rights; adopted at San José 22 November 1969; entered into force 18 July 1978.
[124] See, e.g., BBC, 'Ethics: Religion and Abortion', undated but accessed 1 February 2019, at http://bbc.in/2Epr2MG.
[125] Human Rights Committee, General Comment 36 on the right to life, para. 8.
[126] Ibid.
[127] Ibid., citing Human Rights Committee, *Mellet v. Ireland*, Communication No. 2324/2013, Views adopted on 31 March 2016, paras. 7.4–7.8; and Concluding Observations on Ireland (2014), para. 9.
[128] On 25 May 2018, voting in a referendum supported removing the constitutional ban on abortion and was signed in to law on 18 September 2018. This means that Ireland now recognises the equal right to life of the mother and the unborn. See Health (Regulation of Termination of Pregnancy) Act 2018 (Act 31 of 2018), at http://bit.ly/2BAEitd. The repeal of the Eighth Amendment of the Constitution of Ireland is supplemented by the Thirty-Sixth Amendment, which stipulates that 'Provision may be made by law for the regulation of termination of pregnancy'. The constitutional change followed an earlier legislative change in 2013, which saw the adoption of The Protection of Life During Pregnancy Act 2013 (Act No. 35 of 2013). The Act defined the circumstances and processes within which abortion in Ireland could be legally performed. The Act gave effect in statutory law to the terms of the Constitution as interpreted by the Supreme Court in the 1992 judgment in *Attorney General v. X* (the 'X case') until it was superseded by the 2018 Act.

and they should revise their abortion laws accordingly'.[129] Whether this reflects customary law is open to interrogation. This could be said to sustain the view that any restrictions on abortion would be unlawful whereas in State practice there are upper limits set on when an abortion is considered lawful. This issue is discussed in detail in Chapter 11.

Suicide and Euthanasia

2.52 Arguably, on the basis that everyone has an inherent right to life, that right should comprise an entitlement to choose when to end one's life. Thus, for example, the Human Rights Committee explicitly acknowledges 'the central importance to human dignity of personal autonomy'.[130] Nonetheless, there are limits to be imposed on any 'right to die'. In particular, the Committee declares that States Parties to the ICCPR 'should take adequate measures, without violating their other Covenant obligations, to prevent suicides, especially among individuals in particularly vulnerable situations,'[131] including individuals deprived of their liberty.'[132] UN General Assembly Resolution 46/119, adopted without a vote in 1991,[133] contained in an Annex the 'Principles for the Protection of Persons with Mental Illness and for the Improvement of Mental Health Care'. Principle 1(5) states that 'every person with a mental illness shall have the right to exercise all civil, political, economic, social and cultural rights', while Principle 8(2) provides that 'every patient shall be protected from harm'. These principles may not align consistently given the existence of a general right of personal autonomy.

2.53 In the case of *Fernandes de Oliveira* v. *Portugal*, the Grand Chamber of the European Court of Human Rights found two 'distinct albeit related positive obligations' under the right to life as protected in Article 2 of the European Convention on Human Rights: the duty 'to put in place a regulatory framework compelling hospitals to adopt appropriate measures for the protection of patients' lives' and the duty 'to take preventive operational

---

[129] Human Rights Committee, General Comment 36 on the right to life, para. 8, citing its General Comment No. 28: Article 3 (The Equality of Rights between Men and Women), 29 March 2000, para. 10. See also, e.g., Human Rights Committee Concluding Observations on Argentina (2010), para. 13; Concluding Observations on Jamaica (2011), para. 14; and Concluding Observations on Madagascar (2007), para. 14. In Argentina, for instance, in August 2018, the Senate did not pass legislation to allow elective abortion up to 14 weeks of pregnancy. Since 1921, abortion has been legal in Argentina only when a pregnancy is the result of rape or a woman's life is in peril. Up to 500,000 abortions are said to take place each year in Argentina, and unsafe abortion is claimed to be 'a leading cause' of maternal death (although this claim is disputed). 'Catholic Church v Women's Rights in Argentina', Editorial, *The Lancet*, vol. 392, no. 10,147 (18 August 2018), at http://bit.ly/2GZEkkK, p. 532. But see also Letter from P. M. Kioko and P. R. Meana, 'Abortion in Argentina', *The Lancet*, vol. 393, no. 10, 173 (23 February 2019), at http://bit.ly/2NlZaMb, p. 745.

[130] Human Rights Committee, General Comment 36 on the right to life, para. 9.

[131] Ibid., citing Human Rights Committee, Concluding Observations on Ecuador, UN doc. CCPR/C/79/Add.92, 18 August 1998, para. 11.

[132] Human Rights Committee, General Comment 36 on the right to life, para. 9. See, *supra*, Paragraphs 2.43–2.44.

[133] UN General Assembly Resolution 46/119 ('The protection of persons with mental illness and the improvement of mental health care'), adopted without a vote on 17 December 1991.

measures to protect an individual from another individual or, in particular circumstances, from himself'.¹³⁴ The case concerned a suicide by a voluntary in-patient in a mental health institution who had a history of mental health problems, including an earlier attempted suicide.

2.54 The Court reiterated that, where a person is detained by the authorities, a variety of factors will be taken into account in order to establish whether the authorities knew or ought to have known that the life of a particular individual was subject to a real and immediate risk, thereby triggering the duty to take appropriate and specific preventive measures. These factors commonly include a history of mental health problems; the gravity of the mental condition; previous attempts to commit suicide or self-harm, suicidal thoughts or threats, and signs of physical or mental distress.¹³⁵ The Court found that

> the authorities do have a general operational duty with respect to a voluntary psychiatric patient to take reasonable measures to protect him or her from a real and immediate risk of suicide. The specific measures required will depend on the particular circumstances of the case, and those specific circumstances will often differ depending on whether the patient is voluntarily or involuntarily hospitalised. Therefore, this duty, namely to take reasonable measures to prevent a person from self-harm, exists with respect to both categories of patient. However, the Court considers that in the case of patients who are hospitalised following a judicial order, and therefore involuntarily, the Court, in its own assessment, may apply a stricter standard of scrutiny.¹³⁶

2.55 So-called 'mercy deaths', 'mercy killings', assisted suicide, or euthanasia are more complex legally, and, where they are permissible, must be subjected to strict control to prevent abuse. Indeed, it appears that under international law those States that comprehensively prohibit – and even criminalise – such activities do not, per se, violate the right to life. In the context of the ICCPR, the Human Rights Committee does not condemn States Parties 'that allow medical professionals to provide medical treatment or the medical means in order to facilitate the termination of life of afflicted adults, such as the terminally ill, who experience severe physical or mental pain and suffering and wish to die with dignity'.¹³⁷

2.56 Where States do so allow, however, they 'must ensure the existence of robust legal and institutional safeguards to verify that medical professionals are complying with the free, informed, explicit and, unambiguous decision of their patients, with a view to protecting patients from pressure and abuse'.¹³⁸ The Committee does not address the role of others who

---

[134] European Court of Human Rights, *Fernandes de Oliveira v. Portugal*, Judgment (Grand Chamber), 31 January 2019, para. 103.
[135] Ibid., para. 115.
[136] Ibid., para. 124.
[137] Human Rights Committee, General Comment 36 on the right to life, para. 9, citing Committee on Economic, Social and Cultural Rights, General Comment No. 14 ('The Right to the Highest Attainable Standard of Health (Art. 12)', 2000, para. 25 ('attention and care for chronically and terminally ill persons, sparing them avoidable pain and enabling them to die with dignity').
[138] Human Rights Committee, General Comment 36 on the right to life, para. 9, citing the Committee's Concluding Observations on Netherlands (2009), para. 7.

assist a person to take his or her own life, which in many countries is prosecutable as a form of homicide.

Accidents

2.57 As a further part of their duty to protect the lives of persons under their jurisdiction, States are obligated to minimise the risk of traffic and industrial accidents.[139] According to the World Health Organization (WHO), approximately 1.35 million people die each year as a result of road traffic crashes.[140] Road traffic injuries are the leading cause of death for those aged five to twenty-nine years.[141] The threat is also growing. In 2004, WHO stated that for the ten leading causes of the global burden of disease and injury, road traffic accidents had risen from ninth place in 1990 to an expected third place by 2020.[142]

2.58 That said, as Steven Pinker has noted, in the United States road traffic deaths reduced from 24 deaths per 100 million vehicle miles in 1921 to 1 in 2015.[143] That demonstrates that actions can be taken to significantly reduce the risk to individuals, whether they be drivers and passengers in vehicles or on motorcycles or pedestrians. In 2015, the 2030 Agenda for Sustainable Development set the 'ambitious' target of halving the global number of deaths and injuries from road traffic crashes by 2020,[144] which are said by WHO to cost 'most countries' 3 per cent of their gross domestic product (GDP).[145]

2.59 A study in the early 1990s sought to evaluate the effect of potential risk factors on fatality in motor vehicle traffic accidents.[146] The study found that the deleterious effect of alcohol use remained significant for male car drivers after controlling for speed and seatbelt use. Speed was the strongest risk factor of fatality for both motorcycles and motorcars and for both sexes and seemed to be more critical for motorcyclists than motorcar drivers. The protective effect of seatbelt use was unchanged after adjustment for alcohol and speed. The effectiveness of helmet use for male motorcyclists was dependent upon the speed at the time of the accidents, being protective up to 50 kilometres per hour but ineffective at higher speeds.[147]

---

[139] Human Rights Committee General Comment 36 on the right to life, para. 26, citing European Court of Human Rights, *Öneryildiz* v. *Turkey*, Judgment, 30 November 2004, para. 71.
[140] WHO, 'Road Traffic Injuries: Key Facts', 7 December 2018, at http://bit.ly/2SHtXZW.
[141] A total of 93 per cent of the world's fatalities on roads are reported to occur in low- and middle-income countries, even though these countries have approximately 60 per cent of the world's vehicles. WHO, 'Road Traffic Injuries: Key Facts'.
[142] WHO, 'World Report on Road Traffic Injury', *International Journal of Injury Control and Safety Promotion*, January 2004, p. 2.
[143] S. Pinker, *Enlightenment Now!*, Allan Lane, United States, 2018, p. 177.
[144] Target 3.6 is that 'by 2020, halve the number of global deaths and injuries from road traffic accidents'. See United Nations, 'SDG Goal 3: Ensure Healthy Lives and Promote Well-Being for All at All Ages', at http://bit.ly/2Saye30.
[145] WHO, 'Road Traffic Injuries: Key Facts'.
[146] A. Shibata and K. Fukuda, 'Risk Factors of Fatality in Motor Vehicle Traffic Accidents', *Accident Analysis Prevention*, vol. 26, no. 3 (June 1994), pp. 391–7.
[147] Ibid.

2.60 Drugs can also significantly increase the risk of accidents, depending on the substance that is used. For example, the risk of a fatal crash occurring among those who have used amphetamines is about five times the risk of someone who has not.[148] These findings indicate that preventive measures by each State must include legislation restricting vehicle speeds, prohibiting driving under the influence of alcohol or drugs, and obligating seatbelt use, along with dissemination and enforcement measures.

2.61 In the *Marius Alexandru and Marinela Ştefan* case before the European Court of Human Rights,[149] the applicants, a married couple, were driving on a main road when a tree on the roadside became uprooted and fell on their car. The applicants suffered multiple injuries, and three other occupants of the car died. The Court did not rule out that, in certain circumstances, acts and omissions of the authorities in the context of policies to ensure safety in public places could violate Article 2 of the Convention. Nevertheless, where a State Party had adopted a protective legal framework tailored to the different public spaces, an error of judgment on the part of an individual player or negligent coordination among professionals would not be enough to engage the responsibility of the State under the right to life.

2.62 Applying these principles to the facts of the case, the Court found that the government of the respondent State – Romania – had national legislation in place concerning the safety of national roads and, in particular, the maintenance of the trees bordering them. In addition, standards, including in the realm of forestry law, had been promulgated for the prevention of accidents caused by roadside trees. While problems in the implementation of a national regulatory framework will be the subject of particular scrutiny by the Court, no serious concerns existed with respect to Romania at the relevant time.[150]

2.63 Industrial accidents – more correctly termed unintentional injuries in the workplace[151] – have also reduced hugely over the last few decades as health and safety laws have come into force in most States and been further elaborated. They remain, however, a major source of mortality and morbidity, especially in developing nations. In 2017, a publication by the Workplace Safety and Health Institute found that in 2014 occupational mortality in high-income countries was of the order of 3.8 per 100,000 workers, while in low- and middle-income countries of the African Region, it was 21.1. These figures were unchanged from four years previously.[152] Pinker recalls that in the United States annual deaths per hundred thousand workers dropped from more than sixty in 1910 to between three and four in 2015.[153] He ascribes much of the earlier reduction to the introduction of

---

[148] WHO, 'Road Traffic Injuries: Key Facts'.
[149] European Court of Human Rights, *Marius Alexandru and Marinela Ştefan v. Romania*, Judgment (Fourth Section), 24 March 2020 (rendered final on 24 July 2020).
[150] Ibid., paras. 105–7.
[151] See, e.g., Pinker, *Enlightenment Now!*, p. 186.
[152] P. Hämäläinen, J. Takala, and T. B. Kiat, *Global Estimates of Occupational Accidents and Work-Related Illnesses 2017*, Workplace Safety and Health Institute, Singapore, 2017, p. 8.
[153] Pinker, *Enlightenment Now!*, p. 187.

The Content of the Right to Life

employers' liability and workers compensation, 'a simple change in the law brought over from Europe'.[154]

2.64 Industrial accidents may have international as well as national effects. One of the most dramatic examples is the explosion at the Chernobyl nuclear power plant in the spring of 1986. On 26 April, Reactor Four at the Chernobyl nuclear power plant in northern Ukraine near the border with Belarus began to fail. A power surge led to explosions that blew the 1,000-ton cover off the top of the reactor.[155] According to a report published 20 years after the disaster, almost one-third of the reactor's 190 tons of fuel was distributed over the reactor building and surrounding areas, while up to 2 per cent was ejected into the atmosphere.[156]

2.65 WHO estimated that the total radioactivity from Chernobyl was two hundred times that of the combined releases from the atomic bombs dropped on Hiroshima and Nagasaki.[157] Two radionuclides – iodine-131 and caesium-137 – were particularly significant for the radiation dose they delivered to the public. Xenon gas, iodine, and caesium, as well as many tonnes of radioactive fuel, were released as a result of the accident, most of which was deposited close by as dust and debris. In addition, lighter material was carried by wind over Belarus, Russia, and Ukraine, as well as over Scandinavia and other regions across Europe.[158]

2.66 The 1992 Convention on the Transboundary Effects of Industrial Accidents, which was adopted under the auspices of the UN Economic Commission for Europe (UNECE), obligates its parties to 'take appropriate measures ... to protect human beings and the environment against industrial accidents by preventing such accidents as far as possible, by reducing their frequency and severity and by mitigating their effects'.[159] The tenth meeting of the Conference of the Parties to the UNECE Convention was held on 4–6 December 2018 in Geneva. It concluded with the adoption of a long-term strategy for the Convention until 2030, strengthening alignment with the Sendai Framework for Disaster Risk Reduction 2015–30[160] and the UN Sustainable Development Goals.

---

[154] Ibid., p. 186.
[155] BBC, 'The Chernobyl Accident: What Happened', 5 June 2000, at http://bit.ly/2NTDLZp.
[156] I. Fairlie and D. Sumner, *The other Report on Chernobyl (TORCH): An Independent Scientific Evaluation of Health and Environmental Effects 20 Years after the Nuclear Disaster Providing Critical Analysis of a Recent Report by the International Atomic Energy Agency (IAEA) and the World Health Organization (WHO)*, 2006, Summary, at http://bit.ly/2q4Vt2U.
[157] See, e.g., WHO, *Health Consequences of the Chernobyl Accident*, Summary Report, 1995, at http://bit.ly/2J7wbtq, p. 3; and also Welcome Address by Susanne Weber-Mosdorf, Assistant Director General, WHO, at the Chernobyl 20th Anniversary Meeting in Kiev, 24 April 2006, at http://bit.ly/2PaL2sF.
[158] See, e.g., World Nuclear Association, 'Chernobyl Accident 1986', updated November 2016, at http://bit.ly/2PaLc3f.
[159] Art. 3(1), Convention on the Transboundary Effects of Industrial Accidents; adopted at Helsinki 17 March 1992; entered into force 19 April 2000. The Convention had forty-one parties as of writing and two signatories (Canada and the United States). See the UN Treaty Section web page on adherence to the Convention, at http://bit.ly/2SbCzCS.
[160] The Sendai Framework for Disaster Risk Reduction 2015–30 outlines four priorities for action to prevent disasters and reduce existing disaster risks: (i) understanding disaster risk; (ii) strengthening disaster risk governance to manage disaster risk; (iii) investing in disaster reduction for resilience; and (iv) enhancing

Disasters

2.67 Disasters may be natural or man-made, including as a result of an industrial accident. A disaster ascribed to human factors that should have been prevented by the government is likely to be deemed to be a violation of human rights, but so too may be a failure to respond effectively to any disaster where death results, engendering a violation of the right to life. According to the Human Rights Committee, States Parties to the ICCPR 'should also develop, when necessary, contingency plans and disaster management plans designed to increase preparedness and address natural and man-made disasters'.[161] Such disasters include 'hurricanes, tsunamis, earthquakes, radioactive accidents and massive cyberattacks resulting in disruption of essential services'.[162]

2.68 In 2016, after several years of work led by its Special Rapporteur on the issue, Eduardo Valencia-Ospina, the ILC adopted its Draft Articles on the Protection of Persons in the Event of Disasters.[163] Draft Article 3(a) defines a disaster for the purpose of the Draft Articles as follows: 'a calamitous event or series of events resulting in widespread loss of life, great human suffering and distress, mass displacement, or large-scale material or environmental damage, thereby seriously disrupting the functioning of society'. Draft Article 5 provides that 'persons affected by disasters are entitled to the respect for and protection of their human rights in accordance with international law'.

2.69 The ILC recommended that the UN General Assembly convene a diplomatic conference to elaborate a convention on the basis of the Draft Articles. The Assembly in turn adopted Resolution 71/141 on 19 December 2016, requesting governments to submit comments on the ILC's recommendation.[164] In December 2018, the Assembly again called for comments from States on the recommendation and decided to address the issue in a further two years' time, in 2020.[165] It is unclear whether a Convention will be adopted in the near to medium term. In 2011, The Brookings–Bern Project on Internal Displacement published the Inter-Agency Steering Committee Operational Guidelines on the Protection of Persons in Situations of Natural Disasters. The Guidelines stated:

> A human rights-based approach provides the framework and necessary standards for humanitarian assistance activities. It grounds the basis for humanitarian action in

disaster preparedness for effective response, and to 'Build Back Better' in recovery, rehabilitation, and reconstruction. The Framework was adopted at the Third UN World Conference on Disaster Risk Reduction in Sendai, Japan, on 18 March 2015. See UN Office for Disaster Risk Reduction (UNISDR), 'Sendai Framework for Disaster Risk Reduction 2015–2030', at http://bit.ly/2UZaoJk.

[161] Human Rights Committee, General Comment 36 on the right to life, para. 26.
[162] Ibid.
[163] *Draft Articles on the Protection of Persons in the Event of Disasters*, 2016, Adopted by the ILC at its Sixty-eighth Session, in 2016, and submitted to the UN General Assembly in the Commission's report covering the work of that session (UN doc. A/71/10), para. 48, at http://bit.ly/2tsTFCw.
[164] See, e.g., G. Bartolini, 'The Draft Articles on "The Protection of Persons in the Event of Disasters": Towards a Flagship Treaty?', *EJIL Talk*, blog post, 2 December 2016, at http://bit.ly/2DVuU6y.
[165] UN General Assembly Resolution 73/209 ('Protection of Persons in the Event of Disasters'), adopted without a vote on 20 December 2018, paras. 3 and 4. On 19 November 2020, the General Assembly's Sixth Committee decided to recommend that the Assembly defer consideration of the agenda item on the protection of persons in the event of disasters to its seventy-sixth session in 2021.

universal principles, such as human dignity and non-discrimination, as well as a set of universally accepted human rights. Those affected by the disaster thus become individual rights holders who can claim rights from particular duty bearers rather than simply being passive beneficiaries and recipients of charity.[166]

The Guidelines further declared that 'the life, physical integrity and health of persons exposed to imminent risks created by natural disasters, including in particular of persons with specific needs, should be protected, to the maximum extent possible, wherever those persons may be located'.[167]

Pollution

2.70 The failure to tackle pollution may also violate the right to life.[168] As WHO observes, outdoor air pollution is a major environmental health problem affecting those in low-, middle-, and high-income countries. Such ambient air pollution in both cities and rural areas was estimated to cause 4.2 million premature deaths worldwide in 2016, a level of mortality 'due to exposure to small particulate matter of 2.5 microns or less in diameter (PM2.5), which cause cardiovascular and respiratory disease, and cancers'.[169] The WHO Air Quality Guideline values for PM2.5 are set at an annual mean of 10 $\mu g/m^3$ and a 25 $\mu g/m^3$ 24-hour mean. Such fine particulate matter is small enough to pass through the lungs into the bloodstream, and has been linked to heart disease, stroke, and lung cancer. 'There is also evidence that exposure exacerbates asthma and may increase the chances of diabetes, neurodegenerative diseases such as dementia[,] and babies born with low birth weights.'[170] In September 2018, it was reported that new scientific evidence had found that particles of air pollution travel through a pregnant woman's lungs and lodge in her placenta.[171]

2.71 The vast majority of the world population – 6.76 billion of the total 7.8 billion people – are said to be living with excessive air pollution.[172] In September 2016, the United Nations found that 92 per cent of the world's population were living in places where pollution levels exceeded recommended limits. In his January 2019 report, David Boyd, UN Special Rapporteur on human rights and the environment, cited findings by WHO that 'air pollution causes 7 million premature deaths annually, including the deaths of more than 600,000 children' to support his claim that this amounts to an 'egregious violation of the right to life'.[173]

---

[166] *IASC Operational Guidelines on the Protection of Persons in Situations of Natural Disasters*, The Brookings – Bern Project on Internal Displacement, United States, 2011, p. 2.
[167] Ibid., p. 15.
[168] See Chapter 18 or a further discussion of this issue.
[169] WHO, 'Ambient (Outdoor) Air Quality and Health: Key Facts', 2 May 2018, at http://bit.ly/2NccKBK.
[170] K. Lay, 'Millions Breathing Unsafe, Polluted Air on the Way to Doctor's Surgery', *The Times*, 11 February 2019, at http://bit.ly/2TXMU7o.
[171] D. Carrington, 'Air Pollution Particles Found in Mothers' Placentas', *The Guardian*, 16 September 2018, at http://bit.ly/2TWoZ8h.
[172] UN, 'Vast Majority of World – 6.76 Billion People – Living with Excessive Air Pollution – UN Report', 27 September 2016, at http://bit.ly/2SZgDj4.
[173] 'Issue of Human Rights Obligations Relating to the Enjoyment of a Safe, Clean, Healthy and Sustainable Environment', Report of the Special Rapporteur on Human Rights and the Environment, UN doc. A/HRC/

2.72 One of the most contaminated urban areas in recent times has been Bangkok. At the end of January 2019, for instance, 437 schools were closed in the Thai capital to protect children from pollution. The air in the city, which has a population of ten million, was measured at 175 $\mu g/m^3$ on 30 January 2019.[174] But one rating of the world's most contaminated cities on an annually averaged basis adjudged that twenty-six of the fifty most polluted cities worldwide in 2019 were in India. The most polluted city was Ghaziabad, whose average pollution level was 110 $\mu g/m^3$ but with monthly values that ranged between 23.9 $\mu g/m^3$ in February and 239.5 $\mu g/m^3$ in December.[175]

Environmental Damage

2.73 More broadly, as the Human Rights Committee has observed,[176] environmental degradation,[177] climate change, and unsustainable development 'constitute some of the most pressing and serious threats to the ability of present and future generations to enjoy the right to life'.[178] The Committee believes that the obligations of States Parties to the ICCPR under international environmental law 'should thus inform the contents of article 6 of the Covenant', while the obligation of States Parties to respect and ensure the right to life 'should also inform their relevant obligations under international environmental law'.[179] The choice of language by the Committee – 'should', not 'shall' – is equivocal, indicating that a violation will not necessarily, or even probably, occur without a serious breach of environmental law.

2.74 That said, the Committee goes on to affirm that implementation of 'the obligation to respect and ensure the right to life, and in particular life with dignity, depends, inter alia, on measures taken by States parties to preserve the environment and protect it against harm, pollution and climate change caused by public and private actors'.[180] This appears inconsistent with the earlier position taken, but the Committee then recommends that States Parties to the ICCPR

   40/55, 8 January 2019, para. 52, citing WHO, 'Burden of Disease from the Joint Effects of Household and Ambient Air Pollution for 2016', May 2018.
[174] J. Fullerton, 'Bangkok Sends Drones to Clean Out the Smog', *The Times*, 1 February 2019, at http://bit.ly/2S9TcyN.
[175] IQAir, 'World's Most Polluted Cities 2019 (PM2.5)', at http://bit.ly/37qum7N.
[176] Human Rights Committee, General Comment 36 on the right to life, para. 62.
[177] African Commission on Human and Peoples' Rights, *Social and Economic Rights Action Center (SERAC) and Center for Economic and Social Rights (CESR) v. Nigeria*, Views, 27 October 2001, para. 67, at http://bit.ly/2V8Noct.
[178] Human Rights Committee, General Comment 36 on the right to life, para. 62, citing the Preamble to the Declaration of the UN Conference on the Human Environment, 17 June 1972 (hereinafter, 1972 Stockholm Declaration), para. 1; Principle 1 of the Rio Declaration on Environment and Development, 14 June 1992; and the Preamble to the UN Framework Convention on Climate Change, 9 May 1992.
[179] Human Rights Committee, General Comment 36 on the right to life, para. 62, citing the Preamble to the Paris Agreement, UN doc. FCCC/CP/2015/L.9, 12 December 2015. The Preamble acknowledges that since climate change 'is a common concern of humankind', parties to the Paris Agreement 'should, when taking action to address climate change, respect, promote and consider their respective obligations on human rights'.
[180] Human Rights Committee, General Comment 36 on the right to life, para. 62.

should therefore ensure sustainable use of natural resources, develop and implement substantive environmental standards, conduct environmental impact assessments and consult with relevant States about activities likely to have a significant impact on the environment, provide notification to other States concerned about natural disasters and emergencies and cooperate with them, provide appropriate access to information on environmental hazards and pay due regard to the precautionary approach.[181]

2.75 As Malgosia Fitzmaurice has recalled,[182] the link between human rights and the environment was first made in the 1972 Stockholm Declaration: 'Both aspects of man's environment, the natural and the man-made, are essential to his well-being and to the enjoyment of basic human rights – even the right to life itself.'[183] Whether there is an autonomous right to a healthy environment is debated. The first human rights treaty to reflect such a right was the 1981 African Charter on Human and Peoples' Rights, though it was phrased in collective rather than individual terms. Thus Article 24 stipulates that 'all peoples shall have the right to a general satisfactory environment favourable to their development'. This provision was tested in the landmark case before the African Commission of *SERAC v. Nigeria*. In its views on the case in 2001, the Commission found not only a violation of Article 24 but also of the right to life, in part because the

> pollution and environmental degradation to a level humanly unacceptable has made it living in the Ogoni land a nightmare. The survival of the Ogonis depended on their land and farms that were destroyed by the direct involvement of the government. These and similar brutalities not only persecuted individuals in Ogoniland but also the whole of the Ogoni community as a whole. They affected the life of the Ogoni society as a whole.[184]

2.76 In the Americas, the 1988 San Salvador Protocol to the Inter-American Convention on Human Rights[185] imposes an individual human right to a healthy environment on its States Parties. Article 11(1) provides that 'everyone shall have the right to live in a healthy environment and to have access to basic public services'. There is, however, no right of individual petition before the Inter-American Court on this right. In accordance with paragraph 2, States Parties are obligated to 'promote the protection, preservation, and improvement of the environment'.

2.77 In fact, a serious violation of a State's customary or conventional environmental law obligations that results in the loss of life will invariably constitute a violation of its duty to

---

[181] Ibid., citing Principles 1, 2, 11, 15, 17, 18 to the 1992 Rio Declaration on Environment and Development; and the 1998 Convention on Access to Information, Public Participation in Decision-Making and Access to Justice in Environmental Matters; signed at Aarhus, Denmark, 25 June 1998; entered into force 30 October 2001.
[182] M. Fitzmaurice, 'Environmental Degradation', chap. 28 in D. Moeckli, S. Shah, and S. Sivakumaran (eds.), *International Human Rights Law*, Oxford University Press, Oxford, 2010, pp. 622–3.
[183] 1972 Stockholm Declaration, para. 1, at http://bit.ly/2tuJOvX.
[184] *SERAC and CESR v. Nigeria*, Views, 27 October 2001, para. 67.
[185] Additional Protocol to the American Convention on Human Rights in the Area of Economic, Social and Cultural Rights; adopted at San Salvador, 17 November 1988; entered into force 16 November 1999. As of 1 May 2021, sixteen States were party to the Protocol. See the list of signatures and ratifications at http://bit.ly/2TW2aBv.

50   *Overview of the Right to Life under International Law*

respect and protect the right to life. Environmental law obligations potentially include the duty to halt the 'discharge of toxic substances or of other substances and the release of heat, in such quantities or concentrations as to exceed the capacity of the environment to render them harmless ... in order to ensure that serious or irreversible damage is not inflicted upon ecosystems'.[186] A customary rule also exists whereby States have 'the responsibility to ensure that activities within their jurisdiction or control do not cause damage to the environment of other States or of areas beyond the limits of national jurisdiction'.[187] This would of course have extraterritorial implications for the right to life, as Chapter 3 discusses.[188]

Disease and Ill Health

2.78 The prevalence of life-threatening diseases, such as heart disease, cancer, AIDS, tuberculosis, or malaria, may give rise to a violation of the right to life, depending on the legislative and programmatic actions and responses of the government. In its 2012 Concluding Observations on Kenya, the Human Rights Committee stated its regret regarding 'the continued reports of high rates of deaths resulting from AIDS and the unequal access to appropriate treatment for those infected with HIV'. The Committee also regretted 'reports of HIV/AIDS prevalence among homosexuals which is partly attributable to the laws that criminalize consensual same-sex relationships and the societal stigmatization of this group that hampers access to treatment and medical care by this group'.[189]

2.79 Malaria still occurs in almost 100 States and is particularly prevalent in sub-Saharan Africa and South Asia. An estimated 207 million people suffered from the disease in 2012, of whom approximately 627,000 died. About 90 per cent of these deaths were in sub-Saharan Africa, with 77 per cent among children under the age of 5.[190] Pinker repeats the claim that, in the past, malaria killed half of the people who had ever lived,[191] but between 2000 and 2015, rates dropped by at least 45 per cent, saving 6 million lives.[192] As part of this effort, the Gates Foundation committed US$258 million in 2005 for malaria research and

---

[186] Principle 1, 1972 Stockholm Declaration.
[187] Principle 21, 1972 Stockholm Declaration.
[188] The South Korean government has held talks with China, where much of the pollution affecting South Korea originates, to establish an early warning system. Chinese local governments have agreed to order cars operated by civil servants off the roads on critical days and to reduce output at coal-fired power stations. A number of South Korean factories have also volunteered to minimise operations at times of intense pollution. R. Lloyd Parry, 'China Under Fire as South Korea Chokes on "Fine Dust" Pollution', *The Times*, 29 January 2019, at http://bit.ly/2S8tknb.
[189] Human Rights Committee, Concluding Observations on Kenya, UN doc. CCPR/C/KEN/CO/3, 31 August 2012, para. 9; see also General Comment 36 on the right to life, para. 62.
[190] Bill and Melinda Gates Foundation, 'Malaria: Strategy Overview', at http://gates.ly/2VhTvK5.
[191] Pinker, *Enlightenment Now!*, p. 66.
[192] Swiss Tropical and Public Health Institute, 'Malaria and the UN Sustainable Development Goals (SDGs) 2030', Scientific Fact Sheet, 16 April 2018, at http://bit.ly/2STk4IT. Pinker suggests a 60 per cent drop over the same period.

development, including funding to support R&D on a malaria vaccine, new drugs, and improved mosquito control methods.[193]

2.80 The third Sustainable Development Goal is to 'ensure healthy lives and promote wellbeing for all at all ages'. One of the targets for this Goal is to 'by 2030, end the epidemics of AIDS, tuberculosis, malaria and neglected tropical diseases and combat hepatitis, water-borne diseases and other communicable diseases'.[194] But the *World Malaria Report 2018*, published in November 2018, found that 'after an unprecedented period of success in global malaria control', progress had stalled. Data in 2015–17 showed that 'no significant progress in reducing global malaria cases was made in this period. There were an estimated 219 million cases and 435,000 related deaths in 2017.'[195]

2.81 Eleven high-burden countries (Burkina Faso, Cameroon, the Democratic Republic of Congo, Ghana, India, Mali, Mozambique, Niger, Nigeria, Tanzania, and Uganda) account for more than 70 per cent of global malaria cases and deaths. By 2017, ten of these countries, all of them in sub-Saharan Africa, were not on track to meet the global targets.[196] The resistance of people to anti-malarial drugs and of mosquitoes to insecticides are considered major factors behind this stalling of progress.[197] In one of the most affected States, Burkina Faso, researchers are preparing to release so-called gene drive mosquitoes into the wild for the first time, by 2024. Gene drive involves developing a genetically modified mosquito in the laboratory that can kill off its own species by spreading a faulty gene.[198]

The Right to Life and Non-discrimination

2.82 The relationship between the right to life and the prohibition of discrimination is more complex than might instinctively be presumed. The African Commission on Human and Peoples' Rights has affirmed that any deprivation of life that results from a

---

[193] Bill and Melinda Gates Foundation, 'Gates Foundation Commits $258.3 Million for Malaria Research and Development', 2005, at http://gates.ly/2Eqjl8S.
[194] See World Health Organization, 'Sustainable Development Goals (SDGs): Target 3.3', at http://bit.ly/2GHExcR.
[195] WHO, *The World Malaria Report 2018*, 19 November 2018, available at http://bit.ly/2U6CL8k.
[196] Ibid., p. 52.
[197] In 2017, *The Economist* reported that 'fingers are ... being pointed at a decline in a technique known as indoor residual spraying (IRS). This involves coating the interior walls of buildings in malaria-prone areas with insecticide, to kill mosquitoes that land on them. The report says that the proportion of people at risk of malaria who are protected by IRS has fallen from 5.8% in 2010 to 2.9% in 2016. Again, it is unclear why. It may be an unintended consequence of the sensible policy of rotating, over the years, the insecticides used for IRS. This helps suppress the evolution of insecticide-resistance in mosquitoes. But it often means replacing conventional pyrethroid insecticides with more expensive alternatives, which some people cannot afford.' 'The War on Malaria. After Years of Success, Progress against Malaria Is Slowing', *The Economist*, 2 December 2017, at http://econ.st/2SXWlqM.
[198] But Dr Ify Aniebo, a molecular geneticist from Nigeria, asked: 'Will the engineered organism upset the delicate balance of ecosystems, thereby causing new diseases to emerge or prompting already existing illnesses to spread?' Quoted in S. Arie, 'GM Mosquitoes: Playing with God or the Only Way to Wipe Out Malaria?', *Daily Telegraph*, 5 February 2019, at http://bit.ly/2Xl7pgj.

violation of 'the procedural or substantive safeguards in the African Charter, including on the basis of discriminatory grounds or practices, is arbitrary and as a result unlawful'.[199] As a theoretical statement of the law, this is sound. But in practice, such a rule may prove problematic to implement.

2.83 The Black Lives Matter movement,[200] which began in the United States, concerns perceptions that police officers (and others) are far more likely to shoot a person of colour than a white person in the same circumstances.[201] While recognising the shortcomings of the available data, according to the Centers for Disease Control (CDC), of 6,338 deaths at the hands of police that occurred in the United States between 1999 and 2013, blacks were 27.6 per cent of the total while representing only 13.2 per cent of the US population.[202] But if a particular shooting is lawful in the specific circumstances in which it occurs, under international law, the statistically greater likelihood of the police shooting a person of colour in those circumstances would not act so as to render it inevitably unlawful. If, on the other hand, the shooting is unlawful and racial animus is proven, this could turn the homicide into a hate crime and aggravate the violation of human rights.

NON-REFOULEMENT

2.84 The principle of *non-refoulement* is the prohibition on deporting or extraditing a person against their will to the jurisdiction of another State (or the subject of international law) where they are likely to face inhumane treatment or even death. Originally a fundamental norm of refugee law,[203] non-refoulement has since become a human rights

---

[199] African Commission General Comment on the Right to Life, para. 12.

[200] See http://bit.ly/2ErlVeT. According to the Black Lives Matter website, 'In 2013, three radical Black organisers – Alicia Garza, Patrisse Cullors, and Opal Tometi – created a Black-centered political will and movement building project called #BlackLivesMatter. It was in response to the acquittal of Trayvon Martin's murderer, George Zimmerman. ... The project is now a member-led global network of more than 40 chapters. Our members organize and build local power to intervene in violence inflicted on Black communities by the state and vigilantes.' According to one commentator, 'By using the tools of social media, BLM [Black Lives Matter] was the first U.S. social movement in history to successfully use the internet as a mass mobilization device. The recent successes of movements, such as #MeToo, #NeverAgain, and #TimesUp, would be inconceivable had it not been for the groundwork that #BlackLivesMatter laid.' F. L. Roberts, 'How Black Lives Matter Changed the Way Americans Fight for Freedom', blog post, ACLU website, United States, 13 July 2018, at http://bit.ly/2Iyhbsd.

[201] See, e.g., H. Yan, '"Black Lives Matter" Cases: What Happened after Controversial Police Killings', *CNN*, 27 June 2017, at http://cnn.it/2SWqeYr.

[202] CDC, Web-based Injury Statistics Query and Reporting System (WISQUARS™) database, Fatal Injury Reports, 1999–2013, for National, Regional, and States (Legal Intervention Injury, Deaths, and Rates per 100,000 all races), at http://bit.ly/2U4tWfk; cited by Amnesty International United States, *Deadly Force: Police Use of Lethal Force in the United States*, June 2015, at http://bit.ly/2tAdnwg, p. 10.

[203] Writing in 1977, the Office of the UN High Commissioner for Refugees (UNHCR) stated that 'the most essential component of refugee status and of asylum is protection against return to a country where a person has reason to fear persecution. This protection has found expression in the principle of non-refoulement.' UNHCR, 'Note on Non-Refoulement', UN doc. EC/SCP/2, 23 August 1977, at http://bit.ly/2XuAWnU.

treaty rule and is widely agreed to be both a general principle of international law and a customary law norm.[204] It may even constitute a peremptory norm of international law.[205]

2.85 Violating the rule of *non-refoulement*, where the individual is killed by the State into whose jurisdiction he or she is sent, amounts to a violation of the right to life by both the sending and receiving State. A violation of human rights also occurs where a person is handed over to a State in such circumstances by another subject of international law, such as an international organisation. This would be so, at the least where the killing was reasonably foreseeable.

2.86 Under the 1951 UN Convention relating to the Status of Refugees, it is provided that 'no Contracting State shall expel or return ("refouler") a refugee in any manner whatsoever to the frontiers of territories where his life or freedom would be threatened on account of his race, religion, nationality, membership of a particular social group or political opinion'.[206] The Office of the UN High Commissioner for Refugees (UNHCR) 'is of the view that the prohibition of refoulement of refugees, as enshrined in Article 33 of the 1951 Convention and complemented by non-refoulement obligations under international human rights law, ... constitutes a rule of customary international law'.[207]

2.87 The 1984 Convention against Torture[208] was the first global human rights treaty to incorporate the rule of non-refoulement more broadly: According to Article 3(1), 'No State Party shall expel, return ("refouler") or extradite a person to another State where there are substantial grounds for believing that he would be in danger of being subjected to torture.' In its General Comment No. 4 (2017) on the implementation of Article 3 of the Convention, the Committee against Torture declared that

> any person found to be at risk of torture if deported to a given State should be allowed to remain in the territory under the jurisdiction, control or authority of the State party concerned so long as the risk persists.[209] ... Furthermore, the person at risk should never be deported to another State from which the person may subsequently face

---

[204] In January 2017, Bruno Nascimbene declared that 'the very principle of non-refoulement can be recognised as a human right which all the Member States of the international community guarantee as such to individuals.' 'Non-refoulement as a Principle of International Law and the Role of the Judiciary in its Implementation', Dialogue between judges, Proceedings of the Seminar 27 January 2017, Strasbourg, 2017, at http://bit.ly/2EsJhAW, p. 49.

[205] See, e.g., A. Orakhelashvili, *Peremptory Norms in International Law*, Oxford University Press, Oxford, 2006, p. 55. See also, with respect to the application of the rule to refugees, Cartagena Declaration on Refugees, Colloquium on the International Protection of Refugees in Central America, Mexico and Panama, adopted by the Colloquium on the International Protection of Refugees in Central America, Mexico and Panama, held at Cartagena, Colombia, on 19–22 November 1984, at http://bit.ly/2tBgKTm, S. III, para. 5.

[206] Art. 33(1), Convention relating to the Status of Refugees; adopted at Geneva 28 July 1951; entered into force 22 April 1954. As of 1 May 2021, 146 States were party to the Convention.

[207] UNHCR, *Advisory Opinion on the Extraterritorial Application of Non-refoulement Obligations under the 1951 Convention relating to the Status of Refugees and its 1967 Protocol*, 2007, at http://bit.ly/2IunGfo, para. 15.

[208] Convention against Torture and Other Cruel, Inhuman or Degrading Treatment or Punishment; adopted at New York 10 December 1984; entered into force 26 June 1987. As of 1 May 2021, 171 States were party to the Convention.

[209] See, e.g., Committee against Torture, *Aemei v. Switzerland*, UN doc. CAT/C/18/D/34/1995, 29 May 1997, para. 11.

deportation to a third State in which there are substantial grounds for believing that the person would be in danger of being subjected to torture.[210]

2.88 At regional level, the 1969 Inter-American Convention on Human Rights stipulates that 'in no case may an alien be deported or returned to a country, regardless of whether or not it is his country of origin, if in that country his right to life or personal freedom is in danger of being violated because of his race, nationality, religion, social status, or political opinions'.[211] In its 2015 General Comment on the right to life under the African Charter, the African Commission on Human and Peoples' Rights declared that 'States should not violate the principle of non-refoulement, through extradition or other mechanisms, by transferring or returning individuals to circumstances where their lives might be endangered'.[212]

2.89 While there is no specific provision on *non-refoulement* in the European Convention on Human Rights, the leading case before the European Court of Human Rights of *Soering v. United Kingdom*[213] has clearly established that the extradition of a person to another State where he or she may be subject to the death penalty may amount to inhumane treatment by the extraditing state. *Soering* concerned the possible extradition to the United States of a West German national to face trial in Virginia on a murder charge. He complained that, upon conviction, he would be likely to spend many years on death row awaiting execution.

2.90 An important case of recent years on *non-refoulement*, adjudged by the European Court's Grand Chamber, is *Paposhvili v. Belgium*. In 2006, while the applicant, a Georgian national, was in prison, he was diagnosed with chronic lymphocytic leukaemia in Binet stage B, with a very high level of CD38 expression. In 2007, he received a course of chemotherapy. A report prepared the following year by Antwerp University Hospital, where the applicant was being treated, stated that his condition was life-threatening and that, on the basis of the averages observed in 2007, his life expectancy was between three and five years.[214] The applicant had alleged that substantial grounds had been shown for believing that if he had been expelled to Georgia, he would have faced a real risk there of inhuman and degrading treatment, contrary to Article 3 of the Convention, and of a premature death in breach of Article 2. The Grand Chamber held that refoulement would be unlawful in

---

[210] See, e.g., Committee against Torture, General Comment No. 1 (1997) on the implementation of article 3, para. 2; *Avedes Hamayak Korban v. Sweden*, UN doc. CAT/C/21/D/88/1997, 16 November 1998, para. 7; and *Z. T. v. Australia*, UN doc. CAT/C/31/D/142/2000, 19 November 2003. Committee against Torture, General Comment No. 4 (2017) on the implementation of article 3 of the Convention in the context of article 22, UN doc. CAT/C/GC/4, 4 September 2018, para. 12.
[211] Art. 22(8), 1969 Inter-American Convention on Human Rights.
[212] African Commission General Comment on the right to life, para. 40.
[213] European Court of Human Rights, *Soering v. United Kingdom*, Judgment (Plenary of the Court), 7 July 1989.
[214] European Court of Human Rights, *Paposhvili v. Belgium*, Judgment (Grand Chamber), 13 December 2016, paras. 34–36.

situations involving the removal of a seriously ill person in which substantial grounds have been shown for believing that he or she, although not at imminent risk of dying, would face a real risk, on account of the absence of appropriate treatment in the receiving country or the lack of access to such treatment, of being exposed to a serious, rapid and irreversible decline in his or her state of health resulting in intense suffering or to a significant reduction in life expectancy.[215]

The Court, though, considered this as a potential violation of the prohibition on inhumane treatment rather than as one concerning the right to life. Indeed, having found a violation under Article 3 of the European Convention, the Court considered it 'not necessary to examine the complaint under Article 2'.[216]

2.91 The Human Rights Committee's latest view on the application of the rule of *non-refoulement* under Article 6 of the ICCPR was surprisingly equivocal. In its 2004 General Comment No. 31, the Committee had stated that the duty to respect and ensure the Covenant rights 'for all persons in their territory and all persons under their control entails an obligation not to extradite, deport, expel or otherwise remove a person from their territory, where there are substantial grounds for believing that there is a real risk of irreparable harm, such as that contemplated by articles 6 and 7 of the Covenant'. The Committee's 2018 General Comment on the right to life, however, states:

> The obligation not to extradite, deport or otherwise transfer pursuant to article 6 of the Covenant *may* be broader than the scope of the principle of non refoulement under international refugee law, since it *may also require the protection of aliens not entitled to refugee status*. States parties must, however, allow all asylum seekers claiming a real risk of a violation of their right to life in the State of origin access to refugee or other individualized or group status determination procedures that could offer them protection against refoulement.[217]

2.92 This seems to bring into question both the scope *ratione personae* and the effect of the rule of *non-refoulement* under the right to life. Yet, as Nigel Rodley observed, exposing someone to the threat of a violation of the right to life is itself a violation of the prohibition of ill-treatment, as well as presumably of the right to life.[218] Indeed, in its 2003 Views in *Judge v. Canada*, the Human Rights Committee considered that Canada, as a State Party to the ICCPR that had abolished the death penalty,

> violated the author's right to life under article 6, paragraph 1, by deporting him to the United States, where he is under sentence of death, without ensuring that the death

---

[215] Ibid., para. 183.
[216] Ibid., para. 207.
[217] Human Rights Committee, General Comment 36 on the right to life, para. 31 (added emphasis), citing the Committee's Concluding Observations on Tajikistan, UN doc. CCPR/C/TJK/CO/2, 22 August 2013, para. 11; and its Concluding Observations on Estonia, UN doc. CCPR/CO/77/EST, 15 April 2003, para. 13. See also General Comment 36 on the right to life, para. 30.
[218] N. S. Rodley, 'Integrity of the Person', in Moeckli, Shah, and Sivakumaran (eds.), *International Human Rights Law*, p. 229.

penalty would not be carried out. The Committee recognizes that Canada did not itself impose the death penalty on the author. But by deporting him to a country where he was under sentence of death, Canada established the crucial link in the causal chain that would make possible the execution of the author.[219]

THE TRANSFER OF WEAPONS

2.93 The transfer of weapons may also violate the right to life. Just as the transfer of a person to another jurisdiction where it is known or expected that he or she will be killed by the receiving State is a violation of the right to life by both the sending and receiving State, so too is the transfer of weapons to another State where it is known or expected that they will be used in an extrajudicial execution.[220]

2.94 With respect to conventional arms and related ammunition, Article 6(3) of the UN Arms Trade Treaty[221] specifies that a State Party shall not authorise any transfer 'if it has knowledge at the time of authorization that the arms or items would be used in the commission of genocide, crimes against humanity, grave breaches of the Geneva Conventions of 1949, attacks directed against civilian objects or civilians protected as such, or other war crimes as defined by international agreements to which it is a Party'. A transfer contrary to this provision that resulted in death as a consequence of an international crime would violate the right to life.

2.95 With respect to weapons of mass destruction, UN Security Council Resolution 1540 decided that all States 'shall take and enforce effective measures to establish domestic controls to prevent the proliferation of nuclear, chemical, or biological weapons and their means of delivery, including by establishing appropriate controls over related materials'.[222] Accordingly, in its General Comment 36 on the right to life, the Human Rights Committee stipulated that States Parties to the ICCPR 'must take all necessary measures to stop the proliferation of weapons of mass destruction, including measures to prevent their acquisition by non-state actors', and to refrain from transferring them, 'all in accordance with their international obligations'.[223]

THE DUTY TO INVESTIGATE POTENTIALLY UNLAWFUL DEATH

2.96 There is a duty under international law to investigate any potentially unlawful death or enforced disappearance. A failure to do so would usually amount to either a violation of the procedural component of the right to life or a combination of the right to life and the

---

[219] Human Rights Committee, *Judge v. Canada*, Views, 2003, para. 10.6.
[220] See on this issue, e.g., 'Arms' in A. Clapham and S. Marks, *International Human Rights Lexicon*, Oxford University Press, Oxford, 2005, p. 13.
[221] Arms Trade Treaty; adopted at New York 2 April 2013; entered into force 24 December 2014. As of 1 May 2021, 110 States were party to the Treaty.
[222] UN Security Council Resolution 1540, adopted by unanimous vote on 28 April 2004, operative para. 3.
[223] Human Rights Committee, General Comment 36 on the right to life, para. 66, citing inter alia the 1968 Treaty on the Non-proliferation of Nuclear Weapons, the 2017 Treaty on the Prohibition of Nuclear Weapons, the 1971 Biological Weapons Convention, and the 1992 Chemical Weapons Convention.

general duty to respect and ensure human rights. With respect to the ICCPR, in its General Comment 36 on the right to life, the Human Rights Committee has considered the duty to investigate to be 'implicit' in the obligation to protect life, but sees it as 'reinforced by the general duty to ensure the rights recognized in the Covenant', as well as the duty to provide an effective remedy to victims of human rights violations.[224]

2.97 A similar approach was taken in the past by the European Court of Human Rights. In its judgment in the landmark *McCann* case, the Grand Chamber endorsed the view that the obligation to protect the right to life under the Convention, 'read in conjunction with the State's general duty under Article 1 … to "secure to everyone within their jurisdiction the rights and freedoms defined in [the] Convention", requires by implication that there should be some form of effective official investigation when individuals have been killed as a result of the use of force by, inter alios, agents of the State'.[225]

2.98 But for several years now, the European Court has instead considered the duty to investigate to be an integral 'procedural' component of the right to life. Its departure from its earlier practice first occurred in its judgment of 2002 in the *Mastromatteo* case, wherein it 'reiterate[d]' that 'the positive obligations laid down in the first sentence of Article 2 of the Convention ["Everyone's right to life shall be protected by law."] also require by implication that an efficient and independent judicial system should be set in place by which the cause of a murder can be established and the guilty parties punished'.[226]

2.99 The procedural obligation to carry out an effective investigation under Article 2 has thus 'evolved into a separate and autonomous duty'.[227] The same approach is taken by the African Commission on Human and Peoples' Rights: 'The failure of the State transparently to take all necessary measures to investigate suspicious deaths and all killings by State agents and to identify and hold accountable individuals or groups responsible for violations of the right to life constitutes in itself a violation by the State of that right.'[228]

2.100 The Inter-American Court of Human Rights has perceived of a general duty to investigate alleged or suspected human rights violations, including but not limited to the right to life, as inhering in the general duty to respect rights in Article 1(1) of the American Convention on Human Rights. Where there is a breach of the procedural obligation to investigate a suspicious death along with a violation of the prohibition on arbitrary deprivation of life, the Court has framed it as a violation of the right to life in combination

---

[224] Article 2(1) and (3), respectively, of the ICCPR. Human Rights Committee, General Comment 36 on the right to life, para. 27.
[225] European Court of Human Rights, *McCann and others v. United Kingdom*, Judgment (Grand Chamber), 27 September 1995, para. 161.
[226] European Court of Human Rights, *Mastromatteo v. Italy*, Judgment (Grand Chamber), 24 October 2002, para. 89.
[227] European Court of Human Rights, *Janowiec and others v. Russia*, Judgment (Grand Chamber), 21 October 2013, para. 132.
[228] African Commission General Comment on the right to life, para. 15.

with Article 1(1).[229] In other cases, in particular those where the substantive limb of Article 4 was not violated, the Court has examined an alleged violation of the duty to investigate potentially unlawful death under Article 8 of the American Convention, which guarantees the right to a fair trial for the determination of the 'rights and obligations' of any nature.

2.101 The duty to investigate and, 'where appropriate', to 'prosecute such incidents' applies to States Parties to the ICCPR, where 'they know or should have known of potentially unlawful deprivations of life'.[230] This includes where it is alleged that excessive use of force has been used 'with lethal consequences'.[231] The duty to investigate is one that is ongoing and persistent in nature. Thus where a State's compliance with its treaty obligations with respect to arbitrary deprivation of life cannot be considered by a human rights court or treaty body *ratione temporis* (because the use of force occurred prior to the State's adherence to a particular treaty), the duty to investigate may persist, at least for a number of years after the events in question occurred.[232]

2.102 Investigations into an alleged violation of Article 6 of the ICCPR must always be independent, impartial, prompt, thorough, effective, credible, and transparent. They should be undertaken in accordance with relevant international standards, in particular the Minnesota Protocol on the Investigation of Potentially Unlawful Death (2016), and 'must be aimed at ensuring that those responsible are brought to justice'.[233] The Minnesota Protocol was elaborated in 2014–16 by an international group of experts led by the UN Special Rapporteur on extrajudicial, summary, or arbitrary executions and the OHCHR.[234]

2.103 The Protocol applies to the investigation of all potentially unlawful death. As also reflected in Rule 71 of the Nelson Mandela Rules, the duty to investigate does not exist only where the State in question is in receipt of a formal complaint.[235] In the event that a violation is found, 'full reparation must be provided, including, in view of the particular circumstances of the case, adequate measures of compensation, rehabilitation and satisfaction'.[236]

---

[229] Inter-American Court of Human Rights, *Velásquez Rodríguez v. Honduras*, Judgment (Merits), 29 July 1988, para. 188; Inter-American Court of Human Rights, *Godínez Cruz v. Honduras*, Judgment (Merits), 20 January 1989, paras. 175–6, 184, 198.

[230] Human Rights Committee, General Comment 36 on the right to life, para. 27.

[231] Ibid.

[232] According to its judgment in the *Šilih* case, 'there must exist a genuine connection between the death and the entry into force of the Convention in respect of the respondent State for the procedural obligations imposed by Article 2 to come into effect'. European Court of Human Rights, *Šilih v. Slovenia*, Judgment (Grand Chamber), 9 April 2009, para. 163. Based on the 'genuine connection' standard, the European Court of Human Rights has endorsed an indicative limit of ten years. European Court of Human Rights, *Janowiec and others v. Russia*, Judgment (Grand Chamber), para. 146. In its judgment in the *Detention Center of Catia* case, the Inter-American Court of Human Rights found that thirteen years after the events, the duty to investigate persisted. Inter-American Court of Human Rights, *Montero-Aranguren and others (Detention Center of Catia) v. Venezuela*, Judgment, para. 137.

[233] Ibid., para. 27.

[234] *Minnesota Protocol on the Investigation of Potentially Unlawful Death (2016), The Revised United Nations Manual on the Effective Prevention and Investigation of Extra-legal, Arbitrary and Summary Executions*, OHCHR, New York/Geneva, 2017.

[235] Ibid.

[236] Ibid., para. 28.

The Content of the Right to Life

2.104 According to the Protocol, to be effective investigations must, at a minimum, take all reasonable steps to (a) identify the victim(s); (b) recover and preserve all material probative of the cause of death, the identity of the perpetrator(s), and the circumstances surrounding the death; (c) identify possible witnesses and obtain their evidence in relation to the death and the circumstances surrounding the death; (d) determine the cause, manner, place and time of death, and all of the surrounding circumstances. In determining the manner of death, the investigation should distinguish between natural death, accidental death, suicide, and homicide; and (e) determine who was involved in the death and their individual responsibility for the death.[237]

2.105 Critical in the case of a potentially unlawful death during detention is the conduct of an autopsy. The Minnesota Protocol stipulates that 'it will almost always be the case that these aims will be materially assisted in some way by the performance of an autopsy. A decision not to undertake an autopsy should be justified in writing and should be subject to judicial review.'[238]

RIGHTS PERTAINING TO THE DEAD

2.106 Under international law, there is no right, per se, of the dead[239] to the disposal of their bodies in accordance with their personal spiritual, humanist, or religious convictions. There is, however, a longstanding customary rule that the family of a deceased person have the right to dispose of the body in an appropriate manner, such as through burial. In his 1625 work, *De Jure Belli ac Pacis*, Grotius declared that the right of burying the dead already existed in the law of nations.[240] He asserted that the right to burial was explained by the dignity of the human person.[241]

2.107 Such a right of burial, which accrues to the family of the deceased, is not, however, unequivocal. While there are, of course, sound public health reasons for the safe disposal of bodies,[242] whether through cremation or by burial,[243] in certain circumstances these

---

[237] Ibid., para. 25, citing Inter-American Court of Human Rights, *Veliz Franco and others v. Guatemala*, Judgment (Preliminary objections, merits, reparations and costs), 19 May 2014, para. 191.

[238] *Minnesota Protocol on the Investigation of Potentially Unlawful Death* (2016), para. 25.

[239] Death is the 'irreversible cessation of all vital functions, including brain activity. Death is "natural" when it is caused solely by disease and/or the ageing process. It is "unnatural" when its causes are external, such as intentional injury (homicide, suicide), negligence, or unintentional injury (death by accident).' Ibid., Glossary, p. 53.

[240] Grotius, *De Jure Belli ac Pacis*, chap. XIX, book II; see Inter-American Court of Human Rights, *Moiwana Village v. Suriname*, Judgment (Preliminary Objections, Merits, Reparations and Costs), Separate Opinion of Judge Antônio Augusto Cançado Trindade, 15 June 2005, para. 60.

[241] Grotius, *De Jure Belli ac Pacis*, chap. XIX, book II.

[242] That said, as the ICRC has observed, 'contrary to popular belief, dead bodies are a negligible health hazard. After a disaster, the top priority is to look after the living. Rushing to bury the dead diverts resources away from rescue efforts and can make it impossible to identify bodies later.' ICRC, 'Why Dead Bodies Do Not Cause Epidemics', FAQ, 13 November 2013, at http://bit.ly/36BsFne. A dead body is ordinarily defined as the physical remains of an expired human being prior to complete decomposition. Stimmel Law, 'Rights and Obligations as to Human Remains and Burial', 2020, at http://bit.ly/3eZmQ7o.

[243] In Ireland, for instance, by statutory instrument it is stipulated that, in general, no interment is permitted in any burial ground 'unless the body be enclosed in a coffin of wood or some other sufficiently strong

may even run counter to a person's express convictions and/or those of close family members. In Germany, for instance, it is generally prohibited to scatter cremated remains, whether on land or at sea. When remains are nonetheless scattered, this is almost always performed illegally.[244]

2.108 Those subjected to the execution of the death penalty may, however, be buried by the authorities under human rights law. In addition, in many States there is a possibility to disinter bodily remains after burial, should the interests of justice require it. Thus for instance, in Ireland by statute the relevant Minister 'may grant a licence for the exhumation of the body of a deceased person'.[245]

2.109 In many common law countries, a right of burial exists under the common law. That said, in the United States, 'no universal rule exists as to whom the right of burial is granted'.[246] As a San Francisco law firm further explains, the 'right to possession of a dead human body for the purpose of burial is, under ordinary circumstances, in the spouse or other relatives of the deceased'.[247] That said, 'an unrestricted property right does not exist in a dead body. The matter of the disposition of the dead is so involved in the public interest, including the public's health, safety, and welfare, that it is subject to control by law instead of being subject entirely to the desires, whim, or caprice of individuals'.[248]

2.110 Civil law States tend to have detailed, and fairly rigid, rules governing the disposal of human remains. For instance, it is claimed that 'the German way of death is perhaps even more regulated than the German way of life. The German propensity to regulate almost every aspect of daily life carries over into the afterlife, with Germany's funeral industry among the most regulated in the world.'[249] While cremation has become increasingly popular in Germany – owing to the high cost of burial – savings compared to a normal burial are limited by laws that still require a coffin and a burial plot even for 'cremains'. Such onerous laws have led to alleged 'corpse tourism', where the body of the deceased is carried by lorry out of the country and cremated in Czechia, the Netherlands, or Switzerland, 'where the costs are much lower and the laws are more liberal'.[250]

2.111 Wide discretion is accorded to States under international human rights law with respect to the manner of disposal of dead bodies. Rights inhere in close family members

material'. Anyone 'presenting a body for interment in violation of this rule shall be liable to a penalty of €125'. Clause V(i), Statutory Instrument No. 144/2013 – Burial Ground (Amendment) Regulations, 2013, at http://bit.ly/35va4tK. Uncoffined burials are, however, permissible in an area of a burial ground designated exclusively for that purpose. Ibid., Clause V(ii).

[244] 'German Funerals; R.I.P.; Death in Deutschland', German Way, at http://bit.ly/2K2LUio.
[245] S. 46(1), Local Government (Sanitary Services) Act, 1948, at http://bit.ly/32LwRQa.
[246] Stimmel Law, 'Rights and Obligations as to Human Remains and Burial', 2020.
[247] Ibid., citing New Jersey Superior Court, *Sherman v. Sherman*, 330 NJ Super. 638 (Ch. Div., 1999).
[248] Stimmel Law, 'Rights and Obligations as to Human Remains and Burial', 2020, citing Colorado Court of Appeal, *Wolf v. Rose Hill Cemetery Association*, 832 P.2d 1007 (1991).
[249] See, e.g., H. Flippo, *When in Germany, Do as the Germans Do*, 2nd ed., McGraw-Hill Education, New York, 2018.
[250] 'German Funerals; R.I.P.; Death in Deutschland', German Way.

rather than in the deceased and pertain to a duty upon the State to inform the family of the location of the body of a family member, wherever that is known, and to ensure they are given the opportunity to dispose of the body in an appropriate manner. Accordingly, preventing family members from being in a position to honour the express wishes of the deceased without just reason violates fundamental rights to family life.[251]

2.112 This right may, in certain circumstances, exist beyond the family and inhere in the broader community. Thus, for example, the N'djuka people in Suriname have 'specific and complex rituals that must be precisely followed upon the death of a community member'. According to longstanding tradition, 'it is extremely important to have possession of the physical remains of the deceased, as the corpse must be treated in a particular manner during the N'djuka death ceremonies and must be placed in the burial ground of the appropriate descent group. Only those who have been deemed unworthy do not receive an honorable burial.'[252]

2.113 The case of *Moiwana Village* v. *Suriname* concerned inter alia the prevention, by the authorities, of the survivors of an attack on an N'djuka village by State agents from recovering the bodies of their fellow community members. In its judgment in 2005, the Inter-American Court of Human Rights held that this had violated the right to humane treatment enshrined in Article 5(1) of the American Convention on Human Rights.[253] One of the greatest sources of suffering for Moiwana community members is that they do not know what has happened to the remains of their loved ones, and, as a result, they cannot honour and bury them in accordance with fundamental norms of N'djuka culture. The Court found it 'understandable' that community members had been distressed by reports indicating that some of the corpses were burned at a mortuary.[254]

2.114 The case of *Sabanchiyeva* v. *Russia*, before the European Court of Human Rights, concerned the treatment of bodies of insurgents killed during an attack on 13–14 October 2005 against Russian police and Ministry of Interior facilities in the town of Nalchik, in the Republic of Kabardino-Balkariya in the North Caucasus. The applicants alleged, in particular, that the circumstances of identification of their deceased family members had been inhuman and degrading and that the decision not to return the bodies of these persons to their families had been unlawful and disproportionate, in breach of Article 3 (right to freedom from torture and inhuman or degrading treatment), Article 8 (right to private and family life), and Article 9 (right to freedom of thought, conscience and religion).[255]

---

[251] The European Court of Human Rights has held that a woman in a close relationship with a man but to whom she was not married at the relevant time was to be considered to be protected by the right to a private life. European Court of Human Rights, *Sabanchiyeva* v. *Russia*, Judgment (First Section), 6 June 2013, para. 119.
[252] Inter-American Court of Human Rights, *Moiwana Village* v. *Suriname*, Judgment, para. 98.
[253] Ibid., para. 103.
[254] Ibid., para. 100.
[255] European Court of Human Rights, *Sabanchiyeva* v. *Russia*, Judgment (First Section), 6 June 2013, para. 3.

2.115 In its judgment, the Court rejected the argument that Article 3 had been violated by the authorities in Russia. Local facilities for refrigerated storage were indeed insufficient to contain all of the bodies of those killed and even thereafter bodies had to be piled on top of one another for storage in refrigerator wagons. But, the Court said, these lapses resulted from objective logistical difficulties arising from the nature of the events of 13–14 October 2005 and the number of casualties, 'and can hardly be said to have had as their purpose to subject the applicants to inhuman treatment, and in particular, to cause them psychological suffering'.[256] The family members were asked to identify the bodies, albeit in difficult conditions, but thus were not excluded from knowing the truth about the fate of their loved ones. Taken in the round, the Court did not find that the circumstances could give the suffering of the applicants 'a dimension and character distinct from the emotional distress which may be regarded as inevitably caused to any family member of a deceased person in a comparable situation'.[257]

2.116 The applicants also alleged a violation of their right to respect for private and family life based on the authorities' refusal to return the bodies. The Government had maintained that the decision not to return the bodies of the applicants' relatives had been taken pursuant to domestic legislation (the Suppression of Terrorism Act and the Interment and Burial Act) as well as a decree on combating terrorism.[258] The decision was therefore 'in accordance with law', as Article 8(2) of the European Convention requires, and there was thus no contravention of the principle of legality. The Court also accepted that the decision not to return the bodies of those engaged in terrorism might be for a legitimate aim. It cited in this regard a decision by the Russian Constitutional Court whereby the

> burial of those who have taken part in a terrorist act, in close proximity to the graves of the victims of their acts, and the observance of rites of burial and remembrance with the paying of respects, as a symbolic act of worship, serve as a means of propaganda for terrorist ideas and also cause offence to relatives of the victims of the acts in question, creating the preconditions for increasing inter-ethnic and religious tension.[259]

2.117 But, the Court held, the automatic denial to the applicants of any participation in the relevant funeral ceremonies 'or at least some kind of opportunity for paying their last respects to the deceased person' was disproportionate in the circumstances. Russia, it concluded, had 'overstepped any acceptable margin of appreciation in this regard', and there was thus a violation of Article 8 of the European Convention on Human Rights.[260] In light of this holding, the Court did not find it necessary to consider the alleged violation of Article 9 of the Convention, although it did note separately that it had found 'no indication which would enable it to conclude that the legislation in question was directed exclusively against followers of the Islamic faith or that the applicants were treated differently from the

---

[256] Ibid., para. 112.
[257] Ibid., para. 113.
[258] Ibid., para. 116.
[259] Ibid., para. 128.
[260] Ibid., paras. 143–7.

The Content of the Right to Life

people in a relevantly similar situation solely on the basis of their religious affiliation or ethnicity'.[261]

2.118 Under the ICCPR, where the death penalty is imposed, the Human Rights Committee has confirmed that the family must be informed in advance of the date on which a State Party plans to execute the convicted person.[262] Similarly, relatives of individuals deprived of their life by the State must be able to receive the bodily remains, if they so wish.[263] Failure to do so will ordinarily violate the right to freedom from torture or cruel, inhuman, or degrading treatment or punishment under Article 7 of the Covenant.

2.119 Thus, for example, in the case of *Kovaleva and Kozyar* v. *Belarus*, the Committee declared that the 'complete secrecy surrounding the date of the execution and the place of burial, as well as the refusal to hand over the body for burial in accordance with the religious beliefs and practices of the executed prisoner's family' had the effect of 'intimidating or punishing the family by intentionally leaving it in a state of uncertainty and mental distress'.[264] The Committee thus concluded that these elements, cumulatively, and Belarus's subsequent persistent failure to notify the authors of the complaint (the father and sister of the deceased) of the location of Mr Kovalev's grave, amounted to inhuman treatment of the authors.[265]

Rights Pertaining to the Dead under International Humanitarian Law

2.120 The ICRC has determined that a customary rule applicable in all armed conflicts dictates that the dead 'must be disposed of in a respectful manner and their graves respected and properly maintained'.[266] Furthermore, each party to the conflict 'must take all possible measures to prevent the dead from being despoiled. Mutilation of dead bodies is prohibited.'[267] There is a duty in all armed conflicts to recover the dead, but a requirement for survey and clearance of anti-personnel mines or items of unexploded ordnance may reasonably delay the implementation of that duty.[268]

2.121 Detailed treaty rules pertain to respect for the dead in situations of international armed conflict. The 1949 Geneva Conventions specify that, if possible, the dead must be buried and this in accordance with the rites of the religion to which they belonged. They may only be cremated in exceptional circumstances, notably because of imperative reasons of hygiene, on account of the religion of the deceased, or in accordance with

---

[261] Ibid., para. 162.
[262] Human Rights Committee, General Comment 36 on the right to life, para. 56.
[263] Ibid.; and see, e.g., Human Rights Committee, Concluding Observations: Botswana, UN doc. CCPR/C/BWA/CO/1, 24 April 2008, para. 13.
[264] Human Rights Committee, *Kovaleva and Kozyar* v. *Belarus*, Views, UN doc. CCPR/C/106/D/2120/2011, 27 November 2012, para. 11.10.
[265] Ibid.
[266] ICRC Customary IHL Rule 115: 'Disposal of the Dead', at http://bit.ly/2Uuol3I.
[267] ICRC Customary IHL Rule 113: 'Treatment of the Dead', at http://bit.ly/35CDtm9.
[268] See generally ICRC, *The Recovery of Human Remains in Weapon-Contaminated Settings*, Geneva, September 2020.

the express wish of the deceased.[269] In principle, burial should be in individual graves. Collective graves may only be used when circumstances do not permit the use of individual graves or, in case of burial of prisoners of war or civilian internees, because unavoidable circumstances require the use of collective graves.[270] The Geneva Conventions also stipulate that, if it is possible, graves should be grouped according to nationality.[271]

2.122 In situations of non-international armed conflict, the 1977 Additional Protocol II stipulates that it is required 'to search for the dead, prevent their being despoiled, and decently dispose of them'.[272] The rights set out supra in Paragraphs 2.105–2.118 apply also in non-international armed conflict as they do in peacetime. Indeed, case-law cited therein before the European and Inter-American courts pertained to situations of apparent non-international armed conflict. UN Security Council Resolution 2474, adopted on 11 June 2019, calls upon parties to armed conflict 'to take all appropriate measures, to actively search for persons reported missing, to enable the return of their remains, and to account for persons reported missing without adverse distinction'.[273]

2.123 Echoing the right to family life in human rights law,[274] the ICRC has found also that it is a customary rule that family life 'must be respected as far as possible'.[275] This rule holds that all feasible measures must be taken by the authorities to account for missing persons and that there is a duty to inform families of their whereabouts, including those who have been killed, when such information is available.[276] In a 1974 resolution, 'Assistance and cooperation in accounting for persons who are missing or dead in armed conflicts', the UN General Assembly considered that 'the desire to know the fate of loved ones lost in armed conflicts is a basic human need which should be satisfied to the greatest extent possible'.[277]

---

[269] Art. 17, 1949 Geneva Convention I; Art. 120, 1949 Geneva Convention III; Art. 130, 1949 Geneva Convention IV. With respect to the Second Geneva Convention, parties to the conflict are obligated to ensure that burial at sea, 'carried out individually as far as circumstances permit, is preceded by a careful examination, if possible by a medical examination, of the bodies, with a view to confirming death, establishing identity and enabling a report to be made'. Art. 20(1), 1949 Geneva Convention II. If bodies of those killed at sea are on land, then the provisions of Geneva Convention I apply. Art. 20(2), 1949 Geneva Convention II.

[270] Art. 17(1), 1949 Geneva Convention I; Art. 120(5), 1949 Geneva Convention III; and Art. 130(2), 1949 Geneva Convention IV.

[271] Art. 17(3), 1949 Geneva Convention I; Art. 120(4), 1949 Geneva Convention III.

[272] Art. 8, 1977 Additional Protocol II.

[273] UN Security Council Resolution 2474, adopted by unanimous vote on 11 June 2019, operative para. 2. See also UN, 'Security Council Adopts First-Ever Resolution on Persons Reported Missing during Armed Conflict, as Speakers Call for Greater Political Will to Address Problem', UN doc. SC/13835, 11 June 2019, at http://bit.ly/3pFfNpc.

[274] See, in addition to Art. 8, European Convention on Human Rights: Art. 17(1), American Convention on Human Rights; Art. 18(1), African Charter on Human and Peoples' Rights; and Art. 21, Arab Charter on Human Rights.

[275] ICRC Customary IHL Rule 105: 'Respect for Family Life', at http://bit.ly/2IJ9oYL.

[276] See ibid.

[277] UN General Assembly Resolution 3220 (XXIX), adopted on 6 November 1974 by ninety-five votes to nil with thirty-two abstentions, eighth preambular para.

3

Jurisdiction and the Right to Life

INTRODUCTION

3.01 This chapter addresses the jurisdictional aspects of the right to life with respect to both its primary substantive element (the prohibition of arbitrary deprivation of life) and its procedural element (the duty to investigate potentially unlawful death). Consonant with its denotation in other branches of international law, in international human rights law jurisdiction has geographical, material, personal, and temporal aspects.

3.02 Under general international law, jurisdiction is 'the entitlement of a State to assert State authority in relation to persons and things'.[1] As such, it 'reflects the basic principles of state sovereignty, equality of states and non-interference in domestic affairs'.[2] But international human rights law distinguishes itself from the conception of jurisdiction in many other international legal regimes. Ordinarily, international law articulates the outer limits of a State's legal competence vis-à-vis other States 'to make, apply, and enforce rules of conduct upon persons'.[3] Significantly, however, in human rights law jurisdiction serves to encroach upon and restrict the opportunity for States lawfully to perform a wide array of acts within their sovereign competence.

3.03 In addition to preventing certain actions, the substance of human rights law, particularly the right to life, also obligates States to engage in certain conduct. This pertains to peacetime and to situations of armed conflict. Under international humanitarian law, for example, the compulsory universal jurisdiction demanded by the four Geneva Conventions of 1949 – to which all States are party – obligates the extension of jurisdictional reach in domestic penal law beyond what governments might otherwise wish to see and do.[4]

---

[1] A. Orakhelashvili, *Akehurst's Modern Introduction to International Law*, 8th ed., Routledge, London, 2019, p. 213.
[2] M. N. Shaw, *International Law*, 8th ed., Cambridge University Press, Cambridge, 2017, p. 483.
[3] C. Staker, 'Jurisdiction', chap. 11 in M. D. Evans (ed.), *International Law*, 4th ed., Oxford University Press, Oxford, 2014, p. 311.
[4] Under the Geneva Convention IV, each State Party is obligated 'to search for persons alleged to have committed, or to have ordered to be committed' grave breaches of the Convention, and to 'bring such persons, regardless of their nationality, before its own courts'. Art. 146, Geneva Convention Relative to the Protection of Civilian Persons in Time of War; adopted at Geneva 12 August 1949; entered into force 21 October 1950 (hereinafter, 1949 Geneva Convention IV). As of 1 May 2021, 196 States were party to the Convention. In addition, according to the International Committee of the Red Cross, Niue, the 197th State,

The Geographical Basis for Jurisdiction

3.04 The primary basis for jurisdiction in international law is geographical.[5] This is also the case in international human rights law. Jurisdiction *ratione loci* concerns first and foremost the writ of a State over its sovereign territory, whether metropolitan or non-metropolitan. The territory of a State encompasses not only its physical landmass but also its territorial sea (which extends up to twelve nautical miles from the coastal baseline),[6] as well as the airspace above both the land[7] and that territorial sea.[8] States 'may thus legislate for ships off their coasts, and for aircraft in their skies'.[9]

3.05 Such authority does not, however, transform those ships and aircraft, even when flagged or owned by the territorial state, into sovereign territory.[10] It is also a common misconception that the embassies abroad of a State are its sovereign territory, but this is also not the case.[11] There will, however, be exclusive criminal jurisdiction within an embassy for the possessor State (unless consent is given to the territorial State), as well as responsibility under international human rights law for acts committed therein by the possessor State.[12]

3.06 Jurisdiction *ratione loci* may underpin the substance of an international legal obligation. Acts committed at any place under the jurisdiction of a State generally fall within the scope of both customary and conventional international human rights law. This jurisdiction, while primarily applicable to a State's sovereign territory – even in situations where the national authorities do not effectively control all of that territory[13] – may also exist extraterritorially in certain circumstances. Similarly, under international disarmament law, jurisdictional clauses are often employed in order to determine which weapons are to be destroyed under a particular treaty. The 1992 Chemical Weapons Convention, for

---

'remains bound' by New Zealand's ratification of the four Conventions, 'until such time as Niue accedes to the Conventions in its own right'. See http://bit.ly/3mdzdiK.

[5] Shaw, *International Law*, 8th ed., p. 483.
[6] Arts. 2(1) and 3, United Nations (UN) Convention on the Law of the Sea; adopted at Montego Bay 10 December 1982; entered into force 16 November 1994 (hereinafter, UNCLOS). As of 1 May 2021, 168 States were party to the Convention.
[7] Arts. 1 and 2, Convention on International Civil Aviation; adopted and signed at Chicago, 7 December 1944; entered into force 4 April 1947. As of 1 May 2021, 193 States were party to the Convention.
[8] Art. 2(2), UNCLOS. Airspace is generally considered to end at the Kármán Line, set today some 100 kilometres above the earth's surface. But see also on this issue J. C. McDowell, 'The Edge of Space: Revisiting the Karman Line', *Acta Astronautica*, vol. 151 (October 2018), pp. 668–77, at http://bit.ly/37Ux5VS. McDowell argues for a figure of 80 kilometres independent of solar and atmospheric conditions, rather than the 'currently popular' 100 kilometre value. Ibid., p. 676.
[9] Staker, 'Jurisdiction', p. 316.
[10] A. Clapham, *Brierly's Law of Nations*, 7th ed., Oxford University Press, Oxford, 2012, pp. 233–4.
[11] Ibid., p. 207. See also J. J. Paust, 'Non-Extraterritoriality of "Special Territorial Jurisdiction" of the United States: Forgotten History and the Errors of Erdos', Comment, *Yale Journal of International Law*, vol. 24 (1999), pp. 305–28, at 307.
[12] See, *infra*, Paragraph 3.40.
[13] This may be as a result of foreign military occupation or domestic insurgency. European Court of Human Rights, *Catan and others v. Moldova and Russia*, Judgment (Grand Chamber), 19 October 2012, para. 110. This case is discussed *infra* at Paragraph 3.33.

instance, obliges each State Party to 'destroy chemical weapons it owns or possesses, or that are located in any place under its jurisdiction or control'.[14]

3.07 Under Article 2(1) of the International Covenant on Civil and Political Rights[15] (ICCPR), each State Party undertakes 'to respect and to ensure to all individuals within its territory and subject to its jurisdiction the rights recognized in the ... Covenant'. This jurisdictional clause has come to be understood expansively. The 'and' in the clause is construed not as a conjunctive, making the two elements cumulative as its ordinary meaning – and early negotiations – would indicate, but in effect as meaning 'within its territory *or otherwise subject to* its jurisdiction'. As discussed further below, this broad construction was endorsed by the International Court of Justice in its Advisory Opinion in the *Wall* case.[16]

3.08 The interpretation of Article 2 of the ICCPR as applying also to certain extraterritorial acts is especially significant where the right to life is at stake, and particularly where these concern respect for the jus cogens prohibition on arbitrary deprivation of life. Jurisdiction, the Human Rights Committee has stipulated in its General Comment No. 36, extends to persons 'located outside any territory effectively controlled by the State whose right to life is nonetheless affected by its military or other activities in a direct and reasonably foreseeable manner'.[17]

3.09 But the Committee goes further, requiring also that each State Party to the ICCPR 'take appropriate measures to protect individuals against deprivation of life by other States, international organizations and foreign corporations' operating outside their territory but where they are subject to its jurisdiction.[18] With regard to corporations, the Committee cites its Views adopted in 2017 in *Yassin and Others v. Canada*. The case concerned the construction of settlements in the West Bank by a Canadian company and the complaint by a number of Palestinians to the Committee of the violation of several of their rights by Canada. These complaints included cruel, inhuman, or degrading treatment prohibited under Article 7 of the Covenant, but not the right to life. The Committee stated:

> While the human rights obligations of a State on its own territory cannot be equated in all respects with its obligations outside its territory, ... there are situations where a State party has an obligation to ensure that rights under the Covenant are not impaired by extraterritorial activities conducted by enterprises under its jurisdiction. ... That is particularly the

---

[14] Art. I(2), Convention on the Prohibition of the Development, Production, Stockpiling and Use of Chemical Weapons and on their Destruction; adopted at Geneva 3 September 1992; entered into force 29 April 1997. As of 1 May 2021, 193 States were party to the Convention.

[15] International Covenant on Civil and Political Rights; adopted at New York 16 December 1966; entered into force 23 March 1976.

[16] International Court of Justice, *Legal Consequences of the Construction of a Wall in the Occupied Palestinian Territory*, Advisory Opinion, 9 July 2004, para. 109.

[17] Human Rights Committee, General Comment No. 36: Article 6: right to life, UN doc. CCPR/C/GC/36, 3 September 2019 (hereinafter, Human Rights Committee, General Comment 36 on the right to life), para. 63.

[18] Ibid., para. 22.

case where violations of human rights that are as serious in nature as the ones raised in this communication are at stake.'[19]

This is consonant with the universal application to State conduct of jus cogens norms: the prohibition of arbitrary deprivation of life, enforced disappearance, torture, slavery, aggression, and apartheid. These peremptory rules apply without geographical limitation.

The Material Basis for Jurisdiction

3.10 Jurisdiction *ratione materiae* concerns the subject matter of an international legal obligation. Thus, for example, Article 5 of the 1998 Rome Statute of the International Criminal Court[20] (hereinafter, the Rome Statute) stipulates which crimes fall within the jurisdiction of the Court. In a treaty of international human rights law, the subject matter is the rights that are protected thereunder.

3.11 Material jurisdiction is often closely linked with the notion of immunity from prosecution. In its judgment in 2002 in the *Arrest Warrant* case, the International Court of Justice stated that 'it is only where a State has jurisdiction under international law in relation to a particular matter that there can be any question of immunities in regard to the exercise of that jurisdiction'.[21] The immunity from prosecution that certain State officials normally enjoy in the exercise of their functions does not extend, *ratione materiae*, to the commission of international crimes.[22]

The Personal Basis for Jurisdiction

3.12 Jurisdiction *ratione personae* in international criminal law concerns who (or which entity) is to be held responsible for an internationally wrongful act or the commission of an international crime. Under the Rome Statute, the International Criminal Court 'shall

---

[19] Human Rights Committee, *Yassin and others v. Canada*, Views, 26 July 2017, para. 6.5. The complaint failed not on jurisdictional but on causal grounds, on the basis that the nexus between Canada's obligations under the Covenant, the actions of the two Canadian corporations concerned, and the alleged violation of the authors' rights was 'not sufficiently substantiated to render the case admissible'. Ibid., para. 6.7.

[20] Rome Statute of the International Criminal Court; adopted at Rome 17 July 1998; entered into force 1 July 2002 (hereinafter, Rome Statute). As of 1 May 2021, 123 States were party to the Convention.

[21] International Court of Justice, *Case Concerning the Arrest Warrant of 11 April 2000 (Democratic Republic of the Congo v. Belgium)*, Judgment, 14 February 2002, para. 46.

[22] See, e.g., Opinion by Legal Advisory Committee to the Minister of Foreign Affairs of the Republic of Poland on immunities of State officials from foreign criminal jurisdiction, Warsaw, 27 April 2015, p. 14, at http://bit.ly/36Hd6Zn. Such immunity *ratione materiae* is understood as a functional immunity, 'since the protection afforded to persons who enjoy immunity is ultimately granted to them by virtue of the functions or tasks that each of them performs within his or her hierarchical official relationship with the State'. International Law Commission (ILC), 'Second report on the immunity of State officials from foreign criminal jurisdiction, Concepción Escobar Hernández, Special Rapporteur', UN doc. A/CN.4/661, 4 April 2013, paras. 47, 48. Distinct from immunity *ratione materiae* is immunity from prosecution *ratione personae*: applying to the position rather than the functions performed thereunder. The most obvious is immunity given to a head of State (perhaps, 'the oldest form of immunity'). ILC, 'Preliminary Report on Immunity of State Officials from Foreign Criminal Jurisdiction, Roman Anatolevich Kolodkin, Special Rapporteur', UN doc. A/CN.4/601, 29 May 2008, para. 78.

have jurisdiction over natural persons' and therefore not also legal persons (bodies corporate).[23] Among natural persons, the Court 'shall have no jurisdiction over any person who was under the age of 18 at the time of the alleged commission of a crime'.[24]

3.13 In international human rights law, the personal basis for jurisdiction concerns whether an individual, group, or body corporate may be held accountable for a rights violation in addition to or as an alternative to the State. Jurisdiction *ratione personae* also addresses who has *locus standi* to bring a claim of a rights violation (or of another violation of international law) and who is protected under a particular human rights treaty. In the European Court's Grand Chamber judgment in the *Jaloud* case,[25] extraterritorial jurisdiction to the applicant was found on the basis of Dutch control of persons passing through a checkpoint in Iraq.[26]

The Temporal Basis for Jurisdiction

3.14 Jurisdiction *ratione temporis* concerns whether a given act falls within the jurisdiction of a particular court or tribunal based on when it occurred. This is particularly an issue with respect to the date on which a State became party to a particular treaty. In the case of the International Criminal Court, for instance, acts that occurred before a State's adherence to the Rome Statute will not generally fall within the jurisdiction of the Court.[27] In any event, there is no possibility of jurisdiction under the Court prior to 1 July 2002 when the Rome Statute itself entered into force.[28]

3.15 As discussed below,[29] events that took place prior to a State becoming party to a human rights treaty may not be judged thereunder according to the substantive component of the right to life. But the procedural component of the right to life – the duty to investigate suspicious death – may persist for many years, thereby according jurisdiction to a court that it would otherwise not have in a particular case.

3.16 Nonetheless, there may be a situation where the impact on the victim is continuing and accordingly so too is the human rights violation. In its views on the *Lovelace* case, the Human Rights Committee found jurisdiction even though the loss of the complainant's status as a registered member of an Indian group had occurred at the time of her marriage in 1970 and Canada had only accepted the Committee's jurisdiction for individual petitions in 1976. The Committee noted that it was

---

[23] Art. 25(1), Rome Statute.
[24] Art. 26, Rome Statute.
[25] European Court of Human Rights, *Jaloud v. The Netherlands*, Judgment (Grand Chamber), 20 November 2014.
[26] Ibid., para. 152. See also on this issue A. Sari, 'Jaloud v Netherlands: New Directions in Extra-Territorial Military Operations', blog entry, *EJIL: Talk!*, 24 November 2014, at http://bit.ly/2OmcIsR.
[27] Unless the State concerned has made a declaration with the Court Registrar in accordance with Article 12(3) of the Rome Statute.
[28] Paragraph 1 of Article 11 ('Jurisdiction *ratione temporis*') decrees: 'The Court has jurisdiction only with respect to crimes committed after the entry into force of this Statute.'
[29] See, *infra*, Paragraphs 3.51–3.53.

not competent, as a rule, to examine allegations relating to events having taken place before the entry into force of the Covenant and the Optional Protocol. ... In the case of Sandra Lovelace it follows that the Committee is not competent to express any view on the original cause of her loss of Indian status ... at the time of her marriage in 1970 ...

The Committee recognizes, however, that the situation may be different if the alleged violations, although relating to events occurring before 19 August 1976, continue, or have effects which themselves constitute violations, after that date.[30]

Such an ongoing violation occurs, for instance, with respect to enforced disappearance, where the victim of a disappearance has not been duly accounted for.

JURISDICTION UNDER HUMAN RIGHTS TREATIES

Jurisdiction under Global Human Rights Treaties

3.17 Each global and regional human rights treaty has a different scope of application. Article 2(1) of the ICCPR referred to above provides in full as follows:

Each State Party to the present Covenant undertakes to respect and to ensure to all individuals within its territory and subject to its jurisdiction the rights recognized in the present Covenant, without distinction of any kind, such as race, colour, sex, language, religion, political or other opinion, national or social origin, property, birth or other status.

The correct legal interpretation of the salient phrase, 'all individuals within its territory and subject to its jurisdiction' is still disputed, albeit by a tiny minority of States. These States have interpreted the wording as rendering the requirements of presence on sovereign territory and subjection to jurisdiction cumulative. But general State practice and judicial interpretation, including by the International Court of Justice,[31] has determined that they are alternatives.[32]

3.18 In its Advisory Opinion on the *Legal Consequences of the Construction of a Wall in the Occupied Palestinian Territory* (the *Wall* case), the Court observed that the *travaux préparatoires* of the Covenant confirm the Human Rights Committee's broad interpretation of Article 2 of the ICCPR.

These show that, in adopting the wording chosen, the drafters of the Covenant did not intend to allow States to escape from their obligations when they exercise jurisdiction outside their national territory. They only intended to prevent persons residing abroad

---

[30] Human Rights Committee, *Lovelace v. Canada*, Views, 30 July 1981, paras. 10–11.

[31] See, in particular, International Court of Justice, *Legality of the Threat or Use of Nuclear Weapons*, Advisory Opinion, 8 July 1996, para. 25; *Legal Consequences of the Construction of a Wall in the Occupied Palestinian Territory*, Advisory Opinion, 9 July 2004, paras. 107–11; and *Case Concerning Armed Activities on the Territory of the Congo (Democratic Republic of the Congo v. Uganda)*, Judgment, 19 December 2005, paras. 179–80, 211, 217, and 219–20.

[32] Indeed, were it otherwise, the reference to 'subject to its jurisdiction' could further restrict the application of the Covenant to acts or omissions of the territorial State against, or which affected, only certain individuals even when the relevant events occurred on its sovereign territory.

from asserting, vis-à-vis their State of origin, rights that do not fall within the competence of that State, but of that of the State of residence.[33]

The interpretation of Article 2 as applying to certain extraterritorial acts is, as the International Court of Justice observed, reflected in the 'constant practice' of the Human Rights Committee.[34] Thus, for instance, in its General Comment 31, the Committee stated that the wording 'means that a State party must respect and ensure the rights laid down in the Covenant to anyone within the power or effective control of that State Party, even if not situated within the territory of the State Party'.[35]

3.19 Under the broad interpretation of Article 2(1) of the ICCPR, either acts must have occurred on sovereign territory, or a person outside sovereign territory must come within the jurisdiction of a State by other means. Thereby, jurisdiction would, for instance, extend to individuals in territory controlled by a foreign state through military occupation or where a State, in an extraterritorial act, has taken an individual into its custody (whether that be by lawful or unlawful means). According to the Human Rights Committee, Article 2(1) 'also applies to those within the power or effective control of the forces of a State Party acting outside its territory, regardless of the circumstances in which such power or effective control was obtained, such as forces constituting a national contingent of a State Party assigned to an international peace-keeping or peace-enforcement operation'.[36]

3.20 Two States – Israel and the United States – have opposed all extraterritorial application of the ICCPR. In 2013, in its fourth periodic report under the ICCPR, Israel recognised that the applicability of the Covenant to the West Bank 'has been the subject of considerable debate in recent years', noting further that, in its periodic reports under the Covenant, it 'did not refer to the implementation of the Convention in these areas for several reasons, ranging from legal considerations to the practical reality'.[37] It further stated that 'in line with basic principles of treaty interpretation, Israel believes that the Convention, which is territorially bound, does not apply, nor was it intended to apply, to areas beyond a state's national territory'.[38]

3.21 In its Concluding Observations on Israel's fourth periodic report, the Human Rights Committee expressed its regret that Israel 'continues to maintain its position on the non-applicability of the Covenant' to the Occupied Palestinian Territories, given the 'interpretation to the contrary' of Article 2(1), which is 'supported by the Committee's

[33] International Court of Justice, *Legal Consequences of the Construction of a Wall in the Occupied Palestinian Territory*, Advisory Opinion, 9 July 2004, para. 109.
[34] Ibid.
[35] Human Rights Committee, General Comment No. 31: 'The Nature of the General Legal Obligation Imposed on States Parties to the Covenant', UN doc. CCPR/C/21/Rev.1/Add. 13, 26 May 2004 (hereinafter, Human Rights Committee, General Comment No. 31), para. 10. See also S. Joseph and M. Castan, *The International Covenant on Civil and Political Rights: Cases, Materials; and Commentary*, 3rd ed., Oxford University Press, Oxford, 2014, paras. 4.11–4.17.
[36] Human Rights Committee, General Comment No. 31, para. 10.
[37] Fourth Periodic Report of Israel under the ICCPR, UN doc. CCPR/C/ISR/4, 12 December 2013, p. 11, para. 46.
[38] Ibid., para. 48.

established jurisprudence', the jurisprudence of the International Court of Justice, and State practice.[39] In its most recent (fifth) periodic report under the ICCPR, Israel has maintained its position. Thus, in October 2019, it stated that, having 'carefully reviewed the matter in recent years', it 'continue[s] to maintain that the Covenant applies only to a State territory'.[40] It repeated its consistent assertion that the Convention is territorially bound and does not apply to areas beyond a State's national territory.[41]

3.22 In contrast, the United States, in its fourth periodic report under the Covenant issued in 2012, had appeared to soften slightly its opposition to extraterritorial application of the ICCPR. Therein, the United States stated that it was 'mindful' of the Committee's view that States Parties are required to respect and ensure Covenant rights 'to all persons who may be within their territory and to all persons subject to their jurisdiction', and that this included 'anyone within the power or effective control' of a State Party, even if not situated within its territory.[42] The United States was also 'aware' of the jurisprudence in the International Court of Justice, which has found the ICCPR 'applicable in respect of acts done by a State in the exercise of its jurisdiction outside its own territory', as well as the positions on the issue among other States Parties.[43]

3.23 In its Concluding Observations on the fourth periodic report, the Human Rights Committee did not acknowledge an apparent slight shift in position. It called on the United States to interpret the ICCPR 'in good faith' and to 'review its legal position so as to acknowledge the extraterritorial application of the Covenant under certain circumstances'.[44] In its list of issues for inclusion in the United States' fifth periodic report, the Committee asked it to clarify the

> current legal position on the scope of applicability of the Covenant with respect to individuals under its jurisdiction but outside its territory, such as those detained at the Guantánamo Bay facility, those on ships and aircraft registered to the United States that are participating in programmes such as Operation Martillo,[45] and those directly targeted by aircraft and unmanned aerial vehicles operated by the United States.[46]

Indeed, in its fifth periodic report, which it submitted in 2021, the United States reiterated clearly its earlier stance whereby:

---

[39] Human Rights Committee, Concluding Observations on the Fourth Periodic Report of Israel, UN doc. CCPR/C/ISR/CO/4, 21 November 2014, p. 2, para. 5.
[40] Fifth Periodic Report of Israel under the ICCPR, UN doc. CCPR/C/ISR/5, 30 October 2019, para. 22.
[41] Ibid., para. 24.
[42] Fourth Periodic Report of the United States under the ICCPR, UN doc. CCPR/C/USA/4, 22 May 2012, para. 505.
[43] Ibid.
[44] Human Rights Committee, Concluding Observations on the Fourth Periodic Report of the United States, UN doc. CCPR/C/USA/CO/4, 23 April 2014, para. 3(a).
[45] Operation Martillo (Hammer) is a US, European, and Western Hemisphere effort targeting illicit trafficking routes in coastal waters along the Central American isthmus. US Southern Command, 'Operation Martillo', undated but accessed 31 January 2020, at http://bit.ly/2GBWurs (footnote not in original).
[46] Human Rights Committee, List of issues prior to submission of the fifth periodic report of the United States of America, UN doc. CCPR/C/USA/QPR/5, 18 April 2019, para. 4.

The United States has not changed its position that Article 2(1) creates obligations for a State Party only with respect to individuals who are both within the territory of the State Party and within that State Party's jurisdiction. Thus, we do not agree that Article 2(1) creates obligations for a State Party with respect to individuals on State Party-registered ships located beyond that State Party's territorial sea, or on State Party-registered aircraft flying in international airspace or in another State's airspace. Merely being on a ship or aircraft registered in a State (and thereby being generally subject to its exclusive jurisdiction on the high seas, for example) does not constitute being in a State's territory for the purposes of Article 2(1) of the Covenant.[47]

3.24 There have been indications that the United States has opposed the extraterritorial application of the ICCPR specifically and does not maintain this position with respect to the entire corpus of conventional and customary human rights law. Thus, in 2014, in its Concluding Observations on the United States' combined third to fifth periodic reports under the 1984 Convention Against Torture, the Committee against Torture welcomed its 'unequivocal commitment to abide by the universal prohibition of torture and ill-treatment everywhere, including at Bagram and Guantanamo Bay detention facilities, as well as the assurances that United States personnel are legally prohibited under international and domestic law from engaging in torture or cruel, inhuman, or degrading treatment or punishment at all times and in all places'.[48] The Committee noted that the United States had reviewed its position concerning the extraterritorial application of the Convention Against Torture and accepted that

> it applies to 'certain areas beyond' its sovereign territory, and more specifically to 'all places that the State party controls as a governmental authority', noting that it currently exercises such control at 'the United States Naval Station at Guantanamo Bay, Cuba, and over all proceedings conducted there, and with respect to US-registered ships and aircraft'.[49]

3.25 Under Article 2(1) of the 1989 Convention on the Rights of the Child,[50] States Parties are obligated to 'respect and ensure the rights' set out in the Convention 'to each child within their jurisdiction'. There is thus no reference to sovereign territory as in the ICCPR. The Convention is the most widely ratified human rights treaty, with 196 States Parties as of writing.[51] In its General Comment No. 5, the Committee on the Rights of the Child

---

[47] Fifth Periodic Report of the United States under the ICCPR, UN doc. CPR/C/USA/5, 19 January 2021. para. 14 (original footnote omitted in which the United States referred to its fourth periodic report under the ICCPR).
[48] Committee against Torture, Concluding Observations on the combined third to fifth periodic reports of the United States, UN doc. CAT/C/US/CO/3–5, 19 December 2014, para. 10.
[49] Ibid.
[50] Convention on the Rights of the Child; adopted at New York 20 November 1989; entered into force 2 September 1990.
[51] Only the United States of America, a signatory, is not a State Party to the Convention.

reiterated that 'in all circumstances the State which ratified or acceded to the Convention remains responsible for ensuring the full implementation of the Convention throughout the territories under its jurisdiction'.[52] This did not, however, clarify the extent of extraterritorial jurisdiction; indeed, the Comment was not specifically intended to explain the implications of Article 2(1).

3.26 In its Advisory Opinion on the *Wall* case, the International Court of Justice simply stated that based on the wording in Article 2(1) of the Convention on the Rights of the Child, the Convention 'is therefore applicable within the Occupied Palestinian Territory'.[53] Subsequently, the Committee on the Rights of the Child urged Israel 'to abide by its obligations to ensure the full application of the Convention in Israel and in the OPT [Occupied Palestinian Territory], including the West Bank, the Gaza Strip as well as in the Occupied Syrian Golan heights'.[54]

Jurisdiction under Regional Human Rights Treaties

Jurisdiction under the Inter-American Convention on Human Rights

3.27 According to Article 1(1) of the 1969 Inter-American Convention on Human Rights, States Parties must ensure the rights protected therein to 'all persons subject to their jurisdiction'.[55] There is, therefore, no territorial specification in the provision as contained in the ICCPR, although a draft of the Inter-American Convention had proposed to incorporate one.[56] Thus negotiating States had essentially agreed upon 'a broad criterion' that includes not only acts or omissions attributable to the State when committed (or omitted) within sovereign territory, 'but also responsibility for acts or omissions carried out outside State territory but within State jurisdiction, such as the actions of an occupying army or actions taken on diplomatic premises'.[57] In interpreting the provision on jurisdiction, the Inter-American Commission on Human Rights has generally applied an

---

[52] Committee on the Rights of the Child, General Comment No. 5: 'General Measures of Implementation of the Convention on the Rights of the Child (arts. 4, 42 and 44, para. 6)', UN doc. CRC/GC/2003/5, 27 November 2003, para. 41.

[53] International Court of Justice, *Legal Consequences of the Construction of a Wall in the Occupied Palestinian Territory*, Advisory Opinion, para. 113. The Court also held that the Convention applied extraterritorially to a situation of military occupation in its judgment in the *Armed Activities* case in the Democratic Republic of Congo. International Court of Justice, *Case Concerning Armed Activities on the Territory of the Congo (Democratic Republic of the Congo v. Uganda)*, Judgment, 19 December 2005, paras. 217, 219.

[54] Committee on the Rights of the Child, Concluding Observations on the second to fourth periodic reports of Israel, UN doc. CRC/C/ISR/CO/2–4, 4 July 2013, para. 3.

[55] Art. 4(1), American Convention on Human Rights; adopted at San José 22 November 1969; entered into force 18 July 1978.

[56] Inter-American Court of Human Rights, *The Environment and Human Rights (State Obligations in Relation to the Environment in the Context of the Protection and Guarantee of the Rights to Life and to Personal Integrity: Interpretation and Scope of Articles 4(1) and 5(1) in Relation to Articles 1(1) and 2 of the American Convention on Human Rights)*, Advisory Opinion OC-23/17, 15 November 2017, Requested by the Republic of Colombia, para. 77; see also C. Medina, *The American Convention on Human Rights*, Intersentia, Cambridge, 2014, para. 12.

[57] Ibid.

'authority' or 'control' test.[58] This approach has been maintained by the Inter-American Court of Human Rights.

3.28 In its 2017 Advisory Opinion on the Environment and Human Rights, the Inter-American Court affirmed its position whereby the term 'jurisdiction' in Article 1(1) means that the obligation to respect and ensure human rights applies not only to every person within a State Party's territory but also to another 'who is in any way subject to its authority, responsibility or control'.[59] This interpretation, the Court affirmed, 'coincides' with the sense 'the Inter-American Commission has given to the word "jurisdiction" in Article 1(1) of the Convention in its decisions'.[60] In this regard, the Commission had observed that, in international law, 'the bases of jurisdiction are not exclusively territorial'. According to 'inter-American human rights law', the Commission held, 'each American State is obligated ... to respect the rights of all persons within its territory and of those present in the territory of another State but subject to the control of its agents'.[61]

3.29 Previously, the Inter-American Commission had ruled admissible a case that concerned the bombardment by the United States of the Richmond Hill Mental Health Facility during its invasion of Grenada in 1983. The bombardment killed sixteen people.[62] The case concluded with a friendly settlement: a new hospital was built in 1987 to replace the one destroyed by the bombing, and residents of the new facility and the individual petitioners were paid compensation and provided with clothing, food, care, and services.[63] But in providing this reparation for the harm caused, the US Government considered it 'important to note for the record its longstanding position that its actions were entirely in conformance with the law of armed conflict, and that therefore the United States had no legal liability for any damages claimed'.[64] It did not, however, explicitly reject the competence of the Inter-American Commission to address acts committed extraterritorially.

3.30 Thus, as the Inter-American Court has further observed, most of the situations in which extraterritorial application of human rights law has been confirmed 'involve

---

[58] See, e.g., Inter-American Commission on Human Rights, *Report on Terrorism and Human Rights*, OAS doc. OEA/Ser.L/V/II.116, Doc. 5 rev. 1 corr., 22 October 2002, para. 374; see also O. A. Hathaway and others, 'Human Rights Abroad: When Do Human Rights Treaty Obligations Apply Extraterritorially?', *Arizona State Law Journal*, vol. 43 (2011), p. 26.

[59] Inter-American Court of Human Rights, *The Environment and Human Rights*, Advisory Opinion, 2017, para. 73.

[60] Ibid., para. 74, citing inter alia, Inter-American Commission on Human Rights, *Franklin Guillermo Aisalla Molina (Ecuador v. Colombia)*, Admissibility Report No. 112/10, 21 October 2011, para. 91. See also C. M. Cerna, 'Extraterritorial Scope of Human Rights Treaties: The American Convention on Human Rights', in F. Coomans and M. T. Kamminga (eds.), *Extraterritorial Applications of Human Rights Treaties*, Intersentia, Antwerp, 2004, text available at http://bit.ly/2GISYvg.

[61] Inter-American Commission on Human Rights, *Franklin Guillermo Aisalla Molina (Ecuador v. Colombia)*, Admissibility Report, para. 91.

[62] Inter-American Commission on Human Rights, *Case of Disabled Peoples' International and others v. United States*, Report on Admissibility (Case No. 9213), published in Inter-American Commission on Human Rights, *Annual Report 1986–7*.

[63] Inter-American Commission on Human Rights, *Richmond Hill v. United States*, Case No. 9213, Report No. 3/96, OAS doc. OEA/Ser.L/V/II.91 Doc. 7, 1996, para. 4.

[64] Ibid.

military actions or actions by State security forces that indicate "control", "power" or "authority" in the execution of the extraterritorial conduct'.[65] The 'exceptional' situations in which the extraterritorial conduct of a state constitutes the exercise of its jurisdiction, should, the Court said, 'be interpreted restrictively'.[66] But such situations can still occur extraterritorially when a state is either exercising 'authority over a person', or 'when that person is under its effective control'.[67] That effective control may be exercised when it is responsible for activities that cause 'harm and consequent violation of human rights',[68] potentially a very broad casting of jurisdiction.[69]

Jurisdiction under the African Charter on Human and Peoples' Rights

3.31 The 1981 African Charter on Human and Peoples' Rights[70] does not have a jurisdictional clause. Instead, its States Parties recognise the rights, duties, and freedoms enshrined in the Charter and are required to undertake to adopt legislative or other measures to give effect to them.[71] Moreover, 'every individual' is entitled to enjoy the rights and freedoms recognised and guaranteed in the Charter.[72] According to the African Commission on Human and Peoples' Rights, writing in its 2015 General Comment on the right to life under the African Charter:

> A State shall respect the right to life of individuals outside its territory. A State also has certain obligations to protect the right to life of such individuals. The nature of these obligations depends for instance on the extent that the State has jurisdiction or otherwise exercises effective authority, power, or control over either the perpetrator or the victim (or the victim's rights), or exercises effective control over the territory on which the victim's rights are affected, or whether the State engages in conduct which could reasonably be foreseen to result in an unlawful deprivation of life.[73]

In its judgment in the *Armed Activities* case in the Democratic Republic of Congo, the International Court of Justice explicitly held that the African Charter (including the right to life in Article 4) applied extraterritorially to a situation of military occupation.[74]

---

[65] Inter-American Court of Human Rights, *The Environment and Human Rights*, Advisory Opinion, 2017, para. 80.
[66] Ibid., para. 81.
[67] Ibid.
[68] Ibid., para. 104(h).
[69] See, e.g., A. Berkes, 'A New Extraterritorial Jurisdictional Link Recognised by the IACtHR', blog post, *EJIL Talk!*, 28 March 2018, at http://bit.ly/2OgCijc.
[70] Art. 4, African Charter on Human and Peoples' Rights; adopted at Nairobi 27 June 1981; entered into force 21 October 1986 (hereinafter, ACHPR).
[71] Art. 1, ACHPR.
[72] Art. 2, ACHPR.
[73] African Commission on Human and Peoples' Rights, 'General Comment No. 3 on the African Charter on Human and Peoples' Rights: The Right to Life (Article 4)', adopted at Banjul (57th Ordinary Session) November 2015 (hereinafter, African Commission General Comment on the right to life), para. 15.
[74] International Court of Justice, *Case Concerning Armed Activities on the Territory of the Congo (Democratic Republic of the Congo v. Uganda)*, Judgment, 19 December 2005, paras. 217, 219.

Jurisdiction under the Arab Charter on Human Rights

3.32 The jurisdictional clause in the 2004 Arab Charter on Human Rights[75] repeats the formulation employed in the ICCPR. Article 3(1) stipulates that each State Party to the Charter 'undertakes to ensure to all individuals within its territory and subject to its jurisdiction' the rights recognised therein. To date, there has been no jurisprudence on the issue, but the provision may reasonably be interpreted in the same manner, as has the Human Rights Committee with respect to Article 2(1) of the ICCPR.

Jurisdiction under the European Convention on Human Rights

3.33 The 1950 European Convention on Human Rights[76] has seen the most extensive jurisprudence of any of the regional human rights courts on the issue of jurisdiction. When a State Party does not exercise effective control over all of its own territory, it may still be held responsible for a violation of human rights. In its judgment in the *Catan* case, the Grand Chamber of the European Court of Human Rights stated that although Moldova had no effective control over the acts of the self-styled 'Moldavian Republic of Transdniestria', a breakaway entity controlling territory in Transnistria, 'the fact that the region is recognised under public international law as part of Moldova's territory gives rise to an obligation, under Article 1 of the Convention, to use all legal and diplomatic means available to it to continue to guarantee the enjoyment of the rights and freedoms defined in the Convention to those living there'.[77]

3.34 With respect to extraterritorial jurisdiction, the European Court has focused on the notion of a State's 'effective control' over a person located in another state. In its 1995 judgment on preliminary objections in the *Loizidou* case, the Court's Grand Chamber rejected Turkey's preliminary objections *ratione loci*. Turkey, as a respondent state, had claimed that the Court lacked the competence to consider the merits of the case on the grounds that the matters complained of did not fall within Turkish jurisdiction.[78] The Court explicitly took into account the object and purpose of the European Convention in holding that a State Party's responsibility 'may also arise when as a consequence of military action – whether lawful or unlawful – it exercises effective control of an area outside its national territory'.[79]

3.35 In its subsequent judgment in the *Banković* case,[80] however, which concerned the bombing of Radio Televizije Srbije in Belgrade on 23 April 1999 by member States of the

---

[75] Art. 5(1), Arab Charter on Human Rights; adopted at Tunis 22 May 2004; entered into force 15 March 2008.
[76] Convention for the Protection of Human Rights and Fundamental Freedoms; adopted at Rome 4 November 1950; entered into force 3 September 1953.
[77] European Court of Human Rights, *Catan and others v. Moldova and Russia*, Judgment (Grand Chamber), 19 October 2012, para. 110. See, similarly: *Mozer v. Moldova and Russia*, Judgment (Grand Chamber), 23 February 2016, paras. 99–100.
[78] European Court of Human Rights, *Loizidou v. Turkey*, Judgment (Preliminary Objections) (Grand Chamber), 23 March 1995, para. 55.
[79] Ibid., para. 62.
[80] European Court of Human Rights, *Banković and others v. Belgium and others*, Decision on Admissibility (Grand Chamber), 12 December 2001.

North Atlantic Treaty Organization (NATO), the Court held that Article 1 of the Convention 'must be considered to reflect th[e] ordinary and essentially territorial notion of jurisdiction, other bases of jurisdiction being exceptional and requiring special justification in the particular circumstances of each case'.[81] It held that jurisdiction did not exist under the European Convention on Human Rights for the bombing in a country outside the legal space ('*espace juridique*') of the Convention (i.e., in a State, not a party). The Court distinguished its holding in the *Banković* case from other instances where a State Party to the European Convention, 'through the effective control of the relevant territory and its inhabitants abroad as a consequence of military occupation or through the consent, invitation or acquiescence of the Government of that territory, exercises all or some of the public powers normally to be exercised by that Government'.[82]

3.36 The Court also cited other 'exceptional' instances of the extraterritorial exercise of jurisdiction by a State Party that would fall within the Convention. These included 'cases involving the activities of its diplomatic or consular agents abroad and on board craft and vessels registered in, or flying the flag of, that State'.[83] In these specific situations, the Court stated, 'customary international law and treaty provisions have recognised the extraterritorial exercise of jurisdiction by the relevant State'.[84]

3.37 The European Court's reasoning in the *Banković* case has not been expressly overruled and therefore remains authoritative. That said, in its 2007 decision on admissibility in the *Pad* case against Turkey,[85] jurisdiction was founded for the alleged killing in May 1999 of seven Iranian men in north-west Iran by Turkish soldiers after rocket fire from Turkish helicopters. Turkey had admitted to having bombed the area from a helicopter (but denied that its soldiers were present in Iran), asserting that it had suspected that terrorists had been there at the time. A chamber of the European Court considered it unnecessary to determine the exact location of the killings (in Iran or Turkey), 'given that the Government had already admitted that the fire discharged from the helicopters had caused the killing of the applicants' relatives, who had been suspected of being terrorists'.[86]

3.38 It remains the case, though, that the Grand Chamber judgment in *Banković* circumscribes the notion of jurisdiction under the European Convention as far as the inter-State use of force is concerned, precluding its application when there is no physical presence by troops (or law enforcement officials) belonging to a State Party. As such, and notwithstanding the fact that the principle of *stare decisis* does not formally govern the Court's jurisprudence,[87] the European Convention would not appear to apply to the subject matter of certain bombings and missile attacks to which the Inter-American Convention

---

[81] Ibid., para. 61.
[82] Ibid., para. 71.
[83] Ibid., para. 73.
[84] Ibid.
[85] European Court of Human Rights, *Pad and others v. Turkey*, Judgment (Decision on admissibility) (Third Section), 28 June 2007.
[86] Ibid., para. 54.
[87] See on this issue, *infra*, Paragraph 39.07.

and the ICCPR would. But taking custody of a person abroad, even in a country outside the Convention's 'espace juridique', is likely to found its extraterritorial application.[88]

THE PROHIBITION OF ARBITRARY DEPRIVATION OF LIFE

3.39 Acts that may constitute an arbitrary deprivation of life, when committed abroad, may fall to be judged under the various global and regional human rights treaties in a number of scenarios.[89] First, a relevant act that occurs onboard a ship or aircraft will engage the flag state's international responsibility. With respect to the right to life under the ICCPR, this was affirmed by the Human Rights Committee in its General Comment No. 36 on the right to life: 'States parties are also required to respect and protect the lives of all individuals located on marine vessels or aircrafts registered by them or flying their flag.'[90]

3.40 Second, while a consulate or embassy abroad remains sovereign territory belonging to the territorial State, acts by consular or embassy staff that cause the death of a person on the premises (or by government or diplomatic staff visiting from the capital) will potentially engage the international responsibility of that state, in particular under international human rights law.[91] This is akin to a 'functional exercise of sovereignty', in the words of one commentator.[92] In the case of the killing of Jamal Khashoggi on 2 October 2018 in the Saudi Arabian consulate in Istanbul, the 'unjustified use of deadly force' by Saudi officials under the effective control of the State represented a clear violation of the right to life by Saudi Arabia.[93]

---

[88] See, e.g., European Court of Human Rights, *Al-Jedda* v. *United Kingdom*, Judgment (Grand Chamber), 7 July 2011, paras. 84–86; *Öcalan* v. *Turkey*, Judgment (Grand Chamber), 12 May 2005, para. 91; *Al-Saadoon and Mufdhi* v. United Kingdom, Decision on admissibility (Chamber), 30 June 2009. In its decision in the *Al-Saadoon* case, the European Court of Human Rights noted that during 'the first months of the applicants' detention, the United Kingdom was an occupying power in Iraq. The two British-run detention facilities in which the applicants were held were thus under the jurisdiction of the United Kingdom for the purpose of the European Convention. Ibid., para. 87–8. The limitation of jurisdiction under the European Convention over the acts of hostilities in an international armed conflict was affirmed by the Court's Grand Chamber in in 2021. European Court of Human Rights, *Georgia* v. *Russia (II)*, Judgment (Grand Chamber), 21 January 2021, paras. 133-44. For cogent criticism of the holding and its reasoning see M. Milanovic, 'Georgia v. Russia No. 2: The European Court's Resurrection of Bankovic in the Contexts of Chaos', *EJIL: Talk!*, 25 January 2021, at https://bit.ly/345Jaan.

[89] The African Commission on Human and Peoples' Rights has asserted that 'customary international law prohibits, without territorial limitation, arbitrary deprivation of life'. African Commission General Comment on the right to life, para. 14. It is not entirely certain that sufficient *opinio juris* exists among States to sustain this assertion.

[90] Human Rights Committee, General Comment 36 on the right to life, para. 63. See also on this issue, Art. 5(1)(a), Convention against Torture and Other Cruel, Inhuman or Degrading Treatment or Punishment; adopted at New York 10 December 1984; entered into force 26 June 1987. As of 1 May 2021, 171 States were party to the Convention and a further 5 States were signatories.

[91] European Court of Human Rights, *Banković and others* v. *Belgium and others*, Decision on Admissibility (Grand Chamber), 12 December 2001, para. 73.

[92] S. Miller, 'Revisiting Extraterritorial Jurisdiction: A Territorial Justification for Extraterritorial Jurisdiction under the European Convention', *European Journal of International Law*, vol. 20, no. 4 (2010), pp. 1223–46, at 1240.

[93] 'Annex to the Report of the Special Rapporteur on Extrajudicial, Summary or Arbitrary Executions: Investigation into the Unlawful Death of Mr. Jamal Khashoggi', UN doc. A/HRC/41/CRP.1, 19 June 2019, paras. 193, 219, 222. For a 'quite fanciful' scenario akin to the killing of Mr Khashoggi, discussed by an

3.41 Third, the Human Rights Committee also implies that a wilful failure to assist individuals who find themselves in a situation of distress at sea will also amount to arbitrary deprivation of life.[94] International law imposes a general obligation on the master of a vessel to rescue any person who is in danger of being lost at sea, but the duty is qualified by the condition that providing assistance will not pose a serious danger to either the vessel or its crew and passengers.[95] Nonetheless, in the context of counterpiracy operations, the obligation to assist would apply to pirates as well as to hostages. That said, if a pirate 'is in a sinking skiff but continues to shoot at the crew of a ship that attempts to rescue him, the ship is not obliged to rescue that individual. However, if the pirate begins to drown and falls unconscious, and therefore ceases to pose a danger, the master has a duty to rescue him.'[96]

3.42 Fourth, when an individual is deemed to be in the custody of a foreign State, he or she benefits from fundamental human rights protections, including those afforded by the rights to life, to freedom from torture or other forms of inhumane treatment, and to liberty and security. For the application of protective measures against bodily harm, it does not matter whether the taking into custody occurred lawfully or unlawfully, nor whether it occurred during peacetime or a situation of armed conflict (international or non-international in character). This is the case under the ICCPR, the Convention on the Rights of the Child, the European Convention on Human Rights, the Inter-American Convention on Human Rights,[97] and the African Charter on Human and Peoples' Rights. The situation with respect to the Arab Charter on Human Rights is unclear.

3.43 The *Hassan* case before the European Court of Human Rights concerned the treatment of Mr Tarek Hassan after his capture by British troops on 23 April 2003 in Iraq during the Coalition occupation of that country. From that moment, he was 'within the physical power and control of the United Kingdom soldiers and therefore fell within United Kingdom jurisdiction'.[98] The UK Government had formally acknowledged that where State agents operating extraterritorially take an individual into custody, this is a ground of extraterritorial jurisdiction which has been recognised by the Court.[99] However, the United Kingdom also claimed that this basis of jurisdiction should not apply during the active hostilities phase of an international armed conflict, where State agents are operating in territory they are not the occupying power, and where the conduct

---

international lawyer seven years previously, see M. Milanovic, 'Waiting for the Als', *EJIL Talk!*, Published on 6 June 2011, at http://bit.ly/38VzAYb.
[94] Human Rights Committee, General Comment 36 on the right to life, para. 63.
[95] See, e.g., Art. 98, UNCLOS.
[96] A. Priddy and S. Casey-Maslen, *Counterpiracy under International Law*, Academy Briefing No. 1, Geneva Academy of International Humanitarian Law and Human Rights, Geneva, August 2012, Section G, pp. 37–8.
[97] See, e.g., Inter-American Commission on Human Rights, *Coard and others v. United States*, Report No. 109/99 (Case 10.951), 29 September 1999, text available at http://bit.ly/2RNV4Aq. The case concerned the arrest and detention of a number of individuals by the US forces that had invaded Grenada in 1983.
[98] European Court of Human Rights, *Hassan v. United Kingdom*, Judgment (Grand Chamber), 16 September 2014, para. 76.
[99] Ibid.

of the State will instead be subject to the requirements of international humanitarian law.[100]

3.44 The European Court, though, rejected the argument, in part on the basis that it would be inconsistent with the case-law of the International Court of Justice, which had found that international humanitarian and human rights law may apply concurrently. Consonant with the line taken by the International Court of Justice, the European Court determined that it would interpret the Convention, including its Article 1, in harmony with other rules of international law, including humanitarian law.[101]

3.45 Fifth, where a State occupies foreign territory, in particular through the actions of its armed forces, it brings the population under occupation within the protection of the relevant human rights treaty, in particular with respect to the right to life. In this regard, the Human Rights Committee stipulates in its General Comment 36 that States Parties to the ICCPR 'must respect and protect the lives of individuals located in places, which are under their effective control, such as occupied territories, and in territories over which they have assumed an international obligation to apply the Covenant'.[102]

3.46 As jurisprudence before the International Court of Justice cited above demonstrates, the same applies, *mutatis mutandis*, to the Convention on the Rights of the Child and the African Charter on Human and Peoples' Rights.[103] Relevant jurisprudence before the European Court of Human Rights, also cited above, demonstrates that this is also the case with respect to the European Convention on Human Rights. With respect to the Inter-American Convention on Human Rights, the Inter-American Commission on Human Rights' report on the *Coard* case supports the same approach, even though strictly speaking the case was adjudged on the basis of the Charter of the Organization of American States (OAS) and the 1948 American Declaration of the Rights and Duties of Man.

3.47 Where an alleged arbitrary deprivation of life concerns bombing or missile attack by a foreign state, the situation is, as seen, a little more mixed. The ICCPR certainly applies, as demonstrated by the dicta of the International Court of Justice on its Advisory Opinion on the threat or use of nuclear weapons.[104] The Human Rights Committee has since stated that the protection of the right to life 'includes persons located outside any territory effectively controlled by the State, whose right to life is nonetheless impacted by its military or other activities in a direct and reasonably foreseeable manner'.[105] The Committee cites in support of its assertion its Concluding Observations on the fourth periodic report of the United States in 2014, in which it expressed concern about the

---

[100] Ibid.
[101] Ibid., para. 77.
[102] Human Rights Committee, General Comment 36 on the right to life, para. 63.
[103] In the context of the African Charter, the African Commission on Human and Peoples' Rights has stated that an arbitrary deprivation of life will fall within the Charter, inter alia, where a state party has 'effective control over the territory on which the victim's rights are affected'. African Commission General Comment on the right to life, para. 14.
[104] ICJ, *Legality of the Threat or Use of Nuclear Weapons*, Advisory Opinion, 8 July 1996, para. 25.
[105] Human Rights Committee, General Comment 36 on the right to life, para. 63.

practice of targeted killings in extraterritorial counter-terrorism operations using 'drones'. The Committee called on the United States to 'ensure that any use of armed drones complies fully with its obligations under article 6 of the Covenant, including, in particular, with respect to the principles of precaution, distinction and proportionality in the context of an armed conflict'.[106]

3.48 As evidenced by the approach taken by the Inter-American Commission on Human Rights in the Richmond Hill case, the right to life under the Inter-American human rights system would also apply to extraterritorial bombardment or missile attack, even absent physical control of the territory. The same would in all likelihood apply to the African Charter on Human and Peoples' Rights – according to the African Commission, jurisdiction will be founded where a State Party 'engages in conduct which could reasonably be foreseen to result in an unlawful deprivation of life'.[107] But within the context of the European Convention on Human Rights, the decision of the European Court's Grand Chamber in *Banković* as confirmed in *Georgia v. Russia (II)* remains the law, seemingly precluding its applicability, as a general rule, outside the legal space of the Convention for acts in the conduct of hostilities in the context of an international armed conflict.

THE DUTY TO INVESTIGATE POTENTIALLY UNLAWFUL DEATH

3.49 There is a corresponding duty under international law on each State to investigate any potentially unlawful death, as Chapter 2 outlined. Failure to do so would usually amount to a violation of the procedural component of the right to life (or to a violation of the right to life when read in conjunction with the duty to respect and ensure human rights, including the right to a remedy for violation of human rights). The duty applies to any situation where an arbitrary deprivation of life may have occurred, that is to say anywhere on sovereign territory, on territory occupied abroad, or during custody effected extraterritorially. This is so, whether this occurs during peacetime or in a situation of armed conflict. Where, however, the death occurs after custody extraterritorially and there is no evidence of a link with treatment during custody, a duty to investigate will not be sustained.[108]

3.50 Outside the legal space of the European Convention on Human Rights, the duty to investigate alleged violations of the right to life in the conduct of hostilities conducted

---

[106] Human Rights Committee, Concluding Observations on the Fourth Periodic Report of the United States, UN doc. CCPR/C/USA/CO/4, 23 April 2014, para. 9.

[107] African Commission, General Comment on the right to life, para. 14.

[108] In its judgment in the *Hassan* case referred to above, the European Court stated that 'there is no evidence to suggest that Tarek Hassan was ill-treated while in detention, such as to give rise to an obligation on the respondent State under Article 3 to carry out an official investigation. Nor is there any evidence that the United Kingdom authorities were responsible in any way, directly or indirectly, for Tarek Hassan's death, which occurred some four months after he was released from Camp Bucca, in a distant part of the country not controlled by United Kingdom forces. In the absence of any evidence of the involvement of United Kingdom State agents in the death, or even of any evidence that the death occurred within territory controlled by the United Kingdom, no obligation to investigate under Article 2 can arise.' European Court of Human Rights, *Hassan v. United Kingdom*, Judgment (Grand Chamber), para. 63.

Jurisdiction and the Right to Life

extraterritorially and in the absence of military occupation, the duty to investigate also applies to States Parties to the ICCPR, the Convention on the Rights of the Child, the Inter-American Convention on Human Rights, and, seemingly, the African Charter on Human and Peoples' Rights. With respect to the Arab Charter on Human Rights, the situation is uncertain, although since the wording of the jurisdictional clause in the Charter mirrors that of the ICCPR, it may be expected that it will also similarly apply.

3.51 Moreover, the duty to investigate is an obligation that persists after the events that led to an alleged or suspected potentially unlawful death.[109] Under the 2001 Draft Articles on the Responsibility of States for Internationally Wrongful Acts, 'The breach of an international obligation by an act of a State having a continuing character extends over the entire period during which the act continues and remains not in conformity with the international obligation.'[110]

3.52 The *Mocanu* case before the European Court of Human Rights' Grand Chamber in 2014 involved allegations by the applicants that they had been victims of the violent crackdown on anti-government demonstrations in Bucharest in June 1990, but where no effective investigation had been carried out into those events.[111] Romania's adherence to the European Convention only occurred in 1994, and therefore an allegation of a substantive violation of the right to life would fail *ratione temporis*. It was indicated that investigations conducted over approximately nineteen years by the civilian prosecutor's offices and, subsequently, by the military prosecuting authorities, had not made it possible to establish the identity of the perpetrators or the degree of involvement of the security forces.[112] However, the European Court observed:

> International case-law provides examples of cases where the alleged victims of mass violations of fundamental rights, such as the right to life and the right not to be subjected to ill-treatment, have been authorised to wait many years before bringing proceedings at national level and subsequently applying to the international courts, although the admissibility criteria for their applications, with regard to exhaustion of domestic remedies and time-limits for submitting complaints, were similar to those provided for by the Convention.[113]

The Court observed that the majority of the proceedings and the most important procedural measures were carried out after the date at which Romania adhered to the

---

[109] The Inter-American Court of Human Rights has interpreted enforced disappearance as a continuing unlawful act (until the person who has been allegedly subject to such disappearance is accounted for). Inter-American Court of Human Rights, *Blake v. Guatemala*, Judgment (Merits), 24 January 1998, para. 67.

[110] Art. 14(2), Draft Articles on Responsibility of States for Internationally Wrongful Acts, Text adopted by the International Law Commission at its fifty-third session, in 2001, and submitted to the UN General Assembly in UN doc. A/56/10.

[111] European Court of Human Rights, *Mocanu and others v. Romania*, Judgment (Grand Chamber), 17 September 2014, para. 3.

[112] Ibid., para. 155.

[113] Ibid., para. 191, citing Inter-American Commission on Human Rights, *Community of Rio Negro of the Maya Indigenous People and Its Members v. Guatemala*, Report No. 13/2008 of 5 March 2008; Inter-American Court of Human Rights, '*Las Dos Erres*' *Massacre v. Guatemala*, Judgment, 24 November 2009; and Inter-American Court of Human Rights, *García Lucero and others v. Chile*, Judgment, 28 August 2013.

Convention.[114] Consequently, the Court found that it had 'jurisdiction *ratione temporis* to examine the complaints raised by Mrs Mocanu and Mr Stoica under the procedural aspect of Articles 2 and 3 of the Convention, in so far as those complaints relate to the criminal investigation conducted in the present case after the entry into force of the Convention in respect of Romania'.[115]

---

[114] European Court of Human Rights, *Mocanu and others* v. *Romania*, Judgment (Grand Chamber), para. 210.

[115] Ibid., para. 211. See also European Court of Human Rights, *Crăiniceanu and Frumuşanu* v. *Romania*, Judgment (Third Section), 24 April 2012 (rendered final on 24 July 2012), para. 81.

4

The Relationship between the Right to Life and Other Human Rights

INTRODUCTION

4.01 Underpinning all human rights are the notions of dignity and non-discrimination. Thus, the Charter of the United Nations obligates the UN to promote 'universal respect for, and observance of, human rights and fundamental freedoms for all without distinction as to race, sex, language, or religion'.[1] The Universal Declaration of Human Rights stipulates that 'all human beings are born free and equal in dignity and rights'.[2] As a 'foundational' human right and a 'fulcrum', the right to life is of manifest significance to all other human rights.[3] Accordingly, this chapter considers how the right to life interrelates with other human rights.

4.02 The Human Rights Committee has observed that the effective protection of the right to life is 'the prerequisite for the enjoyment of all other human rights', while its content 'can be informed by other human rights'.[4] But the right to life has an especially close connection with certain other fundamental rights. The most obvious, and most proximate, relationship is with the right to freedom from torture and other forms of cruel, inhuman, or degrading treatment or punishment.[5] Also of particular import, however, are the right to

---

[1] Art. 55(c), Charter of the United Nations; adopted at San Francisco 26 June 1945; entered into force 24 October 1945 (hereinafter, UN Charter). As of 1 May 2021, there were 193 UN member States: 49 States were formally party to the UN Charter and a further 144 were admitted to the United Nations on the basis of Article 4 of the UN Charter, having declared their acceptance of the obligations contained in the Charter.

[2] Art. 1, Universal Declaration of Human Rights; adopted by the UN General Assembly on 10 December 1948.

[3] African Commission on Human and Peoples' Rights, General Comment No. 3 on the African Charter on Human and Peoples' Rights: The Right to Life (Article 4), adopted during the 57th Ordinary Session of the Commission held from 4 to 18 November 2015 in Banjul (hereinafter, African Commission General Comment on the right to life), paras. 1 and 5.

[4] Human Rights Committee, General Comment No. 36: Article 6: right to life, UN doc. CCPR/C/GC/36, 3 September 2019 (hereinafter, Human Rights Committee, General Comment 36 on the right to life), para. 2.

[5] As set out, for instance, in Article 7 of the International Covenant on Civil and Political Rights; adopted at New York 16 December 1966; entered into force 23 March 1976 (hereinafter, ICCPR); and the Convention against Torture and Other Cruel, Inhuman or Degrading Treatment or Punishment; adopted at New York 10 December 1984; entered into force 26 June 1987 (hereinafter, CAT). As of 1 May 2021, 173 States were party to the ICCPR while 171 States were party to CAT. The right is given clear voice in the regional human rights treaties, albeit in slightly different formulations. The 1950 European Convention on Human Rights provides: 'No one shall be subjected to torture or to inhuman or degrading treatment or punishment.' Art. 3, Convention for the Protection of Human Rights and Fundamental Freedoms; adopted at Rome by the Council of Europe 4 November 1950; entered into force 3 September 1953. Under the 1969 American Convention on Human

a fair trial, the rights to liberty and to security, the right to privacy, the right of peaceful assembly, and the rights to food and water.[6]

4.03 For children, the right to life is explicitly linked in the Convention on the Rights of the Child with the right to survival and development,[7] as Chapter 22 discusses. The Human Rights Committee also makes the connection between a child's right to life and the obligation in Article 24(1) of the Covenant on Civil and Political Rights (ICCPR) to provide every child to such measures of protection as are required by his or her status as a minor. A wilful or negligent failure to do so will inform the duty to protect life under Article 6(1) of the ICCPR.

THE RELATIONSHIP WITH THE RIGHT TO FREEDOM FROM TORTURE

4.04 Article 7 of the ICCPR stipulates, in part, that 'no one shall be subjected to torture or to cruel, inhuman or degrading treatment or punishment'. As a general rule, it remains true to say that if a State uses unlawful force against a person under its jurisdiction and the victim survives, the question of a violation falls to be considered under Article 7 rather than Article 6 of the Covenant. On an exceptional basis, where the State manifestly seeks to kill a person but does not succeed in doing so, the Committee may find a violation of the right to life. Thus, in its Views in *Chongwe v. Zambia*, adopted on 25 October 2000, the Committee found a violation of the right to life of the author of the communication who was shot and wounded when Zambian police fired at his car while he was on his way to attend a political rally.[8] Zambia did not contest the allegation that it had 'authorised the use of lethal force without lawful reasons, which could have led to the killing of the author'.[9]

4.05 The dividing line between the right to life and the right to freedom from torture in the Covenant is also not distinctly drawn in instances of enforced disappearance. Such actions by State agents, for instance, have lead the Human Rights Committee to hold that both Article 6 and Article 7 are violated (as well as Article 9 on the right to liberty and

---

Rights, 'No one shall be subjected to torture or to cruel, inhuman, or degrading punishment or treatment.' Art. 5(2), American Convention on Human Rights 'Pact of San José'; adopted at San José 22 November 1969; entered into force 18 July 1978. The 1981 African (Banjul) Charter on Human and Peoples' Rights stipulates that 'all forms of exploitation and degradation of man particularly slavery, slave trade, torture, cruel, inhuman or degrading punishment and treatment shall be prohibited'. Art. 5, African Charter on Human and Peoples' Rights; adopted at Nairobi 27 June 1981; entered into force 21 October 1986.

[6] In November 2020, the UN Food and Agriculture Organization (FAO) reported that '3.2 billion people live in agricultural areas with high or very high water shortages or scarcity, of whom 1.2 billion people live in areas with very high water constraints. From the 1.2 billion people, nearly half live in Southern Asia, and about 460 million live in Eastern and South-eastern Asia.' FAO, *The State of Food and Agriculture (SOFA) 2020*, Report, Rome, available at http://bit.ly/37hfZ5l.

[7] Art. 6, Convention on the Rights of the Child; adopted at New York 20 November 1989; entered into force 2 September 1990 (hereinafter, CRC). As of 1 May 2021, 196 States were party to the CRC.

[8] Human Rights Committee, *Chongwe v. Zambia*, Views, UN doc. CCPR/C/70/D/821/1998, 9 November 2000, para. 6.

[9] Ibid., para. 5.2.

security of person and Article 16 on the right to recognition as a person before the law).[10] Moreover, the Committee declared in its General Comment No. 36 on the right to life that during a situation of armed conflict, 'practices inconsistent with international humanitarian law, *entailing a risk* to the lives of civilians and other persons protected by international humanitarian law, ... would also violate article 6 of the Covenant'.[11] This threshold of a risk seems remarkably low.

4.06 That said, a general dividing line between the right to life and the right to freedom from torture or other inhumane treatment does exist based on the consequences for the victim(s), and it similarly persists in the regional human rights mechanisms. As Chapter 2 described,[12] the European Court of Human Rights has held that the right to life as protected in the European Convention on Human Rights[13] may only exceptionally be violated when a person survives the use of potentially deadly force by the State. Its position on the extent of harm that must occur has materially evolved over time, as the following review of jurisprudence illustrates.

4.07 On the face of it, holding that the right to life of a survivor has been violated does not seem compatible with the wording of Article 2(2) of the European Convention on Human Rights. The provision stipulates that 'deprivation of life shall not be regarded as inflicted in contravention' of the article 'when it results from the use of force which is no more than absolutely necessary' in furtherance of a series of legitimate purposes. But in its 2000 judgment in the *Ilhan* case, the European Court's Grand Chamber held that 'the degree and type of force used and the unequivocal intention or aim behind the use of force may, among other factors, be relevant in assessing whether in a particular case the State agents' actions in inflicting injury short of death must be regarded as incompatible with the object and purpose of Article 2 of the Convention'.[14] This object and purpose is generally to protect life, especially against the action – or inaction – of State agents.

4.08 In 2019, the Grand Chamber held that it emerges from the Court's case-law that

> where the victim was not killed but survived and where he or she does not allege any intent to kill, the criteria for a complaint to be examined under this aspect of Article 2 are, firstly, whether the person was the victim of an activity, whether public or private, which by its very nature put his or her life at real and imminent risk and, secondly, whether he or she has suffered injuries that appear life-threatening as they occur. Other factors, such as whether escaping death was purely fortuitous ... or whether the victim was infected with a potentially fatal disease ... may also come into play. The Court's assessment depends on the circumstances.[15]

---

[10] Human Rights Committee, General Comment 36 on the right to life, para. 58.
[11] Ibid., para. 64 (added emphasis).
[12] See, *supra*, paras. 2.14–2.19.
[13] Convention for the Protection of Human Rights and Fundamental Freedoms; adopted at Rome 4 November 1950; entered into force 3 September 1953.
[14] European Court of Human Rights, *Ilhan* v. *Turkey*, Judgment (Grand Chamber), 27 June 2000, para. 76.
[15] European Court of Human Rights, *Nicolae Virgiliu Tănase* v. *Romania*, Judgment (Grand Chamber), 25 June 2019, para. 140.

The Court further avers that, while 'there is no general rule', if the conduct is 'by its very nature' dangerous, putting a person's life 'at real and imminent risk', such as is the case with the application of 'life-threatening violence', then 'the level of injuries sustained may not be decisive and, in the absence of injuries, a complaint in such cases may still fall to be examined under Article 2'.[16]

4.09 In its report of 1998 in the Yaşa case,[17] the European Commission on Human Rights had accepted the principle that Article 2 could apply to the survivor of a serious attack, but in its report had limited its finding of a violation to the failure to investigate a shooting of the applicant that had resulted in life-threatening injuries. (The applicant's uncle had been killed by unknown gunmen, who, the applicant alleged, had also been dispatched by the authorities.) The Commission was 'of the opinion that the failure to make any further or more detailed investigation into the attacks on the applicant and his uncle amounts to a failure to protect the right to life'.[18]

4.10 When the case came before a chamber of the European Court, the Commission's position was explicitly endorsed. In its judgment of early September 1998, the Court held that 'the mere fact that the authorities were informed of the murder of the applicant's uncle gave rise *ipso facto* to an obligation under Article 2 to carry out an effective investigation'. It further affirmed that this duty to investigate arose also with respect 'to the attack on the applicant which, because eight shots were fired at him, amounted to attempted murder'.[19]

4.11 A month later, the Grand Chamber issued its judgment in the landmark case of *Osman v. United Kingdom*. Therein, there was no suggestion that the applicant had been attacked by any agent of the State. The two applicants in the case were British citizens residing in London. The husband of the first was shot dead by a Mr Paul Paget-Lewis on 7 March 1988. Mr Paget-Lewis had developed a sexual attraction to the man's son; the boy was wounded in the shooting that led to his father's death. The two applicants argued that the authorities had failed to comply with their positive obligation to protect life under Article 2(1) of the European Convention on Human Rights. The Court adjudged that, 'having regard to the nature of the right protected by Article 2, a right fundamental in the scheme of the Convention, it is sufficient for an applicant to show that the authorities did not do all that could be reasonably expected of them to avoid a real and immediate risk to life of which they have or ought to have knowledge'.[20]

4.12 In the *Makaratzis* case, the Greek Government explicitly contended that Article 2 did not come into play since the victim was still alive. Although they conceded that the police officers who were involved in the chase of Mr Makaratzis had used their firearms, they had

---

[16] Ibid.
[17] European Commission on Human Rights, *Esref Yaşa v. Turkey*, Report, adopted 8 April 1997.
[18] Ibid., para. 107.
[19] European Court of Human Rights, *Esref Yaşa v. Turkey*, Judgment (Chamber), 2 September 1998, para. 100.
[20] European Court of Human Rights, *Osman v. United Kingdom*, Judgment (Grand Chamber), 28 October 1998, para. 116.

not intended to kill him, but only to force him to stop his car so they could arrest him.[21] A third party given leave to intervene in the case, the Institut de Formation en Droits de l'Homme du Barreau de Paris, considered that it should be possible for Article 2 to apply in a case where the police had made use of potentially lethal force, even if that force did not cause the death of the person who was the target of the police actions. In its view, there should be no waiting for an irreversible violation of the right to life before reviewing the circumstances in which lethal force was used.[22] The Grand Chamber agreed, although it cautioned that the Court's case-law established that 'it is only in exceptional circumstances that physical ill-treatment by State agents which does not result in death may disclose a violation of Article 2 of the Convention'.[23]

4.13 The Court accepted the Greek Government's submission that the police did not intend to kill the applicant. It observed, however, that the fact that he was not killed was 'fortuitous'. A ballistics report found 16 holes in the car caused by bullets following a horizontal or an upward trajectory to the car driver's level. The applicant was injured on the right arm, the right foot, the left buttock, and the right side of the chest, and was hospitalised for nine days.[24] The Court concludes that, irrespective of whether or not the police actually intended to kill him, the applicant was the victim of conduct which, by its very nature, endangered his life, even though he survived the event. Article 2 was thus applicable.[25]

4.14 In its 2005 judgment in the *Acar* case, a chamber of the European Court found a violation of the right to life of two applicants who 'were wounded in the course of a sustained and lethal attack with firearms which resulted in the death of eight of their fellow villagers'. The Court concluded that the applicants 'were the victims of conduct which, by its very nature, put their lives at grave risk, even though, in the event, they survived'.[26]

4.15 In its 2007 judgment in the *Rochela Massacre* case, the Inter-American Court of Human Rights cited the *Acar* judgment in support of its findings of 'extraordinary circumstances that lay a foundation' for a violation of the right to life under the Inter-American Convention with respect to the three survivors of the massacre. The Court reached its decision 'taking into account the force employed, the intent and objective of the use of this force, and the situation in which the victims found themselves'.[27]

4.16 In its 2015 judgment in the *Kitanovski* case, a chamber of the European Court addressed the use of firearms against one of the applicants which did not turn out to be

---

[21] European Court of Human Rights, *Makaratzis v. Greece*, Judgment (Grand Chamber), 20 December 2004, para. 38.
[22] Ibid., para. 43.
[23] Ibid., para. 51.
[24] Ibid., para. 54.
[25] Ibid., para. 55.
[26] European Court of Human Rights, *Acar and others v. Turkey*, Judgment (Fourth Section), 24 May 2005 (as rendered final on 12 October 2005), para. 77.
[27] Inter-American Court of Human Rights, *Rochela Massacre v. Colombia*, Judgment (Merits, Reparations, and Costs), 11 May 2007, paras. 123–5.

lethal. The Court's First Section affirmed that the text of Article 2 of the European Convention, 'read as a whole, demonstrates that it covers not only intentional killing, but also situations where it is permitted to use force which may result, as an unintended outcome, in the deprivation of life'.[28]

4.17 Of course, it is perfectly possible for a violation to occur of both the right to life and the right to freedom from torture or other inhumane treatment. An obvious example is when a detainee is tortured and he or she subsequently dies as a result of his/her injuries. In the *Shuriyya Zeynalov* case, the applicant complained under Articles 2 and 3 of the European Convention on Human Rights that his son had been tortured by agents of the Ministry of National Security of the Nakhchivan Autonomous Republic in Azerbaijan; that he died as a result; and that the domestic authorities had failed to conduct an effective investigation in that regard.[29] In that case, the Court decided to examine the question as to whether the applicant's son was ill-treated in custody separately from the complaint under Article 2 that he died as a result of such alleged ill treatment. It began with an analysis of the substantive aspect of Article 3 and then analysed the 'related complaint' of a violation of the right to life.[30]

4.18 The Court reiterated its established jurisprudence whereby

> where the events in issue lie wholly, or in large part, within the exclusive knowledge of the authorities, as in the case of persons within their control in custody, strong presumptions of fact will arise in respect of injuries occurring during such detention. Where an individual is taken into police custody in good health but is found to be injured afterwards, it is incumbent on the State to provide a plausible explanation of how those injuries were caused, failing which a clear issue arises under Article 3 of the Convention.[31]

4.19 The government had not claimed that the individual in question already had bruises on his body when he was arrested on 24 August 2011. Furthermore, although the forensic expert who examined the victim's body several hours after his death did not refer in his report to any injury or trace of injury, a video-recording of the body filmed before the funeral evidenced serious injuries. The authenticity of the video-recording was not disputed by the authorities, nor did they deny the fact that injuries were visible on the deceased's shoulders, elbows, knees, and buttocks.[32]

4.20 The Court could not exclude that those injuries resulted from acts of torture, although it found insufficient proof in the circumstances to sustain such a finding. Nonetheless, the ill treatment of the applicant's son 'caused him actual bodily injury

---

[28] European Court of Human Rights, *Kitanovski v. North Macedonia*, Judgment (First Section), 22 January 2015, para. 53. See further *Abdulkhadzhiyeva and Abdulkhadzhiyev v. Russia*, Judgment (Third Section), 4 October 2016, paras. 70, 71.
[29] European Court of Human Rights, *Shuriyya Zeynalov v. Azerbaijan*, Judgment (Fifth Section), 10 September 2020, para. 1.
[30] Ibid., para. 34.
[31] Ibid., para. 50.
[32] Ibid., paras. 52–4.

and its consequences must have also caused him considerable mental suffering, diminishing his human dignity'. Accordingly, the Court found a substantive violation of Article 3 of the Convention on the basis of inhuman and degrading treatment.[33]

4.21 With respect to Article 2 of the Convention, the Court noted: 'As a general rule, the mere fact that an individual dies in suspicious circumstances while in custody should raise an issue as to whether the State has complied with its obligation to protect that person's right to life.'[34] The omissions in the forensic examination are particularly relevant in the context of the right to life, the Court stipulated, since the failure to record the injuries meant that the pathologist did not consider whether a causal link could exist between those injuries and the death. While the European Court generally requires proof 'beyond reasonable doubt', in situations where knowledge of the salient events lie wholly or in large part with the authorities, as with detainees, 'strong presumptions of fact' will pertain to injuries and death occurring during detention. Taken together with the obstruction of the investigation by the authorities, their inability to 'convincingly' account for the circumstances of the death led the Court to also find a substantive violation of the right to life.[35]

4.22 A serious, wilful violation by the authorities of the rights pertaining to the dead, such as with respect to the possibility to view and bury the body of a deceased person, may rise to a violation of the prohibition on torture or other forms of cruel, inhuman, or degrading treatment. As discussed in Chapter 2, these rights ordinarily inhere in the family,[36] though under the right to private life, a person who was in a close relationship with a person prior to his or her demise, such as through cohabitation, may also have pertinent rights.[37] Thus a lesser violation by the authorities of rights pertaining to the dead may be addressed under the right to a private and/or family life.

4.23 There has been less consideration in other regional human rights mechanisms of the inter-relationship between the right to life and the right to freedom from inhumane treatment. That said, the Inter-American Court of Human Rights has explicitly followed the path taken by the European Court in certain respects. In its judgment in the *Rochela Massacre* case, the Inter-American Court cited the *Acar* judgment in support of its findings of 'extraordinary circumstances that lay a foundation' for a violation of the right to life under the Inter-American Convention with respect to the three survivors of the massacre. The Court reached its decision 'taking into account the force employed, the intent and objective of the use of this force, and the situation in which the victims found themselves'.[38]

---

[33] Ibid., paras. 60–2.
[34] Ibid., para. 67.
[35] Ibid., paras. 72–6.
[36] There is a general duty to respect the express wishes of a person prior to his or her death but the wishes of the deceased are not binding on surviving family members under international law.
[37] As may, in exceptional circumstances, members of his or her community. See Inter-American Court of Human Rights, *Moiwana Village v. Suriname*, Judgment (Preliminary Objections, Merits, Reparations and Costs), 15 June 2005.
[38] Inter-American Court of Human Rights, *Rochela Massacre v. Colombia*, Judgment (Merits, Reparations, and Costs), 11 May 2007, paras. 123–5.

4.24 While the African Court of Human and Peoples' Rights has yet to take a position on the matter, the African Commission on Human and Peoples' Rights has stated in its General Comment on the right to life under the 1981 African Charter on Human and Peoples' Rights: 'Where a State or its agent has attempted unlawfully to kill a person, but that person survives, where it has unlawfully threatened the life of a person, or where it has forcibly caused a person to disappear and that person's fate remains unknown, in addition to the violation of other rights, a violation of the right to life has occurred.'[39]

THE RELATIONSHIP WITH THE RIGHT TO A FAIR TRIAL

4.25 Where a death penalty case is being prosecuted, a court or human rights treaty body will be especially attentive to due process. Fair trial rights include the right to a fair and public hearing by a competent, independent, and impartial tribunal established by law.[40] Every defendant has the right to be presumed innocent until proved guilty beyond a reasonable doubt. That high evidentiary threshold is particularly important in the case of a capital trial.[41]

4.26 Article 14(3) of the ICCPR sets out other fundamental fair trial rights: the right to be informed promptly and in detail in a language the accused understands of the nature and cause of the charge(s); the availability of adequate time and facilities to prepare a defence and to communicate with counsel of choice; the right to be tried without undue delay; the right to be present at the trial and to a defence in person or through legal assistance of choice; the right to examine, or have examined, witnesses against him and to obtain the attendance and examination of witnesses on his/her behalf under the same conditions as witnesses giving testimony for the prosecution; the right to free assistance of an interpreter; and the right not to be compelled to confess guilt or to self-incriminate. Violation of any of these fair trial rights will routinely render a death sentence arbitrary and therefore also a violation of the right to life.

4.27 There is no overriding right under general international law to be tried before a civilian court even in a capital case, although the risks that a trial before a military court may not respect all fundamental fair trial rights are substantially higher.[42] In the African human rights system, however, the African Commission on Human and Peoples' Rights has stated that a military court may not lawfully impose a death sentence.[43] Under the ICCPR, the general right to a public trial is subject to the possibility of exclusion 'from all or part of a trial for reasons of morals, public order (ordre public) or national security in a democratic society, or when the interest of the private lives of the parties so requires, or to the extent strictly necessary in the opinion of the court in special circumstances where publicity would prejudice the interests of justice'.[44]

---

[39] African Commission General Comment on the right to life, para. 8.
[40] Art. 14(1), ICCPR. See Human Rights Committee, General Comment 36 on the right to life, paras. 41 and 42.
[41] Human Rights Committee, General Comment 36 on the right to life, para. 43.
[42] F. Andreu-Guzmán, *Military Jurisdiction and International Law: Military Courts and Gross Human Rights Violations*, vol. 1, International Commission of Jurists, Geneva, 2004, pp. 74–5.
[43] African Commission General Comment on the right to life, para. 24.
[44] Art. 14(1), ICCPR.

THE RELATIONSHIP WITH THE RIGHTS TO LIBERTY AND SECURITY

4.28 Article 9(1) of the ICCPR stipulates in part that 'everyone has the right to liberty and security of person'. Often considered as a composite right, in reality the rights to liberty and security are two distinct, albeit related, rights. The right to liberty of person concerns 'freedom from confinement of the body' while the right to security of person demands 'freedom from injury to the body and the mind, or bodily and mental integrity'.[45] As the Human Rights Committee has further recalled, the first substantive protection described in the Universal Declaration of Human Rights is the right of 'everyone' to 'life, liberty and security of person'.[46] That indicates not only the 'profound importance' of the rights being protected[47] but also their close inter-relationship.

4.29 The right to personal security obligates States Parties to the ICCPR 'generally to protect individuals from foreseeable threats to life or bodily integrity proceeding from any governmental or private actors'.[48] This clearly links the right to security with the customary law duty to protect life. Indeed, the Human Rights Committee describes the two rights – to life and to security – as 'overlapping'. The right to security, however, 'may be considered broader to the extent that it also addresses injuries that are not life-threatening'.[49] Where death results from a wilful failure to protect, violations of both rights may ordinarily be found.

4.30 Thus, in its Views in *Marcellana and Gumanoy v. The Philippines*, the Committee observed that

> given that the victims were human rights workers and that at least one of them had been threatened in the past, there appeared to have been an objective need for them to be afforded protective measures to guarantee their security by the State. However, there is no indication that such protection was provided at any time. On the contrary, the authors claimed that the military was the source of the threats received by Ms Marcellana, and that the fact-finding team was under constant surveillance during its mission.[50]

Ms Marcellana and Mr Gumanoy were taken out from the vehicles in which the mission was travelling by armed men, at least some of whom were associated with the military. Their dead bodies were later found. The cause of death in each case was gunshot wounds.[51] The Committee stated that violations of, inter alia, Articles 6(1) and 9(1) of the Covenant had occurred.

---

[45] Human Rights Committee, General Comment No. 35: Article 9 (Liberty and Security of Person), UN doc. CCPR/C/GC/35, 16 December 2014, para. 3.
[46] Ibid., para. 2.
[47] Ibid.
[48] Ibid., para. 9.
[49] Ibid., para. 55.
[50] Human Rights Committee, *Marcellana and Gumanoy v. The Philippines*, Views (UN doc. CCPR/C/94/D/1560/2007), 30 October 2008, para. 7.7.
[51] Ibid., paras. 2.3 and 2.4.

4.31 An especially serious violation of the rights to liberty and to security occurs in the case of an enforced disappearance. The archetypal example is where one or more State agents arrest or detain an individual and then maintain him or her incommunicado. The individual is often tortured and may then be either released or killed. Thus the Committee declared, 'extreme forms of arbitrary detention that are themselves life-threatening violate the rights to personal liberty and personal security as well as the right to protection of life, in particular enforced disappearances'.[52]

4.32 The Committee cites in this regard the case of *Mojica v. Dominican Republic*. Therein, the Committee recalled that the rights to liberty and security of person 'may be invoked not only in the context of arrest and detention' but also that States Parties to the ICCPR are barred from tolerating, condoning, or ignoring threats 'made by persons in authority to the personal liberty and security of non-detained individuals within the State party's jurisdiction'. With respect to Article 6(1) of the Covenant, States Parties 'should take specific and effective measures to prevent the disappearance of individuals and establish effective facilities and procedures to investigate thoroughly, by an appropriate impartial body, cases of missing and disappeared persons in circumstances that may involve a violation of the right to life'.[53]

THE RELATIONSHIP WITH THE RIGHTS TO PRIVATE AND TO FAMILY LIFE

4.33 According to Article 8(1) of the European Convention on Human Rights: 'Everyone has the right to respect for his private and family life, his home and his correspondence.' The European Court of Human Rights has considered the relationship between this right and the rights to life and to freedom from torture or other inhuman or degrading treatment protected under the Convention. In this regard, the Court has held that the positive obligations upon the State to 'protect' under Articles 2 or 3 may in some instances be considered either under Article 8 taken alone or in combination with Article 3 of the Convention.[54] This individual or composite set of obligations, the Court has further clarified, can include a duty to maintain and apply in practice an adequate legal framework affording protection against acts of violence by private individuals.[55]

4.34 In the case of *Nicolae Virgiliu Tănase v. Romania*,[56] however, which concerned a car crash in which an individual sustained unintentional life-threatening injuries, the Grand Chamber did not find either Article 3 or Article 8 applicable, but rather it considered the

---

[52] Human Rights Committee, General Comment No. 35: Article 9 (Liberty and security of person), para. 55.
[53] Human Rights Committee, *Mojica v. Dominican Republic*, Views (UN doc. CCPR/C/51/D/449/1991), 15 July 1994, paras. 5.4 and 5.5.
[54] European Court of Human Rights, *Buturugă v. Romania*, Judgment (Fourth Section), 11 February 2020 (rendered final on 11 June 2020), para. 44.
[55] European Court of Human Rights, *Guide on Article 8 of the European Convention on Human Rights: Right to Respect for Private and Family Life, Home and Correspondence*, Updated 30 April 2020, at http://bit.ly/2FnrL4c, para. 32.
[56] European Court of Human Rights, *Nicolae Virgiliu Tănase v. Romania*, Judgment (Grand Chamber), 25 June 2019.

application under the right to life. The applicant was diagnosed, inter alia, with polytrauma, post-traumatic mesentery rupture, and fractured and/or displaced bones and body parts. He underwent three surgical operations, including one involving the removal of part of his intestines, and had required a lower tracheotomy because of respiratory complications. A report on his medical condition noted that his injuries had required between 200 and 250 days of medical care and concluded that their severity had endangered his life.[57] With respect to the prohibition of inhuman or degrading treatment under the European Convention on Human Rights, the Court stated that bodily injuries and physical and mental suffering experienced by an individual following an accident which is merely the result of chance or negligent conduct cannot be considered as the consequence of 'treatment' to which that individual has been 'subjected' within the meaning of Article 3.[58]

4.35 Concerning Article 8, the Court reiterated that the object of the provision is 'essentially that of protecting the individual against arbitrary interference by the public authorities'. There are also, however, 'positive obligations inherent in an effective respect for private life' which may involve the taking of measures 'designed to secure respect for private life even in the sphere of the relations of individuals between themselves'.[59] But, the Court stated, there is nothing in its established case-law to suggest that the scope of private life 'extends to activities which are of an essentially public nature'.[60] While a risk that serious personal harm might occur in the event of an accident clearly existed, that risk 'was minimised by traffic regulations aimed at ensuring road safety for all road users, including through the proper separation of vehicles on the road'. Moreover, the Court observed, the accident 'did not occur as the result of an act of violence intended to cause harm to the applicant's physical and psychological integrity'.[61] Accordingly, the Court did 'not discern any particular aspect of human interaction or contact which could attract the application of Article 8 of the Convention' in the case at hand.[62]

4.36 In the *Cáceres* case,[63] a farming family in Paraguay had complained to the Human Rights Committee that the mass use of agrotoxins by nearby large agrobusinesses had poisoned many local residents and led to the death of their relative, Ruben Portillo Cáceres. In its 2019 Views, the Committee found violations of the family members' rights to life; to privacy, family, and home; and to an effective remedy, noting that the state had failed to adequately enforce environmental regulations and did not properly redress the resulting harms. In January 2011, Mr Portillo Cáceres died after suffering from severe nausea and fever, allegedly because of pesticides and insecticides. Twenty-two other members of Colonia Yeruticreadaen were affected by similar symptoms at the same time. The Committee stated that

---

[57] Ibid., para. 18.
[58] Ibid., para. 123.
[59] Ibid., para. 125.
[60] Ibid., para. 128.
[61] Ibid., para. 130.
[62] Ibid., para. 131.
[63] Human Rights Committee, *Cáceres v. Paraguay*, Views (CCPR/C/126/D/2751/2016), 25 July 2019.

when pollution has direct repercussions on the right to one's private and family life and home, and the adverse consequences of that pollution are serious because of its intensity or duration and the physical or mental harm that it does, then the degradation of the environment may adversely affect the well-being of individuals and constitute violations of private and family life and the home.[64]

4.37 The Court has found that in certain circumstances the procedural obligation under Article 2 to carry out an effective investigation into an alleged violation of the right to life may come into conflict with a State's obligations under Article 8.[65] The case of *Solska and Rybicka v. Poland* concerned the exhumation, in the context of criminal proceedings, of the remains of deceased persons against the wishes of their families. Polish domestic law did not provide a mechanism to review the proportionality of the decision ordering exhumation. As a consequence, the Court held that the interference was not 'in accordance with the law' and thus amounted to a violation of Article 8. More generally, the Court declared that the authorities have to find a 'due balance' between the requirements of an effective investigation as demanded by the procedural element of the right to life and the protection of the right to respect for private and family life of persons affected by the investigation. There may be circumstances, the Court said, 'in which exhumation is justified, despite opposition by the family'.[66]

THE RELATIONSHIP WITH THE RIGHT OF PEACEFUL ASSEMBLY

4.38 The right of peaceful assembly is protected in the ICCPR (in Article 21) and in regional human rights treaties.[67] It does not address directly the use of force to prevent an unlawful gathering nor to disperse one that has already assembled unlawfully. In its General Comment No. 37 on the right of peaceful assembly, adopted in July 2020, the Human Rights Committee observed that the full protection of the right depends on the protection of a range of other rights. 'Use of unnecessary or disproportionate force or other unlawful conduct by State officials during an assembly may', the Committee stated, 'breach articles 6, 7 and 9 of the Covenant'.[68]

4.39 Among the cases cited by the Committee was *Florentina Olmedo v. Paraguay*.[69] The communication concerned an agricultural worker, Blanco Domínguez, who took part in a peaceful demonstration in Paraguay in favour of agrarian reform. On 3 June 2003,

---

[64] Ibid., para. 7.8.
[65] European Court of Human Rights, *Guide on Article 8 of the European Convention on Human Rights: Right to Respect for Private and Family Life, Home and Correspondence*, para. 36, citing *Solska and Rybicka v. Poland*, Judgment (First Section), 20 September 2018, paras. 118–19.
[66] Ibid., para. 121.
[67] See Chapter 14 on the issue of assemblies and the right to life.
[68] Human Rights Committee, General Comment No. 37: Article 21: right of peaceful assembly, UN doc. CCPR/C/GC/37, 27 July 2020 (hereinafter, Human Rights Committee, General Comment 37 on the right of peaceful assembly), para. 98.
[69] Human Rights Committee, *Florentina Olmedo v. Paraguay*, Views (Comm. No. 1828/2008), UN doc. CCPR/C/104/D/1828/2008, 26 April 2012.

around a thousand demonstrators, including Mr Domínguez, converged on the site of the demonstration. They found themselves confronted by considerable numbers of police, anti-riot police, and military personnel. Coming face to face with a police barrier, the demonstrators decided to blockade the road. They were warned that if they did not disperse, the blockade would be cleared by force. But while negotiations were still underway, the prosecutor ordered the road to be cleared. The police use of force was immediate and extremely violent, involving the use of firearms as well as tear gas and water cannons.

4.40 The police beat many of the demonstrators, fired indiscriminately at those who were fleeing, and violently broke into and damaged various nearby houses, severely beating any persons they managed to catch. Both metal-jacketed and rubber-coated bullets were fired 'indiscriminately'.[70] Mr Dominguez had been at the head of the demonstration and, along with other demonstrators, had peacefully surrendered to the police, kneeling down with his hands up. While he was in this position, an officer of the Paraguayan National Police shot him in the back at very close range. After he fell to the ground, he was hit on the head by the police. After undergoing two surgical operations, Blanco Dominguez died on 5 June 2003.[71] In finding a violation of the right to life, the Human Rights Committee reiterated that Paraguay was obligated to protect the life of the demonstrators.[72]

4.41 An 'extreme case', the Committee further recalled in its General Comment No. 37, 'when participants in peaceful assemblies are subjected to unlawful force or conduct as part of a widespread or systematic attack directed against any civilian population' may also amount to a crime against humanity.[73] Under the Rome Statute of the International Criminal Court (ICC), a crime against humanity means acts such as murder or extermination, enforced disappearance, serious instances of arbitrary deprivation of liberty, torture, serious sexual violence, or persecution, when committed as part of and with knowledge of such an attack.[74]

4.42 On 8 February 2018, the Prosecutor of the ICC decided to open a preliminary examination into the situation in Venezuela to analyse alleged crimes in the context of demonstrations and related political unrest.[75] Subsequently, on 27 September 2018, a group of States Parties to the Rome Statute (Argentina, Canada, Chile, Colombia, Paraguay, and Peru) made a referral regarding the situation in Venezuela since 12 February 2014.[76]

---

[70] Ibid., paras. 2.1 and 2.4–2.6.
[71] Ibid., para. 2.7.
[72] Ibid., para. 7.5.
[73] Human Rights Committee, General Comment 37 on the right of peaceful assembly, para. 98.
[74] Art. 7(1), Rome Statute of the International Criminal Court; adopted at Rome 17 July 1998; entered into force 1 July 2002.
[75] ICC, 'Statement of the Prosecutor of the International Criminal Court, Fatou Bensouda, on Opening Preliminary Examinations into the Situations in the Philippines and in Venezuela', The Hague, 8 February 2018, at http://bit.ly/2PpEt6o.
[76] ICC, 'Statement of the Prosecutor of the International Criminal Court, Fatou Bensouda, on the Referral by a Group of Six States Parties Regarding the Situation in Venezuela', The Hague, 27 September 2018, at http://bit.ly/35xa64Y.

4.43 Also potentially amounting to crimes against humanity were abuses committed in Iraq in the period from October 2019 to June 2020 against demonstrators against the authorities. In a joint report, the UN Assistance Mission in Iraq (UNAMI) and the Office of the UN High Commissioner for Human Rights (OHCHR) documented 'patterns of abuses committed by multiple armed actors' that indicated 'the widespread targeting of protesters and persons allegedly critical of political parties and armed groups with various ties to the State, including targeted killings, abductions, disappearances, violent attacks at demonstration sites or elsewhere, including in homes'.[77] The report further stated:

> Live ammunition caused most of the 359 deaths of protesters attributed to the security forces at protest sites, with shrapnel and the direct impact of tear gas canisters responsible for 28 other deaths. Noting the widespread use of live ammunition in situations beyond the narrow scope in which the use of firearms is permitted, many of these killings may amount to arbitrary deprivation of life. Security forces also shot indiscriminately into crowds of protesters and may have intentionally used lethal force without justification.[78]

A report cited by the OHCHR recorded 149 deaths of protesters from 1 to 8 October 2019 and attributed at least 70 per cent to 'shots in the head or chest area'.[79]

THE RELATIONSHIP WITH THE RIGHTS TO FOOD AND TO WATER

4.44 The right to life also interrelates directly with a number of economic and social rights, particularly the rights to food and to water, as Chapter 13 discusses. There is a duty upon every State to exercise due diligence to seek to prevent and address both extreme poverty and starvation. Intentionally seeking to cause starvation, for example by provoking a famine, will violate the right to freedom from cruel or inhuman treatment as well as the right to food. Such illegal conduct may also violate the right to life, particularly (but not only) if the person dies as a result.

4.45 The right to water is sometimes considered within the right to food but it is also increasingly seen as possessing an autonomous existence in international law. The right to water falls within the category of guarantees essential for securing an adequate standard of living, 'particularly since it is one of the most fundamental conditions for survival'.[80] It is, the Committee on Economic, Social and Cultural Rights has further averred, a 'public good fundamental for life and health', one that is 'indispensable for leading a life in human dignity' and a 'prerequisite for the realization of other human rights'.[81] Indeed, the Committee has asserted, the right to water should be seen 'in conjunction with other rights

---

[77] UNAMI and OHCHR, *Human Rights Violations and Abuses in the Context of Demonstrations in Iraq October 2019 to April 2020*, Baghdad, August 2020, p. 7.
[78] Ibid., p. 19 (footnotes omitted).
[79] Ibid.
[80] Committee on Economic, Social and Cultural Rights, General Comment No. 15: The right to water (arts. 11 and 12 of the International Covenant on Economic, Social and Cultural Rights), UN doc. E/C.12/2002/11, 20 January 2003, para. 3.
[81] Ibid., para. 1.

enshrined in the International Bill of Human Rights, foremost amongst them the right to life and human dignity'.[82]

4.46 Under the International Covenant on Economic, Social and Cultural Rights (ICESCR), States Parties explicitly recognise 'the fundamental right of everyone to be free from hunger'.[83] This treaty provision is also a customary law rule applicable to all States. Where a person is in the specific care of the State, the failure to ensure sufficient and appropriate food and water will be a violation of the right to freedom from cruel or inhuman treatment. If that concerns a detainee, it will also breach the duty to treat 'with humanity and with respect for the inherent dignity of the human person' all persons deprived of their liberty.[84] Should the detainee die as a consequence of avoidable deprivation, this will amount to a violation of the right to life.[85]

---

[82] Ibid., para. 3.

[83] Art. 11(2), International Covenant on Economic, Social and Cultural Rights; adopted at New York 16 December 1966; entered into force 3 January 1976. As of 1 May 2021, 171 States were party to the Covenant and a further 4 States were signatories.

[84] Arts. 7 and 10(1), ICCPR.

[85] Human Rights Committee, *Yekaterina Pavlovna Lantsova v. Russia*, Views (UN doc. CCPR/C/74/D/763/1997), 26 March 2002, para. 9.2.

PART II

Major Themes

5

Deaths as a Result of Armed Conflict

INTRODUCTION

5.01 The right to life continues to apply during situations of armed conflict. This fact is reflected in both treaty law and customary international law. While certain human rights treaties do not provide for any derogation from their provisions,[1] or expressly provide for their application during armed conflict,[2] others allow a State Party to derogate from the full observance of certain human rights. But aside from the 1950 European Convention on Human Rights,[3] none permits any derogation from the duties to respect and protect the right to life in all circumstances, including in armed conflict.

The Application of the ICCPR in Armed Conflict

5.02 The 1966 International Covenant on Civil and Political Rights (ICCPR) allows a State Party to take measures derogating from its obligations under the Covenant 'in time of public emergency which threatens the life of the nation and the existence of which is officially proclaimed'.[4] This would potentially apply to an armed conflict of significant intensity.[5] But the ICCPR explicitly excludes the possibility of any derogation pertaining

---

[1] This is the case with respect to the UN Convention on the Rights of the Child; adopted at New York 20 November 1989; entered into force 2 September 1990; and the African Charter on Human and Peoples' Rights; adopted at Nairobi 27 June 1981; entered into force 21 October 1986. See also Art. 4(2), Convention on the Rights of Persons with Disabilities; adopted at New York 13 December 2006; entered into force 3 May 2008.

[2] According to the UN Convention against Torture, 'No exceptional circumstances whatsoever, whether a state of war or a threat of war, internal political instability or any other public emergency, may be invoked as a justification of torture.' Art. 2(2), Convention against Torture and Other Cruel, Inhuman or Degrading Treatment or Punishment; adopted at New York 10 December 1984; entered into force 26 June 1987.

[3] Under the European Convention on Human Rights, it is possible to derogate from the right to life for 'lawful acts of war'. Art. 15, Convention for the Protection of Human Rights and Fundamental Freedoms; adopted at Rome 4 November 1950; entered into force 3 September 1953. As Chapter 6 discusses, it is not settled whether this pertains only to compliance with international humanitarian law applicable to international armed conflict or to compliance with the rules of jus ad bellum (or to both).

[4] Art. 4(1), International Covenant on Civil and Political Rights; adopted at New York 16 December 1966; entered into force 23 March 1976.

[5] 'Not every disturbance or catastrophe qualifies as a public emergency which threatens the life of the nation, as required by article 4, paragraph 1.' Human Rights Committee, General Comment No. 29: Article 4: Derogations during a State of Emergency, adopted on 24 July 2001, UN doc. CCPR/C/21/Rev.1/Add.11, 31 August 2001, para. 3.

to Article 6 on the right to life.[6] Accordingly, in its consideration in 1996 of the application of the right to life to the use of nuclear weapons by one State against another in a situation of international armed conflict, the International Court of Justice observed that 'the protection of the International Covenant of [sic] Civil and Political Rights does not cease in times of war, except by operation of Article 4 of the Covenant whereby certain provisions may be derogated from in a time of national emergency. Respect for the right to life is not, however, such a provision.'[7] The Human Rights Committee has similarly declared: 'Like the rest of the Covenant, article 6 continues to apply also in situations of armed conflict to which the rules of international humanitarian law are applicable, including to the conduct of hostilities.'[8]

5.03 This position has been widely endorsed by State practice and *opinio juris*. Among examples of contrary practice, the United States had been perceived as reluctant to accept the application of international human rights law during armed conflict. In 2012, however, in its fourth periodic report on its implementation of the ICCPR, the United States declared that it 'has not taken the position that the Covenant does not apply "in time of war." Indeed, a time of war does not suspend the operation of the Covenant to matters within its scope of application.'[9]

5.04 Perhaps the only State that has vociferously opposed the application of the Covenant during armed conflict, including the right to life, and which continues to do so today, is Israel. In written comments submitted in February 2020 on the Human Rights Committee's draft General Comment 37 on the right of assembly, Israel stated:

> While there may well be a convergence between the law of armed conflict and international human rights law in some respects, in the current state of international law and state-practice [sic] worldwide, it is Israel's view that the law of armed conflict and international human rights law, which are codified in separate instruments, nevertheless remain distinct and apply in different circumstances.[10]

5.05 Israel's position notwithstanding, it is accepted and recognised by the international community of States as a whole that the right to life is applicable during a situation of armed conflict. The crux of what continues to be disputed concerns the nature and effects of the interrelationship between the right to life and the applicable rules of international humanitarian law, a branch of international law also widely referred to as the law of armed conflict. The nature of the interrelationship is sometimes framed in terms of an either/or question: is the act at issue regulated by international humanitarian law or is it governed by

---

[6] Art. 4(2), ICCPR.
[7] ICJ, *Legality of the Threat or Use of Nuclear Weapons*, Advisory Opinion, 8 July 1996, para. 25.
[8] Human Rights Committee, 'General comment No. 36: Article 6: right to life', UN doc. CCPR/C/GC/36, 3 September 2019, para. 70 (hereinafter, Human Rights Committee, General Comment 36 on the right to life).
[9] Fourth Periodic Report of the United States on its Implementation of the ICCPR, UN doc. CCPR/C/USA/4, 22 May 2012, para. 506.
[10] Comments of Israel on Draft General Comment 37 of the Human Rights Committee, Submitted by the Office of the Deputy Attorney General (International Law), 13 February 2020, para. 21.

international human rights law? This is, however, a mischaracterisation of the legal matter, at the least with respect to the right to life. Given that the right to life applies in all circumstances – whether peacetime or armed conflict – the challenge exists primarily in the *interpretation* of the right to life during armed conflict, rather than in determining whether the right applies.[11]

The Content of the Chapter

5.06 The fundamental interpretative issue on the relationship between the right to life and international humanitarian law is addressed in the next section of the present chapter. Thereafter follows a brief discussion of how armed conflict is defined under international humanitarian and criminal law. The remainder of the chapter considers the application of the right to life during armed conflicts, first with respect to the protection of persons in the power of the enemy and then in the context of the conduct of hostilities. Finally, the duty to investigate alleged violations of the right to life during armed conflict is reviewed.

THE RELATIONSHIP BETWEEN THE RIGHT TO LIFE AND INTERNATIONAL HUMANITARIAN LAW

5.07 During the negotiation of the ICCPR, several States had proposed that the text explicitly provide that killings lawfully perpetrated by the military in time of war would not violate the right to life.[12] Instead, the decision was taken to prohibit 'arbitrary' deprivation of life in all circumstances. This generic formulation comprised 'elements of unlawfulness and injustice, as well as those of capriciousness and unreasonableness'.[13] But its central tenet is to render deprivation of life arbitrary 'as a rule' if it is inconsistent either with international law or with more protective domestic law.[14] This *renvoi* means that rules emanating from other branches of international law than human rights should be applied to help determine whether or not a violation of the right to life has occurred.

5.08 Jus in bello is the branch of international law that regulates conduct during a situation of armed conflict, in particular, but not only by States. In such situations, international humanitarian law is the mainstay of jus in bello, applying specifically to certain acts committed by parties to an armed conflict where those occur with sufficient nexus to that conflict. The Human Rights Committee has stated: 'Use of lethal force consistent with international humanitarian law and other applicable international law norms is, in general, not arbitrary.'[15] This postulate is discussed below. Also potentially

---

[11] This is the case subject to issues of extraterritorial jurisdiction as and where they occur. See Chapter 3 for a more detailed discussion of this issue.
[12] M. J. Bossuyt, *Guide to the 'Travaux Préparatoires' of the International Covenant on Civil and Political Rights*, Martinus Nijhoff, Dordrecht/Boston, 1987, pp. 115–25.
[13] M. Nowak, *UN Covenant on Civil and Political Rights. Commentary*, 2nd rev. ed., Engel, Kehl am Rhein, 2005, p. 111.
[14] Human Rights Committee, General Comment 36 on the right to life, para. 12.
[15] Ibid., para. 64.

relevant during an armed conflict is the law of neutrality, which constrains – or obligates – conduct in international armed conflict by States that are not a party to that conflict. For instance, a State proclaiming neutrality is precluded from providing support to the forces of warring parties in such a conflict.[16] The law of neutrality also contains rules that fall within the realm of jus ad bellum: the law on inter-State use of force.[17]

5.09 In practice, the details of the interrelationship between the right to life and the applicable rules of international humanitarian law are rather more complex and nuanced than is sometimes claimed. In particular, as this chapter discusses, the nature of the relationship hinges in part on which branch of the law of armed conflict is applicable to a particular case or set of facts. So-called Geneva Law is the branch of international humanitarian law that applies to the treatment of persons in the power of the enemy, protecting them against all forms of inhumane treatment. Hague Law concerns the conduct of hostilities – the fighting and related activities, including reconnaissance and logistics – seeking generally to protect civilians as well as, under limited, specific circumstances, combatants while they are fighting.

5.10 The Human Rights Committee has declared that while rules of international humanitarian law 'may be relevant for the interpretation and application' of Article 6 of the ICCPR, 'when the situation calls for their application, both spheres of law are complementary, not mutually exclusive'.[18] This contrasts somewhat with the earlier, but most recent, pronouncement of the International Court of Justice on the issue, wherein it declared that 'some rights may be exclusively matters of international humanitarian law; others may be exclusively matters of human rights law; yet others may be matters of both these branches of international law'.[19] In academic writings, there is much debate – but no general agreement, let alone consensus – on the nature of the interrelationship between the right to life and the applicable rules of international humanitarian law.[20]

5.11 While it is clear that an act that lacks clear nexus to the armed conflict, such as the use of force in law enforcement, is not a matter regulated by international humanitarian law, in its categorisation of the interrelationship, the International Court of Justice did not explain which 'rights' were exclusively matters of international humanitarian law, nor how such an approach would operate in practice. While international humanitarian law has specific rules

---

[16] P. Seger, 'The Law of Neutrality', in A. Clapham and P. Gaeta (eds.), *The Oxford Handbook of International Law in Armed Conflict*, Oxford University Press, Oxford, 2014, p. 248.

[17] See Chapter 6 on the interrelationship between the right to life and jus ad bellum.

[18] Human Rights Committee, General Comment 36 on the right to life, para. 64.

[19] International Court of Justice, *Legal Consequences of the Construction of a Wall in the Occupied Palestinian Territory*, Advisory Opinion, 9 July 2004, para. 106. The dicta were supported in the judgment in the Armed Activities case a year later: *Case Concerning Armed Activities on the Territory of the Congo (Democratic Republic of Congo v. Uganda)*, Judgment, 19 December 2005, para. 216.

[20] For examples of this debate, see, e.g., D. Murray (ed.), *Practitioners' Guide to Human Rights Law in Armed Conflict*, Oxford University Press, Oxford, 2016; G. Oberleitner, *Human Rights in Armed Conflict: Law, Practice, Policy*, Cambridge University Press, Cambridge, 2015; and M. Milanovic, 'The Lost Origins of Lex Specialis: Rethinking the Relationship between Human Rights and International Humanitarian Law', in J. Ohlin (ed.), *Theoretical Boundaries of Armed Conflict and Human Rights*, Cambridge University Press, Cambridge, 2016.

governing the treatment of specified individuals, the rules it lays down do not commonly give rise to 'rights' as such. They sometimes demand specific conduct of a party to an armed conflict. More often, they lay down prohibitions on certain conduct in specified situations. It is more accurate to say that in a situation of armed conflict, the right to life – and particularly what amounts to the 'arbitrary' deprivation of life – is to be interpreted by reference to the rules of international humanitarian law and the rules of other branches of international law. That is so, as and where those rules are applicable and pertinent.

THE EXISTENCE AND CLASSIFICATION OF AN ARMED CONFLICT

5.12 The challenge of interpretation with respect to international humanitarian law pertains, primarily, within and in connection to an ongoing armed conflict.[21] The term 'armed conflict', which has largely supplanted the narrower notion of 'war' since the conclusion of the four Geneva Conventions in 1949,[22] concerns violence between two or more 'parties' to a conflict, which may be State or non-State in nature. According to the 1949 Geneva Conventions and their two Additional Protocols of 1977, two classifications (sometimes called typologies)[23] of armed conflict exist: international armed conflict and armed conflict not of an international character.[24] The latter of the two classifications is more commonly referred to as non-international armed conflict or even just by the acronym 'NIAC'. The scope and forms of both international armed conflict[25] and non-international armed conflict[26] are set out in treaty law, as interpreted by relevant jurisprudence, in particular within the context of international criminal law tribunals. The two classifications, and the subsidiary forms of armed conflict within those classifications, are now considered in turn.

International Armed Conflict

5.13 There are five different forms of international armed conflict: war, active armed conflict, military occupation, proxy armed conflicts, and wars of national liberation. All

---

[21] Certain obligations exist prior to armed conflict, such as the duty to disseminate IHL and the duty to test weapons so as to ensure their compliance with rules on the conduct of hostilities. Other obligations persist after the end of an armed conflict, such as with respect to those originally detained in connection with an armed conflict.

[22] Article 2 common to the four Geneva Conventions of 1949 refers to 'cases of declared war or of any other armed conflict'.

[23] See, e.g., S. Vité, 'Typology of Armed Conflicts in International Humanitarian Law: Legal Concepts and Actual Situations', *International Review of the Red Cross*, vol. 91, no. 873 (March 2009), pp. 69–94, at http://bit.ly/3cl95gh.

[24] References to 'civil war', 'transnational' armed conflict, or 'internationalized' armed conflict, which are occasionally found in scholarship, have no grounding in treaty law and are not reflected in State practice. They should be disregarded in considerations of the application of international law.

[25] See Art. 2 common to the four Geneva Conventions of 1949; and Art. 1(4), Protocol Additional to the Geneva Conventions of 12 August 1949, and Relating to the Protection of Victims of International Armed Conflicts; adopted at Geneva 8 June 1977; entered into force 7 December 1978 (hereinafter, 1977 Additional Protocol I).

[26] See Art. 3 common to the four Geneva Conventions of 1949; and Art. 1(2), Protocol Additional to the Geneva Conventions of 12 August 1949, and Relating to the Protection of Victims of Non-International Armed Conflicts; adopted at Geneva 8 June 1977; entered into force 7 December 1978 (hereinafter, 1977 Additional Protocol II).

108   *Major Themes*

but one of the five – the last, where national liberation movements use force in pursuit of self-determination – involve military action between at least two States. A conflict can, however, still exist even if only one of the two States in opposition is using force against the other. In the case of national liberation movements, they are effectively considered as the armed forces of a State 'in waiting'.

War as International Armed Conflict

5.14 Traditionally, war was declared between two States prior to the outbreak of hostilities. Indeed, the 1907 Hague Convention III on the Opening of Hostilities,[27] a treaty that is still nominally in force, demands that hostilities between States Parties 'must not commence without previous and explicit warning, in the form either of a declaration of war, giving reasons, or of an ultimatum with conditional declaration of war'.[28] Even though all five permanent members of the UN Security Council are States Parties to the 1907 Hague Convention III,[29] the practice of declaring war has fallen into desuetude. The United States, for example, last declared war on another State (Romania) in 1942.[30] There is certainly no obligation to do so under customary international law.

5.15 Since a declaration of war may not be followed by the outbreak of hostilities,[31] it might be thought that the right to life has little or no application prior to any use of armed force. In fact, such a declaration may be recognised as the legal basis for executions to occur in a number of States which have abolished the death penalty only in peacetime. This is an important concern under the aegis of the right to life. The 1989 Second Optional Protocol to the ICCPR on the abolition of the death penalty, for instance, explicitly allows a reservation to be made at the time of adherence providing for the application of the death penalty 'in time of war pursuant to a conviction for a most serious crime of a military nature committed during wartime'.[32] The death penalty must, though, already have been incorporated in domestic legislation. Among the eighty-eight States Parties to the Protocol (as of 1 December 2020), four continue to retain the death penalty during wartime.[33] Many States that are not party to the Protocol also do so.

[27] Convention (III) relative to the Opening of Hostilities; adopted at The Hague 18 October 1907; entered into force 26 January 1910.
[28] Art. 1, 1907 Hague Convention III.
[29] A further thirty-one States are party to the Convention, the most recent adherent being Ukraine, which acceded in 2015. Prior to that, the last adherence was by South Africa, which acceded the Convention back in 1978.
[30] Article I, Section 8, paragraph 11 of the Constitution of the United States of America vests in the US Congress the power 'to declare War'. J. K. Elsea and M. C. Weed, *Declarations of War and Authorizations for the Use of Military Force: Historical Background and Legal Implications*, Congressional Research Service, Washington, DC, 18 April 2014, available at http://bit.ly/3em5qkg, p. 1.
[31] At the end of March 2013, for instance, the Democratic Republic of Korea declared that it was entering a 'state of war' with the Republic of Korea in the south of the peninsula, repudiating the Armistice in place since its signature on 27 July 1953. BBC, 'North Korea Enters "State of War" with South', 30 March 2013, at http://bbc.in/3bdfTwi; and BBC, 'The Korean War Armistice', 5 March 2015, at http://bbc.in/2KazYaE. The declaration of war was not followed by actual hostilities, either against the Republic of Korea or against the United States.
[32] Art. 2, Second Optional Protocol to the International Covenant on Civil and Political Rights, aiming at the abolition of the death penalty; adopted at New York 15 December 1989; entered into force 11 July 1991.
[33] Azerbaijan, Chile, El Salvador, and Greece. Cyprus, Malta, and Spain had made similar reservations under their respective adherence to the Protocol, but each later withdrew them. With respect to several of the

Active International Armed Conflict

5.16 Considerably more common than a declaration of war is the actual outbreak of hostilities between two States, a situation that ordinarily leads to loss of life, sometimes on a massive scale. Hostilities typically take place on land, at sea, and/or in the air, but may also potentially occur in outer space or cyberspace.

5.17 There is no settled threshold of violence for an active international armed conflict to come into existence, but it is generally agreed to be low. According to the International Committee of the Red Cross (ICRC), for example, 'factors such as duration and intensity are generally not considered to enter the equation'.[34] Indeed, in the ICRC's view, 'the mere capture of a soldier or minor skirmishes between the armed forces of two or more States may spark ... an international armed conflict and lead to the applicability' of international humanitarian law, at least 'insofar as such acts may be taken as evidence of genuine belligerent intent'.[35]

5.18 An active international armed conflict exists even if the State being attacked or invaded does not respond with any military action of its own.[36] International humanitarian law both applies to and regulates force that is used unilaterally, and in such a case both States are party to an international armed conflict. Moreover, the fact that in a situation of armed conflict the regime governing one State is not recognised by the government of its enemy does not preclude the application of international humanitarian law.[37] In October 2001, for instance, the Taliban was recognised as the legitimate government of Afghanistan by only three States (Pakistan, Saudi Arabia, and the United Arab Emirates), yet when the United States started bombing Afghanistan, an international armed conflict nonetheless came into existence between those two States.

Military Occupation as International Armed Conflict

5.19 An occupation by one State of some or all of the territory belonging to another is an international armed conflict[38] that brings into play the relevant rules of international humanitarian law.[39] This is the case regardless of whether or not the armed forces of the

---

reserving States, other States Parties have formally objected to their ostensible reservation. For details, see the UN Treaty Collection web page for the Protocol, at http://bit.ly/3acHtsv.

[34] ICRC, 'International Humanitarian Law and the Challenges of Contemporary Armed Conflicts', Report for the 32nd International Conference of the Red Cross and Red Crescent, Geneva, October 2015, at http://bit.ly/2Mzrxch, p. 8.

[35] Ibid.

[36] Art. 2 common to the 1949 Geneva Conventions.

[37] Art. 4(3), Geneva Convention Relative to the Treatment of Prisoners of War; adopted at Geneva 12 August 1949; entered into force 21 October 1950 (hereinafter, 1949 Geneva Convention III).

[38] As set out in the Element of Crimes under the jurisdiction of the International Criminal Court, the term 'international armed conflict' includes military occupation. Elements of Crimes, reproduced from the *Official Records of the Assembly of States Parties to the Rome Statute of the International Criminal Court*, First Session, New York, 3–10 September 2002, part II.B, footnote 34.

[39] These are set out in a number of treaties, most notably the Regulations annexed to the 1907 Hague Convention IV and the 1949 Geneva Convention IV. See in particular Arts. 42–56, Regulations Concerning the Laws and Customs of War on Land Annexed to Convention (IV) respecting the Laws and Customs of War on Land; adopted at The Hague 18 October 1907; entered into force 26 January 1910; and

territorial State violently resist the occupation. According to Article 2 common to each of the four 1949 Geneva Conventions, 'The Convention shall also apply to all cases of partial or total occupation of the territory of a High Contracting Party, even if the said occupation meets with no armed resistance.' Where, however, the territorial State validly consents to the presence of foreign troops on its soil,[40] such as through the conclusion of a Status of Forces Agreement, there is no military occupation and no application of international humanitarian law (unless, for instance, the foreign force is actively supporting the territorial State in its own armed conflict).

Proxy Armed Conflicts

5.20 A proxy armed conflict is one in which one State attacks another not through the medium of its armed forces but through its active support of a non-State armed group. According to the jurisprudence of the International Criminal Tribunal for the former Yugoslavia (ICTY), later endorsed by the International Criminal Court, this occurs where the non-State armed group pursues military action under the foreign State's 'overall control'. The notion denotes situations where the foreign State 'has a role in organising, coordinating or planning the military actions of the military group, in addition to financing, training and equipping or providing operational support to that group'.[41]

Wars of National Liberation

5.21 According to Article 1(4) of the 1977 Additional Protocol I, an international armed conflict may encompass 'armed conflicts in which peoples are fighting against colonial domination and alien occupation and against racist régimes in the exercise of their right of self-determination, as enshrined in the Charter of the United Nations and the Declaration on Principles of International Law concerning Friendly Relations and Co-operation among States in accordance with the Charter of the United Nations'. This is not a rule of customary international law, as the requisite *opinio juris* is lacking.

5.22 That said, where a State is party to the Protocol, a national liberation movement fighting against the State's colonial domination or foreign occupation may make a formal declaration to the Swiss Federal Council – as depositary of the Additional Protocol I – that it will respect the Protocol and the 1949 Geneva Conventions. If the Federal Council validates the declaration, this transforms what could otherwise be a non-international armed conflict into an international armed conflict.[42] This has only occurred once in the history of the Protocol: in the case of Morocco's occupation of Western Sahara, where the

---

Arts. 47–78, Convention (IV) Relative to the Protection of Civilian Persons in Time of War; adopted at Geneva 12 August 1949; entered into force 21 October 1950 (hereinafter, 1949 Geneva Convention IV).

[40] In its judgment in the *Nicaragua* case, the International Court of Justice observed that (military) intervention was 'already allowable at the request of the government of a State'. International Court of Justice, *Case Concerning Military and Paramilitary Activities in and Against Nicaragua (Nicaragua v. United States)*, Judgment (Merits), 27 June 1986, para. 246.

[41] International Criminal Court (ICC), *Prosecutor v. Thomas Lubanga Dyilo*, Judgment (Trial Chamber I), 14 March 2012, para. 541.

[42] Arts. 1(4) and 96(3), 1977 Additional Protocol I.

long-standing conflict between Morocco and the Polisario Front has been considered an international armed conflict since 2015.[43]

Non-international Armed Conflict

5.23 There are different forms of non-international armed conflict, but for the purpose of the application of the right to life, the most important – and broadest – form is one to which both Article 3 common to the four Geneva Conventions and customary international law on the conduct of hostilities apply. Such an 'armed conflict not of an international character' occurs in the territory of one of the States Parties to the Geneva Conventions. As of 1 May 2021, of the total of 197 States recognised by the UN Secretary-General (and, similarly, the Swiss Federal Council), all but one – Niue – were formally party to the four 1949 Geneva Conventions.[44]

5.24 There is no definition of non-international armed conflict in the Conventions themselves, but in the 1977 Additional Protocol II, it is stipulated that 'situations of internal disturbances and tensions, such as riots, isolated and sporadic acts of violence and other acts of a similar nature' are not armed conflicts.[45] A 'genuine' non-international armed conflict must therefore be distinguished from 'a mere act of banditry or an unorganized and short-lived insurrection'.[46]

5.25 Although not necessarily the subject of consensus, a generally accepted – or at least very widely cited – definition of a non-international armed conflict[47] is the one proposed by the ICTY Appeals Chamber in 1995. In its decision on jurisdiction in the *Tadić* case in 1995, the Tribunal referred to 'protracted armed violence between governmental authorities and organized armed groups or between such groups within a State'.[48] The Appeal Chamber effectively held that two criteria determined the existence of a non-international armed conflict: a significant level of armed violence and the involvement of at least one 'organised' armed group in armed struggle, either against a State or against another similarly organised armed group. The employment of the term 'protracted' initially caused some confusion, but the ICTY subsequently clarified that it pertains rather to the 'intensity of the conflict' and not, in line with the word's meaning in ordinary parlance, its longevity.[49]

---

[43] See on this issue K. Fortin, 'Unilateral Declaration by Polisario under API accepted by Swiss Federal Council', *Armed Groups and International Law* blog, 2 September 2015, at http://bit.ly/2NcAolb.
[44] Moreover, according to the ICRC, Niue 'remains bound' by New Zealand's ratification in 1959 of the Geneva Conventions, 'until such time as Niue accedes to the Conventions in its own right'. See http://bit.ly/3mdzdiK.
[45] Art. 1(2), 1977 Additional Protocol II.
[46] J. Pictet (ed.), *Geneva Convention for the Amelioration of the Condition of the Wounded and Sick in Armed Forces in the Field: A Commentary*, ICRC, Geneva, 1952, p. 50.
[47] M. Schmitt (ed.), *Tallinn Manual on the International Law Applicable to Cyber Warfare*, Cambridge University Press, Cambridge, 2013, Commentary on Rule 23, para. 6.
[48] ICTY, *Prosecutor v. Tadić (aka 'Dule')*, Decision on the Defence Motion for Interlocutory Appeal on Jurisdiction (Appeals Chamber) (Case No IT-94-1), 2 October 1995, para. 70.
[49] ICTY, *Prosecutor v. Tadić*, Judgment (Trial Chamber) (Case No IT-94-1-T), 7 May 1997, para. 562.

5.26 Organised armed groups are those imbued with a military-style command-and-control structure, where their members typically possess and use a variety of weapons, and which control a significant logistical capacity giving them the capability to sustain military operations.[50] In its judgment in the *Boškoski* case, an ICTY Trial Chamber summarised in five categories the factors that the Tribunal as a whole had assessed in its jurisprudence in order to determine whether or not any given armed group was sufficiently organised. These were the existence of a command structure for the group; the ability to carry out operations in an organised manner; the level of logistics; the level of intragroup discipline; and (more debatably) whether the armed group was able to 'speak with one voice'.[51] Where, and for such time as, both criteria of conflict intensity and armed group organisational level are met, a non-international armed conflict is ongoing.

5.27 A final point of import is that, within a single State, multiple armed conflicts may exist in parallel as a matter of international law. These conflicts may be solely international or non-international in character, or may be a mix of both classifications. In addition, the same acts of violence may even fall within two simultaneous armed conflicts, such as occurs when a non-State armed group within a State is attacked by another State without the consent of the territorial State.

THE RIGHT TO LIFE AND THE PROTECTION OF PERSONS IN THE POWER OF THE ENEMY

5.28 Geneva Law is the branch of IHL that concerns the protection of persons 'in the power of the enemy'. This is where, for instance, they are formally detained by the authorities of the enemy or because they are on territory controlled by the enemy, in particular as a result of its military occupation of foreign lands. Individuals are protected by Geneva Law, depending on their status under international humanitarian law. As ordinary civilians, they are protected against inhumane treatment at all times when they are residing in occupied territory or are detained for reasons related to the conflict. In contrast, anyone participating directly in hostilities is only protected from attack before such participation and thereafter. Once they are in the power of the enemy, however, such as following capture or where they are otherwise *hors de combat* as a consequence of wounds or sickness, all inhumane treatment is prohibited.

5.29 In all circumstances and in all armed conflicts, a violation of international humanitarian law leading directly or causally to the death of a person would also amount to a violation of human rights law. Thus, for example, the summary execution of any individual while he or she is in the power of the enemy, whether the victim be civilian or a member of the military, is a serious violation of both international humanitarian law and the right to life. This is also the case where a person in the power of the enemy is subjected to physical violence (other than in lawful self-defence) and he or she later dies as

---

[50] S. Casey-Maslen with S. Haines, *Hague Law Interpreted*, Hart, Oxford, 2018, p. 62.
[51] ICTY, *Prosecutor v. Boškoski and Tarčulovski*, Judgment (Trial Chamber II) (Case No IT-04-82-T), 10 July 2008, paras. 199–203.

a result. In either scenario, a violation of the right to life occurs both when the author of the violence belongs to the authorities of the enemy and when the authorities unreasonably fail to prevent the violence at the hands of another (e.g., a private civilian or, in a detention facility, another inmate).

5.30 In case of a foreign military occupation, the Occupying Power is obligated under the 1949 Geneva Convention IV to ensure to 'the fullest extent of the means available to it' that adequate food (and water) and medical supplies are provided to the civilian population.[52] If the resources in the occupied territory are inadequate, the Occupying Power must either bring in the necessary food and medicine to fill the gap or, failing that, must both agree to and facilitate the provision of humanitarian relief.[53] Furthermore, the Occupying Power 'may not requisition foodstuffs, articles or medical supplies available in the occupied territory, except for use by the occupation forces and administration personnel, and then only if the requirements of the civilian population have been taken into account'.[54]

5.31 Any wilful failure by the Occupying Power to meet its obligations to ensure the adequate supply of food and water and medical care in occupied territory not only violates international humanitarian law; it also violates human rights law. Survivors will be likely to have been subjected to inhumane treatment. Where people die as a consequence of a failure by the Occupying Power to meet its obligations, however, a violation of the right to life will have occurred. Similarly, the failure by an enemy power to provide adequate food and water or necessary medical care to any person they are detaining, leading to his or her death, will violate not only international humanitarian law but also the right to life. In each case, the violations occur irrespective of whether an individual is, or is required to be, held responsible under either military law or international criminal law for a war crime.

5.32 Special protection is afforded to combatants in an international armed conflict when they are no longer directly participating in hostilities. For instance, combatant members of the armed forces who are captured by the enemy during an international armed conflict have the right to prisoner-of-war status.[55] A critical element of this status is known as combatant's privilege. This longstanding customary rule precludes a prisoner of war from being put on trial by the power that is detaining him or her for lawful acts of war, such as participating directly in hostilities against the armed forces of that power or killing a member of those armed forces where the fatal act complied with IHL.[56] Nonetheless, should a State that is party to an armed conflict try an enemy soldier from another State for

---

[52] Art. 55, 1949 Geneva Convention IV.
[53] Arts. 55 and 59, 1949 Geneva Convention IV.
[54] Art. 55, 1949 Geneva Convention IV.
[55] Arts. 4–5 and 7, 1949 Geneva Convention III.
[56] As the ICRC has explained, 'Upon capture, combatants entitled to prisoner-of-war status may neither be tried for their participation in the hostilities nor for acts that do not violate' IHL. The ICRC recalls that this is a longstanding rule of customary IHL. Note to Rule 106 of the ICRC Customary IHL Study: 'Conditions for Prisoner-of-War Status', at http://bit.ly/3aXJwlc. As Jens David Ohlin observes, 'the privilege of combatancy transforms, almost magically, what would otherwise be an unlawful act of murder into a lawful killing consistent with jus in bello'. J. D. Ohlin, 'When Does the Combatant's Privilege Apply?', *Opinio Juris*, 1 August 2014, at http://bit.ly/2PwKzlT.

the mere fact of having taken up arms against it (and impose a sentence of death upon conviction), this would not only violate international humanitarian law, it would also violate the right to life on the basis that it was a clear instance of arbitrary deprivation of life.

5.33 In contrast, there is no absolute comprehensive prohibition under international law on the imposition of a death sentence on a person who, in direct connection with a non-international armed conflict, has taken up arms against the State and where he or she has killed another in the course of that action. In addition, in an international armed conflict, a person who does not meet the definition of a combatant, particularly the one set out in Article 4 of the 1949 Geneva Convention III, which reflects customary law, does not enjoy combatant's privilege and thus immunity from prosecution.

5.34 In any armed conflict, however, the execution of any pregnant woman in the power of the enemy will violate the right to life.[57] The imposition of the death penalty – and *a fortiori* the execution of that sentence – on any convicted person who was under eighteen years of age at the time of the commission of the offence will also violate the right to life. So too will the imposition of the death penalty (as well as, inevitably, the execution) of any person of any age after a trial that has not met the requirements of fairness[58] or where the crime for which the defendant was convicted was not among the most serious.[59] This limits potentially permissible death penalty crimes associated with an armed conflict to those involving intentional, unlawful homicide, as is the case in peacetime.[60]

5.35 The applicable rules of international human rights law are more restrictive than is the case under treaty-based international humanitarian law. Under the 1949 Geneva Convention IV, for instance, the Occupying Power may impose the death penalty on a civilian especially protected under that treaty in a case where he or she is guilty either of espionage or of serious acts of sabotage against the military installations of the Occupying Power. This is so even if no one is killed, provided always that such offences were already punishable by death under the domestic law of the occupied territory in force before the occupation began.[61]

5.36 Outside the conduct of hostilities, the use of lethal force by the Occupying Power or its agents during its enforcement of the law must always comply with the rules governing law enforcement as codified in the 1990 UN Basic Principles on the Use of Force and

---

[57] Arguably, so too under customary law will be the execution of a nursing mother, although this prohibition may better be considered as *de lege ferenda*.
[58] That the mere imposition of the death penalty after conviction at the conclusion of an unfair trial violates also the right to life rather than only the right to freedom from inhumane treatment is on the basis that Article 6(2) of the ICCPR only allows the imposition of the death penalty where it is 'not contrary to the provisions' of the Covenant, including those set out in Article 14 on the conduct of a fair trial. The Human Rights Committee cites as illustration of this point its Views of 2003 in the *Kurbanov* case. See Human Rights Committee, *Abduali Ismatovich Kurbanov v. Tajikistan*, Views (UN doc. CCPR/C/79/D/1096/2002), 6 November 2003, esp. paras. 7.4–7.7.
[59] Art. 6(2), ICCPR. See also Human Rights Committee, General Comment 36 on the right to life, paras. 41, 52.
[60] Ibid., para. 35.
[61] Art. 68, Geneva Convention IV.

Firearms by Law Enforcement Officials.[62] According to Basic Principle 9, firearms may only be used where necessary either in self-defence or defence of others against the imminent threat of death or serious injury, or to prevent the impending perpetration of a particularly serious crime involving grave threat to life. Use of firearms with intent to kill can only ever be lawful outside the conduct of hostilities when this is strictly unavoidable in order to protect life, such as with a view to preventing the imminent detonation of a bomb or killing of a hostage. The use of firearms in breach of these rules by the Occupying Power or its agents, such as with a view to protecting only property, will constitute a violation of the right to life.

5.37 Astonishingly, the ICRC in its commentary of 2020 on Article 42 of the 1949 Geneva Convention III suggests that laying anti-personnel mines outside a prisoner-of-war camp might be lawful in certain circumstances.[63] The placing of anti-personnel mines is an intentional lethal use of force and can only be lawful when strictly unavoidable to protect life. Given that use of firearms – and less-lethal weapons in the ICRC's interpretation of the provision – is already considered an 'extreme measure', the ICRC's appreciation of the applicable law is not robust.

THE RIGHT TO LIFE IN THE CONDUCT OF HOSTILITIES

5.38 The International Court of Justice, in its 1996 Advisory Opinion on the legality of the use of nuclear weapons by one State against another in a situation of international armed conflict, held that

> in principle, the right not arbitrarily to be deprived of one's life applies also in hostilities. The test of what is an arbitrary deprivation of life, however, then falls to be determined by the applicable *lex specialis*, namely, the law applicable in armed conflict which is designed to regulate the conduct of hostilities. Thus, whether a particular loss of life, through the use of a certain weapon in warfare, is to be considered an arbitrary deprivation of life contrary to Article 6 of the Covenant, can only be decided by reference to the law applicable in armed conflict and not deduced from the terms of the Covenant itself.[64]

5.39 The Court makes two essential points in its dicta. The first is that the right to life applies to the conduct of hostilities in an international armed conflict and this, without jurisdictional limitation. As the issue was not addressed by any of the States which addressed the Court orally or in writing in the proceedings, the Court decided not to deal with an 'internal' use of nuclear weapons 'by a State within its own boundaries'. There is, however, no evidence to support a contention that the right to life would apply only to

---

[62] Basic Principles on the Use of Force and Firearms by Law Enforcement Officials; adopted by the Eighth UN Congress on the Prevention of Crime and the Treatment of Offenders at Havana, 27 August to 7 September 1990.
[63] ICRC Commentary on Article 42 of the 1949 Geneva Convention III, 2020, para. 2550. See further *infra* Paragraphs 10.19–10.20.
[64] International Court of Justice, *Legality of the Threat or Use of Nuclear Weapons*, Advisory Opinion, 8 July 1996, para. 25.

hostilities in an international armed conflict yet somehow not to those in the context of a non-international armed conflict. Indeed, Article 2(2)(c) of the European Convention on Human Rights explicitly applies the right to life to action taken by a State Party in the repression of an insurrection, which is a form of non-international armed conflict. Moreover, under international custom, the rules of international humanitarian law governing the use of force in the conduct of hostilities are effectively the same, irrespective of the classification of conflict.

5.40 The second essential point made by the International Court of Justice is that in interpreting what amounts to arbitrary deprivation of life during the conduct of hostilities, the rules of international humanitarian law will be determinant. If those rules are violated, so too will be the right to life (at the least in case of a resultant death). If, on the other hand, the use of force complies with the rules of international humanitarian law on the conduct of hostilities, no arbitrary deprivation of life will have occurred. In this, the Human Rights Committee largely concurs with the tenor of the International Court of Justice's 1996 Advisory Opinion. Thus, in its General Comment 36 on the right to life, the Committee declared: 'Use of lethal force consistent with international humanitarian law and other applicable international law norms is, in general, not arbitrary.'[65] The Committee does not disclose in which (exceptional) circumstances it believes that a use of lethal force that complied with international humanitarian law would still be arbitrary and therefore a violation of the right to life.

5.41 The list of international humanitarian law rules applicable to the use of nuclear weapons delineated by the International Court of Justice in its Advisory Opinion was remarkably short. Only two were highlighted by the Court – the principle of distinction and the prohibition of unnecessary suffering:

> The first is aimed at the protection of the civilian population and civilian objects and establishes the distinction between combatants and non-combatants; States must never make civilians the object of attack and must consequently never use weapons that are incapable of distinguishing between civilian and military targets. According to the second principle, it is prohibited to cause unnecessary suffering to combatants: it is accordingly prohibited to use weapons causing them such harm or uselessly aggravating their suffering.

Thus, extrapolating the logic of the Court's approach, one can see that both the targeting of civilians and an indiscriminate attack (i.e., one where no lawful military objective is targeted by an attack) would not only violate international humanitarian law but would also be constitutive of a violation of the right to life. This is so, at the least where a civilian was killed as a result.[66] In addition, one may deduce that the targeting of a combatant with

---

[65] Human Rights Committee, General Comment 36 on the right to life, para. 64.

[66] Case law in the European Court of Human Rights has found a violation of the right to life where potentially lethal force was used in the conduct of hostilities but civilians injured in the attack survived. See, e.g., European Court of Human Rights, *Benzer v. Turkey*, Judgment (Former Second Section), 12 November 2013 (as rendered final on 24 March 2014), paras. 142, 143, and 252(4). The Court declared that it was 'not in doubt that an attack was carried out on the applicants' villages which caused death and destruction. That attack,

an unlawful weapon – one that is of a nature to cause superfluous injury or unnecessary suffering[67] – would similarly violate the right to life (at the least where the combatant died as a result of his or her injuries).

5.42 A more elaborate list of violations of international humanitarian law that would give risk to a violation of the right to life has been compiled by the Human Rights Committee in its General Comment 36 on the right to life:

> Practices inconsistent with international humanitarian law, entailing a risk to the lives of civilians and other persons protected by international humanitarian law, including the targeting of civilians, civilian objects and objects indispensable to the survival of the civilian population, indiscriminate attacks, failure to apply the principles of precaution and proportionality, and the use of human shields, would also violate article 6 of the Covenant.

Thus a civilian does not need to lose his or her life for a violation of the right to life to occur under the ICCPR in the view of the Committee.

5.43 The addition of the principle of proportionality to the non-exhaustive list is especially important insofar as it represents the second of the two fundamental IHL principles/rules (the first being the principle of distinction).[68] It holds that where a lawful military objective is being targeted – and thus the principle of distinction being complied with – an attack[69] must also seek to ensure that the expected incidental harm to civilians (or damage to civilian objects, or the two combined) is not excessive when compared to the military advantage anticipated to result from the attack.[70] The principle regulates decision-making and resultant action at the moment the attack is launched. Accordingly, compliance is not judged at the moment of impact, much less on the basis of the number of civilians actually killed or injured as a result (though this data will potentially be relevant in assessing the reasonableness of the judgment made by the attacker when launching the attack). Where the rule of proportionality is violated by a particular attack and a civilian dies as a consequence, his or her right to life will also have been violated.

---

which caused these three applicants' injuries, was so violent and caused the indiscriminate deaths of so many people that these three applicants' fortuitous survival does not mean that their lives had not been put at risk. The Court is thus satisfied that the risks posed by the attack to these three applicants call for examination of their complaints under Article 2 of the Convention.'

[67] ICRC, Customary IHL Rule 70: 'Weapons of a Nature to Cause Superfluous Injury or Unnecessary Suffering', at http://bit.ly/2CyqlPC.

[68] Surprisingly, the International Court of Justice did not consider the principle of proportionality in attack in its consideration of applicable IHL rules in the context of the 1996 Advisory Opinion.

[69] Contrary to the ordinary meaning of the word, 'attack' in IHL is explicitly defined to also cover defensive actions. According to Article 49(1) of the 1977 Additional Protocol I: '"Attacks" means acts of violence against the adversary, whether in offence or in defence.'

[70] As the ICRC have concluded, under customary international humanitarian law applicable in all armed conflicts, 'Launching an attack which may be expected to cause incidental loss of civilian life, injury to civilians, damage to civilian objects, or a combination thereof, which would be excessive in relation to the concrete and direct military advantage anticipated, is prohibited.' ICRC, Customary IHL Rule 14: 'Proportionality in Attack', at http://bit.ly/2k9mrHh.

5.44 The principle of precautions in attack, similarly applicable in all armed conflicts as determined by the ICRC's study of customary IHL published in 2005, is best understood as a supporting principle, underpinning both the principle of distinction and the principle of proportionality in attack. It holds that in the conduct of military operations, 'constant care must be taken to spare the civilian population, civilians and civilian objects. All feasible precautions must be taken to avoid, and in any event to minimize, incidental loss of civilian life, injury to civilians and damage to civilian objects.'[71]

5.45 In 2012, in its judgment in the *Santo Domingo massacre* case, the Inter-American Court of Human Rights found violations of human rights by applying the duty to take precautions to the non-international armed conflict between Colombia and the non-State armed group, the Colombian Revolutionary Armed Forces.[72] It cited the position of the ICRC on the customary status of the norm in all armed conflict as authoritative.[73] The violation of the principle appears to have been determinative in the Court's finding of a violation of the right to life in those killed by an attack by means of a Second World War–era cluster bomb dropped by the Colombian Air Force.[74]

5.46 The reference by the Human Rights Committee also to attacks on civilian objects as being constitutive of a violation of the right to life is more questionable. The wording of the General Comment could be interpreted to mean that not only an attack on an empty civilian house or a school but also, for instance, one on livestock or even pets held by civilians (all civilian objects under IHL) would all violate the right to life, even though no civilian was killed or even injured. This is not reflective of extant international law.

THE DUTY TO INVESTIGATE POTENTIALLY ARBITRARY DEPRIVATION OF LIFE DURING ARMED CONFLICT

5.47 The procedural duty to investigate potential violations of the right to life persists at all times during armed conflict.[75] This reflects the duty under international humanitarian law to investigate potential violations of the rules espoused thereunder. In particular, as the ICRC has observed, since there is an obligation under international humanitarian law to prosecute war crimes – serious violations of the law that attract individual criminal responsibility – this 'logically presupposes an obligation to investigate'.[76] The practical application of these duties, however, will depend in part on whether a potential violation results from a breach of Geneva Law or Hague Law, a related issue being the feasibility of

---

[71] ICRC Customary IHL Rule 15: 'Principle of Precautions in Attack', at http://bit.ly/2m6mCnj.
[72] Inter-American Court of Human Rights, *Santo Domingo Massacre v. Colombia*, Judgment (Preliminary Objections, Merits and Reparations), 30 November 2012, *esp.* paras. 229–30.
[73] Ibid., para. 216.
[74] Ibid., paras. 228–30.
[75] According to the Minnesota Protocol, the duty to investigate any potentially unlawful death applies to all cases during an armed conflict outside the conduct of hostilities, meaning that it concerns, in particular, cases of detention with sufficient nexus to the armed conflict. *Minnesota Protocol on the Investigation of Potentially Unlawful Death* (2016), para. 16.
[76] ICRC, *Guidelines for Investigating Deaths in Custody*, Geneva, 2013, p. 12.

Deaths as a Result of Armed Conflict

conducting an investigation in the prevailing circumstances. In many instances, a violation of Geneva Law will occur in a territory and/or in a facility under the control of a State, typically making the investigation more straightforward. In contrast, in many instances, a violation of Hague Law will occur when a State is not in effective control of the territory being attacked and where the victims are located. These two branches of international humanitarian law are considered in turn.

5.48 In a situation of international armed conflict, international humanitarian law explicitly addresses the action that must be taken following the death of or serious injury to a prisoner of war or civilian internee specially protected under the 1949 Geneva Convention III and IV, respectively. Where death or serious injury has been caused or is suspected to have been caused by a guard, another prisoner of war, an internee, or indeed any other person, or with respect to any death whose cause is unknown, the discovery of the death 'shall be immediately followed by an official enquiry by the Detaining Power'.[77] More generally, in both international and non-international armed conflict, violence against detainees is prohibited by treaty and customary international humanitarian law 'and can amount to a war crime'.[78] A fortiori this is the case where the detainee dies from injuries sustained during detention. A failure to investigate any death during detention – unless it unquestionably results from natural causes – will violate the procedural component of the right to life.

5.49 In its judgment in the *al-Skeini* case, which concerned the deaths of individuals during or following detention, the European Court of Human Rights' Grand Chamber acknowledged that 'where the death to be investigated under Article 2 [of the European Convention on Human Rights] occurs in circumstances of generalised violence, armed conflict or insurgency, obstacles may be placed in the way of investigators' and that 'concrete constraints may compel the use of less effective measures of investigation or may cause an investigation to be delayed'.[79] 'Nonetheless', the Court concluded, 'the obligation under Article 2 to safeguard life entails that, even in difficult security conditions, all reasonable steps must be taken to ensure that an effective, independent investigation is conducted into alleged breaches of the right to life'.[80] One of the applicants in the *al-Skeini* case was a Colonel in the Basra police force whose son, Baha Mousa, died while in the custody of the British army, three days after having been arrested by soldiers in September 2003. Baha Mousa, who was found to have ninety-three identifiable injuries on his body, died of asphyxiation.[81]

5.50 Investigating deaths that occur during the conduct of hostilities ordinarily poses additional challenges, most obviously where there is a lack of effective control over the territory where the victims are located. Even in such situations, however, there may be

---

[77] Art. 121, 1949 Geneva Convention III; Art. 131, 1949 Geneva Convention IV.
[78] ICRC, *Guidelines for Investigating Deaths in Custody*, Geneva, 2013, p. 12.
[79] European Court of Human Rights, *al-Skeini and others v. United Kingdom*, Judgment (Grand Chamber), 7 July 2011, para. 164.
[80] Ibid.
[81] Ibid., paras. 63, 66.

video or photographic evidence of who has been killed or what has been destroyed during an attack that can contribute to a partially effective investigation. In other situations, access to the area of impact of the attack is possible.

5.51 The *Jaloud* case[82] concerned a shooting to death at a checkpoint in Iraq that was jointly manned at the relevant time by armed Iraqi Civil Defence Corps personnel and Dutch troops. Although arguably a Geneva Law case, as the Iraqi and foreign forces effectively controlled the area at the time in question, it is better considered as a Hague Law incident. A key issue with respect to liability under the European Convention on Human Rights was to determine who had fired the fatal shots: the Iraqi or the Dutch forces. It appears that the calibre of ammunition fired by each differed (NATO 5.56 mm rounds by the Dutch soldiers but 7.62 mm rounds by the Iraqis).

5.52 The European Court noted the applicant's claim that the Royal Military Constabulary attached to the Dutch forces had held the body of Mr Azhar Sabah Jaloud for some hours, yet no autopsy had been performed during that period. The body had been transferred to an Iraqi civilian hospital, where an autopsy had been carried out but without the presence of Royal Military Constabulary officials. The autopsy report, 'such as it was', had been added to the file but not translated.[83] Other forensic evidence, the applicants affirmed, 'had been treated in a similarly careless fashion. In particular, no detailed translation had been made of the report on the bullet fragments removed from the body'.[84]

5.53 The Court observed that the autopsy seems to have been carried out in the absence of any qualified Netherlands official and that nothing is known of the qualifications of the Iraqi pathologist who performed it.[85] Moreover, the Court noted, the pathologist's report 'had serious shortcomings; extremely brief, it was lacking in detail and there were not even any pictures included'.[86] More generally, no alternative arrangement appeared to have been considered for the autopsy, even though the forces of the United States or the United Kingdom in Iraq might have had facilities and qualified personnel available.[87] The Court thus found that the investigation was deficient with respect to the autopsy.[88]

5.54 In the *Benzer* case, which concerned a bombing by the Turkish Air Force of two Kurdish villages in the south-east area of the country, a Turkish prosecutor from Şirnak charged with investigating the case decided that Kurdish Workers' Party (PKK) members had carried out bombing attacks on the ground 'despite the lack of any information in his file to support his conclusion'.[89] A number of prosecutors expressly instructed the *gendarmerie* and the police to investigate the 'killings by members of the PKK', clearly

---

[82] European Court of Human Rights, *Jaloud v. The Netherlands*, Judgment (Grand Chamber), 20 November 2014.
[83] Ibid., para. 169.
[84] Ibid., para. 170.
[85] Ibid., para. 213.
[86] Ibid., para. 214.
[87] Ibid., para. 215.
[88] Ibid., para. 216.
[89] European Court of Human Rights, *Benzer v. Turkey*, Judgment, para. 190.

demonstrating 'that none of them had an open mind as to what might have happened in the applicants' two villages'.[90] When a prosecutor 'finally gave thought to visiting the applicants' two villages some fourteen years after the bombing, he was told by the military that they would not be able to provide security during any such visit to protect the prosecutor'.[91]

5.55 The Court observed that an investigation by the military prosecutor 'also left a lot to be desired', being 'limited to asking the military officials whether any flight had been conducted over the applicants' villages'. The military prosecutor 'did not ask to examine the flight logs personally, and left it to the behest of the military who, in fact, were the suspects in his investigation'.[92] This was crucial evidence, 'which constituted a key element in the possible identification and prosecution of those responsible'.[93] 'Having regard to the abundance of information and evidence showing that the applicants' villages were bombed by the Air Force', the Court was constrained to conclude that the investigation's 'inadequacy' was due to the national investigating authorities' 'unwillingness officially to establish the truth and punish those responsible'.[94]

[90] Ibid., para. 191.
[91] Ibid., para. 195.
[92] Ibid., para. 192.
[93] Ibid., para. 196.
[94] Ibid., para. 197.

6

Jus ad Bellum, Aggression, and the Right to Life

INTRODUCTION

6.01 In its most recent General Comment on the right to life under the 1966 International Covenant on Civil and Political Rights[1] (ICCPR), the Human Rights Committee declared that a State Party to the Covenant that perpetrates aggression leading to fatalities violates the right to life. Thus, according to the Committee: 'States parties engaged in acts of aggression as defined in international law, resulting in deprivation of life, violate ipso facto article 6 of the Covenant.'[2] That implies that potentially an aggressor State may be held responsible under international human rights law for every death caused by its waging of an aggressive war. Further, in such a circumstance, Article 6 of the Covenant could apply not only to civilian but also to military deaths. That is potentially so, irrespective of the party to the armed conflict to which they belong.

6.02 A number of States have rejected or objected to the Human Rights Committee's stance. The starkest is the position of the United States, which it outlined in remarks made in 2017 with respect to the draft of the General Comment. In a blanket assertion, the United States declared that it does 'not believe that the right to life in Article 6 creates obligations with respect to any death that would in some way be caused by any violation of international law'.[3] This includes but is not limited to violations of jus ad bellum.

6.03 The United Kingdom claimed it was not within the mandate of the Committee to address such issues.[4] France, which stated that Article 6 of the ICCPR 'is not intended to

---

[1] International Covenant on Civil and Political Rights; adopted at New York 16 December 1966; entered into force 23 March 1976.
[2] Human Rights Committee, 'General Comment No. 36: Article 6: right to life', UN doc. CCPR/C/GC/36, 3 September 2019, para. 70 (hereinafter, Human Rights Committee, General Comment 36 on the right to life).
[3] 'Observations of the United States of America on the Human Rights Committee's Draft General Comment No. 36 on Article 6 – Right to Life', 6 October 2017, available at http://bit.ly/39y57Ad, para. 20.
[4] 'Human Rights Committee Draft General Comment No. 36 on Article 6 of the International Covenant on Civil and Political Rights, on the Right to Life: Comments of the Government of the United Kingdom of Great Britain and Northern Ireland', undated but accessed October 2017, also available at http://bit.ly/39y57Ad, para. 34.

regulate the use of force between states', called on the Committee 'not to adopt a broad reading of Article 6'.[5] Canada stated simply that it 'would insist on removing' Paragraph 70.[6] More nuanced in its comments on the then draft paragraph was Germany, which pointed out that

> maintaining international peace and security is primarily a matter regulated by the part of international law governing the ius ad bellum, rather than a subject matter treated by human rights law. Notwithstanding the fact that an act of aggression *may entail* or lead to violations of human rights, a clear distinction between the different legal regimes should be maintained in order to allow for an adequate attribution of responsibilities in international law.[7]

6.04 Undeniably, the affirmation by the Human Rights Committee represents a normative development in its position on the interrelationship between international human rights law and jus ad bellum. In its General Comment 6 on the right to life of 1982 (now formally superseded by General Comment 36),[8] it claimed that 'States have the supreme duty to prevent wars, acts of genocide and other acts of mass violence causing arbitrary loss of life. Every effort they make to avert the danger of war, especially thermonuclear war, and to strengthen international peace and security would constitute the most important condition and guarantee for the safeguarding of the right to life.'[9] In its General Comment 6, the Human Rights Committee was not explicitly asserting that aggression violates the right to life of all those killed as a result. That said, the assertion that wars *cause* – as opposed to involve – arbitrary loss of life was already an indication that this might one day become its view.

6.05 This chapter considers the extent to which the affirmation that aggression resulting in loss of life is always a violation of the right to life constitutes *lex lata*. It begins by discussing how contemporary jus ad bellum outlaws aggression within the context of the broader prohibition of inter-State use of force, noting that the prohibition only obliquely refers to the promotion of human rights. The chapter then considers the interrelationship between jus ad bellum (and other bodies of international law) and international human rights law, recognising that this has attracted relatively little comment so far from States (aside from the brief comments cited above), as well as from judicial authorities and leading publicists.

---

[5] 'Commentaires du Gouvernement français à propos du projet d'Observation générale n° 36 sur l'article 6 du Pacte international relatif aux droits civils et politiques, concernant le droit à la vie', undated but accessed October 2017, also available at http://bit.ly/39y57Ad, para. 42.

[6] 'Human Rights Committee, Draft General Comment No. 36 on Article 6 of the International Covenant on Civil and Political Rights – Right to Life: Comments by the Government of Canada', undated but accessed October 2017, also available at http://bit.ly/39y57Ad, para. 22.

[7] 'Submission from Germany on the draft General Comment on Article 6 of the International Covenant on Civil and Political Rights – Right to Life', also available at http://bit.ly/39y57Ad, para. 24 (added emphasis).

[8] Human Rights Committee, General Comment 36 on the right to life, para. 1.

[9] Human Rights Committee, General Comment 6 on the Right to Life, adopted at the Sixteenth Session of the Committee on 30 April 1982, para. 2.

JUS AD BELLUM'S PROHIBITION OF INTER-STATE USE OF FORCE

6.06 The fundamental rule of jus ad bellum is set out in Article 2(4) of the Charter of the United Nations (UN Charter).[10] This article reads in full as follows: 'All Members shall refrain in their international relations from the threat or use of force against the territorial integrity or political independence of any state, or in any other manner inconsistent with the Purposes of the United Nations.' This rule is the cornerstone both of the UN Charter and of modern jus ad bellum.[11]

The Status of the Prohibition

6.07 The prohibition on inter-State use of force in Article 2(4) is a rule of customary international law. It is binding on all UN member States.[12] It constrains all other States also as a general principle of law.[13] But such is the fundamental nature of the prohibition on the use of force, it is also widely considered to be a peremptory (jus cogens) norm of international law. According to the 1969 Vienna Convention on the Law of Treaties,[14] a jus cogens norm is one that is 'accepted and recognized by the international community of States as a whole as a norm from which no derogation is permitted and which can be modified only by a subsequent norm of general international law having the same character'.[15] A peremptory norm 'enjoys a higher rank in the international hierarchy than treaty law and even "ordinary" customary rules'.[16]

6.08 That the prohibition is indeed a peremptory norm of international law appears, implicitly, to be the position of the International Court of Justice. In its judgment in the *Nicaragua* case, the Court cited the view of the International Law Commission, in the course of the Commission's work on the codification of the law of treaties, that 'the law of the Charter concerning the prohibition of the use of force in itself constitutes a conspicuous example of a rule in international law having the character of jus cogens'.[17] This was also the

---

[10] Charter of the United Nations; adopted at San Francisco 26 June 1945; entered into force 24 October 1945. As of 1 May 2021, 193 States were bound directly by the UN Charter.

[11] International Court of Justice, *Case Concerning Armed Activities on the Territory of the Congo (Democratic Republic of Congo v. Rwanda)*, Judgment, 19 December 2005, para. 148.

[12] International Court of Justice, *Case Concerning Military and Paramilitary Activities in and against Nicaragua (Nicaragua v. United States)*, Judgment (Merits), 27 June 1986 (hereinafter, *Nicaragua* judgment), paras. 185, 188, and 190.

[13] Principle 1, *The Declaration on Principles of International Law Concerning Friendly Relations and Co-operation among States*, annexed to UN General Assembly Resolution 2625, adopted without a vote on 24 October 1970.

[14] Vienna Convention on the Law of Treaties; adopted at Vienna 23 May 1969; entered into force 27 January 1980 (hereinafter, VCLT).

[15] Art. 53, VCLT. As at 1 December 2020, only 116 States were party to the Vienna Convention, although most of its provisions are today reflective of customary law. This includes the provisions in Article 53, which contains the 'basic elements of *jus cogens*'. International Law Commission (ILC), 'First report on *jus cogens* by Dire Tladi, Special Rapporteur', UN doc. A/CN.4/693, 8 March 2016, para. 61.

[16] International Criminal Tribunal for the former Yugoslavia (ICTY), *Prosecutor v. Anto Furundžija*, Judgment (Case No. IT-95-17/1-T) (Trial Chamber), 10 December 1998, para. 153.

[17] International Court of Justice, *Nicaragua* judgment, para. 190, citing para. 1 of the commentary of the Commission to Article 50 of its draft Articles on the Law of Treaties, *ILC Yearbook*, 1966-II, p. 247.

position of the two litigants in the *Nicaragua* case: Nicaragua and the United States.[18] It is also the overt position of most leading publicists.[19] Sometimes, however, the jus cogens norm is restricted or specifically directed to the prohibition of aggression and not the inter-State use of force more generally.[20]

The Scope of the Prohibition on Use of Force

6.09 The prohibition pertains only to the use of armed force.[21] Thus, illegal economic warfare, such as through discriminatory trade embargoes, the nationalisation of foreign companies, or the unlawful imposition of tariffs upon imports, does not constitute a prohibited use of force.[22] Force that falls within the scope of the prohibition may be employed from or on land, from or at sea, from or in the air, from or in space, and from or in cyberspace.

6.10 The notion of force is thus not limited in scope to the use of weapons and ammunition that act through the application of kinetic energy, such as bullets, bombs, and missiles. Other weapons also deliver force that is regulated by jus ad bellum, such as by diffusing toxic chemicals or biological agents or directing electromagnetic energy.[23] The term encompasses cyber operations that damage or interrupt the normal operation of computer systems and networks, at the least when these operations result in physical harm to people or objects.[24]

---

[18] International Court of Justice, *Nicaragua* judgment, para. 190.

[19] See, in particular, International Court of Justice, *Nicaragua* judgment, Separate Opinion of ICJ President Nagendra Singh, p. 153; *Case Concerning Oil Platforms (Islamic Republic of Iran v. United States of America)*, Judgment (Merits), 6 November 2003 (hereinafter, *Oil Platforms* judgment), Separate Opinion of Bruno Simma, para. 6; *Oil Platforms* judgment, Separate Opinion of Pieter Kooijmans, para. 46; Y. Dinstein, *War, Aggression and Self-Defence*, 6th ed., Cambridge University Press, Cambridge, 2017, para. 302; A. Orakhelashvili, *Akehurst's Modern Introduction to International Law*, 8th ed., Routledge, London, 2018, p. 54; and O. Corten, *The Law against War*, Hart, Oxford, 2010, p. 200ff. André de Hoogh 'assumed' that the prohibition on the use of armed force is a jus cogens norm. A. de Hoogh, 'Jus Cogens and Armed Force', in M. Weller (ed.), *The Oxford Handbook of the Use of Force in International Law*, Oxford University Press, London, 2015, p. 1164. Christine Gray does not offer her own view but does observe that 'States and commentators generally agree that the prohibition is not only a treaty obligation but also customary law and even *ius cogens*'. C. Gray, *International Law and the Use of Force*, 4th ed., Oxford University Press, Oxford, 2018, p. 32.

[20] 'Those peremptory norms that are clearly accepted and recognized include the prohibitions of aggression, genocide, slavery, racial discrimination, crimes against humanity and torture, and the right to self-determination.' Draft articles on Responsibility of States for Internationally Wrongful Acts, with commentaries; Text adopted by the ILC at its fifty-third session, in 2001, Commentary, para. 5, on draft Article 26; see further Commentary, para. 4, on draft Article 40.

[21] International Court of Justice, *Nicaragua* judgment, para. 247.

[22] J. Crawford, *Brownlie's Principles of Public International Law*, 9th ed., Oxford University Press, Oxford, 2019, p. 717.

[23] S. Casey-Maslen (ed.), *Weapons Under International Human Rights Law*, Cambridge University Press, Cambridge, 2014, p. xx.

[24] See M. Roscini, 'Cyber Operations as a Use of Force', in N. Tsagourias and R. Buchan (eds.), *Research Handbook on International Law and Cyberspace*, Edward Elgar, London, 2015, pp. 233–54; and R. Buchan, 'Cyber Attacks: Unlawful Uses of Force or Prohibited Interventions?', *Journal of Conflict & Security Law*, vol. 17, no. 2 (2012), pp. 211–27.

6.11 The minimum threshold of force falling within the scope of Article 2(4) of the UN Charter (and the corresponding rule under customary international law) is low. The Independent International Fact-Finding Mission on the Conflict in Georgia (Georgia Fact-Finding Mission), for instance, affirmed that the prohibition on use of force 'covers all physical force which surpasses a minimum threshold of intensity'.[25] Arguably, certain law enforcement measures conducted by one State on the territory of another without that territorial State's express consent would not violate the prohibition on inter-State use of force.[26]

Use of Force against a State's Territorial Integrity

6.12 Article 2(4) explicitly prohibits use of force by a UN member State against the territorial integrity of any other State. Thus bombardment of the territory of another State or the use of weapons on or against that territory ordinarily falls within the international legal prohibition on the use of force.[27] Such action may involve the firing of bullets, rockets, shells, or missiles or the dropping of a bomb, and occurs irrespective of whether the force is delivered directly, remotely, or autonomously.

6.13 Military occupation by one State of part of the territory of another also contravenes the prohibition on use of force. This notion encompasses the 'invasion or attack by the armed forces of a State of the territory of another State, or any military occupation, however temporary, resulting from such invasion or attack, or any annexation by the use of force of the territory of another State or part thereof'.[28] There is no need for the territorial State to react militarily to an occupation for that military operation to amount to unlawful inter-State use of force. When foreign military units 'premeditatedly make an unauthorized crossing of the frontier of a State, this may be deemed as an incipient use of force – prompting the application of the prohibition in Article 2(4) – even if no hostilities have erupted as yet'.[29]

6.14 Whether the placement of military forces in areas where sovereignty is contested amounts to unlawful military occupation depends on a number of factors. If a dispute exists as to the precise delineation of a border, parties to the dispute may not be ipso facto violating the prohibition on the use of force by retaining its armed forces already stationed there. If, on the other hand, forces are moved into an area by a State that has no legitimate claim to that area, or if there are competing claims to it, this will violate the prohibition on the inter-State use of force.

---

[25] *Independent International Fact-Finding Mission on the Conflict in Georgia*, Report, Vol. II, September 2009, p. 242. See also Corten, *The Law against War*, p. 55.

[26] Corten, *The Law against War*, pp. 52–5.

[27] Art. 3(b), Definition of Aggression, annexed to UN General Assembly Resolution 3314 (XXIX); adopted without a vote on 14 December 1974 (hereinafter, 1974 Definition of Aggression). See also Art. 8*bis*(2)(b), Rome Statute of the International Criminal Court; adopted at Rome 17 July 1998; entered into force 1 July 2002 (hereinafter, Rome Statute).

[28] Art. 3(a), 1974 Definition of Aggression. See also Article 8*bis*(2)(a), ICC Statute.

[29] Dinstein, *War, Aggression and Self-Defence*, 6th ed., para. 248.

6.15 Thus the duty under international law to resolve disputes without recourse to the use of force applies with respect to border disputes between States. In the Eritrea-Ethiopia Claims Commission Award on jus ad bellum issues, the Commission condemned Eritrea for using force to secure an area (in and around Badme), even though Eritrea 'had a valid claim' to the town. The Commission noted that 'border disputes between States are so frequent that any exception to the prohibition of the threat or use of force for territory that is allegedly occupied unlawfully would create a large and dangerous hole in a fundamental rule of international law'.[30]

6.16 The Commission held Eritrea to have violated the prohibition on inter-State use of force because its armed forces were not in control of Badme when hostilities erupted with Ethiopia. Eritrea had maintained consistently, since securing its independence from Ethiopia in 1993, that Badme was Eritrean territory. It cited colonial treaties between Italy and Ethiopia in justification of its position on this point. It also acknowledged, however, 'that the Badme area had been continuously under Ethiopian authority for a considerable period of time, both before and after independence in 1993'.[31] This meant that an attempt to take the town by force would be unlawful.

Use of Force against a State's Political Independence

6.17 An attack that takes place outside the territory of a State may also violate the prohibition on use of force in international law where it targets another State's political independence. An obvious example, which is included in the 1974 UN Definition of Aggression, is an attack by the armed forces of one State against the land, sea, or air forces of another, but which takes place outside the territory of the victim State.[32] As the Georgia Fact-Finding Mission observed, the wording of the 1974 Definition 'cannot be interpreted narrowly so as to exclude military bases *outside* the territory of the victim State, because a systematic interpretation of this provision shows that land forces outside their own State are the very object of this provision'.[33]

---

[30] Eritrea-Ethiopia Claims Commission, *Partial Award: Jus Ad Bellum – Ethiopia's Claims 1–8*, 19 December 2005, para. 10. See also T. Ruys and F. R. Silvestre, 'The Nagorno-Karabakh Conflict and the Exercise of "Self-Defense" to Recover Occupied Land', blog post, *Just Security*, 10 November 2020, at http://bit.ly/2Vdg2JS. For a contrary view, see, e.g., D. Akande and A. Tzanakopoulos, 'Use of Force in Self-Defence to Recover Occupied Territory: When Is It Permissible?', *EJIL: Talk!*, 18 November 2020, at http://bit.ly/39paQLs. Even these two leading publicists, however, acknowledge that 'there must be some proximity between attack and defence, and that the lapse of time between the two cannot be extended indefinitely'. Moreover, for their argument that '[i]n cases of occupation that result from a use of force, the armed attack has not only occurred but has not ceased' to hold, a clear determination would be needed that the occupying State had indeed committed an act of aggression. Did Armenia commit aggression in 1988? Is Israel's continued occupation of territory of several of its neighbours tantamount to an armed attack?

[31] M. Plaut, 'The Conflict and Its Aftermath', in D. Jacquin-Berdal and M. Plaut (eds.), *Unfinished Business: Ethiopia and Eritrea at War*, Red Sea Press, New Jersey, 2004, p. 93; see S. D. Murphy, 'The Eritrean-Ethiopian War (1998–2000)', George Washington University Law School, Washington, DC, 2016, at http://bit.ly/2KPyqUu, p. 2.

[32] Art. 3(d), 1974 Definition of Aggression.

[33] *Independent International Fact-Finding Mission on the Conflict in Georgia*, Report, Vol. II, p. 264 (original emphasis).

6.18 Another clearly unlawful use of force against a State's political independence would be the assassination of the head of another State or a senior government official anywhere outside that State's metropolitan or non-metropolitan territory. On 3 January 2020, missiles launched from a US Reaper drone struck two vehicles leaving Baghdad's international airport. At least seven people died in the attack, including the commander of Iran's Quds Force, General Qassem Soleimani (who was the specific target of the US attack). The US Department of Defense issued a statement in the aftermath, arguing that the US strike on General Soleimani constituted 'defensive action to protect U.S. personnel abroad', primarily on the basis that General Soleimani 'was actively developing plans to attack American diplomats and service members in Iraq and throughout the region'.[34]

6.19 The use of force in self-defence against a threat that is perceived to be imminent or otherwise temporally proximate is unlawful. Article 51 of the UN Charter makes it clear that an armed attack must have already occurred, and the predominance of *opinio juris* among States rejects anticipatory self-defence as customary law.[35]

Use of Force in Any Other Manner Inconsistent with UN Purposes

6.20 The use of force by any State in its international relations, which is in any manner inconsistent with the Purposes of the United Nations, is also unlawful. This is a catch-all provision that broadens, not narrows, the scope of the general prohibition on the use or threat of force. Its most obvious consequence is to confirm the prohibition on use of force such as to deprive a people of its right to self-determination. This is especially the case where a colonial State uses force to seek to prevent a people under its domination or suzerainty from formally attaining independence.

6.21 Article 1 of the UN Charter sets out the purposes of the United Nations, which include developing 'friendly relations among nations based on respect for the principle of equal rights and self-determination of peoples'[36] and achieving international cooperation in 'promoting and encouraging respect for human rights and for fundamental freedoms for all without distinction as to race, sex, language, or religion'.[37] A mistake is sometimes made to seek to justify unilateral humanitarian intervention on the basis that it is promoting respect for human rights. This is clearly not the state of the law, either under the Charter or under broader international law. Indeed, unilateral use of force is the very antithesis of an effort to achieve 'international cooperation'.

---

[34] US Department of Defense, 'Statement by the Department of Defense', Release, 2 January 2020, at http://bit.ly/38HoPFg.

[35] I. Brownlie, *International Law and the Use of Force by States*, Oxford University Press, Oxford, 1963, p. 278. In 2014, the Non-aligned Movement (whose membership today numbers 120 States) explicitly 'oppose[d] and condemn[ed] ... the adoption of the doctrine of pre-emptive attack'. XVII Ministerial Conference of the Non-aligned Movement, Algiers, 26–29 May 2014, Final Document, para. 26.5.

[36] Art. 1(2), UN Charter.

[37] Art. 1(3), UN Charter.

USE OF FORCE TO DEPRIVE A PEOPLE OF ITS RIGHT TO SELF-DETERMINATION

6.22 In the 1970 Declaration on the Principles of International Law's first principle, which is dedicated to the rules laid down in Article 2(4) of the UN Charter, it is stipulated that 'every State has the duty to refrain from any forcible action which deprives peoples ... of their right to self-determination and freedom and independence'.[38] This includes the use of force against peoples under colonial, racist, or alien domination, most notably those identified by the United Nations as non-self-governing territories.[39]

6.23 With respect specifically to Western Sahara, in 1975, after decolonisation by Spain, the International Court of Justice held in an Advisory Opinion that Western Sahara was not *terra nullius*, signalling that it was not territory belonging to no State that was open to acquisition through the legal process of 'occupation'.[40] The Court referred to the 1960 Declaration on the Granting of Independence to Colonial Countries and Peoples adopted by UN General Assembly, wherein it is stipulated: 'All armed action or repressive measures of all kinds directed against dependent peoples shall cease in order to enable them to exercise peacefully and freely their right to complete independence, and the integrity of their national territory shall be respected.'[41] At the end of its analysis, the Court did not find, with respect to either Morocco or Mauritania, 'legal ties of such a nature as might affect the application of resolution 1514 (XV) in the decolonization of Western Sahara and, in particular, of the principle of self-determination through the free and genuine expression of the will of the peoples of the Territory'.[42] The Court concluded therefore that the people of Western Sahara could exercise their right to self-determination.

6.24 On 31 October 1975, however, Morocco invaded Western Sahara from the north-east and sought to annex the territory. In late February 1976, the Saharan Arab Democratic Republic[43] was declared by the Polisario Front, the military force of the Saharawi people. A sixteen-year-long insurgency ended with a UN-brokered truce in 1991, but a promised referendum on independence is still only slated to take place.[44] The Sahrawi Arab Democratic Republic is a member of the African Union but is not recognised as a State by the United Nations. Nonetheless, in 1979, the UN General Assembly adopted Resolution 34/47 by majority vote in which it deeply deplored 'the aggravation of the

---

[38] Principle 1, para. 6, 1970 Declaration on Principles of International Law.
[39] See, e.g., UN General Assembly Special Committee on Decolonization, 'Ensuring Non-self-governing Territories Can Address Challenges Key to Moving Decolonization Efforts Forward, Secretary-General Tells Regional Seminar', UN doc. GA/COL/3320, 10 May 2018, at http://bit.ly/2DsZqFm.
[40] International Court of Justice, *Western Sahara*, Advisory Opinion, 16 October 1975, para. 79.
[41] Para. 4, Declaration on the Granting of Independence to Colonial Countries and Peoples; adopted under UN General Assembly Resolution 1514 (XV) by ninety votes to zero with nine abstentions (Australia, Belgium, the Dominican Republic, France, Portugal, South Africa, Spain, the United Kingdom, and the United States), 14 December 1960.
[42] ICJ, *Western Sahara*, Advisory Opinion, 16 October 1975, para. 162.
[43] Also termed formally the Sahrawi Arab Democratic Republic or Saharawi Arab Democratic Republic. See, e.g., African Union, 'Saharawi Arab Democratic Republic', at http://bit.ly/2VbKQL9. The Republic – spelt both ways – is a member State of the African Union.
[44] UN Office for the Coordination of Humanitarian Affairs, 'Western Sahara', undated but accessed 1 August 2019 at http://bit.ly/2MnmzPW; and BBC, 'Western Sahara Profile', 14 May 2018, at http://bbc.in/2NcxpYA.

130   *Major Themes*

situation resulting from the continued occupation of Western Sahara by Morocco' and urged Morocco to 'terminate the occupation of the Territory of Western Sahara'.[45]

6.25 Morocco has continued to assert that Western Sahara is sovereign territory. In June 2011, however, Morocco adhered to the 1977 Additional Protocol I to the four Geneva Conventions, which concerns international armed conflicts under jus in bello. Article 1(4) of the Protocol provides that international armed conflicts include those

> in which peoples are fighting against colonial domination and alien occupation and against racist régimes in the exercise of their right of self-determination, as enshrined in the Charter of the United Nations and the Declaration on Principles of International Law concerning Friendly Relations and Co-operation among States in accordance with the Charter of the United Nations.[46]

6.26 On 21 June 2015, the Polisario Front made a declaration on behalf of the people of Western Sahara that it undertook to apply the 1949 Geneva Conventions and 1977 Additional Protocol I to the conflict between it and the Kingdom of Morocco. This was made in accordance with Article 96(3) of the Protocol, which provides: 'The authority representing a people engaged against a High Contracting Party in an armed conflict of the type referred to in Article 1, paragraph 4, may undertake to apply the Conventions and this Protocol in relation to that conflict by means of a unilateral declaration addressed to the depositary.' This was the first time the Swiss Federal Council, as depositary of the Protocol, had accepted such a declaration by a national liberation movement and a non-State entity under international law.[47] It clearly indicates that Western Sahara is a State in waiting in international law, beyond the realm of the African Union.

THE DEFINITION OF AGGRESSION

6.27 Paragraph 70 of the Human Rights Committee's General Comment 36 stipulated that a violation of the right to life resulted from 'acts of aggression as defined in international law'. But not every unlawful use of force constitutes an act of aggression. Thus aggression was defined by the UN General Assembly in 1974 as 'the most serious and dangerous form of the illegal use of force'.[48] Similarly, as the ILC Special Rapporteur has stated, certain peremptory norms, 'most notably the prohibitions of aggression and genocide, by their very nature require an intentional violation on a large scale'.[49]

---

[45] UN General Assembly Resolution 34/47, adopted on 21 November 1979 by eighty-five votes to six with forty-one abstentions, paras. 5 and 6.
[46] Art. 1(4), Protocol Additional to the Geneva Conventions of 12 August 1949, and Relating to the Protection of Victims of International Armed Conflicts (Protocol I), of 8 June 1977 (hereinafter, 1977 Additional Protocol I).
[47] K. Fortin, 'Unilateral Declaration by Polisario under API Accepted by Swiss Federal Council', 2 September 2015, at http://bit.ly/2NcAolb.
[48] 1974 Definition of Aggression, fifth preambular para.
[49] Commentary, para. 8, on draft Article 40, 2001 Draft Articles on State Responsibility.

6.28 Article 3 of the 1974 Definition of Aggression sets out, in a non-exhaustive list, acts that may qualify as an act of aggression:

(a) The invasion or attack by the armed forces of a State of the territory of another State, or any military occupation, however temporary, resulting from such invasion or attack, or any annexation by the use of force of the territory of another State or part thereof;
(b) Bombardment by the armed forces of a State against the territory of another State or the use of any weapons by a State against the territory of another State;
(c) The blockade of the ports or coasts of a State by the armed forces of another State;
(d) An attack by the armed forces of a State on the land, sea or air forces, or marine and air fleets of another State;
(e) The use of armed forces of one State which are within the territory of another State with the agreement of the receiving State, in contravention of the conditions provided for in the agreement or any extension of their presence in such territory beyond the termination of the agreement;
(f) The action of a State in allowing its territory, which it has placed at the disposal of another State, to be used by that other State for perpetrating an act of aggression against a third State;
(g) The sending by or on behalf of a State of armed bands, groups, irregulars or mercenaries, which carry out acts of armed force against another State of such gravity as to amount to the acts listed above, or its substantial involvement therein.

6.29 The term 'aggression' is found in the UN Charter, but not directly in the prohibition on the use of force in Article 2(4). The Purposes of the United Nations, referred to in Article 2(4), are stated to be the taking of effective collective measures for the maintenance of international peace and security, including 'for the suppression of acts of aggression'.[50] Chapter VII of the Charter concerns 'action with respect to threats to the peace, breaches of the peace, and acts of aggression'. As set out in Article 51, an 'armed attack' must occur before a State may exercise its right of self-defence. The terms 'armed attack' and 'aggression' certainly overlap, but they are not synonyms.[51] The excessive use of force in self-defence, where the right of self-defence lawfully exists, does not constitute aggression.

6.30 Within Chapter VII of the UN Charter, Article 39 stipulates the UN Security Council 'shall determine the existence of any threat to the peace, breach of the peace, or act of aggression'. The Council has only rarely declared that a use of force amounted to aggression: in relation to South Africa's attack on Angola in 1976, Southern Rhodesia's attack on Mozambique in 1973, and two Israeli attacks against the Palestine Liberation Organisation in Tunisia, in 1985 and 1988. In Resolution 611 (1988), the Security Council 'condemn[ed] vigorously the aggression, perpetrated on 16 April 1988 against the sovereignty and territorial integrity of Tunisia in flagrant violation of the Charter of the United

---

[50] Art. 1(1), UN Charter.
[51] Dinstein, *War, Aggression and Self-Defence*, 6th ed., para. 549.

Nations, international law and norms of conduct'.[52] This was the last time the Council had decried an act of aggression.[53]

6.31 However, the notion of a 'breach of the peace' under the UN Charter also comprises acts of aggression: aggression 'always constitutes a breach of the peace'.[54] For instance, the Argentinian invasion of the Falkland Islands/Malvinas in 1982 and the Iraqi invasion of Kuwait in 1990 were both condemned in the Security Council as a breach of the peace; both were assuredly acts of aggression. In its Resolution 502, the Council was 'deeply disturbed' at reports of 'an invasion on 2 April 1982 by armed forces of Argentina' and determined 'that there exists a breach of the peace in the region of the Falkland Islands (Islas Malvinas)'.[55] The Council demanded an immediate cessation of hostilities and the 'immediate withdrawal of all Argentine forces from the Falkland Islands (Islas Malvinas)'.[56]

6.32 In its Resolution 660, the Council expressed its alarm at the invasion of Kuwait on 2 August 1990 by the military forces of Iraq and determined 'that there exists a breach of international peace and security as regards the Iraqi invasion of Kuwait'.[57] The Council further condemned the Iraqi invasion of Kuwait and demanded that Iraq 'withdraw immediately and unconditionally all its forces to the positions in which they were located on 1 August 1990'.[58]

IS AGGRESSION LEADING TO LOSS OF LIFE AN ARBITRARY DEPRIVATION OF LIFE?

6.33 In determining whether an act of aggression violates the right to life, the notion of arbitrariness must be interpreted. In its General Comment 36, the Human Rights Committee explains that deprivation of life is 'as a rule' arbitrary 'if it is inconsistent with international law or domestic law'.[59] The reference to other bodies of international law is critical; to hold otherwise would be to denude international law of all its protection. As the General Comment further states: 'A deprivation of life may, nevertheless, be

---

[52] UN Security Council Resolution 611, adopted on 25 April 1988 by fourteen votes to zero with one abstention (the United States), operative para. 1.
[53] R. Kolb, *International Law on the Maintenance of Peace: Jus Contra Bellum*, Edward Elgar, Cheltenham, 2019, p. 116.
[54] N. Krisch, 'Article 39', in B. Simma, D.-E. Khan, G. Nolte, and A. Paulus (eds.), *The Charter of the United Nations: A Commentary*, Vol. II, Oxford University Press, Oxford, 2002, p. 1293, para. 42.
[55] UN Security Council Resolution 502, adopted on 3 April 1982 by ten votes to one (Panama), with four abstentions (China, Poland, Spain, and the Union of Soviet Socialist Republics), second and third preambular paras.
[56] Ibid., operative paras. 1 and 2.
[57] Resolution 660, adopted on 2 August 1990 by fourteen votes to zero (Yemen did not participate in the vote), first and second preambular paras.
[58] Ibid., operative paras. 1 and 2.
[59] Human Rights Committee, General Comment 36 on the right to life, para. 12. The Committee refers in turn to the African Commission on Human and Peoples' Rights' General Comment No. 3 on the African Charter on Human and Peoples' Rights: The Right to Life (Article 4), 2015, para. 12.

Jus ad Bellum, Aggression, and the Right to Life

authorized by domestic law and still be arbitrary.'[60] The issue to determine, therefore, is which bodies of international law inform the interpretation of the notion of an 'arbitrary' deprivation of life.

6.34 What does not appear to be at issue is that the rules of law enforcement clarify when a police officer will engage the responsibility of the State under international human rights law for an arbitrary deprivation of life. As Article 3 of the 1979 UN Code of Conduct for Law Enforcement Officials provides, 'Law enforcement officials may use force only when strictly necessary and to the extent required for the performance of their duty.'[61] The official commentary on the provision further stipulates:

> National law ordinarily restricts the use of force by law enforcement officials in accordance with a principle of proportionality. It is to be understood that such national principles of proportionality are to be respected in the interpretation of this provision. In no case should this provision be interpreted to authorize the use of force which is disproportionate to the legitimate objective to be achieved.[62]

Thus, if the action that leads to death involves unnecessary or disproportionate force on the part of the law enforcement official, the right to life will be violated. In the words of the Inter-American Court of Human Rights: 'When excessive force is used [during a law enforcement operation], any deprivation of life is arbitrary.'[63]

6.35 There is specific regulation of the use of firearms by another soft-law law enforcement instrument: the 1990 Basic Principles on the Use of Force and Firearms by Law Enforcement Officials.[64] Basic Principle 9 states (in part):

> Law enforcement officials shall not use firearms against persons except in self-defence or defence of others against the imminent threat of death or serious injury, to prevent the perpetration of a particularly serious crime involving grave threat to life, to arrest a person presenting such a danger and resisting their authority, or to prevent his or her escape, and only when less extreme means are insufficient to achieve these objectives.

This represents customary international law (see Chapter 7 for further discussion on law enforcement and the right to life). Accordingly, if a law enforcement official uses his or her firearm in circumstances other than those delineated in Basic Principle 9 (for instance, purely to protect property or to shoot an escaping unarmed thief who has not used any

---

[60] Human Rights Committee, General Comment 36 on the right to life, para. 12.
[61] Art. 3, Code of Conduct for Law Enforcement Officials; adopted under UN General Assembly Resolution 34/169; resolution adopted without a vote on 17 December 1979.
[62] Commentary para. (b) on Art. 3, UN Code of Conduct for Law Enforcement Officials.
[63] Inter-American Court of Human Rights, *Montero-Aranguren and others (Detention Centre of Catia) v. Venezuela*, Judgment (Preliminary Objection, Merits, Reparations, and Costs), 5 July 2006, para. 68.
[64] Principle 1, Basic Principles on the Use of Force and Firearms by Law Enforcement Officials; adopted at Havana by the Eighth UN Congress on the Prevention of Crime and the Treatment of Offenders 7 September 1990 (hereinafter, 1990 Basic Principles). In December 1990, the UN General Assembly welcomed the Basic Principles and invited governments to respect them. UN General Assembly Resolution 45/166, adopted without a vote on 18 December 1990, para. 4.

violence) and the target is killed in either case, the deprivation of life will have been arbitrary.

6.36 The right to life, which is non-derogable under the ICCPR, continues to apply during situations of armed conflict, as described in the previous chapter. During an armed conflict, the legality of the use of force in the conduct of hostilities is determined by reference to international humanitarian law (otherwise known as the law of armed conflict). The International Court of Justice has specifically held that 'in principle' Article 6 of the ICCPR 'applies also in hostilities'.[65] In so doing, it rejected the opposition of certain States whereby 'the International Covenant on Civil and Political Rights made no mention of war or weapons, and it had never been envisaged that the legality of nuclear weapons was regulated by that instrument'.[66] Instead, the Court used the rules of international humanitarian law to interpret the notion of 'arbitrary' in Article 6: 'whether a particular loss of life, through the use of a certain weapon in warfare, is to be considered an arbitrary deprivation of life contrary to Article 6 of the Covenant, can only be decided by reference to the law applicable in armed conflict and not deduced from the terms of the Covenant itself'.[67] Thus compliance with, among others, the fundamental jus cogens principles of distinction and proportionality in attack in international humanitarian law, as well as the prohibition of means and methods of warfare of a nature to cause superfluous injury or unnecessary suffering, will inform the interpretation and application of the right to life during combat.

6.37 The same approach applies to international environmental law. The Human Rights Committee has affirmed: 'Implementation of the obligation to respect and ensure the right to life, and in particular life with dignity, depends, inter alia, on measures taken by States parties to preserve the environment and protect it against harm, pollution and climate change caused by public and private actors.'[68] The cornerstone of international environmental law was set out in Principle 21 of the 1972 Stockholm Declaration:[69]

> States have, in accordance with the Charter of the United Nations and the principles of international law, the sovereign right to exploit their own resources pursuant to their own environmental policies, *and the responsibility to ensure that activities within their jurisdiction or control do not cause damage to the environment of other States or of areas beyond the limits of national jurisdiction.*[70]

In its 1996 Advisory Opinion on nuclear weapons, the International Court of Justice declared that the general obligation upon States 'to ensure that activities within their

---

[65] International Court of Justice, *Legality of the Threat of Use of Nuclear Weapons*, Advisory Opinion, 8 July 1996, para. 25.
[66] Ibid., para. 24.
[67] Ibid., para. 25.
[68] Human Rights Committee, General Comment 36 on the right to life, para. 62.
[69] P. Sands and J. Peel, *Principles of International Environmental Law*, 3rd ed., Cambridge University Press, Cambridge, 2012, p. 191.
[70] Principle 21, Declaration of the United Nations Conference on the Human Environment; adopted by the UN Conference on the Human Environment, Stockholm, 5–16 June 1972 (added emphasis).

jurisdiction and control respect the environment of other States or of areas beyond national control is now part of the corpus of international law relating to the environment'.[71] A serious violation of that duty leading to the death of individuals in the other affected State (or States) would also constitute a violation of their right to life.

6.38 In its 2004 judgment in *Öneryildiz v. Turkey*, which concerned the deaths of nine people in a house built on land surrounding a rubbish tip following a methane explosion, the Grand Chamber of the European Court of Human Rights found a violation of the right to life in its substantive limb.[72] The applicant complained that no measures had been taken to prevent an explosion despite an expert report having drawn the authorities' attention to the need to act preventively, as such an explosion was not unlikely. The Court reiterated that its approach to the interpretation of Article 2 on the right to life 'is guided by the idea that the object and purpose of the Convention as an instrument for the protection of individual human beings requires its provisions to be interpreted and applied in such a way as to make its safeguards practical and effective'.[73]

6.39 The Court further reiterated that Article 2 does not solely concern deaths resulting from the use of force by agents of the State but also lays down a positive obligation on States to take appropriate steps to safeguard the lives of those within their jurisdiction.[74] The Court considered 'that this obligation must be construed as applying in the context of any activity, whether public or not, in which the right to life may be at stake, and a fortiori in the case of industrial activities, which by their very nature are dangerous'.[75]

6.40 While Article 2 of the 1950 European Convention on Human Rights does not contain the term 'arbitrary' with respect to its protection of the right to life, the same principle would apply to the interpretation of Article 6 of the ICCPR. Thus, in a case in which the Human Rights Committee gave its views in September 2019, the authors of the complaint alleged a violation by omission of Article 6 with respect, among others, to a man who died while exhibiting symptoms of pesticide poisoning.[76] The Committee observed that 'a narrow interpretation does not adequately convey the full concept of the right to life' and that States Parties 'must take positive action to protect that right'.[77] It was of the view that

> heavily spraying the area in question with toxic agrochemicals ... poses a reasonably foreseeable threat to the authors' lives given that such large-scale fumigation has contaminated the rivers in which the authors fish, the well water they drink and the fruit trees, crops and farm animals that are their source of food. The authors were hospitalized due to poisoning, and the State party has not adduced evidence of any kind to demonstrate that

---

[71] International Court of Justice, *Legality of the Threat of Use of Nuclear Weapons*, Advisory Opinion, 8 July 1996, para. 29.
[72] European Court of Human Rights, *Öneryildiz v. Turkey*, Judgment (Grand Chamber), 30 November 2004, para. 110.
[73] Ibid., para. 69.
[74] Ibid., para. 71.
[75] Ibid.
[76] Human Rights Committee, *Norma Portillo Cáceres and others v. Paraguay*, Views (UN doc. CCPR/C/126/D/2751/2016), 25 July 2019, para. 7.2.
[77] Ibid., para. 7.3.

the results of the blood and urine tests were within the normal range, nor has an alternative explanation been given for the events in question. Furthermore, Mr. Portillo Cáceres died with no explanation from the State party, as an autopsy was never conducted.[78]

The Committee noted that the State Party in question, Paraguay, was bound by the 2001 Stockholm Convention on Persistent Organic Pollutants. The Stockholm Convention, which entered into force on 17 May 2004, is an international environmental law treaty that seeks to eliminate or restrict the production and use of persistent organic pollutants.

6.41 The question therefore is whether the same approach – to interpret the notion of 'arbitrary' based on rules emanating from other branches of international law than human rights – also applies to the rules of jus ad bellum. A priori, there appears to be no valid substantive objection to such an approach, given that there is no suggestion that the application of the right to life in any way affects the content of the rules governing inter-State use of force. It is merely, in the same manner that the International Court of Justice applied the right to life to the use of nuclear weapons *in bello*, interpreting what amounts to arbitrary deprivation of life in the case of a violation of the prohibition on inter-State use of force.

6.42 Moreover, it is not any contravention of jus ad bellum that will suffice to constitute a violation of the right to life: the breach must be serious. Only acts of aggression, in the view of the Human Rights Committee, are enough. No human rights responsibility *ad bellum* will attach to a State that is exercising its inherent right of self-defence, or which is using force pursuant to an authorisation from the UN Security Council acting under Chapter VII of the UN Charter. Moreover, the objections made by States to the ostensible interrelationship between the two branches of international law – those of the United States aside[79] – are largely procedural in nature or relate to the 'mandate' of the Human Rights Committee.

6.43 As noted previously, the legal approach to the protection of the right to life under the 1950 European Convention on Human Rights differs substantially from that taken in other regional and global human rights instruments. Nonetheless, it may be taken to endorse a broad understanding of the fundamental interrelationship between jus ad bellum and international human rights law. Article 2(2) of the European Convention does not prohibit 'arbitrary' deprivation of life, but limits use of force by the State to that which is 'absolutely necessary' (a) in defence of any person from unlawful violence; (b) in order to effect a lawful arrest or to prevent the escape of a person lawfully detained; or (c) in action lawfully taken for the purpose of quelling a riot or insurrection.

6.44 Article 15(2) of the European Convention addresses the use of force in a situation of international armed conflict,[80] specifying that no derogation may be made from Article 2, 'except in respect of deaths resulting from lawful acts of war'. As William Schabas has

---

[78] Ibid., para. 7.5.
[79] The United States' objections fly in the face of International Court of Justice jurisprudence and are not justified by any evidence.
[80] An insurrection, as referred to in Article 2(2)(c), is a form of non-international armed conflict.

Jus ad Bellum, Aggression, and the Right to Life

observed: 'Historically, the term "act of war" had significance in the context of the jus ad bellum.'[81] He concludes that

> to avail of the 'lawful acts of war' exception to killing in the course of armed conflict, the use of force itself must be consistent with international law. In other words, a declaration of derogation from the right to life by a State with respect to the use of force against another State that is not in the exercise of the inherent right of self-defence or authorized by the Security Council would be ineffective.[82]

6.45 Objections to such an understanding are primarily grounded in fear that the European Court of Human Rights could become politicised as a result, rather than any notion that the Court is juridically incompetent to make such a determination. On 11 September 2019, the Grand Chamber held oral hearings on the admissibility of an inter-State claim by Ukraine against Russia regarding Crimea.[83] Marko Milanovic has asked whether the Court should pronounce on whether Ukraine or Russia is the rightful sovereign of Crimea. Affirming that the legal response is not difficult to determine – 'Russia's annexation of Crimea was as clearly illegal as anything can be'[84] – he nonetheless cautions against international human rights bodies pronouncing on 'issues which, while capable of legal determination, are not part of their central mission of human rights protection and may negatively affect that mission'. He even suggests that any such pronouncement 'would provoke [an] intense backlash, even possibly leading to Russia's withdrawal from the Council of Europe'.[85]

6.46 At the oral hearings, the judges asked the two States Parties to the European Convention in dispute whether they believed that the Court should address the issue of sovereignty over Crimea and any UN Charter violations on the part of Russia, in order to establish whether Russia had jurisdiction over Crimea in the sense of Article 1 of the European Convention. Russia responded that the Court should not pronounce itself on the sovereignty dispute between the parties, arguing that this was a purely political issue over which the Court did not have jurisdiction. In contrast, Ukraine called on the Court to rule that Crimea remained Ukrainian territory. It did so on the basis that this would be in accordance with the general position taken within the international community and that the Court needed to define whether the juridical nature of Russia's jurisdiction was territorial or extraterritorial.

6.47 While such a definition may largely be unnecessary, the precise moment at which Russia gained control over Crimea will demand assessment of the facts. Indirectly, it may also call for a legal assessment of when a military occupation existed in the peninsula. The

---

[81] W. Schabas, *The European Convention on Human Rights: A Commentary*, Oxford University Press, Oxford, 2017, p. 601.
[82] Ibid.
[83] European Court of Human Rights, *Ukraine v. Russia* (App. No. 20958/14) (Grand Chamber hearing), 11 September 2019.
[84] M. Milanovic, 'Does the European Court of Human Rights Have to Decide on Sovereignty over Crimea? Part I: Jurisdiction in Article 1 ECHR', blog entry, *EJIL: Talk!*, 23 September 2019, at http://bit.ly/2NWDkAN.
[85] Ibid.

legality of the occupation is irrelevant for any obligations under international humanitarian law, but were the Court to make such a finding, it might be at the least implicit in any finding of jurisdiction that the occupation was unlawful under jus ad bellum.[86]

THE CONSEQUENCES OF AGGRESSION BEING A VIOLATION OF THE RIGHT TO LIFE

6.48 Given the clear statement of the law by the Human Rights Committee, it may be expected that a complaint will be submitted by an applicant in the coming years alleging that a member of her or his family was killed unlawfully because of bombardments or military occupation that constituted acts of aggression. A resident of Nagorno-Karabkah might choose to do so: both Armenia and Azerbaijan have recognised the right of individual petition under the ICCPR. If the military operation violated international humanitarian law, the Committee may decide to dodge the *ad bellum* question. If, however, the operation was conducted in compliance with IHL, it may be constrained to apply its understanding of the breadth of the right to life protected in Article 6 of the ICCPR.

6.49 In its Views, the Human Rights Committee will, it is to be presumed, follow its normal approach to issues of admissibility. If it finds the complaint admissible, with domestic remedies pursued and exhausted, it will assess the case on the merits. It will look at the views of States, judicial and quasi-judicial authorities, and leading publicists, and come to a conclusion. It will consider the position of the UN Security Council (while acknowledging that its finding that aggression has, or has not occurred, is 'a political, not a judicial finding').[87] If the Committee makes an adjudication of legality *ad bellum* in its views rendered on a particular communication from an individual under the ICCPR,[88] there is no possibility of any compensation being awarded. There is rather a determination of whether one or more violations of the Covenant have occurred. Such a view is not formally binding on the State (though it is nonetheless influential).

6.50 If, in contrast, it is a regional human rights court that is issuing a binding judgment, that court may impose a duty to make reparation. Under the European Convention on Human Rights, for instance, if the Court finds that there has been a violation of the Convention, and if the internal law of the State party concerned allows only partial reparation to be made, the Court shall, if necessary, afford just satisfaction to the injured

---

[86] In a further blog post, Milanovic suggests that there is no need for the Court to make a determination of military occupation. He also discusses the problems engendered by alleged violations of human rights by the mass automatic naturalisation of Ukrainian citizens in Crimea by Russia, and respect for the right of each person to enter their own country, which might demand an assessment of the legality of Russian action *ad bellum*. M. Milanovic, 'Does the European Court of Human Rights Have to Decide on Sovereignty over Crimea? Part II: Issues Lurking on the Merits', blog post, *EJIL: Talk!*, 24 September 2019, at http://bit.ly/33XYcop.
[87] Krisch, 'Article 39', in Simma et al., *The Charter of the United Nations: A Commentary*, p. 1294, para. 44.
[88] Art. 5(4), Optional Protocol to the International Covenant on Civil and Political Rights; adopted at New York 16 December 1966; entered into force 23 March 1976.

Jus ad Bellum, Aggression, and the Right to Life 139

party.[89] There is a corresponding obligation on each State Party to 'undertake to abide by the final judgment of the Court in any case to which they are parties'.[90]

6.51 Here, a massive financial award could potentially be made, whether in an inter-State case or to a huge number of applicants in a joined set of individual applications. While such an award is highly unlikely, it is not beyond the realm of the possible. One of a number of objections to such a holding could concern the practicality of adjudicating and implementing the Court's award. That should not, though, be the basis for outright rejection of the notion. It is not, for example, suggested that a finding of genocide or crime against humanity, and a corresponding award of compensation, would not be imposed on the basis purely that its implementation would be administratively demanding.

6.52 Article 1 of the 2001 Draft Articles on State Responsibility stipulates that 'every internationally wrongful act of a State entails the international responsibility of that State'. This includes a duty to pay compensation. Thus the responsible State 'is under an obligation to make full reparation for the injury caused by the internationally wrongful act'.[91] There is State practice for the allocation of financial responsibility for an act of aggression. The UN Compensation Commission (UNCC) was created to address Iraq's financial liability for its 'unlawful invasion and occupation of Kuwait' in 1990. In its Resolution 687, the UN Security Council reaffirmed that Iraq was 'liable under international law for any direct loss, damage – including environmental damage and the depletion of natural resources – or injury to foreign Governments, nationals and corporations as a result of its unlawful invasion and occupation of Kuwait'.[92] The Commission was established in 1991 as a subsidiary organ of the Security Council.[93]

6.53 The UNCC was 'neither a court nor a tribunal with an elaborate adversarial process'.[94] The total compensation it paid out amounted to some $48 billion, which was awarded to approximately 1.5 million successful claimants.[95] Decision 11 of the Commission's Governing Council had limited the possibility of members of the Allied Coalition Armed Forces receiving compensation for loss or injury arising from their involvement in Coalition military operations against Iraq to those held as prisoners of war and whose loss or injury resulted from mistreatment in violation of the law of armed conflict.[96] However, the UNCC's Panel of Commissioners also accepted claims from members of the Kuwaiti Armed Forces for events that occurred during the day of the

---

[89] Art. 41 (Just satisfaction), European Convention on Human Rights.
[90] Art. 46(1), European Convention on Human Rights.
[91] Article 31(1), 2001 Draft Articles on State Responsibility.
[92] UN Security Council Resolution 687, adopted on 3 April 1991 by twelve votes to one (Cuba) with two abstentions (Ecuador and Yemen), operative para. 15.
[93] UN Security Council Resolution 692 (1991), adopted on 20 May 1991 by fourteen votes to zero, with one abstention (Cuba).
[94] UNCC, 'Claims Processing', accessed at http://bit.ly/2U865PM on 3 September 2013 (page no longer online).
[95] UNCC Home Page, at https://uncc.ch/.
[96] The text of the decision is available at http://bit.ly/2UcYZtw.

invasion (2 August 1990) or the days immediately following the invasion. The Panel further accepted claims on behalf of Kuwaiti members of the resistance or other military personnel who remained within Kuwaiti territory and who suffered death or personal injury due to the Iraqi invasion and occupation of Kuwait.[97] These claims encompassed violations of jus ad bellum as well as of jus in bello.

[97] UNCC, 'Recommendations Made by the Panel of Commissioners Concerning Individual Claims for Serious Personal Injury or Death (Category "B" Claims)', UN doc. S/AC.26/1994/1, 26 May 1994, pp. 14–15.

7

The Use of Force in Law Enforcement

INTRODUCTION

7.01 This chapter[1] addresses the use of force for law enforcement as it pertains to the right to life. It discusses definitions of the notions of 'law enforcement' and the 'use of force' and identifies the body of international law that regulates directly such use of force. A violation of the law of law enforcement resulting in death (and potentially also, in exceptional circumstances, serious injury) would usually constitute arbitrary deprivation of life. In the words of the Inter-American Court of Human Rights, 'When excessive force is used [during a law enforcement operation], any deprivation of life is arbitrary.'[2]

7.02 The two key principles underpinning the actual use of force – necessity and proportionality – are described along with the principles of legality and precaution that human rights law adds to the regulation and planning of the use of force in law enforcement. The specific rules governing the use of firearms are then delineated: those that govern their use to incapacitate a suspect (or prisoner in flight) and the rule applicable to discharging a firearm with intent to kill. The design, testing, and use of 'less-lethal' weapons, such as batons, conducted electrical/electric-shock weapons (e.g., Taser), kinetic energy projectiles, and chemical irritants dispersed at a distance (e.g., tear gas) are then considered. Finally, the chapter outlines the human rights law obligation upon law enforcement agencies and officials to prevent harm being inflicted by third parties, based on the duty to protect life.

Definitions

7.03 The term *law enforcement* is often employed but is not formally defined under international law. It is ordinarily understood, however, as the discipline that applies to the prevention and investigation of crimes and the consequent arrest and detention of suspects

---

[1] The author would like to thank Dr Abi Dymond for her detailed contribution to this chapter on less-lethal weapons. Her time was supported by the Economic and Social Research Council [grant ES/N016564/1].
[2] Inter-American Court of Human Rights, *Montero-Aranguren and others (Detention Centre of Catia) v. Venezuela*, Judgment (Preliminary Objection, Merits, Reparations, and Costs), 5 July 2006, para. 68.

by designated State agents.[3] In turn, and in accordance with the official commentary to Article 1 of the 1979 Code of Conduct for Law Enforcement Officials,[4] 'the term "law enforcement officials" includes all officers of the law, whether appointed or elected, who exercise police powers, especially the powers of arrest or detention'.[5] Law enforcement officials include the military, 'whether uniformed or not', as well as other State security forces, whenever and wherever they exercise such powers.[6]

7.04 The term 'use of force' is also not formally defined under international law. In ordinary parlance, force is understood in terms of physics as kinetic energy upon a moving or stationary body and more generally as 'coercion or compulsion, especially with the threat or use of violence'.[7] The use of force in law enforcement combines aspects of both meanings. In that context, a 2017 publication of the United Nations Office on Drugs and Crime (UNODC) and the Office of the United Nations High Commissioner for Human Rights (OHCHR) defined the use of force as 'the use of physical means that may harm a person or cause damage to property'.[8] Physical means, they recall, 'include the use of hands and body by law enforcement officials; the use of any instruments, weapons or equipment, such as batons; chemical irritants such as pepper spray; restraints such as handcuffs; dogs; and firearms'.[9] This should not, though, be interpreted to exclude the action of, for instance, aiming a firearm or electric-shock weapon.[10] Such acts should be considered a use of force under international law, as they are in a number of domestic frameworks.[11]

---

[3] See, e.g., International Committee of the Red Cross, *To Serve and to Protect: Human Rights and Humanitarian Law for Police and Security Forces*, Geneva, March 2014, §3.3. Law enforcement agencies are also bound by the duty under international human rights law to facilitate the enjoyment of the right of peaceful assembly.

[4] Code of Conduct for Law Enforcement Officials; adopted at New York by UN General Assembly Resolution 34/169 (resolution adopted without a vote on 17 December 1979) (hereinafter, 1979 Code of Conduct).

[5] Art. 1, 1979 Code of Conduct.

[6] Ibid.; see, similarly, note 1, Basic Principles on the Use of Force and Firearms by Law Enforcement Officials; adopted at Havana by the Eighth UN Congress on the Prevention of Crime and the Treatment of Offenders, 7 September 1990 (hereinafter, 1990 Basic Principles). In December 1990, the UN General Assembly welcomed the Basic Principles and invited governments to respect them. UN General Assembly Resolution 45/166, adopted without a vote on 18 December 1990, para. 4.

[7] *Oxford English Dictionary*, 'force', definitions 1 and 2. Kinetic energy (KE) is measured in joules and is calculated according to the following equation where $KE = mv^2$, wherein m is mass (in kilograms) and v is the velocity (in metres per second).

[8] UNODC and OHCHR, *Resource Book on the Use of Force and Firearms in Law Enforcement*, Criminal Justice Handbook Series, United Nations, New York, 2017, at http://bit.ly/2wAjBLH, p. 1.

[9] Ibid. According to the Geneva Centre for the Democratic Control of Armed Forces (DCAF), use of force 'is generally understood as any physical constraint, ranging from physical restraint by hand or with a restraining device, to the use of firearms or weapons'. Legislative Guidance Tool for States to Regulate Private Military and Security Companies, DCAF, Geneva, 2016, p. iv, at http://bit.ly/2OAuDdU.

[10] As UNODC and OHCHR recall (*Resource Book on the Use of Force and Firearms in Law Enforcement*, p. 1), the 'actual use of force has the potential to inflict harm, cause (serious) injury, and may be lethal in some instances'. This implies a distinction between threatened and 'actual' discharge of a weapon, both of which may occur in the case of conducted electrical weapons.

[11] See, *infra*, Paragraphs 7.35–7.37.

7.05 In the OHCHR's 2020 United Nations Human Rights Guidance on Less-Lethal Weapons in Law Enforcement, a more detailed definition of the use of force was offered, as follows:

> The use of physical means to coerce or influence behaviour or to damage property. Such means may be kinetic, chemical, electrical or of another kind. The use of force may injure and even, in certain instances, kill. A weapon may be used to apply force without being discharged, for example by pointing it at a person while threatening to discharge it unless the person engages in or refrains from certain behaviour.[12]

Accordingly, the use of force for law enforcement is considered to comprehend acts by law enforcement officials in the performance of their duties that use the threat or use of violence, in particular when seeking to coerce or compel lawful behaviour or prevent crime.[13] This may occur not only by the application of kinetic energy but also through the use of weapons such as those that conduct electricity or diffuse noxious chemicals. Actions by law enforcement officials that seek to compel behaviour in a target, in particular by aiming a weapon prior to discharge, also constitute a use of force.

GENERAL PRINCIPLES OF LAW

7.06 Four general principles of law govern the use of force in law enforcement: legality, precaution, and necessity and proportionality. These principles reflect rules of customary international law. Where the State breaches the principles of legality or precaution, or where a law enforcement official breaches the principles of necessity or proportionality, the right to life of any person harmed as a consequence will ordinarily have been violated. Thus there must be accountability for all use of force by State agents. As the European Court of Human Rights affirmed in its judgment in 2013 in *Douet v. France*, 'it is normally for the Government to provide relevant evidence that the use of force was both proportionate and necessary'.[14]

The Principle of Legality

7.07 To comply with the principle of legality, domestic laws on the use of force for law enforcement purposes must be in place that reflect the principles of necessity and proportionality. As the African Commission on Human and Peoples' Rights recalls in its 2015 General Comment on the right to life under the 1981 African Charter, 'States must adopt a clear

---

[12] *United Nations Guidance on Less-Lethal Weapons in Law Enforcement*, OHCHR, New York/Geneva, 2020, p. 46.
[13] Of course, in practice force may also be used for illegitimate purposes, such as to take revenge on someone or to punish them for perceived earlier transgressions.
[14] European Court of Human Rights, *Douet v. France*, Judgment (Fifth Section), 3 October 2013, para. 30 (author's translation).

legislative framework for the use of force by law-enforcement and other actors that complies with international standards, including the principles of necessity and proportionality.'[15]

7.08 The principle of legality means that force must not be exercised arbitrarily (in the narrow sense of 'not according to law'). As the first principle of the 1990 Basic Principles on the Use of Force and Firearms by Law Enforcement Officials instructs, 'Governments and law enforcement agencies shall adopt and implement rules and regulations on the use of force and firearms against persons by law enforcement officials.'[16] This partially reflects the duty to protect the right to life 'by law', as Article 6(1) of the 1966 International Covenant on Civil and Political Rights[17] requires. This provision, the Human Rights Committee affirms in its 2018 General Comment on the right to life, 'lays the foundation for the obligation of States parties to respect and to ensure the right to life, to give effect to it through legislative and other measures, and to provide effective remedies and reparation to all victims of violations of the right to life'.[18]

7.09 In its judgment in the *Ciorcan* case, the European Court of Human Rights recalled that 'police officers should not be left in a vacuum when performing their duties, whether in the context of a prepared operation or a spontaneous chase of a person perceived to be dangerous: a legal and administrative framework should define the limited circumstances in which law-enforcement officials may use force and firearms, in the light of the international standards which have been developed in this area'.[19] As the UN Special Rapporteur on extrajudicial, summary or arbitrary executions observed in his 2014 report to the Human Rights Council: 'The first step of securing the right to life is ... the establishment of an appropriate legal framework for the use of force by the police, which sets out the conditions under which force may be used in the name of the State and ensuring a system of responsibility where these limits are transgressed.'[20]

7.10 In its 2018 General Comment on the right to life, the Human Rights Committee affirms that a deprivation of life may be authorised by domestic law 'and still be arbitrary':[21] 'The notion of "arbitrariness" is not to be fully equated with "against the law", but must be interpreted more broadly to include elements of inappropriateness, injustice, lack of predictability, and due process of law ... as well as elements of reasonableness, necessity, and proportionality.'[22] For, as the UN Special Rapporteur on extrajudicial, summary or arbitrary executions noted in 2014, while 'many States have reformed their laws during the last few

---

[15] African Commission on Human and Peoples' Rights (ACmnHPR), 'General Comment No. 3 on the African Charter on Human and Peoples' Rights: Article 4, the Right to Life', adopted in November 2015, para. 27, at http://bit.ly/1JCH8Mc.
[16] Principle 1, 1990 Basic Principles.
[17] International Covenant on Civil and Political Rights; adopted at New York 16 December 1966; entered into force 23 March 1976.
[18] Human Rights Committee, 'General Comment No. 36: Article 6: right to life', UN doc. CCPR/C/GC/36, 3 September 2019 (hereafter, Human Rights Committee, General Comment 36 on the right to life), para. 4.
[19] European Court of Human Rights, *Ciorcan and others* v. *Romania*, Judgment (Third Section), 27 January 2015 (rendered final on 27 April 2015), para. 107.
[20] Report of the Special Rapporteur on extrajudicial, summary or arbitrary executions, Christof Heyns, UN doc. A/HRC/26/36, 1 April 2014, para. 26 (footnote in original).
[21] Human Rights Committee, General Comment 36 on the right to life, para. 12.
[22] Ibid.

decades to give greater expression to the international rules and standards, in others the laws in force today date (in form or in substance) from the pre-human rights era – in particular from colonial times[23] – or form part of the legacy of former dictatorial regimes'.[24] In Belize and Botswana, for instance, the use of firearms is still potentially lawful under their respective domestic regimes in order purely to protect property.[25] Bhutan allows police officers to fire into the crowd at an unlawful assembly once warning shots have been fired in the air.[26] As discussed herein, these provisions violate international law.

7.11 In some instances, States have not adopted primary legislation governing police use of force. This is the case, for instance, in Indonesia, which restrains police use of force in two regulations issued by the Chief of the Indonesian National Police.[27] Other States have only amended existing legislation to comply with international law after adverse judgments in regional human rights courts. With respect to Bulgaria, for example, in 2014, after criticism by the European Court of Human Rights, particularly by the Court's Grand Chamber in the *Nachova* case,[28] Bulgaria adopted a new law on police use of force to improve its compliance with the international rules governing law enforcement.[29] Once adopted, the legislation must be publicly accessible. There should also be regulations that govern police use of particular weapons.[30]

The Principle of Precaution

7.12 The human rights law principle of precaution requires that the authorities plan law enforcement operations in a manner that minimises the risk of the police having resort to

---

[23] The British Riot Act of 1714, for example, served as a model for many former British colonies. In the case of France, the *Loi du 7 juin 1848 sur les attroupements* (modified in 1943) was likewise copied in France's overseas territories.

[24] Report of the Special Rapporteur on extrajudicial, summary or arbitrary executions, 1 April 2014, para. 31.

[25] See entries for Belize and Botswana on the Law on Police Use of Force Worldwide website, at http://bit.ly/2vkVwut; and http://bit.ly/2Mqf72Z, respectively.

[26] See entry for Bhutan on the Law on Police Use of Force Worldwide website, at http://bit.ly/2UX9GvH.

[27] Regulation No. 1 of 2009 on the Use of Force in Police Action and Regulation No. 8 of 2009 on the Implementation of Human Rights Principles and Standards in the Discharge of Duties of the Indonesian National Police.

[28] The European Court of Human Rights described the 'laxity of the regulations on the use of firearms and the manner in which they tolerated the use of lethal force' and held that the then extant legal framework was 'fundamentally deficient', falling 'well short of the level of protection "by law" of the right to life that is required by the Convention in present-day democratic societies in Europe'. European Court of Human Rights, *Nachova v. Bulgaria*, Judgment (Grand Chamber), 6 July 2005, paras. 99, 100.

[29] Use of force by law enforcement officials is generally regulated by the 2014 Ministry of Interior Act (especially Arts. 85–88). See, e.g., Law on Police Use of Force website, 'Bulgaria', at http://bit.ly/2n3EaNZ.

[30] In its judgment in the *Yaşa* case, the European Court of Human Rights observed 'that at the time of the facts Turkish law lacked any specific provisions on the use of tear-gas grenades during demonstrations, and did not lay down instructions for their utilisation. Given that during the events in Diyarbakir between 28 and 31 March 2006 two persons were killed by tear-gas grenades and that the applicant was injured on the same occasion, it may be deduced that the police officers were able to act very independently and take ill-considered initiatives, which would probably not have been the case if they had been given appropriate training and instructions. In the Court's view, such a situation is incompatible with the level of protection of the physical integrity of individuals which is required in contemporary democratic societies in Europe.' European Court of Human Rights, *Abdullah Yaşa and others v. Turkey* Judgment (Second Section), 16 July 2013, para. 49.

a potentially lethal weapon and thereby lessening the possibility of death or serious injury to a member of the public or law enforcement official. As the UN Special Rapporteur on extrajudicial, summary or arbitrary executions has observed:

> Once a situation arises where the use of force is considered, it is often too late to rescue the situation. Instead, in order to save lives, all possible measures should be taken 'upstream' to avoid situations where the decision on whether to pull the trigger arises, or to ensure that all the possible steps have been taken to ensure that if that happens, the damage is contained as much as is possible.[31]

7.13 The principle of precaution comes from the realm of human rights law rather than from the law of law enforcement. It was first enunciated by the Grand Chamber of the European Court of Human Rights in its 1995 judgment in the *McCann* case, which concerned the killing of suspected terrorists by British military personnel in the course of a law enforcement operation. The Court stated that it was obliged to 'carefully scrutinise ... not only whether the force used by the soldiers was strictly proportionate to the aim of protecting persons against unlawful violence but also whether the anti-terrorist operation was planned and controlled by the authorities so as to minimise, to the greatest extent possible, recourse to lethal force'.[32] Citing the decision in McCann, the Human Rights Committee has affirmed that States Parties to the 1966 Covenant

> are expected to take all necessary measures intended to prevent arbitrary deprivations of life by their law enforcement officials, including soldiers charged with law enforcement missions. These measures include appropriate legislation controlling the use of lethal force by law enforcement officials, procedures designed to ensure that law enforcement actions are adequately planned in a manner consistent with the need to minimize the risk they pose to human life ... and the supplying of forces responsible for crowd control with effective 'less-lethal' means and adequate protective equipment in order to obviate their need to resort to lethal force.[33]

The Inter-American Court of Human Rights has espoused a similar approach, though it has tended to consider the duty of precaution as subsumed within the principle of proportionality.[34]

7.14 As part of the principle of precaution, there is a duty to consider whether a planned operation can be delayed or its details revised to reduce the risks of violence occurring. The

---

[31] Report of the Special Rapporteur on extrajudicial, summary or arbitrary executions, 1 April 2014, para. 63.
[32] European Court of Human Rights, *McCann and others v. United Kingdom*, Judgment (Grand Chamber), 27 September 1995, para. 194.
[33] Human Rights Committee, General Comment 36 on the right to life, para. 13.
[34] In the *Detention Centre of Catia* case against Venezuela, the Inter-American Court of Human Rights declared that 'use of force by the security forces ... should be planned and proportionally limited by the government authorities'. Inter-American Court of Human Rights, *Montero-Aranguren and others (Detention Centre of Catia) v. Venezuela*, Judgment (Preliminary Objection, Merits, Reparations, and Costs), 5 July 2006, para. 67. This official translation is of questionable faith to the original Spanish, which reads: 'El uso de la fuerza por parte de los cuerpos de seguridad estatales ... debe ser planeado y limitado proporcionalmente por las autoridades'. Arguably, a more faithful rendition of the Spanish would be 'must be planned and restricted by the authorities on the basis of proportionality'.

2014 judgment in the *Shchiborshch* case by the European Court of Human Rights concerned a Russian citizen suffering from mental illness that required institutional treatment. Mr Shchiborshch feared that anyone entering his apartment was a burglar and the police had been informed of this fact. The police chose to enter forcibly and storm the kitchen in which he had barricaded himself, in the course of which he sustained injuries that proved fatal. This decision, which did not result from any prior planning and assessment, was hastily taken at the scene even though there was no requirement for urgent action.[35] The Court observed that the Russian authorities had not explained why the police had taken 'actions aimed at securing Mr Shchiborshch's involuntary hospitalisation without being accompanied by qualified medical personnel'.[36] This decision by the authorities reflected a failure to plan a law enforcement operation in accordance with the principle of precaution.

7.15 Similarly, where the use of force is unavoidable, appropriate planning of a medical response is essential. The *Finogenov* case before the European Court of Human Rights concerned the violent resolution by Russian Special Forces of a major hostage crisis at a Moscow theatre. The Court accorded to Russia a 'margin of discretion' in the manner in which they ended the hostage taking, which involved the pumping of a narcotic gas into the theatre before it was stormed, 'even if now, with hindsight, some of the decisions taken by the authorities may appear open to doubt'.[37] The Court nonetheless held that 'the original plan of the rescue and evacuation of the hostages was in itself flawed in many respects'.[38] The Court held that

> the rescue operation was not spontaneous: the authorities had about two days to reflect on the situation and make specific preparations. Second, in this area (evacuation and medical assistance) the authorities should have been in a position to rely on some generally prepared emergency plan, not related to this particular crisis. Third, they had some control of the situation outside the building, where most of the rescue efforts took place (contrary to the situation within the building, which was in the hands of the terrorists). Finally, the more predictable a hazard, the greater the obligation to protect against it: it is clear that the authorities in this case always acted on the assumption that the hostages might have been seriously injured (by an explosion or by the gas), and thus the large number of people in need of medical assistance did not come as a surprise.[39]

The Principle of Necessity

7.16 Necessity is the fundamental principle governing the use of force by law enforcement personnel. Thus Article 3 of the 1979 Code of Conduct stipulates that law enforcement

---

[35] European Court of Human Rights, *Shchiborshch and Kuzmina v. Russia*, Judgment (First Section), 16 January 2014, para. 240.
[36] Ibid., para. 233.
[37] European Court of Human Rights, *Finogenov and others v. Russia*, Judgment (First Section), 20 December 2011, para. 213.
[38] Ibid., para. 252.
[39] Ibid., para. 243.

officials may use force 'only when strictly necessary'. The accompanying official commentary emphasises that any use of force by law enforcement officials 'should be exceptional'. The European Court of Human Rights has held that 'where injuries have been sustained at the hands of the police, the burden to show the necessity of the force used lies on the Government'.[40] The principle of necessity holds that only minimum necessary force in pursuit of a legitimate law enforcement purpose is permissible. Once the need for any force has passed, application of further force will be unlawful. These three elements are addressed in turn.

Minimum Necessary Force

7.17 On the basis that the use of force should be exceptional and may be applied only when strictly necessary, in the overwhelming majority of interactions with members of the public, the police should use non-violent means to enforce the law wherever it is reasonably possible to do so. Thus, according to Principle 4 of the 1990 Basic Principles, 'Law enforcement officials, in carrying out their duty, shall, as far as possible, apply non-violent means before resorting to the use of force and firearms.' Such non-violent means may include verbal persuasion, the presence and authority of a police officer, and positive body language.[41] As the US Department of Justice has stated, 'The ability of a police officer to bring calm to a situation is a core policing skill.'[42]

7.18 The duty to refrain from the use of force other than when necessary reflects the rights to life, to freedom from inhumane treatment, to liberty, and to security. For instance, in its judgment in 2015 in the case of *Bouyid* v. *Belgium*, the Grand Chamber of the European Court of Human Rights reiterated its longstanding position that 'in respect of a person who is ... confronted with law-enforcement officers, any recourse to physical force which has not been made strictly necessary by his own conduct diminishes human dignity and is, in principle, an infringement' of the right to freedom from torture and inhuman or degrading treatment.[43] In the 2020 judgment in *Navalnyy and Gunko*, the arrest by the Russian police of Mr Navalnyy was found by the court to involve degrading treatment:

> From the moment when he was put on his feet until he entered the police station, the police officers' interaction with him consisted in asking whether he would start walking by himself, demanding that he stay still, and threatening to break his arm. ... Nothing in the video-recording suggests that this manner of restraining the first applicant was indispensable for bringing him to the police station.[44]

---

[40] European Court of Human Rights, *Anzhelo Georgiev and others* v. *Bulgaria*, Judgment (Fourth Section), 30 September 2014, para. 67.
[41] M. J. Palmiotto, *Policing: Concepts, Strategies, and Current Issues in American Police Forces*, 3rd ed., CreateSpace Independent Publishing Platform, United States, 2013, p. 245.
[42] US Department of Justice, Investigation of the Ferguson Police Department, Civil Rights Division, 4 March 2015, p. 26, at http://bit.ly/1lV31kb.
[43] European Court of Human Rights, *Bouyid* v. *Belgium*, Judgment (Grand Chamber), 28 September 2015, paras. 88, 100.
[44] European Court of Human Rights, *Navalnyy and Gunko* v. *Russia*, Judgment (First Section), 10 November 2020, para. 45 and see generally paras. 43–9.

7.19 Routine inquiries by law enforcement officials would not normally give rise to a necessity for the use of force. The *Rachwalski and Ferenc* case before the European Court of Human Rights is instructive in this regard. The case concerned the use of force against a group of students following a police inquiry as to an unlocked car in the street. In its judgment, the Court noted that the police officers 'ordered all the applicants out of the house and stood them against a wall, dressed in their night clothes'.[45] It was at that moment that the officers used truncheons on the students. In the Court's opinion,

> the manner of intervention of the police at that stage is particularly open to criticism. It has not been shown or argued that the applicants at that time had behaved in an aggressive manner which would have warranted the use of truncheons against them. Nor has the Court been presented with any evidence to show that at that juncture the applicants had offered any physical resistance. . . . It cannot be ruled out that at that stage the use of force against the applicants was motivated rather by punitive intentions than by any genuine need to break or discourage any physical opposition.[46]

7.20 In finding a violation of the right to freedom from inhumane treatment (under Article 3 of the European Convention on Human Rights), the Court observed that, in its submissions, the respondent Government (Poland) 'did not explain what criteria had been used to assess the necessity of the use of a police team with guard dogs and truncheons to investigate a minor issue of an unlocked car and in the absence of any aggression or behaviour disturbing the public order on the part of the applicants'.[47] The Court further expressed the view that the 'mere fact that the car was left unlocked in front of the house' could not 'in itself constitute a good reason for a heavy-handed police intervention'.[48]

7.21 In any given situation, the judgment of whether the force used by a law enforcement official was necessary or not is to be made based on the information available to that official at the time. Thus, for example, the US Supreme Court observed in the key case of *Graham v. Connor* that 'police officers are often forced to make split-second judgments in circumstances that are tense, uncertain, and rapidly evolving – about the amount of force that is necessary in a particular situation'.[49] Accordingly, a police officer may make an honest mistake and not be held criminally responsible, unless that mistake was manifestly unreasonable in the circumstances. In the *McCann* case, the Grand Chamber of the European Court of Human Rights held that a

> use of force by agents of the State may be justified where it is based on an honest belief which is perceived, for good reasons, to be valid at the time but which subsequently turns out to be mistaken. To hold otherwise would be to impose an unrealistic burden on the

---

[45] European Court of Human Rights, *Rachwalski and Ferenc v. Poland*, Judgment (Fourth Section), 28 July 2009, para. 58.
[46] Ibid.
[47] Ibid., para. 60.
[48] Ibid.
[49] US Supreme Court, *Graham v. Connor*, 490 US 386 (1989), Decided 15 May 1989, at 396–7.

State and its law-enforcement personnel in the execution of their duty, perhaps to the detriment of their lives and those of others.[50]

7.22 Subsequently, this 'honest belief' test has been 'consistently applied by the Court in determining whether the use of lethal force was justified'.[51] As later recalled in its judgment in the *da Silva* case, in a number of cases the European Court 'has expressly stated that as it is detached from the events at issue, it cannot substitute its own assessment of the situation for that of an officer who was required to react in the heat of the moment to avert an honestly perceived danger to his life or the lives of others; rather, it must consider the events from the viewpoint of the person(s) acting in self-defence at the time of those events'.[52]

A Legitimate Law Enforcement Purpose

7.23 According to Article 3 of the 1979 Code of Conduct, law enforcement officials may use force 'only . . . to the extent required for the performance of their duty'. Thus force may only be lawful where it is used for a legitimate law enforcement purpose. Such a purpose includes the arrest of a suspected criminal or the prevention of crime. In any event, there must be lawful grounds for the arrest or physical intervention. In its 2017 judgment in the *Ksenz* case, the European Court of Human Rights reiterated 'its established case-law that the use of force by the police in the course of arrest operations will only not be in breach' of the prohibition of inhumane treatment 'if indispensable and not excessive. The burden to prove this rests on the Government.'[53]

7.24 Where force is exercised as a result of overt ethnic or gender discrimination on the part of the law enforcement official, this will constitute a serious violation of the principle of necessity. This is similarly the case where force is used with a view to extracting bribes. In both cases, the right to freedom from inhumane treatment will be breached. All punitive use of force is unlawful.[54] Where death results from any such unlawful action of the law enforcement official, the violation will be of the right to life.

---

[50] European Court of Human Rights, *McCann and others v. United Kingdom*, Judgment (Grand Chamber), 27 September 1995, para. 200.
[51] European Court of Human Rights, *Armani da Silva v. United Kingdom*, Judgment (Grand Chamber), 30 March 2016, para. 244.
[52] Ibid., para. 245.
[53] European Court of Human Rights, *Ksenz and others v. Russia*, Judgment (Third Section), 12 December 2017, para. 94.
[54] In its 2020 judgment in the *Kukhalashvili* case, the European Court of Human Rights considered that 'the use of lethal force for purely punitive, retaliatory purposes, even if those purposes target alleged members of the criminal underworld, cannot be justified'. European Court of Human Rights, *Kukhalashvili v. Georgia*, Judgment (Fifth Section), 2 April 2020, para. 151. In its 2019 judgment in the *Altony Brooks* case, the US Court of Appeals for the Fourth Circuit stated that 'corrections officers cross the line into an impermissible motive – using force "maliciously" and for the "very purpose of causing harm", . . . when they inflict pain not to induce compliance, but to punish an inmate for intransigence or to retaliate for insubordination'. US Court of Appeals (for the Fourth Circuit), *Altony Brooks v. Lieutenant Johnson and others*, Judgment (Case No. 17–7448), 10 May 2019, p. 15.

7.25 A US Department of Justice investigation in 2014–15 found that the practices of the Ferguson Police Department (FPD) in Missouri 'disproportionately harm African Americans', uncovering 'substantial evidence that this harm stems in part from intentional discrimination in violation of the Constitution'. Notably, this included the use of force against African Americans 'at disproportionately high rates, accounting for 88% of all cases from 2010 to August 2014 in which an FPD officer reported using force'.[55]

7.26 The US Department of Justice initiated an investigation into the Chicago Police Department in Illinois following the fatal shooting of a seventeen-year-old African American, Laquan McDonald, by a white Chicago Police Officer on 20 October 2014.[56] Mr McDonald, who was shot sixteen times by a single officer, was pronounced dead at Mount Sinai Hospital. On 24 November 2015, the officer who fired the sixteen rounds was charged with first-degree murder and other felony crimes.[57] The Department of Justice investigation found that the Chicago Police Department (CPD) had tolerated racially discriminatory conduct that contributed to a 'pattern of unreasonable force'.[58] This pattern 'and systemic deficiencies falls heaviest on the predominantly black and Latino neighborhoods on the South and West Sides of Chicago, which are also experiencing higher crime'.[59] Of all use-of-force incidents for which race was recorded between January 2011 and 18 April 2016,

> black individuals were subject to approximately 76% (19,374) of the uses of force, as compared to whites, who represented only 8% (2,007) of the force incidents. In some categories of force, blacks were even more overrepresented: black individuals were the subject of 80% of all CPD firearm uses and 81% of all Taser contact-stun uses during that time period.[60]

An End to Use of Force When It Is No Longer Necessary

7.27 Once the need for force has passed, such as when a suspect is handcuffed and is not (or no longer) resisting arrest, further force will be unlawful. A 2019 US federal appellate decision concerned a detainee who died in a Birmingham, Alabama, city jail after being shocked in the chest with a Taser in dart mode when he resisted being placed in a new

---

[55] US Department of Justice, *Investigation of the Ferguson Police Department*, 4 March 2015, p. 62, at http://bit.ly/1lV31kb.
[56] US Department of Justice, *Investigation of the Chicago Police Department*, Department of Justice Civil Rights Division and US Attorney's Office for the Northern District of Illinois, 13 January 2017, p. 1, at http://bit.ly/2ilv2Ex.
[57] See, e.g., N. Husain, 'Data: Laquan McDonald Timeline: The Shooting, the Video and the Fallout', *Chicago Tribune*, 20 October 2017, at http://trib.in/2LO7pTI. In October 2018, the officer who fired the fatal shots, Jason Van Dyke, was found guilty of second-degree murder of Mr McDonald and sixteen counts of aggravated battery with a firearm (one for each round fired). In January 2019, Mr Van Dyke was sentenced to six years and nine months in prison for the second-degree murder conviction (second-degree murder in the United States is intentional killing without premeditation). N. Chavez, D. Andone, and M. Baldacci, 'Former Chicago Officer Jason Van Dyke Sentenced to 81 Months for Fatally Shooting Laquan McDonald', CNN, 19 January 2019, at http://cnn.it/2ZSlTp7.
[58] US DOJ, *Investigation of the Chicago Police Department*, pp. 15, 145.
[59] Ibid., p. 144.
[60] Ibid., p. 145.

cell.[61] The detainee was suffering from symptoms of alcohol withdrawal and exhibiting delusional behaviour. The court ruled that a deputy 'clearly crossed' the constitutional line, when, having already shocked the detainee once for five seconds, dropping him to the floor, rendering him motionless, and causing him to urinate on himself, he shocked him again a full eight seconds later in the neck in stun mode. While the officer sought to justify the second shock by the detainee's failure to comply with an order to roll over and be handcuffed, the evidence indicated that he was not responsive because of the effects of the first shock. As the court asked: 'Really, is there any surer indication of a grown man's inability to control his bodily functions than his wetting himself?'[62]

The Principle of Proportionality

7.28 As the official commentary on Article 3 of the 1979 Code of Conduct recalls, domestic law 'ordinarily restricts the use of force by law enforcement officials in accordance with a principle of proportionality'.[63] Article 3 provides that law enforcement officials 'may use force only when strictly necessary and to the extent required for the performance of their duty'. The commentary further stipulates that in no case should this provision 'be interpreted to authorize the use of force which is disproportionate to the legitimate objective to be achieved'. According to Principle 5 of the 1990 Basic Principles, 'Whenever the lawful use of force and firearms is unavoidable, law enforcement officers shall ... act in proportion to the seriousness of the offence and legitimate objective to be achieved.' Thus proportionality sets an upper limit on when minimum necessary force may be lawful, based on a comparison of the threat posed and the harm inflicted on life or limb and to property by the actions taken to repel the threat.[64]

7.29 In a 2012 decision, the African Commission on Human and Peoples' Rights held that

> proportionality requires that the rights of the person threatened (police officers in this case) are measured against those of the deceased persons ... in an objective way, in the light of the prevailing circumstances at the time when the final decision on the use of lethal force is made. The potential taking of life ... is placed on one side of the scale, and, since the right to life is at stake, only the protection of life (that of the police officials) will carry any weight, on the other.[65]

---

[61] US Court of Appeals (for the Eleventh Circuit), *Anthony Piazza and Nyreekis Jarnell Hunter v. Jefferson County, Alabama, and Mike Hale and others*, Judgment (No. 18–10487), 9 May 2019, at http://bit.ly/2mRWrkq; see 'Electronic Control Weapons – AELE Case Summaries', accessed 26 September 2019, at http://bit.ly/2lUsH6p.

[62] *Anthony Piazza v. Jefferson County*, Judgment, 9 May 2019, s. A2.

[63] Thus, for example, in England and Wales, the Police (Conduct) Regulations 2012 stipulate that with respect to use of force, police officers will 'only use force to the extent that it is necessary, proportionate and reasonable in all the circumstances'. Police (Conduct) Regulations 2012, Schedule 2: Standards of Professional Behaviour, at http://bit.ly/2AJLQ1R, Regulation 3.

[64] Proportionality has a specific meaning in the law applicable to law enforcement that is distinct from its meaning in other branches of international law, such as the law of armed conflict/international humanitarian law or the law on inter-State use of force (jus ad bellum). See Chapters 5 and 6 on these issues.

[65] *Noah Kazingachire, John Chitsenga, Elias Chemvura, and Batanai Hadzisi (represented by Zimbabwe Human Rights NGO Forum) v. Zimbabwe*, Decision, 2012, at http://bit.ly/2AySjfQ, para. 116.

7.30 With respect to the right to life as protected in the European Convention on Human Rights, the European Court has affirmed that the 'force used must be strictly proportionate to the achievement of the aims' set out in the three subparagraphs of Article 2(2).[66] These are, namely, to defend any person from unlawful violence; to effect a lawful arrest or prevent the escape of a person lawfully detained; and to quell a riot or insurrection.[67] Concerning arbitrary deprivation of life, as prohibited under the 1969 Inter-American Convention on Human Rights, the Inter-American Court of Human Rights held in its judgment in the *Cruz Sánchez* case that a violation of the right to life would occur when the use of force is 'illegitimate, excessive or disproportionate'.[68]

7.31 The Inter-American Court of Human Rights has also linked the principle of proportionality to the principle of precaution. In the *Detention Centre of Catia* case, the Court declared that 'use of force by the security forces must be exceptional, and must be planned and restricted by the authorities on the basis of proportionality'.[69] In the later *Nadege Dorzema* case, it endorsed this approach, holding that proportionality 'is also related to the planning of preventive measures, since it involves an assessment of the reasonableness of the use of force. Thus, it is useful to analyze the facts rigorously to determine ... whether the violations could have been avoided with the implementation of less harmful measures.'[70]

7.32 The application of proportionality is starkest in relation to potentially lethal weapons, especially firearms. For instance, to 'effectively break up a pub brawl or to stop an escaping thief might be taken to require, in the prevailing circumstances, that a firearm be discharged. But the principle of proportionality will intervene to prevent such use even where it unquestionably amounts to the minimum necessary force in any particular situation.'[71] In this regard, Sir Nigel Rodley argued that Principle 9 of the 1990 Basic Principles, which regulates when firearms may lawfully be used in law enforcement, 'impose[s] a principle of proportionality'.[72]

7.33 With respect to an electric-shock weapon, such as a Taser, national case-law and practice have noted the relevance of proportionality. In *Armstrong v. Village of Pinehurst*,

---

[66] European Court of Human Rights, *Karataş and others v. Turkey*, Judgment (Second Section), 12 September 2017, para. 68.
[67] Art. 2(2)(a) to (c), European Convention on Human Rights.
[68] Inter-American Court of Human Rights, *Cruz Sánchez and others v. Peru*, Judgment (Preliminary Objections, Merits, Reparation, and Costs), 17 April 2015, para. 261. In the original Spanish: 'no cualquier privación de la vida será reputada como contraria a la Convención, sino solo aquella que se hubiera producido de manera arbitraria, por ejemplo por ser producto de la utilización de la fuerza de forma ilegítima, excesiva o desproporcionada'.
[69] Inter-American Court of Human Rights, *Montero-Aranguren and others (Detention Centre of Catia) v. Venezuela*, Judgment (Preliminary Objection, Merits, Reparations, and Costs), 5 July 2006, para. 67.
[70] Inter-American Court of Human Rights, *Nadege Dorzema and others v. Dominican Republic*, Judgment (Merits, Reparations, and Costs), 24 October 2012, para. 87.
[71] S. Casey-Maslen and S. Connolly, *Police Use of Force under International Law*, Cambridge University Press, Cambridge, 2017, p. 93.
[72] N. S. Rodley with M. Pollard, *The Treatment of Prisoners under International Law*, 3rd ed., Oxford University Press, Oxford, 2011, p. 499.

the US Court of Appeals for the Fourth Circuit (for Maryland and the Eastern District of North Carolina) held that 'immediately tasing a non-criminal, mentally ill individual, who seconds before had been conversational, was not a proportional response'.[73] It further stated: 'Force that imposes serious consequences requires significant circumscription.' Electric-shock weapons 'are proportional force only when deployed in response to a situation in which a reasonable officer would perceive some immediate danger that could be mitigated by using the taser'.[74] In October 2016, the US Supreme Court decided not to overturn the ruling in an appellate court that police can use a Taser only if officers are in immediate danger.[75]

USE OF FIREARMS

Definitions and Terminology

7.34 Firearms are defined in the 2001 Firearms Protocol[76] as follows:

> 'Firearm' shall mean any portable barrelled weapon that expels, is designed to expel or may be readily converted to expel a shot, bullet or projectile by the action of an explosive, excluding antique firearms or their replicas. Antique firearms and their replicas shall be defined in accordance with domestic law. In no case, however, shall antique firearms include firearms manufactured after 1899.[77]

According to this broad definition, firearms include handguns, rifles, shotguns, submachine guns, light machine guns, and hand-held grenade launchers. The attachment of the adjective 'portable' excludes heavy weapons.[78] The requirement that the shot, bullet, or projectile be expelled by action of an explosive typically excludes an electric-shock weapon from the definition of a firearm, since the probes through which electricity is passed are projected out of the weapon by gas propulsion.[79]

---

[73] US Court of Appeals for the Fourth Circuit, *Armstrong v. Village of Pinehurst*, Judgment (Case No. 15-1191), 11 January 2016, p. 19.
[74] Ibid., p. 21.
[75] L. Hurley, 'Supreme Court Rejects Taser Excessive Force Case', *Reuters*, 3 October 2016, at http://reut.rs/2O5GgbI.
[76] Protocol against the Illicit Manufacturing of and Trafficking in Firearms, Their Parts and Components and Ammunition, Supplementing the United Nations Convention against Transnational Organized Crime; adopted at New York 31 May 2001; entered into force 3 July 2005. As of 1 May 2021, 119 States were party to the Protocol. A further 10 States were signatories.
[77] Art. 3(a), 2001 Firearms Protocol.
[78] In US federal law, firearms are defined as 'a shot gun or rifle having a barrel of less than eighteen inches in length, or any other weapon, except a pistol or revolver, from which a shot is discharged by an explosive if such weapon is capable of being concealed on the person, or a machine gun, and includes a muffler or silencer for any firearm whether or not such firearm is included within the foregoing definition'. 26 USCA §861(a). Under legislation in force in England and Wales, '"Firearm" means a lethal barrelled weapon of any description from which any shot, bullet or other missile can be discharged.' S. 57, 1968 Firearms Act.
[79] Tasers and other makes of conducted electrical weapons are not considered firearms in the United States. They are legal for law enforcement use in all fifty US states and can be legally owned by private citizens in forty-eight states. 'Taser Laws', accessed 1 December 2020, at http://bit.ly/2n2Flo2. In the United Kingdom, conducted electrical weapons are not defined as firearms but are 'prohibited weapons' under s. 5(1)(b) of the

The Use of Force in Law Enforcement

7.35 In addition to the general principles of necessity and proportionality, which apply to any use of force by a law enforcement official, specific provisions in both the 1979 Code of Conduct and the 1990 Basic Principles cover the use of firearms. While the term *use* unquestionably covers the discharge of firearms, it is not settled whether also brandishing and even possibly unholstering a firearm amounts to use under international law. A number of States define 'use' of firearms in broad terms. In the United Kingdom, for example, where police officers outside Northern Ireland are not routinely armed, an authorised firearms officer 'makes use of a firearm ... by pointing it or by discharging the weapon'.[80] In Denmark, police use of a firearm includes not only discharging a round but also firing a warning shot, or drawing a firearm and threatening someone, with the purpose of ensuring that an order given is followed.[81]

7.36 In its 1995 judgment in *Bailey v. United States*, the US Supreme Court defined the use of a firearm (albeit in relation to drug trafficking for the purpose of the federal criminal code, not by a law enforcement official) as 'active employment'. The Court stated that such active employment 'certainly includes brandishing, displaying, bartering, striking with, and, most obviously, firing or attempting to fire a firearm'.[82] In 2016, the US Department of Justice's Civil Rights Division report on the Baltimore City Police Department implies that an officer pointing a weapon 'at unarmed and innocent civilians to control a scene'[83] amounts to use of force. The Department of Justice Civil Rights Division further observes that 'pointing a gun at an individual for general control is an inappropriate use of a firearm and is a threat of deadly force where the underlying offense, if any, does not justify deadly force being used'.[84] This would distinguish, under US domestic law, the use of a firearm (which includes brandishing and pointing it) from the use of deadly force (which would refer only to the act of discharging a firearm).

7.37 The fact that the 1990 Basic Principles refer both to the use and discharge of firearms indicates that use may also be a broader concept under international law. Thus Principle 11 stipulates that rules and regulations on the use of firearms by law enforcement officials should include guidelines that

(b) Ensure that firearms *are used* only in appropriate circumstances and in a manner likely to decrease the risk of unnecessary harm ...
(e) Provide for warnings to be given, if appropriate, *when firearms are to be discharged.*[85]

1968 Firearms Act as amended ('any weapon of whatever description designed or adapted for the discharge of any noxious liquid, gas or other thing').
[80] Association of Chief Police Officers, *Manual of Guidance on the Management, Command and Deployment of Armed Officers*, 3rd ed., 2011, para. 2.18, and cf. also para. 2.19, at http://bit.ly/2vbFwuN.
[81] F. Z. Olsen, 'The Use of Police Firearms in Denmark', Copenhagen, 2008, p. 2, at http://bit.ly/1jE0jiP.
[82] US Supreme Court, *Bailey v. United States*, 516 US 137 (1995), at 148.
[83] US DOJ, *Investigation of the Baltimore City Police Department*, 10 August 2016, p. 75, at http://bit.ly/2n2Ghl4.
[84] Ibid., p. 79.
[85] Principle 11, 1990 Basic Principles (added emphasis).

7.38 Although a number of national jurisdictions refer to 'lethal force' or 'deadly force', these are not helpful terms in international law owing to their inherent vagueness. They are sometimes used as synonyms for the discharge of firearms, while on other occasions they are used to mean intentional lethal use of firearms. These differing concepts, which are regulated by distinct norms of international law, are simply described hereafter as 'shooting to stop' and 'shooting to kill'. In the former, a round (or possibly, depending on the circumstances, a volley of rounds) is fired at a suspect, typically at his or her main body mass.[86] While death may be the result of this action, it is not the intent, objectively defined. When shooting with intent to kill, a law enforcement official will typically fire single or multiple rounds into the head of the suspect with a view to achieving a fatal outcome.

Shooting to Stop

7.39 The commentary on Article 3 of the 1979 Code of Conduct states, in part, that 'every effort should be made to exclude the use of firearms, especially against children. In general, firearms should not be used except when a suspected offender offers armed resistance or otherwise jeopardizes the lives of others and less extreme measures are not sufficient to restrain or apprehend the suspected offender.'

7.40 More detailed parameters of when it is lawful to discharge a firearm with a view to 'stopping' a suspected or convicted criminal are set out in Principle 9 of the 1990 Basic Principles. Principle 9 states, in part:

> Law enforcement officials shall not use firearms against persons except in self-defence or defence of others against the imminent threat of death or serious injury, to prevent the perpetration of a particularly serious crime involving grave threat to life, to arrest a person presenting such a danger and resisting their authority, or to prevent his or her escape, and only when less extreme means are insufficient to achieve these objectives.

This provision can be taken to reflect customary international law applicable to all States despite considerable variance in domestic legislation and practice.[87] The European Court of Human Rights and the Inter-American Court of Human Rights have both cited the 1990 Basic Principles as authoritative statements of the international rules governing the use of force in law enforcement.[88] According to the Human Rights Committee, all operations of

---

[86] As the College of Policing has recalled, research 'indicates that the accuracy of shots fired under training conditions is generally greater than in operational circumstances. Police officers are normally trained to discharge conventional firearms at the largest part of the subject they can see, which in most cases will be the central body mass.' College of Policing, 'Armed Policing: Accuracy of Shot', last modified 28 June 2018, at http://bit.ly/2LW9T1G. (The College of Policing was established in 2012 as the professional body for all those working for the police service in England and Wales.) Aiming at the legs of a suspect is highly challenging in operational circumstances and may result in a bystander being hit instead.

[87] See, e.g., Law on Police Use of Force website, at www.policinglaw.info.

[88] See, e.g., European Court of Human Rights, *Giuliani and Gaggio v. Italy*, Judgment (Grand Chamber), 24 March 2011, para. 154; European Court of Human Rights, *Benzer v. Turkey*, Judgment (Former Second Section), 12 November 2013, para. 90; Inter-American Court of Human Rights, *Cruz Sánchez and others v. Peru*, Judgment (Preliminary Objections, Merits, Reparation, and Costs), 17 April 2015, para. 264.

law enforcement agents should comply with relevant international standards, 'including' the 1979 Code of Conduct and the 1990 Basic Principles.[89]

Use Against an Imminent Threat of Death or Serious Injury

7.41 The default scenario for the lawful use of firearms is where their use is necessary in self-defence or defence of others against an imminent threat of death or serious injury. In the prevailing circumstances, 'less extreme' means to achieve these objectives must not be reasonably open to the law enforcement official. It is not necessary, though, that the threat posed by the suspect to the law enforcement official or member of the public come 'from the wielding of a firearm'; depending on the situation, a knife, an iron bar, a car being driven at someone, a potentially lethal chokehold, or even a baseball bat might suffice.[90] Under international law, a threat purely to property (e.g., damage or theft of either movable or immovable property) is not sufficient to allow the use of firearms.[91]

7.42 The notion of imminence is not defined in the 1990 Basic Principles. According to the UN Special Rapporteur on extrajudicial, summary or arbitrary executions, 'an imminent or immediate threat' should be considered 'a matter of seconds, not hours'.[92] As the Los Angeles Police Department (LAPD) has observed, *Black's Law Dictionary* defines imminent as 'Near at hand; impending; on the point of happening'.[93] It has been asserted elsewhere by the author that it 'may well be the case' that imminence in the context of the rule in Basic Principle 9 'should be construed as being limited to a second or even a split second'.[94] Thus the unofficial '21-foot rule' used in practice by numerous law enforcement agencies in the United States certainly does not reflect extant international law. According to this 'rule', a dangerous suspect armed with a knife advancing towards a police officer may be shot once he or she comes within twenty-one feet, as if he or she comes any closer and runs at the officer at full pelt, that officer will likely not have the time to draw his or her firearm and shoot twice.[95]

7.43 What amounts to serious injury is also not defined in the 1990 Basic Principles. Arguably, the term 'should be construed narrowly to mean potentially fatal injuries'.[96] As the LAPD recalls, for instance, serious bodily injury is defined in the California Penal Code as including loss of consciousness, concussion, bone fracture, protracted loss or impairment of function of any bodily member or organ, a wound requiring extensive suturing, and serious disfigurement.[97] It is also suggested, however, that the term 'would

---

[89] Human Rights Committee, General Comment on the right to life, para. 13.
[90] Casey-Maslen and Connolly, *Police Use of Force Under International Law*, p. 98.
[91] See also UNODC and OHCHR, *Resource Book on the Use of Force and Firearms in Law Enforcement*, p. 21: 'a threat merely against property cannot justify using firearms against a person'.
[92] Report of the Special Rapporteur on extrajudicial, summary or arbitrary executions, Christof Heyns, UN doc. A/HRC/26/36, 1 April 2014, para. 59.
[93] LAPD, 2015 *Use of Force Year-End Review*, 'The Department's Use of Force Policy', p. 55, at http://bit.ly/2Oh3ITE.
[94] Casey-Maslen and Connolly, *Police Use of Force Under International Law*, p. 98.
[95] See, e.g., E. Conlon, *Blue Blood*, Ebury Press, London, 2011, p. 268.
[96] Casey-Maslen and Connolly, *Police Use of Force Under International Law*, p. 118.
[97] California Penal Code S. 243(f)(4), cited by LAPD, 2015 *Use of Force Year-End Review*, 'The Department's Use of Force Policy', p. 55. In the realm of road traffic safety, the Maximum Abbreviated Injury Scale (MAIS) is used across European Union Member States to determine the severity of injury. European

extend beyond serious bodily harm to encompass rape. The New York state penal code, for instance, specifically defines serious injury justifying use of lethal force to include forcible rape.'[98] Indeed, the term employed in the Basic Principles does not limit the serious injury to that which is inflicted on the body; psychological harm may also be encompassed.[99]

Use Against a Grave Threat to Life

7.44 In truly exceptional circumstances, a firearm may be used even when the threat posed by a suspect is not imminent. Thus Basic Principle 9 also allows the use of firearms, when absolutely necessary, 'to prevent the perpetration of a particularly serious crime involving grave threat to life, to arrest a person presenting such a danger and resisting their authority, or to prevent his or her escape'. There are thus three distinct scenarios for potentially 'shooting to stop' aside from the default scenario of preventing an imminent threat of death or serious injury: (1) to prevent the perpetration of a particularly serious crime involving grave threat to life; (2) to enable a suspect resisting arrest to be arrested if he or she is about to commit a particularly serious crime that involves grave threat to life; and (3) to prevent a suspect resisting arrest from escaping in circumstances where he or she is about to commit a particularly serious crime that involves a grave threat to life.

7.45 In contrast to the default scenario for potentially lawful use of firearms, the threat must be to life alone and not also of serious injury. The threat to life must also be 'grave', meaning it must be both temporally proximate and 'continuous',[100] even though it does not need to be imminent. Thus the mere fact that a suspect 'flees from arrest or escapes from custody does not justify the use of a firearm, unless this person presents an ongoing grave threat to the life of another person that can be realized at any time'.[101] It remains the

Commission, '2016 Road Safety Statistics: What Is Behind the Figures?', Fact Sheet, La Valette, 28 March 2017, at http://bit.ly/2nvmKei. The Abbreviated Injury Scale severity score is an ordinal scale of 1 to 6 (1 indicating a minor injury and 6 being maximal). A casualty that sustains an injury with a score of 3 or higher on the Scale is classified as clinically seriously injured (MAIS3+). This covers 'an injury for which a person is detained in hospital as an inpatient, or any of the following injuries whether or not they are detained in hospital: fractures, concussion, internal injuries, crushings, burns (excluding friction burns), severe cuts, severe general shock requiring medical treatment and injuries causing death 30 or more days after the accident'. UK Department of Transport, 'Estimating Clinically Seriously Injured (MAIS3+) Road Casualties in the UK', *Reported Road Casualties Great Britain: 2015 Annual Report*, p. 7, at http://bit.ly/2diWZrG.

[98] Casey-Maslen and Connolly, *Police Use of Force Under International Law*, p. 119, citing New York State Penal Law, Part I, Title C, Art. 35, at http://bit.ly/1K9ns7O: 'A person may not use deadly physical force upon another person ... unless: ... (b) He or she reasonably believes that such other person is committing or attempting to commit a kidnapping, forcible rape, forcible criminal sexual act or robbery.' The reference to forcible rape would distinguish it from, for example, statutory rape, where sexual relations involve someone below the age of consent who cannot legally consent to having sex, but who engages in sexual relations without the use or threat of physical force being involved.

[99] For a description of the forms of psychological injury accepted under US law, see, e.g., H. Koch and T. Kevan, *Psychological Injury (Personal Injury Practitioner's Library)*, rev. ed., XPL Law, United States, March 2005.

[100] UNODC and OHCHR, *Resource Book on the Use of Force and Firearms in Law Enforcement*, p. 21.

[101] Amnesty International, *Use of Force. Guidelines for Implementation of the UN Basic Principles on the Use of Force and Firearms by Law Enforcement Officials*, Dutch Section, Amsterdam, 2015, p. 31, Guideline 2(c), at http://bit.ly/2LROt61.

case, therefore, that a threat purely to property is not sufficient grounds for the lawful use of firearms.

7.46 It is also not enough for the crime to be perpetrated to be 'serious' (for instance, as demonstrated by the length of imprisonment that may be imposed upon a suspect's conviction); its perpetration must involve a grave threat to life. As the UN Special Rapporteur on extrajudicial, summary or arbitrary executions observed in 2014:

> In the context of arrest or escape, the use of force is often determined purely by the crime the person is suspected to have committed. A typical provision reads as follows: in the prevention of the crimes of burglary, housebreaking or forcible unnatural crimes, among others, 'a person may justify any necessary force or harm, extending, in the case of extreme necessity, even to killing'. Offences that are classified as felonies and crimes such as kidnapping in other cases permit the lethal use of force in effecting arrest or preventing escape. Some countries allow the use of lethal force based on the penalty for the suspected criminal offence; frequently where life imprisonment or imprisonment for 10 years or more is prescribed, but this does not constitute a reliable proxy for the question whether the person concerned is dangerous.[102]

Accordingly, where the act of escaping from lawful custody itself is a serious offence, an order allowing police officers to shoot an escaping suspect or convicted felon would potentially allow the use of firearms against any person trying to escape from lawful custody, not just one who poses a grave threat to life.[103] This would be arbitrary in nature and would not be lawful.

7.47 While the European and Inter-American Courts have both addressed the use of firearms in situations where the threat posed by the suspect was not imminent, they have not directly and specifically assessed the 'grave threat to life' exception, nor have they delineated with sufficient care and clarity the scenarios in which recourse to firearms could be lawful. In the *Nadege Dorzema* case, for example, the Inter-American Court of Human Rights considered that 'even when abstaining from the use of force would have allowed the individuals that were the subject of the State's action to escape, the agents should not have used lethal force against people who did not represent a threat or a real or imminent danger to the agents or third parties'.[104] The Court does not identify the requisite level of the harm that would need to be threatened to justify the discharge of a firearm, although it has endorsed the 1990 Basic Principles as the relevant standards

---

[102] Report of the Special Rapporteur on extrajudicial, summary or arbitrary executions, Christof Heyns, UN doc. A/HRC/26/36, 1 April 2014, para. 95.

[103] Amnesty International, *Use of Force: Guidelines for Implementation of the UN Basic Principles on the Use of Force and Firearms by Law Enforcement Officials*, p. 57 note 39. This is the case with Nigerian Police Force Order 237, for instance, which even allows use of firearms in case of a misdemeanour. Nigerian Federal Police, Force Order 237: Rules for Use in Guidance of Firearms by the Police, §3(d), at http://bit.ly/2vz8sfE.

[104] Inter-American Court of Human Rights, *Nadege Dorzema and others* v. *Dominican Republic*, Judgment (Merits, Reparations, and Costs), 24 October 2012, para. 85(ii). The original Spanish reads: 'aún cuando la abstención del uso de la fuerza hubiera permitido la huida de las personas objeto de la acción estatal, los agentes no debieron emplear la fuerza letal frente a las personas que no representaban una amenaza o peligro real o inminente de los agentes o terceros'.

governing the use of force. In its 2018 General Comment on the right to life, the Human Rights Committee appears to have mistakenly dismissed *in toto* the exceptional 'grave threat to life' basis for a possibly lawful use of firearms.[105]

7.48 In its 2005 judgment in the *Kakoulli* case, a chamber of the European Court reaffirmed that 'the legitimate aim of effecting a lawful arrest can only justify putting human life at risk in circumstances of absolute necessity'. The case concerned the shooting of an unarmed Greek Cypriot man by Turkish soldiers after his unlawful entry into a restricted area controlled by Turkish forces in northern Cyprus. The Court considered that, 'in principle', there 'can be no such necessity where it is known that the person to be arrested poses no threat to life or limb and is not suspected of having committed a violent offence, even if a failure to use lethal force may result in the opportunity to arrest the fugitive being lost'.[106] In the later *Solomou* case, which also concerned shooting by Turkish forces in northern Cyrus of an unarmed man engaged in a demonstration in a prohibited area, the Court stated that 'a potential illegal or violent action from a group of persons cannot, as such, justify the immediate shooting and killing of one or more other individuals who are not themselves posing a threat'.[107]

7.49 Examples of the sort of threat that could amount to a grave threat to life might include a convicted serial killer escaping from a maximum-security prison or a suspected terrorist who was believed to have already committed murder in situations where they were expected to try to kill again in the very near future. In 1997, in the case of *M. D. v. Turkey*, the European Commission on Human Rights considered that the shooting of an escaping terrorist bombing suspect fell within the exception set out in Article 2(2)(b) of the European Convention on Human Rights 'to prevent the escape of a person lawfully detained'.[108] In 2005, the then UN Special Rapporteur on torture and other cruel, inhuman, or degrading treatment or punishment, Manfred Nowak, affirmed that 'for the purpose of arresting a person suspected of having committed murder or a terrorist attack, the police may, of course, use firearms if other less intrusive methods prove ineffective'.[109] In March 2016, in Brussels, Salah Abdeslam, a prime suspect for the planning of the November 2015 Paris terror attacks, was shot by armed police in the leg

---

[105] Human Rights Committee, General Comment 36 on the right to life, para. 12: 'The use of potentially lethal force for law enforcement purposes is an extreme measure . . ., which should be resorted to only when strictly necessary in order to protect life or prevent serious injury from an imminent threat. . . . It cannot be used, for example, in order to prevent the escape from custody of a suspected criminal or a convict who does not pose a serious and imminent threat to the lives or bodily integrity of others.' The Committee cites in support of this position the views of the African Commission on Human and Peoples' Rights in the case of *Kazingachire v. Zimbabwe* (May 2012), paras. 118–20. However, the African Commission only cited the first part of Basic Principle 9 in arriving at its decision, ignoring entirely the second section of the provision.

[106] European Court of Human Rights, *Kakoulli v. Turkey*, Judgment (Fourth Section), 22 November 2005, para. 108.

[107] European Court of Human Rights, *Solomou and others v. Turkey*, Judgment (Fourth Section), 24 June 2008, para. 78.

[108] European Commission on Human Rights, *M. D. v. Turkey*, Decision, 30 June 1997.

[109] 'Torture and Other Cruel, Inhuman or Degrading Treatment, Report of the Special Rapporteur on the Question of Torture, Manfred Nowak', UN doc. E/CN.4/2006/6, 23 December 2005, note 2.

as he left a building that was surrounded by police officers.[110] Belgian State prosecutor Eric Van der Sypt was reported as admitting that Mr Abdeslam was not armed, but stated that he was shot when he did not immediately obey orders when confronted by police.[111]

7.50 Accordingly, in the aftermath of a major incident involving substantial loss of life, such as a terrorist attack, the view expressed by UNODC and OHCHR that 'someone driving through a roadblock, but otherwise posing no apparent immediate danger, should not be killed or fired at'[112] might be open to question. For instance, in December 2015, a French *gendarme* in Paris fired as many as ten shots at a car when a driver refused to stop and then tried to force his car through a roadblock at one of the main entrances of *Les Invalides* on Rue Grenelle in the French capital. The incident took place at the complex where a remembrance ceremony had recently been held for the 130 people killed in the 13 November Islamist attacks across Paris.[113] The driver was not injured, but following his arrest, he was institutionalised in a secure mental health facility.[114]

Use of Firearms during Assemblies

7.51 The use of firearms to disperse an unauthorised but non-violent assembly, such as a public protest or demonstration, is unlawful.[115] Even if a violent assembly, such as a riot, is in progress, firearms may only be used in accordance with the rules set out above, and 'only when less dangerous means are not practicable and only to the minimum extent necessary'.[116] In this regard, Israel's fatal shooting of fifty-nine Palestinian protesters in Gaza in May 2018 was widely criticised. On 13 June 2018, the UN General Assembly, meeting in emergency special session, adopted a resolution deploring 'the use of any excessive, disproportionate and indiscriminate force by the Israeli forces against Palestinian civilians in the Occupied Palestinian Territory, including East Jerusalem, and particularly in the Gaza Strip, including the use of live ammunition against civilian protesters, including children, as well as medical personnel and journalists'.[117] In March 2019, the Independent International Commission of inquiry on the Protests in the Occupied Palestinian Territory presented the report of its detailed findings to the Human Rights Council. The Commission stated: 'Firearms deployed against a human

---

[110] See, e.g., 'Salah Abdeslam: Video of Paris Attacks Suspect Being Shot by Police Marksmen during Raid', *The Independent*, 22 March 2016, at http://ind.pn/2KkogI8.
[111] J. Curtis and T. Wyke, 'Terror Mastermind Salah Abdeslam Escaped Police by Hiding in a Wardrobe Then Walked the Streets of Brussels Freely for Weeks before He Was Captured in Sting Triggered by a Pizza Delivery', *Daily Mail Online*, 20 March 2016, at http://dailym.ai/2Kksik3.
[112] UNODC and OHCHR, *Resource Book on the Use of Force and Firearms in Law Enforcement*, p. 22.
[113] Associated Press, 'Police Open Fire on Car after Driver Tries to Ram Barrier at Paris's Invalides Monument', *Daily Telegraph*, 16 December 2015, at http://bit.ly/2n5g4md.
[114] Reuters, 'L'individu ayant forcé l'entrée des Invalides interné', 16 December 2015, at http://bit.ly/2OE1q1K.
[115] This is the case in Bangladesh, for instance. Police Regulations explicitly authorise dispersal by means of firearms, referring in support to sections 127–8 of the 1898 Criminal Procedure Code (which authorises force to be used to disperse an unlawful assembly). See Law on Police Use of Force Worldwide report on Bangladesh, at http://bit.ly/2LzdYKv.
[116] Principle 14, 1990 Basic Principles.
[117] UN General Assembly, Tenth Emergency Special Session, Resolution ES-10/20 ('Protection of the Palestinian civilian population'), adopted on 13 June 2018 by 120 votes to 8, with 45 abstentions, para. 2.

body are potentially lethal. Even where death is not intended, such as shooting at limbs ("shooting to stop"), it is an extreme measure which should be resorted to only when strictly necessary in order to protect life or prevent serious injury from an imminent threat.'[118]

7.52 Firing on unarmed demonstrators protesting against the regime is unlawful. In Zimbabwe, for instance, amid concerns that the election of 30 July 2018 was being rigged, protesters came onto the streets, with some engaging in destruction of property. The Zimbabwean Army reacted by firing live ammunition, seemingly indiscriminately, killing six people over the course of two days.[119] The United Kingdom condemned 'the excessive use of force by the security forces towards demonstrators', and the UK ambassador to Zimbabwe 'met government ministers … and made clear that the military should be removed from the streets of Harare and the security forces should act with the utmost restraint'.[120]

Shooting to Kill

7.53 A heightened international legal standard applies to the discharge of a firearm with intent to kill. This is set out in the final sentence of Basic Principle 9: 'In any event, intentional lethal use of firearms may only be made when strictly unavoidable in order to protect life.' Thus, preventing serious injury will not allow the intentional taking of life during a law enforcement operation; only the preservation of life (of either a law enforcement official or a member of the public) can suffice. Inherent in the phrase 'strictly unavoidable' is the notion of both imminence and absolute necessity.[121] There must be no other means realistically open to law enforcement personnel to prevent loss of life.

7.54 The standard reflected in 1990 Basic Principle 9 is a norm of customary international law.[122] Moreover, although the standard refers to intentional lethal use of *firearms*, this is extrapolated to all means of force when used to kill, from baseball bats and knives to missiles, grenades, and bombs.[123] In 2014, the UN Special Rapporteur on extrajudicial,

---

[118] Report of the detailed findings of the independent international Commission of inquiry on the protests in the Occupied Palestinian Territory, UN doc. A/HRC/40/CRP.2, 18 March 2019, para. 90.

[119] 'Zimbabwe Death Toll Rises to Six Following Protests', SABC Digital News, 2 August 2018, at http://bit.ly/2Kwbbf5.

[120] J. Flanagan, 'Zimbabwe Election: Harare Streets Cleared before Announcement of Results', *The Times*, 2 August 2018, at http://bit.ly/2Mif1KG.

[121] Human Rights Committee, General Comment 36 on the right to life, para. 12.

[122] See, e.g., Inter-American Court of Human Rights, *Montero-Aranguren and others (Detention Centre of Catia) v. Venezuela*, Judgment (Preliminary Objection, Merits, Reparations, and Costs), 5 July 2006, para. 69. As the African Commission on Human and Peoples' Rights observes, the standard for intentional lethal use of force by law enforcement officials reflects the principle of proportionality while the underlying requirement that all other means are insufficient to achieve that objective reflects the principle of necessary. ACmnHPR, General Comment No. 3 on the African Charter on Human and Peoples' Rights: Article 4, the Right to Life, para. 27.

[123] In its judgment in the 2009 *Alkin* case, a chamber of the European Court of Human Rights affirmed that 'the laying of such indiscriminate and inhumane weapons as anti-personnel landmines, which affect the lives of a disproportionate number of civilians and children, amounts to intentional use of lethal force'. European Court of Human Rights, *Alkin v. Turkey*, Judgment (Second Section), 13 October 2009, para. 30. This is so

summary or arbitrary executions affirmed: 'A common sense understanding of the scope of application of Basic Principle 9 suggests that all weapons that are designed and are likely to be lethal should be covered, including heavy weapons such as bombs and (drone) missiles, the use of which constitutes an intentional lethal use of force.'[124]

7.55 The heightened international legal standard for intentional killing typically concerns two scenarios: a hostage taker who is on the cusp of killing his/her hostage or a suicide (or other) bomber just about to detonate an explosive device. Thus '[i]f a suspect is not honestly believed to be about to pull the trigger of a firearm aimed at a hostage's head, or to detonate a bomb, intentional lethal use of force cannot be said to be strictly unavoidable to protect life'.[125] The European Court of Human Rights has made it clear that although one could infer that the wording of Article 2 of the 1950 European Convention on Human Rights refers only to intentional lethal use of force – 'No one shall be deprived of his life intentionally'[126] – in fact, it encompasses also 'force which may result, as an unintended outcome, in the deprivation of life' (e.g., 'shooting to stop').[127] That said, the Court has addressed the intentional lethal use of force in a number of cases.

7.56 In *McCann*, British soldiers who opened fire on three Irish Republican Army (IRA) operatives in Gibraltar had acknowledged at an earlier inquest that their intent, once they opened fire, was to kill.[128] 'All four soldiers admitted that they shot to kill. They considered that it was necessary to continue to fire at the suspects until they were rendered physically incapable of detonating a device.'[129] The Grand Chamber stated its acceptance that

> the soldiers honestly believed, in the light of the information that they had been given, ... that it was necessary to shoot the suspects in order to prevent them from detonating a bomb and causing serious loss of life .... The actions which they took, in obedience to superior orders, were thus perceived by them as absolutely necessary in order to safeguard innocent lives.[130]

7.57 The *da Silva* case concerned the fatal shooting of Jean-Charles de Menezes in 2005 by firearms officers of London's Metropolitan Police Service (MPS). Mr de Menezes, a Brazilian electrician, was mistaken for a suicide bomber about to detonate explosives on a tube train in the British capital. In fact, the actual bomber was on the south coast of

---

even though most anti-personnel mines are designed to inflict serious wounds rather than to kill, the rationale being that this will require other soldiers to evacuate their injured colleague.

[124] Report of the Special Rapporteur on extrajudicial, summary or arbitrary executions, 1 April 2014, para. 70.
[125] Casey-Maslen and Connolly, *Police Use of Force Under International Law*, p. 100.
[126] Art. 2(1), European Convention on Human Rights.
[127] European Court of Human Rights, *Andronicou and Constantinou v. Cyprus*, Judgment (Chamber), 9 October 1997, para. 171.
[128] As the Court recalled: 'At the inquest, both soldiers stated under cross-examination that once it became necessary to open fire they would continue shooting until the person was no longer a threat. C agreed that the best way to ensure this result was to kill. D stated that he was firing at Savage to kill him and that this was the way that all soldiers were trained.' European Court of Human Rights, *McCann and others v. United Kingdom*, Judgment (Grand Chamber), 27 September 1995, para. 80.
[129] Ibid., para. 199.
[130] Ibid., para. 200.

England, preparing to flee the country.[131] According to the applicant, the definition of self-defence under the law in force in England and Wales is flawed, since the officers who shot Mr de Menezes only had to show that they had an honest belief – as opposed to an honest and objectively reasonable belief – that their use of force was absolutely necessary.[132] In the view of the Government of the United Kingdom, an honest belief did not need 'to be shown to be reasonable by reference to objectively established facts, although the objective reasonableness of the belief would nevertheless be relevant in determining whether or not it was genuinely held'.[133]

7.58 In its 2016 judgment in the case, the Grand Chamber of the Court effectively endorsed the view of the UK government, holding that

> the principal question to be addressed is whether the person had an honest and genuine belief that the use of force was necessary. In addressing this question, the Court will have to consider whether the belief was subjectively reasonable, having full regard to the circumstances that pertained at the relevant time. If the belief was not subjectively reasonable (that is, it was not based on subjective good reasons), it is likely that the Court would have difficulty accepting that it was honestly and genuinely held.[134]

This test of subjective reasonableness reflects accurately the state of international law in adjudging whether a use of force by law enforcement personnel, including intentional lethal use of force, may be lawful.

7.59 As the Grand Chamber of the European Court of Human Rights declared in its 2005 judgment in the *Makaratzis* case, in exceptional circumstances a violation of the right to life may occur even if the target of use of force by law enforcement personnel survives.[135] In that case, multiple officers fired at least two dozen shots, some in automatic mode.[136] Sixteen bullet holes were found in the victim's car. In its earlier judgment in the *Acar* case, the European Court held that relevant factors were 'whether the force used against the applicant was potentially lethal' as well as 'the degree and type of force used, the context in which his life was put at risk and the nature of the impugned conduct of the state officials concerned'.[137] In the *Rochela Massacre* case, the Inter-American Court of Human Rights cited the *Acar* judgment in support of its findings of 'extraordinary circumstances that lay a foundation for a violation' of the right to life under the 1969 American Convention on Human Rights, 'taking into account the force employed, the intent and objective of the use of this force, and the situation in which the victims found themselves'.[138]

---

[131] See, e.g., BBC, 'Profile: Hussain Osman', 9 July 2007, at http://bbc.in/2IW3DpB.
[132] *Armani da Silva v. United Kingdom* (App. No. 5878/08), application lodged on 21 January 2008.
[133] *Armani da Silva v. United Kingdom*, Judgment (Grand Chamber), 30 March 2016, para. 208.
[134] Ibid., para. 248.
[135] European Court of Human Rights, *Makaratzis v. Greece*, Judgment (Grand Chamber), 20 December 2004, paras. 51, 52.
[136] See *infra* with respect to use of firearms in automatic firing mode.
[137] European Court of Human Rights, *Acar and others v. Turkey*, Judgment (Fourth Section), 24 May 2005, paras. 78, 79.
[138] Inter-American Court of Human Rights, *Rochela Massacre v. Colombia*, Judgment (Merits, Reparations, and Costs), 11 May 2007, paras. 123–25.

Ammunition

7.60 In the shooting of Mr de Menezes, the firearms officers used hollow-point rounds rather than full-metal-jacket bullets.[139] This issue was not addressed by the European Court in its judgment in the *da Silva* case. As their name suggests, hollow-point rounds do not have a jacket that covers the front of the bullet. Such ammunition therefore expands (or 'mushrooms') when entering the human body, depositing much of its kinetic energy in the first twenty centimetres. This reduces the likelihood that the bullet will pass through ('overpenetrate' or 'through-and-through' penetrate) the body of the target, potentially wounding or even killing an unintended third party.

7.61 The use of bullets 'which expand or flatten easily in the human body'[140] is not only prohibited as a means of warfare in the conduct of hostilities under the law of armed conflict; when used with the requisite *mens rea*, it is punishable as a war crime under the 1998 Rome Statute of the International Criminal Court.[141] This prohibition does not apply to law enforcement operations.[142]

7.62 In fact, law enforcement officials often use expanding ammunition also in submachine guns, carbines, and rifles. Indeed, increasingly, such bullets are routinely used by law enforcement officials in all of their firearms around the world in order to minimise the risk to the general public who may be bystanders during a confrontation between the police and an armed suspect. In 1998, the New York City Police Department (NYPD) became 'almost the last' US law enforcement agency to change from full-metal-jacket to hollow-point rounds. They did so following a two-year period in which fifteen bystanders were struck by full-metal-jacket bullets fired by police officers; of these, five were hit by bullets that had passed through other people, and two were hit by bullets that had passed through objects.[143] Within Europe, expanding bullets are used more or less routinely by police forces in, among others, Austria, Belgium, Denmark, Finland, France, Germany, the Netherlands, Norway, Spain, Sweden, Switzerland, Turkey, and the United Kingdom.

7.63 Moreover, given the risk of overpenetration from full-metal-jacket rounds fired from both handguns and rifles, the duty of precaution under international human rights law could be interpreted to require that police and other law enforcement officials be

---

[139] See, e.g., S. Wright, 'De Menezes: Police Used Special "Hollow-Point" Bullets Designed to Kill Instantly', *Daily Mail*, last updated 15 October 2007, at http://dailym.ai/2O4eiNy.

[140] These include soft-point and open-tip match rounds.

[141] Art. 8(2)(b)(xix), ICC Statute (applicable in international armed conflict) and Art. 8(2)(e)(xv), ICC Statute (in non-international armed conflict).

[142] In 2005, the International Committee of the Red Cross (ICRC) inaccurately asserted that 'expanding bullets commonly used by police in situations other than armed conflict are fired from a pistol and therefore deposit much less energy than a normal rifle bullet or a rifle bullet which expands or flattens easily. Police forces therefore do not normally use the type of expanding bullet that is prohibited for military rifles.' ICRC Study of Customary International Humanitarian Law, Rule 77: 'Expanding Bullets', at http://bit.ly/2n4Acol.

[143] M. Cooper, 'New York Police Will Start Using Deadlier Bullets', *New York Times*, 9 July 1998, at http://nyti.ms/2OoSMt5.

equipped with appropriate expanding ammunition.[144] This standard may not yet represent international *lex lata* but could be *de lege ferenda*. As of writing, it seemingly remained the case that 'no application has yet been brought to a human rights court or other human rights mechanism by an innocent bystander hit by a police full-metal-jacket bullet that overpenetrated through the target. Were such a case to arise, an applicant might have an arguable case for a violation of his or her right to life.'[145]

Modes of Firing

7.64 There are three main modes of firing on many rifles and submachine guns: single shot, burst, and fully automatic mode. Single shot or semi-automatic mode fires a single round each time the trigger is pulled without the need for reloading. Burst mode involves the firing of multiple rounds (e.g., two or three) with one pull of the trigger. In fully automatic mode, when the trigger is depressed, the weapon will continue firing until the magazine is empty or the trigger is released, whichever is sooner.[146] Only semi-automatic mode should be used in law enforcement operations.[147]

7.65 In its judgment in the *Nachova* case, the Grand Chamber of the European Court of Human Rights found that grossly excessive force had been used, in part because of the use of a rifle in automatic mode, which 'could not possibly have aimed with any reasonable degree of accuracy using automatic fire'.[148] In its 2015 judgment in the *Kitanovski* case, a chamber of the European Court referred to the holding in *Nachova* and affirmed that 'it is absolutely impossible to aim with a reasonable degree of accuracy using automatic fire'.[149] In its 2020 judgment in the *Kukhalashvili* case, the Court declared that 'having recourse to automatic weapons within the close confines of the prison walls would necessarily have meant that the risk of causing fatalities was inordinately high, owing to such weapons being used in close proximity to the prison population'.[150]

---

[144] Thus certain bullets intended to cause maximum injury in big game hunting would not be lawful for use against human targets. See also R. Sanchez, 'Brutal Message in Bullet's Hollow Point', *Washington Post*, 10 January 1994, at http://wapo.st/2vbqKUC.

[145] Casey-Maslen and Connolly, *Police Use of Force Under International Law*, p. 142.

[146] For example, the widely used Heckler and Koch G-36 assault rifle has a model with default settings of single shot, two-shot burst, and fully automatic fire. See, e.g., http://bit.ly/2LOAChq.

[147] In the 1996 case of *Makwati v. State*, the appellant was a member of the Special Support Group (SSG) of the Botswana Police Service. Several police officers had been assaulted during the night, and the following day, the appellant and others went to look for persons who had assaulted their colleagues. The appellant was in possession of an AK-47 assault rifle. When he sought to arrest a suspect, this man brushed aside the appellant's firearm and ran away. The appellant fired three shots from his AK-47 in automatic mode from behind the deceased, all of which struck him. There were no warning shots fired, it was during daylight, and there were many police officers surrounding the deceased's yard. The court held that the appellant had gone far beyond the limited protection afforded by domestic law in shooting dead the suspect with an assault rifle in automatic mode. The appellant was convicted of manslaughter by the Court of Appeal of Botswana. *Makwati v. State* 1996 BLR 682.

[148] European Court of Human Rights, *Nachova v. Bulgaria*, Judgment (Grand Chamber), 6 July 2005, para. 108.

[149] European Court of Human Rights, *Kitanovski v. North Macedonia*, Judgment (First Section), 22 January 2015, para. 56.

[150] European Court of Human Rights, *Kukhalashvili v. Russia*, Judgment (Fifth Section), 2 April 2020, para. 153.

7.66 In South Africa, one of the most notorious incidents of recent years involving police use of force was the fatal shooting of thirty-four striking miners by officers of the South African Police Service (SAPS) and the injury of more than seventy others in August 2012. The events took place at Marikana in the North West Province.[151] The Commission of Inquiry that was subsequently established to investigate the tragedy reported that in the main volley of fire, SAPS officers fired off three hundred rounds in eight seconds, some using rifles in fully automatic mode. One expert witness, Lieutenant-Colonel Classen, testified that this was 'grossly negligent', while the policing expert called by SAPS said that in his view automatic rifle fire 'has no place' in law enforcement.[152]

7.67 In their joint report of 2016, the UN Special Rapporteurs on the rights to freedom of peaceful assembly and of association (Maina Kiai), and on extrajudicial, summary or arbitrary executions (Christof Heyns) stated that automatic firearms should not be used under any circumstances in the policing of assemblies.[153] In its General Comment No. 37 on the right of peaceful assembly, adopted in July 2020, the Human Rights Committee stated that 'it is never lawful to fire indiscriminately or to use firearms in fully automatic mode when policing an assembly'.[154] Indeed, any discharge of a firearm in fully automatic mode during a law enforcement operation would amount to a violation of international human rights law because each shot must be targeted at a specific individual and justified in the circumstances.

Warning Shots

7.68 The firing of warning shots is controversial owing to the risk of harming innocent bystanders, and State practice in law enforcement in this regard is mixed. Principle 10 of the 1990 Basic Principles requires law enforcement officials to 'identify themselves as such and give a clear warning of their intent to use firearms, with sufficient time for the warning to be observed, unless to do so would unduly place the law enforcement officials at risk or would create a risk of death or serious harm to other persons, or would be clearly inappropriate or pointless in the circumstances of the incident'. Such a warning could, though, be verbal and not necessarily involve discharge of the weapon.

7.69 In some countries, such as Brazil or the United States, warning shots are generally discouraged or even prohibited.[155] In Nigeria, an Order (revised in 2019) stated that 'under no circumstance will warning shots be fired over the head of persons violently

---

[151] See generally *Marikana Commission of Inquiry: Report on Matters of Public, National and International Concern Arising Out of the Tragic Incidents at the Lonmin Mine in Marikana, in the North West Province*, 31 March 2015, available at http://bit.ly/2Kh8JN.
[152] Ibid., p. 258.
[153] 'The Proper Management of Assemblies', Joint report of the Special Rapporteur on the rights to freedom of peaceful assembly and of association, Maina Kiai, and the Special Rapporteur on extrajudicial, summary or arbitrary executions, Christof Heyns, UN doc. A/HRC/31/66, 4 February 2016, para. 67(e).
[154] Human Rights Committee, General Comment No. 37: Article 21: right of peaceful assembly, UN doc. CCPR/C/GC/37, 27 July 2020, para. 88.
[155] The NYPD Guidelines on the Use of Firearms, for instance, stipulate simply that 'police officers shall not fire warning shots'. See, e.g., *NYPD Annual Firearms Discharge Report 2012*, 2013, at http://on.nyc.gov/2AA7OnG.

assembled'.[156] In 1998, an article in a US journal, *Law and Order*, examined the danger, value, and legality of police use of warning shots 'to gain compliance from a suspect'.[157] It noted that many police departments had had in place a policy against warning shots for years, owing to concern that a warning shot might result in unintended injury or death to a suspect or bystander. On the other hand, the authors argued that there is 'evidence that a safely placed warning shot can shock a suspect into compliant behaviour that precludes shooting the suspect'.[158]

7.70 In January 2017, the National Consensus Policy on Use of Force was published, a policy supported by eleven professional law enforcement bodies in the United States. While acknowledging that warning shots are 'inherently dangerous', the Policy proposes that they be permitted when they have 'a defined target'; 'the use of deadly force is justified'; the warning shot 'will not pose a substantial risk of injury or death to the officer or others'; and 'the officer reasonably believes that the warning shot will reduce the possibility that deadly force will have to be used'.[159] Despite being termed a consensus policy, the provisions on warning shots remain controversial among US law enforcement personnel.[160]

7.71 In other national jurisdictions, such as Denmark, Germany, Greece, Israel, the Netherlands, Switzerland, Tunisia, or Turkey, for instance, police officers may be required (or at least authorised) in certain circumstances to fire a warning shot before firing on an individual.[161] The 2001 European Code of Police Ethics also endorses the use of warning shots. According to the official commentary on a provision concerning police use of force, 'if lethal weapons are deemed necessary, they should not be used beyond what

---

The California Department of Justice's 2015 *Law Enforcement Policy & Procedures Manual*, states that 'generally, warning shots or shots fired for the purpose of summoning aid are discouraged and may not be discharged unless the agent reasonably believes that they appear necessary, effective and reasonably safe'. California Department of Justice's March 2015 *Law Enforcement Policy & Procedures Manual*, §304.1.2 (Warning Shots), at http://bit.ly/2c9eBF9. In contrast, LAPD policy provides that 'warning shots shall only be used in exceptional circumstances where it might reasonably be expected to avoid the need to use deadly force. Generally, warning shots shall be directed in a manner that minimizes the risk of injury to innocent persons, ricochet dangers and property damage.' LAPD, 2015 *Use Of Force Year-End Review*, 'The Department's Use of Force Policy', p. 55. With respect to counterpiracy law enforcement operations, the US Coast Guard and the Department of Homeland Security have observed that a warning shot 'means a signal to a vessel to stop. The term does not include shots fired as a signal that the use of deadly force is imminent, a technique that should not be employed.' US Coast Guard and the Department of Homeland Security, 'Guidance on Self-Defense or Defense of Others by U.S. Flagged Commercial Vessels Operating In High Risk Waters', Port Security Advisory (3–09), 18 June 2009, para. 2(i), p. 2.

[156] See the Nigeria profile on the Laws on the Rights of Peaceful Assembly Worldwide, at http://bit.ly/2mUM5QP. Capital letters in original.

[157] D. E. Mulroy and J. Santiago, 'Warning Shots Revisited', *Law and Order*, vol. 46, no. 4 (April 1998), pp. 96–9.

[158] Ibid.

[159] *National Consensus Policy on Use of Force*, January 2017, p. 4, at http://bit.ly/2KqszlC. See also in this regard Martin Kaste, 'Police Warning Shots May Be in for a Comeback', NPR, 28 March 2017, at http://n.pr/2vpxqhg.

[160] See, e.g., K. Johnson, 'Should Cops Be Able to Fire Warning Shots in Tense Situations? Even Police Sharply Disagree', *USA Today*, 25 October 2017, at http://usat.ly/2lkuoL9.

[161] 2004 Act on Police Activities, s. 17(2).

is considered strictly necessary – shoot to warn before shoot to wound and do not wound more than is strictly necessary'.[162]

7.72 The 2007 judgment by a chamber of the European Court of Human Rights in the *Bakan* case addressed the use of warning shots by a Turkish *gendarme* against a fleeing suspect that missed and ricocheted, killing an innocent bystander. Turkish law required warning shots and then shooting at the legs, before 'free' shooting was permissible.[163] A chamber of the European Court found that the killing in this case was accidental and noted as a salient fact that the *gendarme* had not used his assault rifle in automatic mode.[164] Two years later, in its judgment in the *Kallis and Androulla Panayi* case, also against Turkey, the Court, citing Basic Principle 10, gave its 'opinion' that 'opening of fire should, whenever possible, be preceded by warning shots'.[165] This stance was approved by the Court's Grand Chamber in 2011 in its judgment in the *Giuliani and Gaggio* case.[166]

7.73 In sum, however, there is no clear rule under international law that determines whether or not a warning shot is required (where feasible), or, in the alternative, is unlawful. Wherever it is reasonably possible to do so, a verbal warning should precede any discharge of a firearm.

USE OF LESS-LETHAL WEAPONS

Terminology and Definitions

7.74 There is no internationally agreed definition of the term 'less-lethal weapon', though there is a general understanding that any such weapons are 'less lethal' by comparison to firearms. Earlier international instruments, such as the 1990 Basic Principles, do not employ the term, referring instead to 'non-lethal weapons' or 'non-lethal incapacitating weapons'.[167] The more modern nomenclature of less-lethal weapon is, though, explicitly used in Human Rights Council Resolution 38/11, adopted without a vote in July 2018, on the 'promotion and protection of human rights in the context of peaceful protests'.[168] The resolution does not, however, define less-lethal weapons. In the UN Guidance on Less-Lethal Weapons in Law Enforcement (2020), the following definition is offered:

> Weapons designed or intended for use on individuals or groups of individuals and which, in the course of expected or reasonably foreseen use, have a lower risk of causing death or serious injury than firearms. Less-lethal ammunition may be fired from conventional

---

[162] *European Code of Police Ethics*, adopted by the Committee of Ministers of the Council of Europe on 19 September 2001, official commentary on para. 37, available at http://bit.ly/2LWjS7a.
[163] European Court of Human Rights, *Bakan v. Turkey*, Judgment (Second Section), 12 June 2007, para. 34.
[164] Ibid., paras. 54–5.
[165] European Court of Human Rights, *Kallis and Androulla Panayi v. Turkey*, Judgment (Fourth Section), 27 October 2009, para. 62.
[166] European Court of Human Rights, *Giuliani and Gaggio v. Italy*, Judgment (Grand Chamber), 24 March 2011, para. 177.
[167] Principle 2, 1990 Basic Principles.
[168] UN Human Rights Council Resolution 38/11, adopted without a vote on 6 July 2018, paras. 13, 15, and 16.

firearms. For the purpose of this Guidance, the term includes conventional firearms when they are used to discharge less-lethal ammunition, but not when they are used to discharge conventional bullets or other ammunition that would be likely to result in life-threatening injuries.[169]

The Inter-American Commission on Human Rights has observed that the category of weapons considered 'non-lethal' or 'less lethal' could 'encompass a whole range of devices from rubber and rubber-coated bullets, tear gas, electric shock dart guns (tasers), water cannons, plastic bullets, to high sound and heat devices, and others'.[170]

General Considerations

7.75 Less-lethal weapons are those which are intended, designed, and/or used on individuals to reduce the risk of death or serious injury when compared to the effects of firearms using 'live' ammunition. As the Human Rights Council has cautioned, 'even less-lethal weapons can result in a risk to life'.[171] When used appropriately, however, less-lethal weapons can serve to protect the right to life. Thus the 1990 Basic Principles urge governments and law enforcement agencies to

> equip law enforcement officials with various types of weapons and ammunition that would allow for a differentiated use of force and firearms. These should include the development of non-lethal incapacitating weapons for use in appropriate situations, with a view to increasingly restraining the application of means capable of causing death or injury to persons.[172]

The Human Rights Committee's General Comment 36 on the right to life calls on States Parties to the International Covenant on Civil and Political Rights (ICCPR) to 'take all necessary measures intended to prevent arbitrary deprivations of life by their law enforcement officials, including soldiers charged with law enforcement missions. These measures include . . . the supplying of forces responsible for crowd control with effective "less-lethal" means and adequate protective equipment in order to obviate their need to resort to lethal force."[173]

7.76 Regional human rights courts have taken a stricter stance than the Human Rights Committee, typically adjudging a violation of the right to life in circumstances when it finds that law enforcement officials should have been equipped with appropriate less-lethal weapons and instead had recourse only to firearms. Thus the Inter-American Commission on Human Rights has noted that States

---

[169] *United Nations Guidance on Less-Lethal Weapons in Law Enforcement* (2020), p. 45.
[170] Inter-American Commission on Human Rights, *Gross Human Rights Violations in the Context of Social Protests in Nicaragua*, OAS doc. OEA/Ser.L/V/II, Doc. 86, 21 June 2018, para. 96, at http://bit.ly/2KAO1Jp.
[171] UN Human Rights Council Resolution 38/11, 6 July 2018, para. 15. Similarly, the Inter-American Commission on Human Rights has recalled that 'almost all use of force', including the use of less-lethal weapons, 'may cause serious injury or even the death of a person'. Inter-American Commission on Human Rights, *Gross Human Rights Violations in the Context of Social Protests in Nicaragua*, 2018, para. 96.
[172] Principle 2, 1990 Basic Principles.
[173] Human Rights Committee, General Comment 36 on the right to life, para. 13.

have an obligation to provide their police with the means, weaponry and equipment that will enable them to use nonlethal force in the procedures they follow to lawfully deter and suppress violence and crime. Within the region, there have been multiple cases in which the right to life was violated by members of the state security forces. These deaths could have been avoided had the members of the state security forces been equipped with nonlethal means of deterrence and adequate protective equipment, rather than relying strictly on firearms to perform their assigned function.[174]

7.77 In its judgment in the *Güleç* case, the European Court of Human Rights similarly regretted that *gendarmes* in Turkey 'used a very powerful weapon because they apparently did not have truncheons, riot shields, water cannon, rubber bullets or tear gas'.[175] The Court further observed that the lack of such equipment was 'all the more incomprehensible and unacceptable' because the province where the use of force occurred was 'in a region in which a state of emergency has been declared, where at the material time disorder could have been expected'.[176]

Design and Testing

7.78 Where law enforcement officials are duly equipped with less-lethal weapons, the weapons must have already been appropriately designed and tested, and the officials trained in their lawful and proper use prior to deployment. This falls within the broader duty to adopt legislation on use of force by law enforcement officials as well as governing regulations and standing operating procedures (SOPs). Thus, in its Resolution 38/11, the Human Rights Council encouraged States 'to make appropriate protective equipment and less-lethal weapons available to their officials exercising law enforcement duties in order to decrease their need to use weapons of any kind, while pursuing efforts to regulate and establish protocols for the training and use of less-lethal weapons'.[177]

7.79 The 1990 Basic Principles stipulate: 'The development and deployment of non-lethal incapacitating weapons should be carefully evaluated in order to minimize the risk of endangering uninvolved persons, and the use of such weapons should be carefully controlled.'[178] Certain weapons will be inherently unlawful; examples include spiked or electrified batons[179] and blinding lasers.[180] Such weapons are not, though, rendered unlawful by the right to life, but are of a nature to cause excessive injury without fulfilling

---

[174] Inter-American Commission on Human Rights, *Report on Citizen Security and Human Rights*, OAS doc. OEA/Ser.L/V/II, Doc. 57, 31 December 2009, para. 115.
[175] European Court of Human Rights, *Güleç v. Turkey*, Judgment, 27 July 1998, para. 71.
[176] Ibid.
[177] UN Human Rights Council Resolution 38/11, 6 July 2018, para. 15.
[178] Principle 3, 1990 Basic Principles.
[179] European Commission Council Regulation No. 1236/2005 concerning trade in certain goods which could be used for capital punishment, torture, or other cruel, inhuman, or degrading treatment or punishment (as amended.), 27 June 2005.
[180] 1995 Protocol IV on blinding laser weapons to the 1980 Convention on Certain Conventional Weapons.

a legitimate law enforcement objective. They thus fall within the prohibition on inhumane treatment or punishment, such as contained in Article 7 of the ICCPR.

7.80 Testing will determine both whether the weapons are fit for purpose and identify factors that will endanger the life or well-being of the targets of their use. The Human Rights Committee has stated:

> While preferable to more lethal weapons, States parties should ensure that 'less-lethal' weapons are subject to strict independent testing and evaluate and monitor the impact on the right to life of weapons such as electro-muscular disruption devices ('Tasers), ... rubber or foam bullets, and other attenuating energy projectiles, ... which are designed for use or are actually used by law enforcement officials, including soldiers charged with law enforcement missions.[181]

Similarly, UNODC and the OHCHR have advocated thorough testing of less-lethal weapons by means of a process that is conducted 'independently from corporate interest'. In particular, 'data and information about capabilities and functions, as provided by manufacturers should not be accepted without independent testing prior to the introduction of the instrument to the law enforcement agency'.[182]

Controlling Use

7.81 The result of testing should feed directly into regulations and SOPs and related training. The Inter-American Commission on Human Rights, for instance, has noted that 'when using less lethal weapons, one should bear in mind ... the design or characteristics of the weapon'.[183] Likewise, the 1990 Basic Principles stipulate that the use of less-lethal weapons 'should be carefully controlled'.[184] With respect to the right to life, a number of weapons raise particular concerns as it is relatively straightforward to use them in a way that would imperil life. These weapons – police batons, electric-shock weapons, kinetic energy projectiles, and chemical irritants dispersed at a distance – are discussed in turn.

Police Batons

7.82 The baton or truncheon is the police officer's most common less-lethal weapon.[185] Designs vary widely: in shape (in addition to traditional, straight batons, side-handled batons are increasingly common); material (earlier designs of wood have been largely replaced by rubber, plastic, or metal), length; and weight. These vectors substantially influence the consequent amount of striking power that can be generated. Side-handled batons, for instance, can generate up to nine times the striking power of conventional

---

[181] Human Rights Committee, General Comment 36 on the right to life, para. 14.
[182] UNODC and OHCHR, *Resource Book on the Use of Force and Firearms in Law Enforcement*, pp. 74–5.
[183] Inter-American Commission on Human Rights, *Situation of Human Rights in Venezuela*, OAS doc. OEA/Ser.L/V/II, Doc. 209, 31 December 2017, para. 225, at http://bit.ly/2nbTbgL.
[184] Principle 3, 1990 Basic Principles.
[185] One survey found that nine in ten law enforcement officials carry one. M. Schlosser, 'Don't Forget about Your Baton', *Police: The Law Enforcement Magazine*, 10 October 2016, at http://bit.ly/2vkuT93 (accessed 31 July 2018).

straight batons, while 'a baton that is too light or too small may cause an officer to strike a subject repeatedly to effectively control a suspect. ... While a heavier baton is more likely to cause injury, this risk is reduced when strikes are properly delivered to an approved target area on the body and is more likely to be effective in a single strike.'[186]

7.83 Certain parts of the body are particularly vulnerable to baton strikes, leading to a greater risk of death or serious injury. For example, blows to the head, neck, and throat, spine, kidneys, and solar plexus could result in 'significant injury with bruising and rupture of internal organs, including the heart, liver, spleen, or kidneys or a head injury'.[187] Indeed, Portuguese Police Regulations prohibit baton strikes to certain areas of the body such as the head, neck, or spine 'in view of their potential lethal consequences, unless there is a potentially lethal threat'. The 2006 Peruvian Human Rights Manual for Police similarly instructs officers to avoid baton strikes to the head, neck, and thorax.[188] Other means of using a baton than a strike are also potentially lethal, with neck holds presenting a 'high risk of serious injury or death as a result of large blood vessel or airway compression'.[189]

7.84 The *Perişan* case before the European Court of Human Rights concerned the death of numerous inmates at Diyarbakir prison from multiple injuries and fractures, in particular of the skull and ribs, resulting from baton strikes (as well as the impact from other blunt instruments). In addition to the eight who were killed in this way, a further six sustained life-threatening injuries. The Court found there had been a violation of the right to life with respect to all fourteen victims on the basis that the force used by officers had not been 'absolutely necessary' in the circumstances.[190]

7.85 In Uganda, the 2003 conviction and death sentence of prison warder Absolom Omolo Owiny was upheld on appeal in 2008. Mr Owiny was convicted of the murder of Wanok Michael after the appellant 'tortured and beat him up with a baton until he became unconscious. Later the same day, the deceased died from his injuries.'[191] The 2011 case of *United States v. Matthew Dean Moore and Melvin Williams* concerned the beating to death of Raymond Robair. Officer Williams was charged with 'unreasonably kicking Robair and striking him with his police baton while acting as a New Orleans Police

---

[186] As cited in AELE, *Assault and Battery: Baton/Nightstick*, undated, at http://bit.ly/2AOie30. Similarly, a study by the Canadian Police Research Centre of the pros and cons of the baton in common use noted that 'the small size of the baton is unable to generate enough kinetic energy to cause effective control of a violent subject. This increases the likelihood of continued multiple strikes[,] ... increasing (risks) ... to both the subject and the officer.' Canadian Police Research Centre, TR-02-2003 *Collapsible Baton Officer Safety Unit Edmonton Police Service*, Report, 2003, p. 10.

[187] J. J. Payne-James et al., 'Clinical Forensic Medicine: History and Development', in M. M. Stark (ed.), *Clinical Forensic Medicine: A Physician's Guide*, Humana Press, New York, 2005, p. 19.

[188] UNODC and OHCHR, *Resource Book on the Use of Force and Firearms in Law Enforcement*, p. 82.

[189] G. M. Vilke, 'Neck Holds', in D. L. Ross and T. C. Chan (eds.), *Forensic Science and Medicine: Sudden Deaths in Custody*, Humana Press, New York, 2006, pp. 15–27.

[190] European Court of Human Rights, *Perişan and others v. Turkey*, Judgment (Second Section), 20 May 2010, paras. 86–9. See also with respect to use of batons European Court of Human Rights, *R. R. and R. D. v. Slovakia*, Judgment (Third Section), 1 September 2020.

[191] *Absolom Omolo Owiny v. Uganda*, Criminal Appeal No. 321 of 2003, [2008] UGCA 2, Judgment of 7 April 2008, at http://bit.ly/2LW8qZY.

Department police officer, wilfully depriving Robair of his right to be free from the use of unreasonable force by a law enforcement officer'.[192] The defendants appealed against their convictions and sentence. In February 2013, the US Court of Appeals for the Fifth Circuit (covering Louisiana, Mississippi, and Texas) upheld the decision of the district court.[193]

7.86 In the United Kingdom, a jury in the Inquest into the death of Ian Tomlinson, who was on his way from work at the time of the G20 demonstrations in London in 2009, returned a verdict of 'unlawful killing'. They found that Ian Tomlinson was 'fatally injured ... as a result of a baton strike from behind and a push in the back by a police officer which caused Mr Tomlinson to fall heavily. Both the baton strike and the push were excessive and unreasonable. Mr Tomlinson ... was complying with police instructions to leave. ... He posed no threat.'[194] A subsequent court case acquitted the officer who had used force of a charge of manslaughter.[195] A Metropolitan Police Disciplinary Panel, though, found the officer guilty of gross negligence.[196]

Electric-Shock Weapons

7.87 Projectile electric-shock weapons are devices capable of applying, at a distance, an electric-shock to a target via one or more projectiles. The most common brand name is Taser.[197] The projectiles are most commonly wired darts, or 'probes', though other variants exist. The electric shock in a projectile electric-shock weapon is devised with a view to engendering neuro-muscular incapacitation. However, simply drawing and aiming the red-dot laser of the weapon on a suspected (often referred to as 'red-dotting') may prevent an encounter with law enforcement from escalating into a violent and perhaps even life-threatening event. Certain other electric-shock weapons can also produce a non-incapacitating electric-shock when pressed directly against the body (referred to as 'drive-stun' mode).

7.88 The OHCHR has stated that 'among other uses, conducted electrical weapons are used by law enforcement officials to incapacitate, at a distance, individuals posing an imminent threat of injury (to others or to themselves)'.[198] Electric-shock weapons thus may be used as a less-lethal alternative to firearms in situations where firearms would be

---

[192] US Court of Appeals (for the Fifth Circuit), *United States* v. *Matthew Dean Moore and Melvin Williams*, Government Brief (Case No. 11-30877), at http://bit.ly/2nbO5kz.
[193] US Court of Appeals (for the Fifth Circuit), *United States* v. *Matthew Dean Moore and Melvin Williams*, Judgment (Case No. 11–30877), 11 February 2013, at http://bit.ly/2vl17AT.
[194] INQUEST, 'Jury's Verdict of Unlawful Killing at Inquest into Death of Ian Tomlinson Vindicates Family and Public Concern', 3 May 2011, available at http://bit.ly/2vq5laD (accessed 31 July 2018).
[195] R. S. Bray, 'Paradoxical Justice: The Case of Ian Tomlinson', *Journal of Law and Medicine*, vol. 21, no. 2 (2013), pp. 447–72.
[196] P. Walker, 'Ian Tomlinson Case: PC Simon Harwood Guilty of Gross Misconduct', *The Guardian*, 17 September 2012, at http://bit.ly/2nbXwAz.
[197] The term Taser is sometimes used erroneously to refer to all electric-shock weapons, but it is a brand name of an electric-shock weapon produced by Axon (formerly Taser International). See: Axon, 'Taser International, Inc. Trademark Policy and Use Guidelines', January 2016, at http://bit.ly/2nlndC1.
[198] United Nations Human Rights Guidance on Less-Lethal Weapons in Law Enforcement (2020), para. 7.4.3, citing US Court of Appeals (for the Fourth Circuit), *Armstrong* v. *Village of Pinehurst*, Judgment, 11 January 2016, pp. 19, 21.

lawful,[199] though they require careful training to ensure the distance between the two probes fired into the target's skin is sufficient to result in neuro-muscular incapacitation. Thick clothing may also prevent an effective electrical current from passing into the body.[200] Electric-shock weapons are also used in certain situations of imminent threat of harm, where the use of firearms would be unlawful.

7.89 A number of cases have been documented where individuals have died following the application of projectile electric-shock weapons, though the risk of death and serious injury from the weapon is considered 'low to very low'.[201] A study by Reuters identified 1,042 deaths involving projectile electric-shock weapons in the United States, of which, in cases where autopsy findings were available, the weapon was listed as a cause of death or a contributory factor in 160.

7.90 In *Heston v. City of Salinas and Taser International Inc. and Others*, which concerned the death of Robert Heston after repeated and prolonged Taser discharges, a federal jury found Taser International liable for failure to warn that 'prolonged exposure to electric-shock from the device ... poses a risk of cardiac arrest in a person against whom the device is deployed'.[202] International good practice calls for an automatic cut-off to be incorporated into every electric-shock weapon after five seconds.[203] Another potential risk from the use of electric-shock weapons may be to a foetus. It has been reported that 'spontaneous abortion has been linked' to the discharge of an electric-shock weapon, 'although the strength of the association is uncertain'.[204]

---

[199] United Nations Human Rights Guidance on Less-Lethal Weapons in Law Enforcement (2020), para. 7.4.3.
[200] In *Arnold v. Buck*, the Taser was initially used in an attempt to stop a man who was believed to have a knife from making good his escape. Although the Taser was fired, the weapon was ineffective leading to the officers then discharging a firearm against the individual. US District Court for Connecticut, *Arnold v. Buck*, Judgment (Case No. 3:11-cv-1343 (VLB)), 2 August 2013, at http://bit.ly/2AFvd76.
[201] Defence Scientific Advisory Council Sub-Committee on the Medical Implications of Less-Lethal Weapons (DOMILL), 'Statement on the Medical Implications of Use of the Taser X26 and M26 Less-Lethal Systems on Children and Vulnerable Adults', Doc. Dstl/BSC/27/01/11 dated 4 April 2011 (amended 27 January 2012), United Kingdom, at http://bit.ly/2LRXRHs (accessed 5 August 2018).
[202] L. Wilson, 'The Implication of Taser Failure to Warn Liability for Police Misconduct Lawsuits', *Law Report*, vol. 10, no. 6 (2011), pp. 1–9. See further US District Court for the Northern District of California (San José Division), *Betty Lou Heston and others v. City of Salinas and others*, Judgment (Case No. C 05-03658 JW), 30 January 2009, at http://bit.ly/2AHN39B.
[203] United Nations Human Rights Guidance on Less-Lethal Weapons in Law Enforcement (2020), para. 7.4.4. The case of *Family Members of Anastasio Hernández-Rojas, Petitioners v. United States*, in which the deceased had been beaten and shocked multiple times, was before the Inter-American Commission on Human Rights as of writing. The petitioners affirm that the Taser's log recorded that it was activated 'at least four times. ... This log recorded that the first and second administrations lasted five seconds, the third thirteen seconds, and the fourth for twelve seconds.' *Family Members of Anastasio Hernandez-Rojas v. United States*, Complaint, March 2016, submitted on behalf of the Petitioners, Inter-American Commission on Human Rights, p. 26, at http://bit.ly/2LYHnwB. In its response, the US Department of State noted that under a 2017 settlement agreement, the US Government provided US$1 million to the Estate of Mr. Hernández Rojas. 'Hernandez Rojas v. United States, Pet. No. P-524-16, Response of the United States, Sept. 12, 2017', at http://bit.ly/2mTn1tu.
[204] DOMILL, 'Statement on the Medical Implications of Use of the Taser X26 and M26 Less-Lethal Systems on Children and Vulnerable Adults'.

7.91 Death may also result from secondary injuries resulting from the use of an electric-shock weapon. This is particularly the case when the victim of the shock is on a high wall or on top of a building. For example, in July 2014, a homeless man with mental health issues was shocked by a Taser while he was sitting on top of a rooftop billboard in Los Angeles. LAPD officers tried to grab him but he fell to the ground, missing an airbag that had been placed for his protection. He suffered serious head injuries and died later. A subsequent inquiry found that the officer's discharge of his Taser departed from LAPD policy and training, which generally discourages use against an individual who is in danger of falling 'which would likely result in death or serious bodily injury'.[205]

7.92 The electrical discharge from a Taser can also ignite flammable substances. In 2016, Devon and Cornwall Police in the United Kingdom paid compensation to the parents of a man who was set alight after being struck by a Taser discharge (albeit without accepting any liability for the death). Andrew Pimlott, a thirty-two-year-old man, had doused himself in fuel and was holding a lit match when the weapon was fired at him outside his parents' house in Plymouth in April 2013. He died a few days afterwards from severe burns. An inquest found the Taser was the most likely cause of the fuel igniting. A police spokesman said: 'Whilst the outcome of the inquest in 2015 did indicate that the Taser was the most likely cause of the ignition, no criticism was levied at the force or the officer, and confirmed the officer had used his Taser in accordance with national training.'[206]

Kinetic Impact Projectiles

7.93 Kinetic impact projectiles cover a range of less-lethal projectiles that are launched from firearms and are designed to be effective by the force of the kinetic energy they impart when they impact the body. Projectiles come in a range of calibres and sizes and encompass a range of ammunition usually made of plastic, rubber, or wood. 'Rubber-coated' bullets are composed of a metal core coated in rubber. There are also 'bean-bag rounds' (fabric pillows filled with metal pellets). Weapons can typically deliver either a single projectile at a time or multiple projectiles simultaneously.

7.94 A 2016 review conducted by two non-governmental human rights organisations, the International Network of Civil Liberties Organisations and Physicians for Human Rights, considered 1,925 people who had suffered injury as a result of being struck by kinetic impact projectiles. Of these, 53 died from their injuries and 294 suffered permanent disability, most often loss of sight.[207] A 2001 joint study by scientists, academics, and law enforcement personnel in the United States, which tested 80 different types of kinetic impact munition, identified their 'general inaccuracy'. They also noted the 'large variations' in the momentum they imparted, noting that 'the human effect' of the variation

---

[205] 'Skid Row Residents Criticize LAPD after Death of Mentally Ill Man', *Los Angeles Times*, 2 July 2014, at http://lat.ms/2OM8VUf. See also US District Court for the District of Oregon, *Snauer v. City of Springfield and Officer E. Sether*, Findings and Recommendations (Case No. 09-CV-6277-TC), 1 October 2010, at http://bit.ly/2vGoKjP.
[206] BBC, 'Andrew Pimlott: Police Pay Family of Taser Death Man', 17 August 2016, at http://bbc.in/2GTRePw.
[207] International Network of Civil Liberties Organisations and Physicians for Human Rights, *Lethal in Disguise: The Health Consequences of Crowd Control Weapons*, 2016, at http://bit.ly/2vkLCc6.

'could range from ineffective to tragic'.[208] The inaccuracy of many projectiles combined with a high kinetic energy imparted to the human target increases the risk of death not only to the target but also to bystanders.

7.95 Especial concern exists with respect to rubber-coated bullets. According to UNODC and the OHCHR, there are 'particular risks attached to the use of rubber coated metal bullets, which are conceived to be less-lethal but are still potentially lethal and carry a high risk of serious injury to a person depending on the body part hit'.[209] In its 2020 judgment in the *Andreea-Marusia Dumitru* case, the European Court of Human Rights noted that the applicant, a fifteen-year-old girl at the time of the police operation, had arrived in Bucharest hospital in a state of haemorrhagic shock. She had a thirty square centimetre wound in the right of her abdomen and had suffered massive internal and external haemorrhaging, serious physical damage to her liver, and a ruptured diaphragm, and several of her ribs had been broken. During emergency surgery, the doctors removed ten rubber bullets and a fragment of a cartridge shell fired by the police from her stomach, and were forced to ablate part of her liver.[210]

7.96 In its 2018 report on social protests in Nicaragua, the Inter-American Commission on Human Rights identified a 'pattern identified with regard to the infliction of severe injuries by state agents ... (by) shooting of rubber bullets by anti-riot squad personnel straight at young demonstrators, sometimes aiming for their eyes'. They noted that 'the Commission considers that the acts of violence aimed directly at the vital organs of people who did not pose an imminent threat to the lives of the State security agents constitute arbitrary use of force and, where they resulted in deaths, extrajudicial executions'.[211]

7.97 The 1984 case of *Stewart v. United Kingdom* concerned the death of a thirteen-year-old boy, Brian Stewart, who was hit on the head with a plastic bullet (known as a baton round). It was reported that the soldier was hit by a missile as he fired, causing him to move the weapon away from its intended trajectory and unintentionally hit Brian Stewart. The Court found that the force used was 'no more than absolutely necessary in action lawfully taken for the purpose of quelling a riot' under Article 2 of the European Convention on Human Rights, in a situation where soldiers were 'confronted with a hostile and violent crowd of 150 persons who were attacking them with stones and other missiles'.[212]

---

[208] Applied Research Laboratory, Pennsylvania State University, and Los Angeles Sheriff's Department, *The Attribute Based Evaluation of Less than Lethal, Extended Range, Impact Munitions*, United States, 2001, available at http://bit.ly/2ngvF25.
[209] UNODC and OHCHR, *Resource Book on the Use of Force and Firearms in Law Enforcement*, p. 94.
[210] European Court of Human Rights, *Andreea-Marusia Dumitru v. Romania*, Judgment (Fourth Section), 31 March 2020, para. 11.
[211] Inter-American Commission on Human Rights, *Gross Human Rights Violations in the Context of Social Protests in Nicaragua*, 2018, para. 108.
[212] European Commission on Human Rights, *Kathleen Stewart v. United Kingdom*, Decision on Admissibility, 10 July 1984.

Chemical Irritants Dispersed at a Distance

7.98 The most widely used chemical irritant dispersed at a distance is CS[213] (either micronised powder or pyrotechnically generated smoke), which is typically discharged either in the form of projectiles or from grenades shot from a launcher. Tear gas is often used to describe CS and other lachrymatory agents used by police forces. Death may result either from the effects of inhalation of the chemical irritant on a vulnerable person[214] or from the kinetic impact on the body of the grenade housing the irritant.[215] A stampede may also occur when irritants are used against a crowd in enclosed areas, such as a football stadium, without the possibility of escape. In such cases, the consequences may be lethal.[216] The 1992 Chemical Weapons Convention[217] prohibits the use of riot control agents such as tear gas as a method of warfare, but makes an explicit exception for their use for law enforcement, 'including domestic riot control'.[218]

THE DUTY TO PROTECT

7.99 Beyond the duty to respect the right to life of those individuals they encounter, law enforcement agencies and officials also have a duty of due diligence to protect all individuals within their jurisdiction from harm.[219] As the Minnesota Protocol on the Investigation of Potentially Unlawful Death (2016) recalls, this is

> particularly the case where state officials have specific information about threats against one or more identified individuals; or where there is a pattern of killings where victims are linked by political affiliation, sex, sexual orientation or gender identity, religion, race or ethnicity, caste, or social status.[220]

7.100 The obligation on the State to protect individuals in their relations with others was first confirmed by the European Court on Human Rights in its 1998 judgment in the *Osman* case. The Court set out three criteria to determine whether a violation of

---

[213] 2-chlorobenzalmalononitrile.

[214] In October 2015, it was reported that an eight-month-old Palestinian baby had died after inhaling teargas in a village near Bethlehem. The baby, Ramadan Mohammad Faisal Thawabta, was said by the Palestinian Ministry of Health to have suffocated inside his family home in Beit Fajjar, a village south of Bethlehem. K. Shuttleworth, 'Baby Dies in West Bank after Inhaling Teargas, Says Palestinian Ministry', *The Guardian*, 30 October 2015, at http://bit.ly/2M2K3Jj.

[215] European Court of Human Rights, *Abdullah Yaşa and others v. Turkey*, Judgment (Second Section), 16 July 2013, para. 29.

[216] See, e.g., 'Sheriff's Acknowledge Using Fire-Starting Pyrotechnic Tear Gas Against Dorner', CBS Los Angeles, 13 February 2013.

[217] Convention on the Prohibition of the Development, Production, Stockpiling and Use of Chemical Weapons and on Their Destruction; adopted at Geneva 3 September 1992; entered into force 29 April 1997.

[218] Art. II(9), 1992 Chemical Weapons Convention.

[219] See, e.g., Human Rights Committee, General Comment No. 31 on The Nature of the General Legal Obligation Imposed on States Parties to the Covenant, UN doc. CCPR/C/21/Rev.1/Add.13, 26 May 2004, para. 8.

[220] *Minnesota Protocol on the Investigation of Potentially Unlawful Death (2016)*, OHCHR, New York/Geneva, 2017, para. 8(b).

the right to life had occurred: was the victim threatened in a real and immediate way; did the authorities know this (or ought they have known it); and did they take reasonable measures to counter that risk?[221] The three criteria are cumulative in application, meaning that if law enforcement officials have failed to take reasonable measures to counter a real and immediate risk that was known or should have been known, that would engage the responsibility of the State for a violation of the right to life.

7.101 In the United Kingdom, the *Ebrahimi* case sheds further light on the domestic obligation of the duty on law enforcement officials to protect the vulnerable. Bijan Ebrahimi, a person with mental disabilities, was beaten to death and set alight on a Bristol estate by his neighbour Lee James in July 2013, who wrongly believed he was a paedophile. A 'collective failure' by Avon and Somerset Police and Bristol City Council was identified, along with institutional racism in which both parties 'repeatedly sided' with the Iranian national's abusers, who had targeted him for 'racist abuse and victimisation'.[222] Following a report by the then Independent Police Complaints Commission,[223] two police community support officers (PCSOs) and two police officers were dismissed by Avon and Somerset Police and two were convicted of 'misconduct in public office' and sentenced to terms of imprisonment.[224]

7.102 In its judgment in the 2017 *Tagayeva* case,[225] a chamber of the European Court of Human Rights found that Russia had failed to take reasonable measures to prevent a terrorist attack (the Beslan school siege of 2004 in North Ossetia). The authorities had learned of a planned attack on an educational institution in the region but had not stepped up security (indeed it had been reduced), nor had they warned schools, teachers, or pupils of the danger. As has been noted, 'the Court concluded unanimously that the information available to the Russian authorities was clear about the nature, imminence and location of the attack, and therefore Russia was under an obligation to take measures to prevent the taking of hostages'.[226] Russia was not granted leave to appeal the decision to the Grand Chamber.[227]

---

[221] European Court of Human Rights, *Osman v. United Kingdom*, Judgment, 28 October 1998. See J.-F. Akandji-Kombe, *Positive Obligations under the European Convention on Human Rights: A Guide to the Implementation of the European Convention on Human Rights*, Human Rights Handbooks, No. 7, Council of Europe, at http://bit.ly/2M5MaMy, pp. 25–6.

[222] BBC, 'Bijan Ebrahimi Murder: Bristol City Council Calls for Fresh Probe', 15 January 2018, at http://bbc.in/2AEVKli.

[223] The IOPC has since been renamed the Independent Office for Police Conduct. See its official website at www.policeconduct.gov.uk.

[224] Ibid. See also T. Cork, 'Disgraced Policeman Jailed for Gross Misconduct over Ebrahimi Murder Case Remains Defiant and Said "The Jury Got It Wrong"', *Bristol Live*, 26 February 2018, at http://bit.ly/2vEldoV.

[225] European Court of Human Rights, *Tagayeva and others v. Russia*, Judgment (First Section), 13 April 2017.

[226] S. Galani, 'Hostages and Human Rights at the European Court of Human Rights: The Tagayeva and Others v Russia Case', University of Bristol Law School Blog, Posted 8 May 2017, at http://bit.ly/2vE1Blo.

[227] BBC, 'Beslan Siege: Russia "Will Comply" with Critical Ruling', 20 September 2017, at http://bbc.in/2OM9bmr.

8

Counterterrorism

INTRODUCTION

8.01 This chapter describes how the duty on States to respect and protect the right to life applies to counterterrorism operations. The 2005 Council of Europe Convention on the Prevention of Terrorism describes its purpose as follows: 'to enhance the efforts of Parties in preventing terrorism and its negative effects on the full enjoyment of human rights, in particular the right to life'.[1]

8.02 According to Statista, there were 32,836 fatalities from terrorism in 2018, the highest recorded annual figure for its data consolidation in the thirteen-year period 2006–18.[2] In early 2020, the UN Counter-Terrorism Committee Executive Directorate (CTED) reported that, despite losing territory it once controlled and the death of its leader, the Islamic State 'posed, and is likely to continue to pose, a significant global challenge, maintaining a diminished, but enduring presence in Iraq and the Syrian Arab Republic, as well as a network of regional and national affiliates'. Other terrorist groups, the report continued, 'including those affiliated with Al-Qaida, also continued to pose a threat, seeking to exploit conditions conducive to the spread of violent extremism, which can be conducive to the spread of terrorism, in States suffering from political instability and ongoing or unresolved armed conflicts'.[3]

8.03 The chapter begins by defining – to the extent possible, given dispute as to the issue among States – the terms 'terrorism' and 'counterterrorism'. It then discusses how the duty to respect and protect life, especially with regard to the jus cogens prohibition on arbitrary deprivation of life, affects the legality of counterterrorism operations under global human rights treaties and standards. The corresponding treatment of counterterrorism operations under regional treaties and standards is then considered. The final section of the chapter

---

[1] Art. 2, Convention on the Prevention of Terrorism; adopted at Warsaw 16 May 2005; entered into force 1 June 2007. As of 1 May 2021, 40 States were party to the Convention and a further 8 were signatories.
[2] Statista, 'Number of Fatalities Due to Terrorist Attacks Worldwide between 2006 and 2018', October 2019, at http://bit.ly/2Cygb4T.
[3] 'Report to the Counter-Terrorism Committee on the Activities and Achievements of the Counter-Terrorism Committee and Its Executive Directorate during the Period from 2018 to 2019', Annex 1 to Letter dated 5 February 2020 from the Chair of the Security Council Committee established pursuant to resolution 1373 (2001) concerning counter-terrorism addressed to the President of the Security Council, UN doc. S/2020/99, 5 February 2020, para. 5.

looks at rules restricting the use of force in counterterrorism in a situation of armed conflict.

The Definition of Terrorism and Counterterrorism

8.04 International law does not seek to define what is considered purely domestic terrorism, that is to say, terrorism in which the victims and perpetrators are of the same nationality and the acts constituting a terrorist offence all take place in the country of their nationality. Thus, for instance, the 1997 Terrorist Bombings Convention stipulates: 'This convention shall not apply where the offence is committed within a single State, the alleged offender and the victims are nationals of that State, the alleged offender is found in the territory of that State and no other State has a basis ... to exercise jurisdiction.'[4]

8.05 This means, in effect, that States may cast domestic terrorism in broad terms. That said, in its General Comment 37 on the right of peaceful assembly as set out in the International Covenant on Civil and Political Rights (ICCPR),[5] the UN Human Rights Committee stated: 'While acts of terrorism must be criminalised in conformity with international law, the definition of such crimes must not be overbroad or discriminatory and must not be applied so as to curtail or discourage the exercise of the right of peaceful assembly.... The mere act of organising or participating in a peaceful assembly cannot be criminalized under anti-terrorism laws.'[6] As an illustration, the Committee cited its 2018 Concluding Observations on Bahrain's initial State Party report on its implementation of the Covenant:

> The Committee acknowledges the State party's need to adopt measures to combat terrorism. However, it is concerned that the Act on the Protection of Society from Acts of Terrorism (Act No. 58 of 2006) includes an overly broad definition of terrorism that provides too much room for interpretation and may result in violations of the right to freedom of expression, association and assembly. The Committee is also concerned about reports of the extensive use of the Act outside the scope of terrorism, including against human rights defenders and political activists, and of violations of article 14 of the Covenant [on fair trial rights] in the context of trials based on the Act.[7]

8.06 There is, however, no consensus as to the definition of 'international terrorism' in international law. Indeed, for the last two decades, the conclusion of the Comprehensive Convention on International Terrorism has been stymied by, primarily, lack of agreement as to the parameters of the term. Major sticking points include whether the acts of groups

---

[4] Art. 3, International Convention for the Suppression of Terrorist Bombings; adopted at New York 15 December 1997; entered into force 23 May 2001. As of 1 May 2021, of the 197 States recognised by the UN Secretary-General, 170 were party to the Convention and a further 2 were signatories.
[5] Art. 21, International Covenant on Civil and Political Rights; adopted at New York 16 December 1966; entered into force 23 March 1976. As of 1 May 2021, 173 States were party to the ICCPR.
[6] Human Rights Committee, General Comment No. 37: Article 21: right of peaceful assembly, UN doc. CCPR/C/GC/37, 27 July 2020, para. 68 (footnote omitted).
[7] Human Rights Committee, Concluding Observations on the Initial Report of Bahrain, UN doc. CCPR/C/BHR/CO/1, 15 November 2018, para. 29.

182 Major Themes

fighting against foreign military occupation or engaged in an armed struggle for independence from colonial rule are to be considered terrorist in nature. For others, the acts of armed forces of States should not fall within the scope of the Convention.[8]

8.07 In 2018, before the UN General Assembly, Saudi Arabia, speaking on behalf of the Organization of Islamic Cooperation, committed to resolving outstanding issues. Noting that terrorism contradicts the principles of Islam, it called for more dialogue, but added that it is vital to distinguish between terrorism and the legitimate rights of people to resist foreign occupation, 'a distinction duly observed in international law'.[9] The Gambia, speaking for the African Group, said that any act of terrorism is a flagrant violation of international law. The Gambia supported the work done so far in drafting the Comprehensive Convention but said that the text should not deny people their right to self-determination. El Salvador, speaking on behalf of the Community of Latin American and Caribbean States, described the lack of a definition for terrorism as an 'unjustifiable legal gap'.[10]

8.08 That said, the general contours of the crime of international terrorism are well known. In the first counterterrorism treaty adopted by States under UN auspices, the 1979 Hostage-Taking Convention in its preamble called for 'effective measures for the prevention, prosecution and punishment of all acts of taking of hostages, as manifestations of international terrorism'.[11] It defined the crime of hostage-taking substantively as

> Any person who seizes or detains and threatens to kill, to injure or to continue to detain another person (hereinafter referred to as the 'hostage') in order to compel a third party, namely, a State, an international intergovernmental organization, a natural or Juridical person, or a group of persons, to do or abstain from doing any act as an explicit or implicit condition tor the release of the hostage commits the offence of taking of hostages ('hostage-taking') within the meaning of this Convention.[12]

Thus, the core elements of the crime of hostage-taking under the 1979 Convention were stipulated to be acts or threats of violence with a view to compelling a change of conduct on the part of a State (or other subject of international law).

8.09 An alternative intent for international terrorism to that of changing State behaviour was indicated in the 1997 Terrorist Bombings Convention. Thereunder, States Parties are obligated to 'adopt such measures as may be necessary' to criminalise acts within the scope of the Convention, 'in particular where they are intended or calculated to provoke a state

---

[8] See, e.g., M. Hmoud, 'Negotiating the Draft Comprehensive Convention on International Terrorism: Major Bones of Contention', *Journal of International Criminal Justice*, vol. 4, no. 5 (November 2006), pp. 1031–43.
[9] UN, 'Fight against International Terrorism Impeded by Stalemate on Comprehensive Convention, Sixth Committee Hears as Seventy-Third Session Begins', UN doc. GA/L/3566, 3 October 2018, at http://bit.ly/3aDkHfg.
[10] Ibid.
[11] International Convention Against the Taking of Hostages; adopted at New York 17 December 1979; entered into force 3 June 1983 (hereinafter, 1979 Hostage-Taking Convention). As of 1 May 2021, 176 States were party to the Convention and a further 2 States were signatories.
[12] Art. 1(1), 1979 Hostage-Taking Convention.

of terror in the general public or in a group of persons or particular persons'.[13] This centres on the notion of terrorism as the intentional killing of civilians.[14] But the Terrorist Bombings Convention also deems as terrorist attacks on the military infrastructure of the State. In adhering to it, Pakistan issued a declaration whereby nothing in the Convention 'shall be applicable to struggles, including armed struggle, for the realization of right of self-determination launched against any alien or foreign occupation or domination, in accordance with the rules of international law'. Many States objected to this apparent reservation.[15] Finland, for instance, was 'of the view that the declaration amounts to a reservation as its purpose is to unilaterally limit the scope of the Convention'. Finland further considered the declaration 'to be in contradiction with the object and purpose of the Convention, namely the suppression of terrorist bombings wherever and by whomever carried out'.[16]

8.10 A comprehensive definition was, however, concretising around the targeting of civilians, as reflected in the 1999 Terrorist Financing Convention.[17] In Article 2(1)(b), it is stipulated that an offence pertains to any act

> intended to cause death or serious bodily injury to a civilian, or to any other person not taking an active part in the hostilities in a situation of armed conflict, when the purpose of such act, by its nature or context, is to intimidate a population, or to compel a government or an international organization to do or to abstain from doing any act.

The challenges to the acceptance of the definition were again, though, evident. Egypt, for instance, made a declaration upon its ratification of the Convention whereby 'Egypt does not consider acts of national resistance in all its forms, including armed resistance against foreign occupation and aggression with a view to liberation and self-determination, as terrorist acts within the meaning of article 2, paragraph 1, subparagraph (b), of the Convention.'[18]

8.11 The definition in Article 2 of the draft Comprehensive Convention on International Terrorism, as elaborated in 2005, reads as follows:

> 1. Any person commits an offence within the meaning of the present Convention if that person, by any means, unlawfully and intentionally, causes:
>   (a) Death or serious bodily injury to any person; or

---

[13] Art. 5, 1997 Terrorist Bombings Convention.
[14] See 'A More Secure World: Our Shared Responsibility', Report of the High-level Panel on Threats, Challenges and Change, in UN doc. A/59/565, 2 December 2004, paras. 160, 164.
[15] Australia, Austria, Canada, Denmark, Finland, France, Germany, India, Ireland, Israel, Italy, Japan, Moldova, the Netherlands, New Zealand, Norway, Poland, Russia, Spain, Sweden, United Kingdom, and the United States.
[16] Declaration of Finland, 17 June 2003, at http://bit.ly/2YbSI1g.
[17] International Convention for the Suppression of the Financing of Terrorism; adopted at New York 9 December 1999; entered into force 10 April 2002. As of 1 May 2021, 189 States were party to the Convention and a further 2 States were signatories.
[18] Declaration of Egypt, at http://bit.ly/2FAC4So.

(b) Serious damage to public or private property, including a place of public use, a State or government facility, a public transportation system, an infrastructure facility or to the environment; or
(c) Damage to property, places, facilities or systems referred to in paragraph 1(b) of the present article resulting or likely to result in major economic loss;
when the purpose of the conduct, by its nature or context, is to intimidate a population, or to compel a Government or an international organization to do or to abstain from doing any act.
2. Any person also commits an offence if that person makes a credible and serious threat to commit an offence as set forth in paragraph 1 of the present article.
3. Any person also commits an offence if that person attempts to commit an offence as set forth in paragraph 1 of the present article.

This definition retains the broadest notion of international terrorism outside the conduct of hostilities by armed forces or groups in an armed conflict.[19] It effectively comprises the attacking of any person or any property beyond a minimum threshold of violence. As an example, any foreign national engaged in the 'Yellow Vest' movement that paralysed France in 2019 and who daubed graffiti on a national monument could potentially be considered an international terrorist under the definition.

8.12 In 2011, the Appeals Chamber of the Special Tribunal for Lebanon, an ad hoc mechanism created in relation to the bombing that killed former Lebanese Prime Minister Rafik Hariri on 14 February 2005, issued a decision in which it claimed that international terrorism during peacetime was already defined under customary international law and that it comprised the following three key elements:

(a) the perpetration of a criminal act (such as murder, kidnapping, hostage-taking, or arson), or threatening such an act;
(b) the intent to spread fear among the population or to coerce a national or international authority to take some action or to refrain from taking it; and
(c) when the act involves a transnational element.[20]

Yet, given that the adoption of the Comprehensive Convention on International Terrorism remains precluded by lack of agreement on the definition, the holding by the Special Tribunal for Lebanon was not persuasive.[21] Indeed, in the Tribunal's own judgment against four accused, issued in August 2020, the Trial Chamber affirmed not only that the Appeals Chamber's 'lengthy (41 page)' consideration of the 'apparent existence of a customary international law definition of terrorism' was '*obiter dicta*', the Trial Chamber was also 'not convinced that one exists'.[22]

---

[19] Art. 20(2), Draft Comprehensive Convention on International Terrorism (2005).
[20] Special Tribunal for Lebanon, *Interlocutory Decision on the Applicable Law: Terrorism, Conspiracy, Homicide, Perpetration*, Cumulative Charging (Case No. STL-11-01/I), 16 February 2011, para. 85.
[21] See, e.g., M. Milanovic, 'Special Tribunal for Lebanon Delivers Interlocutory Decision on Applicable Law', *EJIL Talk!*, published on 16 February 2011, at http://bit.ly/3gb00Zo.
[22] Special Tribunal for Lebanon, *Prosecutor v. Salim Jamil Ayyash and others*, Judgment (Case No. STL-11-01/T/TC), 18 August 2020, para. 6192. See also on this issue the Separate Opinion of Judge Janet Nosworthy, who

8.13 Correspondingly, it is also the case that no accepted definition of 'counterterrorism' exists in international law. Writing in 2006, Javier Ruperez, the Executive Director of CTED, observed that 'in order to conclude the accelerating effort to develop a global counter-terrorist policy led by the United Nations, it would be helpful to have both the [Comprehensive] convention and the definition'.[23] Nonetheless, the UN Security Council has long had a Counter-Terrorism Committee (CTC), established in the wake of the 11 September 2001 terrorist attacks in the United States. The CTC works to develop the ability of UN member States to prevent terrorist acts within their borders and across regions. The CTC is assisted by CTED, which carries out the policy decisions of the Committee, conducts expert assessments of each member State, and facilitates the provision of technical assistance in counterterrorism.[24] In its 2020 report to the UN Security Council, CTED noted: 'Efforts to ensure compliance with international human rights obligations while countering terrorism continued to be a priority concern for Member States and the Counter-Terrorism Committee.'[25]

8.14 As a working definition of counterterrorism, the US Department of Defense uses the following: 'Activities and operations taken to neutralize terrorists and their organizations and networks in order to render them incapable of using violence to instil fear and coerce governments or societies to achieve their goals.'[26] The UN Global Counter-Terrorism Strategy, which was adopted in 2006 under UN General Assembly Resolution 60/288,[27] is composed of four pillars – namely, addressing the conditions conducive to the spread of terrorism, measures to prevent and combat terrorism, measures to build States' capacity to prevent and combat terrorism and to strengthen the role of the UN system in that regard, and measures to ensure respect for human rights for all and the rule of law as the fundamental basis for the fight against terrorism.

8.15 In the annexed Plan of Action to the Global Counter-Terrorism Strategy, UN member States resolved 'to recognize that international cooperation and any measures that we undertake to prevent and combat terrorism must comply with our obligations under international law, including the Charter of the United Nations and relevant international conventions and protocols, in particular human rights law, refugee law and international humanitarian law'.[28]

---

asserts, but without adducing sufficient evidence, that the definition was *de lege ferenda* as custom as of 2005. See paras. 124–5.

[23] J. Ruperez, 'The United Nations in the Fight Against Terrorism', January 2006, at http://bit.ly/3h8XHqH.
[24] United Nations, 'The United Nations Security Council Counter-Terrorism Committee', at http://bit.ly/2EdkvHq.
[25] 'Report to the Counter-Terrorism Committee on the activities and achievements of the Counter-Terrorism Committee and its Executive Directorate during the period from 2018 to 2019', para. 19.
[26] 'Counterterrorism', in US Department of Defense, *DOD Dictionary of Military and Associated Terms*, as of November 2019, Washington, DC, at http://bit.ly/34cGg58, p. 53.
[27] UN General Assembly Resolution 60/288, adopted without a vote on 20 September 2006.
[28] Plan of Action, annexed to UN General Assembly Resolution 60/288, para. 3.

COUNTERTERRORISM UNDER GLOBAL STANDARDS

8.16 Notwithstanding the lack of agreed or accepted definitions of terrorism and counterterrorism, there is a duty upon every State to exercise due diligence to seek to prevent both international and domestic terrorism. This duty must be fulfilled in accordance with international human rights law, in particular respect for the right to life. In its General Comment 36 on the right to life,[29] the Human Rights Committee reminds 'all States' – not merely States Parties to the ICCPR – of their 'responsibility as members of the international community to protect lives and to oppose widespread or systematic attacks on the right to life', including 'international terrorism'.[30]

8.17 In its 2017 judgment in the *Tagayeva* case,[31] the European Court of Human Rights held that there existed a duty upon States Parties to the European Convention on Human Rights to prevent terrorism. It found for the first time that a State – Russia – had failed to meet its due diligence obligations under the right to life in this regard. The case concerned the siege at the school in Beslan in early September 2004, which ended with the deaths of more than three hundred teachers and children as a result of the storming of the school. The pupils and their teachers had been taken hostage by the Riyadus-Salikhin Reconnaissance and Sabotage Battalion of Chechen Martyrs,[32] an Islamist armed group designated as terrorist by the UN Security Council on 4 March 2003.[33]

8.18 The applicants had argued that the Russian authorities had known of a real and immediate threat to life but had failed to take reasonable preventive measures available to them.[34] In September 2014, two counterterrorism experts from the United Kingdom had produced a report following a request from the European Human Rights Advocacy Centre (EHRAC), the applicants' representatives.[35] The experts concluded that, while no security measures could serve as a guarantee against the attackers' success, the presence of security personnel on the roads and at potential targets would have acted as a deterrent and could have impeded the attackers. They considered that the fact that a group of more than 30 armed terrorists had been able to travel along the local roads to Beslan, having encountered only one police roadblock manned by a single officer, demonstrated 'the extent of failure of the authorities to act upon the information available to them'.[36]

---

[29] Human Rights Committee, General Comment No. 36: Article 6: right to life, United Nations (UN) doc. CCPR/C/GC/36, 3 September 2019 (hereinafter, Human Rights Committee, General Comment 36 on the right to life).

[30] Human Rights Committee, General Comment 36 on the right to life, para. 70.

[31] European Court of Human Rights, *Tagayeva and others* v. *Russia*, Judgment (First Section), 13 April 2017 (as rendered final on 18 September 2017).

[32] Mapping Militant Organizations, 'Riyadus-Salikhin Reconnaissance and Sabotage Battalion of Chechen Martyrs', Center for International Security and Cooperation (CISAC), Stanford University, last modified August 2018, at http://stanford.io/321r8F1.

[33] List at http://bit.ly/321NkyH.

[34] *Tagayeva and others* v. *Russia*, Judgment, para. 478.

[35] Ibid., para. 436.

[36] Ibid., para. 439.

8.19 In its assessment, the Court confirmed that it was 'acutely conscious of the difficulties faced by modern States in the fight against terrorism and the dangers of hindsight analysis'. In its role as the body tasked with supervising the human rights obligations under the European Convention on Human Rights, the Court 'would need to differentiate between the political choices made in the course of fighting terrorism, that remain by their nature outside of such supervision, and other, more operational aspects of the authorities' actions that have a direct bearing on the protected rights'.[37] For the Court to find a violation of the positive obligation to protect life, 'it must be established that the authorities knew, or ought to have known at the time, of the existence of a real and immediate risk to the life of identified individuals from the criminal acts of a third party and that they failed to take measures within the scope of their powers which, judged reasonably, might have been expected to avoid that risk'.[38] This obligation may apply, the Court declared, 'not only to situations concerning the requirement of personal protection of one or more individuals identifiable in advance as the potential target of a lethal act, but also in cases raising the obligation to afford general protection to society'.[39]

8.20 Against this background, the Court found that the information known to the authorities before the taking of hostages by the Riyadus-Salikhin Reconnaissance and Sabotage Battalion of Chechen Martyrs at Beslan school confirmed the existence of a real and immediate risk to life. At least several days in advance the authorities had sufficiently specific information about a planned terrorist attack in the areas in the vicinity of the Malgobek District in Ingushetia and targeting an educational facility on 1 September. The intelligence information likened the threat to major attacks undertaken in the past by the Chechen separatists, which had resulted in heavy casualties. A threat of this kind clearly indicated a real and immediate risk to the lives of the potential target population, including a vulnerable group of schoolchildren.[40] In the face of a threat 'of such magnitude, predictability, and imminence', it could reasonably be expected 'that some preventive and protective measures would cover all educational facilities in the districts concerned and include a range of other security steps, in order to detect, deter and neutralise the terrorists as soon as possible and with minimal risk to life'.[41]

8.21 Although some preventive measures were taken, these were inadequate. The terrorists were, the Court recalled, 'able to successfully gather, prepare, travel to and seize their target, without encountering any preventive security arrangements. No single sufficiently high-level structure was responsible for the handling of the situation, evaluating and allocating resources, creating a defence for the vulnerable target group and ensuring effective containment of the threat and communication with the field teams.'[42] In the

---

[37] Ibid., para. 481.
[38] Ibid., para. 482.
[39] Ibid.
[40] Ibid., para. 491.
[41] Ibid., para. 486.
[42] Ibid., para. 491.

prevailing circumstances, the Court found there had been a breach of the positive obligations under Article 2 of the Convention in respect of all applicants in the case.[43]

8.22 In addition to operational measures, there must also be an appropriate domestic legal framework in place. Thus, in interpreting the right to life under the ICCPR, the Human Rights Committee has declared that States Parties 'must enact a protective legal framework that includes effective criminal prohibitions on all manifestations of violence or incitement to violence that are likely to result in deprivation of life', such as 'terrorist attacks'.[44] The Committee notes that the criminal sanctions attached to such crimes 'must be commensurate with their gravity', while also remaining compatible with all the provisions of the Covenant.[45]

8.23 Counterterrorism operations must of course comply with the right to life, in particular the prohibition on arbitrary deprivation of life. This is especially pertinent to the use of firearms and *a fortiori* the use of explosive munitions. The standards for use of potentially or intentionally lethal force in all law enforcement operations are codified in the 1990 Basic Principles on the Use of Force and Firearms by Law Enforcement Officials,[46] specifically its Principle 9. This standard, which reflects customary international law applicable to all State use of force in counterterrorism outside the conduct of hostilities in an armed conflict, provides in full:

> Law enforcement officials shall not use firearms against persons except in self-defence or defence of others against the imminent threat of death or serious injury, to prevent the perpetration of a particularly serious crime involving grave threat to life, to arrest a person presenting such a danger and resisting their authority, or to prevent his or her escape, and only when less extreme means are insufficient to achieve these objectives. In any event, intentional lethal use of firearms may only be made when strictly unavoidable in order to protect life.

Thus an imminent threat to life or of serious injury will allow a law enforcement official to use a firearm to stop a terrorist suspect where other, less extreme means are insufficient. According to the UN Special Rapporteur on extrajudicial, summary or arbitrary executions, 'an imminent or immediate threat' should be considered 'a matter of seconds, not hours'.[47] This is the default scenario for the use of potentially lethal force.

8.24 In addition, in exceptional circumstances, a threat to life that is temporally proximate but not necessarily imminent, but where less hazardous means are inadequate, may also

---

[43] Ibid., para. 493.
[44] Human Rights Committee, General Comment 36 on the right to life, para. 20.
[45] Ibid.
[46] Basic Principles on the Use of Force and Firearms by Law Enforcement Officials; adopted at Havana by the Eighth UN Congress on the Prevention of Crime and the Treatment of Offenders 7 September 1990 (hereinafter, 1990 Basic Principles). In December 1990, the UN General Assembly welcomed the Basic Principles and invited governments to respect them. UN General Assembly Resolution 45/166, adopted without a vote on 18 December 1990, para. 4.
[47] Report of the Special Rapporteur on extrajudicial, summary or arbitrary executions, Christof Heyns, UN doc. A/HRC/26/36, 1 April 2014, para. 59.

justify recourse to the use of firearms. In both scenarios, the intent must be to incapacitate (stop) the terrorist suspect, but not to kill him or her. The Basic Principles also stipulate that 'exceptional circumstances such as internal political instability or any other public emergency may not be invoked to justify any departure from these basic principles'.[48]

8.25 Where it is absolutely necessary to kill a terrorist suspect, most notably when he or she is about to detonate a bomb or kill a hostage and no alternative course of action exists to prevent this occurring, it may be lawful to shoot with intent to kill. Intentional lethal use of force must be strictly unavoidable in order to protect life. The use of an explosive munition – mine, grenade, shell, or bomb – is to be considered an intentional lethal use of force. Thus, in 2014, the UN Special Rapporteur on extrajudicial, summary or arbitrary executions affirmed: 'A common sense understanding of the scope of application of Basic Principle 9 suggests that all weapons that are designed and are likely to be lethal should be covered, including heavy weapons such as bombs and (drone) missiles, the use of which constitutes an intentional lethal use of force.'[49]

COUNTERTERRORISM UNDER REGIONAL STANDARDS

8.26 The issue of counterterrorism has been addressed to varying extents in the interpretation and application of regional instruments. This is especially the case in the jurisprudence of the European Court of Human Rights and the work of the Inter-American Commission on Human Rights and the Inter-American Court of Human Rights. They apply, explicitly or implicitly, the standards set out in Basic Principle 9 to all law enforcement counterterrorism operations. The legal situation is more complex in a situation of armed conflict, and the European Court has struggled with the interrelationship between the right to life and international humanitarian law, especially where the respondent State denies the existence of an armed conflict (see the section below, 'Counterterrorism in the Conduct of Hostilities').

European Court of Human Rights' Jurisprudence

8.27 At the regional level, the 1950 European Convention on Human Rights[50] does not explicitly address counterterrorism. Under Article 2(2) of the Convention, deprivation of life shall not be regarded as a violation of the right to life when it results

from the use of force which is no more than absolutely necessary:

(a) in defence of any person from unlawful violence;
(b) in order to effect a lawful arrest or to prevent the escape of a person lawfully detained;
(c) in action lawfully taken for the purpose of quelling a riot or insurrection.

---

[48] Principle 8, 1990 Basic Principles.
[49] Report of the Special Rapporteur on extrajudicial, summary or arbitrary executions, 1 April 2014, para. 70.
[50] Convention for the Protection of Human Rights and Fundamental Freedoms; adopted at Rome 4 November 1950; entered into force 3 September 1953.

The notion of an insurrection may be considered to encompass an armed conflict not of an international character in the sense of Article 3 common to the four Geneva Conventions of 1949.

8.28 The European Court of Human Rights has addressed counterterrorism operations under the right to life in its judgments in a number of important cases, in particular *McCann v. United Kingdom* (1995); *Finogenov v. Russia* (2012); *Cangöz v. Turkey* (2016); *Armani da Silva v. United Kingdom* (2016); *Tagayeva v. Russia* (2017, a case discussed above with respect to one aspect of the judgment, prevention of a terrorist attack); and *Satybalova v. Russia* (2020).

The McCann Case

8.29 The Grand Chamber's 1995 judgment in the *McCann* case[51] is one of the European Court's most important and influential decisions. The case – the Court's first on the right to life – concerned the shooting to death by British soldiers of three members of the Irish Republican Army (IRA) in Gibraltar in 1988. The British soldiers had opened fire believing that the IRA members were about to remotely detonate a bomb. In fact, no bomb had yet been placed and it would have been detonated by a timing device, not by remote control. The Court accepted, however, that the soldiers honestly believed at the time of their use of force that it was necessary to shoot the suspects 'in order to prevent them from detonating a bomb and causing serious loss of life'.[52]

8.30 The Court held that the use of lethal force by agents of the State to achieve one of the aims set out in Article 2(2) of the European Convention on Human Rights 'may be justified ... where it is based on an honest belief which is perceived, for good reasons, to be valid at the time but which subsequently turns out to be mistaken'.[53] 'To hold otherwise', the Grand Chamber said, 'would be to impose an unrealistic burden on the State and its law-enforcement personnel in the execution of their duty, perhaps to the detriment of their lives and those of others'.[54]

8.31 Yet although it did not find a violation of the right to life for the use of lethal force, the Court also stated that it was obligated to 'carefully scrutinise ... not only whether the force used by the soldiers was strictly proportionate to the aim of protecting persons against unlawful violence but also whether the anti-terrorist operation was planned and controlled by the authorities so as to minimise, to the greatest extent possible, recourse to lethal force'.[55] This enunciation of a precautionary principle demanded thus that the Court ask 'whether the anti-terrorist operation as a whole was controlled and organised in a manner which respected the requirements of Article 2 ... and whether the information and instructions given to the soldiers which, in effect, rendered inevitable the use of lethal

---

[51] European Court of Human Rights, *McCann and others v. United Kingdom*, Judgment (Grand Chamber), 27 September 1995.
[52] Ibid., para. 200.
[53] Ibid.
[54] Ibid.
[55] Ibid., para. 194.

force, took adequately into consideration the right to life of the three suspects'.[56] The Court proceeded to answer these two questions in the negative.

The Finogenov Case

8.32 Members of the armed group that took over the school in Beslan in 2004 had occupied the Dubrovka theatre in Moscow on 23 October 2002, with several dozen heavily armed militants taking around a thousand people hostage. In resolving the crisis using force, Russian special forces first pumped a narcotic gas (in all likelihood, a derivative of the opiate, fentanyl) into the auditorium and then stormed the building. In addition to killing the hostage-takers, 129 or more of the hostages died, most as a result of choking on their own vomit or having suffocated as a result of a swollen tongue.[57]

8.33 As in its judgment in *McCann*, the European Court did not find a violation of the right to life on the basis of an unlawful use of force by the Russian authorities. The hostage-taking had come as a surprise 'so the military preparations for the storming had to be made very quickly and in full secrecy'; the Court further noted that the authorities were not in control of the situation inside the theatre. 'In such a situation', the Court accepted that 'difficult and agonising decisions' had to be made. It was prepared to grant the authorities 'a margin of appreciation, at least in so far as the military and technical aspects of the situation are concerned', even though, 'with hindsight', some of the decisions 'may appear open to doubt'.[58]

8.34 Following the Grand Chamber's approach in *McCann*, the precautionary principle was critical to a holding of a violation of the right to life by the European Court's First Section in *Finogenov*. It asked 'whether the authorities took all necessary precautions to minimise the effects of the gas on the hostages, to evacuate them quickly and to provide them with necessary medical assistance'.[59] The lack of adequate planning and preparation; the refusal to tell the medical staff outside and in nearby hospitals which toxic chemical it had used;[60] and the delay of an hour in evacuating the victims led the Court to hold that they had not.[61] Moreover, the duty to assist the injured applies even if the person or persons are themselves suspected offenders.[62]

The Cangöz Case

8.35 In 2005, the applicants' seventeen relatives were killed by members of the security services in south-east Turkey in contested circumstances.[63] The national investigating

---

[56] Ibid., para. 201.
[57] European Court of Human Rights, *Finogenov and others v. Russia*, Judgment (First Section), 20 December 2011 (as rendered final on 4 June 2012), paras. 24, 101.
[58] Ibid., para. 213.
[59] Ibid., para. 237.
[60] Ibid., paras. 254, 255, 257.
[61] Ibid., para. 266.
[62] S. Casey-Maslen and S. Connolly, *Police Use of Force under International Law*, Cambridge University Press, Cambridge, 2017, p. 96.
[63] European Court of Human Rights, *Cangöz and others v. Turkey*, Judgment (Second Section), 26 April 2016.

authorities had concluded that the deceased were members of an outlawed organisation who had been killed when the security forces returned their fire after coming under attack. But the security forces had been aware for a considerable time of their presence in the area and that their intention was to hold a meeting, not to engage in acts of violence. Despite this advance notice, there was no evidence that alternative, non-fatal methods to arrest them had been considered. The Court therefore had 'strong doubts' about whether lethal force had been necessary.[64]

8.36 Citing its decision in *McCann*, the Court's Second Section reiterated that law enforcement personnel 'in a democratic society are expected to show a degree of caution in the use of firearms even when dealing with dangerous terrorists'.[65] The government did not provide any evidence that 'clear instructions had been issued by those planning the operation as to how to capture and detain the suspects alive or as to how to negotiate a peaceful surrender'. That failure, in the opinion of the Court, 'must have increased the risk to the lives of any who might have been willing to surrender'.[66] In addition, the Turkish Government had claimed that 'the soldiers had responded to the terrorists with the same kind of weapons, namely assault rifles'. But in the autopsy report, the injuries on most of the bodies were said to have been caused by explosives. Video footage examined by the Court showed such extensive injuries that the Court deemed it 'impossible' that they could have been caused by assault rifles.[67]

8.37 The Court found that the investigation by the authorities 'was so manifestly inadequate and left so many obvious questions unanswered' that it could not rely on the conclusion reached at its completion.[68] As a consequence, the Court found that Turkey had failed to discharge its burden of proving that the killing of the applicants' seventeen relatives constituted a use of force which was no more than absolutely necessary or that it was a proportionate means of achieving the purposes advanced by them.[69] It concluded therefore that Turkey had violated the right to life of the applicants' seventeen relatives in its substantive aspect.

The Armani da Silva Case

8.38 This case concerned the intentional killing in 2007 by the Metropolitan Police of a suspected terrorist who was in fact an entirely innocent individual: a Brazilian electrician, Jean-Charles de Menezes, living and working in London. He was mistakenly believed to be a suicide bomber about to detonate explosives on a tube train in the British capital. The Grand Chamber did not find the United Kingdom responsible for a violation of Article 2 of the European Convention on Human Rights, holding that the principal question to be addressed in such a situation was whether the officer had 'an

---

[64] Ibid., para. 113.
[65] Ibid., para. 106.
[66] Ibid., para. 109.
[67] Ibid., para. 120.
[68] Ibid., para. 138.
[69] Ibid.

honest and genuine belief that the use of force was necessary'.[70] In its assessment, the Court 'will have to consider whether the belief was subjectively reasonable, having full regard to the circumstances that pertained at the relevant time'.[71]

8.39 What is surprising in the case is that neither the applicant nor the Court in its judgment addressed the legal implications of the manifest, significant failings in the State counterterrorism operation that led to the fatal shooting of Mr de Menezes. The failure by officers engaged in the surveillance operation to determine whether or not Mr de Menezes was one of the suspected terrorists appears to have been a critical factor that led to his wrongful shooting. Given the importance of the issue, better surveillance should have been ensured, consonant with the United Kingdom's duty of precaution under the right to life. This should have been a key determinant in assessing whether the United Kingdom had violated Mr de Menezes's right to life.

The Tagayeva Case

8.40 Some of the facts of this case were considered above.[72] In ending the hostage-taking crisis at the school in Beslan, Russia used very high levels of force, employing tanks, armoured personnel carriers equipped with large-calibre machine guns, and soldiers using portable grenade launchers and flame-throwers.[73] Many of the bodies were charred beyond recognition. On 17 September 2004, seventy-three bodies were taken to a forensic laboratory for identification through DNA testing.[74] The experts' report commissioned by EHRAC acknowledged that the situation faced by the Russian authorities, once the terrorists had reached their target, was a terrible one. The possibility of a peaceful outcome of the hostage-taking appeared minimal. The authorities were therefore required to make extraordinarily difficult and agonising decisions in a highly fluid situation.[75]

8.41 If the first explosions had been triggered by the detonation of an improvised explosive device (IED) placed by the terrorists, and they had started to shoot at the fleeing hostages, the authorities had no option but to launch a rescue operation. The intervention ended with massive loss of life, with accounts differing as to the use of flame-throwers and tank cannon fire. The experts stressed that these were military weapons destined to neutralise buildings with enemy combatants within. In their view, if these weapons had indeed been used at a time when hostages had still been within the building, it would have been unjustifiable.[76]

8.42 Overall, the Court found that the evidence supported a 'prima facie complaint that the State agents used indiscriminate weapons upon the building while the terrorists and

---

[70] European Court of Human Rights, *Armani da Silva v. United Kingdom*, Judgment (Grand Chamber), 30 March 2016, para. 248.
[71] Ibid.
[72] See, *supra*, Paragraph 8.17 *et seq*.
[73] *Tagayeva and others v. Russia*, Judgment, paras. 86–8, 94–5.
[74] Ibid., para. 104.
[75] Ibid., para. 444.
[76] Ibid., para. 446.

hostages were intermingled'. Accordingly, the Court stated, 'it seems impossible that it could be ensured that the risk to the hostages could be avoided or at least minimised'.[77] That said, the Court draws a distinction between 'routine police operations' and situations of large-scale counterterrorist operations.[78] The Court noted that Russia's Suppression of Terrorism Act

> remained silent not only on the types of weapons and ammunition that could be used, but also on the rules and constraints applicable to this choice. It did not incorporate in any clear manner the principles of using force that should be no more than 'absolutely necessary', such as the obligations to decrease the risk of unnecessary harm and exclude the use of weapons and ammunition that carried unwarranted consequences.[79]

8.43 The operation was aimed at saving lives and re-establishing law and order. Therefore, the commanders were obligated to consider the lives of more than one thousand people held by the terrorists, including hundreds of children. 'The hostages, who had been left exhausted by more than fifty hours of detention in stressful conditions, without access to food or water, clearly constituted a vulnerable group', the Court said. 'The acute danger of the use of indiscriminate weapons in such circumstances should have been apparent to anyone taking such decisions.'[80] The Court declared that 'errors of judgment or mistaken assessments, unfortunate in retrospect, will not in themselves entail responsibility under Article 2', but 'use of explosive and indiscriminate weapons, with the attendant risk for human life, cannot be regarded as absolutely necessary in the circumstances'. Accordingly, the Court held, there has been a violation of Article 2 of the European Convention on Human Rights by the State agents, 'on account of the massive use of lethal force'.[81]

The Satybalova Case

8.44 Particular constraints on the use of force occur when a terrorist suspect is in custody. On the evening of 2 May 2010, Marat Satybalov and six friends were driving to the countryside for a barbecue in two cars. On the way there, Mr Satybalov and two others who were driving together in one car stopped at a pharmacy in the village of Dylym in Dagestan to get painkillers.[82] The pharmacist thought that Mr M. G. looked suspicious 'with his long beard' and called the police.[83] Police officers from the Kazbekovskiy district police station arrived and searched him at gunpoint. They then approached the passengers in the car. The commander of the officers, Major A. S., dragged Mr Satybalov out of the car by his beard and hit him on the head with the butt of his machine gun. The officers then subjected Mr Satybalov and his two friends to beatings, hitting them with the butts of

---

[77] Ibid., para. 589.
[78] Ibid., para. 595.
[79] Ibid., para. 598.
[80] Ibid., para. 607.
[81] Ibid., paras. 609, 610.
[82] European Court of Human Rights, *Satybalova v. Russia*, Judgment (Third Section), 30 June 2020, para. 6.
[83] Ibid., para. 7.

their machine guns and kicking them. Then they took them to the police station without telling them the reasons for their detention.[84]

8.45 At the station, the three men were taken to the courtyard and subjected to beatings. They were punched, kicked, and hit with the butts of machine guns. They were then taken inside and asked repeatedly 'why they had long beards'. Major A. S. repeatedly pulled Mr Satybalov's beard, beat him, and continued to ask him about his beard. He filmed the ill treatment of the three men on his phone while insulting them. The three men were released the next day after having been fined for failure to obey police orders.[85]

8.46 Mr Satybalov's health worsened over the coming days. In the early hours of 6 May 2010, the applicants and their relatives took Mr Satybalov back to Khasavyurt hospital, where he immediately underwent emergency surgery. He had lost a lot of blood owing to internal bleeding following the beatings on 2 May 2010. Doctors performed further emergency surgery and informed the applicants that Mr Satybalov was in a critical condition. He had punctured lungs, broken ribs, and damage to his heart and arteries. His kidneys were severely damaged and had stopped functioning. On 7 May 2010, Mr Satybalov died in hospital.[86]

8.47 The Court reiterated that the obligation on the authorities to account for the treatment of an individual in custody is particularly stringent where that individual dies. In the absence of an adequate explanation, the Court can draw inferences which may be unfavourable for the respondent Government.[87] In fact, the Government neither disputed the ill-treatment of Mr Satybalov, nor that he had died as a result of the injuries inflicted during that ill-treatment.[88] Given that the authorities had failed to provide any explanation or justification for the use of force by the police against Mr Satybalov which led to his death, the Court held that his death could be attributed to the State and that Russia had violated his right to life.[89] Having found a violation of the right to life, as a result of the severity of the beatings, the Court went on to also hold that Russia had violated the prohibition on torture in Article 3 of the European Convention on Human Rights.[90]

The Inter-American Human Rights System

8.48 According to Article 4(1) of the 1969 American Convention on Human Rights, 'Every person has the right to have his life respected. . . . No one shall be arbitrarily deprived of his life.'[91] This includes suspected or convicted terrorists.

---

[84] Ibid., paras. 8–10.
[85] Ibid., paras. 11–16.
[86] Ibid., paras. 19–20.
[87] Ibid., para. 69.
[88] Ibid., para. 68.
[89] Ibid., paras. 69–70.
[90] Ibid., paras. 76–7.
[91] Art. 4, American Convention on Human Rights; adopted at San José 22 November 1969; entered into force 18 July 1978 (added emphasis).

8.49 The Inter-American Commission on Human Rights addressed both terrorism and counterterrorism in an important report in 2002.[92] The Commission observed that 'in situations where a state's population is threatened by violence, the state has the right and obligation to protect the population against such threats ... and in so doing may use lethal force in certain situations'. Citing Basic Principle 9 of the 1990 UN Basic Principles on the Use of Force and Firearms, the Commission stated that this 'includes, for example, the use of lethal force by law enforcement officials where strictly unavoidable to protect themselves or other persons from imminent threat of death or serious injury'.[93] 'Unless such exigencies exist', the Commission said, 'use of lethal force may constitute an arbitrary deprivation of life or a summary execution; that is to say, the use of lethal force must be necessary as having been justified by a state's right to protect the security of all'.[94]

8.50 The Inter-American Convention Against Terrorism was adopted by members of the Organization of American States (OAS) in 2002, entering into force in July 2003.[95] Its purposes, as set out in Article 1, are to 'prevent, punish, and eliminate terrorism'. It is explicit that the measures carried out by the States Parties under the Convention 'shall take place with full respect for the rule of law, human rights, and fundamental freedoms'.[96] The Convention does not, however, regulate the use of force in counterterrorism operations nor discuss the treatment of suspected or convicted terrorists.

8.51 The Inter-American Court of Human Rights has, however, issued a number of important judgments on specific counterterrorism operations, in particular in the cases of *Neira Alegría v. Peru*[97] (1995) and *Cruz Sánchez v. Peru*[98] (2015).

The Neira Alegría Case

8.52 This case concerned the violent repression of riots by the Peruvian military that took place on 18–19 June 1986 at the San Juan Bautista prison. Hundreds of prisoners in the Blue Pavilion area of the prison rioted, seized hostages, and armed themselves with weapons. To resolve the situation the State's naval forces demolished the building and blew down the prison walls with explosives. In total, 111 people died, of whom 97 could not be identified, including the three victims in this case. Each of the three had been charged with terrorist offences. Amnesty International alleged that summary executions of surrendered rioters occurred at the prison after its storming.[99] It was further suggested that the

---

[92] Inter-American Commission on Human Rights, *Report on Terrorism and Human Rights*, Organization of American States (OAS) doc. OEA/Ser.L/V/II.116 Doc. 5 rev. 1 corr., 22 October 2002, at http://bit.ly/318A2RC.
[93] Ibid., para. 87.
[94] Ibid., para. 88.
[95] Inter-American Convention Against Terrorism; adopted at Bridgetown 3 June 2002; entered into force 10 July 2003. Text available at http://bit.ly/2Q8b7HK. As of 1 May 2021, twenty-four States were party to it and a further ten were signatories. See http://bit.ly/3gcOrke.
[96] Art. 15(1), 2002 Inter-American Convention Against Terrorism.
[97] Inter-American Court of Human Rights, *Neira Alegría v. Peru*, Judgment (Merits), 19 January 1995.
[98] Inter-American Court of Human Rights, *Cruz Sánchez v. Peru*, Judgment (Preliminary Objections, Merits, Reparations, and Costs), 17 April 2015.
[99] *Neira Alegría v. Peru*, Judgment, para. 43.

final explosion that demolished the prison occurred not while an attack was in progress but afterwards, as a result of the blasting of the columns that sustained the building.[100]

8.53 The Court concluded that Víctor Neira-Alegría, Edgar Zenteno-Escobar, and William Zenteno-Escobar lost their lives due to the effects of the crushing of the violent uprising by the forces of the Government and as a consequence of disproportionate use of force.[101] The Court accepted that those detained in the Blue Pavilion of the San Juan Bautista Prison were 'highly dangerous and in fact armed', but held that this did not justify the amount of force that was used.[102] Indeed, a minority report by the Peruvian Congressional Commission on the operation found that 'the military force used was disproportionate in relationship to the actual danger present, and no precautionary measures were put into effect to reduce the human cost of crushing the riot'.[103] The Inter-American Court held that the right to life of each of the three men had been violated.[104]

The Cruz Sánchez Case

8.54 The case concerned the taking as hostages on 17 December 1996 of 379 people – Peruvian citizens and foreign nationals – by a commando of the Tupac Amaru Revolutionary Movement (MRTA) at the residence of the Ambassador of Japan in Lima. Several hostages were subsequently released in the course of talks with mediators. On 22 April 1997, the residence was stormed by the Peruvian military. All of the MRTA members who had seized the residence died; according to the official account, this occurred during fighting with State forces. The petitioners, however, alleged that in fact a number of guerrillas who had surrendered and who were in the effective custody of the State were summarily executed.[105]

8.55 The Inter-American Commission on Human Rights declared the petition admissible in 2004 and in 2011, it concluded that the Peruvian State was responsible for the violation of the rights to life, due process, and judicial protection.[106] In 2015, the Inter-American Court of Human Rights issued its judgment in the case, finding Peru responsible for the unlawful killing of MRTA member Eduardo Nicolás Cruz Sánchez. The Court reiterated that the duty to protect the right to life applies to every State institution responsible for security, including the police and armed forces.[107] The use of lethal force must be minimised, its constraints must be set down in law, and force used must never exceed that which is 'absolutely necessary' to repel violence or confront a threat.[108]

---

[100] Ibid., para. 52.
[101] Ibid., para. 72.
[102] Ibid., para. 74.
[103] Ibid., para. 62.
[104] Ibid., para. 76.
[105] Inter-American Commission on Human Rights, *Eduardo Nicolas Cruz Sanchez and Herma Luz Melendez Cueva v. Peru*, Report No. 13/04 (Case 136/03), OAS doc. OEA/Ser.L/V/II.122 Doc. 5 rev. 1 (2004).
[106] Inter-American Commission on Human Rights, *Eduardo Nicolas Cruz Sanchez and others v. Peru*, Report No. 66/10 (Case 12.444) (Merits), 31 March 2011, para. 5.
[107] Inter-American Court of Human Rights, *Cruz Sánchez v. Peru*, Judgment, 2015, para. 259.
[108] Ibid., para. 263.

8.56 The Court said that the right to life laid down in the Inter-American Convention was to be interpreted in the light of the 1990 Basic Principles on the Use of Force and Firearms.[109] At the same time, given the existence of a non-international armed conflict between Peru and the MRTA at the salient time, the Court acknowledged the application of Common Article 3 to the 1949 Geneva Conventions,[110] which prohibits the murder of those no longer taking an active part in hostilities.

8.57 The operation, at least in its early stages when fighting was occurring between the detainees and the naval ground forces, seems to have been considered as amounting to the conduct of hostilities under IHL. The Court held, though, that the overall operation was subject to the human rights precautionary principle enunciated by the European Court of Human Rights, as discussed previously.[111] In this regard, the authorities did not appear to have seriously considered the possibility that MRTA members could be captured, much less to have actively planned for this eventuality. The focus, they declared, was put squarely on rescuing the hostages.[112] Evaluating the forensic evidence and relevant testimony on the events related to the death of Eduardo Nicolás Cruz Sánchez, the Court considered that his death occurred after he had come within the custody of the State.[113] As a consequence, Peru had violated Mr Sánchez's right to life, as interpreted in the light of Common Article 3.[114]

African Charter on Human and Peoples' Rights

8.58 The 1981 African Charter on Human and Peoples' Rights does not specifically address the issue of counterterrorism.[115] In 2015, the African Commission on Human and Peoples' Rights adopted its General Comment on the right to life under Article 4 of the African Charter on Human and Peoples' Rights.[116] The General Comment stipulates that 'organised crime and terrorism can pose significant threats to the enjoyment of the right to life and require a robust State response, but one that at all times takes into account the requirements of international human rights law'.[117]

8.59 The same year, the Commission adopted its *Principles and Guidelines on Human and Peoples' Rights while Countering Terrorism in Africa*. Therein the African Commission

---

[109] Ibid., para. 264.
[110] Ibid., para. 270. See, e.g., Art. 3, Convention (IV) relative to the Protection of Civilian Persons in Time of War; adopted at Geneva 12 August 1949; entered into force 21 October 1950.
[111] Inter-American Court of Human Rights, *Cruz Sánchez v. Peru*, Judgment, 2015, para. 283. Although the Inter-American Court cited the European Court of Human Rights' judgment in the *Finogenov* case in this regard, that decision had not considered the application of international humanitarian law at any point.
[112] Ibid., paras. 285, 286.
[113] Ibid., para. 313.
[114] Ibid., para. 316.
[115] African Charter on Human and Peoples' Rights; adopted at Nairobi 27 June 1981; entered into force 21 October 1986.
[116] African Commission on Human and Peoples' Rights, General Comment No. 3 on the African Charter on Human and Peoples' Rights on the right to life (Article 4), adopted during its 57th Ordinary Session, Banjul, The Gambia, November 2015.
[117] Ibid., para. 2.

reiterated that the prohibition on arbitrary deprivation of life 'applies in the context of human rights abuses resulting from acts of terrorism and counterterrorism'. It also reaffirmed that the standard for lethal force is that laid down in Principle 9 of the 1990 Basic Principles on the Use of Force and Firearms.[118] In addition, counterterrorism operations must be 'strictly proportionate to the aim of protecting individuals against violence and be planned and controlled by the authorities so as to minimise, to the greatest extent possible, recourse to lethal or non-lethal force'.[119]

Arab Charter on Human Rights

8.60 The 2004 Arab Charter on Human Rights does not address the issue of terrorism or counterterrorism.[120] The 1998 Arab Convention on the Suppression of Terrorism had determined that 'all cases of struggle by whatever means, including armed struggle, against foreign occupation and aggression for liberation and self-determination, in accordance with the principles of international law, shall not be regarded as an offence'.[121] There is no mention of constraints imposed on the use of force in counterterrorism operations.

ASEAN Convention on Counter Terrorism

8.61 The 2007 Association of South-East Asian Nations (ASEAN) Convention on Counter Terrorism lays down a 'framework for regional cooperation to counter, prevent and suppress terrorism in all its forms and manifestations and to deepen cooperation among law enforcement agencies and relevant authorities of the Parties in countering terrorism'.[122] It is stipulated that any person taken into custody 'shall be guaranteed fair treatment, including enjoyment of all rights and guarantees in conformity with the laws of the Party in the territory of which that person is present and applicable provisions of international law, including international human rights law'.[123] The first preambular paragraph reaffirms the commitment of ASEAN Member States 'to protect human rights'. There is no mention of constraints imposed on the use of force in counterterrorism operations.

COUNTERTERRORISM IN THE CONDUCT OF HOSTILITIES

8.62 For several years, regional human rights courts struggled to interpret the right to life in a situation of armed conflict, in particular with respect to the application of international

---

[118] African Commission on Human and Peoples' Rights, *Principles and Guidelines on Human and Peoples' Rights while Countering Terrorism in Africa*, adopted by the African Commission during its 56th Ordinary Session in Banjul, Gambia (21 April to 7 May 2015), available at http://bit.ly/2FG8bjE, p. 17.
[119] Ibid.
[120] Arab Charter on Human Rights; adopted at Tunis 22 May 2004; entered into force 15 March 2008.
[121] Art. 2(a), Arab Convention on the Suppression of Terrorism; adopted at Cairo 22 April 1998; entered into force 7 May 1999.
[122] Art. I, ASEAN Convention on Counter Terrorism; adopted at Cebu City, The Philippines, 13 January 2007; entered into force 27 May 2011.
[123] Art. VIII(1), ASEAN Convention on Counter Terrorism.

humanitarian law. The European Court of Human Rights, for instance, seemed to develop a hybrid set of rules that adapted international humanitarian law rules and terminology to that of human rights protection and law enforcement rules. In a number of cases, it accepted that law enforcement rules should apply to the exclusion of international humanitarian law in conflict zones on the basis that, in particular, the governments of Russia and Turkey did not acknowledge the existence of an armed conflict within, respectively, Chechnya and the south-east.[124] Legal reasoning by the Court has since improved but it has still to articulate clearly how it perceives the relationship between respect for and protection of the right to life and international humanitarian law rules on targeting and use of force.

CASE LAW OF THE EUROPEAN COURT OF HUMAN RIGHTS

8.63 In its 2005 judgment in the *Isayeva* case, which concerned the bombing of a convoy of civilians escaping from the village of Katyr-Yurt on 30 January 2000, the Court noted that no martial law and no state of emergency had been declared in Chechnya at the time, and that no derogation had been made under Article 15 of the European Convention on Human Rights.[125] That much is true, but this is only part of the legal narrative. Indeed, the Court had overtly 'accepted' that the situation in Chechnya at the relevant time 'called for exceptional measures by the State in order to regain control over the Republic and to suppress the illegal armed insurgency'.[126] Moreover, Article 15 to which the Court referred speaks of 'lawful acts of war', whereas the situation in Chechnya at the time was a non-international armed conflict. Such an armed conflict is better considered as an insurrection under Article 2(2)(c) of the European Convention on Human Rights (as the Court had implicitly recognised) and no derogation is either possible or necessary.

8.64 The regional commander of Russian forces in Chechnya testified that his 'main aim had been to restore constitutional order in the western districts ... by disarming the illegal armed groups and, if they offered resistance, by eliminating them, i.e. conducting the military stage of the counter-terrorist operation'.[127] But since Russia denied the existence of any armed conflict in Chechnya, the Court decided instead to pursue Russia's contorted attempt to justify its actions as some form of ordinary law enforcement. 'The operation in question therefore has to be judged against a normal legal background', the Court concluded.[128]

---

[124] The European Court of Human Rights has delivered around 280 judgments finding violations of the European Convention on Human Rights which took place against the background of counterterrorism in the 1990s, in particular in connection with the conflict between Turkish security forces and the Kurdish Workers' Party (PKK). European Court of Human Rights (Press Unit), 'Armed Conflicts', Fact Sheet, March 2020, at http://bit.ly/2FBxHq1, p. 3. To date, the Court has delivered more than 250 judgments finding violations of the European Convention on Human Rights in connection with the armed conflict in Chechnya. About 60% of the applications concern enforced disappearance; other issues include killing and injuries to civilians, destruction of homes and property, indiscriminate use of force, use of landmines, illegal detention, torture, and inhuman conditions of detention. Ibid., p. 10.
[125] European Court of Human Rights, *Isayeva v. Russia*, Judgment (App. No. 57950/00) (First Section), 24 February 2005, para. 191.
[126] Ibid., para. 180.
[127] Ibid., para. 66.
[128] Ibid., para. 191.

8.65 Despite rejecting the relevance of international humanitarian law, the Court proceeded to apply a term derived from that body of international law to denote the illegality of the gravity ordnance FAB-250 and FAB-500 bombs dropped by the Russian air force. Use of such 'indiscriminate' weapons 'in a populated area, outside wartime and without prior evacuation of the civilians', is, the Court said, 'impossible to reconcile with the degree of caution expected from a law-enforcement body in a democratic society'.[129] For sure, in the context of the conduct of hostilities in armed conflict, international humanitarian law would not consider these two bombs to be inherently indiscriminate and therefore incapable of lawful use.

8.66 That reality notwithstanding, the 'massive use of indiscriminate weapons', the Court concluded, 'stands in flagrant contrast' with the aim of protecting people from unlawful violence under Article 2(2)(a) of the European Convention on Human Rights. It 'cannot be considered compatible with the standard of care prerequisite to an operation of this kind involving the use of lethal force by State agents'.[130] The Court held accordingly that Russia had violated its obligation 'to protect' the right to life of the applicant and her son Zelimkhan Isayev (both of whom survived) and her three nieces, Zarema Batayeva, Kheda Batayeva, and Marem Batayeva (all of whom were killed).[131]

8.67 A better analysis by the Court's First Section would have followed the lines of argument put forward on the basis of third-party expertise, applying international humanitarian law principles and rules on discrimination and proportionality in attack to the bombing and Russia's duty to respect the right to life. Human Rights Watch, for instance, was cited by the applicant for its 2003 report on the conflict in which it stated that 'Russian forces appear to have deliberately bombed, shelled, or fired upon civilian convoys, causing significant civilian casualties. ... The frequency of the attacks on fleeing civilians left many civilians trapped in areas of active conflict, contributing indirectly to the high death toll of the conflict.'[132] The application of international humanitarian law would not have changed the outcome of the case, but would have served to ground it more solidly in the rules applicable to use of force in the conduct of hostilities in an armed conflict. These rules would have been delineated in order to interpret what was no more than 'absolutely necessary' in the quelling of the insurrection.

8.68 In its 2011 judgment in the *Esmukhambetov* case, also pertaining to the conflict in Chechnya but in relation to earlier events in September 1999, the European Court considered that 'the indiscriminate bombing of a village inhabited by civilians – women and children being among their number – was manifestly disproportionate to the achievement of the purpose ... invoked by the Government': that of, once again, protecting people from unlawful violence.'[133] According to the Russian Government, in early

---

[129] Ibid.
[130] Ibid.
[131] Ibid., para. 201.
[132] Ibid., para. 113.
[133] European Court of Human Rights, *Esmukhambetov and others v. Russia*, Judgment (First Section), 29 March 2011, para. 150.

September 1999, the military body responsible for counterterrorism in Chechnya had received information to the effect that a 'concentration of members of illegal armed groups' and a terrorist training camp had been identified within Shelkovskiy state farm. The information further indicated that a number of large-scale terrorist attacks, including hostage-taking, were being prepared. Given the 'impossibility' of using ground troops in the area, the decision was taken to launch 'a pinpoint missile strike by air forces'.[134] The civilian casualties in the case were ascribed to collateral damage.

8.69 This time the European Court explicitly referred to international humanitarian law rules as being relevant to the case, specifically the 1977 Additional Protocol II, which governs certain high-intensity non-international armed conflicts and to which Russia had adhered already in 1989. But again it eschewed assessment of those rules, preferring to cite the failure of the authorities to consider 'at all comprehensively the limits and constraints on the use of indiscriminate weapons within a populated area', and citing its earlier judgment in *Isayeva* in support of this holding.[135] There was also, the Court said, 'no evidence that at any stage of the operation any measures were taken in order to avoid, or at least to minimise, the risk to the lives of the residents'. In these circumstances, the Court declared, it 'cannot but conclude that the authorities failed to exercise appropriate care in the organisation and control of the operation of 12 September 1999'.[136] In this case, the Court could rather have cited the customary humanitarian law duty to take feasible precautions to protect civilians in order to sustain a holding that Russia's action had clearly been more than 'absolutely necessary' in the quelling of the insurrection in Chechnya.

8.70 In its 2013 judgment in *Benzer v. Turkey*,[137] the European Court of Human Rights addressed the bombing of a village in the south-east of the country in March 1994 by the Turkish armed forces. Turkey had sought, unpersuasively, to put the blame on the shoulders of the Kurdish Workers' Party (PKK) for the deaths and injuries caused as a result of its actions. This time the Court not only referred to international humanitarian law in its summary of relevant international materials,[138] it also explicitly applied that body of law. 'In any event', the Court stated, 'an indiscriminate aerial bombardment of civilians and their villages cannot be . . . reconcilable with any of the grounds regulating the use of force' in Article 2(2) of the European Convention on Human Rights, 'or, indeed, with the customary rules of international humanitarian law or any of the international treaties regulating the use of force in armed conflicts'.[139]

8.71 In its judgment in *Benzer*, in assessing the legality of counterterrorist action, the Court edged closer to using international humanitarian law, where applicable, as a critical

---

[134] Ibid., para. 21.
[135] Ibid., para. 149.
[136] Ibid.
[137] European Court of Human Rights, *Benzer and others v. Turkey*, Judgment (Second Section), 12 November 2013 (as rendered final on 24 March 2014).
[138] Ibid., para. 89. Albeit, the reference was only to Common Article 3, which does not apply to the conduct of hostilities, but which would govern the failure to assist the survivors.
[139] Ibid., para. 184.

reference to interpreting the right to life under the European Convention on Human Rights in an armed conflict. Indeed, the Court's Grand Chamber had already endorsed this approach in theory in its 2009 judgment in the *Varnava* case.[140] Therein, the Court had stated: 'Article 2 must be interpreted in so far as possible in light of the general principles of international law, including the rules of international humanitarian law which play an indispensable and universally accepted role in mitigating the savagery and inhumanity of armed conflict.'[141]

8.72 Thus, if applicable international humanitarian law is violated in particular circumstances, the Court should have no difficulty in concluding that action taken was not absolutely necessary for suppressing an insurgency. If, however, action by the State complies with applicable international humanitarian law, the Court will need to consider – and should make explicit – whether the precautionary measures it has discerned in Article 2(2) in counterterrorism operations during peacetime apply also during the conduct of hostilities in a situation of armed conflict.

Case Law of the Inter-American Court of Human Rights

8.73 The Inter-American Court of Human Rights had already in 2006 accepted the potential for international humanitarian law to interpret rights protected under the Convention, in its judgment in the *Case of the Ituango Massacres*.[142] In that case, the acts of terrorism were perpetrated by paramilitary groups of which the State was not only aware but that also involved the active participation of State agents in a number of instances.[143]

8.74 Arguably, however, to date the key jurisprudence in the Inter-American Court on counterterrorism operations during armed conflict is the *Santo Domingo Massacre*. The case concerned the dropping by the Colombian Air Force of a Second World War–era cluster bomb containing six explosive submunitions on the hamlet of Santo Domingo on 13 December 1998. The attack killed seventeen civilians, including four boys and two girls, and injured twenty-seven others (including five girls and four boys).

8.75 The Court found a violation of human rights by applying the international humanitarian law duty to take precautions to the non-international armed conflict between Colombia and the non-state armed group, the Colombian Revolutionary Armed Forces (FARC).[144] The Court had also taken 'note' that domestic judicial and administrative bodies had considered that the State 'failed to comply with the principle of distinction'

---

[140] European Court of Human Rights, *Varnava and others* v. Turkey, Judgment (Grand Chamber), 18 September 2009.
[141] Ibid., para. 185.
[142] Inter-American Court of Human Rights, *Case of the Ituango Massacres v. Colombia*, Judgment (Preliminary Objections, Merits, Reparations and Costs), 1 July 2006, para. 179.
[143] Ibid., para. 133.
[144] Inter-American Court of Human Rights, *Santo Domingo Massacre v. Colombia*, Judgment (Preliminary Objections, Merits and Reparations), 30 November 2012, para. 216.

when executing the operation.[145] Colombia had sought to attribute the deaths to a truck bomb placed by FARC guerrillas,[146] a claim rejected by the Court.[147] The Court said that given the lethal capacity and limited precision of the device used, its launch over the hamlet was contrary to the customary law duty of precautions in attack. Based in particular on this finding, the Court found a violation of the right to life of those who were killed and a violation of the prohibition on inhumane treatment of the injured.[148]

8.76 In its submissions to the Court, Colombia had entered a preliminary objection in relation to the alleged violations of the rights to life, personal integrity, property, and freedom of movement and residence, 'because these were matters relating to the presumed violation of norms of international humanitarian law'.[149] Colombia explicitly recognised the existence of an armed conflict and argued that resultant violations and responsibilities 'could not be determined by the Court, because the latter does not have competence to make the type of declarations that relate to the application of international humanitarian law, because "the law of war" does not fall within its competences'.[150]

8.77 The Court, however, explicitly rejected this argument, pointing out that it can, as it has in other cases,

> interpret the obligation and the rights contained in the American Convention in light of other treaties. In this case, by using IHL as a supplementary norm of interpretation to the treaty-based provisions, the Court is not making a ranking between normative systems, because the applicability and relevance of IHL in situations of armed conflict is evident. This only means that the Court can observe the regulations of IHL, as the specific law in this area, in order to make a more specific application of the provisions of the Convention when defining the scope of the State's obligations.[151]

8.78 The Court's decision in the *Sánchez* case has already been discussed. The approach it would take in that case is consistent with its reasoning in the *Santo Domingo Massacre* case three years later. It differs markedly from the approach taken by the European Court in Finogenov, which was also an instance of hostage-taking linked to an armed conflict. In its judgment in *Sánchez*, the Inter-American Court explicitly adopted an analysis that interpreted the right to life through the lens of international humanitarian law. Thus, it stated that 'the parties and the Inter-American Commission have agreed that the Court should interpret the scope of the provisions of the American Convention in this case in light of the relevant provisions of international humanitarian law since the events occurred in the context of a non-international armed conflict'.[152] The Court agreed to pursue this

---

[145] Ibid., para. 213.
[146] Ibid., paras. 6, 138, 183.
[147] Ibid., para. 210.
[148] Ibid., para. 230.
[149] Ibid., para. 16.
[150] Ibid.
[151] Ibid., para. 24.
[152] Inter-American Court of Human Rights, *Cruz Sánchez v. Peru*, Judgment, 2015, para. 267.

line, applying in particular Common Article 3 and customary IHL.[153] It further indicated that analysis of the possible violation of Article 4 of the American Convention must consider, among others, the principle of distinction, the principle of proportionality, and the principle of precautions in attack.[154] This reasoning is robust.

8.79 Where, potentially, the Court's approach is open to question is on the basis that it went on to consider the hostage rescue operation as one in the conduct of hostilities to which Common Article 3 was also applicable, while also applying the precautionary principle governing a situation of law enforcement to the operation as a whole.[155] Arguably, a better approach would have been to consider the entire operation as one of law enforcement, just as the European Court did in its judgment in *Finogenov*. The government's stated aim was to save the hostages not eliminate the Tupac Amaru hostage takers. In such a scenario, the rules on the use of potentially or intentionally lethal force would be those laid down in the 1990 Basic Principle 9.

8.80 If, in contrast, the rescue operation were indeed a situation of hostilities, considerable incidental death and injury to the hostages could have been deemed lawful under the international humanitarian law rule of proportionality in attack. There would also be no obligation to minimise the risk of death of the hostage takers, as is the case in a law enforcement operation. In any event, the outcome of the case – that Mr Sánchez was the subject of an extrajudicial execution[156] – would not have differed. Whether the judgment of the Court would have been different in relation to the other two deceased hostage takers, Herma Luz Meléndez Cueva and Víctor Salomón Peceros Pedraza,[157] is moot.

African Commission on Human and Peoples' Rights

8.81 In its 2015 General Comment on the Right to Life, the African Commission on Human and Peoples' Rights stated: 'The right to life continues to apply during armed conflict. During the conduct of hostilities, the right to life needs to be interpreted with reference to the rules of international humanitarian law. In all other situations the intentional deprivation of life is prohibited unless strictly unavoidable to protect another life or other lives.'[158]

8.82 The African Commission further observes that international humanitarian law 'does not prohibit the use of force in hostilities against lawful targets (for example combatants or civilians directly participating in hostilities) if necessary from a military perspective, provided that, in all circumstances, the rules of distinction, proportionality and precaution in attack are observed'.[159] But, the Commission cautioned, any violation of international

---

[153] Ibid., para. 270.
[154] Ibid., para. 273.
[155] Ibid., paras. 276, 277, 283.
[156] Ibid., para. 319.
[157] Ibid., paras. 342, 343.
[158] African Commission on Human and Peoples' Rights, General Comment No. 3 on the African Charter on Human and Peoples' Rights on the right to life (Article 4), 2015, para. 13.
[159] Ibid., para. 32.

humanitarian law 'resulting in death, including war crimes, will be an arbitrary deprivation of life'.[160]

Human Rights Committee

8.83 Most recently, in its General Comment 36 on the right to life, the Human Rights Committee has recalled that Article 6 of the ICCPR continues to apply in situations of armed conflict to which the rules of IHL are applicable, including to the conduct of hostilities.[161] According to the Committee, the use of lethal force 'consistent with international humanitarian law and other applicable international law norms is, in general, not arbitrary'.[162]

8.84 This largely reflects the position advanced by the International Court of Justice in its 1996 Advisory Opinion on the Legality of the Threat or Use of Nuclear Weapons.[163] Therein, the Court has stated that 'whether a particular loss of life, through the use of a certain weapon in warfare, is to be considered an arbitrary deprivation of life contrary to Article 6 of the Covenant, can only be decided by reference to the law applicable in armed conflict and not deduced from the terms of the Covenant itself'. The use of the words 'in general' by the Human Rights Committee, though, suggests that space may exist to find a violation of the right to life even when IHL rules are complied with, including in a counterterrorism operation in a situation of armed conflict.

8.85 The Human Rights Committee further observes that 'practices inconsistent with international humanitarian law, entailing a risk to the lives of civilians and other persons protected by international humanitarian law', including the targeting of civilians or civilian objects would also violate Article 6 of the Covenant. The Committee called on States Parties to disclose whether 'less harmful alternatives were considered', a possible invocation of the precautionary duty under international human rights law.[164]

---

[160] Ibid.
[161] Human Rights Committee, General Comment 36 on the right to life, para. 64, citing General Comment No. 31 (2004) on the nature of the general legal obligation imposed on States parties to the Covenant, para. 11; and General Comment No. 29 (2001) on derogations from provisions of the Covenant during a state of emergency, para. 3.
[162] Human Rights Committee, General Comment 36 on the right to life, para. 64.
[163] International Court of Justice, *Legality of the Threat or Use of Nuclear Weapons*, Advisory Opinion, 8 July 1996, para. 25.
[164] Ibid. The Committee refers to the principle in paragraph 13 of the General Comment, citing the European Court of Human Rights' judgment in the *McCann* case in support.

9

The Death Penalty

INTRODUCTION

9.01 This chapter describes the legality of both the imposition and execution of the death penalty under the right to life. Judicially sanctioned killing as a sentence following conviction at the issue of a criminal trial is regulated in detail by international human rights law under treaty, custom, and general principles of law. Key judicial decisions at the regional and national levels are also cited as subsidiary means for the determination of rules of law.

9.02 Amnesty International has reported that 106 States had completely abolished the death penalty by the end of 2018 and of the 197 States recognised by the Secretary-General of the United Nations (UN) 'more than two-thirds are abolitionist in law or practice'.[1] Among the 'retentionist' States, thirty-four are known to have executed one or more persons in 2010 through the end of 2019: Afghanistan, Bahrain, Bangladesh, Belarus, Botswana, Chad, China, Egypt, Equatorial Guinea, India, Indonesia, Iran, Iraq, Japan, Jordan, Kuwait, Malaysia, Myanmar, Nigeria, North Korea, Oman, Pakistan, Palestine, Saudi Arabia, Singapore, Somalia, South Sudan, Sudan, Syria, Thailand, United Arab Emirates, the United States, Vietnam, and Yemen.

9.03 According to Amnesty International, a total of fifty-four States imposed the death penalty in 2018; that year, most known executions occurred in China, Iran, Saudi Arabia, Vietnam, and Iraq 'in that order'.[2] For several years now, while China executes the most people in absolute terms, Iran 'probably' has a higher per capita execution rate.[3]

THE DEATH PENALTY UNDER GLOBAL STANDARDS

9.04 The imposition and execution of the death penalty were first regulated by human rights treaty in the 1966 International Covenant on Civil and Political Rights[4] (ICCPR),

---

[1] Amnesty International, 'Death Penalty', 2019, at http://bit.ly/37i8SHU. This is an increase of seven from April 2014 when 99 of 197 States had completely abolished the death penalty. R. Hood and C. Hoyle, *The Death Penalty: A Worldwide Perspective*, 5th ed., Oxford University Press, Oxford, 2015, p. 16.
[2] Amnesty International, 'Death Penalty', 2019, at http://bit.ly/37i8SHU.
[3] Hood and Hoyle, *The Death Penalty: A Worldwide Perspective*, 5th ed., p. 75.
[4] International Covenant on Civil and Political Rights; adopted at New York 16 December 1966; entered into force 23 March 1976. As of 1 May 2021, 173 States were party to it.

under paragraphs 2, 4, 5, and 6 of Article 6.[5] States Parties that have not abolished the death penalty are permitted to impose a death sentence 'only for the most serious crimes' and 'in accordance with the law in force at the time of the commission of the crime'.[6] The death penalty shall not be imposed for crimes committed by those under eighteen years of age at the time of the commission of the offence, and it shall not be executed on pregnant women.[7] These stipulations reflect customary international law applicable to all States.[8] They are also generally reflected in treaty rules of international humanitarian law.[9]

9.05 Under Article 4(2) of the ICCPR, no derogation is possible under any of the provisions in Article 6. The Covenant as a whole does not prohibit the making of reservations, but under treaty and customary law on the law of treaties, reservations that are incompatible with the object and purpose of a treaty are invalid.[10] This issue arose with respect to Pakistan's purported reservations to the Covenant's rules on the imposition of the death penalty whereby, among others, the provisions of Article 6 'shall be so applied to the extent that they are not repugnant to the Provisions of the Constitution of Pakistan and the Sharia laws'.

9.06 A number of States Parties to the ICCPR objected to this reservation (and others that Pakistan made in a similar vein). The Netherlands, for instance, 'considers that reservations of this kind must be regarded as incompatible with the object and purpose of the Covenant and would recall that, according to customary international law, as codified in the Vienna Convention on the Law of Treaties, reservations incompatible with the object and purpose of a treaty shall not be permitted'.[11] Canada, noting that Article 6 was non-

---

[5] A proposal by Colombia and Uruguay during the elaboration of the Covenant to outlaw the death penalty was defeated by a vote of fifty-one votes to nine with twelve abstentions. Only Brazil, Colombia, the Dominican Republic, Ecuador, Finland, Italy, Panama, Uruguay, and Venezuela voted in favour. See generally 'Draft International Covenants on Human Rights', UN doc. A/2929, 1 July 1955, at http://bit.ly/3kEtWPC.

[6] Art. 6(2), ICCPR.

[7] Art. 6(5), ICCPR. The treaty rule was 'inspired by humanitarian considerations and by consideration for the interests of the unborn child'. 'Draft International Covenants on Human Rights', UN doc. A/2929, 1 July 1955, 'Article 6', at p. 85, para. 10.

[8] With respect to the prohibition on imposing the death penalty on child offenders, see, e.g., Inter-American Commission on Human Rights, *Napoleon Beazley v. United States*, Decision (Case 12.412), Report No. 101/03, 29 December 2003, paras. 47, 48, citing with approval its earlier views in *Michael Domingues v. United States*, Decision (Case 12.285), Report 62/02, paras. 84, 85.

[9] See, *infra*, Paragraphs 9.38–9.44. As discussed therein, however, in one international humanitarian law treaty, it is prohibited only to execute the death penalty on child offenders rather than to impose it.

[10] Art. 19(c), Vienna Convention on the Law of Treaties; adopted at Vienna 23 May 1969; entered into force 27 January 1980.

[11] Communication by The Netherlands of 30 June 2011 related to the reservations made by Pakistan upon ratification of the ICCPR on 23 June 2010, text available at http://bit.ly/37osGKf. See similarly the communications objecting to the reservations made by Pakistan by Australia (28 June 2011); Austria (24 June 2011); Belgium (28 June 2011); Canada (27 June 2011); Czech Republic (20 June 2011); Denmark (28 June 2011); Estonia (21 June 2011); Finland (28 June 2011); France (24 June 2011); Germany (28 June 2011); Greece (22 June 2011); Hungary (28 June 2011); Ireland (23 June 2011); Italy (28 June 2011); Latvia (29 June 2011); Norway (29 June 2011); Poland (20 June 2011); Portugal (28 June 2011); Slovak Republic (23 June 2011); Spain (9 June 2011); Sweden (22 June 2011); Switzerland (28 June 2011); and the United States (29 June 2011). The communication by the United Kingdom (28 June 2011) was a little more vague as to the grounds on which it was objecting to the purported reservations by Pakistan.

derogable, stated that 'reservations which consist of a general reference to national law or to the prescriptions of the Islamic Sharia constitute, in reality, reservations with a general, indeterminate scope'.[12] Poland stated that it 'considers that reservations aimed at limitation or exclusion of the application of treaty norms stipulating non-derogable rights are in opposition with the purpose of this treaty. On these grounds, the reservations made with regard to Articles 6 and 7 of the Covenant are impermissible.'[13] Subsequently, in a communication received on 20 September 2011, the Government of Pakistan notified the UN Secretary-General that it had decided to withdraw the reservation it had made upon ratification to Article 6 (and to a number of other provisions in the ICCPR).

The Status of the Death Penalty under International Law

The Status of the Death Penalty under General International Law

9.07 The imposition and execution of the death penalty are not, per se, prohibited by any rule of general international law. There is neither a general customary prohibition of the death penalty nor does it violate a general principle of international law, although the obligation of progressive abolition of the death penalty is *de lege ferenda*.[14] This reflects the material aspect of not only the right to life but also of the prohibition on torture or other forms of inhumane treatment. Thus, for instance, in declaring the death penalty unconstitutional in 1995, South Africa's Constitutional Court decided that it was incompatible both with the prohibition on cruel, inhuman, or degrading punishment and with a 'culture of respect for human life and dignity' that made the rights to life and to dignity cornerstones of the South African Constitution. 'Everyone, including the most abominable of human beings, has the right to life, and capital punishment is therefore unconstitutional.'[15] In the United States, Colorado and then, in March 2021, Virginia became the twenty-second and twenty-third states to abolish capital punishment since it was reinstated by a Supreme Court decision in 1976.[16]

THE PROHIBITION OF THE MANDATORY DEATH SENTENCE

9.08 Domestic laws providing for the *mandatory* imposition of a death sentence for any offence are arbitrary in nature.[17] This is because they do not allow for the sentence to be

---

[12] Communication by Canada related to the reservations made by Pakistan upon ratification of the ICCPR, 27 June 2011.
[13] Communication by Poland related to the reservations made by Pakistan upon ratification of the ICCPR, 20 June 2011.
[14] Already in 1982, in its General Comment 6 on the right to life, the Human Rights Committee had referred to abolition as being 'desirable'. Human Rights Committee, General Comment No. 6: Article 6 (Right to life), 1982, para. 6.
[15] Constitutional Court of South Africa, *State v. T. Makwanyane and M. Mchunu*, [1995] CCT/3/94, ZACC3, *esp*. paras. 222, 267, 275, 278, 281–82, 392. See also Hood and Hoyle, *The Death Penalty: A Worldwide Perspective*, 5th ed., p. 89.
[16] D. K. Li, 'Colorado Abolishes the Death Penalty', NBC News, 22 March 2020, at http://nbcnews.to/3qXyIfz.
[17] Human Rights Committee, General Comment No. 36: Article 6: the right to life, UN doc. CCPR/C/GC/36, 3 September 2019 (hereinafter, Human Rights Committee, General Comment 36 on the right to life), para. 37.

appealed to a higher court or for the personal circumstances of the convicted person to be taken into account by the court.[18] Both of these rights are also integral to the conduct of a fair trial, making the mandatory death penalty for any offence, no matter how serious, inherently unlawful.

9.09 When they have done so, domestic and regional courts have tended to strike down mandatory death sentences on the basis that they are unconstitutional, sometimes on the basis that they violate the right to life but more often because they are deemed to contravene the right to freedom from inhumane treatment or punishment or to violate fair trial rights (or indeed both).[19] For instance, in its 1983 judgment in *Mithu v. State of Punjab*,[20] the Indian Supreme Court stated that 'the last word on the question of justice and fairness does not rest with the legislature'. It is 'for the courts to decide whether the procedure prescribed by a law for depriving a person of his life or liberty is fair, just and reasonable'. The Court held that 'a standardized mandatory sentence, and that too in the form of a sentence of death, fails to take into account the facts and circumstances of each particular case. It is those facts and circumstances which constitute a safe guideline for determining the question of sentence in each individual case.'

9.10 In its 1987 judgment in *Sumner v. Shuman*,[21] the US Supreme Court held that the mandatory death sentence at issue in Nevada violated the US Constitution, striking down the last vestiges of the mandatory death penalty in the United States.[22] The statute in question, according to the Supreme Court, 'precluded a determination whether any relevant mitigating circumstances justified imposing on him [Mr Shuman] a sentence less than death'.[23] And although 'a sentencing authority may decide that a sanction less than death is not appropriate in a particular case, the fundamental respect for humanity underlying the Eighth Amendment [to the US Constitution, which prohibits cruel and unusual punishment] requires that the defendant be able to present any relevant mitigating evidence that could justify a lesser sentence'.[24]

9.11 In a 2001 judgment in the consolidated cases of *Spence v. The Queen* and *Hughes v. The Queen*, the Eastern Caribbean Court of Appeal held that the mandatory nature of

---

[18] 'Capital punishment and the implementation of the safeguards guaranteeing protection of the rights of those facing the death penalty: Yearly supplement of the Secretary-General to his quinquennial report on capital punishment', UN doc. A/HRC/42/28, 28 August 2019, para. 22.

[19] In its 2007 judgment in *Kafantayeni v. Attorney General*, for instance, the Malawi High Court unanimously agreed that the mandatory death penalty in Malawian law violated the right of every person under Section 19 of the Constitution to protection against being subjected to inhuman and degrading treatment or punishment and the right of an accused person under Section 42(2)(f) of the Constitution to a fair trial. The plaintiff had also argued that the mandatory death penalty violated his right to life, also explicitly protected under the Constitution, but the Court did not endorse this. Malawi High Court, *Kafantayeni v. Attorney General*, Constitutional Case No. 12 of 2005 [2007] MWHC 1.

[20] Supreme Court of India, *Mithu v. State of Punjab*, Judgment (Criminal Appeal No. 745 of 1980), 7 April 1983.

[21] US Supreme Court, *Sumner v. Shuman*, Judgment (Case No. 86-246), 22 June 1987.

[22] Most mandatory death sentences in the United States had already been struck down by the Supreme Court in its judgment in *Woodson v. North Carolina* (1976) 426 US 280.

[23] US Supreme Court, *Sumner v. Shuman*, Judgment (Case No. 86-246), 22 June 1987, p. 78.

[24] Ibid., p. 85.

The Death Penalty

the imposition of the death penalty was unconstitutional on the grounds that it amounted to inhuman or degrading punishment expressly prohibited by the constitutions of Saint Vincent and Saint Lucia.[25] In so holding, the judgment also referred obliquely to the notion of a fair trial: 'a court must have the discretion to take into account the individual circumstances of an individual offender and offense in determining whether the death penalty can and should be imposed, if the sentencing is to be considered rational, humane and rendered in accordance with the requirements of due process'.[26]

9.12 The Eastern Caribbean Court of Appeal cited and rejected the 1995 holding in the Belize Court of Appeal in *Lauriano v. Attorney General of Belize*,[27] wherein the existence of the prerogative of mercy was deemed to provide the necessary flexibility to the mandatory sentencing system. The Court of Appeal declined to follow that approach on the basis that the prerogative of mercy 'is a non-judicial power which is exercised after the lawful sentence of the court has been imposed. ... The constitutionality of the sentence cannot be based on the subsequent exercise of mercy.'[28]

9.13 The Court of Appeal also referred to, but did not discuss in detail, the Views expressed by the Human Rights Committee in 2000 in the case of *Eversley Thompson v. St. Vincent*, in which it considered that

> such a system of mandatory capital punishment would deprive the author of the most fundamental of rights the right to life, without considering whether this exceptional form of punishment is appropriate in the circumstances of his or her case. The existence of the right to seek pardon or commutation, as required by article 6, para 4 of the Covenant, does not secure adequate protection to the right to life, as these discretionary measures by the executive are subject to a wide range of other considerations compared to judicial review in all aspects of a criminal case.[29]

Saint Vincent had argued that that the death sentence was only mandatory in its domestic law for murder – the most serious crime under the law – and that this in itself meant that it was a proportionate sentence.[30]

9.14 In 2018, in its consolidated judgment in the cases of *Jabari Sensimania Nervais v. The Queen* and *Dwayne Omar Severin v. The Queen*,[31] the Caribbean Court of Justice held that a section of the Offences Against the Person Act in Barbados was unconstitutional because

---

[25] Eastern Caribbean Court of Appeal, *Spence and Hughes v. The Queen*, Crim. App. Nos. 20 of 1998 and 14 of 1997, Judgment, 2 April 2001. See further on the two cases, J. Harrington, 'The Challenge to the Mandatory Death Penalty in the Commonwealth Caribbean', American Journal of International Law, vol. 98, no. 1 (January 2004), pp. 126–40.
[26] Eastern Caribbean Court of Appeal, *Spence and Hughes v. The Queen*, Judgment, para. 43.
[27] Court of Appeal of Belize, *Lauriano v. Attorney General of Belize* (1995) 3 Bz LR 77.
[28] Eastern Caribbean Court of Appeal, *Spence and Hughes v. The Queen*, Judgment, para. 35. See in this sense Human Rights Committee, General Comment 36 on the right to life, para. 37.
[29] Human Rights Committee, *Eversley Thompson v. St. Vincent*, Views, U.N. Doc. CCPR/C/70/D/806/1998, 18 October 2000, para. 8.2.
[30] Ibid.
[31] Caribbean Court of Justice, *Jabari Sensimania Nervais v. The Queen* and *Dwayne Omar Severin v. The Queen*, Judgment, 27 June 2018 [2018] CCJ 19 (AJ).

it provided for a mandatory sentence of death. The Court stated that 'the principle of a fair trial must be accorded to the sentencing stage too and also includes the right to appeal or apply for review by a higher court prescribed by law. The right to a fair trial as an element of protection of the law is one of the corner stones of a just and democratic society, without which the rule of law and public faith in the justice system would inevitably collapse.'[32]

9.15 In its 2009 judgment in *Attorney General v. Susan Kigula*,[33] the Supreme Court of Uganda agreed with the argument of the respondents that a fair trial, as provided for in the Constitution, included the possibility of pleading mitigation in relation to sentencing. In its judgment, the Supreme Court stated: 'A trial does not stop at convicting a person. The process of sentencing a person is part of the trial. This is because the court will take into account the evidence, the nature of the offence and the circumstances of the case in order to arrive at an appropriate sentence.'[34] The Supreme Court further held that the pre-determined sentence 'is inconsistent with the principle of equality before and under the law. Not all murders are committed in the same circumstances, and all murderers are not necessarily of the same character.'[35]

The Prohibition of the Death Penalty under Treaty Law

9.16 A significant number of States are bound by treaty law not to execute any person within their jurisdiction at either global or regional level, or both. At the global level, this concerns the Second Optional Protocol to the ICCPR,[36] to which eighty-eight States were a party as of this writing. That said, under Article 2(1) of the Second Optional Protocol, a State may make a reservation when ratifying or acceding to the Protocol allowing for the application of the death penalty 'in time of war pursuant to a conviction for a most serious crime of a military nature committed during wartime'. Of the States Parties to the Second Optional Protocol, five (Azerbaijan, Brazil, Chile, El Salvador, and Greece) had sought to do so as of writing, although objections to El Salvador's purported reservation by several other States Parties were made on the grounds that it did not comply with the Protocol's explicit requirements.[37] Greece is prohibited from applying the death penalty by its membership in the European Union and the Charter of Fundamental Rights and as a State Party to the European Convention on Human Rights (as discussed later).

---

[32] Ibid., para. 49.
[33] Supreme Court of Uganda, *Attorney General v. Susan Kigula and 417 others* (Constitutional Appeal No. 3 of 2006) [2009] UGSC 6 (21 January 2009).
[34] Ibid., pp. 41, 45.
[35] Ibid., p. 43.
[36] Second Optional Protocol to the International Covenant on Civil and Political Rights, aiming at the abolition of the death penalty; adopted at New York 15 December 1989; entered into force 11 July 1991.
[37] See Art. 2(2), Second Optional Protocol to the ICCPR. Thus Austria, Finland, France, Germany, Ireland, Italy, the Netherlands, Norway, Poland, Portugal, Spain, Sweden, Switzerland, and Togo all objected to El Salvador's reservation on the basis that the national military laws were not communicated to the depositary at the time of making the reservation and that the reservation was not limited to the crimes cited in Article 2(1) of the Protocol. Finland also objected to Brazil's reservation on the basis that the national military laws were not communicated to the depositary at the time of making the reservation.

9.17 There is also a specific treaty law prohibition on the imposition of the death penalty on child offenders.[38] Article 6(5) of the ICCPR specifies that the death penalty 'shall not be imposed for crimes committed by persons below eighteen years of age'. This provision applies both in peacetime and in a situation of armed conflict.[39] In 1993, France communicated to the UN Secretary-General as depositary its objection to the reservation made at the time of its ratification of the Covenant by the United States relating to Article 6(5). France considered that this reservation was not valid, 'inasmuch as it is incompatible with the object and purpose of the Convention'.[40] The US reservation to Article 6(5) of the ICCPR was, however, explicitly made subject to its domestic Constitutional constraints. In 2005, the US Supreme Court held that the execution of child offenders violated the US Constitution.[41]

9.18 Article 37(a) of the Convention on the Rights of the Child[42] provides: 'Neither capital punishment nor life imprisonment without possibility of release shall be imposed for offences committed by persons below eighteen years of age.'[43] Only the United States (a signatory) was not party to the Convention as of writing. Nonetheless, as Chapter 22 describes, a 2019 report by Amnesty International recorded a total of 145 executions of child offenders in 10 States between 1990 and April 2019: China, the Democratic Republic of Congo, Iran, Nigeria, Pakistan, Saudi Arabia, South Sudan, Sudan, the United States, and Yemen.[44]

The Legality of the Re-establishment of the Death Penalty

9.19 Once a State has abolished the death penalty, it is arguably unlawful to reinstitute this sentence in domestic law. According to the Human Rights Committee, 'States parties to the Covenant that have abolished the death penalty, through amending their domestic laws, becoming parties to the Second Optional Protocol to the Covenant or adopting

---

[38] As noted, *infra*, at Paragraph 13.03, this is a customary norm. See also N. Peterson, 'Life, Right to, International Protection', *Max Planck Encyclopedia of Public International Law*, last updated October 2012, at http://bit.ly/2u2adEK.

[39] This is despite the fact that one international humanitarian law treaty limits the prohibition to execution of the death penalty and not also its imposition as sentence. See, *infra*, Paragraphs 9.38–9.44 for the pertinent rules of international humanitarian law.

[40] Communication of France, 4 October 1993, at http://bit.ly/2SEcEpX.

[41] In 2005, the US Supreme Court ruled by five to four majority that the Eighth and Fourteenth Amendments to the Constitution (prohibiting cruel and unusual punishments, and the denial of life to any person without due process of law, respectively) forbade the imposition of the death penalty on offenders who were under 18 years of age when they committed a capital crime. US Supreme Court, *Roper v. Simmons*, No. 03-633, 1 March 2005.

[42] Convention on the Rights of the Child; adopted at New York 20 November 1989; entered into force 2 September 1990.

[43] According to Article 5(3) of the African Charter on the Rights and Welfare of the Child, 'Death sentence shall not be pronounced for crimes committed by children'. African Charter on the Rights and Welfare of the Child; adopted at Addis Ababa 1 July 1990; entered into force 29 November 1999. As of 1 February 2020, 49 States were party to the Charter, leaving Morocco (a non-signatory), and the Democratic Republic of Congo, the Sahrawi Arab Democratic Republic, Somalia, South Sudan, and Tunisia (all signatories) outside the Charter's purview.

[44] Amnesty International, 'Executions of Juveniles since 1990 as of April 2019', 2019, at http://bit.ly/2Fcsn9i. According to the UN Secretary-General, as of September 2018 children were also on death row in Bangladesh and the Maldives. 'Question of the death penalty', Report of the UN Secretary-General, UN doc. A/HRC/39/19, 14 September 2018, para. 39, citing reporting by Amnesty International.

another international instrument obligating them to abolish the death penalty, are barred from reintroducing it.'[45] Abolition of the death penalty, the Committee affirms, is 'legally irrevocable'.[46] Hard evidence for this assertion is, however, rather elusive. Among global and regional human rights treaties, only the 1969 Inter-American Convention on Human Rights contains such a stipulation.[47] Indeed, there is no reference cited by the Committee itself to illustrate its own holding. It is true that Article 6(2) refers to 'countries which have not abolished the death penalty', implying that the possibility of imposing the death penalty is denied to any such State. But this construction is a rather frail basis on which to found such an important legal principle.[48]

9.20 The Gambia is an example of a State that abolished the death penalty (in 1993), subsequently reinstated it (in 1995),[49] but then later abolished it again. The death penalty was last used under President Yahya Jammeh in 2012, when nine soldiers were executed by firing squad.[50] In February 2018, a moratorium on the application of the death penalty was instituted, along with commutation of extant death sentences to life imprisonment. The Gambia then ratified the Second Optional Protocol to the ICCPR on 28 September 2018 (having signed it on 20 September 2017). In its Concluding Observations on the Gambia in 2018, the Human Rights Committee was concerned, however, that the death penalty was still provided for in the Constitution.[51]

Progressive Abolition as an Emerging Customary Norm

9.21 There is stronger evidence to support the emergence of a customary norm in favour of the progressive abolition of the death penalty.[52] Article 6(6) of the ICCPR stipulates that nothing in Article 6 'shall be invoked to delay or to prevent the abolition of capital punishment by any State Party to the ... Covenant'. In 1971, the UN General Assembly adopted its Resolution 2857, by majority vote, in which it affirmed that 'in order to fully guarantee the right to life', the main objective to be pursued is the progressive restriction of the number of capital offences 'with a view to the desirability of abolishing this punishment in all countries'.[53] In the Second Optional Protocol to the ICCPR, the preamble

---

[45] Human Rights Committee, General Comment 36 on the right to life, para. 34.
[46] Ibid.
[47] Art. 4(3), American Convention on Human Rights; adopted at San José 22 November 1969; entered into force 18 July 1978.
[48] But see on this point the Individual Opinion of Fausto Pocar in Human Rights Committee, *Chitat Ng v. Canada*, Views (Comm. No. 469/1991), UN doc. CCPR/C/49/D/469/1991, 7 January 1994.
[49] See, e.g., A. Novak, 'Rule of Law, and the Death Penalty in The Gambia', *Premium Times*, 3 August 2013, at http://bit.ly/37gFnGo.
[50] Agence France-Presse, 'Gambia Suspends Death Penalty in Step towards Abolition', *The Guardian*, 19 February 2018, at http://bit.ly/2ut2twp.
[51] Human Rights Committee, Concluding Observations on The Gambia in the absence of its second periodic report, UN doc. CCPR/C/GMB/CO/2, 30 August 2018, para. 27.
[52] For examples of actions taken at regional and national levels in this sense, see, e.g., 'Capital punishment and the implementation of the safeguards guaranteeing protection of the rights of those facing the death penalty: Yearly supplement of the Secretary-General to his quinquennial report on capital punishment', UN doc. A/HRC/30/18, 16 July 2015, paras. 11–15.
[53] UN General Assembly Resolution 2857, adopted on 20 December 1971 by fifty-nine votes to one with fifty-eight abstentions, para. 3.

notes that Article 6 of the ICCPR 'refers to abolition of the death penalty in terms that strongly suggest that abolition is desirable'.[54] In 2016, in his report to the UN General Assembly, the UN Special Rapporteur on extrajudicial, summary or arbitrary executions stated that 'authorities with decision-making power concerning the death penalty should recognize that the world is moving in that direction, requiring at least the progressive abolition of the death penalty'.[55]

9.22 A year earlier, the UN Secretary-General had repeated his view that the death penalty 'has no place in the twenty-first century'.[56] In the light of the evolution of international human rights law and jurisprudence and State practice, he said, 'the imposition of the death penalty is incompatible with fundamental tenets of human rights, in particular human dignity, the right to life and the prohibition of torture or other cruel, inhuman or degrading treatment or punishment'. In its General Comment 36 on the right to life, the Human Rights Committee made its strongest statement on the issue to date, whereby

> Article 6, paragraph 6 reaffirms the position that States parties that are not yet totally abolitionist should be on an irrevocable path towards complete eradication of the death penalty, de facto and de jure, in the foreseeable future. The death penalty cannot be reconciled with full respect for the right to life, and abolition of the death penalty is both desirable . . . and necessary for the enhancement of human dignity and progressive development of human rights.[57]

Women

9.23 There is no general prohibition on the imposition and execution of the death penalty on women.[58] Article 6(5) of the ICCPR specifically prohibits the carrying out of the death penalty on pregnant women. This rule is reflective of customary law. It is also contained in international humanitarian law treaty rules applicable during armed conflict. The rule does not, however, preclude the execution of the death sentence once the child has been born, at the least after a period of nursing the baby (a rule that is, at the least, *de lege ferenda*).

The Application of the Death Penalty

9.24 Where it is potentially lawful, the death penalty must still be applied in strict accord with certain rules. In particular, the sentence may only be imposed for the 'most serious

---

[54] Second Optional Protocol to the ICCPR, third preambular para.
[55] 'Report of the Special Rapporteur on extrajudicial, summary or arbitrary executions', UN doc. A/71/372, 2 September 2016, para. 42. See also C. Heyns and T. Probert 'The right to life and the progressive abolition of the death penalty', in *Moving Away From the Death Penalty: Argument, Trends and Perspectives*, Office of the UN High Commissioner for Human Rights (OHCHR), Geneva, 2014.
[56] 'Capital punishment and the implementation of the safeguards guaranteeing protection of the rights of those facing the death penalty: Yearly supplement of the Secretary-General to his quinquennial report on capital punishment', 2015, para. 55.
[57] Human Rights Committee, General Comment 36 on the right to life, para. 50.
[58] A woman will be equally protected as would a man if she had committed a capital offence while under eighteen years of age.

crimes', it must not be applied in a discriminatory manner, and there must be an opportunity for the condemned to seek clemency or pardon. Violation of any of those rules will render the death penalty unlawful, in particular as a violation of the right to life.

The 'Most Serious Crimes'

9.25 Article 6(2) of the ICCPR states that a sentence of death 'may be imposed only for the most serious crimes in accordance with the law in force at the time of the commission of the crime'. The Human Rights Committee interprets the term 'most serious crimes' as pertaining 'only to crimes of extreme gravity' that involve 'intentional killing'.[59] Crimes not resulting directly and intentionally in death, such as attempted murder, corruption and other economic and political crimes, armed robbery, piracy, abduction, and drug and sexual offences, although potentially serious in nature, can 'never' serve as the basis, within the framework of Article 6, for the imposition of the death penalty.[60] Moreover, the Committee has affirmed, 'a limited degree of involvement or of complicity in the commission of even the most serious crimes, such as providing the physical means for the commission of murder, cannot justify the imposition of the death penalty'.[61]

9.26 Under no circumstances may the death penalty ever be applied as a sanction against conduct whose very criminalisation violates the Covenant.[62] The Committee cites as examples adultery, homosexuality, apostasy, the establishment of political opposition groups, and offending a head of State.[63]

9.27 It is noteworthy that the 1998 Rome Statute of the International Criminal Court, which judges senior military and political figures and officials for international crimes that may involve the killing of hundreds or even thousands of people, does not allow the death penalty to be imposed on anyone who is convicted.[64]

A Fair Trial

9.28 Fair trial rights include the right to a fair and public hearing by a competent, independent, and impartial tribunal established by law.[65] Every defendant shall have the right to be presumed innocent until proved guilty beyond a reasonable doubt. That high threshold is particularly important in the case of a capital trial.[66] Article 14(3) of the ICCPR sets out other fundamental fair trial rights: the right to be informed promptly and in detail in a language he or she understands of the nature and cause of the charge against him or her; the availability of adequate time and facilities to prepare a defence and to

---

[59] Human Rights Committee, General Comment 36 on the right to life, para. 35.
[60] Ibid.
[61] Ibid.
[62] Ibid., para. 36.
[63] Ibid. The Committee stipulates in this regard that States Parties which retain the death penalty for such offences commit a violation of their obligations under Article 6 as well as when read in conjunction with Article 2(2) of the Covenant, 'as well as of other provisions of the Covenant'.
[64] Art. 77(1), Rome Statute of the International Criminal Court; adopted at Rome 17 July 1998; entered into force 1 July 2002.
[65] Art. 14(1), ICCPR.
[66] Human Rights Committee, General Comment 36 on the right to life, para. 43.

communicate with counsel of choice; the right to be tried without undue delay; the right to be present at the trial and to a defence in person or through legal assistance of choice; the right to examine, or have examined, witnesses against him or her and to obtain the attendance and examination of witnesses on his or her behalf under the same conditions as witnesses giving testimony for the prosecution; the right to free assistance of an interpreter; and the right not to be compelled to confess guilt or to self-incriminate. Violation of any of these fair trial rights will render a death sentence arbitrary.

9.29 There is no overriding right under general international law to be tried before a civilian court in a capital case, although the risks that a trial before a military court may not respect all fundamental fair trial rights are substantially higher.[67] In the African human rights system, however, the African Commission on Human and Peoples' Rights has stated that a military court may not lawfully impose a death sentence.[68] Under the ICCPR, the general right to a public trial is subject to the possibility of exclusion 'from all or part of a trial for reasons of morals, public order (ordre public) or national security in a democratic society, or when the interest of the private lives of the parties so requires, or to the extent strictly necessary in the opinion of the court in special circumstances where publicity would prejudice the interests of justice'.[69]

9.30 As noted previously, violation of the fair trial guarantees provided for in Article 14 of the Covenant in proceedings that result in the imposition of the death penalty renders the sentence arbitrary in nature, and in violation of Article 6 of the Covenant. In its General Comment 36 on the right to life, the Human Rights Committee detailed as instances of such violations: use of forced confessions; the inability of the accused to question relevant witnesses; the lack of effective representation involving confidential attorney-client meetings during all stages of the criminal proceedings, including during criminal interrogation, preliminary hearings, trial, and appeal; a failure to respect the presumption of innocence which may manifest itself in the accused being placed in a cage or handcuffed during the trial; lack of an effective right of appeal; the lack of adequate time and facilities for the preparation of the defence and the inability to access legal documents essential for conducting the legal defence or appeal; lack of suitable interpretation; a failure to provide accessible documents and procedural accommodation for persons with disabilities; excessive and unjustified delays in the trial or the appeal process; and a lack of independence or impartiality of the trial or appeal court.[70]

9.31 The Committee has determined that other serious procedural flaws, not explicitly covered by Article 14 of the Covenant, 'may nonetheless' render the imposition of the

---

[67] F. Andreu-Guzmán, *Military Jurisdiction and International Law: Military Courts and Gross Human Rights Violations*, vol. 1, International Commission of Jurists, Geneva, 2004, pp. 74–5.
[68] African Commission on Human and Peoples' Rights (ACmnHPR), 'General Comment No. 3 on the African Charter on Human and Peoples' Rights: The Right to Life (Article 4)', adopted at Banjul (57th Ordinary Session) November 2015 (hereinafter, African Commission General Comment on the right to life), para. 24.
[69] Art. 14(1), ICCPR.
[70] Human Rights Committee, General Comment 36 on the right to life, para. 41.

death penalty contrary to Article 6.[71] It cites, as an example, a failure to promptly inform detained foreign nationals of their right to consular notification pursuant to the 1963 Vienna Convention on Consular Relations, resulting in the imposition of the death penalty.[72]

Discriminatory Application of the Death Penalty

9.32 The fundamental rule of non-discrimination applies to all trials but is especially significant in a capital trial. As the UN Secretary-General has reported:

> The application of the death penalty often also violates the right to equality and the principle of non-discrimination. The decision about whether to sentence a convict to death or to lesser punishment is often arbitrary and does not necessarily follow predictable, rational criteria. In that judicial lottery, the odds are often stacked against the poor, minorities and other common targets of discrimination, including women, foreign nationals and lesbian, gay, bisexual, transgender and intersex persons.[73]

9.33 In one study in the mid-1990s in Philadelphia in the United States, it was concluded that the likelihood of receiving a death sentence in a capital case was 3.9 times higher if the defendant was black. The results were obtained after analysis and control for case differences such as the severity of the crime and the background of the defendant.[74] Racial bias persists in the US criminal justice system, in terms of both the race of the victim as well as that of the defendant. Writing in early 2020, one analyst stated that, 'blacks who kill whites – a rare event – are the most likely offenders to receive the death penalty'. However, 'regardless of the perpetrator's race, those who kill whites are more likely to face capital charges, receive a death sentence, and die by execution than those who murder blacks'.[75] In 2020, President Donald Trump had the macabre distinction of, for the first time in US history, enabling the federal government to execute more American civilians in a single year than all the states of the Union combined. All three individuals who were executed after he lost the presidential election were black.[76]

The Right to Seek Clemency

9.34 Article 6(4) of the ICCPR stipulates that anyone sentenced to death 'shall have the right to seek pardon or commutation of the sentence. Amnesty, pardon or commutation of

---

[71] Ibid., para. 42.
[72] Art. 36(1)(b), Vienna Convention on Consular Relations; adopted at Vienna 24 April 1963; entered into force 19 March 1967.
[73] 'Capital punishment and the implementation of the safeguards guaranteeing protection of the rights of those facing the death penalty: Yearly supplement of the Secretary-General to his quinquennial report on capital punishment', 2015, para. 55.
[74] See 'The Death Penalty in Black and White: Who Lives, Who Dies, Who Decides', *Death Penalty Information Center*, blog post, 4 June 1998, at http://bit.ly/2OKJDrp.
[75] D. S. Medwed, 'Black Deaths Matter: The Race-of-Victim Effect and Capital Punishment', *Northeastern University School of Law Research Paper No. 367-2020*, Posted on SSRN, 30 January 2020, at http://bit.ly/2OPMeQF.
[76] E. Pilkington, 'Donald Trump Has Executed More Americans than All States Combined, Report Finds', *The Guardian*, 16 December 2020, at http://bit.ly/37qiILj.

the sentence of death may be granted in all cases'. The Human Rights Committee has stated that no category of sentenced persons 'can be a priori excluded from such measures of relief, nor should the conditions for attainment of relief be ineffective, unnecessarily burdensome, discriminatory in nature or applied in an arbitrary manner'.[77] Thus, the inadmissibility of the possibility to seek relief from the execution of the death sentence will make its imposition arbitrary.

Persons with Disabilities

9.35 There is no general rule of international law that prohibits the imposition of the death penalty on a person with a disability. That said, the Human Rights Committee has held that States Parties to the ICCPR 'must refrain from imposing the death penalty on individuals who face special barriers in defending themselves on an equal basis with others, such as persons whose serious psycho-social and intellectual disabilities impeded their effective defense, ... and on persons that have limited moral culpability. They should also refrain from executing persons that have diminished ability to understand the reasons for their sentence.'[78] A death sentence imposed on a person whose mental state precluded an effective defence will be a violation of Article 6 of the Covenant, while the execution of the sentence on someone whose mental state degrades significantly later (beyond the obvious distress of the convicted person at his or her impending death) is likely to violate the prohibition on inhumane treatment or punishment codified in Article 7 of the ICCPR.[79]

9.36 In the United States, Alfred Bourgeois, who had been on death row for 15 years, was executed by the federal government. Mr Bourgeois's appeal claimed he had an IQ of 75 and was intellectually disabled. Lower courts allegedly relied on their own non-expert judgment and stereotypes of people with intellectual disabilities. Justices Elena Kagan and Sonia Sotomayor dissented from the majority's rejection of Bourgeois' stay application, arguing that it was unconstitutional to carry out the death sentence under the Federal Death Penalty Act's prohibition on executing people with intellectual disabilities.[80] As of writing, Lisa Montgomery, the first female death row inmate in the United States in almost six decades, was awaiting her execution for murder. One of her attorneys stated: 'Mrs Montgomery's case presents compelling grounds for clemency, including her history as a victim of gang-rape, incest and child sex trafficking, as well as her severe mental illness.'[81]

---

[77] Human Rights Committee, General Comment 36 on the right to life, para. 47. See similarly Art. 4(6), Inter-American Convention on Human Rights.

[78] Human Rights Committee, General Comment 36 on the right to life, para. 49. The African Commission on Human and Peoples' Rights has taken a similar position. See African Commission General Comment on the right to life, para. 25; and see, *infra*, Paragraph 9.57.

[79] According to Safeguard 3 of the UN Safeguards the death sentence shall not be carried out on 'persons who have become insane'. Safeguards guaranteeing protection of the rights of those facing the death penalty; approved by Economic and Social Council Resolution 1984/50 of 25 May 1984. See Hood and Hoyle, *The Death Penalty: A Worldwide Perspective*, 5th ed., p. 257ff.

[80] S. Kimball Stephenson, 'Second US Federal Prisoner Executed in Two Days Despite Intellectual Disability', *Jurist*, 13 December 2020, at http://bit.ly/30QDnxM.

[81] 'US Judge Briefly Stays Execution of Only Female Death Row Inmate', *The Guardian*, 20 November 2020, at http://bit.ly/3ad64kx.

9.37 The intellectually disabled tend to have a lesser capacity to understand the meaning and consequences of their actions and are therefore much less likely to be deterred by threats of punishment. They are also more vulnerable as suspects in the criminal justice system.[82] Hood and Hoyle cite the US case of Earl Washington, whose IQ was assessed in the range of 69.[83] After sixteen years on death row, he was pardoned after DNA evidence demonstrated that he was not guilty of the offences of rape and murder for which he had been convicted. The suspect was only able to identify the scene of the crime after police took him there three times. Psychological analyses of Mr Washington reported that, to compensate for his disability, he would politely defer to any authority figure with whom he came into contact. Thus, when police officers asked him leading questions in order to obtain a confession, he complied and offered affirmative responses in order to gain their approval.[84]

9.38 The case of R. S. v. *Trinidad and Tobago*,[85] cited by the Human Rights Committee in its General Comment 36, concerned a man on death row who was believed to be suffering from a mental illness. A psychiatrist who interviewed the author of the communication concluded in an affidavit that he was 'experiencing auditory hallucinations and is probably suffering from severe mental illness that may be significantly affecting his ability to think and behave normally'. He recommended a detailed examination of his mental status to determine the extent and nature of the disorder.[86] The author of the complaint to the Committee claimed that to issue a warrant for the execution of a mentally incompetent prisoner was in violation of customary international law and a violation of the right to life protected under the Covenant.[87] As it was not claimed that Mr R. S. was mentally incompetent at the time the death penalty was imposed, but only later when the warrant for execution was issued (and that his mental state at that time was obvious to those around him), the Committee concluded that the issuing of the warrant violated Article 7 of the Covenant.[88] The Committee did not have detailed information regarding the author's state of mental health at earlier stages of the proceedings and thus was not in a position to decide whether the author's rights under Article 6 were also violated.[89]

The Death Penalty under International Humanitarian Law

9.39 International humanitarian law prohibits the imposition or execution of the death penalty against certain persons convicted and sentenced in connection with an armed

---

[82] Hood and Hoyle, *The Death Penalty: A Worldwide Perspective*, 5th ed., p. 240.
[83] Ibid., p. 241.
[84] National Registry of Exonerations, 'Earl Washington', Newkirk Center for Science & Society at University of California Irvine, the University of Michigan Law School, and Michigan State University College of Law, United States, accessed 16 February 2020 at http://bit.ly/2SwOi2A.
[85] Human Rights Committee, *R. S. v. Trinidad and Tobago*, Views (UN doc. CCPR/C/74/D/684/1996), 2 April 2002.
[86] Ibid., para. 2.6.
[87] Ibid., para. 6.1.
[88] Ibid., para. 7.2.
[89] Ibid.

The Death Penalty

conflict. The applicable treaty rules are, however, somewhat inconsistent both within the same classification of armed conflict and between different classifications of armed conflict. In its study of customary international humanitarian law, the International Committee of the Red Cross (ICRC) neither dedicated a rule to the death penalty nor explicitly clarified whether any of the treaty rules had crystallised as custom. The international humanitarian law rules do not, however, amend or otherwise detract from those described above under the right to life and which apply at all times – both in peacetime and during armed conflict.

9.40 In international armed conflict, prisoners of war 'must at all times be humanely treated. Any unlawful act or omission by the Detaining Power causing death or seriously endangering the health of a prisoner of war in its custody is prohibited'.[90] Under 'combatant's privilege', no prisoner of war may be convicted of any offence, much less sentenced to death, for the fact of having engaged in hostilities against the detaining power, as long as he or she has complied with the rules of international humanitarian law while participating directly in hostilities. Thus even the fact of having killed many enemy soldiers during combat will not allow a lawful conviction of a combatant enjoying prisoner-of-war status as long as the acts of killing each complied with international humanitarian law.

9.41 A combatant may be convicted – and sentenced to death, unless domestic law did not already provide for that penalty – for having committed a serious violation of international humanitarian law, where the conduct amounted to a war crime. Examples could be the wilful targeting and killing of civilians or soldiers *hors de combat* during the conduct of hostilities. A prisoner of war may also be sentenced for the wilful killing of a prison guard or another prisoner during his or her detention. In contrast, a prisoner of war who attempts to escape and is recaptured before having made good his escape is liable only to a disciplinary punishment for this act, 'even if it is a repeated offence'.[91]

9.42 Further under the provisions of 1949 Geneva Convention III, if a prisoner of war is convicted after appeals have been denied, or if a sentence pronounced on a prisoner of war in the first instance is a death sentence, the Detaining Power must, as soon as possible, address a communication to the Protecting Power detailing the precise wording of the finding and the sentence; attaching a summary report of any preliminary investigation and of the trial, emphasising in particular the elements of the prosecution and the defence; and including notification, where applicable, of the establishment where the sentence will be served (or executed).[92]

9.43 Civilians in the territories of parties to an international armed conflict, including in occupied territory, 'shall at all times be humanely treated, and shall be protected

---

[90] Art. 13, Convention Relative to the Treatment of Prisoners of War; adopted at Geneva 12 August 1949; entered into force 21 October 1950 (hereinafter, 1949 Geneva Convention III). Prisoner-of-war status is guaranteed to combatants and certain other individuals and groups. See Art. 4, 1949 Geneva Convention III, along with Chapter 7 of this work.
[91] Art. 93, 1949 Geneva Convention III.
[92] Art. 107, 1949 Geneva Convention III.

especially against all acts of violence or threats thereof'.[93] Under the 1949 Geneva Convention IV, in a situation of military occupation, 'the death penalty may not be pronounced against a protected person who was under eighteen years of age at the time of the offence'.[94] The 1977 Additional Protocol I provides more narrowly that 'the death penalty for an offence related to the armed conflict shall not be executed on persons who had not attained the age of eighteen years at the time the offence was committed'.[95] This rule applies to all persons convicted for an offence related to the armed conflict, whether or not they enjoyed protected status under the Geneva Conventions and Additional Protocol 1. It is narrower than – and today is in breach of – the rule that exists in customary international human rights law whereby no death sentence shall be imposed in any circumstances on a person who was under eighteen at the time of the commission of the offence.

9.44 The 1977 Additional Protocol I requires that parties to a conflict 'endeavour, to the maximum extent feasible' to avoid imposing the death penalty on pregnant women or mothers having dependent infants for any offence related to the armed conflict. In any event, the death penalty may not be executed on such women.[96] Internees in a military occupation who are recaptured after having escaped, or when attempting to escape, will be liable only to disciplinary punishment in respect of this act, even if it is a repeated offence.[97]

9.45 In any non-international armed conflict, 'violence to life and person, in particular murder of all kinds, mutilation, cruel treatment and torture' is prohibited against any detainee held in connection with the conflict, whether he or she be military or civilian.[98] According to the 1977 Additional Protocol II, the imposition of the death penalty on pregnant women or mothers of young children is prohibited.[99] Unusually, this provision is stricter than the corresponding provision pertaining to women in a situation of international armed conflict. Moreover, under Common Article 3, 'the passing of sentences and the carrying out of executions without previous judgment pronounced by a regularly constituted court, affording all the judicial guarantees which are recognized as indispensable by civilized peoples' is a serious violation of

---

[93] Art. 27, Geneva Convention Relative to the Protection of Civilian Persons in Time of War; adopted at Geneva 12 August 1949; entered into force 21 October 1950 (hereinafter, 1949 Geneva Convention IV).
[94] Art. 68(4), 1949 Geneva Convention IV.
[95] Art. 77(5), Protocol Additional to the Geneva Conventions of 12 August 1949, and relating to the Protection of Victims of International Armed Conflicts; adopted at Geneva 8 June 1977; entered into force 7 December 1978 (hereinafter, 1977 Additional Protocol I).
[96] Art. 76(3), Additional Protocol I.
[97] Art. 120, 1949 Geneva Convention IV.
[98] Article 3 common to the four 1949 Geneva Conventions. See, e.g., Geneva Convention Relative to the Protection of Civilian Persons in Time of War; adopted at Geneva 12 August 1949; entered into force 21 October 1950. See also Art. 4, Protocol additional to the Geneva Conventions of 12 August 1949, and relating to the protection of victims of non-international armed conflicts; adopted at Geneva 8 June 1977; entered into force 7 December 1978 (hereinafter, 1977 Additional Protocol II).
[99] Art. 6(4), 1977 Additional Protocol II.

The Death Penalty

international humanitarian law. The imposition of a death sentence at the issue of an unfair trial is a war crime within the jurisdiction of the International Criminal Court.[100]

THE DEATH PENALTY UNDER REGIONAL STANDARDS

9.46 There is a wide variance in the standards that apply to the death penalty under regional human rights treaties. In Europe, the death sentence has been in effect outlawed by the European Court of Human Rights. The African human rights system is moving in that direction, following jurisprudence in recent years. Severe restrictions are imposed on the death penalty by the Inter-American human rights systems. But the 2004 Arab Charter on Human Rights[101] infringes customary international law on the death penalty in a number of respects, particularly with regard to the possibility it foresees of executing child offenders.

The Death Penalty under the European Convention on Human Rights

9.47 Article 2 of the 1950 European Convention on Human Rights[102] protects the right to life. Paragraph 1 provides that no one shall be deprived of his life intentionally 'save in the execution of a sentence of a court following his conviction of a crime for which this penalty is provided by law'.[103] In 1983, Protocol No. 6 to the Convention concerning the Abolition of the Death Penalty was adopted at Strasbourg, outlawing the death penalty in general but allowing for its application 'in respect of acts committed in time of war or of imminent threat of war', where existing domestic law allowed for this exception.[104] In 2002, Protocol No. 13 to the Convention concerning the abolition of the death penalty in all circumstances removed that exception.[105]

9.48 In its 2003 judgment in the *Öcalan* case, a Chamber of the European Court stated that a de facto abolition of the death penalty in Europe had developed into a de jure abolition in forty-three of the forty-four States parties to the European Convention.[106] It

---

[100] Art. 8(2)(c)(iv), ICC Statute. In the corresponding elements of crimes, the Court is asked to consider whether 'in the light of all relevant circumstances, the cumulative effect of factors with respect to guarantees deprived the person or persons of a fair trial'. Elements of Crimes, *Official Records of the Assembly of States Parties to the Rome Statute of the International Criminal Court, First session, New York, 3–10 September 2002*, p. 34.
[101] Arab Charter on Human Rights; adopted at Tunis 22 May 2004; entered into force 15 March 2008.
[102] Convention for the Protection of Human Rights and Fundamental Freedoms; adopted at Rome 4 November 1950; entered into force 3 September 1953.
[103] Art. 2(1), European Convention on Human Rights.
[104] Arts. 1 and 2, Protocol No. 6 to the European Convention on Human Rights concerning the Abolition of the Death Penalty; adopted at Strasbourg 28 April 1983; entered into force 1 March 1985. As of 1 May 2021, 46 States were party to the Protocol while 1 (the Russian Federation) was a signatory.
[105] Art. 1, Protocol No. 13 to the European Convention on Human Rights concerning the abolition of the death penalty in all circumstances removed that exception; adopted at Vilnius 3 May 2002; entered into force 1 July 2003. As of 1 May 2021, forty-four States were party to the Protocol while one (Armenia) was a signatory. Neither Azerbaijan nor the Russian Federation is a signatory.
[106] European Court of Human Rights, *Öcalan v. Turkey*, Judgment (First Section), 12 March 2003, para. 195.

can 'also be argued', the Court said, 'that the implementation of the death penalty can be regarded as inhuman and degrading treatment contrary to Article 3'.[107] The Court did not reach any firm conclusion on that point given that, on the facts of the case, Article 3 had been violated by the imposition of a death sentence following an unfair trial.[108]

9.49 In 2010, in its judgment in the *Al-Saadoon* case,[109] a Chamber of the Court asserted that the position had 'evolved' since then. The Court considered that the wording of the second sentence of Article 2(1) no longer acted 'as a bar to its interpreting the words "inhuman or degrading treatment or punishment" in Article 3 as including the death penalty'.[110] It may be taken that the imposition and execution of the death penalty are now prohibited to any State Party to the European Convention since that decision. Moreover, the EU Charter of Fundamental Rights stipulates in its Article 2(2) that 'no one shall be condemned to the death penalty, or executed'.[111]

The Death Penalty under the American Convention on Human Rights

9.50 According to the 1969 American Convention on Human Rights: 'Every person has the right to have his life respected. This right shall be protected by law and, in general, from the moment of conception. No one shall be arbitrarily deprived of his life.'[112] Article 4 of the Convention allows for the death penalty in broadly similar terms to the ICCPR. According to paragraph 2:

> In countries that have not abolished the death penalty, it may be imposed only for the most serious crimes and pursuant to a final judgment rendered by a competent court and in accordance with a law establishing such punishment, enacted prior to the commission of the crime. The application of such punishment shall not be extended to crimes to which it does not presently apply.

In its report in 2000 on a series of death row cases in Jamaica, the Inter-American Commission on Human Rights held the mandatory death penalty to be a violation of the right to life under the Convention:

> Imposing a mandatory death penalty for all crimes of capital or multiple non-capital murders prohibits a reasoned consideration of each individual case to determine the propriety of the punishment in the circumstances. By its nature, then, this process eliminates a reasoned basis for sentencing a particular individual to death, and fails to allow for rational and proportionate connections between individual offenders, their offenses, and the punishment imposed on them. Implementing the death penalty in

---

[107] Ibid., para. 198.
[108] Ibid. See similarly on this point the dicta in the Grand Chamber: European Court of Human Rights, Öcalan v. *Turkey*, Judgment (Grand Chamber), 12 May 2005, paras. 164, 165.
[109] European Court of Human Rights, *Al-Saadoon and Mufdhi* v. *United Kingdom*, Judgment (Fourth Section), 2 March 2010.
[110] Ibid., para. 120.
[111] Art. 2(2), European Union Charter of Fundamental Rights, incorporated into EU law by Article 6(1) of the Consolidated version of the Treaty on European Union.
[112] Art. 4(1), American Convention on Human Rights.

this manner therefore results in the arbitrary deprivation of life, within the ordinary meaning of that term and in the context of the object and purpose of Article 4(1) of the Convention.'[113]

9.51 Paragraph 3 of Article 4 provides that the death penalty shall not be re-established in States that have abolished it, the only regional human rights treaty to have such a provision. Under Article 4(4), in no case may capital punishment be inflicted for political offences or related common crimes. Article 4(5) prohibits the imposition of the death penalty on those who, at the time the crime was committed, were either under eighteen years of age or over seventy years.[114] In addition, the death penalty may not be executed on a pregnant woman. Finally, every person condemned to death 'shall have the right to apply for amnesty, pardon, or commutation of sentence, which may be granted in all cases. Capital punishment shall not be imposed while such a petition is pending decision by the competent authority.'[115]

9.52 A Protocol to the American Convention on Human Rights to Abolish the Death Penalty, was adopted at Asunción on 8 June 1990. A total of thirteen States were party to the Protocol as of writing,[116] which obligates them to 'not apply the death penalty in their territory to any person subject to their jurisdiction'.[117] Akin to the exceptions provided for in both the Second Optional Protocol to the ICCPR and the Protocol 6 to the European Convention on Human Rights, however, when adhering to the Protocol to the Inter-American Convention, States are permitted to continue to apply the death penalty to the most serious crimes committed in wartime.[118] To date, both Brazil and Chile have chosen to do so.[119]

The Death Penalty under African Human Rights Standards

9.53 The African Charter on Human and Peoples' Rights (the 'Banjul Charter') enshrines the right to life for 'every human being' as follows: 'Human beings are inviolable. Every human being shall be entitled to respect for his life and the integrity of his person. No one may be arbitrarily deprived of this right.'[120] There is no provision in the Banjul Charter explicitly allowing for the death penalty. Nonetheless, in 2013 the African Commission stated that the imposition of the death penalty to the 'most serious crimes' would not

---

[113] Inter-American Commission on Human Rights, Report No. 41/00 (Cases 12.023 (Desmond McKenzie), 12.044 (Andrew Downer and Alphonso Tracey), 12.107 (Carl Baker), 12.126 (Dwight Fletcher), and 12.146 (Anthony Rose)), Jamaica, 13 April 2000, para. 196.
[114] This is the only human rights treaty in force which prohibits the execution of the elderly.
[115] Art. 4(6), Inter-American Convention on Human Rights.
[116] Argentina, Brazil, Chile, Costa Rica, Dominican Republic, Ecuador, Honduras, Mexico, Nicaragua, Panama, Paraguay, Uruguay, and Venezuela. See http://bit.ly/2Sz5O4S.
[117] Art. 1, Protocol to the American Convention on Human Rights to Abolish the Death Penalty; adopted at Asuncion 8 June 1990; entered into force 28 August 1991.
[118] Ibid., Art. 2.
[119] See the respective declarations at http://bit.ly/2Sz5O4S.
[120] Art. 4(1), African Charter on Human and Peoples' Rights; adopted at Nairobi 27 June 1981; entered into force 21 October 1986.

constitute a violation of the right to life.[121] Such crimes would encompass those where the crime is intentional and involves the use of violence or firearms resulting in the death of another as in the case of murder.[122]

9.54 Two years later, in its decision in *Ping* v. *Botswana*, the Commission affirmed that it would 'itself be arbitrary, given its previous decisions with respect to the death penalty', were it 'suddenly to determine that the practice of the death penalty in Africa would in all cases be a violation of Article 4'.[123] 'However', the Commission declared, given the 'evolution of international human rights law and jurisprudence, and State practice', it considered it 'increasingly difficult to envisage a case in which the death penalty can be found to have been applied in a way that is not in some way arbitrary'.[124] As a result, the Commission concluded, 'it is difficult to conceive that, if called upon in future to do so, that the Commission will find that the death penalty, however it is executed, is any longer compatible with the African Charter'.[125] Most recently, in its decision in November 2019 in *Ally Rajabu* v. *Tanzania*, the African Court reaffirmed that the mandatory death penalty does not uphold the requirements of fairness and due process guaranteed under Article 7(1) of the Charter, thereby rendering the death penalty contrary to Article 4 of the Charter.[126]

9.55 In its 2015 General Comment on the right to life under the Charter, the African Commission on Human and Peoples' Rights noted that it had, on several occasions, passed resolutions calling on States to abolish the death penalty or to establish a moratorium 'in line with the continental and global trend'.[127] One of these resolutions is No. 136 of 2008, which urged States Parties to the African Charter that still retain the death penalty 'to observe a moratorium on the execution of death sentences with a view to abolishing the death penalty'.[128] The 'vast majority' of African States have, according to the African Commission, now abolished the death penalty in law or in practice.[129] International law, the African Commission further affirms, 'requires those States that have not yet abolished the death penalty to take steps towards its abolition in order to secure the rights to life and to dignity, in addition to other rights such as the right to be free from torture, and cruel, inhuman or degrading treatment'.[130]

---

[121] African Commission on Human and Peoples' Rights, *Kobedi* v. *Botswana*, Decision, 2011, para. 202.
[122] Ibid., para. 205.
[123] African Commission on Human and Peoples' Rights, *Interights & Ditshwanelo* v. *Botswana*, Decision (Comm. No. 319/06), adopted in Banjul, during the 57th Ordinary Session of the African Commission, 4–18 November 2015, para. 66.
[124] Ibid.
[125] Ibid.
[126] African Court of Human and Peoples' Rights, *Ally Rajabu and others* v. *Tanzania*, Decision (App. No. 007/2015), 28 November 2019, paras. 112–14.
[127] African Commission General Comment on the right to life, para. 22.
[128] African Commission on Human and Peoples' Rights, 'Resolution 136 Calling on State Parties to Observe a Moratorium on the Death Penalty', ACHPR/Res.136(XXXXIV)08, Resolution adopted at Abuja 24 November 2008, at http://bit.ly/39xjILx.
[129] African Commission General Comment on the right to life, para. 22.
[130] Ibid., para. 22.

9.56 States that have abolished the death penalty in law 'shall not reintroduce it', according to the African Commission,[131] although evidence is not adduced to support that assertion. The same is true of the affirmation that States with moratoria on the death penalty 'must take steps to formalise abolition in law, allowing no further executions'.[132]

9.57 In its General Comment on the right to life under the Banjul Charter, the African Commission on Human and Peoples' Rights has stated: 'If, for any reason, the criminal justice system of a State does not, at the time of trial or conviction, meet the criteria of Article 7 of the African Charter [on fair trial rights] or if the particular proceedings in which the penalty is imposed have not stringently met the highest standards of fairness, then the subsequent application of the death penalty will be considered a violation of the right to life.'[133] In its 1998 decision in *International Pen* v. *Nigeria*, the Commission had stated: 'Given that the trial which ordered the executions itself violates Article 7, any subsequent implementation of sentences renders the resulting deprivation of life arbitrary and in violation of Article 4.'[134] Military courts, the Commission has affirmed, 'shall not have the power to impose the death penalty'.[135]

9.58 Reflecting general international law, the African Commission has stated that the execution of pregnant women or children[136] will always amount to a violation of the right to life.[137] Its assertion that nursing mothers may not be executed reflects the customary international rule that is *de lege ferenda*. More progressively, the Commission holds a similar view with respect to the 'elderly' or 'persons with psycho-social or intellectual disabilities'.[138] No definition is offered for these disparate categories. The 2016 Protocol to the African Charter on Human and Peoples' Rights on the Rights of Older Persons in Africa defines 'older persons' as those aged sixty years and above.[139] The Convention on the

---

[131] Ibid., para. 23.
[132] Ibid.
[133] Ibid., para. 24.
[134] African Commission on Human and Peoples' Rights, *International PEN, Constitutional Rights Project, Civil Liberties Organisation and Interights (on behalf of Ken Saro-Wiwa Jnr.)* v. *Nigeria*, Decision (Comm. Nos. 137/94, 139/94, 154/96 and 161/97), 31 October 1998, para. 103.
[135] African Commission General Comment on the right to life, para. 24.
[136] It is clear that by 'children' is meant child offenders, even if they are now adults. This is confirmed by the dictum in the previous paragraph whereby 'the death penalty shall not be imposed for crimes committed by children'.
[137] African Commission General Comment on the right to life, para. 25.
[138] In its 2019 judgment in *Madison* v. *Alabama*, the US Supreme Court held that the Eighth Amendment to the US Constitution may permit executing a prisoner even if he cannot remember committing his crime, but it may prohibit executing a prisoner who suffers from dementia or another disorder rather than psychotic delusions. *Madison* v. *Alabama*, Judgment (Docket No. 17-7505), 27 February 2019. Vernon Madison was sixty-eight years old when his case came before the Court, a long-time death-row inmate who was convicted of capital murder more than twenty years earlier. Multiple strokes had left him with vascular dementia. He could no longer see, walk independently, or control his bladder. According to his petition for review, a psychologist's examination found that he can no longer remember the alphabet past the letter G or name the previous president of the United States. M. Ford, 'The Cruelty of Executing the Sick and Elderly: Two Controversial Cases in Alabama Reveal a Disturbing Trend in the Death Penalty in America', *New Republic*, 27 February 2018, at http://bit.ly/39wPTuD.
[139] Art. 1, Protocol to the African Charter on Human and Peoples' Rights on the Rights of Older Persons in Africa; adopted at Addis Ababa 31 January 2016; not yet in force.

Right of Persons with Disabilities describes persons with disabilities, for the purpose of the Convention, as including 'those who have long-term physical, mental, intellectual or sensory impairments which in interaction with various barriers may hinder their full and effective participation in society on an equal basis with others'.[140] Speaking at the Ninth Session of the Conference of States Parties to the Convention on the Right of Persons with Disabilities in 2016, Paul Deany, Program Officer at the non-governmental Disability Rights Fund, said that psycho-social disability remained 'one of the most challenging and misunderstood areas of disability'; it could be 'episodic, invisible and often not well identified'.[141]

The Death Penalty under the Arab Charter on Human Rights

9.59 The 2004 Arab Charter on Human Rights has a general provision enshrining the protection of the right to life. Under Article 5(1), 'Every human being has an inherent right to life.' Paragraph 2 stipulates further that 'this right shall be protected by law. No one shall be arbitrarily deprived of his life.' No derogation from Article 5 may be made.[142] Three provisions are dedicated to the death penalty, which are, overall, the least progressive by far of those incorporated in the regional human rights treaties. Article 6 provides:

> The death penalty shall be inflicted only for the most serious crimes in accordance with the law in force at the time of the commission of the crime. Such a penalty can only be carried out pursuant to a final judgment rendered by a competent court. Anyone sentenced to death shall have the right to seek pardon or commutation of the sentence.

9.60 Article 7(1) does not comply with customary international law. It provides that the death penalty 'shall not be inflicted on a person under 18 years of age, unless otherwise provided by the law in force at the time of the commission of the crime'. This ostensibly allows a State to derogate in its national law from the customary international law prohibition on executing children and potentially also allows the execution of a death sentence once the convicted person has attained the age of eighteen.

9.61 Paragraph 2 of Article 7 stipulates that the death penalty 'shall not be carried out on a pregnant woman prior to her delivery or on a nursing mother within two years from the date on which she gave birth. In any case, the interests of the infant shall prevail'. To date, there has been no jurisprudence under the Charter that could elucidate further the regional standards.

---

[140] Art. 1, Convention on the Rights of Persons with Disabilities; adopted at New York 13 December 2006; entered into force 3 May 2008. As of 1 May 2021, 181 States and the European Union were party to the Convention and a further 9 States were signatories.

[141] 'Psychosocial Disability: One of the Most Misunderstood Areas of Disability', Disability Rights Fund, 2016, at http://bit.ly/2SCy05w.

[142] Art. 4(2), 2004 Arab Charter on Human Rights.

THE METHOD OF EXECUTION

The Normative Framework

9.62 An execution that uses a method that is cruel or inhuman does not necessarily, per se, violate the right to life but will certainly violate the prohibition on torture or other forms of cruel, inhuman, or degrading treatment or punishment. That said, in its General Comment 36 on the right to life, the Human Rights Committee asserted that a failure to respect Article 7 of the Covenant in the execution of the death penalty 'would inevitably render the execution arbitrary in nature and thus also in violation of article 6'.[143] In its earlier General Comment No. 20 on Article 7 of the ICCPR, the Committee had stated that, when imposing capital punishment, the execution of the sentence 'must be carried out in such a way as to cause the least possible physical and mental suffering'.[144] Asphyxiation, stoning, and – according to certain determinations – also death by hanging have been found to violate the right to freedom from inhumane treatment or punishment. The legality of the use of firing squads is contested.

9.63 In its judgment in *Jabari* v. *Turkey* in 2000,[145] the European Court held that the risk of death by stoning for an Iranian national who had fled Iran after a relationship with a married man precluded her return to Iran.[146] The order for deportation would, if executed, have given rise to a violation of Article 3 (prohibition of torture) of the European Convention on Human Rights.[147] In April 2019, the UN High Commissioner for Human Rights urged the Government of Brunei to halt the entry into force of its revised Penal Code, which would enshrine in legislation the death penalty for offences such as rape, adultery, sodomy, extramarital sexual relations for Muslims, robbery, and insult or defamation of the Prophet Mohammad, among others, and allows death by stoning: 'cruel and inhuman punishments that seriously breach international human rights law'.[148] In its Views in *Ng* v. *Canada*,[149] the Human Rights Committee found that the method of execution by cyanide gas asphyxiation amounted to cruel, inhuman, and degrading treatment: the author of the complaint had alleged, without rebuttal, that asphyxiation by cyanide gas may cause prolonged suffering and agony and may take more than ten minutes.[150]

---

[143] Human Rights Committee General Comment 36 on the right to life, para. 40.
[144] Human Rights Committee, General Comment No. 20 on Article 7 of the ICCPR, UN doc. CCPR/C/21/Add.3, 10 March 1992, para. 6.
[145] European Court of Human Rights, *Jabari* v. *Turkey*, Judgment (Fourth Section), 11 July 2000.
[146] See also in support of the illegality of 'death by stoning' the Joint opinion by Mr A. Mavrommatis and Mr W. Sadi (dissenting) in Human Rights Committee, *Chitat Ng* v. *Canada*, Views (UN doc. CCPR/C/49/D/469/1991), 5 November 1993: 'We do not believe that, on the basis of the material before us, execution by gas asphyxiation could constitute cruel and inhuman treatment within the meaning of article 7 of the Covenant. A method of execution such as death by stoning, which is intended to and actually inflicts prolonged pain and suffering, is contrary to article 7.'
[147] European Court of Human Rights, *Jabari* v. *Turkey*, Judgment, paras. 41–3.
[148] 'Bachelet URGES Brunei to Stop Entry into Force of "Draconian" New Penal Code', news release, OHCHR, Geneva, 1 April 2019, at http://bit.ly/2SokQeP.
[149] Human Rights Committee, *Chitat Ng* v. *Canada*, Views adopted on 5 November 1993.
[150] Ibid., para. 16.3.

9.64 In its decision in the *Kobedi* case, the African Commission declared its view that

> the execution of a death sentence by hanging may not be compatible with respect for the inherent dignity of the individual and the duty to minimize unnecessary suffering, because it is a notoriously slow and painful means of execution. If carried out without appropriate attention to the weight of the person condemned because hanging can result either in slow and painful strangulation, because the neck is not immediately broken by the drop, or, at the other extreme, in the separation of the head from the body.[151]

In contrast, in its 2009 judgment in *Attorney General v. Susan Kigula*,[152] the Supreme Court of Uganda was 'inclined to the view that the pain and suffering experienced during the hanging process is inherent in the punishment of the death penalty which has been provided for in the constitution. We would therefore not say it is unconstitutional.'[153]

9.65 In its 2019 judgment in *Bucklew v. Precythe*,[154] the US Supreme Court held that the Eighth Amendment to the US Constitution does not guarantee a prisoner a 'painless' death. Moreover, the Court declared, traditionally accepted methods of execution are not necessarily unconstitutional because an arguably more humane method becomes available. Mr Bucklew had argued that, regardless of whether the lethal injection protocol in place in Missouri would cause excruciating pain for all prisoners, it would cause him severe pain because he had a particular medical condition.[155]

9.66 The legality of death by firing squad is debated, in particular in the United States, as a result of restrictions on the procurement of drugs from pharmaceutical companies.[156] In February 2017, the US Supreme Court had denied the request by Thomas Arthur, an Alabama death-row prisoner, to be shot to death rather than be subjected to the risk of a painful death from secret, experimental lethal-injection drugs.[157] But in her dissenting opinion, Supreme Court Justice Sonia Sotomayor condemned the decision for tacitly endorsing execution methods that could be considered cruel or inhumane in violation of

---

[151] African Commission on Human and Peoples' Rights, *Kobedi v. Botswana*, Decision, 2011, para. 169.
[152] Supreme Court of Uganda, *Attorney General v. Susan Kigula and 417 others* (Constitutional Appeal No. 3 of 2006) [2009] UGSC 6 (21 January 2009).
[153] Ibid., p. 62.
[154] US Supreme Court, *Bucklew v. Precythe*, 587 US ___ (2019).
[155] Mr Bucklow had a disease known as cavernous haemangioma, which causes vascular tumours – clumps of blood vessels – to grow in his head, neck, and throat. His complaint alleged that this condition could prevent the pentobarbital from circulating properly in his body, that the use of a chemical dye to flush the intravenous line could cause his blood pressure to spike and his tumours to rupture, and that pentobarbital could interact adversely with his other medications.
[156] See, e.g., S. Moran, 'A Modest Proposal: The Federal Government Should Use Firing Squads to Execute Federal Death Row Inmates', *University of Miami Law Review*, vol. 74, no. 1 (November 2019); J. P. Williams, 'The Return of the Firing Squad', *US News*, 3 March 2017, at http://bit.ly/38rdHQK.
[157] US Supreme Court, *Thomas D. Arthur v. Jefferson S. Dunn, Commissioner, Alabama Department of Corrections, and others*, Petition for Writ of Certiorari to the US Court of Appeals for the Eleventh Circuit (Case No. 16–602), 580 US ___ (2017), 21 February 2017.

the US Constitution. At the same time, Justice Sotomayor observed that States in the United States have used a number of different methods of execution – hanging, electrocution, the gas chamber, and lethal injection – but have abandoned each one as science has demonstrated that the method 'causes unconstitutional levels of suffering'.[158] The execution of Mr Arthur is said to have lasted about thirty minutes, a substantially longer period of time than would typically be the case.[159]

9.67 In 1879, the Supreme Court in *Wilkerson v. Utah*[160] had permitted an execution by firing squad while observing that the Eighth Amendment forbade gruesome methods of execution such as disembowelling, quartering, public dissection, and burning alive. This case has not been overruled. Professor Phyllis Goldfarb of George Washington University has contested the assertion that death by firing squad is 'pain- and botch-free', noting some marksmen miss the heart and hit other parts of the body, while others fire prematurely. 'The condemned dies from blood loss and loses consciousness when blood supplied to the brain drops precipitously. Even when the people in the firing squad hit their target as intended, it may take at least a couple of minutes for the condemned to die and sometimes much longer.'[161]

9.68 In Vietnam, during the French colonial period, the guillotine was the most popular method of execution. Following independence in 1945, the Democratic Republic of Vietnam decided to change to execution by firing squad.[162] This requirement was set out in Vietnam's Code of Criminal Procedure: 'The death sentence is executed by shooting (firing squad).'[163] In 2010, the Law on Criminal Execution changed the lawful method of execution to lethal injection.[164] This stipulation has applied since 1 November 2011, according to the terms of an implementing decree.[165] The decision to change the method of execution to lethal injection was, according to the government, with a view to inflicting less pain on the condemned person as well as to reduce the negative psychological impact on the executioners.[166]

9.69 It is reported that, in North Korea, the vast majority of executions occur by firing squad. This 'often involves three shooters firing three rounds each into the body of the condemned person'.[167] Certain executions are said to have been carried out by anti-aircraft

---

[158] Dissenting Opinion of Justice Sotomayor, in ibid., p. 13.
[159] J. Jarvie, 'Murderer Known as "Houdini of Death Row" Executed in Alabama', *Los Angeles Times*, 25 May 2017, at http://lat.ms/2HkMRxF.
[160] US Supreme Court, *Wilkerson v. Utah*, 99 US 130 (1879).
[161] Cited in Williams 'The Return of the Firing Squad'.
[162] Kien Tran and Cong Giao Vu, 'The Changing Nature of Death Penalty in Vietnam: A Historical and Legal Inquiry', *Societies*, 12 August 2019.
[163] Art. 259(3), 2003 Code of Criminal Procedure.
[164] Art. 59(1), 2010 Law on Criminal Execution.
[165] Degree 82/2011/N-CP of 19 September 2011.
[166] Prime Ministerial Decision No. 01/2004/QD-TTg on the List of State Secret Information of the People's Courts, 2004, at http://bit.ly/2uwxpMd.
[167] BBC, 'North Korea: Hundreds of Public Execution Sites Identified, Says Report', 11 June 2019, at http://bbc.in/38oMXjz.

guns, ripping the body of the victims to shreds.[168] In February 2020, a North Korean trade official was reportedly shot to death after visiting a public bath while he was meant to be in quarantine as a coronavirus precaution.[169]

[168] See, e.g., J. Sharman, 'North Korean Defector "Forced to Watch 11 Musicians Executed with Anti-Aircraft Guns"', *The Independent*, 21 September 2017, at http://bit.ly/37n3sLJ; and C. Hughes, 'Inside Kim Jong-Un's Feared Inner-Circle: North Korean Despot Has Teenage Sex Slaves Plucked from School, Enjoys £1,000 a-Time Lunches and Forces Upper Class Elite to Watch Horrific Executions', *Daily Mirror*, last updated 30 September 2018, at http://bit.ly/2SlP1U3. On the other hand, allegations reported in the media that at least one condemned person was killed by hungry dogs appears to have been either a bizarre form of satire or fake news.

[169] 'Reports: Kim Jong-Un Executed North Korea Official Who Used Public Bath While in Coronavirus Quarantine', *National Post*, 13 February 2020, at http://bit.ly/31OFZ56.

10

Deaths in Custody

INTRODUCTION

10.01 This chapter describes the duty of States to prevent and investigate deaths that occur while a person is in their formal custody or is otherwise being detained by the authorities. When a person is held in a place of detention, the risks of him or her being killed or seriously harmed, whether at the hands of warders or by other inmates, are acute. In addition, a detainee may decide to commit suicide, whether as a consequence of mental health issues, the broader circumstances of incarceration, or directly as a result of his or her treatment while in detention. Inadequate provision of medical care, food, or water may also contribute to premature death. Of course, detainees can and do also die from natural causes.[1]

10.02 The chapter begins by discussing the notions of custody and detention. It then discusses the duty to prevent deaths occurring during detention, under both global and regional standards. While the focus is on State prisons, police stations, and other detention facilities, the right to life in privately run detention centres is also considered. The legality of the use of potentially lethal force against a person escaping from custody is then addressed. Finally, the duty to investigate deaths occurring in custody is outlined.

The Definition of Custody and Detention

10.03 There is no agreed definition under international law of either *custody* or *detention*, although the terms are well understood as overlapping forms of deprivation of liberty. These may or may not conform with the right to liberty and its core prohibition of arbitrary deprivation of liberty. The Inter-American Commission of Human Rights has defined the notion of 'deprivation of liberty' in broad terms, as follows:

> Any form of detention, imprisonment, institutionalization, or custody of a person in a public or private institution which that person is not permitted to leave at will, by order of or under de facto control of a judicial, administrative or any other authority, for

---

[1] The International Committee of the Red Cross (ICRC) defines a death as natural 'when it is caused solely by disease and/or the aging process'. ICRC, *Guidelines for Investigating Deaths in Custody*, Geneva, 2013, p. 8.

reasons of humanitarian assistance, treatment, guardianship, protection, or because of crimes or legal offenses.[2]

The Commission clarifies that, as a category, detainees include those who are deprived of their liberty 'because of crimes or infringements or noncompliance with the law, whether they are accused or convicted'. Also encompassed are those under the 'custody and supervision' of institutions, such as secure psychiatric hospitals and other establishments for persons with physical, mental, or sensory disabilities; institutions for children and the elderly; and centres for migrants, refugees, or asylum seekers.[3]

10.04 In criminal law procedure, custody is generally considered the formal detention of an individual by organs of the State (police or judiciary), particularly one that follows an arrest.[4] Under the 1966 International Covenant on Civil and Political Rights[5] (ICCPR), it is stipulated: 'It shall not be the general rule that persons awaiting trial shall be detained in custody.'[6] Article 9 of the ICCPR more broadly refers to the notions of arbitrary detention and arbitrary deprivation of liberty as if they are to be considered synonyms. The wording of the 1984 Convention against Torture[7] (CAT) implies a similar understanding of the notion of custody and detention. Thus, CAT provides: 'When a State, pursuant to this article, has taken a person into custody, it shall immediately notify the States referred to in article 5, paragraph 1, of the fact that such person is in custody and of the circumstances which warrant his detention.'[8]

10.05 National criminal laws endorse an understanding under international law of custody as a formalised type of detention, even though the precise appreciation of the two terms may differ from State to State. Under domestic law in the United States, for instance, the fact of being detained is broad in scope, and does not necessarily indicate that a detainee has been arrested or will be formally taken into custody by a law enforcement official. According to the federal US Criminal Code, whoever escapes or attempts to escape from 'any custody under or by virtue of any process issued under the laws of the United States by any court, judge, or magistrate judge, or from the custody of an officer or employee of the United States pursuant to lawful arrest' commits an offence.[9] In a similar vein, in India, when the police or another law enforcement agency holds someone under

---

[2] Inter-American Commission on Human Rights, 'Revision of the United Nations Standard Minimum Rules for the Treatment of Prisoners', UN doc. UNODC/CCPCJ/EG.6/2014/INF/2, 8 October 2013, p. 3.
[3] Ibid.
[4] *Custody* also means, more broadly, 'in the care of'. This broader sense applies to its employment in the Elements of Crime of the crime against humanity of torture under Article 7(1)(f) of the 1998 Rome Statute of the International Criminal Court: ('Such person or persons were in the custody or under the control of the perpetrator'). 'Elements of Crimes', *Official Records of the Assembly of States Parties to the Rome Statute of the International Criminal Court*, First session, New York, 3–10 September 2002, Part II(B).
[5] International Covenant on Civil and Political Rights; adopted at New York 16 December 1966; entered into force 23 March 1976. As of 1 May 2021, 173 States were party to the ICCPR.
[6] Art. 9(3), ICCPR.
[7] Convention against Torture and Other Cruel, Inhuman or Degrading Treatment or Punishment; adopted at New York 10 December 1984; entered into force 26 June 1987. As of 1 May 2021, 171 States were party to CAT.
[8] Art. 6(4), CAT.
[9] 18 US Code §751 ('Prisoners in custody of institution or officer'), available at http://bit.ly/2vhvf2P.

suspicion of an illegal act but has not charged them with a crime, this is known as detention. Under Indian criminal law, custody is a second stage of an arrest of a suspect, usually prior to a trial. Police custody means the individual is held in a police cell, while in case of judicial custody, he or she is held in prison.[10]

THE DUTY TO PREVENT DEATHS IN CUSTODY UNDER GLOBAL STANDARDS

10.06 States are obligated to respect and protect the lives of all detainees. Arbitrary deprivation of life by State agents will be unlawful inside a detention facility just as it is outside. This applies to all State-run facilities and all facilities whose management the State contracts out to the private sector, whereby the private company and its staff are acting as agents of the State. In this regard, under the International Law Commission's (ILC's) 2001 Draft Articles on Responsibility of States for Internationally Wrongful Acts, 'the conduct of a person or entity which is not an organ of the State … but which is empowered by the law of that State to exercise elements of the governmental authority shall be considered an act of the State under international law, provided the person or entity is acting in that capacity in the particular instance'.[11] Indeed, the official commentary on the article specifies that 'in some countries private security firms may be contracted to act as prison guards and in that capacity may exercise public powers such as powers of detention and discipline pursuant to a judicial sentence or to prison regulations'.[12]

10.07 Consonant with the general law of law enforcement, all use of force by warders in any custodial facility, whether State-run or privately managed, must be both necessary and proportionate. This means, as Chapter 7 has described, that any use of force must be the minimum necessary in the circumstances, must be undertaken in pursuit of a legitimate law enforcement purpose, and that force may be employed only for as long as is necessary. Where it is necessary, the force used must also be proportionate to the threat or the harm to be avoided.

10.08 These requirements are largely reflected in the soft-law Nelson Mandela Rules, which were adopted by unanimous vote by the UN General Assembly in 2015. Rule 82(1) stipulates that, in a prison, 'prison staff shall not, in their relations with the prisoners, use force except in self-defence or in cases of attempted escape, or active or passive physical resistance to an order based on law or regulations. Prison staff who have recourse to force must use no more than is strictly necessary and must report the incident immediately to the prison director.'[13] Precautionary measures must be taken in any custodial facility to

---

[10] P. Sepaha, 'Difference between Detention, Arrest and Custody', *Law Colloquy*, 18 July 2018, at http://bit.ly/38CS7Z7.

[11] Art. 5: Conduct of persons or entities exercising elements of governmental authority, *Draft articles on Responsibility of States for Internationally Wrongful Acts*, Text adopted by the Commission at its fifty-third session, in 2001, and submitted to the UN General Assembly in UN doc. A/56/10 (hereinafter, ILC Draft Articles on State Responsibility).

[12] Commentary, para. 2, on Article 5, ILC Draft Articles on State Responsibility.

[13] Rule 82(1), UN Standard Minimum Rules for the Treatment of Prisoners (the Nelson Mandela Rules), adopted by UN General Assembly Resolution 70/175; the resolution was adopted by unanimous vote on 17 December 2015.

minimise the risks of death or serious injury, including the equipping of warders with appropriate less-lethal weapons.[14] The carrying of personal weapons by law enforcement officials in custodial settings is, however, prohibited.[15]

10.09 With respect to compliance with Article 6(1) of the ICCPR, the Human Rights Committee has stated: 'Loss of life occurring in custody, in unnatural circumstances, creates a presumption of arbitrary deprivation of life by State authorities, which can only be rebutted on the basis of a proper investigation which establishes the State's compliance with its obligations under article 6.'[16] The onus is thus placed on the State to justify, through an effective and impartial investigation, that it is not legally responsible for the death of a person in custody (or, potentially, another form of detention). Accordingly, in its Views in the *Khadzhiyev* case, where it found that the right to life of the deceased had been violated by Turkmenistan, the Human Rights Committee drew attention to the fact that the State Party concerned had 'not presented evidence establishing that a prompt and thorough investigation took place that would rebut the author's allegations that Ms. Muradova was killed due to the torture she sustained while in custody'.[17]

10.10 In the event that one detainee kills another, if the State either failed to exercise due diligence to prevent the death (or if it subsequently fails to investigate its circumstances and take the appropriate prosecutorial action), the victim's right to life will have been violated.[18] The European Court of Human Rights has held that where the authorities 'knew or ought to have known at the time of the existence of a real and immediate risk to the life of an identified individual by a third party or himself' they are obligated to 'take measures within the scope of their powers which, judged reasonably, might have been expected to avoid that risk'.[19] However, even where no such knowledge exists, 'there are certain basic precautions which police officers and prison officers should be expected to take in all cases in order to minimise any potential risk to protect the health and well-being of the arrested person'.[20] This reflects general international law as being inherent in the duty to protect the right to life of any person under a State's jurisdiction.

10.11 In the *Mižigárová* case[21] cited by the European Court with respect to precautionary measures, the applicant's husband, Mr Ľubomír Šarišský, had been arrested on suspicion of bicycle theft. In the version provided by the Slovak government, Mr Šarišský had written

---

[14] *United Nations Human Rights Guidance on Less-Lethal Weapons in Law Enforcement*, Office of the UN High Commissioner for Human Rights (OHCHR), Geneva/New York, 2020, para. 2.6.

[15] Ibid., para. 6.2.1.

[16] Human Rights Committee, 'General Comment No. 36: Article 6: right to life, UN doc. CCPR/C/GC/36, 3 September 2019 (hereinafter, Human Rights Committee, General Comment 36 on the right to life), para. 61.

[17] Human Rights Committee, *Khadzhiyev v. Turkmenistan*, Views (UN doc. CCPR/C/122/D/2252/2013), 6 April 2018, para. 7.4.

[18] *The Minnesota Protocol on the Investigation of Potentially Unlawful Death* (2016), Office of the UN High Commissioner for Human Rights, New York/Geneva, 2017, para. 8(c).

[19] European Court of Human Rights, *Keller v. Russia*, Judgment (First Section), 17 October 2013 (rendered final on 17 February 2014), para. 82.

[20] Ibid.

[21] European Court of Human Rights, *Mižigárová v. Slovakia*, Judgment (Fourth Section), 14 December 2010 (rendered final on 14 March 2011).

a suicide note while in police custody and then grabbed a police officer's gun during formal interview and shot himself. The Court doubted the official version of events, even referring in its judgment to the 'inherent improbability of the theory', but held that even if it were true, there were no compelling reasons as to why the interrogation of a non-violent suspect had been entrusted to an armed police officer. Moreover, at the time of Mr Šarišský's death, regulations in force required Slovakian police officers to secure their service weapons before interrogation in order to avoid any 'undesired consequences'.[22]

10.12 Under Article 10(1) of the ICCPR, all persons deprived of their liberty 'shall be treated with humanity and with respect for the inherent dignity of the human person'. Accordingly, detainees in custodial or other detention facilities must be provided with adequate food, water, shelter, clothing, and medical care.[23] Article 10 of the ICCPR further requires that those who have been accused but not convicted must, 'save in exceptional circumstances', be held separately from those convicted 'and shall be subject to separate treatment appropriate to their status as unconvicted persons'.[24] For their protection, accused children must be detained separately from adults 'and brought as speedily as possible for adjudication'.[25]

Deaths in Custody under International Humanitarian Law

10.13 International humanitarian law prohibits violence against anyone detained in connection with an armed conflict. In situations of international armed conflict, prisoners of war 'must at all times be humanely treated. Any unlawful act or omission by the Detaining Power causing death or seriously endangering the health of a prisoner of war in its custody is prohibited'.[26] In addition, prisoners of war 'must at all times be protected, particularly against acts of violence'. They are further entitled 'in all circumstances to respect for their persons and their honour'.[27] Civilians in the territories of parties to an international armed conflict, including in occupied territory, 'shall at all times be humanely treated, and shall be protected especially against all acts of violence or threats thereof'.[28] These are treaty and customary rules binding on all States.

10.14 In any non-international armed conflict, 'violence to life and person, in particular murder of all kinds, mutilation, cruel treatment and torture', is prohibited against any detainee held in connection with the conflict, whether he or she be military or civilian.[29] The provision does not explicitly require that detainees be protected but

---

[22] Ibid., para. 89.
[23] See, e.g., Rules 19, 21, 22, and 27, Nelson Mandela Rules.
[24] Art. 10(2)(a), ICCPR.
[25] Art. 10(2)(b), ICCPR.
[26] Art. 13, Geneva Convention Relative to the Treatment of Prisoners of War; adopted at Geneva 12 August 1949; entered into force 21 October 1950 (hereinafter, 1949 Geneva Convention III). Prisoner-of-war status is guaranteed to combatants and certain other individuals as delineated in Article 4 of 1949 Geneva Convention III.
[27] Art. 14, 1949 Geneva Convention III.
[28] Art. 27, Geneva Convention Relative to the Protection of Civilian Persons in Time of War; adopted at Geneva 12 August 1949; entered into force 21 October 1950 (hereinafter, 1949 Geneva Convention IV).
[29] Article 3 common to the four 1949 Geneva Conventions. See also Art. 4, Protocol additional to the Geneva Conventions of 12 August 1949, and relating to the protection of victims of non-international armed conflicts;

this may be taken as implicit. According to the 1977 Additional Protocol II, all the wounded, sick, and shipwrecked, whether or not they have taken part in an armed conflict falling within the scope of application of the Protocol, 'shall be respected and protected'.[30]

Use of Force Against a Person Escaping from Custody

10.15 Under the 1990 UN Basic Principles on the Use of Force and Firearms by Law Enforcement Officials, law enforcement officials, 'in their relations with persons in custody or detention, shall not use force, except when strictly necessary for the maintenance of security and order within the institution, or when personal safety is threatened'.[31] Specific rules apply to the use of force against a person escaping from custody. As noted above, under Rule 82(1) of the Nelson Mandela Rules, staff may use force in a case of attempted escape from a prison, but that force must be no more than is strictly necessary.

10.16 This notion of strict necessity has been understood to incorporate the principle of proportionality. In its judgment in the *Nachova* case, the Grand Chamber of the European Court of Human Rights stated that 'the use of lethal force by police officers may be justified in certain circumstances. However, any use of force must be "no more than absolutely necessary", that is to say it must be strictly proportionate in the circumstances.'[32] Under the 1990 Basic Principles, a firearm may only be used, where necessary, against an escaping detainee presenting an 'immediate' threat to life or of serious injury to another or where he or she constitutes an ongoing grave threat to life that is not imminent.[33] The Human Rights Committee has stated that all operations of law enforcement officials should comply with the 1990 Basic Principles.[34] The authoritative nature of the Principles has also been endorsed by judgments of the European and Inter-American Courts of Human Rights.[35]

10.17 Potentially more complex is the use of firearms against an escaping enemy military detainee in the context of an armed conflict. In an international armed conflict, the 1949 Geneva Convention III stipulates that the use of weapons against prisoners of war who are escaping or attempting to escape 'shall constitute an extreme measure, which shall always

---

adopted at Geneva 8 June 1977; entered into force 7 December 1978 (hereinafter, 1977 Additional Protocol II). As of 1 May 2021, 169 States were party to the Protocol.

[30] Art. 7(1), 1977 Additional Protocol II.

[31] Principle 15, Basic Principles on the Use of Force and Firearms by Law Enforcement Officials, adopted by the Eighth UN Congress on the Prevention of Crime and the Treatment of Offenders, Havana, Cuba, 27 August to 7 September 1990 (hereinafter, 1990 Basic Principles). The Basic Principles were 'welcomed' by UN General Assembly Resolution and governments 'invited' to respect them. UN General Assembly Resolution 45/166, adopted without a vote on 18 December 1990, para. 4. Today the Basic Principles reflect customary law.

[32] European Court of Human Rights, *Nachova v. Bulgaria*, Judgment (Grand Chamber), 6 July 2005, para. 94.

[33] Principles 16 and 9, 1990 Basic Principles. Principle 16 refers to an 'immediate' threat while Principle 9 determines that the threat must be 'imminent'. The differing use of term should not be considered to imply a distinct time scale.

[34] Human Rights Committee, General Comment 36 on the right to life, para. 13.

[35] See, e.g., European Court of Human Rights, *Benzer v. Turkey*, Judgment (Former Second Section), 12 November 2013 (as rendered final on 24 March 2014), para. 90; Inter-American Court of Human Rights, *Cruz Sánchez and others v. Peru*, Judgment (Preliminary Objections, Merits, Reparation, and Costs), 17 April 2015, para. 264.

be preceded by warnings appropriate to the circumstances'.[36] In its 1960 commentary on the provision, the International Committee of the Red Cross (ICRC) stipulated that these warnings may either be verbal (using, for instance, a whistle or bell) or may be made by means of a warning shot.[37] Surprisingly, however, the ICRC commentary of the time appeared to endorse a broad use of firearms, arguing: 'One cannot require the Detaining Power to reinforce the sentry units indefinitely at the expense of its active combat forces. The only remaining alternative is therefore to adopt very strict measures in order to intimidate prisoners of war.'[38] The commentary further stated: 'In any case, if the guards or sentinels have to open fire on prisoners of war, they should first aim low, unless they are themselves in imminent danger, so as to avoid inflicting fatal wounds.'[39]

10.18 This rule must today be interpreted in light of the rules governing the use of firearms in the 1990 Basic Principles. Indeed, in its 2020 commentary on Article 42, the ICRC stated: 'Any use of firearms against a person is potentially lethal irrespective of what is being aimed at (e.g. legs, knees or chest). .... "Shoot to wound", such as aiming low (e.g. at legs) cannot be considered as a warning or as a preventive step; it is an actual use of potentially lethal force, which is strictly limited under Article 42.'[40]

10.19 Only upon a successful escape would a detained prisoner of war become targetable under the far more permissive IHL rules governing the use of force in the conduct of hostilities.[41] This is consonant with the limited State practice existing on the issue. The United States, for instance, considers that the use of tear gas against rioting or escaping prisoners of war is not a violation of the 1992 Chemical Weapons Convention.[42] The Convention explicitly prohibits the use of riot control agents as a method of warfare[43] but allows their use for law enforcement.[44]

---

[36] Art. 42, 1949 Geneva Convention III.
[37] ICRC Commentary on Article 42 of the 1949 Geneva Convention III, p. 247, at http://bit.ly/37s3mn5. The 'essential thing', the ICRC states, 'is that the warnings must be clearly perceived and understood by those to whom they are addressed. The number of warnings is not stipulated, but it will be noted that the Convention uses the plural form, which necessarily implies at least two warnings; the figure of three is generally considered as statutory.'
[38] Ibid.
[39] Ibid. Aiming at the lower limbs is not generally accepted as good law enforcement practice owing to the risk of missing the target and hitting an unintended bystander. Most (though not all) law enforcement agencies around the world train their officers to aim at the main body mass of a target.
[40] ICRC Commentary on Article 42 of the 1949 Geneva Convention III, 2020, at http://bit.ly/3hvie99, para. 2548 (footnote omitted).
[41] See ICRC, *International Humanitarian Law and the Challenges of Contemporary Armed Conflicts*, Report for the 32nd International Conference of the Red Cross and Red Crescent, Geneva, October 2015, p. 36.
[42] US Department of Defense, *Department of Defense Law of War Manual*, Washington DC, June 2015 (Updated December 2016), para. 9.22.6.1. For details of other relevant State practice along the same lines, see E. Hoffberger-Pippan, 'Non-Lethal Weapons and International Law: A Three-Dimensional Perspective', PhD thesis, Johannes Kepler University, Linz, Austria, 2018, pp. 100–101.
[43] Art. I(5), Convention on the Prohibition of the Development, Production, Stockpiling and Use of Chemical Weapons and on their Destruction; adopted at Geneva 3 September 1992; entered into force 29 April 1997 (hereinafter, 1992 Chemical Weapons Convention).
[44] Art. II(9), 1992 Chemical Weapons Convention.

240   *Major Themes*

10.20 In its commentary of 2020 on Article 42 of Geneva Convention III, the ICRC suggests that laying anti-personnel mines outside a prisoner-of-war camp might be lawful in circumstances where prisoners are informed of their presence:

> Where the Detaining Power has placed anti-personnel mines outside a prisoner-of-war camp without marking them or informing the prisoners of their presence, this may – depending on the circumstances – amount to the use of weapons without warning against an escaping prisoner. Placing such mines in these conditions may also amount to violations of other international rules governing their use.[45]

The placing of anti-personnel mines is an intentional lethal use of force and can only be lawful in international law when strictly unavoidable to protect life.[46] Given that use of firearms – and less-lethal weapons in the organisation's interpretation of the provision[47] – is already considered an 'extreme measure', the ICRC's appreciation of the applicable law is not reliable. One hundred and sixty-four States are party to the Anti-Personnel Mine Ban Convention, which outlaws the use of the weapons in all circumstances. Moreover, a total ban on the use of anti-personnel mines is *de lege ferenda* under customary international law.[48]

10.21 In a non-international armed conflict, law enforcement rules governing the use of firearms would apply to all detainees seeking to escape. The precautionary principle under international human rights law would also apply, requiring that less-lethal weapons be available and that they be used to prevent an escape,[49] except where the use of firearms was both necessary and proportionate in the circumstances. In its judgment in *Nachova*, the European Court held that an escaping suspect (at least when he or she does not pose a grave threat to life) may not be shot 'even if a failure to use lethal force may result in the opportunity to arrest the fugitive being lost'.[50] The case concerned two deserters from the military rather than escaping military detainees, but the principle is generally applicable.

PREVENTING DEATHS IN CUSTODY UNDER REGIONAL STANDARDS

Deaths in Custody under the European Convention on Human Rights

10.22 Article 2 of the 1950 European Convention on Human Rights[51] protects the right to life. The obligation set out in Article 2(1) to protect 'by law' the right to life 'enjoins the States [parties] not only to refrain from the intentional and unlawful taking of life, but also

---

[45] ICRC Commentary on Article 42 of the 1949 Geneva Convention III, 2020, para. 2550.
[46] See, *supra*, Paragraph 8.25.
[47] ICRC Commentary on Article 42 of the 1949 Geneva Convention III, 2020, para. 2526.
[48] See further Chapter 15 of this work on the Convention and customary law.
[49] See, e.g., Hoffberger-Pippan, 'Non-Lethal Weapons and International Law: A Three-Dimensional Perspective', p. 141.
[50] European Court of Human Rights, *Nachova* v. *Bulgaria*, Judgment (Grand Chamber), 6 July 2005, para. 95.
[51] Convention for the Protection of Human Rights and Fundamental Freedoms; adopted at Rome 4 November 1950; entered into force 3 September 1953.

lays down a positive obligation on the States to take appropriate steps to safeguard the lives of those within their jurisdiction'.[52] In order to establish whether or not a State Party to the European Convention has complied with its obligation to protect the life of a detainee under Article 2, the Court will assess whether the authorities 'did everything reasonably possible, in good faith and in a timely manner, to try to avert the fatal outcome'.[53]

10.23 Given that persons in custody 'are in a vulnerable position and that the authorities are under a duty to protect them', the European Court of Human Rights has held that 'as a general rule, the mere fact that an individual dies in suspicious circumstances while in custody should raise an issue as to whether the State has complied with its obligation to protect that person's right to life'.[54] This does not go as far as does the Human Rights Committee in imposing a rebuttable presumption of State responsibility where a detainee dies in custody. That said, the Court has determined that it is incumbent on a State party to the European Convention 'to account for any injuries suffered in custody, an obligation which is particularly stringent when an individual dies'.[55] Moreover, where the circumstances of an applicant's death 'lie wholly within the exclusive knowledge of the authorities', as is often the case with a detainee, the Court will consider that 'the burden of proof is on the Government to provide a satisfactory and convincing explanation of their version'.[56]

10.24 In its 2020 judgment in the *Cantaragiu* case,[57] the Court noted that the applicant's brother, a former judo champion who was only twenty-one years of age at the time, was in good health when he was taken into the custody of the police. During his detention, he died as a result of a rupture of his duodenum, 'a clear sign of ill-treatment'. In such circumstances, the Court held, 'there is a strong presumption that the death occurred as a result of the actions of the authorities, which must provide an adequate explanation of those actions in order to refute the presumption'. No such explanation, the Court declared, was given either domestically or by the respondent government (Moldova) during the case proceedings.[58]

10.25 The *Shchokin* case against Ukraine concerned the death of a prisoner, the applicant's son, during his imprisonment in a penal colony. His death followed acts of 'torture', including a violent sexual assault, inflicted on him by inmates (with the possible involvement of a prison officer).[59] In holding Ukraine responsible for a violation of the right to life, the Court took into account not only the prisoner's general vulnerability as a detainee

---

[52] European Court of Human Rights, *Mustafayev v. Azerbaijan*, Judgment (Fifth Section), 4 May 2017 (rendered final on 4 August 2017), para. 53.
[53] European Court of Human Rights, *Mammadov and others v. Azerbaijan*, Judgment (Fifth Section), 21 February 2019 (rendered final on 21 May 2019), para. 137.
[54] European Court of Human Rights, *Mustafayev v. Azerbaijan*, Judgment, para. 53.
[55] Ibid., para. 54.
[56] European Court of Human Rights, *Mammadov and others v. Azerbaijan*, Judgment, para. 139.
[57] European Court of Human Rights, *Cantaragiu v. Moldova*, Judgment (Second Section), 24 March 2020.
[58] Ibid., para. 29.
[59] European Court of Human Rights, *Yuriy Illarionovich Shchokin v. Ukraine*, Judgment (Fifth Section), 3 October 2013 (rendered final on 3 January 2014), para. 38.

but also the particular risk of reprisals against him that existed following an earlier escape he had effected from the colony.[60]

10.26 Particular attention must be paid to the welfare of children in detention. In its judgment in the *Çoşelav* case, the Court took into account a number of factors that led to the suicide of a juvenile detainee. The boy, who was by common agreement suffering from significant psychological troubles, had already tried to take his own life twice (and had been reprimanded by prison guards for doing so). He had sought help from the prison staff, which had not been forthcoming. More generally, he was also a child held within an adult prison in contradiction with general international standards.[61]

10.27 In its 2020 judgment in the *Fabris* case, the European Court of Human Rights recalled that with respect to acts of self-harming by an adult detainee, the authorities have a positive obligation to act where they knew or should have known that a real and immediate risk existed of suicide.[62] The case concerned the voluntary inhalation of kitchen cooking gas by a drug addict with mental health issues. On the basis of the facts of the case, the Court did not find a substantive or procedural violation of the right to life under the European Convention. In its judgment in *Jeanty*,[63] which concerned an allegation by the applicant (who survived) that the authorities had taken insufficient steps to prevent his suicide, the Court decided to consider the matter in the context of the right to life. In rejecting his claim of a violation of the right to life, the Court held that the respondent State, Belgium, had taken all reasonable steps taking into account the 'unpredictability of human behaviour'.[64]

10.28 Numerous cases have addressed poor conditions in prisons in States Parties to the European Convention on Human Rights, though when they have not resulted in, or seriously threatened to cause, the death of a detainee, they have been considered under Article 3 as either inhuman or degrading treatment and not as a potential violation of the right to life. The Court has considered treatment to be 'inhuman' because it was premeditated, it was applied for hours at a stretch, and it caused either actual bodily injury or intense physical and mental suffering. It has deemed treatment to be 'degrading' because it aroused in the victims a feeling of fear, anguish, and inferiority.[65] In considering whether a particular form of treatment is 'degrading', the Court does not always require that the object be to humiliate the person concerned.

10.29 In its judgment in *Kalashnikov*, the Court accepted that the authorities had not sought to debase the applicant. But he had been incarcerated with as many as twenty or

---

[60] Ibid.
[61] European Court of Human Rights, *Çoşelav v. Turkey*, Judgment (Second Section), 9 October 2012 (as rendered final on 18 March 2013), paras. 32, 57, 65–69.
[62] European Court of Human Rights, *Fabris and Parziale v. Italy*, Judgment (First Section), 19 March 2020, para. 76.
[63] European Court of Human Rights, *Jeanty v. Belgium*, Judgment (Third Section), 31 March 2020.
[64] Ibid., para. 79.
[65] European Court of Human Rights, *Kalashnikov v. Russia*, Judgment (Third Section), 15 July 2002 (rendered final on 15 October 2002), para. 95.

more other inmates in a cell designed for eight (and with only eight beds), where sleep was significantly impeded, and where, although the cell was lacking adequate ventilation, inmates were permitted to smoke. There was also a persistent infestation of insects in the cell. The conditions in the cell, from which inmates were only allowed to escape for two hours a day, led to the detainee suffering from various skin diseases and fungal infections. The Court held that the conditions in which he was held 'must have caused him considerable mental suffering, diminishing his human dignity and arousing in him such feelings as to cause humiliation and debasement'.[66]

10.30 The *Pocasovschi and Mihaila* case[67] concerned conditions in a Moldovan prison whose electricity and water had been cut off by the separatist 'Moldavian Republic of Transdniestria'. The Court found a violation of Article 3 because although the municipal authority which ordered the utilities to be cut had been controlled by separatists, the prison itself had been under full Moldovan Government control. The Court also agreed with findings in domestic courts that the men had been held in inhuman conditions between September 2002 and April 2004, owing to a lack of water, electricity, food, and warmth. Notably, the Bender Court of Appeal had found that, following the prison's disconnection from the utilities, the prison administration was no longer able to offer food or medical treatment for tuberculosis that was of adequate quality (both applicants were ill with tuberculosis at the relevant time).[68]

10.31 In contrast, in *Gagiu v. Romania*, the detainee at the centre of the case had been given treatment only for bronchial pneumonia even though he also suffered from chronic hepatitis.[69] The treatment recommended for him by two surgeons and an in-house medical specialist was not authorised by the prison authorities.[70] He was finally hospitalised for cirrhosis of the liver but died the following day. Rejecting the government's objections on the basis that the deceased had not suffered violence during his incarceration, the Court found a violation of the right to life by Romania.[71]

Deaths in Custody under the American Convention on Human Rights

10.32 According to the 1969 American Convention on Human Rights: 'Every person has the right to have his life respected. This right shall be protected by law and, in general, from the moment of conception. No one shall be arbitrarily deprived of his life.'[72] Under Article (2) of the Convention, 'no one shall be subjected to torture or to cruel, inhuman, or

---

[66] Ibid., paras. 97–8.
[67] European Court of Human Rights, *Pocasovschi and Mihaila v. Moldova and Russia*, Judgment (Second Section), 29 May 2018 (rendered final on 29 August 2018).
[68] Ibid., paras. 34, 58, 64.
[69] European Court of Human Rights, *Gagiu v. Romania*, Judgment (Third Section), 24 February 2009 (rendered final on 24 May 2009), para. 59.
[70] Ibid., para. 61.
[71] Ibid., paras. 55, 63, 64.
[72] Art. 4(1), American Convention on Human Rights; adopted at San José 22 November 1969; entered into force 18 July 1978.

degrading punishment or treatment. All persons deprived of their liberty shall be treated with respect for the inherent dignity of the human person.'

10.33 The conditions in prisons in a number of countries in the Americas are exceptionally dangerous to life. Brazil, for instance, which has the third-largest prison population in the world after the United States and China,[73] faces huge challenges in complying with its duty to respect and protect the rights of those it detains.[74] In August 2019, the Inter-American Commission on Human Rights condemned the massacre that took place at a prison in the municipality of Altamira, in the state of Pará. At least sixty-two people died, including sixteen who were decapitated, as a result of violence between two rival gangs within the facility. The Commission called on the Brazilian State to 'take all necessary measures to ensure that events of this kind do not happen again'.[75] The Commission also warned, 'with profound concern, that these deaths ... happened in a context marked by repeated acts of violence in Brazil's penitentiaries, which suffer high levels of overcrowding and appalling conditions of detention'.[76]

10.34 The case of *Montero-Aranguren and others (Detention Center of Catia)* before the Inter-American Court of Human Rights concerned the alleged extrajudicial execution of thirty-seven detainees at the Detention Centre of Catia in Caracas on 27 November 1992. It was claimed that guards from the Centre itself, along with National Guard troops and the Metropolitan Police, intervened in massive numbers, firing indiscriminately at the detainees. It was further alleged that the detainees were enduring inhuman conditions of detention at the time.[77] On 4 April 2006, at the beginning of the public hearings convened by the Court, Venezuela announced that it had come to 'express the acknowledgement of the facts, to ... honour the memory of those that have died, to acknowledge the truth and to seek justice. The State considers that it is its obligation to acknowledge all the facts as charged, this is a formal admission.'[78]

10.35 In its judgment, the Inter-American Court stated that overcrowding had been an important contributing factor to violence at the Detention Centre, since prisoners would fight each other for a minimum living space of their own. Many prisoners were in cells that housed two or even four times as many inmates as they were designed for, meaning that the available space for each inmate was approximately thirty square centimetres.[79] The overcrowding also caused hygiene problems, with pervasive filth and smells, along with

---

[73] World Prison Brief, 'Highest to Lowest – Prison Population Total', accessed 25 January 2020, at http://bit.ly/2GknSKk. Brazil's total prison population was said at the time to be 746,532.

[74] R. Muggah, C. Taboada, and Dandara Tinoco, 'Q&A: Why Is Prison Violence So Bad in Brazil?', *Americas Quarterly*, 2 August 2019, at http://bit.ly/2RNHpZ5.

[75] IACmnHR, 'IACHR Condemns Massacre with More than 60 Dead in Brazilian Prison', Press Release, Washington, DC, 5 August 2019, at http://bit.ly/30Uus3S.

[76] Ibid.

[77] Inter-American Court of Human Rights, *Montero-Aranguren and others (Detention Center of Catia) v. Venezuela*, Judgment (Preliminary Objection, Merits, Reparations and Costs), 5 July 2006, para. 3.

[78] Ibid., para. 40.

[79] The Court held that this reality amounted per se to cruel, inhuman, or degrading treatment. Ibid., para. 91.

insect infestations.[80] Conditions were so poor that the centre was regarded by the Venezuelan government as one of the worst prisons of the country, with drug, alcohol, and even weapons smuggling a common occurrence. Violence and maltreatment were prevalent, both as a result of power struggles among the detainees and at the hands of the guards.[81] Prison guards were underpaid, untrained, and, therefore, prone to corruption.[82]

10.36 The Court set out clearly its understanding of the legality of the use of force and firearms in its judgment, noting that when excessive force is used against detainees, any deprivation of life is arbitrary.[83] The Court stated that the use by law enforcement officers of firearms and lethal force must be generally forbidden and can only be justified in extraordinary cases where it is absolutely necessary for the circumstances. The Court recalled the tenets of Principle 9 of the 1990 Basic Principles in its judgment, noting that the existence of violence, drugs, and weapons in a detention facility did not in and of itself justify recourse to lethal force.[84] The measures to be adopted by the State to ensure security and safety must prioritise prevention over a repressive system, the Court said.[85]

Deaths in Custody under African Human Rights Standards

10.37 The African Charter on Human and Peoples' Rights (the 'Banjul Charter') enshrines the right to life for 'every human being' as follows: 'Human beings are inviolable. Every human being shall be entitled to respect for his life and the integrity of his person. No one may be arbitrarily deprived of this right.'[86] In its General Comment on the right to life under the Banjul Charter, the African Commission on Human and Peoples' Rights has stated: 'Any deprivation of life resulting from a violation of the procedural or substantive safeguards in the African Charter, including on the basis of discriminatory grounds or practices, is arbitrary and as a result unlawful.'[87]

10.38 The African Commission has further decreed that where a person dies in State custody, 'there is a presumption of State responsibility and the burden of proof rests upon the State to prove otherwise through a prompt, impartial, thorough and transparent investigation carried out by an independent body'.[88] This 'heightened responsibility', the Commission affirms, 'extends to persons detained in prisons, in other places of detention

---

[80] Inter-American Court of Human Rights, *Montero-Aranguren and others (Detention Center of Catia) v. Venezuela*, Judgment, para. 60(9).
[81] Ibid., para. 60(11).
[82] Ibid., para. 60(15).
[83] Ibid., para. 68.
[84] Ibid., paras. 69, 70.
[85] Ibid., para. 71.
[86] Art. 4(1), African Charter on Human and Peoples' Rights; adopted at Nairobi 27 June 1981; entered into force 21 October 1986.
[87] African Commission on Human and Peoples' Rights, 'General Comment No. 3 on the African Charter on Human and Peoples' Rights: The Right to Life (Article 4)', adopted at Banjul (57th Ordinary Session) November 2015 (hereinafter, African Commission General Comment on the right to life), para. 12.
[88] Ibid., para. 37.

(official and otherwise), and to persons in other facilities where the State exercises heightened control over their lives'.[89] This position was reaffirmed in 2017 in Commission Resolution 375.[90] Previously, in its 2014 Luanda Guidelines, the Commission had framed the responsibility of the State in slightly different terms, noting that given the control the State exercises over persons held in police custody or pre-trial detention, States 'shall provide a satisfactory explanation, and make available information on the circumstances surrounding custody or detention, in every case of death or serious injury of persons who are deprived of their liberty'.[91]

10.39 Under the Robben Island Guidelines, the Commission urges States Parties to the Banjul Charter to take steps to ensure that the treatment of all persons deprived of their liberty is in conformity with international standards, 'guided by the UN Standard Minimum Rules for the Treatment of Prisoners'[92] (now revised and termed the Nelson Mandela Rules). Nelson Mandela himself famously wrote in his autobiography that 'no one truly knows a nation until one has been inside its jails'. In South Africa, at the end of March 2017, the country's 236 operational prisons had only 119,134 bed spaces available for an average inmate population of 160,280. Prisons in urban areas had the worst overcrowding rates.[93] Violence and ill treatment are said to be common while in prison, including as a result of prevailing gang culture, and sexual abuse is also reportedly a common phenomenon, 'linked to overcrowding rates and understaffing'.[94]

10.40 The prison system includes two privately-run prisons: the Kutama Sinthumule Correctional Centre (run by the US company, GEO Group), and Mangaung Correctional Centre (managed by G4S). Allegations of torture, including electrocuting inmates, have been made against G4S prison workers.[95] In December 2019, Justice and Correctional Services Minister Ronald Lamola expressed concern after learning of the 'disturbing allegations'.[96]

---

[89] Ibid.

[90] 'Reaffirming the State's heightened level of responsibility to protect the rights of those it places in its custody, and particularly the presumption of State responsibility for deaths occurring in custody.' Resolution on the Right to Life in Africa, Doc. ACHPR/Res.375(LX)2017, adopted by the African Commission on Human and Peoples' Rights at its 60th Ordinary Session held in Niamey from 8 to 22 May 2017, tenth preambular para.

[91] *Guidelines on the Conditions of Arrest, Police Custody and Pre-Trial Detention in Africa* ('Luanda Guidelines'), adopted by the African Commission on Human and Peoples' Rights (the Commission) during its 55th Ordinary Session in Luanda, from 28 April to 12 May 2014, para. 20.

[92] *Resolution on Guidelines and Measures for the Prohibition and Prevention of Torture, Cruel, Inhuman or Degrading Treatment or Punishment in Africa* ('The Robben Island Guidelines'), 2nd ed., 2008, para. 33.

[93] G. Makou, I. Skosana, and R. Hopkins, 'Factsheet: The State of South Africa's Prisons', *AfricaCheck*, last updated 12 June 2018, at http://bit.ly/36prPI7.

[94] D. Thulani and S. Gear, 'South Africa', 2017 Annual Report, *Prison Insider*, at http://bit.ly/2RtahXB.

[95] Ibid. See also, e.g., 'Mangaung Prison Is a Private Hell', *Mail & Guardian*, 25 October 2013, at http://bit.ly/38QEnu3.

[96] E. Naki, 'Private Prison in Bloem Has Minister "Concerned" after Allegations of Torture', *The Citizen*, 2 December 2019, at http://bit.ly/2NUAs7l.

Deaths in Custody under the Arab Charter on Human Rights

10.41 The 2004 Arab Charter on Human Rights[97] has a general provision enshrining the protection of the right to life. Under Article 5(1), 'every human being has an inherent right to life'. Paragraph 2 stipulates further: 'This right shall be protected by law. No one shall be arbitrarily deprived of his life.' No derogation from Article 5 may be made.[98] Article 8(1) prohibits 'physical or mental torture' and 'cruel, inhuman or degrading treatment or punishment', but no provision in the Charter explicitly protects detainees or establishes minimum conditions of detention. To date, there has been no jurisprudence under the Charter that could elucidate such regional standards.

THE DUTY TO INVESTIGATE DEATHS IN CUSTODY

The Normative Framework

10.42 The duty under international law to investigate any suspicious death, including in custody or other forms of detention, is today firmly part of both global and regional treaties and standards. Sometimes seen as arising from a combination of the right to life and the general duty to respect and ensure human rights, increasingly the duty to investigate is considered as a procedural component integral to the right to life. With respect to the ICCPR, the Human Rights Committee has considered the duty to be 'implicit' in the obligation to protect, but sees it as 'reinforced by the general duty to ensure the rights recognized in the Covenant' (Article 2(1)), when read in conjunction with Article 6(1) on the right to life, as well as the duty to provide an effective remedy to victims of human rights violations (Article 2(3) of the ICCPR).[99]

10.43 A similar approach was taken in the past by the European Court of Human Rights. In its judgment in the landmark *McCann* case, the Grand Chamber endorsed the view that the obligation to protect the right to life under the Convention,

> read in conjunction with the State's general duty under Article 1 . . . to 'secure to everyone within their jurisdiction the rights and freedoms defined in [the] Convention', requires by implication that there should be some form of effective official investigation when individuals have been killed as a result of the use of force by, inter alios, agents of the State.[100]

10.44 For two decades now, the European Court has considered the duty to investigate to be a procedural component of the right to life. Its departure from earlier practice occurred in its judgment in the *Mastromatteo* case wherein it 'reiterate[d]' that 'the positive obligations laid down in the first sentence of Article 2 of the Convention ["Everyone's right to life

---

[97] Arab Charter on Human Rights; adopted at Tunis 22 May 2004; entered into force 15 March 2008.
[98] Art. 4(2), 2004 Arab Charter on Human Rights.
[99] Human Rights Committee, General Comment 36 on the right to life, para. 27.
[100] European Court of Human Rights, *McCann and others v. United Kingdom*, Judgment (Grand Chamber), 27 September 1995, para. 161.

shall be protected by law"] also require by implication that an efficient and independent judicial system should be set in place by which the cause of a murder can be established and the guilty parties punished'.[101] The procedural obligation to carry out an effective investigation under Article 2 has 'evolved into a separate and autonomous duty'.[102] The same line is taken by the African Commission on Human and Peoples' Rights: 'The failure of the State transparently to take all necessary measures to investigate suspicious deaths and all killings by State agents and to identify and hold accountable individuals or groups responsible for violations of the right to life constitutes in itself a violation by the State of that right."[103]

10.45 In the words of the Human Rights Committee, 'an important element of the protection afforded to the right to life by the Covenant is the obligation on the States parties [to the ICCPR], where they know or should have known of potentially unlawful deprivations of life, to investigate and, where appropriate, prosecute such incidents'.[104] This includes where it is alleged that excessive use of force has been used 'with lethal consequences'.[105] The duty to investigate is ongoing in nature. Thus, where a State's compliance with its treaty obligations with respect to arbitrary deprivation of life cannot be considered by a human rights court or treaty body *ratione temporis* (because the use of force occurred prior to the State's adherence to a particular treaty), the duty to investigate may persist, at least for a number of years after the events in question occurred.[106]

10.46 As noted previously, the Committee has held that the presumption of arbitrary deprivation of life by the State when loss of life occurs in custody in unnatural circumstances 'can only be rebutted on the basis of a proper investigation which establishes the State's compliance with its obligations under article 6'.[107] Such investigations of potentially unlawful deprivations of life should be undertaken in accordance with relevant international standards, including the Minnesota Protocol on the Investigation of Potentially Unlawful Death (2016) issued by the United Nations, and 'must be aimed at ensuring that those responsible are brought to justice'.[108] Investigations into an alleged

---

[101] European Court of Human Rights, *Mastromatteo v. Italy*, Judgment (Grand Chamber), 24 October 2002, para. 89.
[102] European Court of Human Rights, *Janowiec and others v. Russia*, Judgment (Grand Chamber), 21 October 2013, para. 132.
[103] African Commission General Comment on the Right to Life, para. 15.
[104] Human Rights Committee, General Comment 36 on the right to life, para. 27.
[105] Ibid.
[106] According to its judgment in the *Šilih* case, 'there must exist a genuine connection between the death and the entry into force of the Convention in respect of the respondent State for the procedural obligations imposed by Article 2 to come into effect'. European Court of Human Rights, *Šilih v. Slovenia*, Judgment (Grand Chamber), 9 April 2009, para. 163. Based on the 'genuine connection' standard, the European Court of Human Rights has endorsed an indicative limit of ten years. European Court of Human Rights, *Janowiec and others v. Russia*, Judgment (Grand Chamber), para. 146. In its judgment in the *Detention Center of Catia* case, the Inter-American Court found that thirteen years after the events, the duty to investigate persisted. Inter-American Court of Human Rights, *Montero-Aranguren and others (Detention Center of Catia) v. Venezuela*, Judgment, para. 137.
[107] Ibid., para. 29.
[108] Ibid., para. 27.

violation of Article 6 must always be independent, impartial, prompt, thorough, effective, credible, and transparent. In the event that a violation is found, 'full reparation must be provided, including, in view of the particular circumstances of the case, adequate measures of compensation, rehabilitation and satisfaction'.[109]

10.47 The Minnesota Protocol on the Investigation of Potentially Unlawful Death (2016) is a soft-law instrument whose elaboration by an international group of experts was led by the Special Rapporteur on extrajudicial, summary or arbitrary executions, along with the Office of the UN High Commissioner for Human Rights.[110] The Protocol applies to the investigation of all 'potentially unlawful death', which includes situations where the death occurred when a person 'was detained by, or was in the custody of, the State, its organs, or agents'. This comprises 'all deaths of persons detained in prisons, in other places of detention (official and otherwise) and in other facilities where the State exercises heightened control over their life', such as psychiatric hospitals, institutions for children and the elderly, and centres for migrants, stateless people, or refugees.[111]

10.48 According to the Protocol, a State's duty to investigate is triggered 'where it knows or should have known of any potentially unlawful death, including where reasonable allegations of a potentially unlawful death are made'.[112] The Protocol emphasises that, as reflected in Rule 71 of the Nelson Mandela Rules, the duty to investigate does not exist only where the State is in receipt of a formal complaint.[113] The Protocol stipulates that, to be effective, investigations must, at a minimum, take all reasonable steps to (a) identify the victim(s); (b) recover and preserve all material probative of the cause of death, the identity of the perpetrator(s), and the circumstances surrounding the death; (c) identify possible witnesses and obtain their evidence in relation to the death and the circumstances surrounding the death; (d) determine the cause, manner, place and time of death, and all of the surrounding circumstances. In determining the manner of death, the investigation should distinguish between natural death, accidental death, suicide, and homicide; and (e) determine who was involved in the death and their individual responsibility for the death.[114]

10.49 Distinguishing between suicide and homicide is particularly important in case of death in custody as there may be a temptation on the part of the authorities (or other inmates) to seek to disguise an unlawful killing as a suicide. Alternatively, inadequate attention may be accorded, because of the cost in time and money, to an investigation of a suspicious death. Critical in the case of a death during detention is, therefore, the conduct of an autopsy. The Minnesota Protocol stipulates: 'It will almost always be the

---

[109] Ibid., para. 28.
[110] *Minnesota Protocol on the Investigation of Potentially Unlawful Death (2016), The Revised United Nations Manual on the Effective Prevention and Investigation of Extra-legal, Arbitrary and Summary Executions*, OHCHR, New York/Geneva, 2017.
[111] Ibid., para. 2(b).
[112] Ibid., para. 15.
[113] Ibid.
[114] Ibid., para. 25, citing Inter-American Court of Human Rights, *Veliz Franco and others v. Guatemala*, Judgment (Preliminary objections, merits, reparations and costs), 19 May 2014, para. 191.

case that these aims will be materially assisted in some way by the performance of an autopsy. A decision not to undertake an autopsy should be justified in writing and should be subject to judicial review."[115]

10.50 Even if an autopsy is conducted, its conclusions (and the conclusions of the broader investigation) must take into account all the available evidence. In the *Zhumbaeva* case before the Human Rights Committee,[116] the authorities had claimed that Mr Zhumbaeva had committed suicide by hanging. Certain forensic evidence, however, suggested otherwise. On 24 October 2004, the victim and his wife had been asked to follow police officers to Bazarkorgon police station in Kyrgyzstan after a quarrel that was qualified as a public disturbance. The victim was kept in custody, while his wife was released. She was later called back to the station by the police, where she saw her husband's dead body lying on the floor.

10.51 Testimony by an ambulance doctor called to the police station indicated that the victim did not have strangulation marks indicating a hanging but, rather, red finger marks on his neck. A forensic professional who examined the victim's body in the presence of doctors and two of the victim's relatives found scratches on the eyebrow, under the chin, on the neck, and on the right upper arm, as well as a bloody wound on the left side of the neck. The forensic expert stated that the wounds could appear from something hard such as fingernails or a wrist, but that examination of body tissues indicated that the victim died of mechanical asphyxiation, which could have been caused by hanging from a soft fabric. In response to questioning as to whether manual strangulation could have been the cause of the victim's death, it was said that no scratches had been found on the cervical fabrics or skin but that the fracture of the horn of the thyroid could have resulted from pressure by hands.[117]

10.52 Mr Zhumbaeva's mother complained to the Human Rights Committee, claiming that her son had died in police custody as a result of excessive and unnecessary use of force by police officers. He was, she said, was in good physical and mental health before being taken into custody and, according to his wife, did not possess any sports trousers with which he had allegedly hanged himself. The trousers were never forensically examined and, due to the victim's high alcohol level at the time of death, it was argued that he had neither the physical capacity nor the time to hang himself. In its Views on the case, the Human Rights Committee observed that Kyrgyzstan had not explained the basis on which it was concluded that the victim had committed suicide in police custody. The testimony by the forensic expert and the ambulance doctor, allied to the fact that the concerned police officer had proffered three different versions of the victim's death while another police officer's testimony had not even been considered, led the Committee to conclude that Kyrgyzstan was responsible for arbitrary deprivation of Mr Zhumbaeva's life.[118]

---

[115] *Minnesota Protocol on the Investigation of Potentially Unlawful Death* (2016), para. 25.
[116] Human Rights Committee, *Turdukan Zhumbaeva v. Kyrgyzstan*, Views (UN doc. CCPR/C/102/D/1756/2008), 19 July 2011.
[117] Ibid., para. 8.3.
[118] Ibid., para. 8.8.

The Duty to Investigate during Armed Conflict

10.53 The duty to investigate exists also during armed conflict.[119] In situations of international armed conflict, treaty law explicitly requires that every death of, or serious injury to, a prisoner of war or civilian internee that is caused or suspected to have been caused by a guard, another prisoner of war, or internee, or indeed any other person, as well as any death the cause of which is unknown, 'shall be immediately followed by an official enquiry by the Detaining Power'.[120] In both international and non-international armed conflict, violence against detainees is prohibited by treaty and customary international humanitarian law 'and can amount to a war crime'.[121]

10.54 The obligation under international humanitarian law to prosecute war crimes, as the ICRC avers, 'logically presupposes an obligation to investigate'.[122] Indeed, one of the rules identified by the ICRC in its study of customary international humanitarian law, published in 2005, was that 'States must investigate war crimes allegedly committed by their nationals or armed forces, or on their territory, and, if appropriate, prosecute the suspects. They must also investigate other war crimes over which they have jurisdiction and, if appropriate, prosecute the suspects.'[123] The ICRC affirms that the rule applies in all armed conflicts.

10.55 With respect to other suspected violations that do not amount to a war crime, a duty to investigate can be inferred also from the duty to respect and to ensure respect for the 1949 Geneva Conventions in all circumstances.[124] In addition, the 1977 Additional Protocol I[125] obligates all States Parties to take measures necessary to suppress all breaches of the Geneva Conventions or of the Protocol 'which result from a failure to act when under a duty to do so'.[126]

10.56 The right to life continues to apply during situations of armed conflict, including the duty to investigate potentially unlawful death. In its judgment in the *Case of the 'Mapiripán Massacre'*, the Inter-American Court of Human Rights recognised the 'difficult circumstances of Colombia' given the armed conflict existing at the relevant time, but declared that 'no matter how difficult' the conditions were, they 'do not release a State Party to the American Convention of its obligations'.[127] When a State 'conducts or tolerates

---

[119] According to the Minnesota Protocol, the duty to investigate any potentially unlawful death applies to all cases during an armed conflict outside the conduct of hostilities, meaning that it concerns, in particular, cases of detention with sufficient nexus to the armed conflict. *Minnesota Protocol on the Investigation of Potentially Unlawful Death* (2016), para. 16.
[120] Art. 121, 1949 Geneva Convention III; Art. 131, 1949 Geneva Convention IV.
[121] ICRC, *Guidelines for Investigating Deaths in Custody*, p. 12.
[122] Ibid.
[123] ICRC Customary IHL Rule 158: 'Prosecution of War Crimes', at http://bit.ly/37FdYin.
[124] Art. 1 common to the four 1949 Geneva Conventions.
[125] Art. 87, Protocol Additional to the Geneva Conventions of 12 August 1949, and relating to the Protection of Victims of International Armed Conflicts; adopted at Geneva 8 June 1977; entered into force 7 December 1978 (hereinafter, 1977 Additional Protocol I).
[126] Art. 86(1), 1977 Additional Protocol I.
[127] Inter-American Court of Human Rights, *Case of the 'Mapiripán Massacre'* v. *Colombia* Judgment (Merits, Reparations, and Costs), 15 September 2005, para. 238.

actions leading to extra-legal executions, not investigating them adequately and not punishing those responsible, as appropriate, breaches the duties to respect rights ... and to ensure their free and full exercise'.[128] And as the UN Special Rapporteur on extrajudicial, summary or arbitrary executions has observed, 'Armed conflict and occupation do not discharge the State's duty to investigate and prosecute human rights abuses. The right to life is non-derogable regardless of circumstance.'[129]

10.57 In its judgment in the *al-Skeini* case, the European Court of Human Rights' Grand Chamber cited both preceding statements.[130] It later acknowledged that 'where the death to be investigated under Article 2 [of the European Convention on Human Rights] occurs in circumstances of generalised violence, armed conflict or insurgency, obstacles may be placed in the way of investigators' and that 'concrete constraints may compel the use of less effective measures of investigation or may cause an investigation to be delayed'.[131] 'Nonetheless', the Court concluded, 'the obligation under Article 2 to safeguard life entails that, even in difficult security conditions, all reasonable steps must be taken to ensure that an effective, independent investigation is conducted into alleged breaches of the right to life'.[132]

10.58 By 'effective' is meant that the investigation 'is capable of leading to a determination of whether the force used was or was not justified in the circumstances and to the identification and punishment of those responsible'.[133] But this is an obligation of means, not result:

> The authorities must take the reasonable steps available to them to secure the evidence concerning the incident, including, inter alia, eyewitness testimony, forensic evidence and, where appropriate, an autopsy which provides a complete and accurate record of injury and an objective analysis of clinical findings, including the cause of death. Any deficiency in the investigation which undermines its ability to establish the cause of death or the person or persons responsible will risk falling foul of this standard.[134]

In the *al-Skeini* case, the sixth applicant was a Colonel in the Basra police force whose son, Baha Mousa, was twenty-six years old when he died while in the custody of the British army, three days after having been arrested by soldiers on 14 September 2003. Baha Mousa, who was found to have ninety-three identifiable injuries on his body, died of asphyxiation.[135]

10.59 The *Jaloud* case[136] concerned not a death in custody but a shooting to death at a checkpoint jointly manned by armed Iraqi Civil Defence Corps (ICDC) personnel and

---

[128] Ibid.
[129] Report of the UN Special Rapporteur on extrajudicial, summary or arbitrary executions, Philip Alston, UN doc. E/CN.4/2006/53, 8 March 2006, para. 36.
[130] European Court of Human Rights, *al-Skeini and others v. United Kingdom*, Judgment (Grand Chamber), 7 July 2011, paras. 93, 94.
[131] Ibid., para. 164.
[132] Ibid.
[133] Ibid., para. 166.
[134] Ibid.
[135] Ibid., paras. 63, 66.
[136] European Court of Human Rights, *Jaloud v. The Netherlands*, Judgment (Grand Chamber), 20 November 2014.

Dutch troops. That said, the approach taken by the European Court towards the investigation is equally applicable to a death in detention in certain respects. A key issue was to determine who had fired the fatal shots: the Iraqi or the Dutch forces. It appears that the calibre of ammunition fired by each differed (NATO 5.56 mm rounds by the Dutch soldiers but 7.62 mm rounds by the Iraqis). The European Court noted the applicant's claim that the Royal Military Constabulary attached to the Dutch forces had held the body of Mr Azhar Sabah Jaloud for some hours, yet no autopsy had been performed during that period. The body had been transferred to an Iraqi civilian hospital, where an autopsy had been carried out but without the presence of Royal Military Constabulary officials. The autopsy report, 'such as it was', had been added to the file but not translated.[137] Other forensic evidence, the applicants affirmed, 'had been treated in a similarly careless fashion. In particular, no detailed translation had been made of the report on the bullet fragments removed from the body.'[138]

10.60 The Court observed that the autopsy seems to have been carried out in the absence of any qualified Netherlands official and that nothing is known of the qualifications of the Iraqi pathologist who performed it.[139] Moreover, the Court noted, the pathologist's report 'had serious shortcomings; extremely brief, it was lacking in detail and there were not even any pictures included'.[140] More generally, no alternative arrangement appeared to have been considered for the autopsy, even though the US or UK forces might have had facilities and qualified personnel available.[141] The Court thus found that the investigation was deficient with respect to the autopsy.[142]

---

[137] Ibid., para. 169.
[138] Ibid., para. 170.
[139] Ibid., para. 213.
[140] Ibid., para. 214.
[141] Ibid., para. 215.
[142] Ibid., para. 216.

11

Abortion

INTRODUCTION

11.01 This chapter describes how the duty on States to respect and protect the right to life applies to terminations of pregnancy. Worldwide, tens of millions of abortions are said to take place each year.[1] In France, for instance, where the annual incidence rate is of the order of almost 15 per 1,000 women, elective abortion is a common reproductive health event, comprising more than 210,000 procedures each year. Indeed, it has been calculated that two in five of all women in France will undergo an abortion in the course of their reproductive life.[2] In the United States, in 2016, 623,471 legal induced abortions were reported to the Centers for Disease Control at a rate of 11.6 abortions per 1,000 women aged 15–44 years. The abortion ratio was 186 abortions per 1,000 live births.[3]

11.02 The decision whether or not to have an abortion can have far-reaching personal and familial consequences. Aborting a pregnancy may be a criminal offence, both for the pregnant woman who undergoes an abortion and for anyone who performs it. While most States allow medical (or surgical) abortion[4] under varyingly defined but limited circumstances, as of 1 August 2020, of the 193 member States of the United Nations, 23 were said to have national laws that render abortion illegal, even in extreme circumstances when the

---

[1] The National Right to Life Educational Trust Fund, 'Contribution to the General Discussion in preparation for General Comment No. 36 (Article 6 of the ICCPR: Right to life)', New York, June 2015, p. 2.

[2] C. Moreau, J. Trussell, J. Desfreres, and N. Bajos, 'Medical versus Surgical Abortion: The Importance of Women's Choice', *Contraception*, vol. 84, no. 3 (September2011), pp. 224–9.

[3] Centers for Disease Control (CDC), 'CDCs Abortion Surveillance System FAQs', last reviewed 25 November 2019, at http://bit.ly/31XCnOr. According to a 2013 report by the UN Department of Economic and Social Affairs, nine States have a higher reported abortion rate than the United States: Bulgaria, Cuba, Estonia, Georgia, Kazakhstan, Romania, Russia, Sweden, and Ukraine. UNDESA (Population Division), *World Abortion Policies 2013*, at http://bit.ly/2Y6A5M5.

[4] A medical abortion uses medication to end a pregnancy. In the United Kingdom, the treatment typically involves the taking of two different medicines: mifepristone (which blocks the hormone needed for pregnancy to grow) and misoprostol, which causes the body to expel the pregnancy from the womb. Misoprostol causes the softening and opening of the cervix and contractions of the womb, so that the pregnancy can pass through the vagina. This approach is said to be the safest option with a pregnancy of no more than nine weeks and six days for most people. Marie Stopes UK, 'At Home Abortion Pills', 2019, at http://bit.ly/3kN59Ki. With a surgical abortion, the pregnancy is removed vaginally by a doctor using a suction method. This is offered in the United Kingdom at up to twenty-three weeks and six days of pregnancy (the legal limit, as discussed below, is twenty-four weeks). Most of those who abort their pregnancy will experience some bleeding and cramping afterwards. Marie Stopes UK, 'Surgical Abortion', 2019, at http://bit.ly/30ZHv5G.

mother's life is in imminent peril.[5] The precise number is contested. For although legislation may preclude the possibility of abortion, the broader principle of necessity in criminal law[6] may demand intervention to prevent a pregnant woman or girl dying from complications during pregnancy, even if that requires an abortion.[7] In any event, the overall tendency is towards liberalisation: in recent decades, dozens of States worldwide have eased their constraints on abortion in domestic law.[8] But as is the case with end-of-life decisions (see Chapter 18 on euthanasia and suicide), abortion remains a highly charged and controversial issue morally, politically, and religiously, as well as legally.

11.03 The chapter continues by defining the term 'abortion'. It then discusses how the duty to respect and protect life affects its legality, first under global human rights standards. In this regard, in its General Comment 36 on the right to life under the 1966 International Covenant on Civil and Political Rights[9] (ICCPR),[10] the UN Human Rights Committee addresses abortion in some detail. This is a key normative reference but it is also a contested one; indeed, the Committee received more comments from organisations on the legality of abortion during its drafting of the General Comment than it did on any other single aspect of the right to life. The differing treatment of abortion under regional standards is then discussed. The final section of the chapter looks at the evolving State practice on abortion.

The Definition of Abortion

11.04 Global human rights treaties do not directly address the issue of abortion, much less define it. Thus, for instance, there is no language on abortion in either the 1948 Universal Declaration of Human Rights[11] or the ICCPR.

---

[5] According to the Center for Reproductive Rights in 2020 the following 23 UN member States did not allow an abortion under any circumstances: Andorra, Republic of Congo, Dominican Republic, Egypt, El Salvador, Gabon, Haiti, Honduras, Iraq, Jamaica, Lao People's Democratic Republic (Lao PDR), Madagascar, Malta, Marshall Islands, Mauritania, Nicaragua, Palau, Philippines, San Marino, Senegal, Sierra Leone, Suriname, and Tonga, as well as two territories of the Netherlands, Aruba and Curaçao. Center for Reproductive Rights, 'The World's Abortion Laws', 2020, at http://bit.ly/3kHyRQV and http://bit.ly/3iEiOBG. The law in the Marshall Islands and Palau is said to be unclear. UNDESA has claimed that both States allow abortion to save the pregnant woman's life. UNDESA, *World Abortion Policies 2013*.

[6] The defence of necessity may apply when a doctor performs an abortion (i.e., commits a criminal act) during an emergency in order to prevent a greater harm from happening. See, e.g., 'Necessity', *Justia*, 2020, at http://bit.ly/346tKUI.

[7] UNDESA suggests that this is the case in Andorra and San Marino. For UNDESA, in 2011 only the following UN member States would not allow an abortion in extreme circumstances to save a pregnant woman's life: Chile, Dominican Republic, El Salvador, Malta, Nicaragua, and South Sudan. The Center for Reproductive Rights believes that legislation in South Sudan now allows an abortion to be performed to save the life of a pregnant woman. Center for Reproductive Rights, 'The World's Abortion Laws', 2020.

[8] Center for Reproductive Rights, 'The World's Abortion Laws', 2020.

[9] International Covenant on Civil and Political Rights; adopted at New York 16 December 1966; entered into force 23 March 1976. As of 1 May 2021, 173 States were party to the ICCPR.

[10] Human Rights Committee, General Comment No. 36: Article 6: right to life, UN doc. CCPR/C/GC/36, 3 September 2019 (hereinafter, Human Rights Committee, General Comment 36 on the right to life).

[11] Universal Declaration of Human Rights; approved by UN General Assembly Resolution 217 A, adopted on 10 December 1948.

11.05 The term abortion is ordinarily defined as 'the deliberate termination of a human pregnancy'. The *Oxford English Dictionary* definition goes on to clarify, reflecting the law in force in many countries, that this is 'most often performed during the first 28 weeks of pregnancy'. A termination of a human pregnancy that occurs naturally is known as a miscarriage.[12] The killing of a foetus after delivery as a baby, whether that delivery occurs naturally or as a deliberate result of human intervention, is infanticide.

THE STATUS OF ABORTION UNDER INTERNATIONAL LAW

11.06 There is no general right of a pregnant woman to an abortion under customary international law, even within a minimal number of weeks. Nor, however, is there any rule generally prohibiting abortion. In both cases, there is insufficient *opinio juris* to credibly assert the existence of a rule as a matter of custom. Thus the Human Rights Committee has stipulated that, subject to a number of caveats (discussed later), States Parties to the ICCPR '*may* adopt measures designed to regulate voluntary termination of pregnancy'.[13]

11.07 There are a customary rule and a general principle of law whereby the option of abortion must be offered to a pregnant woman or girl whose life is in imminent threat or will be in grave peril if she takes the pregnancy to full term. This reflects the practice in the overwhelming majority of States.[14] To act otherwise is to contravene the jus cogens prohibition on arbitrary deprivation of life. The norm whereby a woman or girl who is carrying a pregnancy that has a fatal foetal abnormality has the right to be granted access to an abortion appears to be *de lege ferenda* – if it has not already crystallised as custom – in international law.[15] To deny that right could amount to the infliction of cruel, inhuman, or degrading treatment on the pregnant woman or girl. A right to be granted access to an abortion in case of either rape or incest is probably *de lege ferenda* in customary law, but is less certain, based on the relative lack of *opinio juris*.

11.08 There is a particular risk that a foetus with physical or intellectual disabilities will be the subject of an abortion but there is no international rule prohibiting an abortion in such circumstances. The issue is not addressed in the 2006 Convention on the Rights of Persons with Disabilities.[16] That does not mean, however, that a foetus is entirely unprotected

---

[12] Amnesty International reports that, in El Salvador, women who have had miscarriages have been charged with aggravated homicide, a charge which can bring a sentence of up to fifty years' imprisonment. Amnesty International, 'How Some of the World's Most Restrictive Abortion Laws Turn Women into Criminals', undated, at http://bit.ly/3iKx1wU.

[13] Human Rights Committee, General Comment 36 on the right to life, para. 8 (added emphasis).

[14] Seemingly, as of 2020, this would concern only Chile, Dominican Republic, El Salvador, Malta, and Nicaragua.

[15] In terms of State practice, according to UNDESA, between 1996 and 2011 the Bahamas, Benin, Burkina Faso, Chad, Colombia, Eritrea, Ethiopia, Fiji, Guinea, Jordan, Mexico, Monaco, Nepal, Niger, Oman, Sudan, Swaziland, Switzerland, and Togo all amended their national laws to allow for abortion in case of foetal impairment. During the same period, only Iraq tightened its laws to preclude such a possibility. UNDESA, *World Abortion Policies 2013*.

[16] Convention on the Rights of Persons with Disabilities; adopted at New York 13 December 2006; entered into force 3 May 2008.

ABORTION UNDER GLOBAL STANDARDS

11.09 The Convention on the Rights of the Child (CRC), to which each bar one of 197 States recognised by the UN Secretary-General is party, defines a child as 'a child means every human being below the age of eighteen years'.[17] The reference to a 'human being' is generally interpreted as excluding a foetus. For instance, in adhering to the CRC in 1991, the United Kingdom stated that it 'interprets the Convention as applicable only following a live birth'.[18] In adhering to the Convention three years later, Luxembourg made an interpretive declaration specific to the right to life whereby Article 6 of the CRC 'presents no obstacle to implementation of the provisions of Luxembourg legislation concerning . . . prevention of back-street abortion and the regulation of pregnancy termination'.[19]

11.10 That said, the ninth preambular paragraph to the CRC does refer to the need of the child, by reason of his or her physical and mental immaturity, to 'special safeguards and care, including appropriate legal protection, before as well as after birth'. The wording cites and reproduces, in quotation marks, the language of the Declaration on the Rights of the Child adopted by the erstwhile League of Nations in 1924. The text was subsequently cited verbatim in the preamble to the Declaration on the Rights of the Child endorsed by the UN General Assembly in 1959.[20]

11.11 In signing the CRC in January 1990, Ecuador made the following statement: 'In signing the Convention on the Rights of the Child, Ecuador reaffirms . . . [that it is] especially pleased with the ninth preambular paragraph of the draft Convention, which pointed to the need to protect the unborn child, and believed that that paragraph should be borne in mind in interpreting all the articles of the Convention.'[21] More forceful still was the Holy See, which appended a declaration to its adherence to the CRC in April 1990:

> The Holy See recognizes that the Convention represents an enactment of principles previously adopted by the United Nations, and once effective as a ratified instrument, will safeguard the rights of the child before as well as after birth, as expressly affirmed in the 'Declaration of the Rights of the Child' . . . and restated in the ninth preambular paragraph

---

[17] Art. 1, Convention on the Rights of the Child; adopted at New York 20 November 1989; entered into force 2 September 1990.
[18] Interpretative declaration of the United Kingdom, 16 December 1991, at http://bit.ly/2E7Bf2v.
[19] Declaration of Luxembourg, 7 March 1994, at http://bit.ly/2E7Bf2v.
[20] 1959 Declaration on the Rights of the Child, adopted on 20 November 1959 by unanimous vote in UN General Assembly Resolution 1386 (XIV).
[21] Declaration of Ecuador, 26 January 1990, at http://bit.ly/2E7Bf2v.

of the Convention. The Holy See remains confident that the ninth preambular paragraph will serve as the perspective through which the rest of the Convention will be interpreted, in conformity with article 31 of the Vienna Convention on the Law of Treaties.[22]

11.12 In interpreting the right to life under the ICCPR, the Human Rights Committee has put the life of the pregnant woman or girl at the centre of its protection. Thus it stipulates in General Comment 36: 'Although States parties may adopt measures designed to regulate voluntary termination of pregnancy, those measures must not result in violation of the right to life of a pregnant woman or girl, or her other rights under the Covenant.'[23] The Committee implies that 'restrictions on the ability of women or girls to seek abortion that jeopardize their lives' are likely to violate the right to life, even if they survive. States Parties should also, the Committee declares, 'effectively protect the lives of women and girls against the mental and physical health risks associated with unsafe abortions'.[24] In 2014, it was estimated that approximately twenty-two million unsafe abortions take place worldwide each year, with between 4.7 and 13.2 per cent of maternal deaths attributed to unsafe abortion.[25] To comply with the right to life, the Human Rights Committee declares, States Parties to the ICCPR 'must provide safe, legal and effective access to abortion where the life and health of the pregnant woman or girl is at risk'.[26]

11.13 If restrictions subject women or girls to undue 'physical or mental pain or suffering', then a violation of Article 7 of the Covenant (the prohibition on torture or cruel, inhuman or degrading treatment) is more likely than would be a violation of the right to life. This will occur 'most notably where the pregnancy is the result of rape or incest or where the pregnancy is not viable'.[27] On this latter point, the Committee cites its Views of 2016 in the case of *Mellet v. Ireland*.[28] The communication was made in 2013 on behalf of Amanda Mellet, a woman who was denied access to an abortion in Ireland in 2011 after learning her pregnancy involved a fatal foetal impairment and found the prospect of continuing her pregnancy unbearable. At the time, Ireland's abortion laws were among the most

[22] Declaration of the Holy See, 20 April 1990, at http://bit.ly/2E7Bf2v.
[23] Human Rights Committee, General Comment 36 on the right to life, para. 8.
[24] Ibid.
[25] L. Say, D. Chou, A. Gemmill, Ö Tunçalp, A. B. Moller, J. Daniels, A. M. Gülmezoglu, M. Temmerman, and L. Alkema, 'Global Causes of Maternal Death: A WHO Systematic Analysis', *Lancet Global Health*, vol. 2, no. 6 (June 2014), pp. 323–33.
[26] Human Rights Committee, General Comment 36 on the right to life, para. 8.
[27] Ibid. A 'non-viable pregnancy' means there is no chance of a live-born baby or the foetus does not have a chance to survive even when born alive. Depending on the stage of pregnancy, viability means different things. Before six weeks, it can mean that human chorionic gonadotropin (hCG) levels are increasing normally. hCG is a hormone produced by the placenta during its implantation process in the uterus. After six weeks, a normal foetal heart indicates a viable pregnancy. A foetal heart with no heartbeat at any point is called foetal demise. Between six and about twenty-four weeks, a non-viable pregnancy is when a baby delivered has no chance of survival, even if there is still a heartbeat in the uterus. After that time, a viable pregnancy is when a baby has a chance to survive outside of the womb. However, some countries without adequate neo-natal care consider non-viable at less than about twenty-eight weeks' gestation. See, e.g., ConceiveAbilities, 'The Difference between Viable and Non-Viable Pregnancy', blog entry, 19 March 2019, at http://bit.ly/2PWIAF2.
[28] Human Rights Committee, *Mellet v. Ireland*, Views, UN doc. CCPR/C/116/D/2324/2013, 17 November 2016.

restrictive in the world, with abortion permitted only when there was a risk to the life of a pregnant woman. Indeed, since 1983 (and until new legislation adopted in 2018 following a national referendum on the question), Article 40.3.3 of the Constitution of Ireland had placed 'the right to life of the unborn' on an equal footing with the right to life of pregnant women.

11.14 The Committee recalled in its Views that 'the fact that a particular conduct or action is legal under domestic law does not mean that it cannot infringe article 7 of the Covenant'.[29] Indeed, the Committee observed, Ireland's domestic legal framework had 'subjected the author to conditions of intense physical and mental suffering'. Her physical and mental anguish was 'exacerbated by not being able to continue receiving medical care and health insurance coverage for her treatment from the Irish health-care system'. She was obliged, the Committee observed, 'to choose between continuing her non-viable pregnancy or travelling to another country while carrying a dying foetus, at her personal expense and separated from the support of her family, and returning while not fully recovered'. To this was added the 'shame and stigma' associated with the criminalisation of abortion of a fatally ill foetus, 'the fact of having to leave the baby's remains behind and later having them unexpectedly delivered to her by courier', and Ireland's refusal to provide her with the necessary and appropriate post-abortion and bereavement care.[30]

11.15 Taken together, the Committee concluded, the facts of the treatment of Ms Mellet and her personal circumstances amounted to cruel, inhuman, or degrading treatment in violation of Article 7 of the ICCPR.[31] The Center for Reproductive Rights remarked that 'this ground-breaking ruling marks the first time that, in response to an individual complaint, an international human rights court or committee has recognized that by criminalizing abortion a state has violated a woman's human rights'.[32]

11.16 Already in its 2014 Concluding Observations on the fourth periodic report of Ireland on its implementation of the ICCPR (also cited in General Comment 36), the Committee had called on the Irish Government to 'revise its legislation on abortion, including its Constitution, to provide for additional exceptions in cases of rape, incest, serious risks to the health of the mother, or fatal foetal abnormality'.[33] Following a national referendum, the possibility of lawful abortion in Ireland was significantly broadened by Statute.[34] Since 1 January 2019, a termination has been permitted in the following circumstances: where there is a grave risk to the life of, or a grave risk of serious harm to the health of, a pregnant woman (this is to be adjudged through examination by two medical practitioners); where there is an immediate and serious risk to life or of serious harm to the health of a pregnant woman (based on an examination by one medical practitioner); where two medical

---

[29] Ibid., para. 7.4.
[30] Ibid.
[31] Ibid., para. 7.6.
[32] Center for Reproductive Rights, 'Mellet v. Ireland', 7 August 2016, at http://bit.ly/2XZ3Iic.
[33] Human Rights Committee, Concluding Observations on Ireland, UN doc. CCPR/C/IRL/CO/4, 19 August 2014, para. 9.
[34] Health (Regulation of Termination of Pregnancy) Act 2018.

practitioners agree in good faith that a condition affecting the foetus is likely to lead to the death of the foetus either before or within twenty-eight days of birth; or where it has been duly certified that the term of the pregnancy has not exceeded twelve weeks.[35]

11.17 The UN Committee on the Elimination of Discrimination against Women has also addressed the issue of abortion. In its General Recommendation 35, issued in 2017, it states that violations of women's sexual and reproductive health and rights, such as criminalisation of abortion, denial or delay of safe abortion and post-abortion care, and forced continuation of pregnancy, 'are forms of gender-based violence that, depending on the circumstances, may amount to torture or cruel, inhuman or degrading treatment'.[36]

11.18 The Committee has also engaged directly with States Parties to the 1979 Convention on the Elimination of All Forms of Discrimination against Women[37] (CEDAW) on the issue of abortion. In 2018, the Committee stated that the United Kingdom was violating the rights of women in Northern Ireland by unduly restricting their access to abortion. In the report of its dedicated inquiry on the issue, published in March 2018, the Committee found that the United Kingdom was responsible for 'grave violations' of rights under CEDAW, on the basis that the criminal law in force in Northern Ireland compels women to carry pregnancies to full term in cases of severe foetal impairment, including fatal foetal abnormality, and cases of rape or incest, thereby subjecting them to severe physical and mental anguish. This, the Committee on the Elimination of Discrimination against Women affirmed, constitutes gender-based violence against women. It also found that the violations were 'systematic', given the deliberate criminalisation of abortion and a 'highly restrictive policy on access to abortion', which compels women to carry pregnancies to full term, to travel outside Northern Ireland to undergo legal abortion, or to self-administer abortifacients.[38]

11.19 In October 2019, the Committee on the Elimination of Discrimination against Women discussed the fourth periodic report of Andorra on its implementation of the Convention. During the interactive dialogue with the authorities, Committee experts raised concerns about access to abortion and reiterated a recommendation made in previous Concluding Observations that the government should legalise abortion under certain circumstances (as of this writing, abortion remained wholly illegal in Andorra).[39] The Committee called on the authorities to amend Article 108 of the Penal Code to

---

[35] Ss. 9–12, Health (Regulation of Termination of Pregnancy) Act 2018.
[36] Committee on the Elimination of Discrimination against Women, General Recommendation No. 35 on gender-based violence against women, updating general recommendation No. 19, UN doc. CEDAW/C/GC/35, 14 July 2017, para. 18.
[37] Convention on the Elimination of All Forms of Discrimination against Women; adopted at New York 18 December 1979; entered into force 3 September 1981. As of 1 May 2021, 189 States were parties to CEDAW and a further 2 (Palau and the United States) were signatories.
[38] Inquiry concerning the United Kingdom of Great Britain and Northern Ireland under article 8 of the Optiona Protocol to the Convention on the Elimination of All Forms of Discrimination against Women. Report of the Committee, UN doc. CEDAW/C/OP.8/GBR/1, 6 March 2018, para. 83.
[39] Women who receive an abortion within Andorra can face up to six months of house arrest; doctors who perform the procedure can be sentenced to up to three years in prison and be barred from practicing medicine for up to five years. M. Bernhard, 'Andorra's Abortion Rights Revolution: Push to Legalize

decriminalise abortion, at the very least in cases where a threat existed to the mother's physical and mental health; the woman had been raped or was a victim of incest; or when the foetus was not viable.[40] In its subsequent Concluding Observations, the Committee expressed its concern that Andorra had taken no measures to amend its legislation in order to decriminalise abortion under certain circumstances. It remained concerned by the interpretation of the right to life in the Constitution as a limitation on women's sexual and reproductive health rights.[41]

11.20 The global COVID-19 pandemic that erupted in 2020 impacted access to abortion. In July 2020, in a submission to the Committee on the Elimination of Discrimination against Women with respect to Russia, Human Rights Watch noted that Russian law allows an abortion to be performed during the first twelve weeks of pregnancy for any reason. Yet, it noted, 'women's access to safe abortion care in Moscow became a serious issue in March 2020, after the Minister of Health declared that "non-urgent" procedures would be postponed to avoid the overcrowding of hospitals due to COVID-19'.[42] This, the organisation said, 'led to hospitals turning down women seeking abortion procedures, while access to cancer treatment and procedures for other conditions continued'.[43]

11.21 Human Rights Watch cited a report by the rights group *Nasiliyu.Net* ('No to violence'), which claimed that many hospitals in Moscow were denying women access to safe abortion procedures, telling them that absent a 'direct threat to life and health', abortion procedures will not be carried out during the pandemic.[44] This policy decision by the authorities may, it suggested, be 'an attempt to curb women's rights, by coercing women to carry out births rather than terminate their pregnancies'. In early May 2020, Human Rights Watch further observed, the Russian Orthodox Church called on the government to suspend abortions altogether during the pandemic.[45]

ABORTION UNDER REGIONAL STANDARDS

11.22 The issue of abortion has been addressed to varying extents in the interpretation and application of regional instruments. This is especially the case in the jurisprudence of the

---

Abortion Could Tip Country into Constitutional Crisis, Opponents Say', *Politico*, 22 October2019, at http://politi.co/2JmBbPa.

[40] 'Committee on the Elimination of Discrimination against Women Discusses Access to Abortion and Gender Stereotypes in Dialogue with Andorra', news release, 23 October 2019, at http://bit.ly/30YQeVK.

[41] Committee on the Elimination of Discrimination against Women, Concluding Observations on Andorra, UN doc. CEDAW/C/AND/CO/4, 13 November 2019, para. 35.

[42] 'Murashko: Russia Will Postpone Non-Urgent Scheduled Operations', *Ria Novosti*, 30 March 2020 (Russian original), at http://bit.ly/30YjTOI.

[43] Human Rights Watch, 'Submission to the Committee on the Elimination of Discrimination against Women on Russia', 3 July 2020, at http://bit.ly/31310sF.

[44] T. Lokshina (Human Rights Watch), 'Denying Women Abortion Access in Moscow', Commentary, 28 April 2020, at http://bit.ly/2PU5tsD.

[45] Human Rights Watch, 'Submission to the Committee on the Elimination of Discrimination against Women on Russia', 3 July 2020.

European Court of Human Rights and the work of the Inter-American Commission on Human Rights and the Inter-American Court.

European Court of Human Rights' Jurisprudence

11.23 At the regional level, the 1950 European Convention on Human Rights does not explicitly address abortion.[46] The European Court of Human Rights has even sidestepped, on a number of occasions, the question of when in the life cycle Convention protection begins. In its 2004 judgment in *Vo v. France*,[47] the Court's Grand Chamber held that it was 'neither desirable, nor even possible as matters stand, to answer in the abstract the question whether the unborn child is a person for the purposes of Article 2 of the Convention ("*personne*" in the French text)'.[48] The case concerned a mix-up in a hospital with another patient with the same surname, resulting in the applicant's amniotic sack being punctured. This made an abortion necessary for health reasons. The applicant had argued that the unintentional killing of her child should have been classified as manslaughter. The Court, however, did not find a violation of the right to life. It referred to legal regimes in other contracting States, noting the third-party intervention whereby, in the criminal law of England and Wales, it was well established that the unborn were not treated as legal persons for the purpose of the common-law rules of murder or manslaughter.[49]

11.24 The issue of the rights of the unborn was again raised in the *Evans* case,[50] adjudged by the Grand Chamber in 2007. The applicant, who was suffering from ovarian cancer, had undergone in-vitro fertilisation with her then partner before having her ovaries removed. Six embryos were created and put in safe storage. When the couple's relationship ended, her ex-partner withdrew his consent for the embryos to be used, not wishing to be the genetic parent of the applicant's child. National law consequently required that the eggs be destroyed. The applicant complained that this would prevent her from ever having a child to whom she would be genetically related and further that this amounted to a violation of the embryo's right to life. The Grand Chamber held that the issue of when the right to life began came within the 'margin of appreciation' accorded to States Parties in their implementation of the European Convention, given the 'absence of any European consensus on the scientific and legal definition of the beginning of life'.[51]

11.25 The European Court has, however, adjudicated whether a right exists to an abortion exists in certain circumstances in compliance with the rights to life and to private and

---

[46] Convention for the Protection of Human Rights and Fundamental Freedoms; adopted at Rome 4 November 1950; entered into force 3 September 1953.
[47] European Court of Human Rights, *Vo v. France*, Judgment (Grand Chamber), 8 July 2004.
[48] Ibid., para. 85.
[49] In Attorney-General's Reference (No. 3, 1994), the House of Lords had concluded that injury of the unborn without a live birth could not lead to a conviction for murder, manslaughter, or indeed any other violent crime. Ibid., para. 73.
[50] European Court of Human Rights, *Evans v. United Kingdom*, Judgment (Grand Chamber), 10 April 2007.
[51] Ibid., para. 54.

family life (Article 8) in its judgment in *A, B, and C v. Ireland*.[52] One of the applicants ('C') was in remission from a rare form of cancer[53] and, unaware that she was pregnant, underwent check-ups contraindicated in pregnancy. She learnt that her pregnancy could provoke a relapse and believed it put her life at risk. In its judgment, the Grand Chamber observed that the protection accorded under Irish domestic law to the right to life of the unborn and the restrictions on lawful abortion in Ireland 'were based on profound moral and ethical values to which the Convention afforded a significant margin of appreciation'. A 'broad margin', the Court further held, referring to its earlier judgments in *Vo* and in *Evans*, 'was specifically accorded to determining what persons were protected by Article 2 of the Convention'. Moreover, as the Court expressly acknowledged, it had not yet addressed 'the substantive issue of the regulation of abortion'.[54]

11.26 The third applicant complained under Article 2 that abortion was not available in Ireland even in a life-threatening situation because of the failure to implement Article 40.3.3 of the Constitution (cited previously).[55] The Court, though, observed that, as was the case for the first and second applicants, there was no legal impediment to C travelling abroad for an abortion, nor did she claim that any other impediment intervened to prevent her travelling to England for an abortion. In such circumstances, the Court concluded, there was no evidence of any relevant risk to the third applicant's life and her complaint under Article 2 of the Convention had to be rejected as 'manifestly ill-founded'.[56] Instead, the Court deemed that her complaint that she was required to travel abroad for an abortion, resulting from her fear for her life (see below), fell to be examined under Article 8 of the Convention.[57]

11.27 The Court adjudged that Article 8 'cannot ... be interpreted as conferring a right to abortion'.[58] This is a very clear statement of law. That said, the Court noted 'a consensus amongst a substantial majority of the Contracting States of the Council of Europe towards allowing abortion on broader grounds than accorded under Irish law'.[59] In particular, it said, an abortion was justified on health and well-being grounds in some forty States Parties to the European Convention. Moreover, only three States – Andorra, Malta, and San Marino – had more restrictive access to abortion services than Ireland at the time, prohibiting as they did abortion in all circumstances, regardless of the risk to the woman's life.[60] Given, however, that the option lawfully existed to seek and obtain an abortion abroad, the Court did not consider that this consensus decisively narrowed the broad

---

[52] European Court of Human Rights, *A, B, and C v. Ireland*, Judgment (Grand Chamber), 16 December 2010.
[53] Ibid., paras. 23 and 24.
[54] Ibid., para. 185.
[55] Ibid., para. 157.
[56] Ibid., paras. 158, 159.
[57] Ibid., para. 158.
[58] Ibid., para. 214.
[59] Ibid., para. 235.
[60] Andorra subsequently allowed for abortion to save the pregnant woman or girl's life. According to UNDESA, while San Marino's legislation on abortion did not expressly allow abortion to be performed to save the life of a woman, general principles of criminal law allowed abortion to be performed for that reason on the ground of necessity.

margin of appreciation accorded to Ireland.[61] Thus the Court held that the prohibition in its domestic law 'struck a fair balance between the right of the first and second applicants to respect for their private lives and the rights invoked on behalf of the unborn'.[62]

11.28 Applicant 'C', however, had a rare form of cancer. When she discovered she was pregnant, she feared for her life, as she believed that her pregnancy increased the risk of her cancer returning and that she would not obtain treatment for that cancer in Ireland while pregnant.[63] The Court considered that any such risk to her life caused by her pregnancy 'clearly concerned fundamental values and essential aspects of her right to respect for her private life'. Contrary to Ireland's claim, she did not need to further substantiate the alleged medical risk, since there appeared to be no effective domestic procedure for establishing that risk.[64]

11.29 Article 40.3.3 of the Irish Constitution, as interpreted by the Irish Supreme Court in the X case, provided that an abortion could be available in Ireland if a real and substantial risk to the life of the mother, including a risk of self-harm, were established that could only be avoided by a termination of the pregnancy. But no criteria or procedures had been laid down in Irish law, whether in legislation, by case law, or otherwise, by which the risk was to be determined, 'leading to uncertainty as to its precise application'. Accordingly, the Court concluded that the authorities had failed to comply with their positive obligation to respect C's private life and held that Article 8 of the European Convention on Human Rights had been violated.[65]

The Inter-American Human Rights System

11.30 According to Article 4(1) of the 1969 American Convention on Human Rights, 'every person has the right to have his life respected. This right shall be protected by law and, *in general, from the moment of conception*. No one shall be arbitrarily deprived of his life.'[66] In its judgment in *Artavia Murillo and others ('In Vitro Fertilization')* v. *Costa Rica*, the Inter-American Court of Human Rights considered under which circumstances an embryo could be considered a person for the purposes of Article 4(1). The Court concluded that 'conception' occurred legally at the moment when the embryo becomes implanted in the uterus and not before.[67] It further held that the words 'in general' in paragraph 1 of the article entailed 'that the protection of the right to life under this provision is not absolute, but rather gradual and incremental according to its development'.[68]

11.31 On 29 April 2013, hours after the Salvadoran Supreme Court had denied an abortion for a woman with serious complications in her pregnancy, the Inter-American Court of

[61] European Court of Human Rights, A, B, and C v. Ireland, Judgment, para. 236.
[62] Ibid., para. 241.
[63] Ibid., para. 250.
[64] Ibid.
[65] Ibid., paras. 267, 268.
[66] Art. 4, American Convention on Human Rights; adopted at San José 22 November 1969; entered into force 18 July 1978 (added emphasis).
[67] Inter-American Court of Human Rights, *Artavia Murillo and others ('In Vitro Fertilization')* v. *Costa Rica*, Judgment (Preliminary objections, merits, reparations and costs), 28 November 2012, para. 264.
[68] Ibid.

Human Rights granted precautionary measures. It ordered El Salvador officials to allow her medical team to take all necessary steps to preserve the life and health of 'Beatriz', a twenty-two-year-old Salvadoran woman who was five months pregnant and suffering from complications related to lupus and kidney disease. Beatriz was carrying a non-viable anencephalic foetus (one without a brain). She had requested authorisation for medical personnel to perform an abortion without fear of criminal prosecution.[69] Subsequent to the ruling, a caesarean section was performed in the twenty-sixth week of pregnancy.[70]

11.32 El Salvador is one of seven States in Latin America and the Caribbean in which abortion was prohibited in all circumstances by law. According to data from Citizens' Association for the Decriminalization of Therapeutic, Ethical and Eugenic Abortion of El Salvador, between 2000 and 2011, 129 women were prosecuted in El Salvador for abortion or aggravated homicide, with sentences upon conviction ranging between two and forty years in prison.[71] In 2017, in its report on admissibility, the Inter-American Commission on Human Rights held that the case against El Salvador should proceed, inter alia on the basis of violations of Beatriz's rights to life and to freedom from inhumane treatment.[72]

11.33 Later in 2017, the Inter-American Commission issued a general statement on abortion, noting consistent information pointing to the close relationship between poverty, unsafe abortions, and high maternal mortality rates.[73] The Commission underscored that laws criminalising abortion in all circumstances 'have a negative impact on women's dignity and their rights to life, to personal integrity, and to health, as well as on their general right to live free from violence and discrimination'. Criminalising abortion in cases where the woman's life is at risk and when the pregnancy results from rape or incest 'imposes a disproportionate burden on the exercise of women's rights and creates a context that facilitates unsafe abortions and high rates of maternal mortality'.[74]

African Charter on Human and Peoples' Rights and the Maputo Protocol

11.34 The 1981 African Charter on Human and Peoples' Rights does not address the issue of abortion.[75] In 2015, the African Commission on Human and Peoples' Rights adopted its General Comment on the right to life under Article 4 of the African Charter on Human

---

[69] Center for Reproductive Rights, 'Inter-American Court of Human Rights Orders El Salvador Government to Allow Pregnant Woman with Critical Complications Access to Life-saving Health Care', press release, 30 May 2013, at http://bit.ly/31PoPVm.
[70] 'IACHR Demands Explanations from El Salvador over Beatriz Case', Center for Justice and International Law, 8 April 2015, at http://bit.ly/30WVB7Q.
[71] Ibid.
[72] Inter-American Commission on Human Rights, *Beatriz v. El Salvador*, Report on Admissibility (Petition 2003-13), Report No. 120/17, OAS doc. OEA/Ser.L/V/II.164 Doc. 141, 7 September 2017.
[73] Inter-American Commission on Human Rights, 'IACHR Urges All States to Adopt Comprehensive, Immediate Measures to Respect and Protect Women's Sexual and Reproductive Rights', press release 165/17, 23 October 2017, at http://bit.ly/31XIDWq.
[74] Ibid.
[75] African Charter on Human and Peoples' Rights; adopted at Nairobi 27 June 1981; entered into force 21 October 1986.

and Peoples' Rights.[76] The General Comment does not address the issue of abortion. The 1990 African Charter on the Rights and Welfare of the Child defines a child as 'every human being below the age of 18 years'.[77]

11.35 Article 14(2)(c) of the 2003 Protocol on the Rights of Women in Africa[78] (the 'Maputo Protocol') explicitly requires that 'medical abortion' be available 'in cases of sexual assault, rape, incest, and where the continued pregnancy endangers the mental and physical health of the mother or the life of the mother or the foetus'.[79] The case of *Igohozo v. Prosecution*[80] before the High Court of Rwanda concerned the alleged drugging and rape of a thirteen-year-old girl, as a result of which she became pregnant. This led to depression, stigma, and shame, with the girl unable to continue with her education. She desired to terminate her pregnancy at all costs, even at the risk of losing her life. The High Court granted her the right to an abortion, reversing the decision by a court of first instance, holding that her age meant that she could not have lawfully consented to intercourse. In its judgment, the Court cited Article 14(2)(c) of the Maputo Protocol.

Arab Charter on Human Rights

11.36 The 2004 Arab Charter on Human Rights does not address the issue of abortion.[81]

STATE PRACTICE

11.37 In 1994, 179 States signalled a commitment to prevent unsafe abortions and reduce maternal mortality by endorsing the International Conference on Population and Development Programme of Action (ICPD).[82] The Sustainable Development Goals (SDGs) do not encompass an explicit call for changes to overly restrictive abortion laws. Two targets are, however, cited as relevant. Target 3.7 is that by 2030, universal access will be ensured to sexual and reproductive health care services, including services for family planning, information, and education. In addition, the Target is that reproductive health services should be integrated by that date into national strategies and programmes. Target 5.6 is to ensure, again by 2030, universal access to sexual and reproductive health and reproductive rights.

---

[76] African Commission on Human and Peoples' Rights, General Comment No. 3 on the African Charter on Human and Peoples' Rights on the right to life (Article 4), adopted during its 57th Ordinary Session, Banjul, The Gambia, November 2015.
[77] Art. 2, African Charter on the Rights and Welfare of the Child; adopted at Addis Ababa 1 July 1990; entered into force 29 November 1999.
[78] Protocol to the African Charter on Human and Peoples' Rights on the Rights of Women in Africa; adopted at Maputo 11 July 2003; entered into force 25 November 2005. As of 1 August 2020, forty-two States were party to the Protocol and another ten States were signatories.
[79] Art. 14(2)(c), Maputo Protocol.
[80] High Court of Rwanda, *Igohozo v. Prosecution* [2016] 3 RLR.
[81] Arab Charter on Human Rights; adopted at Tunis 22 May 2004; entered into force 15 March 2008.
[82] Center for Reproductive Rights, 'Accelerating Progress: Liberalization of Abortion Laws Since ICPD', Fact Sheet 2020, at http://bit.ly/3axlka2, p. 1.

11.38 Several dozen States have amended their national laws to loosen the restrictions on abortion in recent decades. In the last twenty-five years, according to the Center for Reproductive Rights, eighteen States have overturned comprehensive prohibitions on abortion, amending national legislation to permit abortion under various circumstances.[83] Most of the eighteen reformed their laws to permit abortion when the woman's health is at risk and on specific enumerated grounds, particularly when the pregnancy results from rape or incest. Five States – Bhutan, Chile, Iran, Micronesia, and Somalia – reformed their laws to permit abortion only to save the life of the woman, where the foetus is not viable, or on grounds of the pregnancy having resulted from rape or incest.[84] In December 2020, Argentina was poised to decriminalise abortion up to fourteen weeks' pregnancy after legislation was passed by the lower house of its parliament.[85]

11.39 There has been some tightening of restrictions on abortion in a small number of States. For instance, in the United States, in 2019 Louisiana passed a bill to ban abortions after a foetal heartbeat is detected, making the state the ninth that year to pass abortion restrictions that could challenge the constitutional right first established by the US Supreme Court in its 1973 judgment in *Roe* v. *Wade*[86] (as reaffirmed but amended by its 1992 judgment in *Planned Parenthood* v. *Casey*).[87] Alabama has changed its laws to prohibit abortions in nearly all cases. Georgia, Kentucky, Louisiana, Missouri, Mississippi, and Ohio passed 'heartbeat' bills that effectively prohibit abortions after six to eight weeks of pregnancy, when doctors can usually start detecting a foetal heartbeat. Utah and Arkansas voted to limit the procedure to the middle of the second trimester.[88] As of writing, however, the legality of the decision in *Roe* v. *Wade* was due to come once again before the US Supreme Court.

11.40 In England, Scotland, and Wales, a pregnant girl or woman can legally have an abortion at up to twenty-three weeks and six days of pregnancy, in accordance with the 1967 Abortion Act, as amended by The Human Fertilisation and Embryology Bill, which entered into force on 1 April 1991.[89] Twenty-four weeks is the currently accepted point at

---

[83] Angola, Bhutan, Burkina Faso, Central African Republic, Chile, Colombia, DR Congo, Eswatini, Iran, Lesotho, Mauritius, Micronesia, Monaco, Nepal, Niger, Sao Tome and Principe, Somalia, and Togo.

[84] Center for Reproductive Rights, 'Accelerating Progress: Liberalization of Abortion Laws Since ICPD', Fact Sheet, p. 2.

[85] U. Goñi and T. Phillips, 'Argentina's Lower House Passes Bill to Allow Abortion', *The Guardian*, 11 December 2020, at http://bit.ly/2LCYDc1.

[86] US Supreme Court, *Jane Roe and others* v. *Henry Wade, District Attorney of Dallas County*, 410 US 113, Decided 22 January 1973. The Court held that the Fourteenth Amendment to the US Constitution, which prohibits any State from depriving 'any person of life, liberty, or property, without due process of law', granted each pregnant woman the right to choose an abortion within certain circumstances.

[87] In *Planned Parenthood* v. *Casey*, the US Supreme Court partially reaffirmed its 1973 judgment in *Roe* v. *Wade*, determining that abortion was legal until the foetus reaches viability, usually set at between twenty-four and twenty-eight weeks. US Supreme Court, *Planned Parenthood of Southeastern Pennsylvania and others* v. *Robert P. Casey and others*, 505 US 833, Decided 29 June 1992.

[88] K. K. Rebecca Lai, 'Abortion Bans: 9 States Have Passed Bills to Limit the Procedure This Year', *New York Times*, last updated 29 May 2019, at http://nyti.ms/3awJ3XP.

[89] Department of Health and Social Care, Abortion Statistics, England and Wales: 2019. Summary information from the abortion notification forms returned to the Chief Medical Officers of England and Wales. January

which the foetus is considered viable outside the mother's body.[90] In Northern Ireland, however, as noted previously, access to abortion is limited, as the 1967 Act was not extended to this region.

[90] to December 2019, London, 11 June 2020, at http://bit.ly/2Y405KY, p. 3. The Human Fertilisation and Embryology Act reduces the upper limit for an abortion from twenty-eight weeks.

Ibid. A baby born at twenty-four weeks would generally require considerable medical intervention, potentially including mechanical ventilation and other invasive treatments followed by a lengthy stay in a neo-natal intensive care unit (NICU), possibly also requiring tubal assistance with eating and breathing. In the hands of experienced specialists, babies born slightly earlier may have a chance at survival. Babies born at twenty-three weeks may survive in a state-of-the-art NICU, but the odds of survival are much lower. A 2015 study also showed that babies born at twenty-two weeks may have a small chance at survival, but death or serious health issues are more probable. K. Danielsson, 'Premature Birth and Survival Statistics', *VeryWell Family*, 20 April 2020, at http://bit.ly/31TdovT. See also M. Ye Hee Lee, 'Setting the Record Straight on Measuring Fetal Age and the "20-Week Abortion"', *Washington Post*, 26 May 2015, at http://wapo.st/3fU6Q5a.

12

Euthanasia and Suicide

INTRODUCTION

12.01 Does the right to life also comprise the right to seek to choose the time and manner of one's death? Euthanasia and suicide – the decision by a person to end or take his or her life, with or without assistance – are highly controversial on moral, personal, philosophical, and religious levels, as is their treatment in national and international law. A 2016 review of domestic criminal law in 192 nations found that in 25 suicide was illegal, with a further 20 sanctioning those who attempt suicide with a term of imprisonment. The vast majority of countries criminalise the aiding, abetting, or encouraging of suicide, though the nature and sanction of the actions that are illegal vary.[1]

12.02 Many religions prohibit, or at least stigmatise, the taking of one's own life, as they do with the unlawful taking of another's.[2] Public opinion across different nations, however, remains deeply divided on the issue, with advocacy groups active on both sides of the argument.[3] Moreover, even if one does not oppose euthanasia per se, there are unquestionably significant practical concerns in ensuring that any decision to die is truly a voluntary one; that it is not a transitory wish that treatment or support could overcome; and that any person assisting a person's death has that person's genuine and informed consent to do so.

---

[1] B. L. Misharaa and D. N. Weisstubb, 'The Legal Status of Suicide: A Global Review', *International Journal of Law and Psychiatry*, vol. 44 (January–February 2016), pp. 54–74.

[2] Although the Bible does not prohibit suicide, Augustine of Hippo argued in his noted fifth century CE work *On the City of God against the Pagans* that it violated the Sixth Commandment, 'Thou shalt not kill'. Building on Augustine's thought, Thomas Aquinas declared in the thirteenth century CE that suicide was 'altogether wrong' for three reasons: it runs counter to the natural inclination to cherish oneself; it injures the community to which each man belongs; and it wrongs God, who alone has power over life and death. N. M. Gorsuch, *The Future of Assisted Suicide and Euthanasia*, Princeton University Press, Princeton, 2006, pp. 26, 27.

[3] In the United States, for instance, Compassion & Choices (formerly, the Hemlock Society) 'envision[s] a society that affirms life and accepts the inevitability of death, embraces expanded options for compassionate dying, and empowers everyone to choose end-of-life care that reflects their values, priorities, and beliefs'. Compassion & Choices, 'About Us', 2020, at http://bit.ly/2P5rNyZ. In contrast, Human Life International is 'the world's largest global pro-life apostolate, with an active network in over 100 countries'. Human Life International, 'About Us', 2020, at http://bit.ly/3hJ7Kmj. Despite both groups preaching compassion, there appears to be little love lost between the two bodies. See, e.g., B. Clowes, 'The Fractured History of the Hemlock Society', Human Life International, 18 June 2020, at http://bit.ly/3hMUA7W.

12.03 This chapter describes how the right to life applies to and restrains both euthanasia (active and passive, as well as voluntary, non-voluntary, and involuntary) and suicide, including assisted suicide. It begins by discussing the definition of these terms along with a summary of relevant data on prevalence and main causes or motivations. A sharp distinction is to be emphasised between those notions and that of abortion (the intentional killing of a foetus in the womb; the subject of the previous chapter) and that of so-called mercy killings in Germany from the late 1930s and early 1940s. The Nazis killed tens of thousands of children and adults with disabilities within its broader extermination programme. The chapter then discusses in turn the contemporary global and regional human rights treaty regulation of State Party duties with respect to suicide and euthanasia. A final section considers the legal practice of States, which continues to evolve, gradually, towards the decriminalisation of both suicide and euthanasia.

THE DEFINITION, CAUSES, AND PREVALENCE OF SUICIDE

12.04 Suicide is the intentional taking of one's own life by one's own hand. It is, in the words of the World Health Organization (WHO), a 'serious global public health issue'. Almost 800,000 people die as a result of suicide every year, which equates to one suicide somewhere in the world every forty seconds. This puts the action of killing oneself intentionally among the top twenty leading causes of death globally, with more deaths annually due to suicide than to armed conflict, breast cancer, malaria, or homicide.[4]

12.05 The link between suicide and psycho-social disabilities such as depression and alcohol addiction is said to be 'well established' in high-income nations, but almost four-fifths of suicides occur in low- and middle-income countries. Globally, suicide is the third leading cause of death in those between fifteen and nineteen years of age.[5] Suicide is far more common in boys and men than it is in girls and women – at 13.7 per 100,000, the global age-standardised suicide rate is considerably higher in males than it is in females (7.5 per 100,000).[6]

12.06 As WHO records, many suicides occur impulsively in moments of crisis, such as following a breakdown in ability to deal with financial problems, distress at the ending of a close relationship, or as a result of chronic pain and illness. In addition, experiencing armed conflict, natural disaster, violence, abuse, or suffering loss of family are strongly associated with suicidal behaviour.[7] Suicide rates are high among vulnerable groups who experience discrimination, such as refugees and migrants; indigenous peoples; lesbian, gay, bisexual, transgender, intersex (LGBTI) persons; and prisoners.[8] Ingestion of pesticide (used in one in five instances globally), hanging, and self-inflicted gunshot wounds are among the most common methods of suicide.

---

[4] WHO, *Suicide in the World: Global Health Estimates*, Geneva, 2019, available at http://bit.ly/39AZLoy, p. 1.
[5] WHO, 'Suicide: Key Facts', 2 September 2019, at http://bit.ly/3310r8r.
[6] WHO, *Suicide in the World: Global Health Estimates*, p. 9. The suicide mortality rate as defined as the number of suicide deaths in a year, divided by the population, and multiplied by 100,000.
[7] WHO, 'Suicide: Key Facts'.
[8] Ibid.

Assisted Suicide

12.07 In practice, a person's suicide may often be assisted in some form, in particular by a doctor. The World Medical Association (WMA) defines physician-assisted suicide as referring to 'cases in which, at the voluntary request of a patient with decision-making capacity, a physician deliberately enables a patient to end his or her own life by prescribing or providing medical substances with the intent to bring about death'.[9] The role of the physician in any suicide is particularly controversial. In its 2019 Declaration on Euthanasia and Physician-Assisted Suicide, adopted by the 70th World Medical Assembly in Tbilisi, the WMA reiterated 'its strong commitment to the principles of medical ethics and that utmost respect has to be maintained for human life'. 'Therefore', the Declaration stated, the Association 'is firmly opposed to euthanasia and physician-assisted suicide'. Less controversially, it further declared, 'No physician should be forced to participate in euthanasia or assisted suicide, nor should any physician be obliged to make referral decisions to this end.'[10]

12.08 That said, in Oregon, physician-assisted suicide was legalised after a referendum in the state in 1993 narrowly approved it (51 per cent in favour to 49 per cent against).[11] This was the first statute[12] to provide for medically assisted death.[13] Subsequently, it has been legalised within eight other states and the District of Columbia across the United States.[14] Internationally assisted suicide or euthanasia or both have been decriminalised in the state of Victoria in Australia and in Belgium, Canada, Colombia, Luxembourg, The Netherlands, and Switzerland.[15] In February 2020, Portugal's parliament voted to develop a new law to make euthanasia and assisted suicide legal.[16] But euthanasia remains a crime in Oregon (as it does in every US state),[17] even though, as one opponent of assisted dying has observed, the distinction between the two may be perceived by some as slender: 'What, for example, is the supposed difference between a doctor handing a lethal pill to a patient; placing the pill on the patient's tongue; and dropping it down the patient's throat?'[18]

---

[9] WMA *Declaration on Euthanasia and Physician-Assisted Suicide*, adopted by the 70th WMA General Assembly, Tbilisi, Georgia, October 2019, at http://bit.ly/3gfM8O4.

[10] Ibid.

[11] In November 1997, a measure was placed on the general election ballot to repeal the Death with Dignity Act. Voters chose to retain the Act by a margin of 60 per cent to 40 per cent. State of Oregon, 'Oregon's Death with Dignity Act (DWDA), Frequently Asked Questions', last updated 1 January 2020, at http://bit.ly/3jRCkMl.

[12] Oregon Revised Statutes Chap. 127.800–127.897.

[13] D. A. Jones, C. Gastman, and C. MacKellar, 'Introduction', in *Euthanasia and Assisted Suicide: Lessons from Belgium*, Cambridge University Press, Cambridge, 2017, p. 1.

[14] In 2008, Washington state adopted a similar law to Oregon followed by Vermont (2013); California (2016); Colorado (2016); Washington, DC (2017); Hawaii (2018); New Jersey (2019); and Maine (2019). In 2009, Montana's Supreme Court endorsed physician-assisted suicide. For up-to-date records of the situation in each state, see, e.g., the Death With Dignity website, at http://bit.ly/3k5v2EX.

[15] My Death My Decision, 'Assisted Dying In Other Countries', 2018, at http://bit.ly/3jUjCUp.

[16] BBC, 'Portugal MPs in Move to Legalise Euthanasia', 21 February 2020, at http://bbc.in/2PluFb2. In March 2021, however, the Constitutional Court overturned the law decriminalising euthanasia, saying it was too imprecise.

[17] State of Oregon, 'Oregon's Death with Dignity Act (DWDA), Frequently Asked Questions', last updated 1 January 2020, at http://bit.ly/3jRCkMl.

[18] J. Keown, *Euthanasia, Ethics and Public Policy: An Argument Against Legalisation*, 2nd ed., Cambridge University Press, Cambridge, 2018, p. 18.

12.09 The US Supreme Court has held that there is no constitutional 'right' to assisted suicide in the United States, nor even a right to commit suicide that is protected under the Fourteenth Amendment to the Constitution. In its 1997 judgment in *Washington v. Glucksberg*,[19] the Court unanimously held that such a right was not protected by the due process clause. To determine otherwise, the Court declared, would be to run counter to 'a consistent and almost universal tradition that has long rejected the asserted right', and which 'continues explicitly to reject it today, even for terminally ill, mentally competent adults'.[20]

EUTHANASIA

The Definition of Euthanasia

12.10 Although there is no 'universally agreed definition',[21] euthanasia is the act of deliberately ending a person's life in order to relieve pain or suffering. The Belgian Act Concerning Euthanasia defines euthanasia as 'the act which intentionally terminates the life of a person at his/her request and which is carried out by an individual other than the person in question'.[22] In active euthanasia, a person directly and deliberately causes another's death. Voluntary active euthanasia occurs at the request of the person who dies.[23]

12.11 Non-voluntary euthanasia occurs when the person is unconscious or otherwise unable to make a meaningful choice between living and dying (e.g., a baby or a person with acute intellectual disabilities), and an appropriate person decides on their behalf. Non-voluntary euthanasia also covers instances where the prevailing law does not regard a child as legally competent to take such a decision. Involuntary euthanasia occurs when the person who dies makes the choice to live but is killed anyway.[24]

12.12 In most States, euthanasia is punishable as murder.[25] Passive euthanasia is the withdrawal of life-support from a very seriously ill patient in a hospital with the expectation that he or she will die naturally within a proximate period. Passive euthanasia has been deemed lawful in a number of States, including in the United Kingdom by a 1993 judgment by the House of Lords. The *Bland* case[26] concerned a victim of the Hillsborough Stadium disaster

---

[19] US Supreme Court, *Washington v. Glucksberg*, 521 US 702 (1997), decided 26 June 1997.
[20] Ibid, p. 723.
[21] Keown, *Euthanasia, Ethics and Public Policy: An Argument Against Legalisation*, p. 9.
[22] S. 2, 2002 Act Concerning Euthanasia; unofficial English translation with amendments through 2014 available as Appendix III to Jones, Gastman, and MacKellar (eds.), *Euthanasia and Assisted Suicide: Lessons from Belgium*, pp. 305–15. The wording of the definition in the 2002 Belgian Euthanasia Act ('carried out by an individual other than the person in question') demonstrates that the Act does not regulate assisted suicide but, as Herman Nys observes, assisting a suicide was not expressly criminalised in existing Belgian law. H. Nys, 'A Discussion of the Legal Rules on Euthanasia in Belgium Briefly Compared with the Rules in Luxembourg and the Netherlands', chap. 1 in ibid., pp. 7–25, at 10.
[23] BBC, 'Forms of Euthanasia', 2014, at http://bbc.in/39Atzl4.
[24] Ibid.
[25] Keown, *Euthanasia, Ethics and Public Policy: An Argument Against Legalisation*, p. 10.
[26] *Airedale NHS Trust v. Bland* [1993] AC 789 House of Lords.

in 1989 who, as a result of being crushed, was in a persistent vegetative state.[27] Mr Bland, who had been in that state for three years, was being kept alive by life-support machines. While his brain stem was still functioning, which controlled his heartbeat, breathing, and digestion, he had no hope of recovery. The hospital, with the consent of his parents, applied for a declaration that it might lawfully discontinue all life-sustaining treatment and medical support measures, including by terminating ventilation and nutrition and hydration by artificial means.

12.13 Lord Goff declared:

> the law draws a crucial distinction between cases in which a doctor decides not to provide, or to continue to provide for his patient treatment or care which could or might prolong his life and those in which he decides, for example by administering a lethal drug, actively to bring his patient's life to an end. As I have already indicated, the former may be lawful, either because the doctor is giving effect to his patient's wishes by withholding the treatment or care, or even in certain circumstances in which ... the patient is incapacitated from stating whether or not he gives his consent. But it is not lawful for a doctor to administer a drug to his patient to bring about his death, even though that course is prompted by a humanitarian desire to end his suffering, however great that suffering may be.[28]

As Keown observes, however, this alleged crossing of the Rubicon to which Lord Goff later refers is of questionable legal coherence.[29] An omission, as well as an act, can amount to an unlawful killing[30] – that starving a baby to death constitutes murder is a testament to this.

12.14 Thus a broader understanding of euthanasia encompasses both the intentional termination of a patient's life by act (such as a lethal injection) and the intentional termination of life by omission (passive euthanasia).[31] Excluded from such a definition, however, is the notion of double effect when pain-relieving drugs will also have the effect of shortening the patient's life. Lord Goff referred to

> the established rule that a doctor may, when caring for a patient who is, for example, dying of cancer, lawfully administer painkilling drugs despite the fact that he knows that an incidental effect of that application will be to abbreviate the patient's life. Such a decision may properly be made as part of the care of the living patient, in his best interests; and, on this basis, the treatment will be lawful. Moreover, where the doctor's treatment of his patient is lawful, the patient's death will be regarded in law as exclusively caused by the injury or disease to which his condition is attributable.[32]

---

[27] Distinct from a coma, when a patient is unconscious and seemingly asleep, in PVS a patient has wake/sleep cycles, though without awareness. Keown, *Euthanasia, Ethics and Public Policy: An Argument Against Legalisation*, pp. 11–12.
[28] [1993] 1 All ER 821, at 867.
[29] Keown, *Euthanasia, Ethics and Public Policy: An Argument Against Legalisation*, pp. 13–14.
[30] R v. Miller [1983] 2 AC 161 House of Lords.
[31] Keown, *Euthanasia, Ethics and Public Policy: An Argument Against Legalisation*, p. 11.
[32] [1993] 1 All ER 821, at 868.

Major Themes

Eugenics and Euthanasia

12.15 In *The Republic*, written about 375 BCE, Plato set out his vision of the creation of a greater society, which would be achieved by ensuring that the members of the upper classes procreated while reproduction by those in the lower classes was discouraged. Two and a half thousand years later, science would be employed to further a philosophical claim for selective breeding. One possible interpretation of Darwinist evolutionary theory is that, since nature weeds out the weakest of the species, elimination of the weak is, by definition, simply reinforcing natural selection. In his landmark 1871 work *The Descent of Man*, Darwin himself lamented that the humanitarian impulse of 'civilised men' to 'build asylums for the imbecile, the maimed, and the sick' has allowed the 'weak' members of civilised society to 'propagate their kind'. It is 'surprising', we went on, 'how soon ... care wrongly directed ... leads to the degeneration of a domestic race'.[33]

12.16 Darwin explicitly regretted that 'the reckless, degraded and often vicious members of society tend to increase at a quicker rate than the provident and generally virtuous members', citing among others the views of the English social and political philosopher, William Rathbone Greg, whereby 'the careless, squalid, unaspiring Irishman multiplies like rabbits'.[34] His views on other races are even more repugnant. In 1883, Darwin's cousin, Francis Galton, coined the term *eugenics* – literally meaning 'good creation' – to describe the 'science of improving stock' with a view to giving 'the more suitable races or strains of blood a better chance of prevailing over the less suitable'.[35]

12.17 Galton's views, supported by those of Social Darwinists, would be influential, especially in the United States.[36] In 1896, Connecticut made it illegal for people with epilepsy or who were 'feeble-minded' to marry.[37] Indeed, while most attention has, justly, focused on the horrors of the Nazi's euthanasia programme, it is easy to forget that eugenics was prevalent as social policy in the United States in the 1920s and 1930s. No fewer than forty-one states enacted laws providing for the forced sterilisation of 'feeblemindedness', a concept that denoted those with certain intellectual disabilities or who exhibited forms of moral 'degeneracy'.[38]

12.18 In 1927, the constitutionality of Virginia's Eugenical Sterilization Act, promulgated in 1924 (and in force until 1979),[39] came before the US Supreme Court in *Buck v. Bell*.[40]

---

[33] C. Darwin, *The Descent of Man*, 2nd ed., 1879, Penguin Classics, London, 2004, p. 159; see also Gorsuch, *The Future of Assisted Suicide and Euthanasia*, p. 34.

[34] Darwin, *The Descent of Man*, p. 164, citing W. R. Greg, 'On the Failure of "Natural Selection" in the Case of Man', *Fraser's Magazine* (September 1868), pp. 353–62. See further on Greg's views and his role in the creation of 'Social' Darwinism: I. Budil, 'Alfred Russel Wallace, William Rathbone Greg and the Origin of Social Darwinism', *West Bohemian Historical Review*, February 2014, pp. 59–74, available at http://bit.ly/308RYeq.

[35] F. Galton, *Inquiries into Human Faculty and Its Development*, 1883; see Gorsuch, *The Future of Assisted Suicide and Euthanasia*, p. 34.

[36] 'Social Darwinism', *History*, last updated 21 August 2018, at http://bit.ly/2X9Belj.

[37] 'Eugenics', *History*, updated 28 October 2019, at http://bit.ly/3jPdDA3.

[38] Gorsuch, *The Future of Assisted Suicide and Euthanasia*, p. 34.

[39] G. Carlton, 'Virginia Ran A Secret Eugenics Program That Didn't End Until 1979', *Medium*, 18 April 2018, at http://bit.ly/3jZGlOM.

[40] US Supreme Court, *Buck v. Bell*, 274 US 200 (1927), decided 2 May 1927; text available at http://bit.ly/3jNe2TP.

Euthanasia and Suicide 275

The Virginia State Colony of Epileptics and Feeble Minded was a facility for persons with disabilities founded 'partly to provide care for a vulnerable population and partly to remove it from the gene pool, by sequestering those individuals during their fertile years'.[41] As Andrea DenHoed records, Carrie Buck arrived at the Colony at the same time as its superintendent, Dr Albert Priddy, was seeking to transform the institution into one where the unfit could be committed for a short time, sterilised, and then released back into the general population, safe in the assurance that they could never reproduce.

12.19 Ms Buck had been officially declared a middle-grade 'moron'. This designation, which was based on an assessment of IQ, placed her above 'idiot' and 'imbecile' in the scale of the time, just below 'normal'. Morons were considered particularly dangerous in prevailing thought: they were smart enough to pass undetected and possibly breed with their superiors. Moreover, Ms Buck had already had a child as an unmarried teenager, thereby demonstrating the 'differential fecundity' said to be rife among the mentally deficient.[42] (In fact, she had been raped by her foster mother's nephew.[43])

12.20 Counsel for Ms Buck argued that compulsory sterilisation violated the fourteenth amendment to the US Constitution, which forbids states from denying any person 'life, liberty or property, without due process of law' or to 'deny to any person within its jurisdiction the equal protection of the laws'. Mr Whitehead recalled the Court's own precedent of *Munn v. Illinois*, in which it had defined the meaning of 'deprivation of life' as extending 'to all those limbs and faculties by which life is enjoyed'. The operation of salpingectomy (the surgical removal of one or both fallopian tubes), Ms Buck's Counsel contended, 'clearly comes within the definition. It is a surgical operation consisting of the opening of the abdominal cavity and the cutting of the Fallopian tubes with the result that sterility is produced.'[44] If the Act was validated, he concluded, in 'place of the constitutional government of the fathers we shall have set up Plato's Republic'.[45]

12.21 In response, Mr Strode, Counsel for the defendant, declared that a surgical operation was 'required for the protection of the individual and of society'.[46] The operation, he affirmed, 'can only be illegal when performed against the will or contrary to the interest of the patient'. He went on to argue that she could not determine the matter for herself 'both because being not of full age her judgment is not to be accepted ... and because she is further incapacitated by congenital mental defect'.[47]

12.22 In his brief judgment validating the Virginian law, Supreme Court Justice Oliver Wendall Holmes Jr declared: 'It is better for the world, if instead of waiting to execute

---

[41] A. DenHoed, 'The Forgotten Lessons of the American Eugenics Movement', *The New Yorker*, 27 April 2016, at http://bit.ly/3hE3C6U.
[42] Ibid.
[43] N. Antonios and C. Raup, 'Buck v. Bell (1927)', *Embryo Project Encyclopedia*, 1 January 2012, at http://bit.ly/2CLMiyn.
[44] *Buck v. Bell*, 274 US 200 (1927), at 201.
[45] Ibid., pp. 202–3.
[46] Ibid., pp. 203–4.
[47] Ibid., p. 204.

degenerate offspring for crime, or to let them starve for their imbecility, society can prevent those who are manifestly unfit from continuing their kind.'[48] In a further holding, similarly memorable for its squalid brutality, Justice Holmes asserted that 'three generations of imbeciles are enough'.[49] Thousands of Virginians,[50] and many more elsewhere in the United States, underwent the procedure before the practice was brought to an end.

12.23 The Nazis adopted eugenics as a scientific underpinning of their racist ideology, drawing on the US experience. Hitler even wrote directly to Madison Grant, the American author of *Passing of the Great Race*, in which Grant advocated the sterilisation of 'undesirables', describing the 1916 eugenics tract as 'his Bible'.[51] The Nazis began with coercive sterilisation of 'life unworthy of life', then moved on to kill 'impaired' children in hospitals, and later 'impaired' adults taken from psychiatric hospitals. The killing was carried out in specially designed centres using carbon monoxide as the lethal agent.[52] Thus, before creating the extermination camps for the Jews, Gypsies, and the political opponents of national socialism, the Nazis established 'a policy of direct medical killing: that is, killing arranged within medical channels, by means of medical decisions, and carried out by doctors and their assistants'. They called the programme 'Euthanasia'.[53]

12.24 There were also German authors to which the Nazis could turn for ideological inspiration and 'scientific' underpinning for their extermination programme. In his 1895 work, *Das Recht auf den Tod* ('The Right to Death'), Adolf Jost argued that ultimately a person's life – and especially their death – belonged to the State. To keep the State, a social organism, fit and healthy, the State must kill.[54] In *The Permission to Destroy Life Unworthy of Life*, a 1920 joint publication by a German lawyer and a professor of psychiatry, it was advocated that killing 'empty shells of human beings' was not to be equated with other types of killing, as such people were 'already dead'. War only accentuated the need to do so, given that the best of youth died in combat, leaving those with the worst genes, who did not fight, to proliferate freely, 'accelerating biological and cultural degeneration'.[55]

12.25 Doctors got the message, even though it was sometimes passed subliminally. One such, interviewed by Robert Jay Lifton for his noted 1986 work, *The Nazi Doctors: Medical Killing and the Psychology of Genocide*, heard Rudolf Hess declare at a mass meeting in 1934 that national socialism was 'nothing but applied biology'.[56] By the end of the 1930s,

[48] Ibid., p. 207.
[49] Ibid.
[50] In total, 7,325 individuals were reportedly sterilised in Virginia under its prevailing legislation. Of those, about half were deemed 'mentally ill', while the remainder were deemed 'mentally deficient'. Approximately 62 per cent of those sterilised were female. L. Kaelber, 'Virginia', University of Vermont, 2012, at http://bit.ly/3geu4Us.
[51] Gorsuch, *The Future of Assisted Suicide and Euthanasia*, p. 36; S. Kühl, *Nazi Connection: Eugenics, American Racism, and German National Socialism*, Oxford University Press, Oxford, 2002, p. 85.
[52] R. J. Lifton, *The Nazi Doctors: Medical Killing and the Psychology of Genocide*, Basic Books, New York, 1986.
[53] Ibid.
[54] See ibid., p. 46.
[55] Ibid., p. 47.
[56] Ibid., p. 31.

the Nazis were killing thousands of children with physical and/or intellectual disabilities, beginning with newborns and the very young, before turning to elder children and later adults. Even after 1941, when Hitler put an end to the 'euthanasia' programme after a public backlash spearheaded by a few courageous Catholic and Protestant religious leaders,[57] children continued to be killed. As one doctor explained, 'there was no killing, strictly speaking. ... People felt this is not murder, it is a putting-to-sleep'.[58]

GLOBAL TREATY REGULATION OF SUICIDE AND EUTHANASIA

12.26 Under treaty law, the ICCPR does not refer to either suicide or euthanasia at any point in its text. That said, there is a duty set out in Article 6(1) to protect life by law. That could be taken to denote the need for States to prohibit attempted suicide and to criminalise those who would seek to assist suicide. In fact, in its General Comment 36 on the right to life, the Human Rights Committee acknowledges 'the central importance to human dignity of personal autonomy', implying surreptitiously that there might indeed exist a 'right to die'.[59]

12.27 With respect to suicide, the Committee focuses on a recommendation to States Parties to the Covenant that they 'should take adequate measures, without violating their other Covenant obligations, to prevent suicides'. This is, the Committee held, especially important for persons in 'particularly vulnerable situations', such as individuals deprived of their liberty.[60] In its supporting reference, the Committee cites its own Concluding Observations on Ecuador from 1998, in which it expressed concern about the very high number of suicides of young females referred to in Ecuador's State Party report, 'which appear in part to be related to the prohibition of abortion'.[61] The Committee regretted Ecuador's 'failure to address the resulting problems faced by adolescent girls, in particular rape victims, who suffer the consequences of such acts for the rest of their lives'. This, the Committee concluded, was incompatible with the rights to life and to freedom from inhumane treatment, among other Covenant rights.[62]

---

[57] The Bishop of Munster was an especially powerful advocate. Focusing on the killing of the elderly, he wrote in terms everyday Germans could understand: 'Poor unproductive people if you wish, but does this mean they have lost their right to live?' Ibid., p. 96.

[58] Ibid., pp. 56–7, 89.

[59] Human Rights Committee, 'General comment No. 36. Article 6: right to life', UN doc. CCPR/C/GC/36, 3 September 2019 (hereinafter, Human Rights Committee, General Comment No. 36), para. 9.

[60] The 2015 Nelson Mandela Rules cover the risk of suicide only scantily. In its Rule 30, a physician or other qualified health care professional is to 'see, talk with and examine every prisoner as soon as possible following his or her admission and thereafter as necessary', paying particular attention to 'identifying any signs of psychological or other stress brought on by the fact of imprisonment, including, but not limited to, the risk of suicide'. UN General Assembly Resolution 70/175: United Nations Standard Minimum Rules for the Treatment of Prisoners (the Nelson Mandela Rules), adopted without a vote on 17 December 2015. There is, of course, also a risk that prison authorities or individual custodial officers may seek to conceal a violent death as a suicide. See, e.g., Human Rights Committee, *Turdukan Zhumbaeva v. Kyrgyzstan*, Views (UN doc. CCPR/C/102/D/1756/2008), 19 July 2011.

[61] Human Rights Committee, Concluding Observations on Ecuador, UN doc. CCPR/C/79/Add.92, 18 August 1998, para. 11.

[62] Ibid.

12.28 Concerning euthanasia, the Committee is more circumspect. It notes that afflicted adults, such as the terminally ill, who experience severe physical or mental pain and suffering, may wish 'to die with dignity'. But the General Comment focuses not so much on whether the practice of euthanasia is compatible or not with the Covenant per se, but on whether 'robust legal and institutional safeguards' are in place 'to verify that medical professionals are complying with the free, informed, explicit and unambiguous decision of their patients, with a view to protecting patients from pressure and abuse'.[63]

12.29 In so doing, the Committee cites its 2009 Concluding Observations on the report of the Netherlands, a State that allows euthanasia under certain conditions. The Committee reiterated its concern, expressed in previous Concluding Observations on that State Party, at 'the extent' of euthanasia and assisted suicides in the Netherlands. Under the 2002 Dutch Law on the Termination of Life on Request and Assisted Suicide,[64] the Committee recalled, 'although a second physician must give an opinion, a physician can terminate a patient's life without any independent review by a judge or magistrate to guarantee that this decision was not the subject of undue influence or misapprehension'.[65] The Committee again urged the Netherlands to review the legislation 'in light of the Covenant's recognition of the right to life'.[66] In October 2020, however, the Netherlands extended the possibility of euthanasia also to children aged between one and twelve after months of highly charged political debate. The Dutch Minister of Health, Hugo de Jonge, said a change in regulations was necessary to help 'a small group of terminally ill children who agonise with no hope, and unbearable suffering'. In supporting the change in parliament, Mr De Jonge cited a report showing overwhelming support for a change in the law among doctors.[67]

12.30 In its written submission of 2015 in preparation for the General Comment 36 on the right to life, The National Right to Life Educational Trust Fund, a non-governmental organisation based in New York, had urged the Committee to go much further and affirm that the right to life 'should be interpreted to guard against physician-assisted suicide and euthanasia'.[68] The Fund argued that laws permitting euthanasia discriminate by denying the right to life of the disabled, sick, and elderly. They also observed that the legalisation of euthanasia 'has, in practice, led to the killing[69] of some persons who are influenced by pressure, coercion, and mental illness' and that it 'has, in some places, led to the killing of

---

[63] Human Rights Committee, General Comment 36 on the right to life, para. 9.
[64] An English version of the text is available at http://bit.ly/39FQaNl.
[65] Human Rights Committee, Concluding Observations on the Netherlands, UN doc. CCPR/C/NLD/CO/4, 25 August 2009, para. 7.
[66] Ibid.
[67] D. Bofey, 'Dutch Government Backs Euthanasia for Under-12s', *The Guardian*, 14 October 2020, at http://bit.ly/2SWlW16. In 2019, there were 6,361 cases of euthanasia in the Netherlands, amounting to just over 4 per cent of total deaths in the country. Of those, 91 per cent were for terminal medical conditions, while the remainder involved severe psychiatric illness.
[68] National Right to Life Educational Trust Fund, 'Contribution to the General Discussion in preparation for General Comment No. 36 (Article 6 of the ICCPR: Right to life)', June 2015, p. 3.
[69] As Keown observes, some advocates of euthanasia object to the use of the word 'kill' on the basis of its emotive overtones. Keown, *Euthanasia, Ethics and Public Policy: An Argument Against Legalisation*, pp. 1–2, note 3.

Euthanasia and Suicide

patients without an explicit, voluntary request'. Prohibiting euthanasia is, the Fund asserted, 'necessary to prevent these obvious violations of the right to life and to safeguard the most vulnerable members of society'.[70]

REGIONAL TREATY REGULATION OF SUICIDE AND EUTHANASIA

The European Convention on Human Rights

12.31 At the regional level, the 1950 European Convention on Human Rights[71] does not directly address either euthanasia or suicide. Both issues have, though, come before the European Court of Human Rights on numerous occasions. With respect to euthanasia, as of writing a leading case remained *Pretty v. United Kingdom*, a Chamber judgment of 2002.[72] The applicant was dying of motor neurone disease, a degenerative disease affecting the muscles for which there is no cure. Given that the final stages of the disease are both distressing and undignified, Ms Pretty wished to be able to control how and when she died. But the nature of her disease precluded her from committing suicide alone and she specifically wanted her husband to help her. Although attempting to commit suicide had been decriminalised in the United Kingdom in 1961 (as discussed later), assisting a suicide remained a criminal offence. She complained that her husband had not been guaranteed freedom from prosecution if he helped her to die.

12.32 The Court, however, held that there had been no violation of the right to life of the Convention. Article 2 cannot, the Court said, 'without a distortion of language, be interpreted as conferring the diametrically opposite right, namely a right to die; nor can it create a right to self-determination in the sense of conferring on an individual the entitlement to choose death rather than life'.[73] The Court accordingly found that 'no right to die, whether at the hands of a third person or with the assistance of a public authority, can be derived from Article 2 of the Convention'.[74] The Court did, though, consider that, without negating the principle of sanctity of life protected under the Convention, in 'an era of growing medical sophistication combined with longer life expectancies', many were 'concerned that they should not be forced to linger on in old age or in states of advanced physical or mental decrepitude which conflicted with strongly held ideas of self and personal identity'.[75]

12.33 The Court has generally deferred to national courts and legislatures on whether euthanasia or assisted suicide should be permitted or criminalised. It has, however, shown willingness to find a violation of the Convention when procedural requirements have not been followed or, as in the *Koch* case,[76] when the authorities or domestic courts have

---

[70] Ibid., p. 4.
[71] Convention for the Protection of Human Rights and Fundamental Freedoms; adopted at Rome by the Council of Europe 4 November 1950; entered into force 3 September 1953.
[72] European Court of Human Rights, *Pretty v. United Kingdom*, Judgment (Fourth Section), 29 April 2002.
[73] Ibid., para. 39.
[74] Ibid., para. 40.
[75] Ibid., para. 65.
[76] European Court of Human Rights, *Koch v. Germany*, Judgment (Fifth Section), 19 July 2012.

largely declined to consider a case on its merits. In *Koch*, the applicant's wife, a quadriplegic, unsuccessfully applied for authorisation to obtain a lethal dose of a drug that would have enabled her to commit suicide at home in Germany. An administrative appeal by the applicant and his wife was lodged and dismissed. In the meantime, in February 2005, they both went to Switzerland, where the wife committed suicide with the help of the association, Dignitas.[77] The applicant subsequently complained that the refusal of the German domestic courts to examine the merits of his complaint had infringed his right to respect for private and family life.

12.34 The Court found a violation of the applicant's procedural rights under Article 8 (governing respect for private and family life) on the basis of the courts' refusal to examine the merits of his complaint. It did not, however, find a substantive violation of the right, holding that it was for the domestic courts to examine the merits of a case, in particular in light of the fact that no consensus existed among Council of Europe member States as to whether to allow any form of assisted suicide.

12.35 In its earlier judgment in *Haas*[78] (cited in the *Koch* decision), a chamber of the Court had nonetheless acknowledged that an individual's right to decide in which way and at which time his or her life should end formed part of the right to respect for private life within the meaning of Article 8.[79] This was, however, subject to a person being in a position freely to form his or her own will and to act accordingly. The Court was also 'sympathetic' to the applicant's 'wish to commit suicide in a safe and dignified manner and without unnecessary pain and suffering, particularly given the high number of suicide attempts that are unsuccessful and which frequently have serious consequences for the individuals concerned and for their families'.[80] In the situation at hand, the applicant's claim failed because Switzerland's requirement of a prescription, issued on the basis of a thorough psychiatric assessment, was, the Court held, an appropriate means to ensure that a person's decision to end his or her life did in fact reflect free will. The Court was not persuaded that it had been impossible for Mr Haas to find a specialist willing to assist him, as he had claimed.[81]

12.36 As of writing, the *Mortier* case against Belgium was before the Court awaiting its judgment. In April 2012, an oncologist, Dr Wim Distelmans, killed Ms Godelieva De Troyer, a Belgian citizen who was not terminally ill, because of 'untreatable depression'. He had received consent from three other physicians who had no previous material involvement in her care to do so. Ms De Troyer's doctor of more than twenty years had denied her request to be euthanised in September 2011, but after a reported €2,500

---

[77] Dignitas also made a third-party submission in the *Koch* case, arguing that a person's decision to determine the manner of ending his or her life was part of the right to self-determination protected by Article 8. A state party should only regulate the right of an individual who independently decided on the time or methods of his or her demise in order to prevent hasty and insufficiently considered actions. *Koch v. Germany*, para. 40.
[78] European Court of Human Rights, *Haas v. Switzerland*, Judgment (First Section), 20 January 2011.
[79] Ibid., para. 51.
[80] Ibid., para. 56.
[81] Ibid., paras. 57–61.

Euthanasia and Suicide 281

donation to Life End Information Forum, an organisation Dr Distelmans had co-founded, he carried out her request to die because of the depression.[82]

12.37 The donation gives rise to an apparent conflict of interest, according to the application before the Court. Moreover, no one contacted the applicant before his mother's death even though, Mr Mortier says, her depression was not only largely the result of a relationship break-up, but also due to her feelings of distance from her family.[83] In late 2018, the Court gave notice of the application to the Belgium Government and put questions to the parties under Article 2 (the right to life), Article 8 (the right to respect for private and family life), and Article 35 (admissibility criteria).

12.38 With respect to suicide in a custodial setting, the standards under the European Convention are clear. In its March 2020 judgment in the *Fabris* case, the Court recalled that, with respect to acts of self-harming by an adult detainee, the authorities have a positive obligation to act where they knew or should have known that a real and immediate risk existed of suicide.[84] In its judgment in *Jeanty*,[85] adopted later the same month, which concerned an allegation by the applicant (who survived) that the authorities had taken insufficient steps to prevent his suicide, the Court decided to consider the matter in the context of the right to life. In rejecting his claim of a violation of the right to life, the Court held that the respondent State, Belgium, had taken all reasonable steps taking into account the 'unpredictability of human behaviour'.[86]

Other Regional Human Rights Treaties

12.39 The 1969 American Convention on Human Rights does not directly address either euthanasia or suicide.[87] As of writing, a case that concerns suicide – *Paola Guzman Albarracín v. Ecuador* – was before the Inter-American Court. Paola Guzman was an adolescent public-school student who was raped and sexually abused by the vice-principal of her school. The abuse led to a pregnancy and then to a second abuse by her school doctor. As a result of the violence inflicted upon her, she committed suicide three days after her sixteenth birthday.[88]

12.40 In its report on the merits of the case of October 2018,[89] the Inter-American Commission on Human Rights concluded that the Ecuadorian State was responsible for

---

[82] Alliance Defending Freedom, 'Mortier v. Belgium', blog post, 8 January 2019, at http://bit.ly/3jUoUw3.
[83] Ibid.
[84] European Court of Human Rights, *Fabris and Parziale v. Italy*, Judgment (First Section), 19 March 2020, para. 76.
[85] European Court of Human Rights, *Jeanty v. Belgium*, Judgment (Third Section), 31 March 2020.
[86] Ibid., para. 79.
[87] American Convention on Human Rights; adopted at San José 22 November 1969; entered into force 18 July 1978.
[88] Center for Reproductive Rights, 'Center Argues Milestone Case at Inter-American Court of Human Rights: Seeking to Protect Girls from Sexual Violence in Schools', 29 January 2020, at http://bit.ly/3hQyPUF.
[89] Inter-American Commission on Human Rights, *Paola del Rosario Guzmán Albarracín and Relatives v. Ecuador*, Report No. 110/18 (Case 12,678), Merits, 5 October 2018.

violations of Ms Albarracín's rights to life, personal integrity, autonomy, private life, and dignity; her right to enjoy special protection from the State as a child; her right to equality and non-discrimination; her rights to education and health; and her right to live without violence. In October 2003, Ms Albarracín's mother had initiated a private criminal prosecution against the vice principal of the school for sexual harassment, rape, and instigation to suicide. The alleged crime of instigation of suicide, however, would not be permitted to go to trial.[90]

12.41 The Inter-American Commission established that 'for months' Ms Albarracín was 'a victim of violence as a woman and girl, including sexual violence, and that that situation was so severe that it led her to commit suicide'.[91] Moreover, after she had swallowed white phosphorus pellets, the school doctor in question, Raúl David Ortega, decided that

> it was very late and there was nothing to be done; instead of calling an ambulance immediately to attempt a transfer to a health center that did have the resources to respond to Paola's situation, that doctor deemed it more of a priority to apprise the Vice Principal and the Inspector General, Luz Arellano de Azán, of the situation. ... [N]one of the three public servants took the necessary steps to have Paola immediately driven to a hospital to receive the emergency treatment she needed. From statements made by Paola's classmates, it transpires that the three public servants waited for her mother to arrive and for her to look after Paola's transfer to hospital, thereby losing at least 30 minutes that might have saved her life.[92]

'Accordingly', the Commission concluded, 'the acts and omissions of these public servants, who had the added duty of caring for Paola in a school environment, contributed to the victim's demise, thereby making the State also internationally responsible for what happened that day'.[93]

12.42 The African Charter does not address the act of suicide nor of euthanasia but does incorporate the right to dignity as a distinct human right.[94] Neither the 2004 Arab Charter[95] nor the non-binding Human Rights Declaration issued by the Association of South-East Asian Nations (ASEAN) in 2012[96] addresses either euthanasia or suicide. Within the Islamic world, the Qur'an makes it clear that life is sacred, and only Allah can give life or take it away.[97] It is thus wrong for any person, even a patient or doctor, to end or request to end a life before Allah does, because it would go against Allah's plan for that life.[98] Whoever commits suicide with something will be punished with the same thing in the hell-fire.[99]

[90] Ibid., paras. 9 and 10.
[91] Ibid., para. 143.
[92] Ibid., para. 153.
[93] Ibid., para. 154.
[94] 'Every individual shall have the right to the respect of the dignity inherent in a human being and to the recognition of his legal status.' Art. 5, African Charter on Human and Peoples' Rights; adopted at Nairobi 27 June 1981; entered into force 21 October 1986.
[95] Arab Charter on Human Rights; adopted at Tunis 22 May 2004; entered into force 15 March 2008.
[96] ASEAN Human Rights Declaration, adopted by the Heads of State/Government of ASEAN member States at Phnom Penh, Cambodia, 18 November 2012, at http://bit.ly/329wakp.
[97] 'It is not possible for one to die except by permission of Allah.' *Qur'an* 3:145.
[98] BBC, 'Euthanasia', at http://bbc.in/33c2Eer.
[99] Hadith Bukhari 78.647.

THE PREVENTION OF SUICIDE

12.43 The UN Sustainable Development Goals do not address euthanasia, but they do set a target for a reduction in suicides. SDG Target 3.4 holds that, by 2030, States should have reduced by one-third premature mortality from non-communicable diseases through prevention and treatment and promote mental health and well-being. Indicator 3.4.2 for the target is the suicide mortality rate. Few believe that criminalising attempted suicide is an effective means to reduce suicides; the response is both social and economic in nature, with a public health approach at its heart.

The Domestic Legal Regulation of Suicide

12.44 Domestic legal regimes continue to evolve towards decriminalisation of suicide. Most recently, Singapore amended its Penal Code, repealing Section 309 (Attempt to commit suicide); the new legal regime entered into force on 1 January 2020.[100] In Africa, Zambia repealed the law that criminalised suicide back in 1967, decreeing: 'The rule of law whereby it is an offence against the common law for a person to kill himself is hereby abrogated.' As a consequence, there are no legal consequences for suicide attempts in Zambia, and survivors of a suicide attempt are not liable to judicial penalties.[101]

12.45 The United Kingdom abrogated laws criminalising and penalising attempted suicide in 1961[102] – one of the last European nations to do so[103] – though several of its former colonies in Africa maintain pre-colonial legislation that renders attempted suicide an offence. In the Gambia, for example, the criminal code, which dates back to 1933, stipulates that 'any person who attempts to kill himself is guilty of a misdemeanour'.[104] (Stricter penalties exist for those who assist a suicide, with the criminal code prescribing life imprisonment.)[105] Similar provisions exist in Ghana, Kenya, Malawi, Nigeria, Tanzania, and Uganda, among others.[106]

12.46 But certain States not only criminalise attempted suicide; they persistently imprison the offenders. In Malaysia, prosecutions of attempted suicides are said usually to result in sentences of up to several months' imprisonment.[107] In Saudi Arabia, a Jordanian national was given a month in jail and sixty lashes in 2018 for threatening

---

[100] R. Tan, 'Attempted Suicide Is No Longer a Crime in Singapore', *Samaritans of Singapore*, January 2020, at http://bit.ly/2P2IwTt.

[101] M. Adinkrah, 'Anti-Suicide Laws in Nine African Countries: Criminalization, Prosecution and Penalization', *African Journal of Criminology and Justice Studies*, vol. 9, no. 1 (May 2016), pp. 279–92, at 286.

[102] 1961 Suicide Act (9 & 10 Eliz 2 c 60), available at http://bit.ly/30789c7.

[103] G. Holt, 'When Suicide Was Illegal', BBC News, 3 August 2011, at http://bbc.in/3jTH7NA.

[104] 1933 Criminal Code of The Gambia (as amended), available at http://bit.ly/2PhOHU9, s. 206.

[105] Ibid., s. 205.

[106] See for details Adinkrah, 'Anti-Suicide Laws in Nine African Countries: Criminalization, Prosecution and Penalization'.

[107] 'Suicide: A Tragedy or a Crime?', *Lex; in breve*, UMLR, 30 January 2019, at https://bit.ly/2NVEBem; M. Bradley (MARQUE Lawyers), 'The Long History of Criminalising Suicide', *Lexology*, 6 August 2019, at http://bit.ly/3fcOaNw.

to kill himself.[108] North Korea criminalises suicide by imposing penalties on the family members of the suicide victim.[109]

Domestic Regulation of Euthanasia and Physician-Assisted Suicide

The Belgian Euthanasia Act

12.47 The Belgian Euthanasia Act was adopted on 28 May 2002. It allows an adult and, following a 2014 amendment, an 'emancipated minor' (following a decision by a judge) to request euthanasia.[110] The request by any person must be 'expressed in a recurring manner which is voluntary, well considered and is not the result of any external pressure'.[111] The patient must further be 'medically futile condition of constant and unbearable physical or mental suffering that can not be alleviated, resulting from a serious and incurable disorder caused by illness or accident'.[112]

12.48 The notions of physical suffering and mental suffering are alternative (but not necessarily disjunctive), meaning that severe psycho-social disabilities in the absence of physical pain may suffice. This has, according to Hermann Nys, led to 'relatively common acceptance of euthanasia on [sic] the request of psychiatric patients'.[113] In contrast, patients in a late stage of dementia are not entitled to be euthanised, despite efforts by different political parties to broaden the scope of the legislation. This is because an advance directive (i.e., a request) by a person prior to suffering from late-stage dementia must be 'irreversibly unconscious according to the current state of medical science', meaning in practice a persistent vegetative state.[114] This has led to people in early-stage dementia seeking, and being granted, euthanasia.[115]

12.49 Etienne Montero alleges that the notion of incurable disorder – seemingly an objective notion – is in fact imprecise and is even, despite this imprecision, exceptionally permissive. He argues that it covers rheumatism and arthritis, as well as diabetes, given that multiple disorders taken together may be deemed sufficiently serious.[116] Increasingly, he cautions, euthanasia is being approved for the elderly who suffer from various ailments related to old age, such as those with polyarthritis (thereby reducing their mobility), failing

---

[108] M. Nabbout, 'Expat in Saudi Arabia Sentenced to Jail for Threatening to Commit Suicide', Step Feed, 1 February 2018, at http://bit.ly/2P6MriC.
[109] S. A. Margaret, F. Azida, and L. M. Nge, 'Suicidal Prevention Using Jurisdiction', *International Journal of Business, Economics and Law*, vol. 1 (2012), pp. 98–103, at http://bit.ly/3gfZlqk.
[110] There is no minimum age stipulated in the Belgian legislation. In contrast, in the corresponding law in the Netherlands, a minimum age of twelve years is fixed.
[111] S. 3(1), 2002 Belgian Euthanasia Act.
[112] Ibid. English translation of the Act available at http://bit.ly/2KQHT0E.
[113] Nys, 'A Discussion of the Legal Rules on Euthanasia in Belgium Briefly Compared with the Rules in Luxembourg and the Netherlands', p. 16.
[114] Ibid., pp. 21, 22.
[115] E. Montero, 'The Belgian Experience of Euthanasia Since Its Legal Implementation in 2002', chap. 2 in Jones, Gastman, and MacKellar (eds.), *Euthanasia and Assisted Suicide: Lessons from Belgium*, pp. 26–48, at 35.
[116] Ibid., p. 30.

eyesight, and hearing impairment.'[117] This evolution from 'an exceptional practice and an ethical transgression' towards the 'normalisation' of euthanasia 'makes it necessary seriously to consider the logic *that operates in the dynamics of law-making and implementation*'.[118]

12.50 Also particularly controversial is the euthanasia of children. In 2016 and 2017, Belgian physicians gave lethal injections to three children under eighteen years of age. Only minimal details were provided in the 2018 report from the Federal Control and Evaluation Commission on Euthanasia (FCECE) – the State body that regulates euthanasia in Belgium. One boy was seventeen years of age, but Belgian doctors also ended the lives of a nine-year-old and an eleven-year-old. These were the first cases concerning children under the age of twelve anywhere in the world, a member of the FCECE told the *Washington Post* in an interview. The nine-year-old had a brain tumour.[119]

12.51 According to the 2002 Belgian Act, the lethal act must be performed by a physician.[120] Before carrying it out, another physician must be consulted regarding the serious and incurable disorder,[121] although that physician's view is not binding.[122] Where the disorder is not terminal, a second physician (psychiatrist or specialist in the condition in question) must be consulted. In such a case, at least one month must elapse between the request and the act of euthanasia. In any event, under the express terms of the Belgian Act, no physician is under an obligation to practice euthanasia on anyone.[123]

The Oregon Act

12.52 In 1997, Oregon enacted the Death with Dignity Act (hereinafter, the Oregon Act), allowing terminally ill Oregonians to end their lives through the voluntary self-administration of a lethal dose of medication, expressly prescribed by a physician for that purpose. The advantage, to physicians, of assisting suicide over performing euthanasia is said to be psychological, as they typically do not witness the suicide of the patients they assist, thereby potentially lessening the impact upon them.[124]

12.53 The Act outlines four specific patient requirements to participate. A patient must be at least eighteen years of age, a resident of the state of Oregon,[125] capable of making and communicating health care decisions to health care practitioners, and diagnosed with a terminal illness that will lead to death within six months. The attending and consulting

---

[117] Ibid., p. 31.
[118] Ibid., p. 46 (original emphasis).
[119] C. Lane, 'Children Are Being Euthanized in Belgium', *Washington Post*, 7 August 2018, at http://wapo.st/2FsCWYA.
[120] S. 4(2), 2002 Belgian Euthanasia Act.
[121] S. 3((2)3), 2002 Belgian Euthanasia Act.
[122] Nys, 'A Discussion of the Legal Rules on Euthanasia in Belgium Briefly Compared with the Rules in Luxembourg and the Netherlands', p. 17.
[123] S. 14, 2002 Belgian Euthanasia Act.
[124] D. P. Sulmasy, 'Ethics and the Psychiatric Dimensions of Physician-Assisted Suicide', chap. 3 in Jones, Gastman, and MacKellar (eds.), *Euthanasia and Assisted Suicide: Lessons from Belgium*, pp. 49–64, at 52.
[125] Among the justifications of residence are an Oregon driving licence, registration to vote in the state, owing or leasing property in the state, and the filing of a state tax return for the most recent tax year.

physicians must determine if a patient meets these requirements and report that fact to the Oregon Health Authority at the time a prescription is written.[126]

12.54 The Act's implementation, as of 2015, was ascribed primarily not to the search for relief from pain but rather as a consequence of loss of autonomy, loss of dignity, decreased ability to enjoy life, loss of control of bodily functions, and being a burden on others.[127] Similarly, in its latest report, issued in 2020 but covering the calendar year 2019, the Public Health Division's Center for Health Statistics observed: 'As in previous years, the three most frequently reported end-of-life concerns were decreasing ability to participate in activities that made life enjoyable (90%), loss of autonomy (87%) and loss of dignity (72%).'[128]

12.55 The 2020 Report stated that 188 people died in 2019 from ingesting the prescribed medications, including eighteen who had received prescriptions in earlier years. The characteristics of these patients 'were similar to those in previous years: most patients were aged 65 years or older (75%) and most had cancer (68%)'.[129] Since the law was passed in 1997, a total of 2,518 people have received prescriptions under the Act and 1,657 people (66 per cent) have died from ingesting the medications.[130]

12.56 Following a revision to the relevant legislation, since the beginning of 2020 patients have been made exempt from any waiting period that exceeds their life expectancy. Patients with less than fifteen days to live are exempt from the fifteen-day waiting period between the first and second oral requests for medication. Patients with less than forty-eight hours to live are exempt from the forty-eight-hour waiting period between the patient's written request and the writing of the lethal prescription.[131]

The Judgment of the Montana Supreme Court in the *Baxter* Case

12.57 While other US states adopted legislation to decriminalise physician-assisted suicide, at the end of 2009 Montana's Supreme Court declared the practice not unlawful in its Opinion in the *Baxter* case.[132] The case is notable for the Court's explicit finding of a right to die with dignity, which encompassed seeking the assistance of a physician to do so. Montana law states that a person commits deliberate homicide if 'the person purposely or knowingly causes the death of another human being'. This could apply to the acts of a physician. At the same time, the Montana Constitution determined that the 'dignity of the human being is inviolable'.[133]

---

[126] State of Oregon Public Health Division Center for Health Statistics, 'Oregon Death with Dignity Act: 2019 Data Summary', issued on 25 February 2020, at http://bit.ly/3fdT7FR, p. 4.
[127] Sulmasy, 'Ethics and the Psychiatric Dimensions of Physician-Assisted Suicide', p. 50.
[128] 'Oregon Death with Dignity Act: 2019 Data Summary', p. 6.
[129] Ibid., p. 3.
[130] Ibid., p. 5.
[131] State of Oregon, 'Oregon's Death with Dignity Act (DWDA), Frequently Asked Questions', Last updated 1 January 2020.
[132] Supreme Court of Montana, *Baxter* v. *Montana*, Opinion of the Court (Case DA 09–0051), decided 31 December 2009, available at http://bit.ly/3hQZsJ8.
[133] Art. II(4) Constitution of Montana, at http://bit.ly/3ggKop7.

12.58 The first plaintiff in the case, Robert Baxter, had been diagnosed as terminally ill with lymphocytic leukaemia. Mr Baxter was planning to end his life by self-administering and ingesting a legal dose of medication that his doctor would prescribe. His doctors, who were co-plaintiffs, filed a suit seeking to prevent a resultant criminal prosecution. The district court had held that under Montana's Constitution, a competent, terminally ill patient has a right to die with dignity, which includes protecting the patient's doctor from prosecution under the state's homicide statutes.

12.59 Justice W. William Leaphart delivered the Opinion of the Supreme Court of Montana, affirming the holding of the district court. Justice Leaphart noted that suicide was not a crime under state law.[134] He then assessed whether the consent of the patient to his doctor's assistance in dying could constitute a statutory defence to a homicide charge against the doctor.[135] He adjudged that a terminally ill patient who was a mentally competent adult at the salient time could grant consent to doctors providing aid in him or her. A further statutory hurdle to overcome was that such consent would be ineffective if it was against public policy to allow the conduct or the harm that results. The court found no indication in the law that such assistance provided by a physician to a terminally ill and mentally competent adult patient contravened public policy. It was neither disruptive to public peace nor did it physically endanger others in the view of the Court: 'Each stage of the physician-patient interaction is private, civil, and compassionate.'[136]

12.60 The state's Terminally Ill Act already provided that terminally ill patients are entitled to autonomous, end-of-life decisions, even if enforcing those decisions involves direct acts by a doctor. The Terminally Ill Act confers on terminally ill patients a right to have their end-of-life wishes followed, even if it requires that a doctor participate by withdrawing or withholding treatment. There was, the Court said, nothing in the statute to indicate it was against public policy to honour those same wishes when the patient is conscious and able to vocalise the decision and carry it out himself with self-administered medication and with no immediate or direct assistance from a physician.[137]

12.61 Justice James C. Nelson concurred in the court's analysis and further concluded 'that physician assistance in dying is protected by the Montana Constitution as a matter of privacy and a matter of individual dignity'.[138] The Constitution, he held, also firmly protects physician assistance in dying. But, he cautioned, the case was not about a 'right to die'. Indeed, the notion that there is such a 'right', he stated, 'is patently absurd, if not downright silly'. The only 'right' guaranteed to a terminally ill patient 'is the right to preserve his personal autonomy and his individual dignity, as he sees fit, in the face of an

---

[134] *Baxter v. Montana*, Opinion of the Court, para. 11.
[135] Ibid., para. 12.
[136] Ibid., paras. 18, 23.
[137] Ibid., para. 30.
[138] Ibid., para. 59.

ultimate destiny that no power on earth can prevent'.[139] Significantly, he declared, the only right in Montana's Constitution that is 'inviolable' is the right of human dignity.[140]

12.62 A dissenting opinion was rendered by Justice Jim Rice. He recalled that the prohibition against homicide protects and preserves human life, is the ultimate recognition of human dignity, and is a foundation for modern society, as it has been for thousands of years. Based on this foundation, Justice Rice opined, Anglo-American law, encompassing the law of Montana, has prohibited the enabling of suicide for more than seven hundred years.[141] An underlying flaw of the court's analysis, he said, is its failure to distinguish between the doctor's basic intention in the assisted-suicide case from the doctor's intention while providing treatment in other cases. A physician providing palliative care, 'even in cases where the treatment arguably contributes to the patient's death, lacks the requisite mental state to be charged under homicide statutes'.[142]

12.63 Under state law, he affirmed, physicians who assist in suicide are subject to criminal prosecution regardless of whether the patient survives or dies. If the patient survives, the doctor may be prosecuted under aiding or soliciting suicide. If the patient dies, the doctor may be prosecuted under the homicide statutes. It is very clear, he concluded, that a patient's consent to the efforts of the doctor is meaningless under these statutes.

The Judgment of the Canadian Supreme Court in the *Carter* Case

12.64 In 2015, Canada's Supreme Court rendered its decision in *Carter* v. *Canada (Attorney General)*.[143] The Court concluded that the prohibition on physician-assisted dying was 'void insofar as it deprives a competent adult of such assistance where (1) the person affected clearly consents to the termination of life; and (2) the person has a grievous and irremediable medical condition (including an illness, disease or disability) that causes enduring suffering that is intolerable to the individual in the circumstances of his or her condition'.[144]

12.65 The Court recalled that Section 7 of the 1982 Canadian Charter of Rights and Freedoms, which is part and parcel of Canada's Constitution, stipulates: 'Everyone has the right to life, liberty and security of the person and the right not to be deprived thereof except in accordance with the principles of fundamental justice.'[145] The Court noted that the trial judge in the case found that the prohibition on physician-assisted dying had the effect of forcing some individuals to take their own lives prematurely, for fear that they would be incapable of doing so when they reached the point where suffering was intolerable. On that basis, she found that the right to life was engaged.[146] The Supreme Court saw 'no basis for interfering with the trial judge's conclusion on this point'. The evidence of

---

[139] Ibid., para. 66.
[140] Ibid., para. 83.
[141] Ibid., para. 96.
[142] Ibid., para. 97.
[143] Supreme Court of Canada, *Carter* v. *Canada (Attorney General)*, 2015 SCC 5, decided 6 February 2015, text of the judgment available at http://bit.ly/3hUay01.
[144] Ibid., para. 4.
[145] Ibid., para. 54.
[146] Ibid., para. 57.

premature death was not challenged before the Court. It was therefore established, the Court concluded, 'that the prohibition deprives some individuals of life'.[147]

12.66 The Court did not agree that

> the existential formulation of the right to life requires an absolute prohibition on assistance in dying, or that individuals cannot 'waive' their right to life. This would create a 'duty to live', rather than a 'right to life', and would call into question the legality of any consent to the withdrawal or refusal of lifesaving or life-sustaining treatment. The sanctity of life is one of our most fundamental societal values. Section 7 is rooted in a profound respect for the value of human life. But s. 7 also encompasses life, liberty and security of the person during the passage to death.[148]

John Keown was among a number of pro-life commentators who criticised the judgment. He alleged that 'the Supreme Court's misunderstanding in *Carter* of the key principle of the sanctity of life and of the right to life is by itself sufficient to vitiate the judgment'. Notwithstanding his harsh assessment, *Carter* has determined that physician-assisted suicide is not a criminal offence in Canada.

12.67 A year later, the Canadian Parliament passed Bill C-14, also legalising voluntary euthanasia. But in a significant departure from the criteria established in the *Carter* judgment, the law requires that the individual seeking to die be in an 'advance state of irreversible decline' and that natural death has already become 'reasonably foreseeable'. By 'implication', it is observed, 'this excludes not only individuals with physical conditions that are not advanced or terminal, but also persons with capacity who suffer from serious and incurable mental illnesses or psychiatric conditions, even if they are grievous and irremediable and cause intolerable suffering to the individual'.[149] This exclusion is, Watts and Solomon have argued, unconstitutional.[150]

12.68 Subsequently, a Quebec Superior Court judge struck down the requirement that a person's natural death must be 'reasonably foreseeable' before she or he could be eligible for medical assistance in dying.[151] Quebec Superior Court Justice Christine Baudouin had determined the provision was an infringement on the right to life, liberty, and security of the person under the Charter of Rights and Freedoms.[152] The 'reasonably foreseeable' criterion was excised from the law for people in Quebec as of 12 March 2020. But as of this writing, the Quebec government backed away from its plan to allow medically assisted death also for people with mental illness until it has held more extensive consultations on the issue.[153]

---

[147] Ibid., para. 58.
[148] Ibid., para. 63.
[149] M. Watts and D. Solomon, 'Bill C-14 and Its Deviation from Carter 2015', *Osler*, 18 July 2016, at http://bit.ly/2P9IpWf.
[150] Ibid.
[151] J. Downie, 'A Watershed Month for Medical Assistance in Dying', *Policy Options*, 20 September 2019, at http://bit.ly/3ghxGoS.
[152] B. Shingler, 'Montrealers Who Challenged Assisted Dying Laws See Ruling as "Ray of Hope"', *CBC News*, last updated 12 September 2019, at http://bit.ly/2D8s7dT.
[153] B. Shingler, 'Quebec Suspends Plan to Make Assisted Dying Open to People with Mental Illness', *CBC News*, posted 27 January 2020, at http://bit.ly/313TptX.

12.69 In slight contrast, in the course of proceedings in *Lamb* v. *Canada*, a case before the British Colombia Supreme Court, an expansive interpretation of 'reasonably foreseeable' death emerged, but with the criterion retained. Julia Lamb, a young British Columbia woman with a degenerative neuromuscular disorder, feared exclusion from the category of those who could seek medical assistance to end her life prematurely. The Attorney General of Canada submitted evidence to the court from an expert witness, Dr Madeline Li, affirming that Ms Lamb did in fact meet the legal requirements for assisted dying. To meet the 'reasonably foreseeable' criterion, the expert declared, she would have only to express the requisite intent to end preventive care and refuse treatment for the inevitable ensuing infection. As a result, Ms Lamb and the British Columbia Civil Liberties Association that supported her case sought an adjournment.[154]

Legislative Change in New Zealand

12.70 In October 2020, New Zealanders voted in a binding national referendum to legalise euthanasia and assisted suicide. The measures, which take effect in November 2021, will apply to adults who have terminal illnesses and who are likely to die within six months, where they are enduring 'unbearable' suffering.[155]

Prospective Legislative Change in Ireland

In September 2020, the 'Bill entitled an Act to make provision for assistance in achieving a dignified and peaceful end of life to qualifying persons and related matters' passed its second reading in the lower chamber of the Irish Parliament, the Dáil Éireann.[156] The bill, which has been tabled by People Before Profit TD (Member of Parliament) Gino Kenny, aims to enable citizens to die with medical assistance if they are suffering from a terminal illness. If the bill became law, the roles of two medical practitioners, one of whom would have to be independent, would be central to the entire process. The independent practitioner would not be able to be a relative, partner, or colleague of the first practitioner (who would likely be the person's own doctor).[157]

---

[154] Downie, 'A Watershed Month for Medical Assistance in Dying'.
[155] 'New Zealanders Vote to Legalise Euthanasia in Binding Referendum', *France24*, 30 October 2020, at http://bit.ly/31VsJwz.
[156] Houses of the Oireachtas, 'Dying with Dignity Bill 2020 (Bill 24 of 2020)', at http://bit.ly/3qcBqgA.
[157] 'Explainer: Everything You Need to Know about the Assisted Dying Bill Set to Come Before the Dáil. New Legislation Could Soon See Assisted Dying Legalised in Ireland', *The Journal.ie*, 29 September 2020, at http://bit.ly/2VgESZA.

13

Poverty and Starvation

INTRODUCTION

13.01 This chapter describes how the duty on States to respect, protect, and fulfil the right to life applies to the prevalence and the alleviation of poverty and the prevention of starvation. The UN Guiding Principles on Extreme Poverty and Human Rights, adopted by the Human Rights Council in 2012, stated that poverty 'is a cause of preventable death, ill-health, high mortality rates and low life expectancy, not only through greater exposure to violence but also material deprivation and its consequences, such as lack of food, safe water and sanitation'.[1] Furthermore, people living in poverty 'are often exposed to both institutional and individual risks of violence and threats to their physical integrity from State agents and private actors, causing them to live in constant fear and insecurity'. Law enforcement officials 'often profile and deliberately target persons living in poverty', while women and girls living in poverty are particularly affected by gender-based violence and typically deprived of the protection to which they have a right.[2]

13.02 In its General Comment 36 on the right to life under the 1966 International Covenant on Civil and Political Rights (ICCPR),[3] the UN Human Rights Committee stated: 'The duty to protect life also implies that States parties should take appropriate measures to address the general conditions in society that may give rise to direct threats to life or prevent individuals from enjoying their right to life with dignity. ... These general conditions may include ... hunger and malnutrition and extreme poverty.'[4] Thus the Human Rights Committee conceives of socio-economic rights, such as the right to an adequate standard of living and the right to food, as potentially giving rise – at least in extreme cases – to binding obligations under the right to life.

13.03 In his 2017 report to the UN General Assembly, the Special Rapporteur on extreme poverty and human rights criticised a widespread failure to respect the purported

---

[1] UN Guiding Principles on Extreme Poverty and Human Rights, adopted without a vote under Human Rights Council Resolution 21/11, 27 September 2012, para. 63.
[2] Ibid.
[3] Art. 21, International Covenant on Civil and Political Rights; adopted at New York 16 December 1966; entered into force 23 March 1976. As of 1 May 2021, 173 States were party to the ICCPR and a further 6 States were signatories.
[4] Human Rights Committee, General Comment No. 36: Article 6: right to life, UN doc. CCPR/C/GC/36, 3 September 2019, para. 26 (footnote omitted).

indivisibility of civil and political rights and economic, social, and cultural rights.[5] When 'the situation of people living in poverty is addressed in development or human rights frameworks', he wrote, 'their civil and political rights are often completely ignored, explicitly excluded from the analysis or mentioned only in passing'.[6] The right to life, the Special Rapporteur further asserted, is

> an excellent illustration of the reluctance of many human rights bodies at the international level to implement the principle of indivisibility. While the Inter-American Court of Human Rights and constitutional courts in countries as diverse as Colombia, India and Kenya have interpreted the right to life in ways that acknowledge the indivisibility of the two sets of rights, the great majority of national and international human rights bodies prefer to keep the two sets of rights rigidly separated from one another.[7]

13.04 This chapter continues with a discussion of the meaning of the terms 'poverty' and 'starvation' under international law. It then discusses how the duty to respect and protect life under global human rights treaties and standards imposes obligations on States to alleviate poverty and prevent starvation. The corresponding treatment of these duties under regional treaties and standards is then considered. The final section of the chapter looks at how these duties apply in a situation of armed conflict.

The Definition of Poverty and Starvation

13.05 Neither 'poverty' nor indeed 'extreme poverty' is formally defined under international law. Under the International Covenant on Economic, Social and Cultural Rights (ICESCR), States Parties 'recognize the right of everyone to an adequate standard of living for himself and his family, including adequate food'.[8] One might therefore construe poverty as inevitably representing in human rights terms an 'inadequate' standard of living, delineated by the lack of family resources to purchase minimally sufficient food and water and clothing and to benefit from the protection afforded by some form of housing, however rudimentary.

13.06 In 2001, in a statement on the issue, the Committee on Economic, Social and Cultural Rights stated that poverty was 'a human condition characterized by the sustained or chronic deprivation of the resources, capabilities, choices, security and power necessary for the enjoyment of an adequate standard of living and other civil, cultural, economic, political and social rights'.[9] The 2015 Human Development Report, published by the UN

---

[5] *Vienna Declaration and Programme of Action*, adopted by the World Conference on Human Rights, Vienna, 25 June 1993, UN doc. A/CONF. 157/24 (Part 1), chap. III), Part 1, para. 5.
[6] Report of the Special Rapporteur on extreme poverty and human rights, Philip Alston, UN doc. A/72/502, 4 October 2017, Summary.
[7] Ibid., para. 42.
[8] Art. 11(1), International Covenant on Economic, Social and Cultural Rights; adopted at New York 16 December 1966; entered into force 3 January 1976. As of 1 May 2021, 171 States were party to the Covenant and a further 4 States were signatories.
[9] Committee on Economic, Social and Cultural Rights, 'Poverty and the International Covenant on Economic, Social and Cultural Rights: Statement Adopted by the Committee on Economic, Social and Cultural Rights on 4 May 2001', UN doc. E/C.12/2001/10, 10 May 2001, para. 8.

Development Programme (UNDP), defined human poverty more generally 'by many dimensions of impoverishment: deprivation of a long and healthy life, of knowledge, of a decent standard of living, and of participation'.[10]

13.07 One of the World Bank Group's two core goals is to end 'extreme poverty' (the other being to promote shared prosperity).[11] It defines extreme poverty as pertaining to those who live on the equivalent in purchasing power parity (PPP) of US$1.90 a day or less.[12] Globally, extreme poverty so defined has rapidly declined, with World Bank estimates suggesting that the number fell from 1.9 billion in 1990 to about 736 million in 2015. But the number of people living in extreme poverty has been rising in Sub-Saharan Africa, comprising more than half of the extreme poor in 2015. Forecasts indicate that by 2030, nearly nine in ten of the extremely impoverished worldwide will be found in Sub-Saharan Africa.[13] The full impact of the global COVID-19 pandemic on poverty rates remained to be laid bare, as of writing, but a report by the World Bank in October 2020 claimed that the pandemic could drive up to forty million people into extreme poverty in Africa in 2020, erasing at least five years of progress in fighting poverty.[14]

13.08 According to the Special Rapporteur on extreme poverty and human rights, however, the income-centred approach of the World Bank 'fail[s] to capture the complexity of extreme poverty and its wide-ranging impact on human rights'. UNDP's *Human Development Report 2019*[15] applies instead a Multidimensional Poverty Index (MPI), developed in collaboration with the Oxford Poverty and Human Development Initiative. The MPI identifies multiple deprivations at the household and individual level in health, education, and standard of living, using micro data from household surveys.[16] The global MPI covers 101 countries, home to 77 per cent of the world's population, or 5.7 billion people. Some 23 per cent of these people (1.3 billion), it assessed in 2019, are 'multidimensionally' poor.[17]

13.09 Starvation is ordinarily defined as 'suffering or death caused by lack of food'.[18] It is therefore an acute shortage of nutrition in a person – a dangerous level of hunger – that seriously endangers health and also, potentially, life. In 2015, UN member States committed to the 2030 Agenda for Sustainable Development, which recognised the importance of 'looking beyond hunger'. The Sustainable Development Goals seek not only to eradicate

[10] UNDP, 2000 *Human Development Report*, UNDP, New York, 2000, p. 17.
[11] The World Bank, 'Poverty', 2020, at http://bit.ly/31Ibh57.
[12] F. Ferreira, D. Mitchell Jolliffe, and E. Beer Prydz, 'The International Poverty Line Has Just Been Raised to $1.90 a Day, but Global Poverty Is Basically Unchanged. How Is That Even Possible?', World Bank Blogs, 4 October 2015, at http://bit.ly/2E52sUd.
[13] D. Wadhwa, 'The Number of Extremely Poor People Continues to Rise in Sub-Saharan Africa', World Bank Blogs, 19 September 2018, at http://bit.ly/3hiaqHF.
[14] The World Bank, 'World Bank Confirms Economic Downturn in Sub-Saharan Africa, Outlines Key Polices Needed for Recovery', Washington, DC, 8 October 2020, at http://bit.ly/3qko2Eu.
[15] UNDP, *Human Development Report 2019: Beyond Income, Beyond Averages, Beyond Today: Inequalities in Human Development in the 21st Century*, New York, 2019.
[16] UNDP, 'What Is the Multidimensional Poverty Index?', undated but 2019, at http://bit.ly/31eJLpx.
[17] UNDP, *Human Development Report 2019*, p. 68.
[18] *Oxford English Dictionary* definition.

all forms of malnutrition but also to ensure access for all to safe, nutritious, and sufficient food all year round.[19]

13.10 According to the *State of Food Security and Nutrition in the World* (2020), however, published jointly by several UN agencies, more than 690 million people were blighted by hunger in 2019, an increase of nearly 60 million in 5 years. Most of the world's undernourished – 381 million – are found in Asia.[20] In 2020, the Special Rapporteur on the right to food concluded that, despite the Sustainable Development Goal of 'zero hunger' and malnutrition by 2030, the realisation of the right to food remained a 'distant, if not impossible, reality for far too many'.[21]

POVERTY AND STARVATION UNDER GLOBAL STANDARDS

13.11 There is a duty upon every State to exercise due diligence to seek to prevent and address both extreme poverty and starvation. Intentionally inflicting starvation upon a person or group of individuals, for example by provoking a famine, will violate the right to freedom from cruel or inhuman treatment as well as the right to food; it may also violate the right to life, in particular – but not only – if a person dies as a result.

13.12 The right to water is sometimes considered within the right to food but it is also increasingly seen as possessing an autonomous existence in international law. The right to water falls within the category of guarantees essential for securing an adequate standard of living, 'particularly since it is one of the most fundamental conditions for survival'.[22] It is, the Committee on Economic, Social and Cultural Rights has further averred, a 'public good fundamental for life and health', one that is 'indispensable for leading a life in human dignity' and a 'prerequisite for the realization of other human rights'.[23] Indeed, the Committee has asserted, the right to water should be seen 'in conjunction with other rights enshrined in the International Bill of Human Rights, foremost amongst them the right to life and human dignity'.[24] In November 2020, the UN Food and Agriculture Organization (FAO) reported that '3.2 billion people live in agricultural areas with high or very high water shortages or scarcity, of whom 1.2 billion people live in areas with very high water constraints. From the 1.2 billion people, nearly half live in Southern Asia, and about 460 million live in Eastern and South-eastern Asia'.[25]

---

[19] Sustainable Development Goal (SDG) 2, Targets 2.1 and 2.2.
[20] *State of Food Security and Nutrition in the World* (2020), United Nations, Rome, 2020, at http://bit.ly/3iVPy9u.
[21] 'Critical perspective on food systems, food crises and the future of the right to food, Report of the Special Rapporteur on the right to food', UN doc. A/HRC/43/44, 21 January 2020, para. 3.
[22] Committee on Economic, Social and Cultural Rights, General Comment No. 15: The right to water (arts. 11 and 12 of the International Covenant on Economic, Social and Cultural Rights), UN doc. E/C.12/2002/11, 20 January 2003, para. 3.
[23] Ibid., para. 1.
[24] Ibid., para. 3.
[25] FAO, *The State of Food and Agriculture* (SOFA) 2020, Report, Rome, available at http://bit.ly/37hfZ5l.

Poverty and Starvation

13.13 Under the ICESCR, States Parties explicitly recognise 'the fundamental right of everyone to be free from hunger',[26] but this is also a customary rule applicable to all States. Where a person is in the specific care of the State, the failure to ensure sufficient and appropriate food and water will be a violation of the right to freedom from cruel or inhuman treatment. If that concerns a detainee, it will also breach the duty to treat 'with humanity and with respect for the inherent dignity of the human person' all persons deprived of their liberty.[27] Should the detainee die as a consequence of avoidable deprivation of food and water, this will amount to a violation of the right to life.[28]

13.14 Article 9 of the ICESCR provides that States Parties 'recognize the right of everyone to social security'. In its General Comment on this provision, the Committee on Economic, Social and Cultural Rights notes that social security, 'through its redistributive character, plays an important role in poverty reduction and alleviation'.[29] In 2006, it was estimated that about four-fifths of the global population lacked access to formal social security. Of these, one-fifth were living in extreme poverty.[30]

13.15 Under the 1989 Convention on the Rights of the Child, States Parties recognise the right of the child to the 'enjoyment of the highest attainable standard of health' and commit, in particular, to taking appropriate measures to combat disease and malnutrition, including 'through the provision of adequate nutritious foods and clean drinking water'.[31] States Parties further recognise 'the right of every child to a standard of living adequate for the child's physical, mental, spiritual, moral and social development'.[32] In its General Comment on this provision, the Committee on the Rights of the Child stated: 'The many risks and protective factors that underlie the life, survival, growth and development of the child need to be systematically identified in order to design and implement evidence-informed interventions that address a wide range of determinants during the life course.'[33]

13.16 Under the Convention on the Rights of Persons with Disabilities (CRPD), States Parties recognise that persons with disabilities 'have the right to the enjoyment of the highest attainable standard of health without discrimination on the basis of

---

[26] Art. 11(2), ICESCR.
[27] Arts. 7 and 10(1), ICCPR.
[28] Human Rights Committee, *Yekaterina Pavlovna Lantsova v. Russia* Views, UN doc. CCPR/C/74/D/763/1997, 15 April 2002, para. 9.2.
[29] Committee on Economic, Social and Cultural Rights, General Comment No. 19: The right to social security (Article 9), UN doc. E/C.12/GC/19, 4 February 2008, para. 3.
[30] Ibid., para. 7, citing M. Cichon and K. Hagemejer, 'Social Security for All: Investing in Global and Economic Development. A Consultation', in Discussion Paper 16, Social Protection Series, International Labour Organization (ILO) Social Security Department, Geneva, 2006.
[31] Art. 24(1)(c), Convention on the Rights of the Child; adopted at New York 20 November 1989; entered into force 2 September 1990. As of 1 May 2021, 196 States were party to the Convention and the United States was a signatory.
[32] Art. 27(1), Convention on the Rights of the Child.
[33] Committee on the Rights of the Child, General Comment No. 15 (2013) on the right of the child to the enjoyment of the highest attainable standard of health (Article 24), UN doc. CRC/C/GC/15, 17 April 2013, para. 16.

disability'.[34] States Parties further recognise the right of persons with disabilities 'to an adequate standard of living for themselves and their families, including adequate food, clothing and housing'.[35]

13.17 In its General Comment on the right of children with disabilities, concluded the year of the adoption of the CRPD, the Committee on the Rights of the Child recalled that 'poverty is both a cause and a consequence of disability' and affirmed that 'most of the causes of disabilities, such as war, illness and poverty, are preventable'.[36] The Committee noted that the 'inherent right to life, survival and development is a right that warrants particular attention where children with disabilities are concerned'.[37] In its 2016 General Comment on women and girls with disabilities, the Committee on the Rights of Persons with Disabilities observed that, as a consequence of discrimination, 'women represent a disproportionate percentage of the world's poor'. Poverty, the Committee further noted, 'is both a compounding factor and the result of multiple discrimination'.[38]

13.18 In 2018, the UN General Assembly adopted by majority vote the Declaration on the Rights of Peasants and Other People Working in Rural Areas.[39] The Declaration noted in its preamble that peasants and other people working in rural areas 'suffer disproportionately from poverty, hunger and malnutrition'.[40] In its Article 13(4), the Declaration stipulated: 'In States facing high levels of rural poverty and in the absence of employment opportunities in other sectors, States shall take appropriate measures to establish and promote sustainable food systems that are sufficiently labour-intensive to contribute to the creation of decent employment.' While not legally binding, the Declaration 'aims to address the multiple forms of discrimination against peasants, who are primary victims of extreme poverty and hunger'.[41]

---

[34] Art. 25, Convention on the Rights of Persons with Disabilities; adopted at New York 13 December 2006; entered into force 3 May 2008. As of 1 May 2021, 181 States were party to the Convention while a further 9 States were signatories. Also a party to the Convention is the European Union.

[35] Art. 28(1), Convention on the Rights of Persons with Disabilities.

[36] Committee on the Rights of the Child, 'General Comment No. 9 (2006): The rights of children with disabilities', UN doc. CRC/C/GC/9, 27 February 2007, para. 1.

[37] Ibid., para. 31.

[38] Committee on the Rights of Persons with Disabilities, General Comment No. 3 (2016) on women and girls with disabilities, UN doc. CRPD/C/GC/3, 25 November 2016, para. 59.

[39] UN General Assembly Resolution 73/165: 'United Nations Declaration on the Rights of Peasants and Other People Working in Rural Areas', adopted on 17 December 2018 by 121 votes to 8 (Australia, Guatemala, Hungary, Israel, New Zealand, Sweden, the United Kingdom, and the United States), with 54 abstentions (Albania, Andorra, Argentina, Armenia, Austria, Belgium, Bosnia and Herzegovina, Brazil, Bulgaria, Cameroon, Canada, Colombia, Croatia, Cyprus, Czechia, Denmark, Estonia, Ethiopia, Fiji, Finland, France, Georgia, Germany, Greece, Honduras, Iceland, Ireland, Italy, Japan, Kiribati, Latvia, Lesotho, Liechtenstein, Lithuania, Malta, Montenegro, Netherlands, Norway, Palau, Poland, Republic of Korea, Romania, Russia, Samoa, San Marino, Singapore, Slovakia, Slovenia, Spain, the former Yugoslav Republic of Macedonia, Turkey, Tuvalu, Ukraine, and Vanuatu).

[40] UN Declaration on the Rights of Peasants and Other People Working in Rural Areas, eighth preambular para.

[41] C. Dommen and C. Golay, 'Switzerland's Foreign Policy and the United Nations Declaration on the Rights of Peasants', Research Brief, Geneva Academy of International Humanitarian Law and Human Rights, Geneva, August 2020, p. 1.

POVERTY AND STARVATION UNDER REGIONAL STANDARDS

13.19 The related issues of poverty and starvation have been addressed to varying extents in the interpretation and application of regional instruments. The Inter-American Commission on Human Rights and the Inter-American Court of Human Rights have been especially prominent in this regard, though increasingly the European Court of Human Rights is also becoming active.[42] The medium- and long-term impacts of the global COVID-19 pandemic that erupted in 2020 are likely to stimulate new cases and further action regarding these fundamental human rights concerns.

The Inter-American Human Rights System

13.20 According to Article 4(1) of the 1969 American Convention on Human Rights, 'every person has the right to have his life respected.... No one shall be arbitrarily deprived of his life.'[43] The Inter-American Commission on Human Rights addressed the issue of poverty in a dedicated 2017 report, 'Report on Poverty and Human Rights in the Americas'.[44] The Commission considers that poverty 'represents a human rights problem resulting in an impediment to the enjoyment and exercise of human rights on a true equal basis by the individuals, groups and communities living with it'.[45] In certain cases, the Commission affirmed, poverty 'also involves violations of human rights for which the State may bear international responsibility'.[46]

13.21 The Inter-American Commission acknowledges that poverty 'may vary in both intensity to the point of being extreme and in terms of duration by becoming chronic', but considers that States 'have the obligation to remove obstacles to the enjoyment and exercise of human rights by persons, groups, and collectives living in this situation'. The State, the Commission affirms, 'must also create the necessary conditions to ensure a dignified life for those living in situations of poverty until its eradication'.[47]

13.22 In 2015, in its judgment in *Gonzales Lluy v. Ecuador*,[48] the Inter-American Court considered poverty as one of the factors that combined to give rise to the discrimination suffered by the victim, Ms Talía Gonzales Lluy, who was infected by HIV when she was three years old. For the first time, the Court used the concept of 'intersectionality' in its

---

[42] In recent years, the European Court of Human Rights has developed 'a significant jurisprudence' that 'illustrates the added value' of the ECHR in the field of poverty. L. Lavrysen, 'Strengthening the Protection of Human Rights of Persons Living in Poverty under the ECHR', *Netherlands Quarterly of Human Rights*, vol. 33, no. 3 (September 2015), pp. 293–325.

[43] Art. 4, American Convention on Human Rights; adopted at San José 22 November 1969; entered into force 18 July 1978 (added emphasis).

[44] Inter-American Commission on Human Rights (Unit on Economic, Social and Cultural Rights), 'Report on Poverty and Human Rights in the Americas', Approved by the Inter-American Commission on 7 September 2017, Organization of American States (OAS) doc. OEA/Ser.L/V/II.164 Doc. 147, 2017.

[45] Ibid., para. 2.

[46] Ibid.

[47] Ibid., para. 94.

[48] Inter-American Court of Human Rights, *Gonzales Lluy and others v. Ecuador*, Judgment (Preliminary Objections, Merits, Reparations and Costs), 1 September 2015.

analysis of discrimination, holding that a confluence of multiple intersecting vulnerability factors and risks of discrimination had associated with her status as a child, a female, a person living in poverty, and someone living with HIV.[49]

13.23 Article 4 of the Convention guarantees not only the right of every human being not to be arbitrarily deprived of life, but also, the Court recalled, 'the obligation of the State to take the necessary measures to establish an adequate legal framework to dissuade any threat to the right to life'.[50] The 'negative obligation to not harm life was violated' when Ms Lluy's blood 'was contaminated by a private entity'.[51] The harm to Ms Lluy's health, 'owing to the severity of the illness involved and the risks that the victim may face at different moments of her life', constituted a violation of the right to life, 'in view of the danger of death that the victim has faced, and may face in the future, owing to her illness'.[52] In his Concurring Opinion, Judge MacGregor Poisot observed that an 'essential element of the right to health is its interdependence with the right to life and the right to personal integrity'.[53]

13.24 The Court has further held that the right to life also encompasses guarantees ensuring the conditions necessary for a dignified existence. In its judgment in 1999 in the *Street Children* case, the Inter-American Court affirmed that

> the fundamental right to life includes not only the right of every human being not to be deprived of his life arbitrarily, but also the right that he [or she] will not be prevented from having access to the conditions that guarantee a dignified existence. States have the obligation to guarantee the creation of the conditions required in order that violations of this basic right do not occur.[54]

Thus, the Inter-American Commission has observed, 'it is possible to state that poverty, particularly extreme poverty, may constitute, in certain circumstances, a violation of the right to life, interpreted broadly'.[55]

13.25 This interpretation echoed in the Inter-American Court's judgments in the *Yakye Axa, Sawhoyamaxa, and Xákmok Kásek Indigenous Communities* cases, in which it found that Paraguay had not taken the necessary measures to ensure a life with dignity, having failed to guarantee the provision of, among other things, water, food, health, and education to the members of these indigenous communities. In the first of these cases, adjudged in 2005, the Court found that the State had 'abridged' the right to life of the members of the Yakye Axa Community 'for not taking measures regarding the conditions that affected their possibility of having a decent life'. However, in the case of alleged responsibility for the death of sixteen individuals named in the complaint, the Court did not have 'sufficient

---

[49] Ibid., para. 290.
[50] Ibid., para. 169.
[51] Ibid., para. 190.
[52] Ibid.
[53] Concurring Opinion of Judge Eduardo Ferrer MacGregor Poisot, para. 21.
[54] Inter-American Court of Human Rights, 'Street Children' (Villagran-Morales and others) v. Guatemala, Judgment (Merits) 19 November 1999, para. 144.
[55] Inter-American Commission on Human Rights, 'Report on Poverty and Human Rights in the Americas', 2017, para. 196.

evidence to establish the causes of [their] deaths' and could not therefore hold that their right to life had been specifically violated.[56]

13.26 In its subsequent judgment in 2006 in the *Sawhoyamaxa* case, the Court clarified that it was 'clear' that a State cannot be held responsible 'for all situations in which the right to life is at risk'.[57] 'Taking into account the difficulties involved in the planning and adoption of public policies and the operational choices that have to be made in view of the priorities and the resources available', the Court said, the positive obligations upon the State must be interpreted without imposing upon the authorities 'an impossible or disproportionate burden'.[58] In order for this positive obligation to arise, the Court held,

> it must be determined that at the moment of the occurrence of the events, the authorities knew or should have known about the existence of a situation posing an immediate and certain risk to the life of an individual or of a group of individuals, and that the necessary measures were not adopted within the scope of their authority which could be reasonably expected to prevent or avoid such risk.[59]

One such risk may emanate from a situation of extreme poverty.[60]

13.27 In contrast to its earlier decision with respect to the *Yakye Axa*, however, in its judgment in the *Sawhoyamaxa* case, the Court did hold that the right to life of specific individuals had been violated. It had found as matters of fact that on the estates on which they lived, the members of the Sawhoyamaxa community were mired in extreme poverty, a situation characterised by 'poor health conditions and medical care, the working conditions of exploitation to which they were subjected, and the restrictions imposed on them to own crops and cattle and to exercise freely their traditional subsistence activities'.[61] Moreover, the Court considered that for a considerable time the State had had 'full knowledge about the actual risk and vulnerability situation' to which they were exposed, 'especially children, pregnant women and the elderly', as well as about their mortality rates.[62] The failure of the Paraguayan authorities to address life-threatening conditions and to ensure existence with a minimum of human dignity engaged the responsibility of the State for violation of the right to life.

European Court of Human Rights' Jurisprudence

13.28 At regional level, the 1950 European Convention on Human Rights[63] does not explicitly address either poverty or starvation as such. Under Article 2(1) of the Convention, however,

---

[56] Inter-American Court of Human Rights, *Yakye Axa Indigenous Community v. Paraguay*, Judgment (Merits, Reparations and Costs), 17 June 2005, paras. 176, 177, 178.
[57] Inter-American Court of Human Rights, *Sawhoyamaxa Indigenous Community v. Paraguay*, Judgment (Merits, Reparations and Costs), 29 March 2006, para. 155.
[58] Ibid.
[59] Ibid.
[60] Ibid., para. 154.
[61] Ibid., para. 73(61).
[62] Ibid., para. 159.
[63] Convention for the Protection of Human Rights and Fundamental Freedoms; adopted at Rome 4 November 1950; entered into force 3 September 1953.

everyone's right to life shall be protected by law. No one shall be deprived of his life intentionally (save in a set of circumstances expounded in the remainder of the article). It is uncontested, for example, that starvation to death of a detainee constitutes a violation of the right to life.

13.29 The European Court of Human Rights has addressed poverty and malnutrition (rather than starvation) in judgments in a number of important cases, including under the right to life, but more often as inhuman or degrading treatment. This is especially so in a situation where a person was in the care of State, such as in the *Nencheva* case[64] (2013), or is incarcerated awaiting trial, as in the *Dudchenko* case (2017), or following criminal conviction. Where ill treatment results from the conduct of private actors, including family members, the ordinary threshold for protection under Articles 2 or 3 applied by the European Court – actual or constructive knowledge of a temporally proximate threat to life or of serious injury – will ordinarily be used to assess whether a rights violation has occurred.

13.30 The *Nencheva* case concerned the deaths of fifteen children and young adults between December 1996 and March 1997 in a home at Dzhurkovo in Bulgaria for children and youth with physical and psychosocial disabilities. Their deaths were the result of the effects of cold and shortages of food, medicine, and other basic necessities. The manager of the home, observing the problems, had sought on several occasions, unsuccessfully, to incite action by those public institutions with direct responsibility for funding the home. The Court found a violation of right to life through the failure of the authorities to protect the lives of the vulnerable children placed in their care from a serious and immediate threat.

13.31 The food in the care home was rather insufficient, of poor quality, and with little variety. Supper had been stopped because of the lack of available food. Staff at the home and local residents had provided, on a voluntary basis, staple food items such as green beans and potatoes, so that the children would not find themselves going a whole day without eating a meal.[65] At domestic level, the Court of Appeal had held that, in the instance of most of the deaths, the lack of adequate food and the extremely difficult living conditions had contributed to the complication of diseases from which the youth were suffering and had accelerated the end of their lives.[66] The European Court recalled that the children and young adults in the home were vulnerable people with severe mental and physical disorders who had been either abandoned by their parents or placed with their parents' consent. 'All were therefore entrusted to the care of the State in a specialised public establishment and were, especially given their particular vulnerability, under the exclusive control of the authorities'.[67]

---

[64] European Court of Human Rights, *Nencheva and others v. Bulgaria*, Judgment (Fourth Section), 18 June 2013 (as rendered final on 16 December 2013).
[65] Ibid., para. 30.
[66] Ibid., para. 52.
[67] Ibid., para. 119.

13.32 The Court noted that a 'crucial' element in the case was that the tragic events in the home where the children were held 'was not sudden, punctual, and unforeseen, as in the case of an event of force majeure to which the State might not be able to respond'. The deaths followed one another over a period of several months.[68] There was clear evidence that the authorities had failed to take prompt, concrete, and adequate measures to prevent the deaths. The lack of reaction over a period of several months to the director's alerts concerning the situation at the home and an apparent lack of prompt and appropriate medical assistance indicate that the authorities did not act, despite having specific knowledge about the real and imminent risks to the lives of the residents at the home. Moreover, the Court noted, no official explanation had been provided for these failures.[69]

13.33 The *Dudchenko* case[70] concerned, among other things, the conditions of the applicant's detention on remand in a series of prisons in Russia and during his transportation to and between detention facilities. From 9 to 12 October 2006, the applicant was transferred by train from Murmansk to Vologda but was given no food, receiving his first meal on 13 October 2006.[71] The Court reiterated its holding in earlier cases that 'the clear insufficiency of food given to an applicant may in itself raise an issue under Article 3 of the Convention'.[72] There is no need to prove any intent on the part of the authorities to humiliate the detainee for a violation to be found.[73]

13.34 The case of *Z and others v. United Kingdom*[74] was also not a right to life case but one similarly concerning an allegation of inhuman and degrading treatment. In its judgment, the Grand Chamber addressed the conditions in which the four applicants – all children – had been brought up and the ill-treatment inflicted on them by their parents. The applicants' family had been referred to the social services in 1987. At that time, child Z was reported to be stealing food at night.[75] From then on, and until they were placed in emergency care, the children lived in filthy conditions, were malnourished, and showed signs of psycho-social problems. Children Z and A were said to be taking food from waste bins at the school.[76]

13.35 The child psychiatrist who examined them stated that 'it was the worst case of neglect and emotional abuse' she had encountered in her career.[77] The children's representatives complained that the local authorities had not taken adequate steps to protect them from the severe negligence and abuse they had suffered and that this

---

[68] Ibid., para. 122.
[69] Ibid., para. 124.
[70] European Court of Human Rights, *Dudchenko v. Russia*, Judgment (Third Section), 7 November 2017 (as rendered final on 5 March 2018).
[71] Ibid., para. 61.
[72] Ibid., para. 130, citing European Court of Human Rights, *Kadiķis v. Latvia* (No. 2), Judgment (Third Section), 4 May 2006, para. 55.
[73] *Kadiķis v. Latvia* (No. 2), Judgment, para. 56.
[74] European Court of Human Rights, *Z and others v. United Kingdom*, Judgment (Grand Chamber), 10 May 2001.
[75] Ibid., para. 10.
[76] Ibid., para. 16.
[77] Ibid., para. 40.

constituted a violation of Article 3 of the European Convention. The treatment of the children had been brought to the attention of the local authority, which was under a statutory duty to protect them, in October 1987, but they were only taken into emergency care more than four years later, at the insistence of the mother, at the end of April 1992.

13.36 The Court stated that there was no doubt as to 'the failure of the system to protect these applicant children from serious long-term neglect and abuse'.[78] Article 3 of the Convention, the Court stated,

> requires States to take measures designed to ensure that individuals within their jurisdiction are not subjected to torture or inhuman or degrading treatment, including such ill-treatment administered by private individuals. . . . These measures should provide effective protection, in particular, of children and other vulnerable persons and include reasonable steps to prevent ill-treatment of which the authorities had or ought to have had knowledge.[79]

African Charter on Human and Peoples' Rights

13.37 The 1981 African Charter on Human and Peoples' Rights does not specifically address the issue of poverty or starvation.[80] In 2015, the African Commission on Human and Peoples' Rights adopted its General Comment on the right to life under Article 4 of the African Charter on Human and Peoples' Rights.[81] The General Comment addresses starvation only with respect to detainees, stipulating that 'when the State deprives an individual of liberty, its control of the situation yields a heightened level of responsibility to protect that individual's rights. This includes a positive obligation to … provide the necessary conditions of a dignified life, including food [and] water.'[82] Under Article 5 of the African Charter, 'Every individual shall have the right to the respect of the dignity inherent in a human being'.

Arab Charter on Human Rights

13.38 The 2004 Arab Charter on Human Rights[83] is unusual among regional human rights treaties in that it addresses the issue both of poverty and starvation. It is stipulated that the right to development 'is a fundamental human right' and that all States Parties must 'take measures to ensure this right'.[84] They must seek, 'at the international level, to eliminate

---

[78] Ibid., para. 74.
[79] Ibid., para. 73.
[80] African Charter on Human and Peoples' Rights; adopted at Nairobi 27 June 1981; entered into force 21 October 1986.
[81] African Commission on Human and Peoples' Rights, General Comment No. 3 on the African Charter on Human and Peoples' Rights on the right to life (Article 4), adopted during its 57th Ordinary Session, Banjul, The Gambia, November 2015, para. 36.
[82] Ibid., para. 2.
[83] Arab Charter on Human Rights; adopted at Tunis 22 May 2004; entered into force 15 March 2008.
[84] Art. 37, Arab Charter on Human Rights.

poverty'.[85] In addition, everyone 'shall have the right to an adequate standard of living for himself and his family, ensuring well-being and a decent life, including adequate food, clothing, housing, services and a right to a safe environment'.[86] States Parties are obligated to take 'appropriate measures within their available resources to ensure the realization of this right'.[87]

ASEAN Declaration on Human Rights

13.39 The 2012 Association of South-East Asian Nations (ASEAN) Declaration on Human Rights[88] addresses both poverty and starvation. According to Article 28(a): 'Every person has the right to an adequate standard of living for himself or herself and his or her family including ... the right to adequate and affordable food, freedom from hunger and access to safe and nutritious food.' In addition, ASEAN member States 'should adopt meaningful people-oriented and gender-responsive development programmes aimed at poverty alleviation'.[89]

POVERTY AND STARVATION IN ARMED CONFLICT

13.40 International humanitarian law does not address poverty as such but it does prohibit deliberate starvation of civilians as a method of warfare in any armed conflict and further requires that all detainees be treated humanely, including through the provision of adequate food and water. The nutritional needs of the civilian population living under occupation and other basic necessities (e.g., food, shelter) must be met by the occupying power, either directly or indirectly (by allowing in humanitarian relief).

13.41 Failure to comply with these obligations will result, in particular when it causes death, in a corresponding violation of the right to life. Depending on the circumstances, including the level of intent on the perpetrator, a war crime may have been committed. But the commission of an international crime is not a prerequisite for a violation of the right to life.

Intentional Starvation of Civilians

13.42 The intentional starvation of the civilian population as a method of warfare is outlawed by treaty and by customary law in all armed conflict. In contrast, the starvation of combatants is not prohibited. Under Article 54(1) of the 1977 Additional Protocol I[90]

---

[85] Ibid.
[86] Art. 38, Arab Charter on Human Rights.
[87] Ibid.
[88] ASEAN Declaration on Human Rights, adopted by the Heads of State/Government of ASEAN member States at Phnom Penh, 18 November 2012.
[89] Art. 36, ASEAN Declaration on Human Rights.
[90] Protocol Additional to the Geneva Conventions of 12 August 1949, and relating to the Protection of Victims of International Armed Conflicts (Protocol I); adopted at Geneva 8 June 1977; entered into force 7 December 1978. As of 1 May 2021, 174 States were party to Additional Protocol I.

(applicable in international armed conflict), 'starvation of civilians as a method of warfare is prohibited'. This is, according to the commentary by the International Committee of the Red Cross (ICRC), where starvation is used as 'a weapon to annihilate or weaken the population'.[91]

13.43 It is further prohibited 'to attack, destroy, remove or render useless objects indispensable to the survival of the civilian population, such as food-stuffs, agricultural areas for the production of food-stuffs, crops, livestock, drinking water installations and supplies and irrigation works', but this is only so where this is done 'for the specific purpose of denying them for their sustenance value to the civilian population or to the adverse Party'.[92] The ICRC explains that 'the verbs "attack", "destroy", "remove" and "render useless" are used in order to cover all possibilities, including pollution, by chemical or other agents, of water reservoirs, or destruction of crops by defoliants'.[93]

13.44 A similar prohibition is instituted by the 1977 Additional Protocol II,[94] which applies to certain high-intensity non-international armed conflicts. According to Article 14 (Protection of objects indispensable to the survival of the civilian population): 'Starvation of civilians as a method of combat is prohibited. It is therefore prohibited to attack, destroy, remove or render useless for that purpose, objects indispensable to the survival of the civilian population such as food-stuffs, agricultural areas for the production of food-stuffs, crops, livestock, drinking water installations and supplies and irrigation works.' In its corresponding commentary on this provision, the ICRC observes that the term 'starvation' means 'the action of subjecting people to famine, i.e., extreme and general scarcity of food'.[95]

13.45 At the time, the prohibition on using starvation against civilians, and the specific protection given to objects indispensable to the survival of the population, were 'new rules supplementing and developing existing law'.[96] The ICRC commentary, which was published in 1987, a decade after the adoption of the two Protocols, maintained the view that this was a progressive development of international humanitarian law. In its later study of customary international humanitarian law, however, published in 2005, the ICRC determined that the prohibition had crystallised as a customary rule. Thus Rule 53, applicable in all armed conflict, holds that the 'use of starvation of the civilian population as a method of warfare is prohibited'.[97] Under the 1998 Rome Statute of the International Criminal Court (ICC), 'intentionally using starvation of civilians as a method of warfare' is punishable as a war crime under the jurisdiction of the ICC in all armed conflicts.[98]

---

[91] ICRC Commentary on Art. 54(1), 1977 Additional Protocol I, 1987, para. 2090, at http://bit.ly/3iXSdzA.
[92] Art. 54(2), 1977 Additional Protocol I.
[93] ICRC Commentary on Art. 54(2), 1977 Additional Protocol I, 1987, para. 2101, at http://bit.ly/3iXSdzA.
[94] Protocol Additional to the Geneva Conventions of 12 August 1949, and relating to the Protection of Victims of Non-International Armed Conflicts (Protocol II); adopted at Geneva 8 June 1977; entered into force 7 December 1978. As of 1 May 2021, 169 States were party to Additional Protocol II.
[95] ICRC Commentary on Art. 14, 1977 Additional Protocol II, 1987, para. 4791, at http://bit.ly/3gjLQ8e.
[96] Ibid., para. 4793.
[97] At http://bit.ly/2BNHBAi.
[98] Art. 8(2)(b)(xxv) and 8(2)(e)(xix), Rome Statute of the International Criminal Court; adopted at Rome 17 July 1998; entered into force 1 July 2002.

13.46 Where combatants or civilians are detained by an adverse party in any armed conflict, they must be given adequate food and water; provided with clothing and medical care, if necessary; and protected from the elements. Thus, with respect to captured combatants in an international armed conflict, according to 1949 Geneva Convention III on the Treatment of Prisoners of War, 'the basic daily food rations shall be sufficient in quantity, quality and variety to keep prisoners of war in good health and to prevent loss of weight or the development of nutritional deficiencies. . . . Sufficient drinking water shall be supplied to prisoners of war'.[99] The ICRC's new (2020) commentary on this provision in the 1949 Geneva Convention III stipulates that the 'detaining Power must ensure that the food and water provided to prisoners of war is sufficient to meet their health needs and takes into account their habitual diet, as well as the labour on which individual prisoners are employed'.[100]

13.47 Prisoners must have access to drinking water twenty-four hours a day.[101] The World Health Organization (WHO) estimates that a person requires between 2.5 and 3 litres of drinking water per day under most conditions.[102] Dehydration can, as the ICRC observes, 'lead to severe illness and may in some cases be fatal'.[103] Deliberately denying prisoners access to sufficient drinking water may amount to a grave breach of the Convention, which is a war crime.[104] It may also, depending on the circumstances, constitute a crime against humanity.

13.48 As a Trial Chamber of the International Criminal Tribunal for the former Yugoslavia (ICTY) held in its 2013 judgment in the *Prlić* case, the deliberate deprivation of food and water with intent to cause serious bodily harm and leading to the death of a detainee constitutes wilful killing as a war crime.[105] The Prosecution alleged that

> the conditions of confinement at Dretelj Prison were harsh and unsanitary due to overcrowding, poor ventilation, the lack of beds and bedding, sanitation facilities, food and water, and that the HVO often made detainees eat amid cruel and humiliating conditions. It further allege[d] that, in mid-July [1993], at least one Muslim detainee died after not receiving any food or water.[106]

In its judgment, the Trial Chamber established that 'throughout their detention at Dretelj Prison, the detainees suffered from hunger and thirst. The Chamber also established that on 16 July 1993, a Muslim detainee died of dehydration when HVO [Bosnian Croat] soldiers deprived the detainees of food and water'.[107]

---

[99] Art. 26, Convention (III) relative to the Treatment of Prisoners of War; adopted at Geneva 12 August 1949; entered into force 21 October 1950.
[100] ICRC Commentary on Art. 26, 1949 Geneva Convention III, 2020, para. 2106, at http://bit.ly/3l62ewx.
[101] Ibid., para. 2128.
[102] Ibid., citing WHO, *How Much Water Is Needed in Emergencies; Technical Notes on Drinking-Water, Sanitation and Hygiene in Emergencies*, Geneva, July 2013.
[103] ICRC Commentary on Art. 26, 1949 Geneva Convention III, 2020, para. 2128.
[104] Ibid.
[105] See, e.g., ICTY, *Prosecutor v. Prlić*, Judgment (Trial Chamber) (Case No. IT-04-74-T), Vol. 4, 29 May 2013, para. 1017.
[106] ICTY, *Prosecutor v. Prlić*, Judgment (Trial Chamber) (Case No. IT-04-74-T), Vol. 3, 29 May 2013, para. 56.
[107] ICTY, *Prosecutor v. Prlić*, Judgment, Vol. 4, para. 285.

13.49 In the case of armed conflict not of an international character, according to Common Article 3 to the four 1949 Geneva Conventions each Party to the conflict must in all circumstances and 'as a minimum' treat humanely all those taking no active part in the hostilities. Violence against detainees is strictly prohibited. This includes 'members of armed forces who have laid down their arms and those placed *hors de combat* by sickness, wounds, detention, or any other cause'.[108] There must further be no adverse distinction in treatment 'founded on race, colour, religion or faith, sex, birth or wealth, or any other similar criteria'.[109]

13.50 Considering the 'purpose of the prohibition of violence to life and person', which is to ensure 'humane treatment of persons not or no longer actively participating in hostilities', the ICRC affirms that the prohibition 'must also be understood as comprising omissions under certain circumstances'.[110] The ICRC cites the specific example of 'letting persons under one's responsibility starve to death by failing to provide food' as being 'irreconcilable with the requirement of humane treatment'.[111] The obligations set out in Common Article 3 represent, in the words of the International Court of Justice, 'a minimum yardstick'[112] for all armed conflicts.

13.51 The specific requirement to provide all persons deprived of their liberty with adequate food is also part of customary IHL.[113] Thus ICRC Customary Rule 118, which applies in all armed conflicts, stipulates: 'Persons deprived of their liberty must be provided with adequate food, water, clothing, shelter and medical attention.'[114] As the ICRC further explains, with regard to international armed conflicts, the term 'detainee' here

> includes combatants who have fallen into the hands of the adverse party, civilian internees, and security detainees. In non-international armed conflicts, it includes persons who have taken a direct part in hostilities and who have fallen into the power of the adverse party, as well as those detained on criminal charges or for security reasons, provided that a link exists between the situation of armed conflict and the deprivation of liberty. The term 'detainees' as used [here] ... covers all persons thus deprived of their liberty.[115]

13.52 A broader obligation to assist the civilian population exists where they are under foreign occupation (i.e., in a situation of international armed conflict). Thus, according to the 1949 Geneva Convention IV on the Protection of Civilians,

---

[108] Art. 3(1) common to the four Geneva Conventions of 1949.
[109] Ibid.
[110] ICRC Commentary on Art. 3, 1949 Geneva Convention III, para. 629, at http://bit.ly/34mhUpo.
[111] Ibid.
[112] ICJ, *Case Concerning Military and Paramilitary Activities in and against Nicaragua* (Nicaragua v. United States), Judgment (Merits), 27 June 1986, para. 218. In 1995, ICTY approved this finding. See ICTY, *Prosecutor v. Tadić (aka 'Dule')*, Decision on the Defence Motion for Interlocutory Appeal on Jurisdiction (Appeals Chamber) (Case No IT-94-1), 2 October 1995, paras. 98 and 117.
[113] ICRC Commentary on Art. 26, 1949 Geneva Convention III, para. 2112, at http://bit.ly/3l62ewx.
[114] ICRC Customary IHL Rule 118: 'Provision of Basic Necessities to Persons Deprived of Their Liberty', at http://bit.ly/2YmIoTS.
[115] Ibid., 'Note'.

to the fullest extent of the means available to it, the Occupying Power has the duty of ensuring the food and medical supplies of the population; it should, in particular, bring in the necessary foodstuffs, medical stores and other articles if the resources of the occupied territory are inadequate. The Occupying Power may not requisition foodstuffs, articles or medical supplies available in the occupied territory, except for use by the occupation forces and administration personnel, and then only if the requirements of the civilian population have been taken into account.[116]

In his 1958 commentary on the provision, Jean Pictet of the ICRC noted that the Occupying Power 'is placed under an obligation to ensure, to the fullest extent of the means available to it, the food and medical supplies of the population'.[117] The inclusion of the phrase 'to the fullest extent of the means available to it' demonstrates, however, that the negotiators 'did not wish to disregard' the 'material difficulties' with which the occupying power might be confronted in wartime, such as financial and transport problems, but that it was still obligated to use 'all the means at its disposal'. Referring back to the Second World War, he observed: 'During recent conflicts thousands of human beings suffered from starvation during the occupation of the country.'

---

[116] Art. 55, Convention (IV) relative to the Protection of Civilian Persons in Time of War; adopted at Geneva 12 August 1949; entered into force 21 October 1950.

[117] J. Pictet, Commentary on Art. 55(1), 1949 Geneva Convention IV, ICRC, 1958, at http://bit.ly/34k3ciR.

14

Assemblies, Demonstrations, and Protests

INTRODUCTION

14.01 This chapter describes the duty of States to respect and protect the right to life in the context of assemblies, including demonstrations, marches, and protests. The right to assembly peacefully is a fundamental human right – 'a fundamental right in a democratic society', in the words of the European Court of Human Rights.[1] As Article 19, an international non-governmental organisation dedicated to freedom of expression, has observed:

> Throughout history, protests have played a crucial role in overcoming severe repression and demanding democratic and accountable governments – such as the fight against colonialism, labour struggles and strikes, the civil rights movement, anti-apartheid and anti-communism movements, the fall of communism, women challenging patriarchy, anti-war and anti-capitalist mobilisations, protests against 'stolen elections' – and often become a default political action of how society seeks to change social, political and economic systems.[2]

14.02 But assemblies, particularly those involving protest against the regime in general or certain specific actions, may be violently repressed by the security forces, including by use of lethal force. Other citizens may violently oppose the message that is being disseminated by participants in an assembly, leading to death or serious injury – actions that may be tolerated by the authorities, if not actively encouraged. In both cases, however, the responsibility of the State will be engaged and the right to life may be violated, as this chapter explores. For, as the UN Special Rapporteurs on freedom of assembly and on extrajudicial executions observed in 2016, States not only have an obligation to refrain from violating the rights of individuals involved in an assembly, but must also ensure the rights of those who participate in, or are affected by an assembly, including by facilitating an enabling environment within which the assembly can proceed peacefully.[3]

---

[1] This statement, made in its 2003 judgment in the *Djavit An* case, has been reiterated by the Court on a number of occasions. European Court of Human Rights, *Djavit An v. Turkey*, Judgment (Third Section), 20 February 2003 (as rendered final on 9 July 2003), para. 56. See, e.g., *Kudrevičius and others v. Lithuania*, Judgment (Grand Chamber), 15 October 2015, para. 91.
[2] Article 19, 'The "Right to Protest": Background Paper', Report, 2015, at http://bit.ly/3iuWhau, p. 4.
[3] Joint Report of the Special Rapporteur on the Rights to Freedom of Peaceful Assembly and of Association and the Special Rapporteur on Extrajudicial, Summary or Arbitrary Executions on the Proper Management of Assemblies, UN doc. A/HRC/31/66, 4 February 2016, para. 13.

14.03 This chapter continues with a discussion of the definition of assembly under international human rights law before considering the status of the right of peaceful assembly under international law. It then discusses the duty to respect and protect life in the context of assemblies, under both global and regional standards. General Comment 37 on the right of peaceful assembly, adopted by the UN Human Rights Committee in July 2020,[4] is an important normative reference in this regard. Tactics in the policing of assemblies, such as arrest, dispersal, or containment, are reviewed, along with the weapons and methods that are most often used in pursuit of those tactics. The legality of the use of potentially lethal force against participants is addressed both in peacetime and, finally, within a situation of armed conflict.

The Definition of an Assembly

14.04 There is no universally agreed definition under international law of an assembly. The 1948 Universal Declaration of Human Rights had merely proclaimed that 'everyone has the right to freedom of peaceful assembly and association'.[5] Likewise, in Article 21 of the 1966 International Covenant on Civil and Political Rights (ICCPR), it is stipulated simply that 'the right of peaceful assembly shall be recognized'.[6]

14.05 In its General Comment 37, the Human Rights Committee defines a peaceful assembly falling within the scope of Article 21 as 'the non-violent gathering by persons for specific purposes, principally expressive ones'.[7] The reference to 'persons' reflects the view of the Committee that the right of an individual acting alone to demonstrate and protest is not protected within the scope of Article 21, but rather through Article 19(2) on freedom of expression.[8] Thus, as the General Comment further clarifies, the right of peaceful assembly is an individual right that is exercised collectively, inherent to which is 'an associative element'.[9]

---

[4] Human Rights Committee, General comment No. 37 (2020) on the right of peaceful assembly (Article 21), UN doc. CCPR/C/GC/37, 17 September 2020 (hereinafter, Human Rights Committee, General Comment 37 on the right of peaceful assembly).

[5] Art. 20(1), Universal Declaration of Human Rights; approved by UN General Assembly Resolution 217 A, adopted on 10 December 1948 by forty-eight votes to zero with eight abstentions (Byelorussian Soviet Socialist Republic, Czechoslovakia, Poland, Saudi Arabia, Ukrainian Soviet Socialist Republic, Union of South Africa, Union of Soviet Socialist Republics, and Yugoslavia).

[6] Art. 21, International Covenant on Civil and Political Rights; adopted at New York 16 December 1966; entered into force 23 March 1976. As of 1 May 2021, 173 States were party to the ICCPR.

[7] Human Rights Committee, General Comment 37 on the right of peaceful assembly, para. 4.

[8] Ibid., para. 13. The General Comment refers to Committee jurisprudence in which it observed that the author of the complaint 'was, on the evidence found by the domestic courts, acting alone. In the Committee's view, the author has not advanced sufficient elements to show that an "assembly", within the meaning of article 21 of the Covenant, in fact existed.' *Patrick Coleman* v. *Australia*, Views (Comm. No. 1157/2003), UN doc. CCPR/C/87/D/1157/2003, 10 August 2006, para. 6.4. See further on this issue Amnesty International, *The Right to Freedom of Assembly*, AI doc. IOR 40/1842/2020, London, 2020, para. 2.2.3.

[9] Ibid.

THE STATUS OF THE RIGHT UNDER INTERNATIONAL LAW

14.06 The right of peaceful assembly is a norm of customary international law binding on all States and a general principle of law. In addition to its recognition in the ICCPR, it is also incorporated in other global human rights instruments. Under the Convention on the Rights of the Child, to which every State bar one is party, the right of the child to freedom of peaceful assembly is explicitly recognised.[10] Under the 1965 International Convention on the Elimination of All Forms of Racial Discrimination, States Parties undertake to guarantee the right of everyone, without distinction as to race, colour, or national or ethnic origin, to freedom of peaceful assembly.[11] In 2018, in the preamble to its Resolution 38/11 on the promotion and protection of human rights in the context of peaceful protests, the UN Human Rights Council recognised the rights to freedom of peaceful assembly, expression, and association as 'human rights guaranteed to all'.[12] This statement was repeated in a corresponding resolution on the right of assembly in 2020, similarly adopted by the Council without a vote.[13]

14.07 In addition to being incorporated within the ICCPR, the right of peaceful assembly is systematically reflected in regional instruments. Under the 1950 European Convention on Human Rights, 'everyone has the right to freedom of peaceful assembly'.[14] According to the 1969 American Convention on Human Rights: 'The right of peaceful assembly, without arms, is recognized.'[15] The 1981 African Charter on Human and Peoples' Rights provides that 'every individual shall have the right to assemble freely with others'.[16] A specific obligation relating to participation of children in peaceful assemblies is found in the 1990 African Charter on the Rights and Welfare of the Child.[17] The 2004 Arab Charter on Human Rights also protects the right of assembly, though only for 'citizens'.[18] Under the soft-law Association of Southeast Asian Nations (ASEAN) Human Rights Declaration of 2012, 'every person has the right to freedom of peaceful assembly'.[19]

---

[10] Art. 15(1), Convention on the Rights of the Child; adopted at New York 20 November 1989; entered into force 2 September 1990.

[11] Art. 5(d)(ix), International Convention on the Elimination of All Forms of Racial Discrimination; adopted at New York 21 December 1965; entered into force 4 January 1969 (hereinafter, CERD). As of 1 May 2021, 182 States were party to CERD.

[12] Human Rights Council Resolution 38/11: 'The promotion and protection of human rights in the context of peaceful protests', adopted without a vote on 6 July 2018, seventh preambular para.

[13] Human Rights Council Resolution 44/20: 'The promotion and protection of human rights in the context of peaceful protests', adopted without a vote on 17 July 2020, seventh preambular para.

[14] Art. 11(1), Convention for the Protection of Human Rights and Fundamental Freedoms; adopted at Rome 4 November 1950; entered into force 3 September 1953.

[15] Art. 15, American Convention on Human Rights; adopted at San José 22 November 1969; entered into force 18 July 1978.

[16] Art. 11, African Charter on Human and Peoples' Rights; adopted at Nairobi 27 June 1981; entered into force 21 October 1986.

[17] Art. 8, African Charter on the Rights and Welfare of the Child; adopted at Addis Ababa 1 July 1990; entered into force 29 November 1999.

[18] Art. 24(6), Arab Charter on Human Rights; adopted at Tunis 22 May 2004; entered into force 15 March 2008.

[19] ASEAN Human Rights Declaration, adopted at Phnom Penh 18 November 2012, para. 24.

14.08 The right of peaceful assembly is also a general principle of law, as reflected in the near ubiquity of its constitutional guarantee at the domestic level. Indeed, more States reflect the right of peaceful assembly in their Constitutions than do the right to life: of the 193 UN member States all but nine[20] guarantee the right of peaceful assembly (compared to 157 that guarantee the right to life). It does not, though, appear that the right of peaceful assembly is a peremptory norm of international law. In its noted discussion of rights *erga omnes*[21] in its judgment in the *Barcelona Traction* case, the Court had included the 'principles and rules concerning the basic rights of the human person'[22] but it did not expressly deem the right of peaceful assembly to fall within their scope.

THE RIGHT TO LIFE IN THE CONTEXT OF ASSEMBLIES: GLOBAL STANDARDS

14.09 The right of peaceful assembly must be respected without discrimination as to race, nationality, or ethnic background, as well as gender and age. Persons with disabilities have the right to equal enjoyment of the right of peaceful assembly[23] (even though, surprisingly, this is not made explicit in the Convention on the Rights of Persons with Disabilities).[24] The political opinion of the assembly participants is not a legitimate basis for discrimination in the duty on States to respect and right the right,[25] except insofar as they advocate

---

[20] Australia, Brunei Darussalam, Djibouti, France, Israel, San Marino, Saudi Arabia, the United Kingdom, and Yemen. Argentina safeguards the rights to petition the authorities and to associate for useful purposes, though it does not use the term 'assembly'.

[21] The International Law Commission (ILC) has determined that 'peremptory norms of general international law (*jus cogens*) give rise to obligations owed to the international community as a whole (obligations *erga omnes*), in which all States have a legal interest'. ILC, *Report of the International Law Commission*, Seventy-first session, UN doc. A/74/10, 2019, chap. V, Conclusion 17(1).

[22] International Court of Justice, *Barcelona Traction, Light and Power Company Ltd. (Belgium v. Spain)*, Judgment, 5 February 1970, para. 34.

[23] In his 2014 report to the Human Rights Council, the UN Special Rapporteur on the right of peaceful assembly noted that persons with 'disabilities frequently face difficulty in staging peaceful assemblies due to limitations related to their disabilities. Those obstacles include the inability to gain access to the forms and notification procedures (for example, due to a lack of regulations or forms in Braille or other accessible formats) and to Government offices where a notification of assembly may be lodged.' Report of the Special Rapporteur on the rights to freedom of peaceful assembly and of association, Maina Kiai, UN doc. A/HRC/26/29, 14 April 2014, para. 34.

[24] Convention on the Rights of Persons with Disabilities; adopted at New York 13 December 2006; entered into force 3 May 2008 (hereinafter, CRPD). Under Article 4(1) of the Convention, States Parties 'undertake to ensure and promote the full realization of all human rights and fundamental freedoms for all persons with disabilities without discrimination of any kind on the basis of disability'. Moreover, as Article 3(c) articulates, one of the principles of the Convention is the 'full and effective participation and inclusion' of persons with disabilities in society. But the omission of a specific reference to the right of peaceful assembly is nonetheless striking. A leading disability rights advocate describes the 'historically rooted misrepresentation of disability as a mere social and medical theme as reflected even within the UN disability framework itself. Hence, he remarks, 'the emphasis has been on economic, social and cultural rights instead of civil and political rights'. In addition, within the United Nations its Disability Rights Department was 'for decades located in the Division for Social Policy and Development with no counterpart in the [human rights] machinery'. Email from Dagnachew Wakene, Africa Regional Officer, Disability Rights Promotion International, 12 August 2020.

[25] Human Rights Committee, General Comment 37 on the right of peaceful assembly, para. 25.

national, racial, or religious hatred that constitutes incitement to discrimination, hostility, or violence.[26] The obligation to deny enjoyment of the right in such cases pertains not only to that conduct when it is criminalised under domestic law, but also to situations where an assembly is organised with a view to inciting the commission of international crimes, such as aggression,[27] genocide, crimes against humanity, or war crimes.

14.10 Under Article 6(1) of the ICCPR, no one shall be arbitrarily deprived of his life. As covered in Chapter 1, this rule is not only of a customary nature; it is also a peremptory norm of international law. The Human Rights Committee has clarified that the deprivation of life of individuals through acts or omissions that violate provisions of the Covenant other than Article 6 'is, as a rule, arbitrary in nature'.[28] This includes, the Committee further indicates, 'the use of force resulting in the death of demonstrators exercising their right to freedom of assembly'.[29] Such a claim may, however, go a little too far. If the police disperse an assembly where they have no right to do so, using minimal force, but a protester attacks an officer putting his life in imminent danger, subsequent use of force by a law enforcement official to prevent the officer from being killed but which proves to be lethal would not necessarily constitute an arbitrary deprivation of life.

14.11 That is not to question that, whether or not participants in an assembly are entitled to enjoy the right of peaceful assembly in the prevailing circumstances, their right to life must always be respected and protected. An unlawful but peaceful assembly may, in certain circumstances, be dispersed – such as where disruption is 'serious and sustained'[30] – but in seeking to disperse such an assembly, '[l]ethal force clearly has no role to play'.[31] Thus firearms must never be used simply to disperse an assembly.[32] Moreover, their use against an unarmed demonstrator who offers no resistance to law enforcement officials is likely to violate the right to life or (if he or she survives) at the least the right to freedom from torture or other inhumane treatment.

14.12 The case of *Florentina Olmedo v. Paraguay*[33] before the Human Rights Committee concerned an agricultural worker, Blanco Domínguez, who took part in a peaceful demonstration in Paraguay in favour of agrarian reform. On 3 June 2003, around one thousand demonstrators, including Mr Domínguez, converged on the site of the demonstration. They found themselves confronted by considerable numbers of police, anti-riot police, and military personnel. Coming face to face with a police barrier, the demonstrators decided

---

[26] Art. 20(2), ICCPR.
[27] Art. 20(1), ICCPR.
[28] Human Rights Committee, General Comment No. 36: Article 6: right to life, UN doc. CCPR/C/GC/36, 3 September 2019 (hereinafter, Human Rights Committee, General Comment 36 on the right to life), para. 17.
[29] Ibid., citing Report of the Special Rapporteur on extrajudicial, summary or arbitrary executions, Christof Heyns, UN doc. A/HRC/26/36, 1 April 2014, para. 75.
[30] Human Rights Committee, General Comment 37 on the right of peaceful assembly, para. 85.
[31] Report of the Special Rapporteur on extrajudicial, summary or arbitrary executions, Christof Heyns, UN doc. A/HRC/26/36, 1 April 2014, para. 75.
[32] Human Rights Committee, General Comment 37 on the right of peaceful assembly, para. 88.
[33] Human Rights Committee, *Florentina Olmedo v. Paraguay*, Views (Comm. No. 1828/2008), UN doc. CCPR/C/104/D/1828/2008, 26 April 2012.

to blockade the road. They were warned that, if they did not disperse, the blockade would be cleared by force. But while negotiations were still underway, the prosecutor ordered the road to be cleared. The police use of force was immediate and violent, involving the use of tear gas,[34] firearms, and water cannons.

14.13 The police beat many of the demonstrators, fired indiscriminately at those who were fleeing, and violently broke into and damaged various nearby houses, beating severely any persons they managed to catch. Both metal-jacketed and rubber-coated bullets were fired 'indiscriminately'.[35] Mr Dominguez had been at the head of the demonstration and, along with other demonstrators, had peacefully surrendered to the police, kneeling down with his hands up. While he was in this position, an officer of the Paraguayan National Police shot him in the back at very close range. After he fell to the ground, he was hit on the head by the police. After undergoing two surgical operations, Blanco Dominguez died on 5 June 2003.[36] In finding a violation of the right to life, the Human Rights Committee reiterated Paraguay's obligation to protect the life of the demonstrators.[37]

14.14 While it has focused considerable attention on safeguarding the right to life in the context of assemblies by restricting the use of firearms, the Human Rights Committee has also been critical of the employment of less-lethal weapons in certain circumstances. In its General Comment 36 on the right to life, the Committee declared that States Parties to the ICCPR 'should not resort to less-lethal weapons in situations of crowd control that can be addressed through less harmful means, especially situations involving the exercise of the right to peaceful assembly'.[38] In doing so, it cited its Concluding Observations on Sweden's fifth periodic report on the implementation of the ICCPR, in which it recommended that 'during demonstrations, the State party should ensure that no equipment that can endanger human life is used'.[39] In its General Comment 37 on the right of peaceful assembly, suggesting the potential illegality of certain less-lethal weapons that could not readily be targeted at specific individuals, the Committee stated that 'less-lethal weapons affecting an area, such as tear gas and water cannon, tend to have indiscriminate effects'.

14.15 At the same time, the Committee has underscored the general role and value of less-lethal weapons in law enforcement as being less hazardous to life than are conventional firearms. In General Comment 36, it declared that States Parties to the ICCPR are expected to take 'all necessary measures' to prevent arbitrary deprivation of life by their

---

[34] The term 'tear gas' is used to describe a variety of lachrymatory agents used by police forces in certain countries. The most widely used chemical irritant dispersed at a distance is 'CS' (either micronised powder or pyrotechnically generated CS particles), which is typically discharged either in the form of projectiles or from grenades shot from a launcher. Office of the United Nations High Commission for Human Rights (OHCHR), *United Nations Human Rights Guidance on Less-Lethal Weapons in Law Enforcement*, New York/Geneva, July 2020 (hereinafter, UN Human Rights Guidance on Less-Lethal Weapons), para. 7.3.1.
[35] Human Rights Committee, *Florentina Olmedo v. Paraguay*, Views, paras. 2.1 and 2.4–2.6.
[36] Ibid., para. 2.7.
[37] Ibid., para. 7.5.
[38] Human Rights Committee, General Comment 36 on the right to life, para. 14.
[39] Human Rights Committee, Concluding Observations on Sweden, UN doc. CCPR/CO/74/SWE, 24 April 2002, para. 10.

law enforcement officials. These measures include 'supplying forces responsible for crowd control with effective, less-lethal means and adequate protective equipment in order to obviate their need to resort to lethal force'.[40] In General Comment 37, it is stipulated that 'all law enforcement officials responsible for policing assemblies must be suitably equipped, including where needed with appropriate and fit-for-purpose less-lethal weapons and protective equipment'. In 2020, the Office of the UN High Commissioner for Human Rights (OHCHR) issued the United Nations Human Rights Guidance on Less-Lethal Weapons in Law Enforcement, which observed that less-lethal weapons 'have an important role in law enforcement'.[41] The UN Human Rights Guidance on Less-Lethal Weapons is further discussed later in this chapter.

14.16 Three of the 1990 Basic Principles on the Use of Force and Firearms by Law Enforcement Officials specifically address the use of force in the context of assemblies.[42] In a section entitled – somewhat inappropriately given part of its content – 'Policing unlawful assemblies', Principle 12 first recalls that 'everyone is allowed to participate in lawful and peaceful assemblies'.[43] Principle 13 then stipulates that 'in the dispersal of assemblies that are unlawful but non-violent, law enforcement officials shall avoid the use of force or, where that is not practicable, shall restrict such force to the minimum extent necessary'.[44] The denotation of dispersal as the primary or even the only tactic to address an unlawful assembly, including one where acts of violence are being perpetrated by some of the participants, may today be seen as anachronistic. Alternative tactics that may be preferable from a policing as well as a human rights perspective, such as targeted arrest and/or containment, are discussed later.

14.17 Principle 14, which concerns the dispersal of 'violent' assemblies, decrees that law enforcement officials 'may use firearms only when less dangerous means are not practicable and only to the minimum extent necessary'. This might appear to countenance the use of firearms as a means of dispersal, reflecting law and practice that persists in a small minority of States,[45] but stands in contrast to the position of the Human Rights Committee and a number of UN Special Rapporteurs, among others. Principle 14 goes on, however, to explicitly restrict the use of firearms to those outlined in Principle 9 of the 1990 Basic Principles; to wit, where there also exists either an imminent threat of death or serious injury or a grave (but temporally proximate) threat to life.

---

[40] Human Rights Committee, General Comment No. 36, para. 13.
[41] UN Human Rights Guidance on Less-Lethal Weapons, para. 1.1.
[42] Basic Principles on the Use of Force and Firearms by Law Enforcement Officials; adopted at Havana by the Eighth UN Congress on the Prevention of Crime and the Treatment of Offenders 7 September 1990 (hereinafter, 1990 Basic Principles). In December 1990, the UN General Assembly welcomed the Basic Principles and invited governments to respect them. UN General Assembly Resolution 45/166, adopted without a vote on 18 December 1990, para. 4.
[43] Principle 12, 1990 Basic Principles.
[44] By 'unlawful', it is not clear whether that is in breach of domestic law or international law, or both.
[45] This is explicitly the case in, for instance, Bangladesh, Bhutan, the Democratic Republic of Congo, Fiji, Namibia, Niger, Nigeria, and Pakistan. See for details country entries in the Law on Police Use of Force Worldwide online repository, at https://policinglaw.info.

Assemblies, Demonstrations, and Protests

14.18 The Independent International Commission of Inquiry on Syria was established on 22 August 2011 by the Human Rights Council through its Resolution S-17/1. The mandate of the Commission is to investigate all alleged violations of international human rights law since March 2011 in the Syrian Arab Republic. In its first report in November 2011, the Commission stated:

> According to individual testimonies, including those of defectors who have acknowledged their role in policing and quelling the protests, State forces shot indiscriminately at unarmed protestors. Most were shot in the upper body, including in the head. Defectors from military and security forces told the commission that they had received orders to shoot at unarmed protesters without warning. In some instances, however, commanders of operations ordered protesters to disperse and issued warnings prior to opening fire. In some cases, non-lethal means were used prior to or at the same time as live ammunition.[46]

14.19 In finding that Syria had violated the right to life, the Commission observed:

> Governments have an obligation to maintain public order. They bear the ultimate responsibility for protecting individuals under their jurisdiction, including those participating in public assemblies and exercising their right to freedom of expression. In the Syrian Arab Republic, the high toll of dead and injured is the result of the excessive use of force by State forces in many regions. Isolated instances of violence on the part of demonstrators do not affect their right to protection as enshrined in international human rights law.[47]

THE RIGHT TO LIFE IN THE CONTEXT OF ASSEMBLIES: REGIONAL STANDARDS

14.20 The right to life in the context of assemblies has also been addressed to varying extents in the interpretation and application of regional instruments. This is especially the case in the jurisprudence of the European Court of Human Rights and the work of the Inter-American Commission on Human Rights. To date, it has been rather less so, at least in relative terms, in the case law of the Inter-American Court of Human Rights, the African Commission on Human and Peoples' Rights, and the African Court of Human and Peoples' Rights.

European Court of Human Rights' Jurisprudence

14.21 The European Court of Human Rights has adjudicated a number of important cases involving assemblies and the right to life. In its 2011 judgment in *Giuliani and Gaggio*,[48] the Court's Grand Chamber addressed the use of deadly force by a *carabiniere* (Italian military police officer) in a violent demonstration during the G8 Summit in Genoa in Italy

---

[46] Report of the independent international commission of inquiry on the Syrian Arab Republic, UN doc. A/HRC/S-17/2/Add.1, 23 November 2011, para. 41.
[47] Ibid., paras. 86, 87.
[48] European Court of Human Rights, *Giuliani and Gaggio v. Italy*, Judgment (Grand Chamber), 24 March 2011.

in July 2001. Two jeeps of *carabinieri* were travelling from an area of earlier contention, during which one of the vehicles was suddenly surrounded by rioters and the police attacked by stones, sticks, and iron bars. One of the rioters, Carlo Giuliani, tried to throw a fire extinguisher at officers, despite a warning from one *carabiniere* not to do so. The officer stated that he perceived an imminent threat to his own life and bodily integrity and to that of his colleagues. He fired his weapon at Mr Giuliani, killing him.[49]

14.22 The Court held concluded that the killing could be justified on the basis that it was action that was no more than absolutely necessary in the circumstances in defence of a person from unlawful violence, as permitted by Article 2(2)(a) of the European Convention on Human Rights. This holding made it 'unnecessary' for the Court to consider whether the use of force was also unavoidable 'in action lawfully taken for the purpose of quelling a riot or insurrection', as allowed under subparagraph (c) of the same provision.[50] In fact, it is exceptionally hard to conceive of a situation whereby the use of a firearm against an individual that was unjustified in the particular circumstances 'would somehow become lawful merely because it took place against the backdrop of a riot'.[51] Theft of or damage to property does not constitute lawful grounds for the use of firearms under international law.

14.23 Indeed, dispersal of participants even amid a riot through the use of firearms has been specifically condemned by the European Court, among others in its judgment in *Güleç* v. *Turkey*.[52] The case concerned spontaneous and unauthorised demonstrations and attacks on public buildings in the town of Idil. The applicant's son was hit and killed from a ricochet bullet that had been fired by a *gendarme* with a view to dispersing the demonstrators. The Court accepted the Commission's earlier assessment of the demonstration as being one that was 'far from peaceful' and which could constitute a riot within the meaning of Article 2(2)(c) of the Convention.[53] But it held that the authorities should have provided their law enforcement officials with alternatives to firearms to disperse the assembly, a clear reflection of the precautionary principle that has underpinned the protection of the right to life in European Court jurisprudence since the *McCann* judgment in 1995.[54]

14.24 As the Court stated in its judgment in the *Güleç* case:

> The gendarmes used a very powerful weapon because they apparently did not have truncheons, riot shields, water cannon, rubber bullets or tear gas. The lack of such equipment is all the more incomprehensible and unacceptable because the province of

---

[49] Ibid., paras. 21–7.
[50] Ibid., paras. 194, 196.
[51] S. Casey-Maslen and S. Connolly, *Police Use of Force under International Law*, Cambridge University Press, Cambridge, 2017, p. 196.
[52] European Court of Human Rights, *Güleç* v. *Turkey*, Judgment (Chamber), 27 July 1998.
[53] Ibid., para. 68.
[54] European Court of Human Rights, *McCann and others* v. *United Kingdom*, Judgment (Grand Chamber), 27 September 1995, para. 194. See also European Court of Human Rights, *Tagayeva and others* v. *Russia*, Judgment (First Section), 13 April 2017, para. 574.

Şırnak, as the Government pointed out, is in a region in which a state of emergency has been declared, where at the material time disorder could have been expected.[55]

Moreover, the Court noted, the Turkish government had produced no evidence to support its assertion during the case pleadings that terrorists were among the demonstrators. If proven, such a fact might, the Court said, have justified recourse to conventional firearms.[56]

14.25 But death has also resulted from the use of less-lethal weapons, as the jurisprudence of the European Court demonstrates. On this issue, the approach of the Court is evolving. In *Stewart v. United Kingdom*, a case before the erstwhile European Commission on Human Rights in 1985, the applicant's son had died after being struck on the head by a plastic bullet fired by a British soldier serving in Northern Ireland. The Commission accepted the domestic finding of fact by Lord Justice Jones in the High Court on 12 March 1982 that 'the soldier who fired the baton round was trained and experienced in its use; that he intended no injury to the applicant's son; that he aimed at a rioter standing next to him[;] and that a blow on the shoulder from a missile disturbed his aim with the result that Brian Stewart was hit on the head by the baton round'.[57]

14.26 The Commission noted that the use of the plastic baton round in Northern Ireland had given rise to 'much controversy' and acknowledged that it is 'a dangerous weapon which can occasion serious injuries and death, particularly if it strikes the head'. But, the Commission also observed, 'information provided by the parties concerning casualties, compared with the number of baton rounds discharged, shows that the weapon is less dangerous than alleged'.[58] This latter holding is unsound. The inaccuracy of the plastic baton round means that many would be discharged and miss their targets, so a high proportion of rounds fired compared to serious injuries sustained would be expected. This does not sustain a finding of relative safety. Indeed, subsequently, the acknowledged dangers resulting from the plastic baton round of the time led to its replacement[59] and ultimately to the development and procurement of a less hazardous munition, the attenuating energy projectile (AEP).[60] Even the AEP, however, 'has not been designed for use as a crowd control technology'.[61]

14.27 In the 2011 judgment in *Giuliani and Gaggio* cited previously, the Court rejected an argument by the applicants that the *carabinieri* should have been equipped with less-lethal

---

[55] European Court of Human Rights, *Güleç v. Turkey*, Judgment (Chamber), 27 July 1998, para. 71.
[56] Ibid.
[57] European Commission on Human Rights, *Stewart v. United Kingdom*, Report of the Commission, 2 July 1985, para. 21.
[58] Ibid., para. 28.
[59] See, e.g., D. Hughes, K. Maguire, F. Dunn, S. Fitzpatrick, and L. G. Rocke, 'Plastic Baton Round Injuries', *Emergency Medical Journal*, vol. 22 (2005); pp. 111–12, at http://bit.ly/3gHFVL3; D. Hambling, 'The Deadly Truth about Rubber Bullets', *Forbes*, 8 June 2020, at http://bit.ly/3fM9dHb.
[60] See College of Policing, 'Armed Policing: Attenuating Energy Projectiles', last modified 30 January 2020, at http://bit.ly/3ixK1po.
[61] *ACPO Attenuating Energy Projectile (AEP) Guidance*, Amended 16 May 2005, available at http://bit.ly/3kEXsWu.

weapons firing rubber bullets.[62] Officers did have tear gas available to them and the Court acknowledged that in 'general terms, there is room for debate as to whether law-enforcement personnel should also be issued with other equipment of this type, such as water cannons and guns using non-lethal ammunition'. However, it held, this was not relevant in the case at hand, since death had occurred 'not in the course of an operation to disperse demonstrators and control a crowd of marchers, but during a sudden and violent attack' which posed 'an imminent and serious threat to the lives of three carabinieri'.[63]

14.28 A 2018 judgment by a chamber of the Court[64] concerned the use of rubber bullets against participants in a demonstration by trade union members. The applicant, Kadri Kılıcı, was a Turkish national and a member of a trade union whose members were civil servants from local authorities. The case concerned a march in March 2009, during which Mr Kılıcı was wounded as a result of police firing rubber bullets to disperse the participants. About two hundred members of various trade unions, including Mr Kılıcı's, had gathered in Beyoğlu in Istanbul and began walking towards Haliç, a neighbouring district, where the Fifth World Water Forum was being held. This was the intended scene of the protest. The applicant claimed that the police attacked the demonstrators while they were already dispersing and that he had been injured by a rubber bullet. Police reports on the incident claimed that, as the demonstrators were in the process of dispersing, a number of individuals had thrown objects at the police, justifying their forcible response.

14.29 The Court did not exclude that the right to life could be applied to the use of rubber bullets given the risk to life from these munitions, especially when fired at close range. But in the circumstances of the case, it decided instead to consider the injuries to Mr Kılıcı under the right to freedom from torture or inhuman or degrading treatment (i.e., Article 3 of the European Convention).[65] The Court acknowledged, however, that although the injuries to the applicant were minor, they could have been far more serious and that, moreover, the risk of serious injury increases if the munitions are not used appropriately.[66] The Court noted the lack of protocols issued by the authorities on the use of rubber bullets during demonstrations or on their appropriate use in general.[67] It found a violation of Article 3.[68]

14.30 Another less-lethal weapon whose lawful use has been adjudicated by the European Court in the context of assemblies is tear gas. A fatality may arise from either the toxic effects of the gas, especially when it is fired in a closed environment, or from the physical trauma resulting from being struck by a tear-gas canister. The latter was the case in *Ataykaya v. Turkey*.[69] On 29 March 2006, in the early afternoon, on leaving his workplace, Tarık Ataykaya found himself in the middle of a demonstration. The government,

---

[62] European Court of Human Rights, *Giuliani and Gaggio v. Italy*, Judgment (Grand Chamber), 24 March 2011, para. 216.
[63] Ibid.
[64] European Court of Human Rights, *Kılıcı v. Turkey*, Judgment (Second Section), 27 November 2018.
[65] Ibid., para. 22.
[66] Ibid., para. 32.
[67] Ibid., para. 34.
[68] Ibid., para. 39.
[69] European Court of Human Rights, *Ataykaya v. Turkey*, Judgment (Second Section), 22 July 2014.

accepting that Mr Ataykaya had not taken part in the demonstration but had just been passing by, explained that the police had fired a large number of tear-gas grenades to disperse the group of demonstrators.

14.31 Mr Ataykaya was struck on the head by one of the grenades and died a few minutes later.[70] The autopsy performed the next day at a public hospital concluded that death was caused by 'a haemorrhage and brain damage inflicted by a firearm projectile (tear-gas grenade)'. The autopsy report further observed that the 'characteristics of the projectile's point of entry show that it had not been fired from a short distance',[71] indicating the high level of kinetic energy deposited by these canisters even when fired over a considerable distance.

14.32 The Court set as its task to examine 'not only whether the use of potentially lethal force against the applicant's son was legitimate but also whether the operation was regulated and organised in such a way as to minimise to the greatest extent possible any risk to his life'.[72] No expert opinion had been ordered by the authorities to establish how the grenade had been fired, the Court observed. This was of distinct concern given that it seems that the shot had been 'direct, following a flat trajectory, rather than a high-angle shot'.[73] The Court held that since 'it has clearly not been established that the lethal force used against the applicant's son did not go beyond what was "absolutely necessary"', the right to life had been violated in its substantive limb.[74]

14.33 The Yaşa case,[75] whose judgment was cited by the Court in *Ataykaya*, arose from the same set of facts, though Mr Yaşa was injured rather than killed as a result of being struck by a tear-gas canister. In the judgment in that case, the Court had stated that the government

> ought to have conducted the requisite investigations to ascertain how the grenade had been shot, preferably with the help of an expert. Since the Government have failed to produce evidence to refute the applicant's contentions, the Court accepts that the shot was direct and followed a flat trajectory. In the Court's view, firing a tear-gas grenade along a direct, flat trajectory by means of a launcher cannot be regarded as an appropriate police action as it could potentially cause serious, or indeed fatal injuries, whereas a high-angle shot would generally constitute the appropriate approach, since it prevents people from being injured or killed in the event of an impact.[76]

The Court likewise observed that, at the time of the facts, Turkish law lacked any specific provisions on the use of tear-gas grenades during demonstrations, and did not lay down instructions for their use.[77]

---

[70] Ibid., para. 7.
[71] Ibid., para. 8.
[72] Ibid., para. 46.
[73] Ibid., para. 56.
[74] Ibid., para. 59.
[75] European Court of Human Rights, *Abdullah Yaşa v. Turkey*, Judgment (Second Section), 16 July 2013.
[76] Ibid., para. 48.
[77] Ibid., para. 49.

14.34 The Court found a violation of Article 3 in the *Yaşa* case.[78] This was similarly the case in the later *Süleyman Çelebi* v. *Turkey*,[79] adjudged in 2016, which concerned the indiscriminate use of tear gas (and water cannon) during a demonstration.[80] Several people reported being hospitalised as a result of the effects of inhaling the gas (and from separate beatings by the police using batons).[81] The Court condemned the chilling effect on the right of peaceful assembly of the use of excessive force by the authorities.[82]

The Inter-American Human Rights System

14.35 There is a duty to protect as well as to respect the rights of participants in an assembly. This encompasses a duty to protect demonstrators from violence 'by persons who may hold the opposite opinion', as the Inter-American Commission on Human Rights has explicitly recognised.[83] The consequences for breaching this duty may be significant and far-reaching. Thus, the Commission has stated, 'historically within the region', the failure to comply with the dual obligations of respect and protection 'has triggered episodes of mass violence, which have in turn caused serious violations of these rights and violations of the State's obligations with respect to other human rights, especially the rights to life, physical integrity and personal liberty and security'.[84] Similarly, as the Inter-American Commission's Special Rapporteur for Freedom of Expression has observed, 'analysis of the rights involved in demonstrations and protests must also take into account the fact that improper responses by the State may affect not … other fundamental rights, such as the rights to life, physical integrity, personal safety, and the right to liberty'.[85]

14.36 The Commission has recalled that the general principles on the use of force, applied to the context of protests and demonstrations, 'require that the security operations be carefully and meticulously planned by persons with experience and training specifically for this type of situation and under clear protocols for action'.[86] In this regard, it has underscored that 'potentially lethal force cannot be used merely to maintain or restore public order or to protect legal interests less valuable than life, such as property'. Reflecting the 1990 Basic Principles, and specifically Principle 9, it has stipulated that 'only the

---

[78] Ibid., para. 51.
[79] European Court of Human Rights, *Süleyman Çelebi and others* v. *Turkey*, Judgment (Second Section), 24 May 2016.
[80] Ibid., paras. 79–80.
[81] Ibid., para. 65.
[82] Ibid., para. 112.
[83] Inter-American Commission on Human Rights, *Annual Report* 2007, chap. IV, para. 259.
[84] Inter-American Commission on Human Rights, *Report on Citizen Security and Human Rights*, Organization of American States (OAS) doc. OEA/Ser.L/V/II, Doc. 57, 31 December 2009, para. 192.
[85] Office of the Special Rapporteur for Freedom of Expression of the Inter-American Commission on Human Rights, Edison Lanza, *Protest and Human Rights: Standards on the rights involved in social protest and the obligations to guide the response of the State*, OAS doc. OEA/SER.L/V/II and CIDH/RELE/INF.22/19, September 2019, para. 26.
[86] Ibid., para. 107, citing Inter-American Commission on Human Rights, *Annual Report* 2015, chap. IV A, para. 79.

protection of life and physical integrity from imminent threats can be a legitimate aim for the use of such force'.[87]

14.37 Prohibiting officers who might come into contact with demonstrators from carrying firearms and conventional ammunition is a precautionary step that has proven to be, the Commission avers, 'the best measure to prevent lethal violence and deaths in the context of social protests'.[88] Accordingly, it believes that firearms and conventional ammunition 'should be excluded from operations to control social protests'.[89] That said, the Commission has accepted that operations 'may include' having officers with firearms and conventional ammunition 'somewhere outside the radius of action of the demonstration for those exceptional cases in which there is a situation of actual, serious, and imminent risk to persons that makes their use warranted'.[90]

14.38 With respect to less-lethal weapons, it has asserted that 'a bright line cannot be drawn between lethal and non-lethal weapons',[91] given that, as the UN Special Rapporteur on extrajudicial executions wrote in 2014, 'almost any use of force against the human person can under certain circumstances lead to loss of life or serious injury'.[92] Empirical evidence, the Inter-American Commission's Rapporteur stated,

> shows that in many cases harm to physical integrity has been caused by the misuse of these types of weapons. This is the case of rubber bullets fired at close range and into the upper part of the body, tear gas fired directly at people, irritating gases used against children or the elderly, or electric shock devices used against people with heart conditions.[93]

Therefore, he declares, 'consideration should be given not only to the design or features of the weapon, but also to other factors relating to its use and control'.[94] Reflecting the concerns of the UN Human Rights Committee noted above, the particular tendency of tear gas to engender 'indiscriminate impact' in the context of social protests is remarked upon.[95]

14.39 In recent years, the Inter-American Commission has expressed significant and repeated concern about the situation of human rights in Venezuela, in particular in relation to the policing of assemblies. At the end of 2017, the Commission published a devastating critique of actions by the authorities in Venezuela. '[T]hose who

---

[87] *Protest and Human Rights: Standards on the rights involved in social protest and the obligations to guide the response of the State*, para. 116.
[88] Inter-American Commission on Human Rights, *Annual Report 2015*, chap. IV A, para. 82.
[89] *Protest and Human Rights: Standards on the rights involved in social protest and the obligations to guide the response of the State*, para. 117.
[90] Inter-American Commission on Human Rights, *Annual Report 2015*, chap. IV A, para. 82.
[91] *Protest and Human Rights: Standards on the rights involved in social protest and the obligations to guide the response of the State*, para. 121.
[92] Report of the UN Special Rapporteur on extrajudicial, summary or arbitrary executions, Note by the Secretary-General, UN doc. A/69/265, 6 August 2014, para. 69.
[93] *Protest and Human Rights: Standards on the rights involved in social protest and the obligations to guide the response of the State*, para. 121.
[94] Ibid.
[95] Ibid., para. 122.

demonstrate and publicly express their opinions', the Commission wrote, 'suffer severe repercussions that violate other human rights', including 'physical assault and aggression, arbitrary detention, criminalization in military courts, torture and other mistreatment, rape, and even death'.[96] Estimates reported by the Commission for just four months in 2017 indicated that 133 people had been killed, 4,000 injured, and more than 5,000 arbitrarily detained.[97] According to available information, 'the high numbers of dead and injured are the result of use of firearms and excessive deployment of less-lethal weapons, such as tear gas and bird shot'.[98]

14.40 While the security forces were responsible for many of the deaths, demonstrators were also killed by armed pro-government militia groups known as *colectivos*.[99] Under international law, the State is responsible for the conduct of a person or group of persons 'if the person or group of persons is in fact acting on the instructions of, or under the direction or control of, that State in carrying out the conduct'.[100] As the official commentary on this provision observes: 'Most commonly, cases of this kind will arise where State organs supplement their own action by recruiting or instigating private persons or groups who act as "auxiliaries" while remaining outside the official structure of the State.'[101]

14.41 The situation in Venezuela further deteriorated significantly in 2018, leading to the involvement of the International Criminal Court (ICC). On 8 February 2018, the ICC Prosecutor decided to open a preliminary examination into alleged crimes in the context of demonstrations and related political unrest.[102] On 27 September 2018, a group of States Parties to the Rome Statute[103] from the Americas (Argentina, Canada, Chile, Colombia, Paraguay, and Peru), made an unprecedented referral of the situation in Venezuela since 12 February 2014, alleging that crimes against humanity had been committed, particularly during assemblies.[104] The Office of the Prosecutor of the ICC has been considering allegations 'that State security forces frequently used excessive force to disperse and put down demonstrations, and arrested and detained thousands of actual or perceived members of the opposition, a number of whom would have been allegedly subjected to serious abuse and ill-treatment in detention'.[105]

---

[96] Inter-American Commission on Human Rights, Democratic Institutions, the Rule of Law and Human Rights in Venezuela, Country Report, OAS doc. OEA/Ser.L/V/II. doc. 209, 31 December 2017, para. 191.
[97] Ibid., para. 193.
[98] Ibid., para. 213.
[99] Ibid., para. 210.
[100] ILC, Draft Articles on the Responsibility of States for Internationally Wrongful Acts, 2001, Art. 8: 'Conduct directed or controlled by a State'.
[101] Commentary, para. 2, on Draft Article 8.
[102] Statement of the Prosecutor of the International Criminal Court, Fatou Bensouda, on opening Preliminary Examinations into the situations in the Philippines and in Venezuela, 8 February 2018, at http://bit.ly/2PpEt6o.
[103] Rome Statute of the International Criminal Court; adopted at Rome 17 July 1998; entered into force 1 July 2002.
[104] English translation of the referral, at http://bit.ly/31OgFMO, para. 2.1.
[105] ICC, Preliminary examination: Venezuela I, at http://bit.ly/3iBrxVo.

Assemblies, Demonstrations, and Protests

14.42 In July 2020, the UN High Commissioner for Human Rights published a report on its Office's investigation into possible violations of the right to life in Venezuela.[106] Based on an OHCHR analysis of open sources, from 1 January to 31 May 2020, 1,324 individuals, including nine women, were reportedly killed in the context of security operations.[107] The report did acknowledge, however, that from July 2019 to May 2020, '[w]hile some restrictions to the right to peaceful assembly were documented, security officers generally showed restraint, and in most cases, complied with international norms and standards on crowd management'.[108]

African Commission on Human and Peoples' Rights

14.43 In 2015, the African Commission on Human and Peoples' Rights adopted its General Comment on the right to life under Article 4 of the African Charter on Human and Peoples' Rights. Therein it stipulated:

> The right to assemble and to demonstrate is integral to democracy and human rights. Even if acts of violence occur during such events participants retain their rights to bodily integrity and other rights and force may not be used except in accordance with the principles of necessity and proportionality. Firearms may never be used simply to disperse an assembly.[109]

14.44 Previously, on 25 March 2011, the African Court on Human and Peoples' Rights ordered provisional measures against Libya in a case presented by the African Commission. The Commission had alleged that demonstrations in Benghazi and other cities and towns on 19 February 2011 were 'violently supressed by security forces who opened fire at random on the demonstrators killing and injuring many people'.[110] The provisional measures ordered by the Court demanded that Libya 'immediately refrain from any action that would result in loss of life or violation of physical integrity of persons, which could be a breach of the provisions of the African Charter on Human and Peoples' Rights or of other international human rights instruments to which it is a party'.[111]

14.45 More recently, in the case of Sudan, the African Commission issued a statement in February 2019 at its 25th Extraordinary Session, in which it expressed its deep concern about the human rights situation following the protests that began in December 2018 due

---

[106] 'Outcomes of the investigation into allegations of possible human right violations of the human rights to life, liberty and physical and moral integrity in the Bolivarian Republic of Venezuela', Report of the United Nations High Commissioner for Human Rights, UN doc. A/HRC/44/20, 2 July 2020.
[107] Ibid., para. 35.
[108] Ibid., para. 23.
[109] African Commission on Human and Peoples' Rights, General Comment No. 3 on the African Charter on Human and Peoples' Rights on the right to life (Article 4), adopted during its 57th Ordinary Session, Banjul, The Gambia, November 2015, para. 28.
[110] African Court of Human and Peoples' Rights, *African Commission on Human and Peoples' Rights v. Libya*, Order for Provisional Measures (App. No. 004/2011), 25 March 2011, para. 2.
[111] Ibid., para. 25.

324   *Major Themes*

to a rise in the price of bread and fuel as well as other essential goods.[112] The Commission noted its concern at 'the use of excessive and disproportionate force to disperse protests, resulting in the deaths and injuries of several protestors' and its alarm at 'reports that security forces fired live ammunition and tear gas into hospital premises, where protestors were taking shelter'.[113] In the Resolution, the Commission called on Sudan to 'refrain from the use of excessive and disproportionate force against protestors and, more generally, take the necessary measures to guarantee the security and safety of its population'.[114]

14.46 On 4 March 2020, the Commission adopted Resolution 437 in which it called for a study on the use of force by law enforcement officials in Africa.[115] The study, which had not been published as of writing, was expected to address the use of force during public order policing, especially in the context of demonstrations and protests.

TACTICS AND WEAPONS IN THE POLICING OF ASSEMBLIES

14.47 As noted previously, the standard tactic in earlier decades – and still in many States – is to disperse what the national or local authorities consider to be an unlawful assembly. This is increasingly understood to be an inappropriate tactic in many instances, not only because of the impact on the enjoyment of the right of peaceful assembly but also because it may render the policing of the assembly participants more difficult. Dispersing protesters risks fragmenting a large assembly into many smaller groups, complicating the task of policing. For this reason, some police forces use an approach of targeted arrests of violent individuals, for instance using snatch squads of specially trained officers, as well as containment – a tactic that holds groups of violent or potentially violent individuals within a closed cordon of officers. These tactics are discussed in turn.

Dispersal

14.48 The 1990 Basic Principles referred only to dispersal as the means for addressing an unlawful assembly, whether the assembly as a whole was 'peaceful' or 'violent'. No definition of either term was proffered at the time but in its General Comment 37, the Human Rights Committee indicated that a violent assembly was one in which violence by participants was 'manifestly widespread', unless the violence emanated from the authorities or *agents provocateurs* acting on their behalf.[116] In contrast, isolated instances of

---

[112] African Commission on Human and Peoples' Rights, Resolution on the Human Rights Situation in the Republic of The Sudan, ACHPR/Res. 413 (EXT.OS/XXV), adopted at the Commission's 25th Extraordinary Session in Banjul, The Gambia, on 5 March 2019.
[113] Ibid., preambular paras. 6 and 7.
[114] Ibid., operative para. 2(iv).
[115] African Commission on Human and Peoples' Rights, Resolution on the Need to Prepare a Study on the Use of Force by Law Enforcement Officials in Africa, ACHPR/Res. 437 (EXT.OS/XXVI1) 2020, adopted at the Commission's 27th Extraordinary Session in Banjul, 4 March 2020, operative decision (i).
[116] Human Rights Committee, General Comment 37 on the right of peaceful assembly, Unedited Version, paras. 18, 19.

violent conduct by participants 'will not suffice to taint an entire assembly as non-peaceful'.[117]

Tear Gas

14.49 The most common means of dispersal is either police charges or the use of chemical irritants, particularly tear gas. The dangers of tear gas have already been described in some detail above. A report by the OHCHR in August 2020 stated: 'From 25 to 28 October [2019], and on 1 November and 7 November, Iraqi Security Forces reportedly killed at least 12 protesters at the entrance to Jumhuriyah bridge [in Baghdad] by firing tear gas canisters horizontally at short range, resulting in lethal impact wounds to the head and torso of victims.'[118] In addition to the risk of blunt force trauma resulting from being struck by a tear-gas canister, the means and location of deployment of the gas are also significant in influencing the likely extent of harm on those affected. In confined spaces, without the possibility of exit, individuals may be overcome by the toxic chemical effects. A stampede may be created. To minimise the risk of protesters moving forward towards police lines, increasing the likelihood of violent clashes leading to injury, tear gas should normally be fired by police in the open and in front of violent protesters, not behind them.

14.50 The UN Human Rights Guidance on Less-Lethal Weapons, published in 2020, observes: 'In certain cases, the consequences of using chemical irritants may be lethal,'[119] such as when they are dispersed in confined spaces and result in high levels of exposure. Pyrotechnic projectiles containing chemical irritants may result in death if the round burns near combustible material and causes a fire.'[120] The use of tear gas can 'temporarily cause breathing difficulties, nausea, vomiting, irritation of the respiratory tract, tear ducts and eyes, spasms, chest pains, dermatitis or allergies'.[121] In large doses, however, 'it can cause necrosis of the tissue in the respiratory tract and the digestive system, pulmonary oedema and internal bleeding'.[122]

14.51 Tear gas may be combined with other measures to provoke widespread violations of fundamental human rights. In Guinea, on 28 September 2009, a stampede was caused in a stadium in Conakry as a result of an assault by a combined force of several hundred Presidential Guard troops known as 'red berets', *gendarmes* working with the Anti-Drug and Anti-Organized Crime unit, officers from the Anti-Riot Police, and dozens of civilian-clothed irregular militias. The stadium was packed with tens of thousands of

---

[117] Ibid., para. 19.
[118] Human Rights Violations and Abuses in the Context of Demonstrations in Iraq October 2019 to April 2020, OHCHR and UNAMI, Baghdad, August 2020, at http://bit.ly/34TIoPF, p. 61.
[119] Y. Karagama and others, 'Short-Term and Long-Term Physical Effects of Exposure to CS Spray', *Journal of the Royal Society of Medicine*, vol. 96, no. 4 (2003), pp. 172–4; M. Crowley, *Chemical Control*, Palgrave, London, 2015, p. 48. See also R. J. Haar and others, 'Health Impacts of Chemical Irritants Used for Crowd Control: A Systematic Review of the Injuries and Deaths Caused by Tear Gas and Pepper Spray', *BMC Public Health*, vol. 17 (2017).
[120] UN Human Rights Guidance on Less-Lethal Weapons, para. 7.3.3 (footnote in original).
[121] Ibid., para. 7.3.5.
[122] Ibid.

peaceful pro-democracy supporters protesting the military regime and Captain Moussa Dadis Camara's presumed candidacy in the forthcoming presidential elections. Forces entered the stadium, sealing off most exits, after Anti-Riot Police fired tear gas into the stadium.[123]

14.52 The UN-mandated international commission on inquiry found that many people suffocated or were trampled to death in crowd stampedes, which were compounded by the use of tear gas.[124] Although the precise number of those killed will never be known, as the authorities covered up the scale of the fatalities, at least eighty-nine persons were reported missing subsequently.[125] The Commission on Inquiry found that crimes against humanity had been committed, including that of murder, torture, and enforced disappearance.[126]

Organised Dispersal

14.53 If dispersal is determined to be required, a steady move forward by police officers in formation and equipped with suitable personal protective equipment (PPE), such as dedicated helmets, body armour, and large shields, can be effective. To be safe, however, the tactic demands intensive scenario-based training and a high level of discipline. To be lawful, batons may be used against specific individuals only when strictly necessary and in an appropriate manner. Lack of discipline by the participating officers may create panic or merely redistribute a problem.[127]

Targeted Arrest

14.54 The UN Human Rights Guidance on Less-Lethal Weapons stipulates that the use of less-lethal weapons to disperse an assembly 'should be considered a measure of last resort'. 'Before approving dispersal', the Guidance provides, 'law enforcement agencies should seek to identify any violent individuals and isolate them from the other participants. This may enable the main assembly to continue'.[128] Such targeted arrests are, according to the Human Rights Committee, 'more proportionate measures' than dispersal.[129] That said, as the General Comment also recalls: 'Indiscriminate mass arrest[s] prior to, during or following an assembly, are arbitrary and thus unlawful.'[130]

---

[123] Human Rights Watch, 'Guinea: September 28 Massacre Was Premeditated', 27 October 2009, at http://bit.ly/33Tpp70.
[124] Report of the International Commission of Inquiry mandated to establish the facts and circumstances of the events of 28 September 2009 in Guinea, UN doc. S/2009/693, annex, paras. 62, 84.
[125] Ibid., para. 198.
[126] Ibid., para. 199.
[127] Casey-Maslen and Connolly, *Police Use of Force under International Law*, pp. 199–200.
[128] UN Human Rights Guidance on Less-Lethal Weapons, para. 6.3.3, citing Joint report of the Special Rapporteur on the rights to freedom of peaceful assembly and of association and the Special Rapporteur on extrajudicial, summary or arbitrary executions on the proper management of assemblies, UN doc. A/HRC/31/66, para. 52. See also Human Rights Council Resolution 25/38, para. 9.
[129] Human Rights Committee, General Comment 37 on the right of peaceful assembly, para. 85.
[130] Ibid., para. 82.

Containment

14.55 Containment (better known colloquially as 'kettling')[131] is where the police encircle and close in a section of the participants in an assembly. Containment allows the police to maintain control over a public order situation and, if applied appropriately, minimises the risk of injury to all concerned. The use of kettling in law enforcement is normally traced back to the actions of the German police in Hamburg in 1986 during a protest against nuclear weapons.[132] It is regularly performed at football matches where violence between rival fans is expected. An added advantage for the police is that, 'unlike dispersal, their use of force is essentially defensive: if members of the contained gathering attempt to break out of the containment then it is they who must attack, not the police'.[133]

14.56 According to the Human Rights Committee, containment 'may be used only where it is necessary and proportionate to do so, in order to address actual violence or an imminent threat emanating from that section'.[134] 'Particular care' must, though, be taken 'to contain, as far as possible, only people linked directly to violence and to limit the duration of the containment to the minimum necessary'.[135]

14.57 The legality of the tactic was earlier tested before the European Court of Human Rights in *Austin v. United Kingdom*.[136] The case did not concern the right to life, but the right to liberty and particularly the prohibition on arbitrary deprivation of liberty. The application centred on a challenge to the decision by the Metropolitan Police Service to contain a group of several thousand people at Oxford Circus in London during the May Day protests in 2001. The police, perceiving a risk of violence and disorder (which did occur), imposed a cordon under the common-law power in England and Wales to 'keep the peace'. The applicants to the European Court – one protester and three bystanders caught up in the containment – had lost their challenge to the decision in the House of Lords in 2009.

14.58 The Court's Grand Chamber adjudged that the cordon, which lasted for up to seven hours, did not constitute an arbitrary deprivation of liberty within Article 5 of the European Convention on Human Rights. According to the European Court,

> the police must be afforded a degree of discretion in taking operational decisions. Such decisions are almost always complicated and the police, who have access to information

---

[131] The etymology of the term is unclear. It has been suggested that originates in the idea that steam is confined to a small area of a boiling kettle. Another suggestion is that the word is from German, in which 'Kessel' (the everyday word for a kettle) has an older sense of a semi-circular ring of hunters driving game before them. The best-known example of the military sense is the Stalingrad Kessel of 1942, so called at the time by the German forces besieging the Russian city. M. Quinion, 'Kettling', 2011, at http://bit.ly/2DNSVAB.
[132] Casey-Maslen and Connolly, *Police Use of Force under International Law*, p. 205.
[133] P. A. J. Waddington and M. Wright, 'Police Use of Force, Firearms and Riot-Control', in T. Newburn (ed.), *Handbook of Policing*, 2nd ed., Routledge, London, 2011, p. 472.
[134] Human Rights Committee, General Comment 37 on the right of peaceful assembly, para. 84.
[135] Ibid.
[136] European Court of Human Rights, *Austin and others v. United Kingdom*, Judgment (Grand Chamber), 15 March 2012.

and intelligence not available to the general public, will usually be in the best position to make them. ... Police forces in the Contracting States face new challenges, perhaps unforeseen when the Convention was drafted, and have developed new policing techniques to deal with them, including containment or 'kettling'. Article 5 cannot be interpreted in such a way as to make it impracticable for the police to fulfil their duties of maintaining order and protecting the public, provided that they comply with the underlying principle of Article 5, which is to protect the individual from arbitrariness.'[137]

The European Court's judgment, in this case, has been widely criticised. Particularly surprising is that not only did the Court not believe that arbitrary deprivation of liberty had occurred; it did not even accept that there had been any deprivation of liberty. As David Mead remarked in a blog entry on the decision: 'It is hard not to see how being held for up to seven hours without access to food or water, without shelter or perhaps suitable clothing on a wet, windy day was not depriving someone of their liberty. In common sense terms, what more was needed?'[138]

ASSEMBLIES DURING ARMED CONFLICT

14.59 The right of peaceful assembly ordinarily persists during armed conflict. Under a number of treaties, however, in particular the ICCPR, the right is derogable. That said, the Human Rights Committee has stated that States Parties to the Covenant 'must not rely on derogation from the right of peaceful assembly if they can attain their objectives by imposing restrictions in terms of article 21'.[139] That provision in the Covenant stipulates: 'No restrictions may be placed on the exercise of this right other than those imposed in conformity with the law and which are necessary in a democratic society in the interests of national security or public safety, public order (ordre public), the protection of public health or morals or the protection of the rights and freedoms of others.'[140]

14.60 Where an assembly proceeds during a situation of armed conflict, the question arises as to which bodies of law govern the use of force. While human rights law will always apply, in interpreting and applying the right to life it is debated as to whether the notion of arbitrariness is to be determined primarily by reference to international humanitarian law or by the rules governing law enforcement. This is especially significant if firearms are used against assembly participants, given the permissiveness of international humanitarian law.

14.61 A key issue will be whether assembly participants are deemed to be taking a direct part in hostilities. It is irrelevant for the purposes of this issue whether the situation of armed conflict is international or non-international in character. IHL treaties apply the

---

[137] Ibid., para. 56.
[138] D. Mead, 'The Right to Protest Contained by Strasbourg: An Analysis of Austin v. UK & the Constitutional Pluralist Issues It Throws Up', UK Constitutional Law Group, 16 March 2012. See also Report of the Special Rapporteur on the Rights to Freedom of Peaceful Assembly and of Association, Maina Kiai. Addendum: Mission to the UK, UN doc. A/HRC/23/39/Add.1, 17 June 2013, paras. 36–8.
[139] Human Rights Committee, General Comment 37 on the right of peaceful assembly, para. 96.
[140] Art. 21, ICCPR.

rule in both classifications of armed conflict[141] and the International Committee of the Red Cross's (ICRC's) study of customary international humanitarian law published in 2005 held that the rule was of a customary nature and that it was applicable to all armed conflict. Thus, under Rule 6, 'civilians are protected against attack, unless and for such time as they take a direct part in hostilities'.[142]

14.62 But while the existence and application of the rule to all armed conflicts appear uncontested, certain aspects of the interpretation of the rule are keenly debated. The ICRC issued Interpretive Guidance on the notion of direct participation in hostilities in 2009, following several years of animated debate in expert working groups.[143] It was generally agreed that the notion comprised three cumulative components – that the enemy must be at risk of harm or its civilian population must be actually harmed ('threshold of harm'), that the participation of an individual must lead through a direct chain of actions to attaining that threshold ('direct causation'), and that the action must be of a nature to[144] assist one party to an armed conflict to the detriment of an adverse party (belligerent nexus). But there is where agreement largely ends.

14.63 The ICRC's Interpretive Guidance set the threshold of harm at a low level; certainly lower than it did in its 1987 commentaries on the two 1977 Additional Protocols to the Geneva Conventions. Therein the ICRC had declared that '"direct" participation means acts of war which by their nature or purpose are likely to cause actual harm to the personnel and equipment of the enemy armed forces'.[145] In 2009, however, the ICRC asserted that to meet the threshold of harm, the act need only be likely to 'adversely affect the military operations or military capacity of a party to an armed conflict'.[146] In the Guidance, the ICRC explicitly recognised the concerns of some of the experts it consulted 'that the criterion of "adversely affecting" military operations or military capacity was too wide and vague and could be misunderstood to authorize the killing of civilians without any military necessity', but disregarded them.[147]

---

[141] Art. 51 (3), Protocol Additional to the Geneva Conventions of 12 August 1949, and relating to the Protection of Victims of International Armed Conflicts (Protocol I); adopted at Geneva 8 June 1977, entered into force 7 December 1978 (hereinafter, 1977 Additional Protocol I); and Art. 13(3), Protocol additional to the Geneva Conventions of 12 August 1949, and relating to the protection of victims of non-international armed conflicts (Protocol II); adopted at Geneva 8 June 1977, entered into force 7 December 1978 (hereinafter, 1977 Additional Protocol II).

[142] ICRC Customary International Humanitarian Law Rule 6: 'Civilians' Loss of Protection from Attack', at http://bit.ly/2UBUTKx.

[143] N. Melzer, *Interpretive Guidance on the Notion of Direct Participation in Hostilities under International Humanitarian Law*, ICRC, Geneva, 2009.

[144] There is some confusion in the guidance as to whether intent is to be assessed subjectively or objectively on the basis of the facts.

[145] ICRC Commentary on the two 1977 Additional Protocols to the Geneva Conventions, at http://bit.ly/30PnnD8, para. 1944.

[146] *Interpretive Guidance on the Notion of Direct Participation in Hostilities under International Humanitarian Law*, p. 46.

[147] Ibid., p. 47, note 99. It did so on the basis of the protective element in Section IX of its Guidance, whereby 'the kind and degree of force which is permissible against persons not entitled to protection against direct attack must not exceed what is actually necessary to accomplish a legitimate military purpose in the prevailing circumstances'.

14.64 In a 2014 report on the use of force, the ICRC recognised that 'it is not entirely clear in international law which situations in the context of an armed conflict are governed by the conduct of hostilities paradigm and which are covered by the law enforcement paradigm'.[148] In particular, the report notes that 'situations of civilian unrest (such as riots) may arise while combat operations against the adversary are taking place. Sometimes the two situations of violence may even intermingle, for instance when fighters are hiding among rioting civilians or demonstrators. In such cases, it may become difficult to distinguish fighters from rioting civilians and to identify the relevant applicable paradigm.'[149]

14.65 The report, which narrated discussions from an expert meeting organised by the ICRC, looked at violent assemblies in some detail. In a rather surprising statement, it was asserted that 'riots are generally not considered as amounting to direct participation in hostilities, regardless of how violent they might be and of the reasons for which the civilian population reacts violently'.[150] It is further claimed, citing the ICRC's own Interpretive Guidance on direct participation in hostilities, that 'riots which are not specifically designed to cause directly the required threshold of harm in support of a party to the conflict and to the detriment of another, fall outside the conduct of hostilities paradigm and are to be dealt with under the law enforcement paradigm'.[151]

14.66 This stance appears to confuse the position taken by the Interpretive Guidance. The reasons for which the civilian population reacts (whether or not that reaction is violent) are, in the view of the ICRC as expressed in 2009, critical. Thus the Guidance gives the example of large numbers of unarmed civilians who deliberately gather on a bridge in order to prevent the passage of governmental ground forces in pursuit of an insurgent group. In such a case, the Interpretive Guidance stipulates that those assembly participants 'would probably have to be regarded as directly participating in hostilities'.[152] They would thus become a lawful target under IHL rules governing the conduct of hostilities and could potentially be shot and killed without warning.

14.67 The ICRC Report on the Use of Force also discussed which rule would apply to a 'riot' (i.e., a violent assembly). The fictitious case study the experts considered was one in which 'fighters take advantage of the riot and attack the soldiers with rifles. Some contend that fighters instrumentalized the population and incited it to demonstrate in order to hide in the crowd and to conduct an attack.'[153] The report noted:

> The vast majority of experts agreed that in [such] situations . . . the classical legal analysis is that the two paradigms of the conduct of hostilities and law enforcement apply in parallel. The conduct of hostilities paradigm is applicable to the use of force against fighters while

---

[148] G. Gaggioli, *Expert Meeting: The Use of Force in Armed Conflicts Interplay Between the Conduct of Hostilities and Law Enforcement Paradigms*, ICRC, Geneva, 2014, p. 1.
[149] Ibid.
[150] Ibid., p. 24.
[151] Ibid., p. 25.
[152] Ibid., p. 81.
[153] Gaggioli, *Expert Meeting: The Use of Force in Armed Conflicts Interplay Between the Conduct of Hostilities and Law Enforcement Paradigms*, p. 24.

the law enforcement paradigm remains applicable as regards the use of force against rioting civilians.

Thus 'fighters who are in the crowd can be targeted on sight if the IHL prohibitions of indiscriminate attacks and of attacks in violation of the principles of proportionality and precaution are respected. Incidental damage among the civilians is thus not prohibited, provided it is not excessive in relation to the concrete and direct military advantage anticipated.'[154]

14.68 This is not, however, readily reconciled with the ICRC's position in the other area of major contention in the 2009 Interpretive Guidance – how members of non-State armed groups are to be considered: as civilians or as 'combatants'.[155] State practice, the ICRC declared in its study of customary law published in 2005, is 'not clear' as to the situation of members of armed opposition groups.[156] In its later Interpretive Guidance, however, the ICRC argued that in non-international armed conflict, 'organized armed groups constitute the armed forces of a non-State party to the conflict and consist only of individuals whose continuous function it is to take a direct part in hostilities ("continuous combat function")'.[157] This is so, whether or not the individuals are armed, and potentially allows them to be killed on sight even while they are shopping or sleeping (or standing, unarmed, in an assembly amid groups of civilians). The concept of continuous combat function is highly controversial.[158]

14.69 The issue was at the forefront of the considerations by the UN Commission of Inquiry into the protests in Gaza in the Occupied Palestinian Territory that began in March 2018.[159] According to an interpretation of the law that accepts the notion of continuous combat function, military members of Hamas present in the crowd protesting near the fence surrounding Gaza could be targeted with lethal force without warning. Civilians in the crowd would be protected, as such, from direct attack, but the international humanitarian law rule of proportionality in attack would potentially admit that

---

[154] Ibid., p. 25.
[155] Strictly speaking, the international legal notion of combatant only exists in international armed conflict. ICRC Customary Customary International Humanitarian Law Rule 3: 'Definition of Combatants', at http://bit.ly/2GYnRfC.
[156] Ibid.
[157] N. Melzer, *Interpretive Guidance on the Notion of Direct Participation in Hostilities*, ICRC, Geneva, 2009 (hereinafter, ICRC Interpretive Guidance on DPH), chap. II.
[158] It is certainly not the case, as Michael Schmitt has argued, that 'consensus exists that organized armed groups may be targeted' and rather that only 'a persistent controversy surrounds whether *any* members of the group continue to benefit from the prohibition on targeting civilians'. M. N. Schmitt, 'International Humanitarian Law and the Conduct of Hostilities', chap. 7 in B. Saul and D. Akande (eds.), *The Oxford Guide to International Humanitarian Law*, Oxford University Press, Oxford, 2020, p. 157 (added emphasis). Indeed, writing in the same volume, Hill-Cawthorne is more cautious on the issue: 'It might be argued that it is now accepted that the law of NIAC does not prohibit the targeting of members of armed opposition groups on the basis of that status alone.' Hill-Cawthorne, 'Persons Covered by International Humanitarian Law: Main Categories', in Saul and Akande (eds.), *The Oxford Guide to International Humanitarian Law*, p. 106.
[159] 'Report of the detailed findings of the independent international Commission of inquiry on the protests in the Occupied Palestinian Territory', UN doc. A/HRC/40/CRP.2, 18 March 2019.

a number may lawfully suffer incidental harm when Hamas fighters were being duly targeted as long as the expected harm to civilians was not 'excessive'.

14.70 The Commission report explicitly acknowledged that the notion of continuous combat function 'has been the object of criticism'. It stated tactfully that it 'does not opine on the recognition of CCF [continuous combat function], nor its lawfulness as an IHL-based status', before proceeding, implicitly, to do just that. It noted, correctly, that continuous combat function does not appear anywhere in an IHL treaty and concludes, also correctly, that the concept 'remains unsettled when assessed as custom'.[160] In such circumstances, the Commission stated, while legal approaches 'accepted by only a small group of countries are not necessarily wrong', they are 'best not applied ... until there is further acceptance by the international community'.[161] The Commission concluded that during a situation of armed conflict, demonstrations are to be managed according to the rules governing law enforcement. International human rights law, the Commission affirmed, 'prohibits the targeting of individuals in the crowd with lethal force if based purely on their membership in an armed group'.[162]

14.71 In the summary of its findings, the report by the Commission stated that even had it accepted the 'continuous combat function', with its 'permissive approach to targeting members of armed groups', it believes that the Israeli Security Forces would have had 'difficulty' in complying with the principles of precautions and proportionality in the attack.

> Given the proximity, even intermingling, of armed group members with the demonstrating civilian crowd, harm to civilians is not only foreseeable, but nearly impossible to avoid. Indeed the more than 1,500 demonstrators wounded by shrapnel attest to the danger of civilians being injured by mistake, by ricochets, by bullet fragmentation and by shots going through one body to enter another, when snipers fire high-velocity live ammunition into a demonstrating crowd.[163]

14.72 The better view is that the notion of continuous combat function, an ICRC construct, does not represent the state of the law. As the Commission had noted, it is not found in the two 1977 Additional Protocols (or anywhere else in an IHL treaty). Its formal adoption by States could potentially increase the loss of life by a significant margin, not only among military members of armed opposition groups but also generally among the civilian population. The low standard of feasibility set out under precautionary measures in an international armed conflict, whereby a party to the conflict must only do 'everything feasible to verify that the objectives to be attacked are neither civilians nor civilian objects',[164] if applied also to situations of non-international armed conflict, would not

---

[160] Ibid., para. 105.
[161] Ibid.
[162] Ibid., para. 106.
[163] Ibid., para. 696.
[164] Art. 57(2)(a)(i), 1977 Additional Protocol I.

mitigate the risk.[165] It may be, however, that international human rights law requires a higher standard in such a situation, given the jus cogens nature of the prohibition on arbitrary deprivation of life.[166]

14.73 In its General Comment 37, the Human Rights Committee partially addressed the issue of targeting those participating directly in hostilities when participating also in an assembly. The paragraph bears reproduction in full:

> In a situation of armed conflict, the use of force during peaceful assemblies remains regulated by the rules governing law enforcement and the Covenant continues to apply.[167] Civilians in an assembly are protected from being targeted with lethal force unless and for such time as they take a direct part in hostilities, as that term is understood under international humanitarian law (IHL). In such a circumstance, they may be targeted only to the extent they are not otherwise protected under international law from attack. Any use of force under applicable IHL is subject to the rules and principles of distinction, precautions in attack, proportionality, military necessity and humanity. In all decisions on the use of force, the safety and protection of assembly participants and the broader public should be an important consideration.[168]

The paragraph sidesteps the issue of whether members of an organised armed group ordinarily retain their civilian protection against attack. It is also unclear whether an assembly in which fighters are participating is to be considered peaceful. A 'peaceful' assembly, the Committee explains, 'stands in contradistinction to one characterized by widespread and serious violence'.[169] In addition, the 'conduct of specific participants in an assembly may be deemed violent if authorities can present credible evidence that, before or during the event, . . . the participants have violent intentions and plan to act on them'.[170] A State might instinctively impute violent intentions to a member of an organised armed group. The Committee further provides that the carrying by participants of weapons 'is not necessarily sufficient to deem those participants' conduct violent'.[171] That is unlikely to be the position taken by many States confronting fighters in such a situation.

---

[165] In its judgment in the *Kupreškić* case, the ICTY endorsed the view, subsequently confirmed by the ICRC in its customary IHL study, that the precautionary rules applied also in non-international armed conflict as a matter of custom. International Tribunal for the Prosecution of Persons Responsible for Serious Violations of International Humanitarian Law Committed in the Territory of the Former Yugoslavia since 1991 (ICTY), *Prosecutor v. Zoran Kupreškić and others*, Judgment (Case No. IT-95-16-T) (Trial Chamber), 14 January 2000, paras. 49 and 132.

[166] Inter-American Court of Human Rights, *Case of the 'Street Children' (Villagrán-Morales) v. Guatemala*, Judgment (Merits), 19 November 1999, para. 139. See also 'Fourth report on peremptory norms of general international law (*jus cogens*) by Dire Tladi, Special Rapporteur', UN doc. A/CN.4/727, 31 January 2019, para. 128.

[167] Human Rights Committee, General Comment 36 on the right to life, para. 64.

[168] Human Rights Committee, General Comment 37 on the right of peaceful assembly, Unedited Version, para. 97 (footnote in original).

[169] Ibid., para. 15.

[170] Ibid., para. 19.

[171] Ibid., para. 20.

15

Arms Control and Disarmament

INTRODUCTION

15.01 This chapter describes how the obligations upon States under arms control and disarmament law impact on and intersect with their duties to respect and protect the right to life. In its General Comment No. 36 on the right to life in Article 6 under the 1966 International Covenant on Civil and Political Rights (ICCPR),[1] the UN Human Rights Committee declared that States Parties to the Covenant must take 'all necessary measures' to stop the proliferation of weapons of mass destruction and, recalling an earlier General Comment on the right to life, 'must also respect their international obligations to pursue in good faith negotiations in order to achieve the aim of nuclear disarmament under strict and effective international control'.[2]

15.02 This chapter considers the inter-relationship between the right to life and arms control and disarmament more broadly, encompassing also prohibitions and restrictions on conventional weapons as well as those pertaining to weapons of mass destruction. It offers definitions of both 'arms control' and 'disarmament' in the absence of agreement under international law as to the scope of each term. It then considers obligations under global arms control and disarmament treaties, first with respect to specific weapons of mass destruction and then with respect to conventional weapons. The use of weapons is addressed separately from disarmament duties and other arms control obligations. The relationship between the UN Arms Trade Treaty,[3] and the right to life is accorded further distinct treatment. Controls imposed on weapons at the regional level by treaty or judicial decision are then reviewed.

15.03 The Human Rights Committee also affirmed in its General Comment 36 that 'the development of autonomous weapon systems lacking in human compassion and judgment raises difficult legal and ethical questions concerning the right to life, including

---

[1] International Covenant on Civil and Political Rights; adopted at New York 16 December 1966; entered into force 23 March 1976. As of 1 May 2021, 173 States were party to the ICCPR and a further 6 were signatories.

[2] Human Rights Committee, 'General Comment No. 36: Article 6: right to life', UN doc. CCPR/C/GC/36, 3 September 2019 (hereinafter, Human Rights Committee, General Comment 36 on the right to life), para. 66, citing Human Rights Committee, General Comment No. 14: Article 6 (Right to life), 1984 (hereinafter, Human Rights Committee, General Comment 14 on the right to life), para. 7.

[3] Arms Trade Treaty, adopted at New York 2 April 2013; entered into force 24 December 2014. As of 1 May 2021, 110 States were party to the Treaty.

The Definition of Arms Control and Disarmament

15.04 There is no agreed definition of either 'arms control' or 'disarmament' under international law, although both terms are used widely. The term 'disarmament' has often been used as a generic term for all forms of control on weapons under international law,[5] but disarmament as a discipline is better understood, as it is in this chapter, as more narrowly pertaining to the elimination of weapons, particularly through the destruction of stockpiles. For instance, the North Atlantic Treaty Organization (NATO) defines disarmament as 'the act of eliminating or abolishing weapons (particularly offensive arms) either unilaterally (in the hope that one's example will be followed) or reciprocally. It may refer either to reducing the number of arms, or to eliminating entire categories of weapons.'[6] More narrowly in this chapter, the term *disarmament* is used to denote comprehensive elimination of a weapon, including the destruction of deployed and stockpiled weapons.

15.05 The term 'arms control' was first coined in the 1950s in the context of the arms race between the Soviet Union and the United States.[7] In that context, it was employed to describe ceilings or phased mutual reductions in the level of armaments agreed upon between the two superpowers. Since then, its meaning has evolved to denote the range of restraints short of comprehensive elimination that are imposed under international law upon weapons. Thus it is today a broad term, considerably broader than disarmament, which describes prohibitions and restrictions on the development, production, stockpiling, deployment, testing, transfer, and use of both conventional weapons and weapons of mass destruction.[8] This is how Jozef Goldblat understood the term in his seminal work on arms control, the last edition of which was published in 2002,[9] and it is how it is understood in this chapter. Disarmament is therefore subsumed as a category of arms control.

GLOBAL PROHIBITIONS ON THE USE OF WEAPONS

15.06 The international legal regulation of the use of weapons is fragmented. Prohibitions and restrictions on the use of all weapons in the conduct of hostilities in a situation of

---

[4] Human Rights Committee, General Comment 36 on the right to life, para. 65.
[5] J. Kierulf, *Disarmament under International Law*, Djof Publishing, Denmark, 2017, p. 5.
[6] NATO, 'Arms Control, Disarmament and Non-Proliferation in NATO', last updated 16 March 2020, at http://bit.ly/2ND8I41.
[7] J. Borrie and T. Caughley, 'Viewing Weapons Through a Humanitarian Lens: From Cluster Munitions to Nukes?' *Irish Studies in International Affairs*, vol. 25 (2014), pp. 23–43.
[8] See, e.g., NATO, 'Arms Control, Disarmament and Non-Proliferation in NATO', Last updated 16 March 2020, at http://bit.ly/2ND8I41.
[9] J. Goldblat, *Arms Control: The New Guide to Negotiations and Agreements*, Sage, Thousand Oaks, CA, 2002.

armed conflict are imposed by international humanitarian law.[10] Prohibitions and restrictions on the use of all weapons in law enforcement, which fall outside the scope of application of international humanitarian law, are derived from the interpretation of certain human rights, in particular the right to life and the right to freedom from torture and other forms of cruel, inhuman, or degrading treatment or punishment.[11] There are also comprehensive prohibitions on the use of a small number of specific weapons, applicable at all times and in all circumstances, which are imposed by global disarmament treaties. These concern anti-personnel mines, cluster munitions, and nuclear weapons. As discussed later in this chapter, chemical weapons are an exceptional case in this regard, while the prohibition on the use of biological weapons is implicit.

15.07 According to the Human Rights Committee, 'the threat or use of weapons of mass destruction, ... which are indiscriminate in effect and are of a nature to cause destruction of human life on a catastrophic scale, is incompatible with respect for the right to life and may amount to a crime under international law'.[12] This sweeping statement needs some context and clarification. The term 'weapon of mass destruction' is generally taken to refer to a small group of weapons with a very high lethality rate over a wide area: biological weapons, chemical weapons, and nuclear weapons. It was used in this sense in UN Security Council Resolution 1540, adopted in 2004.[13] The first preambular paragraph affirms that the proliferation of nuclear, chemical, and biological weapons constitutes a threat to international peace and security, while the second refers to the need for all UN member States to prevent the proliferation of all weapons of mass destruction in all its aspects.[14]

15.08 In its *Dictionary of Military and Associated Terms*, the US Department of Defense defines WMD as 'chemical, biological, radiological, or nuclear weapons capable of a high order of destruction or causing mass casualties, excluding the means of transporting or propelling the weapon where such means is a separable and divisible part from the weapon'.[15] This definition excludes toxic chemicals used as 'less-lethal' weapons, particularly tear gas, which do not cause widespread death, although they can certainly be lethal and may violate the right to life.[16] Conventional weapons are generally considered to be defined in the negative as all those that are not designated as weapons of mass destruction.

[10] See, e.g., with respect to all conventional weapons, Arts. 35 and 51(4)(b) and (c), Protocol Additional to the Geneva Conventions of 12 August 1949, and relating to the Protection of Victims of International Armed Conflicts; adopted at Geneva 8 June 1977; entered into force 7 December 1978 (hereinafter, 1977 Additional Protocol I).

[11] 1979 Code of Conduct for Law Enforcement Officials, adopted by UN General Assembly Resolution 34/169, adopted without a vote, 17 December 1979; UN Basic Principles on the Use of Force and Firearms by Law Enforcement Officials, welcomed by the UN General Assembly in its Resolution 45/166, adopted without a vote, 14 December 1990. See also United Nations Human Rights Guidance on Less-Lethal Weapons in Law Enforcement, Office of the UN High Commissioner for Human Rights (OHCHR), New York/Geneva, 2020.

[12] Human Rights Committee, General Comment 36 on the right to life, para. 66.

[13] UN Security Council Resolution 1540, adopted by unanimous vote on 28 April 2004.

[14] Also potentially covered by the term are radiological weapons. These are weapons, sometimes called 'dirty bombs', that use conventional explosives to disperse radiation and may kill significant numbers of people, but which do not involve a nuclear explosion.

[15] US Department of Defense (DOD), *DOD Dictionary of Military and Associated Terms*, January 2020, p. 230.

[16] See on this issue Chapter 7.

15.09 In its affirmation in General Comment 36, the Human Rights Committee refers 'particularly' to nuclear weapons. The capability of nuclear weapons to destroy entire cities, especially those whose explosive yield comparative to conventional explosives is measured in the millions of tons (megatons), is unparalleled in any other weapon as yet devised by humankind. In its General Comment 14, adopted in 1984, the Committee stated: 'It is evident that the designing, testing, manufacture, possession and deployment of nuclear weapons are among the greatest threats to the right to life which confront mankind today. This threat is compounded by the danger that the actual use of such weapons may be brought about, not only in the event of war, but even through human or mechanical error or failure.'[17]

Prohibitions on the Use of Weapons in the Conduct of Hostilities

15.10 The law of armed conflict/international humanitarian law imposes both general and specific prohibitions on the use of weapons in the conduct of hostilities in a situation of armed conflict. Many of these rules are of a customary nature and apply to all weapons, whether conventional in nature or capable of mass destruction. Any use of a weapon that is prohibited by international humanitarian law in the conduct of hostilities, at the least when it results in death, will ordinarily also amount to a violation of the right to life. This is so, because deprivation of life 'is, as a rule, arbitrary if it is inconsistent with international law'.[18]

General Prohibitions on the Use of Weapons

15.11 There are two general prohibitions on the use of weapons under international humanitarian law. Those that are 'of a nature to cause superfluous injury or unnecessary suffering' and those that are 'inherently indiscriminate' may not be used as a means of warfare, whether in international armed conflict or in armed conflict not of an international character (non-international armed conflict). These customary rules apply to conventional weapons and weapons of mass destruction alike.

15.12 The prohibition on use of weapons of a nature to cause superfluous injury or unnecessary suffering was first incorporated as such in the 1977 Additional Protocol I.[19] However, its antecedents trace back to 1868 and the Saint Petersburg Declaration adopted that year, which outlawed the anti-personnel use of exploding bullets in warfare between contracting States.[20] This specific prohibition exists to this day and is reflected in customary law (applicable in all armed conflict).[21] But arguably the Saint Petersburg Declaration is more significant for the fundamental principles of the law of war it espoused. In the

---

[17] Human Rights Committee, General Comment 14 on the right to life, para. 7.
[18] Human Rights Committee, General Comment 36 on the right to life, para. 12.
[19] Art. 35(2), 1977 Additional Protocol I.
[20] Declaration Renouncing the Use, in Time of War, of Explosive Projectiles Under 400 Grammes Weight; adopted at Saint Petersburg 11 December 1868; entered into force the same day.
[21] International Committee of the Red Cross (ICRC) Customary IHL Rule 78: 'Exploding Bullets', at http://bit.ly/2EpZ5Hi.

preamble to the Declaration, it was stipulated that the only 'legitimate object' that States should endeavour to accomplish through warfare is 'to weaken the military forces of the enemy'. This is, the Declaration affirms, an objective that 'would be exceeded by the employment of arms which uselessly aggravate the sufferings of disabled men, or render their death inevitable'. The first of these principles reflects civilian immunity from attack (a notion that would not be incorporated in a binding international humanitarian law treaty for another century), while the second prohibits weapons that inflict gratuitous harm on soldiers.

15.13 Thus the human focus of protection of the second principle are combatants, constituting one of the rare international humanitarian law rules that protect soldiers while they are directly participating in hostilities. In addition to violating international humanitarian law, using a weapon that is of a nature to cause superfluous injury or unnecessary suffering against a combatant[22] may also violate his or her right to life.[23] This is so, potentially even if death does not ultimately result.[24] Of course, any use of such illegal weapons against civilians would similarly be prohibited.

15.14 The principle of civilian immunity from attack also evoked by the Saint Petersburg Declaration – the principle of distinction – is not only of a customary nature but is likewise also a norm of jus cogens. That 'the basic rules of international humanitarian law' are peremptory norms of international law was reiterated by the International Law Commission in its study of the question, which it submitted to the UN General Assembly in 2019.[25] According to the 'Basic Rule' in the 1977 Additional Protocol I, 'in order to ensure respect for and protection of the civilian population and civilian objects, the Parties to the conflict shall at all times distinguish between the civilian population and combatants and between civilian objects and military objectives and accordingly shall direct their operations only against military objectives'.[26]

15.15 The prohibition on inherently indiscriminate weapons in international humanitarian law, which derives from the principle of distinction, was also first incorporated as such in the 1977 Additional Protocol I. Therein it is stipulated that indiscriminate attacks are prohibited.[27] Such attacks, the Protocol stipulates, include those which employ a means of combat that 'cannot be directed at a specific military objective' and those that employ a means of combat 'the effects of which cannot be limited' and are, in each case, 'of

---

[22] See, e.g., Weapons Law Encyclopedia, 'Superfluous Injury or Unnecessary Suffering', LAST updated 30 November 2013, Geneva Academy of International Humanitarian Law and Human Rights, at http://bit.ly/3lnvpeQ.
[23] A lawful reprisal using a prohibited weapon, in response to and with a view to ending an earlier serious violation of international humanitarian law, may exceptionally not violate that body of law. See on this issue, e.g., S. Casey-Maslen with S. Haines, *Hague Law Interpreted: The Conduct of Hostilities under the Law of Armed Conflict*, Hart, Oxford, 2018, chap. 15, sect. III.
[24] See on this issue *supra* Paragraphs 2.14–2.19.
[25] Annex to the text of the draft conclusions on peremptory norms of general international law (jus cogens), adopted by the ILC on first reading, in UN doc. A/74/10, 2019, at http://bit.ly/3hwjqJk, point (d).
[26] Art. 48, 1977 Additional Protocol I.
[27] Art. 51(4), 1977 Additional Protocol I.

a nature to strike military objectives and civilians or civilian objects without distinction'.[28] These two rules identify the scope of the prohibition on inherently indiscriminate weapons: either a weapon cannot be targeted with sufficient accuracy (such as an early variant of the Scud missile or some improvised rockets used in armed conflicts in Bosnia and Herzegovina or Palestine) or its effects cannot be limited in time and space (as is the case with biological weapons). In either case, the weapon is inherently indiscriminate and may never be used in the conduct of hostilities. International humanitarian law reiterates: 'In any armed conflict, the right of the Parties to the conflict to choose methods or means of warfare is not unlimited.'[29]

Specific Prohibitions on the Use of Weapons

15.16 Most of the customary prohibitions on specific weapons as a means of warfare can be linked to either of the general prohibitions or, in a number of instances, to both. Those whose use is comprehensively prohibited on the basis that they are of a nature to cause superfluous injury or unnecessary suffering are, in addition to exploding bullets, expanding bullets[30] and blinding laser weapons.[31] Those whose use is comprehensively prohibited on the basis that they are inherently indiscriminate are, as noted previously, biological weapons[32] and early Scud missiles (the R-11 Zemlya),[33] modified air bombs used against Bosnian forces in Sarajevo in the early 1990s,[34] as well as a number of rockets fired by Palestinian forces during the 2014 Gaza conflict (Fajr-5, J-80, M75, and R-160).[35]

15.17 Those whose specific prohibition, first in treaty law and then in customary law, can be ascribed to both general prohibitions are, most notably, chemical weapons[36] and poison (and poisoned weapons)[37]. The original prohibition on the use of 'projectiles the sole object of which is the diffusion of asphyxiating or deleterious gases' was incorporated in

---

[28] Art. 51(4)(b) and (c), 1977 Additional Protocol I.
[29] Art. 35(1), 1977 Additional Protocol I. This is a distinct customary rule even though it was not recognised as such by the ICRC in its study of customary international humanitarian law, published in 2005.
[30] According to ICRC Customary IHL Rule 77 ('Expanding Bullets'), '[t]he use of bullets which expand or flatten easily in the human body is prohibited'. At http://bit.ly/3gvLivK. It may be, but is not certain, that the United States is in a position to claim persistent objector status to this rule.
[31] According to ICRC Customary IHL Rule 86 ('Blinding Laser Weapons'), '[t]he use of laser weapons that are specifically designed, as their sole combat function or as one of their combat functions, to cause permanent blindness to unenhanced vision is prohibited'. At http://bit.ly/2FYEhau.
[32] According to ICRC Customary IHL Rule 73 ('Biological Weapons'), '[t]he use of biological weapons is prohibited'. At http://bit.ly/2HaDz7i. It is arguable that the original treaty prohibition of 'bacteriological methods of warfare' in 1925 was motivated also by a desire to spare combatants. Protocol for the Prohibition of the Use of Asphyxiating, Poisonous or Other Gases, and of Bacteriological Methods of Warfare, adopted at Geneva 17 June 1925; entry into force 8 February 1928.
[33] Casey-Maslen, *Hague Law Interpreted: The Conduct of Hostilities under the Law of Armed Conflict*, p. 21.
[34] ICTY, *Prosecutor v. Dragomir Milošević*, Judgment (Trial Chamber III) (Case No IT-98-29/1-T), 12 December 2007, paras. 92, 93, 97.
[35] Report of the detailed findings of the independent commission of inquiry established pursuant to Human Rights Council Resolution S-21/1, UN Doc A/HRC/29/CRP.4, 22 June 2015, para. 97.
[36] According to ICRC Customary IHL Rule 74 ('Chemical Weapons'), '[t]he use of chemical weapons is prohibited'. At http://bit.ly/2UHjYDz.
[37] According to ICRC Customary IHL Rule 72 ('Poison and Poisoned Weapons'), '[t]he use of poison or poisoned weapons is prohibited'. At http://bit.ly/2Xhoc4m.

1899 Hague Declaration IV,2.[38] In concluding the agreement, the negotiating States declared in the preamble that they were 'inspired by the sentiments which found expression in the Declaration of Saint Petersburg'. The indiscriminate nature of chemical weapons and poison, however, also helps explain their comprehensive prohibition as a means or method of warfare.

15.18 Any use in the conduct of hostilities of biological weapons, blinding laser weapons, chemical weapons, expanding or exploding bullets, or the use of any inherently indiscriminate weapons will violate international humanitarian law. It will also violate the right to life (or at least, if the injuries to a survivor are not life-threatening, the prohibition on inhumane treatment in international human rights law). In most instances, use will also amount to an international crime. Under the Rome Statute of the International Criminal Court[39] (Rome Statute), the following are punishable as war crimes under the jurisdiction of the Court:

> Employing weapons which use microbial or other biological agents, or toxins, whatever their origin or method of production (biological weapons)[40]
> Employing asphyxiating, poisonous or other gases, and all analogous liquids, materials, or devices (chemical weapons)[41]
> Employing bullets which expand or flatten easily in the human body, such as bullets with a hard envelope which does not entirely cover the core or is pierced with incisions (expanding bullets)[42]
> Employing poison or poisoned weapons[43]
> Employing laser weapons specifically designed, as their sole combat function or as one of their combat functions, to cause permanent blindness to unenhanced vision – that is, to the naked eye or to the eye with corrective eyesight devices (blinding laser weapons)[44]

A further war crime in the Rome Statute prohibiting weapons whose *primary* effect is to injure by fragments undetectable by X-rays in the human body[45] criminalises the use of an illegal weapon that does not exist and has never done so. Many weapons, of course, have such secondary effects.

---

[38] Declaration (IV,2) concerning Asphyxiating Gases; adopted at The Hague 29 July 1899; entered into force 4 September 1900.
[39] Rome Statute of the International Criminal Court; adopted at Rome 17 July 1998; entered into force 1 July 2002.
[40] Art. 8(2)(b)(xxvii) and (2)(e)(xvi), ICC Statute, applicable in international and non-international armed conflict, respectively.
[41] Art. 8(2)(b)(xviii) and (2)(e)(xiv), ICC Statute, applicable in international and non-international armed conflict, respectively.
[42] Art. 8(2)(b)(xix) and (2)(e)(xv), ICC Statute, applicable in international and non-international armed conflict, respectively.
[43] Art. 8(2)(b)(xvii) and (2)(e)(xiii), ICC Statute, applicable in international and non-international armed conflict, respectively.
[44] Art. 8(2)(b)(xxix) and Art. 8(2)(e)(xviii), ICC Statute, applicable in international and non-international armed conflict, respectively.
[45] Art. 8(2)(b)(xxviii) and Art. 8(2)(e)(xvii), ICC Statute, applicable in international and non-international armed conflict, respectively.

Prohibitions on the Use of Weapons in Law Enforcement

15.19 Few non-explosive weapons are comprehensively prohibited for use in law enforcement. Indeed, two whose use is outlawed as a means of warfare may legitimately be used in law enforcement under the relevant rules and conditions:[46] tear gas (a chemical weapon used as a means of riot control to disperse violent gatherings)[47] and expanding bullets, which are used routinely by many law enforcement agencies in order to minimise the risk to bystanders.[48]

15.20 Set out in the 2020 UN Human Rights Guidance on Less-Lethal Weapons, the following non-exhaustive list identifies less-lethal weapons and related equipment whose anti-personnel use would inevitably violate international human rights law:

- Spiked batons
- Blinding laser weapons
- Directed energy weapons liable to cause serious injury[49]

These less-lethal weapons have no legitimate role or purpose in law enforcement and therefore are inherently inhumane. Depending on the circumstances, their use in law enforcement might also fall to be considered under the right to life. The use of blinding laser weapons is also unlawful in the conduct of hostilities in armed conflict.

15.21 Among lethal weapons, few may ever be used lawfully in law enforcement. Landmines, for instance, have no legitimate role. In the past, they were used by certain States to prevent smuggling,[50] though such conduct by a State clearly violates the right to life. While firearms may be used in exceptional circumstances, for instance where strictly necessary to confront an imminent threat of death or serious injury, rounds may be discharged only in semi-automatic mode. The use of firearms in burst or fully automatic mode will not be lawful in law enforcement operations.[51] In its General Comment 37 on the right of peaceful assembly, adopted in July 2020, the Human Rights Committee stated: 'It is never lawful to fire indiscriminately or to use firearms in fully automatic mode when policing an assembly.'[52]

GLOBAL DISARMAMENT OBLIGATIONS

15.22 Strictly speaking, there are only five global disarmament treaties. These concern biological weapons, chemical weapons, and, most recently, nuclear weapons, as well as,

---

[46] See on these issues Chapter 7.
[47] Human Rights Committee, General Comment No. 37: Article 21: right of peaceful assembly, UN doc. CCPR/C/GC/37, 27 July 2020 (hereinafter, General Comment 37 on the right of peaceful assembly), para. 87.
[48] Expanding ammunition, such as soft-point or hollow-point bullets, expand and deposit more kinetic energy in the body they first strike thereby reducing the risks of overpenetration.
[49] *United Nations Human Rights Guidance on Less-Lethal Weapons in Law Enforcement*, OHCHR, New York/Geneva, 2020, para. 5.1.
[50] See, e.g., Associated Press, 'Assad Troops Plant Land Mines on Syria-Lebanon Border', *Haaretz*, 1 November 2011, at http://bit.ly/2QrOlKS.
[51] See on this issue Chapter 7.
[52] Human Rights Committee, General Comment 37 on the right of peaceful assembly, para. 88.

Biological Weapons

15.23 The 1971 Convention on the Prohibition of the Development, Production and Stockpiling of Bacteriological (Biological) and Toxin Weapons and on Their Destruction was adopted on 16 December 1971 and entered into force on 26 March 1975. The Convention was based on the longstanding treaty law prohibition on bacteriological warfare in situations of international armed conflict, adopted in 1925. This early prohibition is cited in the Preamble to the Biological Weapons Convention. As of 1 May 2021, 183 of the total of 197 States recognised by the UN Secretary-General were party to the Biological Weapons Convention. Four other States were signatories (Egypt, Haiti, Somalia, and Syria), while ten had still to sign (Chad, Comoros, Djibouti, Eritrea, Israel, Kiribati, Micronesia, Namibia, South Sudan, and Tuvalu).

15.24 The preamble to the 1971 Convention notes the determination of the States Parties, 'for the sake of all mankind, to exclude completely the possibility of bacteriological (biological) agents and toxins being used as weapons'. The States Parties further declare 'that such use would be repugnant to the conscience of mankind and that no effort should be spared to minimise this risk'. Under Article I, States Parties undertake never in any circumstances to 'develop, produce, stockpile or otherwise acquire or retain' biological weapons. Thus, despite the preambular paragraphs, the Convention does not explicitly prohibit use. In 1996, however, the Final Declaration of the Fourth Review Conference of the Convention clarified that use is 'effectively prohibited under Article I of the Convention'.[54]

15.25 Although the ICRC customary rule prohibiting use of biological weapons applies to situations of armed conflict, any use of biological weapons in any circumstances, including peacetime, would amount to a serious violation of international law. Biological agents include anthrax, botulinum toxin, tularaemia, plague, Q fever, ricin, smallpox, and staphylococcal toxins.

15.26 A prohibition on transfer is contained in a dedicated provision separate from the other general undertakings. Under Article III of the Convention, each State Party

---

[53] According to the 1969 Vienna Convention on the Law of Treaties, a treaty 'does not create either obligations or rights for a third State without its consent'. Art. 34, Vienna Convention on the Law of Treaties; adopted at Vienna 23 May 1969; entered into force 27 January 1980. As of 1 May 2021, 116 States were party to the Convention. Most of its provisions, however, codify customary law, including this fundamental rule of the law of treaties.

[54] Fourth Review Conference of the Parties to the 1971 Biological Weapons Convention, Geneva, 25 November–6 December 1996, UN doc. BWC/CONF.4/9, Final Declaration, Commentary on Article I, para. 3.

Arms Control and Disarmament

'undertakes not to transfer to any recipient whatsoever, directly or indirectly ... any of the agents, toxins, weapons, equipment or means of delivery' set out in Article I. Any such prohibited transfer would not only amount to a violation of the Convention; it would also violate the customary law of arms control. In its Resolution 1540 (2004), the UN Security Council affirmed that the proliferation of biological weapons or their means of delivery constitutes a threat to international peace and security.[55] A transfer to another State which then used a biological weapon resulting in a fatality would constitute a violation of the right to life not only by the State that used it but, potentially, also by the transferring State.[56]

15.27 It is not prohibited to transfer biological agents or toxins where they are of appropriate types and quantities for prophylactic, protective, or other peaceful purposes. The wording of the exception in Article I is reinforced in Article X(1), according to which States Parties 'undertake to facilitate, and have the right to participate in, the fullest possible exchange of equipment, materials, and scientific and technological information for the use of bacteriological (biological) agents and toxins for peaceful purposes'. The term 'exchange' encompasses transfers, including of relevant vaccines and antibiotics, and related research.

Chemical Weapons

15.28 The 1992 Convention on the Prohibition of the Development, Production, Stockpiling and Use of Chemical Weapons and on Their Destruction was adopted by the Conference on Disarmament in Geneva on 3 September 1992, entering into force on 29 April 1997.[57] The improvement in superpower relations in the late 1980s, the chemical attack by Saddam Hussein's regime on the Kurds in Halabja in 1988, the publicity given to the threat of chemical warfare during the Gulf War, and a bilateral US–Soviet agreement to refrain from further production and to destroy most of their chemical weapons stockpiles 'all gave impetus to the Convention negotiations'.[58]

15.29 After its formal adoption by the Conference on Disarmament, the Chemical Weapons Convention was opened for signature on 13 January 1993 in Paris. During the three-day signing conference, 130 States signed the Convention, a record for a disarmament treaty. As of 1 May 2021, 193 States were party to the Convention, leaving only the Democratic People's Republic of Korea, Egypt, Israel (a signatory), and South

---

[55] UN Security Council Resolution 1540 (2004), adopted by unanimous vote on 28 April 2004, first preambular para.
[56] Whether the transferring State had also violated the right to life would depend on whether it had cause to suspect that the agent it was transferring would be so used as a weapon.
[57] As noted previously, the use of certain chemical agents as a means of warfare, such as chlorine or sulphur mustard, had first been prohibited almost one hundred years earlier, at the First Hague Peace Conference in 1899. But it failed to prevent massive use of chemical weapons in the First World War, despite the main protagonists (Belgium, France, Germany, and the United Kingdom, among others) all being party to it.
[58] Organisation for the Prohibition of Chemical Weapons (OPCW), 'Origins of the Chemical Weapons Convention and the OPCW', Fact Sheet No. 1, The Hague, November 2017, at http://bit.ly/2U3Bwt6, p. 2.

Sudan as States which were not party. The Chemical Weapons Convention is the most widely ratified arms control and disarmament treaty in history.

15.30 Under Article I(1) of the Convention, chemical weapons mean the following: toxic chemicals and their precursors, munitions and devices specifically designed to cause death or other harm through the toxic properties of those toxic chemicals, and equipment specifically designed for use directly in connection with the employment of those munitions and devices. Under Article II(1), toxic chemicals are defined as any chemical 'which through its chemical action on life processes can cause death, temporary incapacitation or permanent harm to humans or animals', while precursors are 'any chemical reactant which takes part at any stage in the production by whatever method of a toxic chemical. This includes any key component of a binary or multicomponent chemical system.'

15.31 Excluded from the scope of the definition are toxic chemicals where they are intended for purposes not prohibited under the Convention, as long as the types and quantities of those chemicals 'are consistent with such purposes'. Purposes not prohibited include industrial, agricultural, research, medical, and pharmaceutical activities, as well as those directly related to protection against toxic chemicals and chemical weapons. This excludes from the scope of the prohibition, among others, all research and development of chemicals and their precursors, as long as this is dedicated to peaceful purposes.

15.32 Under Article I(1) of the Convention, each State Party undertakes never under any circumstances:

(a) To develop, produce, otherwise acquire, stockpile or retain chemical weapons, or transfer, directly or indirectly, chemical weapons to anyone;
(b) To use chemical weapons;
(c) To engage in any military preparations to use chemical weapons;
(d) To assist, encourage or induce, in any way, anyone to engage in any activity prohibited to a State Party under this Convention.

In addition to these broad prohibitions, the use of riot control agents (e.g., tear gas) as a method of warfare is explicitly outlawed.[59] That said, the use of certain chemical agents, including riot control agents, for the purpose of law enforcement – as long as their types and quantities are consistent with such use – is not prohibited. The Chemical Weapons Convention is the only disarmament law treaty to have such an exemption for law enforcement.[60]

15.33 The prohibition on transfer, directly or indirectly, of chemical weapons to anyone renders illegal any export of chemical weapons (importation is covered by the prohibition on acquisition). The ban on indirect transfer outlaws the export of parts and components of chemical weapons, particularly prohibited toxic chemicals and their precursors. In its Resolution 1540 (2004), the UN Security Council affirmed that the proliferation of chemical weapons or their means of delivery constitutes a threat to international peace

[59] Art. I(5), Chemical Weapons Convention.
[60] Art. II(9)(d), Chemical Weapons Convention.

and security.[61] The undertaking never under any circumstances to assist, encourage or induce, in any way, anyone is said to outlaw 'any action which contributes to prohibited activities'.[62]

15.34 Toxic chemicals under the Chemical Weapons Convention include mustard gas, phosgene, ricin, sarin, and VX (venomous agent X). These are set out in Schedules to the Convention. Also addressed are precursors, which comprise, for instance, chlorosarin (for the production of sarin) and methylphosphonyl difluorides (used to produce sarin and soman as a binary chemical weapon). Such agents must be destroyed where they have no legitimate peaceful purpose or, at the least, strictly controlled (very small samples may be retained in certain circumstances for the development of vaccines or antidotes). The standard method for the destruction of toxic chemicals is closed incineration in specially designed chambers.[63]

15.35 Chlorine, which is not a scheduled toxic chemical, is widely used to disinfect tap water, and it is therefore lawful to store and sell it for such purposes. Nonetheless, chlorine can be used as a chemical weapon and even at low concentrations can inflict permanent lung damage.[64] Chlorine was first used in warfare by German forces in the First World War, in which one-third of the 15,000 soldiers subjected to the 1915 gas attack near the town of Ypres died. In Syria, an Organisation for the Prohibition of Chemical Weapons (OPCW)[65] fact-finding mission investigating the use of chlorine gas in June 2014 concluded that the chemical agent had been used not only in that instance but also in earlier attacks.[66]

15.36 In 2015, UN Security Council Resolution 2209 condemned the use of chlorine in attacks in Syria, noting that this was the 'first ever documented instance of the use of toxic chemicals as weapons within the territory' of a State Party to the Chemical Weapons Convention. This was not only a violation of IHL but also a war crime and potentially also a crime against humanity. If, indeed, the Syrian armed forces were responsible, it also amounted to a violation of the right to life by Syria.

15.37 In March 2018, Russian operatives attempted to assassinate a Russian military intelligence defector resident in the United Kingdom using a toxic chemical agent – Novichok. The UK government claimed that this had violated the customary law prohibition on inter-State use of force codified in Article 2(4) of the UN Charter.[67] This was also

---

[61] UN Security Council Resolution 1540 (2004), adopted by unanimous vote 28 April 2004, first preambular para.
[62] W. Krutzsch and R. Trapp, *A Commentary on the Chemical Weapons Convention*, Martinus Nijhoff, The Netherlands, 1994, p. 15.
[63] S. Casey-Maslen and T. Vestner, *A Guide to International Disarmament Law*, Routledge, United Kingdom, 2019, para. 7.39.
[64] See, e.g., 'Syria Chlorine Attack Claims: What This Chemical Is and How It Became a Weapon', *The Conversation*, 7 September 2016, at http://bit.ly/2zjSzvp.
[65] The OPCW was established by the Chemical Weapons Convention to monitor and ensure its implementation.
[66] OPCW, 'OPCW Fact Finding Mission: "Compelling Confirmation" That Chlorine Gas Used as Weapon in Syria', The Hague, 10 September 2014, at http://bit.ly/2JzTbSe.
[67] 'Salisbury Incident', Statement by the Prime Minister (Mrs Theresa May), in *Hansard* HC Vol 637 (14 March 2018), at http://bit.ly/2Q8OhL.

the first use by one State Party of a prohibited chemical agent on the territory of another and was in clear violation of the Chemical Weapons Convention. It constituted a violation of the right to life by Russia with respect to Mr Sergei Skripal, his daughter Yulia, a police officer Detective Sergeant Nick Bailey (all of whom survived but were fortunate to do so), and Ms Dawn Sturgess (who died).[68] The United Kingdom could have launched an inter-State case under Article 33 of the European Convention on Human Rights with a view to securing justice for the victims, but chose not to do so.

Anti-personnel Mines

15.38 The Convention on the Prohibition of the Use, Stockpiling, Production, and Transfer of Anti-Personnel Mines and on their Destruction was the first disarmament treaty to be concluded that comprehensively outlawed a conventional weapon. Adopted by a specially convened diplomatic conference in Oslo on 18 September 1997, the Anti-Personnel Mine Ban Convention entered into force on 1 March 1999.

15.39 The proxy wars of the Cold War and the national liberation struggles for decolonisation had seen widespread use of anti-personnel mines, with landmines used by both regular armed forces and non-state armed groups. Many types of anti-personnel mines were designed to maim military personnel rather than to kill them, so additional human resources would be taken up with the transportation of casualties for medical attention. In fact, very often civilians were the victims (and sometimes the targets). In 1994, the International Committee of the Red Cross (ICRC) estimated, on the basis of its field data and that of other humanitarian organisations, that an average of two thousand people each month were being killed or injured by anti-personnel mines, terming the global problem of mine injuries 'an epidemic'.[69]

15.40 In contrast to the Biological and Chemical Weapons Conventions, however, there was no prior comprehensive prohibition of the use of anti-personnel mines. At the time, the international legal regulation of the use of landmines was set out in a protocol annexed to an international humanitarian law treaty adopted under UN auspices in 1980. The Convention on Certain Conventional Weapons (CCW)[70] had a series of Protocols attached to it. The Protocol on Prohibitions or Restrictions on the Use of Mines, Booby-Traps and Other Devices (CCW Protocol II) prohibited the targeting of civilians using anti-personnel (or anti-vehicle) mines, as well as their indiscriminate use, but this merely reaffirmed treaty and customary rules on the conduct of hostilities, and specifically the

---

[68] BBC, 'Novichok Victim Dawn Sturgess' Daughter Challenges Coroner', 14 July 2020, at http://bbc.in/31yv6Wk.
[69] ICRC, 'Anti-personnel Mines: Overview of the Problem', FAQ, Geneva, 2 November 2009, at http://bit.ly/2TscIt7.
[70] Convention on Prohibitions or Restrictions on the Use of Certain Conventional Weapons Which May Be Deemed to Be Excessively Injurious or to Have Indiscriminate Effects; adopted at Geneva 10 October 1980; entered into force 2 December 1983. As of 1 May 2021, a total of 125 States were party to the CCW.

application of the principle of distinction.[71] Moreover, the Protocol did not apply to non-international armed conflicts, in the context of which the overwhelming majority of anti-personnel mines were being used in the early 1990s.

15.41 The First Review Conference of the CCW saw the adoption of an amended Protocol II that tightened restrictions on anti-personnel mines (and extended the Protocol's scope of application to non-international armed conflicts) but still fell considerably short of the total prohibition that an increasing number of States were seeking.[72] At the closing of the Conference on 3 May 1996, Canada invited other interested States to come to Ottawa that autumn in order to discuss the path towards a total global prohibition on anti-personnel mines. The International Strategy Conference: Towards a Global Ban on Anti-Personnel Mines was held in Ottawa on 3–5 October 1996. In the final session, Canada's Minister of Foreign Affairs, Lloyd Axworthy, surprised assembled States by inviting them to return to Ottawa before the end of 1997 to sign a treaty comprehensively outlawing anti-personnel mines. Minister Axworthy's initiative would become known as the Ottawa Process.

15.42 The negotiation of the Anti-Personnel Mine Ban Convention was therefore a stand-alone process outside the Conference on Disarmament that had successfully negotiated and adopted the Chemical Weapons Convention in 1992. The Conference on Disarmament took decisions by consensus, which would have precluded the negotiation of a total prohibition, and in any event, was deadlocked following the disputed conclusion of the Comprehensive Nuclear-Test-Ban Treaty (CTBT) in 1996.[73] Overcoming opposition by the United States to a comprehensive prohibition on all anti-personnel mines in all circumstances, on 18 September 1997 the ninety negotiating States concluded the Anti-Personnel Mine Ban Convention at a specially convened diplomatic conference in Oslo.[74] Its core obligations were largely modelled on the Chemical Weapons Convention, but it went beyond that Convention's narrow disarmament focus to also institute obligations to conduct mine clearance within specified deadlines[75] and, indirectly, to assist mine victims.[76]

15.43 The Convention has attracted widespread adherence, with 164 States Parties as of 1 May 2021. That said, key military States remain formally outside its purview, notably China, India, Pakistan, the Russian Federation, and the United States. Moreover, while most States not party have refrained from the use of anti-personnel mines in recent years,

---

[71] Arts. 3(2) and (3), Protocol on Prohibitions or Restrictions on the Use of Mines, Booby-Traps and Other Devices; adopted at Geneva 10 October 1980; entered into force 2 December 1983.
[72] The Conference also adopted the treaty prohibition on blinding laser weapons, in 1995, in CCW Protocol IV.
[73] The CTBT was drafted in the Conference on Disarmament but could not be adopted as a result of opposition by India. The text of the treaty was forwarded by Australia to the UN General Assembly where it was adopted by 158 votes to 3 (Bhutan, India, and Libya), with 5 abstentions.
[74] ICRC, *The Ottawa Treaty Explained*, Geneva, 1998, available at http://bit.ly/31Cq4IN, p. 4.
[75] Under Article 5 of the Convention, each State must complete clearance of mined areas containing anti-personnel mines located on territory anywhere under its jurisdiction or control within ten years of becoming a party to the Convention.
[76] Under Article 6(3), 'Each State Party in a position to do so shall provide assistance for the care and rehabilitation, and social and economic reintegration, of mine victims.' There is thus no obligation on each State Party to assist victims located on territory anywhere under its jurisdiction or control.

at the end of January 2020, the United States announced a major reversal of its policy on landmines, declaring that their use outside the Korean peninsula would now be possible.[77] Accordingly, the prohibition on the use of anti-personnel mines in the Convention does not yet constitute a customary rule, though it is *de lege ferenda*. This means that while a State Party to the Convention that uses anti-personnel mines that kill or seriously injure any person will violate not only the Convention itself but likely also the right to life, the same is not necessarily true for a State not party. Jurisprudence on this issue in the European Court of Human Rights is discussed later in this chapter.

15.44 During the lifetime of the Convention – twenty-one years since it entered into force as of this writing – the treaty prohibition on new use has been violated by at least one State Party: Yemen. In 2011–12, at Bani Jarmooz (a location north of the capital, Sana'a), Yemen's armed forces used anti-personnel mines during the uprising that led to the ousting of then-president Ali Abdullah Saleh. In November 2013, the office of Yemen's prime minister admitted that a 'violation' of the Convention had occurred in 2011.[78] This was not only a violation of the Anti-Personnel Mine Ban Convention but also a violation of the duty to respect and protect life. Yemen is a State Party to the 2004 Arab Charter on Human Rights.[79] Article 5(1) of the Charter stipulates that every human being has an inherent right to life. According to paragraph 2, the right 'shall be protected by law. No one shall be arbitrarily deprived of his life'.

15.45 In addition, serious accusations of use by State armed forces have been levelled at States Parties South Sudan,[80] Turkey,[81] and Ukraine.[82] In its monitoring report, issued towards the end of 2019, the International Campaign to Ban Landmines's (ICBL's) *Landmine Monitor* publication stated that there had been no allegations of use of anti-personnel mines by States Parties over the last three years and that only two States not party (Myanmar and Syria) had used anti-personnel mines.[83] Indiscriminate use by those two States is a violation of the right to life with respect to anyone killed or seriously injured as a result.

---

[77] N. Egel, 'The Trump Administration Approved the U.S. Use of Land Mines. That's a Step Back for Global Campaigns to Ban Their Deployment', *Washington Post*, 11 February 2020, at http://wapo.st/2UjRzmB.

[78] Human Rights Watch, 'Memo to Delegates: Yemen's Compliance with the Mine Ban Treaty: The Case of Bani Jarmooz', 8 April 2014 at http://bit.ly/32D3zSA.

[79] Arab Charter on Human Rights; adopted at Tunis 22 May 2004; entered into force 15 March 2008.

[80] International Campaign to Ban Landmines (ICBL), 'Concern at Reported Use of Antipersonnel Mines in South Sudan: South Sudanese Authorities Should Confirm or Deny the Claimed Use of Antipersonnel Mines', 31 March 2015, at http://bit.ly/2JVspW3.

[81] See, e.g., ICBL, 'Spotlight on Turkey', 19 February 2014, at http://bit.ly/38cKB6L.

[82] In 2016, the OHCHR reported that the Ukrainian armed forces had used anti-personnel mines. OHCHR, 'Report on the Human Rights Situation in Ukraine 16 February to 15 May 2016', at http://bit.ly/2IldoNv, para. 14. In contrast, the ICBL's Landmine Monitor stated in 2019 that it 'has received no credible information that Ukrainian government forces used antipersonnel mines in violation of the Mine Ban Treaty since 2014 and into 2019'. Landmine Monitor, 'Ukraine: Mine Ban Policy', last updated 7 October 2019, at http://bit.ly/398O33o.

[83] *Landmine Monitor Report 2019*, ICBL – Cluster Munition Coalition (CMC), Geneva, 2019, at http://bit.ly/2x1jSgr, p. 8.

Cluster Munitions

15.46 Cluster munitions were developed and used in the Second World War. But it was their use on an unprecedented scale by the United States during the Vietnam War, especially during its bombing of the Lao People's Democratic Republic (Laos), where 260 million submunitions were dropped over the country, that marked out the weapons as being especially hazardous to civilians. Also heavily affected were – and still are – Cambodia and Vietnam. More recently, Soviet forces used air-dropped and rocket-delivered cluster munitions on a wide scale in Afghanistan in the 1980s. Israel fired several million submunitions into southern Lebanon during its invasion of the country in 2006. These explosive munitions are designed to kill personnel or destroy vehicles, including tanks. Whereas anti-personnel mines are often designed to maim, submunitions are typically designed to kill.

15.47 In 1974, a group of countries led by Sweden had called for the prohibition of a number of anti-personnel weapons including 'cluster warheads', and these proposals were subsequently discussed in the diplomatic conferences that resulted in the two 1977 Additional Protocols to the Geneva Conventions and the CCW. When the CCW was adopted in 1980, however, it contained no measures on cluster munitions. The renewed use of the weapons in Afghanistan in 2001–2, this time by the United States, and then in Iraq in 2003, underlined problems associated with the accuracy and reliability of a weapon intended to saturate areas with explosive force, and increased disquiet among national policy-makers in a number of States Parties to the CCW.[84] Israel's use in Lebanon proved to be a tipping point in the decisions by many States.

15.48 In a process led by Norway, the Convention on Cluster Munitions was adopted in Dublin on 30 May 2008, entering into force on 1 August 2010. As was the case with the Anti-Personnel Mine Ban Convention, the 2008 Convention on Cluster Munitions was negotiated at an ad hoc diplomatic conference convened outside UN auspices, as agreement to prohibit those weapons within the CCW's consensus-based framework proved impossible. As of 1 May 2021, 110 States were party to the Convention on Cluster Munitions.

15.49 Similar to the 1997 Anti-Personnel Mine Ban Convention, States adhering to the Convention on Cluster Munitions must never under any circumstances use, develop, produce, acquire, stockpile, retain, or transfer cluster munitions. They are also generally prohibited from assisting, encouraging, or inducing anyone to undertake any activity prohibited by its provisions. None of these prohibitions has yet crystallised as customary law.

15.50 The Convention on Cluster Munitions defines a cluster munition as 'a conventional munition that is designed to disperse or release explosive submunitions each weighing less than 20 kilograms, and includes those explosive submunitions'.[85] Cluster munitions are typically deployed by aircraft or artillery with a canister or dispenser that disperses explosive submunitions. The Convention applies also to explosive bomblets that are specifically

---

[84] V. Wiebe, J. Borrie, and D. Smyth, 'Introduction', in G. Nystuen and S. Casey-Maslen (eds.), *The Convention on Cluster Munitions: A Commentary*, Oxford University Press, Oxford, 2010, paras. 0.21, 0.22.
[85] Art. 2(2), Convention on Cluster Munitions.

designed to be dispersed or released directly from dispensers fixed to aircraft.[86] All landmines are excluded from the scope of the Convention on Cluster Munitions, as are munitions or submunitions designed to dispense flares, smoke, pyrotechnics, or chaff, as well as munitions or submunitions designed to produce electrical or electronic effects.[87]

15.51 There have been no serious allegations of the use of cluster munitions by any State Party to the Convention. States not party, however, in particular Saudi Arabia and possibly also other members of its erstwhile coalition with the United Arab Emirates against Houthi forces, have used cluster munitions in the armed conflicts in Yemen. Human Rights Watch has stated that it has recorded Saudi air strikes using cluster munitions dating back to 2009.[88] In December 2016, the organisation reported that eighteen coalition attacks using cluster munitions since 2015 had killed at least eighteen civilians and injured seventy-four more.[89] As of writing, air strikes using cluster munitions by the Saudi-led coalition have been recorded since May 2017.[90]

15.52 On 17 December 2009, the United States used at least five ship- or submarine-launched cruise missiles, each containing 166 BLU-97 submunitions, in an attack on al-Ma'jalah in Yemen's southern Abyan governorate that killed 55 people, including 41 civilians. Amnesty International published a series of photographs showing the remnants of the cruise missile, including the propulsion system, a BLU-97 submunition, and the payload ejection system, the latter of which is unique to the TLAM-D cruise missile.[91] These attacks in Yemen involved manifold violations of the right to life by, at least, Saudi Arabia and the United States.

Nuclear Weapons

15.53 Nuclear weapons are comprehensively prohibited by the 2017 Treaty on the Prohibition of Nuclear Weapons. The Treaty, which was adopted by a UN diplomatic conference in New York on 7 July 2017, entered into force on 22 January 2021, following its ratification by fifty States. The Treaty prohibits not just the use of nuclear weapons and other nuclear explosive devices[92] but also any threatening to

---

[86] Art. 1(2), Convention on Cluster Munitions.
[87] Art 2(2)(a) and (b), Convention on Cluster Munitions.
[88] Human Rights Watch, 'Yemen: Cluster Munitions Harm Civilians', 31 May 2015, at http://bit.ly/32sdPox.
[89] Human Rights Watch, 'Brazil-Made Cluster Munitions Wound Children', 23 December 2016, at http://bit.ly/32ub4vE.
[90] OHCHR, 'The Situation of Human Rights in Yemen, Including Violations and Abuses since September 2014', UN doc. A/HRC/36/33, 5 September 2017, p. 9.
[91] Cluster Munition Monitor, 'Yemen: Cluster Munition Ban Policy', last updated 2 August 2018, at http://bit.ly/3jg0VJN.
[92] These are devices that involve a nuclear explosion but which have not been weaponised. The first hydrogen (thermonuclear) device test-detonated was exploded by the United States over Enewetak atoll in the Marshall Islands at the beginning of November 1952. The device which contained 65 tons of heavy hydrogen and weighed 82 tons, was housed in a refrigeration system that itself took 6 weeks to assemble. The top of the mushroom cloud following the detonation stabilised at a height of 41 kilometres, spreading out to a diameter of more than 160 kilometres. T. Downing, 1983: *The World at the Brink*, Little, Brown, London, 2018, p. 7.

use such weapons or devices.[93] None of the nuclear-armed States or the so-called 'umbrella' States has adhered to the Treaty.

15.54 In 1996, the International Court of Justice unanimously held that there exists 'an obligation to pursue in good faith and bring to a conclusion negotiations leading to nuclear disarmament in all its aspects under strict and effective international control'. This evokes but goes beyond the obligation in Article VI of the Treaty on the Non-Proliferation of Nuclear Weapons (NPT), to which five of the nine nuclear-armed States (the five permanent members of the UN Security Council) are party.[94] That provision obligates all States Parties to the NPT to 'pursue negotiations in good faith on effective measures relating to cessation of the nuclear arms race at an early date and to nuclear disarmament'.[95]

OTHER GLOBAL ARMS CONTROL OBLIGATIONS

15.55 Other global arms control obligations concern, in particular, the testing of nuclear weapons, and controls on transfer with a view to precluding either proliferation of weapons of mass destruction or serious violations of international humanitarian law or human rights. The NPT prohibits transfers of nuclear weapons or other nuclear explosive devices to any State (or any other recipient) other than the five nuclear-weapon States designated under the Treaty.[96] Such a transfer would be incompatible with the protection of the right to life. As the Human Rights Committee has stipulated, States Parties to the ICCPR 'must take all necessary measures to stop the proliferation of weapons of mass destruction, including measures to prevent their acquisition by non-State actors'.[97]

15.56 The explosive testing of nuclear weapons has significant implications for the right to life. The last atmospheric test occurred in October 1980 in a desert area in China's far west.[98] Any atmospheric (i.e., above-ground) detonation of nuclear weapons would violate a customary law rule that prohibits all explosive testing other than that conducted underground. Even if no one were killed as a result of an explosion, the long-term health and environmental effects resulting from a test detonation would likely amount also to violations of the right to life. The lives of millions around the world have already been prematurely curtailed by atmospheric testing conducted since the 1950s by China, Russia, the United Kingdom, and the United States. Others have been badly affected by uranium mining or during the clean-up of nuclear accidents. Indeed, some areas of the world will

---

[93] Art. 1(1)(d), Treaty on the Prohibition of Nuclear Weapons; adopted at New York 7 July 2017; entered into force 22 January 2021.
[94] Art. VI, Treaty on the Non-Proliferation of Nuclear Weapons; opened for signature at London, Moscow, and Washington, DC, 1 July 1968; entered into force 5 March 1970. As of 1 May 2021, 190 States were party to the NPT.
[95] As recalled by the Human Rights Committee in its General Comment 36 on the right to life, para. 66.
[96] Arts. I and IX(3), NPT.
[97] Human Rights Committee, General Comment 36 on the right to life, para. 66.
[98] A. Gale, 'North Korea's Threat: The History of Aboveground Nuclear Tests', *Wall Street Journal*, 22 September 2017, at http://on.wsj.com/34GgHcK.

352   *Major Themes*

remain uninhabitable for hundreds of years as a result of radioactive contamination. In the South Pacific, for instance, parts of the Marshall Islands are still more radioactive than is either Chernobyl or Fukushima after the respective accidents at the nuclear power plants in 1986 and 2011.

15.57 It may also be the case that a general rule prohibiting all explosive testing of nuclear weapons or other nuclear explosive devices including underground has now crystallised as customary law. The only State to have detonated nuclear explosive devices in the last two decades has been the Democratic People's Republic of Korea (North Korea). Indeed, only North Korea is known to have test-detonated a nuclear explosive device since 1998: first in 2006 and then a further five times through to September 2017, making it the only nation to have tested nuclear weapons in the twenty-first century.[99] North Korea has been sharply condemned by the UN Security Council as a result, beginning with its very test detonation.[100] The very widespread adherence to the CTBT – 168 ratifying states and 16 signatories – is further evidence of State practice towards a customary prohibition.

The Arms Trade Treaty and the Right to Life

15.58 The UN Arms Trade Treaty,[101] which restricts the transfer of most conventional weapons by its 110 States Parties (as of writing), was negotiated within the United Nations. The annual value of the trade in conventional arms is counted in the tens of billions of dollars. In 2019, exports of conventional weapons amounted to more than US$27 billion according to the Stockholm International Peace Research Institute (SIPRI). The ATT was adopted by the UN General Assembly[102] after a consensus agreement at the UN diplomatic conference convened to negotiate it failed to conclude it. Three States – Iran, North Korea, and Syria – blocked the Treaty's adoption (and again voted against its adoption in the General Assembly).

15.59 The ATT explicitly prohibits transfers of conventional weapons within its scope in a number of scenarios: where a UN embargo is in place; where it would violate a State Party's disarmament treaty obligations, or where the weapons would be used to commit genocide, crimes against humanity, or certain war crimes, including attacks on civilians protected as such.[103] In addition, where a proposed export of conventional weapons within the Treaty's scope would undermine peace and security, or where an 'overriding risk' exists that the weapons would be used to 'commit or facilitate' a 'serious violation' of either

---
[99] T. Rauf, '"Unfinished Business" on the Anniversary of the Comprehensive Nuclear-Test-Ban Treaty', Commentary, SIPRI, Stockholm, 26 September 2016, at http://bit.ly/3gweO5b.

[100] In its Resolution 1718 (2006), the UN Security Council, acting under Chapter VII of the UN Charter, condemned the nuclear test by North Korea on 9 October 2006 'in flagrant disregard of its relevant resolutions', on the basis that such a test would 'represent a clear threat to international peace and security', and demanded that North Korea 'not conduct any further nuclear test'. UN Security Council Resolution 1718, adopted by unanimous vote on 14 October 2006, operative paras. 1 and 2.

[101] Arms Trade Treaty; adopted at New York 2 April 2013; entered into force 24 December 2014 (hereinafter, ATT).

[102] UN General Assembly Resolution 67/234B, adopted by 154 votes to 3, with 23 abstentions.

[103] Art. 6, ATT.

international humanitarian law or of international human rights law, the export must not be authorised.[104] For the purpose of the legal analysis under the Arms Treaty Treaty, a single violation of the right to life in this regard would be sufficient to constitute a serious violation of international human rights law.[105]

15.60 A transfer of weapons where there existed a clear and substantial risk that they would be used in arbitrary deprivation of life would itself constitute a violation of the right to life. As such, international law has evolved since the 1995 application of *Tugar v. Italy* before the erstwhile European Commission on Human Rights.[106] The applicant was trained as a deminer by the Mines Advisory Group, a non-governmental organisation that conducts mine clearance operations in affected countries, including Iraq. In 1982, the Iraqi Minister of Foreign Affairs agreed to a contract with an Italian company for the supply to Iraq of 5.75 million anti-personnel mines. In a judgment on 20 February 1991, the Brescia Court found the company responsible for illegal arms trafficking to Iraq. In April 1993, the applicant was seriously injured by an anti-personnel mine of Italian origin while clearing mines in Iraq.

15.61 The applicant argued that Italy's supply to Iraq of 'lethal weapons' amounted to a failure to comply with its positive obligations to 'protect the right to life' under Article 2 of the 1950 European Convention on Human Rights.[107] He cited the European Court of Human Rights' judgment in the *Soering* case in which the United Kingdom was prevented from extraditing a German national to the United States where he would face the death penalty on the basis that the prolonged detention on death row would constitute inhumane treatment.[108] Mr Tugar asserted by analogy that his right to life would be violated by his exposure by Italian authorities to the risk of 'indiscriminate' use of anti-personnel mines by Iraq.

15.62 In its decision, the Commission observed that no right to have the transfer of arms regulated or other such measures taken by a State Party to the European Convention on Human Rights is 'as such guaranteed by the Convention'. It considered that the circumstances of the *Tugar* case were 'entirely different from those prevailing in extradition or expulsion cases' and denied any immediate relationship between the mere supply, even if not properly regulated, of weapons and the possible 'indiscriminate' use thereof in a third country. 'In conclusion, the Commission finds that the injuries suffered by the applicant are exclusively attributable to Iraq, and that the use of anti-personnel mines – even if

---

[104] Art. 7(1)(a) and (b)(i) and (ii) and Art. 7(3), ATT.
[105] S. Casey-Maslen and A. Clapham, Commentary on Article 7, in S. Casey-Maslen, A. Clapham, G. Giacca, and S. Parker, *The Arms Trade Treaty: A Commentary*, Oxford University Press, Oxford, 2016, para. 7.50.
[106] European Commission on Human Rights, *Tugar v. Italy*, Decision (Admissibility) (First Chamber), 18 October 1995.
[107] Convention for the Protection of Human Rights and Fundamental Freedoms; adopted at Rome 4 November 1950; entered into force 3 September 1953.
[108] European Court of Human Rights, *Soering v. United Kingdom*, Judgment (Plenary), 7 July 1989. According to paragraph 85 of the judgment, the Court held that 'in so far as a measure of extradition has consequences adversely affecting the enjoyment of a Convention right, it may, assuming that the consequences are not too remote, attract the obligations of a Contracting State under the relevant Convention guarantee'.

delivered by Italy – made by Iraq can in no way engage any responsibility of the Italian Government under Article 2 (Art. 2) of the Convention."[109]

15.63 This was questionable law at the time but is certainly not robust today. The ATT demands that exports of conventional weapons within its scope be effectively regulated.[110] The notion of State responsibility under international law is set out by the International Law Commission (ILC) in its 2001 Draft Articles on State Responsibility for Internationally Wrongful Acts.[111] Article 16 provides:

> A State which aids or assists another State in the commission of an internationally wrongful act by the latter is internationally responsible for doing so if:
>
> (a) that State does so with knowledge of the circumstances of the internationally wrongful act; and
> (b) the act would be internationally wrongful if committed by that State.

15.64 In the case brought by Bosnia and Herzegovina against Serbia and Montenegro, the International Court of Justice found that Article 16 represented customary international law and asserted that the threshold for a finding of complicity in genocide by a State required that 'at the least its organs were aware that genocide was about to be committed or was under way. . . . In other words, an accomplice must have given support in perpetrating the genocide with full knowledge of the facts.'[112] Thus a State that transfers weapons to another State knowing that they would be used to arbitrarily deprive one or more persons of their life would itself be responsible for a violation of the right to life.

15.65 In the case of *Ilaşcu v. Moldova and Russia*, the Grand Chamber of the European Court observed that large quantities of weapons from the 14th Army's arsenal appeared to have been transferred voluntarily to the Transdniestrian separatists, who had, moreover, been able to secure further arms, unopposed by the Russian military.[113] The Russian Government had observed during the court proceedings, without a hint of irony, that the Moldovan Government was the only legitimate government of Moldova. As Transdniestrian territory was an integral part of the Republic of Moldova, only the latter, it claimed, could be held responsible for acts committed in that territory.[114] The European Court, however, held that Russia's responsibility was also engaged in respect of unlawful acts committed by the Transdniestrian separatists, 'regard being had to the military and

---

[109] European Commission on Human Rights, *Tugar v. Italy*, Decision, 18 October 1995.
[110] Art. 5, ATT.
[111] Draft articles on responsibility of States for internationally wrongful acts, adopted by the ILC at its fifty-third session, August 2001.
[112] International Court of Justice, *Case Concerning the Application of the Convention on the Prevention and Punishment of the Crime of Genocide (Bosnia and Herzegovina v. Serbia and Montenegro)*, Judgment, 26 February 2007, para. 432; see also paras. 420–1.
[113] European Court of Human Rights, *Ilaşcu and others v. Moldova and Russia*, Judgment (Grand Chamber), 8 July 2004, paras. 57–9.
[114] Ibid., para. 305.

political support it gave them to help them set up the separatist regime and the participation of its military personnel in the fighting'.[115]

15.66 While the case concerned, inter alia, Articles 3 and 5 of the European Convention on Human Rights (for the treatment of Romanian nationals), and not the legality of the transfer of weapons, the principle whereby a State may be held responsible for violations of human rights on the basis of the military support it provides to another State, including by the transfer of weapons, is a marked progression from the holding in *Tugar* a decade earlier.

15.67 Otherwise at the regional and bilateral level, a number of arms control or disarmament agreements have been concluded, which also have clear implications for the right to life. Thus, for example, the 2010 Central African Convention for the Control of Small Arms and Light Weapons (better known as the 2010 Kinshasa Convention)[116] stipulates that small arms and light weapons, their ammunition, and parts and components may only be lawfully transferred in a limited number of situations: either where they are necessary in order to maintain law and order, where they are needed for defence or national security purposes. They may also be moved into another jurisdiction where forces possessing such weapons participate in peacekeeping operations abroad and only when such operations are conducted under the aegis of the UN, the African Union, the Economic Community of Central African States, or other regional or sub-regional organisations of which a State Party is a member.[117]

15.68 States Parties are required to prohibit any transfer of small arms and light weapons, their ammunition, and parts and components to non-state armed groups (Article 4). As of 1 May 2021, eight States were party to the Kinshasa Convention and three States were signatories, the latest State to ratify being Equatorial Guinea in December 2019.[118] A violation by a State Party of the prohibition of transfers in the Kinshasa Convention would engage the transferring State's responsibility under international law, including human rights law.

15.69 To date, however, the *Tugar* case aside, human rights courts have largely been uninvolved in adjudicating the legality of transfers of weapons under regional human rights treaties. The European Court of Human Rights has, though, addressed the use of weapons and associated protective measures in a number of other judgments. For instance, in its judgment of 2006 in *Paşa and Erkan Erol*, the Court held that the placement of warning signs and two rows of barbed wire around a minefield near a village in an area normally used for pasture did not comply with the State's positive obligation under Article 2 to protect life.[119]

---

[115] Ibid., para. 382.
[116] Central African Convention for the Control of Small Arms and Light Weapons, their Ammunition and all Parts and Components that can be used for their Manufacture, Repair and Assembly; adopted at Kinshasa 30 April 2010; entered into force 8 March 2017.
[117] Art. 3(2), Kinshasa Convention.
[118] Angola, Cameroon, the Central African Republic, Chad, Congo, Equatorial Guinea, Gabon, and Sao Tome and Principe are States Parties. Burundi, Democratic Republic of the Congo, and Rwanda are signatories.
[119] European Court of Human Rights, *Paşa and Erkan Erol v. Turkey*, Judgment (Second Section), 12 December 2006 (as rendered final on 23 May 2007), paras. 32–8.

15.70 In its judgment in *Albekov v. Russia*, which concerned a failure to clear landmines, the European Court of Human Rights held that

> having regard to the State's failure to endeavour to locate and deactivate the mines, to mark and seal off the mined area so as to prevent anybody from freely entering it, and to provide the villagers with comprehensive warnings concerning the mines laid in the vicinity of their village, the Court finds that the State has failed to comply with its positive obligation under Article 2 of the Convention to protect [life].[120]

15.71 The 1981 African Charter on Human and Peoples' Rights does not specifically address arms control and disarmament.[121] In 2015, the African Commission on Human and Peoples' Rights adopted its General Comment on the right to life under Article 4 of the African Charter on Human and Peoples' Rights.[122] The General Comment addresses the importance of the availability of less-lethal weapons, as an alternative to firearms during law enforcement, and raises significant concerns as to the legality of autonomous weapons, but does not otherwise address arms control or disarmament.[123]

15.72 To date, neither the Inter-American Commission on Human Rights nor the Inter-American Court of Human Rights has pronounced on the legality under the American Convention on Human Rights of arms exports.

---

[120] European Court of Human Rights, *Albekov and others v. Russia*, Judgment (Third Section), 9 October 2008 (as rendered final on 6 April 2009), para. 90.
[121] African Charter on Human and Peoples' Rights; adopted at Nairobi 27 June 1981; entered into force 21 October 1986.
[122] African Commission on Human and Peoples' Rights, General Comment No. 3 on the African Charter on Human and Peoples' Rights on the right to life (Article 4), adopted during its 57th Ordinary Session, Banjul, The Gambia, November 2015.
[123] Ibid., paras. 30, 35.

16

Enforced Disappearance

INTRODUCTION

16.01 This chapter describes how the duty of States to respect and protect the right to life applies to enforced disappearance. As the UN Human Rights Committee recalled in its General Comment 36 on the right to life under the 1966 International Covenant on Civil and Political Rights (ICCPR),[1] enforced disappearance 'constitutes a unique and integrated series of acts and omissions representing a grave threat to life'.[2] In rather more emotive terms, the Office of the UN High Commissioner for Human Rights (OHCHR) has observed: 'A disappearance has a doubly paralysing impact: on the victims, frequently tortured and in constant fear for their lives, and on their families, ignorant of the fate of their loved ones, their emotions alternating between hope and despair, wondering and waiting, sometimes for years, for news that may never come.'[3]

16.02 The key elements in an enforced disappearance are the detention or abduction of an individual, followed by a refusal to acknowledge his or her whereabouts and confirm his or her well-being. A deprivation of liberty followed by 'a refusal to acknowledge that deprivation of liberty or by concealment of the fate of the disappeared person, in effect removes that person from the protection of the law and places his or her life at serious and constant risk'.[4] Thus an enforced disappearance does not mean that the victim is dead (although often that is the case, or it later occurs, or it is assumed to have occurred).

16.03 In any event, the State is accountable for an enforced disappearance.[5] A State is likely to be found to have violated the duty to protect life, as codified in Article 6(1) of the ICCPR.[6] That said, '[u]nder no circumstances should families of victims of enforced

---

[1] International Covenant on Civil and Political Rights; adopted at New York 16 December 1966; entered into force 23 March 1976. As of 1 May 2021, 173 States were party to the ICCPR and a further 6 States were signatories.
[2] Human Rights Committee, 'General Comment No. 36: Article 6: right to life', UN doc. CCPR/C/GC/36, 3 September 2019 (hereinafter, Human Rights Committee, General Comment 36 on the right to life), para. 58.
[3] OHCHR, Enforced or Involuntary Disappearances, Fact Sheet 6/rev.3, Geneva, 2009, p. 1.
[4] Human Rights Committee, General Comment 36 on the right to life, para. 58.
[5] Ibid.
[6] This is cast in broader terms than was identified by the OHCHR in 2009, which characterised the right to life as being violated by an enforced disappearance only when the disappeared person is killed. OHCHR, Enforced or Involuntary Disappearances, Fact Sheet 6/rev.3, Geneva, 2009, p. 3.

disappearance be obliged to declare them dead in order to be eligible for reparation'.[7] In its Views in *Prutina and others v. Bosnia and Herzegovina*, which it cited in General Comment 36, the Human Rights Committee held that for a State which is investigating disappearances conducted on its territory to oblige families of disappeared persons to have the family member declared dead in order to be eligible for compensation, while the investigation is ongoing, was a breach of Article 2(3) of the Covenant (on the right to a remedy), read in conjunction with Articles 6, 7, and 9 on the rights to life, freedom from torture, and liberty and security of person, respectively.[8]

16.04 In his partly dissenting opinion in the *Prutina* case, Committee member Fabián Salvioli asserted that there was 'a more flagrant and obvious violation', namely, the requirement by the State that the relative of a disappeared person must apply for a death certificate in order to obtain a benefit or compensation. The violation inheres in the fact that it obliges the relative to recognise the death of the disappeared person, 'even though that person's fate is uncertain'.[9] This, Mr Salvioli affirmed, constitutes cruel and inhuman treatment within the meaning of Article 7 of the ICCPR.[10] This reflects the approach that is increasingly taken by human rights bodies with respect to the family members of a disappeared person.

16.05 In its Views of 2015 in *Katwal v. Nepal*, the Human Rights Committee observed that, while the ICCPR does not explicitly use the term 'enforced disappearance' in any of its articles, enforced disappearance 'constitutes a unique and integrated series of acts that represents continuing violation of various rights recognized in that treaty'.[11] Enforced disappearance, the Committee stipulates in its General Comment 36, results in a violation of the right to life as well as of other rights recognised in the ICCPR – in particular, the prohibition of torture or cruel, inhuman, or degrading treatment or punishment (Article 7); the rights to liberty and security of person (Article 9); and the right to recognition as a person before the law (Article 16).[12] There may also be, as further illustrated later in this chapter, a failure to ensure a remedy for a human rights violation (Article 2(3)). In addition, in one of the cases the Committee cites in its General Comment 36 – *Bousroual v. Algeria* – reference is also made to the right of all persons deprived of their liberty to be treated with humanity and with respect for the inherent dignity of the human person (Article 10 of the ICCPR).[13]

16.06 In that case, Ms. Louisa Bousroual, an Algerian national, had submitted the communication on behalf of her husband, Salah Saker (also an Algerian national), who

---

[7] Human Rights Committee, General Comment 36 on the right to life, para. 58.
[8] Human Rights Committee, *Prutina and others v. Bosnia and Herzegovina*, Views (UN docs. CCPR/C/107/D/1917/2009,1918/2009,1925/2009, and 1953/2010), 28 March 2013, para. 9.6.
[9] Ibid., Individual opinion of Committee member Fabián Salvioli (partly dissenting), para. 6.
[10] Ibid.
[11] Human Rights Committee, *Katwal v. Nepal*, Views (UN doc. CCPR/C/113/D/2000/2010), 1 April 2015, para. 11.3.
[12] Ibid.
[13] Human Rights Committee, *Bousroual v. Algeria*, Views (UN doc. CCPR/C/86/992/2001), 30 March 2006, para. 9.2.

had been missing for almost six years following his arrest in May 1994. The Algerian authorities acknowledged that he had been arrested by police and detained for questioning on suspicion of membership of an illegal group. They affirmed that he had subsequently been transferred to the military branch of the judicial police for further questioning. They also claimed that he had been released a day later and was subsequently a fugitive from justice.[14] On 29 July 1995, a criminal court in Constantine had rendered a judgment in absentia – and in secret – for Mr Saker's membership in an illegal group. He was convicted and sentenced to death.[15] The Committee noted that Algeria had not rebutted the fact that Mr Saker had been unaccounted for since at least 29 July 1995. As the authorities had not provided any information or evidence relating to the victim's release (much less his well-being), the Committee found a violation of Article 6(1) of the ICCPR for its failure to protect the life of Mr Saker.[16]

16.07 This chapter continues with a discussion of the definition(s) of enforced disappearance under international law. It then considers the international legal status of the prohibition of enforced disappearance. Thereafter, attention is paid as to how the duty to respect and protect life under global human rights treaties and standards imposes obligations upon States with respect to enforced disappearance. The corresponding treatment of these duties under regional treaties and standards is then assessed. The final section of the chapter looks at how the prohibition of enforced disappearance applies in a situation of armed conflict.

The Definition of Enforced Disappearance

16.08 Enforced disappearance is defined in slightly different terms in international human rights treaty and under international criminal law. Under Article 2 of the 2006 International Convention for the Protection of All Persons from Enforced Disappearance (CPED), enforced disappearance is stated to be

> the arrest, detention, abduction or any other form of deprivation of liberty by agents of the State or by persons or groups of persons acting with the authorization, support or acquiescence of the State, followed by a refusal to acknowledge the deprivation of liberty or by concealment of the fate or whereabouts of the disappeared person, which place such a person outside the protection of the law.[17]

Thus, under the CED definition, those engaging in the enforced disappearance must be agents of the State.

---

[14] Ibid., para. 4.4.
[15] Ibid., paras. 4.4 and 5.5.
[16] Ibid., para. 9.11.
[17] International Convention for the Protection of All Persons from Enforced Disappearance; adopted at New York 20 December 2006; entered into force 23 December 2010 (hereinafter, CPED). As of 1 May 2021, sixty-three States were party to the CPED and a further forty-eight were signatories.

16.09 A seemingly broader definition of enforced disappearance as a crime against humanity is expounded in the 1998 Rome Statute of the International Criminal Court. Thereunder, the 'enforced disappearance of persons' means

> the arrest, detention or abduction of persons by, or with the authorization, support or acquiescence of, a State or a political organization, followed by a refusal to acknowledge that deprivation of freedom or to give information on the fate or whereabouts of those persons, with the intention of removing them from the protection of the law for a prolonged period of time.[18]

According to this definition, an enforced disappearance does not need to be committed by a State agent. A 'political organisation', which includes an armed group opposing the authorities or at least independent of them, may also be held responsible for enforced disappearance as a crime against humanity. It may well be that this is the definition to be applied under customary law. That said, CPED also obligates each State Party to take 'appropriate measures to investigate' acts defined in Article 2 of the Convention where they are 'committed by persons or groups of persons acting without the authorization, support or acquiescence of the State'.[19] One may consider the difference between the two definitions as, therefore, rather one of nuance than of substance.[20]

THE STATUS UNDER INTERNATIONAL LAW OF THE PROHIBITION OF ENFORCED DISAPPEARANCE

16.10 Although the CPED has, thus far, attracted a relatively low level of adherence since its adoption in 2006, with only sixty-three States Parties as of this writing, the prohibition of enforced disappearance is undoubtedly one that has crystallised as a rule of customary law. The Convention stipulates unequivocally that 'no one shall be subject to enforced disappearance'.[21] The CPED further clarifies: 'No exceptional circumstances whatsoever, whether a state of war or a threat of war, internal political instability or any other public emergency, may be invoked as a justification for enforced disappearance.'[22] As discussed further, the customary prohibition of enforced disappearance applies not only in peacetime but also in a situation of armed conflict.

16.11 There is also strong evidence that the prohibition has attained the status of a peremptory norm of international law (jus cogens). In this regard, the Special Rapporteur of the International Law Commission (ILC) on the question of peremptory norms noted in his fourth report in January 2019: 'The *jus cogens* nature of the prohibition

---

[18] Art. 7(2)(i), Rome Statute of the International Criminal Court; adopted at Rome 17 July 1998; entered into force 1 July 2002.
[19] Art. 3, CPED.
[20] The requirement under the Rome Statute that the removal of the victim of enforced disappearance from the protection of the law be for 'a prolonged period of time' potentially narrows the scope of the actus reus of the offence for the purposes of international criminal law.
[21] Art. 1(1), CPED.
[22] Art. 1(2), CPED.

of enforced disappearance has received a large degree of support.'[23] In a statement issued in 2013, the Committee on Enforced Disappearance noted the 'character *erga omnes* of the State's obligations' under the CPED.[24] The ILC has determined: 'Peremptory norms of general international law (*jus cogens*) give rise to obligations owed to the international community as a whole (obligations *erga omnes*), in which all States have a legal interest.'[25]

16.12 The strongest support for the peremptory nature of the prohibition has come from jurisprudence in the Americas, both at the regional level and in domestic courts and in State practice. Thus, for instance, in its judgment on the merits in the *Goiburú* case, the Inter-American Court of Human Rights declared in 2006 that 'the prohibition of the forced disappearance of persons and the corresponding obligation to investigate and punish those responsible has attained the status of *jus cogens*'.[26] But already in 1987, in Section 702(c) of the Restatement of the Law, Third, Foreign Relations Law of the United States, published by the American Law Institute, the prohibition of 'causing disappearance of individuals' was described as a norm of jus cogens.[27] In 1992, the US Court of Appeals for the Ninth Circuit cited the Third Restatement in its judgment in *Siderman de Blake* as evidence in this regard.[28]

ENFORCED DISAPPEARANCE AND THE RIGHT TO LIFE UNDER GLOBAL STANDARDS

16.13 There is a duty upon every State to exercise due diligence to seek to prevent and address enforced disappearance, in particular through the conduct of an effective investigation and appropriate sanction of any wrongdoing. Thus, for instance, States Parties to the ICCPR 'must', the Human Rights Committee has held, 'take adequate measures to prevent the enforced disappearance of individuals, and conduct an effective and speedy inquiry to establish the fate and whereabouts of persons who may have been subject to enforced disappearance'.[29] Softening the holding of the Inter-American Court of Human Rights in the *Goiburú* case, they '*should* also ensure', the Committee declares, 'that the

---

[23] ILC, Fourth report on peremptory norms of general international law (jus cogens) by Dire Tladi, Special Rapporteur, UN doc. A/CN.4/727, 31 January 2019, para. 125.

[24] Committee on Enforced Disappearance, 'Statement on the *Ratione Temporis* Element in the Review of Reports Submitted by States Parties under the International Convention for the Protection of All Persons from Enforced Disappearance', Geneva, 2013, at http://bit.ly/2ElNRDR, para. 5.

[25] ILC, *Report of the International Law Commission*, Seventy-first session, UN doc. A/74/10, 2019, chap. V, Draft Conclusion 17(1).

[26] Inter-American Court of Human Rights, *Goiburú and others v. Paraguay*, Judgment (Merits, Reparations and Costs), 22 September 2006, para. 84.

[27] In 1990, Daniel Murphy termed the jus cogens norms delineated in Section 702 of the Third Restatement as 'certainly a safe list'. D. T. Murphy, 'The Restatement (Third)'s Human Rights Provisions: Nothing New, But Very Welcome', *International Lawyer*, vol. 24 (1990), p. 917, at 922.

[28] US Court of Appeal (for the Ninth Circuit), *Siderman de Blake v. Argentina*, Judgment, 965 F.2d 699 (1992), Decided 22 May 1992, p. 717. The Ninth Circuit considers appeals from district courts in the states of Alaska, Arizona, California, Hawaii, Idaho, Montana, Nevada, Oregon, and Washington.

[29] Human Rights Committee, General Comment 36 on the right to life, para. 58. The problem of enforced disappearance had been raised by the Committee in its General Comment No. 6. Human Rights Committee, General Comment No. 6: Article 6 (Right to life), 1982, para. 4.

enforced disappearance of persons is punished with appropriate criminal sanctions, and introduce prompt and effective procedures for cases of disappearance to be investigated thoroughly by independent and impartial bodies'.[30]

16.14 Such investigatory bodies should 'as a rule' operate within the ordinary criminal justice system.[31] In this regard, the Human Rights Committee cited its Views in 1990 in *Herrera Rubio v. Colombia*. Therein the Committee had noted that there was reason to believe that the Colombian military was responsible for the deaths of Josh Herrera and Emma Rubio de Herrera and that, in any event, a thorough investigation was needed 'by an appropriate impartial body'.[32] The Colombian authorities had claimed that the two killings had been duly investigated and that no evidence was found to support charges against any military personnel. The investigation was therefore closed by order of the Attorney-General delegate for the Armed Forces in 1984. In a letter he wrote the following year to the Attorney-General of Colombia, he stated that the dossier was closed 'because it was established that no member of the armed forces took part in those events'.[33]

16.15 In a statement issued in 2016, the Committee on Enforced Disappearance stated that 'with a view to ensuring a fair trial before an independent and impartial court', it has recommended in its Concluding Observations to States Parties, as and when relevant, 'that all cases of enforced disappearance remain expressly outside military jurisdiction and be investigated and prosecuted by, or under control of, civil authorities and tried only by ordinary courts'.[34] The Committee referred specifically to the 1994 Inter-American Convention on Forced Disappearance of Persons whose Article IX stipulates that 'persons alleged to be responsible for the acts constituting the offence of forced disappearance of persons may be tried only in the competent jurisdictions of ordinary law in each State, to the exclusion of all other special jurisdictions, particularly military jurisdictions'.[35] Taking into account 'the progressive development of international law' as well as the provisions of the CPED, the Committee on Enforced Disappearance reaffirmed that military jurisdiction 'ought to be excluded in cases of gross human rights violations, including enforced disappearance'.[36]

16.16 The treatment of enforced disappearance under the ICCPR is clearly illustrated by the Views of the Human Rights Committee in *El Boathi v. Algeria*, which it adopted in

---

[30] Ibid. (added emphasis).
[31] Ibid.
[32] Human Rights Committee, *Joaquín David Herrera Rubio and others v. Colombia*, Views (UN doc. CCPR/C/OP/2), 2 November 1987, para. 10.3.
[33] Ibid., para. 6.1.
[34] Committee on Enforced Disappearance, Statement on Enforced Disappearance and Military Jurisdiction, Geneva, 2016, at http://bit.ly/2YnUDzx, para. 5.
[35] Art. IX, Inter-American Convention on Forced Disappearance of Persons; adopted at Belem do Para, Brazil 9 June 1994; entered into force 28 March 1996. Mexico made a reservation to Article IX when adhering to the Convention, but in 2014 informed the depositary that it was withdrawing its reservation. See http://bit.ly/3aPIqJ3.
[36] Committee on Enforced Disappearance, Statement on Enforced Disappearance and Military Jurisdiction, 2016, para. 10.

2017.³⁷ Brahim El Boathi, born in 1965, was married and the father of two children. He was employed as a soldier at the Bouzareah barracks. On 17 January 1994, he took a bus to go to work. He was arrested at a police checkpoint in a neighbourhood in Oued Koriche municipality in Algiers wilaya (governorate). His family has not seen him since then.³⁸ The Algerian authorities stated that the period in question was a complex one for Algeria, which involved many instances of disappearance, but did not address the specifics of the case or the complaint by the author (Mr El Boathi's mother).³⁹

16.17 The Committee noted that, at the Oued Koriche police station, Officer A. Z. told the prosecutor of Baïnem court in Algiers that he had arrested Mr El Boathi, but the same officer later told the author that he had arrested and killed her son. The Committee took note of the many contradictory pieces of information regarding his fate, including a refusal on 2 May 2000 to issue a disappearance decision, implying that the Algerian authorities still believed him to be alive at that time. The Committee concluded that, in the light of the statements by Officer A. Z. and the many years since Mr El Boathi's disappearance, it is highly likely that notwithstanding the absence of a body, he had been the victim of summary execution by Officer A. Z. or he had died in detention. The authorities had produced no evidence to indicate that it had fulfilled its obligation to protect the life of Mr El Boathi, and the Committee thus found that Algeria had failed in this duty in violation of Article 6(1) of the Covenant.⁴⁰

16.18 The Committee acknowledged the degree of suffering caused by being detained without contact with the outside world for an indefinite period. It noted that the author of the complaint and the rest of Mr El Boathi's family have never received any information on his fate or place of detention. In the absence of any explanation from the Algerian authorities, the Committee considered that this disappearance constitutes a violation of Article 7 of the Covenant with regard to Brahim El Boathi. In addition, owing to the anguish and distress caused to the author and her family by the disappearance of Mr El Boathi, they were also held to be the subject of a violation of Article 7.⁴¹

16.19 With regard to the alleged violation of Article 9 of the ICCPR, which protects the rights to liberty and to security of person, the Committee noted the author's allegations that Mr El Boathi was arbitrarily arrested, without a warrant, and was not formally charged or brought before a judicial authority before which he could have challenged the lawfulness of his detention. In the absence of any information from the authorities on those issues, the Committee considered that 'due weight' must be given to the author's allegations, thus finding a violation also of Article 9 with regard to Mr El Boathi.⁴²

---

[37] Human Rights Committee, *El Boathi v. Algeria*, Views (UN doc. CCPR/C/119/D/2259/2013), 17 March 2017.
[38] Ibid., para. 2.1.
[39] Ibid., paras. 4.1–4.5.
[40] Ibid., para. 7.5.
[41] Ibid., para. 7.6.
[42] Ibid., para. 7.9.

16.20 The Committee further held that Mr El Boathi's enforced disappearance more than twenty-three years previously had removed him from the protection of the law and deprived him of his right to be recognised as a person before the law, in violation of Article 16 of the Covenant. The Committee affirms that the intentional removal of a person from the protection of the law for a prolonged period of time 'constitutes a refusal to recognize him or her as a person before the law, particularly if the efforts of his or her relatives to obtain access to potentially effective remedies have been systematically impeded'. In this case, Algeria had not provided 'any convincing explanation concerning the fate or whereabouts of Brahim El Boathi' despite the multiple requests addressed to the authorities by the author of the complaint.[43]

16.21 Finally, there had also been a violation of Article 2(3) of the Covenant on the right to a remedy, on the basis that a failure by a State Party to investigate allegations of violations 'could, in itself, give rise to a separate breach of the Covenant'. The family of Mr El Boathi had informed the competent authorities, including the public prosecutor of Algiers court, of his disappearance, but Algeria had not initiated an 'in-depth, thorough and impartial investigation into the disappearance' as the Covenant and general international law required, and the author of the complaint had received only 'vague and contradictory' information.[44] Given that it had found violations of Mr El Boathi's rights to life and freedom from torture by Algeria, however, the Committee did not deem it necessary to consider separately the claims in relation to the violation of Article 10(1) of the Covenant: the obligation to treat with humanity and with respect for the inherent dignity of the human person anyone deprived of his or her liberty.[45] The facts, however, clearly evidenced that a violation of this duty had also occurred in this case.

16.22 In 2019, the Committee on Enforced Disappearances issued a set of guiding principles on the search for disappeared persons.[46] The first of the sixteen principles is that the search for a disappeared person 'should be conducted under the presumption that he or she is alive'. This is so, regardless of the circumstances of the disappearance, the date on which the disappearance began, and when the search is launched.[47] Significantly for the scope of application *ratione temporis* of the right to life, Principle 7 states that the search 'is a continuing obligation'. Thus the search for a disappeared person 'should continue until his or her fate and/or whereabouts have been determined with certainty'.[48]

16.23 This has implications for the application of human rights treaties. As discussed later, while a State may become party to a particular treaty after the initial disappearance took place, the fact that the duty to investigate is an ongoing and continuing obligation means that a treaty body or regional human rights court may have jurisdiction to hear a complaint.

---

[43] Ibid., para. 7.10.
[44] Ibid., para. 7.11.
[45] Ibid., para. 7.9.
[46] Committee on Enforced Disappearances, *Guiding Principles for the Search for Disappeared Persons*, UN doc. CED/C/7, 8 May 2019 (hereinafter, 2019 Guiding Principles for the Search for Disappeared Persons).
[47] Principle 1, 2019 Guiding Principles for the Search for Disappeared Persons.
[48] Principle 7(1), 2019 Guiding Principles for the Search for Disappeared Persons.

That said, according to Article 35(1) of the CPED, the Committee on Enforced Disappearance has 'competence solely in respect of enforced disappearances which commenced after the entry into force' of the CPED.

16.24 The 2019 Guiding Principles also address the form and nature of the required investigation. Principle 4 stipulates that the search should follow a 'differential approach'. By this is meant that searches must take account of relative risks and vulnerabilities.[49] Thus, for instance, a search for disappeared children and adolescents should take into account their 'extreme vulnerability' and officials 'should respect the principle of the best interests of the child at all stages of the search'.[50] In cases involving adolescent girls and women who have disappeared, all stages of the search should be conducted with a gender perspective.[51]

16.25 Further, in cases involving disappeared persons who are members of indigenous peoples or other ethnic or cultural groups, there is a need to consider and respect specific cultural patterns. An effective search should involve the provision of translators of the languages of the communities and bicultural interpreters.[52] In cases involving disappeared persons who are members of the lesbian, gay, bisexual, transgender, and intersex (LGBTI) community; who have disabilities; or who are older persons, the bodies responsible for the search should take account of their particular needs and vulnerabilities.[53]

16.26 Also of great importance for observance of the right to life is the need for the search to be 'independent and impartial'.[54] As a consequence, the 'entities responsible for the search' should be 'independent and autonomous' and 'should perform all their duties in compliance with the principle of due process'. All staff should demonstrate 'independence, impartiality, professional competence' and should have the ability to carry out their work using 'a differential approach, sensitivity and moral integrity'.[55] Consonant with the procedural element of the right to life, as the Minnesota Protocol on the Investigation of Potentially Unlawful Death (2016) recalls, international law requires that investigations be prompt, effective and thorough, independent and impartial, and transparent.[56]

ENFORCED DISAPPEARANCE UNDER REGIONAL STANDARDS

16.27 The issue of enforced disappearance has been addressed especially by the Inter-American Commission on Human Rights and the Inter-American Court of Human Rights as well as, albeit to a less extent, by the European Court of Human Rights. There has been

---

[49] Principle 4(1), 2019 Guiding Principles for the Search for Disappeared Persons.
[50] Principle 4(2), 2019 Guiding Principles for the Search for Disappeared Persons.
[51] Principle 4(3), 2019 Guiding Principles for the Search for Disappeared Persons.
[52] Principle 4(4), 2019 Guiding Principles for the Search for Disappeared Persons.
[53] Principle 4(5), 2019 Guiding Principles for the Search for Disappeared Persons.
[54] Principle 15, 2019 Guiding Principles for the Search for Disappeared Persons.
[55] Principle 15(1), 2019 Guiding Principles for the Search for Disappeared Persons.
[56] *The Minnesota Protocol on the Investigation of Potentially Unlawful Death (2016)*, OHCHR, New York/Geneva, 2017, para. 22.

relatively scant treatment of the issue in the African human rights system and little if any by the dedicated normative standards in the Arab world and across South-East Asia.

The Inter-American Human Rights System

16.28 According to Article 4(1) of the 1969 American Convention on Human Rights, 'Every person has the right to have his life respected. ... No one shall be arbitrarily deprived of his life.'[57] In the view of the Inter-American Commission on Human Rights, the fact that a person is disappeared over an extended period of time and in a context of violence is sufficient to conclude that the person was deprived of his life in violation of the right to life recognised in Article 4 of the 1969 Convention.[58] The 1994 Inter-American Convention on the Forced Disappearance of Persons prohibits enforced disappearance as 'a grave and abominable offence against the inherent dignity of the human being' and states that it 'violates numerous non-derogable and essential human rights enshrined in the American Convention on Human Rights'.[59]

16.29 On 30 August 2019 – the International Day of Victims of Enforced Disappearance – the Inter-American Commission remembered the victims 'whose fate remains unknown' and called on States in the region 'to take all necessary measures ... to prevent, investigate, and punish the practice of this serious human rights violation in their territory, and to implement comprehensive reparation for the victims'.[60] It called on regional States to adhere to the 1994 Inter-American Convention on the Forced Disappearance of Persons (to which only 15 of 34 States in the Americas were party as of 1 May 2021).[61]

16.30 In its judgment on the merits of 2013 in *Osorio Rivera and Family Members v. Peru*, the Inter-American Court of Human Rights reiterated that the prohibition of enforced disappearance was a peremptory norm of international law.[62] The case concerned a forced disappearance by the Peruvian army following the detention of Jeremías Osorio Rivera in April 1991 in the – mistaken – belief that he was fighting for the guerrilla group Shining Path (*Sendero Luminoso*). The army later disseminated false information regarding his whereabouts to his family.

16.31 Mr. Osorio Rivera's family never heard from him after his arrest. They filed a criminal complaint against Lieutenant Tello Delgado, the leader of the 'Palmira Plan of Operations' ostensibly responsible for the disappearance. The State's military court

---

[57] Art. 4, American Convention on Human Rights; adopted at San Jose 22 November 1969; entered into force 18 July 1978.
[58] Cited in Inter-American Court of Human Rights, *Osorio Rivera and Family Members v. Peru*, Judgment (Preliminary objections, merits, reparations and costs), 26 November 2013, para. 160.
[59] 1994 Inter-American Convention on the Forced Disappearance of Persons, third and fourth preambular paras.
[60] Inter-American Commission on Human Rights, 'On the International Day of the Victims of Enforced Disappearances, the IACHR Calls on States to Comply with Their International Obligations', press release, 30 August 2019, at http://bit.ly/3hlkoso.
[61] List of signatories and ratifications at http://bit.ly/3aPIqJ3.
[62] Inter-American Court of Human Rights, *Osorio Rivera and Family Members v. Peru*, Judgment, para. 112.

dismissed the case in 1996 because of the lack of a confirmed link between Mr. Osorio Rivera's disappearance and the Lieutenant. On 27 August 2013, Peru's Supreme Court held that a judgment acquitting Lieutenant Tello Delgado would not be annulled. The next day, the Inter-American Court conducted a hearing of the case.

16.32 The complainants alleged the State had violated the right to life of Mr Osorio Rivera 'by failing to comply with the obligation to respect and to ensure this right, as a result of the incomplete investigation into the enforced disappearance'.[63] In the case of Article 4 of the American Convention, the Court considers that, 'owing to the nature of enforced disappearance, the victim is in an aggravated situation of vulnerability, which gives rise to the risk that several different rights may be violated, including the right to life'.[64] In addition, the Inter-American Court has established that enforced disappearance 'has frequently included the execution of those detained, in secret and without any type of trial, followed by the concealment of the corpse in order to erase any material trace of the crime and to ensure the impunity of those who committed it, which signifies a violation of the right to life recognized in Article 4 of the Convention'.[65] In the case at hand, the Court found a violation of Mr Osorio Rivera's right to life by Peru.[66]

European Court of Human Rights' Jurisprudence

16.33 At regional level, the 1950 European Convention on Human Rights[67] does not explicitly address enforced disappearance as such. Under Article 2(1) of the Convention, however, everyone's right to life shall be protected by law. In earlier jurisprudence, the European Court of Human Rights was reluctant to find a violation of the right to life in a case of enforced disappearance. More recently, however, the Court applies a presumption of a violation of the substantive limb of Article 2 of the European Convention on Human Rights when the victim has last been seen alive in life-threatening circumstances and the respondent State fails to provide convincing explanations as to his or her fate and whereabouts.[68]

16.34 In 1998, a chamber of the Court considered an application in *Kurt* v. *Turkey* that asserted a violation of Article 2 on the basis that her son's disappearance occurred in a context which was 'life-threatening'.[69] The Commission had found that in the absence of any evidence as to the fate of Üzeyir Kurt subsequent to his detention, 'it would be inappropriate to draw the conclusion that he had been a victim of a violation

---

[63] Ibid., para. 161.
[64] Ibid., para. 169.
[65] Ibid.
[66] Ibid., para. 171.
[67] Convention for the Protection of Human Rights and Fundamental Freedoms; adopted at Rome 4 November 1950; entered into force 3 September 1953.
[68] European Court of Human Rights, *Bazorkina* v. *Russia*, Judgment (First Section), 27 July 2006, paras. 110–12; see Council of Europe Commissioner for Human Rights, *Missing Persons and Victims of Enforced Disappearance in Europe*, issue paper, 2016, at http://bit.ly/2EnIWlr, p. 38.
[69] European Court of Human Rights, *Kurt* v. *Turkey*, Judgment (Chamber), 25 May 1998.

of Article 2'.[70] The Court was also dismissive of the claim by the applicant, noting that it rested 'entirely on presumptions deduced from the circumstances of her son's initial detention bolstered by more general analyses of an alleged officially tolerated practice of disappearances and associated ill-treatment and extra-judicial killing of detainees in the respondent State'. The Court found these arguments unpersuasive and also rejected the applicant's argument that there existed a practice of violation of the right to life on the basis that the evidence did not substantiate that claim.[71] Instead, the Court preferred to consider the applicant's assertions that Turkey had failed in its obligation to protect her son's life under the prohibition of arbitrary detention protected in Article 5 of the European Convention on Human Rights.[72]

16.35 In 2005, in its judgment in *Toğcu v. Turkey*, the Court found that it was unable to reach a conclusion as to who might have been responsible for the disappearance of Ender Toğcu. It follows, therefore, the Court declared, 'that there has been no violation of Article 2 of the Convention on that account'.[73] The Court also rejected the applicant's claim that the failure of the authorities to take reasonable steps to investigate or to protect his son, whose forced disappearance had been reported to them, disclosed a failure to comply with the obligation under Article 2 to take positive steps to protect the right to life.[74] Instead, the Court found it 'more appropriate, in the circumstances of this case' to consider the issue under the procedural obligation of the right to life to carry out an effective investigation.[75]

16.36 In contrast, in its judgment in *Aslakhanova and others v. Russia*, issued in 2012, the European Court established that the applicants' family members 'must be presumed dead following their unacknowledged detention by State agents'. The 'liability for their presumed deaths', the Court held, 'rests with the respondent State'. Noting that the Russian government did not seek to rely on any grounds for the justification of the deaths, the Court found violations of the right to life in respect of eight individuals named in the application.[76] In this case, the pattern of enforced disappearances in Chechnya at the salient time was a factor taken into account by the Court.

16.37 Whether the failure by the authorities to provide a plausible explanation as to a detainee's fate, in the absence of a body, raises issues under Article 2 depends on the circumstances of the case, and in particular on the existence of sufficient circumstantial evidence that the detainee must be presumed to have died in custody.[77] In this regard, the period of time since a person was detained, although not decisive, is a relevant factor: the

---

[70] Ibid., para. 105.
[71] Ibid., para. 108.
[72] Ibid., para. 109.
[73] European Court of Human Rights, *Toğcu v. Turkey*, Judgment (Second Section), 31 May 2005, para. 102.
[74] Ibid., paras. 103, 105.
[75] Ibid., para. 105.
[76] European Court of Human Rights, *Aslakhanova and others v. Russia*, Judgment (First Section), 18 December 2012, para. 118.
[77] European Court of Human Rights, *Timurtas v. Turkey*, Judgment (First Section), 13 June 2000, para. 82.

longer the passage of time, the greater the weight to be attached to other elements of circumstantial evidence.[78]

16.38 A disappearance that occurs in life-threatening circumstances obligates the State to take operational measures to protect the right to life of the disappeared person. Thus, in its 2005 judgment in *Koku*, the Court found that in the circumstances, following his disappearance, the life of the applicant's brother was 'at more real and immediate risk than other persons at that time'. Accordingly, the action to be expected from the authorities was 'to take preventive operational measures to protect his life which was at risk from the criminal acts of other individuals'.[79]

16.39 Any negligence on the part of the investigating authorities in the face of real and imminent threats to a specific individual's life emanating from State agents acting outside their legal duties may violate the positive obligation to protect life. In its judgment in *Gongadze*, the Court found that complaints that had been made by the late Mr Gongadze, 'and subsequent events revealing the possible involvement of State officials in his disappearance and death, were neglected or simply denied for a considerable period of time without proper investigation'. The lack of reaction to the alleged involvement of the police in the disappearance when information about such a possibility was public meant that there had been a substantive violation of Article 2 of the Convention.[80]

16.40 In its judgment in the *Varnava* case,[81] the Grand Chamber of the European Court explicitly reviewed jurisprudence in the Inter-American Court of Human Rights and the Human Rights Committee on jurisdiction *ratione temporis*, where a State had become party to the relevant treaty after the initial disappearance had taken place. It recalled that the Chamber of the Court, in its consideration of the case, had excluded from its examination any allegations of violations based on facts occurring before the date of ratification of the right of an individual petition by Turkey on 28 January 1987. It noted, though, that the Grand Chamber in the fourth inter-State case had found that the disappearance of some 1,485 Greek Cypriots disclosed a situation of continuing violation under Article 2 in so far as the authorities of the respondent State had failed to conduct an effective investigation aimed at clarifying the whereabouts and fate of the persons who had gone missing in life-threatening circumstances. It found no reason to differ as concerned the nine missing men in this case, and concluded that to the extent that there was a continuing obligation under Article 2, it had competence *ratione temporis*.[82]

16.41 The Grand Chamber in *Varnava* recalled that general international law, as codified in Article 28 of the 1969 Vienna Convention on the Law of Treaties, held that the provisions of a treaty do not bind a Contracting Party in relation to any act or fact which

---

[78] European Court of Human Rights, *Taniş and others v. Turkey*, Judgment (Fourth Section), 2 August 2005.
[79] European Court of Human Rights, *Koku v. Turkey*, Judgment (Second Section), 31 May 2005, para. 132.
[80] European Court of Human Rights, *Gongadze v. Ukraine*, Judgment (Second Section), 8 November 2005, paras. 170 and 171.
[81] European Court of Human Rights, *Varnava and others v. Turkey*, Judgment (Grand Chamber), 18 September 2009.
[82] Ibid., para. 121.

took place, or any situation which ceased to exist, before the date the relevant State became party to it.[83] In its analysis, the Court distinguished the substantive obligations under Article 2 and the procedural duty to investigate. It recalled its earlier jurisprudence, whereby the procedural obligation arises when individuals have gone missing in life-threatening circumstances and underscored that this duty is not confined to cases where it is apparent that the disappearance was caused by an agent of the State.[84]

16.42 Turkey had also sought to sustain that the missing men had to be presumed dead long before any temporal jurisdiction arose in 1987; thus there was no 'disappearance' to be investigated after that date.[85] The Court, however, distinguished a factual presumption from the legal consequences that may flow from it. 'Even if there was an evidential basis which might justify finding that the nine missing men died in or closely after the events in 1974, this would not dispose of the applicants' complaints concerning the lack of an effective investigation.'[86] Moreover, the Court held,

> where disappearances in life-threatening circumstances are concerned, the procedural obligation to investigate can hardly come to an end on discovery of the body or the presumption of death; this merely casts light on one aspect of the fate of the missing person. An obligation to account for the disappearance and death, and to identify and prosecute any perpetrator of unlawful acts in that connection, will generally remain.[87]

African Charter on Human and Peoples' Rights

16.43 The 1981 African Charter on Human and Peoples' Rights does not specifically address the issue of enforced disappearance.[88] In 2015, the African Commission on Human and Peoples' Rights adopted its General Comment on the right to life under Article 4 of the African Charter on Human and Peoples' Rights.[89] The General Comment stipulates that where a State or its agent has 'forcibly caused a person to disappear and that person's fate remains unknown, in addition to the violation of other rights, a violation of the right to life has occurred'.[90]

Arab Charter on Human Rights

16.44 The 2004 Arab Charter on Human Rights[91] does not address enforced disappearance.

---

[83] Ibid., para. 130.
[84] Ibid., para. 136.
[85] Ibid., para. 141.
[86] Ibid., para. 144.
[87] Ibid., para. 145.
[88] African Charter on Human and Peoples' Rights; adopted at Nairobi 27 June 1981; entered into force 21 October 1986.
[89] African Commission on Human and Peoples' Rights, General Comment No. 3 on the African Charter on Human and Peoples' Rights on the right to life (Article 4), adopted during its 57th Ordinary Session, Banjul, The Gambia, November 2015.
[90] Ibid., para. 8.
[91] Arab Charter on Human Rights; adopted at Tunis 22 May 2004; entered into force 15 March 2008.

ASEAN Declaration on Human Rights

16.45 The 2012 Association of South-East Asian Nations (ASEAN) Declaration on Human Rights[92] does not address enforced disappearance. In commenting on the 'flawed' Declaration, Human Rights Watch stated that it 'fails to include several key basic rights and fundamental freedoms, including the right to freedom of association and the right to be free from enforced disappearance'.[93]

ENFORCED DISAPPEARANCE IN ARMED CONFLICT

16.46 The prohibition on enforced disappearance in the CPED applies at all times, including armed conflict, and in all circumstances. As noted previously, the Convention makes it explicit that '[n]o exceptional circumstances whatsoever, whether a state of war ... or any other public emergency ... may be invoked as a justification for enforced disappearance'.[94] Surprisingly, when adhering to the Convention Norway introduced an apparent reservation whereby 'whether and to what extent the various provisions of the Convention apply in situations of armed conflict will depend on an interpretation of the provision in question in the light of international humanitarian law'.[95] This is not a robust appreciation of the rules set out in the CPED, which apply on an independent basis in a situation of armed conflict.

16.47 In fact, international humanitarian law treaties do not address enforced disappearance as such. Nevertheless, as the International Committee of the Red Cross (ICRC) observed in its study of customary international humanitarian law published in 2005, enforced disappearance 'violates, or threatens to violate', a range of customary international humanitarian law rules, 'most notably' the prohibitions of arbitrary deprivation of liberty, torture and other cruel or inhuman treatment, and murder. As noted previously, the ICRC determined that a customary rule existed in all armed conflict whereby 'enforced disappearance is prohibited'.[96]

16.48 Already in 1981, the Twenty-Fourth International Conference of the Red Cross had considered that enforced disappearances 'imply violations of fundamental human rights such as the right to life, freedom and personal safety, the right not to be subjected to torture or cruel, inhuman or degrading treatment, the right not to be arbitrarily arrested or detained, and the right to a just and public trial'.[97] The Resolution had urged governments 'to endeavour to prevent forced or involuntary disappearances and to undertake and

---

[92] ASEAN Declaration on Human Rights, adopted by the Heads of State/Government of ASEAN Member States at Phnom Penh, 18 November 2012.
[93] Human Rights Watch, 'Civil Society Denounces Adoption of Flawed ASEAN Human Rights Declaration', 19 November 2012, at http://bit.ly/32fKeal.
[94] Art. 1(2), CPED.
[95] Declaration of Norway upon ratification of the CPED, at http://bit.ly/3aQ2Pos.
[96] ICRC, Customary IHL Rule 98: 'Enforced Disappearance', at http://bit.ly/3l2j2EC.
[97] Resolution II: 'Forced or involuntary disappearances', adopted at the 24th International Conference of the Red Cross, Geneva, 1981, third preambular para. The text of the resolution is available at http://bit.ly/32jWCGB.

complete thorough inquiries into every case of disappearance occurring in their territory'.[98]

16.49 In its judgment in the *Osorio Rivera* case, referred to previously, the Inter-American Court noted that the Inter-American Commission on Human Rights had indicated 'that the circumstances surrounding the arrest and transfer of Jeremías Osorio Rivera and the way in which information on his whereabouts was released were consistent with the *modus operandi* for enforced disappearances used by the security forces during the internal armed conflict in Peru'.[99] The Court noted that the ICRC had established that the prohibition of arbitrary deprivation of liberty is a rule of customary international humanitarian law, applicable to both international and non-international armed conflicts.[100]

16.50 The Inter-American Court further concluded that the actions of the army following the detention 'were in line with the *modus operandi* for enforced disappearances committed by State agents during the relevant period as part of the counterinsurgency strategy, without his whereabouts being known to date'.[101] The Court held that the disappearance of Mr. Osorio Rivera took place 'in the context of a pattern of selective enforced disappearances', which placed him in 'a serious situation of vulnerability and risk of suffering irreparable harm to his personal integrity and his life'.[102]

16.51 The European Court of Human Rights has held that disappearances, particularly those that take place during a situation of armed conflict, call for a less rigid interpretation of time limits on applications to the Court. In its judgment in the *Er* case,[103] referring to the decision in *Varnava*, a chamber of the Court stated: 'The serious nature of disappearances is such that the standard of expedition expected of the relatives cannot be rendered too rigorous in the context of Convention protection.'[104]

16.52 The *Er* case concerned the disappearance in July 1995 of a Turkish family's forty-four-year-old father and brother following a military operation in their village. The applicants alleged that Ahmet Er had been arrested on 14 July 1995 following a clash between the Turkish security forces and the Kurdish Workers' Party (PKK) and taken to the local *gendarmerie* station. They did not see him subsequently. The Turkish government, however, claimed that Mr Er had not in fact been taken into custody on that day but rather had helped soldiers find landmines planted by terrorists in the area and had been released the following day.

16.53 In his eyewitness statement, given in October 1995, the elderly uncle of the family said that he had been taken on 14 July with Ahmet to the *gendarmerie* station, where they

---

[98] Ibid., operative para. 3.
[99] Inter-American Court of Human Rights, *Osorio Rivera and Family Members v. Peru*, Judgment, para. 103.
[100] ICRC, Customary IHL Rule 99: 'Deprivation of Liberty', at http://bit.ly/3aNTNRM. Surprisingly, the Court did not refer to ICRC Customary IHL Rule 98 on enforced disappearances.
[101] Inter-American Court of Human Rights, *Osorio Rivera and Family Members v. Peru*, Judgment, para. 154.
[102] Ibid., para. 168.
[103] European Court of Human Rights, *Er v. Turkey*, Judgment (Second Section), 31 July 2012.
[104] Ibid., para. 57.

had been tied to a pole, beaten, and left until the next morning. He also alleged that they had been doused with hot water and that Ahmet had had the bones in his feet broken with a stone. On his release, he had seen Ahmet being dragged unconscious along the ground by a group of soldiers. A fellow villager also testified that he had seen Ahmet, handcuffed, being taken in a military vehicle from the *gendarmerie* station to the commando unit. The gendarmerie officers confirmed in December 1995 that they had taken Ahmet and his uncle to the station, but denied any allegations of torture; they said they had released the two men the next day.

16.54 The applicants, the Court found, had done all that could be expected of them to assist the authorities, could not therefore be criticised for waiting nine years before lodging their complaint about their relative's disappearance.[105] The Court therefore declared this part of the applicants' complaint admissible. The Court observed that Mr Er's disappearance fitted in with the pattern of disappearances of large numbers of persons in south-east Turkey between 1992 and 1996. In its examination of a number of those disappearances, the Court concluded that the disappearance of a person in that region during that period 'could be regarded as life-threatening'.[106] Moreover, the lack of any documentary evidence relating to Ahmet Er's detention at the *gendarmerie* station increased the risk to his life in the context of the situation in the south-east at the time of his disappearance.[107] Noting that the authorities had failed to account for what happened during Mr Er's detention and that they did not rely on any ground of justification for a possible use of lethal force by their agents, it followed that liability for his death was attributable to Turkey. Accordingly, the Court found a violation of Article 2 of the Convention in its substantive aspect.[108]

---

[105] Ibid., paras. 55–6.
[106] Ibid., para. 77.
[107] Ibid., para. 78.
[108] Ibid., para. 79.

17

Accidents, Disease, and Natural Disasters

INTRODUCTION

17.01 This chapter considers how the right to life may be violated by the failure to tackle disease and natural disasters or to prevent and address accidents. Under customary as well as treaty international law, there is a duty to protect and fulfil as well as respect life. But the view of certain human rights bodies on the action required of States to comply with these duties with respect to accidents, disease, and disasters differs materially, as this chapter considers.

17.02 Thus, with respect to the right to life under the 1966 International Covenant on Civil and Political Rights[1] (ICCPR), the Human Rights Committee has affirmed only that 'the duty to protect life also implies that States parties should take appropriate measures to address the general conditions in society that may give rise to direct threats to life or prevent individuals from enjoying their right to life with dignity'. These include 'pervasive traffic and industrial accidents' and 'the prevalence of life-threatening diseases, such as AIDS, tuberculosis and malaria'.[2] Furthermore, the Committee has declared, States Parties to the ICCPR 'should also develop, when necessary, contingency plans and disaster management plans designed to increase preparedness and address natural and manmade disasters that may adversely affect enjoyment of the right to life, such as hurricanes, tsunamis, earthquakes, radioactive accidents and massive cyberattacks resulting in disruption of essential services'.[3]

17.03 This is a surprisingly weak formulation, with the consistent employment of hortatory language suggesting that no unequivocal duty obligates a State Party to the Covenant to exercise due diligence in tackling disease, natural disasters, and accidents. In fact, international human rights law, in particular the right to life, is considerably more demanding. Foreseeable threats to life demand action from the authorities, and it must be action that is of a minimum level of competence. Indeed, while the response of individual States with respect to the global COVID-19 pandemic that erupted in 2020 will be litigated for many

---

[1] International Covenant on Civil and Political Rights; adopted at New York 16 December 1966; entered into force 23 March 1976.
[2] Human Rights Committee, General Comment No. 36: Article 6: right to life, UN doc. CCPR/C/GC/36, 3 September 2019 (hereinafter, Human Rights Committee, General Comment 36 on the right to life), para. 26.
[3] Ibid.

years to come,[4] it is clear that a negligent failure in any State to take action reasonably expected to reduce risk and to protect both the public and health care workers – and *a fortiori* the deliberate spreading by the authorities of falsehoods about the disease that lead to its greater propagation – engage the international responsibility of the State.

17.04 With respect to the right to life under the 1981 African Charter on Human and Peoples' Rights,[5] the African Commission on Human and Peoples' Rights better reflects extant international law. Its General Comment issued in 2015 'proceeds from an understanding that the Charter envisages the protection not only of life in a narrow sense, but of dignified life. This requires a broad interpretation of States' responsibilities to protect life. Such actions extend to . . . humanitarian responses to natural disasters, famines, outbreaks of infectious diseases, or other emergencies.'[6]

17.05 That said, the African Commission's 2015 General Comment does not explicitly address the issue of accidents, even though the rates of, for instance, road traffic death in Africa are the highest in the world on a regional basis. In 2016, they stood at 26.6 per 100,000 people, which compares to a global rate of 18.2 per 100,000 people.[7] The General Comment does, though, refer to the State's 'positive duty to protect individuals and groups from real and immediate risks to their lives caused either by actions or inactions of third parties'.[8]

17.06 The remainder of this chapter addresses, in turn, the prevention and repression of disease, the reduction of and response to accidents of varying nature, and preparedness and responses to natural disasters. In each case, a State must reflect international good practice in preventive and reparative measures while tailoring its actions appropriately to the prevailing domestic context. While approaches between States may reasonably differ, and honest mistakes may be made that would not contravene the right to life even if fatalities result, negligent acts or omissions, as well as recklessness, may be constitutive of a violation.

THE PREVENTION AND REPRESSION OF DISEASE

17.07 Disease is ordinarily defined as 'a disorder of structure or function in a human, animal, or plant, especially one that produces specific symptoms or that affects a specific

---

[4] In November 2020 in France, for instance, the public prosecutor announced that a criminal investigation into whether the public officials who orchestrated France's response to the COVID-19 crisis committed offences, including manslaughter and endangering lives, would be split into four inquiries. Reuters, 'Paris Prosecutor Advances Criminal Investigation into COVID-19 Crisis Handling', 10 November 2020, at http://reut.rs/37BFvCG.

[5] African Charter on Human and Peoples' Rights; adopted at Nairobi 27 June 1981; entered into force 21 October 1986.

[6] African Commission on Human and Peoples' Rights, 'General Comment No. 3 on the African Charter on Human and Peoples' Rights: The Right to Life (Article 4)', adopted at Banjul (57th Ordinary Session) November 2015 (hereinafter, African Commission General Comment on the right to life), para. 3.

[7] World Health Organization (WHO), *Global Status Report on Road Safety 2018*, Geneva, 2018, at http://bit.ly/2UwBysY, p. 8.

[8] African Commission General Comment on the right to life, para. 41.

location and is not simply a direct result of physical injury'.[9] In turn, pathology is the 'science of the causes and effects of disease'.[10] That said, as Jackie Leach Scully has observed, what is generally considered as a disease may change over time, 'partly as a result of increasing expectations of health, partly due to changes in diagnostic ability, but mostly for a mixture of social and economic reasons'.[11] Thus, as she notes, osteoporosis was recognised as a disease by the World Health Organization (WHO) only in 1994, after being considered for a long time as an unavoidable part of normal ageing.[12]

17.08 In contrast, for much of the twentieth century, homosexuality was viewed in the United States and many other countries as an 'endocrine disturbance requiring hormone treatment' and later as an 'organic mental disorder treatable by electroshock and sometimes neurosurgery'. It was not officially depathologised by the American Psychiatric Association until 1974, which removed it from the list of disease states in its Fourth Edition of the Diagnostic and Statistical Manual of Mental Disorders.[13] Whether children diagnosed with attention deficit hyperactivity disorder (ADHD) – or attention deficit disorder (ADD), as it is also widely termed today – are suffering from a disease or a behavioural problem (or even a disability) continues to be disputed.[14] According to the Centers for Disease Control (CDC) in the United States, ADHD is one of the most common neurodevelopmental disorders of childhood.[15]

17.09 According to WHO, as of 2016 the ten deadliest diseases in the world were coronary artery disease (CAD), strokes, respiratory illness, chronic obstructive pulmonary disease (COPD), cancers, diabetes, Alzheimer's disease, diarrhoea, tuberculosis (TB), and cirrhosis (see Figure 17.1).[16] None is mentioned by the Human Rights Committee's General Comment 36 on the right to life. For several of these diseases, exercise and a healthy diet with reasonable limits on alcohol intake and abstaining from smoking remain the best means of prevention. This calls for information and awareness campaigns, as well as, arguably, dissuasive rates of taxation. But a due margin of discretion will be accorded to States under international human rights law as to how they manage their public health.

17.10 Among other diseases, even though it is not one of the ten greatest killers globally, malaria remains deadly, especially in developing countries. In 2020, coronavirus became a headline killer in many countries, officially claiming the lives of 3.5 million people by the end of May 2021,[17] although it was estimated that total deaths might have killed as many as

---

[9] Definition of 'disease' in the *Oxford English Dictionary*.
[10] Definition of 'pathology' in the *Oxford English Dictionary*.
[11] J. L. Scully, 'What Is a Disease?', *EMBO Reports*, vol. 5, no. 7 (July 2004), pp. 650–3, at http://bit.ly/38MWMuU, at 650.
[12] Ibid.
[13] Ibid.
[14] Ibid.; and see, e.g., D. Bernstein, 'Is ADHD a Disease? That's Not the Right Question', blog entry, ADDitude, last updated 6 November 2019, at http://bit.ly/3pzGlI8.
[15] CDC, 'What Is ADHD?', at http://bit.ly/2KcZrUp.
[16] WHO, 'The Top 10 Causes of Death', Fact Sheet, Geneva, 24 May 2018, at http://bit.ly/3nuCnid.
[17] See 'COVID-19 Dashboard', maintained by the Center for Systems Science and Engineering (CSSE) at Johns Hopkins University in the United States, at http://bit.ly/3lBMD7T.

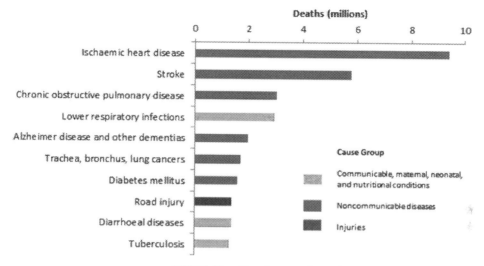

FIGURE 17.1 WHO's Top Ten Causes of Death, 2016

12 million people over that time.[18] Both diseases demanded specific actions as preventive measures distinct from those noted above.[19] Moreover, malaria was expected to kill more people in Sub-Saharan Africa this year than COVID-19 because of lockdowns and a shift in funding that has disrupted efforts to tackle the disease. Young children were likely to account for most of a top-end estimate of 100,000 excess deaths from the preventable disease in 2020, according to WHO.[20]

17.11 Malaria, an acute infectious disease caused by parasites called plasmodia and spread by the female anopheles mosquito, still occurs in almost 100 States. It is particularly prevalent in Sub-Saharan Africa and South Asia. An estimated 207 million people suffered from the disease in 2012, of whom approximately 627,000 died. About 90 per cent of these deaths were in Sub-Saharan Africa, with 77 per cent among children under the age of 5.[21] Between 2000 and 2015, rates dropped by at least 45 per cent, saving 6 million lives.[22]

---

[18] 'Tracking covid-19 excess deaths across countries', *The Economist*, 11 May 2021, at https://econ.st/3hN7mGM.
[19] Obesity was, however, said to be a major contributing factor to morbidity in the case of coronavirus, which directs authorities towards efforts to reduce calorific intake. This is partly explained by reference to immune cells from obese people being less effective at killing viruses and cancer cells. See, e.g., L. Lynch, 'Obesity and COVID-19 – Why the Increased Risk?', Science Foundation Ireland, 2020, at http://bit.ly/2UBjxK3.
[20] J. Flanagan, 'Malaria a Bigger Killer than Coronavirus in Sub-Saharan Africa', *The Times*, 1 December 2020, at http://bit.ly/37mLSd1 (subscription required).
[21] Bill and Melinda Gates Foundation, 'Malaria: Strategy Overview', at http://gates.ly/2VhTvK5.
[22] Swiss Tropical and Public Health Institute, 'Malaria and the UN Sustainable Development Goals (SDGs) 2030', Scientific Fact Sheet, 16 April 2018, at http://bit.ly/2STk4IT. Pinker suggests a 60 per cent drop over the same period.

17.12 No vaccine against malaria yet exists.[23] The most promising candidate to date, until recently, was the RTS,S vaccine developed by the pharmaceutical company, GlaxoSmithKline.[24] The vaccine, which has been under development since 1987, has evidenced in tests a prevention rate of four in ten cases of malaria and three in ten severe cases among children who received all four doses.[25] As of writing, a pilot rollout was underway in Ghana, Kenya, and Malawi.[26] As of early December 2020, however, a new potential vaccine developed by the Jenner Institute was preparing for phase-three clinical trials in Burkina Faso, Kenya, Mali, and Tanzania.[27] Otherwise, sprays and mosquito-proof bed nets treated with insecticide have proven to be the most effective means of prevention, though the destruction of larvae by environmental management, the use of larvicides or mosquito larvae predators, and the destruction of adult mosquitoes are broader measures that governments could be reasonably expected to undertake.[28]

17.13 The third Sustainable Development Goal (SDG) is to 'ensure healthy lives and promote wellbeing for all at all ages'. One of the targets for SDG 3 is, by 2030, to 'end the epidemics of AIDS, tuberculosis, malaria and neglected tropical diseases and combat hepatitis, water-borne diseases and other communicable diseases'.[29] Coordinated action can certainly be effective.[30] But the *World Malaria Report 2018*, published in November 2018, found that 'after an unprecedented period of success in global malaria control', progress had stalled. Data in 2015–17 showed that 'no significant progress in reducing global malaria cases was made in this period. There were an estimated 219 million cases and 435,000 related deaths in 2017'.[31]

17.14 Eleven high-burden countries (Burkina Faso, Cameroon, the Democratic Republic of Congo, Ghana, India, Mali, Mozambique, Niger, Nigeria, Tanzania, and Uganda) account for more than 70 per cent of global malaria cases and deaths. By 2017, ten of these countries, all of them in Sub-Saharan Africa, were not on track to meet the global targets.[32]

---

[23] The Gates Foundation committed US$258 million in 2005 for malaria research and development, including funding to support R&D on a malaria vaccine, new drugs, and improved mosquito control methods. Bill and Melinda Gates Foundation, 'Gates Foundation Commits $258.3 Million for Malaria Research and Development', 2005, at http://gates.ly/2Eqjl8S.

[24] The vaccine is designed to stop the Plasmodium falciparum malaria parasite from entering the liver, preventing the subsequent deadly blood stages.

[25] 'Malaria Vaccination: A Major Milestone', editorial in *The Lancet: Infectious Diseases*, vol. 19, no. 6 (1 June 2019), p. 559, at http://bit.ly/35jnFkK.

[26] M. van den Berg, B. Ogutu, N. K. Sewankambo, N. Biller-Andorno, and M. Tanner, 'RTS,S Malaria Vaccine Pilot Studies: Addressing the Human Realities in Large-Scale Clinical Trials', *Trials*, vol. 20 (2019), article 316, at http://bit.ly/3f7E4PC.

[27] T. Whipple and F. Elliott, 'Malaria Vaccine Another Success Story for Jenner Institute Team behind COVID Jab', *The Times*, 5 December 2020, at http://bit.ly/2L4FmzT (subscription required).

[28] See, e.g., European Centre for Disease Prevention and Control (ECDC), 'Prevention and Control Measures for Malaria', at http://bit.ly/2UxNRFi.

[29] See http://bit.ly/2GHExcR.

[30] See, e.g., G. Gachelin, P. Garner, E. Ferroni, J. P. Verhave, and A. Opinel, 'Evidence and Strategies for Malaria Prevention and Control: A Historical Analysis', *Malaria Journal*, vol. 17 (2018), article 96, at http://bit.ly/3f3kJiB.

[31] WHO, *The World Malaria Report 2018*, 19 November 2018, available at http://bit.ly/2U6CL8k.

[32] Ibid., p. 52.

Accidents, Disease, and Natural Disasters 379

Resistance of people to anti-malarial drugs and of mosquitoes to insecticides are considered major factors behind this stalling of progress. To comply with the right to life, each affected State must have a plan in place to reduce transmission of the disease and to protect the most vulnerable.

17.15 In any event, early diagnosis and treatment are a critical aspect of reducing the number of deaths from malaria. Longer-term approaches aside from vaccination are also being trialled. In one of the most affected States, Burkina Faso, researchers have been preparing to release so-called gene drive mosquitoes into the wild for the first time, by 2024. Gene drive involves developing a genetically-modified mosquito in the laboratory that can kill off its own species by spreading a faulty gene.[33]

17.16 In mid-November 2019, COVID-19 (caused by a specific form of coronavirus, SARS-CoV-2) was identified in Wuhan province in China. The virus has been tracked back, with some confidence, to horseshoe bats, although the precise date and manner of its zoonotic crossing to humans are not known as of this writing.[34] Moreover, given that horseshoe bats are not endemic to the area of Wuhan where COVID-19 was first detected in a human patient, it is widely speculated that an intermediary animal, possibly a pangolin, may have been involved in its transmission to humans.[35] A global study of the origins of SARS-CoV-2, convened by WHO, was up and running in November 2020.[36]

17.17 Since COVID-19 is caused by a virus, antibiotics are ineffective in its treatment.[37] Social distancing and the wearing of masks significantly reduce its transmission but do not stop it. Regular, thorough hand-washing with soap or hand sanitiser are effective in minimising the risk of a person contracting the virus.[38] As of this writing, however, a number of potentially highly effective vaccines were being rolled out following regulatory approval. Their development has been achieved in record time, following extensive human testing.[39] But their availability came not a moment too soon. As of early December 2020, more than 1.5 million were known to have died from COVID-19.

---

[33] S. Arie, 'GM Mosquitoes: Playing with God or the Only Way to Wipe Out Malaria?', *Daily Telegraph*, 5 February 2019, at http://bit.ly/2Xl7pgj.

[34] 'The Coronavirus's Origins Are Still a Mystery; We Need a Full Investigation', editorial opinion, *Washington Post*, 14 November 2020, at http://wapo.st/2UyyFb2. See also S. Boseley, 'Origin Story: What Do We Know Now about Where Coronavirus Came From?', *The Guardian*, 12 December 2020, at http://bit.ly/3nsW3mU.

[35] T. Burki, 'The Origin of SARS-CoV-2', *The Lancet: Infectious Diseases*, vol. 20, no. 9 (1 September 2020), pp. 1018–19, at http://bit.ly/3pAKw6L. A coronavirus found in pangolins is said to be close, genetically, to SARS-CoV-2. 'The Coronavirus's Origins Are Still a Mystery; We Need a Full Investigation', Editorial Opinion, *Washington Post*.

[36] WHO, 'WHO-Convened Global Study of the Origins of SARS-CoV-2', Geneva, 5 November 2020, at http://bit.ly/3pxqGJx. See also L. Mullin, 'The WHO Is Hunting for the Coronavirus's Origins; Here Are the New Details', *National Geographic*, 6 November 2020, at http://on.natgeo.com/3lFlyAD.

[37] WHO, 'Coronavirus Disease (COVID-19) Advice for the Public: Mythbusters', 2020, at http://bit.ly/36I1qaK.

[38] See, e.g., D. Berning Sawa, 'Hand Sanitizer or Hand Washing: Which Is Better against Coronavirus?', *The Guardian*, 4 March 2020 (as corrected on 6 April 2020), at http://bit.ly/3nrE3Jo.

[39] See, e.g., A. McKeever, 'Dozens of COVID-19 Vaccines Are in Development; Here Are the Ones to Follow', *National Geographic*, 13 November 2020, at http://on.natgeo.com/2K5icJc. It often takes ten to fifteen years to bring a vaccine to market; the fastest-ever – the vaccine for mumps – required four years in the 1960s. Vaccines typically go through a three-stage clinical trial process before they are sent to regulatory agencies for

380   Major Themes

A total of more than 65 million people were tested and found to have contracted the virus (countless others with symptoms were not tested or were asymptomatic).[40] The global hit to economic activity was exceptionally dire, estimated to reach tens of trillions of dollars in 2020 and beyond.[41] As a guide, the entire European Union Internal Market is worth some €15 trillion annually. The economic impact was pushing tens of millions of people into poverty, with significant concomitant consequences for their life expectancy and well-being.

17.18 Some of the worst affected States saw misinformation and falsehoods propagated by their leaders, seemingly for domestic political reasons. In Brazil, for instance, President Jair Bolsonaro famously dismissed coronavirus as a 'little flu' amid a plethora of inaccurate claims and assertions.[42] The online data website, Statista, even had a graph summarising by month the number of false or misleading statements made by the Brazilian president.[43] By August 2020, according to their assessment, he made seventy-five statements about COVID-19 containing information that was deemed fake or distorted. This was a reduction from the previous month when around one hundred of his statements on the global pandemic were considered incorrect or misleading. While of course not all of the deaths in Brazil are attributable to his actions, a considerable minority might be causally linked, which would make him potentially responsible for the violation of the right to life of thousands of people. As of mid-December 2020, more than 182,000 Brazilians were killed by the virus, giving the country the second-highest level of mortality in absolute terms in the world.[44] He was widely condemned for sluggishness in planning to vaccinate Brazilians, with a front-page editorial in the *Folha de São Paulo* terming Bolsonaro's inaction 'homicidal negligence', claiming Brazilians had been 'abandoned by the government' and that they were condemned to 'watch in distress' as vaccination began elsewhere.[45]

17.19 But, as of writing, the world's highest death toll in absolute terms occurred in the United States. By the end of May 2021, at least 590,000 people were recorded across the

   approval. Phase 1 checks the safety of the vaccine and whether it triggers an immune response in healthy humans. Phase 2 widens the testing pool to include groups of people who may have the disease or are more likely to catch it, to gauge the vaccine's effectiveness. Phase 3 expands the pool up to the thousands to make sure the vaccine is safe and effective among a wider array of people. Ibid. See also D. Sridhar, 'It's Not Just the Vaccine. There Are Many Causes for Hope in the Fight against COVID', *The Guardian*, 16 November 2020, at http://bit.ly/392N7k7.
[40] 'COVID-19 Dashboard' maintained by the CSSE at Johns Hopkins University, as of 5 December 2020.
[41] See, e.g., S. Nagarajan, 'The Coronavirus Pandemic Could Cost the Global Economy a Nightmarish $82 Trillion over 5 years, a Cambridge Study Warns', *Business Insider*, 20 May 2020, at http://bit.ly/2IwN4SL.
[42] 'The *Irish Times*' View on Coronavirus in Brazil: A Death Every Minute', *Irish Times*, 8 June 2020, at http://bit.ly/3nnNiKu.
[43] 'Brazil: Bolsonaro's Fake Statements on the Novel Coronavirus by Month 2020', published by Statista Research Department, 14 September 2020, at http://bit.ly/2IFIRfq.
[44] 'COVID-19 Dashboard', Global Deaths, as of 16 December 2020; and see H. Kalout, 'Bolsonaro's Failed Diplomacy Leaves Brazil Isolated as Pandemic Rages', *Foreign Policy*, 7 July 2020, at http://bit.ly/3f5lms7; and C. Paz, 'What Bolsonaro's COVID-19 Case Tells Us about Trump's', *The Atlantic*, 3 October 2020, at http://bit.ly/3kxsgrb.
[45] Cited in T. Phillips, 'Bolsonaro Branded "Homicidally Negligent" over Brazil's Vaccine Planning', *The Guardian*, 13 December 2020, at http://bit.ly/3afaUh0.

world's wealthiest nation as having died of COVID-19. A public health system more likely to be encountered in a developing nation and widespread obesity – 42.4 per cent of the population in 2017–18 were classified as obese[46] – meant that the country was always going to be hit hard by the virus. Conspiracy theories and falsehoods about even the existence of the virus rampant on social media were reinforced by acts and statements from the national leadership, especially US President Donald J. Trump. Among a litany of misstatements and misrepresentations, President Trump had claimed, falsely, that a CDC study had shown that '85 percent of the people wearing masks catch' the virus. In one press conference, he had even called for injected disinfectants to treat the virus.[47] In an interview in October 2020, Dr Anthony Fauci, the director of the National Institute of Allergy and Infectious Diseases in the United States, told CBS News' flagship documentary programme *60 Minutes* that he was 'absolutely not' surprised that Donald Trump had contracted coronavirus.[48]

17.20 President Trump's opponent in the November 2020 presidential elections, Democratic candidate Joe Biden, also did not escape criticism. Fact checkers at PolitiFact found, for instance, that despite a claim from Mr Biden to the contrary, Mr Trump could not have prevented every COVID-19 death in the United States had he 'done his job from the beginning'. As public health experts observed, 'a more robust handling of the pandemic would likely have seen the country's death count significantly reduced, but not to zero'.[49] As the incoming US president, the nation's forty-sixth, Joe Biden was obligated to take swift and effective action to bring the virus under control. By mid-December 2020, 16.7 million people were known to have the virus across the country.[50]

17.21 International organisations may also be responsible under human rights law for the propagation of disease. Thus the responsibility of the United Nations for an outbreak of cholera in Haiti in 2010 has been invoked by the UN Special Rapporteur on extreme poverty and human rights. In his annual report to the UN General Assembly in 2016, Philip Alston noted that cholera arrived in Haiti in October 2010, soon after the arrival of a new contingent of UN peacekeepers from a cholera-infected region (Nepal). The scientific evidence, he declared, pointed 'overwhelmingly' to the peacekeeping mission being the source of the outbreak. As of mid-2016, 9,145 Haitians died and almost 780,000 were infected.[51]

[46] CDC, 'Adult Obesity Facts', last reviewed on 29 June 2020, at http://bit.ly/2HaYomE.
[47] C. Paz, 'All the President's Lies about the Coronavirus', *The Atlantic*, 2 November 2020, at http://bit.ly/38Rop2O; see also RMIT ABC Fact Check, 'Donald Trump Has Made Many False Coronavirus Claims, But Some of Joe Biden's Are Wide of the Mark Too', *ABC News*, last updated 29 October 2020, at http://ab.co/3lDmpBZ; and BBC, 'Coronavirus: Trump "Can't Imagine Why" US Disinfectant Calls Spiked', 28 April 2020, at http://bbc.in/35IwAQd.
[48] J. Lapook, 'Fauci Admits Administration Has Restricted His Media Appearances, Says He's Not Surprised Trump got COVID', *60 Minutes*, CBS News, 19 October 2020, at http://cbsn.ws/3f4uNYL; see also H. Sullivan, 'Global Report: Fauci "Absolutely Not" Surprised Trump got COVID; Biden Warns Virus Worsening', *The Guardian*, 19 October 2020, at http://bit.ly/3t4P4xc.
[49] RMIT ABC Fact Check, 'Donald Trump Has Made Many False Coronavirus Claims, But Some of Joe Biden's Are Wide of the Mark Too'.
[50] 'COVID-19 Dashboard', cases by country/region/sovereignty, as of 16 December 2020.
[51] 'Report of the Special Rapporteur on extreme poverty and human rights', UN doc. A/71/367, 26 August 2016, Summary.

17.22 In rejecting the validity of a claim for compensation against the organisation, in 2013 the Under-Secretary-General for Legal Affairs recalled the UN's immunity from prosecution in domestic courts and appeared to attribute the cause of the outbreak to the aftermath of an earlier earthquake.[52] The same year, however, the former UN High Commissioner for Human Rights, Navanethem Pillay, called publicly for the Haitian victims to be compensated.[53] Moreover, as the Special Rapporteur on extreme poverty and human rights recalls, the UN in Haiti claims 'to ensure that its peacekeeping operations and their personnel operate within the normative framework of international human rights law and are held accountable for alleged violations'.[54] The Special Rapporteur concluded that 'strong grounds' existed for the issuance of an apology and the acceptance of responsibility.[55]

17.23 In December 2016, then UN Secretary-General Ban Ki-moon admitted that the UN had caused the outbreak, ending six years of refusing to accept causal responsibility, and acknowledged that it had left 'a blemish' on the reputation of the organisation.[56] But he stopped short of a full apology, let alone accepting any legal responsibility. In May 2020, in a letter to the UN Secretary-General, António Guterres, numerous UN special rapporteurs criticised the organisation for making 'illusory' promises to the Haitian people, noting that after pledging US$400 million to address the cholera outbreak, the UN had raised just $21 million and spent 'a pitiful' $3 million. 'This is a deeply disappointing showing following the loss of 10,000 lives', the rapporteurs declared.[57] As Chapter 33 describes, the UN is bound by customary human rights norms, in particular the duty to respect and protect life. The negligence of the organisation determines its responsibility for a massive number of violations of the right to life with respect to the cholera outbreak in Haiti.

ACCIDENT PREVENTION AND REDUCTION

17.24 Accidents will happen, runs the cliché. Indeed, without accidents, there would be no Darwinian evolution, as Michael Yarus pointed out in his 2018 work *Life from an RNA World – The Ancestor Within*.[58] But within the scope of its duty to protect life, a State must make all reasonable efforts to prevent and reduce accidents in territory under its jurisdiction. This demands the adoption of legislation on safety standards across the spectrum of human activity and to undertake practical measures to implement and ensure respect for those standards.

---

[52] Ibid., para. 28, citing Letter dated 21 February 2013 from the Under Secretary General for Legal Affairs, Patricia O'Brien, to Brian Concannon, Director, Institute for Justice and Democracy in Haiti.
[53] 'Report of the Special Rapporteur on extreme poverty and human rights', UN doc. A/71/367, para. 38.
[54] Ibid., para. 48, citing letter dated 25 November 2014 from Assistant Secretary General Pedro Medrano Rojas, Senior Coordinator for the Cholera Response in Haiti, addressed to the special procedures mandate holders, para. 57.
[55] 'Report of the Special Rapporteur on extreme poverty and human rights', UN doc. A/71/367, para. 79.
[56] E. Pilkington and B. Quinn, 'UN Admits for First Time That Peacekeepers Brought Cholera to Haiti', *The Guardian*, 1 December 2016, at http://bit.ly/3kFwBsm.
[57] E. Pilkington, 'UN Response to Haiti Cholera Epidemic Lambasted by Its Own Rights Monitors', *The Guardian*, 4 May 2020, at http://bit.ly/3lEkzk5.
[58] M. Yarus, *Life from an RNA World – The Ancestor Within*, Harvard University Press, Cambridge, MA, 2010.

17.25 Road and rail accidents and industrial accidents can be especially deadly, sometimes involving multiple casualties. WHO reported that the number of road traffic deaths globally has continued to rise steadily, attaining 1.35 million in 2016, the most recent year for which data were available as of writing. That said, the rate of death relative to the size of the world's population has remained constant.[59] WHO categorised progress to realise SDG Target 3.6 – which called for a 50 per cent reduction in the number of road traffic deaths by 2020 – remained 'far from sufficient'.[60]

17.26 Moreover, as WHO observed, road traffic accidents have become the eighth leading cause of death for all age groups. 'More people now die as a result of road traffic injuries than from HIV/AIDS, tuberculosis or diarrhoeal diseases.' Road traffic accidents have also become the leading cause of death for children and young adults aged five to twenty-nine years, 'signalling a need for a shift in the current child and adolescent health agenda which, to date, has largely neglected road safety'.[61] Furthermore, variation in death rates across regions and countries 'also corresponds with differences in the types of road users most affected'. Certain 'vulnerable' road users – pedestrians, cyclists, and motorcyclists – represent more than half of all global road traffic deaths.[62] This demands a tailored road safety strategy in every country in the world, involving, in particular the ministries of transportation and health.

17.27 In a judgment in March 2020 in *Marius Alexandru and Marinela Ștefan v. Romania*,[63] a chamber of the European Court of Human Rights assessed the responsibility of the authorities for a car accident. Ms Stefan is the daughter and sister of three people who were killed in an accident that occurred on 6 August 2007 when a tree beside the road fell on the car in which they were travelling. A police investigation was launched on the basis of possible charges of involuntary manslaughter against the driver, Ms Stefan's father.[64]

17.28 The European Court criticised the excessively long period of the investigations into the causes of the accident – eight and a half years – and a series of 'irregularities' that began with the initial police inquiry.[65] It held that the procedural element of the right to life had been violated as a consequence. But it rejected the application for a finding of a violation of the substantive element of the right to life. There were in place regulations governing the maintenance of trees bordering highways. With respect to the practical measures taken, the Court held that these were within the margin of appreciation of the national authorities.[66] In a partially dissenting opinion, however, Judge Pinto de Albuquerque disapproved of the approach taken by the Court, fearing that the margin of appreciation

---

[59] WHO, *Global Status Report on Road Safety 2018*, Geneva, 2018, Summary, p. 2.
[60] Ibid.
[61] Ibid., p. 3.
[62] Ibid., p. 6.
[63] European Court of Human Rights, *Marius Alexandru and Marinela Ștefan v. Romania*, Judgment (Fourth Section), 24 March 2020.
[64] Ibid., para. 6.
[65] Ibid., paras. 88–93.
[66] Ibid., paras. 104–9.

ceded to the State 'risked denuding the right to life of its substance'.[67] He referred to expert opinions whereby the trees had been left to stand for too long (given their specific type) and holding that the trimming had been conducted in a negligent manner, leading to instability in the trees' root systems.[68]

17.29   The worst industrial accident in history occurred on 3 December 1984, when some forty tons of methyl isocyanate escaped from the Union Carbide plant in Bhopal, India. The gas drifted over the densely populated neighbourhoods around the plant, killing thousands of people immediately and creating a panic as tens of thousands of others attempted to flee Bhopal. The final death toll was reported by the authorities at 5,295, while an estimated 25,000 died over the course of the following days. Half a million survivors have suffered respiratory problems, eye irritation, or blindness. Since methyl isocyanate is twice as heavy as air, children were affected most.[69]

17.30   In the decades since the disaster, Union Carbide Corporation (UCC), its former Indian subsidiary (Union Carbide India), its current owner, DowDuPont, the state government of Madhya Pradesh, and the central Indian government have all sought to evade responsibility for the disaster and its clean-up. UCC settled in 1989 for US$470 million in damages, with each gas-exposed person getting 25,000 Indian rupees (roughly $2,200 at the time), but under the terms of the settlement, UCC continued to deny liability for the incident. Yet a plant operator had told government investigators that months before the leak, managers shut down a refrigeration unit that was intended to keep the methyl isocyanate tank cool enough to prevent accidents. One of the three safety systems in place had been out of service for weeks; the other had broken down days before the accident.[70]

17.31   In 2012, the Indian Supreme Court ordered the city to install pipes to bring in clean water from the Narmada River. But the pipes coming into some houses run through sewers, and on rainy days, dirt and faeces mingle with the clean water. Following a survey indicating twenty other communities where the water was contaminated, in March 2018 the Supreme Court ordered the city to lay down sewage and drainage networks for the entire city. A Greenpeace report estimated that a full clean-up would cost US$30 million over four years. Writing in July 2018, Apoorva Mandavilli stated that the Bhopal disaster of thirty-four years ago was, 'in fact, still unfolding'.[71]

17.32   Among industrial workplaces, offshore oil rigs are especially hazardous.[72] On 6 July 1988, an American oil rig in the North Sea, Piper Alpha, exploded, killing 167 men. The primary cause of the accident was found to be maintenance work carried out simultaneously on one of

---

[67] European Court of Human Rights, *Marius Alexandru and Marinela Ştefan v. Romania*, Judgment (Fourth Section), Partially dissenting opinion of Judge Pinto de Albuquerque, p. 31.
[68] Ibid., p. 33, citing also the expert opinion referred to in para. 44 of the judgment.
[69] A. Mandavilli, 'The World's Worst Industrial Disaster Is Still Unfolding', *The Atlantic*, 10 July 2018, at http://bit.ly/3fbbQ6A.
[70] Ibid.
[71] Ibid.
[72] 'The Dangers of Offshore Oil Rigs', Maritime Injury Guide, Posted on 30 July 2014, at http://bit.ly/3lJosBg.

the high-pressure condensate pumps and on a safety valve, which led to a leak in condensates.[73] The total insured loss was about £1.7 billion, making it one of the costliest man-made catastrophes in history. The accident forced the offshore industry to pay more attention to safety issues. A public inquiry into the accident began in November 1988, which was published in November 1990. The report made 106 recommendations for changes to North Sea safety procedures.[74] Issues concerned the management of change (design issues), personal safety over process safety (fire water pumps on manual start to protect divers), isolation and permits for maintenance (pump started before maintenance complete), handover (inadequate transfer of information between crews, shifts, and disciplines), safety culture (complacency), and emergency response (evacuation). The remains of Piper Alpha toppled into the sea on 28 March 1989.[75]

17.33 Some of the lessons of the Piper Alpha disaster, however, were not learned or implemented. On 20 April 2010, methane gas shot up a Deepwater Horizon oil well in the Gulf of Mexico, igniting from a spark in the rig's engines. The explosion killed eleven workers on the rig, and the incident resulted in the worst oil spill in US history. By the time the well was sealed in September 2010, an estimated 4.9 million barrels of oil had leaked into the Gulf of Mexico. Ten years on, it was found that some long-lived species of wildlife would be harmed for generations.[76] The investigatory commission created by the Obama administration to investigate the spill found that a series of lapses in safety had contributed to the disaster, many of which traced back to a culture both within BP and the industry more broadly that did not value safety enough. It was reported in 2020 that the full impacts of the spill were not yet known.[77]

17.34 A new agency in the United States, the Bureau of Safety and Environmental Enforcement, was created to track and enforce offshore drilling safety issues, something that had been handled by the same agency that approved leases to oil companies. The Bureau announced new safety rules for offshore operations in 2016. These include a requirement that blowout protectors – the piece that had failed at Deepwater Horizon – be inspected by a third party, rather than self-certified by the drilling companies. But subsequently many of the new rules, as well as other safety practices put in place after the disaster, were weakened. In 2019, the Trump administration revoked the requirement for independent safety certification for blowout protectors and bi-weekly testing.[78]

17.35 The Chernobyl nuclear power plant disaster in Ukraine on 26 April 1986 could have been by far the worst disaster in history, effectively rendering much of the European

---

[73] 'Piper Alpha Platform, North Sea', Offshore Technology, at http://bit.ly/3kHLeuY.
[74] Ibid.
[75] F. Macleod and S. Richardson, 'Piper Alpha: The Disaster in Detail', *The Chemical Engineer*, 6 July 2018, at http://bit.ly/3IJEgHj.
[76] J. Meiners, 'Ten Years Later, BP Oil Spill Continues to Harm Wildlife – Especially Dolphins', *National Geographic*, 17 April 2020, at http://on.natgeo.com/3kHM8rm.
[77] A. Borunda, 'We Still Don't Know the Full Impacts of the BP Oil Spill, 10 Years Later', *National Geographic*, 20 April 2020, at http://on.natgeo.com/3fbH7X8.
[78] Ibid.

continent uninhabitable.[79] As it is, the clean-up of the area surrounding the plant is expected to continue for decades, while parts of the surrounding environment may remain uninhabitable for thousands of years.[80] While the official report was of only thirty immediate deaths, these figures are unpersuasive, and a far higher death toll over the medium and long term is far more credible.

17.36 The accident was the result of a flawed reactor design that was operated with inadequately trained personnel. The resulting steam explosion and fires released at least 5 per cent of the radioactive reactor core into the environment, with the deposition of radioactive materials in many parts of Europe.[81] The explosions released four hundred times as much radioactive fallout as the bomb the United States dropped on Hiroshima in 1945.[82] The 1991 report by the State Committee on the Supervision of Safety in Industry and Nuclear Power on the root cause of the accident found that while the operators had placed their reactor in a dangerously unstable condition, virtually guaranteeing an accident, they had not violated vital operating policies and principles, 'since no such policies and principles had been articulated'.[83] These myriad failures invoked the responsibility of the authorities for violations of the right to life and, with respect to those who survived but who contracted thyroid cancer as a consequence of the disaster, the prohibition on inhumane treatment.

THE PREVENTION AND PREPAREDNESS FOR NATURAL DISASTERS

17.37 A disaster is defined by the International Law Commission (ILC) as 'a calamitous event or series of events resulting in widespread loss of life, great human suffering and distress, mass displacement, or large-scale material or environmental damage, thereby seriously disrupting the functioning of society'.[84] In turn, disaster preparedness refers to measures taken to prepare for and reduce the effects of disasters. That is, as the International Federation of Red Cross and Red Crescent Societies (IFRC), the world's largest humanitarian network, further explains, 'to predict and, where possible, prevent

---

[79] S. Kramer, 'A Chernobyl "Suicide Squad" of Volunteers Helped Save Europe – Here's Their Amazing True Story', Business Insider, 26 April 2018, at http://bit.ly/32TFKaF. See also R. E. Webb, 'Chernobyl: What Could Have Happened', *Ecologist*, vol. 16, nos. 4–5 (1986), pp. 167–8.
[80] E. Blakemore, 'The Chernobyl Disaster: What Happened, and the Long-Term Impacts', *National Geographic*, 17 May 2019, at http://on.natgeo.com/3nrYEgG.
[81] World Nuclear Association, 'Chernobyl Accident 1986', updated April 2020, at http://bit.ly/3fccK2B.
[82] Kramer, 'A Chernobyl "Suicide Squad" of Volunteers Helped Save Europe – Here's Their Amazing True Story'.
[83] World Nuclear Association, 'Chernobyl Accident 1986'.
[84] Para. 3(a) of International Law Commission (ILC) Draft Articles on the Protection of Persons in the Event of Disasters, 2016, adopted by the ILC at its sixty-eighth session in 2016, and submitted to the UN General Assembly in UN doc. A/71/10, para. 48 (hereinafter, ILC Draft Articles on the Protection of Persons in the Event of Disasters). The Draft Articles elaborated by the ILC explicitly exclude response to a disaster where it is governed by the rules of international humanitarian law. Art. 18(2), ILC Draft Articles on the Protection of Persons in the Event of Disasters.

disasters, mitigate their impact on vulnerable populations, and respond to and effectively cope with their consequences'.[85]

17.38 Today, we can predict with greater accuracy than ever before especially dangerous hurricanes, winter storms, and floods. 'We know which areas are prone to earthquakes and tornadoes or susceptible to wildfires, and we can tell hours in advance whether a tsunami will hit our shores.'[86] But this faster warning will only be as effective as the disaster preparedness plans that are put in action. As the 2016 ILC Draft Articles on the Protection of Persons in the Event of Disasters recall: 'The affected State has the duty to ensure the protection of persons and provision of disaster relief assistance in its territory, or in territory under its jurisdiction or control.'[87]

17.39 In late December 2004, one of the deadliest tsunamis in history killed hundreds of thousands of people in the Indian Ocean region. Deaths were recorded as far away as Somalia, Seychelles, and South Africa. *The Lancet* estimated that 'around 1.8 million people were displaced and about 460,000 homes damaged or destroyed. Even a decade on, many of those figures are still semi-provisional. It was just too big to ever assess the full truth.'[88] One of the immediate lessons from the disaster was that humanitarian aid should invest more in prevention and go beyond the provision of food, medicine, and immediate needs.[89] There were also fundamental changes in the way major disasters are handled within the UN. This included the creation of a special regional fund from which WHO can dispense up to $175,000 immediately upon request with a phone call or email.[90]

17.40 In a blog entry on The World Bank website, also in 2014, Abhas Jha identified three key lessons from the disaster.[91] The first was that 'putting resources into hazard mitigation and emergency preparedness is perhaps the best investment a country can make'. He recalled that a sophisticated early warning system has been developed at a cost of more than US$400 million across 28 nations. With 101 sea-level gauges, 148 seismometers, and 9 buoys, the Indian Ocean Tsunami Warning System can send alerts to countries' tsunami warning centres within 10 minutes of a quake. The second relates to the importance of building strong institutional coordination and adequate financing mechanisms. He noted that the government of Indonesia established the National

---

[85] IFRC, 'Disaster Preparedness', at http://bit.ly/2IRF52s.
[86] H. Levin, 'How to Prepare for a Natural Disaster – Emergency Preparedness Plan', MoneyCrashers, 14 October 2020, at http://bit.ly/3f8OT3U.
[87] Art. 10(1), ILC Draft Articles on the Protection of Persons in the Event of Disasters.
[88] 'Remembering the Indian Ocean Tsunami', Special Report, *The Lancet*, vol. 384 (13 December 2014), at http://bit.ly/38SvZo5.
[89] S. Briceño, '10 Lessons Learned from the South Asia Tsunami of 26 December 2004', UN Office for Disaster Risk Reduction (UNDRR), posted 7 January 2005, available at http://bit.ly/3nzNp5L.
[90] 'Remembering the Indian Ocean Tsunami', Special Report, *The Lancet*. See also 'A Decade after Indian Ocean Tsunami, Lessons Learned', UNDRR Regional Office for Asia and Pacific, Updated 26 December 2014, at http://bit.ly/3pGuFTV.
[91] A. Jha, 'Three Key Lessons from the 2004 Tsunami', blog entry, *The World Bank*, 23 December 2014, at http://bit.ly/36Q15CS.

Agency for Disaster Management in the aftermath of the disaster, 'which has emerged as a tremendously capable institution'. The third lesson is the need to put communities at the centre of the reconstruction process. In 'Aceh', he said, 'community-led recovery through participatory mapping of risks, local investment planning, and owner-driven reconstruction of housing enabled local communities to thrive again, and in the long term, become more resilient and safer'.[92]

17.41 In turn, learning in developing communities affected by natural disasters is of value to Western nations struggling with COVID-19 as the civil society Communicating with Disaster-Affected Communities (CDAC) Network[93] observed in mid-November 2020. As FanMan Tsang, the Network's Director of Common Services: Capacity Bridging and Technology, affirmed: 'To build trust it involves taking effort to understand the communication networks communities already trust. Within this, there are built-in mechanisms that ensure voices from every part of society are heard, and that their influence makes a meaningful change to the way authorities behave so that their needs, as perceived by themselves, are included.'[94]

17.42 He noted that technology must be used in a coordinated and focused way, for otherwise it could easily miss data concerning the vulnerable. As a case in point, at the start of the national lockdown in the United Kingdom, 'homeless people were absent from consideration until a chance intervention by a homeless expert, who happened to be in the office of the Prime Minister when the lockdown was instigated, ensured they were'.[95] In contrast, in many countries that were already in the midst of a humanitarian relief operation, effective mechanisms were swiftly implemented during the onset of the COVID-19 crisis. Often, they were already being used to address outbreaks of disease such as the Ebola virus, refugee relief operations, or reconstruction work.[96]

17.43 In the 2016 ILC Draft Articles on the Protection of Persons in the Event of Disasters it was stipulated that 'the inherent dignity of the human person shall be respected and protected in the event of disasters'.[97] Draft Article 5 provided that 'persons affected by disasters are entitled to the respect for and protection of their human rights in accordance with international law'. In its commentary on the provision, the ILC noted that it 'serves as a reminder of the duty of States to ensure compliance with all relevant human rights obligations applicable both during the disaster and the pre-disaster phase'. The Commission recognised 'an intimate connection between human rights and the principle of human dignity reflected in draft article 4, reinforced by the close proximity of the two

---

[92] Ibid.
[93] CDAC Network, 'About the CDAC Network', at http://bit.ly/32WzgrA.
[94] F. Tsang, 'How Hard-Fought Lessons from the Last Decade of Humanitarian Assistance in Crisis Situations Can Help the Global Response to COVID-19 Be More Responsive to the Needs of Real People on the Ground', blog entry, 16 November 2020, at http://bit.ly/3fcbvRc.
[95] Ibid.
[96] Ibid.
[97] Draft Article 4, ILC Draft Articles on the Protection of Persons in the Event of Disasters.

draft articles'.[98] As the Commission duly observed: 'A particularly relevant right is the right to life, as recognized in article 6, paragraph 1, of the International Covenant on Civil and Political Rights if a State is refusing to adopt positive measures to prevent or respond to disasters that cause loss of life.'[99]

17.44 The Commission decided to recommend to the UN General Assembly the elaboration of a treaty on the basis of the Draft Articles. However, this recommendation has not been acted upon by States, as of this writing.

---

[98] ILC Draft Articles on the Protection of Persons in the Event of Disasters, commentary para. 1 on Draft Article 5.

[99] Ibid., commentary para. 6. It was further determined by the ILC that 'response to disasters shall take place in accordance with the principles of humanity, neutrality and impartiality, and on the basis of non-discrimination, while taking into account the needs of the particularly vulnerable'. Draft Article 6, ILC Draft Articles on the Protection of Persons in the Event of Disasters.

18

Pollution and Climate Change

INTRODUCTION

18.01 This chapter considers whether, and if so how, the right to life may be violated by pollution and, at the least, a wilful failure to seek to tackle climate change. In this regard, with respect to the right to life under the 1966 International Covenant on Civil and Political Rights[1] (ICCPR), the Human Rights Committee has affirmed: 'Implementation of the obligation to respect and ensure the right to life, and in particular life with dignity, depends, inter alia, on measures taken by States parties to preserve the environment and protect it against harm, pollution and climate change caused by public and private actors.'[2]

18.02 In interpreting the right to life under the 1981 African Charter on Human and Peoples' Rights,[3] the General Comment issued by the African Commission on Human and Peoples' Rights in 2015 'proceeds from an understanding that the Charter envisages the protection not only of life in a narrow sense, but of dignified life. This requires a broad interpretation of States' responsibilities to protect life. Such actions extend to preventive steps to preserve and protect the natural environment.'[4]

18.03 The State's 'positive duty to protect individuals and groups from real and immediate risks to their lives caused either by actions or inactions of third parties' encompasses, the African Commission further affirms, 'preventive steps to preserve and protect the natural environment'.[5] In its earlier ruling of 27 May 2002, the Commission had held that a decision to allow massive oil pollution in Ogoniland in the pursuit of economic development could not be considered reasonable in light of its effects on the enjoyment of the rights to life, health, food, and water.[6] With respect to the right to life, the use of

---

[1] International Covenant on Civil and Political Rights; adopted at New York 16 December 1966; entered into force 23 March 1976.
[2] Human Rights Committee, General Comment No. 36: Article 6: right to life, UN doc. CCPR/C/GC/36, 3 September 2019 (hereinafter, Human Rights Committee, General Comment 36 on the right to life), para. 62.
[3] African Charter on Human and Peoples' Rights; adopted at Nairobi 27 June 1981; entered into force 21 October 1986.
[4] African Commission on Human and Peoples' Rights, 'General Comment No. 3 on the African Charter on Human and Peoples' Rights: The Right to Life (Article 4)', adopted at Banjul (57th Ordinary Session) November 2015 (hereinafter, African Commission General Comment on the Right to Life), para. 3.
[5] Ibid., para. 41.
[6] African on Human and Peoples' Rights, *Social and Economic Rights Action Centre and Centre for Economic and Social Rights v. Nigeria*, Decision (Comm. No. 155/96 (2001)), 27 May 2002.

Pollution and Climate Change

force was a basis for the Commission's holding as well as the environmental damage. In the salient paragraph, it was stated:

> The Security forces were given the green light to decisively deal with the Ogonis, which was illustrated by the wide spread terrorisations and killings. The pollution and environmental degradation to a level humanly unacceptable has made it living in the Ogoni land a nightmare. The survival of the Ogonis depended on their land and farms that were destroyed by the direct involvement of the Government. These and similar brutalities not only persecuted individuals in Ogoniland but also the whole of the Ogoni Community as a whole. They affected the life of the Ogoni Society as a whole.[7]

INTERNATIONAL ENVIRONMENTAL LAW AND THE RIGHT TO LIFE

18.04 A serious violation of international environmental law leading to death is ipso facto violative also of the right to life. This includes also the situation where environmental pollution in one State affects the environment and the population in another.

18.05 In 2012, the Human Rights Council established the mandate for the UN Independent Expert on human rights and the environment.[8] Mr John Knox was appointed the first Independent Expert. In his final report, in January 2018, Mr Knox, redesignated in 2015 as Special Rapporteur on the issue of human rights obligations relating to the enjoyment of a safe, clean, healthy and sustainable environment, observed: 'A safe, clean, healthy and sustainable environment is necessary for the full enjoyment of a vast range of human rights, including the rights to life, health, food, water and development.'[9] As he recalled, in 2010, the General Assembly recognised – albeit in a resolution that was not unanimously supported – 'the right to safe and clean drinking water and sanitation as a human right that is essential for the full enjoyment of life and all human rights'.[10] He called upon the General Assembly to adopt a similar resolution that recognises the right to a safe, clean, healthy and sustainable environment, 'another right that is essential for the full enjoyment of life and all human rights'.[11]

18.06 David R. Boyd was appointed as the new Special Rapporteur on 1 August 2018. In his report of January 2019, he noted that in twelve States, the courts have ruled that the right to

---

[7] Ibid., para. 67.
[8] Human Rights Council Resolution 19/10, adopted without a vote on 22 March 2012, operative para. 2.
[9] Report of the Special Rapporteur on the issue of human rights obligations relating to the enjoyment of a safe, clean, healthy and sustainable environment, UN doc. A/HRC/37/59, 24 January 2018, para. 2.
[10] UN General Assembly Resolution 64/292, adopted on 28 July 2010 by 122 votes to nil with 41 abstentions, operative para. 1. The States abstaining were Armenia, Australia, Austria, Bosnia and Herzegovina, Botswana, Bulgaria, Canada, Croatia, Cyprus, Czechia, Denmark, Estonia, Ethiopia, Greece, Guyana, Iceland, Ireland, Israel, Japan, Kazakhstan, Kenya, Latvia, Lesotho, Lithuania, Luxembourg, Malta, Moldova, The Netherlands, New Zealand, Poland, the Republic of Korea, Romania, Slovakia, Sweden, Tanzania, Trinidad and Tobago, Turkey, Ukraine, United Kingdom, United States, and Zambia. Many of the abstentions were motivated by an oral revision to operative paragraph 1 just prior to the draft resolution's adoption from 'declared' to 'recognised'.
[11] Report of the Special Rapporteur on the issue of human rights obligations relating to the enjoyment of a safe, clean, healthy and sustainable environment, UN doc. A/HRC/37/59, para. 14.

a healthy environment is an essential element of the right to life and an enforceable, constitutionally protected right.'[12] Building on the work of his predecessor, he argued: 'Surely if there is a human right to clean water, there must be a human right to clean air. Both are essential to life, health, dignity and wellbeing.'[13] He observes that 'air pollution causes 7 million premature deaths annually, including the deaths of more than 600,000 children'.[14] But he then asserts, without proffering supporting evidence or analysis, that 'these staggering and almost incomprehensible statistics represent an egregious violation of the right to life'.[15] This claim does not accurately represent international human rights law.

18.07 In the *Cáceres* case,[16] a farming family in Paraguay had complained to the Human Rights Committee that the mass use of agrotoxins by nearby large agrobusinesses had poisoned many local residents and led to the death of their relative, Ruben Portillo Cáceres. In its 2019 Views, the Committee found violations of the family members' rights to life; to privacy, family, and home; and an effective remedy, noting that the state had failed to adequately enforce environmental regulations and did not properly redress the resulting harms. In January 2011, Mr Portillo Cáceres died after suffering from severe nausea and fever, allegedly because of pesticides and insecticides. Twenty-two other members of Colonia Yeruticreadaen were affected by similar symptoms at the same time. The Committee stated that

> heavily spraying the area in question with toxic agrochemicals – an action which has been amply documented ... – poses a reasonably foreseeable threat to the authors' lives given that such large-scale fumigation has contaminated the rivers in which the authors fish, the well water they drink and the fruit trees, crops and farm animals that are their source of food. The authors were hospitalized due to poisoning, and the State party has not adduced evidence of any kind to demonstrate that the results of the blood and urine tests were within the normal range, nor has an alternative explanation been given for the events in question. Furthermore, Mr. Portillo Cáceres died with no explanation from the State party, as an autopsy was never conducted.[17]

18.08 Regional human rights courts have also addressed the relevance of environmental protection to the right to life. The case of *Öneryildiz v. Turkey* concerned the deaths of nine people as a consequence of a methane explosion. They were living in a house built on

---

[12] Issue of human rights obligations relating to the enjoyment of a safe, clean, healthy and sustainable environment: Report of the Special Rapporteur, UN doc. A/HRC/40/55, 8 January 2019, para. 14. The Special Rapporteur cites as examples in his report only four States: India, Ireland, Nigeria, and Pakistan. He also cites in support his earlier research published in 2011: D. R. Boyd, 'The Implicit Constitutional Right to a Healthy Environment', *Review of European Community and International Environmental Law*, vol. 20, no. 2 (July 2011), pp. 171–9.

[13] Issue of human rights obligations relating to the enjoyment of a safe, clean, healthy and sustainable environment: Report of the Special Rapporteur, UN doc. A/HRC/40/55, para. 44.

[14] Ibid., para. 52.

[15] Ibid.

[16] Human Rights Committee, *Cáceres v. Paraguay*, Views (CCPR/C/126/D/2751/2016), 25 July 2019.

[17] Ibid., para. 7.5.

land that surrounded a rubbish tip. The applicant complained that no measures had been taken to prevent an explosion despite an expert report having drawn the authorities' attention to the need to act preventively, as such an explosion was not unlikely. In its 2004 judgment, the Grand Chamber of the European Court of Human Rights found a violation of the right to life in its substantive limb.[18] The Court reiterated that its approach to the interpretation of Article 2 on the right to life 'is guided by the idea that the object and purpose of the Convention as an instrument for the protection of individual human beings requires its provisions to be interpreted and applied in such a way as to make its safeguards practical and effective'.[19]

18.09 The Court further reiterated that Article 2 does not solely concern deaths resulting from the use of force by agents of the State but also lays down a positive obligation on States to take appropriate steps to safeguard the lives of those within their jurisdiction.[20] The Court considered 'that this obligation must be construed as applying in the context of any activity, whether public or not, in which the right to life may be at stake, and a fortiori in the case of industrial activities, which by their very nature are dangerous'.[21]

18.10 While Article 2 of the 1950 European Convention on Human Rights does not contain the term 'arbitrary' with respect to its protection of the right to life, the same principle would apply to the interpretation of Article 6 of the ICCPR. Thus, in a case in which the Human Rights Committee gave its views in September 2019, the authors of the complaint alleged a violation by the omission of Article 6 with respect, among others, to a man who died while exhibiting symptoms of pesticide poisoning.[22] The Committee observed that 'a narrow interpretation does not adequately convey the full concept of the right to life' and that States Parties 'must take positive action to protect that right'.[23] It was of the view that

> heavily spraying the area in question with toxic agrochemicals ... poses a reasonably foreseeable threat to the authors' lives given that such large-scale fumigation has contaminated the rivers in which the authors fish, the well water they drink and the fruit trees, crops and farm animals that are their source of food. The authors were hospitalized due to poisoning, and the State party has not adduced evidence of any kind to demonstrate that the results of the blood and urine tests were within the normal range, nor has an alternative explanation been given for the events in question. Furthermore, Mr. Portillo Cáceres died with no explanation from the State party, as an autopsy was never conducted.[24]

The Committee noted that the State Party in question, Paraguay, was bound by the 2001 Stockholm Convention on Persistent Organic Pollutants. The Stockholm Convention,

---

[18] European Court of Human Rights, *Öneryildiz v. Turkey*, Judgment (Grand Chamber), 30 November 2004, para. 110.
[19] Ibid., para. 69.
[20] Ibid., para. 71.
[21] Ibid.
[22] Human Rights Committee, *Norma Portillo Cáceres and others v. Paraguay*, UN doc. CCPR/C/126/D/2751/2016, 20 September 2019, para. 7.2.
[23] Ibid., para. 7.3.
[24] Ibid., para. 7.5.

which entered into force on 17 May 2004, is an international environmental law treaty that seeks to eliminate or restrict the production and use of persistent organic pollutants.

18.11 The cornerstone of international environmental law was set out in Principle 21 of the 1972 Stockholm Declaration:[25]

> States have, in accordance with the Charter of the United Nations and the principles of international law, the sovereign right to exploit their own resources pursuant to their own environmental policies, *and the responsibility to ensure that activities within their jurisdiction or control do not cause damage to the environment of other States or of areas beyond the limits of national jurisdiction.*[26]

In its 1996 Advisory Opinion on nuclear weapons, the International Court of Justice declared that the general obligation upon States 'to ensure that activities within their jurisdiction and control respect the environment of other States or of areas beyond national control is now part of the corpus of international law relating to the environment'.[27] Thus, a serious violation of that duty leading to the death of individuals in the other affected State or States would also constitute a violation of their right to life.

POLLUTION AND THE RIGHT TO LIFE OF CHILDREN

18.12 Pollution has a significant and growing impact on the lives of children. According to WHO, lower respiratory infections are among the largest causes of mortality in children, accounting for 15.5 per cent of deaths in 2015. Exposure to pollution and other environmental harms in childhood can have lifelong consequences, including an increase in the likelihood of cancer and other diseases.[28]

18.13 The most important environmental risks are household air pollution from exposure to smoke from cookstoves, ambient air pollution, and second-hand tobacco smoke.[29] Together, ambient and household air pollution contribute to seven million premature deaths annually, including the deaths of approximately 600,000 children.[30] In September 2018, it was reported that new scientific evidence found that particles of air pollution can travel through a pregnant woman's lungs and lodge in her placenta.[31]

---

[25] P. Sands and J. Peel, *Principles of International Environmental Law*, 3rd ed., Cambridge University Press, Cambridge, 2012, p. 191.

[26] Principle 21, Declaration of the United Nations Conference on the Human Environment; adopted by the UN Conference on the Human Environment, Stockholm, 5–16 June 1972 (added emphasis).

[27] ICJ, *Legality of the Threat of Use of Nuclear Weapons*, Advisory Opinion, 8 July 1996, para. 29.

[28] Report of the Special Rapporteur on the issue of human rights obligations relating to the enjoyment of a safe, clean, healthy and sustainable environment, UN doc. A/HRC/37/59, 24 January 2018, para 41(b).

[29] WHO, *Don't Pollute My Future! The Impact of the Environment on Children's Health*, Geneva, 2017, p. 2.

[30] 'Issue of human rights obligations relating to the enjoyment of a safe, clean, healthy and sustainable environment. Report of the Special Rapporteur', UN doc. A/HRC/40/55, 8 January 2019, para. 26, citing WHO, 'Burden of disease from the joint effects of household and ambient air pollution for 2016', May 2018.

[31] D. Carrington, 'Air Pollution Particles Found in Mothers' Placentas', *The Guardian*, 16 September 2018, at http://bit.ly/2TWoZ8h.

18.14 In the United Kingdom, a new inquest into the death of an asthmatic nine-year-old girl began at the end of November 2020, after a medical report suggested a direct link between her illness and poor air quality near her home, not far from a busy road. Ella Adoo-Kissi-Debrah became the first person in the United Kingdom – and possibly in the world – to have 'air pollution' formally listed as a cause of death by the coroner at the issue of an inquest.[32] The coroner recorded that air pollution exposure was a cause of Ms Adoo-Kissi-Debrah's death, alongside acute respiratory failure and severe asthma. She was exposed, he said, to nitrogen dioxide and particulate matter pollution in excess of WHO guidelines, the principal source of which was traffic emissions. He said there was a failure to reduce limits to legal limits, which possibly contributed to her death, and her mother was not given information about the potential to exacerbate asthma.[33] Indeed, given the prior judicial warnings about air pollution that were seemingly ignored by the authorities,[34] a violation of her right to life has likely occurred.

18.15 Makuch et al. argue with respect to the right to life under the Convention on the Rights of the Child[35] (CRC) that 'Article 6 on the right to life provides the most substantial legal argument for the environmental rights of the child. If you cannot breathe clean air, drink clean water, and so on, how can you live?'[36] In other respects, however, the provisions in the CRC on environmental pollution are weak. While under Article 24(1) States Parties recognise the right of the child to the enjoyment of the highest attainable standard of health, in implementing this right, they are only constrained to take 'into consideration the dangers and risks of environmental pollution'. That said, in its General Comment on the article (No. 15, 2013), the Committee on the Rights of the Child declared that States 'should take measures to address the dangers and risks that local environmental pollution poses to children's health in all settings'.[37]

18.16 Air pollution in a number of States is so severe that it may amount to a violation of the child's right to life. In mid-December 2019, State authorities warned people to wear face masks or stay indoors after very high levels of air pollution returned to Bangkok following months of relatively clean air. The national Pollution Control Department

---

[32] H. Cockburn, 'Ella Kissi-Debrah Inquest: Coroner Says Air Pollution Contributed to Death of Nine-Year-Old in Landmark Ruling', *The Independent*, 16 December 2020, at http://bit.ly/3ah1QY3; and C. Marshall, 'Rosamund Adoo-Kissi-Debrah: "Did Air Pollution Kill My Daughter?"', BBC, 29 November 2020, at http://bbc.in/2JllkAD.

[33] S. Laville, 'Girl's Death Contributed To by Air Pollution, Coroner Rules in Landmark Case', *The Guardian*, 16 December 2020, at http://bit.ly/2IUVVhd.

[34] F. Harvey, 'Air Pollution: UK Government Loses Third Court Case as Plans Ruled "Unlawful"', *The Guardian*, 21 February 2018, at http://bit.ly/2KTteBV; and S. Laville, 'Landmark Inquest to Rule If Air Pollution Killed London Pupil', *The Guardian*, 30 November 2020, at http://bit.ly/308n3bw.

[35] Convention on the Rights of the Child; adopted at New York 20 November 1989; entered into force 2 September 1990.

[36] K. E. Makuch, S. Zaman, and M. R. Aczel, 'Tomorrow's Stewards: The Case for a Unified International Framework on the Environmental Rights of Children', *Health and Human Rights Journal*, 12 June 2019, at http://bit.ly/35r42aB.

[37] Committee on the Rights of the Child, 'General Comment No. 15 (2013) on the right of the child to the enjoyment of the highest attainable standard of health', UN doc. CRC/C/GC/15, 17 April 2013, para. 49.

issued the warning when the amount of hazardous PM 2.5 dust particles[38] exceeded designated safe levels in three areas in the capital. Air pollution had forced the closure of some schools in Bangkok earlier in the year.[39] The safe threshold in Thailand is set at 50 μg (micrograms) per cubic metre of air, which is higher than the recognised safe level in many other nations.[40] One website recorded Luanda, the Angolan capital, as the most polluted city in the world in 2019. Its PM 2.5 level was 182 μg per cubic metre.[41]

CLIMATE CHANGE AND THE RIGHT TO LIFE

18.17 As the UN Special Rapporteur on human rights and the environment has observed: 'Climate change is having a major impact on a wide range of human rights today, and could have a cataclysmic impact in the future unless ambitious actions are undertaken immediately.'[42] Among the rights being 'threatened and violated', he further notes, are the rights to life, health, food, water and sanitation, a healthy environment, an adequate standard of living, housing, property, self-determination, development, and culture.[43]

18.18 As the Special Rapporteur recalls, climate change has many direct and indirect effects on the full enjoyment of the right to life.[44] Climate-related deaths are caused by extreme weather events, heatwaves, floods, droughts, wildfires, water-borne and vector-borne diseases, malnutrition, and air pollution. Globally, at least 150,000 premature deaths annually by 2012 were linked to climate change.[45]

18.19 In 2019, the Human Rights Committee considered a communication on the right to life authored by an individual who was contesting the legality of his deportation from New Zealand to Kiribati in 2015.[46] Mr Teitiota did so on the basis that he had been constrained to flee the island of Tarawa in the Republic of Kiribati by the effects of climate change and sea-level rise. Attempts to combat sea-level rise have largely been ineffective, according to Teitiota. Inhabitable land on Tarawa has eroded, resulting in a housing crisis and land disputes that have caused numerous fatalities. Kiribati has thus become an untenable and violent environment for the author and his family.[47]

---

[38] PM 2.5 is particulate matter 2.5 micrometres or less in diameter.
[39] 'Air Pollution Soars in Thai Capital Bangkok, Authorities Issue Warning', CAN, 19 December 2019, at http://bit.ly/2QGYGIX.
[40] A. Wipatayotin, 'Dust Pollution Surges in Greater Bangkok', *Bangkok Post*, 30 September 2019, at http://bit.ly/2MUHlVD.
[41] STC, 'World's Most and Least Polluted Cities', 27 August 2019, at http://bit.ly/3605VFY.
[42] 'Human rights obligations relating to the enjoyment of a safe, clean, healthy and sustainable environment, Note by the Secretary-General', UN doc. A/74/161, 15 July 2019, para. 26.
[43] Ibid.
[44] Ibid., para. 29.
[45] Ibid., citing DARA and the Climate Vulnerable Forum, *Climate Vulnerability Monitor: A Guide to the Cold Calculus of a Hot Planet*, 2nd ed., DARA, 2012.
[46] Human Rights Committee, *Ioane Teitiota v. New Zealand*, Views (Comm. No. 2728/2016), UN doc. CCPR/C/127/D/2728/2016, 7 January 2020.
[47] Ibid., para. 2.1.

18.20 New Zealand's Immigration and Protection Tribunal rejected his claim for asylum, although it did not exclude the possibility that environmental degradation could 'create pathways into the Refugee Convention or protected person jurisdiction'.[48] The author of the communication accepted that his experiences were common to people throughout Kiribati. He believed that the government was powerless to stop the sea-level rise. Internal relocation was, he said, not possible.[49]

18.21 With respect to the ICCPR, the Tribunal noted that the right to life must be interpreted broadly. The Tribunal accepted that the right to life involves a positive obligation of the state to fulfil the right by taking programmatic steps to provide for the basic necessities for life. However, the author could not point to any act or omission by the government of Kiribati indicating a risk that he would be arbitrarily deprived of his life within the scope of Article 6 of the Covenant. The Tribunal considered that Kiribati was active on the international stage concerning the threats of climate change, as demonstrated by its 2007 Programme of Action. Moreover, it observed, the author could not establish that there was a sufficient degree of risk to his life, or that of his family, at the relevant time.[50]

18.22 In assessing whether the communication was admissible, the Human Rights Committee considered that the author had sufficiently demonstrated that, due to the impact of climate change and associated sea-level rise on the habitability of Kiribati and on the security situation in the islands, he faced a real risk of impairment to his right to life under Article 6 of the ICCPR as a result of New Zealand's decision to remove him to the Republic of Kiribati.[51] The Committee then moved to consider communication on its merits. It recalled its position in General Comment 36 on the right to life, wherein it had declared that States Parties to the Covenant 'must allow all asylum seekers claiming a real risk of a violation of their right to life in the State of origin access to refugee or other individualized or group status determination procedures that could offer them protection against *refoulement*'.[52]

18.23 The Committee observed that the State Party had 'thoroughly considered and accepted the author's statements and evidence as credible, and that it examined his claim for protection separately under both the Refugee Convention and the Covenant'.[53] There had therefore been no vitiation of process. The Committee also noted the Tribunal's statement that the author appeared to allege not a risk of harm specific to him, but rather a general risk faced by everyone in Kiribati. The Committee held that the author had not demonstrated 'clear arbitrariness or error in the domestic authorities' assessment as to whether he faced a real, personal and reasonably foreseeable

---

[48] Ibid., para. 2.2.
[49] Ibid., para. 2.5.
[50] Ibid., para. 2.9.
[51] Ibid., para. 8.6.
[52] Ibid., para. 9.3, citing General Comment 36 on the right to life, para. 31.
[53] Human Rights Committee, *Ioane Teitiota v. New Zealand*, Views, para. 9.6.

risk of a threat to his right to life as a result of violent acts resulting from overcrowding or private land disputes in Kiribati'.[54]

18.24 Furthermore, the information provided to the Committee did not indicate that when the author was returned to Kiribati (in 2015), there was a real and reasonably foreseeable risk that he would be exposed to a situation of indigence, deprivation of food, and extreme precarity that could threaten his right to life, including his right to a life with dignity. The Committee therefore considered that the author had failed to establish that the assessment of the domestic authorities 'was clearly arbitrary or erroneous in this regard, or amounted to a denial of justice'.[55]

18.25 The Committee rejected Mr Teitiota's claim of a violation of the right to life on the facts.[56] But it also expressed the view that 'without robust national and international efforts, the effects of climate change in receiving states may expose individuals to a violation of their rights under articles 6 or 7 of the Covenant, thereby triggering the non-refoulement obligations of sending states'. Furthermore, the Committee declared, 'given that the risk of an entire country becoming submerged under water is such an extreme risk, the conditions of life in such a country may become incompatible with the right to life with dignity before the risk is realized'.[57]

18.26 There were two dissenting opinions among the Human Rights Committee. Professor Vasilka Sancin addressed New Zealand's conclusion that the available evidence did not support the author's contention that he could not obtain potable water. She observed, though, that '"potable water" should not be equated with "safe drinking water". Water can be designated as potable, while containing microorganisms dangerous for health, particularly for children.'[58] She opined that the burden lay with New Zealand, in order to comply with its positive duty to protect life from risks arising from known natural hazards, to demonstrate that the author and his family would in fact enjoy access to safe drinking (or even potable) water in Kiribati.[59]

18.27 A second dissenting opinion was provided by Duncan Laki Muhumuza of Uganda. Ambassador Laki would also have found a violation of the author's right to life. He asserted that although deaths were seemingly 'not occurring with regularity', it 'would indeed be counterintuitive to the protection of life, to wait for deaths to be very frequent and considerable; in order to consider the threshold of risk as met'.[60] He stated that it 'should be sufficient'

> that the child of the author has already suffered significant health hazards on account of the environmental conditions. It is enough that the author and his family are already

---

[54] Ibid., para. 9.7.
[55] Ibid., para. 9.9.
[56] Ibid., para. 10.
[57] Ibid., para. 9.11.
[58] Human Rights Committee, *Ioane Teitiota v. New Zealand*, Views, Annex 1: Individual opinion of Committee member Vasilka Sancin (dissenting), para. 3.
[59] Ibid., para. 5.
[60] Human Rights Committee, *Ioane Teitiota v. New Zealand*, Views, Annex 2: Individual opinion of Committee member Duncan Laki Muhumuza (dissenting), para. 5.

facing significant difficulty in growing crops and resorting to the life of subsistence agriculture on which they were largely dependent. Considering the author's situation and his family, balanced with all the facts and circumstances of the situation in the author's country of origin, reveals a livelihood short of the dignity that the Convention seeks to protect. . . . New Zealand's action is more like forcing a drowning person back into a sinking vessel, with the 'justification' that after all there are other voyagers on board. Even as Kiribati does what it takes to address the conditions; for as long as they remain dire, the life and dignity of persons remains at risk.[61]

18.28 While the dissenting opinions do not represent the current state of international law, they prefigure the evolution that is bound to come in the next three decades as the dramatic effects of climate change become even more pronounced and visible. In some ocean basins, sea-level rise has been as much as twenty centimetres since the start of the satellite record in 1993, and the rise is increasing ever more rapidly. In the United States, almost 40 per cent of the population live in relatively densely populated coastal areas, where sea level plays a role in flooding, shoreline erosion, and hazards from storms. Globally, eight of the world's ten largest cities are said to be near a coast.[62]

18.29 The most recent special report from the Intergovernmental Panel on Climate Change (in 2018) predicted a rise in ocean levels of between twenty-six and seventy-seven centimetres by 2100, with temperatures warming 1.5°C. Analysis based on North American Space Agency (NASA) and European data predicts a rise of sixty-five centimetres by the end of this century if the current trajectory continues.[63] But there are also increasingly dramatic forecasts of even higher rises in sea levels. An academic analysis published by *Nature* in October 2019 noted that under higher emissions scenarios, twenty-first-century rise may approach or in the extremes exceed two metres, in the case of early-onset Antarctic ice sheet instability.[64] Summer ice loss in the Arctic was also pushing record levels as of July 2020.[65]

---

[61] Ibid., paras. 5 and 6.
[62] R. Lindsey, 'Climate Change: Global Sea Level', NOAA, Climate.gov, United States, 14 August 2020, at http://bit.ly/3k8msVc.
[63] C. Nunez, 'Sea Level Rise, Explained', *National Geographic*, 19 February 2019, at http://on.natgeo.com/2RqcJNO.
[64] S. A. Kulp and B. H. Strauss, 'New Elevation Data Triple Estimates of Global Vulnerability to Sea-Level Rise and Coastal Flooding', *Nature*, 29 October 2019, at http://go.nature.com/2RmeyLD.
[65] A. Freedman, 'Arctic Sea Ice Is in a Downward Spiral, and May Break a Record in 2020', *Washington Post*, 20 July 2020, at http://wapo.st/2FkIUfb.

19

Autonomous Use of Force

INTRODUCTION

19.01 This chapter considers whether the autonomous use of force is compatible with respect for and protection of the right to life. The development of artificial intelligence has given rise to autonomy from human beings in the decision to target individuals with force and the ability to kill them. While weapons systems incorporating features of automaticity of action and reaction have existed for many years, the ever-increasing sophistication – and phenomenal speed – of decision-making by machine mean that both as a means of warfare and in law enforcement, autonomous weapons systems may become commonplace in years to come. Indeed, the informal architect of the US Department of Defense's first policy on autonomous weapons systems has claimed that the rise of artificial intelligence 'will transform warfare'.[1] Whether that is desirable or ethical[2] is not considered hereunder; this chapter focuses on whether the use of autonomous weapons systems can comply with the right to life, and, if so, under which circumstances.

19.02 In this regard, with respect to the right to life under the 1966 International Covenant on Civil and Political Rights[3] (ICCPR), the UN Human Rights Committee has affirmed that 'the development of autonomous weapon systems lacking in human compassion and judgment raises difficult legal and ethical questions concerning the right to life, including questions relating to legal responsibility for their use'.[4] The Committee affirmed that 'such weapon systems should not be developed and put into operation, either in times of war or

---

[1] P. Scharre, *Army of None: Autonomous Weapons and the Future of War*, W. W. Norton, New York, 2018, p. 5.
[2] For one view of the ethical issues, see the paper submitted by the International Committee of the Red Cross (ICRC) in 2018 in the context of the discussions under the auspices of the UN Convention on Certain Conventional Weapons. Therein, the ICRC argues: 'Ethical issues are at the heart of the debate about the acceptability of autonomous weapon systems. It is precisely anxiety about the loss of human control over weapon systems and the use of force that goes beyond questions of the compatibility of autonomous weapon systems with our *laws* to encompass fundamental questions of acceptability to our *values*.' ICRC, 'Ethics and Autonomous Weapon Systems: An Ethical Basis for Human Control?', Group of Governmental Experts of the High Contracting Parties to the Convention on Prohibitions or Restrictions on the Use of Certain Conventional Weapons Which May Be Deemed to Be Excessively Injurious or to Have Indiscriminate Effects, UN doc. CCW/GGE.1/2018/WP.5, 29 March 2018, Executive Summary (original emphasis).
[3] International Covenant on Civil and Political Rights; adopted at New York 16 December 1966; entered into force 23 March 1976.
[4] Human Rights Committee, General Comment No. 36: Article 6: right to life, UN doc. CCPR/C/GC/36, 3 September 2019 (hereinafter, Human Rights Committee, General Comment 36 on the right to life), para. 65.

in times of peace, unless it has been established that their use conforms with article 6 and other relevant norms of international law'.[5]

19.03 Thus the Committee did not consider autonomous weapon systems to be inherently unlawful; rather, it noted the requirement that their use be confirmed to comply with, in particular, international human rights law and international humanitarian law. The duty to review new weapons for their potential compliance with international humanitarian law and other salient branches of international law is a customary rule[6] that was first codified in the 1977 Additional Protocol I to the four Geneva Conventions of 1949.[7]

19.04 In August 2020, Human Rights Watch asserted that 'the challenge of killer robots [fully autonomous lethal weapons systems], like climate change, is widely regarded as a grave threat to humanity that deserves urgent multilateral action'.[8] In support of this assertion, it refers to the endorsement by the Minister for Foreign Affairs of both France and Germany of an 'Alliance for Multilateralism'[9] declaration concerning lethal autonomous weapons systems. Presented during the UN General Assembly on 26 September 2019, with the support of several other nations including Canada, Chile, Ghana, Mexico, and Singapore, the declaration's explicit support for the 'Eleven Principles' elaborated by the Group of Governmental Experts (GGE) created under the UN Convention on Certain Conventional Weapons[10] (CCW)

---

[5] Ibid., citing Report of the Special Rapporteur on extrajudicial, summary or arbitrary executions, Christof Heyns, UN doc. A/HRC/23/47, 9 April 2013, paras. 113–14.

[6] M. Schmitt, 'Autonomous Weapon Systems and International Humanitarian Law: A Reply to the Critics', *Harvard National Security Journal*, Features Online (2013), at http://bit.ly/34b9uzF, p. 28.

[7] Art. 36, Protocol Additional to the Geneva Conventions of 12 August 1949, and relating to the Protection of Victims of International Armed Conflicts (Protocol I); adopted at Geneva 8 June 1977; entered into force 7 December 1978. See S. Casey-Maslen, N. Corney, and A. Dymond-Bass, 'The Review of Weapons under International Humanitarian Law and Human Rights Law', chap. 14 in S. Casey-Maslen (ed.), *Weapons under International Human Rights Law*, Cambridge University Press, Cambridge, 2014, pp. 411–47, at 412 and 420–4. See also, in this regard, K. Lawand, 'Reviewing the Legality of New Weapons, Means and Methods of Warfare', *International Review of the Red Cross*, vol. 88, no. 864 (December 2006), pp. 925–30, at 929. Surprisingly, in its guide to the review of new weapons, also published in 2006, the ICRC made no mention of international human rights law, indicating that among rules of international law only international humanitarian law is relevant to such a review: 'The relevant rules include general rules of IHL applying to all weapons, means and methods of warfare, and particular rules of IHL and international law prohibiting the use of specific weapons and means of warfare or restricting the methods by which they can be used.' ICRC, *A Guide to the Legal Review of New Weapons, Means and Methods of Warfare: Measures to Implement Article 36 of Additional Protocol I of 1977*, Geneva, January 2006, section 1.2, pp. 10–11. More recently, the Stockholm International Peace Research Institute (SIPRI) was incorrect in its claim that 'it remains a matter of debate whether a state should give consideration to international human rights law (IHRL) in the review process'. V. Boulanin and M. Verbruggen, *Article 36 Reviews: Dealing with the challenges posed by emerging technologies*, Report, SIPRI, Stockholm, December 2017, at http://bit.ly/2EHf3gq, p. 5. Indeed, that statement appears to be contradicted later in the same publication: 'IHRL also forms part of the corpus of international law that needs to be considered in the conduct of an Article 36 review.' Ibid., p. 30.

[8] Human Rights Watch, 'Stopping Killer Robots: Country Positions on Banning Fully Autonomous Weapons and Retaining Human Control', 10 August 2020, at http://bit.ly/2SmLJyQ, p. 1.

[9] See generally Alliance for Multilateralism, 'What Is the "Alliance for Multilateralism"?', at http://bit.ly/3ljc4uv.

[10] Convention on Prohibitions or Restrictions on the Use of Certain Conventional Weapons Which May Be Deemed to Be Excessively Injurious or to Have Indiscriminate Effects; adopted at Geneva 10 October 1980; entered into force 2 December 1983. As of 1 May 2021, a total of 125 states were party to the CCW.

'marked the first time such a high-level group has acknowledged concerns' over fully autonomous weapons systems.[11] The Eleven Principles include the stipulation that 'human responsibility for decisions on the use of weapons systems must be retained since accountability cannot be transferred to machines. This should be considered across the entire life cycle of the weapons system.'[12]

19.05 In September 2020, the influential Non-Aligned Movement (NAM)[13] expressed its view, in a Working Paper submitted on its behalf by Venezuela in the context of the discussions under CCW auspices, that 'Lethal Autonomous Weapon Systems (LAWS) raise several ethical, legal, moral and technical, as well as international peace and security-related questions which should be thoroughly deliberated and examined in the context of conformity to international law including international humanitarian law and international human rights law.'[14] The NAM further declared that it was 'pleased' that, while divergences remained, a 'general sense has developed' among States Parties to the CCW 'that all weapons, including those with autonomous functions, must remain under the direct control and supervision of humans at all times and must comply with international law, including International Humanitarian Law and International Human Rights Law'.[15]

19.06 With respect to the right to life under the 1981 African Charter on Human and Peoples' Rights,[16] the General Comment issued by the African Commission on Human and Peoples' Rights in 2015 was similarly normative. The General Comment declares that 'any machine autonomy in the selection of human targets or the use of force should be subject to meaningful human control. The use of such new technologies should follow the established rules of international law.'[17] This effectively outlaws the use of fully autonomous weapons systems, deeming them incompatible with the right to life. There has also been opposition from a great number of artificial intelligence (AI) and robotics researchers. In an Open Letter published on the Future of Life Institute, the signatories

---

[11] Human Rights Watch, 'Stopping Killer Robots: Country Positions on Banning Fully Autonomous Weapons and Retaining Human Control', p. 1.

[12] Alliance for Multilateralism, 'Declaration by the Alliance for Multilateralism on Lethal Autonomous Weapons Systems (LAWS)', 2019, at http://bit.ly/36pxcuF.

[13] Of the 197 States recognised by the Secretary-General of the United Nations, the NAM has 120 member States: 53 in Africa, 39 in Asia, 26 in Latin America and the Caribbean, and 2 in Europe. There are 17 observers. 'Members and Other Participants of NAM Movement', at http://bit.ly/2G8FEUe. In May 2020, referring to the COVID-19 global pandemic, the UN Secretary-General stated: 'With two thirds of UN Member States, the Non-Aligned Movement has a critical role to play in forging global solidarity.' UN, 'Non-Aligned Movement Has Critical Role to Play in Galvanizing Global Solidarity to Fight COVID-19 Pandemic, Secretary-General Tells Online Summit', UN Press release SG/SM/20072, 4 May 2020, at http://bit.ly/3cFQKw6.

[14] Working paper by the Bolivarian Republic of Venezuela on behalf of the Non-Aligned Movement (NAM) and Other States Parties to the Convention on Certain Conventional Weapons (CCW), UN doc. CCW/GGE.1/2020/WP.5, 14 September 2020, at http://bit.ly/2HsxB51, para. 2.

[15] Ibid., para. 21.

[16] African Charter on Human and Peoples' Rights; adopted at Nairobi 27 June 1981; entered into force 21 October 1986.

[17] African Commission on Human and Peoples' Rights, 'General Comment No. 3 on the African Charter on Human and Peoples' Rights: The Right to Life (Article 4)', adopted at Banjul (57th Ordinary Session) November 2015, para. 35.

declare that 'we believe that AI has great potential to benefit humanity in many ways, and that the goal of the field should be to do so. Starting a military AI arms race is a bad idea, and should be prevented by a ban on offensive autonomous weapons beyond meaningful human control.'[18]

19.07 There are four main concerns about autonomous use of force under the right to life. First, it is questioned whether an autonomous weapons system is, or will ever be, capable of accurately identifying as a target only those individuals who may be lawfully targeted with force in the circumstances prevailing at the time. Second, it is interrogated whether a decision to use potentially lethal force may lawfully be left to a computer algorithm rather than to a human being. Third, it is unclear whether such a system is able to function in a manner that enables a person to be safely arrested with the minimum necessary use of force in a law enforcement operation or allows the acceptance of a surrender by a person participating directly in hostilities during an armed conflict, as the law of armed conflict/international humanitarian law requires. Fourth, if a machine violates the applicable law, who is to be held accountable and on what legal basis?

19.08 Discussions on the issue of regulation of lethal autonomous weapons systems (deliberately, if ironically, attracting the acronym 'LAWS') have been ongoing for several years in the context of the CCW. But these discussions have not crystallised in an agreement to negotiate a treaty to at least constrain, and possibly prohibit, such weapons systems as a means of warfare beyond the elaboration of the Eleven Principles.[19] Moreover, the CCW has never been used as a forum to regulate the use of force in law enforcement. Indeed, the Eleven Guiding Principles, published in an annex to the report on the 2019 Session of the GGE considering the question under the auspices of the CCW, mention neither human rights nor situations of law enforcement.[20]

19.09 This chapter moves next to consider the definitions of autonomy and a fully autonomous weapon/lethal autonomous weapons system. The chapter then looks briefly at machine autonomy and the types of autonomous weapons systems that have either been procured and deployed or which are known to be under development. It considers their legality both under the right to life during peacetime or in law enforcement during armed conflict and as a means of warfare in the conduct of hostilities during and in connection with an armed conflict.

KEY DEFINITIONS

19.10 There is not – or at least not yet – an agreed definition under international law of either a fully autonomous weapon or a lethal autonomous weapons system. In November 2019, the

---

[18] 'Lethal Autonomous Weapons Pledge', Open Letter available with list of signatories at http://bit.ly/3lbqP2l. As of 1 October 2020, the pledge had been signed by 247 organisations and 3,253 individuals.
[19] Traditionally, the States Parties to the CCW take all their substantive decisions by consensus.
[20] 'Draft Report of the 2019 session of the Group of Governmental Experts on Emerging Technologies in the Area of Lethal Autonomous Weapons Systems', UN doc. CCW/GGE.1/2019/CRP.1/Rev.2, 21 August 2019, at http://bit.ly/2FWKhB2, Annex IV, p. 13.

report on discussions in the CCW noted that no consensus existed among States Parties as to even the desirability of agreeing upon a definition. The report stated that 'the concept of autonomy being a spectrum, ... the difficulty of defining a clear point between semi- and fully autonomous systems was underlined'.[21]

19.11 *Autonomy* ordinarily means 'freedom from external control or influence'.[22] Aptly enough, as the *Oxford English Dictionary* recalls, the etymology of the word is from the Greek αυτονομος, which means 'having its own laws'.[23] Or, in the rather wordier definition of autonomy proposed by the US Department of Defense in the context of weapons systems: 'Autonomy is the computational capability for intelligent behavior that can perform complex missions in challenging environments with greatly reduced need for human intervention, while promoting effective man-machine interaction.'[24]

19.12 More straightforward was the Department of Defense's proposed definition in 2012 of a (fully) autonomous weapons system: 'a weapon system that, once activated, can select and engage targets without further intervention by a human operator'.[25] The definition, the Department of Defense confirmed, 'includes human-supervised autonomous weapon systems that are designed to allow human operators to override operation of the weapon system, but can select and engage targets without further human input after activation'.[26] The definition, 'elegant in its simplicity', was praised by Brazil as being of 'great usefulness'[27] (although it wrongly ascribed the origin of the definition to a joint report of June 2020 by the Stockholm International Peace Research Institute (SIPRI) and the International Committee of the Red Cross (ICRC)).[28] Brazil went on to offer its own, more 'comprehensive' definition of a lethal autonomous weapons system in its paper on definitions of August 2020:

> An intelligent weapon system with autonomous operation mode (i.e., without human input after activation) capable of recognizing patterns in combat environments, and of learning to operate and make decisions regarding the critical functions of target identification, tracking, locking-on and engaging based on uploaded databases, acquired experiences and its own calculations and conclusions.

It is not certain, however, that this definition adds great clarity. In particular, are these capabilities to be regarded as alternatives or as cumulative prerequisites?

[21] 'Report of the 2019 session of the Group of Governmental Experts on Emerging Technologies in the Area of Lethal Autonomous Weapons Systems: Addendum', UN doc. CCW/GGE.1/2019/3/Add.1, 8 November 2019, at http://bit.ly/342atly, para. 14.
[22] *Oxford English Dictionary* definition.
[23] Ibid.
[24] K. Kearns, 'DoD Autonomy Roadmap', NDIA 19th Annual Science and Engineering Technology Conference, 21 March 2018, at http://bit.ly/2FMt4Kv, p. 4.
[25] Department of Defense, 'Autonomy in Weapon Systems', *Directive No. 3000.09*, Washington, DC, 21 November 2012 (as revised 8 May 2017), at http://bit.ly/342w3q1, pp. 13–14.
[26] Ibid.
[27] V. Boulanin, N. Davison, N. Goussac, and M. Peldán Carlsson, *Limits on Autonomy in Weapon Systems: Identifying Practical Elements of Human Control*, Report, SIPRI/ICRC, Geneva, June 2020, available at http://bit.ly/341R2JO.
[28] 'LAWS and human control: Brazilian proposals for working definitions', UN doc. CCW/GGE.1/2020/WP.4, 19 August 2020, at http://bit.ly/3jaEOVx, para. 4.

19.13 The United Kingdom's definition of an autonomous weapons system is different from that of most other States and has not evolved over time. In 2011, the then UK Ministry of Defence doctrine on unmanned aerial systems declared that autonomous systems 'will, in effect, be self-aware and their response to inputs indistinguishable from, or even superior to, that of a manned aircraft. As such, they must be capable of achieving the same level of situational understanding as a human.'[29] Without that higher level of awareness, the United Kingdom regarded a system as 'automated'. As Scharre observed, the differing UK stance was 'not a product of sloppy language', it was 'a deliberate choice'. It enabled the United Kingdom to claim that autonomous weapons systems 'do not, and may never, exist'.[30]

19.14 In 2017, in its later Joint Doctrine Publication, the Ministry of Defence similarly distinguished between automated and autonomous systems. Reiterating the glossary incorporated in its 2011 doctrine, an automated (or automatic) system was one that, 'in response to inputs from one or more sensors, is programmed to logically follow a predefined set of rules in order to provide an outcome. Knowing the set of rules under which it is operating means that its output is predictable.'[31] In contrast, an autonomous system

> is capable of understanding higher-level intent and direction. From this understanding and its perception of its environment, such a system is able to take appropriate action to bring about a desired state. It is capable of deciding a course of action, from a number of alternatives, without depending on human oversight and control, although these may still be present. Although the overall activity of an autonomous unmanned aircraft will be predictable, individual actions may not be.[32]

AUTONOMOUS WEAPONS SYSTEMS UNDER DEVELOPMENT OR IN USE

19.15 Fully autonomous weapons systems require the integration of several core elements: a mobile combat platform (e.g., aircraft, ship, or ground vehicle), sensors to scrutinise the platform's surroundings, processing systems to classify objects discovered by the sensors, and algorithms directing the platform to initiate attack when an allowable target is detected.[33] Maziar Homayounnejad identifies three main advantages to such systems as a means of warfare: the ability to operate without communications links (arguably a strategic as well as a tactical/operational benefit), the speed and responsiveness of machine action relative to human performance (human neuromuscular response has a critical delay of 0.25 seconds), and minimal costs and resources (including allocation of

---

[29] UK Ministry of Defence, *The UK Approach to Unmanned Aircraft Systems*, Joint Doctrine Note 2/11, London, 2011, at http://bit.ly/3d25sgS, para. 206.
[30] Scharre, *Army of None: Autonomous Weapons and the Future of War*, p. 110.
[31] UK Ministry of Defence, *Unmanned Aircraft Systems*, Joint Doctrine Publication 0-30.2, August 2017, at http://bit.ly/30FNHPx, para. 2.5 and table 2.3.
[32] Ibid.
[33] M. T. Klare, 'Autonomous Weapons Systems and the Laws of War', *Arms Control Today*, March 2019, at http://bit.ly/342Bx4c.

human resources to maintenance and oversight but without a pilot or other operator who can be killed or captured).[34]

19.16 It is sometimes claimed that no fully autonomous systems have yet been deployed. But this is not accurate. While it is true that 'very few truly autonomous robotic weapons are in active combat use', many armed forces employ close-in naval defence weapons such as the US Phalanx system that can fire autonomously when a ship is under attack by enemy planes or missiles.[35] 'Yet', Michael Klare observes, 'such [automated] systems cannot independently search for and strike enemy assets on their own, and human operators are always present to assume control if needed'.[36] An exception is the Israeli Harpy airborne anti-radiation unmanned aircraft, which can loiter for several hours over a certain area to search for and destroy enemy radar installations.[37] Termed 'a rather rudimentary autonomous munition' by one commentator, the Harpy detects and engages specific radar-emitting objects within tight spatial and temporal boundaries defined by deploying commanders.[38]

19.17 Also rudimentary, but nonetheless autonomous in lethal action, is the CBU-105 cluster munition produced by the United States. The munition is dropped from an aircraft. As it approaches the target area, the outer casing opens to release ten BLU-108 submunitions. Each submunition contains four sensor-fuzed projectiles called skeets, which are then released. An infrared seeker on each skeet scans for targets on the ground while a laser-ranging device calculates the range for release timing. In contrast to a loitering munition such as the Harpy, a skeet can only 'hover with its sensor active for a few seconds before firing'.[39] Once it has locked onto a target, the skeet fires copper penetrators on the top of the target. A shrapnel ring released along with it causes damage in the immediate area around the target.[40] The US-produced weapons were used by Saudi Arabia in the armed conflict in Yemen, leading to specific criticism from Human Rights Watch on the basis of the risk they pose to civilians.[41]

19.18 An exemption specifically designed to permit this type of munition was, however, included in the 2008 Convention on Cluster Munitions.[42] Article 2(2)(c) of the Convention excludes from the definition of a prohibited cluster munition:

> A munition that, in order to avoid indiscriminate area effects and the risks posed by unexploded submunitions, has all of the following characteristics:

---

[34] M. Homayounnejad, 'Lethal Autonomous Weapon Systems Under the Law of Armed Conflict', PhD thesis, King's College London, 2018, s. 1.2.2, pp. 20–1.
[35] Klare, 'Autonomous Weapons Systems and the Laws of War'.
[36] Ibid.
[37] Scharre, *Army of None: Autonomous Weapons and the Future of War*, pp. 5, 47, 48.
[38] Homayounnejad, 'Lethal Autonomous Weapon Systems Under the Law of Armed Conflict', s. 2.4, p. 45.
[39] Scharre, *Army of None: Autonomous Weapons and the Future of War*, p. 52.
[40] NRP (a defence analyst who retains anonymity on the website), 'CBU-105 Sensor Fuzed Weapon: USAF's Ultimate Tank-buster', *Defencyclopedia*, 12 June 2015, at http://bit.ly/2SrYA3b.
[41] B. Brumfield and S. Shelbayah, 'Report: Saudi Arabia Used U.S.-Supplied Cluster Bombs in Yemen', *CNN*, updated 4 May 2015, at http://cnn.it/3irzWu5; Human Rights Watch, 'Technical Briefing Note: Cluster Munition Use in Yemen', 14 February 2016, at http://bit.ly/3cLb3YV.
[42] Convention on Cluster Munitions; adopted at Dublin 30 May 2008; entered into force 1 August 2010.

(i) Each munition contains fewer than ten explosive submunitions;
(ii) Each explosive submunition weighs more than four kilograms;
(iii) Each explosive submunition is designed to detect and engage a single target object;
(iv) Each explosive submunition is equipped with an electronic self-destruction mechanism;
(v) Each explosive submunition is equipped with an electronic self-deactivating feature[.]

Neither Saudi Arabia nor the United States is party to the Convention on Cluster Munitions, but many of the US allies within the North Atlantic Treaty Organization (NATO) are. The United Kingdom, for instance, has assisted Saudi Arabia in its targeting during the armed conflict in Yemen. Under the Convention on Cluster Munitions, the United Kingdom is prohibited from assisting any other State in engaging in conduct that the Convention prohibits to a State party, which includes the use of outlawed cluster munitions.[43]

19.19 Within the general context of weapon systems, both munitions and delivery platforms are likely to emerge from development as autonomous in years to come. These will not only be individual weapons systems. With a view to overwhelming military defences (including autonomous defensive systems), swarms of autonomous weapons systems are likely to be deployed and fielded. The US armed forces, for instance, are engaged in a 'Cluster Swarm' project to develop a missile warhead that dispenses a swarm of small unmanned aerial vehicles that fan out to locate and destroy vehicles with explosively formed penetrators.[44] It is undoubtedly the case that other militarily powerful States, in particular China and Russia, are engaged in similar research.

19.20 Paul Scharre observes that while the mechanisation of the industrial revolution enabled the creation of machines that were physically stronger and faster than human beings, the 'AI revolution is enabling the *cognitization* of machines, creating machines that are smarter and faster than humans for narrow tasks'.[45] 'Yet', he cautions, 'computers still fall short of humans in understanding context and interpreting meaning. AI programs today can identify objects in images, but can't draw these individual threads together to understand the big picture.'[46] Indeed, as he remarks, 'robots have one major disadvantage. By removing the human from the vehicle, they lose the most advanced cognitive processor on the planet: the human brain.'[47]

---

[43] Art. 1(1)(c), Convention on Cluster Munitions.
[44] Z. Kallenborn, 'Swarms of Mass Destruction: The Case for Declaring Armed and Fully Autonomous Drone Swarms as WMD', Modern War Institute, 28 May 2020, at http://bit.ly/3cKFDSE; and D. Hambling, 'U.S. Army's New Drone Swarm May Be a Weapon of Mass Destruction', Forbes, 1 June 2020, at http://bit.ly/2GqVRUz.
[45] Scharre, *Army of None: Autonomous Weapons and the Future of War*, p. 5.
[46] Ibid., p. 6.
[47] Ibid., p. 13.

THE ABILITY TO IDENTIFY TARGETS ACCURATELY

19.21 In their 2012 report, *Losing Humanity: The Case against Killer Robots*, Human Rights Watch and The International Human Rights Clinic (IHRC) at Harvard Law School stated, with respect to fully autonomous weapons systems, that 'the rule of distinction, which requires armed forces to distinguish between combatants and non-combatants, poses one of the greatest obstacles to fully autonomous weapons complying with international humanitarian law. Fully autonomous weapons would not have the ability to sense or interpret the difference between soldiers and civilians, especially in contemporary combat environments.'[48] This is a powerful claim. It basically asserts that every fully autonomous weapons system is inherently indiscriminate, at least as far as the targeting of persons is concerned. It is, however, far from certain that it is factually or legally accurate.

19.22 Michael N. Schmitt, a leading publicist specialising in IHL, took issue with the report in a 2013 features article in the *Harvard National Security Journal*,[49] affirming that 'much of *Losing Humanity* is either counter-factual or counter-normative'.[50] With respect to the claim that autonomous weapons systems are inherently indiscriminate, Schmitt writes:

> What Human Rights Watch appears to have missed is that even an autonomous weapon system that is completely incapable of distinguishing a civilian from a combatant or a military objective from a civilian object can be lawful per se. Not every battlespace contains civilians or civilian objects. When they do not, a system devoid of any capacity to distinguish protected persons and objects from lawful military targets can be used without endangering the former. Typical examples would include the employment of such systems for an attack on a tank formation in a remote area of the desert or from warships in areas of the high seas far from maritime navigation routes. The inability of the weapon systems to distinguish bears on the legality of their use in particular circumstances (such as along a roadway on which military and civilian traffic travels), but not their lawfulness per se.[51]

19.23 Schmitt further attests that 'Human Rights Watch's apprehension is also counter-factual'. He does so on the basis that military technology

> has advanced well beyond simply being able to spot an individual or object. Modern sensors can, inter alia, assess the shape and size of objects, determine their speed, identify the type of propulsion being used, determine the material of which they are made, listen to the object and its environs, and intercept associated communications or other electronic emissions. They can also gather additional data on other objects or individuals in the area and, depending on the platform with which they are affiliated, monitor a potential target

---

[48] Human Rights Watch and IHRC, *Losing Humanity: The Case against Killer Robots*, Washington, DC, 2012, at http://bit.ly/34c4kCP, p. 30.
[49] M. N. Schmitt, 'Autonomous Weapon Systems and International Humanitarian Law: A Reply to the Critics', *Harvard National Security Journal Features*, 5 February 2013, pp. 1–37, at http://bit.ly/34b9uzF.
[50] Ibid., p. 3.
[51] Ibid., p. 11.

for extended periods in order to gather information that will enhance the reliability of identification and permit target engagement when the target is relatively isolated.

He suggests that software in autonomous weapon systems 'is likely to be developed' that enables individuals to be visually identified, 'thereby enabling precision during autonomous "personality strikes" against specified persons'. 'These and related technological capabilities', he concludes, 'auger against characterization of autonomous weapon systems as unlawful per se solely based on their autonomous nature'.[52]

19.24 Thus the case is argued that such systems may lawfully be used now, at least in certain environments free of civilians and civilian objects, and that they may, in time to come, be capable of deployment in environments in which civilians and/or civilian objects are present. Indeed, under international humanitarian law, the standard of reliability that a lawful military objective is indeed being targeted is low. According to the article on precautions in attack in the 1977 Additional Protocol I, those who plan or decide upon an attack must 'do everything feasible to verify that the objectives to be attacked are neither civilians nor civilian objects and are not subject to special protection but are military objectives'.[53]

19.25 Although this rule is not included in the 1977 Additional Protocol II, given that such precautionary measures underpin respect for the fundamental principle of distinction, it may reasonably be considered to form part of the corpus of customary law. Indeed, in its judgment in the *Galić* case, a trial chamber of the International Criminal Tribunal for the former Yugoslavia (ICTY) held: 'The practical application of the principle of distinction requires that those who plan or launch an attack take all feasible precautions to verify that the objectives attacked are neither civilians nor civilian objects, so as to spare civilians as much as possible.'[54]

19.26 While not formally defined in international law, the ICRC study of customary international humanitarian law rules observes that the obligation to take all 'feasible' precautions 'has been interpreted by many States as being limited to those precautions which are practicable or practically possible, taking into account all circumstances ruling at the time, including humanitarian and military considerations'.[55] The feasibility standard is thus far below the threshold of a standard to take all 'necessary' or even all 'possible' measures to ensure that an intended target is a lawful military objective. The US Department of Defense has asserted that, under customary international law, 'no legal presumption of civilian status exists for persons or objects, nor is there any rule inhibiting commanders or other military personnel from acting based on the information available to him or her in doubtful cases'.[56] For the Department of Defense, the key issue is rather one

[52] Ibid.
[53] Art. 57(2)(a)(i), 1977 Additional Protocol I.
[54] ICTY, *Prosecutor* v. *Galić*, Judgment (Trial Chamber) (Case No. IT-98-29-T), 5 December 2003, para. 58.
[55] ICRC Customary IHL Rule 15: ('Principle of Precautions in Attack'), at http://bit.ly/2m6mCnj, text and accompanying note 20.
[56] US Department of Defense, *Law of War Manual*, updated December 2016, Washington, DC, §5.4.3.2, pp. 200–1.

of good faith: 'The requirement that military commanders and other decision-makers make decisions in good faith based on the information available to them recognizes that decisions may be made when information is imperfect or lacking, which will often be the case during armed conflict.'[57]

19.27 Given the weakness of the IHL standard, Maziar Homayounnejad argues that it is necessary to elevate the precautionary rule codified in the Additional Protocol I to a 'full' international humanitarian law/law of armed conflict principle. Currently, respect for the precautionary rule is not, formally at least, part of the prohibition on indiscriminate attacks. It is crucial, he states, that this involves US/NATO forces developing and applying 'a broader precautionary principle' for lethal autonomous weapons systems.[58]

19.28 At the same time, recalling the 'technologically agnostic nature of Article 57' (of the 1977 Additional Protocol I), Homayounnejad suggests that if an autonomous weapons system 'is able to verify targets more accurately than manned or remotely-piloted systems, because it uses a wider range of sensors and sources (including spectrums that are imperceptible to the human senses)', and if it processes the information 'faster and without the fears and frailties of human imperfections', this 'may obligate the use' of such an autonomous weapons system.[59] This latter assertion, however, goes too far. Just as there is no requirement under international humanitarian law/law of armed conflict to use precision-guided munitions,[60] there is no requirement to apply the best means of intelligence gathering where that is not practically possible in the circumstances.

THE LEGALITY OF ALGORITHMS IN THE USE OF FORCE

19.29 The standard of accuracy required by international humanitarian law/law of armed conflict of an attack is also low. Although it is not certain where precisely that standard falls,[61] long-range artillery and aerial bombardment, where shells or bombs are likely to fall more than 1,000 metres away from intended targets (that are lawful military objectives), have typically been considered indiscriminate. That said, it may prove to be the case that

---

[57] Ibid., §5.3.2, p. 197.
[58] Ibid., p. 272.
[59] Ibid., p. 250.
[60] US Department of Defense, *Law of War Manual*, updated December 2016, §5.2.3.2, citing also the military manuals of Australia, Canada, and Germany.
[61] The holding in the *Gotovina* case by an ICTY trial chamber that shells fired from long-range artillery must fall within two hundred metres of a lawful military objective in an urban environment or be deemed indiscriminate was explicitly overturned by the Appeals Chamber. ICTY, *Prosecutor v. Ante Gotovina and Mladen Markač*, Judgment (Trial Chamber I) (Case No IT-06-90-T), 15 April 2011, para. 1898; ICTY, *Prosecutor v. Ante Gotovina and Mladen Markač*, Judgment (Appeals Chamber) (Case No. IT-06-90-A), 20 November 2012, esp. paras. 61, 66, and 67. But, controversially, the Appeals Chamber did not determine where the correct standard was set. An amicus curiae brief to the Court had suggested four hundred metres as the appropriate standard. ICTY, *Prosecutor v. Gotovina* (Appeals Chamber) (Case No IT-06-90-A), Application and Proposed Amicus Curiae Brief Concerning the 15 April 2011 Trial Chamber Judgment and Requesting that the Appeals Chamber Reconsider the Findings of Unlawful Artillery Attacks during Operation Storm, p. 21.

Autonomous Use of Force

a far smaller circular error probable is the actual threshold in law.[62] For rifle fire, the upper legal threshold is likely counted rather in the dozens of metres at most, while for mortar shells this may be 100 metres in many instances.[63] If a computer algorithm can ensure compliance with such parameters in the use of force, its deployment may be permissible under *in bello* rules.

19.30 In contrast, the use of force in law enforcement is under far stricter legal constraints. While armed police officers do frequently fire at a person and miss, the human rights law precautionary principle applicable to law enforcement operations dictates that a shot should not be fired where it is probable that the target will not be successfully hit and especially where the risk to bystanders is significant. In any event, using a firearm can only be lawful in law enforcement where it is necessary to prevent an imminent threat of death or serious injury (or, exceptionally, to prevent a grave and temporally proximate threat to life from materialising) and where other, less harmful weapons would not be effective.[64]

19.31 Honest mistakes are permissible if they are reasonable in the circumstances. But the aim of opening fire in such circumstances must be to incapacitate, not kill, the criminal suspect. A tighter standard applies where the intent is to kill (for instance, to prevent a suicide or remote bomber from detonating his explosive device). This can only ever be lawful where it is strictly unavoidable to protect life.[65] These same rules would apply *in toto* to any autonomous weapons system.

THE ABILITY TO ACCEPT A SURRENDER OR ENABLE AN ARREST

19.32 Any person who submits and ends unlawful action during a law enforcement operation must be capable of being arrested. This implies that either autonomous weapons systems must be capable of arresting a suspect safely – typically without any use of force unless the suspect resists violently – or the system must be directly supported by police officers or other law enforcement officials who can themselves make the arrest. Their absence would not justify the use of force, especially the use of potentially lethal force.

19.33 In any armed conflict, whether international or non-international in character, a person clearly expressing an intent to surrender is *hors de combat* and may no longer – if he or she was previously directly participating in hostilities – be lawfully targeted. As the 1977 Additional Protocol I specifies, a person is *hors de combat* if he or she clearly expresses an intention to surrender, provided that he or she abstains from any hostile act and does not attempt to escape.[66] This rule applies as a matter of custom in all armed conflict.[67] As

---

[62] S. Casey-Maslen with S. Haines, *Hague Law Interpreted: The Conduct of Hostilities under the Law of Armed Conflict*, Hart, Oxford, 2018, p. 158.
[63] Ibid., pp. 159–60.
[64] Basic Principle 9, UN Basic Principles on the Use of Force and Firearms by Law Enforcement Officials; adopted at Havana, Cuba, 7 September 1990; and welcomed by the UN General Assembly, in Resolution 45/166, adopted without a vote on 18 December 1990, para. 4.
[65] Basic Principle 9, UN Basic Principles on the Use of Force and Firearms by Law Enforcement Officials.
[66] Art. 41(2)(b), 1977 Additional Protocol I.
[67] ICRC Customary IHL Rule 47: ('Attacks against Persons Hors de Combat'), at http://bit.ly/3ornohg.

Yoram Dinstein has observed, in a non-international armed conflict, the basis of the prohibition on denial of quarter in the 1977 Additional Protocol II – the order that there will be no survivors from an attack – is that '*au fond*, the idea is that fighters must be given the chance to surrender'.[68]

19.34 It has always been hard to conceive of how a surrender may be taken during an aerial attack, whether that be manned or unmanned in nature. Moreover, how long must a person seeking to surrender wait? A loitering munition could be there for days. But any movement away from the place where the person is standing could be interpreted as an attempt to escape, rendering him or her once more liable to lawful targeting and thus to being killed outright.

ACCOUNTABILITY FOR VIOLATIONS

19.35 There are undoubtedly challenges in ensuring accountability when a sensor or algorithm incorrectly identifies a person or an object as a legitimate target and death, injury, or damage results to an individual who is protected from the use of force. The weapons system which caused that harm can be destroyed, but a fundamental principle of both international human rights law and international humanitarian law is that there must be institutional and personal accountability for unlawful use of force.

19.36 In this regard, it is important to distinguish State responsibility from individual criminal responsibility. Where a violation of international humanitarian law has occurred, the State that deployed the system will be responsible for an internationally wrongful act. The same applies in case of a violation of the right to life, whether that occurs in peacetime or during a situation of armed conflict. More challenging is individual criminal responsibility. Dinstein suggests that those who design and activate a fully autonomous weapons system '*might* be held accountable if their creations do not comply with' international humanitarian law rules,[69] but that is hardly a reassuring statement. Indeed, as Ted Piccone asks, 'Where should responsibility for errors of design and use lie in the spectrum between 1) the software engineers writing the code that tells a weapons system when and against whom to target an attack, 2) the operators in the field who carry out such attacks, and 3) the commanders who supervise them?'[70]

19.37 There are certainly potential problems with attribution but that too is the case with cyber operations, which are generally considered legal under international humanitarian law. Schmitt acknowledges the particular challenges of compliance with the international humanitarian law principle of proportionality in attack, but appears to sympathise with the view that 'those who take the decision to employ the systems will be responsible for any foreseeable consequences, including violations of international humanitarian law, as they are

---

[68] Y. Dinstein, *Non-international Armed Conflicts in International Law*, Cambridge University Press, Cambridge, 2014, para. 433.

[69] Y. Dinstein, *The Conduct of Hostilities under the Law of International Armed Conflict*, 3rd ed., Cambridge University Press, Cambridge, 2016, para. 264 (added emphasis).

[70] T. Piccone, 'Order from Chaos: How Can International Law Regulate Autonomous Weapons?', Brookings, 10 April 2018, at http://brook.gs/36svsky.

with respect to other weapons and tactics'.[71] Bonnie Docherty accepts that military commanders or operators 'could be found guilty if they deployed a fully autonomous weapon with the intent to commit a crime'. It would, however, she states, 'be legally challenging and arguably unfair to hold an operator responsible for the unforeseeable actions of an autonomous robot'.[72] In 2013, the UN Special Rapporteur on extrajudicial, summary or arbitrary executions stated simply that the deployment of lethal autonomous weapons systems 'may be unacceptable because no adequate system of legal accountability can be devised'.[73]

CONCLUDING REMARKS

19.38 The US Department of Defense asserted starkly in late 2016: 'The law of war does not specifically prohibit or restrict the use of autonomy to aid in the operation of weapons.'[74] This is an accurate assessment of international humanitarian law / the law of armed conflict. It may well be, however, that at least a majority of States are moving towards some form of binding regulation of weapons incorporating artificial intelligence, in particular by prohibiting those autonomous weapons that are not subject to some form of human control in targeting and especially the release of munitions or other weapons against identified targets.[75]

19.39 In October 2020, Human Rights Watch and the IHRC at Harvard Law School published a report entitled New Weapons, Proven Precedent, setting out 'elements of and models for a treaty on killer robots'.[76] The report, authored by Bonnie Docherty, concluded that negotiating a treaty on fully autonomous weapons 'is a challenging but feasible endeavor'.[77] The core of the treaty would be on ensuring that all weapons, whether used as a means of warfare or in law enforcement, would be under 'meaningful human control'[78] and would 'prohibit weapons systems that lack such control'.[79]

---

[71] M. N. Schmitt, 'International Humanitarian Law and the Conduct of Hostilities,' chap. 7 in B. Saul and D. Akande (eds.), *The Oxford Guide to International Humanitarian Law*, Oxford University Press, Oxford, 2020, p.173.

[72] B. Docherty, 'The Need for and Elements of a New Treaty on Fully Autonomous Weapons', Human Rights Watch and IHRC, Washington, DC, June 2020, at http://bit.ly/3l1PXbu, p. 2.

[73] 'Report of the Special Rapporteur on extrajudicial, summary or arbitrary executions, Christof Heyns', UN doc. A/HRC/23/47, 9 April 2013, Summary.

[74] US Department of Defense, *Law of War Manual*, updated December 2016, §6.5.9.2: 'No Law of War Prohibition on the Use of Autonomy in Weapon Systems'.

[75] The US Department of Defense policy issued in 2012 stated: 'It is DoD policy that ... [a]utonomous ... weapon systems shall be designed to allow commanders and operators to exercise appropriate levels of human judgment over the use of force.' Department of Defense, 'Autonomy in Weapon Systems', *Directive No. 3000.09*, §4. But as Scharre observes, that policy does not prohibit even fully autonomous weapons systems. Scharre, *Army of None: Autonomous Weapons and the Future of War*, p. 75.

[76] Human Rights Watch and IHRC at Harvard Law School, *New Weapons, Proven Precedent. Elements of and Models for a Treaty on Killer Robots*, Washington, DC, October 2020.

[77] Ibid., p. 24.

[78] See further Human Rights Watch and IHRC, 'Killer Robots and the Concept of Meaningful Human Control', Memorandum to Convention on Conventional Weapons (CCW) Delegates, 11 April 2016, at http://bit.ly/2HhJfjJ.

[79] Human Rights Watch and IHRC, *New Weapons, Proven Precedent: Elements of and Models for a Treaty on Killer Robots*, p. 4.

19.40 Many will believe that such a normative development would be an unequivocal global good, keeping the decision to kill in the hands of human beings and inhibiting a burgeoning arms race. Others may wonder if, given the pitiful lack of respect for international humanitarian law rules on the conduct of hostilities and the widespread, discriminatory use of force by the police that has given rise to the Black Lives Matter movement, machines could not do even a little better. Yes, they lack human judgment and compassion, but machines also do not fear, and they lack venomous hatred and contempt for others who are different.

20

Slavery

INTRODUCTION

20.01 Chattel slavery is as old as humanity, although today the practice is rare. Between 1500 and 1875, an estimated 12.5 million slaves were traded across the Atlantic by Brazil, Britain, Denmark and the Baltic nations, France, the Netherlands, Portugal, Uruguay, and the United States.[1] The last nation in the world to formally abolish slavery was Mauritania, in 1981, although tens of thousands of people – said to be mostly from the minority Haratine or Afro-Mauritanian groups – still live as bonded labourers there in what is often termed 'modern slavery'.[2]

20.02 Under the 1966 International Covenant on Civil and Political Rights (ICCPR), it is stipulated that 'no one shall be held in slavery; slavery and the slave-trade in all their forms shall be prohibited'.[3] The distinct prohibition of slavery is not only a customary rule of international law, it is also a peremptory norm of international law (jus cogens).[4] Slavery has been famously described as 'social death',[5] but this chapter considers whether, and in which circumstances, it may also constitute a violation of the right to life.

The Prohibition of the Slave Trade and Slavery

20.03 The prohibition of the slave trade in international law is one of the longest-standing goals of the international community of States. The Congress of Vienna, which in 1814–15 brought together the great European powers with a view to bringing peace to Europe in the wake of the Napoleonic Wars,[6] included in its Final Act the Declaration XV.[7] The

---

[1] Slave Voyages, 'Trans-Atlantic Slave Trade – Estimates', at http://bit.ly/3eaYjLK.
[2] 'The Unspeakable Truth about Slavery in Mauritania', *The Guardian*, 8 June 2018, at http://bit.ly/2Jrgjqd.
[3] Art. 8(1), International Covenant on Civil and Political Rights; adopted at New York 16 December 1966; entered into force 23 March 1976.
[4] Annex to the text of the draft conclusions on peremptory norms of general international law (jus cogens), adopted by the international Law Commission (ILC) on first reading, in UN doc. A/74/10, 2019, at http://bit.ly/3hwjqJk, point (f). See also Commentary to Art. 40(3)–(5), ILC Draft Articles on the Responsibility of States for Internationally Wrongful Acts, in UN doc. A/56/10, 2001, pp. 283–4.
[5] O. Patterson, *Slavery and Social Death: A Comparative Study*, Harvard University Press, Boston, 1982.
[6] See, e.g., S. Ghervas, 'What Was the Congress of Vienna?', *History Today*, vol. 64, no. 9 (September 2014), at http://bit.ly/2qOjJrU.
[7] Declaration of the Powers regarding the abolition of the Slave Trade; adopted at Vienna 8 February 1815.

'Declaration of the Powers regarding the abolition of the Slave Trade' affirmed that the trading in slaves as chattels 'has been considered, by just and enlightened men of all ages, as repugnant to the principles of humanity and universal morality'.

20.04 The signatories proclaimed 'in the name of their Sovereigns, their wish of putting an end to a scourge, which has so long desolated Africa, degraded Europe, and afflicted humanity',[8] while also stipulating that the Declaration could 'not prejudge the period that each particular Power may consider as most advisable for the definitive Abolition of the Slave Trade'. They called for this to be 'a subject of negotiation between the Powers'.[9] Another seventy-five years would elapse, however, before a formal treaty ending the slave trade would be adopted.

20.05 The Slave Trade and Importation into Africa of Firearms, Ammunition, and Spirituous Liquors (General Act of Brussels) was signed at Brussels on 2 July 1890 after months of deliberation. Article V of the General Act required each signatory State, within one year of signature, to 'enact or propose' legislation criminalising, as a grave offence against the person 'the organizers and abettors of slave-hunting, ... those guilty of mutilating male adults and children, and ... all persons taking part in the capture of slaves by violence'. Further to be criminalised as an offence against individual liberty were the actions of 'the carriers and transporters of, and ... dealers in, slaves'. The Act, which had been negotiated by seventeen powers of the time,[10] was motivated by 'the firm intention of putting an end to the crimes and devastations engendered by the traffic in African slaves, of efficiently protecting the aboriginal population of Africa, and of securing for that vast continent the benefits of peace and civilization'.[11]

20.06 The 1919 Convention of Saint-Germain-en-Laye, which supplemented and revised the 1890 Brussels Act, was adopted under the aegis of the League of Nations. This Convention included an undertaking by its signatories to 'endeavour to secure the complete suppression of slavery in all its forms and of the slave trade by land and sea'.[12] In June 1924, a Temporary Slavery Commission was appointed by the Council of the League of Nations. The Commission elaborated a draft of an international convention outlawing slavery. But in early September 1925, Great Britain itself proposed a draft Protocol, which, after significant revision, would become the Convention to Suppress the Slave Trade and Slavery.[13] The Convention was amended by a Protocol of 7 December 1953 to reflect the fact that neither the League of Nations nor the Permanent International Court of Justice still existed. As of

---

[8] Act No. XV – Declaration of the Powers, on the Abolition of the Slave Trade, of 8 February 1815 (Transl. from French original), reproduced in *Hansard*, Vol. 32 (1 February to 6 March 1816), p. 200.
[9] Ibid., p. 201.
[10] Austro-Hungary, Belgium, Denmark, France, Germany, Great Britain, Italy, the Independent Congo State, the Netherlands, Norway, Persia, Portugal, Russia, Spain, Sweden, Turkey, the United States, and Zanzibar. A. Le Ghait, 'The Anti-Slavery Conference', *The North American Review*, vol. 154, no. 424 (March 1892), University of Northern Iowa, United States, pp. 287–96, at 289.
[11] Preambular paragraph to The Slave Trade and Importation into Africa of Firearms, Ammunition, and Spirituous Liquors (General Act of Brussels).
[12] Art. 11, Convention of Saint-Germain-en-Laye; signed on 10 September 1919.
[13] Convention to Suppress the Slave Trade and Slavery; signed at Geneva, 25 September 1926.

1 May 2021, the 1926 Slavery Convention (as amended) has attracted ninety-nine States Parties.[14] Kazakhstan was the most recent State to adhere to the Convention, in 2008.

20.07 The substantive heart of the 1926 Slavery Convention is found in its second article, according to which the States Parties undertake,

> each in respect of the territories placed under its sovereignty, jurisdiction, protection, suzerainty or tutelage, so far as they have not already taken the necessary steps:
> (a) To prevent and suppress the slave trade;
> (b) To bring about, progressively and as soon as possible, the complete abolition of slavery in all its forms.

20.08 As noted previously, slavery is explicitly prohibited in the ICCPR. This followed a provision in the 1948 Universal Declaration of Human Rights whereby 'no one shall be held in slavery or servitude; slavery and the slave trade shall be prohibited in all their forms'.[15] The International Convention on the Protection of the Rights of All Migrant Workers and Members of Their Families provides that 'no migrant worker or member of his or her family shall be held in slavery or servitude'.[16]

20.09 The 2006 Convention on the Rights of Persons with Disabilities reflects the Universal Declaration of Human Rights' formulation on slavery.[17] Interconnections and correlations between physical and psychological disability, legal capacity, and slavery were apparent in chattel slavery.[18] These remain pertinent in the case of modern slavery and human trafficking.[19] As US Department of Justice guidance says, for example, 'Victims of human trafficking may develop disabilities from abuse at the hands of their traffickers, and individuals with disabilities may be targeted by traffickers because they are vulnerable.'[20]

20.10 Slavery is similarly prohibited under each of the regional human rights treaties. The prohibition had already been included in the 1950 European Convention on Human Rights[21] and the illegality of the practice was subsequently reflected in the 1969 Inter-American

---

[14] See the UN Treaty Section list of parties and signatories, at http://bit.ly/2wNoB2Z.

[15] Art. 4, Universal Declaration of Human Rights; adopted at Paris by UN General Assembly Resolution 217, 10 December 1948.

[16] Art. 11(1), International Convention on the Protection of the Rights of All Migrant Workers and Members of their Families; adopted at New York 18 December 1990; entered into force 1 July 2003. In addition, the Convention includes a preambular reference to 'the Slavery Conventions'.

[17] Art. 27(2): 'States Parties shall ensure that persons with disabilities are not held in slavery or in servitude.'

[18] See 'The Hauntings of Slavery: Colonialism and the Disabled Body in the Caribbean', in S. Grech and K. Soldatic (eds.), Disability and the Global South: The Critical Handbook, Springer, Switzerland, 2016, pp.379–91; and D. H. Boster, African American Slavery and Disability: Bodies, Property, and Power in the Antebellum South, 1800–1860, Routledge, New York, 2013.

[19] The United States Department of State has noted that 'persons with disabilities remain one of the groups most at risk of being trafficked'. See Trafficking in Persons Report 2012, June 2012, at http://bit.ly/2JnX5zZ.

[20] Human Trafficking Task Force E-Guide; developed in partnership by the US Department of Justice's Office for Victims of Crime (OVC), at https://bit.ly/2kGJ4zv.

[21] 'No one shall be held in slavery or servitude.' Art. 4(1), Convention for the Protection of Human Rights and Fundamental Freedoms; adopted at Rome by the Council of Europe 4 November 1950; entered into force 3 September 1953.

Convention on Human Rights,[22] the 1981 African Charter on Human and Peoples' Rights,[23] and the 2004 Arab Charter on Human Rights.[24] Enslavement is also prohibited by the 1990 Cairo Declaration on Human Rights in Islam.[25]

20.11 This chapter continues with a discussion of the definition of 'slavery', as well as reference to the term 'modern slavery' or 'practices similar to slavery'. The prohibition of enslavement as a war crime in a situation of armed conflict and as a crime against humanity are also reflected in the legal analysis. The chapter concludes by considering the extent to which slavery is a violation of the right to life.

THE DEFINITION OF SLAVERY

20.12 The definition of slavery in the 1926 Slavery Convention remains authoritative under international law.[26] According to Article 1(1) of the Convention, 'slavery is the status or condition of a person over whom any or all of the powers attaching to the right of ownership are exercised'.

20.13 By a person's status is meant his or her status under the law. In its 2008 judgment in the *Tang* case, the High Court of Australia stated simply: 'Status is a legal concept.'[27] Not only did laws in force in many nations prior to the 1926 Slavery Convention not prohibit enslavement; in several instances they actually regulated the treatment of slaves as lesser categories of human beings, allowing, for example, corporal violence and punishment that would be manifestly unlawful if carried out upon citizens. Thus the Temporary Slavery Commission observed that the 'most important measure for the gradual abolition of slavery is that the status of slavery should no longer be recognised in the eye of the law'.[28]

---

[22] 'No one shall be subject to slavery or to involuntary servitude, which are prohibited in all their forms, as are the slave trade and traffic in women.' Art. 6(1), American Convention on Human Rights; adopted at San José 22 November 1969; entered into force 18 July 1978.

[23] 'All forms of exploitation and degradation of man particularly slavery, slave trade ... shall be prohibited.' Art. 5, African Charter on Human and Peoples' Rights; adopted at Nairobi 27 June 1981; entered into force 21 October 1986.

[24] 'Slavery and slave trade in all their forms shall be prohibited and punishable by law. No one shall, under any circumstances, be held in slavery or in servitude.' Art. 10(1), Arab Charter on Human Rights; adopted at Tunis 22 May 2004; entered into force 15 March 2008.

[25] According to Art. 11(a): 'Human beings are born free, and no one has the right to enslave, humiliate, oppress or exploit them, and there can be no subjugation but to Allah the Almighty.' However, it is also stipulated that the right set out in the Declaration are subject to sharia law, which did not outlaw all forms of slavery. See, e.g., D. Ze'evi, 'Slavery', in J. L. Esposito (ed.), *The Oxford Encyclopedia of the Islamic World*, Oxford University Press, Oxford, 2009, text reproduced at http://bit.ly/2J1DN42. The 1990 Declaration also asserts, in Art. 10(b), that colonialism 'of all types' is 'one of the most evil forms of enslavement'.

[26] See, e.g., Inter-American Court of Human Rights, *Hacienda Brasil Verde Workers* v. *Brazil*, Judgment (Preliminary Objections, Merits, Reparations and Costs), 20 October 2016, para. 268.

[27] High Court of Australia, *R.* v. *Tang*, [2008] HCA 39, para. 25.

[28] Report of the Temporary Slavery Commission adopted in the course of its Second session, 13–25 July 1925, League of Nations doc. A.19.1925, 25 July 1925, p. 3; see J. Allain, *The Law and Slavery*, Brill, Leiden, 2015, pp. 435–6.

20.14 The inclusion of the words 'or condition' in the Convention definition significantly broaden it. These words were inserted late in the drafting process.[29] As the High Court of Australia recalled, since 'the legal status of slavery did not exist in many parts of the world, and since it was intended that it would cease to exist everywhere, the evident purpose of the reference to "condition" was to cover slavery de facto as well as de jure'.[30] The mere fact, therefore, that the law might not appear to allow a certain treatment to be meted out is not sufficient grounds, on its own, to exclude a person from coming within the international legal definition of slavery. It is the reality of the status of people, not just their theoretical standing, which counts.

20.15 To own something is to hold a formal title over it. To become a lawful owner of a chattel (meaning an item of property other than freehold land or other immutable property), one typically has to purchase it (or the materials from which it is then made); to gather or collect it (when it does not belong to any other person or entity); or to be gifted it by another, lawful owner. Herein, then, clearly lies the notion of the slave as 'chattel'. Slaves, once they have been procured (through birth to another slave or their capture, kidnap, or purchase), were then either kept or traded on or gifted in much the same way as one would, for example, a head of cattle or a kitchen tool.[31]

20.16 The notion of 'powers attaching to a right of ownership' further broadens the definition. A slave is not limited to a person who is, according to the law, 'owned' by a 'lawful' owner, but extends to a person who is subject to any or all of the *powers* attaching to a right of ownership. These powers are, generally speaking, to possess a thing (or rent it out); to store it away (or put it on show); to use it (or abuse it); to adapt or improve it as the possessor sees fit (or even to destroy it); and to keep it, sell it, or gift it away. In short, the powers attaching to a right of ownership focus on the notion of control, for, broadly speaking, the owner decides what he or she would like to do with a chattel.

20.17 In a 2012 soft-law instrument, the *Bellagio-Harvard Guidelines* on the Legal *Parameters of Slavery* it is stated:

> In cases of slavery, the exercise of 'the powers attaching to the right of ownership' should be understood as constituting control over a person in such a way as to significantly deprive that person of his or her individual liberty, with the intent of exploitation through the use, management, profit, transfer or disposal of that person.[32]

Jean Allain remarks:

> Slavery, after all, is not pretty; it is [a] nasty business where control tantamount to possession is achieved through violence. In such instances, personal liberty is lost; the free will of the person has been taken away, transferred from the slave to the owner – the

---

[29] See, e.g., J. Allain, *The Law and Slavery*, Brill, Leiden, 2015, pp. 401–3.
[30] High Court of Australia, *R. v. Tang*, [2008] HCA 39, para. 25.
[31] Possession is not a prerequisite for ownership: one may, for instance, own an apartment (but not live in it) or own a car (but not keep it in the driveway or garage, much less actually drive it).
[32] Bellagio-Harvard Guidelines on the Legal Parameters of Slavery, adopted on 3 March 2012 by the Members of the Research Network on the Legal Parameters of Slavery, Guideline 2.

slaveholder. Once this is achieved, the slave can then be exploited, their labour used, their sexual autonomy disregarded, all at the whim of the person who now possess[es] the enslaved.[33]

20.18 In sum, therefore, a slave, as defined under international law, is a person whose legal status or personal situation is more akin to that of an object than a person, such is the extent and duration of control over her or his life exerted by another. This control, which is generally maintained through the threat or use of force backed by law, manifests itself in extreme forms of exploitation and ill-treatment, typically generating significant financial reward for the slave-holder.

20.19 Modern slavery (or 'practices similar to slavery') focuses on the notion of exploitation but is far broader than is the concept of slavery under the 1926 definition. An important dividing line between slavery and practices similar to slavery is the reason for the condition in which a person finds himself or herself. Where a person's vulnerability is exploited for financial reasons or on the basis purely of emotional or psychological control, this will not amount to slavery as defined under international law. Where, on the other hand, protracted labour or performance of services (including sexual services) is extracted by use of force, especially when this occurs in a confined area without hope of release or free movement, such exploitation may fall within the ambit of the international legal definition of slavery.

20.20 Thus, for example, in its 2005 judgment in *Siliadin* v. *France*, the European Court of Human Rights held that the applicant had not been 'enslaved' because her employers, although exercising significant control over her, had not had 'a genuine right of legal ownership over her reducing her to the status of an "object"'.[34] The applicant, a Togolese national who had come to France in 1994 hoping to study, was made to work instead as a domestic servant in a private home in Paris. Her passport was confiscated and she worked for several years without pay, fifteen hours a day, without a day off. The applicant had complained of having been a domestic slave. The Court held that the criminal law in force at the time had not protected her sufficiently but concluded that rather than slavery, the applicant had been held in servitude – a 'particularly serious form of denial of freedom'[35] – in violation of Article 4 of the European Convention on Human Rights.[36]

Sexual Enslavement

20.21 In November 2018, in its judgment in the *López Soto* case,[37] the Inter-American Court of Human Rights found Venezuela responsible for acts of torture and sexual slavery committed against Linda Loaiza López Soto in violation of the 1969 American Convention on

---

[33] Allain, *The Law and Slavery*, p. 510.
[34] European Court of Human Rights, *Siliadin* v. *France*, Judgment (Second Section), 26 July 2005, para. 122.
[35] Ibid., para. 123.
[36] Ibid., paras. 123–9.
[37] Inter-American Court of Human Rights, *López Soto and others* v. *Venezuela*, Judgment (Merits, Reparation, and Costs), 26 September 2018.

Human Rights, the 1985 Inter-American Convention to Prevent and Punish Torture, and the 1994 Inter-American Convention on the Prevention, Punishment and Eradication of Violence against women ('Convention of Belem do Para').

20.22 On 27 March 2001, Ms López Soto, who at that time was eighteen years old, was kidnapped by a private individual who kept her deprived of liberty for almost four months. During that period Ms López Soto was subjected to physical, verbal, psychological, and sexual violence, including forced administration of alcohol, drugs, and medicines; deprivation of food; repeated acts of vaginal and anal rape, at times with objects; beatings that caused her injuries, facial bruises, and severe damage of her auditory chambers, thorax, abdomen, nose, and jaw; and more. Due to the multiple injuries she suffered, Ms López Soto was hospitalized for almost one year and underwent fifteen surgical operations. On 19 July 2001, she was freed by police officers and firefighters.

20.23 The Inter-American Commission had earlier found that the forms of physical violence and sexual violation that she had suffered had had a deep and irreversible impact on her life.[38] Despite these abuses, and notwithstanding threats to her life, the Court did not expressly assess whether her right to life had been violated through her sexual enslavement. It did, however, conclude that Venezuela had violated Ms López Soto's rights to juridical personality, personal integrity, freedom from torture, freedom from slavery, personal liberty, a fair trial, dignity, autonomy and private life, freedom of movement and residence, judicial protection, and equality before the law.

SLAVERY AS A VIOLATION OF THE LAW OF ARMED CONFLICT

20.24 Surprisingly, perhaps, given the strong historical link between war and enslavement, a specific treaty prohibition on slavery and the slave trade is only found in one contemporary law of armed conflict treaty,[39] the 1977 Additional Protocol II to the Geneva Conventions.[40] Article 4 of that Protocol provides protection to '[a]ll persons who do not take a direct part or who have ceased to take part in hostilities, whether or not their liberty has been restricted'. When the Protocol applies, its prohibition on slavery and the slave trade 'in all their forms' governs acts 'at any time and in any place whatsoever' within the relevant State's territory.

20.25 On the basis of its assessment of State practice, the International Committee of the Red Cross (ICRC) believes that the prohibition of slavery and the slave trade in

---

[38] Ibid., para. 1.
[39] The Lieber Code, which was issued to the Union soldiers during the American Civil War, had stipulated that 'private citizens are no longer murdered, enslaved, or carried off to distant parts'. 1863 Instructions for the Government of Armies of the United States in the Field, General Order No. 100 (Lieber Code), §23; cf. also §§42–3 and 58.
[40] Art. 4(2)(f), Protocol Additional to the Geneva Conventions of 12 August 1949, and relating to the protection of victims of non-international armed conflicts (Protocol II); adopted at Geneva 8 June 1977; entered into force 7 December 1978. The Protocol applies only to certain non-international armed conflicts: those between a state and an organised armed group that exercises effective control over territory.

all their forms is also a customary norm of international humanitarian law.[41] The ICRC observes that the military manuals and the legislation of many states prohibit slavery and the slave trade.[42] The customary prohibition of slavery and the slave trade binds all States and all armed opposition groups when they are party to any armed conflict.[43]

SLAVERY AS AN INTERNATIONAL CRIME

Slavery as a War Crime

20.26 During armed conflict, slavery and deportation to slave labour are prohibited as war crimes under customary international law, in connection with an armed conflict whether it is international or non-international in character.[44] Already in 1945, the Nuremberg Charter stipulated that deportation to slave labour was a war crime.[45] Almost fifty years later, the prosecutor of the International Criminal Tribunal for the former Yugoslavia (ICTY) charged a Bosnian Serb prison commander, Milorad Krnojelac, with slavery as a violation of the laws or customs of war during the armed conflicts that broke out in Bosnia and Herzegovina in 1992.[46]

20.27 Although Mr Krnojelac was acquitted of the charge, the acquittal was for want of evidence and not because the Tribunal did not believe that slavery linked to an armed conflict could not amount to a war crime.[47] Indeed, in the earlier *Kunarac* case, the ICTY Trial Chamber held that 'the prohibition against slavery in situations of armed conflict is an inalienable, non-derogable and fundamental right, one of the core rules of general customary and conventional international law'.[48] Moreover, the ICRC asserts that even though slavery per se is not contained as a war crime in the Rome Statute of the International Criminal Court,[49] it would fall under the prohibition of cruel treatment or as an outrage upon personal dignity.[50]

---

[41] ICRC Study of Customary International Humanitarian Law, Rule 94, at http://bit.ly/2kIohsm.
[42] Ibid., citing in evidence the military manuals of Canada, France, Israel, the Netherlands, New Zealand, Senegal, and the United States; and the legislation of Armenia, Australia, Belgium, Canada, China, Congo, Croatia, France, Ireland, Kenya, Mali, the Netherlands, New Zealand, Niger, Norway, the Philippines, the United Kingdom, and the United States.
[43] See ibid.
[44] ICRC Study of Customary International Humanitarian Law, Rule 156, at https://bit.ly/2pOOWqp.
[45] Article 6, Nuremberg Charter.
[46] ICTY, *Prosecutor v. Milorad Krnojelac*, Judgment (Trial Chamber) (Case No. IT-97-25-T), 15 March 2002, para. 10.
[47] Ibid., para. 64. Mr Krnojelac was also charged with enslavement as a crime against humanity.
[48] ICTY, *Prosecutor v. Kunarac*, Judgment (Trial Chamber) (Case No. IT-96-23-T & IT-96-23/1-T), 22 February 2001, para. 353.
[49] Rome Statute of the International Criminal Court; adopted at Rome 17 July 1998; entered into force 1 July 2002 (Rome Statute).
[50] ICRC Study of Customary International Humanitarian Law, Rule 156: (iv) Other serious violations of international humanitarian law committed during a non-international armed conflict, point (v).

Sexual Slavery as a War Crime

20.28 A specific war crime of sexual slavery is included in the Rome Statute, applicable to both international and non-international armed conflicts.[51] In January 2017, in its judgment in the *Ntaganda* case, the ICC extended its jurisdiction over sexual slavery as a war crime to encompass acts committed against *members of a conflict party's own armed forces*.[52] This was a controversial holding – one that was not widely expected to survive on appeal. But in June 2017, the ICC Appeals Chamber confirmed that the Court did indeed have jurisdiction over alleged war crimes of sexual slavery of child soldiers within Bosco Ntaganda's *Forces Patriotiques pour la Libération du Congo*, a non-state armed group operating in the Democratic Republic of Congo.[53]

Slavery as a Crime against Humanity

20.29 When it is committed as part of a widespread or systematic attack directed against a civilian population, enslavement is a crime against humanity.[54] Enslavement had already been identified as a crime against humanity under the 1945 Charter of the International Military Tribunal (Nuremberg Charter),[55] as well as in the 1946 International Military Tribunal for the Far East (Tokyo Charter) adopted in the aftermath of the Second World War.[56]

20.30 Fritz Sauckel, the Nazi Plenipotentiary for the Mobilisation of Workers, was convicted by the Nuremberg Tribunal of crimes against humanity for his use of slave labour. He was condemned, in particular, for having forced more than five million workers from occupied Europe into labour, either in Germany itself or in the territories it occupied. According to one of his orders, 'all the men must be fed, sheltered and treated in such a way as to exploit them to the highest possible extent at the lowest conceivable degree of expenditure'.[57] Camps such as Auschwitz in Poland and Buchenwald in central Germany became administrative centres of huge networks of forced labour camps. Auschwitz III supplied forced labourers to a synthetic rubber plant owned by the German company, I. G. Farben. Prisoners in the concentration camps were literally worked to death.[58]

20.31 A crime against humanity may be committed within or outside a situation of armed conflict, a legal reality that is duly reflected in the Rome Statute. The Statute grants to the

---

[51] Art. 8(2)(b)(xxii) and (e)(vi), respectively.
[52] ICC, 'Ntaganda case: ICC Trial Chamber VI rejects challenge to jurisdiction over two war crimes counts', press release ICC-CPI-20170104-PR1267, 4 January 2017, at http://bit.ly/2sxATck.
[53] ICC, 'Ntaganda case: ICC Appeals Chamber confirms the Court's jurisdiction over two war crimes counts', press release ICC-CPI-20170615-PR1313, 15 June 2017, at http://bit.ly/2sefggq.
[54] Crimes against humanity are cruel or inhumane acts committed as part of a widespread or systematic attack against civilians. The term was first coined in 1915 by the governments of France, Great Britain, and Russia in a declaration condemning mass killings of Armenians in the Ottoman Empire.
[55] Art. 6, Nuremberg Charter.
[56] Art. 5(c), Tokyo Charter.
[57] Trial International, 'Fritz Sauckel', last modified 8 June 2016, at http://bit.ly/2JaBurr.
[58] 'Forced Labor', United States Holocaust Memorial Museum, 2018, at http://bit.ly/243uUrn.

Court potential jurisdiction over enslavement as a crime against humanity,[59] defining such enslavement as 'the exercise of any or all of the powers attaching to the right of ownership over a person and includes the exercise of such power in the course of trafficking in persons, in particular women and children'.[60] The first part of the definition is derived from that set out in the 1926 Slavery Convention, while the second part identifies scenarios that may be captured by that definition. As William Schabas has noted, there is a clear overlap between enslavement and sexual slavery as crimes against humanity.[61]

Sexual Slavery as a Crime against Humanity

20.32 The Rome Statute also grants the Court potential jurisdiction over the specific crime against humanity of sexual slavery.[62] A specific element of the crime is again that the perpetrator exercised 'any or all of the powers attaching to the right of ownership' over another and gives examples of such powers: purchasing, selling, lending, or bartering or by imposing a 'deprivation of liberty'. With respect to the sexual aspect of slavery, the substantive element of the crime is that the perpetrator 'caused such person or persons to engage in one or more acts of a sexual nature'.[63] Such acts are clearly broader in scope than rape and would not be limited to those involving penetration of the victim.[64]

SLAVERY AND THE RIGHT TO LIFE

20.33 In addition to its specific prohibition, slavery could also be seen as a violation of the foundational right to life in certain circumstances. In most cases, the treatment meted out to those who are deemed, legally, to have been enslaved is a violation of the prohibition on torture as well as the prohibition on enslavement. That said, those enslaved may be killed, in order to try to cover up the crimes that have been committed. Moreover, the analogy between slavery and enforced disappearance, whose victims 'are frequently tortured and in constant fear of being killed',[65] is also pertinent. A case need not involve the death of an individual to found such a violation, as Chapter 2 of this work has outlined.

---

[59] Art. 7(1)(c), Rome Statute.

[60] Art. 7(2)(c), Rome Statute. One of the corresponding elements of crime is that 'the perpetrator exercised any or all of the powers attaching to the right of ownership over one or more persons, such as by purchasing, selling, lending or bartering such a person or persons, or by imposing on them a similar deprivation of liberty'. Element 1 of Article 7(1)(c): Crime against humanity of enslavement, in *Official Records of the Assembly of States Parties to the Rome Statute of the International Criminal Court*, First session, New York, 3–10 September 2002, Part II.B.

[61] W. Schabas, *An Introduction to the International Criminal Court*, 4th ed., Cambridge University Press, Cambridge, 2012, p.115.

[62] Art. 7(2)(g), ICC Statute.

[63] Elements 1 and 2 of Article 7(1)(g): Crime against humanity of sexual slavery.

[64] Rape as a war crime is defined in the ICC Elements of Crime as follows: 'The perpetrator invaded the body of a person by conduct resulting in penetration, however slight, of any part of the body of the victim or of the perpetrator with a sexual organ, or of the anal or genital opening of the victim with any object or any other part of the body.'

[65] Amnesty International, 'Disappearances: Overview', at http://bit.ly/1U5UOcu.

20.34 Furthermore, dignity, not just physical existence, is at the heart of the enjoyment of the right to life.[66] The 'social death' of enslavement is clearly an abnegation of a dignified life. As the Human Rights Committee has stated with respect to Article 6 of the ICCPR: 'The right to life is a right that should not be interpreted narrowly. It concerns the entitlement of individuals to be free from acts and omissions that are intended or may be expected to cause their unnatural or premature death, as well as to enjoy a life with dignity.'[67]

20.35 The Islamic State enslaved many people during its reign of terror in Iraq and Syria, especially Yazidi women.[68] As a non-State armed group, the Islamic State is obligated to respect jus cogens norms, including the prohibitions on arbitrary deprivation of life and enslavement. The Independent International Commission of Inquiry on Syria affirmed in 2016 that the policy of enslavement of Yazidi women amounted to not only crimes against humanity but also genocide.[69] According to Bill Wiley, Executive Director of the Commission for International Justice and Accountability, which seeks the prosecution of Islamic State commanders for slavery as genocide: 'IS fighters didn't take it upon themselves to rape these women and girls. There was a carefully executed plan to enslave, sell, and rape Yazidi women presided over by the highest levels of the IS leadership. And in doing so, they were going to eradicate the Yazidi group by ensuring there were no more Yazidi children born.'[70] The Islamic State sought to justify slavery through the issuance of articles, sermons, and fatwas interpreting Islamic law that argued how enslavement was in accordance with Islam.[71] The impact on the girls and women who were enslaved by the Islamic State continues to be devastating.[72]

20.36 In contrast, the notion of 'modern slavery' seems indistinct. It is a catch-all concept for a wide range of practices similar to slavery, many of which, while clearly violative of human rights, do not amount to slavery as traditionally understood and do not contravene the right to life. While a range of estimates exist, one holds that 45.8 million people are in 'some form' of modern slavery in 167 countries.[73]

---

[66] See, e.g., W. Moka-Mubelo, 'Human Rights and Human Dignity', in *Reconciling Law and Morality in Human Rights Discourse. Philosophy and Politics – Critical Explorations*, vol. 3 (2017), Springer, Cham; though for a more nuanced view, see also C. McCrudden, 'Human Dignity and Judicial Interpretation of Human Rights', *European Journal of International Law*, vol. 19, no.4 (1 September 2008), pp.655–724, at http://bit.ly/2sx6PNU.

[67] Human Rights Committee, General Comment No. 36: Article 6: right to life, UN doc. CCPR/C/GC/36, 3 September 2019, para. 3.

[68] N. Al-Dayel and A. Mumford, 'ISIS and Their Use of Slavery', International Center for Counter-Terrorism – The Hague, 27 January 2020, at http://bit.ly/3ockmp5.

[69] Independent International Commission of Inquiry on Syria, '"They came to destroy": ISIS Crimes Against the Yazidis', UN doc. A/HRC/32/CRP.2, 15 June 2016.

[70] Associated Press, 'Investigators Build Case for IS Crimes Against Yazidis', VOA, 21 May 2020, at https://bit.ly/2Visolu.

[71] Ibid.; and see also N. Al-Dayel, A. Mumford, and K. Bales, 'Not Yet Dead: The Establishment and Regulation of Slavery by the Islamic State', *Studies in Conflict & Terrorism*, 2020, at http://bit.ly/3fQI4EM.

[72] See, e.g., G. Vale, 'Liberated, Not Free: Yazidi Women after Islamic State Captivity', *Small Wars & Insurgencies*, vol. 31, no. 3 (2020), pp. 511–39.

[73] P. Southwell, M. Brewer, and B. Douglas-Jones, *Human Trafficking and Modern Slavery Law and Practice*, Bloomsbury Professional, London, 2018, p. 417, s. 15.1.

20.37 Under the 2015 Modern Slavery Act in the United Kingdom, a person commits an offence if he or she 'holds another person in slavery or servitude and the circumstances are such that the person knows or ought to know that the other person is held in slavery or servitude'.[74] Also an offence under the Act is 'forced or compulsory labour'.[75] It is further specified that references to holding a person in slavery or servitude or requiring a person to perform forced or compulsory labour are to be construed in accordance with Article 4 of the European Convention on Human Rights.[76]

---

[74] S. 1(1)(a), 2015 Modern Slavery Act. Text of the Act at http://bit.ly/34JywHt.
[75] S. 1(1)(b), 2015 Modern Slavery Act.
[76] Ss. 1(2) and 13(1), 2015 Modern Slavery Act.

PART III

The Protection of At-Risk Groups and Individuals

21

Women

INTRODUCTION

21.01 This chapter describes the content and protection of the right to life of women under international law. Under treaty law, a woman is generally considered to be any female of the age of eighteen years or more, unless majority is attained earlier under domestic law. Girls generally attain majority at the age of eighteen, though a number of States set a lower age in their domestic law.[1] Eighteen years is the age at which the protections afforded by the UN Convention on the Rights of the Child[2] (CRC) generally cease.[3] A small number of States set their age of majority at greater than eighteen years.[4]

21.02 The 1966 International Covenant on Civil and Political Rights[5] (ICCPR) refers explicitly to the rights of women in a number of provisions but does not specify either a minimum or maximum age when legally a girl becomes a woman.[6] Its Article 3 stipulates, however, that States Parties 'undertake to ensure the equal right of men and women to the enjoyment of all civil and political rights' set out in the Covenant.[7] Taking

---

[1] See Chapter 25 for the discussion of the definition of a child under international law.
[2] Art. 1, Convention on the Rights of the Child; adopted at New York 20 November 1989; entered into force 2 September 1990 (hereinafter, CRC). As of 1 May 2021, 196 States were party to the CRC. Only the United States, a signatory, was a State not party.
[3] A notable exception to the general rule is the prohibition on sentencing to death any person (boy or girl, man or woman) who was under eighteen years of age at the time of commission of the capital offence. This prohibition exists even though the defendant may now be an adult. Art. 37, CRC.
[4] For example, when adhering to the CRC, Cuba declared that, under the national law in force, 'majority is not attained at 18 years of age for purposes of the full exercise of civic rights'. Declaration of Cuba with respect to Article 1 of the CRC, available at http://bit.ly/2Q3VBw7. The age of majority in Algeria is nineteen years and one day. 'La Police Algérienne', at http://bit.ly/3fqO1H9. In 2018, Japan's parliament adopted a law lowering the age of majority to eighteen from twenty; this will take effect on 1 April 2022. BBC, 'Coming of Age: Why Adults in Japan Are Getting Younger', 13 June 2018, at http://bbc.in/2OjmSu7. Within the United States, in the state of Mississippi, the age of majority is twenty-one; two other American states (Alabama and Nebraska) set the age over eighteen: at nineteen years in each case.
[5] International Covenant on Civil and Political Rights; adopted at New York 16 December 1966; entered into force 23 March 1976.
[6] Furthermore, Article 23(2) provides that the right of men and women 'of marriageable age' to marry and to found a family shall be recognised, but without specifying a minimum age.
[7] Thus the references in the Covenant to 'he' or 'his' should be construed to mean 'he or she' or 'his or her'.

into account the references to 'child' and 'children' in the ICCPR, 'women' should best be understood in that instrument consonant with the definition in Article 1 of the CRC.

21.03 Other treaties may similarly consider that a girl only becomes a woman at eighteen years of age but may decide to extend their scope of application to pertain also to girls. The 1979 Convention on the Elimination of All Forms of Discrimination against Women[8] (CEDAW) does not formally define women for the purpose of the Convention.[9] That said, in its General Recommendation 28 on the core obligations under Article 2 of the Convention, issued in 2010, the UN Committee on the Elimination of Discrimination against Women observes that States Parties 'in particular are obliged to promote the equal rights of girls since girls are part of the larger community of women'.[10]

21.04 At the regional level, the 2003 Protocol to the African Charter on Human and Peoples' Rights on the Rights of Women in Africa also defines 'women' broadly, determining the term to encompass 'persons of female gender, including girls'.[11] In contrast, the 1994 Inter-American Convention on the Prevention, Punishment, and Eradication of Violence against Women[12] (Belém do Pará Convention) does not define who falls within its scope of application.[13] Jurisprudence, however, such as in the *Cotton Field* case discussed as follows, has applied the legal protection afforded by the Convention also to girls. With respect to the 1969 American Convention on Human Rights,[14] however, the Inter-American Court has considered that, in general, by 'child' is understood 'any individual who has not attained 18 years of age'.[15] This implies that any female of eighteen years or more is to be considered a woman.

---

[8] Convention on the Elimination of All Forms of Discrimination against Women; adopted at New York 18 December 1979; entered into force 3 September 1981. As of 1 May 2021, 189 States were party to CEDAW and a further 2 (Palau and the United States) were signatories, making it one of the most widely ratified human rights treaties.

[9] CEDAW refers in one provision to the 'organization of programmes for girls and women who have left school prematurely'. Art. 10(f), CEDAW. In its General Recommendation 36, which it issued in 2017, the Committee on the Elimination of Discrimination against Women declared that all States Parties to the Convention 'have an obligation to protect girls and women from any form of discrimination that denies them access to all levels of education and to ensure that, where that occurs, they have recourse to avenues of justice'. Committee on the Elimination of Discrimination against Women, General Recommendation No. 36 (2017) on the right of girls and women to education, UN doc. CEDAW/C/GC/36, 27 November 2017, para. 7.

[10] Committee on the Elimination of Discrimination against Women, General Recommendation No. 28 on the core obligations of States parties under article 2 of the Convention on the Elimination of All Forms of Discrimination against Women, UN doc. CEDAW/C/GC/28, 16 December 2010, para. 21.

[11] Art. 1(k), Protocol to the African Charter on Human and Peoples' Rights on the Rights of Women in Africa; adopted on 1 July 2003; entered into force 25 November 2005.

[12] Inter-American Convention on the Prevention, Punishment, and Eradication of Violence against Women; adopted at Belém do Pará, Brazil, 9 June 1994; entered into force 3 May 1995.

[13] All the members of the Organization of American States (OAS) are party to the Convention, except Canada and the United States.

[14] American Convention on Human Rights; adopted at San José 22 November 1969; entered into force 18 July 1978.

[15] Inter-American Court of Human Rights, *Case of the Massacres of El Mozote and Nearby Places* v. *El Salvador*, Judgment (Merits, reparations, and costs), 25 October 2012, para. 150 note 183.

THE RIGHT TO LIFE OF WOMEN UNDER GLOBAL STANDARDS

The ICCPR

21.05 Each woman under the jurisdiction of a State Party to the ICCPR benefits from the protection of the right to life afforded by its Article 6 to every person. This right is non-derogable in toto.[16] As discussed in Chapter 1 of this work, customary international law has long stipulated that every human being has the right to life without discrimination as to sex or gender. As stipulated in the 1993 Declaration on the Elimination of Violence against Women, women are entitled to the equal enjoyment and protection of all human rights, including the right to life.[17] Further, the prohibition of arbitrary deprivation of life of any person, including any woman,[18] codified in Article 6(1) of the ICCPR, has attained the status of a peremptory norm of international law (jus cogens).[19]

21.06 The duty to respect the right to life means that a State Party to the ICCPR – or any other State – may not arbitrarily deprive any woman of her life. The duty to protect life by law, codified in Article 6(1) of the ICCPR, requires that certain acts be criminalised for everyone under a State's jurisdiction. These include all acts of gender-based violence directed against women, but especially those that endanger life. Thus, for instance, the Human Rights Committee has stated in its General Comment 36 on the right to life: 'Femicide, which constitutes an extreme form of gender-based violence that is directed against girls and women, is a particularly grave form of assault on the right to life.'[20] At the same time, the criminalisation of certain acts must not serve to put the lives of women at unnecessary risk. In this regard, the Human Rights Committee also declared in the General Comment that restrictions on the ability of women or girls to seek abortion must not jeopardise their lives. It has further called upon States Parties to the ICCPR to 'effectively protect the lives of women and girls against the mental and physical health risks associated with unsafe abortions'.[21]

21.07 In accordance with Article 6(5) of the ICCPR, a sentence of death shall not be carried out on a pregnant woman. This codifies what has become a customary rule applicable to all States in all circumstances.[22] Its customary nature is supported by the rule's incorporation in regional human rights treaties in Africa and the Americas, as well as

---

[16] Art. 4(2), ICCPR.
[17] Art. 3(a), 1993 Declaration on the Elimination of Violence against Women, proclaimed by UN General Assembly Resolution 48/104 of 20 December 1993. Diane Otto complains about 'the masculinity of the universal subject of human rights law whose rights are fully promoted and explicitly protected' with 'gender dualism' similarly being reinforced by the comparative approach measuring women's equality against men's enjoyment of rights. D. Otto, 'Women's Rights', chap. 16 in D. Moeckli, S. Shah, and S. Sivakumaran (eds.), *International Human Rights Law*, 3rd ed., Oxford University Press, Oxford, 2017, pp. 309, 311.
[18] Human Rights Committee, 'General comment No. 36. Article 6: right to life', UN doc. CCPR/C/GC/36, 3 September 2019 (hereinafter, Human Rights Committee, General Comment 36 on the right to life), para. 3.
[19] See Chapter 1 for a discussion of the peremptory status of the norm.
[20] Human Rights Committee, General Comment 36 on the right to life, para. 61.
[21] Ibid., para. 8. See further Chapter 11 on abortion and the right to life.
[22] Extrajudicial, summary or arbitrary executions: Report by the Special Rapporteur, UN doc. E/CN.4/1998/68, 23 December 1997, para. 117.

in the Arab Charter on Human Rights, each of which explicitly outlaws the execution of pregnant women. The practice is similarly outlawed in both international and non-international armed conflict by international humanitarian law treaties that enjoy widespread ratification (see further below). In Europe, the death penalty, in general, has been all but outlawed by State practice and by jurisprudence in the European Court of Human Rights.[23]

21.08 The prohibition on executing a pregnant woman may also constitute a peremptory norm of international law. In his fourth report on jus cogens norms of January 2019, the Special Rapporteur of the International Law Commission (ILC) did not discuss whether the rule had developed into a peremptory norm.[24] But given virtually uniform practice at the domestic, regional, and international level, including among States that retain the death penalty, a strong case can be made for the norm's elevation to jus cogens. Under domestic law, only one State in the world – Saint Kitts and Nevis – allows a pregnant woman to be executed,[25] and this appears to be largely a theoretical possibility. The last execution there was in 2008 – of a man, convicted of killing his wife.[26]

21.09 With particular respect to the right to life, in its General Committee 28 issued in 2000, the Human Rights Committee stated that, when reporting on their implementation of Article 6, States Parties to the ICCPR should provide data on pregnancy- and childbirth-related deaths of women (typically formulated as the maternal mortality ratio; see below).[27] States Parties should also give information on any measures they have taken to ensure that women 'do not have to undergo life-threatening clandestine abortions'[28] and report on 'measures to protect women from practices that violate their right to life, such as female infanticide, the burning of widows and dowry killings'.[29] The Committee also wishes to have information on the 'particular impact on women of poverty and deprivation that may pose a threat to their lives'.[30]

CEDAW

21.10 Violence against women, whether at the hands of the State or at the hands of private individuals, including family members, continues to be 'pervasive' around the world.[31] This is partially the result of inadequacies in domestic law. In many States, legislation addressing

---

[23] ECtHR, *Al-Saadoon and Mufdhi v. United Kingdom*, Judgment (Fourth Section), 2 March 2010, para. 120.
[24] ILC, 'Fourth report on peremptory norms of general international law (jus cogens) by Dire Tladi, Special Rapporteur', UN doc. A/CN.4/727, 31 January 2019.
[25] Cornell Center on the Death Penalty Worldwide, 'Pregnant Women', last updated 25 January 2012, at http://bit.ly/38GaQEq.
[26] A. Bright, 'India Uses Death Penalty: 5 Other Places Where It's Legal but Rare', *Christian Science Monitor*, 29 August 2012, at http://bit.ly/3250xLY.
[27] Human Rights Committee, General Comment No. 28: Article 3 (The equality of rights between men and women), 29 March 2000, para. 10.
[28] See further Chapter 11 on abortion.
[29] Human Rights Committee, General Comment 28 on equality of rights, para. 10.
[30] Ibid.
[31] Otto, 'Women's Rights', p. 310.

gender-based violence against women is 'non-existent, inadequate or poorly implemented'.[32] Surprisingly, CEDAW itself does not explicitly refer in its substantive provisions to the right of women to freedom from violence.[33] In its General Recommendation 12 on violence against women, however, issued in 1989, the Committee on the Elimination of Discrimination against Women affirmed that the Convention requires its States Parties to act to protect women against violence of any kind occurring within the family, at the workplace, or in any other area of social life.[34]

21.11 In 1992, in its General Recommendation 19, also addressing violence against women, the Committee reaffirmed that discrimination against women includes gender-based violence – that is, 'violence which is directed against a woman because she is a woman or that affects women disproportionately'. It further confirmed that such violence constitutes a violation of women's rights.[35] Gender-based violence, the Committee later recalled, 'takes multiple forms, including acts or omissions intended or likely to cause or result in death'.[36] Deaths resulting from such violence include 'murders, killings in the name of so-called "honour" and forced suicides'.[37]

21.12 In 2017, the Committee declared that State practice and *opinio juris* over the twenty-five years since the issuance of its General Recommendation 19 'suggest that the prohibition of gender-based violence against women has evolved into a principle of customary international law', further asserting that the Recommendation was 'a key catalyst for that process'.[38] States Parties to CEDAW will be responsible, the Committee declared in 2017 in its General Recommendation 35 on gender-based violence against women, 'should they fail to take all appropriate measures to prevent, as well as to investigate, prosecute, punish and provide reparations for, acts or omissions by non-State actors that result in gender-based violence against women'.[39] This includes actions taken by corporations operating extraterritorially.[40]

21.13 Moreover, as the Committee on the Elimination of Discrimination against Women affirmed, a woman's right to a life free from gender-based violence 'is indivisible from and interdependent on other human rights, including the rights to life, health, liberty and security of the person, equality and equal protection within the family, freedom from torture,

---

[32] Committee on the Elimination of Discrimination against Women, General Recommendation No. 35 on gender-based violence against women, updating General Recommendation No. 19, 2017, para. 7.
[33] Otto, 'Women's Rights', p. 317.
[34] Committee on the Elimination of Discrimination against Women, General Recommendation No. 12: Violence against women, 1989, first preambular para. The Committee referred specifically to Articles 2, 5, 11, 12, and 16 of the Convention as underpinning those duties.
[35] CEDAW Committee, General Recommendation No. 19: Violence against women, 1992, para. 6. See further CEDAW Committee, General Recommendation No. 35 on gender-based violence against women, updating General Recommendation No. 19, UN doc. CEDAW/C/GC/35, 26 July 2017, para. 1.
[36] Committee on the Elimination of Discrimination against Women, General Recommendation No. 35 on gender-based violence against women, para. 14.
[37] Ibid., footnote 17.
[38] Ibid., para. 2.
[39] Ibid., para. 24(2).
[40] Ibid.

cruel, inhumane or degrading treatment, and freedom of expression, movement, participation, assembly and association'.[41] In 2019, the UN Special Rapporteur on violence against women, its causes and consequences regretted the fact that General Recommendation 35, which 'provides the most advanced standards on violence against women and provides an updated road map for preventing and combating violence against women', had benefited from only 'limited dissemination within the United Nations system and beyond'.[42]

21.14 The Committee on the Elimination of Discrimination against Women has established jurisprudence on the right to life of women, and specifically their right to protection against unlawful violence. Its 2007 Views on a submission made on behalf of Fatma Yildirim, who was stabbed to death by her husband, concerned the duties upon a State Party to prevent gender-based violence directed against women. The Committee considered that the failure by the authorities in Austria to have detained Ms Yildirim's husband, Irfan, even after many threats that he would kill her for leaving him, was a breach of the State's due diligence obligation to protect her. In response to Austria's claim that his arrest seemed 'disproportionately invasive', the Committee declared 'that the perpetrator's rights cannot supersede women's human rights to life and to bodily integrity'.[43] Acknowledging that Mr Yildirim had been prosecuted to the full extent of the law for killing Ms Yildirim, the Committee nonetheless concluded that Austria had violated its obligations under CEDAW to protect her life and her physical and mental integrity.[44]

THE RIGHT TO LIFE OF WOMEN UNDER REGIONAL STANDARDS

21.15 While all the main regional human rights treaties offer legal protection to women, including protection of their right to life, they do not, for the most part, specifically protect the right of life of women. The notable exception is the 2003 Protocol on the Rights of Women in Africa (commonly referred to as the Maputo Protocol), which entered into force in 2005. The Maputo Protocol to the African Charter has been widely ratified, with 42 States Parties as of 1 May 2021 and a further 10 signatories.[45] Only three African nations had neither signed nor adhered to it: Botswana, Egypt, and Morocco.[46]

---

[41] Ibid., para. 15.
[42] Report of the Special Rapporteur on violence against women, its causes and consequences, UN doc. A/HRC/41/42, 20 June 2019, para. 40.
[43] Committee on the Elimination of Discrimination against Women, *Vienna Intervention Centre against Domestic Violence and the Association for Women's Access to Justice on behalf of Banu Akbak, Gülen Khan, and Melissa Özdemir v. Turkey*, Views (Comm. No. 6/2005), UN doc. CEDAW/C/39/D/6/2005, 1 October 2007 (hereinafter, *Fatma Yildirim v. Austria*), para. 12.1.5, citing its Views in *A. T. v. Hungary*, Comm. No. 2/2003, 26 January 2005, para. 9.3.
[44] Committee on the Elimination of Discrimination against Women, *Fatma Yildirim v. Austria*, para. 12.1.6. The Committee referred specifically to Article 2 (a) and (c) to (f) and Article 3 of CEDAW, read in conjunction with Article 1 of the Convention and General Recommendation 19, and her corresponding rights to life and to physical and mental integrity.
[45] The signatory States were Burundi, Central African Republic, Chad, Eritrea, Madagascar, Niger, the Sahrawi Arab Democratic Republic, Somalia, South Sudan, and Sudan.
[46] This compares to 54 of the 55 African Union member States that were party to the African Charter on Human and Peoples' Rights as of 1 May 2021. Only Morocco was a State not party.

The Right to Life of Women under the Maputo Protocol

21.16 The Maputo Protocol stipulates in its Article 4 that 'every woman shall be entitled to respect for her life and the integrity and security of her person'.[47] The 2017 judgment by the Economic Community of West African States (ECOWAS) Court of Justice in the *Dorothy Chioma Njemanze* case against Nigeria concerned the violation of a range of rights protected under the Protocol, including the provisions in Article 4 (though not directly the right to life).[48] The second, third, and fourth plaintiffs in the case were abducted by a number of individuals in a white bus (allegedly branded as the Abuja Environmental Protection Board (AEPB) and the Society against Prostitution and Child Labour). They were then unlawfully detained in inhuman conditions and sexually and physically assaulted by officials of the AEPB. When the first plaintiff, Ms Njemanze, tried to secure the release of her friends, she was herself threatened and harassed physically and sexually by AEPB officials, as well as by Nigerian police officers and army personnel. The judgment in this case was the first ruling by the regional ECOWAS Court that directly applied the provisions of the Maputo Protocol.[49]

21.17 It is provided in the Maputo Protocol that 'in those countries where the death penalty still exists', States Parties must ensure that a sentence of death is not executed 'on pregnant or nursing women'.[50] A similar prohibition is not, though, found in the African Charter on Human and Peoples' Rights itself. The Protocol further obligates its States Parties to take 'all appropriate measures to protect the reproductive rights of women', specifically by 'authorising medical abortion in cases of sexual assault, rape, incest, and where the continued pregnancy endangers the mental and physical health of the mother or the life of the mother or the foetus'.[51]

The Right to Life of Women under the American and Belém do Pará Conventions

21.18 According to the 1969 American Convention on Human Rights: 'Every person has the right to have his life respected. This right shall be protected by law and, in general, from the moment of conception. No one shall be arbitrarily deprived of his life.'[52] The Convention specifically addresses the rights of women only twice. In one provision, it is stipulated that capital punishment shall not be applied to pregnant women.[53] Separately, it is provided that the trafficking of women is prohibited in all its forms.[54]

---

[47] Art. 4(1), Maputo Protocol.
[48] ECOWAS Court of Justice, *Dorothy Chioma Njemanze and three others v. Federal Republic of Nigeria*, Judgment (Case No. ECW/CCJ/APP/17/14), 12 October 2017.
[49] S. Omondi, E. Waweru, and D. Srinivasan, 'Breathing Life into the Maputo Protocol: Jurisprudence on the Rights of Women and Girls in Africa', *Equality Now*, Nairobi, 2018, p.24, available at http://bit.ly/2Qvoosc.
[50] Art. 4(2)(j), Maputo Protocol. As discussed below, it is not certain that the prohibition on executing nursing women has yet crystallised as a rule of customary international law.
[51] Art. 14(2)(c), Maputo Protocol.
[52] Art. 4(1), American Convention on Human Rights.
[53] Art. 4(5), American Convention on Human Rights.
[54] Art. 6(1), American Convention on Human Rights.

21.19 Article 1 of the Belém do Pará Convention stipulates that violence against women shall be understood as 'any act or conduct, based on gender, which causes death or physical, sexual or psychological harm or suffering to women, whether in the public or the private sphere'. Article 2 further clarifies that violence against women

> shall be understood to include physical, sexual and psychological violence:
>
> a. that occurs within the family or domestic unit or within any other interpersonal relationship, whether or not the perpetrator shares or has shared the same residence with the woman, including, among others, rape, battery and sexual abuse;
> b. that occurs in the community and is perpetrated by any person, including, among others, rape, sexual abuse, torture, trafficking in persons, forced prostitution, kidnapping and sexual harassment in the workplace, as well as in educational institutions, health facilities or any other place; and
> c. that is perpetrated or condoned by the State or its agents regardless of where it occurs.

21.20 In 2009, the Inter-American Court of Human Rights decided the case of one murdered woman and two murdered girls, whose partially decomposed bodies were found in a cotton field in Ciudad Juárez, Mexico, on 6 November 2001. The deaths occurred in the context of widespread violence against women across many regions of Mexico, in particular in Ciudad Juárez. Family members contacted law enforcement officials on behalf of Ms Ramos, Ms González, and Ms Herrera, respectively, after they had not returned home from work at the end of the day. However, their cases were dismissed, with law enforcement officers joking that they were 'probably with their boyfriends'.[55] Indeed, the Inter-American Commission alleged that when each disappearance was reported, 'the next of kin received comments from State officials regarding their daughter's behaviour, which, in their opinion, influenced the subsequent lack of official action'.[56]

21.21 In the view of one commentator, the 'importance of this case is undisputable as it embraces a gender perspective' with a judgment that 'represents at least symbolic progress toward the protection of women's rights'.[57] The Inter-American Commission had called upon the Court to declare Mexico responsible for violation of numerous rights under the Inter-American Convention, including the right to life. Mexico acknowledged that, during the first stage of the investigations, from 2001 to 2003, 'irregularities' occurred – without specifying their nature and extent – but also claimed that the irregularities had

---

[55] Inter-American Court of Human Rights, *González and others ('Cotton Field') v. Mexico*, Judgment (Preliminary Objection, Merits, Reparations, and Costs), 16 November 2009 (hereinafter, *Cotton Field* judgment), paras. 196–200.
[56] Ibid., para. 196.
[57] J. I. Acosta López, 'The Cotton Field Case: Gender Perspective and Feminist Theories in the Inter-American Court of Human Rights Jurisprudence', *Revista Colombiana de Derecho Internacional*, vol. 21 (2012), pp. 17–54, at 18, 51.

been fully rectified. The authorities denied any violations of the right to life had occurred as State agents 'did not take part in any of the three murders'.[58]

21.22 The Inter-American Commission had also urged the Court to hold Mexico responsible for failure to comply with the obligations arising from Article 7 of the Belém do Pará Convention, specifically the duty in paragraph (b) of the article to 'apply due diligence to prevent, investigate and impose penalties for violence against women'. In response, the State argued that the Court did not have jurisdiction to determine violations of that Convention on the basis that the Court may only interpret and apply the Inter-American Convention and other instruments that 'expressly' grant it jurisdiction.[59] Mexico asserted that each Inter-American treaty requires a specific declaration granting jurisdiction to the Court. The Court, however, rejected this interpretation of the Inter-American Convention, concluding that 'the combination of the systematic and teleological interpretations, the application of the principle of effectiveness, added to the sufficiency of the literal criterion', in the case, allowed the Court to confirm its compulsory jurisdiction to examine potential violations also of Article 7 of the Belém do Pará Convention.[60]

21.23 In its judgment in the *Cotton Field* case, with respect to alleged violations of the right to life, the Court noted that despite the denial by Mexico of 'any kind of pattern in the motives for the murders of women in Ciudad Juárez', the State had told the Committee on the Elimination of Discrimination against Women 'that "they are all influenced by a culture of discrimination against women based on the erroneous idea that women are inferior"'.[61] After reviewing the available evidence, the Court concluded that murders in Ciudad Juárez were to be generally considered as '"gender-based murders of women", also known as femicide'.[62] The Court identified a corresponding pattern of inadequate investigation of such murders, citing a statement by the UN Special Rapporteur on the independence of judges and lawyers in 2002. Following a visit to Ciudad Juárez in 2001, the Special Rapporteur 'was amazed to learn of the total inefficiency, incompetency, indifference, insensitivity and negligence of the police who investigated these cases'.[63] More broadly, the Court found widespread support for the notion that the failure to solve the crimes was 'a very important characteristic of the killings of women in Ciudad Juárez'.[64] Moreover, even when suspects were identified and successfully prosecuted, sentences imposed for the intentional murder of women averaged no more than fifteen years' imprisonment, even though most of the killings had been committed with aggravating circumstances.[65]

---

[58] Inter-American Court of Human Rights, *Cotton Field* judgment, para. 20.
[59] Ibid., paras. 31 and 35.
[60] Ibid., para. 77.
[61] Ibid., para. 132.
[62] Ibid., para. 143.
[63] Ibid., para. 150, citing Report of the mission of the Special Rapporteur on the independence of judges and lawyers, UN doc. E/CN.4/2002/72/Add.1, 24 January 2002, para. 161.
[64] Inter-American Court of Human Rights, *Cotton Field* judgment, para. 158.
[65] Ibid., para. 160.

21.24 The three young women at the centre of the *Cotton Field* case, Ms Ramos, Ms González, and Ms Herrera, who variously disappeared between late September and late October 2001, were said to be of 'humble origins'.[66] Their bodies, which evidenced particular brutality by the perpetrators of the killings, were suggestive of prior rape and abuse with extreme cruelty.[67] Mexico claimed that the state of decomposition of the bodies precluded a determination of the cause of death.[68] On 18 November 2005, however, the Argentine Forensic Anthropology Team performed a second autopsy on the remains of one of the three victims, Esmeralda Herrera. The team found that the original autopsy performed by the state pathologist had not respected the basic principles of a post-mortem examination, with the result that 'it did not achieve the objectives of a forensic autopsy'.[69]

21.25 In adjudging the alleged violation of the right to life of the three murder victims, the Court recalled that the right to life 'plays a fundamental role' in the American Convention, 'since it is the essential assumption for the exercise of the other rights'. States are obligated to ensure the existence of the conditions necessary to obviate violations 'of this inalienable right' and, in particular, 'to prevent violations by its agents'. Article 4 of the Convention requires States Parties to take 'all appropriate measures to protect and preserve the right to life'.[70] Mexico, however, had failed to show that it had made reasonable efforts in the circumstances to find the victims alive. It had not acted promptly 'during the first hours and days following the reports of the disappearances', which had resulted in a loss of valuable time. In addition, 'the attitude of the officials towards the victims' next of kin, suggesting that the missing persons' reports should not be dealt with urgently and immediately', led the Court to conclude that unjustified delays had followed the filing of the reports. These facts revealed that the State 'did not act with the required due diligence to prevent the death and abuse suffered by the victims'.[71]

21.26 Furthermore, the State had not proven that it had taken the requisite measures, including through the adoption of laws or standards, or to ensure that the officials in charge of receiving reports of missing persons had both the capacity and the sensitivity to understand the seriousness of the phenomenon of violence against women and the willingness to act immediately.[72] Based on these conclusions, the Court held that Mexico had violated the rights to life and personal integrity protected under the American Convention, as well as the obligations established in Article 7(b) and (c) of the Belém do Pará Convention of Claudia Ivette González, Laura Berenice Ramos Monárrez, and Esmeralda Herrera Monreal.[73]

---

[66] Ibid., para. 168.
[67] Ibid., para. 210.
[68] Ibid., para. 211.
[69] Ibid., para. 218.
[70] Ibid., para. 245.
[71] Ibid., para. 284.
[72] Ibid., para. 285.
[73] Ibid., para. 286.

21.27 Problems of gender-based violence directed against women, including domestic violence, were seemingly exacerbated during the responses to the global COVID-19 pandemic in 2020. In April 2020, the Inter-American Commission on Human Rights called upon member States of the Organization of American States (OAS) to incorporate a gender perspective in their responses to COVID-19 and to combat sexual and domestic violence affecting women in this context. The Commission stated it was deeply alarmed by reports of an increase in domestic violence following the measures of social confinement and isolation adopted by the authorities to contain the spread of coronavirus in the region, noting, in particular, significant increases in Brazil and the United States.[74]

The Right to Life of Women under the European Convention on Human Rights

21.28 Article 2(1) of the 1950 European Convention on Human Rights[75] stipulates simply that 'everyone's right to life shall be protected by law'. No specific provision safeguards the life or physical integrity of women. The Convention does, though, prohibit discrimination against women on the basis of sex, as is the case with the ICCPR, proclaiming, 'The enjoyment of the rights and freedoms set forth in [the] Convention shall be secured without discrimination on any ground',[76] including sex or gender.[77] In addition to respecting the right to life of women, States Parties to the European Convention on Human Rights must also exercise due diligence in ensuring their protection from third parties, including the spouse or partner of a woman. As discussed previously, the Committee on the Elimination of Discrimination against Women has long considered that violence against women, including domestic violence, is a form of discrimination against women. As a consequence, where 'general and discriminatory judicial passivity' exists that mainly affects women, even where the passivity is unintentional, the European Court is likely to consider that violence 'may be regarded as gender-based violence', which is 'a form of discrimination against women'.[78]

The Protection of Women from Domestic Violence

21.29 Jurisprudence on the protection of women against domestic violence within the European Court of Human Rights has not been entirely consistent (as of writing), but it

---

[74] Inter-American Commission on Human Rights, 'The IACHR Calls on Member States to Adopt a Gender Perspective in the Response to the COVID-19 Pandemic and to Combat Sexual and Domestic Violence in This Context', press release, Washington, DC, 11 April 2020, at http://bit.ly/31RYeIW.

[75] Convention for the Protection of Human Rights and Fundamental Freedoms; adopted at Rome by the Council of Europe, 4 November 1950; entered into force 3 September 1953 (hereinafter, European Convention on Human Rights).

[76] Art. 14, European Convention on Human Rights.

[77] 'Articles 2, 3 and 14: Equal access to justice in the case-law of the European Court of Human Rights on violence against women', Research and Library division, Directorate of the Jurisconsult, European Court of Human Rights, 2015, at http://bit.ly/3eaqnos, p. 4. In this regard, the European Court of Human Rights observed back in 1985 that 'the advancement of the equality of the sexes is today a major goal in the member States of the Council of Europe'. European Court of Human Rights, *Abdulaziz, Cabales and Balkandali v. United Kingdom*, Judgment (Plenary of the Court), 28 May 1985, para. 78.

[78] European Court of Human Rights, *Opuz v. Turkey*, Judgment (Third Section), rendered final on 9 September 2009, para. 200.

may be evolving towards an enhanced duty of protection upon the State. The first case adjudged by the Court on the nature of the specific duty to protect against domestic violence was *Kontrová v. Slovakia*, in 2007.[79] The Court reiterated its view expressed in earlier cases that not every alleged risk to life entails for the authorities an obligation to take operational measures to prevent that risk from materialising. Under the so-called *Osman* test, enunciated in a judgment in 1998, a positive obligation to act exists when the authorities 'knew or ought to have known' at the time of a 'real and immediate risk' to the life of a specific individual from the criminal acts of a third party.[80] A violation of the Convention would occur if the authorities failed to take measures within the scope of their powers which, judged reasonably, might have been expected to avoid that risk.[81] Thus, in its judgment in the *Kontrová* case, the Court was applying the *Osman* test directly to issues of domestic violence.

21.30 In its 2020 judgment in *Tërshana v. Albania*,[82] the Court's Second Section rejected the claim of a survivor of an acid attack by a former partner that her right to life had been violated by the authorities on the basis of its failure to protect her against the attack. It did so because 'it does not appear that the applicant at any time before the attack brought to the authorities' attention any risks posed to her life by her former husband, which would have triggered the authorities' positive obligation to take preventive measures or other reasonable steps to protect the applicant's life'.[83]

21.31 The Court did, however, find a violation of the procedural element of the right to life insofar as the investigation by the Albanian authorities was inadequate. The Court noted that between 2006 and 2012, international reports indicated that violence against women 'was under-reported, under-investigated, under-prosecuted, and under-sentenced'. The reports further suggested that the police and prosecuting authorities 'manifested an ineffectual approach to violence against women on the ground of "social attitude and cultural values" and that a climate of leniency or impunity prevailed towards perpetrators of violence against women'.[84] The Court considered that the circumstances of the attack had 'the hallmarks of a form of gender-based violence', which 'should have incited the authorities to react with special diligence in carrying out the investigative measures. Whenever there is a suspicion that an attack might be gender motivated, it is particularly important that the investigation is pursued with vigour.'[85]

21.32 A common problem in cases of alleged domestic violence is that a woman who has been attacked is pressured by her husband or partner to withdraw a criminal complaint. This was the situation in *Opuz*, a case adjudged by the European Court

---

[79] 'Articles 2, 3 and 14: Equal access to justice in the case-law of the European Court of Human Rights on violence against women', p. 6.
[80] As developed by the Court in *Osman v. United Kingdom*, Judgment, 28 October 1998, para. 116; see *Kurt v. Austria*, Judgment (Fifth Section), Separate Opinion of Judge Hüseynov, para. 2.
[81] European Court of Human Rights, *Kontrová v. Slovakia*, Judgment (Fourth Section), 31 May 2007, para. 50.
[82] European Court of Human Rights, *Tërshana v. Albania*, Judgment (Second Section), 4 August 2020.
[83] Ibid., paras. 151, 152.
[84] Ibid., para. 156.
[85] Ibid., para. 160.

in 2009.[86] The Court considered whether the authorities had been justified in not pursuing criminal proceedings against a violent husband after the withdrawal of complaints against him by the victims (the applicant – his wife – and her mother). The husband later fatally shot the applicant's mother as she attempted to help Ms Opuz flee the matrimonial home. For years prior to that, the husband had assaulted both his wife and her mother, with their injuries sometimes rising to the level of life-threatening. Although criminal proceedings had been brought against the husband for a range of offences, which included death threats, serious assault, and even attempted murder, in at least two instances, the prosecutions were discontinued after the women withdrew their complaints, allegedly under pressure from the applicant's husband.

21.33 For the fatal shooting of the applicant's mother – an act the husband had justified as a means to protect his honour – he was convicted of murder and sentenced to life imprisonment. He was, however, released pending appeal whereupon he renewed his threats against the applicant. She sought the authorities' protection, but it was not until seven months later, and only after a request from the Court for information, that they took active measures to protect her. The Court reiterated the *Osman* test it had endorsed in its *Kontrová* judgment, though it also observed that 'the more serious the offence or the greater the risk of further offences, the more likely that the prosecution should continue in the public interest, even if victims withdraw their complaints'.[87]

21.34 The 2019 chamber judgment in the *Kurt* case[88] concerned an allegation by the applicant that the Austrian authorities had failed to protect her and her children from her violent husband. The particular failure to protect her son's physical integrity against her husband, she argued, had resulted in him murdering their son, specifically on the basis they had not taken her husband into pre-trial detention after he had allegedly attacked and raped her and beaten the children.[89] In its judgment, the Court reiterated that 'vulnerable individuals in particular are entitled to State protection'.[90] But in rejecting the applicant's claim, the Court also confirmed its earlier holdings that 'the scope of the positive obligation must be interpreted in a way which does not impose an impossible or disproportionate burden on the authorities'.[91]

21.35 In his Separate Opinion to the Court's judgment in *Kurt*, however, Judge Latif Hüseynov stated that situations of domestic violence should be considered *differently* from the norm because they often constitute 'not just an isolated incident, but rather a continuous practice of intimidation and abuse'. Therefore, he asserted, State authorities

> should react, with due diligence, to each and every act of domestic violence and take all necessary measures to make sure that such acts do not lead to more serious consequences. It follows that the duty to prevent and protect comes into play when the risk to life is

---

[86] European Court of Human Rights, *Opuz v. Turkey*, Judgment (Third Section), rendered final on 9 September 2009.
[87] Ibid., para. 139.
[88] European Court of Human Rights, *Kurt v. Austria*, Judgment (Fifth Section), 4 July 2019.
[89] Ibid., paras. 12–22 and 48.
[90] Ibid., para. 63.
[91] Ibid., para. 69.

present, even if it is not imminent. In other words, in a domestic violence case, the positive obligation to protect life can be violated even where the risk to life is not immediate.[92]

Judge Hüseynov affirmed that the 2017 judgment by the Court's First Section in the *Talpis* case[93] had given 'hope that the Court was ready to deviate from an incident-based understanding of domestic violence' and to either 'reconsider the application of the Osman test to the particular situation of domestic violence, or at least to interpret the concept of immediate risk flexibly'.[94]

21.36 The test laid down in *Talpis* comprised an obligation on the authorities to 'take account of the recurrence of successive episodes of violence within the family unit'.[95] This approach was explicitly followed by the Court in its judgment in *Volodina v. Russia*, issued by another chamber five days after the judgment in *Kurt*.[96] The Court further observed that Russia remains one of only a few member States whose national legislation does not provide victims of domestic violence with measures of protection comparable to 'restraining orders', 'protection orders', or 'safety orders', which aim to safeguard a victim by requiring the abusive spouse or partner to leave a shared residence and to abstain from approaching or contacting their victim.[97] On 4 November 2019, the *Kurt* case was referred to the Court's Grand Chamber for its consideration.[98]

The Istanbul Convention

21.37 The Council of Europe Convention on preventing and combating violence against women and domestic violence,[99] better known as the Istanbul Convention, is a treaty adopted by the Council of Europe in 2011. The Council of Europe has declared that violence against women, including domestic violence, 'is one of the most serious forms of gender-based violations of human rights in Europe that is still shrouded in silence'.[100] The Convention is particularly noteworthy 'both for its encapsulation of best practices in combating violence against women and for its confirmation that all forms of violence against women, including domestic violence, are human rights violations for which States are responsible'.[101]

---

[92] *Kurt v. Austria*, Judgment (Fifth Section), Separate Opinion of Judge Hüseynov, para. 4.
[93] European Court of Human Rights, *Talpis v. Italy*, Judgment (First Section), 2 March 2017.
[94] *Kurt v. Austria*, Judgment (Fifth Section), Separate Opinion of Judge Hüseynov, para. 5.
[95] *Talpis v. Italy*, Judgment (First Section), para. 122.
[96] European Court of Human Rights, *Volodina v. Russia*, Judgment, 9 July 2019, para. 86.
[97] Ibid., paras. 88, 89.
[98] See also the third-party intervention in January 2020 by Grevio, a body established under the Council of Europe Convention on preventing and combating violence against women and domestic violence. 'Kurt v. Austria: GREVIO Submits First Written Observations', Council of Europe, Strasbourg, 22 January 2020, at http://bit.ly/33qBQXa. On GREVIO, see, *infra*, Paragraph 21.41.
[99] Council of Europe Convention on preventing and combating violence against women and domestic violence; adopted at Istanbul 11 May 2011; entered into force 1 August 2014 (hereinafter, Istanbul Convention).
[100] Council of Europe, Explanatory Report to the Council of Europe Convention on preventing and combating violence against women and domestic violence, undated but accessed 10 July 2020, at http://bit.ly/3ebRLek.
[101] B. C. Meyersfeld, 'The Council of Europe Convention on Preventing and Combating Violence Against Women and Domestic Violence', *International Legal Materials*, vol. 51, no. 1 (February 2012), pp. 106–32.

21.38 The Convention, which entered into force in 2014,[102] defines violence against women as 'a violation of human rights and a form of discrimination against women and shall mean all acts of gender-based violence that result in, or are likely to result in, physical, sexual, psychological or economic harm or suffering to women, including threats of such acts, coercion or arbitrary deprivation of liberty, whether occurring in public or in private life'.[103] The implementation of the Convention, 'in particular measures to protect the rights of victims', must occur 'without discrimination on any ground such as sex, gender, race, colour, language, religion, political or other opinion, national or social origin, association with a national minority, property, birth, sexual orientation, gender identity, age, state of health, disability, marital status, migrant or refugee status, or other status'.[104]

21.39 The Istanbul Convention does not explicitly protect the right to life, although parties must refrain from engaging in any act of violence against women and ensure that State authorities, officials, and agents comply with this obligation.[105] In addition, parties are obligated to take 'the necessary legislative and other measures to exercise due diligence to prevent, investigate, punish and provide reparation for acts of violence covered by the scope of this Convention that are perpetrated by non-State actors'.[106] Article 12 of the Convention contains the general obligation to prevent violence against women, with Articles 13 to 16 outlining this obligation more specifically by calling for detailed preventive measures in the area of awareness raising, education, training, and perpetrator treatment programmes.[107]

21.40 The Convention further incorporates the customary principle of *non-refoulement*, including where a threat to life exists, obligating parties to 'take the necessary legislative or other measures to respect the principle of non-refoulement in accordance with existing obligations under international law'.[108] Parties are required to take the necessary measures to ensure that women victims of violence 'who are in need of protection, regardless of their status or residence, shall not be returned under any circumstances to any country where

---

[102] As of 1 December 2020, the Istanbul Convention had been ratified by 34 States. In March 2021, however, Turkey announced its withdrawal. Council of Europe, 'Turkey's announced withdrawal from the Istanbul Convention endangers women's rights', 22 March 2021, at https://bit.ly/3wcoE3U. The Convention also provides for EU accession, which would require the consent of the European Parliament. On 28 November 2019, the European Parliament adopted a resolution calling on the European Union Council to urgently conclude the process of EU adherence. European Parliament, 'EU Accession to the Council of Europe Convention on Preventing and Combating Violence against Women ("Istanbul Convention")/2016-03', 24 June 2020, at http://bit.ly/38ItQC8. In addition, Canada, the Holy See, Japan, Kazakhstan, Mexico, Tunisia, and the United States, non-members of the Council of Europe, may also adhere to the Convention.
[103] Art. 3(a), Istanbul Convention.
[104] Art. 4(3), Istanbul Convention.
[105] Art. 5(1), Istanbul Convention.
[106] Art. 5(2), Istanbul Convention.
[107] See generally M. Hester and S.-J. Lilley, *Preventing Violence against Women: Article 12 of the Istanbul Convention. A collection of papers on the Council of Europe Convention on preventing and combating violence against women and domestic violence*, Council of Europe, September 2014, at http://bit.ly/3eiwfV8.
[108] Art. 61(1), Istanbul Convention.

their life would be at risk or where they might be subjected to torture or inhuman or degrading treatment or punishment'.[109]

21.41 In a novel approach to oversight of treaty compliance, a group of experts on action against violence against women and domestic violence ('GREVIO') is established under specific provisions in the Istanbul Convention to monitor its implementation.[110] In addition to receiving State reports, GREVIO may organise, in cooperation with the national authorities and with the assistance of independent national experts, country visits, if it deems the information obtained from States Parties to be insufficient or if urgent issues arise that require on-site clarification.[111] Speaking in May 2019 at an event organised by UN Women on the Convention's implementation, Zita Gurmai, a member of the Hungarian National Assembly and the Parliamentary Assembly of the Council of Europe, said, 'Since its entry into force in 2014, the Convention has contributed to saving hundreds of lives ... and set high legislative and policy standards.'[112] At the same time, the event concluded that five years since the Convention's entry into force, 'progress remains slow in fully eliminating violence against women and girls'.[113]

The Right to Life of Women under the Arab Charter on Human Rights

21.42 The 2004 Arab Charter on Human Rights[114] has a general provision enshrining the protection of the right to life, including for women. Under Article 5(1), 'every human being has an inherent right to life'. Paragraph 2 of the article stipulates further: 'This right shall be protected by law. No one shall be arbitrarily deprived of his life.' No derogation from respect for Article 5 may be made.[115] Under Article 7(2) of the Charter, the death penalty 'shall not be carried out on a pregnant woman prior to her delivery or on a nursing mother within two years from the date on which she gave birth. In any case, the interests of the infant shall prevail.' The article as a whole is not included in the list of non-derogable provisions under the Charter.

21.43 Under Article 3(3) of the Arab Charter: 'Men and women are equal in human dignity, in rights and in duties, within the framework of the positive discrimination established in favour of women by Islamic Shari'a and other divine laws, legislation and international instruments. Consequently, each State Party to the present Charter shall undertake all necessary measures to guarantee the effective equality between men and women.' According to Article 33(2) of the Charter: 'All forms of violence and abusive treatment in the relations between family members, especially towards women and children, shall be prohibited. The State and society undertake to provide outstanding

---

[109] Art. 61(2), Istanbul Convention.
[110] Art. 66(1), Istanbul Convention.
[111] Art. 66(9), (13), and (14), Istanbul Convention.
[112] UN Women, 'High-Level Meeting Urges Effective Enforcement of the Istanbul Convention to Eradicate Violence against Women', 6 May 2019, at http://bit.ly/2ZTZSHr.
[113] Ibid.
[114] Arab Charter on Human Rights; adopted at Tunis 22 May 2004; entered into force 15 March 2008.
[115] Art. 4(2), 2004 Arab Charter on Human Rights.

Protection of Women against Violence in the ASEAN Region

21.44 The Declaration on the Elimination of Violence against Women in the Association of South-East Asian Nations (ASEAN) Region was adopted by the ASEAN Ministerial Meeting on 30 June 2004. In the preamble to the non-binding Declaration, ASEAN members recognised that violence against women 'both violates and impairs their human rights and fundamental freedoms, limits their access to and control of resources and activities, and impedes the full development of their potential'.[116] In the operative text, member States undertake to ensure that their domestic laws serve to prevent violence against women and to enhance the protection and recovery of survivors, including through measures to investigate, prosecute, and punish the perpetrators. This is so, whether violence occurs in the home, in the workplace, in the community, or in custody.[117]

21.45 The 2012 ASEAN Human Rights Declaration, which is also non-binding, stipulates that the rights of women 'are an inalienable, integral and indivisible part of human rights and fundamental freedoms'.[118] The Declaration further declares: 'Every person has an inherent right to life which shall be protected by law. No person shall be deprived of life save in accordance with law.'[119] In the preamble to the Declaration, ASEAN members reaffirmed the importance of ASEAN's efforts in promoting human rights, including through the Declaration on the Elimination of Violence against Women in the ASEAN Region.

THE DEATH PENALTY

The Normative Framework

21.46 There is no general prohibition on the imposition and execution of the death penalty on women. Under customary international law, it is prohibited to execute – though not necessarily to impose – a sentence of death upon a pregnant woman. For a State to act otherwise amounts to an arbitrary deprivation of life. The prohibition is codified in the ICCPR[120] and in several regional instruments. As noted previously, under the Maputo Protocol, in those countries where the death penalty still exists, States Parties must ensure that a sentence of death is not executed 'on pregnant or nursing women'.[121] The Arab Charter stipulates that the death penalty may not be carried out on a pregnant

---

[116] Declaration on the Elimination of Violence against Women in the ASEAN Region; adopted by the ASEAN Ministerial Meeting, 30 June 2004, at http://bit.ly/2O8dqtm, fourth preambular para.
[117] Ibid., operative para. 4.
[118] ASEAN Human Rights Declaration, adopted by the Heads of State/Government of ASEAN member States at Phnom Penh, Cambodia, 18 November 2012, at http://bit.ly/329wakp, para. 4.
[119] Ibid., para. 11.
[120] Article 6(5) of the ICCPR specifies that the death penalty 'shall not be carried out on pregnant women'.
[121] Art. 4(2)(j), Maputo Protocol.

woman or on a nursing mother within two years of her giving birth.[122] Under the American Convention on Human Rights, capital punishment will not be applied to pregnant women.[123] The European Convention stipulates: 'No one shall be deprived of his life intentionally save in the execution of a sentence of a court following his conviction of a crime for which this penalty is provided by law.'[124] The reference to *his* life and *his* conviction should, though, be considered generically to cover also women and not to outlaw per se the execution of women. In any event, however, all capital punishment is today effectively unlawful under the European Convention.[125]

21.47 A specific treaty rule prohibiting the execution of a nursing mother binds States Parties to the Maputo Protocol (and the African Charter on Human and Peoples' Rights more generally)[126] as well as the Arab Charter, but may not yet have crystallised in customary international law. Such a rule is, though, *de lege ferenda* and is underpinned and supported by widespread State practice. In its General Comment 36 on the right to life, the Human Rights Committee repeated the rule in the ICCPR prohibiting the execution of a pregnant woman but did not elaborate on any specific illegality of the death penalty once she has given birth.[127] The International Committee of the Red Cross (ICRC) did not find that the various treaty prohibitions on executing nursing mothers in relation to any armed conflict (discussed later) codified a rule of customary international humanitarian law.[128]

The Death Penalty under International Humanitarian Law

21.48 Under 'combatant's privilege', no prisoner of war – a combatant captured during an international armed conflict – may be convicted of any offence, much less sentenced to death, for the fact of having engaged in hostilities against the detaining power, as long as he or she has complied with the rules of international humanitarian law while participating directly in hostilities.[129] This customary rule applies to female combatants just as it does to

---

[122] Art. 7(2), 2004 Arab Charter on Human Rights.
[123] Art. 4(5), Inter-American Convention on Human Rights.
[124] Art. 2(1), European Convention on Human Rights.
[125] See on this issue Chapter 13.
[126] In its 2015 General Comment on the right to life under the African Charter, African Commission on Human and Peoples' Rights states: 'Whatever the offence or the circumstances of the trial, the execution of . . . nursing women . . . will always amount to a violation of the right to life.' African Commission on Human and Peoples' Rights, 'General Comment No. 3 on the African Charter on Human and Peoples' Rights: The Right to Life (Article 4)', adopted at Banjul (57th Ordinary Session), November 2015, para. 25.
[127] Human Rights Committee, General Comment 36 on the right to life, para. 48.
[128] ICRC Customary IHL Rule 134: 'Women', at http://bit.ly/2Tj990S.
[129] As Switzerland has observed, in an international armed conflict, combatants 'may take part in licit acts of war, for which they may not be subjected to criminal prosecution or brought to court ("combatants' privileges")'. Swiss Federal Department of Foreign Affairs, *The ABC of International Humanitarian Law*, 3rd rev. ed., Bern, 2018, at http://bit.ly/38PwyWq, p. 16. The rule is of a customary nature. 'Upon capture, combatants entitled to prisoner-of-war status may neither be tried for their participation in the hostilities nor for acts that do not violate international humanitarian law. This is a long-standing rule of customary international humanitarian law.' International Committee of the Red Cross (ICRC), Customary IHL Rule 106: 'Conditions for Prisoner-of-War Status', at http://bit.ly/3aXJwlc. See further Articles 87 and 99, Convention (III) relative to the Treatment of Prisoners of War; adopted at Geneva 12 August 1949; entered into force 21 October 1950.

male combatants. Also in relation to a situation of international armed conflict, the 1977 Additional Protocol I requires that parties to a conflict 'endeavour, to the maximum extent feasible' to avoid imposing the death penalty on pregnant women or mothers having dependent infants for any offence related to the armed conflict. In any event, the Protocol provides, the death penalty may not be executed on such women.[130]

21.49 In a situation of non-international armed conflict, the 1977 Additional Protocol II prohibits even the imposition of the death penalty on pregnant women or mothers of young children.[131] Unusually, this provision is stricter than the corresponding provision pertaining to women applicable in a situation of international armed conflict. Moreover, under Common Article 3 to the four 1949 Geneva Conventions, 'the passing of sentences and the carrying out of executions without previous judgment pronounced by a regularly constituted court, affording all the judicial guarantees which are recognized as indispensable by civilized peoples', is a serious violation of international humanitarian law. The imposition of a death sentence at the culmination of an unfair trial is a war crime within the jurisdiction of the International Criminal Court.[132]

WOMEN'S RIGHT TO LIFE IN ARMED CONFLICT

21.50 Prior to 1945, Otto observes, international law took a 'paternalistic or "protective" approach to women, treating them as the property, extension, or dependants of men'.[133] Thus, for example, at the turn of the twentieth century, the law of armed conflict referred to the protection of 'family honour and rights' during occupation.[134] With women now members in most armed forces, and some serving on the front line as soldiers, the legal and practical situation has since changed markedly and women are understood to have specific protection as bearers of individual rights and entitlements.

21.51 Under the 1949 Geneva Convention IV, in the territories of the parties to an international armed conflict and to occupied territories, 'Women shall be especially protected against any attack on their honour, in particular against rape, enforced prostitution, or any form of indecent assault.'[135] In the two 1977 Additional Protocols, specific

---

[130] Art. 76(3), Protocol Additional to the Geneva Conventions of 12 August 1949, and relating to the Protection of Victims of International Armed Conflicts; adopted at Geneva 8 June 1977; entered into force 7 December 1978 (hereinafter, 1977 Additional Protocol I).
[131] Art. 6(4), 1977 Additional Protocol II.
[132] Art. 8(2)(c)(iv), Rome Statute of the International Criminal Court; adopted at Rome 17 July 1998; entered into force 1 July 2002 (Rome Statute). In the corresponding elements of crimes, the Court is asked to consider whether, 'in the light of all relevant circumstances, the cumulative effect of factors with respect to guarantees deprived the person or persons of a fair trial'. Elements of Crimes, *Official Records of the Assembly of States Parties to the Rome Statute of the International Criminal Court, First session, New York, 3–10 September 2002*, p. 34.
[133] Otto, 'Women's Rights', p. 312.
[134] Art. 46, Regulations concerning the Laws and Customs of War on Land, annexed to Convention (IV) respecting the Laws and Customs of War on Land; adopted at The Hague, 18 October 1907; entered into force 26 January 1910. This repeated the provision incorporated as Article 46 in the Regulations annexed to Convention (II) with Respect to the Laws and Customs of War on Land adopted at The Hague, 29 July 1899.
[135] Art. 27, Convention (IV) Relative to the Protection of Civilian Persons in Time of War; adopted at Geneva, 12 August 1949; entered into force 21 October 1950.

protection is afforded to women civilians and those *hors de combat*. The Additional Protocol I (applicable to international armed conflict) stipulates that women 'shall be the object of special respect and shall be protected in particular against rape, forced prostitution and any other form of indecent assault'.[136] The 1977 Additional Protocol II (applicable to certain non-international armed conflicts) provides that outrages upon personal dignity, in particular humiliating and degrading treatment, rape, enforced prostitution, and any form of indecent assault 'remain prohibited at any time and in any place whatsoever'.[137]

21.52 What has not changed has been the widespread targeting of women civilians by parties to armed conflict, often on a systematic basis, for rape, sexual enslavement, and murder. While rape will typically be considered as torture, gang rape and rape followed by further violence to the victim may also fall to be considered as violations of the right to life.[138] In addition to constituting war crimes,[139] sexual violence may also, depending on the circumstances, amount to crimes against humanity[140] and even genocide.[141,142]

21.53 Within the United Nations, the Office of the Special Representative of the UN Secretary-General on Sexual Violence in Conflict was established in 2010 pursuant to Security Council Resolution 1888 (2009).[143] In April 2017, the Secretary-General appointed Ms Pramila Patten of Mauritius as the third Special Representative. Within the UN system, the Special Representative chairs the UN Action Against Sexual Violence in Conflict (UN Action), a network that unites the work of 15 UN entities[144] whose goal is said to be nothing less than 'ending sexual violence during and in the wake of conflict'.[145]

---

[136] Art. 75(2)(b), 1977 Additional Protocol I.
[137] Art. 4(2), 1977 Additional Protocol II.
[138] For a discussion of the application of the right to life to rape victims under the Indian Constitution, see, e.g., K. I. Vibhute, 'Victims of Rape and Their Right to Live with Human Dignity and to Be Compensated: Legislative and Judicial Responses in India', *Journal of the Indian Law Institute*, vol. 41, no. 2 (April–June 1999), pp. 222–36, at 227–28. See further G. Binion, 'Human Rights: A Feminist Perspective', *Human Rights Quarterly*, vol. 17, no. 3 (August 1995), pp. 509–26.
[139] Art. 8(2)(b)(xxii) and (2)(e)(vi), Rome Statute.
[140] Art. 7(1)(g), Rome Statute.
[141] Art. 6(b), Rome Statute. See on this issue International Criminal Tribunal for Rwanda (ICTR), *Prosecutor v. Athanase Seromba*, Judgment (Case No. ICTR-2001-66-A), 12 March 2008, para. 46.
[142] See further on this issue, e.g., Amnesty International, *Rape and Sexual Violence: Human Rights Law and Standards in the International Criminal Court*, London, 2011, at http://bit.ly/2ZRi18B, esp. pp. 38–40.
[143] UN Security Council Resolution 1888, adopted by unanimous vote on 30 September 2009, para. 4.
[144] UN member entities comprise the Department of Peacebuilding and Political Affairs (DPPA), the UN Entity for Gender Equality and the Empowerment of Women (UN Women), the UN Population Fund (UNFPA), the UN Development Programme (UNDP), the Joint UN Program on HIV/AIDS (UNAIDS), the Department of Peace Operations (DPO), the Office of the UN High Commissioner for Refugees (UNHCR), Office of the Special Representative of the Secretary-General for Children and Armed Conflict, the Office of the High Commissioner for Human Rights (OHCHR), the World Health Organization (WHO), the Office for the Coordination of Humanitarian Affairs (OCHA), the UN Children's Fund (UNICEF), the UN Office on Drugs and Crime (UNODC), the UN Office for Disarmament Affairs (UNODA), and the International Organization for Migration (IOM).
[145] UN, 'The Office of the Special Representative of the Secretary-General on Sexual Violence in Conflict (OSRSG-SVC)', undated but accessed 9 July 2020, at http://bit.ly/32qliN7.

21.54 In his annual report to the UN Security Council covering 2018, the UN Secretary-General noted that it remained difficult to ascertain the exact prevalence of conflict-related sexual violence. This is due to a range of challenges, including under-reporting resulting from the intimidation and stigmatization of survivors, as well as restrictions on access for UN staff. Nonetheless, while non-State actors were responsible for the majority of incidents of sexual violence he recorded, State actors were also implicated in country situations he listed, with national armed forces, police, or other security forces being listed in the Democratic Republic of Congo, Myanmar, Somalia, South Sudan, Sudan, and Syria.[146] Conflict-related sexual violence, along with killing, pillaging and the illicit exploitation of natural resources, continued to function as both a driver and a result of forced displacement.[147] In response to the report, the Security Council adopted Resolution 2467 whose preamble expressed 'deep concern at the full range of threats and human rights violations and abuses experienced by women and girls in armed conflict and post-conflict situations', recognising that women and girls 'are particularly at risk and are often specifically targeted and at an increased risk of violence in conflict and post-conflict situations'.[148]

21.55 In Myanmar in 2018, amid the genocide being perpetrated by the Myanmar army (Tatmadaw), the independent International Fact-Finding Mission on Myanmar reported that the so-called clearance operations (a systematic process of driving out hundreds of thousands of Rohingya from Myanmar beginning in August 2017) represented 'a human rights catastrophe'. Thousands of Rohingya were, the Fact-Finding Mission affirmed, killed or injured during these operations. Information collected by the Fact-Finding Mission suggests that an estimate of 'up to 10,000 deaths' is credible. In Min Gyi, a village in Rakhine state near the border with Bangladesh, 'women and girls were taken to nearby houses, gang raped, then killed or severely injured'.[149] Elsewhere in Rakhine state, 'mothers were gang raped in front of young children, who were severely injured and in some instances killed'.[150]

21.56 On 8 August 2019, the Fact-Finding Mission published a report affirming its earlier conclusion 'that Myanmar incurs State responsibility under the prohibition against genocide'.[151] The report referred to 'continued concerns regarding conflict-related sexual violence', identifying cases 'between April 2018 and July 2019 where Tatmadaw soldiers subjected women and, in one case, a girl to sexual violence, including rape, gang rape and attempted rape, as well as forced nudity, leading to them being ostracized by their

---

[146] 'Conflict-Related Sexual Violence: Report of the United Nations Secretary-General', UN doc. S/2019/280, 29 March 2019, paras. 11 and 12.
[147] Ibid., para. 15.
[148] UN Security Council Resolution 2467 (2019), adopted by unanimous vote on 23 April 2019, tenth preambular para.
[149] Report of the Independent International Fact-Finding Mission on Myanmar, UN doc. A/HRC/39/64, 12 September 2018, para. 36.
[150] Ibid., para. 38.
[151] Report of the Independent International Fact-Finding Mission on Myanmar, UN doc. A/HRC/42/50, 8 August 2019, para. 18.

communities and government authorities'.[152] In January 2020, the International Court of Justice imposed provisional measures on Myanmar in a contentious case brought by The Gambia. The Gambia contends that Myanmar's military and security forces and persons or entities acting on its instructions or under its direction and control have been responsible for killings, rape, and other forms of sexual violence, torture and other cruel treatment, all with the intent to destroy the Rohingya group, in whole or in part.[153]

21.57 The extent of the problem confronting the international community with respect to sexual violence, especially in armed conflict, was exacerbated by the outbreak of the global COVID-19 pandemic in 2020. On 18 June 2020, a Joint Statement by European Union High Representative for Foreign Affairs and Security Policy, Josep Borrell, the UN Special Representative on Sexual Violence in Conflict, on the occasion of the International Day for the Elimination of Sexual Violence in Conflict declared:

> The pandemic poses a significant threat to the maintenance of peace and security, as well increased risks of violence. It entails particularly devastating risks for women and girls in fragile and conflict-affected contexts and creates an environment that may worsen violence against women and children, including sexual violence and intimate partner violence. Victims of conflict-related sexual violence are amongst those bearing the brunt of the pandemic.[154]

MATERNAL MORTALITY

21.58 Aside from deaths as a result of violence, many women die as a result of complications during and following pregnancy and childbirth, most of which are either preventable or treatable.[155] The major complications that account for nearly three quarters of all maternal deaths are severe bleeding (generally after childbirth), infections (usually after childbirth), high blood pressure during pregnancy (pre-eclampsia and eclampsia), and complications from delivery; unsafe abortion is also a significant cause of maternal mortality. The remainder of deaths are caused by or associated with infections, such as malaria, or related to chronic conditions like cardiac diseases or diabetes.[156]

Maternal Health and the Right to Life

21.59 In 2011, in its landmark decision in *Alyne da Silva Pimentel*,[157] the Committee on the Elimination of Discrimination against Women found that Brazil had violated the right to

---

[152] Ibid., para. 60.
[153] International Court of Justice, *Application of the Convention on the Prevention and Punishment of the Crime of Genocide (The Gambia v. Myanmar)*, Order, 23 January 2020, para. 29.
[154] Joint Statement by EU High Representative for Foreign Affairs and Security Policy, Josep Borrell, and UN Special Representative on Sexual Violence in Conflict, Pramila Patten, on the Occasion of the International Day for the Elimination of Sexual Violence in Conflict, Brussels/New York, 18 June 2020, at http://bit.ly/2CoRgjJ.
[155] World Health Organization (WHO), 'Maternal Mortality', 19 September 2019, at http://bit.ly/2Cp7Ujd.
[156] Ibid.
[157] Committee on the Elimination of Discrimination against Women, *Alyne da Silva Pimentel v. Brazil*, Views (Comm. No. 17/2008), 27 September 2011, at http://bit.ly/3iPEGuQ.

health protected by CEDAW. Surprisingly, the Committee did not also find a violation of the right to life, despite this being claimed by the deceased's mother. The case concerned a Brazilian woman of African descent who died from pregnancy-related causes after her local health centre misdiagnosed her symptoms and delayed providing her with emergency obstetric care. Although she showed symptoms of a high-risk pregnancy, the doctor at the private health clinic she attended sent her home. After her condition worsened during the following two days, she returned to the clinic. By that time, the doctors were unable to detect a foetal heartbeat. Delivery was induced six hours later, producing a stillborn foetus. Surgery to extract her placenta was performed fourteen hours later, although good medical practice determined it should have occurred immediately after the delivery was induced.[158]

21.60 Owing to the steady deterioration in her physical health, she was transferred to a higher-tier public health care institution, but she had to wait more than eight hours before transfer to the General Hospital in Nova Iguacu. She died after waiting more than twenty-one hours for medical attention, leaving behind her five-year-old daughter.[159]

21.61 As the complaint against the State highlighted, '4,000 maternal deaths occur each year in Brazil, representing one third of all maternal deaths in Latin America'.[160] Moreover, a disproportionately high number of victims are among vulnerable groups, 'especially women of African descent'.[161] Brazil had argued that Ms. da Silva Pimentel Teixeira's death was non-maternal and that the probable cause of her death was a digestive haemorrhage.[162] It had also sought to evade responsibility on the basis that the clinic was private, not State, but the Committee rejected that argument on the basis of acknowledged 'shortcomings in the system used to contract private health services and, by extension, the inspection and control thereof'. The Committee noted that

> the State is directly responsible for the action of private institutions when it outsources its medical services and that, furthermore, the State always maintains the duty to regulate and monitor private health-care institutions. In line with article 2(e) of the Convention, the State party has a due diligence obligation to take measures to ensure that the activities of private actors in regard to health policies and practices are appropriate.[163]

21.62 The Committee found violations of the right to access health care and to effective judicial protection in the context of non-discrimination.[164] The Views of the CEDAW

---

[158] 'Case of Alyne da Silva Pimentel Teixeira ("Alyne") v. Brazil', Fact Sheet, Center for Reproductive Rights, New York, at http://bit.ly/2CpQflw, p. 2.
[159] Ibid.
[160] Committee on the Elimination of Discrimination against Women, *Alyne da Silva Pimentel v. Brazil*, Views, 2011, para. 5.1.
[161] Committee on the Elimination of Discrimination against Women, Concluding Observations on Brazil, August 2007, paras. 11 and 35.
[162] Committee on the Elimination of Discrimination against Women, *Alyne da Silva Pimentel v. Brazil*, Views, 2011, para. 7.3.
[163] Ibid., para. 7.5.
[164] Ibid., paras. 7.5 and 7.8. See further J. Bueno de Mesquita and E. Kismödi, 'Maternal Mortality and Human Rights: Landmark Decision by United Nations Human Rights Body', *Bulletin of the World Health Organization*, vol. 90 (2012), p. 79.

Committee clearly recognise that States 'have an immediate and enforceable human rights obligation to address and reduce maternal mortality'.[165] But the absence of a finding of a violation also of the right to life – indeed the Committee's failure to address this element of the complaint in any depth – is puzzling. This is especially so, given the serious risk of death occurring from a failure to ensure the provision of adequate maternal care. Indeed, the Committee had expressly held that Ms da Silva Pimentel Teixeira's death was 'maternal', noting further that 'the lack of appropriate maternal health services has a differential impact on the right to life of women'.[166]

21.63 Writing the year before the Committee on the Elimination of Discrimination against Women issued its Views in the *Alyne da Silva Pimentel* case, two leading commentators were claiming that preventable maternal mortality 'also often represents a violation of a woman's right to life'.[167] They note that while women in developed countries have only a 1-in-2,800 chance of dying in childbirth – a 1-in-8,700 chance in some countries – women in Africa have a 1-in-20 chance. In several countries, they record, the lifetime risk is greater than 1 in 10.[168] There is, they declare, 'no single cause of death and disability for men between the ages of 15 and 44 that is close to the magnitude of maternal death and disability'.[169]

Maternal Health and the Sustainable Development Goals

21.64 Sustainable Development Goal (SDG) 3 aims to ensure healthy lives and promote well-being for all, at all ages. One of the targets is, by 2030, to reduce the global MMR to less than 70 per 100,000 live births.[170] This is a very ambitious target, given current realities. The global MMR in 2017 was estimated at 211 maternal deaths per 100,000 live births, down from 342 in 2000. Thus estimates for 2017 (the latest year for which reliable data were available as of writing) indicated some 295,000 maternal deaths globally. This is a 35 per cent drop compared to the estimated total in 2000 of 451,000 maternal deaths.[171] But the reduction masks huge inequalities between nations, with rates varying dramatically depending on the developmental status of the country in which the woman gives birth. In 2017, in low-income countries, the MMR was assessed at some 462 per 100,000 live

---

[165] 'Case of Alyne da Silva Pimentel Teixeira ("Alyne") v. Brazil', Fact Sheet, Center for Reproductive Rights, New York, p. 2.
[166] Committee on the Elimination of Discrimination against Women, *Alyne da Silva Pimentel v. Brazil*, Views, 2011, paras. 7.3 and 7.6. The claim by the Center for Reproductive Rights that this is effective recognition that the right to life is violated in such cases is not persuasive. 'Case of Alyne da Silva Pimentel Teixeira ("Alyne") v. Brazil', Fact Sheet, Center for Reproductive Rights, New York, p. 3.
[167] P. Hunt and J. Bueno de Mesquita, *Reducing Maternal Mortality: The Contribution of the Right to the Highest Attainable Standard of Health*, University of Essex and UN Population Fund (UNFPA), Colchester, 2010, at http://bit.ly/3ebvzRy, p. 3.
[168] Ibid., p. 4.
[169] Ibid.
[170] SDG 3, Health Target 3.1. In September 2015, Agenda 2030 set out seventeen Sustainable Development Goals that States have committed to achieving.
[171] *Trends In Maternal Mortality 2000 to 2017. Estimates by WHO, UNICEF, UNFPA, World Bank Group and the United Nations Population Division*, WHO, Geneva, 2019.

births. This compares to an average of 11 per 100,000 live births across high-income countries.[172]

21.65 For millions of women to die when '88–98% of maternal deaths'[173] are probably preventable is, in the words of two medical commentators, 'obscene'.[174] To reduce the MMR, the key is ensuring access to high-quality care during pregnancy and during and after childbirth. The presence of skilled health professionals 'can make the difference between life and death for the mother as well as for the baby'. Immediately after childbirth, an injection of oxytocics – an agent, known as a uterotonic or ecbolic, used to induce contraction or greater tonicity of the uterus – effectively reduces the risk of bleeding. Infection after childbirth can be eliminated through good hygiene, and if early signs of infection are recognised and treated swiftly. Pre-eclampsia can be detected and managed before the onset of convulsions (eclampsia) and other life-threatening complications, for instance through the use of drugs such as magnesium sulphate. According to the World Health Organization (WHO), to avoid maternal deaths, it is also vital to prevent unwanted pregnancies.[175]

21.66 In sum, where a State has a high maternal mortality ratio (MMR; of 40 or above per 100,000 live births), it is obligated to take systemic action with a view to reducing the rate of maternal mortality. A failure to do so is likely to found a violation of the right to life, at the least where a woman dies as a result of inadequate health care. In addition, where, within a country, members of minorities face similarly high levels of risk – especially where there are significant national inequalities and minority women are subject to discrimination in the provision of health care – action must be taken to redress their lack of access in order to comply with the State's duty to respect and protect the right to life. Within any State, negligent action by a health care provider that is a causal factor in a maternal death may also amount to a violation of the right to life.

---

[172] WHO, 'Maternal Mortality', 19 September 2019. Even among developed nations, however, there is considerable variance in the MMR. Women in the United States, for instance, 'face a far greater risk of dying from childbirth complications than in many other wealthy countries'. E. Kumler Kaplan, 'Reducing Maternal Mortality', *New York Times*, 5 March 2019, at http://nyti.ms/2ZknJB7. In December 2018, the United States signed into law the Preventing Maternal Deaths Act, which provides federal grants to states to investigate the deaths of women who die within a year of being pregnant. The MMR in the United States of between 14 and 18 per 100,000 births compares to Sweden, where the rate is 4, and England, which registers 9 deaths per 100,000 births. African American women face similar rates of death as those of women delivering in some developing countries, with rates of more than 40 per 100,000 births. Centers for Disease Control, 'Pregnancy Mortality Surveillance System', page last reviewed 4 February 2020, at http://bit.ly/2CmT9O9. Moreover, the MMR in America has more than doubled in less than 20 years. M. C. Lu, 'Reducing Maternal Mortality in the United States', *JAMA*, American Medical Association, United States, 25 September 2018, at http://bit.ly/2W5guuO. One of the reasons ascribed to the big jump in deaths is the greater use of delivery by caesarean section for non-medical reasons. Kumler Kaplan, 'Reducing Maternal Mortality', *New York Times*.

[173] 'Maternal Mortality: Helping Women Off the Road to Death', *WHO Chronicle*, vol. 40 (1986), pp. 175–83, at http://bit.ly/3iLh7mO, at p. 177.

[174] O. M. R. Campbell and W. J. Graham (on behalf of The Lancet Maternal Survival Series steering group), 'Strategies for Reducing Maternal Mortality: Getting On with What Works', *The Lancet*, vol. 368, no. 9543 (7 October 2006), pp. 1284–99, at http://bit.ly/3ebLrmZ, at p. 1297.

[175] Ibid.

22

Children

INTRODUCTION

22.01 This chapter describes the content and protection of the right to life of children under international law.[1] The notion that a child has rights is long-standing: the 1924 Declaration of the Rights of the Child, adopted by the League of Nations,[2] was the first international instrument explicitly acknowledging the existence of children's rights.[3] But the Declaration did not, in fact, institute legally binding rights, detailing instead a series of five principles for action by adults to support and protect children, none of which explicitly called for the protection of life. In 1959, the UN General Assembly adopted the Declaration of the Rights of the Child, which stipulated that every child 'shall be protected against all forms of neglect, cruelty and exploitation'.[4] Again, however, a child's right to life was not overtly guaranteed. In 1989, however, the Convention on the Rights of the Child[5] (CRC) – the most widely ratified human rights treaty in history – specified, for the first time in a global human rights instrument, that every child has the right to life.

The Definition of a Child

22.02 Under Article 1 of the CRC, a child is defined as every human being below the age of eighteen, unless, under applicable domestic law, the age of majority is attained earlier. The age of majority is the age at which a child becomes an adult in the eyes of the law. In most cases, this coincides with the age at which a person is allowed to vote in national

---

[1] The author would like to thank Ms Sanskriti Sanghi, LL.M candidate at the University of Cambridge, for her extensive background research for this chapter.
[2] Declaration of the Rights of the Child; adopted at Geneva by the Fifth Assembly of the League of Nations 28 February 1924. The text of the Declaration was elaborated by the International Save the Children Union, the forerunner to the international non-governmental organisation (NGO), Save the Children.
[3] Office of the United Nations High Commissioner for Human Rights (OHCHR), *Legislative History of the Convention on the Rights of the Child*, Vol. I, New York/Geneva, 2007, p.3.
[4] Principle 9, Declaration of the Rights of the Child; proclaimed by UN General Assembly Resolution 1386 (XIV), adopted without a vote on 20 November 1959 (hereinafter, 1959 UN Declaration of the Rights of the Child).
[5] Convention on the Rights of the Child; adopted at New York 20 November 1989; entered into force 2 September 1990 (hereinafter, CRC).

elections.[6] Most States set the age of majority at eighteen, though some set it earlier, while in a very small minority of States children legally become adults at an age greater than eighteen years.

22.03 Worldwide, the lowest age of majority is set in Iran, where, in the words of the Committee on the Rights of the Child established to oversee implementation of the CRC, it 'remains set at predefined ages of puberty, namely 9 lunar years for girls and 15 lunar years for boys'. This results, the Committee observes, in girls and boys above those ages 'being deprived of the protections under the Convention'.[7] Other national exceptions to an age of majority at eighteen years include Yemen, where it continues to be fifteen. This is despite discussions in parliament in recent years about the possibility of raising it to eighteen.[8] In Saudi Arabia, although legislation ostensibly defines a child as anyone under eighteen,[9] a judge has the power to set a different age.[10] Within Europe, only Scotland (a country within the United Kingdom and therefore not an independent State as of writing) sets majority below eighteen – at sixteen years of age.[11] Previously, Nepal's statutory age of majority was also sixteen,[12] but in 2018 this was raised by law to eighteen.[13]

22.04 Upon adherence to the CRC in 1995, Botswana entered a reservation whereby it 'does not consider itself bound' by the provisions of Article 1 insofar as they 'may conflict with the Laws and Statutes of Botswana'.[14] As of 2018, however, the Children's Act defined a child as 'any person who is below the age of 18 years'. The Act did, though, explicitly allow other domestic laws to set a different age where this 'has or would have the effect of harming the child's emotional, physical, psychological or moral well-being, or of prejudicing the exercise of the rights and freedoms of others, national security, the public interest, public safety, public order, public morality or public health'.[15] In this regard, Botswana conceded in its third national report in 2018 under the CRC that 'some challenges' persisted in harmonising the definitions of the child in other laws.[16]

---

[6] The ages at which a child is allowed by law to, for instance, marry, enter into contracts, join the armed forces, or drink alcohol (where this is permissible for any person) may also be different.
[7] Committee on the Rights of the Child, Concluding Observations on the combined third and fourth periodic reports of Iran, UN doc. CRC/C/IRN/CO/3–4, 14 March 2016, para. 27.
[8] Committee on the Rights of the Child, Concluding Observations on the fourth periodic report of Yemen, UN doc. CRC/C/YEM/CO/4, 25 February 2014, paras. 9, 27.
[9] See, e.g., the Child Protection Act. Third and fourth periodic reports of Saudi Arabia under the CRC, UN doc. CRC/C/SAU/3–4, 8 April 2015, para. 70.
[10] Committee on the Rights of the Child, Concluding Observations on the combined third and fourth periodic reports of Saudi Arabia, UN doc. CRC/C/SAU/CO/3–4, 25 October 2016, para. 13.
[11] S. 1, 1991 Age of Legal Capacity (Scotland) Act.
[12] S. 2(A) of the 1992 Children's Act states that every human being below the age of 16 is a child. Third to fifth periodic reports of Nepal under the CRC, UN doc. CRC/C/NPL/3–5, 23 December 2013, para. 49.
[13] S. 2(j), Act Relating to Children 2018, Act No. 23 of 2075 B.S.
[14] Declaration of Botswana with respect to Article 1 of the CRC, available at http://bit.ly/2Q3VBw7.
[15] Combined second and third reports submitted by Botswana under the CRC, UN doc. CRC/C/BWA/2–3, 27 November 2018, para. 41.
[16] Ibid., para. 42. As discussed later in this chapter, Botswana has entered a reservation to provision in the African Charter on the Rights and Welfare of the Child as the age of eighteen defining the end of childhood. See, *infra*, Paragraph 25.21. To date, it is the only African State to do so.

22.05 Under international law, eighteen is the maximum age at which the protections afforded by the CRC cease. There are, though, a number of States that set majority in their domestic law later than that. When adhering to the CRC, Cuba, for instance, declared that under its domestic law, 'majority is not attained at 18 years of age for purposes of the full exercise of civic rights'.[17] Upon its adherence to the CRC in 1995, Liechtenstein had similarly made a declaration concerning Article 1 of the Convention, noting that under its domestic legislation 'children come of age with 20 years'. On 1 October 2009, however, Liechtenstein informed the UN Secretary-General that it was withdrawing that declaration.[18]

22.06 The age at which a child begins to receive the protections afforded by international law remains controversial. The preamble to the 1959 UN Declaration of the Rights of the Child had called for the child to receive 'appropriate legal protection, before as well as after birth'.[19] This phrasing is cited verbatim in the preamble to the CRC.[20] The wording of the text in Article 6 of the CRC, however, implies that a child is protected under the Convention only from birth. Prior to that, there is not a human being for the purposes of international law but rather a foetus (from eight weeks after fertilisation) or, at earlier stages, first a fertilised egg (zygote and then blastocyst) and then, at about two weeks after fertilisation, an embryo.[21] During the negotiation of the CRC, however, the Holy See stated that it recognised that the rights of the child 'began before birth'. It affirmed 'that a child and its life existed from the moment of conception which was the transmission of life in marriage to which the mission of transmitting life was exclusively entrusted. Consequently, a conceived child was entitled to rights. Human life shall absolutely be respected and protected from the moment of conception.'[22]

22.07 Such a broad interpretation of a child under the CRC, in which the protections guaranteed by the Convention begin before a child is born, is shared by only a small number of other States Parties, in particular those in the Americas.[23] When adhering to the Convention in 1990, Argentina declared that Article 1 of the Convention 'must be interpreted to the effect that a child means every human being from the moment of conception up to the age of eighteen'.[24] Upon its adherence to the CRC the same year, Guatemala affirmed that its Constitution establishes that the State 'guarantees and

---

[17] Declaration of Cuba with respect to Article 1 of the CRC, available at http://bit.ly/2Q3VBw7.
[18] Declaration of Liechtenstein with respect to Article 1 of the CRC, available at http://bit.ly/2Q3VBw7.
[19] 1959 UN Declaration of the Rights of the Child, Third preambular para.
[20] CRC, Ninth preambular para.
[21] Of course, that does not imply that a foetus in the womb, an embryo, or a fertilised egg is not entitled to protection under domestic law, only that they are not covered by the protections afforded under the CRC.
[22] Report of the working group on a draft convention on the rights of the child, UN doc. E/CN.4/1988/28, 6 April 1988, para. 25.
[23] Under the 1969 American Convention on Human Rights, every person has the right to have their life respected. It is further provided that 'this right shall be protected by law and, in general, from the moment of conception'. Art. 4(1), American Convention on Human Rights; adopted at San José 22 November 1969; entered into force 18 July 1978. With respect to family planning and the voluntary termination of pregnancy, see, *infra*, Paragraph 25.15.
[24] Declaration of Argentina with respect to Article 1 of the CRC, available at http://bit.ly/2Q3VBw7.

protects human life from the time of its conception'.[25] *Stricto sensu*, though, this is a statement of fact as to the tenets of domestic law rather than an interpretive declaration of Article 6 for the purposes of international law. In sum, the CRC should be understood to protect the rights of the child only from birth.

THE RIGHT TO LIFE OF CHILDREN UNDER GLOBAL STANDARDS

22.08 Each child under the jurisdiction of a State Party to the 1966 International Covenant on Civil and Political Rights[26] (ICCPR) benefits from the protection of the right to life afforded by its Article 6 to every human being. This right is non-derogable in toto.[27] As discussed in Chapter 1 of this work, that every human being has the right to life has long reflected customary international law. Further, the prohibition of arbitrary deprivation of life of any person, including any child,[28] as codified in Article 6(1) of the ICCPR, has attained the status of a peremptory norm of international law (jus cogens).

22.09 The ICCPR refers explicitly to the rights of children in a number of provisions but does not define the notion; nor does it specify either a minimum or maximum age of majority. Today, the term as employed in the ICCPR should best be understood consonant with the definition in Article 1 of the CRC. Article 24(1) of the ICCPR entitles every child 'to such measures of protection as are required by his status as a minor on the part of his family, society and the State'. The Human Rights Committee has determined that this obligates the taking of 'special measures designed to protect the life of every child, in addition to the general measures required by article 6'.[29]

22.10 The formulation of the right to life under the CRC differs materially from that set out in the ICCPR in a number of aspects. Article 6(1) of the CRC provides simply: 'States Parties recognize that every child has the inherent right to life.' The provision reiterates the customary nature of the right of every child to life[30] and certainly comprises a duty 'to respect', even though there is no explicit prohibition on the arbitrary deprivation of life of any child. There is also no specific requirement that the right of each child to life must be 'protected by law', as is set out in Article 6(1) of the ICCPR.

---

[25] Declaration of Guatemala with respect to Article 1 of the CRC, available at http://bit.ly/2Q3VBw7.
[26] International Covenant on Civil and Political Rights; adopted at New York 16 December 1966; entered into force 23 March 1976.
[27] Art. 4(2), ICCPR.
[28] Human Rights Committee, General Comment No. 36: Article 6: right to life, UN doc. CCPR/C/GC/36, 3 September 2019 (hereinafter, Human Rights Committee, General Comment 36 on the right to life), para. 3.
[29] Ibid., para. 60, citing: Human Rights Committee, General Comment No. 17, para. 1; General Comment No. 32, paras. 42–44; *Prutina v. Bosnia and Herzegovina*, Views (Comm. No. 1917/2009), 28 March 2013, para. 9.8; and Concluding Observations on Benin (2015), para. 19. When taking special measures of protection, the Human Rights Committee further provides that States Parties to the ICCPR should be guided by the provisions in the CRC governing the best interests of the child and the need to ensure the survival and development of all children as well as their well-being. Human Rights Committee, General Comment 36 on the right to life, para. 60.
[30] Under the CRC, the right to life is the only right of the child that is described as 'inherent'.

22.11 Instead, the right to life of every child as protected under the CRC explicitly comprises an obligation on each State Party to 'ensure to the maximum extent possible the survival and development of the child'.[31] This provision, which combines core elements of the broader international legal duties 'to protect' and 'to fulfil' human rights, demands positive action to promote not only continued physical existence but also the enjoyment of both a fully developed and a dignified life. Upon the Convention's adoption in 1989, and despite the view expressed to the contrary during its elaboration,[32] the obligation in Article 6(2) of the CRC represented a progressive development of international law.

22.12 The reference to survival in Article 6(2) comprises 'the right to have positive steps taken to prolong the life of the child'.[33] It has become, in the words of one authority, a 'term of art' within children's rights, whose recognition 'would clearly expand the range of positive measures required to be taken on behalf of the child'.[34] Requiring that States Parties to the CRC only seek to ensure the survival of children within their jurisdiction would, however, have been considered too limited an obligation by many of the negotiating States. Thus, during the drafting of the Convention, India, in particular, was consistently of the view that the right to survival should be supplemented by the notion of healthy development, given that children can survive 'in very poor conditions'.[35] The duty to promote the development of children, the importance of which had already been stressed in both the 1924 Declaration of the Rights of the Child and the 1959 UN Declaration of the Rights of the Child, was therefore a logical complement to the duty to ensure to the maximum extent possible their survival. While a precise definition of the notion of development is elusive, in its General Comment No. 5 on the implementation of the CRC the Committee on the Rights of the Child declared that it expected States Parties to interpret the notion in Article 6 'in its broadest sense as a holistic concept, embracing the child's physical, mental, spiritual, moral, psychological and social development'.[36]

22.13 Taken together, the obligations in Article 6(2), which are now of a customary nature, impose a broad set of duties on the State. These include the duty to take measures to reduce infant mortality, including through action to ensure adequate nutrition and to tackle disease and cure illness, as well as to minimise the incidence of infanticide and other acts of violence

---

[31] Art. 6(2), CRC.

[32] During the drafting of the Convention, however, Venezuela feared that the inclusion of paragraph 2 in Article 6 would diminish the scope of the right to life protected in other instruments. 'Report of the working group on a draft convention on the rights of the child', UN doc. E/CN.4/1988/28, 6 April 1988, para. 24.

[33] Report of the working group on a draft convention on the rights of the child, 6 April 1988, para. 19; see N. Peleg and J. Tobin, Commentary on Article 6, in J. Tobin (ed.), *The UN Convention on the Rights of the Child: A Commentary*, Oxford Commentaries on International Law, Oxford University Press, Oxford, 2019, pp. 196–7.

[34] P. Alston, 'The Unborn Child and Abortion Under the Draft Convention on the Rights of the Child', *Human Rights Quarterly*, vol. 12 (1990), pp. 156–78, at 159.

[35] See, e.g., 'Report of the working group on a draft convention on the rights of the child', UN doc. E/CN.4/1988/28, 6 April 1988, para. 17.

[36] Committee on the Rights of the Child, 'General measures of implementation of the Convention on the Rights of the Child', General Comment No. 5, UN doc. CRC/GC/2003/5, 27 November 2003, para. 12 (hereinafter, Committee on the Rights of the Child, General Comment 5).

against children. Requisite action to promote the good health of children involves among many other actions, limiting access to narcotics and controlling pollution. Each of these threats to life is particularly grave in the case of a child.[37] Implementation measures with respect to development, in the view of the Committee on the Rights of the Child, 'should be aimed at achieving the optimal development for all children'.[38] The duty to ensure to the maximum extent possible every child's survival and development imposes a stricter duty than the standard of due diligence that exists under the ICCPR with respect to the protection of every person's right to life.[39] In addition, as discussed in more detail later in this chapter,[40] the imposition of the death penalty on anyone convicted of committing any crime when under eighteen years of age is unlawful, as a matter of customary law.[41]

22.14 There is no provision for derogation from any of the rights set out in the CRC, but equally there is no specific consideration as to whether the right to life may be subject to limitations by reservation, as long as any reservation did not extend beyond the dictates of the customary law of treaties.[42] None of the 196 States Parties to the CRC,[43] however, has made any reservation purporting to restrict the overall scope of the right to life of children. That said, a small number of States made formal declarations concerning Article 6 when adhering to the Convention, particularly with respect to aspects of family planning, reproductive health, and the voluntary termination of pregnancies.

22.15 China, the world's most populous State, with more than 270 million children, declared upon adherence to the CRC in 1992[44] that it would implement Article 6 of the Convention only to the extent that it accords with the provisions of Article 25 of the Chinese Constitution concerning family planning[45] and in conformity with the provisions of Article 2 of the Law on Minor Children.[46] The Committee on the Rights of the Child

---

[37] Thus the 1990 World Declaration on the Survival, Protection and Development of Children identified a number of elements that are hazardous to a child's physical survival, including malnutrition, disease, lack of clean water, inadequate sanitation, and the effects of the drug problem. *World Declaration on the Survival, Protection and Development of Children*, adopted at the World Summit for Children, New York, 30 September 1990, para. 6.

[38] Committee on the Rights of the Child, General Comment No. 5, para. 12.

[39] According to the Human Rights Committee, States Parties to the ICCPR are 'under a due diligence obligation to undertake reasonable positive measures, which do not impose on them disproportionate burdens, ... in response to reasonably foreseeable threats to life originating from private persons and entities, whose conduct is not attributable to the State'. Human Rights Committee, General Comment 36 on the right to life, para. 21.

[40] See, *infra*, Paragraphs 25.44–25.46.

[41] See Art. 37(a), CRC. Article 6(5) of the ICCPR had already specified that the death penalty 'shall not be imposed for crimes committed by persons below eighteen years of age'.

[42] According to the 1969 Vienna Convention on the Law of Treaties, a state may, when signing or adhering to a treaty, formulate a reservation unless 'the reservation is incompatible with the object and purpose of the treaty'. Art. 19(c), Vienna Convention on the Law of Treaties; adopted at Vienna 23 May 1969; entered into force 27 January 1980. This provision reflects customary international law.

[43] Only the United States, a signatory, is a State not party to the Convention.

[44] Declaration of China with respect to Article 6 of the CRC, available at http://bit.ly/2Q3VBw7.

[45] Article 25 stipulates that 'the state promotes family planning so that population growth may fit the plan for economic and social development'.

[46] Under the Law, as revised in 2006, Article 2 stipulates simply that a child attains the age of majority at eighteen years of age.

has called on China on several occasions to 'immediately withdraw its reservation to article 6 of the Convention in order to promote and safeguard the inherent right to life of every child'.[47] France confirmed upon its ratification of the Convention that Article 6 'cannot be interpreted as constituting any obstacle to the implementation of the provisions of French legislation relating to the voluntary interruption of pregnancy'.[48] Luxembourg declared that Article 6 'presents no obstacle to implementation of the provisions of Luxembourg legislation concerning sex information, the prevention of back-street abortion and the regulation of pregnancy termination'.[49] Similarly, Tunisia declared that Article 6 'shall not be interpreted in such a way as to impede the application of Tunisian legislation concerning voluntary termination of pregnancy'.[50]

22.16 In its 2018 General Comment on the right to life under the ICCPR, the Human Rights Committee stated: 'Although States parties may adopt measures designed to regulate voluntary terminations of pregnancy, such measures must not result in violation of the right to life of a pregnant woman or girl, or her other rights under the Covenant.'[51]

The Right to a Life with Dignity

22.17 As is the case under other global and regional human rights treaties,[52] the right to life of a child as protected by the CRC is to be interpreted broadly. This incorporates the notion of a life with dignity,[53] which encompasses, at its core, the protection of physical and psychological integrity. In its General Comment No. 21 on children living in the streets, the Committee on the Rights of the Child stated that the need to protect the most vulnerable 'definitely requires an interpretation of the right to life that encompasses the minimum conditions for a life with dignity'.[54]

22.18 In its interpretation of Article 19 of the CRC, which concerns the protection of children from violence, abuse, or neglect, the Committee on the Rights of the Child has stated that it is a 'fundamental' assumption that the concept of dignity 'requires that every child is recognized, respected and protected as a rights holder and as a unique and valuable human being with an individual personality, distinct needs, interests and

---

[47] Committee on the Rights of the Child, Concluding Observations on the combined third and fourth periodic reports of China, UN doc. CRC/C/CHN/CO/3–4, 29 October 2013, para. 7(a).
[48] Declaration of France with respect to Article 6 of the CRC, available at http://bit.ly/2Q3VBw7.
[49] Declaration of Luxembourg with respect to Article 6 of the CRC, available at http://bit.ly/2Q3VBw7.
[50] Declaration of Tunisia with respect to Article 6 of the CRC, available at http://bit.ly/2Q3VBw7.
[51] Human Rights Committee, General Comment 36 on the right to life, para. 8.
[52] In its 2018 General Comment on the right to life under the ICCPR, the Human Rights Committee stated that 'the right to life is a right which should not be interpreted narrowly. It concerns the entitlement of individuals ... to enjoy a life with dignity'. Human Rights Committee, General Comment 36 on the right to life, para. 3.
[53] The Preamble to the CRC opens with the 'recognition of the inherent dignity and of the equal and inalienable rights of all members of the human family' as the 'foundation of freedom, justice and peace in the world'. CRC, First preambular para.
[54] Committee on the Rights of the Child, General Comment No. 21 on Children in Street Situations, UN doc. CRC/C/GC/21, 21 June 2017, para. 29 (hereinafter, Committee on the Rights of the Child, General Comment 21 on children living in the streets).

privacy'.[55] The 'absolute' right to dignity precludes the practice of torture, as well as corporal punishment and other forms of cruel or degrading punishment,[56] and discriminatory treatment on grounds of, inter alia, race, colour, sex, religion, or birth.[57]

22.19 The notion of dignity is comprised within, but is not synonymous with, the concept of a child's development. Infringing on a child's dignity may impede its ability to develop to the fullest extent, but, under international law, the scope of a child's right to development is broader. This right has been described by one authority as 'a composite right that aims to ensure the child's abilities to fulfil her or his human potential to the maximum during childhood and adulthood alike'.[58] In recent years, there has been increasing emphasis on the importance of 'nurturing care' to a child's development. In 2018, the WHO published a major report with the involvement of UNICEF, the World Bank, and other agencies, in which it affirmed: 'Nurturing care is not only important for promoting young children's development. It also protects them from the worst effects of adversity by lowering their stress levels and encouraging emotional and cognitive coping mechanisms. Nurturing care is especially important for children with development difficulties and disabilities, as well as for preventing the maltreatment of children.'[59] A number of academics suggested in 2020 that this new framework, with its focus on 'thriving' as well as surviving, calls for changes to UNICEF's approach to early child development:

> In addition to requiring support for child health and nutrition, thriving also includes the ability of children to form relationships, learn, take on responsibilities, and ultimately to establish a family, provide economic stability, and contribute to society. To build the broader skills of thriving, children require opportunities for responsive relationships and opportunities to explore and learn, within a secure and safe context.[60]

22.20 In his discussion (and attempted abnegation) of a human right to dignity, Conor O'Mahony explicitly rejected the notion of dignity as engaging a sense of autonomy.[61] He cites the 1991 case of 'X', a fourteen-year-old girl in Ireland who was raped and became pregnant. Evidence indicated clearly that she would commit suicide if she were not

---

[55] Committee on the Rights of the Child, 'General Comment No. 13: The right of the child to freedom from all forms of violence', UN doc. CRC/C/GC/13, 18 April 2011, para. 3(c) (hereinafter, Committee on the Rights of the Child, General Comment 13 on freedom from violence).

[56] Ibid., paras. 17 and 61. See also, e.g., M. D. A. Freeman, 'Upholding the Dignity and Best Interests of Children: International Law and the Corporeal Punishment of Children', *Law and Contemporary Problems*, vol. 73 (Spring 2010), pp. 211–51, at http://bit.ly/2Zxghkz.

[57] See Art. 2(1), CRC; Art. 2(1), ICCPR.

[58] N. Peleg, *The Child's Right to Development*, thesis submitted to University College London for the degree of Doctor of Philosophy, London, November 2012, at http://bit.ly/357S5Gh; and N. Peleg, *The Child's Right to Development*, Cambridge University Press, Cambridge, July 2019.

[59] World Health Organization, UNICEF, and World Bank Group, *Nurturing Care for Early Childhood Development: A Framework for Helping Children Survive and Thrive to Transform Health and Human Potential*, WHO, Geneva, 2018, p. 11.

[60] M. M. Black, C. K. Lutter, and A. C. B. Trude, 'All Children Surviving and Thriving: Re-envisioning UNICEF's Conceptual Framework of Malnutrition', Comment, *Lancet Global Health*, vol. 8 (June 2020), at http://bit.ly/2XqMtFs.

[61] C. O'Mahony, 'There Is No Such Thing as a Right to Dignity', *International Journal of Constitutional Law*, vol. 10, no.2 (30 March 2012), pp. 551–74, at esp. 568–69.

allowed to travel to the United Kingdom for an abortion. In a landmark judgment in 1992, the Irish Supreme Court established the right of Irish women to an abortion if a pregnant woman's life was at risk because of pregnancy, including where that risk of death emanated from a likely suicide.[62] But, O'Mahony affirmed, to allow the abortion constitutes 'an attack on the dignity of the unborn child (as expressly protected by the Irish Constitution) as the child is clearly not receiving equal treatment and respect'. In his view, 'it is entirely irrelevant that the child was begotten by rape' since there is 'an irreconcilable conflict between the dignity of the unborn child and the autonomy-as-dignity of the mother'.[63]

22.21 O'Mahony argued that the 'only logically satisfactory way' to resolve the case would be 'either to decide that the unborn does not have an inherent human dignity' or 'to cease classifying autonomy as an aspect of human dignity itself, and to view it instead as a right which flows from human dignity but which may not be exercised in a manner which infringes on the dignity of another'.[64] In the instant case, however, that stance confused conflicts within a domestic regime with the interpretation and application of international law. Consonant with the definition of a child in the global human rights treaties, the Human Rights Committee has made it clear that it prioritises the protection of a future mother over an unborn child (as indeed did the Irish Supreme Court in its 1992 judgment in the 'X' case). In its General Comment 36 on the right to life, the Committee stated that the right to life under the ICCPR impels States Parties to provide 'safe, legal and effective access to abortion where the life and health of the pregnant woman or girl is at risk, and where carrying a pregnancy to term would cause the pregnant woman or girl substantial pain or suffering, most notably where the pregnancy is the result of rape or incest or is not viable'.[65] Following a national referendum, the possibility of lawful abortion in Ireland was regulated (and broadened) under the Health (Regulation of Termination of Pregnancy) Act 2018.[66]

THE RIGHT TO LIFE OF CHILDREN UNDER REGIONAL STANDARDS

22.22 While all the main regional human rights treaties offer protection to children, including for their right to life, they do not, for the most part, specifically protect the

---

[62] *Attorney General v. X* [1992] 1 IR 1. Chief Justice Finlay stated as follows: 'I am satisfied that the test proposed on behalf of the Attorney General that the life of the unborn could only be terminated if it were established that an inevitable or immediate risk to the life of the mother existed, for the avoidance of which a termination of the pregnancy was necessary, insufficiently vindicates the mother's right to life.'

[63] Ibid., p. 569.

[64] Ibid.

[65] Human Rights Committee, General Comment 36 on the right to life, para. 8, citing its views in *Mellet v. Ireland* (Comm. No. 2324/2013, 31 March 2016), paras. 7.4–7.8; and Concluding Observations on Ireland (2014), para. 9.

[66] The Act, which entered into force on 1 January 2019, allows for a termination in the following circumstances: where there is a serious to the life or of serious harm to the health of a pregnant woman (adjudged through examination by two medical practitioners); where there is an immediate serious risk to life or of serious harm to the health of a pregnant woman (based on an examination by one medical practitioner); where two medical practitioners agree in good faith that a condition affecting the foetus is likely to lead to the death of the foetus either before, or within 28 days of birth; or where it has been duly certified that the term of the pregnancy has not exceeded 12 weeks. Ss. 9–12, Health (Regulation of Termination of Pregnancy) Act 2018.

right of life of children. The primary exception is the African Charter on the Rights and Welfare of the Child, adopted in 1990 by the erstwhile Organization of African Unity,[67] a regional institution replaced in 2002 by the African Union. Article V(1) of the Charter, which has been very widely ratified by the African States,[68] explicitly protects the 'inherent' right to life of every child, defined therein as any human being, without exception, under the age of eighteen.[69]

The Right to Life of Children under the European Convention on Human Rights

The Special Protection of Children

22.23 Article 2(1) of the 1950 European Convention on Human Rights[70] stipulates simply: 'Everyone's right to life shall be protected by law.' No specific provision safeguards the life or physical integrity of children. That said, the European Court of Human Rights has found that the prohibition on ill treatment under Article 3 of the Convention imposes on the State the 'inherent' duty to adopt special measures to safeguard children.[71] Given that this duty results, in part, from the 'particularly vulnerable nature of children',[72] *a fortiori* it should apply also to the protection of the right to life by States Parties to the European Convention, including against the acts of private individuals.

22.24 In fact, as of writing, jurisprudence on this issue within the European Court of Human Rights was mixed, in particular in the context of domestic violence. The 2019 chamber judgment in the *Kurt* case[73] concerned an allegation by the applicant that the Austrian authorities had failed to protect her and her children from her violent husband (referred to in the proceedings as 'E'). The particular failure to protect her son's physical integrity against E, she argued, resulted in her husband murdering their son, specifically on the basis they had not taken E into pre-trial detention after he had allegedly attacked and raped her and beaten the children.[74] In its judgment rejecting the applicant's claim, the Court reiterated: 'Children and other vulnerable individuals in particular are entitled to State protection.'[75] But the Court also confirmed its earlier holdings that 'the scope of

---

[67] African Charter on the Rights and Welfare of the Child; adopted at Addis Ababa 1 July 1990; entered into force 29 November 1999.
[68] Of the 55 member States of the African Union, 49 were party to the Charter on the Rights and Welfare of the Child as of 1 December 2020. Only the Democratic Republic of Congo, Morocco, the Sahrawi Arab Democratic Republic, Somalia, South Sudan, and Tunisia were not parties to the Charter at that date (all but Morocco were signatory States).
[69] Botswana has formally declared that it does not consider itself bound by the definition of a child under Article II of the 1990 Charter.
[70] Convention for the Protection of Human Rights and Fundamental Freedoms; adopted at Rome by the Council of Europe 4 November 1950; entered into force 3 September 1953.
[71] European Court of Human Rights, *O'Keeffe v. Ireland*, Judgment (Grand Chamber), 28 January 2014, para. 146.
[72] Ibid.
[73] European Court of Human Rights, *Kurt v. Austria*, Judgment (Fifth Section), 4 July 2019.
[74] Ibid., paras. 12–22 and 48.
[75] Ibid., para. 63.

the positive obligation must be interpreted in a way which does not impose an impossible or disproportionate burden on the authorities'.[76]

22.25 The so-called *Osman* test within the European Court of Human Rights holds that the right to life is violated if the authorities 'knew or ought to have known' at the relevant time of 'a real and immediate risk' to a specific individual from the criminal acts of a third party, and they failed to take 'reasonable measures' to avoid or minimise that risk.[77] This applies to all persons, whether child or adult. In his Separate Opinion to the Court's judgment in *Kurt*, however, Judge Hüseynov stated that situations of domestic violence should be considered differently from the norm because they often constitute 'not just an isolated incident, but rather a continuous practice of intimidation and abuse'. Therefore, he asserted, State authorities

> should react, with due diligence, to each and every act of domestic violence and take all necessary measures to make sure that such acts do not lead to more serious consequences. It follows that the duty to prevent and protect comes into play when the risk to life is present, even if it is not imminent. In other words, in a domestic violence case, the positive obligation to protect life can be violated even where the risk to life is not immediate.[78]

22.26 Judge Hüseynov affirmed that the 2017 judgment by the Court's First Section in the *Talpis* case[79] had given 'hope that the Court was ready to deviate from an incident-based understanding of domestic violence and reconsider the application of the Osman test to the particular situation of domestic violence, or at least to interpret the concept of immediate risk flexibly'.[80] The test laid down in *Talpis* comprised an obligation on the authorities to 'take account of the recurrence of successive episodes of violence within the family unit'.[81] This approach was explicitly followed by the Court in *Volodina v. Russia*, the judgment of which was issued by another chamber five days after the Fifth Section's judgment in *Kurt*.[82] On 4 November 2019, the judgment in the *Kurt* case was referred to the Grand Chamber of the European Court for its consideration.

The Right to Life of Children under the American Convention on Human Rights

The Definition of a Child

22.27 As noted above,[83] Article 4(1) of the American Convention on Human Rights protects the right to life 'in general' from 'the moment of conception'. The phrase 'in general' was incorporated in the treaty text 'with the specific purpose of reconciling the

---

[76] Ibid., para. 69.
[77] As developed by the Court in *Osman v. United Kingdom*, Judgment, 28 October 1998, para. 116; see *Kurt v. Austria*, Judgment (Fifth Section), Separate Opinion of Judge Hüseynov, para. 2.
[78] *Kurt v. Austria*, Judgment (Fifth Section), Separate Opinion of Judge Hüseynov, para. 4.
[79] European Court of Human Rights, *Talpis v. Italy*, Judgment (First Section), 2 March 2017.
[80] *Kurt v. Austria*, Judgment (Fifth Section), Separate Opinion of Judge Hüseynov, para. 5.
[81] *Talpis v. Italy*, Judgment (First Section), para. 122.
[82] European Court of Human Rights, *Volodina v. Russia*, Judgment, 9 July 2019, para. 86.
[83] See, supra, Paragraph 25.07 and note 23.

possibility that domestic law would allow abortion and that the proposal to eliminate it would not be accepted'.[84] In its judgment in *Artavia Murillo and others ('In Vitro Fertilization') v. Costa Rica*, the Inter-American Court of Human Rights considered under which circumstances an embryo could be considered a person for the purposes of Article 4(1). The Court concluded that 'conception' occurred legally at the moment when the embryo becomes implanted in the uterus and not before.[85] It further held that the words 'in general' in paragraph 1 of the article entailed 'that the protection of the right to life under this provision is not absolute, but rather gradual and incremental according to its development'.[86]

22.28 But Cecilia Medina, a former judge at the Inter-American Court of Human Rights, believes that the ambit of the provision is even further restricted, arguing that a foetus which 'has not been removed from the mother's womb is dependent on her, is not a person, and therefore cannot have its own rights, but rather has rights through the mother'.[87] She affirms that the foetus is not imbued with Conventional rights; rather, Article 4(1) imposes upon the State an obligation to protect. According to this understanding, the protection of the foetus occurs 'indirectly through the protection of the mother'.[88] Medina concludes that 'with the purpose of protecting the mother, and taking into consideration that the circumstances in which a pregnancy is terminated can present a high degree of risk to the life of the mother, the State must regulate those circumstances in order to protect her health'.[89]

22.29 The situation is different when the foetus is no longer dependent on the mother 'and one could assume with a degree of certainty that it would survive upon being removed from the mother's womb'.[90] In such a case, although still a foetus, under the Inter-American Convention on Human Rights it has become 'legally a human being to whom the right of life established in Article 4(1) … applies'.[91] But the argument that the Inter-American Convention 'requires the State to criminalize abortion altogether' is 'profoundly erroneous'.[92]

22.30 With respect to the age of majority, the Inter-American Court has considered that, in general, by 'child' is understood 'any individual who has not attained 18 years of age'.[93] The

---

[84] C. Medina, *The American Convention on Human Rights. Crucial Rights and Their Theory and Practice*, Intersentia, Cambridge, 2014, p. 46, para. 8.
[85] Inter-American Court of Human Rights, *Artavia Murillo and others ('In Vitro Fertilization') v. Costa Rica*, Judgment (Preliminary objections, merits, reparations and costs), 28 November 2012, para. 264.
[86] Ibid.
[87] Medina, *The American Convention on Human Rights. Crucial Rights and Their Theory and Practice*, p. 48, para. 10.
[88] Ibid., pp. 48–9, para. 11.
[89] Ibid., p. 49, para. 11.
[90] Ibid., p. 49, para. 12.
[91] Ibid.
[92] Ibid., p. 50, para. 13.
[93] Inter-American Court of Human Rights, *Case of the Massacres of El Mozote and Nearby Places v. El Salvador*, Judgment (Merits, reparations and costs), 25 October 2012, para. 150 note 183, citing its Advisory Opinion OC-17/02 of 28 August 2002 (Juridical Status and Human Rights of the Child), para. 42; and *Case of Furlan and Family v. Argentina*, Judgment (Preliminary objections, merits, reparations and costs), 31 August 2012, para. 123.

duty to protect under Article 19 of the Inter-American Convention applies only to 'minor' children, which may be taken to defer to the age of majority under domestic law where that occurs before eighteen years.[94]

The Right of the Child to Special Protection

22.31 The 1969 American Convention on Human Rights stipulates: 'Every minor child has the right to the measure of protection required by his condition as a minor on the part of his family, society, and the state.'[95] In a 2002 Advisory Opinion on the Juridical Condition and Human Rights of the Child, requested by the Inter-American Commission, the Inter-American Court held that States Parties have the duty to adopt 'all positive measures required to ensure protection of children against mistreatment, whether in their relations with public authorities, or in relationships among individuals or with non-governmental entities'.[96] The Court adduced as evidence provisions from the CRC, determinations by the Committee on the Rights of the Child, and judgments of the European Court of Human Rights regarding the obligations of States to protect children against violence, including in the family.[97]

22.32 In its 1999 judgment in the *Case of the 'Street Children' (Villagrán Morales and others) v. Guatemala*,[98] the Inter-American Court of Human Rights had determined that the specific protection obligations in the Convention 'imply the existence of an additional, complementary right of children, supported by the specificity of these obligations. Thus, the protective measures referred to in Article 19 of the Convention should include ... the guarantee of the child's survival and development.'[99] The Court further stated that when States violate the rights of at-risk children, such as 'street children', it renders them victims 'of a double aggression':

> First, such States do not prevent them from living in misery, thus depriving them of the minimum conditions for a dignified life and preventing them from the 'full and harmonious development of their personality', even though every child has the right to harbor a project of life that should be tended and encouraged by the public authorities so that it may develop this project for its personal benefit and that of the society to which it belongs. Second, they violate their physical, mental and moral integrity and even their lives.[100]

---

[94] The term used in Article 19 of the Spanish authentic version of the American Convention is simply 'niño'.
[95] Art. 19, Inter-American Convention on Human Rights.
[96] Inter-American Court of Human Rights, *Juridical Condition and Human Rights of the Child*, Advisory Opinion OC-17/2002, 28 August 2002, para. 87.
[97] Inter-American Commission on Human Rights, *The Rights of the Child in the Inter-American Human Rights System*, 2nd ed., Organization of American States (OAS) doc. OEA/Ser.L/V/II.133 Doc. 34, 29 October 2008, para. 24, at http://bit.ly/35a9dLW.
[98] Inter-American Court of Human Rights, *Case of the 'Street Children' (Villagrán Morales and others) v. Guatemala*, Judgment (Merits), 19 November 1999.
[99] Ibid., para. 196; see also Inter-American Commission on Human Rights, *The Rights of the Child in the Inter-American Human Rights System*, 2nd ed., 2008, para. 129.
[100] Inter-American Court of Human Rights, *Case of the 'Street Children' (Villagrán Morales and others) v. Guatemala*, Judgment (Merits), para. 191.

22.33 In its 2012 judgment in the *El Mozote Massacres* case, the Inter-American Court reiterated that 'cases in which children are victims of human rights violations are especially serious'. This is because children 'are holders of the rights established in the American Convention, and also possess the special measures of protection established in its Article 19, which must be defined according to the particular circumstances of each specific case'.[101] The adoption of special measures for the protection of children includes 'measures relating to non-discrimination, the prohibition of torture, and the conditions that must be observed in cases in which children are deprived of liberty'.[102] The Court found El Salvador responsible for executions perpetrated by the Salvadoran Armed Forces in massacres committed over a period of three days in December 1981, in violation of Article 4 of the American Convention. In addition, the Court stated,

> it has been proved that there were a considerable number of children among the executed victims, so that, in their regard, the violations of the right to life also occurred in relation to Article 19 of the Convention. This violation was aggravated with regard to the children, and also to the women who were pregnant.[103]

The Prohibition on Imposing the Death Penalty on Children

22.34 Under Article 4(5) of the Inter-American Convention, capital punishment 'shall not be imposed upon persons who, at the time the crime was committed, were under 18 years of age'. The United States is a signatory but not a State Party to the Convention. On 19 February 2002, the Inter-American Commission on Human Rights received a petition on behalf of Napoleon Beazley, an African American youth on death row in Texas. Mr Beazley was seventeen years of age at the time of the offence (murder) for which he had been sentenced to death. Despite precautionary measures adopted by the Inter-American Commission on 27 February 2002 requesting a stay of execution pending the outcome of the proceedings before it, Mr Beazley was executed on 28 May 2002.[104]

22.35 In its submission to the Commission, the United States observed that it had entered a reservation to the corresponding provision under Article 6(5) of the ICCPR whereby it 'reserves the right, subject to its Constitutional constraints, to impose capital punishment on any person (other than a pregnant woman) duly convicted under existing or future laws permitting the imposition of capital punishment, including such punishment for crimes committed by persons below eighteen years of age'.[105] The Inter-American Commission, however, approved its earlier holding that not only was the prohibition codified in Article 4(5) of the Inter-American Convention reflected in customary international law; it was also

---

[101] Inter-American Court of Human Rights, *Case of the Massacres of El Mozote and Nearby Places v. El Salvador*, Judgment, para. 150.
[102] Ibid.
[103] Ibid., para. 156.
[104] Inter-American Commission on Human Rights, *Napoleon Beazley v. United States*, Decision (Case 12.412), Report No. 101/03, 29 December 2003, paras. 1, 12.
[105] Reservation available on the UN Treaty Section website at http://bit.ly/37osGKf.

a peremptory norm of international law (jus cogens).[106] While, as discussed later,[107] the affirmation at the time that the prohibition was a norm of jus cogens was not established, the claim made for its customary nature is well-founded. In such a case, however, the United States was, at the period in question, in a strong position to claim persistent objector status to that customary norm.[108]

The Right to Life of Children under African Human Rights Standards

General Protection of the Child's Right to Life

22.36 The African Charter on Human and Peoples' Rights (the 'Banjul Charter') enshrines the right to life for 'every human being' as follows: 'Human beings are inviolable. Every human being shall be entitled to respect for his life and the integrity of his person. No one may be arbitrarily deprived of this right.'[109] Article 18(3) of the Banjul Charter imposes an obligation upon States Parties to 'ensure the protection of the rights of the woman and the child as stipulated in international declarations and conventions'. In other respects, however, the Charter does not specifically address the rights of children.

Specific Protection of the Child's Right to Life

22.37 But as noted previously, Article V of the 1990 African Charter on the Rights and Welfare of the Child (entitled 'Survival and Development') explicitly protects the 'inherent' right to life of every child. It does so in the following manner:

1. Every child has an inherent right to life. This right shall be protected by law.
2. State Parties to the present Charter shall ensure, to the maximum extent possible, the survival, protection and development of the child.
3. Death sentence shall not be pronounced for crimes committed by children. Recalling the provisions of Article 6(2) of the CRC, but making explicit the duty to protect the child as well as to ensure his or her survival and development, the 1990 African Charter does not create 'new' rights for children but rather emphasises 'the holistic approach that must be followed in the promotion and protection of the rights and welfare of the child'.[110]

---

[106] Inter-American Commission on Human Rights, *Napoleon Beazley v. United States*, Decision, citing with approval its earlier views in *Michael Domingues v. United States*, Decision (Case 12.285), Report 62/02, paras. 84, 85.

[107] See, *infra*, paras. 25.44–25.45.

[108] See Inter-American Commission on Human Rights, *Napoleon Beazley v. United States*, Decision, para. 30. See also J. A. Green, *The Persistent Objector Rule in International Law*, Oxford University Press, Oxford, 2018, pp. 82–3, 110–11, 199–201. Persistent objection does not exist with respect to a jus cogens norm. 'Fourth report on peremptory norms of general international law (*jus cogens*) by Dire Tladi, Special Rapporteur', International Law Commission, UN doc. A/CN.4/727, 31 January 2019, para. 28.

[109] Art. 4(1), African Charter on Human and Peoples' Rights; adopted at Nairobi 27 June 1981; entered into force 21 October 1986.

[110] T. Kaime, 'The Struggle For Context in the Protection of Children's Rights: Understanding the Core Concepts of the African Children's Charter', *Journal of Legal Pluralism*, no. 58 (2008), pp. 33–68, at 53, at http://bit.ly/366VhUf.

Special Protection of Children

22.38 Article 21 of 1990 African Charter on the Rights and Welfare of the Child further requires States Parties to take

> all appropriate measures to eliminate harmful social and cultural practices affecting the welfare, dignity, normal growth and development of the child and in particular:
>
> (a) those customs and practices prejudicial to the health or life of the child; and
> (b) those customs and practices discriminatory to the child on the grounds of sex or other status.

The African Committee of Experts on the Rights and Welfare of the Child, established in 2001,[111] has defined as 'harmful' all practices that imperil the life of children; undermine their dignity; or are prejudicial to their health, to their mental or physical integrity, or to their growth and development, 'regardless of their being condoned by a society, culture, religion, or tradition'.[112] The Committee cites as examples of common harmful practices in Africa child trafficking, sexual exploitation, early marriage, illicit adoption, exploitative child labour, and child enrolment in armed forces.[113]

22.39 The case of *Michelo Hunsungule* v. *Uganda*[114] before the African Committee on the Rights and Welfare of the Child concerned events between 2001 and 2005 in northern Uganda, in particular relating to a non-international armed conflict between Uganda and the Lord's Resistance Army (LRA). Article XXII of the 1990 African Charter obligates States Parties to 'take all necessary measures to ensure that no child shall take a direct part in hostilities' and further, in accordance with their obligations under international humanitarian law, to 'protect the civilian population in armed conflicts' and to take 'all feasible measures to ensure the protection and care of children who are affected by armed conflicts'.[115] In its decision on the Communication, the African Committee held that Article XXII had been violated as a result of acts or omissions on the part of Uganda, including voluntary enlistment of children into the Ugandan People's Defence Force (UPDF).[116] For although the 'general response' of the UPDF to the abduction of children and their recruitment into the LRA was to rescue them from captivity and promote their rehabilitation and reintegration, there were also said to be instances where children were recruited into the UPDF.[117] It was asserted that 'in some instances rescued children were

---

[111] The existence and mandate of the African Committee of Experts on the Rights and Welfare of the Child is set out in Articles 32–46 of the African Charter on the Rights and Welfare of the Child.

[112] African Committee of Experts on the Rights and Welfare of the Child, 'General Comment No. 2 on Article 6 of the African Charter on the Rights and Welfare of the Child', Doc. ACERWC/GC/02, adopted by the Committee at its 23rd Ordinary Session, 7–16 April 2014, para. 30.

[113] Ibid.

[114] African Committee of Experts on the Rights and Welfare of the Child, *Michelo Hunsungule and others (on Behalf of Children in Northern Uganda)* v. *The Government of Uganda*, Decision (Comm. 1/2005), 15–19 April 2013, available at http://bit.ly/37lRqCC.

[115] Arts. 22(2) and (3), African Charter on the Rights and Welfare of the Child.

[116] African Committee of Experts on the Rights and Welfare of the Child, *Michelo Hunsungule and others (on Behalf of Children in Northern Uganda)* v. *The Government of Uganda*, Decision, para. 60.

[117] Ibid., para. 6.

taken to the frontline in order to support intelligence gathering against the LRA', which 'exposed the children to danger and a violation of their rights'.[118]

22.40 Also relevant to the protection of the right to life of children in Africa is the African Union's 2003 Protocol to the African Charter on Human and People's Rights on the Rights of Women in Africa[119] (the 'Maputo Protocol'). The Maputo Protocol explicitly applies to girls as well as to adult women.[120] According to its Article 4(1), 'every woman shall be entitled to respect for her life and the integrity and security of her person'. As discussed in Chapter 11, the case of *Igohozo* v. *Prosecution*[121] before the High Court of Rwanda concerned the alleged drugging and rape of a thirteen-year-old girl, who then became pregnant. This led to depression, stigma, and shame, with the girl unable to continue with her education. She desired to terminate her pregnancy at all costs, even at the risk of losing her life.

22.41 The High Court granted her the right to an abortion, reversing the decision by a court of first instance, holding that her age meant that she could not have lawfully consented to intercourse. In its judgment, the Court cited Article 14(2)(c) of the Maputo Protocol, which requires States Parties to take 'all appropriate measures to protect the reproductive rights of women', specifically by 'authorising medical abortion in cases of sexual assault, rape, incest, and where the continued pregnancy endangers the mental and physical health of the mother or the life of the mother or the foetus'. Although not referred to in the judgment, the case also concerned the protection of life and integrity of person, as protected by Article 4 of the Maputo Protocol.[122]

The Right to Life of Children under the Arab Charter on Human Rights

General Protection of the Child's Right to Life

22.42 The 2004 Arab Charter on Human Rights[123] has a general provision enshrining the protection of the right to life, including for children, but also provides specifically for the right of children to special protection. Under Article 5(1), 'every human being has an inherent right to life'. Paragraph 2 stipulates further that 'this right shall be protected by law. No one shall be arbitrarily deprived of his life.' No derogation from Article 5 may be made.[124]

Special Protection of Children

22.43 Article 33 recognises the right of the child to 'special protection', with paragraph 3 of the provision obligating States Parties to 'take all appropriate legislative, administrative

---

[118] Ibid.
[119] Protocol to the African Charter on Human and Peoples' Rights on the Rights of Women in Africa; adopted at Maputo 11 July 2003; entered into force 25 November 2005. As of 1 May 2021, 42 States were party to the Protocol and another ten were signatories.
[120] Art. 1(k), Maputo Protocol.
[121] High Court of Rwanda, *Igohozo* v. *Prosecution* [2016] 3 RLR.
[122] S. Omondi, E. Waweru, and D. Srinivasan, 'Breathing Life into the Maputo Protocol: Jurisprudence on the Rights of Women and Girls in Africa', *Equality Now*, Nairobi, 2018, p. 82, available at http://bit.ly/2Qvoosc.
[123] Arab Charter on Human Rights; adopted at Tunis 22 May 2004; entered into force 15 March 2008.
[124] Art. 4(2), 2004 Arab Charter on Human Rights.

and judicial provisions to ensure the protection, survival and well-being of children in an atmosphere of freedom and dignity'. A child is not defined under the Arab Charter, but is probably best understood in the same terms as the CRC. As noted previously,[125] a number of Arab States set the age of majority at less than eighteen years.

The Prohibition on Imposing the Death Penalty on Children

22.44 Article 7(1) provides that the death penalty 'shall not be inflicted on a person under 18 years of age', but incorporates a significant caveat whereby this prohibition only applies 'unless otherwise provided by the law in force at the time of the commission of the crime'. This caveat is not consistent with States Parties' obligations under the CRC or under general international law. In this regard, Article 43 of the Arab Charter specifies that nothing in the Charter 'shall be interpreted as impairing the rights and freedoms ... set out in international or regional instruments of human rights that the State Parties have signed or ratified, including ... children's rights'.

THE DEATH PENALTY

The Normative Framework

22.45 Indeed, under customary international law it is prohibited merely to impose (and thus *a fortiori* to carry out) the death penalty on any person who was under eighteen years of age at the time a capital offence was committed.[126] For a State to act otherwise would be to violate general international law. The prohibition is codified in both the ICCPR[127] and the CRC.[128] The imposition of the death penalty on those under eighteen years of age is also prohibited by international humanitarian law applicable during armed conflict. The 1949 Geneva Convention IV on the protection of civilians provides that 'the death penalty may not be pronounced against a protected person who was under eighteen years of age at the time of the offence'.[129] The 1977 Additional Protocol I, also applicable to situations of international armed conflict, provides that 'the death penalty for an offence related to the armed conflict shall not be executed on persons who had not attained the age of eighteen years at the time the offence was committed'.[130] In its 1987 commentary on the provision,

---

[125] See, supra, para. 25.03.
[126] Inter-American Commission on Human Rights, *Napoleon Beazley* v. *United States*, Decision, citing with approval its views in *Michael Domingues* v. *United States*, Decision (Case 12.285), Report 62/02 para. 84. See also N. Peterson, 'Life, Right to, International Protection', *Max Planck Encyclopedia of Public International Law*, last updated October 2012, at http://bit.ly/2u2adEK.
[127] Article 6(5) of the ICCPR specifies that the death penalty 'shall not be imposed for crimes committed by persons below eighteen years of age'.
[128] Article 37(a) of the CRC provides that 'neither capital punishment nor life imprisonment without possibility of release shall be imposed for offences committed by persons below eighteen years of age'.
[129] Art. 68(4), Convention (IV) relative to the Protection of Civilian Persons in Time of War; adopted at Geneva 12 August 1949; entered into force 21 October 1950.
[130] Art. 77(5), Protocol Additional to the Geneva Conventions of 12 August 1949, and relating to the Protection of Victims of International Armed Conflicts (Protocol I); adopted at Geneva 8 June 1977; entered into force 7 December 1978.

the International Committee of the Red Cross stated that 'with regard to time of armed conflict and offences related to conflicts, it can be said that the death penalty for persons under eighteen years of age is ruled out completely'.[131] With respect to the non-international armed conflicts within its scope, the 1977 Additional Protocol II similarly prohibits the imposition of the death penalty on anyone under eighteen years of age at the time of the offence.[132]

22.46 In its 2002 decision in *Michael Domingues v. United States*,[133] the Inter-American Commission on Human Rights had held for the first time that the prohibition was not only of a customary nature but that it had become a norm of jus cogens. It reaffirmed this position in the subsequent *Napoleon Beazley* case. This affirmation was not persuasive as a matter of international law.[134] State practice (described as follows) is mixed such that while general practice and *opinio juris* favours the existence of a customary norm, it is not so extensive as to amount to a norm accepted and recognised 'by the international community of States as a whole'.[135] In this regard, the prohibition was not considered as a jus cogens norm by the Special Rapporteur of the International Law Commission (ILC) in his (admittedly non-exhaustive) list of such norms published in early 2019.[136] That said, none of the States that retain the death penalty for those under eighteen years of age at the time of the commission of the offence appears today to be entitled to persistent objector status to the existence of the customary rule. The United States' reservation to Article 6(5) of the ICCPR was explicitly made subject to its domestic Constitutional constraints. In 2005, the US Supreme Court found that the execution of child offenders violated the US Constitution.[137]

22.47 Even among States that prohibit the imposition of the death penalty on those under eighteen years of age, though, there may be challenges in some in the implementation in practice of the rule. In particular, the lack of a comprehensive birth registration system in a number of developing nations means that it may not be possible to determine with certainty the age of a young defendant at his or her trial. Both the Committee on the Rights of the Child and the Human Rights Committee have stated that if there is no reliable and conclusive evidence that the individual was eighteen years of age or more at the time at

---

[131] ICRC commentary on Article 77 of the 1977 Additional Protocol I, 1987, para. 3202, at http://bit.ly/37qwSJq.
[132] Art. 6(4), Protocol Additional to the Geneva Conventions of 12 August 1949, and relating to the Protection of Victims of Non-International Armed Conflicts (Protocol II); adopted at Geneva 8 June 1977; entered into force 7 December 1978.
[133] Case 12.285, Report No. 62/02.
[134] See also on this issue Green, *The Persistent Objector Rule in International Law*, pp. 203, 216.
[135] Art. 53, 1969 Vienna Convention on the Law of Treaties. See also Second report on jus cogens by Dire Tladi, Special Rapporteur, International Law Commission, UN doc. A/CN.4/706, 16 March 2017, para. 74.
[136] Fourth report on peremptory norms of general international law (jus cogens) by Dire Tladi, Special Rapporteur, para. 39.
[137] In 2005, the US Supreme Court ruled by five to four majority that the Eighth and Fourteenth Amendments to the Constitution (prohibiting cruel and unusual punishments, and the denial of life to any person without due process of law, respectively) forbade the imposition of the death penalty on offenders who were under eighteen years of age when they committed a capital crime. US Supreme Court, *Roper v. Simmons*, No. 03-633, 1 March 2005.

Children

which the crime was committed, the benefit of the doubt shall be accorded to the defendant and the death penalty shall not be imposed.[138]

State Practice

22.48 Despite the customary rule, a 2019 report by Amnesty International has recorded numerous instances of the execution of children worldwide between 1990 and April 2019, documenting 145 executions of child offenders in 10 States: China, the Democratic Republic of Congo, Iran, Nigeria, Pakistan, Saudi Arabia, South Sudan, Sudan, the United States, and Yemen.[139] Iran has executed twice as many child offenders as the other nine States combined; at the time of this writing, it had executed ninety-seven children since 1990. Mirroring its age of majority, boys of fifteen lunar years of age and girls of nine lunar years or more may be executed for a range of domestic crimes, including adultery or sodomy.[140] Among those to be put to death in Iran in 2019 was Zeinab Sekaanvand, the fifth child offender to be executed that year. Convicted of murdering her husband at the age of seventeen, her detention and trial were marred by claims she was a victim of domestic violence and that she had been coerced into making a false confession while being denied access to a lawyer. Commenting on the execution of Ms Sekaanvand, Michelle Bachelet, the UN High Commissioner for Human Rights, said: 'The bottom line is that she was a juvenile at the time the offence was committed, and international law clearly prohibits the execution of juvenile offenders.'[141]

22.49 During the last three decades, however, several States have changed their domestic law to exclude the practice of executing children. This includes, along with the United States, the Democratic Republic of Congo, Kuwait, and Sudan.[142] Even in Iran, the rate of execution of child offenders has slowed since 2013, when the law was changed to give

---

[138] Human Rights Committee, General Comment 36 on the right to life, para. 48; Committee on the Rights of the Child, General Comment No. 10 (2007): Children's Rights in Juvenile Justice, UN doc. CRC/C/GC/10, 25 April 2007, paras. 35 and 39.

[139] Amnesty International, 'Executions of Juveniles since 1990 as of April 2019', 2019, at http://bit.ly/2Fcsn9i. According to the UN Secretary-General, as of September 2018 children were also on death row in Bangladesh and the Maldives. 'Question of the death penalty', Report of the UN Secretary-General, UN doc. A/HRC/39/19, 14 September 2018, para. 39, citing reporting by Amnesty International.

[140] 'Situation of human rights in the Islamic Republic of Iran', Report of the UN Secretary-General, UN doc. A/HRC/37/24, September 2019, para. 15.

[141] V. Wood, 'Iran Executed Seven Children Last Year, Says UN as 90 Remain on Death Row', *The Independent*, 24 October 2019, at http://bit.ly/2ueBTXf.

[142] As noted previously, the US Supreme Court held in 2005 that the Constitution forbade the imposition of the death penalty on offenders who were under eighteen years at the time of the commission of the crime. In the Democratic Republic of Congo, Articles 2 and 9 of the 2009 Law on Child Protection (Law No. 09/001 of 10 January 2009) provide that individuals cannot be sentenced to death for crimes committed while under the age of eighteen. In Sudan, the 2010 Child Act prohibited the imposition of a death sentence against an individual under the age of eighteen. See the Death Penalty Worldwide Database maintained by Cornell University, available at http://dpw.law.cornell.edu/search.cfm. In addition, in March 2017, Kuwait formally abolished the death penalty for all offenders under the age of eighteen. 'Question of the death penalty', Report of the UN Secretary-General, UN doc. A/HRC/39/19, 14 September 2018, para. 39.

judges the discretion to exempt children from the death penalty if they did not understand the nature of their actions.[143]

INFANTICIDE

The Normative Framework

22.50 Infanticide is a long-standing practice whereby parents murder unwanted babies and infants.[144] Today, the crime is committed especially against girls or children with disabilities. The failure by State authorities to exercise due diligence to prevent and repress infanticide is a violation of the right to life. Thus, in its General Comment 36 on the right to life under the ICCPR, the Human Rights Committee stated that States Parties to the Covenant 'must enact a protective legal framework which includes effective criminal prohibitions on all manifestations of violence or incitement to violence that are likely to result in a deprivation of life', specifically including infanticide.[145] The extent of the problem is significant in several States. It is claimed, for instance, that in Senegal, where access to birth control is limited and abortion is generally unlawful, almost one in five incarcerated women in 2015 were in prison either awaiting trial or following conviction for infanticide.[146]

State Practice

22.51 The problem of infanticide is particularly prevalent with respect to girls, with killings often being disguised and falsely reported as still births with a view to evading possible prosecution.[147] In 2016, in the report of a first global study on female infanticide, conducted by a Delhi-based non-governmental organisation, the Asian Centre for Human Rights, it was concluded that the preference for sons over daughters in patrilineal societies was a major reason for female infanticide in many countries around the world. The dowry

---

[143] Wood, 'Iran Executed Seven Children Last Year, Says UN as 90 Remain on Death Row'.

[144] An infant is not formally defined in international law but is generally considered to be a child below one year of age. The practice of infanticide has occurred throughout history and is prevalent in other animal species. See, e.g., S. Newman, 'Infanticide', *Aeon*, 27 November 2017, at http://bit.ly/39ByodN. A number of religions condemn the practice. For example, the Prophet Muhammed is credited with stemming the practice of burying girl infants alive in the Middle East, an act of murder which is condemned as such in the Qur'an. See, e.g., A. Giladi, 'Some Observations on Infanticide in Medieval Muslim Society', *International Journal of Middle East Studies*, vol. 22, no. 2 (May 1990), pp. 185–200, at 186. Thus, in the Qur'an, Surah 17 v 31 states: 'You shall not kill your children for fear of want. We will provide for them and for you. To kill them is a grievous sin.' BBC, 'Female Infanticide', Ethics Guide, at http://bbc.in/36hOSWh. See also 'Muhammed: Legacy of a Prophet', PBS News, 2002, at http://to.pbs.org/3foqopK.

[145] Human Rights Committee, General Comment 36 on the right to life, para. 20, citing its Concluding Observations on Madagascar (2007), para. 17.

[146] Newman, 'Infanticide'; A. Gaestel, 'Why Infanticide Is a Problem in Senegal', *NPR*, 3 October 2018, at http://n.pr/2tjdnDZ. See also H. Moseson, R. Ouedraogo, S. Diallo, and A. Sakho, 'Infanticide in Senegal: Results from an Exploratory Mixed-Methods Study', *Sexual and Reproductive Health Matters*, vol. 27, no. 1 (2019), pp. 203–14.

[147] *World Report on Violence against Children*, UN, New York, 2006, chap. 3, p. 52.

system in South Asia, which makes daughters 'an unaffordable economic burden', has also contributed to female infanticide, the report concluded.[148]

22.52 Despite efforts to change the practice, such as through its 'Care for Girls' campaign, infanticide in mainland China, particularly of girls and children with disabilities, has remained 'pervasive' in the words of the Committee on the Rights of the Child.[149] In its 2013 Concluding Observations on China, the Committee urged the authorities to adopt comprehensive legal and policy measures to address the underlying factors for infanticide; ensure more effective and consistent application and enforcement of laws against infanticide in all provinces and prefectures; and to improve ways to count, verify, and register every birth.[150]

22.53 Infanticide has also been widely practised in India. The 2006 Report of the independent expert for the UN study on violence against children observed that a study in India, interviewing one thousand women about pregnancy outcomes, found that 41 per cent of early neo-natal female deaths were due to female infanticide.[151] To try and tackle the economic causes of the problem, the Indian state of Tamil Nadu has offered parents money to help look after daughters, with an annual sum paid throughout a daughter's education, followed by a lump sum on her twentieth birthday, either for use as a dowry or to fund further education.[152]

22.54 The inherent right to life is, as the Committee on the Rights of the Child has observed, particularly at risk where children with disabilities are concerned.[153] They are more vulnerable to infanticide than other children, since 'some cultures view a child with any form of disability as a bad omen that may "tarnish the family pedigree" and, accordingly, a certain designated individual from the community systematically kills children with disabilities. These crimes often go unpunished or perpetrators receive reduced sentences.'[154] In its 2012 thematic study on the issue of 'violence against women and girls and disability', the Office of the UN High Commissioner for Human Rights (OHCHR) reported that girls with disabilities are more likely to be victims of infanticide than boys with comparable disabilities.[155] The Committee on the Rights of the Child has urged States Parties to the CRC to enforce laws that 'ensure appropriate punishment to all those who directly or indirectly violate the right to life, survival and development of children with disabilities'.[156]

---

[148] *Female Infanticide Worldwide: The Case for Action by the UN Human Rights Council*, Asian Centre for Human Rights, New Delhi, June 2016, p. 1.
[149] Committee on the Rights of the Child, Concluding Observations on the combined third and fourth periodic reports of China, UN doc. CRC/C/CHN/CO/3-4, 29 October 2013, para. 33.
[150] Ibid., para. 34(a), (b), and (c).
[151] *World Report on Violence against Children*, UN, New York, 2006, chap. 3, p. 52.
[152] BBC, 'Female Infanticide', archived file, at http://bbc.in/36hOSWh.
[153] Committee on the Rights of the Child, 'General Comment No. 9 (2006): The rights of children with disabilities', UN doc. CRC/C/GC/9, 27 February 2007, para. 31.
[154] Ibid.
[155] 'Thematic study on the issue of violence against women and girls and disability. Report of the Office of the United Nations High Commissioner for Human Rights', UN doc. A/HRC/20/5, 30 March 2012, para. 24.
[156] Committee on the Rights of the Child, 'General Comment No. 9 (2006): The rights of children with disabilities', para. 31.

INFANT MORTALITY

The Normative Framework

22.55 Besides cases of infanticide, many babies die during and following birth, owing to a range of causes and factors. The first twenty-eight days of life – the neo-natal period – is the most vulnerable time for a child's survival.[157] In its General Comment on the right of children to enjoy the highest attainable standard of health (Article 24 of the CRC), the Committee on the Rights of the Child has observed that a 'significant number of infant deaths occur during the neonatal period, related to the poor health of the mother prior to, and during, the pregnancy and the immediate post-partum period, and to suboptimal breastfeeding practices'.[158]

22.56 The infant mortality rate is defined as the number of deaths of children under one year of age, expressed per one thousand live births.[159] Article 6(2) of the CRC obligates each of its 196 States Parties to ensure to the maximum extent possible the survival of every child within its jurisdiction. Article 24 further requires States Parties to 'pursue full implementation' of the right to the highest attainable standard of health by taking appropriate measures to diminish infant and child mortality.[160] Neither provision, though, specifies maximum levels of infant mortality nor stipulates minimum targets for reductions over time. In its General Comment on the implementation of child rights in early childhood, the Committee on the Rights of the Child urged States Parties 'to take all possible measures to improve perinatal care for mothers and babies, reduce infant and child mortality and create conditions that promote the wellbeing of all young children'.[161] According to the Human Rights Committee, measures required by the right to life under the ICCPR to protect the right to life include 'where necessary' campaigns for improving access to treatments in order to reduce both maternal and infant mortality.[162]

22.57 The UN Sustainable Development Goals (SDGs) are politically, but not legally, binding. They do, however, offer valuable guidance on what States should consider as targets for domestic as well as international achievement. SDG 3, which concerns 'good health and well-being', encompasses action to reduce infant mortality. Its Target 3.2 for child mortality more broadly is to end, by 2030, preventable deaths of newborns and children under five years of age, with all nations aiming to reduce neonatal mortality to at

---

[157] UNICEF, 'Neonatal Mortality', September 2019, at http://bit.ly/36u95YM.
[158] Committee on the Rights of the Child, 'General Comment No. 15 (2013) on the right of the child to the enjoyment of the highest attainable standard of health', UN doc. CRC/C/GC/15, 17 April 2013, para. 18 (hereinafter, Committee on the Rights of the Child, General Comment No. 15).
[159] Organization for Economic Co-operation and Development (OECD), 'Infant mortality rates', *OECD Data*, 2018, at http://bit.ly/2QHCUhQ.
[160] Art. 24(1)(a), CRC.
[161] Committee on the Rights of the Child, General Comment No. 7 (2005): Implementing Child Rights in Early Childhood, UN doc. CRC/C/GC/7/Rev.1, 20 September 2006, para. 10.
[162] Human Rights Committee, General Comment 36 on the right to life, para. 26, citing its Concluding Observations on the Democratic Republic of Congo (2006), para. 14.

least as low as 12 deaths per 1,000 live births and to reduce mortality among those under 5 to at least as low as 25 deaths per 1,000 live births.

State Practice

22.58 There is a challenging route to be traversed if the world is to meet SDG Target 3.2. Globally, median infant mortality rates in 2018 were estimated by the UN to amount to almost 29 deaths per 1,000.[163] In its 2019 report on progress towards SDG Target 3.2, the United Nations stated:

> The under-5 mortality rate has fallen by 49 per cent – from 77 deaths per 1,000 live births in 2000 to 39 deaths in 2017. The total number of under-5 deaths dropped from 9.8 million in 2000 to 5.4 million in 2017. Half of those deaths occurred in Sub-Saharan Africa, and another 30 per cent in Southern Asia. Almost half (2.5 million) of the total number of under-5 deaths took place in the first month of life – the most crucial period for child survival. The global neonatal mortality rate fell from 31 deaths per 1,000 live births in 2000 to 18 deaths in 2017 – a 41 per cent reduction.[164]

If, however, the SDG target for mortality among those under five years of age is met, the UN has calculated that the lives of an additional ten million children will have been saved by 2030. Key to such an achievement will be 'vaccinations, exclusive breastfeeding, proper nutrition, appropriate treatment of common childhood infections, as well as reductions in air pollution and access to safely managed drinking water and sanitation'.[165]

DISEASE, ILLNESS, AND SUBSTANCE ABUSE

The Normative Framework

22.59 Diseases, illnesses, and substance abuse can kill children of any age, although babies and infants are especially at risk. In this regard, Article 24 of the CRC calls for the provision of medical assistance and health care to all children 'with emphasis on the development of primary health care' and the combatting of disease and malnutrition.[166] Surprisingly, however, vaccination is not specifically cited as a measure to be taken, despite it being 'widely recognized as one of the world's most successful and cost-effective health interventions, saving millions of lives'.[167]

22.60 Article 33 of the Convention further obligates States Parties to take 'all appropriate measures, including legislative, administrative, social and educational measures, to protect children from the illicit use of narcotic drugs and psychotropic substances'. In the

---

[163] Estimates generated by the UN Inter-agency Group for Child Mortality Estimation in 2019, downloaded from http://data.unicef.org, last updated 19 September 2019.
[164] *The Sustainable Development Goals Report 2019*, United Nations, New York, 2019, p. 27.
[165] Ibid.
[166] Art. 24(1)(b) and (c), CRC.
[167] *The Sustainable Development Goals Report 2019*, p. 27.

context of the ICCPR, the Human Rights Committee has referred to the duty to protect life as implying that States Parties to the Covenant 'should take appropriate measures to address the general conditions in society that may give rise to direct threats to life or prevent individuals from enjoying their right to life with dignity', which include 'extensive substance abuse'.[168]

State Practice

22.61 The UN reported in 2019 that the proportion of children who received the required three doses of the diphtheria-tetanus-pertussis (DTP3) vaccine increased from 72 per cent in 2000 to 85 per cent in 2015, but then remained unchanged between 2015 and 2017. This meant that almost twenty million children did not receive the vaccine during the first year of life, 'putting them at serious risk of potentially fatal diseases'.[169] To prevent measles, two vaccine doses are needed. Coverage by the second dose (MCV2), given during the second year of a child's life or upon school-entry age, increased from 15 per cent in 2000 to 59 per cent in 2015 and 67 per cent in 2017. 'This progress, while dramatic', is, the UN noted, 'still insufficient to prevent measles outbreaks'.[170] In Nigeria, UNICEF reported that pneumonia killed a child every three minutes in 2019, and claimed that two million children in the country could die in the 2020s – the highest number of any country in the world and more than one-fifth of childhood deaths from pneumonia globally – unless more is done to fight the disease. According to UNICEF, malnutrition, air pollution, and lack of access to vaccines and antibiotics were the main drivers of preventable deaths from pneumonia.[171]

22.62 The UN also attested to an 'acceleration'[172] of programmes to prevent, test, and treat human immunodeficiency virus (HIV)[173] and acquired immunodeficiency syndrome (AIDS). As a result, the incidence of HIV among adults (fifteen to forty-nine years of age) in Sub-Saharan Africa declined by around 37 per cent from 2010 to 2017.[174] But progress has been slower elsewhere, with some sub-regions even seeing an increase in HIV incidence: Western Asia (53 per cent), Central Asia (51 per cent), and Europe (22 per cent). Global HIV incidence among adults declined by 22 per cent between 2010 and 2017, which is 'well short of the progress required to meet the 2020 and 2030 targets'.[175] The largest decline in incidence by age group was among children up to fourteen years of age

---

[168] Human Rights Committee, General Comment 36 on the right to life, para. 26.
[169] *The Sustainable Development Goals Report 2019*, p. 27.
[170] Ibid.
[171] UNICEF Nigeria, 'Two Million Children in Nigeria Could Die in the Next Decade Unless More Is Done to Fight Pneumonia', press release, Abuja, 30 January 2020, at http://uni.cf/2S9A8mi.
[172] *The Sustainable Development Goals Report 2019*, p. 28.
[173] As the Centers for Disease Control (CDC) explain, 'HIV is a virus spread through certain body fluids that attacks the body's immune system, specifically the CD4 cells, often called T cells. Over time, HIV can destroy so many of these cells that the body can't fight off infections and disease.' CDC, 'About HIV/AIDS', undated but accessed on 2 January 2020, at http://bit.ly/2Fg5O3o.
[174] *The Sustainable Development Goals Report 2019*, p. 28.
[175] Ibid.

(registering a 37 per cent drop in 2010–17), reflecting increased provision of anti-retroviral medications to prevent mother-to-child HIV transmission.[176]

22.63 Disappointing results have been registered in recent years with respect to malaria, probably the world's single biggest killer of all time.[177] Malaria, which is caused by parasites transmitted to people through the bites of infected female Anopheles mosquitoes, is both preventable and curable.[178] But after more than a decade of steady gains against the disease, no significant advances were made between 2015 and 2017 in reducing the number of cases worldwide.[179] In 2017, an estimated 219 million cases of malaria were reported, resulting in 435,000 deaths. Sub-Saharan Africa continues to carry the heaviest burden, accounting for more than 90 per cent of all malaria cases worldwide, 'and the toll is rising'.[180] From 2016 to 2017, approximately 3.5 million more malaria cases were reported in the ten most affected African countries. Children under 5 years of age are the most vulnerable to the disease, accounting for 61 per cent (266,000) of malaria deaths worldwide.[181] There is not yet an effective malaria vaccine on the market, with the most promising to date until recently the RTS,S vaccine developed by the pharmaceutical conglomerate, GlaxoSmithKline.[182] The vaccine, which has been under development since 1987, has evidenced in tests a prevention rate of four in ten cases of malaria and three in ten severe cases among children who received all four doses.[183] As of early December 2020, however, a new potential vaccine developed by the Jenner Institute was preparing for phase-three clinical trials in Burkina Faso, Kenya, Mali, and Tanzania.[184]

22.64 With respect to substance abuse deaths among children, data is far scarcer. Collectively, smoking, alcohol, and illicit drug use are estimated to result – in some cases directly, but overwhelmingly indirectly – in the death of 11.8 million people (child and adult) each year. This is greater than the number of deaths from all cancers.[185] But figures for substance abuse deaths are not reliably disaggregated between children and adults. Within the United States, for instance, the American Academy of Family

---

[176] Ibid.
[177] However, oft-repeated claims that malaria has killed half of all the more than 100 billion people who have ever lived have been debunked by statistical analysis. See, e.g., R. Pomeroy, 'Has Malaria Really Killed Half of Everyone Who Ever Lived?', blog entry, *Real Clear Science*, 3 October 2019, at http://bit.ly/2swpNbC.
[178] World Health Organization (WHO), 'Malaria: Key Facts', 27 March 2019, at http://bit.ly/2QhoJB9.
[179] That said, since 2007 nine states have been certified by the WHO Director-General as having eliminated malaria: the United Arab Emirates (2007), Morocco (2010), Turkmenistan (2010), Armenia (2011), the Maldives (2015), Sri Lanka (2016), Kyrgyzstan (2016), Paraguay (2018), and Uzbekistan (2018). Countries that have had at least three consecutive years without a local case of malaria can apply for the WHO certification of malaria elimination. WHO, 'Malaria: Key Facts'.
[180] *The Sustainable Development Goals Report 2019*, p. 28.
[181] Ibid.
[182] The vaccine is designed to stop the *Plasmodium falciparum* malaria parasite from entering the liver, preventing the subsequent deadly blood stages.
[183] 'Malaria Vaccination: A Major Milestone', editorial in *The Lancet: Infectious Diseases*, vol. 19, no. 6 (1 June 2019), p. 559, at http://bit.ly/35jnFkK.
[184] T. Whipple and F. Elliott, 'Malaria Vaccine Another Success Story for Jenner Institute Team behind COVID Jab', *The Times*, 5 December 2020, at http://bit.ly/2L4FmzT (subscription required).
[185] H. Ritchie and M. Roser, 'Drug Use', *Our World in Data*, December 2019, at http://bit.ly/2ZIYJlv.

Physicians (AAFP) has observed that amid the ongoing opioid crisis,[186] it is 'surprising' how little research has been done on opioid-related deaths in young people. While the 2017 National Survey on Drug Use and Health estimated that about 769,000 children aged 12 to 17 misused opioids and about 14,000 had used heroin over the course of the previous year, the survey did not consider how many children might have died from using these drugs as a result.[187] Researchers trawled databases to identify 8,986 children and adolescents who died from opioid poisonings in the United States between 1999 and 2016. Of these, almost four-fifths occurred among non-Hispanic whites and almost three quarters of the total deaths were boys.[188]

22.65 It is asserted that, among other factors, the extent to which a neighbourhood is perceived as disorganised or disordered or is an area characterised by vandalism, abandoned buildings, graffiti, noise, and dirt may influence levels of substance use among adolescents.[189] Children living in the streets are particularly susceptible to substance abuse, although again robust data are acutely lacking.[190] The UN Office on Drugs and Crime (UNODC) has reported that a systematic review and meta-analysis of studies on substance use among children living in the streets in resource-constrained settings found that inhalants[191] were the most common substance used, with pooled analysis[192] putting lifetime prevalence of their use among street-involved children and youth at 47 per cent.[193]

VIOLENCE AGAINST CHILDREN

22.66 Violence against children, whether at the hands of the State or at the hands of private individuals, including family members, continues to be highly prevalent. The particular circumstances of children affect both the nature and the extent of that violence. Circumstances such as living in the streets or being in a place of detention are key factors in a heightened risk to bodily integrity, while the existence of an armed conflict may lead to their recruitment by the State armed forces or non-State armed groups or their

---

[186] Opioids are a class of drugs that include heroin, synthetic opioids such as fentanyl, and pain relievers available legally by prescription, such as oxycodone, hydrocodone, codeine, and morphine. National Institute on Drug Abuse, 'Opioids', undated but accessed 2 January 2020, at http://bit.ly/2QIF69b. Opioids are believed to have killed directly almost 110,000 people worldwide in 2017. See again Ritchie and Roser, 'Drug Use'.

[187] M. Devitt, 'New Research Finds Rise in Pediatric Deaths from Opioids', AAFP, 18 January 2019, at http://bit.ly/2QgqvCA.

[188] Ibid.

[189] UN Office on Drugs and Crime (UNODC), 'Drugs and Age', Booklet 4, World Drug Report 2018, UNODC, Vienna, June 2018, p. 34.

[190] Ibid., pp. 19–20.

[191] Inhalants include paint thinner, petrol, paint, correction fluid, and glue.

[192] A pooled analysis is a statistical technique for combining the results, in this case the prevalence from multiple epidemiological studies, to arrive at an overall estimate of the prevalence.

[193] UNODC, 'Drugs and Age', Booklet 4, p. 20, citing L. Embleton et al., 'The Epidemiology of Substance Use among Street Children in Resource-Constrained Settings: A Systematic Review and Meta-analysis', Addiction, vol. 108, no. 10 (2013), pp. 1722–33.

Children

separation from the family.[194] In addition to the protection afforded to children by Article 6 of the CRC, Article 37(a) codifies the jus cogens prohibition on torture, as well as the customary international law prohibition of other forms of cruel, inhuman, or degrading treatment or punishment.

Children Living on the Street

The Normative Framework

22.67 While children living in the streets is a long-standing and serious phenomenon, there is no specific protection afforded to them under the CRC. At the same time, it must be readily acknowledged that 'street children' or 'children living on the street' are neither a clearly defined population nor one that is homogenous.[195] Even the correct moniker to apply is controversial. Thus, in her 2012 report to the Human Rights Council on the issues raised for the protection of such children, the UN High Commissioner for Human Rights discussed a number of terms and definitions in use, including 'children working and/or living on the street', 'children in street situations', and 'children with street connections'.[196] Each term, the High Commissioner affirmed, has 'the potential to offer distinctive insights and to encourage new avenues of research'.[197]

22.68 But whatever term is applied, a common theme, as the Swiss NGO Terre des Hommes observed in a sectoral policy paper, is that children living in the streets have their most basic rights disregarded, rendering them especially vulnerable to a range of threats to their life and bodily integrity.[198] Indeed, from a rights perspective, the UN High Commissioner for Human Rights attests, the 'greatest challenge faced by a child in a street situation is being recognized and treated as a rights holder'.[199] As a consequence, without appropriate support and assistance, 'children in street situations have a greatly reduced quality of life and life expectancy. They are exposed to all sorts of abuse – physical, psychological and social. In the absence of viable alternatives, it is more than likely that daily reality for these children will be maltreatment and crime.'[200] This includes acts by de facto death squads operating either within, or with the complicity of, law enforcement agencies. In its 2000 Concluding Observations on Colombia, the Committee on the Rights of the Child stated that in the light of Article 6 and other related provisions in the

---

[194] See, e.g., Committee on the Rights of the Child, 'General Comment No. 6 (2005): Treatment of unaccompanied and separated children outside of their country of origin', UN doc. CRC/GC/2005/6, 1 September 2005, paras. 23–4.

[195] S. L. de Moura, 'The Social Construction of Street Children: Configuration and Implications', *British Journal of Social Work*, vol. 32 (2002), pp. 353–67, at 356.

[196] 'Report of the United Nations High Commissioner for Human Rights on the protection and promotion of the rights of children working and/or living on the street', UN doc. A/HRC/19/35, 11 January 2012, para. 12.

[197] Ibid.

[198] Terre des Hommes, 'Children in Street Situations: Sectoral Policy', 2010, at http://bit.ly/2SUDqfv.

[199] 'Report of the United Nations High Commissioner for Human Rights on the protection and promotion of the rights of children working and/or living on the street', para. 22.

[200] Terre des Hommes, 'Children in Street Situations: Sectoral Policy', p. 10.

CRC,[201] it was deeply concerned at the multiple instances of 'social cleansing' of street children and at the 'persistent impunity of the perpetrators of such crimes'. The Committee urged the Colombian authorities to protect children against 'social cleansing' and to 'ensure that judicial action be taken against the perpetrators of such crimes'.[202]

22.69 In its General Comment No. 21 (2017) on children in street situations the Committee again recognised that such children are at risk of extrajudicial killings by State agents as well as 'murder by adults or peers, including murder linked to so-called vigilante justice, and association with/targeting by criminal individuals and gangs'.[203] Children living in the streets are also exposed to 'potentially life-threatening conditions associated with hazardous forms of child labour, traffic accidents, substance abuse, commercial sexual exploitation and unsafe sexual practices; and death due to lack of access to adequate nutrition, health care and shelter'.[204]

22.70 In its 2017 General Comment on the issue, the Committee cited the 1999 judgment of the Inter-American Court of Human Rights in the *Villagran Morales* case, whereby the right to life of children in street situations 'extends not only to civil and political rights but also to economic, social and cultural rights. The need to protect the most vulnerable people – as in the case of street children – definitely requires an interpretation of the right to life that encompasses the minimum conditions for a life with dignity.'[205] States parties' obligations under Article 6 of the CRC, the Committee affirms,

> necessitate careful attention being given to the behaviours and lifestyles of children, even if they do not conform to what specific communities or societies determine to be acceptable under prevailing cultural norms for a particular age group. Programmes can only be effective when they acknowledge the realities of children in street situations. Interventions should support individual children in street situations to achieve their optimal development, maximizing their positive contribution to society.[206]

State Practice

22.71 Yet, in the words of Save the Children, 'so little is known about the welfare of street children that we do not even know in any certain terms how many there are. Global estimates vary widely – from tens of millions to 100 million'.[207] This frequently cited global estimate of more than 100 million children living in the streets has been questioned, including by the High Commissioner for Human Rights. In 2012, she concluded that

---

[201] These include Article 20(1), which stipulates that a 'child temporarily or permanently deprived of his or her family environment, or in whose own best interests cannot be allowed to remain in that environment, shall be entitled to special protection and assistance provided by the State'.

[202] Committee on the Rights of the Child, Concluding Observations on Colombia, UN doc. CRC/C/15/Add.137, 16 October 2000, paras. 34 and 35.

[203] Committee on the Rights of the Child, General Comment 21 on children living in the streets, para. 29.

[204] Ibid.

[205] Ibid.

[206] Ibid., para. 31.

[207] F. Shaheen, J. Glennie, A. Lenhardt, and J. M. Roche, *The Children the World Chooses to Forget*, report, The Save the Children Fund, London, 2016, p. 39, at http://bit.ly/2QiAFmc.

global estimates of the number of such children 'have no basis in fact, and we are no closer today to knowing how many children worldwide are working and/or living in the streets'.[208] That said, a 'growing global population, together with increasing inequalities and migration, suggest that numbers are generally increasing, including in richer regions. The number and flow of children onto the streets of a given city or country may fluctuate significantly according to changes in socio-economic and cultural-political contexts, availability of protection services and patterns of urbanization.'[209]

22.72 Despite the plethora of threats to the lives of well-being of children living in the streets, progress can be, and is, made albeit on a relatively small scale. In 2012, the High Commissioner for Human Rights concluded her study with examples and criteria of good practice.[210] She cited the benefits of local policies designed in close consultation with civil society, academia, and community groups, such as in Rio de Janeiro, around railway stations in India, and as part of Canada's Homelessness Partnering Strategy to make a range of services available to young persons with street connections. In addition, in Ethiopia, in 2008–9, the Consortium for Street Children partnered with Ethiopia's Police University College and UNICEF to train police trainers, who subsequently trained 36,000 police officers throughout the country. Outreach support on the street by social street workers trained in child-centred approaches is being increasingly used as a participatory approach to building relationships with children over time in their own spaces in cities as diverse as Kinshasa, Mexico City, New Delhi, and Brussels.[211]

Children Associated with Gangs

The Normative Framework

22.73 Children living on the street are particularly vulnerable to joining or being targeted by gangs.[212] This is especially the case with elder boys, whose likelihood of being killed as a result is exceptionally high. In its 2019 Global Study on Homicide,[213] UNODC concludes:

> Men and male adolescents aged 15–29 are at the highest risk of homicide globally. This is largely due to the situation in the Americas, where the drivers of homicidal violence are frequently gangs and organized crime, and injuries from firearms are the most frequent cause of death – factors that are known to favour the prevalence of young men as victims and perpetrators.[214]

---

[208] 'Report of the United Nations High Commissioner for Human Rights on the protection and promotion of the rights of children working and/or living on the street', para. 12.
[209] Ibid.
[210] Ibid., para. 37.
[211] Ibid.
[212] Committee on the Rights of the Child, General Comment 21 on children living in the streets, para. 29.
[213] UNODC, *Global Study on Homicide*, 2019, executive summary, at http://bit.ly/2ZOL5gt.
[214] Ibid., p. 23. Regrettably, UNODC does not disaggregate in its reporting on data between children (those under the age of eighteen) and adults (all others).

22.74 Despite a reduction over recent years, El Salvador still has one of the highest murder rates in the world.[215] In its 2018 Concluding Observations on El Salvador, the Committee on the Rights of the Child noted the overall reduction in the number of homicides, but remained deeply concerned by the very high number of killings (4,094 recorded between 2010 and 2017), which mostly affected boys.[216] The Committee noted action taken by the authorities to address the issue of *maras* (youth gangs), in particular the adoption of the 'Safe El Salvador' (El Salvador Seguro) Plan, but pointed to the 'extremely high number of killings and disappearances affecting children, most of them committed by maras, and the vulnerability of boys as young as 5 years old and girls as young as 12 to being recruited by maras'.[217] It expressed further concern at the classification of members of *maras* as terrorists, 'which implies that assisting the rehabilitation of children seeking to leave those groups is a criminal act'.[218]

22.75 The Committee's General Comment No. 20 (2016) on the implementation of the rights of the child during adolescence[219] specifically addressed the issue of gangs. The Committee recognised that recruitment into gangs 'often provide social support, a source of livelihood, protection and a sense of identity in the absence of opportunities to achieve such goals through legitimate activities'.[220] The Committee recommended that States place greater emphasis on developing 'comprehensive public policies that address the root causes of juvenile violence and gangs', rather than resorting to 'aggressive law enforcement approaches'.[221]

State Practice

22.76 According to a 2014 report published by the Overseas Development Institute (ODI) in London, research from low-income urban communities in Brazil and the United States where gang violence is prevalent suggests the following factors reduce the probability of a young man's involvement in gangs:

1. Having a valued, stable relationship or multiple relationships with people (a parent, a grandparent, a female partner) whom they would disappoint by becoming involved with gangs.
2. Having access to alternative identities or some other sense of self that was positively valued by the young man and by those in his social setting, particularly the male peer

---

[215] In August 2019, the Minister of Justice stated that El Salvador's homicide rate had fallen to an average of about 4.4 killings a day since June, about half of the 2018 levels. The country of 6.5 million people recorded 3,340 killings in 2018, or about 9 a day. The bloodiest year of 2015 saw 6,425 homicides, or 17.6 a day. Associated Press, 'El Salvador's Murder Rate Falls to Half of Last Year's, Now It's 4.4 per Day: Minister', *Global News* (Canada), 16 August 2019, at http://bit.ly/2MQzSHb.
[216] Committee on the Rights of the Child, Concluding Observations on the combined fifth and sixth periodic reports of El Salvador, UN doc. CRC/C/SLV/CO/5–6, 29 November 2018, para. 15(a).
[217] Ibid., para. 22(a).
[218] Ibid., para. 22(e).
[219] Committee on the Rights of the Child, 'General Comment No. 20 (2016) on the implementation of the rights of the child during adolescence', UN doc. CRC/C/GC/20, 6 December 2016.
[220] Ibid., para. 83.
[221] Ibid.

group (e.g. being a good student, being a good athlete, having musical skills, having a good job).
3. Being aware of the risks associated with the violent version of masculinity promoted by gang members; and finding an alternative male peer group that provides positive reinforcement for non-gang-involved male identities.
4. Finding an alternative male peer group that provides positive reinforcement for non-gang-involved male identities.[222] Taking into account experiences around the world, the Committee on the Rights of the Child has recommended investing in prevention activities for at-risk adolescents, including through interventions to encourage adolescents to leave gangs, the rehabilitation and reintegration of gang members, programmes and measures of restorative justice, and the creation of municipal alliances against crime and violence, with an emphasis on the school, the family, and social inclusion.[223]

Domestic Violence

The Normative Framework

22.77 The preamble to the CRC affirms that the family is 'the fundamental group of society and the natural environment for the growth and well-being of all its members and particularly children'.[224] While in most instances that is the case, as the World Health Organization's (WHO's) 2002 World Report on Violence and Health[225] attested, it is also true to say that children are abused and neglected by their parents or other caregivers throughout the world. Child abuse includes physical, sexual, and psychological abuse, as well as neglect.[226] Thus, Article 19(1) of the CRC obligates States Parties to take 'all appropriate legislative, administrative, social and educational measures to protect the child from all forms of physical or mental violence, injury or abuse, neglect or negligent treatment, maltreatment or exploitation, including sexual abuse, while in the care of parent(s), legal guardian(s) or any other person who has the care of the child'. Paragraph 2 of the article stipulates that such protective measures 'should, as appropriate, include effective procedures for the establishment of social programmes to provide necessary support for the child and for those who have the care of the child, as well as for other forms of prevention and for identification, reporting, referral, investigation, treatment, and follow-up of instances of child maltreatment described heretofore, and, as appropriate, for judicial involvement'.

22.78 In its General Comment No. 13 (2011) on the right of the child to freedom from all forms of violence, the Committee on the Rights of the Child recognizes that 'much of the

---

[222] R. Marcus, 'Poverty and Violations of Children's Right to Protection in Low- and Middle-Income Countries: A Review of Evidence', ODI, London, 2014, para. 5.6.5, at http://bit.ly/39EU4Wr.
[223] Committee on the Rights of the Child, General Comment No. 20 (2016) on the implementation of the rights of the child during adolescence, para. 83.
[224] CRC, Fifth preambular para.
[225] E. G. Krug, L. L. Dahlberg, J. A. Mercy, A. B. Zwi, and R. Lozano (eds.), *World Report on Violence and Health*, WHO, Geneva, 2002.
[226] See ibid., chap. 3.

violence experienced by children, including sexual abuse, takes place within a family context and stresses the necessity of intervening in families if children are exposed to violence by family members'.[227] Accordingly, implementation of Article 19 of the CRC and related provisions may, in certain cases, demand that the child be taken out of the family for his or her own protection and well-being.[228]

22.79 The jurisprudence of the European Court of Human Rights on domestic violence was summarised previously.[229] The Grand Chamber's judgment in the *Kurt* case will be watched with keen interest. The 2011 Council of Europe Convention on preventing and combating violence against women and domestic violence (Istanbul Convention),[230] to which thirty-four member States were party as of 1 December 2020,[231] contains specific provisions concerning children as direct victims of physical, sexual, or psychological violence in a domestic setting. Article 18(1) stipulates that States Parties 'shall take the necessary legislative or other measures to protect all victims from any further acts of violence'. In so doing, they shall ensure that measures are 'based on an integrated approach which takes into account the relationship between victims, perpetrators, children and their wider social environment'.[232]

State Practice

22.80 While figures should be treated with caution, according to UNICEF, 'every year, as many as 275 million children worldwide become caught in the crossfire of domestic violence and suffer the full consequences of a turbulent home life'.[233] The WHO *Global status report on violence prevention 2014*, which assessed progress since the 2002 WHO report, observes that children who suffer physical abuse 'may manifest a variety of internal and external injuries that can be life threatening':[234]

> Abusive head trauma is a common cause of injuries in very young children. Skull fractures, retinal haemorrhaging, subdural haematomas, neurological disabilities, cortical blindness and seizures are some of the common injuries related to abusive head trauma .... Injuries that are unexplained or inconsistent with the history provided by the child or a caregiver may also suggest abuse.

---

[227] Committee on the Rights of the Child, General Comment 13 on freedom from violence, para. 72(d).
[228] K. Sandberg, 'Children's Right to Protection under the CRC', chap. 2 in A. Falch-Eriksen and E. Backe-Hansen (eds.), *Human Rights in Child Protection: Implications for Professional Practice and Policy*, Springer, Switzerland, August 2018, pp. 15–38, at 16, available at http://bit.ly/2QokoxT.
[229] See, supra, paras. 25.23–25.25.
[230] Council of Europe Convention on preventing and combating violence against women and domestic violence; adopted at Istanbul 11 May 2011; entered into force 1 August 2014 (hereinafter, Istanbul Convention).
[231] Albania, Andorra, Austria, Belgium, Bosnia and Herzegovina, Croatia, Cyprus, Denmark, Estonia, Finland, France, Georgia, Germany, Greece, Iceland, Ireland, Italy, Luxembourg, Malta, Monaco, Montenegro, the Netherlands, North Macedonia, Norway, Poland, Portugal, Romania, San Marino, Serbia, Slovenia, Spain, Sweden, Switzerland, and Turkey. Turkey announced its withdrawal from the Convention in March 2021. The updated list is available at http://bit.ly/35jfS6y.
[232] Art. 18(3), Istanbul Convention.
[233] UNICEF, 'Domestic Violence against Children', *State of the World's Children* 2007, text available at http://uni.cf/39CCGBy.
[234] WHO, *Global Status Report on Violence Prevention 2014*, Geneva, 2014, p. 13.

But, as UNICEF has observed, the consequences of domestic violence are not limited to the immediate victims:

> [They] can span generations. The effects of violent behaviour tend to stay with children long after they leave the childhood home. Boys who are exposed to their parents' domestic violence are twice as likely to become abusive men as are the sons of non-violent parents. Furthermore, girls who witness their mothers being abused are more likely to accept violence in a marriage than girls who come from non-violent homes.[235]

Violence in Educational Establishments

The Normative Framework

22.81 As is the case in the home, schools and other educational establishments are supposed to be safe spaces for children without the occurrence of violence. But while this is true in the majority of cases, it is far from always being so.[236] In its General Comment 13 on the right of the child to be free from all forms of violence, the Committee on the Rights of the Child noted its awareness of 'widespread and intense violence applied against children in State institutions and by State actors including in schools', which 'may amount to torture and killing of children'.[237] Accordingly, SDG Target 4(a) includes the aim to 'provide safe, non-violent, inclusive and effective learning environments for all'. A thematic indicator focuses on the 'percentage of students experiencing bullying, corporal punishment, harassment, violence, sexual discrimination and abuse'. In addition to the relevant provisions in Article 19, noted previously, Article 28(2) of the CRC obligates States Parties to take 'all appropriate measures to ensure that school discipline is administered in a manner consistent with the child's human dignity and in conformity with the ... Convention'.

State Practice

22.82 Although violence in educational establishments 'is one of the most visible forms of violence against children',[238] its global prevalence is not even the subject of a broad-brush estimate. National and regional studies have, though, given an indication of the scale. A study in Ireland, for instance, found that 44 per cent of Irish teenagers were subjected to violence at school, with bullying and physical fights said to be a 'pervasive part of young people's education' in the country.[239] In a regional study for Europe by the WHO, 'Health Behaviour in School-aged Children', it was found that an average of almost one in five

---

[235] UNICEF, 'Domestic Violence against Children'.
[236] A link is sometimes made between violence in the home and subsequent violence in school. See, on this issue, Constitutional Rights Foundation, *Causes of School Violence*, United States, 1997, at http://bit.ly/39uXrPz. Data and information on causation and the interrelationship are currently lacking.
[237] Committee on the Rights of the Child, General Comment 13 on the right to freedom from violence, para. 3(i).
[238] Council of Europe, 'Violence in Schools', 2019, at http://bit.ly/2ugtwdJ.
[239] A. McMahon, 'Report Finds 44% of Irish Teens Subjected to Violence at School', *The Irish Times*, 6 September 2018, at http://bit.ly/39BUA7x.

eleven-year-old boys had been involved in a physical fight at least three times over the preceding twelve months. The average figure, though disguised huge national variations, with Francophone Belgium and Armenia registering more than one in three boys of that age so involved, while Portugal had one in nine and Finland had only one in ten.[240]

22.83 With respect to the Americas, in 2015 the Inter-American Commission on Human Rights issued a report entitled 'Violence, Children and Organized Crime'.[241] The Commission concluded 'that the levels of violence in the region's schools, whether between peers or inflicted by faculty members on students, are alarming and need urgently to be addressed'.[242] States, the Commission affirmed, 'should ensure that education and schools do not reproduce stereotypes based on gender, socioeconomic background, ethnic origin, or other factors, or perpetuate exclusion and discrimination, abuse, or violence. On the contrary, States should encourage the educational process to be inclusive and foster the human rights of, and protection for, children.'[243]

Enlistment in Armed Forces or Groups

The Normative Framework

22.84 During situations of armed conflict or other armed violence, including terrorist violence, children are vulnerable to recruitment. The international legal situation with respect to non-State armed groups is clear: no children under eighteen years of age may be recruited by virtue of the 2000 Optional Protocol to the CRC on the involvement of children in armed conflict. According to Article 4(1), 'armed groups that are distinct from the armed forces of a State should not, under any circumstances, recruit or use in hostilities persons under the age of 18 years'.[244] Not so unequivocal as to the minimum age are the corresponding provisions governing voluntary recruitment into State armed forces. By virtue of Article 3(1), States Parties are obligated only to raise the minimum age to one that is greater than fifteen years, albeit 'recognizing that under the Convention persons under 18 are entitled to special protection'. Under international humanitarian and criminal law, recruitment or use in armed conflict of children under fifteen years of age is a war crime.[245]

22.85 In its Resolution 2427 (2018), the UN Security Council strongly condemned 'all violations of applicable international law involving the recruitment and use of children by

---

[240] WHO, 'Bullying and Physical Fighting among Adolescents', Fact Sheet, Geneva, 15 March 2016, p. 3, at http://bit.ly/2FfyycF.
[241] Inter-American Commission on Human Rights, *Violence, Children and Organized Crime*, Report, OAS doc. OEA/Ser.L/V/II. Doc. 40/15, 11 November 2015, at http://bit.ly/2SPvVGk.
[242] Ibid., para. 535.
[243] Ibid., para. 536.
[244] Optional Protocol to the Convention on the Rights of the Child on the involvement of children in armed conflict; adopted at New York 25 May 2000; entered into force 12 February 2002. As of 1 January 2020, 170 States were party to the Protocol.
[245] Article 8(2)(b)(xxvi) and Article 8(2)(e)(vii) of the ICC Statute provide that 'conscripting or enlisting children under the age of fifteen years' into armed forces or armed groups constitute a war crime in international and non-international armed conflict, respectively.

parties to armed conflict'.[246] The slightly awkward formulation of its condemnation reflected the fact that four of the five permanent members of the Council – China, France, the United Kingdom, and the United States – continue to recruit children into their armed forces.[247] The Council stressed the need 'to pay particular attention to the treatment of children associated or allegedly associated with all non-State armed groups, including those who commit acts of terrorism, in particular by establishing standard operating procedures for the rapid handover of these children to relevant civilian child protection actors'.[248] It further emphasised that children 'who have been recruited in violation of applicable international law by armed forces and armed groups and are accused of having committed crimes during armed conflicts should be treated primarily as victims of violations of international law'.[249]

State Practice

22.86 In his latest report on children and armed conflict, which covers 2018, the UN Secretary-General stated that in Afghanistan the United Nations had 'verified the recruitment and use of 45 boys and 1 girl, with some of the children recruited as young as 8, who were used for combat, at checkpoints, to plant improvised explosive devices, to carry out suicide attacks or other violations, or for sexual exploitation. At least 22 boys were killed during their association.'[250] Most of the instances of recruitment and use of children as soldiers were in non-State armed groups, although the Afghan Army continued to use a number of children to participate directly in hostilities.[251] In Syria, the UN verified the recruitment and use of 806 children (670 boys, 136 girls), more than one-fifth of whom were younger than fifteen years of age, and 94 per cent of whom were used in combat roles. The majority of the children (313) were recruited and used by Kurdish People's Protection Units (YPG/YPJ) operating under the umbrella of the Syrian Democratic Forces.[252] In most cases, recruitment occurred without accountability, but in the Central African Republic, the UN Secretary-General reported that two anti-balaka leaders had been

---

[246] UN Security Council Resolution 2427, adopted by consensus on 9 July 2018, Operative para. 1.
[247] For China, France, and the United States, the minimum age for voluntary recruitment is seventeen years. Other States that are believed to accept children aged seventeen years into their armed forces include Algeria, Australia, Austria, Azerbaijan, Cabo Verde, Cuba, Cyprus, the Democratic People's Republic of Korea, Germany, Guinea-Bissau, Ireland, Israel, Italy, Luxembourg, Malaysia, New Zealand, the Philippines, São Tomé and Príncipe, Saudi Arabia, Turkmenistan, and the United Arab Emirates. The United Kingdom continues to recruit children at the age of sixteen years, with parental consent, the only European nation to do so. Other States that continue to recruit children aged sixteen years into their armed forces include Brazil, Canada, Chile, the Dominican Republic, Egypt, El Salvador, India, Jordan, Pakistan, and Singapore. The situation with respect to Oman remains unclear. See http://bit.ly/2SLXZKV. Iran, a signatory to the Optional Protocol, appears to allow voluntary enlistment into the *Basij* at fifteen years of age.
[248] UN Security Council Resolution 2427, Operative para. 19.
[249] Ibid., Operative para. 20.
[250] 'Children and armed conflict: Report of the Secretary-General', UN doc. A/73/907-S/2019/509, 20 June 2019, para. 18.
[251] Ibid., para. 28.
[252] Ibid., para. 174.

arrested and transferred to the International Criminal Court (ICC) for crimes, including the recruitment and use of children younger than fifteen years of age.[253]

22.87 More generally, as the Committee on the Rights of the Child has observed in its General Comment No. 24:

> When under the control of such groups, children may become victims of multiple forms of violations: conscription, military training, being use in hostilities and/or terrorist acts, including suicide attacks, forced to carry out executions, used as human shields, or being victims of abduction, sale, trafficking, child marriages, or exploitation to carry out dangerous tasks, such as spying, manning check points, conducting patrols, or transporting military equipment. It has been reported that non-State armed groups or terrorist and violent extremist organization also force children to commit acts of violence against their own families or within their own communities to demonstrate loyalty and to discourage future defection.[254]

NEGLECT AND EXPLOITATION

Children in the Workplace

The Normative Framework

22.88 There is no comprehensive prohibition on children being engaged in work, either under the CRC or in general international law. Under Article 32(1) of the CRC, States Parties recognise 'the right of the child to be protected from economic exploitation and from performing any work that is likely to be hazardous or to interfere with the child's education, or to be harmful to the child's health or physical, mental, spiritual, moral or social development'. The International Labour Organization (ILO) Convention on the Worst Forms of Child Labour[255] stipulates, in its Article 1, that each State Party 'shall take immediate and effective measures to secure the prohibition and elimination of the worst forms of child labour as a matter of urgency'. For the purposes of the Convention, the worst forms of child labour comprise all forms of slavery or practices similar to slavery, including forced or compulsory labour; the use, procuring, or offering of a child for prostitution; the use, procuring, or offering of a child for the production and trafficking of drugs; and work which, by its nature or the circumstances in which it is carried out, is likely to harm the health, safety, or morals of children.[256]

---

[253] Ibid., para. 40. On 20 February 2019, ICC Pre-Trial Chamber II decided to join the cases of *The Prosecutor* v. *Alfred Yekatom* and *The Prosecutor* v. *Patrice-Edouard Ngaïssona*. ICC, 'ICC Pre-Trial Chamber II Joins Yekatom and Ngaïssona Cases', Press Release No. ICC-CPI-20190220-PR143, 20 February 2019, at http://bit.ly/2sKHmED.

[254] Committee on the Rights of the Child, 'General Comment No. 24 (2019), Children's rights in the child justice system', UN doc CRC/C/GC/24, 18 September 2019, para. 98.

[255] Worst Forms of Child Labour Convention, ILO Convention No. 182, adopted at Geneva 17 June 1999; entered into force 19 November 2000. As of 1 May 2021, 186 States members of the ILO had adhered to the Convention, leaving only Tonga outside. Of the 193 UN member States, Andorra, Bhutan, Liechtenstein, Micronesia, Monaco, Nauru, and the Democratic People's Republic of Korea are not also members of the ILO. The only non UN member State which is a member of the ILO is the Cook Islands.

[256] Art. 3, ILO Convention 182.

State Practice

22.89 According to ILO estimates, half of all children engaged in some form of labour (75 million from a total of 151 million, as of 2016) are involved in hazardous work that directly endangers their health, safety, and moral development.[257] In the past, ILO has estimated that 22,000 children were killed every year at work, but these figures date back to 2011 when global estimates of child labourers were very much higher than they are today (115 million engaged in hazardous child labour, from a total of 215 million child labourers).[258]

22.90 In her 2006 work on child rights in India, Asha Bajpai argued that no single cause explains the prevalence of child labour. While the nature and extent of poverty in a country do evidence an 'intimate' link with child labour, the specific circumstances of child labour are influenced by many other factors. The phenomenon inheres 'in the cycle of poverty, unemployment, underemployment, and low wages caused by inequitable distribution of resources and economic policies'.[259] Thus SDG Target 8.7, which includes the aim to 'secure the prohibition and elimination of the worst forms of child labour, including recruitment and use of child soldiers, and by 2025 end child labour in all its forms', is wholly unrealistic.

POLLUTION AND THE RIGHT TO LIFE OF CHILDREN

The Normative Framework

22.91 Pollution has a significant and growing impact on the lives of children, as Chapter 18 describes. According to WHO, lower respiratory infections are among the largest causes of mortality in children, accounting for 15.5 per cent of deaths in 2015. The most important environmental risks are household air pollution from exposure to smoke from cookstoves, ambient air pollution, and second-hand tobacco smoke.[260] Together, ambient and household air pollution contribute to seven million premature deaths annually, including the deaths of approximately 600,000 children.[261]

22.92 Makuch et al. argue that 'Article 6 on the right to life provides the most substantial legal argument for the environmental rights of the child. If you cannot breathe clean air, drink clean water, and so on, how can you live?'[262] In other respects, however, the provisions in the CRC on environmental pollution are weak. While under Article 24(1),

---

[257] ILO, *Global Estimates of Child Labour*, 2016, table 1, at http://bit.ly/2rNEUga.
[258] ILO, *Handbook on Hazardous Labour*, Geneva, 2011, p. 7, at http://bit.ly/37BG5yL.
[259] A. Bajpai, *Child Rights in India: Law, Policy, and Practice*, Oxford University Press, Oxford, 2006.
[260] WHO, *Don't Pollute My Future! The Impact of the Environment on Children's Health*, Geneva, 2017, p. 2.
[261] 'Issue of human rights obligations relating to the enjoyment of a safe, clean, healthy and sustainable environment. Report of the Special Rapporteur', UN doc. A/HRC/40/55, 8 January 2019, para. 26, citing WHO, 'Burden of disease from the joint effects of household and ambient air pollution for 2016', May 2018.
[262] K. E. Makuch, S. Zaman, and M. R. Aczel, 'Tomorrow's Stewards: The Case for a Unified International Framework on the Environmental Rights of Children', *Health and Human Rights Journal*, 12 June 2019, at http://bit.ly/35r42aB.

States Parties recognise the right of the child to the enjoyment of the highest attainable standard of health, in implementing this right, they are only constrained to take 'into consideration the dangers and risks of environmental pollution'. That said, in its General Comment on the article (No. 15, 2013), the Committee on the Rights of the Child declared that States 'should take measures to address the dangers and risks that local environmental pollution poses to children's health in all settings'.[263]

State Practice

22.93 In a number of States, air pollution is so severe that it may amount to a violation of children's right to life. In mid-December 2019, State authorities warned people to wear face masks or stay indoors after choking air pollution returned to Bangkok, following months of relatively clean air. The national Pollution Control Department issued a warning when the amount of hazardous PM 2.5 dust particles[264] exceeded designated safe levels in three areas in the capital. Air pollution had forced the closure of some schools in Bangkok earlier in the year.[265] The safe threshold in Thailand is set at 50 μg (microgrammes) per cubic metre of air, which is higher than the recognised safe level in many other nations.[266] One website recorded Luanda, the Angolan capital, as the most polluted city in the world in 2019. Its PM 2.5 level was 182 μg per cubic metre.[267]

22.94 As noted in Chapter 18, in the United Kingdom, a new inquest into the death of an asthmatic nine-year-old girl began at the end of November 2020, after a medical report suggested a direct link between her illness and poor air quality near her home, not far from a busy road. Ella Adoo-Kissi-Debrah could become the first person in the United Kingdom – and possibly the world – to have 'air pollution' formally listed as a cause of death.[268] If this were to occur, given prior judicial warnings about air pollution that were ignored by the authorities,[269] a violation of her right to life might have occurred.

---

[263] Committee on the Rights of the Child, General Comment No. 15, para. 49.
[264] PM 2.5 is particulate matter 2.5 micrometres or less in diameter.
[265] 'Air Pollution Soars in Thai Capital Bangkok, Authorities Issue Warning', CAN, 19 December 2019, at http://bit.ly/2QGYGIX.
[266] A. Wipatayotin, 'Dust Pollution Surges in Greater Bangkok', *Bangkok Post*, 30 September 2019, at http://bit.ly/2MUHlVD.
[267] STC, 'World's Most and Least Polluted Cities', 27 August 2019, at http://bit.ly/3605VFY.
[268] C. Marshall, 'Rosamund Adoo-Kissi-Debrah: "Did Air Pollution Kill My Daughter?"', BBC, 29 November 2020, at http://bbc.in/2JllkAD.
[269] F. Harvey, 'Air Pollution: UK Government Loses Third Court Case as Plans Ruled "Unlawful"', *The Guardian*, 21 February 2018, at http://bit.ly/2KTteBV; and S. Laville, 'Landmark Inquest to Rule If Air Pollution Killed London Pupil', *The Guardian*, 30 November 2020, at http://bit.ly/308n3bw.

23

Racially Motivated Killings

INTRODUCTION

23.01 This chapter describes the duty of States to respect and protect the right to life by preventing and prosecuting racially motivated killings.[1] The centrality of race to the protection of fundamental human rights, including the right to life, is evident from the wording of the 1945 Charter of the United Nations[2] (UN Charter). One of the purposes of the global organisation is stated to be to achieve international cooperation in 'promoting and encouraging respect for human rights and for fundamental freedoms for all without distinction as to race'.[3] The development of the Charter was predominantly a reaction to the 'untold sorrow' wrought by the Second World War, in which the Holocaust perpetrated against more than five million Jews[4] and the extermination of hundreds of thousands of Roma[5] demonstrated the enormities of racially motivated killings both within and outside armed conflicts.

23.02 The continued perpetration of racially motivated killings on a widespread scale and in a systematic manner was addressed in 1994 by a General Recommendation of the Committee on the Elimination of Racial Discrimination in connection with the proposed establishment of an international tribunal to prosecute crimes against humanity. Therein, the Committee expressed its alarm 'at the increasing number of racially and ethnically motivated massacres and atrocities occurring in different regions of the world'.[6]

23.03 Massacres and atrocities have been perpetrated on every continent: against Tutsis in Rwanda; against Bosnian Muslims in Bosnia and Herzegovina; against Uighurs in China,[7]

---

[1] The author would like to acknowledge the contribution to this chapter of Alvin Cheung Yui Yin, a graduate in jurisprudence at Oxford University.
[2] Charter of the United Nations; adopted at San Francisco 26 June 1945; entered into force 24 October 1945 (hereinafter, UN Charter).
[3] Art. 1(3), UN Charter.
[4] 'Holocaust Facts: Where Does the Figure of 6 Million Victims Come From?', *Haaretz*, 26 January 2020, at http://bit.ly/2DqU7sW.
[5] US Holocaust Memorial Museum (Washington, DC), 'Genocide of European Roma (Gypsies), 1939–1945', *Holocaust Encyclopedia*, undated but accessed 1 August 2020 at http://bit.ly/39McFQB.
[6] Committee on the Elimination of Racial Discrimination (CERD Committee), 'General Recommendation XVIII on the establishment of an international tribunal to prosecute crimes against humanity', forty-fourth session (1994), first preambular para.
[7] R. Asat and Y. Diamond, 'The World's Most Technologically Sophisticated Genocide Is Happening in Xinjiang', Argument, *Foreign Policy*, 15 July 2020, at http://bit.ly/3ghUxR2.

among many others. In Iraq, on 16 March 1988, Iraqi Air Force aircraft supported by artillery dropped the nerve agent Sarin and mustard gas on the Kurdish town of Halabja in the north of the country. Thousands of people – mainly women and children – died that day, with up to 12,000 believed to have lost their lives since as a result of the effects of the chemical weapons.[8] In March 2010, the Supreme Iraqi Criminal Tribunal recognised the attack, which took place within the *al-Anfal* campaign against the Kurds during the Iran–Iraq War, as an act of genocide.[9]

THE DEFINITION OF RACE AND RACIAL DISCRIMINATION

23.04 There is no agreed-upon definition of 'race' under international law.[10] The 1948 Genocide Convention refers in its definition of 'genocide' (a term which itself was constructed from the Latin word for 'race' or 'tribe')[11] to 'a national, ethnical, racial or religious group'.[12] As Robert Cryer et al. observe, with respect to the four groups in the Convention, it is difficult to attribute a distinct meaning to each, since they overlap considerably.[13] During the negotiation of the Convention in the Sixth Committee of the UN General Assembly, Sweden (which had proposed the term's inclusion) had acknowledged that 'the concept' of a racial group was 'often ill-defined'.[14] Belgium and Uruguay, with support from Egypt, suggested that the words 'ethnical' and 'racial' were in fact synonyms, while Haiti believed that 'intermingling between races in certain regions had made the problem of race so complicated that it might be impossible, in certain cases, to

---

[8] H. de Bretton-Gordon, 'Remembering Halabja Chemical Attack', *Aljazeera*, 16 March 2016, at http://bit.ly/2tAfFir.
[9] United Press International, '1988 Kurdish Massacre Labeled Genocide', 8 March 2010, at http://bit.ly/3aqXagL.
[10] *Race* is defined by the *Oxford English Dictionary* as 'any of the (putative) major groupings of mankind, usually defined in terms of distinct physical features or shared ethnicity, and sometimes (more controversially) considered to encompass common biological or genetic characteristics'. The *Cambridge English Dictionary* refers to 'a group of people who share the same language, history, characteristics, etc.' See http://bit.ly/372HE96.
[11] International Court of Justice (ICJ), *Case Concerning Application of the Convention on the Prevention and Punishment of the Crime of Genocide (Bosnia and Herzegovina v. Serbia and Montenegro)*, Judgment, 26 February 2007, para. 193.
[12] Art. II, Convention on the Prevention and Punishment of the Crime of Genocide; adopted at Paris 9 December 1948; entered into force 12 January 1951 (hereinafter, 1948 Genocide Convention). As of 1 May 2021, 152 States were party to the 1948 Genocide Convention.
[13] R. Cryer, D. Robinson, and S. Vasiliev, *An Introduction to International Criminal Law and Procedure*, 4th ed., Cambridge University Press, Cambridge, 2019, p. 211. They endorse the approach by the International Criminal Tribunal for the former Yugoslavia (ICTY) in its judgment in the *Krstić* case whereby the four terms 'describe a single phenomenon, roughly corresponding to what was recognised, before the second world war, as "national minorities", rather than to refer to several distinct prototypes of human groups'. ICTY, *Prosecutor v. Krstić*, Judgment (Case No. IT-98-33-T; Trial Chamber), 2 August 2001, para. 556. To 'differentiate each of the named groups on the basis of scientifically objective criteria', the Trial Chamber went on to say, would be 'inconsistent with the object and purpose of the Convention', as evidenced by the travaux préparatoires. Ibid. See Cryer et al., *An Introduction to International Criminal Law and Procedure*, 4th ed., p. 222.
[14] UN doc. A/C.6/SR.75, 15 October 1948, at 115. See F. Martin, 'The Notion of "Protected Group" in the Genocide Convention and its Application', in P. Gaeta (ed.), *The UN Genocide Convention: A Commentary*, Oxford University Press, Oxford, 2009, p. 115.

consider a given group as a racial group, although it could not be denied classification as an ethnical group'.[15]

23.05 In the 1965 International Convention on the Elimination of All Forms of Racial Discrimination[16] (CERD), the term 'racial discrimination' is defined broadly as 'any distinction, exclusion, restriction or preference based on race, colour, descent, or national or ethnic origin which has the purpose or effect of nullifying or impairing ... human rights'.[17] In its order of provisional measures against Myanmar in January 2020 to prevent further atrocities against the Rohingya, the International Court of Justice referred to a 2016 report by the UN High Commissioner for Human Rights, which stated that Rohingya Muslims 'self-identify as a distinct ethnic group with their own language and culture, and claim a longstanding connection to Rakhine State'.[18] The case, which was ongoing as of writing, concerns the contention by The Gambia that Myanmar's military and security forces have been responsible for killings, rape and other forms of sexual violence, torture, beatings, cruel treatment, and the destruction of or denial of access to food, shelter, and other essentials of life, all with the intent to destroy the Rohingya group, in whole or in part.[19]

THE STATUS OF THE PROHIBITION ON RACIAL DISCRIMINATION UNDER INTERNATIONAL LAW

23.06 International human rights law, international humanitarian law, and refugee law, as well as international criminal law, all confirm the illegality of racial discrimination. The prohibition on racial discrimination is not only of a customary nature. In 2019, the Special Rapporteur of the International Law Commission (ILC) on peremptory norms of general international law (jus cogens) referred to 'ample State practice recognizing the prohibition of apartheid and racial discrimination as a peremptory norm of general international law'.[20]

---

[15] UN doc. A/C.6/SR.75, pp. 115–16.

[16] International Convention on the Elimination of All Forms of Racial Discrimination; adopted at New York 21 December 1965; entered into force 4 January 1969 (hereinafter, CERD). As of 1 May 2021, 182 States were party to CERD.

[17] Art. 1(1), CERD. In its General Recommendation XXIX of 2002, the CERD Committee reconfirmed its 'consistent' view that the term 'descent' in Article 1(1) of the Convention 'does not solely refer to "race" and has a meaning and application which complement the other prohibited grounds of discrimination'. It strongly reaffirmed that 'discrimination based on "descent" includes discrimination against members of communities based on forms of social stratification such as caste and analogous systems of inherited status which nullify or impair their equal enjoyment of human rights'. Committee on the Elimination of Racial Discrimination, 'General Recommendation XXIX on Article 1(1) of the Convention (Descent)', sixty-first session (2002), sixth and seventh preambular paras.

[18] International Court of Justice, *Application of the Convention on the Prevention and Punishment of the Crime of Genocide (The Gambia v. Myanmar)*, Order, 23 January 2020, para. 14, citing 'Situation of human rights of Rohingya Muslims and other minorities in Myanmar', UN doc. A/HRC/32/18, 29 June 2016, para. 3.

[19] International Court of Justice, '*Application of the Convention on the Prevention and Punishment of the Crime of Genocide (The Gambia v. Myanmar)*, Request for the indication of provisional measures', Summary 2020/1, 23 January 2020, at http://bit.ly/31apobM.

[20] 'Fourth report on peremptory norms of general international law (*jus cogens*) by Dire Tladi, Special Rapporteur', UN doc. A/CN.4/727, 31 January 2019, para. 94.

23.07 The jus cogens norm thus comprises the policy of apartheid, practised in Southern Africa from the late 1940s to the early 1990s,[21] and analogous practices. Thus the 1973 International Convention on the Suppression and Punishment of Apartheid defines *apartheid* broadly to include 'similar policies and practices of racial segregation and discrimination as practised in southern Africa'.[22] Prohibited acts include denial to a member or members of a racial group or groups of the right to life and the deliberate imposition on a racial group or groups of living conditions calculated to cause its or their physical destruction in whole or in part.[23] The ILC Special Rapporteur recalled that in 1984, the UN Security Council described apartheid and racial discrimination as 'a crime against the conscience and dignity of mankind' and as 'incompatible with the rights and dignity of man'.[24]

RACIALLY MOTIVATED KILLINGS UNDER GLOBAL STANDARDS

23.08 A racially motivated killing will often involve a violation of the right to life that engages the international responsibility of the State. This is certainly the case if a State agent is the perpetrator, at the least where the killing occurs outside the conduct of hostilities in an international armed conflict. Where racially motivated killings by State organs or agents are widespread, depending on the circumstances crimes against humanity and even acts of genocide may also have occurred. Where a private citizen kills a person with racial malice, if the State either failed to exercise due diligence to prevent the death[25] or if it subsequently fails to investigate the circumstances of the death and take the appropriate prosecutorial action, the victim's right to life will have been violated by the State.[26] To meet the demands of international law, an investigation into any potentially unlawful death must give due consideration to any suspected racial animus.[27]

23.09 Article 6(1) of the 1966 International Covenant on Civil and Political Rights[28] (ICCPR) decrees that the inherent right to life 'shall be protected by law' and that no one 'shall be arbitrarily deprived of his life'. According to the Human Rights Committee, this legal protection of the right to life 'must apply equally to all individuals and provide them with effective guarantees against all forms of discrimination'. As a consequence, any

---

[21] 'Apartheid', *History*, Updated 3 March 2020, at http://bit.ly/3ojq8MU.
[22] International Convention on the Suppression and Punishment of the Crime of Apartheid; adopted at New York 30 November 1973; entered into force 18 July 1976. As of 1 May 2021, 109 States were party to the Convention. See http://bit.ly/3k1daeo.
[23] Art. II, International Convention on the Suppression and Punishment of the Crime of Apartheid.
[24] UN Security Council Resolution 473, adopted by unanimous vote on 13 June 1980, para. 3.
[25] European Court of Human Rights, *Nachova v. Bulgaria*, Judgment (Grand Chamber), 6 July 2005, paras. 162–8; see also *B. S. v. Spain*, Judgment, 24 July 2012, paras. 58–9 and *X v. Turkey*, Judgment, 9 October 2012, para. 62.
[26] *The Minnesota Protocol on the Investigation of Potentially Unlawful Death* (2016), Office of the UN High Commissioner for Human Rights, New York/Geneva, 2017, para. 8(c).
[27] European Court of Human Rights, *Nachova v. Bulgaria*, Judgment (Grand Chamber), paras. 153, 161.
[28] International Covenant on Civil and Political Rights; adopted at New York 16 December 1966; entered into force 23 March 1976. As of 1 May 2021, 173 States were party to the ICCPR.

deprivation of life which is 'based on discrimination in law or fact is ipso facto arbitrary in nature'.[29]

23.10 CERD does not explicitly prohibit racially motivated killings. That said, such a prohibition must be taken as implicit given that States Parties are bound to adopt 'immediate and positive measures' to eradicate all acts of racial discrimination and must criminalise 'all acts of violence or incitement to such acts against any race or group of persons of another colour or ethnic origin'.[30]

23.11 The 1984 Convention against Torture defines the term 'torture' as encompassing any act by which severe, physical or mental pain or suffering is intentionally inflicted on a person 'for any reason based on discrimination of any kind'.[31] Paragraph 1 of Article 2 of the Convention obligates each State Party to take 'effective legislative, administrative, judicial or other measures to prevent acts of torture in any territory under its jurisdiction'. In its General Comment on the article, the Committee against Torture emphasised that 'the discriminatory use of mental or physical violence or abuse is an important factor in determining whether an act constitutes torture' and that the protection of minority individuals or populations, especially at risk of torture, is a part of the obligation to prevent torture or ill treatment.[32]

International Refugee Law

23.12 Under international refugee law, the risk of being killed on the basis of one's race may give rise to a right to asylum. According to the 1951 Refugee Convention, a refugee includes any person who, owing to a 'well-founded fear' of being persecuted for reason of race, is outside the country of his nationality and is unable or, owing to such fear, unwilling to avail himself of the protection of that country.[33] The broad meaning given to racial discrimination under CERD 'can be considered valid also for the purposes of the 1951 Convention'.[34] The 1951 Convention's 'notion of race includes not only persons at risk by reason of their membership in a particular racial category, but also other groups such as Jews and Roma defined by physical, linguistic,

---

[29] Human Rights Committee, 'General comment No. 36 (2018) on article 6 of the International Covenant on Civil and Political Rights, on the right to life', UN doc. CCPR/C/GC/36, 30 October 2018 (hereinafter, Human Rights Committee, General Comment No. 36), para. 61. The Human Rights Committee further avers that a 'particular connection' exists in the ICCPR between Articles 6 and Article 20, which prohibits any propaganda for war and certain forms of advocacy constituting incitement to discrimination, hostility, or violence. Ibid., para. 59.

[30] Art. 4(a), CERD.

[31] Art. 1(1), Convention against Torture and Other Cruel, Inhuman or Degrading Treatment or Punishment; adopted at New York 10 December 1984; entered into force 26 June 1987 (hereinafter, CAT). As of 1 May 2021, 171 States were party to CAT.

[32] Committee against Torture, General Comment No. 2: 'Implementation of article 2 by States parties', UN doc. CAT/C/GC/2, 24 January 2008, paras. 20 and 21.

[33] Art. 1(A)(2), Convention relating to the Status of Refugees; adopted at Geneva 28 July 1951; entered into force 22 April 1954 (hereinafter, 1951 Refugees Convention). As of 1 May 2021, 146 States were party to the 1951 Refugees Convention.

[34] G. Goodwin-Gill, *The Refugee in International Law*, 2nd ed., Clarendon Press, Oxford, 1996, p. 43.

or cultural distinctiveness'.[35] As Hathaway and Foster aver, a broad interpretation of race 'is not only historically defensible' but also 'consistent with the modern disavowal of race as a biological or scientific category, and the recognition that "race" is a socially constructed notion'.[36] For sure, persecution on the basis of race is 'all too frequently the background to refugee movements in all parts of the world'.[37]

International Humanitarian Law

23.13 International humanitarian law prohibits racial discrimination against any person who is in the power of the enemy, whether that occurs in the course of an international armed conflict or a non-international armed conflict. An unlawful killing of such a person in an armed conflict that occurred with racial animus would be subject to particular opprobrium. But in the conduct of hostilities in international armed conflict, the intentional killing of a lawful enemy military target (combatant or civilian participating directly in hostilities), even if it occurs as a direct result of racial hatred, would not amount to a violation of international humanitarian law.

23.14 Part II of the 1949 Geneva Convention IV[38] concerns the general protection of populations against certain consequences of war during international armed conflict. Therein, it is stipulated that the provisions, which are intended 'to alleviate the sufferings caused by war', cover 'the whole of the populations of the countries in conflict, without any adverse distinction based, in particular, on race'.[39] During a situation of foreign military occupation, all 'protected persons' who are civilians must be treated 'with the same consideration by the Party to the conflict in whose power they are, without any adverse distinction based, in particular, on race'.[40] Under the 1977 Additional Protocol I to the Geneva Conventions, persons in the power of a party to an international armed conflict 'and who do not benefit from more favourable treatment under the Conventions or under this Protocol shall be treated humanely in all circumstances and shall enjoy, as a minimum, the protection provided by this Article without any adverse distinction based upon race [or] colour'.[41]

23.15 In any non-international armed conflict, according to Article 3 common to the four Geneva Conventions, each party to the conflict must treat all those taking no active part in the hostilities 'humanely, without any adverse distinction founded on race [or] colour'.[42]

---

[35] J. C. Hathaway and M. Foster, *The Law of Refugee Status*, 2nd ed., Cambridge University Press, Cambridge, 2014, p. 394.
[36] Ibid., p. 395.
[37] Goodwin-Gill, *The Refugee in International Law*, 2nd ed., p. 43.
[38] Geneva Convention Relative to the Protection of Civilian Persons in Time of War; adopted at Geneva 12 August 1949; entered into force 21 October 1950 (hereinafter, Geneva Convention IV).
[39] Art. 13, Geneva Convention IV.
[40] Art. 27, Geneva Convention IV.
[41] Art. 75(1), Protocol Additional to the Geneva Conventions of 12 August 1949, and relating to the Protection of Victims of International Armed Conflicts (Protocol I); adopted at Geneva 8 June 1977; entered into force 7 December 1978.
[42] Art. 3, Geneva Convention IV.

In its 2016 commentary on the provision, the International Committee of the Red Cross (ICRC) stated: 'For persons falling within the protective scope of common Article 3, it makes no difference whether they are directly selected for inhumane treatment, or whether their inhumane treatment is the indirect consequence of general policies.'[43] In any non-international armed conflict within the scope of the 1977 Additional Protocol II, the provisions of the Protocol 'shall be applied without any adverse distinction founded on race [or] colour'.[44] A policy of targeting members of ethnic minorities, even where they are directly participating in hostilities and therefore lawful military targets under international humanitarian law, may be unlawful on the basis that it is an arbitrary deprivation of life.

Racially Motivated Killings under International Criminal Law

23.16 According to the 1948 Genocide Convention, as well as the 1998 Rome Statute of the International Criminal Court, and under customary law, the killing of members of a national, ethnical, racial, or religious group with intent to destroy that group, in whole or in part, constitutes genocide.[45] Crimes against humanity encompass murder and extermination when committed as part of a widespread or systematic attack directed against any civilian population, with knowledge of the attack.[46] The crime against humanity of persecution is laid down in Article 7(1)(h) of the Statute. The legal elements of this crime include that the perpetrator is severely deprived, contrary to international law, one or more persons of fundamental rights and that he or she targeted such person or persons by reasons of the identity of a group based, inter alia, on racial or ethnic grounds.[47] Thus, as the International Criminal Court has stated, persecution requires the targeting of a person on the basis of discriminatory grounds, noting that this 'materially distinct element also sets persecution apart from the underlying crimes against humanity'.[48]

23.17 With respect to any crimes under the jurisdiction of the International Criminal Court, the Court's Rules of Procedure and Evidence stipulate that in its determination of a sentence following conviction, an aggravating circumstance is where the crime was committed for any motive involving discrimination, including on grounds of race or colour.[49] In 2014, Germain Katanga was found guilty of being an accessory to the commission of 'very serious crimes under particularly cruel conditions and in

---

[43] ICRC Commentary on Article 3 of the 1949 Geneva Convention I, para. 573, at http://bit.ly/2FZaenV.
[44] Art. 2(1), Protocol additional to the Geneva Conventions of 12 August 1949, and relating to the protection of victims of non-international armed conflicts (Protocol II); adopted at Geneva 8 June 1977; entered into force 7 December 1978.
[45] Art. II, 1948 Genocide Convention; Art. 6(1), Rome Statute of the International Criminal Court; adopted at Rome 17 July 1998; entered into force 1 July 2002 (Rome Statute); ICTY, *Prosecutor v. Krstić*, Judgment (Case No. IT-98-33-T; Trial Chamber), para. 541.
[46] Art. 7, Rome Statute.
[47] ICC, *Elements of Crimes*, The Hague, 2011, p. 10, reproduced from *Official Records of the Assembly of States Parties to the Rome Statute of the International Criminal Court, First session, New York, 3–10 September 2002*.
[48] ICC, *Prosecutor v. Bosco Ntaganda*, Judgment (Case No. ICC-01/04-02/06) (Trial Chamber VI), 8 July 2019, para. 1206.
[49] ICC, *Rules of Procedure and Evidence*, 2nd ed., The Hague, 2013, Rule 145(2)(b)(v), read in conjunction with Art. 21(3), ICC Statute.

a discriminatory manner'. The crimes, which stemmed from an attack in February 2003 on civilians in Bogoro village in the east of the Democratic Republic of the Congo, were murder, both as a war crime and as a crime against humanity; attack against a civilian population as a war crime; and destruction and pillaging as a war crime.[50] Mr Katanga was initially sentenced by the International Criminal Court to a term of imprisonment of twelve years.[51]

RACIALLY MOTIVATED KILLINGS UNDER REGIONAL STANDARDS

Racially Motivated Killings under the European Convention on Human Rights

23.18 Article 2 of the 1950 European Convention on Human Rights[52] protects the right to life. Under Article 14, which concerns the prohibition of discrimination, enjoyment of the rights and freedoms set out in the Convention 'shall be secured without discrimination on any ground such as sex ... race, colour, ... national or social origin, association with a national minority'.[53] Article 14 'has no independent existence since it has effect solely in relation to the enjoyment of the rights and freedoms' safeguarded by the Convention.[54] As the European Court of Human Rights has explained, discrimination is 'treating differently, without an objective and reasonable justification, persons in relevantly similar situations'.[55] Racial discrimination, which includes discrimination on account of a person's ethnic origin, 'is a particularly invidious kind of discrimination and, in view of its perilous consequences, requires from the authorities special vigilance and a vigorous reaction'.[56]

23.19 A leading case on racially motivated killings is *Nachova and others v. Bulgaria*.[57] The Grand Chamber judgment in 2005 is a key decision on police use of force both for Bulgaria and across the region, but the case also concerned alleged racial discrimination.

---

[50] ICC, *Prosecutor v. Germain Katanga*, Decision on Sentence (Case No. ICC-01/04-01/07) (Trial Chamber II), 23 May 2014, para. 143.

[51] On 13 November 2015, after Mr Katanga had served two-thirds of his twelve-year sentence, a Panel of three Judges of the ICC Appeals Chamber reviewed the sentence and decided to reduce it by three years and eight months. ICC, 'Germain Katanga's Sentence Reduced and To Be Completed on 18 January 2016', press release no. ICC-CPI-20151113-PR1174, 13 November 2015, at http://bit.ly/2Tzary8. In March 2019, however, three years after the designated date for his release by the ICC, he was in a Congolese jail, with his trial by a Congolese military court on charges additional to those for which he was convicted in The Hague having 'stalled'. W. Wakabi, 'Defense Lawyer Asks ICC Judges to Stop Katanga's Trial in DRC', *International Justice Monitor*, 1 March 2019, at http://bit.ly/35YCucB.

[52] Convention for the Protection of Human Rights and Fundamental Freedoms; adopted at Rome 4 November 1950; entered into force 3 September 1953.

[53] Art. 14, ECHR.

[54] European Court of Human Rights, *Molla Sali v. Greece*, Judgment (Merits) (Grand Chamber), 19 December 2018, para. 123.

[55] European Court of Human Rights, *Mižigárová v. Slovakia*, Judgment (Merits and Just Satisfaction; Fourth Section), 14 December 2010, para. 114.

[56] Ibid.

[57] European Court of Human Rights, *Nachova and others v. Bulgaria*, Judgment (Grand Chamber), 6 July 2005, para. 55.

The Court referred to the Council of Europe's European Commission against Racism and Intolerance, which had expressed concern regarding racially motivated police violence, particularly against Roma, in a number of European countries, including Bulgaria. It cited testimony by a neighbour of one of the victims, who reported that a senior police officer had shouted at him, immediately after the shooting had occurred, 'You damn Gypsies!' But, the Court held, 'while such evidence of a racial slur being uttered in connection with a violent act should have led the authorities in this case to verify Mr M. M.'s statement, that statement is in itself an insufficient basis for concluding that the respondent State is liable for a racist killing'.[58]

23.20 That said, the Court did conclude that

> the authorities' duty to investigate the existence of a possible link between racist attitudes and an act of violence is an aspect of their procedural obligations arising under Article 2 of the Convention, but may also be seen as implicit in their responsibilities under Article 14 of the Convention taken in conjunction with Article 2 to secure the enjoyment of the right to life without discrimination.[59]

The Grand Chamber further considered that

> any evidence of racist verbal abuse being uttered by law enforcement agents in connection with an operation involving the use of force against persons from an ethnic or other minority is highly relevant to the question whether or not unlawful, hatred-induced violence has taken place. Where such evidence comes to light in the investigation, it must be verified and – if confirmed – a thorough examination of all the facts should be undertaken in order to uncover any possible racist motives.[60]

23.21 In practice, of course, as the Court explicitly noted in its 2014 judgment in *Abdu v. Bulgaria*, 'it is often extremely difficult to prove racist motivation'. Accordingly, the level of obligation on the State to investigate possible racist overtones to an act of violence is one of means rather than of result. Thus 'the authorities must take all reasonable measures having regard to the circumstances of the case'.[61] Further in its judgment, the Court criticised the prosecuting authorities in Bulgaria for concentrating their investigations on whether Mr Abdu and his friend (another Sudanese man) or two Bulgarian youths had started a fight. They did not question an eyewitness on any exchanges he might have heard during the fight or question the two youths about any possible racist motivation for their acts. 'Yet right from the beginning of the investigation the applicant had claimed that he suffered racist insults, and the police report described the two Bulgarians as skinheads, well-known for their extremist, racist ideology.'[62]

---

[58] Ibid., para. 153.
[59] Ibid., para. 161.
[60] Ibid., para. 153.
[61] European Court of Human Rights, *Abdu v. Bulgaria*, Judgment (Merits and Just Satisfaction; Fourth Section), 11 March 2014, para. 45.
[62] Ibid., para. 49.

Racially Motivated Killings under the American Convention on Human Rights

23.22 According to the 1969 American Convention on Human Rights: 'Every person has the right to have his life respected. This right shall be protected by law and, in general, from the moment of conception. No one shall be arbitrarily deprived of his life.'[63] By virtue of Article 1(1) of the Convention, States Parties undertake to respect the rights and freedoms recognised therein and 'to ensure to all persons subject to their jurisdiction the free and full exercise of those rights and freedoms, without any discrimination for reasons of race [or] color'. In its 1993 judgment in the *Aloeboetoe* case, the Inter-American Court of Human Rights held that a racial motive for killings of members of the Saramaka tribe by agents of the Republic of Suriname, which had previously been put forward by the Inter-American Commission, had 'not been duly proved'.[64] While acknowledging that the victims of the killings by soldiers all belonged to the Saramaka tribe, the Court held that 'this circumstance of itself does not lead to the conclusion that there was a racial element to the crime'.[65]

23.23 Under the 1994 Inter-American Convention to Prevent, Punish and Eradicate Violence against Women, States Parties are obligated to 'take special account of the vulnerability of women to violence by reason of among others, their race or ethnic background'.[66] In September 2019, the Inter-American Commission on Human Rights condemned 'the prevalence of murders and other forms of violence against Garifuna women in Honduras, due to their gender and ethno-racial origin'.[67] The Commission called on the authorities to 'eradicate the structural causes that accentuate discrimination and violence against women, particularly those who belong to Afro-descendant ... and indigenous communities'.[68]

Racially Motivated Killings under African Human Rights Standards

23.24 The African Charter on Human and Peoples' Rights (the 'Banjul Charter') enshrines the right to life for 'every human being' as follows: 'Human beings are inviolable. Every human being shall be entitled to respect for his life and the integrity of his person. No one may be arbitrarily deprived of this right.'[69] In its General Comment on the right to

---

[63] Art. 4(1), American Convention on Human Rights; adopted at San José 22 November 1969; entered into force 18 July 1978.
[64] Inter-American Court of Human Rights, *Aloeboetoe and others* case, Judgment (Reparations), 10 September 1993, para. 84.
[65] Ibid., para. 82.
[66] Art. 9, Inter-American Convention on the Prevention, Punishment, and Eradication of Violence against Women; adopted at Belém do Pará, Brazil, 9 June 1994; entered into force 5 March 1995 (hereinafter, Belém do Pará Convention).
[67] Inter-American Commission on Human Rights, 'IACHR Condemns the Prevalence of Murders and Other Forms of Violence against Garifuna Women in Honduras', press release no. 238/19, 24 September 2019, at http://bit.ly/2R3klGE.
[68] Ibid.
[69] Art. 4(1), African Charter on Human and Peoples' Rights; adopted at Nairobi 27 June 1981; entered into force 21 October 1986.

Racially Motivated Killings

life under the Banjul Charter, the African Commission on Human and Peoples' Rights stated: 'Any deprivation of life resulting from a violation of the procedural or substantive safeguards in the African Charter, including on the basis of discriminatory grounds or practices, is arbitrary and as a result unlawful.'[70]

Racially Motivated Killings under the Arab Charter on Human Rights

23.25 The 2004 Arab Charter on Human Rights[71] has a general provision enshrining the protection of the right to life. Under Article 5(1), 'every human being has an inherent right to life'. Paragraph 2 stipulates further: 'This right shall be protected by law. No one shall be arbitrarily deprived of his life.' No derogation from Article 5 may be made.[72] Under Article 3(1) of the Charter, each State Party 'undertakes to ensure to all individuals within its territory and subject to its jurisdiction the right to enjoy all the rights and freedoms' recognised therein, without any distinction on grounds of race or colour.

THE ACTIONS OF LAW ENFORCEMENT PERSONNEL

The Normative Framework

23.26 Law enforcement personnel are obligated to respect fundamental human rights, including the right to life. Article 2 of the 1979 UN Code of Conduct for Law Enforcement Officials[73] stipulates that in 'the performance of their duty, law enforcement officials shall respect and protect human dignity and maintain and uphold the human rights of all persons'. The official commentary on this provision holds that among the relevant international instruments are the ICCPR and CERD. In its General Recommendation XIII on the training of law enforcement officials in the protection of human rights, the Committee on the Elimination of Racial Discrimination stated that compliance by States Parties with their obligations under CERD to refrain from racial discrimination and to ensure the right to security of person and protection by the State against violence or bodily harm 'very much depends upon national law enforcement officials who exercise police powers'.[74] The Committee called on States Parties to review and improve the training of law enforcement officials so that the standards of the Convention as well as the 1979 UN Code of Conduct 'are fully implemented'.[75]

---

[70] African Commission on Human and Peoples' Rights, 'General Comment No. 3 on the African Charter on Human and Peoples' Rights: The Right to Life (Article 4)', adopted at Banjul (57th Ordinary Session), November 2015 (hereinafter, African Commission General Comment on the right to life), para. 12.
[71] Arab Charter on Human Rights; adopted at Tunis 22 May 2004; entered into force 15 March 2008.
[72] Art. 4(2), 2004 Arab Charter on Human Rights.
[73] Code of Conduct for Law Enforcement Officials; adopted at New York by UN General Assembly Resolution 34/169 (resolution adopted without a vote on 17 December 1979; hereinafter, 1979 UN Code of Conduct).
[74] Committee on the Elimination of Racial Discrimination, General Recommendation XIII on the training of law enforcement officials in the protection of human rights, adopted at the forty-second session (1993), paras. 1 and 2.
[75] Ibid., para. 3.

23.27 As Chapter 7 observed, force exercised as a result of overt ethnic discrimination on the part of a law enforcement official will constitute a serious violation of the principle of necessity. The European Court of Human Rights has long held that any recourse to physical force which has not been made strictly necessary by a person's own conduct diminishes human dignity and is, in principle, a violation of the right to freedom from torture and inhuman or degrading treatment.[76]

State Practice

23.28 Where racial discrimination is prevalent in any society, one may expect to find instances of racially motivated killings among law enforcement personnel. In 2018, the Inter-American Commission on Human Rights published a report entitled *African Americans, Police Use of Force, and Human Rights in the United States*.[77] The Commission has stated on a number of occasions that police shootings of unarmed African Americans represent 'a disturbing pattern of excessive force on the part of police officers towards African Americans and other persons of color'.[78] Such acts spurred the creation of the civil society 'Black Lives Matter' movement within the United States.[79] In its 2018 report, the Inter-American Commission found 'a pattern of discriminatory and excessive use of force by police against African Americans' and concluded 'that this pattern places the United States in violation of its obligation under international law to protect the rights to life, personal integrity, and equality before the law'.[80] In its list of issues for inclusion in the United States' fifth periodic report under the ICCPR, published in April 2019, the Human Rights Committee asked the US government to indicate the steps it is taking 'to limit excessive use of force by law enforcement officials against civilians, particularly those belonging to racial minorities'.[81]

23.29 In 2015, the city of Chicago agreed to pay US$5.5 million in reparations to fifty-seven victims of Jon Burge, a commander in the city's police force. Officer Burge had led a group of detectives accused of torturing more than one hundred suspects, mostly African Americans but also some Hispanics, between 1972 and 1991, in order to extract confessions. His alleged victims were shocked with cattle prods, smothered with typewriter covers, and had guns shoved in their mouths. Mr Burge was dismissed in 1993 and sentenced to prison

---

[76] European Court of Human Rights, *Bouyid v. Belgium*, Judgment (Grand Chamber), 28 September 2015, paras. 88, 100.
[77] Inter-American Commission on Human Rights, *African Americans, Police Use of Force, and Human Rights in the United States*, report approved by the Commission on 26 November 2018, Washington, DC.
[78] Ibid., p. 47.
[79] See https://blacklivesmatter.com/. 'The Black Lives Matter Global Network is a chapter-based, member-led organization whose mission is to build local power and to intervene in violence inflicted on Black communities by the state and vigilantes.' 'About', at http://bit.ly/2ErlVeT.
[80] Inter-American Commission on Human Rights, *African Americans, Police Use of Force, and Human Rights in the United States*, para. 310.
[81] Human Rights Committee, 'List of issues prior to submission of the fifth periodic report of the United States of America', UN doc. CCPR/C/USA/QPR/5, 18 April 2019, para. 14.

in 2011 for lying in a civil case about his actions, though statutes of limitations precluded criminal charges for the alleged torture.[82]

23.30 In 2017, the Civil Rights Division of the US Department of Justice published a report on the Chicago Police Department (CPD) finding 'numerous incidents where CPD officers chased and shot fleeing persons who posed no immediate threat to officers or the public. Such actions are constitutionally impermissible'.[83] While not all of these cases involved racial discrimination, between January 2011 and 18 April 2016, black individuals were the subject of 80 per cent of all CPD firearm uses.[84] The CPD's 'pattern or practice of unreasonable force and systemic deficiencies', the report found, 'falls heaviest on the predominantly black and Latino neighborhoods on the South and West Sides of Chicago, which are also experiencing higher crime'.[85] The Department of Justice cited the example of one CPD officer who posted photographs on social media of two slain black men, in the front seats of a car, bloodied, covered in glass, accompanied by the statement, 'Hopefully one of these pictures will make the black lives matter activist organization feel a whole lot better!'[86]

23.31 In January 2019, Jason Van Dyke, a former Chicago police officer who had shot and killed black teenager Laquan McDonald while on duty in 2014, was sentenced to six years and nine months in prison for his actions. The police officer was convicted in October 2018 of second-degree murder and sixteen counts of aggravated battery with a firearm. Officer Van Dyke, who fired sixteen shots in fifteen seconds, had argued he had acted in self-defence after Mr McDonald had lunged at him with a knife. But footage from a police dashcam showed Mr McDonald walking away from police when he was shot.[87]

23.32 Frustrations among African Americans at seemingly systemic racially aggravated use of force and harassment by law enforcement personnel boiled over following the killing of George Floyd on 25 May 2020 in Minneapolis. Mobile phone footage of the arrest showed a white police officer, Derek Chauvin, kneeling on Mr Floyd's neck while he was pinned to the ground. Officer Chauvin, age forty-four, was subsequently charged with murder and was convicted at trial in Minneapolis. Transcripts of police bodycam footage show that Mr Floyd said more than twenty times he could not breathe as he was restrained by four officers.[88] There were demonstrations against racially motivated police brutality all across

---

[82] Associated Press, 'Ex-Chicago Police Commander Linked to Torture of More Than 100 Suspects Dies', *The Guardian*, 20 September 2018, at http://bit.ly/3oxmUn8.

[83] US Department of Justice Civil Rights Division and US Attorney's Office Northern District of Illinois, *Investigation of the Chicago Police Department*, Washington, DC, 13 January 2017, p. 25.

[84] Ibid., p. 145.

[85] Ibid., p. 144. In an article published in early 2020, a US anthropologist claimed that police torture in Chicago has been transformed through legal precedent, activism, and resulting legislation to emerge as a medical condition. L. Ralph, 'Torture without Torturers', *Current Anthropology*, vol. 61, no. 21 (February 2020), at http://bit.ly/2R4KXXH.

[86] US Department of Justice Civil Rights Division and US Attorney's Office Northern District of Illinois, *Investigation of the Chicago Police Department*, p. 147.

[87] N. Chavez, D. Andone, and M. Baldacci, 'Former Chicago Officer Jason Van Dyke Sentenced to 81 Months for Fatally Shooting Laquan McDonald', CNN, 19 January 2019, at http://cnn.it/2ZSlTp7.

[88] BBC News, 'George Floyd: What Happened in the Final Moments of His Life', 16 July 2020, at http://bbc.in/2XjO2WB.

the United States – in all fifty states and the District of Columbia – including in cities and rural communities that are predominantly white. A poll for the media outlet ABC suggested that three quarters of Americans felt that the killing of Mr Floyd was part of a broader problem with how African Americans are treated by police.[89] In addition, across 260 cities and towns in the United Kingdom, thousands defied COVID-19 related lockdowns to join the largest anti-racism rallies since the slavery era.[90] Speaking during an urgent debate in the UN Human Rights Council on racism and excessive use of force in policing on 17 June 2020, UN High Commissioner for Human Rights Michelle Bachelet said, 'Too little has changed over too many years.'[91]

ROMA

Context

23.33 The Romani, better known as Roma, are an Indo-Aryan ethnic group. A genomic study completed in 2012 indicated that the Roma came from a single group that left northwestern India about 1,500 years ago.[92] In 2016, India's Minister for External Affairs said that the Roma were 'India's children'.[93] Today, the Roma live mostly in Europe and the Americas and are traditionally itinerant; numbering some eleven million, the Roma are Europe's largest minority.[94] As noted previously, during the Second World War, the Nazis sought to exterminate Roma across Europe. The *Porajmos*, as the Roma term it, was one of the largest mass killings in history, with hundreds of thousands murdered as a result of the 'racial' threat they were deemed to pose to Aryan blood.[95]

The Normative Framework

23.34 In its General Recommendation XXVII on discrimination against Roma, the Committee on the Elimination of Racial Discrimination called on States Parties to CERD to take measures to prevent the use of illegal force by the police against Roma, in particular in connection with arrest and detention.[96] They further encouraged the recruitment of members of Roma communities into police and other law enforcement

---

[89] H. Cheung, 'George Floyd Death: Why US Protests Are So Powerful This Time', BBC News, 8 June 2020, at http://bbc.in/39Tjy2M.
[90] A. Mohdin and G. Swann, 'How George Floyd's Death Sparked a Wave of UK Anti-racism Protests', *The Guardian*, 29 July 2020, at http://bit.ly/2DllzZg.
[91] UN News, '"I Am My Brother's Keeper", Philonise Floyd Tells UN Rights Body, in Impassioned Plea for Racial Justice', 16 June 2020, at http://bit.ly/2Dc4eSG.
[92] S. N. Bhanoo, 'Genomic Study Traces Roma to Northern India', *New York Times*, 10 December 2012, at http://nyti.ms/2v3flcr.
[93] Indo-Asian News Service, 'Romas Are India's Children: Sushma Swaraj', India.com, 12 February 2016, at http://bit.ly/2R3A1tk.
[94] Bhanoo, 'Genomic Study Traces Roma to Northern India'.
[95] See generally I. Hancock, 'Romanies and the Holocaust: A Re-evaluation and Overview', chap. 17 in D. Stone (ed.), *The Historiography of the Holocaust*, Palgrave Macmillan, London, 2004, pp. 383–96.
[96] Committee on the Elimination of Racial Discrimination, 'General Recommendation XXVII on discrimination against Roma', adopted at its fifty-seventh session (2000), para. 13.

agencies.[97] With respect to the duty to 'ensure protection of the security and integrity of Roma', the Committee called simply for measures to be adopted to prevent racially motivated acts of violence against them.[98] Within Europe, however, the European Court of Human Rights has held that the Roma require special protection because 'as a result of their turbulent history and constant uprooting the Roma have become a specific type of disadvantaged and vulnerable minority'.[99]

State Practice

23.35 Roma have continued to be subject to widespread racial discrimination.[100] In a number of European countries, Roma are at particular risk of being killed or seriously injured, both at the hands of law enforcement officials and from members of the general public. The *Lăcătuş and others* case[101] concerned an attack on Roma homes in a village in September 1993 by a mob of villagers and the local police, during which the applicants' partner and father were beaten to death. In a bar, three Roma (two brothers and another man) had begun to argue with a non-Rom. The verbal confrontation became physical and ended with the death of Cheţan Crăciun, who had come to the aid of his father. The three Roma fled the scene and sought refuge in a neighbour's house. An angry crowd arrived at the house and demanded they come out. Among the crowd were members of the local police force, including the chief of police and a sergeant. When the brothers refused to come out, the crowd set fire to the house. As the fire engulfed the house, they tried to flee but were caught by the mob, who beat and kicked them with stakes and clubs; they both died later that evening. The third Roma man remained in the house, where he died in the fire. It appears that the police officers present at the scene did nothing to stop the attacks.

23.36 The *Moldovan and others* case[102] originated from the same facts. Again, the applicants were Romanian nationals of Roma origin.[103] The applicants alleged that after the deaths the police encouraged the crowd to destroy other Roma properties: in total, thirteen Roma houses in the village were completely destroyed. Hounded from their village and homes, the applicants were obliged to live in cellars, hen houses, and stables. Following

---

[97] Ibid., para. 15.
[98] Ibid., para. 12.
[99] European Court of Human Rights, *D. H. and others v. Czech Republic*, Judgment (Grand Chamber), 13 November 2007, para. 182.
[100] Writing in a British newspaper in 2016, a Roma activist and a Roma filmmaker said: 'What is most painful about being a Roma today is that often people do not see anything wrong in insulting us. When Roma go to the police with complaints of violence or harassment they often say these complaints are not taken seriously enough. Abusing other ethnic minorities is rightly seen as racist and is not tolerated, but abusing Roma is often seen as acceptable.' K. Barsony and D. J. LeBas, 'Before You Make Another Offhand Remark about Roma and Travellers in the UK, We'd Like to Tell You This', *The Independent*, 2 August 2016, at http://bit.ly/3an3WEn.
[101] European Court of Human Rights, *Lăcătuş and others v. Romania*, Judgment (Third Section), 13 November 2012.
[102] European Court of Human Rights, *Moldovan and others v. Romania*, Judgment No. 2 (Former Second Section), 12 July 2005.
[103] Ibid., paras. 17–19.

criminal complaints brought by the applicants, some were awarded damages ten years later. While the Court could not examine the applicants' complaints about the destruction of their houses and possessions or their expulsion from the village, because those events took place before Romania's adherence to the European Convention on Human Rights in June 1994, it found violations concerning the complaints about the applicants' subsequent living conditions and noted that the applicants' ethnicity had been decisive in the excessive length and result of the domestic proceedings.[104]

23.37 The *Guerdner* case[105] concerned the shooting to death of a twenty-six-year-old Roma man during his flight from police custody in France in May 2008. On 18 August 2009, an investigating magistrate issued a dismissal order against the *gendarme* who had fired the fatal shots:

> The use of weapons was at that time the only means available to the gendarme to stop the flight of Joseph Guerdner and prevent his escape.
> Although the death of a man must be regretted and one must sympathise with his family's pain, it appears that all the conditions for the use of weapons were met in this case (clear case of flight, prior commission of a criminal offence, warning, and impossibility of otherwise detaining the fugitive).[106]

Following an appeal, the *gendarme* was charged with the crime of violence leading to unintended death but was ultimately acquitted, as he was deemed to have followed the laws and rules in force at the time in France.[107]

23.38 The European Court, however, found that 'it was clear from the circumstances of the case that the latter was unarmed and that, hindered [by being handcuffed], he could hardly have posed an immediate threat to the life or physical integrity of others'.[108] Moreover, the Court was of the view that given the presence of a number of *gendarmes* when Mr Guerdner fled, a chase was a viable option instead of the resort to potentially lethal force.[109] The Court did not suggest, though, that the *gendarme* had opened fire out of racial malice. In considering whether the investigation into his death met international legal standards, the Court was also not persuaded by the applicants' claim that the judicial authorities had conducted first the investigation and then the trial with hostility towards travellers, the community of which Joseph Guerdner was a member.[110]

23.39 Racial enmity was also alleged to be behind the non-fatal shooting of a Roma by the Bulgarian police in 1999. Vasil Sashov Petrov was believed by two police officers to have been stealing hens and in the course of a night-time chase he was fired upon and hit once. The Court determined that the facts should be examined under the protection of the right to life under the European Convention even though it accepted that the officers had not

---

[104] European Court of Human Rights, 'Roma and Travellers', Fact Sheet, April 2019, p. 2.
[105] European Court of Human Rights, *Guerdner v. France*, Judgment (Fifth Section), 17 April 2014.
[106] Ibid., para. 30.
[107] Ibid., paras. 31–3.
[108] Ibid., para. 71.
[109] Ibid., para. 72.
[110] Ibid., para. 85.

intended to kill him. In reaching its decision, the Court noted that at least one of the officers fired directly at the applicant, seemingly from only four metres away, and said that it could not 'overlook' the fact that the applicant had suffered 'a serious and, albeit temporarily, life-threatening injury'. Also of relevance was the fact that when the officers took the applicant to the hospital, they did not mention to the doctor who took charge of him that they had used firearms against the patient. This seemingly contributed to the doctor failing to realise that the wound had been caused by a firearm, which significantly increased the risk to the applicant's life.[111]

23.40 With respect to the decision to open fire, the Court reiterated that

> the legitimate aim of effecting a lawful arrest can only justify putting human life at risk in circumstances of absolute necessity; there is no such necessity where it is known that the person to be arrested poses no threat to life or limb and is not suspected of having committed a violent offence, even if a failure to use lethal force may result in the opportunity to arrest the fugitive being lost.[112]

While the officers could have reasonably suspected that the applicant had committed an offence, it was never alleged that they had reason to believe that the offence involved violence, that the suspect was dangerous, or that if not arrested he would represent a danger to them or third parties.[113] Moreover, the available evidence – chiefly the medical experts' findings that the applicant was shot from the front at a short distance and was intoxicated – suggested that the officers could have arrested him without using their firearms.[114]

23.41 But while Mr Petrov's right to life had been violated by the excessive use of force against him, he also alleged that the police had chosen to do so on account of his ethnic origin, bringing also into play Article 14 of the European Convention.[115] The Court, though, found that the available evidence in the present case suggested that the officers were not aware he was a Rom when they fired at him. However, even if they had been so aware, the Court believed it was 'not possible to speculate on whether or not that had any bearing on their perception of the applicant and their decision to use firearms'. Given the permissive nature of Bulgarian law at the time, the two officers might have acted as they did 'regardless of the ethnicity of the person concerned'. Moreover, the Court stated, 'there is no indication, and it has not been alleged by the applicant, either before the domestic authorities or before the Court, that the officers uttered racial slurs at any point during the events in question'.[116] The Court held that it had not been established that racist attitudes played a role in events leading up to the shooting of the applicant.[117]

---

[111] European Court of Human Rights, *Vasil Sashov Petrov v. Bulgaria*, Judgment (Fifth Section), 10 June 2010, para. 40.
[112] Ibid., para. 45.
[113] Ibid., para. 48.
[114] Ibid., para. 49.
[115] Ibid., para. 63.
[116] Ibid., para. 69.
[117] Ibid., para. 70.

KURDS

Context

23.42 The Kurds are an Iranian ethnic group native to a mountainous region of Western Asia known as Kurdistan, which spans the north-west of Iran, the south-east of Turkey, northern Iraq, northern Syria, and south-western Armenia. Between twenty-five and thirty-five million Kurds constitute the fourth-largest ethnic group in the Middle East, but they have never obtained statehood even though, after the defeat of the Ottoman Empire in the First World War, the victorious Western allies had made provision for a Kurdish State in the 1920 Treaty of Sevres. Kurds adhere to a number of different religions and creeds, although the majority are Sunni Muslims.[118]

The Normative Framework

23.43 The human rights of Kurds, especially in Iraq and in Turkey, have been forcibly repressed in many instances. Indeed, it is asserted that discriminatory violence against Kurds in Turkey has become normalised through 'decades of State policy that denied the existence of a distinctive Kurdish identity ... combined with limitations on political participation and a crackdown on freedom of association'.[119] Despite holding Turkey responsible for violations of the rights to life and to freedom from torture in relation to the treatment of its Kurdish minority, the European Court of Human Rights has come in for heavy criticism for 'failing to take effective action' to stem widespread violations and abuses.[120] Dilek Kurban argued that, in particular, the Court 'could have done more in cases of right to life and torture, a trend that deepened as the ECHR's oversight of State violence and infringements of minority rights in Turkey grew'.[121]

23.44 One issue has been whether international humanitarian law is applicable. Turkey has always denied that any armed conflict has occurred on its territory, despite the facts on the ground in the south-east of the country indicating otherwise since at the least the 1990s and arguably the mid-1980s.[122] In earlier case-law, the European Court typically skirted the issue, referring instead to 'serious disturbances [which] have raged in the south-east of Turkey between the security forces and the members of the PKK (Workers' Party of Kurdistan)'.[123]

23.45 In its 2004 judgment in the *Ahmet Özkan* case, however, the Court observed: 'Since approximately 1985, serious disturbances have occurred in the south-east of Turkey, involving

---

[118] BBC, 'Who Are the Kurds?', 15 October 2019, at http://bbc.in/2GeEp2B.
[119] K. Yildiz and S. Breau, *The Kurdish Conflict: International Humanitarian Law and Post-Conflict Mechanisms*, 1st ed., Routledge, Abingdon, 2010, p. 16.
[120] DEMTUREUROPE Project, 'The ECHR and Human Rights Violations against Kurds in Turkey', 9 October 2018, at http://bit.ly/3ohZKTg.
[121] Ibid.
[122] See, e.g., International Committee of the Red Cross (ICRC), *The Use of Force in Armed Conflicts: Interplay between the Conduct of Hostilities and Law Enforcement Paradigms*, Expert Meeting, Geneva, 2013, p. 76.
[123] European Court of Human Rights, *Menteş v. Turkey*, Judgment (Grand Chamber), 28 November 1997, para. 12.

armed conflict between the security forces and members of the PKK.'[124] But despite this finding it did not address, at least not directly, the application of international humanitarian law. This is so, even though the applicants had alleged that the military operation on 20 February 1993 had been conducted to terrorise and humiliate the population of Ormanıçı and noting that 'collective punishment was an inhuman form of punishment proscribed even under the law of armed conflict'.[125] The Court spoke more ambiguously of the 'callous disregard displayed by the security forces as to the possible presence of civilian casualties', which, it held, 'amounted to a breach of the Turkish authorities' obligation to protect life under Article 2 of the Convention'.[126]

23.46 In its 2013 judgment in the *Benzer* case, the Court went a step further, directly applying international humanitarian law rules to the bombing by aircraft belonging to the Turkish military of two Kurdish villages in the south-east of the country in March 1994. As a result of the bombing, thirteen people in Koçağili village and twenty-five people in Kuşkonar village lost their lives. Most of the dead were children, women, or the elderly.[127] The Court observed that the Government had limited their submissions to denying that the applicants' villages were bombed by aircraft, and had not sought to justify the killings under Article 2(2) of the European Convention. In any event, the Court said, 'an indiscriminate aerial bombardment of civilians and their villages ... cannot be reconcilable with ... the customary rules of international humanitarian law'.[128]

23.47 The Court held that the attacks had violated the right to life of those killed by the bombing, as well as those severely injured but who survived (which included three of the applicants).[129] The attack that caused those three applicants' injuries was, the Court declared, 'so violent and caused the indiscriminate deaths of so many people that these three applicants' fortuitous survival does not mean that their lives had not been put at risk'. The Court was thus satisfied that the risks posed by the attack to these three applicants called for an examination of their complaints under Article 2 of the Convention protecting the right to life.[130]

23.48 Outside areas of the conduct of hostilities, the use of force by the security forces will be regulated by law enforcement rules. This is especially the case in the context of assemblies, even if they include acts of violence by some of the participants.[131] Thus, in its 1998 judgment

---

[124] European Court of Human Rights, *Ahmet Özkan v. Turkey*, Judgment (Second Section), 6 April 2004, para. 85.
[125] Ibid., para. 332.
[126] Ibid., para. 308. See similarly, European Court of Human Rights, *Akkum and others v. Turkey*, Judgment (First Section), 24 March 2005, para. 252.
[127] European Court of Human Rights, *Benzer v. Turkey*, Judgment (Former Second Section), 12 November 2013, para. 11.
[128] Ibid., para. 184.
[129] Ibid., para. 185.
[130] Ibid., para. 143.
[131] This approach is consistent with the Human Rights Committee's latest General Comment on the right of peaceful assembly under the ICCPR: 'In a situation of armed conflict, the use of force during peaceful assemblies remains regulated by the rules governing law enforcement and the Covenant continues to apply.' Human Rights Committee, General Comment No. 37: Article 21: right of peaceful assembly, UN doc. CCPR/C/GC/37, 17 September 2020, para. 97.

in the *Güleç* case, which concerned Turkish security forces firing live rounds into groups of protesters, some of whom were engaged in serious acts of violence, a chamber of the Court deemed the lack of availability of an alternative to firearms 'unacceptable'. The Court found the failure to equip *gendarmes* with truncheons, riot shields, water cannon, rubber bullets, or tear gas 'all the more incomprehensible and unacceptable because the province of Şırnak, as the Government pointed out, is in a region in which a state of emergency has been declared, where at the material time disorder could have been expected'.[132]

State Practice

23.49 Attacks against Kurds in Turkey have originated both in the actions of State agents and by private citizens. The *Yaşa* case concerned the death of Mr Haşim Yaşa, who was killed on 14 June 1993. Mr Eşref Yaşa, the deceased's nephew, was the applicant who complained that they had both been victims of armed attacks because they sold the pro-Kurdish newspaper *Özgür Gündem*. 'The attacks were part of a campaign orchestrated against that and other newspapers with the connivance or even the direct participation of State agents', according to the application to the European Court.[133] The government maintained that no evidence existed to support the applicant's contention that members of the security forces were responsible for the attacks on him and his uncle.[134]

23.50 The European Commission on Human Rights had determined that it had not been proven beyond reasonable doubt that agents of the security forces or police were involved in the shooting of either the applicant or his uncle. But it did find that the government had been or should have been aware that those involved in its publication and distribution feared they were falling victim to a concerted campaign that was 'tolerated, if not approved, by State agents'.[135] The Commission considered that the right to life had been violated only in that the authorities had failed to carry out an adequate criminal investigation into the facts of the case.[136]

23.51 Before the Court, the applicant asked the Court to follow the Commission's opinion that there had been a procedural violation of the right to life but also to find a substantive violation on the basis that the assault he had suffered and his uncle's murder had been carried out by State agents.[137] He had hoped that the production to the Court of a report produced for the Turkish Prime Minister's Office would be sufficient to tip the balance in his favour. The report analysed 'a series of events, such as murders carried out under orders, the killings of well-known figures or supporters of the Kurds and deliberate acts by a group of "informants" supposedly serving the State'.[138] Instead, the Court considered that 'notwithstanding the serious concerns to which it gives rise', the report did not enable the

---

[132] European Court of Human Rights, *Güleç* v. *Turkey*, Judgment (Chamber), 27 July 1998, para. 71.
[133] European Court of Human Rights, *Yaşa* v. *Turkey*, Judgment (Chamber), 2 September 1998, paras. 6 and 7.
[134] Ibid., para. 30.
[135] Ibid., para. 34.
[136] Ibid., para. 81.
[137] Ibid., para. 82.
[138] Ibid., para. 46.

perpetrators of the attacks on the applicant and his uncle 'to be identified with sufficient precision'.[139]

23.52 With respect to the duty to investigate, the Court took into account the fact that the prevailing climate at the time in that region of Turkey might have impeded the search for conclusive evidence in the domestic criminal proceedings. Nonetheless, the Court said, 'circumstances of that nature cannot relieve the authorities of their obligations under Article 2 to carry out an investigation, as otherwise that would exacerbate still further the climate of impunity and insecurity in the region and thus create a vicious circle'.[140] In addition, the Court was 'struck' by the apparent exclusion from the outset the possibility that State agents might have been implicated in the attacks.[141] Given the circumstances in which allegations of harassment and violence of those involved in the Kurdish newspaper were being made, it was 'incumbent' on the authorities to consider whether State agents 'may have been implicated in the attacks'.[142]

23.53 In any event, a failure to investigate effectively alleged violence against Kurds by private citizens will also engage the responsibility of the State. In this sense in 2016, the Committee on the Elimination of Racial Discrimination expressed its concern at 'reports of incidents of hate crimes, including physical attacks targeting individuals on the basis of their ethnic origin, such as Kurds'.[143] The Committee was 'further concerned that cases of hate speech and hate crimes are not always adequately and effectively investigated and that those responsible are not prosecuted and punished'.[144]

23.54 While attention has focused on the treatment by Turkey of Kurds inside its territory, there have also been occasions where significant force has been used in neighbouring Iraq, in Iran,[145] and especially in the context of Operation Peace Spring in late 2019, in Syria.[146] There has also been violence between rival Kurdish groups.

23.55 The *Issa* case concerned alleged unlawful arrest, detention, ill treatment, and subsequent killing of the applicant's relatives in the course of a military operation conducted by the Turkish Army against the PKK in northern Iraq in April 1995.[147] The applicants were Iraqi Kurdish shepherdesses who earned their living by shepherding sheep in the valleys and hills surrounding their village in Sarsang province near the Turkish

---

[139] Ibid., para. 96.
[140] Ibid., para. 104.
[141] Ibid., para. 105.
[142] Ibid., para. 106.
[143] CERD Committee, Concluding Observations on Turkey, UN doc. CERD/C/TUR/CO/4-6, 11 January 2016, para. 23.
[144] Ibid.
[145] See the *Pad* case referred to in Chapter 3, in Paragraph 3.32.
[146] See, e.g., Agence France-Presse, '"Operation Peace Spring": Turkey Launches Attack on Syrian Kurds', *Outlook India*, 9 October 2019, at http://bit.ly/2DcwuEN.
[147] European Court of Human Rights, *Issa and others v. Turkey*, Judgment (Second Section), 30 March 2005, para. 4.

border. Their deceased relatives were likewise employed.[148] Four shepherdesses were walking in front of seven shepherds when they met Turkish soldiers. The soldiers abused the eleven shepherds, hitting them with their rifle butts, kicking them, and slapping them on the face. They separated the women from the men and told the women to return to the village before taking the men away. The four applicants returned to the village and told the other villagers what had happened.[149]

23.56 On 3 April 1995, the Turkish army withdrew from the area around the village and the village men set off in the direction of Spna to look for the seven shepherds who had gone missing. In an area close to where the seven shepherds had last been seen with the Turkish soldiers they found the bodies of Ismail Hassan Sherif, Ahmad Fatah Hassan, Abdulkadir Izat Khan Hassan, Sarabast Abdulkadir Izat, and Abdulrahman Mohammad Sherriff. The bodies had several bullet wounds and had been badly mutilated – ears, tongues, and genitals were missing. The bodies were taken to the main road and from there to Azadi hospital in Dohuk, where autopsies were conducted.[150]

23.57 Turkey confirmed that a military operation involving its forces took place in northern Iraq between 19 March 1995 and 16 April 1995, but denied that any Turkish soldiers were present in the area indicated by the applicants.[151] For the government, the mere presence of Turkish armed forces for a limited time and for a limited purpose in northern Iraq was not synonymous with 'jurisdiction'. Turkey did not exercise effective control of any part of Iraq, and it had to be concluded, the government alleged, that Turkey could not be held responsible for the acts imputed to it.[152]

23.58 The essential question, the Court held, was whether at the relevant time Turkish troops conducted operations in the area where the killings took place.[153] In holding that their presence could not be established beyond reasonable doubt, the Court declared that it could not 'overlook' the fact that the area where the applicants' relatives were killed was the scene of fierce fighting between PKK militants and Kurdistan Democratic Party (KDP) peshmergas.[154]

---

[148] Ibid., para. 12.
[149] Ibid., para. 15.
[150] Ibid., para. 19.
[151] Ibid., para. 25.
[152] Ibid., para. 58.
[153] Ibid., para. 76.
[154] Ibid., para. 79.

24

LGBTI Persons

INTRODUCTION

24.01 This chapter looks at the right to life of LGBTI persons. Lesbian, gay, bisexual, trans, and intersex persons are at particular risk of being targeted because of their gender or sexual preference. Discrimination against LGBTI persons could be based on sexual orientation (to whom someone is attracted), gender identity (how people define themselves, irrespective of biological sex), gender expression (how gender is expressed, through clothing, hair, or make-up), or sex characteristics (for example, genitals, chromosomes, reproductive organs, or hormone levels.)[1]

24.02 A person's sexual orientation refers to who they are attracted to and with whom they form relationships. Sexual orientations include lesbian (women who are attracted to women); gay (usually men who are attracted to other men); bisexual (attracted to men and women); pansexual (attracted to individuals, regardless of gender); and asexual (not sexually attracted to anyone). Transgender (or trans) people are individuals whose gender identity or gender expression is different from typical expectations of the gender they were assigned at birth. Not all transgender people identify as male or female; some identify as more than one gender or no gender at all. Being transgender has nothing to do with a person's sexual orientation: you can be a trans man and be gay, or be a trans woman and be lesbian. When someone is born with sex characteristics that differ from what is typically seen as female or male traits, they are known as intersex. For instance, in some cases, a person's body has both male and female characteristics. Another instance is where a person's chromosomal make-up is neither typically male nor female. These characteristics might be present at birth or become more apparent during or after puberty.[2]

24.03 With respect to gender identity, the term cisnormativity – the 'cis' prefix being the antonym of the 'trans' prefix[3] – has been used to describe 'the expectation that all people

---

[1] Amnesty International, 'LGBTI Rights', undated but accessed 24 October 2020, at http://bit.ly/3jsdAZA.
[2] Ibid.
[3] From the Latin, 'trans' (across, on the other side of); 'cis' (on this side of). Inter-American Commission on Human Rights, *Violence against Lesbian, Gay, Bisexual, Trans and Intersex Persons in the Americas*, OAS doc. OAS/Ser.L/V/II.rev.1, Doc. 36, Washington, DC, 12 November 2015, para. 31.

are cissexual [or cisgender], that those assigned male at birth always grow up to be men and those assigned female at birth always grow up to be women'.[4]

24.04 Discrimination can result in LGBTI persons being attacked and even murdered as a result of this enmity. The UN Special Rapporteur on extrajudicial, summary or arbitrary executions has noted that LGBT persons are 'especially vulnerable' to extrajudicial killings.[5] In a 2015 report to the Human Rights Council, the Office of the UN High Commissioner for Human Rights (OHCHR) noted that hate-motivated killings of LGBT individuals have been documented in all regions. The killings and related patterns of violence included the murder of transsexual women in Uruguay and of black lesbian women in South Africa. In an assault in Chile, a gay man was beaten and killed by neo-Nazis, who burned him with cigarettes and carved swastikas into his body.[6]

24.05 The Transrespect versus Transphobia Worldwide Project recorded 369 cases of reported killings of trans and gender-diverse people between 1 October 2017 and 30 September 2018. The majority of the murders occurred in Brazil (167), Mexico (71), the United States (28), and Colombia (21). Between 1 January 2008 and 30 September 2018, the project observed a total of 2,982 reported cases in 72 countries.[7] The Trans Murder Monitoring (TMM) project monitors, collects, and analyses reports of homicides of trans and gender-diverse people worldwide. It recorded a further 331 cases of reported killings of trans and gender-diverse people between 1 October 2018 and 30 September 2019.[8]

24.06 Same-sex sexual activity is a crime in seventy States,[9] and in nine of these – Afghanistan, Brunei, Iran, Iraq, Mauritania, Pakistan, Saudi Arabia, Sudan, and Yemen – the penal code prescribes the death penalty as a possible judicial sanction.[10] The Human Dignity Trust reports that Northern Nigeria and parts of Somalia also provide for the death penalty for homosexuality.[11] Even where laws are not enforced, 'their very existence reinforces prejudice against LGBTI people, leaving them feeling like they have no protection against harassment, blackmail and violence'.[12]

---

[4] G. R. Bauer, R. Hammond, R. Travers, M. Kaay, K. Hohenadel, and M. Boyce, '"I Don't Think This Is Theoretical; This Is Our Lives": How Erasure Impacts Health Care for Transgender People', *Journal of the Association of Nurses in AIDS Care*, vol. 20, no. 5 (2009), pp. 348–61.

[5] Report of the Special Rapporteur on extrajudicial, summary or arbitrary executions, Addendum: Follow-up country recommendations: Colombia, UN doc. A/HRC/20/22/Add.2, 15 May 2012, para. 51.

[6] OHCHR, 'Discrimination and violence against individuals based on their sexual orientation and gender identity', Report of the Office of the United Nations High Commissioner for Human Rights, UN doc. A/HRC/29/23, 4 May 2015, para. 36.

[7] Transrespect versus Transphobia Worldwide Project, 'Trans Day of Remembrance (TDoR) 2018', press release, TGEU, 12 November 2018, at http://bit.ly/30m8VMu.

[8] Transrespect versus Transphobia Worldwide Project, 'TMM Update Trans Day of Remembrance 2019', press release, TGEU, 11 November 2019, at http://bit.ly/37AsXgj.

[9] For an overview of the countries where lesbian, gay, bisexual, and transgender people are criminalised, see, e.g., Human Dignity Trust, 'Map of Countries That Criminalise LGBT People', at http://bit.ly/2TlDCDn.

[10] Amnesty International, 'LGBTI Rights'.

[11] Human Dignity Trust, 'Map of Countries that Criminalise LGBT People'.

[12] Amnesty International, 'LGBTI Rights'.

24.07 The chapter looks first at the right to life of LGBTI persons under global standards. This comprises extrajudicial executions by State agents, the failure to exercise due diligence in protecting LGBTI persons, and the imposition of the death penalty for homosexual activity. The chapter then considers the right to life of LGBTI persons under regional standards, in particular the Inter-American and European human rights systems.

THE RIGHT TO LIFE OF LGBTI PERSONS UNDER GLOBAL STANDARDS

24.08 In 2015, the UN General Assembly adopted resolution 69/182 in which it urged all States to 'ensure the effective protection of the right to life of all persons, and to conduct, when required by obligations under international law, prompt, exhaustive and impartial investigations into all killings', including those targeted at persons 'because of their sexual orientation or gender identity'.[13] In 2011, the Human Rights Council had adopted a resolution on human rights, sexual orientation, and gender identity in which it expressed its 'grave concern' over acts of violence, in all regions of the world, committed against individuals because of their sexual orientation and gender identity.[14] In 2016, the Council adopted a further resolution in which it strongly deplored such acts of violence and discrimination, and appointed an Independent Expert on protection against violence and discrimination based on sexual orientation and gender identity.[15]

24.09 As of this writing, the Independent Expert was Victor Madrigal-Borloz of Costa Rica, who took up the position on 1 January 2018. In his 2019 report to the Human Rights Council, Mr Madrigal-Borloz recalled the widespread appreciation that collection and proper management of relevant data are essential in order to adequately address violence and discrimination. That said, 'as a result of barriers created by criminalization, pathologization, demonization and other institutional drivers for stigmatization', he noted that no reliable estimates existed regarding the world population affected by violence based on sexual orientation and/or gender identity.[16]

24.10 The Independent Expert recalled his shock at hearing 'a high-level officer responsible for the formulation of public policy in a country with a population in the tens of millions'

---

[13] UN General Assembly Resolution 69/182, adopted on 18 December 2014 by 122 votes to 0 with 66 abstentions, para. 6(b).

[14] Human Rights Council Resolution 17/19: 'Human rights, sexual orientation and gender identity', adopted on 17 June 2011, fourth preambular para. The resolution was narrowly adopted by twenty-three votes to nineteen, with three abstentions. States voting against the resolution were Angola, Bahrain, Bangladesh, Cameroon, Djibouti, Gabon, Ghana, Jordan, Malaysia, Maldives, Mauritania, Moldova, Nigeria, Pakistan, Qatar, Russia, Saudi Arabia, Senegal, and Uganda. Those abstaining were Burkina Faso, China, and Zambia.

[15] Human Rights Council Resolution 32/2: 'Protection against violence and discrimination based on sexual orientation and gender identity', adopted on 30 June 2016, operative paras. 2 and 3. The resolution was again narrowly adopted, this time by a vote of twenty-three to eighteen, with six abstentions. States voting against the resolution were Algeria, Bangladesh, Burundi, China, Congo, Côte d'Ivoire, Ethiopia, Indonesia, Kenya, Kyrgyzstan, Maldives, Morocco, Nigeria, Qatar, Russia, Saudi Arabia, Togo, and the United Arab Emirates. Those abstaining were Botswana, Ghana, India, Namibia, the Philippines, and South Africa.

[16] 'Data collection and management as a means to create heightened awareness of violence and discrimination based on sexual orientation and gender identity', Report of the Independent Expert on protection against violence and discrimination based on sexual orientation and gender identity, UN doc. A/HRC/41/45, 14 May 2019, para. 12.

claim that his country's population of LGBT and gender-diverse persons 'could not exceed 300 or so'. 'Given the evidence of violence and discrimination against these populations and communities, maintaining such a level of ignorance without seeking an appropriate evidence base, and applying such a personal preconception and prejudice to public policy' were, 'in the opinion of the mandate holder, tantamount to criminal negligence'.[17]

The ICCPR

24.11 The 1966 International Covenant on Civil and Political Rights[18] (ICCPR) does not specifically refer to LGBTI persons. That said, it is stipulated that each State Party to the Covenant 'undertakes to respect and to ensure to all individuals within its territory and subject to its jurisdiction the rights recognized in the ... Covenant, without distinction of any kind, such as ... sex ... or other status'.[19] Thus, as the Human Rights Committee has confirmed in its General Comment 36, the right to life must be respected and ensured 'without distinction of any kind', including 'sexual orientation or gender identity'.[20] In this regard, the Committee referred to its 2011 Concluding Observations on the third periodic report of Iran on implementation of the ICCPR, in which the Committee expressed its concern that 'members of the lesbian, gay, bisexual, and transgender community face harassment, persecution, cruel punishment and even the death penalty'.[21]

24.12 Each LGBTI person under the jurisdiction of a State Party to the ICCPR thus benefits from the full protection of the right to life afforded by Article 6. This right, which belongs to every person, is non-derogable.[22] As discussed in Chapter 1 of this work, that every human being has the right to life – without distinction of any kind – has long reflected customary international law. Furthermore, the jus cogens prohibition of arbitrary deprivation of life codified in Article 6(1) of the Covenant protects all persons, whatever their gender or sexual orientation.

24.13 The duty to respect the right to life means that a State Party to the ICCPR – and indeed any other State – may not arbitrarily deprive any LGBTI person of their life, whether that occurs directly or through the actions of a State agent. The duty to protect life (by law), codified in Article 6(1) of the Covenant, requires specific measures of protection for LGBTI persons. As the Human Rights Committee has stated: 'The duty to protect the right to life requires States parties to take special measures of protection towards persons in vulnerable situations whose lives have been placed at particular risk because of specific threats or pre-existing patterns of violence.'[23] Such persons, the Committee expressly

---

[17] Ibid.
[18] International Covenant on Civil and Political Rights; adopted at New York 16 December 1966; entered into force 23 March 1976.
[19] Art. 2(1), ICCPR.
[20] Human Rights Committee, 'General comment No. 36. Article 6: right to life', UN doc. CCPR/C/GC/36, 3 September 2019 (hereinafter, Human Rights Committee, General Comment 36 on the right to life), para. 61.
[21] Human Rights Committee, Concluding Observations: Islamic Republic of Iran, UN doc. CCPR/C/IRN/CO/3, 29 November 2011, para. 10.
[22] Art. 4(2), ICCPR.
[23] Ibid, para. 23 (footnote omitted).

recalls, may include lesbian, gay, bisexual, transgender, and intersex persons.[24] In its 2003 Concluding Observations on El Salvador, the Committee expressed concern at 'the incidents of people being attacked, or even killed, on account of their sexual orientation' – though it referred only to Article 9 on the right to security and not also to Article 6 – as well as at 'the small number of investigations mounted into such illegal acts'.[25]

The Death Penalty

24.14 The Committee has made it explicit that 'under no circumstances can the death penalty ever be applied as a sanction against conduct the very criminalization of which violates the Covenant'. This includes homosexuality according to General Comment 36,[26] but also encompasses sexual activities by other LGBTI persons. States Parties that retain the death penalty for such 'offences', the Committee affirms, violate their obligations under Article 6 of the ICCPR, 'read alone and in conjunction with article 2 (2) of the Covenant, as well as of other provisions of the Covenant'.[27] The prohibition on executing LGBTI persons on the basis of their gender or sexual identity is not only a customary rule; it is also a peremptory norm of international law.

24.15 Amnesty International has stated that it has had no reports of executions under anti-homosexuality laws in the past few years.[28] But in April 2019, Brunei introduced a law making sex between men punishable by stoning to death. The following month, however, Sultan Hassanal Bolkiah extended a moratorium on the death penalty to cover the new legislation.[29] In October 2019, Ugandan members of parliament pressed for the death penalty to be imposed for homosexual acts.[30]

THE RIGHT TO LIFE OF LGBTI PERSONS UNDER REGIONAL STANDARDS

The Inter-American Human Rights System

24.16 The American Convention on Human Rights[31] does not specifically protect LGBTI persons, but it is clear that their right to life must be protected without discrimination. In

---

[24] Ibid. The Committee makes reference in this regard to its 2010 Concluding Observations on the sixth periodic report of Colombia in which it noted the particular vulnerability of certain groups to being attacked, including LGBT persons. Human Rights Committee, Concluding Observations: Colombia, UN doc. CCPR/C/COL/CO/6, 4 August 2010, para. 12.

[25] Human Rights Committee, Concluding Observations: El Salvador, UN doc. CCPR/CO/78/SLV, 22 August 2003, para. 16.

[26] Human Rights Committee, General Comment 36 on the right to life, para. 36.

[27] Ibid.

[28] BBC, 'Brunei Stoning: Which Places Have the Death Penalty for Gay Sex?', 3 April 2019, at http://bbc.in/3dQrKTm.

[29] BBC, 'Brunei Says It Won't Enforce Death Penalty for Gay Sex', 6 May 2019 at http://bbc.in/3dTLsNR. Lesbian sex carries a penalty of forty strokes of the cane and/or a maximum of ten years' imprisonment.

[30] J. Burke and S. Okiror, 'Ugandan MPs Press for Death Penalty for Homosexual Acts', *The Guardian*, 15 October 2019, at http://bit.ly/3eos1mH.

[31] American Convention on Human Rights; adopted at San José 22 November 1969; entered into force 18 July 1978.

2015, the Inter-American Commission on Human Rights published a landmark report, *Violence against Lesbian, Gay, Bisexual, Trans and Intersex Persons in the Americas.*[32] The report concluded that violence against LGBTI persons was 'pervasive throughout the Americas' and that Organization of American States (OAS) member States had failed to exercise due diligence to 'prevent, investigate, sanction and provide reparations to acts of violence committed against LGBTI persons'.[33] In addition, in several cases documented by the Inter-American Commission, 'the lifeless bodies of LGBT persons show signs of torture, mutilation of their genitalia; and their bodies have been quartered and marked with signs that indicate high levels of prejudice'.[34]

24.17 Eleven OAS Member States in the Commonwealth Caribbean maintain laws criminalising private, consensual, adult sexual activity, and one of these States has legislation that criminalises cross-dressing, which has an impact on the lives of trans persons.[35] Even though prosecutions under these laws are not common, the Commission observed that 'this type of legislation contributes to an environment that condones discrimination, stigmatization, and violence against LGBT persons'.[36]

24.18 The Commission's 2015 Report describes multiple forms of lethal and non-lethal violence against LGBTI persons, including violations of the right to life in the form of extrajudicial executions by State actors, or with their acquiescence, and killings by non-State actors. Data collection and analysis by the Commission between 1 January 2013 and 31 March 2014 suggested that the majority of the victims of killings and other serious acts of violence were gay men and trans women, or persons perceived as such. 'Illegal and arbitrary detention', the report stated, 'is another significant concern in the context of police abuse against LGBT persons'.[37] Latin American organisations cited by the Commission reported that the life expectancy of trans women in the region was between thirty and thirty-five years of age. According to the data collected by the Commission, four-fifths of trans persons killed during a fifteen-month period were thirty-five years of age or younger.[38]

24.19 In 2018, Inter-American Commission issued a report on the situation of LGBTI persons in the Americas. While concluding that levels of physical, psychological, and sexual violence towards this community had remained 'constant' in the intervening three years, the Commission found significant progress had been made towards protecting, recognising, and guaranteeing their rights in various countries in the region. These changes had taken place 'through legislative processes, legal decisions, and public policy-making and have led to greater recognition of LGTBI people's rights by advancing the

---

[32] Inter-American Commission on Human Rights, *Violence against Lesbian, Gay, Bisexual, Trans and Intersex Persons in the Americas*, OAS doc. OAS/Ser.L/V/II.rev.1, Doc. 36, Washington, DC, 12 November 2015.
[33] Ibid., Executive Summary, para. 1.
[34] Ibid., Executive Summary, para. 2.
[35] Ibid., Executive Summary, para. 4.
[36] Ibid.
[37] Ibid., para. 8.
[38] Ibid., para. 16.

agenda of equality and non-discrimination so as to ensure that these people can live their lives free of the risk of violence, terror, and poverty'.[39]

24.20 The Commission called upon all OAS member States to respect and apply the standards contained in 2017 Advisory Opinion of the Inter-American Court of Human Rights,[40] which referred to the right of persons to have their self-perceived gender identity recognised and to the rights of LGBTI persons to equal marriage. In the Opinion, the Court considered it important to provide a frame of reference 'for the effective protection of the rights of such persons who have historically been victims of structural discrimination, stigmatization, diverse types of violence, and violations of their fundamental rights'.[41] The Opinion stressed that, owing to the acts of violence it described, the violation of the right to equality and non-discrimination of LGBTI persons[42] 'results in the concurrent violation of other rights and provisions of the [American] Convention, such as, and above all, the right to life and to physical integrity'.[43]

24.21 The Court referred to its 2012 judgment in the case of *Atala Riffo and Daughters v. Chile*,[44] in which it awarded custody of her children to a lesbian mother; the Supreme Court of Chile had previously granted custody to her ex-husband in 2005, on the basis, inter alia, that Ms Atala Riffo's relationship put the development of her children at risk: 'the alleged "risk for the integral development of the girls from which they must be protected" due to "the potential confusion over sexual roles that could be caused in them by the absence from the home of a male father and his replacement by another person of the female gender"'.[45] This was the first case adjudged by the Inter-American Court concerning the rights of LGBTI persons under the American Convention on Human Rights.[46]

The European Human Rights System

24.22 Under the European Convention on Human Rights, it is stipulated: 'The enjoyment of the rights and freedoms set forth in [the] Convention shall be secured without discrimination on any ground such as sex ... or other status.'[47] This applies, naturally, to the rights to life and to freedom from torture and other inhuman or degrading treatment or

---

[39] Inter-American Commission on Human Rights, *Advances and Challenges towards the Recognition of the Rights of LGBTI Persons in the Americas*, OAS doc. OEA/Ser.L/V/II.170, Doc. 184, Washington DC, 7 December 2018.
[40] Inter-American Court of Human Rights, 'Gender Identity, and Equality and Non-Discrimination of Same-Sex Couples', Advisory Opinion OC-24/17, 24 November 2017 (opinion requested by Costa Rica), at http://bit.ly/34pflm4.
[41] Ibid., para. 33.
[42] Arts. 1(1) and 24, ACHR.
[43] Inter-American Court of Human Rights, 'Gender Identity, and Equality and Non-Discrimination of Same-Sex Couples', Advisory Opinion OC-24/17, para. 47.
[44] Inter-American Court of Human Rights, *Atala Riffo and Daughters v. Chile*, Judgment (Merits, Reparations and Costs), 24 February 2012.
[45] Ibid., para. 97.
[46] Loyola Law School, 'Atala Riffo and Daughters v. Chile', Los Angeles, 2020, at http://bit.ly/3e2HFhy.
[47] Art. 14, Convention for the Protection of Human Rights and Fundamental Freedoms; adopted at Rome 4 November 1950; entered into force 3 September 1953.

punishment under Articles 2 and 3 of the Convention. Cases have, however, focused on Article 3 of the Convention, as the LGBTI applicants survived the treatment they received, whether at the hands of State agents or private individuals.

24.23 In June 2006, the applicants in *M.C. and C.A. v. Romania*[48] participated in an annual gay march in Bucharest. On their way home in the subway, they were attacked by a group of six young men and a woman. The attackers punched and kicked them, shouting homophobic slurs at them. The applicants complained that the investigation into the attack against them had been inadequate, alleging in particular that the authorities had not taken into account the fact that the offences against them had been motivated by hatred against homosexuals. The European Court of Human Rights recalled the 2010 Council of Europe Recommendation to member States on measures to combat discrimination on grounds of sexual orientation or gender identity,[49] which had noted 'a growing amount of evidence demonstrating that a significant number of LGBTI persons in Council of Europe member States experience physical violence, harassment or assault because of their real or perceived sexual orientation and gender identity'.

24.24 The Court observed that even though the scope of a Contracting State's positive obligations 'might differ between cases where treatment contrary to Article 3 has been inflicted through the involvement of State agents and cases where violence has been inflicted by private individuals', the requirements pertaining to an official investigation were 'similar'.[50] For an investigation to be regarded as 'effective', the Court stated, 'it should in principle be capable of leading to the establishment of the facts of the case and to the identification and punishment of those responsible. This is not an obligation as to the results to be achieved but as to the means to be employed.'[51] The Court noted that 'at no point did the authorities initiate criminal inquiries against the alleged culprits'. It recalled its earlier jurisprudence[52] whereby 'the failure to open criminal inquiries – albeit when ill-treatment was inflicted by State agents – may compromise the validity of the evidence collected during the preliminary stages of investigation'.[53] But it saw 'no reason to find otherwise in the circumstances of the present case, where the ill-treatment was perpetrated by private individuals but the investigation fell under the State's positive obligations in respect of Article 3'.[54]

24.25 In its judgment in *Aghdgomelashvili and Japaridze v. Georgia*,[55] the European Court stated: 'When investigating violent incidents, such as ill-treatment, State

---

[48] European Court of Human Rights, *M.C. and C.A. v. Romania*, Judgment (Fourth Section), 12 April 2016 (as rendered final on 12 July 2016).
[49] Committee of Ministers of the Council of Europe, Recommendation CM/Rec(2010)5, adopted on 31 March 2010.
[50] European Court of Human Rights, *M.C. and C.A. v. Romania*, Judgment, para. 111.
[51] Ibid.
[52] e.g. European Court of Human Rights, *Poede v. Romania*, Judgment (Fifth Section), 15 September 2015, paras. 52–53.
[53] European Court of Human Rights, *M.C. and C.A. v. Romania*, Judgment, para. 122.
[54] Ibid.
[55] European Court of Human Rights, *Aghdgomelashvili and Japaridze v. Georgia*, Judgment (Fifth Section), 8 October 2020.

authorities have a duty to take all reasonable steps to unmask possible discriminatory motives, which the Court concedes is a difficult task.' The Court further declared that the obligation on a State Party to the European Convention to investigate possible discriminatory motives for a violent act 'is an obligation to use best endeavours, and is not absolute'.[56] The authorities must, the Court said, 'do whatever is reasonable in the circumstances to collect and secure the evidence, explore all practical means of discovering the truth and deliver fully reasoned, impartial and objective decisions, without omitting suspicious facts that may be indicative of violence induced by, for instance, racial or religious intolerance, or violence motivated by gender-based discrimination'.[57]

24.26 The case concerned allegations of degrading treatment by Georgian police of members of an LGBTI rights organisation in Tbilisi, including strip searches, threats, and insults. The Court shared the view of the applicants in the case that the strip searches had no investigative value whatsoever, 'and that their sole purpose was to make the applicants and the other women feel embarrassed and humiliated and thus punish them for their association with the LGBT community'.[58] The homophobic comments made by the female police officers in the course of the searches can, the Court stated, be taken as additional proof of the abusive purpose of the acts.[59]

24.27 The Court recalled: 'Since interference with human dignity strikes at the very essence of the Convention, any conduct by law-enforcement officers vis-à-vis an individual which diminishes human dignity constitutes a violation of Article 3 of the Convention.'[60] The Court emphasised that 'treating violence and brutality with discriminatory intent, irrespective of whether they are perpetrated by State agents or private individuals, on an equal footing with cases that have no such overtones would be to turn a blind eye to the specific nature of acts that are particularly destructive of fundamental rights'.[61] 'A failure to make a distinction in the way situations that are essentially different are handled', the Court concluded, 'may constitute unjustified treatment irreconcilable with Article 14 of the Convention'.[62]

24.28 As of this writing, a number of cases were pending before the Court on alleged violation of Article 3 of the Convention against LGBTI persons. The case of *Lapunov v. Russia* concerns allegations by the applicant that he was abducted, imprisoned, and subjected to ill treatment by State agents in Chechnya in March 2017 on the grounds of his homosexuality.[63] During detention, he alleges that guards

---

[56] Ibid., para. 38.
[57] Ibid.
[58] Ibid., para. 48.
[59] Ibid.
[60] Ibid., para. 42.
[61] Ibid., para. 44.
[62] Ibid.
[63] European Court of Human Rights, *Lapunov v. Russia* (Appl. No. 28834/19), Communicated on 14 November 2019, at http://bit.ly/2HvuJVh.

armed with water pipes beat him up saying that they were punishing him for his homosexuality and for him having sexual intercourse with Chechens. One of the perpetrators tried to abuse him sexually, but the applicant resisted. Dozens of strokes with water pipe had been administered by the perpetrators on the applicant, particularly on his buttocks. The perpetrators hit his hand with a piece of water pipe. The blood from the hand stained the cell wall.[64]

[64] Ibid., para. 20.

25

Persons with Disabilities

INTRODUCTION[1]

25.01 Persons with disabilities have been described by the World Health Organization (WHO) as 'the largest minority group in the world'.[2] In 2011, WHO and The World Bank estimated that persons with disabilities represented at least 15 per cent of the world's population.[3] They are particularly vulnerable to violence, abuse, and neglect, all of which may result in death, yet they have been largely sidelined in the international discourse on violence.[4] Among persons with disabilities, the elderly figure disproportionately, as relative rates of disabilities encountered by people increase with age, augmenting risk factors.[5] Among other manifestations of 'multiple discrimination' figure prominently children, women, people living with multiple disabilities, and members of ethnic minorities with disabilities.[6] States may offer specific legal protection to persons with disabilities through the Constitution, in dedicated legislation, and/or by mainstreaming protection in broader laws.[7]

25.02 This chapter describes the content and protection of the right to life of persons with disabilities under international law. It begins by discussing the definition of the term 'persons with disabilities' under international law: the way in which disability and persons with disabilities have been referred to in domestic and international law and in relevant

---

[1] The author would like to thank Dr Dagnachew B. Wakene for his insightful comments on a draft of this chapter.
[2] WHO and World Bank, *World Report on Disability*, 2011.
[3] Ibid.
[4] WHO, *Violence against Adults and Children with Disabilities*, at http://bit.ly/2Rckgo8.
[5] WHO and World Bank, *World Report on Disability*, 2011.
[6] In the preamble to the Convention on the Rights of Persons with Disabilities (CRPD), States Parties express their concern about 'the difficult conditions faced by persons with disabilities who are subject to multiple or aggravated forms of discrimination on the basis of race, colour, sex, language, religion, political or other opinion, national, ethnic, indigenous or social origin, property, birth, age or other status'. Convention on the Rights of Persons with Disabilities; adopted at New York 13 December 2006; entered into force 3 May 2008, preambular para. (p).
[7] In Ecuador, Articles 47 and 48 of the 2008 Constitution, however, recognise the rights of persons with disabilities. According to Article 48(7), abandonment of persons with disabilities is punishable by law as is 'any action leading to any kind of abuse, inhuman and degrading treatment, or discrimination because of their disability'. The 1992 Disability Discrimination Act of Australia and the 2018 Rights of Persons with Disabilities Act in Fiji both offer specific protection to persons with disabilities.

concepts and practice have all changed fundamentally over past decades. The chapter then considers the protection of the right to life of persons with disabilities, first under global human rights treaties and subsequently in regional treaties and standards. The legalities of imposing and executing the death penalty on persons with disabilities are then assessed. Thereafter, specific attention is paid to the protection of the right to life of persons with disabilities in situations of armed conflict and finally other man-made humanitarian emergencies and natural disasters. Particular vulnerabilities of women, girls, boys, and the elderly with disabilities to violence and abuse – and to all persons with disabilities at the hands of law enforcement personnel, including in custodial settings – are emphasised throughout.

The Definition of Persons with Disabilities

25.03 Under treaty law, Article 1 of the Convention on the Rights of Persons with Disabilities (CRPD) defines persons with disabilities as 'includ[ing] those who have long-term physical, mental, intellectual or sensory impairments which in interaction with various barriers may hinder their full and effective participation in society on an equal basis with others'.[8] The phrase 'interaction with various barriers' in this definition marks a major departure from earlier approaches to disability in that, under the CRPD, disability derives not primarily from an individual's impairment and/or medical condition, but essentially operates as a consequence of environmental, social, cultural, and attitudinal barriers. Under the 'social' and 'rights-based' models of disability, individuals are not inherently 'disabled': physical, sensory, psychosocial, or intellectual impairments that anyone might experience are turned into disabilities due primarily to socio-environmental and institutional (in general, systemic) barriers that hinder their opportunities for participation, inclusion, and effective interaction in society.[9]

25.04 As of 1 May 2021, 181 States, along with the entire European Union,[10] were parties to the CRPD. Despite the Convention's very widespread adherence, however, it is not certain that the definition in Article 1 has attained the status of customary international law (at least not verbatim). Indeed, in the Preamble to the Convention, it is acknowledged that disability is an 'evolving concept'.[11] It is also explicit in Article 1 that the definition is not exhaustive. A particular issue pertains to the requirement that impairments be of a 'long-term' nature in order to be termed a 'disability' per se. This qualifier narrows considerably the scope of the term 'persons with disabilities', thereby restricting who is

---

[8] Art. 1, CRPD. On the day it was opened for signature, the CRPD attracted 82 signatories: the highest number in history for a UN Convention.

[9] G. Quinn and T. Degener, *Human Rights and Disability*, United Nations, New York and Geneva, 2002, p. 14.

[10] The European Union was the first regional integration organization to become a party to a human rights treaty when it formally confirmed its adherence in 2010. A. Broderick and D. Ferri, *International and European Disability Law and Policy. Text, Cases and Materials*, Cambridge University Press, Cambridge, 2019, p. 3.

[11] In the negotiation of the CRPD, several States had proposed to not include a definition in the Convention 'in order to prioritise flexibility and the need for a dynamic interpretation over time'. Broderick and Ferri, *International and European Disability Law and Policy. Text, Cases and Materials*, p. 65.

Persons with Disabilities

entitled to protection under the CRPD.[12] State practice may, though, act to broaden the definition in customary law. It has already done so in regional treaty law. Thus, the 2018 Protocol to the African Charter on Human and Peoples' Rights on the Rights of Persons with Disabilities in Africa[13] largely reproduces the definition in Article 1 of the CRPD, but, significantly, omits the phrase 'long-term'. The Protocol had not entered into force as of 1 May 2021.[14]

25.05 The 1966 International Covenant on Civil and Political Rights[15] (ICCPR) does not refer to persons with disabilities at any point (or indeed in any alternative formulation). Other treaties tended to talk of the 'disabled'. The 1989 Convention on the Rights of the Child – the most widely ratified human rights treaty in history and the first UN human rights treaty to have explicitly mentioned disability in its original text – refers to the specific rights of 'mentally or physically disabled' children in one article,[16] though it does not define the notion of 'disabled'. In 1975, however, the Declaration on the Rights of Disabled Persons, adopted by the UN General Assembly, had defined 'disabled person' as meaning 'any person unable to ensure by himself or herself, wholly or partly, the necessities of a normal individual and/or social life, as a result of deficiency, either congenital or not, in his or her physical or mental capabilities'.[17] In 1983, the International Labour Organization (ILO) Vocational Rehabilitation and Employment (Disabled Persons) Convention defined the term 'disabled person' as meaning 'an individual whose prospects of securing, retaining and advancing in suitable employment are substantially reduced as a result of a duly recognised physical or mental impairment'.[18] In this way, appreciation of disability in international law was progressing from an approach that focused solely on individual 'incapacities' or medical conditions to one that spotlights external barriers and the resulting disproportionate denial or loss of opportunities for meaningful participation by persons with disabilities compared to non-disabled persons.[19]

---

[12] Thus, for instance, as Claudia Moreno has observed, 'Developmental disAbilities' – conditions and disorders affecting cognitive, physical, communication, social, emotional, and adaptive development – 'can affect individuals on a temporary or a lifelong basis'. C. L. Moreno, 'Developmental Disabilities', chap 7 in A. Gitterman (ed.), *Handbook of Social Work Practice with Vulnerable and Resilient Populations*, 2nd ed., Columbia University Press, New York, 2001, pp. 205–23, at 205.

[13] Protocol to the African Charter on Human and Peoples' Rights on the Rights of Persons with Disabilities in Africa; adopted at Addis Ababa 29 January 2018; not yet in force.

[14] The Protocol will enter into force thirty days after the fifteenth ratification. As of 1 December 2020, nine States had signed the Protocol (Angola, Burkina Faso, Cameroon, Central African Republic, Gabon, Mali, Rwanda, South Africa, and Togo) and none had yet ratified or acceded to it.

[15] International Covenant on Civil and Political Rights; adopted at New York 16 December 1966; entered into force 23 March 1976.

[16] Art. 23(1), Convention on the Rights of the Child; adopted at New York 20 November 1989; entered into force 2 September 1990. Therein it is stipulated that States Parties 'recognize that a mentally or physically disabled child should enjoy a full and decent life, in conditions which ensure dignity, promote self-reliance and facilitate the child's active participation in the community'.

[17] UN General Assembly Resolution 3447 (XXX), adopted without a vote on 9 December 1975, operative para. 1.

[18] Art. 1, ILO Vocational Rehabilitation and Employment (Disabled Persons) Convention, 1983 (No. 159). Convention 159 entered into force on 20 June 1985. As of 1 December 2020, 84 States had ratified the Convention. See http://bit.ly/2JnIYwa.

[19] In their 2016 work, *Human Rights and Disability*, Quinn and Degener defined the 'human rights model of disability' as one that 'focuses on the inherent dignity of the human being and subsequently, but only if

528   *The Protection of At-Risk Groups and Individuals*

25.06 Indeed, the language and terminology used to describe persons with disabilities have fundamentally changed over the last eighty years, both in domestic law and practice as well as in international law, particularly human rights law. The traditional medical model, which focuses on the incapacities of the individual – or even their 'disorders' and 'abnormalities' – has now been replaced by a range of social and human-rights-based models, as indicated in the CRPD. According to these models, disabilities are viewed as impediments to social participation owing to environmental, attitudinal, or other barriers in communities and societies.[20] Gone are references to the 'mentally retarded'[21] and, at least in the English language, the 'handicapped',[22] which connotes disability as an object of charity and alms, while relegating persons with disabilities to permanent socio-economic dependents.[23]

25.07 The legacy of earlier nomenclature persists in other branches of international law. In particular, leading treaties of the law of armed conflict adopted decades ago, but which remain applicable, often reflect belittling, if not pejorative, vocabulary. Thus, for example, the 1949 Geneva Conventions referred to civilians 'suffering from mental disease'.[24] Mental 'disorder' was said to be an 'unquestionable' case giving rise to the right of prisoners of war to direct repatriation.[25] By 1977, however, the terminology was evolving. The Additional Protocol I to the Geneva Conventions thus offers protection to the sick, who are defined as encompassing persons with 'mental disorder or disability'.[26]

25.08 Since the adoption of the CRC in 1989, and even following the conclusion of the CRPD in 2006, discourse on disability has continued to advance. For instance, reference

---

necessary, on the person's medical characteristics. It places the individual centre stage in all decisions affecting him or her and, significantly, locates the main "problem" outside the person and in society. The "problem" of disability under this model stems from a lack of responsiveness by the State and civil society to the difference that disability represents. It follows that the State has a responsibility to tackle socially created obstacles in order to ensure full respect for the dignity and equal rights of all persons.' Quinn and Degener, *Human Rights and Disability*, p. 14.

[20] Broderick and Ferri, *International and European Disability Law and Policy. Text, Cases and Materials*, p. 16. Despite criticisms, Broderick and Ferri emphasise that the social model 'remains the dominant paradigm in understanding disability'. Ibid., p. 17.

[21] See, for example, the Declaration on the Rights of Mentally Retarded Persons, proclaimed by UN General Assembly Resolution 2856 (XXVI) of 20 December 1971.

[22] That said, the French authentic text of the CRPD uses the term 'personnes handicapées' for persons with disabilities; the Convention's formal title in French is Convention relative aux droits des personnes handicapées. Thus the French origins of the non-governmental organisation Handicap International, which advocates for the rights of persons with disabilities, helps explains the usage of the term in its title. In 2018, the organisation was formally renamed Humanity and Inclusion. Handicap International, 'Handicap International dévoile sa nouvelle identité visuelle', press release, 24 January 2018, at http://bit.ly/2WeNfW7.

[23] Broderick and Ferri, *International and European Disability Law and Policy. Text, Cases and Materials*, p. 5.

[24] Art. 91, Convention (IV) Relative to the Protection of Civilian Persons in Time of War; adopted at Geneva 12 August 1949; entered into force 21 October 1950.

[25] Article 110 and Model Agreement Concerning Direct Repatriation and Accommodation in Neutral Countries of Wounded and Sick Prisoners of War, Convention (III) relative to the Treatment of Prisoners of War; adopted at Geneva 12 August 1949; entered into force 21 October 1950.

[26] Art. 8(a), Protocol Additional to the Geneva Conventions of 12 August 1949, and relating to the Protection of Victims of International Armed Conflicts; adopted at Geneva 8 June 1977; entered into force 7 December 1978 (hereinafter, 1977 Additional Protocol I).

to 'psycho-social' disabilities is preferred in the human rights sphere to the term 'mental illness',[27] with conditions giving rise to such psycho-social disabilities as depression, schizophrenia, post-traumatic stress disorder, and bipolar disorder. Intellectual disabilities encompass cognitive and learning disabilities.[28] That said, the American Psychiatric Association's (APA's) landmark publication remains the *Diagnostic and Statistical Manual of Mental Disorders*. The glossary of technical terms in the Manual's latest edition, DSM-5, published in 2013,[29] does not consider the notion of disability.[30]

25.09 At the regional level, the 1950 European Convention on Human Rights[31] does not directly address persons with disabilities, nor does the 1969 American Convention on Human Rights.[32] The 1994 Belém do Pará Convention in the Inter-American human rights system, however, explicitly demands that special account be taken of women subjected to violence 'who are disabled'.[33] The African Charter on the Rights and Welfare of the Child, adopted in 1990 by the erstwhile Organization of African Unity, guarantees the right of every child 'who is mentally or physically disabled' to 'special measures of protection'.[34] The 2003 Protocol to the African Charter on Human and Peoples' Rights on the Rights of Women in Africa dedicates an entire article to the 'special protection of women with disabilities',[35] though the Protocol does not define the term.[36] The African Union Convention for the Protection and Assistance of Internally Displaced Persons in Africa (Kampala Convention) specifically obligates special protection for and assistance to internally displaced persons, including persons with disabilities.[37]

---

[27] The term 'mental' in the definition in the CRPD has been interpreted broadly by the CRPD Committee to stand in contradistinction to the notion of legal capacity. CRPD Committee, General Comment No. 1: Article 12: Equal recognition before the law, UN doc. CRPD/C/GC/1, 19 May 2014, para. 13.

[28] Broderick and Ferri, *International and European Disability Law and Policy. Text, Cases and Materials*, p. 6.

[29] APA, *Diagnostic and Statistical Manual of Mental Disorders*, 5th ed. (DSM-5), American Psychiatric Publishing, Washington, DC, 2013.

[30] For a brief critique of DSM-5 (though not from a disabilities perspective), see, e.g., E. Shorter, 'DSM-5 Will Be the Last', blog entry, *OUPblog*, 14 May 2013, at http://bit.ly/2Op3kUS.

[31] Convention for the Protection of Human Rights and Fundamental Freedoms; adopted at Rome by the Council of Europe 4 November 1950; entered into force 3 September 1953 (hereinafter, European Convention on Human Rights).

[32] American Convention on Human Rights; adopted at San José 22 November 1969; entered into force 18 July 1978.

[33] Art. 9, Inter-American Convention on the Prevention, Punishment, and Eradication of Violence against Women; adopted at Belém do Pará, Brazil, on 9 June 1994; entered into force 3 May 1995 (Belém do Pará Convention).

[34] Art. 13(1), African Charter on the Rights and Welfare of the Child; adopted at Addis Ababa 1 July 1990; entered into force 29 November 1999.

[35] Art. 23, Protocol to the African Charter on Human and Peoples' Rights on the Rights of Women in Africa; adopted on 1 July 2003; entered into force 25 November 2005.

[36] With the adoption of the 2018 Protocol to the African Charter on Human and Peoples' Rights on the Rights of Persons with Disabilities in Africa, the term in the 2003 Protocol should follow the definition of the later instrument and 'include those who have physical, mental, psycho-social, intellectual, neurological, developmental or other sensory impairments which in interaction with environmental, attitudinal or other barriers hinder their full and effective participation in society on an equal basis with others'. Art. 1, 2018 Protocol on the Rights of Persons with Disabilities in Africa.

[37] Art. 9, African Union Convention for the Protection and Assistance of Internally Displaced Persons in Africa; adopted at Kampala 23 October 2009; entered into force 6 December 2012 (Kampala Convention). As of

25.10 Under the 2004 Arab Charter, States Parties undertake to ensure 'that mentally or physically disabled persons should enjoy a decent life, in conditions which ensure dignity, promote self-reliance and facilitate their active participation in society'.[38] With respect to south-east Asia, the non-binding Human Rights Declaration issued by the Association of South-East Asian Nations (ASEAN) in 2012 provides that the rights of persons with disabilities 'are an inalienable, integral and indivisible part of human rights and fundamental freedoms'.[39]

THE RIGHT TO LIFE OF PERSONS WITH DISABILITIES UNDER GLOBAL STANDARDS

The ICCPR

25.11 Each person with a disability or disabilities under the jurisdiction of a State Party to the ICCPR benefits from the protection of the right to life afforded by Article 6. This right, which belongs to every person, is non-derogable.[40] As discussed in Chapter 1 of this work, that every human being has the right to life – without distinction 'of any kind'[41] – has long reflected customary international law. In this way, the jus cogens prohibition of arbitrary deprivation of life codified in Article 6(1) of the Covenant protects all men, women, and children with disabilities.

25.12 The duty to respect the right to life means that a State Party to the ICCPR – and indeed any other State – may not arbitrarily deprive any person with disabilities of his, her, or their life, whether that occurs directly or through the actions of a State agent. This is a particular concern with respect to use of force by law enforcement officials and officials in custodial settings, as discussed later in this chapter. The duty to protect life (by law), codified in Article 6(1) of the ICCPR, requires specific measures of protection for a person with disabilities, as set out by the Human Rights Committee in its General Comment 36 on the right to life.[42] Therein the Committee stated, referring to the corresponding provision on the right to life in the CRPD, that 'persons with disabilities, including psychosocial or intellectual disabilities, are also entitled to specific measures of protection so as to ensure their effective enjoyment of the right to life on an equal basis with others'.[43] Such protection measures 'must', the Committee declared, 'include the provision of reasonable accommodation when necessary to ensure the right to life, such as ensuring access of persons with disabilities to essential facilities and

---

1 December 2020, thirty-one of fifty-five African nations had adhered to the Kampala Convention and a further thirteen were signatories.

[38] Art. 40(1), Arab Charter on Human Rights; adopted at Tunis 22 May 2004; entered into force 15 March 2008.
[39] ASEAN Human Rights Declaration, adopted by the Heads of State/Government of ASEAN member States at Phnom Penh, Cambodia, 18 November 2012, at http://bit.ly/329wakp, para. 4.
[40] Art. 4(2), ICCPR.
[41] Human Rights Committee, 'General comment No. 36. Article 6: right to life', UN doc. CCPR/C/GC/36, 3 September 2019 (hereinafter, Human Rights Committee, General Comment 36 on the right to life), para. 3.
[42] Human Rights Committee, General Comment 36 on the right to life, para. 24.
[43] Ibid, citing Art. 10, CRPD.

services'.[44] Among conditions listed in the General Comment as threatening or preventing enjoyment of the right to life with dignity include gun violence, the prevalence of life-threatening diseases, extreme poverty, and homelessness – all major factors in causing disabilities and/or disproportionately impacting persons with disabilities around the world.[45]

25.13 The right to life must further, the Committee emphasised, be respected and ensured without distinction of any kind, including disability and albinism. Legal protection for the right to life must apply equally to all individuals and provide them with effective guarantees against all forms of discrimination, including multiple and intersectional forms of discrimination. Any deprivation of life based on discrimination in law or in fact is ipso facto arbitrary in nature.[46]

The CRPD

25.14 The CRPD explicitly protects the right to life of every person with disabilities in its Article 10. The provision reads as follows: 'States Parties reaffirm that every human being has the inherent right to life and shall take all necessary measures to ensure its effective enjoyment by persons with disabilities on an equal basis with others.' The reference to the right to life being 'inherent' reaffirms its customary nature. The duty to take 'all necessary measures' to ensure its effective enjoyment by persons with disabilities is potentially far-reaching in nature and extent.

25.15 Among persons with disabilities, women and girls are especially at risk.[47] The notion of 'multiple discrimination' is explicitly recognised in Article 6 of the CRPD, which delineates a duty to take effective measures to address the problem.[48] Thus, for example, in 2014, in its Concluding Observations on Mexico's initial report, the Committee on the Rights of Persons with Disabilities[49] (CRPD Committee) observed that women and girls with disabilities, especially those from indigenous communities, are often the victims of violence and abuse.[50] The Committee urged Mexico to 'implement existing legislative

---

[44] Human Rights Committee, General Comment No. 36, para. 24, citing Arts. 5(3) and 9, CRPD. As discussed further later in this chapter, the notion of 'reasonable accommodation', which originated in the CRPD, is an important advance in the protection of persons with disabilities. As a matter of historical interest, temples and other buildings were being built with access for persons with disabilities in ancient Greece as early as the fourth century BCE. D. Sneed, 'The Architecture of Access: Ramps at Ancient Greek Healing Sanctuaries', *Antiquity*, vol. 94, no. 376 (August 2020), pp. 1015–29.

[45] Human Rights Committee, General Comment No. 36, para. 26.

[46] Ibid., para. 61.

[47] They are also greater in number than men, particularly in low- and middle-income countries, where women are estimated to comprise up to three quarters of persons with disabilities. UN Women, *Making the SDGs Count for Women and Girls with Disabilities*, Issue Brief, New York, 2017, at http://bit.ly/37oSw2t.

[48] According to Article 6(1): 'States Parties recognize that women and girls with disabilities are subject to multiple discrimination, and in this regard shall take measures to ensure the full and equal enjoyment by them of all human rights and fundamental freedoms.'

[49] The CRPD Committee is the body of eighteen independent experts, which monitors implementation of the Convention by its States Parties.

[50] CRPD Committee, Concluding Observations on the initial report of Mexico, UN doc. CRPD/C/MEX/CO/1, 27 October 2014, para. 33.

and policy measures to prevent violence against women and girls with disabilities' and asked that it 'periodically compile data and statistics on the situation of women and girls with disabilities in respect of violence, exploitation and abuse, including femicide'.[51]

25.16 Children with disabilities are said to face 'double prejudice on account of the combined disadvantage accruing to them due to their impairment and age'.[52] Accordingly, the CRPD obligates States Parties to take 'all necessary measures to ensure the full enjoyment by children with disabilities of all human rights and fundamental freedoms on an equal basis with other children'.[53]

25.17 China, the most populous nation on earth, is said to have a high rate of children with disabilities (amounting to around 5 percent of births two decades ago, according to one estimate).[54] Up to 1.2 million children with disabilities are thought to be born every year, of whom some 250,000 babies have disabilities that are obvious at birth. The remainder are children whose disabilities become apparent in the months or years after birth.[55] Children born with disabilities 'or illnesses that may lead to disabilities' may be at risk 'from the first moments of life because their parents or extended family members may consider whether to support the children in their survival'. They may be abandoned predominantly because of fear of the discrimination that many people with disabilities and their families will experience, or owing to the high costs (to the family) of disability.[56] Writing in 2014, Fisher and Shang argued that China needs to establish a system to protect children with disabilities who are abandoned, neglected, or abused by their parents. 'The decision of the life or death of a child should not just be a private family decision', they observe.[57]

25.18 The elderly are also at particular risk. As the UN Special Rapporteur on the rights of persons with disabilities wrote in July 2019, a 'longer lifespan is associated with an increased prevalence of chronic diseases and physical and cognitive impairments, which in interaction with various barriers may result in disabilities'.[58] Within the broad category

---

[51] Ibid., para. 34.
[52] Broderick and Ferri, *International and European Disability Law and Policy. Text, Cases and Materials*, p. 122.
[53] Art. 7(1), CRPD.
[54] Ministry of Health of the People's Republic of China and China Disabled Persons' Federation, 'Notice on printing and distributing "China Action Plan of Promoting the Quality of Newborn Population and Reducing Birth Deficiencies and Disabilities (2002–2010)"', Beijing, 2002. UNICEF reported data from a 2006 survey according to which China had around five million children with disabilities, representing only 1.6 per cent of all children in the country. UNICEF, *Children with Disabilities Atlas 2018*, New York, 2018, at http://bit.ly/3927dsA, chap. 11, p. 144. UNICEF remarks on a 'narrower disability classification criteria used in China', which could help to explain part of the apparent data discrepancies.
[55] Ministry of Health and China Disabled Persons' Federation, 'Notice on printing and distributing "China Action Plan of Promoting the Quality of Newborn Population and Reducing Birth Deficiencies and Disabilities (2002–2010)"'.
[56] K. R. Fisher and X. Shang, 'Protecting the Right to Life of Children with Disabilities in China', *Journal of Social Service Research*, vol. 40, no. 4 (2014), pp. 560–72, at 564, 568, and 569. Costs of disability in China are dominated by medical expenses for which the family is usually responsible, although some employment insurance covers most of the medical costs of employees' children.
[57] Ibid., p. 570.
[58] Report of the Special Rapporteur on the rights of persons with disabilities, UN doc. A/74/186, 17 July 2019, para. 4.

of elderly persons, older women with disabilities 'have consistently worse life prospects and outcomes than older women without disabilities and older men with disabilities'.[59] Older persons with disabilities face significant risks of violence, abuse, and neglect. Abuse occurs both in the community and in institutionalised settings, including hospitals, nursing homes, and other residential settings.[60] According to WHO, 90 per cent of all abusers in community settings are family members.[61] The risk of mortality from abuse and neglect seems to be higher in older adults with greater levels of cognitive impairments.[62]

25.19 Custodial settings hold particular dangers for any person with disabilities, as case-law before the CRPD Committee has highlighted. For those States Parties that have adhered to the Optional Protocol to the CRPD,[63] an individual may make a complaint arguing that his or her rights have been violated. To date, however, jurisprudence before the Committee specifically on Article 10 has been limited. A notable instance of the right to life being cited in a complaint is *Mr. X v. Argentina*, a case on which the Committee rendered its Views in 2014.[64] The author of the complaint was being held in pretrial detention at a federal prison prior to his criminal trial. He had a spinal problem and suffered a stroke while he was in detention, but was refused transfer to house arrest on a number of occasions. He was moved to a prison hospital, but the bathroom serving the facility was inaccessible for a wheelchair.

25.20 The Federal Criminal Court received a report from the Department of Forensic Medicine, which had examined the author during his detention at the Buenos Aires Federal Penitentiary Complex. It stated that a clinical neurosurgical assessment was urgently needed and that the prison hospital did 'not have the infrastructure the patient requires'. Although there was said to be 'no immediate risk of death', his remaining in detention without being able to receive the check-ups or treatments he needed, which included feeding support and psychiatric treatment, 'would severely compromise his clinical status and could endanger his life'.[65] According to the author of the complaint, the authorities had seriously endangered his life and health by confining him in a prison and obliging him to accept outpatient treatment that entailed frequent ambulance transfers.[66]

25.21 In the light of the information at its disposal, the Committee found it did not have sufficient evidence to conclude that either travel to and from the prison in 'a highly sophisticated ambulance with a doctor in attendance' or the conditions of the author's incarceration constituted a violation of the right to life protected in Article 10 of the CRPD.

---

[59] Ibid., para. 9.
[60] Ibid., para. 36.
[61] WHO, 'Elder Abuse: The Health Sector Role in Prevention and Response', Infographic, 2016, at http://bit.ly/2WApGHR.
[62] X. Qi Dong, R. Chen, and M. A. Simon, 'Elder Abuse and Dementia: A Review of the Research and Health Policy', *Health Affairs*, vol. 33, no. 4 (April 2014), pp. 642–9.
[63] As of 1 May 2021, ninety-eight States had adhered to the Protocol.
[64] CRPD Committee, *Mr. X v. Argentina*, Views, UN doc. CRPD/C/11/D/8/2012, 18 June 2014.
[65] Ibid., para. 3.2.
[66] Ibid., para. 8.1.

Instead, the Committee applied the standard of 'reasonable accommodation' in Article 14(2) with respect to persons deprived of their liberty[67] to find a violation of that provision. It held that Argentina was 'under an obligation to provide redress for the breaches of the author's rights under the Convention', which it would need to do 'by making accommodations in his place of detention to ensure his access to prison facilities and services on an equal basis with other prisoners'.[68] More generally, the Committee called on Argentina to 'ensure that, as a consequence of a lack of accessibility or reasonable accommodation, the conditions of detention in which persons with disabilities are held do not become more onerous or cause greater physical and psychological suffering of an extent that would constitute cruel, inhuman or degrading treatment or that would undermine their physical and mental integrity'.[69]

25.22 Following the entry into force of the CRPD, the UN Special Rapporteur on torture and other cruel, inhuman or degrading treatment or punishment called on the UN General Assembly to 'reframe violence and abuse perpetrated against persons with disabilities as torture or a form of ill-treatment'.[70] This, according to the Special Rapporteur, Manfred Nowak, was owing to evidence he had received 'about different forms of violence and abuse inflicted against persons with disabilities – men, women and children'.[71] This concerned especially violence and abuse perpetrated in public institutions, private spheres, and medical settings, which comprised 'unspeakable indignities, neglect, severe forms of restraint and seclusion, as well as physical, mental and sexual violence'. The lack of reasonable accommodation in detention facilities, the Special Rapporteur further affirmed, 'may increase the risk of exposure to neglect, violence, abuse, torture and ill-treatment'.[72]

THE RIGHT TO LIFE OF PERSONS WITH DISABILITIES UNDER REGIONAL STANDARDS

25.23 While all the main regional human rights treaties offer general legal protection that encompasses persons with disabilities, including legal protection of their right to life, they do not, for the most part, specifically protect the right of life of such persons. The notable exception is the Protocol on the Rights of Persons with Disabilities in Africa, a treaty adopted under the auspices of the African Union in 2018 but which has not yet entered into

---

[67] 'States Parties shall ensure that if persons with disabilities are deprived of their liberty through any process, they are, on an equal basis with others, entitled to guarantees in accordance with international human rights law and shall be treated in compliance with the objectives and principles of the present Convention, including by provision of reasonable accommodation.' This picks up on the general provision on equality and non-discrimination in Article 5, paragraph 3, which provides: 'In order to promote equality and eliminate discrimination, States Parties shall take all appropriate steps to ensure that reasonable accommodation is provided.'

[68] CRPD Committee, *Mr. X v. Argentina*, Views, para. 9(a).

[69] Ibid., para. 9(e).

[70] 'Interim Report of the Special Rapporteur on torture and other cruel, inhuman or degrading treatment or punishment, Manfred Nowak', UN doc. A/63/175, 28 July 2008, para. 45.

[71] Ibid., para. 37.

[72] Ibid., para. 38.

force. Already in the African Charter on Human and Peoples' Rights, concluded in 1981, it had been provided that 'the disabled' shall 'have the right to special measures of protection in keeping with their physical or moral needs'.[73] The prohibition of discrimination on the basis of 'other status' in Article 2 of the Charter has been interpreted by the African Commission on Human and Peoples' Rights to encompass disability: a provision 'necessary in eradicating discrimination in all its guises'.[74]

25.24 The 1999 Inter-American Convention on the Elimination of Discrimination against Persons with Disabilities[75] (CIADDIS) does not explicitly protect the right to life. That said, its preamble reaffirms that persons with disabilities 'have the same human rights and fundamental freedoms as other persons; and that these rights, which include freedom from discrimination based on disability, flow from the inherent dignity and equality of each person'.[76] It has been asserted that although CIADDIS does not provide 'a strong tool for the analysis of individual claims' in cases of violations of the rights of persons with disabilities, an 'expansive' interpretation of the Inter-American treaties, particularly the American Convention on Human Rights, by the Inter-American Commission and the Inter-American Court have served to offer protection.[77]

The Right to Life under the 2018 Protocol on the Rights of Persons with Disabilities in Africa

25.25 Article 8 of the Protocol on the Rights of Persons with Disabilities in Africa concerns the right to life. It provides as follows:

1. Every person with a disability has the inherent right to life and integrity.
2. States Parties shall take effective and appropriate measures to ensure:
   a) Protection, respect for life and the dignity of persons with disabilities, on an equal basis with others;
   b) That persons with disabilities have access to services, facilities and devices to enable them to live with dignity and to realise fully their right to life.

In reaffirming the customary right to life of all persons with disabilities, the duty of States Parties to respect, protect, and fulfil that right is also delimited by the article. Article 11

---

[73] Art. 18(4), African Charter on Human and Peoples' Rights; adopted at Nairobi 27 June 1981; entered into force 21 October 1986.

[74] African Commission on Human and Peoples' Rights, *Purohit and Moore v. The Gambia*, Views (Comm. No. 241/2001), May 2003, para. 49; cf. also paras. 45–8.

[75] Inter-American Convention on the Elimination of All Forms of Discrimination Against Persons with Disabilities; adopted at Guatemala City 8 June 1999; entered into force 14 September 2001. As of 1 May 2021, nineteen States were party to the Convention (Argentina, Bolivia, Brazil, Chile, Colombia, Costa Rica, Dominican Republic, Ecuador, El Salvador, Guatemala, Haiti, Honduras, Mexico, Nicaragua, Panama, Paraguay, Peru, Uruguay, and Venezuela). There was also one signatory State, Dominica.

[76] Under Article 1(1) of the Inter-American Convention, the term *disability* 'means a physical, mental, or sensory impairment, whether permanent or temporary, that limits the capacity to perform one or more essential activities of daily life, and which can be caused or aggravated by the economic and social environment'.

[77] D. Guarnizo-Peralta, 'Disability Rights in the Inter-American System of Human Rights: An Expansive and Evolving Protection', *Netherlands Quarterly of Human Rights*, vol. 36, no.1 (1 March 2018), pp. 43–63.

further obligates States Parties to take all appropriate measures 'to eliminate harmful practices perpetrated on persons with disabilities, including witchcraft, abandonment, concealment, ritual killings or the association of disability with omens'.[78]

25.26 Welcoming the adoption of the Protocol in 2018, Catalina Devandas, the UN Special Rapporteur on the rights of persons with disabilities, declared that it 'should lead to considerable improvements in the lives of African people with disabilities'. The Protocol, she said, 'addresses some of the urgent issues that have the most disproportionate impact on people with disabilities, such as poverty, systemic discrimination and harmful practices'.[79] Certainly, the challenge is immense. The United Nations has estimated that there are 80 million people in Africa with disabilities; other estimates put the figure far higher, perhaps as many as 300 million (40 per cent of Africa's 1.2 billion population).[80] Whatever the true number, the life prospects of many of these individuals are bleak. As recalled in 2006, 'some have estimated the life expectancy for a person with a spinal cord injury in a poorer African country at between four months and two years'.[81]

25.27 There is particular concern regarding the right to life of persons with albinism. Albinism is a rare, non-contagious, genetically inherited condition that occurs worldwide regardless of ethnicity or gender, but is especially prevalent in Sub-Saharan Africa.[82] It most commonly results in the lack of melanin pigment in the hair, skin, and eyes (oculocutaneous albinism), causing vulnerability to sun exposure. The preamble to the Protocol on the Rights of Persons with Disabilities in Africa notes the particular alarm of States Parties at 'the maiming or killing of persons with albinism in many parts of the continent'. The physical condition is covered as a sensory impairment under Article 2(e) of the CRPD. In addition to their highly sensitive skin, albinos can have limited visual capacity.[83]

25.28 In June 2015, Ms Ikponwosa Ero was designated as the first UN Independent Expert on the enjoyment of human rights by persons with albinism. She has described persons with albinism as 'a constituency' of persons with disabilities.[84] The right to life and physical integrity of persons with albinism is 'systematically violated', she argues, 'in the

---

[78] Art. 11(1), 2018 Protocol on the Rights of Persons with Disabilities in Africa.
[79] 'African States Affirm the Rights of Persons with Disabilities in a New Landmark Protocol', press release, Geneva, 15 February 2018, at http://bit.ly/30eCfJO.
[80] African Studies Centre Leiden, 'Disability in Africa', University of Leiden, web page last modified on 26 March 2020, at http://bit.ly/3jblfwt.
[81] S. Chalklen, L. Swart, and B. Watermeyer, 'Establishing the Secretarial for the African Decade of Persons with Disabilities', in B. Watermeyer, L. Swart, T. Lorenzo, M. Schneider, and M. Priestley (eds.), *Disability and Social Change: A South African Agenda*, Human Science Research Council Press, South Africa, 2006, p. 96.
[82] See, e.g., E. S. Hong, H. Zeeb, and M. H Repacholi, 'Albinism in Africa as a Public Health Issue', *BMC Public Health*, vol. 6 (2006), pp. 212–19, at http://bit.ly/39chi5A.
[83] S. A. Djoyou Kamga, 'Call for a Protocol to the African Charter on Human and Peoples' Rights on the Rights of Persons with Disabilities in Africa', *African Journal of International and Comparative Law*, vol. 21, no.2 (May 2013), pp. 219–49, p. 230.
[84] Report of the Independent Expert on the enjoyment of human rights by persons with albinism, UN doc. A/72/131, 14 July 2017, para. 8.

context of attacks, killings, mutilations and abandonment'.[85] In her report to the UN General Assembly in July 2019, she observed that persons with albinism in Africa 'generally have a lower life expectancy owing to multiple factors', such as skin cancer, HIV/AIDS, the myth that intercourse with persons with albinism can cure the disease, and harmful practices related to the manifestation of belief in witchcraft.[86] She recalled that hundreds of cases of attacks, including murder, infanticide, mutilation, ritual rape, and trafficking of persons, organs, and body parts, have been reported in twenty-eight countries in Africa in the past decade.[87] As a consequence of her work, the African Union adopted the first Regional Action Plan on Albinism in Africa, covering 2017–21. The Plan set out fifteen specific measures centred around four key pillars: prevention, protection, accountability and equality, and non-discrimination.[88]

The Right to Life of Women with Disabilities under the Inter-American and Belém do Pará Conventions

25.29 According to the 1969 American Convention on Human Rights, 'every person has the right to have his life respected. This right shall be protected by law and, in general, from the moment of conception. No one shall be arbitrarily deprived of his life.'[89] The Inter-American Convention does not specifically address the rights of persons with disabilities, although States Parties 'undertake to respect the rights and freedoms recognized therein and to ensure to all persons subject to their jurisdiction the free and full exercise of those rights and freedoms, without any discrimination' for reason of 'any ... social condition'.[90] Under Article 9 of the Belém do Pará Convention, however, States Parties are obligated to take special account of the vulnerability of women subjected to violence who are disabled.

25.30 In 1997, the Inter-American Commission on Human Rights adjudged a case against Ecuador on behalf of a detainee with a psychosocial disability who died in a social rehabilitation centre.[91] Víctor Rosario Congo, a forty-eight-year-old Ecuadorian man who had been charged with robbery and assault, had been placed in pre-trial detention in the Social Rehabilitation Center in Machala. According to the Commission, when he was incarcerated, Mr Congo behaved in a way 'that suggested mental disorder'. On or about 12 September 1990, he was placed in an isolation cell.[92] Two days later, it appears

---

[85] Of course, if, as is most often the case, attacks are committed by private individuals not agents of the State, whether a violation of the right to life occurs could depend on whether the State had acted with due diligence to prevent and repress such attacks.

[86] Report of the Independent Expert on the enjoyment of human rights by persons with albinism, UN doc. A/74/190, 18 July 2019, para. 15.

[87] Ibid., para. 15.

[88] Report of the Independent Expert on the enjoyment of human rights by persons with albinism on the Regional Action Plan on Albinism in Africa (2017–2021), UN doc. A/HRC/37/57/Add.3, 19 December 2017.

[89] Art. 4(1), Inter-American Convention on Human Rights.

[90] Art. 1(1), Inter-American Convention on Human Rights.

[91] Inter-American Commission on Human Rights, *Víctor Rosario Congo v. Ecuador*, Report 63/99 (Case No. 11.427), 13 April 1999, at http://bit.ly/39odWTZ.

[92] Ibid., paras. 6 and 7.

that he was attacked by a guard at the Rehabilitation Center: the guard 'took advantage of the depressed mental state' of Mr Congo and harassed him by shouting questions over and over at him, 'which clearly made him more demented'. The guard then beat him with a club on the head, inflicting a wound that remained visible post mortem.[93]

25.31 There is no record of Mr. Congo having received any medical treatment. He was returned to the isolation cell, wherein he remained naked and virtually incommunicado. The Center's Director logged that he was being held alone in the isolation cell 'because of his demented state, for he has been urinating, defecating and speaking to himself for some time'.[94] Mr Congo was taken to the Vernaza Hospital only on 25 October 1990. He arrived in a critically dehydrated state and died a few hours after admission. The report on the autopsy performed on his body on 27 October 1990 concluded that he had died of malnutrition, hydro-electrolytic imbalance, and heart and lung failure.[95]

25.32 Based on the definition contained in a 1993 document in the Sub-Commission on Prevention of Discrimination and Protection of Minorities under the erstwhile Commission on Human Rights,[96] the Inter-American Commission concluded that Mr Congo 'must be regarded as mentally disabled'.[97] The Commission determined that the duty of humane treatment for detainees had to be interpreted in light of the UN Principles for the Protection of Persons with Mental Illness and for the Improvement of Mental Health Care, adopted by the UN General Assembly in 1991. The Commission considered that 'a violation of the right to physical integrity is even more serious in the case of a person held in preventive detention, suffering a mental disease, and therefore in the custody of the State in a particularly vulnerable position'.[98]

25.33 In assessing compliance by Ecuador with Mr Congo's right to life, the Commission observed that 'the fact that the State has no special facilities for the admission of prisoners with mental illness does not exempt it from the obligation to provide medical care to the persons in its custody'.[99] In finding a violation of Article 4 of the Convention, the Commission held that Ecuador 'had failed to take the measures in its power to ensure the right to life of a person who, partly because of his state of health and in part owing to injuries inflicted on him by a State agent, was defenceless, isolated, and under its control'.[100]

25.34 The Inter-American Commission on Human Rights has also called upon a State Party to implement precautionary measures to safeguard the lives of persons with

---

[93] Ibid., paras. 8–9.
[94] Ibid., para. 11.
[95] Ibid., paras. 19–20.
[96] UN Sub-Commission on Prevention of Discrimination and Protection of Minorities, Erica Irene Daes, Rapporteur, Principles, Guidelines and Guarantees for the Protection of Persons Detained on Grounds of Mental Ill Health or Suffering from Mental Disorder, UN doc. E/CN.4/Sub.2/1983/17, p. 43.
[97] Inter-American Commission on Human Rights, *Víctor Rosario Congo v. Ecuador*, 13 April 1999, para. 42.
[98] Ibid., para. 67.
[99] Ibid., para. 81.
[100] Ibid., para. 84.

disabilities. In December 2003, it granted a request for precautionary measures to protect the hospital's patients against physical violence and sexual abuse. Mental Disability Rights International (MDRI) had visited the facility, where it found two youths, Julio (aged seventeen) and Jorge (aged eighteen),

> frighteningly thin and locked naked in tiny isolation cells. Holes in the cell floors designed to be latrines were crammed and caked over with excrement. The cells reeked of urine and faeces, and the cell walls were smeared with excrement. Each boy was infested with lice, covered with scars, and spent approximately four hours every other day in an outdoor pen, which was littered with human excrement, garbage, and broken glass.[101]

The Commission called upon Paraguay to adopt all necessary measures to protect the lives, health, and the physical, mental, and moral integrity of the 460 people detained in the institution, with special attention to the situation of women and children; to adopt necessary measures to improve hygiene in the hospital; and to restrict the use of isolation cells in accordance with international standards.[102]

25.35 Disability rights activists had welcomed the Inter-American Commission's decision as 'historic': the 'first time that the Commission called for immediate, life-saving measures to combat ongoing abuses in a psychiatric institution'.[103] Five years on, however, in its decision in 2008 in *Patients at the Neuropsychiatric Hospital v. Paraguay*,[104] after requesting information from the authorities several times, the Commission learned of the deaths of two patients, as well as other acts of sexual abuse and violence at the hospital.[105] A further years later, it was being reported by media in the United States that, due to a lack of funding, the facility – the only state psychiatric hospital in Paraguay – was feeding its patients with donated food and running low on medicine.[106]

25.36 Precautionary measures were also sought – and obtained – in the case of Julio César Cano Molina in Cuba.[107] Mr Molina, who allegedly had 'a mental and intellectual disability', was a forty-five-year-old Afro-descendant incarcerated in the province of Pinar del Río. He had been sentenced to a term of thirty-five years of imprisonment for a range of crimes.[108] In addition to significant physical problems resulting from a car accident, he was said to be suffering from 'epilepsy, psychiatric disorder and a mental disability'. He was

---

[101] A. A. Hillman, 'Protecting Mental Disability Rights: A Success Story in the Inter-American Human Rights System', *Global Disability Rights Now*, Digital Commons, 2005, at http://bit.ly/32iCINI, p. 1.
[102] Ibid., p. 3.
[103] Ibid., p. 1. See also L. Hammes, 'Paraguay: Human Rights for the Mentally Disabled', *NACLA Report on the Americas*, North American Congress on Latin America, vol. 37, no. 5 (March/April 2004).
[104] Inter-American Commission on Human Rights, *Patients at the Neuropsychiatric Hospital v. Paraguay*, Decision on Precautionary Measures (Case No. PM 277-07), 29 July 2008.
[105] Ibid., para. 31.
[106] 'Paraguay's Only Public Psychiatric Hospital Running Low on Supplies', *Fox News*, published 24 June 2013; last updated 19 December 2016, at http://fxn.ws/30ekkD4.
[107] Inter-American Commission on Human Rights, *Matter of Julio César Cano Molina concerning Cuba*, Resolution 24/2014 (Precautionary Measure No. 307-14), 10 September 2014.
[108] Ibid., para. 3.

being held in a punishment cell in 'deplorable conditions', apparently due to the 'stench and nuisances' caused by his diseases, which 'bothered' the rest of the inmates.[109]

25.37 The Commission considered that the serious deterioration of Mr. Molina's health could have an impact on his right to life and personal integrity. It appeared that 'despite a series of purported pathologies caused by a car accident', he was not receiving 'the necessary medical treatment'. The applicants had alleged that his body was swelling, that he suffered from a severe infection, and that he was bleeding from the urethra, requiring specialised medical care and surgery 'that has been recommended since 1995'. The situation was exacerbated by the 'precarious' detention conditions and the lack of adequate food, 'which could worsen his health situation'.[110] The Commission considered 'prima facie' that Mr. Molina's rights to life, personal integrity, and health faced a situation of risk.[111] It decided that Cuba should provide him with specialised medical care, taking into account his particular circumstances and needs, according to his pathological conditions. It further called on the authorities to ensure that his detention conditions 'meet international standards, taking into account his current health situation and mental and intellectual disability'.[112]

25.38 In 2006, the year of the adoption of the CRPD, the Inter-American Court of Human Rights issued its judgment in *Ximenes-Lopes* v. *Brazil*,[113] a case which concerned responsibility for the death of Mr. Damião Ximenes-Lopes in October 1999 in a private psychiatric clinic that operated in Brazil's public health system. Mr. Ximenes-Lopes, a person with a psycho-social disability, had been hospitalised as part of psychiatric treatment in Casa de Reposo Guararapes. He was beaten during his internment, seemingly by staff at the clinic. The Court affirmed that any person in a vulnerable condition is entitled to special protection, recalling that States should 'adopt positive measures, to be determined according to the specific needs of protection of the legal person, either because of his personal condition or the specific situation he is in, such as his disabilities'.[114]

25.39 In its judgment, the Court referred to the particular vulnerability to torture and other types of cruel, inhuman, or degrading treatment of persons with disabilities in psychiatric institutions. 'The vulnerability inherent to people with mental disabilities is', the Court remarked, 'compounded by the high degree of intimacy which is typical of the treatment of psychiatric illnesses, which makes these persons more susceptible to mistreatment when they are hospitalised'.[115] In order to safeguard the right to life, States are responsible for regulating and supervising 'at all times' the services and national programmes of health care

---

[109] Ibid., para. 3(a) and (c).
[110] Ibid., para. 6.
[111] Ibid., para. 8.
[112] Ibid., para. 14.
[113] Inter-American Court of Human Rights, *Ximenes-Lopes* v. *Brazil*, Judgment (Merits, Reparations and Costs), 4 July 2006.
[114] Ibid., para. 103 (footnote omitted).
[115] Ibid., para. 106.

services, 'so that they may deter any threat to the right to life and the physical integrity of the individuals undergoing medical treatment'.[116]

The Right to Life of Persons with Disabilities under the European Convention on Human Rights

25.40 Article 2(1) of the 1950 European Convention on Human Rights[117] provides simply: 'Everyone's right to life shall be protected by law.' No specific provision safeguards the life or physical integrity of persons with disabilities. Indeed, Article 5 of the Convention, which concerns the rights to liberty and to security, expressly allows the lawful detention of persons 'of unsound mind'.[118] The Convention does, however, proclaim: 'The enjoyment of the rights and freedoms set forth in [the] Convention shall be secured without discrimination on any ground.'[119]

Law Enforcement and Persons with Disabilities

25.41 The risk of use of lethal force by law enforcement officials against a person with intellectual or psychosocial disabilities is particularly high.[120] Where they knew or ought to have known that they are confronted with such a person, the police will be expected to act appropriately. A 2014 case concerned a Russian citizen with a psychosocial disability who required institutional treatment. Mr Kirill Shchiborshch feared that anyone entering his apartment was a burglar and the police had been informed of this fact. They chose to enter forcibly, and following a struggle, Mr Shchiborshch was taken to hospital with multiple wounds and comatose. He died without regaining consciousness, having sustained craniocerebral trauma; brain oedema; concussion; slash wounds to the head, body, and extremities; several fractured ribs; and a ruptured jugular vein.[121]

25.42 The Court observed that dealing with individuals with serious mental health issues 'clearly requires special training, the absence of which is likely to render futile any attempted negotiations with a person with a mental disorder as grave as that of Mr Shchiborshch'. The Russian authorities did not explain why the police had taken 'actions aimed at securing Mr Shchiborshch's involuntary hospitalisation without being accompanied by qualified medical personnel'.[122] The Court further regretted that the police used

---

[116] Ibid., para. 99.
[117] Convention for the Protection of Human Rights and Fundamental Freedoms; adopted at Rome by the Council of Europe 4 November 1950; entered into force 3 September 1953 (hereinafter, European Convention on Human Rights).
[118] Art. 5(1)(e), European Convention on Human Rights.
[119] Art. 14, European Convention on Human Rights.
[120] One research paper, published in 2016, estimated that, in the United States, persons with disabilities comprise between one-third and half of all people killed by law enforcement officers. D. M. Perry and L. Carter-Long, 'The Ruderman White Paper on Media Coverage of Law Enforcement Use of Force and Disability: A Media Study (2013–2015) and Overview', March 2016, available at http://bit.ly/3oxyBFZ, pp. 7–8.
[121] European Court of Human Rights, *Shchiborshch and Kuzmina v. Russia*, Judgment (First Section), 16 January 2014 (as rendered final on 2 June 2014), paras. 6–10.
[122] Ibid., para. 233.

force as if they were dealing with any armed offender, without regard to Mr Shchiborshch's delirious state or to the fact that he did not pose an immediate danger to either himself or others. The Russian police chose to storm the kitchen in which Mr Shchiborshch had barricaded himself, in the course of which he sustained injuries that proved lethal. This decision, which was not subject to any preliminary planning and assessment, was hastily taken at the scene without there being any necessity for urgent action.[123]

25.43 In its 2010 judgment in the *Jasinskis* case,[124] the European Court of Human Rights addressed the death in police custody of a forty-three-year-old deaf and mute man, Valdis Jasinskis. Mr Jasinskis had sustained serious – and, according to the post-mortem, ultimately fatal – head injuries falling down a set of stairs after being out with friends. The officers who had attended the scene of the fall had been informed of his disabilities. They took him to the local police station and placed him in a cell for 14 hours as the police officers believed him to be drunk. In finding a violation of his right to life, the Court reiterated that the European Convention on Human Rights obligated States Parties to ensure that persons with disabilities in detention receive treatment consonant with their particular needs. Despite this, Mr Jasinskis had not benefited from 'special care' to guarantee 'such conditions as correspond to his special needs resulting from his disability'.[125]

25.44 More broadly, the Court has held that States must take 'particular measures to provide effective protection of vulnerable persons from ill-treatment of which the authorities had or ought to have had knowledge'.[126] In the *Jasinskis* case, however, the police had not had the applicant medically examined when they took him into custody, as they were specifically required to do by the standards of the European Committee for the Prevention of Torture (CPT). They had not given him the opportunity to tell them about his health, even after he kept knocking on the doors and the walls of the cell. Taking into account that he was both deaf and mute, the police had a clear obligation to at least provide him with a pen and paper to enable him to communicate his concerns.[127] The Court was 'even more concerned by the almost seven hours that passed between the time when the applicant's son "refused to wake up" in the morning and the time when an ambulance was called'. Not getting up for some fourteen hours, the Court observed, 'can hardly be explained by simple drunkenness'.[128]

25.45 In late August 2020, two South African police officers (and subsequently a third) were arrested over the deadly shooting of a sixteen-year-old boy. The family of Nathaniel Julius, who had Down's syndrome, said he had gone out to buy biscuits when he was shot dead in Johannesburg's Eldorado Park suburb. The family said Julius was shot after not answering officers' questions. The failure to respond, however, was due to his disability.

---

[123] Ibid., para. 240.
[124] European Court of Human Rights, *Jasinskis v. Latvia*, Judgment (Third Section), 21 December 2010 (rendered final on 21 March 2011).
[125] Ibid., para. 59.
[126] Ibid.
[127] Ibid., para. 66.
[128] Ibid.

The Independent Police Investigative Directorate (Ipid) arrested the officers and charged them with murder after 'careful consideration of the evidence'. The police had initially claimed that Julius had been caught in a shoot-out between officers and local gangsters.[129] In a message condemning the killing and sympathising with the victim's family, the International Disability Alliance stated:

> The loss of Nathaniel's life in broad daylight is exemplary of the large-scale exclusion and marginalisation faced by persons with disabilities globally. In this century, why are we still advocating for the basic principles that protect the lives of persons with disabilities? Should we not be past this? Why does society continue to view the lives of persons with disabilities as worth less than those without disabilities?[130]

On 10 September 2020, three South African police officers appeared in court over the killing of the teenager. Two of the officers were charged with murder, discharge of a firearm in a public place, being in possession of prohibited ammunition, and defeating the ends of justice. A third suspect was arrested later.[131] Appearing again in court later in September, the officer accused of firing the shot that killed Mr Julies accused her superior of threatening her if she did not corroborate his version of events.[132]

Protection of the Right to Life in Institutional Settings

25.46 The *Nencheva* case[133] concerned the deaths of fifteen children and young adults between December 1996 and March 1997 in a home for youth with physical and psychosocial disabilities. Their deaths were the result of the effects of cold and shortages of food, medicine, and other basic necessities. The manager of the home, observing the problems, had sought on several occasions (but without success) to alert the public institutions with direct responsibility for funding the home and which could have been expected to intervene. The Court found a violation of right to life through the failure of the authorities to protect the lives of the vulnerable children placed in their care from a serious and immediate threat.

25.47 The Court noted that a crucial element in the case was that the tragic events in the Dzhurkovo home where the children were held 'was not sudden, punctual, and unforeseen, as in the case of an event of force majeure to which the State might not be able to respond'. The deaths followed one another over a period of several months.[134] There was clear evidence that the authorities had failed to take prompt, concrete, and adequate

---

[129] BBC, 'Nathaniel Julius: South Africa Police Arrested for Killing Teen', 29 August 2020, at http://bbc.in/2QQn5WN.
[130] A message from the International Disability Alliance on the killing of Nathaniel Julius in South Africa, IDA, 2 September 2020, at http://bit.ly/2EZfuCA.
[131] 'Officers Accused of Killing South African Teen to Appear in Court', *Aljazeera*, 10 September 2020, at http://bit.ly/34vgoAX.
[132] 'Julies Case: Cop Who Fired Fatal Shot Says She Was Threatened by Co-Accused', *Eyewitness News*, 22 September 2020, at http://bit.ly/35DKD8f.
[133] European Court of Human Rights, *Nencheva and others v. Bulgaria*, Judgment (Fourth Section), 18 June 2013 (as rendered final on 16 December 2013).
[134] Ibid., para. 122.

measures to prevent the deaths. The lack of reaction over a period of several months to the director's alerts concerning the situation at the home, along with an apparent lack of prompt and appropriate medical assistance, indicates that the authorities did not act, despite having specific knowledge about the real and imminent risks to the lives of the residents at the home. Moreover, the Court noted, no official explanation had been provided for these failures.[135]

25.48 The *Valentin Câmpeanu* case before the European Court's Grand Chamber concerned the death in 2004 of an eighteen-year-old man in a psychiatric hospital. Abandoned at birth and placed in an orphanage, he had been diagnosed as a young child as being HIV-positive and as suffering from an acute psychosocial disability. The Court found that Mr Câmpeanu had been placed in medical institutions that were not equipped to provide adequate care for his condition, that he had been transferred from one unit to another without proper diagnosis, and that the authorities had failed to ensure his appropriate treatment with anti-retroviral medication.[136]

25.49 Citing the judgment in *Nencheva*, the Grand Chamber recalled that positive obligations to protect the lives of patients arise 'where it is known, or ought to have been known to the authorities in view of the circumstances, that the victim was at real and immediate risk from the criminal acts of a third party'.[137] Referring to the 2010 judgment in *Jasinskis*, the Court stated that where the authorities decide to place and maintain in detention a person with disabilities, 'they should demonstrate special care in guaranteeing such conditions as correspond to any special needs resulting from his disability'.[138] Since the authorities were aware of the lack of personnel, insufficient food, and absence of heating in the hospital where he had been placed, the State had unreasonably put his life in danger.

25.50 A third-party intervener in the case, the Euroregional Center for Public Initiatives (ECPI) had informed the Court that Romania had one of the largest groups of people living with HIV in central and eastern Europe, mainly because between 1986 and 1991, some 10,000 children institutionalised in public hospitals and orphanages had been exposed to the risks of HIV transmission through multiple uses of needles and microtransfusions with unscreened blood.[139] In December 2004, there had been 7,088 cases of AIDS and 4,462 cases of HIV infections registered among children, of whom 3,482 had died of AIDS by the end of 2004. The ECPI alleged that the high incidence of HIV infection among children was due to the treatment to which they had been subjected in orphanages and hospitals. This resulted from a perception that children with disabilities were 'beyond recovery' and 'unproductive' and because the personnel lacked the skills and even interest to provide them with appropriate medical care.[140]

---

[135] Ibid., para. 124.
[136] European Court of Human Rights, *Case of Centre for Legal Resources on Behalf of Valentin Câmpeanu v. Romania*, Judgment (Grand Chamber), 17 July 2014, para. 137.
[137] Ibid., para. 130.
[138] Ibid., para. 131.
[139] Ibid., para. 128.
[140] Ibid.

The Istanbul Convention

25.51 The Council of Europe Convention on preventing and combating violence against women and domestic violence,[141] better known as the Istanbul Convention, was adopted in 2011. The Convention, which entered into force in 2014,[142] must be implemented 'without discrimination on any ground such as ... disability'.[143] The Istanbul Convention does not explicitly protect the right to life, but parties must refrain from any act of violence against women and ensure that State authorities, officials, and agents comply with this prohibition.[144] In addition, parties are obligated to take 'the necessary legislative and other measures to exercise due diligence to prevent, investigate, punish and provide reparation for acts of violence' covered by the Convention and which are perpetrated by non-State actors.[145]

THE RIGHT TO LIFE OF PERSONS WITH DISABILITIES UNDER THE ARAB CHARTER ON HUMAN RIGHTS

25.52 The 2004 Arab Charter on Human Rights has a general provision enshrining the protection of the right to life, including for those with disabilities. Under Article 5(1), 'every human being has an inherent right to life'. Paragraph 2 of the article stipulates further: 'This right shall be protected by law. No one shall be arbitrarily deprived of his life.' No derogation from respect for Article 5 may be made.[146] As noted above, States Parties to the Charter undertake to ensure 'that mentally or physically disabled persons should enjoy a decent life, in conditions which ensure dignity, promote self-reliance, and facilitate their active participation in society'.[147]

25.53 That said, across the Arab world there is a widely held perception that the notion of 'equal protection before the law', as it applies to persons with disabilities extends to a capacity to acquire rights but not a capacity to exercise those rights. During the drafting of the CRPD, more than twenty States in the Arab Group submitted a letter to the Ad Hoc Drafting Committee Chair, 'outlining that they only agreed to the consensus of the CRPD

---

[141] Council of Europe Convention on preventing and combating violence against women and domestic violence; adopted at Istanbul 11 May 2011; entered into force 1 August 2014 (hereinafter, Istanbul Convention).
[142] As of 1 December 2020, the Istanbul Convention had been ratified by thirty-four States. The Convention also provides for EU accession, which would require the consent of the European Parliament. On 28 November 2019, the European Parliament adopted a resolution calling on the European Union Council to urgently conclude the process of EU adherence. European Parliament, 'EU Accession to the Council of Europe Convention on Preventing and Combating Violence against Women ("Istanbul Convention")/2016-03', 24 June 2020, at http://bit.ly/38ItQC8. In addition, Canada, the Holy See, Japan, Kazakhstan, Mexico, Tunisia, and the United States, non-members of the Council of Europe, may also adhere to the Convention.
[143] Art. 4(3), Istanbul Convention.
[144] Art. 5(1), Istanbul Convention.
[145] Art. 5(2), Istanbul Convention.
[146] Art. 4(2), 2004 Arab Charter on Human Rights.
[147] Art. 40(1), Arab Charter on Human Rights; adopted at Tunis 22 May 2004; entered into force 15 March 2008.

on the proviso that "legal capacity" is interpreted as "capacity of rights and not the capacity to act" in line with their domestic legal systems'.[148]

Protection of Persons with Disabilities against Violence in the ASEAN Region

25.54 The 2012 ASEAN Human Rights Declaration, which is non-binding, stipulates that the rights of persons with disabilities 'are an inalienable, integral and indivisible part of human rights and fundamental freedoms'.[149] The Declaration further declares that 'every person has an inherent right to life which shall be protected by law. No person shall be deprived of life save in accordance with law'.[150]

THE DEATH PENALTY

The Normative Framework

25.55 General international law does not comprehensively prohibit the imposition of the death penalty on persons with disabilities. In situations of armed conflict, international humanitarian law does not prohibit the imposition of the death penalty on persons with disabilities, or their execution. A specific prohibition on the execution of persons in all circumstances with severe psycho-social or intellectual disabilities is, however, a customary rule that is, at the least, *de lege ferenda*.

25.56 In 2013, the Inter-American Commission on Human Rights had declared in its report on the *Clarence Allen Lackey* case: 'It is a principle of international law that persons with mental disabilities, either at the time of the commission of the crime or during trial, cannot be sentenced to the death penalty. Likewise, international law also prohibits execution of a person sentenced to death if that person has a mental disability at the time of execution."[151] In 1984, the UN Economic and Social Council (ECOSOC) adopted a resolution on safeguards with respect to the death penalty whereby a capital sentence shall not be carried out on 'persons who have become insane'.[152] But in other respects, the evidence adduced by the Commission in support of its two propositions, which was largely

---

[148] A. L. Pearl, 'Article 12 of the United Nations Convention on the Rights of Persons with Disabilities and the Legal Capacity of Disabled People: The Way Forward?', *Leeds Journal of Law & Criminology*, vol. 1, no. 1 (2013), p. 16. The States were Algeria, Bahrain, Comoros, Djibouti, Egypt, Iraq, Kuwait, Lebanon, Libya, Mauritania, Morocco, Oman, Palestine, Qatar, Saudi Arabia, Somalia, Sudan, Syrian Arab Republic, Tunisia, the United Arab Emirates, and Yemen. See also S. A. D. Kamga, 'A Call for a Protocol to the African Charter on Human and Peoples' Rights on the Rights of Persons with Disabilities in Africa', *African Journal of International and Comparative Law*, vol. 21 no. 2 (2013), p. 228.

[149] ASEAN Human Rights Declaration, adopted by the Heads of State/Government of ASEAN member States at Phnom Penh, Cambodia, 18 November 2012, at http://bit.ly/329wakp, para. 4.

[150] Ibid., para. 11.

[151] Inter-American Commission on Human Rights, *Clarence Allen Lackey and others v. United States*, Merits (Case Nos. 11.575, 12.333, and 12.341), Report No. 52/13, 15 July 2013, para. 213.

[152] Safeguard 3 of the UN Safeguards guaranteeing protection of the rights of those facing the death penalty; approved by ECOSOC Resolution 1984/50 of 25 May 1984. In 1989, ECOSOC *recommended* that UN member States eliminate the death penalty 'for persons suffering from mental retardation or extremely

focused on domestic law in the United States along with reference to the Views of the Human Rights Committee, fell short of the requisite threshold both for *opinio juris*, in the case of customary law, and for general practice across the national laws of States, in the determination of general principles of international law.[153]

25.57 Certainly, as recorded by WHO, people with psycho-social and intellectual disabilities are disproportionately subject to the death penalty where it is still applied.[154] The intellectually disabled tend to have a lesser capacity to understand the meaning and consequences of their actions and are therefore much less likely to be deterred by threats of punishment. They are also more vulnerable as suspects in the criminal justice system.[155] Hood and Hoyle cite the US case of Earl Washington, whose IQ was assessed in the range of 69.[156] After sixteen years on death row, he was pardoned after DNA evidence demonstrated that he was not guilty of the offences of rape and murder for which he had been convicted. The suspect was only able to identify the scene of the crime after police took him there three times. Psychological analyses of Mr Washington reported that to compensate for his disability, he would politely defer to any authority figure with whom he came into contact. Thus, when police officers asked him leading questions in order to obtain a confession, he complied and offered affirmative responses in order to gain their approval.[157]

25.58 The US Supreme Court has purported to preclude the execution of persons with severe intellectual disabilities since 2002. In its judgment in *Atkins* v. *Virginia*, the Court found that executions of 'mentally retarded' criminals are cruel and unusual punishments prohibited by the Eighth Amendment to the US Constitution.[158] The Court observed: 'Mentally retarded persons frequently know the difference between right and wrong and are competent to stand trial. Because of their impairments, however, by definition they have diminished capacities to understand and process information, to communicate, to abstract from mistakes and learn from experience, to engage in logical reasoning, to control impulses, and to understand the reactions of others.'[159] Moreover, defendants with severe intellectual disabilities 'may be less able to give meaningful assistance to

---

limited mental competence, whether at the stage of sentence or execution'. ECOSOC Resolution 1989/64, para. 1(d).

[153] Art. 38(1)(c), 1945 Statute of the International Court of Justice; concluded at San Francisco, 24 October 1945; entered into force 24 October 1945.

[154] Capital punishment and the implementation of the safeguards guaranteeing protection of the rights of those facing the death penalty, Yearly supplement of the Secretary-General to his quinquennial report on capital punishment, UN doc. A/HRC/42/28, 28 August 2019, para. 32.

[155] R. Hood and C. Hoyle, *The Death Penalty: A Worldwide Perspective*, 5th ed., Oxford University Press, Oxford, 2015, p. 240.

[156] Ibid., p. 241.

[157] National Registry of Exonerations, 'Earl Washington', Newkirk Center for Science & Society at University of California Irvine, the University of Michigan Law School, and Michigan State University College of Law, United States, accessed 16 February 2020 at http://bit.ly/2SwOi2A.

[158] US Supreme Court, *Atkins* v. *Virginia*, 536 US 304 (2002), Certiorari to the Supreme Court of Virginia, Case No. 00–8452, 20 June 2002.

[159] Ibid., p. 318.

their counsel and are typically poor witnesses, and their demeanor may create an unwarranted impression of lack of remorse for their crimes'.[160]

25.59 Nonetheless, in 2014, Amnesty International highlighted two States – the United States and Japan – that had executed individuals with psycho-social and intellectual disabilities in the preceding years. The same year, in its judgment in *Hall* v. *Florida*,[161] the Supreme Court narrowed the discretion under which American states may determine whether or not any person convicted of murder has such intellectual disabilities that he or she may not lawfully be executed. Freddie Lee Hall had been tried, convicted, and sentenced to death for the murder in 1978 of Karol Hurst. According to Florida statute, an IQ test score of 70 would in and of itself be sufficient to allow an imposition and execution of a capital offence. This reliance on a test of questionable scientific merit to the exclusion of all other evidence led to an unacceptable risk of a person with severe intellectual disabilities being executed. There are, however, no international standards that define intellectual disability.[162]

25.60 Covering events in 2017, Amnesty International reported that people with 'mental or intellectual disabilities' were executed or remained under sentence of death in several countries, including Japan, the Maldives, Pakistan, Singapore, and the United States.[163] But the US Supreme Court has continued to narrow the discretion of states to execute persons with disabilities. In February 2019, overturning the Texas Court of Criminal Appeals for a second time, the Court ruled that death-row prisoner Bobby James Moore was intellectually disabled and may not be executed.[164] The Court reiterated that, under US law, to make a finding of intellectual disability, a court must see deficits in intellectual functioning – primarily a test-related criterion; adaptive deficits, assessed using both clinical evaluation and individualised measures; and the onset of these deficits while the defendant was still a minor.[165]

25.61 With respect to the ICCPR, in its General Comment 36, the Human Rights Committee has declared that States Parties 'must refrain from imposing the death penalty on individuals who face special barriers in defending themselves on an equal basis with others,

---

[160] Ibid., pp. 320–1.
[161] US Supreme Court, *Hall* v. *Florida*, 572 US 701 (2014), Case No. 12-10882, 27 May 2014.
[162] Cornell Center on the Death Penalty Worldwide, 'Intellectual Disability', undated but accessed 1 July 2020 at http://bit.ly/2ZDeCLV.
[163] Amnesty International, *Death Sentences and Executions 2017, Global Report*, London, at http://bit.ly/3h6fjmP, p. 8.
[164] Death Penalty Information Center, 'U.S. Supreme Court Again Reverses Texas Court's Rejection of Intellectual Disability Claim', posted on 20 February 2019, at http://bit.ly/2ZALYuN. A county court in 2014 had determined that Moore's execution would be unconstitutional. He had failed every grade in school, did not understand the days of the week by the age of thirteen (nor could he tell the time), and even as an adult fell below the standard for being able to live independently. In June 2020, Moore was granted parole after nearly forty years on death row. J. Gill, 'Intellectually Disabled Texas Prisoner Granted Parole after Nearly Four Decades on Death Row in Houston Case', *Houston Chronicle*, 8 June 2020, at http://bit.ly/2CJx3pi.
[165] US Supreme Court, *Bobby James Moore* v. *Texas*, Petition for Writ of Certiorari to the Court of Criminal Appeals of Texas, Case No. 18-443, 586 US ___ (2019) 1, 19 February 2019, at p. 2.

such as persons whose serious psycho-social and intellectual disabilities impeded their effective defence'.[166] States parties should also, the Committee said, 'refrain from executing persons that have diminished ability to understand the reasons for their sentence'.[167] The imposition of a death sentence upon a person whose mental state precluded an effective defence will violate Article 6 of the Covenant, while the execution of a death-row prisoner whose mental state degrades significantly after conviction is likely to violate Article 7 of the ICCPR: the prohibition on inhumane treatment or punishment.[168]

25.62 In January 2019, three UN special rapporteurs[169] urged the authorities in Pakistan to halt the execution of Mr Khizar Hayat, a man with psychosocial disabilities, affirming: 'The imposition of capital punishment on individuals with psychosocial disabilities is a clear violation of Pakistan's international obligations.'[170] At the regional level, the African Commission on Human and Peoples' Rights has stated that 'the execution of ... persons with psycho-social or intellectual disabilities, will always amount to a violation of the right to life'.[171]

THE RIGHT TO LIFE OF PERSONS WITH DISABILITIES IN ARMED CONFLICT

25.63 In the words of the United Nations, persons with disabilities are the 'forgotten victims of armed conflict'.[172] It is certain that, as the UN Secretary-General reported in 2019, armed conflict has a disproportionate impact on persons with disabilities.[173] 'Conflict', the UN Secretary-General noted, 'heightens the risks for persons with disabilities because of destruction and other changes to the physical environment, stress and disruption of essential services. People with disabilities may be unable to flee attacks and are left abandoned and unprotected. Women and girls with disabilities are particularly at risk of violence, exploitation and abuse.'[174]

[166] Human Rights Committee, General Comment 36 on the right to life, para. 49. See also Office of the High Commissioner for Human Rights (OHCHR), 'Death Row: UN expert Urges US Authorities to Stop Execution of Two Persons with Psychosocial Disabilities', press release, Geneva, 17 July 2012.
[167] Human Rights Committee, General Comment 36 on the right to life, para. 49.
[168] Interim Report of the Special Rapporteur on torture and other cruel, inhuman or degrading treatment or punishment, UN doc. A/67/279, 9 August 2012, para. 58.
[169] Ms Agnes Callamard, Special Rapporteur on extrajudicial, summary or arbitrary executions; Ms Catalina Devandas, Special Rapporteur on the rights of persons with disabilities; and Mr Nils Melzer, Special Rapporteur on torture and other cruel, inhuman or degrading treatment or punishment.
[170] OHCHR, 'UN Experts Urge Pakistan to Halt Execution of Person with Disability', Geneva, 13 January 2019, at http://bit.ly/2CGRuTC.
[171] African Commission on Human and Peoples' Rights, General Comment No. 3 on the African Charter on Human and Peoples' Rights: The Right to Life (Article 4), November 2015, para. 25.
[172] UN Enable Fact Sheet, cited in A. Priddy, *Disability and Armed Conflict*, Academy Briefing No. 14, Geneva Academy of International Humanitarian Law and Human Rights, Geneva, April 2019, p. 13. The UN Department of Peace Operations' 2019 Policy on the protection of civilians in UN Peacekeeping has a single reference to the need to plan for the needs of persons with disabilities. UN Department of Peace Operations, *The Protection of Civilians in United Nations Peacekeeping*, Policy, UN doc. Ref. 2019.17, New York, November 2019, para. 37.
[173] 'Protection of civilians in armed conflict: Report of the Secretary-General', UN doc. S/2019/373, 7 May 2019, para. 49.
[174] Ibid.

International Humanitarian Law Rules on the Protection of Persons with Disabilities

25.64 Persons with disabilities are protected under international humanitarian law first and foremost in their capacity as civilians.[175] The principles of distinction and proportionality in attack apply to persons with disabilities, just as they do to any other civilians. This is true under customary law, whether the conflict is international or non-international in character. Thus, for example, in its Resolution 2475, the UN Security Council urged all parties to armed conflict to 'take measures, in accordance with applicable international law obligations to protect civilians, including those with disabilities'. The Council referred specifically to killing and maiming, abduction and torture, and rape and other forms of sexual violence in conflict.[176]

25.65 Civilians with disabilities will be protected from attack by international humanitarian law unless and for such time as they participate directly in hostilities.[177] In international armed conflict, under the 1977 Additional Protocol I, the definition of 'wounded' and 'sick' is explicitly understood to apply to all persons, 'whether military or civilian, who, because of trauma, disease or other physical or mental disorder or disability, are in need of medical assistance or care and who refrain from any act of hostility'.[178]

25.66 Article 3 common to the four 1949 Geneva Conventions formally applies in non-international armed conflict (but also constitutes a minimum level of protection in international armed conflicts).[179] The provision obligates humane treatment of persons in the power of the enemy in all circumstances, which must be ensured without any adverse distinction founded on 'race, colour, religion or faith, sex, birth or wealth, or any other similar criteria'. While disability is not specifically cited as a grounds of prohibited discrimination, it falls within the reference to 'other similar criteria' and therefore a wilful or negligent failure to protect people from violence or to provide them with food, water, and shelter on the basis of the fact of their disabilities would be unlawful. In contrast,

---

[175] The Geneva Academy is highly critical of the treatment of persons with disabilities under international humanitarian law, stating: 'When viewed as a whole, IHL largely reflects the medical and charity approaches to disability by framing persons with disabilities as passive, weak, defective and vulnerable and, as such, in need of special, paternalistic protection.' Ibid., p. 52. At the same time, they concede that this is 'unsurprising considering the time at which most IHL instruments were drafted, long before disability rights discourse had begun to develop'. Ibid. Therefore, it is stated, 'terminology such as "the infirm" should be read as "a person with a disability", cases of mental disease should be read as "persons with psychosocial or intellectual disabilities" and "the blind" as "persons with visual impairments"'. Ibid., p. 53.

[176] UN Security Council Resolution 2475, operative para. 1.

[177] For a discussion of this concept, see Chapter 3.

[178] Art. 8(a), Protocol Additional to the Geneva Conventions of 12 August 1949, and relating to the Protection of Victims of International Armed Conflicts (Protocol I), 8 June 1977; adopted at Geneva 8 June 1977; entered into force 7 December 1978 (1977 Additional Protocol I).

[179] International Court of Justice, *Case Concerning Military and Paramilitary Activities in and Against Nicaragua (Nicaragua v. United States)*, Judgment (Merits) 27 June 1986, para. 218: 'There is no doubt that, in the event of international armed conflicts, these rules also constitute a minimum yardstick, in addition to the more elaborate rules which are also to apply to international conflicts; and they are rules which, in the Court's opinion, reflect what the Court in 1949 called "elementary considerations of humanity."'

special protection of persons with disabilities would not amount to adverse distinction, as is already well established under international human rights law jurisprudence.[180]

The CRPD

25.67 The CRPD dedicates a provision to the protection of persons with disabilities during 'situations of risk and humanitarian emergencies'.[181] According to Article 11, States Parties to the CRPD are obligated to take 'all necessary measures to ensure the protection and safety of persons with disabilities in situations of risk, including situations of armed conflict'. This is a broad-based duty to protect. However, international human rights law tends to consider the duty to protect as one of due diligence, meaning that a State must undertake 'reasonable' or 'reasonably possible' measures. IHL refers to a duty to take only 'feasible' precautions during the conduct of hostilities.[182]

25.68 According to the Geneva Academy of International Humanitarian Law and Human Rights, that the CRPD applies to a State Party's extraterritorial conduct that 'is not controversial and is consistent with the approach of international courts and human rights treaty bodies'.[183] The agreed working methods of the CRPD Committee[184] also provide for a special mechanism for 'early-awareness and urgent-action procedures' with the purpose of 'preventing existing problems within States parties from escalating into full-fledged conflicts or preventing the revival of pre-existing problems'.[185] These mechanisms are also meant to address issues requiring 'immediate attention in order to avoid serious violations of the Convention or to reduce the number or degree of such violations'.[186]

The 2018 Protocol on the Rights of Persons with Disabilities in Africa

25.69 Article 12 of the 2018 Protocol on the Rights of Persons with Disabilities in Africa is entitled 'Situations of Risk'. Under paragraph (a) of the article, States Parties are obligated to take 'specific measures to ensure the protection and safety of persons with disabilities in situations of risk, including situations of armed conflict, forced displacements, humanitarian emergencies and natural disasters'.

---

[180] See, e.g., Committee on the Rights of Persons with Disabilities, *General Comment No. 6 (2018) on equality and non-discrimination*, UN doc. UNCRPD/C/GC/6, paras. 28 and 29.

[181] Although not defined in the CRPD, in Article 1 of the 2018 Protocol to the African Charter on Human and Peoples' Rights on the Rights of Persons with Disabilities in Africa, the term is defined as 'any situation that poses grave risk to the general population, including disasters and all forms of armed conflict'.

[182] Article 11 of the CRPD refers to the duty to take all necessary measures being 'in accordance with their obligations under international law, including international humanitarian law and international human rights law'. This does not diminish the extent of the duty.

[183] *Disability and Armed Conflict*, Geneva Academy of International Humanitarian Law and Human Rights, p. 36.

[184] Committee on the Rights of Persons with Disabilities, *Working Methods of the Committee on the Rights of Persons with Disabilities*, adopted at its fifth session (11–15 April 2011).

[185] Ibid., para. 26.

[186] Ibid.

THE RIGHT TO LIFE OF PERSONS WITH DISABILITIES IN NATURAL AND MAN-MADE DISASTERS

25.70 Natural disasters and disasters resulting from human action other than armed conflict also pose significant threats to persons with disabilities. Unless they occur during an armed conflict, IHL will not be applicable, and international human rights law will be the primary focus of protective duties under international law. The CRPD specifically refers to 'humanitarian emergencies and the occurrence of natural disasters' in recalling the duty of States Parties to 'take, in accordance with their obligations under international law ... all necessary measures to ensure the protection and safety of persons with disabilities in situations of risk'.[187]

25.71 The Inter-Agency Steering Committee (IASC) Task Team on the Inclusion of Persons with Disabilities in Humanitarian Action has drafted guidelines to address the experiences of persons with disabilities in humanitarian disasters. The Guidelines, which were elaborated over the course of three years, were endorsed by the IASC in October 2019 and published in November 2019. They are, the UN proclaims,

> the first humanitarian guidelines to be developed with and by persons with disabilities and their representative organizations in association with traditional humanitarian stakeholders. Based on the outcomes of a comprehensive global and regional multi-stakeholder consultation process, they are designed to promote the implementation of quality humanitarian programmes in all contexts and across all regions, and to establish and increase both the inclusion of persons with disabilities and their meaningful participation in all decisions that concern them.[188]

25.72 Internal displacement is a major consequence of all humanitarian emergencies, including natural and man-made disasters. In May 2020, the UN Special Rapporteur on the human rights of internally displaced persons, Cecilia Jimenez-Damary, dedicated a report to the Human Rights Council on persons with disabilities in the context of internal displacement. She noted that especially at risk of violence or neglect are those internally displaced persons (IDPs), 'with high support needs, such as persons with psychosocial or intellectual disabilities, unaccompanied, separated and orphaned children with disabilities or survivors of severe traumatic events'.[189] Persons with disabilities 'experience violence at much higher rates than others and may experience targeted violence and abuse on the basis of their disability'. These risks can be 'exacerbated' in situations of displacement, including in IDP camps. Loss of assistive devices can also deprive persons with disabilities of independence, forcing them to rely on others and thereby increasing the risk of exploitation and abuse.

---

[187] Art. 11, CRPD.
[188] 'IASC Guidelines, Inclusion of Persons with Disabilities in Humanitarian Action, 2019', posted on 19 November 2019, at http://bit.ly/2SIR58J.
[189] 'Persons with disabilities in the context of internal displacement, Report of the Special Rapporteur on the human rights of internally displaced persons', UN doc. A/HRC/44/41, 14 May 2020, para. 19.

25.73 Among the types of violations brought to the attention of the Special Rapporteur were 'physical, sexual and gender based violence; robbery, bribery and intimidation and coercion; denial of food and essential medicine, harassment, emotional abuse and neglect, often perpetrated by persons known to them'. When violations are perpetrated by caregivers, they are less likely to be reported, thereby fostering impunity. 'Humanitarian crises may have a particularly profound psychological impact on older persons with disabilities and exacerbate mental health and pre-existing cognitive impairments.'[190] Persons with limited mobility and persons living in institutions may be unable to flee from trouble, leaving them exposed to violence or left to survive on their own while others have fled.[191] The Special Rapporteur further recalled that women and the elderly with disabilities also face added stigmatisation and discrimination and protection challenges.[192] She observed that all IDPs with disabilities 'lack visibility in the monitoring of their rights'.[193] They also 'generally lack access to information about available services, protection and reporting mechanisms, and about their own rights'. Lack of information, she recalls, 'can prevent them from accessing vital aid and services'.[194]

25.74 In 2020 and 2021, the global COVID-19 pandemic was severely affecting billions of people directly or indirectly, but persons with disabilities were at particular risk. The IASC has published guidance on risk communication and community engagement (RCCE) with the especially vulnerable during the pandemic. Recommendations included the provision of information in accessible formats, such as braille or using large print, and the employment of multiple forms of communication, such as text captioning or signed videos, text captioning for the hearing impaired, and online materials for people who use assistive technology.[195] The focus thus seemed to be on those with physical disabilities. Also requiring specific consideration, however, are those with psycho-social or intellectual disabilities. Thus, with respect to IDPs, the Special Rapporteur called for specific attention to be given to 'underrepresented and marginalized groups, such as persons with intellectual and psychosocial disabilities, persons with deaf-blindness, women and girls and indigenous or minority groups'.[196]

25.75 In 2020, the European Disability Forum adopted a resolution in its General Assembly 2020 on COVID-19 and the rights of persons with disabilities. The resolution stated that every person

> has the right to immediate, clear and correct information on the pandemic and the measures they and their families should follow. This includes information provided though public websites, mobile applications, information in print, via TV broadcast and

---

[190] Ibid., para. 57.
[191] Ibid., para. 56.
[192] Ibid.
[193] Ibid., para. 24.
[194] Ibid., para. 42.
[195] IASC, 'COVID-19: How to Include Marginalized and Vulnerable People in Risk Communication and Community Engagement', New York, 2020, at http://bit.ly/2ZL6RmU, p. 3.
[196] 'Persons with disabilities in the context of internal displacement, Report of the Special Rapporteur on the human rights of internally displaced persons', UN doc. A/HRC/44/41, 14 May 2020, para. 95.

pre-recorded video, through emergency services and dedicated hotlines for the pandemic, as well as any information provided in person. It is particularly important to ensure persons with disabilities in segregated or institutional settings have access to information, human contact and communication during this time.'[197]

The resolution called for particular respect for the rights of women and girls with disabilities, noting that domestic and gender-based violence had risen during the pandemic, and women and girls with disabilities, who constitute 60 per cent of the population of persons with disabilities in the European Union – around 60 million – 'are at a higher risk of facing violence and abuse, in particular when they have to isolate at home or when they are forced to live in closed-settings such as institutions, psychiatric hospitals and refugee centres'.[198]

---

[197] European Disability Forum (EDF), Resolution on COVID-19 and the Rights of Persons with Disabilities, adopted by the EDF General Assembly 2020, at http://bit.ly/32CsB6E.
[198] Ibid.

26

Older Persons

INTRODUCTION

26.01 This chapter describes the content and protection under international law of the right to life of older persons, considering both global and regional standards. The elderly are especially vulnerable to abuse and neglect, and face, among others, an increasing risk of dementia as they age. While no one can halt the aging process, the special protection to which older persons are entitled enables them to live the remainder of their lives in dignity. In addition, the chapter briefly addresses the legality of the execution of the death penalty on older persons, as well as the legality of euthanasia. (The general aspects of these two issues are dealt with in Chapters 9 and 12, respectively.) This chapter concludes with an analysis of the protection of older persons in situations of armed conflict.

The Definition of an Older Person

26.02 Globally, there is no set international legal definition of an elderly or older person (the two are considered synonyms herein).[1] At the regional level, the 2016 Protocol to the African Charter on Human and Peoples' Rights on the Rights of Older Persons in Africa defines 'older persons' as 'those persons aged sixty (60) years and above'.[2] But the Protocol was adopted against the backdrop of a continent in which the average life expectancy for those born in 2020 was sixty-two years for men and sixty-five years for women. This contrasts with average life expectancy globally, which as of the middle of 2020, was seventy years for men and seventy-five years for women.[3] The

---

[1] The term 'elderly' tends to be used more by medical professionals, while 'older persons' tends to be the language of human rights, but there is no hard and fast rule on this.

[2] Art. 1, Protocol to the African Charter on Human and Peoples' Rights on the Rights of Older Persons; adopted at Addis Ababa 31 January 2016; not yet in force (hereinafter, African Union Protocol on the Rights of Older Persons). Under its Article 26(1), the Protocol will enter into force thirty days after the fifteenth ratification by an African Union member State. As of 1 May 2021, there were two ratifications and fifteen signatories. In 2002, a World Health Organization (WHO) project on the elderly in Africa had proposed to use fifty years as the definition of an older person. WHO, 'Proposed Working Definition of an Older Person in Africa for the MDS Project', 2002, at http://bit.ly/3nzdz9D.

[3] Statista, 'Average Life Expectancy in Africa for Those Born in 2020, by Gender and Region', July 2020, at http://bit.ly/3jT0AR6.

average life expectancy in Western Europe was higher still: seventy-nine years for men and eighty-four years for women.[4]

26.03 In 2006, six Japanese medical professionals, writing in *Geriatrics and Gerontology International*, suggested that 'conventionally, "elderly" has been defined as a chronological age of 65 years or older'.[5] This they linked to Chancellor Bismarck's establishment of eligibility for a pension at sixty-five in the German Empire, more than a century earlier. But given the aging population and generally increasing life expectancy, they recommended that the elderly be defined as those – men or women – older than seventy-five years of age.[6] They appeared, though, to be applying this definition specifically to Japan, where average life expectancy was, at that time, just over eighty-two years of age. As of mid-2020, this had increased to almost eighty-five years.[7]

26.04 While not proposed as a legal definition, the chapter takes as a working definition today the age of sixty-five as the starting point at the global level for an older person, unless relevant instruments set a lower age. An earlier UN rule of thumb of sixty years[8] appears obsolete today. The International Committee of the Red Cross (ICRC) has noted that international humanitarian law 'says nothing about the age at which an individual is considered to be elderly'.[9] The ICRC Commentary on the Fourth Geneva Convention of 1949, published in 1958, states:

> No limit was fixed for 'aged persons'. Should this expression be taken to mean those over 65, as stipulated in the Stockholm Draft? The Conference refrained from naming a definite age, preferring to leave the point to the discretion of Governments. 65 seems, however, to be a reasonable age limit. It is often the age of retirement, and it is also the age at which civilian internees have usually been released from internment by belligerent Powers.[10]

---

[4] Statista, 'Average Life Expectancy in Europe for Those Born in 2020, by Gender and Region', July 2020, at https://bit.ly/2SK62Xe.

[5] H. Orimo, H. Ito, T. Suzuki, A. Araki, T. Hosoi, and M. Sawabe, 'Reviewing the Definition of "Elderly"', *Geriatrics and Gerontology International*, vol. 6, no. 3 (February 2006), pp. 149–58, text available at http://bit.ly/3jLFP6M, at 149.

[6] Ibid., p. 157.

[7] Macrotrends, 'Japan Life Expectancy 1950–2020', accessed 10 October 2020, at http://bit.ly/3nE875x.

[8] Thus, for instance, the Political Declaration adopted at the Second World Assembly on Ageing in Madrid in April 2002 noted: 'We recognize that the world is experiencing an unprecedented demographic transformation and that by 2050 the number of persons aged 60 years and over will increase from 600 million to almost 2 billion and that the proportion of persons aged 60 years and over is expected to double from 10 to 21 per cent. The increase will be greatest and most rapid in developing countries where the older population is expected to quadruple during the next 50 years.' Art. 2, Political Declaration; adopted at Madrid April 2002, at http://bit.ly/3iPgsj3. The Declaration further noted the determination of States 'to enhance the recognition of the dignity of older persons and to eliminate all forms of neglect, abuse and violence'. Art. 5, 2002 Political Declaration.

[9] Françoise Krill, 'The Elderly in Situations of Armed Conflict', address by the ICRC Deputy Director of Operations, Helsinki, September 1999, at http://bit.ly/34L8TVE.

[10] ICRC Commentary on Article 14(1) of 1949 Geneva Convention IV, 1958, at http://bit.ly/3lBHr3n, p. 125.

THE RIGHT TO LIFE OF THE ELDERLY UNDER GLOBAL STANDARDS

The ICCPR

26.05 The 1966 International Covenant on Civil and Political Rights[11] (ICCPR) does not refer explicitly to the rights of older persons. Its Article 3 stipulates, however, that States Parties 'undertake to ensure the equal right of men and women to the enjoyment of all civil and political rights' set out in the Covenant.[12] This applies to men and women of any age, including the elderly. It is further stipulated that the rights recognised in the Covenant must be ensured 'without distinction of any kind' (although age is not explicitly referred to).[13] Under Article 26, discrimination under the law is prohibited 'on any ground', a general exclusion that includes age even though, again, it is not expressly mentioned in the provision.

26.06 Each person under the jurisdiction of a State Party to the ICCPR benefits from the protection of the right to life afforded by its Article 6 to every person, no matter their age.[14] The right is non-derogable *in toto*.[15] That every human being has the right to life without discrimination as to age has long reflected international law. The prohibition of arbitrary deprivation of life of any person, of any age, codified in Article 6(1) of the ICCPR, has attained the status of a peremptory norm of international law (jus cogens).[16]

CEDAW

26.07 The 1979 Convention on the Elimination of All Forms of Discrimination against Women[17] (CEDAW) does not explicitly refer to older persons or the elderly except to require that there be no discrimination in the right to social security, particularly in cases of retirement and old age.[18] That said, in 2010, the UN Committee on the Elimination of Discrimination against Women issued its General Recommendation 27 on older women and the protection of their human rights observing that States Parties 'should take into account the multidimensional nature of discrimination against women and ensure that the principle of gender equality applies throughout women's life cycle, in legislation and in the practical implementation thereof'.[19]

---

[11] International Covenant on Civil and Political Rights; adopted at New York 16 December 1966; entered into force 23 March 1976.
[12] Thus, the references in the Covenant to 'he' or 'his' should be construed to mean 'he or she' or 'his or her'.
[13] Art. 2(1), ICCPR.
[14] Human Rights Committee, General Comment No. 36: Article 6: right to life, UN doc. CCPR/C/GC/36, 3 September 2019 (hereinafter, Human Rights Committee, General Comment 36 on the right to life), para. 61.
[15] Art. 4(2), ICCPR.
[16] See Chapter 1 for a discussion of the peremptory status of the norm.
[17] Convention on the Elimination of All Forms of Discrimination against Women; adopted at New York 18 December 1979; entered into force 3 September 1981. As of 1 May 2021, 189 States were party to CEDAW and a further 2 States (Palau and the United States) were signatories, making it one of the most widely ratified human rights treaties.
[18] Art. 11(1)(e), CEDAW.
[19] Committee on the Elimination of Discrimination against Women, General Recommendation No. 27 on older women and protection of their human rights, UN doc. CEDAW/C/GC/27, 16 December 2010, para. 31.

26.08 The Recommendation noted the obligation upon States Parties 'to draft legislation recognizing and prohibiting violence, including domestic, sexual violence and violence in institutional settings, against older women, including those with disabilities'.[20] States Parties further 'have an obligation to investigate, prosecute and punish all acts of violence against older women, including those committed as a result of traditional practices and beliefs'.[21]

THE ELDERLY AND EUTHANASIA

26.09 In its written submission of 2015 in relation to the elaboration by the Human Rights Committee of its General Comment 36 on the right to life, the National Right to Life Educational Trust Fund, a non-governmental organisation based in New York, had urged the Committee to affirm that the right to life 'should be interpreted to guard against physician-assisted suicide and euthanasia'.[22] The Fund argued that laws permitting euthanasia[23] discriminate by denying the right to life of, among others, the elderly. Indeed, in the case of Belgium, where euthanasia is lawful under certain circumstances, Etienne Montero cautions that the imprecision of the notion of 'incurable disorder' required by the prevailing legislation is increasingly allowing the approval of euthanasia for the elderly who suffer from only ailments related to old age, such as polyarthritis (reducing a person's mobility), failing eyesight, and hearing impairment.[24]

26.10 In contrast, a study by medical professionals in The Netherlands and published in 1997 had concluded that the suggestion that euthanasia or physician-assisted suicide was mainly performed among elderly people in The Netherlands was not supported by research.[25] The study found that between 1984 and 1993, a total of 1,707 cases of euthanasia or physician-assisted suicide were reported to the Public Prosecutor in North Holland. The average age of the female patients to whom euthanasia or physician-assisted suicide was administered was sixty-five years, while for men it was sixty-two. In the younger age groups, euthanasia or physician-assisted suicide was performed relatively more frequently, while the lowest percentage was found in the group aged eighty-five years and over.[26] Almost four-fifths of the total of 1,702 cases (data on five cases were missing) were for persons suffering from a form of cancer.[27] Of these 1,702 cases, 692 (40 per cent) were sixty-

---

[20] Ibid., para. 37.
[21] Ibid.
[22] National Right to Life Educational Trust Fund, 'Contribution to the General Discussion in preparation for General Comment No. 36 (Article 6 of the ICCPR: Right to life)', June 2015, p. 3.
[23] Euthanasia is the intentional termination of life of a competent patient at his or her request, but which carried out by someone other than the patient, while in physician-assisted suicide, drugs and/or advice are provided to a competent patient so that he or she can take his/her own life.
[24] E. Montero, 'The Belgian Experience of Euthanasia Since Its Legal Implementation in 2002', chap. 2 in D. A. Jones, C. Gastman, and C. MacKellar (eds.), *Euthanasia and Assisted Suicide: Lessons from Belgium*, Cambridge University Press, Cambridge, 2017, pp. 26–48, at 31.
[25] B. D. Onwuteaka-Phiupsen, M. T. Muller, and G. Van der Wal, 'Euthanasia and Old Age', *Age and Ageing*, vol. 26 (1997), pp. 487–92.
[26] Ibid., p. 487.
[27] Ibid., p. 489, table 2.

five years of age or older.[28] Indeed, the proportion of euthanasia and physician-assisted suicide among all deaths was, the study found, highest in people aged between twenty-five and forty-four years.[29]

26.11 In its General Comment 36 on the right to life, the Human Rights Committee was cautious on the issue of euthanasia. It declared that States Parties to the ICCPR that

> allow medical professionals to provide medical treatment or the medical means to facilitate the termination of life of afflicted adults, such as the terminally ill, who experience severe physical or mental pain and suffering and wish to die with dignity, must ensure the existence of robust legal and institutional safeguards to verify that medical professionals are complying with the free, informed, explicit and unambiguous decision of their patients, with a view to protecting patients from pressure and abuse.[30]

The Committee thus did not hold euthanasia to be inherently contrary to the right to life, but nor did it explicitly consider the practice, under certain circumstances, to be reflective of a life with dignity.

26.12 A study published by the Gerontological Society of America in 2015 concluded, albeit on the basis of a very small sample,[31] that societal discourse and related behaviour, which devalue the dependent and the old, 'might become internalized by older people', leading them to consider euthanasia or physician-assisted suicide as 'preferable end-of-life options'.[32] Although their knowledge about euthanasia and physician-assisted suicide (and the distinction between the two) was said to be 'patchy', the two medical professionals who conducted and wrote the study identified three 'conflicting discourse strands': self-determination, family involvement, and medicalisation of dying. The 'self determination' discourse strand 'expressed a desire for agency, referring to a right to autonomy, choice, capacity and voluntary decision-making'. One of those interviewed noted that a clear choice was being made 'to have their life end at the moment of their choosing not at the moment of just ordinary life span or a medical person or a religious person'. The participants emphasised, however, that self-determination 'also meant that other people would have different end-of-life wishes'.[33]

THE RIGHT TO LIFE OF OLDER PERSONS UNDER REGIONAL STANDARDS

26.13 While all the main regional human rights treaties offer general legal protection to all, including older persons, and encompassing their right to life, they do not, for the most part, specifically protect their fundamental rights. The most notable exception is the 2016

---

[28] Ibid., p. 490, table 5.
[29] Ibid., p. 491.
[30] Human Rights Committee, General Comment 36 on the right to life, para. 9 (footnotes omitted).
[31] Seven white British people, all over sixty-five years of age, who at the time of interview did not have a known terminal condition or mental health problem, participated in the study. Five participants knew each other from a discussion group about dignity and dying, and two participants were partners.
[32] C. P. T. Lamers and R. R. Williams, 'Older People's Discourses about Euthanasia and Assisted Suicide: A Foucauldian Exploration', *Gerontologist*, vol. 56, no. 6 (2016), pp. 1072–81.
[33] Ibid., p. 1075.

Protocol to the African Charter on Human and Peoples' Rights on the Rights of Older Persons in Africa, a treaty which had not yet entered into force as of writing. In addition, the Protocol to the African Charter on the Rights of Women in Africa, which is in force, provides for the special protection of 'elderly women' (although the term is not defined therein).[34]

26.14 That the right to life applies to all no matter how old they are was confirmed by the Inter-American Court of Human Rights in its 2005 judgment in the *Yakye Axa Indigenous Community* case against Paraguay.[35] The Court declared the following, with respect to the 1969 American Convention on Human Rights:[36]

> As regards the special consideration required by the elderly, it is important for the State to take measures to ensure their continuing functionality and autonomy, guaranteeing their right to adequate food, access to clean water and health care. Specifically, the State must provide care for the elderly with chronic diseases and in terminal stages, to help them avoid unnecessary suffering.[37]

In this case, lack of water and food had caused the death of many older persons, as the Court had explicitly recalled.[38]

26.15 Similarly, in a Recommendation adopted by the Committee of Ministers of the Council of Europe in 2014,[39] it was recognised that 'existing international human rights standards apply to persons at all stages of life'. The Recommendation asserted that they 'form an adequate normative framework for the protection of the human rights of older persons'.[40]

The Right to Life of Older Persons under the 2016 African Union Protocol

26.16 The 2016 Protocol stipulates that States Parties shall 'prohibit and criminalise harmful traditional practices targeted at Older Persons'.[41] The Protocol defines the term 'harmful traditional practices' as meaning 'traditional beliefs, attitudes and practices which violate the fundamental rights of Older persons such as their right to life, dignity and physical integrity'.[42] States Parties also undertake to ensure that 'law enforcement organs at all levels are trained to effectively interpret and enforce policies and legislation to

---

[34] Art. 22, Protocol to the African Charter on the Rights of Women in Africa; adopted at Maputo 1 July 2003; entered into force 25 November 2005.
[35] Inter-American Court of Human Rights, *Yakye Axa Indigenous Community v. Paraguay*, Judgment (Merits, Reparations and Costs), 17 June 2005, para. 175.
[36] American Convention on Human Rights; adopted at San José 22 November 1969; entered into force 18 July 1978.
[37] Inter-American Court of Human Rights, *Yakye Axa Indigenous Community v. Paraguay*, Judgment, para. 175.
[38] Ibid., para. 50.15.
[39] Recommendation CM/Rec(2014)2; adopted by the Committee of Ministers of the Council of Europe on 19 February 2014, at http://bit.ly/3lBz3B5.
[40] Ibid., eleventh preambular para.
[41] Art. 8(1), African Union Protocol on the Rights of Older Persons.
[42] Art. 1, African Union Protocol on the Rights of Older Persons.

protect the rights of Older Persons'.[43] States Parties are further obligated to 'ensure the protection of the rights of Older Women from violence, sexual abuse and discrimination based on gender'.[44] Otherwise, the protection of the right to life of older persons is not accorded special protection in the Protocol.

The Right to Life of Older Persons under the European Convention on Human Rights

26.17 Article 2(1) of the 1950 European Convention on Human Rights[45] stipulates simply that 'everyone's right to life shall be protected by law'. No specific provision safeguards the life or physical integrity of older persons. However, the Convention does proclaim: 'The enjoyment of the rights and freedoms set forth in [the] Convention shall be secured without discrimination on any ground.'[46] This includes age.

26.18 In the 2014 Recommendation of the Committee of Ministers of the Council of Europe it was recalled that 'respect for the dignity of older persons should be guaranteed in all circumstances, including mental disorder, disability, disease and end-of-life situations'.[47] The preamble to the Recommendation stressed that 'all older persons should be able to live their lives in dignity and security, free from discrimination, isolation, violence, neglect and abuse, and as autonomously as possible'.[48]

26.19 In a set of principles annexed to the Recommendation, it was stipulated: 'Member States should protect older persons from violence, abuse and intentional or unintentional neglect. Such protection should be granted irrespective of whether this occurs at home, within an institution or elsewhere.'[49] As the European Court of Human Rights has observed, with an ever-growing number of older persons subject to institutional care, it is important to take into account 'the particular vulnerability of the patients concerned, who often may not be in a position to draw attention to shortcomings in the provision of care on their own initiative'.[50]

26.20 The case of *Dodov* v. *Bulgaria* concerned the disappearance from a State-run nursing home for the elderly of Mrs Stoyanova, the applicant's mother, who suffered from Alzheimer's disease. The applicant alleged that his mother's life had been put at risk through the negligence of the nursing home staff, that the police had not undertaken all necessary measures to search for his mother immediately after her disappearance, and that the ensuing investigation had not resulted in criminal or disciplinary sanctions. The Court found a violation of Article 2 of the Convention, declaring that it was reasonable to assume that

---

[43] Art. 4(3), African Union Protocol on the Rights of Older Persons.
[44] Art. 9(1), Protocol to the African Charter on Human and Peoples' Rights on the Rights of Older Persons.
[45] Convention for the Protection of Human Rights and Fundamental Freedoms; adopted at Rome by the Council of Europe, 4 November 1950; entered into force 3 September 1953 (hereinafter, European Convention on Human Rights).
[46] Art. 14, European Convention on Human Rights.
[47] Committee of Ministers of the Council of Europe, Recommendation CM/Rec(2014)2, fifteenth preambular para.
[48] Ibid., fourteenth preambular para.
[49] Appendix to Recommendation CM/Rec(2014)2, para. 16.
[50] European Court of Human Rights, *Heinisch* v. *Germany*, Judgment (Fifth Section), 21 July 2011, para. 71.

the applicant's mother had died. It further determined that a direct link existed between the failure to supervise the applicant's mother and her disappearance. There had been clear instructions never to leave her unattended.[51] The Court recalled: 'Chains of events that were triggered by a negligent act and led to loss of life may fall to be examined under Article 2.'[52]

26.21 The legal system as a whole had also failed to provide an adequate and timely response as required by the State's obligations under Article 2. The Court found that the facts surrounding the disappearance and presumed death of Mrs Stoyanova had not been established by the authorities; nor was it possible to hold accountable those responsible 'in an effective and timely manner'.[53]

26.22 The Court did not, however, find a violation of the right to life based on the reaction of the police to the applicant's mother's disappearance. The Court observed that the police took a series of steps to try to locate Mrs Stoyanova, which included interviewing witnesses, recording her as missing, and issuing a press release within a week.[54] The applicant had argued that the police should have undertaken intensive searches in the area immediately after his mother's disappearance. However, the Court, while noting that there was 'little doubt that more could have been done by the police', determined that 'the decisive question is whether their reaction was adequate in the circumstances, having regard to the concrete facts and practical realities of daily police work'.[55]

26.23 A further important case on the provision of medical care to the elderly, *Volintiru v. Italy*, was pending before a chamber of the European Court of Human Rights as of writing.[56] In February 2007, at the age of eighty-five, the applicant's mother was rushed to the hospital for hypoglycaemia accompanied by serious neurological damage, a comatose state, a bloodstream infection of the left lung, and a diuretic blockage. Four weeks later, the doctors treating her decided that she should be discharged from the hospital on the basis that although her state of health was still considered serious, her condition appeared stable. On 10 March 2007, she was taken to the casualty department in a coma, dying nine days later. The applicant has complained that her mother did not receive the necessary treatment to protect her life. She also submits that the poor conditions in the hospital caused the infection leading to her mother's death, and complains of the lack of an effective investigation by the authorities into the matter.

THE DEATH PENALTY

The Normative Framework

26.24 There is no prohibition under general international law on the imposition and even the execution of the death penalty on older persons. The situation appears to be distinct

---

[51] Ibid., paras. 6, 70.
[52] Ibid., para. 70.
[53] Ibid., para. 96.
[54] Ibid., para. 101.
[55] Ibid., para. 102.
[56] European Court of Human Rights, *Volintiru v. Italy*, Communicated Case (Appl. No. 8530/08), 19 March 2013.

under regional standards in Africa. In this regard, the African Commission on Human and Peoples' Rights has stated that the execution of the 'elderly' will always amount to a violation of the right to life under the African Charter on Human and Peoples' Rights.[57,58]

26.25 In its 2019 judgment in *Madison v. Alabama*,[59] the US Supreme Court held that the Eighth Amendment to the US Constitution may permit executing a prisoner even if he cannot remember committing his crime, but it may prohibit executing a prisoner who suffers from dementia or another disorder than psychotic delusions. Vernon Madison was sixty-eight years old when his case came before the Court – a long-time death-row inmate who was convicted of capital murder more than twenty years prior. Multiple strokes had left him with vascular dementia. He could no longer see, walk independently, or control his bladder. According to his petition for review, a psychologist's examination found that he could no longer remember the alphabet past the letter G or name the previous president of the United States.[60]

The Death Penalty under International Humanitarian Law

26.26 Under 'combatant's privilege', no prisoner of war – a combatant captured during an international armed conflict – may be convicted of any offence, much less sentenced to death, for the fact of having engaged in hostilities against the detaining power, as long as he or she has complied with the rules of IHL while participating directly in hostilities.[61] This customary rule applies to the elderly just as it does to combatants of a younger age.

26.27 In a situation of non-international armed conflict, Common Article 3 to the four 1949 Geneva Conventions prohibits 'the passing of sentences and the carrying out of executions without previous judgment pronounced by a regularly constituted court, affording all the judicial guarantees which are recognized as indispensable by civilized peoples' is a serious violation of international humanitarian law. Again, this applies to all

---

[57] African Charter on Human and Peoples' Rights; adopted at Nairobi 27 June 1981; entered into force 21 October 1986.
[58] African Commission on Human and Peoples' Rights (ACmnHPR), 'General Comment No. 3 on the African Charter on Human and Peoples' Rights: The Right to Life (Article 4)', adopted at Banjul (57th Ordinary Session), November 2015 (hereinafter, African Commission General Comment on the right to life), para. 25.
[59] US Supreme Court, *Madison v. Alabama*, Judgment (Docket No. 17-7505), 27 February 2019.
[60] M. Ford, 'The Cruelty of Executing the Sick and Elderly: Two Controversial Cases in Alabama Reveal a Disturbing Trend in the Death Penalty in America', *New Republic*, 27 February 2018, at http://bit.ly/39wPTuD.
[61] As Switzerland has observed, in an international armed conflict, combatants 'may take part in licit acts of war, for which they may not be subjected to criminal prosecution or brought to court ("combatants' privileges")'. Swiss Federal Department of Foreign Affairs, *The ABC of International Humanitarian Law*, 3rd rev. ed., Bern, 2018, at http://bit.ly/38PwyWq, p. 16. The rule is of a customary nature. 'Upon capture, combatants entitled to prisoner-of-war status may neither be tried for their participation in the hostilities nor for acts that do not violate international humanitarian law. This is a long-standing rule of customary international humanitarian law.' International Committee of the Red Cross (ICRC), Customary IHL Rule 106: 'Conditions for Prisoner-of-War Status', at http://bit.ly/3aXJwlc. See further Articles 87 and 99, Convention (III) relative to the Treatment of Prisoners of War; adopted at Geneva 12 August 1949; entered into force 21 October 1950.

persons, including the elderly. The imposition of a death sentence at the culmination of an unfair trial in non-international armed conflict is a war crime within the jurisdiction of the International Criminal Court.[62]

THE RIGHT TO LIFE OF THE ELDERLY IN ARMED CONFLICT

26.28 The International Committee of the Red Cross (ICRC) has stated that 'the presence of elderly people among the victims of armed conflict is a relatively recent phenomenon, dating back only to the Second World War'.[63] That said, the ICRC has noted also that the 'plight of the aged has long been neglected', while observing that 'for a very long time the International Red Cross and Red Crescent Movement has been concerned about the plight of the elderly. This concern gave rise to a number of resolutions adopted by various International Conferences of the Red Cross and Red Crescent since 1921.'[64] 'The elderly', the organisation has stated, 'are often left without any means of subsistence' and 'may also be subjected to all sorts of abuse – looting, destruction of their property, threats, physical violence, including rape and sometimes murder – because they belong to a minority or live in particularly remote villages or isolated places'.[65]

26.29 In its study of customary IHL, the ICRC determined: 'The elderly, disabled and infirm affected by armed conflict are entitled to special respect and protection.'[66] The rule, it believes, applies to all armed conflict (although evidence for its application in non-international armed conflict is rather scant). Specific provisions are made under the Fourth Geneva Convention of 1949 for their protection, whereby 'the Parties to the conflict shall endeavour to conclude local agreements for the removal from besieged or encircled areas, of wounded, sick, infirm, and aged persons'.[67] Under the 2002 Madrid Declaration, States pledged 'to protect and assist older persons in situations of armed conflict and foreign occupation'.[68]

[62] Art. 8(2)(c)(iv), Rome Statute of the International Criminal Court; adopted at Rome 17 July 1998; entered into force 1 July 2002 (ICC Statute). In the corresponding elements of crimes, the Court is asked to consider whether, 'in the light of all relevant circumstances, the cumulative effect of factors with respect to guarantees deprived the person or persons of a fair trial'. Elements of Crimes, *Official Records of the Assembly of States Parties to the Rome Statute of the International Criminal Court*, first session, New York, 3–10 September 2002, p. 34.
[63] Françoise Krill, 'The Elderly in Situations of Armed Conflict', Address by the ICRC Deputy Director of Operations, Helsinki, September 1999.
[64] Ibid.
[65] Ibid.
[66] ICRC Customary IHL Rule 138: 'The Elderly, Disabled and Infirm', at http://bit.ly/36PpM4a.
[67] Art. 17, Convention (IV) relative to the Protection of Civilian Persons in Time of War; adopted at Geneva 12 August 1949; entered into force 21 October 1950.
[68] Art. 9, 2002 Madrid Declaration.

27

Journalists

INTRODUCTION

27.01 This chapter[1] considers the right to life of journalists – that is, a person who writes for newspapers, magazines, or news websites, or who prepares news to be broadcast.[2] The risks posed by State agents and non-state actors alike to the safety of journalists, especially those engaged in war reporting or in political journalism that involves uncovering and reporting on corruption or misconduct, are significant.[3] According to Reporters without Borders, forty-nine journalists were killed in the course of their work in 2019, which was the lowest total in sixteen years. The 'historically low' figure, which compares with an annual average of eighty killed during the previous twenty years, was 'above all the result of a fall in the number of journalists killed in war zones'.[4] In 2020, however, the Press Emblem Campaign (PEC) said in its annual report issued in December that eighty-three media workers had been killed in thirty countries around the world. India saw thirteen assassinations, while in Mexico eleven journalists were killed.[5]

27.02 The threat to journalists in zones of armed conflict is a long-standing one. In 2006, the UN Security Council adopted Resolution 1738, in which it expressed its deep concern regarding 'the frequency of acts of violence in many parts of the world against journalists, media professionals and associated personnel in armed conflict, in particular deliberate attacks in violation of international humanitarian law'.[6] The Council explicitly

---

[1] The author would like to thank Nick Cumming-Bruce, a journalist writing for the *New York Times*, for his comments on a draft of this chapter.
[2] This is an ordinary definition of the term; see, e.g., the *Oxford English Dictionary*.
[3] In 2013, Mustafa Haji Abdinur, a Somalia correspondent for the French news agency Agence France-Presse (AFP), spoke before the UN Security Council during an Open Debate on the protection of journalists. 'In showing my face to you and the world, I increase the threat of becoming attacked when I go back home', he said. 'But I am a journalist. They may call me "a dead man walking," but I report the news.' UN Educational, Scientific and Cultural Organization (UNESCO), 'UN Security Council Debates Journalists' Safety', 18 July 2013, at http://bit.ly/3k6Et5Y.
[4] Reporters without Borders, 'RSF Yearly Round-Up: "Historically Low" Number of Journalists Killed in 2019', last updated 17 December 2019, at http://bit.ly/3l5ZQ8M.
[5] PEC, 'India and Mexico Most Dangerous Countries in 2020', press release, Geneva, 10 December 2020.
[6] UN Security Council Resolution 1738, adopted by unanimous vote on 23 December 2006, tenth preambular para.

condemned intentional attacks against journalists in situations of armed conflict and called upon 'all parties to put an end to such practices'.[7]

27.03 In May 2015, the Council adopted Resolution 2222, again by unanimous vote, in which it expressed deep concern at the growing threat to the safety of journalists and other media professionals posed by terrorist groups. It strongly condemned 'incidents of killings, kidnapping and hostage taking committed by' such groups.[8] Under the resolution, the Council requested the UN Secretary-General to include consistently the issue of the safety and security of journalists in his annual reports on the protection of civilians in armed conflict.[9] In his annual report of May 2020 (the latest as of this writing), the UN Secretary-General suggested that the year-on-year drop in the number of journalists killed in armed conflict (down from thirty-five to sixteen) was attributable to the fact that 'fewer journalists were reporting from conflict zones owing to the high degree of insecurity'.[10]

27.04 A UN Plan of Action on the Safety of Journalists and the Issue of Impunity aims to tackle the challenges facing journalists.[11] The Plan resulted from a process that began in 2010 at the instigation of the UN Educational, Scientific and Cultural Organization (UNESCO).[12] In his 2017 report to the UN Security Council on the protection of civilians, the UN Secretary-General had urged UN member States to inform UNESCO 'of the status of judicial enquiries into these killings, strengthen protection for journalists reporting in conflict situations and prevent impunity'.[13] On 11 November 2020, the Spokesperson for the Secretary-General issued a statement on attacks against journalists in conflict zones, reiterating the Secretary-General's deep concern about attacks against journalists and media workers around the world.[14]

27.05 The remainder of the chapter looks at the right to life of journalists first under global standards and then under regional standards. A final section summarises the specific protection afforded under international humanitarian law during situations of armed conflict. In the statement of 11 November 2020, the UN Secretary-General recalled that 'civilians, including civilian journalists engaged in professional missions in areas of armed conflict, must be respected and protected under international humanitarian law'.[15]

[7] Ibid., operative para. 1.
[8] UN Security Council Resolution 2222, adopted by unanimous vote on 27 May 2015, seventeenth preambular para.
[9] Ibid., operative para. 19.
[10] 'Protection of civilians in armed conflict. Report of the Secretary-General', UN doc. S/2020/366, 6 May 2020, para. 16.
[11] A copy of the Plan is available at http://bit.ly/358Q2Fw.
[12] 'UN Plan of Action on the Safety of Journalists and the Issue of Impunity', Office of the UN High Commissioner for Human Rights (OHCHR), at http://bit.ly/3l8n2mK.
[13] 'Protection of civilians in armed conflict. Report of the Secretary-General', UN doc. S/2017/414, 10 May 2017, para. 32.
[14] UN, 'Statement attributable to the Spokesperson for the Secretary-General – on attacks against journalists in conflict zones', New York, 11 November 2020, at http://bit.ly/2IucXSw.
[15] Ibid.

THE RIGHT TO LIFE OF JOURNALISTS UNDER GLOBAL STANDARDS

27.06 The 1966 International Covenant on Civil and Political Rights (ICCPR)[16] does not specifically refer to journalists. That said, it is stipulated that each State Party to the Covenant 'undertakes to respect and to ensure to all individuals within its territory and subject to its jurisdiction the rights recognized in the ... Covenant, without distinction of any kind'.[17] Thus, in its Resolution 2222, the UN Security Council recognised that 'States bear the primary responsibility to respect and ensure the human rights of their citizens, as well as individuals within their territory as provided for by relevant international law'.[18]

27.07 Each journalist under the jurisdiction of a State Party to the ICCPR thus benefits from the full protection of the right to life afforded by Article 6. This right is non-derogable.[19] As discussed in Chapter 1 of this work, that every human being has the right to life – without distinction of any kind – has long reflected customary international law. Furthermore, the jus cogens prohibition of arbitrary deprivation of life codified in Article 6(1) of the Covenant protects all journalists.

27.08 As the Human Rights Committee reiterated in its General Comment 36, the duty to protect the right to life obligates States Parties to the ICCPR to take special measures of protection for those whose lives are at particular risk, including journalists. This is so, whether they are known to be at risk because of specific threats or as a consequence of pre-existing patterns of violence.[20] The Human Rights Committee cited in this regard its Concluding Observations of 2011 on the second periodic report by Serbia, in which the Committee again expressed its concern that journalists 'continue to be attacked, threatened, and murdered'.[21]

27.09 Also cited by the Human Rights Committee was the 2012 report of the UN Special Rapporteur on extrajudicial, summary or arbitrary executions. Therein, the Special Rapporteur considered the mechanisms in place to provide greater protection to the right to life of journalists and concluded that the most immediate problem did not lie with gaps in the international legal framework. 'The challenge is rather to ensure that the established international framework is fully used, and that its norms are reflected in domestic laws and practices', he stated.[22]

27.10 In its forty-fifth ordinary session in September–October 2020, the Human Rights Council adopted a resolution dedicated to the safety of journalists in which it

---

[16] International Covenant on Civil and Political Rights; adopted at New York 16 December 1966; entered into force 23 March 1976.
[17] Art. 2(1), ICCPR.
[18] UN Security Council Resolution 2222, eighth preambular para.
[19] Art. 4(2), ICCPR.
[20] Human Rights Committee, 'General comment No. 36. Article 6: right to life', UN doc. CCPR/C/GC/36, 3 September 2019 (hereinafter, Human Rights Committee, General Comment 36 on the right to life), para. 23.
[21] Human Rights Committee, Concluding Observations on the second periodic report by Serbia, UN doc. CCPR/C/SRB/CO/2, 20 May 2011, para. 21.
[22] Report of the Special Rapporteur on extrajudicial, summary or arbitrary executions, Christof Heyns, UN doc. A/HRC/20/22, 10 April 2012, Summary.

'condemn[ed] unequivocally all attacks, reprisals and violence against journalists and media workers, such as killings, torture, enforced disappearances, arbitrary arrest and arbitrary detention ... in both conflict and non-conflict situations'.[23] The Council called upon States to 'ensure accountability through the conduct of impartial, prompt, thorough, independent and effective investigations into all alleged violence, threats and attacks against journalists and media workers ... within their jurisdiction' and to 'bring perpetrators, including those who command, conspire to commit, aid and abet or cover up such crimes to justice'. It further called upon States to ensure that 'measures to combat terrorism and preserve national security, public order or health are in compliance with their obligations under international law and do not arbitrarily or unduly hinder the work and safety of journalists'.[24]

THE RIGHT TO LIFE OF JOURNALISTS UNDER REGIONAL MECHANISMS

27.11 While the protection afforded by the right to life under regional human rights instruments is similarly general in nature, standards and mechanisms specifically seek to protect journalists. Mechanisms in Africa, the Americas, and Europe have paid particular attention to the protection of journalists, both in peacetime and during armed conflict.

The Protection of Journalists in Europe

27.12 The European Court of Human Rights has addressed several cases concerning the protection of journalists' rights to life and freedom from torture.[25] In 2016, the Council of Europe adopted a Recommendation on the protection of journalists and other media actors, in which it found it 'alarming and unacceptable' that journalists in Europe are 'increasingly being threatened, ... intimidated, arbitrarily deprived of their liberty, physically attacked, tortured and even killed because of their investigative work, opinions or reporting, particularly when their work focuses on the misuse of power, corruption, human rights violations, criminal activities, terrorism and fundamentalism'.[26] The Recommendation declared: 'Given the scale and severity of threats and attacks against journalists and other media actors in Europe and their damaging effects on the functioning of democratic society, far-reaching measures are necessary at the international and national levels in order to strengthen the protection of journalism and the safety of journalists and other media actors, and to eradicate impunity.'[27]

---

[23] Human Rights Council Resolution 45/18: The safety of journalists, adopted without a vote on 6 October 2020, operative para. 1.
[24] Ibid., operative para. 10 (d) and (e).
[25] As generally protected by Articles 2 and 3, Convention for the Protection of Human Rights and Fundamental Freedoms; adopted at Rome by the Council of Europe, 4 November 1950; entered into force 3 September 1953.
[26] Council of Europe Recommendation CM/Rec(2016)4 of the Committee of Ministers to member States on the protection of journalism and safety of journalists and other media actors, adopted by the Committee of Ministers on 13 April 2016, available at http://bit.ly/3mVtM7U, para. 1.
[27] Ibid., para. 5.

27.13 The Guidelines set out in the appendix to the Recommendation stipulated that the conclusions of an investigation into violence perpetrated against a journalist 'must be based on thorough, objective and impartial analysis of all the relevant elements, including the establishment of whether there is a connection between the threats and violence against journalists and other media actors and the exercise of journalistic activities'.[28] Accordingly, where the victim of a killing is a journalist, the European Court of Human Rights, explicitly referring to the Recommendation, now considers it to be 'of utmost importance' to check a possible connection between the crime and the victim's professional activity.[29]

27.14 The *Mazepa* case, adjudged in 2018, concerned the contract killing of Anna Politkovskaya, a well-known investigative journalist in Russia who had addressed violations of human rights in Chechnya in the course of counterterrorism operations in the region. Ms Politkovskaya, who was a strong critic of the actions of Russian President Vladimir Putin, was fatally shot in the lift in her block of flats in Moscow on 7 October 2006.[30] The investigation by the Russian authorities seemingly made little effort to identify who had ordered her murder.

27.15 The earlier case of *Dink* v. *Turkey*[31] concerned the murder of a Turkish journalist of Armenian origin by an extreme nationalist group. Two police departments and one *gendarmerie* department had been informed not only of the likelihood of an assassination attempt but even of the identity of alleged perpetrators, yet none had taken effective action to seek to prevent the crime. The fact that the victim had not sought police protection was not determinative of its necessity in the opinion of the European Court, given that while Mr Dink had been aware of a climate of hostility towards himself, he had had no knowledge of the conspiracy hatched by the group to kill him.[32] The failure to investigate effectively the killing meant that there had been a violation of the procedural element of the right to life in addition to the substantive breach of Turkey's duty to protect his life.

27.16 In *Gongadze* v. *Ukraine*,[33] the failure of the authorities to comply with the procedural duty to investigate meant that the right to life protected by Article 2 of the European Convention had been similarly violated. Georgiy Gongadze was a political journalist who had reported on breaches of democratic principles by the Ukrainian authorities and corruption by high-level State officials.[34] Following his disappearance, his decapitated body was found outside a town in the Kyiv region. Subsequently, the authorities actively impeded the investigation, giving the impression of being more preoccupied with proving that senior State officials had not been involved in the killing of Mr Gongadze than with uncovering the truth about his disappearance and death.[35] The Minister of the Interior of

---

[28] Ibid., para. 19.
[29] European Court of Human Rights, *Mazepa and others* v. *Russia*, Judgment (Third Section), 17 July 2018, para. 73.
[30] Ibid., para. 7.
[31] European Court of Human Rights, *Dink* v. *Turkey*, Judgment (Second Section), 14 September 2010 (rendered final on 14 December 2010).
[32] Ibid., paras. 67–75.
[33] European Court of Human Rights, *Gongadze* v. *Ukraine*, Judgment (Second Section), 8 November 2005 (rendered final on 8 February 2006).
[34] Ibid., para. 9.
[35] Ibid., para. 97.

570   *The Protection of At-Risk Groups and Individuals*

Ukraine announced that the two presumed murderers of Mr Gongadze, identified as drug users, had already died and thus that the case had been solved and could be closed. The Minister claimed that the murder had been spontaneous and without a political motive.[36] Other evidence suggested police officers had killed him.[37]

27.17 The Court observed that the authorities, primarily prosecutors, should have been aware of the vulnerable position in which a journalist who covered politically sensitive topics placed himself at the material time (as evidenced by the death of eighteen journalists in Ukraine since 1991).[38] The fact that the alleged offenders, two of them active police officers, were identified and charged with the kidnap and murder of the journalist a few days after the change in the country's leadership raised 'serious doubts as to the genuine desire of the authorities under the previous government to investigate the case thoroughly'. Accordingly, there had been a violation of the duty to investigate effectively Mr Gongadze's disappearance and violent death.[39]

27.18 As of this writing, investigations were ongoing into the murder of Daphne Caruana Galizia, a Maltese journalist who was killed by a car bomb on 16 October 2017. According to one media report on the assassination, her blog posts 'were a thorn in the side of both the establishment and underworld figures that hold sway in Europe's smallest member State'. Her most recent revelations had accused Malta's prime minister, Joseph Muscat, and two of his closest aides, of misconduct, connecting offshore companies linked to the three men with the sale of Maltese passports and payments from the government of Azerbaijan.[40] On 1 December 2019, following public protests calling for his resignation in relation to the assassination, Prime Minister Muscat announced he was stepping down, and on 13 January 2020 he left office.[41] A few days earlier, the European Parliament, which has been examining the state of the rule of law in Malta, affirmed a worrying lack of progress in investigations into persons of interest around Ms Caruana Galizia's murder.[42]

The Protection of Journalists in the Americas

27.19 In the Americas, the Inter-American Commission on Human Rights published a detailed report on violence against journalists and media workers in 2013.[43] The report,

---

[36] Ibid., para. 50.
[37] Ibid., para. 166.
[38] Ibid., paras. 83, 168.
[39] Ibid., para. 166.
[40] J. Garside, 'Malta Car Bomb Kills Panama Papers Journalist', *The Guardian*, 16 October 2017, at http://bit.ly/2IkKWN9.
[41] '"I've Paid Highest Political Price for a Dark Episode", Says Malta PM', *Euronews*, 11 January 2020, at http://bit.ly/32mjjL6.
[42] Ibid.; and European Parliament resolution of 18 December 2019 on the rule of law in Malta following the recent revelations surrounding the murder of Daphne Caruana Galizia; see also Council of Europe, Parliamentary Assembly Resolution 2293 (2019): Daphne Caruana Galizia's assassination and the rule of law in Malta and beyond – ensuring that the whole truth emerges.
[43] Inter-American Commission on Human Rights, *Violence against Journalists and Media Workers: Inter-American Standards and National Practices on Prevention, Protection and Prosecution of Perpetrators*,

which was compiled by the Commission's Special Rapporteur for Freedom of Expression, described violence against journalists in the Americas as 'an increasingly urgent challenge'. It found that from the beginning of 2010 through to 1 November 2013, at least seventy-eight journalists and media workers were murdered throughout the region for motives that could be connected to the exercise of their profession. Dozens more were disappeared or displaced from their places of work, while hundreds of others received threats or were harassed or attacked in response to their professional activities.[44] The report cited Brazil, Honduras, and Mexico as States of especial concern at the time.[45]

27.20 The report noted the risks emanating from equating journalism with material support to terrorism. It noted that, in 2009, the Commission's Office of the Special Rapporteur for Freedom of Expression and the UN Special Rapporteur on the question had expressed their concern about statements made by Colombian President Álvaro Uribe regarding the journalist Hollman Morris.[46] The president had said in a news conference that Mr Morris had 'shielded himself by his condition as a journalist to be a permissive accomplice to terrorism'. The journalist, a beneficiary of precautionary measures from the Inter-American Commission who had previously been forced to leave the country due to threats against his life, received threatening phone calls following the president's remarks. In their statement, the rapporteurs 'remind[ed] the Colombian State once more that high government officials must abstain from making public statements that stigmatize journalists who are critical of the government and generate an environment of intimidation that gravely affects freedom of expression in the country. This obligation is particularly important in a context of polarization and internal armed conflict, such as Colombia's.'[47]

27.21 In its judgment in 2012 in the *Vélez Restrepo and Family* case,[48] the Inter-American Court of Human Rights held Colombia responsible for having conducted the preliminary investigation into an attack on a journalist by members of the national army through military rather than civilian mechanisms. The Court reiterated its existing view that the military justice system 'is not the competent system of justice to investigate and, as appropriate, prosecute and punish the authors of human rights violations'. The Court clarified that 'the criteria to investigate and prosecute human rights violations before the

---

Report, Organization of American States (OAS) doc. OEA/Ser.L/V/II. CIDH/RELE/INF. 12/13, 31 December 2013.

[44] Ibid., para. 4.
[45] Ibid., para. 14.
[46] Inter-American Commission on Human Rights, 'The Rapporteurs for Freedom of Expression of the UN and of the OAS Express Their Concern Regarding Comments made by High Authorities of the Colombian Government Against Journalists', joint press release, no. R05/09, Geneva/Washington, DC, 9 February 2009, at http://bit.ly/3n2GBxh.
[47] Ibid.; and see Inter-American Commission on Human Rights, *Violence against Journalists and Media Workers: Inter-American Standards and National Practices on Prevention, Protection and Prosecution of Perpetrators*, para. 38.
[48] Inter-American Court of Human Rights, *Vélez Restrepo and Family v. Colombia*, Judgment (Preliminary Objections, Merits, Reparations and Costs), 3 September 2012.

ordinary jurisdiction reside not on the gravity of the violations, but rather on their very nature and on that of the protected juridical right'.[49]

27.22 In this regard, the Inter-American Commission commended the creation in 2012 of a specialised investigative and prosecutorial unit focused on violence against journalists in Mexico. The Office of the Special Prosecutor on Crimes against Freedom of Expression (FEADLE), located within the Office of the Prosecutor General of the Republic, was welcomed as a response to the situation of widespread impunity that exists with regard to crimes against journalists in Mexico.[50] By January 2020, however, the Special Prosecutor's Office had secured just four convictions from 803 investigations into crimes against journalists.[51] Mexico's President López Obrador has been criticised for contributing to a culture of violence against journalists by launching scathing verbal attacks on reporters and news outlets that are critical of his government. After President López Obrador pilloried a story published by the Mexico City–based newspaper *Reforma* in April 2019, the paper's editor received death threats and was a victim of harassment.[52]

27.23 The verbal assaults by US President Donald Trump during his term in office on media outlets in the United States also gave rise to concerns regarding the safety of journalists.[53] In 2020, during the George Floyd protests, on a number of occasions, police even targeted journalists while they were reporting live on television.[54] A Deutsche Welle reporter named Stefan Simons was shot at with rubber-coated bullets and threatened with arrest in Minneapolis in late May 2020.[55] Over the course of that month and the first half of June, the Committee to Protect Journalists (CPJ) recorded at least eighty-nine rubber bullet or projectile incidents, twenty-seven pepper sprayings, and forty-nine tear gassings. While not all of those incidents were directed at the journalists because of their work – sometimes it was simply an issue of being in a crowd that was protesting – there were said to be numerous incidents in which the police targeted journalists. The CPJ called on the police to open investigations into those incidents.[56]

---

[49] Ibid., paras. 239–45.
[50] Inter-American Commission on Human Rights, *Violence against Journalists and Media Workers: Inter-American Standards and National Practices on Prevention, Protection and Prosecution of Perpetrators*, para. 191.
[51] El Financiero, 'Prosecutor for Crimes against Journalists Has Closed 4 of 803 Cases', *Mexico News Daily*, 3 January 2020, at http://bit.ly/3lqzYJ6.
[52] Ibid.
[53] Y. Serhan, 'The "Absurd" New Reality of Reporting from the U.S.', *The Atlantic*, 19 June 2020, at http://bit.ly/32mZ4N8.
[54] See, e.g., M. Safi, C. Barr, N. McIntyre, P. Duncan, and S. Cutler, '"I'm Getting Shot": Attacks on Journalists Surge in US Protests', *The Guardian*, 5 June 2020, at http://bit.ly/2U7S8yR; and US Press Freedom Tracker, at http://bit.ly/3p8MuLd.
[55] 'DW's Stefan Simons on His Confrontation with Minneapolis Police', Deutsche Welle, 31 May 2020, at http://bit.ly/3n4WzXE; 'US Sees over 400 Attacks on Press Freedom in under a Month – But Why?', Deutsche Welle, 19 June 2020, at http://bit.ly/32qobeX.
[56] Ibid.

The Protection of Human Rights Defenders in Africa

27.24 In 2011, the African Commission on Human and Peoples' Rights adopted a resolution on the safety of journalists and media practitioners in Africa, noting that 'killings, attacks and kidnapping of journalists, which are contrary to international humanitarian and human rights law, are often committed in an environment of impunity'.[57] The resolution called upon States Parties to the 1981 African Charter on Human and Peoples' Rights 'and concerned authorities' to 'fulfil their obligation on preventing and investigating all crimes allegedly committed against journalists and media practitioners and also to bring the perpetrators to justice'.[58] It further urged all parties to armed conflicts 'to respect the independence and freedom of journalists and media practitioners to exercise their profession and guarantee their safety and security in accordance with international humanitarian law'.[59]

27.25 The following year, the African Commission issued a resolution on attacks against journalists and media practitioners in Somalia.[60] The resolution expressed the Commission's deep concern at the murder of four journalists in January–April 2012 in Mogadishu and Galkayo, with the death toll then standing at more than thirty journalists over the preceding three years, and at the lack of investigation 'which leaves the perpetrators unpunished'. The Commission condemned the continued killings of journalists in Somalia and called on the Somali authorities 'and all armed groups' to end violations of the right to life against journalists, media practitioners, and media organisations.[61]

The Protection of Journalists in the Arab World

27.26 There are significant threats to the lives of journalists across the Arab world. Indeed, in a UNESCO study of attacks against journalists in 2014–18, *Intensified Attacks, New Defences*,[62] Arab nations were found to be the most dangerous places for journalists, representing 30 per cent (149 journalists) of global killings.[63] Article 5 of the Arab Charter on Human Rights[64] stipulates that 'every human being has an inherent right to life'. It is further specified that 'this right shall be protected by law. No one shall be arbitrarily deprived of his life.'[65]

---

[57] African Commission on Human and Peoples' Rights, Resolution on the Safety of Journalists and Media Practitioners in Africa, ACHPR/Res.185(XLIX)11, adopted by the Commission on 12 May 2011 during its 49th Ordinary Session, held in Banjul on 28 April–12 May 2011, ninth preambular para.
[58] Ibid., operative para. 3.
[59] Ibid., operative para. 4.
[60] African Commission on Human and Peoples' Rights, Resolution on the Attacks against Journalists and Media Practitioners in Somalia, ACHPR/Res.221(LI)2012, adopted by the Commission on 2 May 2012 during its 51st Ordinary Session, held in Banjul from 18 April to 2 May 2012, at http://bit.ly/3n1quA3.
[61] Ibid., paras. (i) and (ii).
[62] UNESCO, *Intensified Attacks, New Defences: Developments in the Fight to Protect Journalists and End Impunity*, Paris, 2019, available at http://bit.ly/3kb7Aos.
[63] See also M. Swart, 'Killings and Attacks against Journalists on the Rise', *Aljazeera*, 2 November 2019, at http://bit.ly/32oG8xL.
[64] Arab Charter on Human Rights; adopted at Tunis 22 May 2004; entered into force 15 March 2008.
[65] Art. 5(2), 2004 Arab Charter on Human Rights.

574   *The Protection of At-Risk Groups and Individuals*

27.27 In 2019, in an Annex to the Report of the Special Rapporteur on extrajudicial, summary or arbitrary executions to the Human Rights Council,[66] Agnès Callamard presented the results of her investigation into the unlawful death of Mr Jamal Khashoggi, a Saudi journalist. 'One of the region's most important journalistic voices, he considered journalism from within, about and for the region to be vital.'[67] Mr Khashoggi was murdered by organs and agents of the Saudi State in the country's consulate in Istanbul on 2 October 2018. Saudi Arabia is subject to the 'peremptory and customary norm' prohibiting extrajudicial killings, she stated, and is obligated to respect the right to life, including by virtue of its adherence to the Arab Charter on Human Rights.[68] Saudi Arabia bears responsibility under international law, she concluded, for the internationally wrongful acts of both his murder and the subsequent failure to investigate the killing effectively.[69]

27.28 In her subsequent report to the Human Rights Council in October 2019, the Special Rapporteur called upon the UN Secretary-General to initiate a follow-up criminal investigation into the killing of Mr Khashoggi 'to build strong files on each of the alleged perpetrators and identify mechanisms for formal accountability, such as an ad hoc or hybrid tribunal'.[70] In addition, as part of the ongoing UN reform process, the Secretary-General should, she stated, 'strengthen system-wide capacity to promote the safety of journalists and ensure that United Nations country teams are fully equipped to implement the United Nations Plan of Action on the Safety of Journalists and the Issue of Impunity at the local level in the countries concerned'.[71]

THE RIGHT TO LIFE OF JOURNALISTS IN SITUATIONS OF ARMED CONFLICT

27.29 During armed conflict, journalists are primarily protected as civilians. According to the 1977 Additional Protocol I, 'journalists engaged in dangerous professional missions in areas of armed conflict shall be considered as civilians'.[72] Thus, as UN Security Council Resolution 1738 recalled, 'journalists, media professionals and associated personnel engaged in dangerous professional missions in areas of armed conflict shall be considered as civilians and shall be respected and protected as such'.[73] This means that they shall not

---

[66] Annex to the Report of the Special Rapporteur on extrajudicial, summary or arbitrary executions: Investigation into the unlawful death of Mr. Jamal Khashoggi, UN doc. A/HRC/41/CRP.1, 19 June 2019.
[67] Ibid., para. 57.
[68] Ibid., para. 197. Saudi Arabia is not a State Party to the ICCPR.
[69] Ibid., para. 219.
[70] Investigation of, accountability for and prevention of intentional State killings of human rights defenders, journalists and prominent dissidents Report of the Special Rapporteur on extrajudicial, summary or arbitrary executions, UN doc. A/HRC/41/36, 4 October 2019, para. 80.
[71] Ibid., para. 81.
[72] Art. 79(1), Protocol Additional to the Geneva Conventions of 12 August 1949, and relating to the Protection of Victims of International Armed Conflicts; adopted at Geneva 8 June 1977; entered into force 7 December 1978 (hereinafter, 1977 Additional Protocol I).
[73] UN Security Council Resolution 1738, operative para. 2. See similarly Security Council Resolution 2222, operative para. 3.

be attacked and that the risk to their lives must be considered in assessing whether an attack is proportionate.[74]

27.30 As is the case with any civilians, however, journalists will lose their status – and thus their immunity from attack – should they participate directly in hostilities, whether in an international or a non-international armed conflict. As the International Committee of the Red Cross (ICRC) observes, the international humanitarian law treaty terminology of taking a 'direct' part in hostilities[75] implies that there can also be 'indirect' participation in hostilities, which does not lead to such loss of protection.[76] Such indirect, 'war-sustaining' activities would, the ICRC stated, include media activities supporting the general war effort, such as political propaganda.[77] Accordingly, a journalist who reflects the government line when reporting on any armed conflict would not be deemed to be participating directly in hostilities and would remain a civilian, protected as such.

27.31 In its 2013 report on violence against journalists, the Inter-American Commission on Human Rights cited the case of the murder in 1988 of journalist Hugo Bustíos Saavedra by a Peruvian military patrol. Mr Bustíos, journalist and correspondent for the magazine *Carretas*, was killed on 24 November 1988 while he was investigating two murders committed during the non-international armed conflict in Peru. The Commission concluded that Mr Bustíos had been extrajudicially executed by agents of the Peruvian State in violation of his right to life.[78] It also found the State responsible for a violation of Article 13 of the Inter-American Convention, which protects freedom of thought and expression, given that it knew that journalists were in the conflict zone and had failed to accord them the necessary protection.[79] The Commission recalled that journalists serve a fundamental role in situations of armed conflict, as 'it is journalists who are risking their lives to bring the public an independent and professional view of what is really happening in areas of conflict'.[80]

27.32 In 2014, a number of human rights organisations sharply criticised the appointment of retired General Daniel Urresti as Minister of the Interior in Peru. General Urresti was under investigation as the alleged mastermind of the murder of Mr Bustíos. On the way to Huanta, Bustíos was attacked with gunfire. Having been hit by a bullet, he lost control of the motorcycle he was driving and fell. The attackers placed an explosive over his injured body, causing his death. Urrestí, an army captain at the time, worked as Head of the S-2 Military Intelligence Branch (Sección de Inteligencia S-2) at the Castropampa base in

---

[74] See Chapter 5 for a general discussion of this issue.
[75] Art. 51(3), 1977 Additional Protocol I; and Art. 13(3), Protocol Additional to the Geneva Conventions of 12 August 1949, and relating to the protection of victims of non-international armed conflicts (Protocol II); adopted at Geneva 8 June 1977; entered into force 7 December 1978.
[76] N. Melzer, *Interpretive Guidance on the Notion of Direct Participation in Hostilities*, ICRC, Geneva, 2009, p. 51.
[77] Ibid.
[78] Inter-American Commission on Human Rights, Hugo Bustíos Saavedra, Report No. 38/97 (Case 10.548), Peru, 16 October 1997, text available at http://bit.ly/3n7ZJtF, para. 60.
[79] Ibid., paras. 76 and 77.
[80] Ibid., para. 73.

Ayacucho.[81] In October 2018, after a nine-year-long investigation, the Third National Criminal Prosecutor's Office declared him innocent of all charges.[82]

27.33 There is a special status for certain journalists embedded within an armed force that is engaged in an international armed conflict. During the conduct of hostilities, all journalists are civilians, but under the 1949 Geneva Convention III, 'war correspondents' who accompany the armed forces (without actually being members thereof) are, upon capture, prisoners of war. This is so, provided that they have received authorisation from the armed forces which they accompany and that they have been provided for that purpose with a duly established identity card.[83] This is a long-standing rule of international humanitarian law.[84] As the ICRC clarifies, however, a distinction must be made between authorised and embedded war correspondents, on the one hand, and all other journalists.[85] Upon falling into the hands of the enemy, the former are prisoners of war, whereas the latter are civilians and may only be interned if absolutely necessary for reasons of security.[86] In any event, detainees must be treated humanely and protected against violence.

---

[81] 'CEJIL, DPLF and WOLA Express Their Concern for the Appointment of Retired General Daniel Urresti as Minister of the Interior in Peru', Washington, DC, 8 July 2014, at http://bit.ly/2I7FLAN.

[82] 'Daniel Urresti es absuelto del asesinato del periodista Hugo Bustíos (VIDEO)', Correo, last updated 4 October 2018, at http://bit.ly/3k9bdeS.

[83] Art. 4(A)(4), Convention (III) relative to the Treatment of Prisoners of War; adopted at Geneva 12 August 1949; entered into force 21 October 1950.

[84] See ICRC Commentary on Article 4 of 1949 Geneva Convention III, 2020, at http://bit.ly/3kaaV7x, para. 1047.

[85] Ibid., para. 1049.

[86] Ibid. See on this issue Arts. 42 and 78, Convention (IV) relative to the Protection of Civilian Persons in Time of War; adopted at Geneva 12 August 1949; entered into force 21 October 1950.

28

Human Rights Defenders

INTRODUCTION

28.01 'Human rights defender' is a term used to describe people who 'individually or with others, act to promote or protect human rights'. Human rights defenders are thus 'identified above all by what they do', as the United Nations has described.[1] Thereby, they are to be distinguished from individuals who are merely exercising their human rights.

28.02 The 1998 UN Declaration on Human Rights Defenders stipulates: 'Everyone has the right, individually and in association with others, to promote and to strive for the protection and realization of human rights and fundamental freedoms at the national and international levels.'[2] Yet, such individuals are at particular risk of being targeted as a result of their work, and the number of reported killings of human rights defenders around the world is said to be rising.[3] As the UN Special Rapporteur on the situation of human rights defenders[4] told the UN General Assembly in October 2020: 'Hundreds of human rights defenders are killed every year because of their work, but these murders are not inevitable or normal.'[5] The civil society organisation Front Line Defenders reported that 304 human rights defenders were murdered because of their work in 2019.[6]

28.03 Mary Lawlor told the UN General Assembly: 'The killing of a human rights defender is a red line no one should cross. States and businesses must do more to protect them.'[7] Across all regions, however, this red line has been crossed, albeit to varying extents. In February 2019, a non-governmental organisation (NGO) submitted a written statement

---

[1] Office of the High Commissioner for Human Rights (OHCHR), *Human Rights Defenders: Protecting the Right to Defend Human Rights*, Fact Sheet No. 29, Geneva, at http://bit.ly/35WZr1Q, p. 2.

[2] Art. 1, Declaration on the Right and Responsibility of Individuals, Groups and Organs of Society to Promote and Protect Universally Recognized Human Rights and Fundamental Freedoms, adopted by UN General Assembly Resolution 53/144, adopted without a vote on 9 December 1998 (hereinafter, 1998 UN Declaration on Human Rights Defenders).

[3] Special Rapporteur on the situation of human rights defenders, Report on the Killings of Human Rights Defenders, Concept Note, OHCHR, 2020.

[4] The Human Rights Commission first established the mandate on the situation of human rights defenders in 2000. The mandate was renewed until 2022 by the Human Rights Council in its Decision 43/115 in 2020.

[5] OHCHR, 'UN Expert Calls for Greater Protection for Human Rights Defenders', press release, New York, 19 October 2020, at http://bit.ly/2GnqScE.

[6] Front Line Defenders, *Global Analysis 2019*, 2020, at http://bit.ly/2GidCWx, p. 7.

[7] OHCHR, 'UN Expert Calls for Greater Protection for Human Rights Defenders'.

to the UN Human Rights Council ahead of its fortieth session alleging that Gulf Cooperation Council (GCC) governments 'regularly target, threaten, imprison, and torture individuals for their human rights activism. Human rights defenders often face reprisals for their work, including ... attacks and threats against family members'.[8] In the Americas, the Inter-American Commission has made clear its serious concern at

> the grave situation of insecurity and danger in which human rights defenders must pursue their work in the hemisphere. Assassinations, forced disappearances, assaults, threats, being identified as enemies or legitimate targets, smear campaigns, legal actions aimed at intimidating them, violation of their homes, and illegal activities targeting defenders – all of these mechanisms used to impede and encumber their work – are part of their day-to-day reality.[9]

The Commission further recalled that 'when a human rights defender is attacked, all those persons for whom he or she works are left without protection'.[10]

28.04 Threats have also been made against UN special rapporteurs, in particular in the Philippines. As Andrew Gilmour, then UN Assistant Secretary-General for Human Rights in New York, observed in 2019, the UN independent expert on the rights of indigenous peoples, Victoria Tauli-Corpuz, was on a Philippines government list of 'terrorists'. This followed the vilification of Agnès Callamard, the Special Rapporteur on extrajudicial, summary or arbitrary executions, whom Philippine President Rodrigo Duterte declared he wanted to 'slap'. He later announced he would like to throw other UN human rights officials to the crocodiles.[11]

28.05 In July 2020, Amnesty International issued an urgent action alert, warning that Afghanistan's human rights community was under intensifying attack from both the authorities and armed groups and that against the backdrop of escalating violence in the country, human rights defenders and activists had been 'largely ignored by the Afghan government and the international community'.[12] The organisation called upon advocates around the world to urge the government of Afghanistan to 'immediately adopt an independent, effective and implementable protection mechanism for [human rights defenders] in the country, to ensure their safety and support'.[13]

28.06 The UN Special Rapporteur on the situation of human rights defenders was planning to dedicate her thematic report, due to be presented at the forty-sixth session of the Human Rights Council in March 2021, to the issue of killings of human rights

---

[8] Americans for Democracy and Human Rights in Bahrain, 'HRC40 Written Statement: The Targeting of Human Rights Defenders in the GCC', 25 February 2019, at http://bit.ly/3jPc4RD.
[9] 'Report on the Situation of Human Rights Defenders in the Americas', OAS doc. OEA/Ser.L/V/II.124, Doc. 5 rev.1, 7 March 2006, at http://bit.ly/3jQalLG, para. 332.
[10] Ibid.
[11] A. Gilmour, 'Human Rights Advocates in Asia Under Attack', OHCHR, New York, 2019, at http://bit.ly/3mL9HBl.
[12] Amnesty International, 'Human Rights Defenders Under Attack', First Urgent Action: Afghanistan, 118/20, AI Index: ASA 11/2680/2020, 10 July 2020, available at http://bit.ly/32jHNEP.
[13] Ibid.

Human Rights Defenders

defenders. In addition to the specific mandate of the Special Rapporteur to protect human rights defenders, also relevant among UN special procedures are the Special Rapporteur on the rights to freedom of peaceful assembly and of association and the Special Rapporteur on the promotion and protection of the right to freedom of opinion and expression.

THE RIGHT TO LIFE OF HUMAN RIGHTS DEFENDERS UNDER GLOBAL STANDARDS

28.07 The 1966 International Covenant on Civil and Political Rights[14] (ICCPR) does not specifically refer to human rights defenders. That said, it is stipulated that each State Party to the Covenant 'undertakes to respect and to ensure to all individuals within its territory and subject to its jurisdiction the rights recognized in the ... Covenant, without distinction of any kind'.[15]

28.08 Each human rights defender under the jurisdiction of a State Party to the ICCPR thus benefits from the full protection of the right to life afforded by Article 6. This right is non-derogable.[16] As discussed in Chapter 1 of this work, that every human being has the right to life – without distinction of any kind – has long reflected customary international law. Furthermore, the jus cogens prohibition of arbitrary deprivation of life codified in Article 6(1) of the Covenant protects all human rights defenders.

28.09 As the Human Rights Committee reiterated in its General Comment 36, the duty to protect the right to life obligates States Parties to the ICCPR to take special measures of protection for those whose lives are at particular risk, including human rights defenders. This is so, whether they are known to be at risk because of specific threats or as a consequence of pre-existing patterns of violence.[17] This duty, which is reflected in the 1998 Declaration on Human Rights Defenders,[18] obligates States to 'take the necessary measures to respond to death threats and to provide adequate protection to human rights defenders, including the creation and maintenance of a safe and enabling environment for defending human rights'.[19]

28.10 Sentencing a human rights defender to death for exercising their right of peaceful assembly is also a clear violation of the prohibition of arbitrary deprivation of life. In 2018, Saudi Arabia's prosecutor was seeking the death penalty against activist Israa al-Ghomgham. She had been arrested in December 2015 along with her husband, Moussa al-Hashem, because of her role in organising peaceful anti-government protests in Qatif in

---

[14] International Covenant on Civil and Political Rights; adopted at New York 16 December 1966; entered into force 23 March 1976.
[15] Art. 2(1), ICCPR.
[16] Art. 4(2), ICCPR.
[17] Human Rights Committee, 'General comment No. 36. Article 6: right to life', UN doc. CCPR/C/GC/36, 3 September 2019 (hereinafter, Human Rights Committee, General Comment 36 on the right to life), para. 23.
[18] Art. 12(2), UN Declaration on Human Rights Defenders.
[19] Human Rights Committee, General Comment 36 on the right to life, para. 53.

the kingdom's Eastern Province in the wake of the Arab Spring. She was also arrested, it was affirmed, because she called for human rights reform and the release of human rights activists.[20] While the demand for the death penalty was rejected, Ms al-Ghomgham was said to be still facing a long prison sentence if convicted by the counterterrorism court before she was due to appear.[21]

THE RIGHT TO LIFE OF HUMAN RIGHTS DEFENDERS UNDER REGIONAL MECHANISMS

28.11 Regional standards and mechanisms also seek explicitly to protect human rights defenders even though the protection afforded by the right to life is similarly general in nature. According to the Council of Europe: 'The existence of mechanisms supporting human rights defenders at international, regional and local level continues to be instrumental in assisting defenders at risk or those who face difficulties in their work, particularly in contexts that tend towards authoritarianism and where the rule of law is not being respected.'[22]

The Protection of Human Rights Defenders in the Americas

28.12 In the Americas, the Executive Secretariat of the Inter-American Commission on Human Rights decided to establish a Unit for Human Rights Defenders in December 2001. A decade later, during its 141st session held in March 2011, the Commission decided to create an Office of the Rapporteur on the Situation of Human Rights Defenders. It did so 'in the interest of giving greater visibility to the important role human rights defenders and justice operators have in building a democratic society in which the rule of law is in full effect'.[23] As a result, the Unit for Human Rights Defenders was turned into the Office of the Rapporteur.[24]

28.13 The Inter-American Commission published a detailed thematic report on the situation of human rights defenders in the region in 2006, observing that human rights defenders were 'frequent victims of violations of the right to life'.[25] The Commission noted that the special impact of attacks on the right to life of human rights defenders lies in their effect beyond the direct victims, having a 'chilling effect that reaches all other human

---

[20] Americans for Democracy and Human Rights in Bahrain, 'HRC40 Written Statement: The Targeting of Human Rights Defenders in the GCC'.
[21] Amnesty International UK, 'Saudi Arabia: "Relief" at Withdrawal of Death Penalty against Female Activist', press release, 1 February 2019, at http://bit.ly/30LJwMC.
[22] 'Human Rights Defenders in the Council of Europe Area: Current Challenges and Possible Solutions. Round-Table with human rights defenders organised by the Office of the Council of Europe Commissioner for Human Rights, Helsinki, 13–14 December 2018', Report, Doc. CommDH(2019)10, Strasbourg, 29 March 2019, para. 45.
[23] Organization of American States (OAS), 'Rapporteurship on Human Rights Defenders and Justice Operators', 2020, at http://bit.ly/323xy7j.
[24] 'Human Rights Defenders in the Council of Europe Area', report, para. 45.
[25] 'Report on the Situation of Human Rights Defenders in the Americas', 2006, para. 148.

rights defenders, directly diminishing their possibilities of exercising their right to defend human rights'.[26]

28.14 The report recalled that the 'absolute prohibition on arbitrary executions and forced disappearances' and the obligation to respect and ensure human rights 'translates, in the case of human rights defenders, among other obligations, into the need to do away with environments incompatible with or dangerous for the protection of human rights'. It is essential, the Commission declared, that States, 'pursuant to their obligations to prevent and protect the right to life, offer adequate protection to human rights defenders, bring about the conditions for eradicating violations by state agents or private persons, and investigate and sanction the violations of that right'.[27]

28.15 A second thematic report was published by the Inter-American Commission in 2011.[28] Therein, the 'close relationship' between the right to life and the exercise of freedom of association was emphasised. This relationship exists on the basis that 'acts against the life of a defender may in turn involve a violation to freedom of association', that is, through a victim's activities to defend and promote human rights.[29] The report cited the Inter-American Court's dicta in *Kawas-Fernández v. Honduras*, in which the Court referred to the duty

> to provide the necessary means for human rights defenders to conduct their activities freely; to protect them when they are subject to threats in order to ward off any attempt on their life or safety; to refrain from placing restrictions that would hinder the performance of their work, and to conduct serious and effective investigations of any violations against them, thus preventing impunity.[30]

28.16 In 2017, the Commission published a further report entitled 'Towards Effective Integral Protection Policies for Human Rights Defenders'.[31] The report cited data provided by civil society organisations, according to which, in 2016, as many as three of every four recorded murders of human rights defenders worldwide occurred in the Americas.[32] Information received by the Commission 'indicates that the killings, assaults, forced disappearances, threats, illegal searches, stigmatizing discourses by high-level authorities in government, criminalization, as well as other forms of financial or administrative restrictions of the work of human rights defenders have

---

[26] Ibid., para. 43, citing Inter-American Court of Hyman Rights, *Huilca Tecse v. Peru*, Judgment (Merits, Reparations and Costs), 3 March 2005, para. 78.

[27] 'Report on the Situation of Human Rights Defenders in the Americas', 2006, para. 45.

[28] Inter-American Commission on Human Rights, 'Second Report on the Situation of Human Rights Defenders in the Americas', OAS doc. OEA/Ser.L/V/II., Doc. 66, 31 December 2011, at http://bit.ly/30Ro6xo.

[29] Ibid., para. 26.

[30] Inter-American Court of Hyman Rights, *Kawas-Fernández v. Honduras*, Judgment (Merits, Reparations and Costs), 3 April 2009, para. 145.

[31] Inter-American Commission on Human Rights, 'Towards Effective Integral Protection Policies for Human Rights Defenders', OAS doc. OEA/Ser.L/V/II., Doc. 207, 29 December 2017, at http://bit.ly/326ETmt.

[32] UN Human Rights Office, 'Inter-American Commission Launch Joint Action Plan on Protection of Human Rights Defenders in the Americas', press release, 25 October 2017, at http://bit.ly/2HZPBEo. See also, e.g., Frontline Defenders, *Annual Report 2016: Stop the Killing of Human Rights Defenders*, 2016, p. 12.

continued'.[33] The Commission observed that only five States in the region – Brazil, Colombia, Guatemala, Honduras, and Mexico – had adopted national protection mechanisms and that, in general, very few public policies had been set in place for the prevention of violence against human rights defenders.[34]

28.17 The Inter-American Commission emphasised that although physical security measures are 'an urgent and necessary response for the immediate and effective protection or human rights defenders', such measures alone do not suffice to properly and effectively guarantee their safety. What is needed is an integral approach in order to 'progressively address the deeper structural problems that accentuate the risks faced by human rights defenders'.[35]

28.18 On 25 October 2017, the Office of the UN High Commissioner for Human Rights (OHCHR) and the Inter-American Commission launched a 'Joint Action Mechanism to contribute to the protection of Human Rights Defenders in the Americas'.[36] Within that framework, the OHCHR and the Inter-American Commission agreed to jointly publish a report on the situation of human rights defenders in the Americas.[37] Due to be made public in late 2019, as of this writing (in 2021), the report has not yet been published.

The Protection of Human Rights Defenders in Europe

28.19 In a roundtable on the issue in Helsinki in December 2018, it was noted that human rights defenders in the Russian Federation 'operated in a hostile environment characterised by instances of physical violence in addition to persistent attacks in public discourse, smear campaigns and open threats against their work'.[38] The situation is said to be 'particularly acute in the North Caucasus, where human rights defenders addressing impunity for serious human rights violations are exposed to serious risks'.[39]

28.20 In Ukraine, human rights defenders, such as anti-corruption activists, journalists, and activists working on the protection of LGBTI rights, have regularly reported physical attacks, intimidation, harassment, or threats.[40] The 'real and dangerous threats' faced to the lives of journalists were said to be 'an alarming phenomenon in many European countries'. Attention was drawn in particular to the killings of investigative journalists

---

[33] Inter-American Commission on Human Rights, 'Towards Effective Integral Protection Policies for Human Rights Defenders', para. 3.
[34] Ibid., para. 6.
[35] Ibid.
[36] On 19 November 2014, the Inter-American Commission and the OHCHR signed a joint declaration to define a general framework to enhance their cooperation.
[37] Joint Report by the Office of the UN High Commissioner for Human Rights and the InterAmerican Commission on Human Rights: 'The Situation of Human Rights Defenders in the Americas', concept note, at http://bit.ly/35UrzTw.
[38] 'Human Rights Defenders in the Council of Europe Area', report, para. 11.
[39] Ibid.
[40] Ibid.

Daphne Caruana Galizia in Malta as well as Ján Kuciak and his fiancé Martina Kušnírová in the Slovak Republic.[41]

28.21 Article 34 of the European Convention on Human Rights allows the European Court of Human Rights to receive applications from NGOs as well as from individuals.[42] The importance of protecting communications from organisations of human rights defenders[43] against unlawful State surveillance has been stressed in a number of cases. For instance, in its 2009 judgment in *Iordachi*, the Court considered that Moldovan law did not provide adequate protection against abuse of power by the State in the field of interception of telephone communications. The interference with the applicants' rights – members of 'Lawyers for Human Rights', a Chișinău-based NGO specialised in the representation of applicants before the Court – was not 'in accordance with the law' and thus breached Article 8 of the Convention on the right to private life.[44] The risk of course is not merely run by those whose communications are being intercepted but also the names of clients or possible applicants may be revealed and these individuals also targeted.

28.22 Within the European Union, the European Instrument for Democracy and Human Rights (EIDHR) funds ProtectDefenders.eu,[45] the EU Human Rights Defenders Mechanism established to provide assistance to defenders at high risk worldwide. ProtectDefenders.eu is a consortium of twelve NGOs active in the field of human rights, offering emergency support and material assistance to human rights defenders in danger, including legal assistance, medical care, and personal security, as well as a programme of temporary relocation for defenders and their families at risk.[46]

The Protection of Human Rights Defenders in Africa

28.23 In Africa, the position of Special Rapporteur on Human Rights Defenders was established by the African Commission on Human and Peoples' Rights under Resolution 69, adopted at the Commission's 35th Ordinary Session held in Banjul, on 21 May to 4 June 2004.[47] In 2018, a Compendium on the legal protection of human rights defenders in Africa was published by the Special Rapporteur on Human Rights Defenders, Commissioner Rémy Ngoy Lumbu, with the assistance of the Centre for Human Rights at the University of Pretoria.[48]

---

[41] Ibid., para. 12.
[42] Art. 34, Convention for the Protection of Human Rights and Fundamental Freedoms; adopted at Rome by the Council of Europe, 4 November 1950; entered into force 3 September 1953.
[43] See, e.g., European Court of Human Rights, *Association for European Integration and Human Rights and Ekimdzhiev v. Bulgaria*, Judgment (Fifth Section), 28 June 2007 (as rendered final on 30 January 2008).
[44] European Court of Human Rights, *Iordachi and others v. Moldova*, Judgment (Fourth Section), 10 February 2009 (as rendered final on 14 September 2009), para. 53.
[45] See http://bit.ly/327bGIi.
[46] 'Human Rights Defenders in the Council of Europe Area', report, para. 49.
[47] See http://bit.ly/3emkHSK.
[48] 'Compendium on the Legal Protection of Human Rights Defenders in Africa', 2018, at http://bit.ly/3jPQ3lJ.

28.24 A year earlier, the Cotonou Declaration on strengthening and expanding the protection of all Human Rights Defenders in Africa was adopted at the second International Symposium on Human Rights Defenders in Africa, held in Benin 27 March–1 April 2017. The Cotonou Declaration observes that reprisals against human rights defenders who communicate or cooperate with sub-regional, regional, and universal human rights mechanisms have been documented in various African States. These reprisals include murders, physical attacks, kidnappings, death threats, and judicial harassment against not only the defenders themselves but also their families. Other forms of police harassment or intimidation are often employed against them.[49] These measures, the Declaration stipulates, 'which aim at silencing human rights defenders and at preventing them from expressing themselves[,] are human rights violations that must be addressed'.[50]

The Protection of Human Rights Defenders in Asia and the Arab World

28.25 Article 43 of the Arab Charter on Human Rights[51] stipulates: 'Nothing in the present Charter shall be interpreted as impairing the rights and freedoms protected by the State Parties' own laws.' This has particular ramifications for human rights defenders. Thus Mohamed Mattar argues that the rule of proportionality must be observed by Arab national laws 'so that any limitations or restrictions on individuals' rights and freedoms are narrowly designed, justifiable, reasonable and only imposed to serve the public interest'.[52] Mattar refers to the 2011 report of the UN Special Rapporteur on the situation of human rights defenders (then Margaret Sekaggya), which stated that for any restriction on the right to freedom of association to be valid, it must meet three criteria: it must be provided by law, it must be necessary in a democratic society, and such limitations may only be imposed in the interest of national security or public safety or public order.[53]

28.26 There are threats to the lives of human rights defenders across the Arab world. In October 2020, Mary Lawlor and Agnès Callamard, along with several other UN experts, called on Iraq to 'immediately investigate the killing and attempted killing of two women human rights defenders and make it safe for everyone who stand up for human rights in the country'.[54] 'Clearly the Iraqi government has little regard for the lives of human rights defenders', the UN experts said. 'Both of these attacks were entirely preventable. Both women had received threats in the past and the State had done nothing to keep them safe.'

---

[49] Ibid., para. 4.
[50] Ibid.
[51] Arab Charter on Human Rights; adopted at Tunis 22 May 2004; entered into force 15 March 2008.
[52] M. Y. Mattar, 'Article 43 of the Arab Charter on Human Rights: Reconciling National, Regional, and International Standards', Harvard Human Rights Journal, vol. 26, no.5 (2013), pp. 91–147, at 116.
[53] Ibid., note 140, citing UN Special Rapporteur on the Situation of Human Rights Defenders, 'Commentary to the Declaration on the Right and Responsibility of Individuals, Groups and Organs of Society to Promote and Protect Universally Recognized Human Rights and Fundamental Freedoms', 2011, pp. 43–4.
[54] OHCHR, 'UN Experts Call on Iraq to Investigate Attacks on Women Human Rights Defenders', press release, Geneva, 2 October 2020, at http://bit.ly/2TQmy8U.

Although all human rights defenders in Iraq face serious risks, the experts said women face multi-layered threats.[55]

28.27 Elsewhere in Asia, the challenges faced by defenders are said to vary, 'with extreme cases being seen in the Philippines – the deadliest country in Asia for defenders, where they are targeted and in some cases killed'.[56] A 2019 report by the International Service for Human Rights described defenders engaged in land rights and environmental rights in the Philippines as being particularly vulnerable to killings and attacks.[57]

---

[55] Ibid.
[56] International Service for Human Rights, 'Asia: ISHR Launches New Report on the Legislative Protection of Human Rights Defenders in Seven Countries', 13 April 2019, at http://bit.ly/385mxpO.
[57] International Service for Human Rights, 'Fighting to Exist: Legislative Protection for Human Rights Defenders in Asia: Legislative Frameworks on the Rights to Freedom of Association, Assembly and Expression in the Seven Jurisdictions in Asia', June 2019, at http://bit.ly/3eiZCbM, p. 15.

29

International Migrants

INTRODUCTION

29.01 The World Health Organization (WHO) provided the following description of the global situation in May 2019: 'More people are on the move now than ever before. There are an estimated 1 billion migrants in the world today of whom 258 million are international migrants.'[1] An international migrant is ordinarily defined as a person who travels to another State, ostensibly in search of a better life, especially through the medium of work opportunities. The Global Compact for Migration follows the practice of excluding refugees from the notion of migrants, noting for instance that 'migrants and refugees are distinct groups governed by separate legal frameworks'.[2]

29.02 A migrant worker is defined by the 1990 Convention on the Protection of the Rights of All Migrant Workers and Members of Their Families (hereinafter, the Migrant Workers Convention) as 'a person who is to be engaged, is engaged or has been engaged in a remunerated activity in a State of which he or she is not a national'.[3] In its *World Migration Report 2020*, published in November 2019, the International Organization for Migration (IOM) estimated the number of international migrants at almost 272 million globally, with nearly two-thirds being labour migrants.[4] India had the largest number of migrants living abroad (17.5 million), followed by Mexico and China (11.8 million and 10.7 million, respectively). The top destination country remained the United States (50.7 million international migrants).[5]

29.03 While migration is a sensitive issue in many countries, as the Special Representative of the Secretary-General of the United Nations on Migration observed in 2017: 'Without migration, societies worldwide would never have achieved their current level of

---

[1] WHO, 'Refugee and Migrant Health: Draft Global Action Plan "Promoting the Health of Refugees and Migrants" (2019–2023)', Geneva, 2019, at http://bit.ly/35cPpdU.

[2] Global Compact for Safe, Orderly and Regular Migration, annexed to UN General Assembly Resolution 73/195, adopted on 19 December 2018 by 152 votes to 5 (Czechia, Hungary, Israel, Poland, and the United States) with 12 abstentions, para. 4. Other sources include asylum seekers and refugees in the total of migrants.

[3] Art. 2(1), International Convention on the Protection of the Rights of All Migrant Workers and Members of Their Families; adopted at New York 18 December 1990; entered into force 1 July 2003. As of 1 May 2021, fifty-six States were party to the Convention and a further twelve were signatories.

[4] IOM, *World Migration Report 2020*, Geneva, November 2019, at http://bit.ly/3pasU14, p. 2.

[5] Ibid., p. 3.

development.'[6] Yet migrants often face heightened threats to their lives and well-being resulting from their legal status of alien in the countries to which they migrate, as well as a consequence of hostility from the local population.[7] This has implications for the duty to protect the right to life, as well as the duty to respect the right to life.

29.04 The Migrant Workers Convention has been ratified by a relatively small number of States – fifty-five as of writing, the lowest of any of the instruments viewed by the Office of the United Nations High Commissioner for Human Rights (OHCHR) as 'core' human rights treaties – reflecting legal, financial, administrative, and political obstacles to adherence among States of reception.[8]

29.05 Legal obstacles concern the 'misconception' that the Migrant Workers Convention 'would limit the sovereign rights of states to decide upon who can enter their territory and for how long they can remain; and, secondly, the equally ubiquitous fear that the Convention would provide for a robust right of family reunification to all migrant workers present in a regular situation in the territory of a state'.[9] In a 2007 monograph, MacDonald and Cholewinski sought to dispel these fears as groundless on the basis that Article 79 of the Migrant Workers Convention provides: 'Nothing in the present Convention shall affect the right of each State Party to establish the criteria governing admission of migrant workers and members of their families.' Under Article 44, a State Party's responsibility in terms of family reunification is limited to taking such measures 'as they deem appropriate to facilitate the reunification of migrant workers with their spouses ... as well with their minor dependent unmarried children'. In language 'as heavily qualified as this', they argue, which leaves 'such a wide discretion' to States, it is 'difficult to see any obligation of any sort, let alone one that could present a serious obstacle to ratification'.[10] Yet, thirteen years on, the level of ratification has barely advanced.

29.06 Financial/administrative obstacles concern the bureaucratic costs and burdens of processing large numbers of incoming migrants. But of greater concern to some States from a political perspective was (and is) the protection afforded by the Convention to unauthorised migrant workers and undocumented family members, even though it was limited in extent. As Beth Lyon opined: 'There seems to be little doubt that by offering protection to unauthorized workers, the framers of the treaty risked what has been to date the result: most countries of migrant employment have shunned the treaty. However, the

---

[6] 'Report of the Special Representative of the Secretary-General on Migration', UN doc. A/71/728, 3 February 2017, at http://bit.ly/3lkc4La, para. 1.

[7] A 2016 report published by the International Labour Organization (ILO), for instance, noted 'several bouts of xenophobic attacks in South Africa against foreign workers, the latest in April/March 2015. One violent outbreak in May 2008 led to the deaths of at least 62 people and the displacement of 100,000 around the country.' M. Buckley, A. Zendel, J. Biggar, L. Frederiksen, and J. Wells, *Migrant Work and Employment in the Construction Sector*, ILO, Geneva, 2016, p. 31.

[8] See generally on this issue E. MacDonald and R. Cholewinski, *The Migrant Workers Convention in Europe: Obstacles to the Ratification of the International Convention on the Protection of the Rights of All Migrant Workers and Members of Their Families: EU/EEA Perspectives*, UNESCO, Paris, 2007.

[9] Ibid., p. 12.

[10] Ibid.

inclusion has been supported by subsequent legal developments and continues to be justified by the humanitarian situation of these workers.'[11]

29.07 Indeed, in 2013 the European Commission published an analysis of the reasons submitted by member States of the European Union for their decision not to ratify the Migrant Workers Convention, which demonstrated that the decision was 'largely driven by political choice rather than by an objective legal scrutiny'.[12] That said, the analysis 'clearly shows that most of the rights enshrined in the ICRMW [Migrant Workers Convention] are already recognised in EU legislation or in other international instruments ratified by EU Member States. The ICRMW clearly distinguishes between the rights of regular and irregular migrants in great detail and is the only Human Rights Convention that does so."[13]

29.08 The remainder of this chapter focuses on the right to life of migrant workers, looking at the global standards and then the regional and national challenges to implementation of the right. The low level of adherence to the Migrant Workers Convention does not impact in any way the content of the right to life as it pertains to migrant workers and their families. Inevitably, however, it does affect the vigour with which its application and implementation is pursued in many countries.

GLOBAL STANDARDS ON THE RIGHT TO LIFE OF MIGRANTS

29.09 The Migrant Workers Convention stipulates simply – and briefly – in its Article 9 that 'the right to life of migrant workers and members of their families shall be protected by law'.[14] While the absence of a reference to the 'inherent' nature of the right to life in Article 9 is striking,[15] it does not affect the broader protection afforded by international law to the right to life of migrant workers, in particular under the 1966 International Covenant on Civil and Political Rights[16] (ICCPR), the 1989 Convention on the Rights of the Child[17] (in

---

[11] B. Lyon, 'The Unsigned United Nations Migrant Worker Rights Convention: An Overlooked Opportunity to Change the "Brown Collar" Migration Paradigm', *New York University Journal of International Law and Politics*, vol. 42 (2010), pp. 389–500, at http://bit.ly/36fZjL3, at 486.

[12] Directorate-General for External Policies of the Union, *Current Challenges in the Implementation of the UN International Convention on the Protection of the Rights of All Migrant Workers and Members of Their Families*, Study, Brussels, July 2013, at http://bit.ly/36lvl8m.

[13] Ibid. See also S. D. Western, S. P. Lockhart, and J. Money, 'Does Anyone Care about Migrant Rights? An Analysis of Why Countries Enter the Convention on the Rights of Migrant Workers and Their Families', *International Journal of Human Rights*, vol. 23, no. 8 (2019), pp. 1276–99.

[14] In addition, it is provided that 'no migrant worker or member of his or her family shall be subjected to torture or to cruel, inhuman or degrading treatment or punishment'. Art. 10, Migrant Worker Convention.

[15] Compare this brief provision with Article 6 of the 1966 International Covenant on Civil and Political Rights; Article 6 of the 1989 Convention on the Rights of the Child; and Article 10 of the 2006 Convention on the Rights of Persons with Disabilities.

[16] Art. 6, International Covenant on Civil and Political Rights; adopted at New York 16 December 1966; entered into force 23 March 1976. As of 1 May 2021, 173 States were party to the ICCPR and a further 6 States were signatories.

[17] Art. 6, Convention on the Rights of the Child; adopted at New York 20 November 1989; entered into force 2 September 1990. As of 1 May 2021, 196 States were party to the Convention and the United States was a signatory.

International Migrants

the case of migrant children), the 2006 Convention on the Rights of Persons with Disabilities[18] (in the case of migrants with disabilities), and of course customary international law.

29.10 In addition, the Migrant Workers Convention grants migrant workers and members of their families the right to receive any medical care that is urgently required for the preservation of their life or avoidance of irreparable harm to their health on the basis of equality of treatment with nationals of the State concerned.[19] Emergency medical care must not be refused by reason of any irregularity with regard to their stay or employment.[20]

29.11 The ICCPR does not specifically refer to migrants.[21] That said, it is stipulated that each State Party to the Covenant 'undertakes to respect and to ensure to all individuals within its territory and subject to its jurisdiction the rights recognized in the ... Covenant, without distinction of any kind'.[22] Accordingly, each migrant in the territory of a State Party to the ICCPR – and thus under its jurisdiction – benefits from the full protection of the right to life afforded by Article 6. This right, which pertains equally to unauthorised as it does authorised migrant workers and to undocumented as well as documented migrants, is non-derogable.[23] That every human being has the right to life – without distinction of any kind – has long reflected customary international law.[24] Furthermore, the jus cogens prohibition of arbitrary deprivation of life codified in Article 6(1) of the Covenant protects all migrants.

29.12 As the Human Rights Committee reiterated in its General Comment 36, the duty to protect the right to life obligates States Parties to the ICCPR to take special measures of protection for those whose lives are at particular risk. This is so, whether they are known to be at risk because of specific threats or as a consequence of pre-existing patterns of violence.[25] Surprisingly, however, the Committee does not cite migrants in general as an obvious category at risk, mentioning only unaccompanied migrant children as potentially falling within the duty to take special measures of protection.[26]

---

[18] Art. 10, Convention on the Rights of Persons with Disabilities; adopted at New York 13 December 2006; entered into force 3 May 2008. As of 1 May 2021, 181 States were party to the CRPD and a further 9 States were signatories. The European Union is also a party to the Convention.

[19] Art. 28, Migrant Workers Convention.

[20] Ibid.; and see OHCHR, 'The International Convention on Migrant Workers and Its Committee', Fact Sheet No. 24 (Rev. 1), New York and Geneva, 2005, at http://bit.ly/3eI6dws, p. 6.

[21] As the Global Compact on Migration recalls, 'Refugees and migrants are entitled to the same universal human rights and fundamental freedoms, which must be respected, protected and fulfilled at all times.' Global Compact on Migration, para. 4.

[22] Art. 2(1), ICCPR.

[23] Art. 4(2), ICCPR.

[24] See Chapter 1 of this work.

[25] Human Rights Committee, 'General comment No. 36. Article 6: right to life', UN doc. CCPR/C/GC/36, 3 September 2019 (hereinafter, Human Rights Committee, General Comment 36 on the right to life), para. 23.

[26] Ibid.

THREATS TO THE LIFE OF MIGRANTS AND INTERNATIONAL ACTION

29.13 Unaccompanied migrant children may indeed 'face further vulnerabilities and can be more exposed to risks, such as gender-based, sexual and other forms of violence and trafficking for sexual or labour exploitation'.[27] But, as the Committee on the Rights of the Child and the Committee on Migrant Workers has also affirmed, at any point during the migratory process, a migrant child's right to life and survival may be at stake owing to, among others, 'violence as a result of organized crime, violence in camps, push-back or interception operations, excessive use of force of border authorities, refusal of vessels to rescue them, or extreme conditions of travel and limited access to basic services'.[28] These same risks pertain to all migrants.

29.14 Under the 2018 Global Compact on Migration, UN member States acknowledge their 'shared responsibilities to one another' and 'an overarching obligation to respect, protect and fulfil the human rights of all migrants, regardless of their migration status'.[29] This followed a call a year earlier by the Special Representative of the Secretary-General on Migration for a 'strong international consensus' to be reached 'on what kind of protections States owe to migrants when their Governments are unable or unwilling to protect them from crises and life-threatening circumstances'.[30]

29.15 One of the areas of focus of the Global Compact is saving the lives of migrants during their journey.[31] Thus Objective 8 of the Global Compact is to 'save lives and establish coordinated international efforts on missing migrants'. In pursuing this objective, UN member States 'commit to cooperate internationally to save lives and prevent migrant deaths and injuries through individual or joint search and rescue operations, standardized collection and exchange of relevant information, assuming collective responsibility to preserve the lives of all migrants, in accordance with international law'.[32] To realise this commitment, States pledged to develop 'procedures and agreements on search and rescue of migrants, with the primary objective of protecting migrants' right to life'.[33]

29.16 Deaths of migrants fleeing the northern coast of Africa across the Mediterranean to Europe increased significantly in 2016.[34] Moreover, a joint report by the Office of the UN

---

[27] Committee on the Rights of the Child and the Committee on the Protection of the Rights of All Migrant Workers and Members of Their Families, Joint General Comment No. 3 (2017) of the Committee on the Protection of the Rights of All Migrant Workers and Members of Their Families and No. 22 (2017) of the Committee on the Rights of the Child on the general principles regarding the human rights of children in the context of international migration, UN doc. CMW/C/GC/3-CRC/C/GC/22, 16 November 2017, para. 40.

[28] Ibid.

[29] Global Compact on Migration, para. 11.

[30] 'Report of the Special Representative of the Secretary-General on Migration', UN doc. A/71/728, para. 23.

[31] For updated data on deaths per month worldwide, see the Missing Migrants Project, which tracks incidents involving migrants, including refugees and asylum-seekers, who have died or gone missing in the process of migration towards an international destination. See http://bit.ly/35cRhDu.

[32] Global Compact on Migration, para. 24.

[33] Ibid., para. 24(a).

[34] See, e.g., United Nations Support Mission in Libya (UNSMIL) and OHCHR, *Desperate and Dangerous: Report on the Human Rights Situation of Migrants and Refugees in Libya*, 20 December 2018, at http://bit.ly/38rXptA.

High Commissioner for Refugees (UNHCR) and the Mixed Migration Centre (MMC) at the Danish Refugee Council, issued in July 2020, suggested that at least 1,750 people died on journeys between West and East Africa and Africa's Mediterranean coast in 2018 and 2019.[35] This equated to more than seventy deaths per month, making it one of the deadliest routes for refugees and migrants in the world.[36] Crossings by migrants between France and the United Kingdom have been steadily increasing since 2013, with a report being published in November 2020 documenting the deaths of almost three hundred migrants since 1999, including thirty-six children, while crossing the Channel.[37]

29.17 Conditions of work for migrant workers if they arrive at their intended destination can also be exceptionally hazardous. Thus, under the Global Compact on Migration, member States committed 'to protect all migrant workers against all forms of exploitation and abuse in order to guarantee decent work and maximize the socioeconomic contributions of migrants in both their countries of origin and destination'.[38] The Special Representative of the Secretary-General on Migration stressed the importance of migrants being able to 'live and work under acceptable conditions'.[39] For, he stated, 'if the rights and dignity of migrant workers are not respected, not only they but also local workers suffer, sometimes finding themselves excluded from whole sectors of employment where minimum standards of pay and conditions of work are not applied'.[40]

29.18 Similarly, in his report to the UN General Assembly in 2016, the UN Special Rapporteur on the human rights of migrants noted that scant attention has been paid to 'the impact of labour market dynamics in destination countries as pull factors for irregular migration'.[41] He called for UN member States to be 'weaned [off] their reliance on cheap labour in specific economic sectors and should ensure labour rights are upheld for all, including documented and undocumented migrants, through the full implementation of sanctions against employers and rigorous labour inspection'. Human rights for all workers, 'whatever their status', will, he declared, lead to 'less labour exploitation, less irregular migration, less migrant smuggling and less loss of life'.[42]

29.19 Beyond the highly significant risk of exploitation, where the safety and security of workplace conditions are not ensured by employers and the authorities, predictably migrants 'at the lower end of the construction wage ladder tend to be at a disproportionately higher

---

[35] UNHCR and MMC, 'On This Journey, No One Cares If You Live or Die': Abuse, Protection, and Justice along Routes between East and West Africa and Africa's Mediterranean Coast, July 2020, at http://bit.ly/3lfTbbV.
[36] UNHCR, 'Thousands of Refugees and Migrants Suffer Extreme Rights Abuses on Journeys to Africa's Mediterranean Coast, New UNHCR/MMC Report Shows', 29 July 2020, at http://bit.ly/2U8Vthh.
[37] See D. Taylor, 'Almost 300 Asylum Seekers Have Died Trying to Cross the Channel since 1999. First Research to Collate Figures Documents the People Who Have Lost their Lives, with Drownings during Sea Crossings on the Rise', The Guardian, 29 October 2020, at http://bit.ly/3k7kunC. The research was conducted by the Institute of Race Relations. See https://irr.org.uk/.
[38] Global Compact on Migration, para. 22.
[39] Report of the Special Representative of the Secretary-General on Migration, UN doc. A/71/728, para. 25.
[40] Ibid.
[41] Report of the Special Rapporteur on the human rights of migrants, UN doc. A/71/285, 4 August 2016, para. 62.
[42] Ibid.

risk of workplace injuries and fatalities'.[43] Notably, this includes the building of major stadia for the world's most lavish sporting events, such as the Federation Internationale de Football Association (FIFA) World Cup. In 2019, nine construction workers were killed in Qatar, with a total of at least thirty-four deaths recorded over six years. Deaths occur both on- and off-site.[44] Hundreds of others die each year on related or other construction projects in Qatar, many as a result of heat stress. In the summer of 2019, hundreds of thousands of migrant workers worked in temperatures of up to 45°C for up to 10 hours a day.[45]

29.20 In January 2020, Amnesty International sharply criticised the fact that migrants building a state-of-the-art stadium for the 2022 football World Cup in Qatar 'are abused and exploited – while FIFA makes huge profits'. Furthermore, if workers complain about their conditions or seek help, they are often intimidated and threatened by their employers.[46] In accordance with Qatar's sponsorship ('*kafala*'), employers seize migrants' passports, preventing them from leaving the country or even from changing jobs. The *kafala* system was ostensibly brought to an end by new legislative provisions adopted in September 2020.[47]

29.21 The Special Rapporteur on the human rights of migrants is an independent expert appointed by the UN Human Rights Council. The mandate was created in 1999 by the erstwhile Commission on Human Rights under Resolution 1999/44. The mandate of the Special Rapporteur covers every State, irrespective of whether a given State has adhered to the Migrant Workers Convention.[48] In a mission in September–October 2019 to Bosnia and Herzegovina, a State Party to the Convention, the Special Rapporteur was concerned to learn that since June of that year, local authorities in Bihać had been relocating those migrants who were staying outside reception centres to a camp at Vucjak, which was located very close to minefields. There was also a high fire and explosion risk at the site, given its former use for landfill.[49]

29.22 The Special Rapporteur found the location of the site to be 'absolutely inappropriate and inadequate for accommodating human beings'.[50] Some eight hundred men and around twenty children, coming mainly from Afghanistan, Iran, and Pakistan, were housed there. Many had been 'escorted' to the site by the local police. There was no running water. Drinking water was provided by the city, with two meals a day delivered by the International Committee of the Red Cross (ICRC) in Bihać. 'The condition of the site

---

[43] Buckley et al., *Migrant Work and Employment in the Construction Sector*, p. x.
[44] P. Pattisson, 'Qatar World Cup: Report Reveals 34 Stadium Worker Deaths in Six Years', *The Guardian*, 16 March 2020, at http://bit.ly/3n6CsZd.
[45] A. Kelly, N. McIntyre, and P. Pattisson, 'Revealed: Hundreds of Migrant Workers Dying of Heat Stress in Qatar Each Year', *The Guardian*, 2 October 2019, at http://bit.ly/3paELMI.
[46] Amnesty International UK, 'Qatar World Cup: The Ugly Side of the Beautiful Game', 27 January 2020, at http://bit.ly/3p7ReRv.
[47] P. Pattisson, 'New Employment Law Effectively Ends Qatar's Exploitative Kafala System', *The Guardian*, 1 September 2020, at http://bit.ly/3p9Dzct.
[48] OHCHR, 'Special Rapporteur on the Human Rights of Migrants', at http://bit.ly/36j7fv5.
[49] Visit to Bosnia and Herzegovina, Report of the Special Rapporteur on the human rights of migrants, UN doc. A/HRC/44/42/Add.2, 12 May 2020, para. 41.
[50] Ibid., para. 43.

was inhuman', he stated. 'There was no electricity, very few sanitation facilities, no warm water for showering and no medical care available. The tents used at the camp were thin and not warm enough for the cold weather in winter.'[51]

29.23 For fear of any loss of life in the forthcoming winter, at the end of his visit the Special Rapporteur urged the authorities to stop forcibly escorting migrants to the Vucjak site and to urgently identify an alternative location, with priority given to children. In his report submitted to the Human Rights Council in May 2020, he was pleased to learn that the site had indeed been dismantled in December 2019 and that, with assistance from IOM, the migrants located at the camp had been transferred to Blažuj, a newly identified reception centre near Sarajevo.[52]

29.24 More recently, migrants have been particularly badly affected by the COVID-19 pandemic. In April 2020, the OHCHR issued guidance on the issue in which it stated: 'Everyone, including all migrants regardless of their migration status, must be taken into account as an integral part of any effective public health and recovery response to COVID-19. Including migrants in the response to this crisis is the only effective way to protect not only migrants' rights, but also to avoid fuelling xenophobia and endangering the health of society as a whole.'[53]

29.25 A research paper by Laura Foley and Nicola Piper concluded that the global health crisis had both amplified existing gender dynamics and created new gender-biased outcomes that disproportionately impacted women migrant workers.[54] For instance, in many countries, women migrant workers comprise the majority of health workers caring for patients, with many others working as cleaners within hospitals and social care settings. These increased interactions with sick patients and greater exposure to coronavirus render them the most at-risk of contracting and spreading the virus.[55]

---

[51] Ibid., para. 42.
[52] Ibid., para. 44.
[53] OHCHR, *COVID-19 and the Human Rights of Migrants: Guidance*, Geneva, April 2020, at http://bit.ly/32rHLdO, p. 1.
[54] L. Foley and N. Piper, COVID-19 and Women Migrant Workers: Impacts and Implications, paper, IOM, Geneva, 2020, at http://bit.ly/3lbNWKq.
[55] Ibid., p. 3.

30

Internally Displaced Persons

INTRODUCTION

30.01 Internally displaced persons (IDPs) are those whose physical safety is under threat as a result of displacement within a State, typically – but not necessarily – the State of their nationality. The term is not formally defined under international law, but according to the 1998 UN Guiding Principles on Internal Displacement, IDPs are 'persons or groups of persons who have been forced or obliged to flee or to leave their homes or places of habitual residence, in particular as a result of or in order to avoid the effects of armed conflict, situations of generalized violence, violations of human rights or natural or human-made disasters, and who have not crossed an internationally recognized state border'.[1] Despite widespread perception, IDPs do not always end up in camps; as the Office for the Coordination of Humanitarian Affairs (OCHA) has observed, most IDPs are taken in by host families, while some find temporary shelter on the move or settle in urban areas. Moreover, IDPs often move several times during their displacement.[2]

30.02 Unless IDPs are foreign nationals who have already been granted refugee status, they are not protected by international refugee law but by international human rights law alone. Should IDPs be caught up in an armed conflict, however, they are also protected by international humanitarian law. This is so, whether they are detained in connection with an armed conflict or are affected by the conduct of hostilities by parties to such a conflict. At the regional level, the African Union Convention for the Protection and Assistance of Internally Displaced Persons in Africa, better known as the Kampala Convention, is the only continental treaty dedicated to the protection of IDPs.[3] It applies both in peacetime and during situations of armed conflict.

---

[1] UN Guiding Principles on Internal Displacement, UN Office for the Coordination of Humanitarian Affairs (OCHA), 1998, text available at http://bit.ly/3kpDjm2, para. 2.
[2] OCHA, 'OCHA on Message: Internal Displacement', 2010, at http://bit.ly/2wMZEXx.
[3] In the Great Lakes region of Africa, the 2007 Protocol on the Protection and Assistance to Internally Displaced Persons 'establishes a legal framework for the protection of IDPs through incorporation of the [1998 UN] Guiding Principles [on Internal Displacement] into domestic law, providing measures aimed at protecting the physical safety and material needs of the displaced, and creating obligations to prevent and address the root causes of displacement'. Walter Kälin, 'The Great Lakes Protocol on Internally Displaced Persons: Responses and Challenges', post, Brookings, 27 September 2007, at http://brook.gs/2Uu4JwN.

30.03 In 2018, the UN launched a global plan to strengthen the protection of IDPs: the Plan of Action for Advancing Prevention, Protection and Solutions for Internally Displaced People (2018–20). As the three-year plan drew to a close, however, it was unclear what practical achievements it had engendered. While all figures should be treated with caution, at the start of 2019, there were 41.3 million IDPs worldwide, according to OCHA: the highest number on record. Of that total, 6.2 million people were displaced within Syria alone.[4] By the end of the year, however, there were said by Norwegian Refugee Council's Internal Displacement Monitoring Centre (IDMC) to be 50.8 million IDPs globally, an apparent increase of 9.5 million over the course of the year.[5]

30.04 This followed the 10.8 million new internal displacements provoked by armed conflict and violence in 2018, according to OCHA.[6] In his 2019 report to the UN Security Council on the protection of civilians, the UN Secretary-General said that forced displacement 'remained a defining feature of conflict in 2018'. It affected, among others, the Central African Republic, the Democratic Republic of Congo, Nigeria, Somalia, South Sudan, Sudan, Syria, and Yemen.[7] Many of those displaced, the Secretary-General observed, 'the majority of whom are women, face significant protection and assistance concerns while the families and communities hosting them, in urban and other areas, are under increasing stress'. Most IDPs will, he further affirms, 'remain displaced for years, without durable solutions that require national leadership and a long-term commitment to address human rights, humanitarian, development, peacebuilding and disaster-risk challenges'.[8]

30.05 IDPs are especially vulnerable to human trafficking, to forced recruitment, to sexual violence, and to falling prey to landmines or unexploded ordnance. IDPs are far more at risk from explosive ordnance than are settled communities because they do not know which areas or which routes are safe and which are not. Some of the typical needs and protection risks that arise in internal displacement include family separation, loss of documentation, freedom of movement in and out of camps, loss of property, and further exposure to the risk of secondary or onward displacement.[9]

GLOBAL STANDARDS PROTECTING THE RIGHT TO LIFE OF IDPS

30.06 The 1966 International Covenant on Civil and Political Rights[10] (ICCPR) does not specifically refer to the internally displaced. That said, it is stipulated that each State Party to the Covenant 'undertakes to respect and to ensure to all individuals within its territory and subject to its jurisdiction the rights recognized in the … Covenant, without

---

[4] 'Protection of civilians in armed conflict. Report of the Secretary-General', UN doc. S/2019/373, 7 May 2019, para. 35.
[5] IDMC, 'Internal Displacement', 2020, at http://bit.ly/3khtDKt.
[6] OCHA, *Global Humanitarian Overview 2020*, New York, 2020, at http://bit.ly/2UgtnAF, p. 13.
[7] 'Protection of civilians in armed conflict. Report of the Secretary-General', UN doc. S/2019/373, para. 35.
[8] Ibid., para. 36.
[9] IDMC, 'Internal Displacement', 2020.
[10] International Covenant on Civil and Political Rights; adopted at New York 16 December 1966; entered into force 23 March 1976.

distinction of any kind'.[11] Accordingly, each IDP in the territory of a State Party to the ICCPR – and thus under its jurisdiction – benefits from the full protection of the right to life afforded by Article 6 whatever their nationality. This right is non-derogable.[12] That every human being has the right to life – without distinction of any kind – has long reflected customary international law.[13] Further, the jus cogens prohibition of arbitrary deprivation of life codified in Article 6(1) of the Covenant protects all IDPs.

30.07 The Human Rights Committee has stated that the duty to protect the right to life requires States Parties to the ICCPR to take special measures of protection towards those in vulnerable situations whose lives are at particular risk because of specific threats or pre-existing patterns of violence. This, the Committee observes, may include displaced persons.[14] A heightened duty to protect the right to life also applies to individuals quartered in 'liberty-restricting State-run facilities', such as certain IDP camps.[15] In its 2006 Concluding Observations on the situation in Kosovo cited in this regard, the Committee had noted its concern: 'Roma, Ashkali and Egyptian internally displaced persons (IDPs) living in camps in lead-polluted areas in north Mitrovica since 1999 have been relocated only recently, although the negative effects on the health of the communities concerned were known since mid-2004.'[16]

30.08 The UN Guiding Principles on Internal Displacement[17] were developed in the 1990s under the aegis of Francis Deng, the then Representative of the UN Secretary-General on internally displaced persons. The content was elaborated by a team of international legal scholars chaired by Walter Kälin, Francis Deng's successor in post. The Guiding Principles were presented to the erstwhile Commission on Human Rights in 1998. Although at their heart soft law, many of the principles espoused therein reflect existing rules of international human rights and humanitarian law. Thus, for instance, they stipulate that, in particular, IDPs must be protected against direct or indiscriminate attacks or other acts of violence, starvation as a method of combat, use as human shields during hostilities, attacks against their camps or settlements, and the use of anti-personnel mines.[18] All of these provisions are binding customary norms.

PROTECTION OF IDPS UNDER INTERNATIONAL HUMANITARIAN LAW

30.09 Additional protection for the displaced is contained in instruments of international humanitarian law. In all armed conflicts, IDPs are protected as civilians.

---

[11] Art. 2(1), ICCPR.
[12] Art. 4(2), ICCPR.
[13] See Chapter 1 of this work.
[14] Human Rights Committee, General Comment No. 36: Article 6: right to life, UN doc. CCPR/C/GC/36, 3 September 2019, para. 23.
[15] Ibid., para. 25.
[16] Human Rights Committee, Concluding Observations on Kosovo (Serbia), UN doc. CCPR/C/UNK/CO/1, 14 August 2006, para. 14.
[17] UN doc. E/CN.4/1998/53/Add.2.
[18] By analogy, protection should also be provided against cluster munition remnants (in particular unexploded submunitions) and other explosive remnants of war.

This is so, unless and for such time as they participate directly in hostilities.[19] When detained or otherwise in the power of a party to the conflict, customary rules dictate their humane treatment in all circumstances and without adverse distinction. Also obligated is respect for fundamental guarantees, which include prohibitions on violence to life and person, outrages upon personal dignity, and the passing of sentences without a fair trial.[20]

30.10 IHL prohibits forced displacement of civilians both by States and by non-State armed groups that are party to an armed conflict, unless the security of the civilians involved or imperative military reasons demands it. This is a rule of customary as well as conventional law.[21] As delineated by the International Committee of the Red Cross (ICRC) in its 2005 Study of Customary IHL, the precise articulation of the rule depends on whether the armed conflict in question is international or non-international in character:

Rule 129.

    A. Parties to an international armed conflict may not deport or forcibly transfer the civilian population of an occupied territory, in whole or in part, unless the security of the civilians involved or imperative military reasons so demand.

    B. Parties to a non-international armed conflict may not order the displacement of the civilian population, in whole or in part, for reasons related to the conflict, unless the security of the civilians involved or imperative military reasons so demand.

30.11 Moreover, in each case, a serious violation of the rule attracts individual criminal responsibility under international criminal law as a war crime.[22] That said, as Erin Mooney observes, the prohibition in non-international armed conflict appears to be broader in scope than is the case in international armed conflict, wherein it is limited to situations of military occupation.[23] In addition, the deportation or forcible transfer of civilians is punishable as a crime against humanity when it is committed as part of a widespread or systematic attack directed against any civilian population, with knowledge of the attack.[24] In March 2014, Islamic State's order to all Kurdish residents to

---

[19] Art. 51(3), Protocol Additional to the Geneva Conventions of 12 August 1949, and relating to the Protection of Victims of International Armed Conflicts (Protocol I); adopted at Geneva 8 June 1977; entered into force 7 December 1978; and Art. 13(3), Protocol Additional to the Geneva Conventions of 12 August 1949, and relating to the protection of victims of non-international armed conflicts (Protocol II); adopted at Geneva 8 June 1977; entered into force 7 December 1978.

[20] International Committee of the Red Cross (ICRC), 'IHL and the Protection of Migrants Caught in Armed Conflict', Geneva, 4 June 2018, available at http://bit.ly/2wkcxYQ.

[21] ICRC Customary IHL Rule 129: 'The Act of Displacement', at http://bit.ly/2Vue9Kj.

[22] ICRC Customary IHL Rule 156: 'Definition of War Crimes', at http://bit.ly/32HjZb2; and Art. 8(2)(b)(viii), and (e)(viii), Rome Statute of the International Criminal Court; adopted at Rome 17 July 1998; entered into force 1 July 2002 (hereinafter, Rome Statute). See also Art. 8(2)(a)(vii), ICC Statute.

[23] E. Mooney, 'Displacement and the Protection of Civilians under International Refugee Law', chap. 8 in H. Willmot, R. Mamiya, S. Sheeran, and M. Weller (eds.), *Protection of Civilians*, 1st ed., Oxford University Press, Oxford, 2016, p. 188.

[24] Art. 7(1)(d), Rome Statute.

leave Tal Akhder village (Ar Raqqah) was deemed to be both a war crime and a crime against humanity by the Independent International Commission of Inquiry on Syria.[25]

30.12 In both international and non-international armed conflicts, State practice, the ICRC observes, 'establishes an exception to the prohibition of displacement in cases where the security of the civilians involved or imperative military reasons (such as clearing a combat zone) require the evacuation for as long as the conditions warranting it exist. This exception is contained in the Fourth Geneva Convention [of 1949] and [the 1977] Additional Protocol II.'[26] This was not the case with respect to displacement forced by Islamic State's actions in Syria.[27]

THE PROTECTION OF IDPS IN AFRICA: THE KAMPALA CONVENTION

30.13 The African Union Convention for the Protection and Assistance of Internally Displaced Persons in Africa (Kampala Convention) was adopted on 23 October 2009, entering into force on 6 December 2012.[28] It is the only continental treaty dedicated to the protection of IDPs. The Kampala Convention applies the definition for IDPs set out in the UN Guiding Principles on Internal Displacement.

30.14 The treaty is devised in an unusual manner insofar as it appears to impose human rights obligations directly on armed groups in addition to those on States. Strictly speaking, however, that is not the case: the State remains the duty bearer under the Convention. In contrast, the Convention does impose obligations directly on international organisations and non-governmental organisations.

30.15 Article 3 of the Convention sets out the general obligations upon its States Parties. In undertaking to 'respect and ensure respect' for the Convention, each State must

   a. Refrain from, prohibit and prevent arbitrary displacement of populations
   b. Prevent political, social, cultural and economic exclusion and marginalisation, that are likely to cause displacement of populations or persons by virtue of their social identity, religion, or political opinion
   c. Respect and ensure respect for the principles of humanity and human dignity of internally displaced persons
   d. Respect and ensure respect and protection of the human rights of internally displaced persons, including humane treatment, non-discrimination, equality, and equal protection of law

---

[25] 'Report of the independent international commission of inquiry on the Syrian Arab Republic', UN doc. A/HRC/27/60, 13 August 2014, paras. 133–5; see Mooney, 'Displacement and the Protection of Civilians under International Refugee Law', p. 191.
[26] ICRC Customary IHL Rule 129: 'The Act of Displacement'.
[27] Report of the independent international commission of inquiry on the Syrian Arab Republic, UN doc. A/HRC/27/60, para. 135.
[28] As of 1 December 2020, thirty-one of fifty-five African States had adhered to the Kampala Convention and a further thirteen were signatories.

Internally Displaced Persons

e. Respect and ensure respect for IHL regarding the protection of internally displaced persons
f. Respect and ensure respect for the humanitarian and civilian character of the protection of and assistance to IDPs, including ensuring that such persons do not engage in subversive activities
g. Ensure individual responsibility for acts of arbitrary displacement, in accordance with applicable domestic and international criminal law
h. Ensure the accountability of non-state actors concerned, including multinational companies and private military or security companies, for acts of arbitrary displacement or complicity in such acts
i. Ensure the accountability of non-state actors involved in the exploration and exploitation of economic and natural resources leading to displacement
j. Ensure assistance to IDPs by meeting their basic needs as well as allowing and facilitating rapid and unimpeded access by humanitarian organisations and personnel
k. Promote self-reliance and sustainable livelihoods among IDPs, provided that such measures shall not be used as a basis for neglecting the protection of and assistance to IDPs, without prejudice to other means of assistance.

It is further stipulated: 'All persons have a right to be protected against arbitrary displacement. The prohibited categories of arbitrary displacement include ... [d]isplacement as a result of harmful practices.'[29] In turn, harmful practices are defined under the Convention as 'all behaviour, attitudes and/or practices which negatively affect the fundamental rights of persons, such as but not limited to their right to life, health, dignity, education, mental and physical integrity and education'.[30]

30.16 Article 7 is entitled 'Protection and Assistance to Internally Displaced Persons in Situations of Armed Conflict'. It is stated in paragraph 3 that the protection and assistance to IDPs under the article is governed by international law and in particular international humanitarian law. The article continues as follows:

4. Members of armed groups shall be held criminally responsible for their acts which violate the rights of IDPs under international law and national law.
5. Members of armed groups shall be prohibited from:
   a. Carrying out arbitrary displacement;
   b. Hampering the provision of protection and assistance to IDPs under any circumstances
   c. Denying IDPs the right to live in satisfactory conditions of dignity, security, sanitation, food, water, health, and shelter; and separating members of the same family
   d. Restricting the freedom of movement of IDPs within and outside their areas of residence

---

[29] Art. IV(4)(e), Kampala Convention.
[30] Art. 1(j), Kampala Convention.

e. Recruiting children or requiring or permitting them to take part in hostilities under any circumstances
  f. Forcibly recruiting persons, kidnapping, abduction, or hostage taking, engaging in sexual slavery and trafficking in persons, especially women and children
  g. Impeding humanitarian assistance and passage of all relief consignments, equipment and personnel to IDPs
  h. Attacking or otherwise harming humanitarian personnel and resources or other materials deployed for the assistance or benefit of IDPs and shall not destroy, confiscate or divert such materials; and
  i. Violating the civilian and humanitarian character of the places where IDPs are sheltered and shall not infiltrate such places.

30.17 In fact, the formulations 'shall be held criminally responsible for their acts' and 'shall be prohibited from' indicate that the obligations under the Kampala Convention remain on the States Parties to prohibit the acts of armed groups and not the armed groups themselves. That said, the text of Article 7 of the Kampala Convention certainly moves towards imposing human rights obligations directly on such groups.

30.18 Of direct normative effect with respect to international organisations and non-governmental organisations is Article VI of the Kampala Convention. Therein it is stipulated: 'In providing protection and assistance to Internally Displaced Persons, international organizations and humanitarian agencies shall respect the rights of such persons in accordance with international law.'[31] Further, international organisations and humanitarian agencies 'shall be bound by the principles of humanity, neutrality, impartiality and independence of humanitarian actors, and ensure respect for relevant international standards and codes of conduct'.[32]

30.19 In December 2019, the IDMC launched a report that declared that internal displacement in Africa had reached unprecedented levels, with nearly seventeen million people living in a situation of displacement within their own countries in Africa by the end of 2018. 'This is the highest figure ever recorded for the continent, and around 40 per cent of the global total.' The scale of displacement, the IDMC declared, 'is likely to continue unabated'[33] – and along with it comes significant threats to the life and well-being of IDPs.

---

[31] Art. VI(2), Kampala Convention.
[32] Art. VI(3), Kampala Convention.
[33] IDMC, 'Internal Displacement in Africa Has Reached Unprecedented Levels', Geneva, 6 December 2019, at http://bit.ly/39kZo1K.

31

Refugees

INTRODUCTION

31.01 A refugee is by definition a person whose safety is under threat. Under global treaty and customary law, a refugee is a person who, owing to a well-founded fear of being persecuted for reasons of race, religion, nationality, membership of a particular social group, or political opinion, is outside the State of his or her nationality and is, as a consequence, unable or unwilling to avail himself or herself of the protection of that State. The notion of persecution comprehends serious harm, notably threats to life or security; of torture or other inhumane treatment; or of a serious act of discrimination.

31.02 Once a person falls within the international legal definition of a refugee, he or she is entitled to make a claim for asylum, meaning shelter from danger. The prohibition in international law of *refoulement* prevents a refugee from being sent back, whether directly or through a third country, to the State from which he or she escaped if he or she will suffer persecution upon or following return. The principle of *non-refoulement* is a rule codified by treaty,[1] as well as one of customary international law.[2] The rule also prohibits the authorities from turning away an asylum seeker at the border.[3] The principle of *non-refoulement* is widely considered to be a rule of jus cogens (a peremptory norm of international law), which is not only binding on all States but is one from which no derogation is possible, even in a situation of armed conflict.[4]

31.03 The Human Rights Committee has stated that the duty to protect the right to life requires States Parties to the 1966 International Covenant on Civil and Political Rights[5] (ICCPR) to take special measures of protection towards persons in vulnerable situations whose lives have been placed at particular risk because of specific threats or pre-existing

---

[1] Art. 33, 1951 Refugees Convention.
[2] E. Mooney, 'Displacement and the Protection of Civilians under International Refugee Law', chap. 8 in H. Willmot, R. Mamiya, S. Sheeran, and M. Weller (eds.), *Protection of Civilians*, 1st ed., Oxford University Press, Oxford, 2016, pp. 194–5.
[3] Ibid., p. 195.
[4] International Law Commission (ILC), Fourth report on peremptory norms of general international law (jus cogens) by Dire Tladi, Special Rapporteur, UN doc. A/CN.4/727, 31 January 2019, paras. 123 and 131–4.
[5] International Covenant on Civil and Political Rights; adopted at New York 16 December 1966; entered into force 23 March 1976.

patterns of violence, which may include refugees.[6] A heightened duty to protect the right to life also applies to individuals quartered in liberty-restricting State-run facilities, such as refugee camps.[7]

A RIGHT TO ASYLUM?

31.04 In 1948, the Universal Declaration of Human Rights had established, in soft law, the right to seek and enjoy – but not necessarily to be granted[8] – asylum from persecution.[9] The right to protection as a refugee was established in treaty law by the 1951 Convention relating to the Status of Refugees[10] (hereinafter, the 1951 Refugees Convention). The centrepiece of the Convention is its definition of a refugee as a person who

> as a result of events occurring before 1 January 1951 and owing to well-founded fear of being persecuted for reasons of race, religion, nationality, membership of a particular social group or political opinion, is outside the country of his nationality and is unable or, owing to such fear, is unwilling to avail himself of the protection of that country.[11]

The 1951 Refugees Convention is thus formally limited to events occurring in Europe prior to 1 January 1951 (i.e., international displacement provoked as a result of the Second World War and the subsequent 'iron curtain' descending over Europe). These temporal and geographical restrictions were removed in a 1967 Protocol on the status of refugees,[12] to which 147 of 197 States were party as of 1 May 2021, but in any event, the right generally to seek and enjoy asylum from persecution on the stipulated grounds is also a rule of customary international law binding on all States.

31.05 The right to seek and enjoy asylum exists for those who leave the country of their nationality and fear to return because of a well-founded fear of persecution. However, this persecution must be on one of five stipulated grounds: race, religion, nationality, membership of a particular social group, or political opinion. While gender is not mentioned as a ground of persecution, it is indirectly covered by the broad notion of a 'particular social group'. According to the Human Rights Committee, in accordance with the duty to respect the right to life, States Parties to the ICCPR must allow 'all asylum seekers

---

[6] Human Rights Committee, General Comment No. 36: Article 6: right to life, UN doc. CCPR/C/GC/36, 3 September 2019, para. 23.
[7] Ibid., para. 25.
[8] R. Boed, 'The State of the Right of Asylum in International Law', *Duke Journal of Comparative and International Law*, vol. 5, no. 1 (1994), at http://bit.ly/2UcuDEN, p. 9.
[9] Art. 14(1), Universal Declaration of Human Rights; adopted at Paris by UN General Assembly Resolution 217, 10 December 1948. Resolution 217 was adopted by forty-eight votes to zero with eight abstentions (Byelorussian SSR, Czechoslovakia, Poland, Saudi Arabia, South Africa, Soviet Union, Ukrainian SSR, and Yugoslavia). Honduras and Yemen did not take part in the vote.
[10] Convention relating to the Status of Refugees; adopted at Geneva 28 July 1951; entered into force 22 April 1954. As of 1 May 2021, 146 States were party to the 1951 Refugees Convention.
[11] Art. I(A)(2), 1951 Refugees Convention.
[12] Protocol relating to the Status of Refugees; adopted at New York 31 January 1967; entered into force 4 October 1967. As of 1 May 2021, 147 States were party to the Protocol. A State does not need to be a party to the 1951 Refugees Convention in order to adhere to its 1967 Protocol.

claiming a real risk of a violation of their right to life in the State of origin access to refugee or other individualized or group status determination procedures that could offer them protection against *refoulement*'.[13] An asylum seeker who has committed an international crime or a serious non-political crime is, however, excluded from refugee status.[14]

31.06 The Arab Charter on Human Rights stipulates: 'Everyone shall have the right to seek political asylum in other countries to escape persecution. This right shall not be enjoyed by persons facing prosecution for an offense under ordinary criminal law. Political refugees shall not be extraditable.'[15] The notion of a political refugee is not defined in the Charter but may be taken to encompass Palestinians seeking asylum. The Arab Convention on Regulating Status of Refugees in the Arab Countries, adopted by the League of Arab States in 1994, has not entered into force for want of ratifications.[16] The huge outflux of Syrians seeking refuge across the region as a result of the armed conflicts that erupted in Syria beginning in 2011 put great strain on neighbouring countries, including on their abilities to determine refugee status.[17]

31.07 The lack of reference to armed conflict in the international legal definition of a refugee means that, ostensibly, fleeing fighting – even when a person's displacement over an international border is forced – is not in and of itself sufficient to guarantee refugee status under the global instruments. In its 1999 judgment in the *Adan* case,[18] the UK House of Lords held, by majority, that while the 1951 Refugee Convention did not exclude group persecution, individuals fleeing armed conflict and seeking asylum needed to show they would be at risk of 'differential impact', over and above the normal risks to life and liberty inherent in the ordinary incidents of civil war.[19] Only in Africa, under the 1969 Organization of African Unity (OAU) Convention (discussed later in this chapter), does that circumstance differ.[20]

31.08 As Chapter 18 describes,[21] in 2019, the Human Rights Committee considered a communication on the right to life authored by a failed asylum seeker who was contesting the legality of his deportation from New Zealand to Kiribati in 2015.[22] Mr Teitiota did so on the basis that he had been constrained to flee the island of Tarawa in the

---

[13] Human Rights Committee, General Comment 36 on the right to life, para. 31.
[14] Art. 1(F), 1951 Refugees Convention.
[15] Art. 28, Arab Charter on Human Rights; adopted at Tunis 22 May 2004; entered into force 15 March 2008.
[16] Text available at http://bit.ly/32pEifX.
[17] See, e.g., K. Mejri, A Comparative Study of Refugee Laws in Arab Countries, Regional Program Political Dialogue South Mediterranean, Mediterranean Dialogue Series No. 16, Konrad Adenauer Stiftung, December 2018, at http://bit.ly/38tl4K7.
[18] UK House of Lords, *Adan v. Secretary of State for the Home Department*, Judgment, 6 April 1998, [1999] 1 AC 293 (HL).
[19] H. Storey, 'Armed Conflict in Asylum Law: The "War-Flaw"', *Refugee Survey Quarterly*, Vol. 31, No.2 (June 2012), pp. 1–32, at 6.
[20] The 1984 Cartagena Declaration on Refugees for the Americas is not a treaty, though it certainly has normative value.
[21] See, supra, Paragraphs 18.17–18.26.
[22] Human Rights Committee, *Ioane Teitiota v. New Zealand*, Views (Comm. No. 2728/2016), UN doc. CCPR/C/127/D/2728/2016, 7 January 2020.

Republic of Kiribati by the effects of climate change and sea-level rise. New Zealand's Immigration and Protection Tribunal had rejected his claim for asylum, although it did not exclude the possibility that environmental degradation could 'create pathways into the Refugee Convention or protected person jurisdiction'.[23]

31.09 The Committee considered the communication taking into account its position in General Comment 36 on the right to life, wherein it had declared that States Parties to the ICCPR 'must allow all asylum seekers claiming a real risk of a violation of their right to life in the State of origin access to refugee or other individualized or group status determination procedures that could offer them protection against *refoulement*'.[24] Ultimately the Committee rejected Mr Teitiota's claim of a violation of the right to life on the facts.[25] But it also expressed the view that 'without robust national and international efforts, the effects of climate change in receiving states may expose individuals to a violation of their rights under articles 6 or 7 of the Covenant, thereby triggering the non-refoulement obligations of sending states'.[26]

REFUGEES AND THE DEATH PENALTY

31.10 The Human Rights Committee does not preclude all extradition from one retentionist State to another where a person being extradited might face the death penalty. Thus, while a refugee could not be sent back to his or her country of origin to face persecution, it might not be excluded that he or she could be sent to a third country, were he or she believed to have committed a capital offence there. That said, it would be contrary to Article 6 of the ICCPR to extradite an individual from a country that had abolished the death penalty to a country in which he or she might face the death penalty.[27] This is so, unless credible and effective assurances against the imposition of the death penalty have been obtained.[28] 'In the same vein', the Committee has affirmed

> the obligation not to reintroduce the death penalty for any specific crime requires States parties not to deport, extradite or otherwise transfer an individual to a country in which he or she is expected to stand trial for a capital offence, if the same offence does not carry the death penalty in the removing State, unless credible and effective assurances against exposing the individual to the death penalty have been obtained.[29]

31.11 The European Court of Human Rights has become considerably more protective of life in its jurisprudence on the death penalty in the last decade. The Court had held in its judgment of 1989 in the *Soering* case[30] that it was not a violation of the right to life to expel

---

[23] Ibid., para. 2.2.
[24] Ibid., para. 9.3, citing General Comment 36 on the right to life, para. 31.
[25] Ibid., para. 10.
[26] Ibid., para. 9.11.
[27] Human Rights Committee, General Comment 36 on the right to life, para. 30.
[28] Ibid., para. 34.
[29] Ibid.
[30] European Court of Human Rights, *Soering v. United Kingdom*, Judgment (Court Plenary), 7 July 1989, para. 103.

a person to face the death penalty since Article 2 of the European Convention of Human Rights[31] did not outlaw capital punishment. However, for those States which are party to Protocol No. 6 to the European Convention concerning the Abolition of the Death Penalty,[32] the European Commission on Human Rights subsequently held that it can be a breach of that protocol to extradite or expel a person to another state where there is a real risk that the death penalty will be imposed.[33] In 2010, however, in its judgment in the *Al-Saadoon* case,[34] a Chamber of the Court asserted that the position had 'evolved' such that the wording of the second sentence of Article 2(1) no longer acted 'as a bar to its interpreting the words "inhuman or degrading treatment or punishment" in Article 3 as including the death penalty'.[35]

31.12 In *A. L. (X. W.) v. Russia*, adjudged by the First Section of the European Court of Human Rights in 2015, a Chinese national sought to avoid being returned to China to face murder charges for the alleged killing of a Chinese police officer in 1996. The Court noted that the parties had not disputed that there was 'a substantial and foreseeable risk that, if deported to China, the applicant might be given the death penalty following trial on the capital charge of murder'. The Court thus concluded that his forcible return to China 'would expose him to a real risk of treatment contrary to Articles 2 and 3 of the Convention and would therefore give rise to a violation of these Articles'.[36] The applicant in that case was not a refugee, but the protection afforded to him would *a fortiori* be granted to a refugee seeking refuge from persecution.

PROTECTION OF REFUGEES UNDER INTERNATIONAL HUMANITARIAN LAW

31.13 Additional protection for asylum seekers and refugees is contained in the instruments of international humanitarian law.[37] In the 1949 Geneva Convention IV,[38] which

---

[31] Art. 2, Convention for the Protection of Human Rights and Fundamental Freedoms; adopted at Rome 4 November 1950; entered into force 3 September 1953.

[32] Protocol No. 6 to the Convention for the Protection of Human Rights and Fundamental Freedoms concerning the Abolition of the Death Penalty; adopted at Strasbourg 28 April 1983; entered into force 1 March 1985. As of 1 May 2021, forty-six States were party to the Protocol and one State (Russia) was a signatory.

[33] See, e.g., European Commission on Human Rights, *Y v. the Netherlands*, Appl. No. 16531/90.

[34] European Court of Human Rights, *Al-Saadoon and Mufdhi v. United Kingdom*, Judgment (Fourth Section), 2 March 2010.

[35] Ibid., para. 120.

[36] European Court of Human Rights, *A.L. (X.W.) v. Russia*, Judgment (First Section), 29 October 2015 (rendered final on 29 January 2016), para. 66.

[37] Mooney observes a 'surprising' lack of enthusiasm among staff at the Office of the United Nations High Commissioner for Refugees (UNHCR) to use international humanitarian law instruments and provisions in practice. Mooney, 'Displacement and the Protection of Civilians under International Refugee Law', p. 195. She questions whether this is part of the institutional turf war competition between UNHCR and the Office for the Coordination of Humanitarian Affairs (OCHA). Ibid., p. 196.

[38] Convention (IV) relative to the Protection of Civilian Persons in Time of War; adopted at Geneva 12 August 1949; entered into force 21 October 1950 (hereinafter, 1949 Geneva Convention IV).

applies to protect civilians in international armed conflict, including to occupied territories, it is stipulated that in applying measures of control under the Convention, 'the Detaining Power shall not treat as enemy aliens exclusively on the basis of their nationality de jure of an enemy State, refugees who do not, in fact, enjoy the protection of any government'.[39] This is a logical measure since if a person is fleeing persecution from his or her own government, he or she can hardly be considered an agent of that government. In addition, evoking the principle of non-refoulement, it is further provided that 'in no circumstances shall a protected person be transferred to a country where he or she may have reason to fear persecution for his or her political opinions or religious beliefs'.[40] Refugees in occupied territory who are not considered protected persons are covered by Article 70(2) of the 1949 Geneva Convention IV.[41]

31.14 Under the 1977 Additional Protocol I,[42] also applicable in international armed conflict, protection as 'protected persons' under international humanitarian law is extended to all those who, 'before the beginning of hostilities', were considered as refugees 'under the relevant international instruments accepted by the Parties concerned or under the national legislation of the State of refuge or State of residence'.[43] This protection occurs 'in all circumstances and without any adverse distinction'.[44]

31.15 There is, however, no corresponding protection for refugees during a situation of non-international armed conflict.[45] They remain, of course, civilians protected from attack. When detained or otherwise in the power of a party to the conflict, customary rules require humane treatment in all circumstances and without adverse distinction. They also require respect for fundamental guarantees, which include the prohibitions on violence to life and person, outrages upon personal dignity, and the passing of sentences without a fair trial.[46]

---

[39] Art. 44, 1949 Geneva Convention IV.
[40] Art. 45, 1949 Geneva Convention IV.
[41] 'Nationals of the Occupying Power who, before the outbreak of hostilities, have sought refuge in the territory of the occupied State, shall not be arrested, prosecuted, convicted or deported from the occupied territory, except for offences committed after the outbreak of hostilities, or for offences under common law committed before the outbreak of hostilities which, according to the law of the occupied State, would have justified extradition in time of peace.'
[42] Protocol Additional to the Geneva Conventions of 12 August 1949, and relating to the Protection of Victims of International Armed Conflicts; adopted at Geneva 8 June 1977; entered into force 7 December 1978 (hereinafter, 1977 Additional Protocol I).
[43] Art. 73, 1977 Additional Protocol I.
[44] Ibid.
[45] V. Muntarbhorn, 'Protection and Assistance for Refugees in Armed Conflicts and Internal Disturbances: Reflections on the Mandates of the International Red Cross and Red Crescent Movement and the Office of the United Nations High Commissioner for Refugees', *International Review of the Red Cross*, no. 265 (July–August 1988), pp. 351–66; H. Obregón Gieseken, 'The Protection of Migrants under International Humanitarian Law', *International Review of the Red Cross*, vol. 99, no. 1 (2017), pp. 121–52, at http://bit.ly/2PAlx35, at 139–40.
[46] International Committee of the Red Cross (ICRC), 'IHL and the Protection of Migrants Caught in Armed Conflict', Geneva, 4 June 2018, available at http://bit.ly/2wkcxYQ.

THE 1969 ORGANIZATION OF AFRICAN UNITY REFUGEES CONVENTION

31.16 The 1969 OAU Refugees Convention[47] is the only regional treaty that grants refugee status to those fleeing armed conflict. Article 1(1) of the Convention repeats the definition in the 1951 Refugees Convention. According to Article 1(2), however, the term 'refugee' shall 'also apply to every person who, owing to external aggression, occupation, foreign domination or events seriously disturbing public order in either part or the whole of his country of origin or nationality, is compelled to leave his place of habitual residence in order to seek refuge in another place outside his country of origin or nationality'.

31.17 Article 2(3) incorporates the principle of *non-refoulement*, applying it to any person, not just any refugee:

> No person shall be subjected by a Member State to measures such as rejection at the frontier, return or expulsion, which would compel him to return to or remain in a territory where his life, physical integrity or liberty would be threatened for the reasons set out in [the definition of a refugee in] Article I, paragraphs 1 and 2.

The peremptory nature of the prohibition on *refoulement* means that even States not party to the 1969 Convention in Africa are duty bound to respect it.

---

[47] OAU Convention Governing the Specific Aspects of Refugee Problems in Africa; adopted at Addis Ababa 10 September 1969; entered into force 20 January 1974. As of 1 May 2021, 46 of 55 African Union members were party to the Convention. Only Djibouti, Eritrea, Madagascar, Mauritius, Morocco, Namibia, the Sahrawi Arab Democratic Republic, Somalia, and Sao Tome and Principe were States not party to the Convention, and all but Morocco were signatories. The UN Treaty Section, however, lists Morocco as having ratified the Convention in 1974. See http://bit.ly/2Tfr9lD.

PART IV

Accountability

32

The Right to Life and State Responsibility

INTRODUCTION

32.01 State responsibility is at the heart of international human rights law whose raison d'être is the protection of the individual against the power of the sovereign. With respect to the right to life, the focus is on accountability for severe ill treatment or a negligent or wilful failure to protect life against specific threats. But while responsibility for arbitrary deprivation of life by State agents remains central, also increasingly demanding of attention is compliance with the duties to protect and fulfil the right to life, by reducing poverty; alleviating hunger, malnutrition, and disease; lowering the rate of accidents; and tackling pollution and climate change. Failure to do so may sustain alleged violations of the right to life and ground the responsibility of culpable States.

32.02 This chapter discusses the notion and content of the responsibility of States for internationally wrongful acts linked to the right to life. A primary reference in this regard is the International Law Commission (ILC) Draft Articles on Responsibility of States for Internationally Wrongful Acts concluded in 2001[1] (hereinafter, the 2001 Draft Articles on State Responsibility). While a number of the draft articles were, in the ILC's own words, a progressive development of international law at the time rather than a codification of custom, two decades later crystallisation as customary law is deemed to have occurred in at least one significant instance. In addition, the ILC Draft Articles on Responsibility of International Organisations, adopted in 2011, also contain a number of additional rules pertaining to State responsibility.[2]

32.03 This chapter first defines the notions of 'State responsibility' and 'internationally wrongful act'. It then describes the fundamental rules of State responsibility before applying them to the different elements and facets of the right to life. In particular, the chapter assesses the extent to which a failure to comply with their duties to respect, protect,

---

[1] Draft articles on Responsibility of States for Internationally Wrongful Acts, with commentaries, 2001; Text adopted by the International Law Commission (ILC) at its fifty-third session, in 2001, and submitted to the UN General Assembly as a part of the Commission's report covering the work of that session, in UN doc. A/56/10, at http://bit.ly/32A3ocT.

[2] ILC, Draft articles on the responsibility of international organizations, adopted by the ILC at its sixty-third session, in 2011, and submitted to the UN General Assembly as a part of the Commission's report covering the work of that session, in UN doc. A/66/10, at http://bit.ly/2YOKPz7 (hereinafter, 2011 Draft Articles on the Responsibility of International Organizations).

and fulfil the right to life of every person within their jurisdiction amounts to an internationally wrongful act. The notion of State responsibility is considered at the global level, including in the International Court of Justice and within UN treaty bodies, and in the regional human rights mechanisms.

THE NOTION OF AN INTERNATIONALLY WRONGFUL ACT

32.04 An internationally wrongful act is, simply put, a violation of a rule of international law by a State that it binds. The rule may be demarcated in a treaty; it may be customary in nature; it may originate in a general principle of law; or it may be a rule discerned by a competent judicial body, such as the International Court of Justice, a regional human rights court, or a domestic court. However, it must be applicable to the State in question. As Article 13 of the 2001 Draft Articles on State Responsibility stipulates: 'An act of a State does not constitute a breach of an international obligation unless the State is bound by the obligation in question at the time the act occurs.'

32.05 A fundamental principle of treaty law is that a State which is not party is not bound by a treaty rule without its consent.[3] Thus it does not constitute an internationally wrongful act if a State acts contrary to a rule in a treaty to which it has not adhered.[4] That said, as discussed further in this chapter, a number of human rights obligations pertaining to the right to life are of a continuing nature. Accordingly, should a State later become party to a salient human rights treaty, ongoing events may overcome an ostensible jurisdictional exclusion *ratione temporis*, enabling a court, tribunal, or human rights treaty body to consider an allegation or a complaint of a violation, the facts of which originated prior to adherence.

32.06 The ILC expressly prefers the term 'internationally wrongful act' to others that have been applied in international law over time, such as 'tort' or, despite its long-standing usage in international law, a 'delict'.[5] The latter term was employed in the Commission's own earlier work on the issue of State responsibility. For instance, in its 1978 report on the issue,

---

[3] According to the 1969 Vienna Convention on the Law of Treaties, a treaty 'does not create either obligations or rights for a third State without its consent'. Art. 34, Vienna Convention on the Law of Treaties; adopted at Vienna 23 May 1969; entered into force 27 January 1980 (hereinafter, VCLT). As of 1 May 2021, 116 States were party to the Convention. Many of its provisions, however, codify customary law, as is the case with this fundamental rule.

[4] There may be difficulty in discerning the 'object and purpose' of a treaty, which should be construed narrowly. It is necessary to do so in order to determine whether a signatory State – or an adhering State prior to the treaty's entry into force – has engaged in acts which would defeat the treaty's object and purpose and therefore commit an internationally wrongful act. See Art. 18, VCLT. Note also that under its Article 73, the provisions of the VCLT 'shall not prejudice any question that may arise . . . from the international responsibility of a State'.

[5] In its 'Observations and submissions' to the Permanent Court of International Justice (PCIJ) in 1937, in the *Phosphates in Morocco* case, the Italian government cited an esteemed German publicist, Heinrich Triepel, who wrote in 1899: 'If at a given time States are internationally obliged to have rules of law with a given content, the State which already has such laws is breaching its obligation if it repeals them and fails to re-enact them, whereas the State which does not yet have such laws breaches its obligation merely by not introducing them; both States thus commit . . . a permanent international delict' ['Völkerrechtliches Dauerdelikt' in German]. PCIJ, *Phosphates in Morocco* case, 1937, PCIJ, Series C, No. 84, p. 494.

the ILC's Special Rapporteur at the time, Roberto Ago, had proposed a draft article whereby 'any internationally wrongful act which is not an international crime ... constitutes an international delict'.[6] In its first judgment, in the *Corfu Channel* case,[7] the International Court of Justice had referred to *corpora delicti*.[8] In his dissenting opinion in the case, Judge Philadelpho Azevedo stated:

> If, for instance, it was required that the violation of an obligation shall be previously established in each case, the drawing up of a complete catalogue of cases of responsibility becomes inevitable. But this would correspond to a less advanced phase, the limitative enumeration of the sources of delicts and quasi-delicts, in accordance with the general tradition of Roman law.[9]

32.07 The term 'internationally wrongful act' has now become generally accepted in international law. But the ILC's chosen expression is itself not perfect, as the Commission has expressly acknowledged. In particular, and despite its meaning in ordinary parlance, the term 'act' is to be understood in this context to comprehend, as and where appropriate, also an 'omission'.[10] This is made explicit in Article 2 of the 2001 Draft Articles on State Responsibility, whereby:

> There is an internationally wrongful act of a State when conduct consisting of an action *or omission*:
>
> (a) is attributable to the State under international law; and
> (b) constitutes a breach of an international obligation of the State.[11]

Certainly, omissions may amount to arbitrary deprivation of life and thereby violate the right to life, such as when the authorities fail to provide food and water to a detainee or omit to ensure the provision of medical treatment and care when needed, resulting in death or a life-threatening or life-altering condition. The failure to investigate potentially unlawful death is, as described further later in this chapter, a violation of the procedural element of the right to life (and inherent to the protection by law that is required of every State).

32.08 The position advanced by the ILC on the two constituent elements of an internationally wrongful act – an act or omission that violates a rule of international law which is applicable to the State in question – has long been accepted as law. The Permanent Court of International Justice in its 1938 judgment in the *Phosphates in Morocco* case effectively identified them as determinative.[12] The International Court of Justice has also

---

[6] Draft Article 19(4) on State Responsibility, in Report of the International Law Commission on the work of its thirtieth session, 8 May–28 July 1978, UN doc. A/33/10, in *Yearbook of the International Law Commission*, 1978, Vol. II, Part 2, Chap. 3.
[7] International Court of Justice (ICJ), *The Corfu Channel Case (United Kingdom v. Albania)*, Judgment (Merits), 9 April 1949.
[8] *The Corfu Channel Case (United Kingdom v. Albania)*, ICJ Report 1949, p. 34.
[9] Ibid., Dissenting Opinion of Judge Azevedo, p. 83.
[10] Commentary, para. 8, on Draft Article 1, 2001 Draft Articles on State Responsibility.
[11] Draft Article 2, 2001 ILC Draft Articles on State Responsibility (added emphasis).
[12] PCIJ, *Phosphates in Morocco* case, Judgment, 1938, PCIJ, Series A/B, No. 74, p. 10, at 28.

referred to the two elements on several occasions. In its judgment in the *United States Diplomatic and Consular Staff in Tehran* case, it held that, in order to establish the responsibility of Iran, 'first, it must determine how far, legally, the acts in question may be regarded as imputable to the Iranian State. Secondly, it must consider their compatibility or incompatibility with the obligations of Iran under treaties in force or under any other rules of international law that may be applicable.'[13]

THE NOTION OF STATE RESPONSIBILITY

32.09 State responsibility describes the circumstances and consequences for a State that violates a primary rule of international law. The rules governing State responsibility are thus often described as secondary rules that apply once an internationally wrongful act has occurred.[14] Draft Article 1 stipulates simply: 'Every internationally wrongful act of a State entails the international responsibility of that State.' As the ILC commentary on this provision explains:

> Article 1 states the basic principle underlying the articles as a whole, which is that a breach of international law by a State entails its international responsibility. An internationally wrongful act of a State may consist in one or more actions or omissions or a combination of both. The term 'international responsibility' covers the new legal relations which arise under international law by reason of the internationally wrongful act of a State.[15]

32.10 The consequences of certain internationally wrongful acts are primarily, if not exclusively, bilateral – that is, between a perpetrator and a victim. The ILC perceives that relationship as primarily one between States – concerning 'only the relations of the responsible State and the injured State *inter se*'[16] – and not, as is the basis of human rights law, between State (perpetrator) and individual (victim). But it later clarifies that the responsibility of the State under Draft Article 1 'covers all international obligations *of* the State and not only those owed *to* other States'.[17] Thus, the ILC declares, 'State responsibility extends, for example, to human rights violations and other breaches of international law where the primary beneficiary of the obligation breached is not a State.'[18]

32.11 That fact does not preclude one State taking action against another State based on an alleged violation of the human rights of one or more of its nationals. This may occur when the individual victim does not have locus standi to bring a claim against the responsible State, but this constraint is not a prerequisite for an inter-state claim of responsibility and reparation. It may also be because the individual whose rights have been violated is a national of the complaining State.

---

[13] International Court of Justice, *United States Diplomatic and Consular Staff in Tehran* case (*United States v. Iran*), Judgment, 24 May 1980, para. 56.
[14] General Commentary, para. 1, 2001 ILC Draft Articles on State Responsibility.
[15] Commentary, para. 1, on Draft Article 1, 2001 Draft Articles on State Responsibility.
[16] Commentary, para. 4, on Draft Article 1, 2001 Draft Articles on State Responsibility.
[17] Commentary, para. 3, on Draft Article 28, 2001 Draft Articles on State Responsibility (original emphasis).
[18] Ibid.

32.12 In its judgment on admissibility in the *Ahmadou Sadio Diallo* case,[19] the International Court of Justice found that Guinea's application to the Court was admissible in so far as it concerns the protection of Mr. Diallo's rights as an individual.[20] A national of Guinea, Mr Diallo alleged that a range of his human rights had been violated, but as an individual, he had no locus standi to bring a claim against the Democratic Republic of Congo before the International Court of Justice. The Court held: 'Owing to the substantive development of international law over recent decades in respect of the rights it accords to individuals, the scope *ratione materiae* of diplomatic protection, originally limited to alleged violations of the minimum standard of treatment of aliens, has subsequently widened to include, *inter alia*, internationally guaranteed human rights.'[21]

32.13 In the arguments it ultimately made before the Court, Guinea maintained that Mr Diallo was the victim in 1988–9 of arrest and detention measures taken by the Congolese authorities in violation of international law, and in 1995–6 of arrest, detention, and expulsion measures also in violation of international law.[22] The Court rejected the claim relating to events in 1988–9, as they had not been presented by Guinea in its Memorial originating the case, but proceeded to address the complaint in relation to the actions of the Congolese authorities in 1995–6 that had been originally alleged. Guinea had argued inter alia that the prohibitions on arbitrary arrest and detention in the 1966 International Covenant on Civil and Political Rights[23] and in the African Charter on Human and Peoples' Rights[24] had been violated by the Congolese authorities with respect to Mr Diallo.

32.14 In reaching its determination that a violation had indeed occurred of the rights to liberty and security, the Court took due account of 'the number and seriousness of the irregularities tainting Mr Diallo's detentions'. These included the fact that he was held for a particularly long time (66 days), and moreover that it appeared that the Congolese authorities had made 'no attempt to ascertain' whether his detention was even necessary.[25] Further, Guinea was justified in arguing that a breach had occurred of Mr Diallo's right to be 'informed, at the time of arrest, of the reasons for his arrest' – a right guaranteed in all cases, irrespective of the grounds for the arrest.[26]

32.15 The consequences for a State of being 'responsible' for an internationally wrongful act are potentially manifold. The 2001 Draft Articles identify a number of these 'legal'

---

[19] International Court of Justice, *Ahmadou Sadio Diallo (Guinea v. Democratic Republic of Congo)*, Judgment (Admissibility), 24 May 2007.
[20] Ibid., para. 96.
[21] Ibid., para. 39.
[22] International Court of Justice, *Ahmadou Sadio Diallo (Guinea v. Democratic Republic of Congo)*, Judgment (Merits), 30 November 2010, para. 21.
[23] Art. 9(1), International Covenant on Civil and Political Rights; adopted at New York 16 December 1966; entered into force 23 March 1976.
[24] Art. 6, African Charter on Human and Peoples' Rights; adopted at Nairobi 27 June 1981; entered into force 21 October 1986.
[25] International Court of Justice, *Ahmadou Sadio Diallo (Guinea v. Democratic Republic of Congo)*, Judgment (Merits), para. 82.
[26] Ibid., para. 84.

consequences. In particular, under Article 30, the State responsible for an internationally wrongful act is under an obligation to cease that act (if it is continuing) and to offer 'appropriate assurances and guarantees of non-repetition, if circumstances so require'.[27] Consonant with the definition of the act in Draft Article 2 as encompassing also an omission, that omission must similarly be rectified by appropriate positive conduct.[28] Thus, if the omission is the failure to conduct an effective investigation into an alleged violation of the right to life, just such an investigation must still be carried out as part of the State's international legal responsibility. The commentary on Article 30 explains that 'assurances are normally given verbally, while guarantees of non-repetition involve something more – for example, preventive measures to be taken by the responsible State designed to avoid repetition of the breach'.[29]

32.16 A 'responsible' State is further obligated 'to make full reparation for the injury caused by the internationally wrongful act'.[30] This is a general principle of law. As stated by the Permanent Court of International Justice in its judgment on jurisdiction in 1927 in the *Factory at Chorzów* case: 'It is a principle of international law that the breach of an engagement involves an obligation to make reparation in an adequate form. Reparation therefore is the indispensable complement of a failure to apply a convention and there is no necessity for this to be stated in the convention itself.'[31] Reparation involves both material and moral damage.[32] 'Material' damage concerns damage to property or other interests of the State and its nationals that is assessable financially. 'Moral' damage includes pain and suffering and the loss of loved ones.[33] As the Draft Articles further clarify: 'Full reparation for the injury caused by the internationally wrongful act shall take the form of restitution, compensation and satisfaction, either singly or in combination.'[34]

32.17 Depending on the character and content of the obligation and on the circumstances of the breach, the responsible State may, according to the Draft Articles, be obligated to another State, to several States, or to the international community as a whole.[35] The reference to several States includes the case in which a breach affects all the other States Parties to a treaty.[36] When an obligation of reparation exists towards a State, reparation is not necessarily owed to that State. While a State's responsibility for the breach of a human rights treaty obligation may exist towards all the other States Parties to the treaty, 'the individuals concerned should be regarded as the ultimate beneficiaries and in that sense as the holders of the relevant rights'.[37] Moreover, the Draft Articles acknowledge that this

---

[27] Art. 30, 2001 Draft Articles on State Responsibility.
[28] Commentary, para. 2, on Draft Article 30, 2001 Draft Articles on State Responsibility.
[29] Commentary, para. 12, on Draft Article 30, 2001 Draft Articles on State Responsibility.
[30] Art. 31(1), 2001 Draft Articles on State Responsibility.
[31] PCIJ, *Factory at Chorzów*, Judgment (Jurisdiction), No. 8, 1927, PCIJ, Series A, No. 9, at http://bit.ly/2GaUDwF, p. 21.
[32] Art. 31(2), 2001 Draft Articles on State Responsibility.
[33] Commentary, para. 5, on Draft Article 31, 2001 Draft Articles on State Responsibility.
[34] Art. 34, 2001 Draft Articles on State Responsibility.
[35] Art. 33(1), 2001 Draft Articles on State Responsibility.
[36] Commentary, para. 2, on Draft Article 33, 2001 Draft Articles on State Responsibility.
[37] Commentary, para. 3, on Draft Article 33, 2001 Draft Articles on State Responsibility.

stipulation is 'without prejudice to any right, arising from the international responsibility of a State, which may accrue directly to any person or entity other than a State'.[38]

32.18 Beyond the possibility for a bilateral claim for a remedy of violation of human rights, in many instances regarding the right to life, any State may be entitled to seek a determination of responsibility of a perpetrator State, even absent a territorial or nationality nexus to the relevant acts. This is so, because internationally wrongful acts that are violations of jus cogens norms are the interest of every State. As the ILC has determined, peremptory norms of international law 'give rise to obligations owed to the international community as a whole (obligations *erga omnes*), in which all States have a legal interest'.[39] In its noted discussion of obligations *erga omnes* in its judgment in the *Barcelona Traction* case, the International Court of Justice had included in an indicative list the 'principles and rules concerning the basic rights of the human person'.[40] As Chapter 1 of this work discusses, the prohibition of arbitrary deprivation of life is a jus cogens norm, and therefore every State has an interest in its observance by every other State.

ACTS ATTRIBUTABLE TO THE STATE

32.19 The Draft Articles consider which acts may be attributed to the State for the purpose of responsibility under international law. The term 'attribution' thus denotes the legal attaching of a given action or omission to a State.[41] A State is, in the words of the ILC, 'a real organized entity, a legal person with full authority to act under international law'.[42] But as the Permanent Court of International Justice noted in an Advisory Opinion of 1923: 'States can act only by and through their agents and representatives.'[43]

32.20 The general rule holds that only the conduct of 'organs of government, or of others who have acted under the direction, instigation or control of those organs, i.e. as agents of the State' may be attributed to the State at the international level.[44] This comprises the three arms of a State – executive, legislative, and judicial – and encompasses acts of local administrative bodies as well as those of central government.[45] Of particular importance for the respect and protection of the right to life are the armed forces, the police, and other

---

[38] Art. 33(2), 2001 Draft Articles on State Responsibility.
[39] Draft Conclusion 17(1) in ILC, *Report of the International Law Commission*, Seventy-first session, UN doc. A/74/10, 2019, chap. V.
[40] International Court of Justice, *Barcelona Traction, Light and Power Company Ltd. (Belgium v. Spain)*, Judgment, 5 February 1970, para. 34.
[41] Commentary, para. 12, on Draft Article 2, 2001 Draft Articles on State Responsibility.
[42] Ibid., para. 5.
[43] PCIJ, *German Settlers in Poland*, Advisory Opinion, 1923, PCIJ, Series B, No. 6, p. 22.
[44] Commentary, para. 2, on Chap. II: Attribution of Conduct to a State, 2001 Draft Articles on State Responsibility.
[45] According to paragraph 1 of Draft Article 4 ('Conduct of organs of a State'): 'The conduct of any State organ shall be considered an act of that State under international law, whether the organ exercises legislative, executive, judicial or any other functions, whatever position it holds in the organization of the State, and whatever its character as an organ of the central Government or of a territorial unit of the State.' Art. 4(1), 2001 Draft Articles on State Responsibility.

law enforcement agencies, including prison and other custodial officers, as well as any other internal or extraterritorial security forces. With respect to the armed forces, according to the 1977 Additional Protocol I, a party to an international armed conflict 'shall be responsible for all acts committed by persons forming part of its armed forces'.[46]

32.21 Moreover, while the structure of a State and the functions of its organs 'are not, in general, governed by international law', the conduct of institutions 'performing public functions and exercising public powers' such as the police is attributable to the State, 'even if those institutions are regarded in internal law as autonomous and independent of the executive government'.[47] For instance, in the United States, there are in total some 18,000 law enforcement agencies at federal, state, county, and local levels.[48] The conduct of the members of each and every one of these agencies can engage the responsibility of the United States under international law.

32.22 This attribution similarly occurs even if members of law enforcement agencies or other security forces acting in the course of their duties go beyond – or even act in flagrant contravention of – the instructions they are given by other State agents.[49] Thus, as the ILC observes, a State 'cannot take refuge' behind provisions of its domestic law or on the basis that instructions given should have prevented the actions or omissions in question or 'ought to have taken a different form'. This is so, the Commission underscores, 'even where the organ or entity in question has overtly committed unlawful acts under the cover of its official status or has manifestly exceeded its competence'.[50]

32.23 This position is also reflected by jurisprudence in regional human rights courts. In its judgment in the *Velásquez Rodríguez* case, the Inter-American Court of Human Rights explicitly held that a breach of the American Convention on Human Rights[51] had occurred 'independent of whether the organ or official has contravened provisions of internal law or overstepped the limits of his authority'. Under international law, the Court recalled, 'a State is responsible for the acts of its agents undertaken in their official capacity and for their omissions, even when those agents act outside the sphere of their authority or violate internal law'.[52]

---

[46] Art. 91, Protocol Additional to the Geneva Conventions of 12 August 1949, and Relating to the Protection of Victims of International Armed Conflicts; adopted at Geneva 8 June 1977; entered into force 7 December 1978 (hereinafter, 1977 Additional Protocol I).

[47] Commentary, para. 6, on Chap. II: Attribution of Conduct to a State, 2001 Draft Articles on State Responsibility.

[48] D. Banks, J. Hendrix, M. Hickman, and T. Kyckelhahn, 'National Sources of Law Enforcement Employment Data', Program Report, US Department of Justice, last updated 4 October 2016, at http://bit.ly/2QySwVh, p. 1.

[49] Draft Article 7 stipulates: 'The conduct of an organ of a State or of a person or entity empowered to exercise elements of the governmental authority shall be considered an act of the State under international law if the organ, person or entity acts in that capacity, even if it exceeds its authority or contravenes instructions.'

[50] Commentary, para. 2, on Article 7, 2001 ILC Draft Articles on State Responsibility.

[51] American Convention on Human Rights; adopted at San José 22 November 1969; entered into force 18 July 1978.

[52] Inter-American Court of Human Rights, *Velásquez-Rodríguez v. Honduras*, Judgment (Merits), 29 July 1988, para. 170.

32.24 There is also State responsibility where paramilitary groups, and *a fortiori* death squads, act under private instruction from an organ or agent of the State. Thus, Draft Article 8 stipulates, 'the conduct of a person or group of persons shall be considered an act of a State under international law if the person or group of persons is in fact acting on the instructions of, or under the direction or control of, that State in carrying out the conduct'. In 1999, prior to the adoption of the Draft Articles, a joint report was elaborated on the situation in East Timor by the UN Special Rapporteur on extrajudicial, summary, or arbitrary executions, the Special Rapporteur on the question of torture, and the Special Rapporteur on violence against women, its causes, and consequences. In the section of the report entitled 'State Responsibility', the Rapporteurs declared:

> While most of the atrocities committed in East Timor must clearly be attributed to pro-integration militia elements, the information gathered and testimonies heard by the Special Rapporteurs leave little doubt as to the direct and indirect involvement of TNI [Indonesian National Army] and police in supporting, planning, assisting and organizing the pro-integration militia groups.
> ... A number of official documents indicating formal cooperation between TNI and militia groups have also been recovered from Indonesian government offices in East Timor.[53]

In the later UN Commission of Inquiry into the atrocities committed in East Timor in 1999, it was stated that 'on 30 August 1999, 78 per cent of the Timorese population voted for emancipation from Indonesian administration in the United Nations-sponsored Popular Consultation. In anticipation of the result, Indonesian security forces unleashed militias upon the population. Wide-scale burning and looting occurred as 1,500 people were killed and hundreds of thousands displaced'.[54]

32.25 Where, however, police or custodial officers are employed by a private company and not an organ of the State, their acts may not be directly attributable to the State unless that company – or the officer personally – is employed, appointed, or contracted by the State. Acts of those engaged or deployed by a private security company that is hired to protect commercial or household property and which is paid by the relevant business(es) or householder(s) will thus not normally constitute acts of the State. That said, the responsibility of the State nonetheless may be engaged if it has failed to duly regulate the private security company and its actions and powers in accordance with its duty to protect as well as respect life.

32.26 More controversially, acts attributable to the State include acts committed by insurrectional movements that later become part of the government of a State or form a new State in part or all of the former State's territory. Article 10 reads as follows:

Article 10. Conduct of an insurrectional or other movement
1. The conduct of an insurrectional movement which becomes the new Government of a State shall be considered an act of that State under international law.

---

[53] 'Situation of human rights in East Timor', UN doc. A/54/660, 10 December 1999, paras. 59, 63.
[54] *Report of the United Nations Independent Special Commission of Inquiry for Timor-Leste*, Geneva, 2 October 2006, at http://bit.ly/2QFf4UE, para. 23.

2. The conduct of a movement, insurrectional or other, which succeeds in establishing a new State in part of the territory of a pre-existing State or in a territory under its administration shall be considered an act of the new State under international law.

3. This article is without prejudice to the attribution to a State of any conduct, however related to that of the movement concerned, which is to be considered an act of that State by virtue of articles 4 to 9.

32.27 Here the ILC's logic is a little harder to fathom. As Gerard Cahin observes, the ILC 'leaves open the question of the moment at which an opposition movement may be characterized as an insurrectional movement'.[55] He suggests that the application of the 1977 Additional Protocol II, which governs certain high-intensity non-international armed conflicts,[56] 'may be a useful starting point'.[57] Instead, the ILC commentary observes more generally:

> A comprehensive definition of the types of groups encompassed by the term 'insurrectional movement' as used in article 10 is made difficult by the wide variety of forms which insurrectional movements may take in practice, according to whether there is relatively limited internal unrest, a genuine civil war situation, an anti-colonial struggle, the action of a national liberation front, revolutionary or counter-revolutionary movements and so on.

32.28 Two points need to be made in respect of this issue. First, there appears to be no good reason why the acts of a non-State armed group that is party to a non-international armed conflict governed by Common Article 3 should be somehow excluded from future responsibility. Even without effective control of territory (required by the 1977 Additional Protocol II for its application) or where one armed group fights another in a failed State (excluded by the scope of application of the Additional Protocol), an armed group can still violate international humanitarian law and commit international crimes (which are violations of jus cogens norms). Second, under the 1977 Additional Protocol I, a national liberation movement engaged in a struggle for decolonisation may be deemed to be a party to an international armed conflict and not a non-international armed conflict.[58] Moreover, the threshold of violence necessary for this form of international armed conflict is widely considered to be far lower than it is for the application of the 1977 Additional Protocol II.[59]

---

[55] G. Cahin, 'Attribution of Conduct to the State: Insurrectional Movements', chap. 19.2 in J. Crawford, A. Pellet, and S. Olleson (eds.), *The Law of International Responsibility*, Oxford Commentaries on International Law, Oxford University Press, Oxford, 2010, p. 248. The decision not to accord any specific legitimacy to national liberation movements has been, as he notes, 'strongly criticized'. See H. Atlam, 'National Liberation Movements and State Responsibility', in M. Spinedi and B. Simma (eds.), *United Nations Codification of State Responsibility*, Oceana Publications, New York, pp. 35–6.

[56] Art. 1, Protocol Additional to the Geneva Conventions of 12 August 1949, and Relating to the Protection of Victims of Non-International Armed Conflicts; adopted at Geneva 8 June 1977; entered into force 7 December 1978 (hereinafter, 1977 Additional Protocol II).

[57] Cahin, 'Attribution of Conduct to the State: Insurrectional Movements', p. 252.

[58] Arts. 1(4) and 96(3), 1977 Additional Protocol I.

[59] See, e.g., S. Casey-Maslen with S. Haines, *Hague Law Interpreted*, Hart, Oxford, 2018, pp. 48–9.

32.29 Furthermore, it is not certain that an insurrectional movement may necessarily even engender an armed conflict under international law. In his seminal commentary on Article 3 in the 1949 Geneva Convention I,[60] Jean Pictet referred to criteria that were 'useful as a means of distinguishing a genuine armed conflict from a mere act of banditry or an *unorganized and short-lived insurrection* or terrorist activities'.[61] With respect to the right to life as protected in the 1950 European Convention on Human Rights, it is specified that deprivation of life shall not be regarded as a violation of the right to life 'when it results from the use of force which is no more than absolutely necessary' in 'action lawfully taken for the purpose of quelling ... an insurrection'.[62] This may comprise both actions of law enforcement and of the conduct of hostilities, with the provision potentially straddling situations of peacetime and situations of non-international armed conflict.

32.30 That does, however, lead to the question of which conduct is to be adjudged as acts of the State that an insurrectional movement later becomes. At the least, this should comprise serious violations of international humanitarian law and violations of jus cogens human rights norms. As the United Nations Mission in South Sudan (UNMISS) stated in 2014:

> The most basic human rights obligations, in particular those emanating from peremptory international law (*ius cogens*) bind both the State and armed opposition groups in times of peace and during armed conflict. In particular, international human rights law requires States, armed groups and others to respect the prohibitions of extrajudicial killing, maiming, torture, cruel inhuman or degrading treatment or punishment, enforced disappearance, rape, other conflict related sexual violence, sexual and other forms of slavery, the recruitment and use of children in hostilities, arbitrary detention as well as of any violations that amount to war crimes, crimes against humanity, or genocide.[63]

32.31 The UN Assistance Mission in Afghanistan (UNAMA) further states that while non-State actors cannot become parties to international human rights treaties, 'non-State actors, including armed groups, are not precluded from being subject to human rights obligations under customary international law. Non-state actors are increasingly deemed to be bound by certain international human rights obligations, particularly those actors exercising *de facto* control over some areas, such as the Taliban.'[64] In its Resolution 1417 (2002), the UN Security Council reiterated that it held the Rassemblement Congolais pour la Démocratie-Goma – a non-State actor but the 'de facto authority' – 'responsible to

---

[60] Convention (I) for the Amelioration of the Condition of the Wounded and Sick in Armed Forces in the Field; adopted at Geneva 12 August 1949; entered into force 21 October 1950.
[61] J. Pictet (ed.), *Geneva Convention for the Amelioration of the Condition of the Wounded and Sick in Armed Forces in the Field: A Commentary*, International Committee of the Red Cross (ICRC), Geneva, 1952, p. 50 (added emphasis).
[62] Art. 2(2)(c), Convention for the Protection of Human Rights and Fundamental Freedoms; adopted at Rome by the Council of Europe, 4 November 1950; entered into force 3 September 1953.
[63] UNMISS, *Conflict in South Sudan: A Human Rights Report*, 8 May 2014, at http://bit.ly/3lpLYqi, para. 18.
[64] UNAMA, *2019 Annual Report on the Protection of Civilians in Armed Conflict in Afghanistan*, Kabul, February 2020, at http://bit.ly/34GCBg6, p. 81.

bring to an end all extrajudicial executions, human rights violations and arbitrary harassment of civilians in Kisangani, and all other areas under [its] control'.[65]

32.32 It may be the case that more than one State may bear responsibility under international law for acts perpetrated in a single territory. This will depend on whether the States in question have jurisdiction *ratione loci, materiae,* and *personae*. As the Grand Chamber of the European Court of Human Rights recalled in its judgment of the *Catan* case against Moldova and Russia: 'The exercise of jurisdiction is a necessary condition for a Contracting State to be able to be held responsible for acts or omissions imputable to it which give rise to an allegation of the infringement of rights and freedoms set forth' in the European Convention on Human Rights.[66] While jurisdiction under the European Convention on Human Rights is primarily limited to a State's own territory, an exception occurs 'when, as a consequence of lawful or unlawful military action, a Contracting State exercises effective control of an area outside that national territory. The obligation to secure, in such an area, the rights and freedoms set out in the Convention, derives from the fact of such control, whether it be exercised directly, through the Contracting State's own armed forces, or through a subordinate local administration.'[67]

32.33 Responsibility potentially pertains also to a situation where a State does not effectively control territory and particularly the non-State actors present therein, whose conduct is alleged to be violating fundamental human rights. Thus, in its judgment in the *Catan* case, the European Court's Grand Chamber stated that although Moldova had no effective control over the acts of the self-styled 'Moldavian Republic of Transdniestria', a breakaway entity controlling territory in Transnistria, 'the fact that the region is recognised under public international law as part of Moldova's territory gives rise to an obligation, under Article 1 of the Convention, to use all legal and diplomatic means available to it to continue to guarantee the enjoyment of the rights and freedoms defined in the Convention to those living there'.[68]

32.34 The fundamental treaty rule has already been invoked whereby a State is not bound by treaty rules (unless they are already of a customary nature) prior to an entry into force of that treaty for that State. But as the ILC commentary recalls, the notion of 'continuing wrongful acts', which owes its origins in international law to Heinrich Triepel, is 'common to many national legal systems'.[69] One such act is enforced disappearance and specifically the general duty to investigate and bring to an end the disappearance. The UN Committee on Enforced Disappearance has 'competence solely in respect of enforced disappearances which commenced after the entry into force' of the 2006 International Convention for the

---

[65] UN Security Council Resolution 1417, adopted by unanimous vote on 14 June 2002, para. 4.
[66] European Court of Human Rights, *Catan and others* v. *Moldova and Russia*, Judgment (Grand Chamber), 19 October 2012, para. 103.
[67] Ibid., para. 106.
[68] Ibid., para. 110. See, similarly, European Court of Human Rights, *Mozer* v. *Moldova and Russia*, Judgment (Grand Chamber), 23 February 2016, paras. 99–100.
[69] Commentary, para. 7, on Draft Article 14, 2001 Draft Articles on State Responsibility.

Protection of All Persons from Enforced Disappearance (CPED).[70] But other human rights fora assert jurisdiction over a continuing duty to investigate a disappearance, even if that occurred before the State in question became party to the relevant treaty.

32.35 Thus, for example, in its 2009 judgment in the *Varnava* case,[71] the Grand Chamber of the European Court explicitly reviewed jurisprudence in the Inter-American Court of Human Rights and the Human Rights Committee on jurisdiction *ratione temporis*, where a State had become party to the relevant treaty after the initial disappearance had taken place. It noted, though, that the Grand Chamber in an inter-State case had found that the disappearance of some 1,485 Greek Cypriots disclosed a situation of continuing violation under Article 2 in so far as the authorities of the respondent State had failed to conduct an effective investigation aimed at clarifying the whereabouts and fate of the persons who had gone missing in life-threatening circumstances. It found no reason to differ regarding the nine missing men in the *Varnava* case and concluded that to the extent that there was a continuing obligation under Article 2, it had competence *ratione temporis*.[72]

32.36 In the *Güzelyurtlu* case,[73] which concerning the murders of several former residents of the self-styled Turkish Republic of Northern Cyprus (TRNC) in the territory of the Republic of Cyprus, the TRNC authorities had initiated their own investigation into the murders. This, the Grand Chamber held, created a 'jurisdictional link' between the applicants and Turkey, resulting in the responsibility of Turkey for the acts and omissions of the 'TRNC' authorities. The Court – and most States – consider that Turkey remains an occupier of the north of Cyprus and the region is therefore under its effective control for the purposes of the European Convention on Human Rights. In addition, the murder suspects had fled to the TRNC, and as a consequence, Cyprus had been prevented from pursuing its own criminal investigation. The Court thus held that Turkey had jurisdiction under the European Convention on Human Rights.[74]

RESPONSIBILITY FOR SERIOUS VIOLATIONS OF JUS COGENS NORMS

32.37 The *Güzelyurtlu* case is also notable for the Court's invocation of the 2001 ILC Draft Articles on State Responsibility, specifically those pertaining to Chapter III of the Draft Articles, which concerns serious breaches of obligations under peremptory norms of general international law. A serious breach of a jus cogens norm is, according to Draft Article 40, 'if it involves a gross or systematic failure by the responsible State to fulfil the obligation'.[75] According to the ILC commentary on the article:

---

[70] Art. 35, International Convention for the Protection of All Persons from Enforced Disappearance; adopted at New York 20 December 2006; entered into force 23 December 2010.
[71] European Court of Human Rights, *Varnava and others v. Turkey*, Judgment (Grand Chamber), 18 September 2009.
[72] Ibid., para. 121.
[73] European Court of Human Rights, *Güzelyurtlu and others v. Cyprus and Turkey*, Judgment (Grand Chamber), 29 January 2019.
[74] Ibid., paras. 191–97.
[75] Art. 40(2), 2001 Draft Articles on State Responsibility.

To be regarded as systematic, a violation would have to be carried out in an organized and deliberate way. In contrast, the term 'gross' refers to the intensity of the violation or its effects; it denotes violations of a flagrant nature, amounting to a direct and outright assault on the values protected by the rule. The terms are not of course mutually exclusive; serious breaches will usually be both systematic and gross. Factors which may establish the seriousness of a violation would include the intent to violate the norm; the scope and number of individual violations; and the gravity of their consequences for the victims.[76]

Thus a single instance of arbitrary deprivation of life or torture would not suffice to invoke Article 40 (and the consequent obligations set out in Draft Article 41, discussed as follows). In contrast, widespread acts of summary execution or torture, such as occurred for instance during the armed conflicts in Syria and Yemen, assuredly would.

ASSISTING ANOTHER STATE TO COMMIT AN INTERNATIONALLY WRONGFUL ACT

32.38 Aiding or assisting another State to commit an internationally wrongful act is also itself an internationally wrongful act. There are specific treaty obligations not to assist another State to violate international law. Indeed, this principle is at the heart of the UN Arms Trade Treaty,[77] where arms may not be transferred by a State Party to any other State where they would be used to commit a range of international crimes, nor where there is an overriding risk they would be used to commit or facilitate a serious violation of international humanitarian law or of international human rights law.[78]

32.39 Draft Article 16, which effectively establishes and delineates a primary rule as well as identifying the secondary consequences, sets two conditions for responsibility under international law in such a case: (a) that the assisting State does so with knowledge of the circumstances of the internationally wrongful act by the assisted State and (b) the act would also be internationally wrongful if committed by the assisting State.[79] In the commentary on the provision, it is suggested that a third condition exists: that the aid or assistance must be given to facilitate the commission of that act.[80] The commentary further asserts that a State is not responsible for aid or assistance 'unless the relevant

---

[76] Commentary, para. 8, on Article 40, 2001 Draft Articles on State Responsibility.
[77] Arms Trade Treaty; adopted at New York 2 April 2013; entered into force 24 December 2014. As of 1 September 2020, 110 States were party to the Treaty.
[78] Art. 7(1) and (3), Arms Trade Treaty; and see also with respect to Art. 6(3) of the Treaty, *infra*, Paragraph 32.40.
[79] Thus Draft Article 16 must be distinguished to a certain degree from prohibitions incorporated in a number of disarmament treaties whereby a State Party may not assist or encourage any other State to engage in conduct that is prohibited to the State Party. It may well be that the State being assisted is not itself prohibited from engaging in certain conduct and therefore does not commit an internationally wrongful act. As an example, under the 1997 Anti-Personnel Mine Ban Convention, a State Party (e.g., the United Kingdom) may not assist, encourage, or induce a State not party (e.g., the United States) to use anti-personnel mines. Art. 1(1)(c), Convention on the Prohibition of the Use, Stockpiling, Production, and Transfer of Anti-Personnel Mines and on their Destruction; adopted at Oslo 18 September 1997; entered into force 1 March 1999. This is so, even though the United States is not prohibited from using anti-personnel mines either by treaty or by custom, given that a customary prohibition has not yet crystallised in international law. See on this issue, *supra*, Paragraph 15.43.
[80] Commentary, para. 3, on Article 16, 2001 Draft Articles on State Responsibility.

State organ intended, by the aid or assistance given, to facilitate the occurrence of the wrongful conduct'.

32.40 This third putative condition miscasts the state of international law and, if validated, would have significantly narrowed the scope of State responsibility in this regard. It has not, however, been reflected in jurisprudence in the International Court of Justice or by subsequent State practice. Thus, in its 2007 judgment in the *Genocide* case, the Court affirmed that Article 16 reflected customary law, but clarified that the key deterring factor was knowledge, not intent: 'There cannot be a finding of complicity against a State unless at the least its organs were aware that genocide was about to be committed or was under way.'[81] 'In other words', the Court held, 'an accomplice must have given support in perpetrating the genocide with full knowledge of the facts'.[82] The 2013 Arms Trade Treaty stipulates the following:

> A State Party shall not authorize any transfer of conventional arms ... if it has knowledge at the time of authorization that the arms or items would be used in the commission of genocide, crimes against humanity, grave breaches of the Geneva Conventions of 1949, attacks directed against civilian objects or civilians protected as such, or other war crimes as defined by international agreements to which it is a Party.[83]

32.41 There are additional consequences when aid or assistance is provided to maintain a serious breach of a jus cogens norm within the meaning of Draft Article 40.[84] Not only is a State internationally responsible for such conduct; there are also other primary obligations imposed by Draft Article 41. Specifically, States 'shall cooperate to bring to an end through lawful means' any serious breach within the meaning of Draft Article 40.[85] This obligation was, however, acknowledged at the time as a potentially progressive development of international law.[86] The ILC has since affirmed that this now reflects customary law.[87] In addition, no State 'shall recognize as lawful a situation created by' such a serious breach.[88] This, the ILC affirmed in 2001, was already recognised by certain courts, State practice, and the practice of the UN Security Council.[89] It is particularly relevant to the

---

[81] International Court of Justice, *Case Concerning the Application of the Convention on the Prevention and Punishment of the Crime of Genocide (Bosnia and Herzegovina v. Serbia and Montenegro)*, Judgment, 26 February 2007, para. 432.
[82] Ibid.
[83] Art. 6(3), Arms Trade Treaty.
[84] Art. 41(2), 2001 Draft Articles on State Responsibility.
[85] Art. 41(1), 2001 Draft Articles on State Responsibility.
[86] Commentary, para. 3, on Article 41, 2001 Draft Articles on State Responsibility.
[87] According to Conclusion 19(1) of draft conclusions on peremptory norms of general international law (jus cogens), adopted by the ILC on first reading in 2019: 'States shall cooperate to bring to an end through lawful means any serious breach by a State of an obligation arising under a peremptory norm of general international law (jus cogens).' See UN doc. A/74/10, August 2019, Chap. V: Peremptory norms of general international law (jus cogens). The ILC Special Rapporteur had earlier declared that 'it would be difficult for the Commission, in 2018, to create the impression that it is in accordance with international law for States not to cooperate to bring to an end situations created by breaches of *jus cogens*'. Fourth report on peremptory norms of general international law (jus cogens) by Dire Tladi, Special Rapporteur, UN doc. A/CN.4/727, 31 January 2019, para. 18.
[88] Art. 41(2), 2001 Draft Articles on State Responsibility.
[89] Commentary, paras. 6–8, on Article 41, 2001 Draft Articles on State Responsibility.

acquisition of territory by an act of aggression. As the Human Rights Committee has asserted: 'States parties engaged in acts of aggression as defined in international law, resulting in deprivation of life, violate ipso facto' Article 6 of the 1966 International Covenant on Civil and Political Rights[90] (ICCPR).[91]

32.42 These obligations are reflected also in the 2011 Draft Articles on the Responsibility of International Organizations. For the purposes of the Draft Articles, an international organization means 'an organization established by a treaty or other instrument governed by international law and possessing its own international legal personality'.[92] A State that aids or assists an international organisation in the commission of an internationally wrongful act by the latter is internationally responsible for doing so if '(a) the State does so with knowledge of the circumstances of the internationally wrongful act; and (b) the act would be internationally wrongful if committed by that State'.[93] In addition, States and international organisations 'shall cooperate to bring to an end through lawful means any serious breach' of a jus cogens norm.[94]

VIOLATIONS OF THE RIGHT TO LIFE THAT CONSTITUTE INTERNATIONALLY WRONGFUL ACTS

32.43 A range of conduct will violate the right to life and thereby constitute an internationally wrongful act. Examples include the most flagrant instances of arbitrary deprivation of life – deliberate extrajudicial executions and other arbitrary killings by State agents, such as the police or the army. This is so whether the killings occur in peacetime or during and in connection with a situation of armed conflict. In this regard, a violation of an international humanitarian law rule, such as the principle of distinction and proportionality in attack, will also amount to arbitrary deprivation of life where it results in death (or was likely or intended to do so) and is therefore constitutive of a violation of the right to life.

32.44 As noted previously, the failure to provide adequate food and water to a detainee or to ensure the provision of appropriate medical care where needed may also amount to arbitrary deprivation of life. This is so, either where the detainee perishes or where he or she suffers life-threatening or life-changing conditions as a result of those failures. In the broader community, a famine, where a State prevents food from being accessed by a civilian population in need, may amount to a crime against humanity. If this occurs during an armed conflict, it may also be a war crime.

32.45 With respect to the prohibition on enforced disappearance – another jus cogens norm – the Human Rights Committee has observed that the deprivation of liberty,

---

[90] International Covenant on Civil and Political Rights; adopted at New York 16 December 1966; entered into force 23 March 1976. As of 1 May 2021, 173 States were party to the ICCPR and a further 6 were signatories.
[91] Human Rights Committee, 'General Comment No. 36: Article 6: right to life', UN doc. CCPR/C/GC/36, 3 September 2019, para. 70.
[92] Art. 2, 2011 Draft Articles on the Responsibility of International Organizations.
[93] Art. 58(1), 2011 Draft Articles on the Responsibility of International Organizations.
[94] Art. 42(1), 2011 Draft Articles on the Responsibility of International Organizations.

followed by a refusal to acknowledge that deprivation of liberty or by concealment of the fate of the disappeared person, in effect removes that person from the protection of the law and places his or her life at serious and constant risk, 'for which the State is accountable'. Such conduct 'results in a violation of the right to life as well as other rights recognized in the Covenant',[95] making an enforced disappearance an internationally wrongful act on a number of grounds.

32.46 The execution of the death penalty after an unfair trial or for a crime that is not 'most serious' will be an internationally wrongful act, as too will be the execution in any circumstance of a pregnant woman or a person who was under eighteen years of age when he or she committed a most serious crime. Both in the case of enforced disappearance and more generally, a violation of the procedural element of the right to life – the duty to investigate potentially unlawful death[96] – is also an internationally wrongful act.

32.47 As noted by the Minnesota Protocol, international law requires that investigations be prompt, effective, thorough, independent, impartial, and transparent.[97] This dictates that the authorities must conduct an investigation as soon as possible and proceed without unreasonable delay. That said, the duty of promptness does not justify a rushed or unduly hurried investigation.[98]

32.48 To meet the requirements of effectiveness and thoroughness, investigators should, to the extent possible, collect and confirm all testimonial, documentary, and physical evidence. Investigations must be capable of ensuring accountability for unlawful death, leading to the identification and, if justified by the evidence and seriousness of the case, the prosecution and punishment of all those responsible.[99] Investigations must, at a minimum, take all reasonable steps to identify the victim or victims; recover and preserve all material probative of the cause of death, the identity of the perpetrator(s) and the circumstances surrounding the death; identify possible witnesses and obtain their evidence in relation to the death and the circumstances surrounding the death; and determine the cause, manner, place and time of death, and all of the surrounding circumstances.[100]

32.49 In determining the manner of death, the investigation should distinguish between natural death, accidental death, suicide, and homicide. It should also seek to determine who was involved in the death and their individual responsibility for the death. An autopsy is, as a general rule, required. In the case of an enforced disappearance, an investigation

---

[95] Ibid., para. 58.
[96] See *Minnesota Protocol on the Investigation of Potentially Unlawful Death (2016), The Revised United Nations Manual on the Effective Prevention and Investigation of Extra-legal, Arbitrary and Summary Executions*, Office of the UN High Commissioner for Human Rights, New York/Geneva, 2017, paras. 2, 8 (c), 9, 15–21.
[97] Ibid., para. 22.
[98] Ibid., para. 23.
[99] Ibid., para. 24.
[100] Ibid., para. 25.

must seek to determine the fate of the disappeared and, if applicable, the location of their remains.[101]

32.50 The investigation must further determine whether a violation has occurred of the right to life. Investigations must seek to identify not only direct perpetrators but also all others who were responsible for the death, including officials in the chain of command who were complicit in the death.[102]

32.51 Investigators and investigative mechanisms must be independent of undue influence. They must be independent institutionally and formally, as well as in practice and perception, at all stages. Investigations must be independent of any suspected perpetrators and the units, institutions, or agencies to which they belong. Investigations of law enforcement killings, for example, must be capable of being carried out free from undue influence that may arise from institutional hierarchies and chains of command. Inquiries into serious human rights violations, such as extrajudicial executions and torture, must be conducted under the jurisdiction of ordinary civilian courts.[103] Investigators must be impartial and must act at all times without bias. They must analyse all evidence objectively. They must consider and appropriately pursue exculpatory as well as inculpatory evidence.[104]

32.52 Finally, investigative processes and outcomes must be transparent, including through openness to the scrutiny of the general public and of victims' families.[105] Any limitations on transparency must be strictly necessary for a legitimate purpose: protecting the privacy and safety of affected individuals, ensuring the integrity of ongoing investigations, or securing sensitive information about intelligence sources or military or police operations. In no circumstances may a State restrict transparency in a way that would conceal the fate or whereabouts of any victim of an enforced disappearance or unlawful killing, or would result in impunity for those responsible.[106]

---

[101] Ibid.
[102] Ibid., para. 26.
[103] Ibid., para. 28.
[104] Ibid., para. 31.
[105] Ibid., para. 32.
[106] Ibid., para. 33.

33

The Right to Life and the Responsibility of International Organisations

INTRODUCTION

33.01 The previous chapter considered State responsibility for internationally wrongful acts linked to the right to life. This chapter looks in turn at the responsibility of international organisations for such acts. A primary reference in this regard is the International Law Commission's (ILC's) Draft Articles on Responsibility of International Organisations for Internationally Wrongful Acts concluded in 2011[1] (hereinafter, the 2011 Draft Articles).[2]

33.02 International organisations are subjects of international law with international personality, denoting that they can contract obligations under international law as well as have obligations imposed upon them. That they are subjects of international law and may undertake obligations on the international plane was affirmed by the International Court of Justice in an Advisory Opinion issued in 1980[3] and is made explicit in the 1986 Vienna Convention on the Law of Treaties between States and International Organizations[4] (VCLTIO).[5] Thus, in the preamble to the VCLTIO, reference is made to 'the specific features of treaties to which international organizations are parties as subjects of international law distinct from States'. It is further noted that 'international organizations possess the capacity to conclude treaties, which is necessary for the exercise

---

[1] ILC, Draft articles on the responsibility of international organizations, adopted by the ILC at its sixty-third session, in 2011, and submitted to the UN General Assembly as a part of the Commission's report covering the work of that session, in UN doc. A/66/10, at http://bit.ly/2YOKPz7 (hereinafter, 2011 Draft Articles).

[2] Article 57 of the 2001 ILC Draft Articles on the Responsibility of States for internationally wrongful acts had stipulated: 'These articles are without prejudice to any question of the responsibility under international law of an international organization, or of any State for the conduct of an international organization.'

[3] International Court of Justice, *Interpretation of the Agreement of 25 March 1951 between the WHO and Egypt*, Advisory Opinion, 20 December 1980, para. 37. A minority of leading commentators question this holding. Jan Klabbers, for instance, commenting on the dicta by the Court, declared that 'it remains unclear which international law and why: there is no plausible theory of obligation'. J. Klabbers, 'The Paradox of International Institutional Law', *International Organisations Law Review*, vol. 5 (2008), pp. 151–73, at 165. See further J. Klabbers, *An Introduction to International Organizations Law*, 3rd ed., Cambridge University Press, Cambridge, 2015, esp. pp. 2, 41, 42, 48, 49.

[4] Vienna Convention on the Law of Treaties between States and International Organizations or between International Organizations; adopted at Vienna 21 March 1986; not yet in force.

[5] See generally on the Convention G. Gaja, 'A "New" Vienna Convention on Treaties between States and International Organizations or between International Organizations: A Critical Commentary', *British Yearbook of International Law*, vol. 58, no. 1 (1987), pp. 253–69.

of their functions and the fulfilment of their purposes'.[6] As of writing, the depositary of the VCLTIO – the Secretary-General of the United Nations – had accepted adherence to the Treaty by 12 international organisations, including the UN itself.[7] The Treaty as a whole has not yet entered into force.[8]

33.03 Adherence by an international organisation to a treaty is an obvious route to the assumption of international legal obligations. But, as the chapter discusses, the primary basis on which an international organisation commits an internationally wrongful act pertaining to the right to life is through a breach of a rule of customary international law. Thus an international organisation may be held responsible for violating the jus cogens prohibition of arbitrary deprivation of life or, at the least where its involvement in the death is suspected or alleged, for a failure to investigate a potentially unlawful death as custom demands.

33.04 The ILC commentary on the 2011 Draft Articles avers that 'like the articles on State responsibility, the ... [2011] draft articles express secondary rules. Nothing in the draft articles should be read as implying the existence or otherwise of any particular primary rule binding on international organizations.'[9] This is, however, not fully persuasive. As Eric David observes with respect to the 2001 Draft Articles, the section on circumstances precluding wrongfulness clarifies primary rules rather than establishing secondary responsibility.[10] Further, in addition to identifying an international organisation's international responsibility for aiding or assisting the commission of an internationally wrongful act, Article 14 of the 2011 Draft Articles effectively prohibits such conduct as a primary rule of international law.

33.05 The ILC commentary on Draft Article 14 cites as an example potentially prohibited aid or assistance the support that was given (and which has continued to be given) by the United Nations Organization Mission in the Democratic Republic of the Congo (MONUC) to the Forces armées de la République démocratique du Congo (FARDC), and the risk of aiding or assisting violations of international humanitarian law (IHL),

---

[6] VCLTIO, tenth and eleventh preambular paras.
[7] The International Atomic Energy Agency (IAEA), the International Civil Aviation Organization, the International Criminal Police Organization, the International Labour Organisation (ILO), the International Maritime Organization (IMO), the Organisation for the Prohibition of Chemical Weapons (OPCW), the Preparatory Commission for the Comprehensive Nuclear-Test-Ban Treaty Organization, the United Nations, United Nations Industrial Development Organization (UNIDO), Universal Postal Union, World Health Organization (WHO), and the World Intellectual Property Organization (WIPO). See Arts. 82, 83, and 84, VCLTIO.
[8] The VCLTIO will enter into force once 35 States have either signed and ratified or acceded to it. As of 1 May 2021, 32 had done so: Albania, Argentina, Australia, Austria, Belarus, Belgium, Bulgaria, Colombia, Croatia, Cyprus, Czechia, Denmark, Estonia, Gabon, Germany, Greece, Hungary, Italy, Liberia, Liechtenstein, Malta, Mexico, Moldova, The Netherlands, Palestine, Senegal, Slovakia, Spain, Sweden, Switzerland, United Kingdom, and Uruguay.
[9] General Commentary para. 3, 2011 Draft Articles on the Responsibility of International Organisations.
[10] E. David, 'Primary and Secondary Rules', chap. 3 in J. Crawford, A. Pellet, and S. Olleson (eds.), *The Law of International Responsibility*, Oxford Commentaries on International Law, Oxford University Press, Oxford, 2010, esp. pp. 29–31.

The Right to Life and the Responsibility of International Organisations 631

human rights law, and refugee law by the FARDC.[11] These risks were laid bare in an internal document issued on 12 October 2009 by the UN Office of Legal Affairs (OLA). Therein, it was stated:

> If MONUC has reason to believe that FARDC units involved in an operation are violating one or the other of those bodies of law and if, despite MONUC's intercession with the FARDC and with the Government of the DRC, MONUC has reason to believe that such violations are still being committed, then MONUC may not lawfully continue to support that operation, but must cease its participation in it completely.[12]

The document added the following:

> MONUC may not lawfully provide logistic or 'service' support to any FARDC operation if it has reason to believe that the FARDC units involved are violating any of those bodies of law. ... This follows directly from the Organization's obligations under customary international law and from the Charter to uphold, promote and encourage respect for human rights, international humanitarian law and refugee law.[13]

33.06 This holding by the OLA that the UN is bound to respect customary human rights, refugee law, and IHL and that international obligations are also directly incumbent on the organisation as originating in the Charter of the United Nations is significant.[14] According to the Charter, one of the purposes of the UN is to 'achieve international cooperation in ... promoting and encouraging respect for human rights and for fundamental freedoms for all without distinction as to race, sex, language, or religion'.[15] Of more direct normative effect, however, is the provision whereby the UN 'shall promote ... universal respect for, and observance of, human rights and fundamental freedoms for all without distinction as to race, sex, language, or religion'.[16] International humanitarian law and refugee law are not mentioned in the Charter, and hence the duty to respect them must come from their existence as custom.

33.07 This chapter continues by defining an international organisation and discussing the notions of 'responsibility' and 'internationally wrongful acts' relevant to such an organisation. The chapter then describes the fundamental rules of responsibility as they pertain to international organisations, before applying those rules to the different components of the right to life. The notion of responsibility is considered both at the global level, including in

---

[11] Commentary para. 6 on Article 14, 2011 Draft Articles.
[12] Para. 11 in Attachment to Note of 12 October 2009 by Ms Patricia O'Brien, Under-Secretary-General for Legal Affairs and UN Legal Counsel, OLA, to Mr Alain Le Roy, Under Secretary-General for Peacekeeping Operations. The document was 'provided' to a journalist of the *New York Times*, which has made a copy available at http://nyti.ms/2Ry52VO. See also J. Gettleman, 'U.N. Told Not to Join Congo Army in Operation', *New York Times*, 9 December 2009, at http://nyti.ms/35FVsYZ.
[13] Para. 12 in Attachment to Note of 12 October 2009 by Ms Patricia O'Brien, Under-Secretary-General for Legal Affairs and UN Legal Counsel, OLA, to Mr Alain Le Roy, Under Secretary-General for Peacekeeping Operations.
[14] Charter of the United Nations; adopted at San Francisco 26 June 1945; entered into force 24 October 1945 (hereinafter, UN Charter).
[15] Art. 1(3), UN Charter.
[16] Art. 55(c), UN Charter.

the International Court of Justice, and in regional human rights mechanisms, specifically the European Court of Human Rights' controversial decision on admissibility in the *Behrami and Behrami* case.

THE DEFINITION OF AN INTERNATIONAL ORGANISATION

33.08 The 2011 Draft Articles define an international organisation as 'an organization established by a treaty or other instrument governed by international law and possessing its own international legal personality'.[17] Indeed, while most international organisations are established by treaty, this is not necessarily the case.[18] The Draft Articles further clarify that international organisations 'may include as members, in addition to States, other entities'.[19] The definition in the 2011 Draft Articles thus differs from the one incorporated in 1986 in the VCLTIO, which provides simply – but more narrowly – that the term international organisation 'means an intergovernmental organization'.[20]

33.09 The commentary on the 2011 Draft Articles observes that the definition proffered therein is 'considered as appropriate for the purposes of the present draft articles and is not intended as a definition for all purposes'.[21] Nonetheless, the VCLTIO definition of an international organisation is overtly criticised by the ILC on three grounds: that it is unclear whether the term 'intergovernmental organization' refers 'to the constituent instrument or to actual membership', on the basis that 'several important international organizations have been established with the participation also of State organs other than governments', and because an 'increasing number' of international organisations include among their membership 'entities other than States as well as States'.[22]

33.10 Thus the notion of an international organisation understood broadly encompasses global organisations, such as the United Nations (of which 193 of 197 States are members), or other treaty-based entities, such as the International Atomic Energy Agency (IAEA),[23] the North Atlantic Treaty Organization (NATO),[24] or the Organisation for the Prohibition

---

[17] Art. 2(a), 2011 Draft Articles.
[18] The commentary provides the example of the Organization of the Petroleum Exporting Countries (OPEC). Commentary para. 4, on Draft Article 2, 2011 Draft Articles on the Responsibility of International Organisations. OPEC is a 'permanent, intergovernmental' organisation, which was created by Iran, Iraq, Kuwait, Saudi Arabia, and Venezuela at the Baghdad Conference on 10–14 September 1960. OPEC, 'Brief History', 2020, at http://bit.ly/33aS4Tb.
[19] Art. 2(a), 2011 Draft Articles.
[20] Art. 2(i), VCLTIO.
[21] Commentary para. 1 on Draft Article 2, 2011 Draft Articles.
[22] Commentary para. 3 on Draft Article 2, 2011 Draft Articles.
[23] The Statute of the IAEA was approved on 23 October 1956 by the 81 States participating in the Conference on the Statute of the International Atomic Energy Agency, held at UN Headquarters in New York. It came into force on 29 July 1957. As of 1 September 2020, 171 States were party to the IAEA Statute. IAEA, 'List of Member States', 2020, at http://bit.ly/35mVG7r.
[24] NATO members are bound by the North Atlantic Treaty, concluded in Washington, DC, in 1949. NATO, 'The North Atlantic Treaty', last updated 10 April 2019, at http://bit.ly/3o94l3j. There were thirty NATO member States as of 1 May 2021. The latest State to join was North Macedonia, which was admitted in 2020. NATO, 'NATO Members', at http://bit.ly/3miDgu2.

of Chemical Weapons (OPCW).[25] The term also extends to regional organisations, such as the African Union,[26] the Council of Europe,[27] or the Organization of American States (OAS), which is vaunted as the world's oldest regional organisation.[28] It also concerns regional economic integration organisations, such as the Association of Southeast Asian Nations (ASEAN),[29] the Economic Community of West African States (ECOWAS),[30] or the European Union.[31]

THE NOTION OF AN INTERNATIONALLY WRONGFUL ACT

33.11 An internationally wrongful act is, simply put, a violation of a rule of international law by an international organisation that it binds. The rule may be demarcated in a treaty (including but not limited to a treaty that has established it); it may be customary in

---

[25] See OPCW, 'About Us: History', 2020, at http://bit.ly/2FmgX6z.
[26] The African Union (AU) is a continental body consisting of the fifty-five member States that make up the countries of the African Continent. It was officially launched in 2002 as a successor to the Organisation of African Unity (OAU, 1963–99). AU, 'About the African Union', 2020, at http://bit.ly/2GUDCY4. The member States are Algeria, Angola, Benin, Botswana, Burkina Faso, Burundi, Cabo Verde, Cameroon, Central African Republic, Chad, Comoros, Republic of the Congo, Democratic Republic of Congo, Côte d'Ivoire, Djibouti, Egypt, Equatorial Guinea, Eritrea, Eswatini, Ethiopia, Gabon, Gambia, Ghana, Guinea, Guinea-Bissau, Kenya, Lesotho, Liberia, Libya, Madagascar, Malawi, Mali, Mauritania, Mauritius, Morocco, Mozambique, Namibia, Niger, Nigeria, Rwanda, São Tomé and Príncipe, Sahrawi Arab Democratic Republic, Senegal, Seychelles, Sierra Leone, Somalia, South Africa, South Sudan, Sudan, Tanzania, Togo, Tunisia, Uganda, Zambia, and Zimbabwe.
[27] Council of Europe: 'Who We Are', 2020, at http://bit.ly/35odNK8. There are forty-seven member States of the Council of Europe: Albania, Andorra, Armenia, Austria, Azerbaijan, Belgium, Bosnia and Herzegovina, Bulgaria, Croatia, Cyprus, Czechia, Denmark, Estonia, Finland, France, Georgia, Germany, Greece, Hungary, Iceland, Ireland, Italy, Latvia, Liechtenstein, Lithuania, Luxembourg, Malta, Moldova, Monaco, Montenegro, the Netherlands, North Macedonia, Norway, Poland, Portugal Romania, Russia, San Marino, Serbia, Slovak Republic, Slovenia, Spain, Sweden, Switzerland, Turkey, Ukraine, and the United Kingdom.
[28] The OAS traces its origins back to the First International Conference of American States, held in Washington, DC, from October 1889 to April 1890. The Conference approved the establishment of the International Union of American Republics, which in 1948 became the OAS. OAS, 'Who We Are', 2020, at http://bit.ly/2RcXhEz. All thirty-five States in the Americas are party to the OAS Charter and are members of the Organization: Antigua and Barbuda, Argentina, The Bahamas, Barbados, Belize, Bolivia, Brazil, Canada, Chile, Colombia, Costa Rica, Cuba, Dominica, the Dominican Republic, Ecuador, El Salvador, Grenada, Guatemala, Guyana, Haiti, Honduras, Jamaica, Mexico, Nicaragua, Panama, Paraguay, Peru, Saint Kitts and Nevis, Saint Lucia, Saint Vincent and the Grenadines, Suriname, Trinidad and Tobago, the United States, Uruguay, and Venezuela.
[29] ASEAN, 'About ASEAN', 2020, at http://bit.ly/3matcDN. ASEAN was established on 8 August 1967 in Bangkok upon the signature of the ASEAN Declaration (Bangkok Declaration) by Indonesia, Malaysia, Philippines, Singapore, and Thailand. Today there are ten member States of ASEAN: Brunei, Cambodia, Indonesia, Lao PDR, Malaysia, Myanmar, the Philippines, Singapore, Thailand, and Vietnam.
[30] ECOWAS was established on 28 May 1975 by the Treaty of Lagos. The organisation has fifteen member States (Benin, Burkina Faso, Cape Verde, Cote d'Ivoire, The Gambia, Ghana, Guinea, Guinea-Bissau, Liberia, Mali, Niger, Nigeria, Sierra Leone, Senegal, and Togo). ECOWAS, 'Basic Information', 2020, at http://bit.ly/2ZqhVWj.
[31] Following the withdrawal of the United Kingdom on 31 January 2020, there are twenty-seven EU member States: Austria, Belgium, Bulgaria, Croatia, Cyprus, Czechia, Denmark, Estonia, Finland, France, Germany, Greece, Hungary, Ireland, Italy, Latvia, Lithuania, Luxembourg, Malta, the Netherlands, Poland, Portugal, Romania, Slovakia, Slovenia, Spain, and Sweden.

nature; it may originate in a general principle of law; or it may be a rule discerned by a competent judicial body, such as the International Court of Justice, a regional human rights court, or even a domestic court. In the words of the International Court of Justice: 'International organizations are subjects of international law and, as such, are bound by any obligations incumbent upon them under general rules of international law, under their constitutions or under international agreements to which they are parties.'[32] Of course, however, the rule must be applicable to the international organisation in question in accordance with international law. As stipulated by Article 5 of the 2011 Draft Articles on the Responsibility of International Organisations, 'the characterization of an act of an international organization as internationally wrongful is governed by international law'.

33.12 A fundamental principle of treaty law that applies also to international organisations is that an international organisation not party to a specific treaty is not bound by a rule contained therein without its consent (or unless it is bound under customary law).[33] Thus for an international organisation to act contrary to a rule in a treaty that it has not joined or which does not formally bind it (for instance, if it is in its constituent instrument) does not constitute an internationally wrongful act.

33.13 The term 'internationally wrongful act' has now become generally accepted as part of the lexicon of international law. As the ILC already recognised in the 2001 Draft Articles on State responsibility, an 'act' in this context is to be understood in this context to potentially encompass also an omission.[34] This is again made explicit in Article 4 of the 2011 Draft Articles, whereby

> There is an internationally wrongful act of an international organization when conduct consisting of an action *or omission*:
>
> (a) is attributable to that organization under international law; and
> (b) constitutes a breach of an international obligation of that organization.[35]

Certainly, omissions may amount to arbitrary deprivation of life and thereby violate the right to life, such as when an international organisation fails to provide food and water to a person it is detaining or omits to ensure the provision of medical treatment and care when needed, resulting in death or a life-threatening or life-altering condition. The failure to conduct an investigation into a death for which an international organisation is potentially responsible is, as noted further later in this chapter, a violation of the procedural element of the right to life. The duty to investigate is inherent to the protection of the right to life that is required under customary law.[36]

---

[32] ICJ, *Interpretation of the Agreement of 25 March 1951 between the WHO and Egypt*, Advisory Opinion, 20 December 1980, para. 37.
[33] According to the 1969 Vienna Convention on the Law of Treaties, a treaty 'does not create either obligations or rights for . . . a third organization without the consent of . . . that organization'. Art. 34, VCLTIO.
[34] Commentary para. 8 on Draft Article 1, 2001 Draft Articles on State Responsibility.
[35] Draft Article 4, 2011 Draft Articles (added emphasis).
[36] On this issue, see Chapter 2.

THE NOTION OF RESPONSIBILITY OF AN INTERNATIONAL ORGANISATION

33.14 The notion of responsibility describes the circumstances and consequences for an international organisation that violates a rule of international law. Draft Article 3 stipulates simply: 'Every internationally wrongful act of an international organization entails the international responsibility of that organization.' This responsibility may be bilateral – that is, with an international organisation (as perpetrator) and injured party (as victim) – but this is not necessarily the case. As the ILC commentary on this provision explains:

> Neither for States nor for international organizations is the legal relationship arising out of an internationally wrongful act necessarily bilateral. The breach of the obligation may well affect more than one subject of international law or the international community as a whole. Thus in appropriate circumstances more than one subject may invoke, as an injured subject or otherwise, the international responsibility of an international organization.[37]

33.15 Beyond the possibility for a bilateral claim against an international organisation for a remedy for a violation of human rights, in many instances regarding the right to life, any State may be entitled to seek a determination of responsibility of a perpetrator organisation, even absent a territorial or nationality nexus to the relevant acts. This is so because internationally wrongful acts that are violations of jus cogens norms are the interest of every State. As the ILC has determined, peremptory norms of international law 'give rise to obligations owed to the international community as a whole (obligations *erga omnes*), in which all States have a legal interest'.[38] In its noted discussion of such obligations *erga omnes* in its judgment in the *Barcelona Traction* case, the International Court of Justice had included in an indicative list the 'principles and rules concerning the basic rights of the human person'.[39] As Chapter 1 of this work discusses, the prohibition of arbitrary deprivation of life is a jus cogens norm, and therefore every State has an interest in its observance by every other State.

33.16 Whether an *erga omnes* obligation is also owed to international organisations is less certain. In its commentary on the 2011 Draft Articles, the ILC leaves the question open. The commentary does observe that 'legal writings concerning the entitlement of international organizations to invoke responsibility in case of a breach of an obligation owed to the international community as a whole mainly focus on the European Union. The views are divided among authors, but a clear majority favours an affirmative solution.'[40] Given that, as noted previously, the UN is obligated under the Charter to promote 'universal respect for, and observance of, human rights and fundamental freedoms for all without distinction', a strong case can be made that it has an *erga omnes* interest in respect for human rights.

---

[37] Commentary para. 5 on Draft Article 3, 2011 Draft Articles.
[38] Draft Conclusion 17(1) in ILC, *Report of the International Law Commission*, Seventy-first Session, UN doc. A/74/10, 2019, chap. V.
[39] ICJ, *Barcelona Traction, Light and Power Company Ltd. (Belgium v. Spain)*, Judgment, 5 February 1970, para. 34.
[40] Commentary para. 8 on Draft Article 49, 2011 Draft Articles.

33.17 The consequences for an international organisation of being found 'responsible' for an internationally wrongful act are potentially manifold. The 2011 Draft Articles identify a number of these 'legal' consequences. In particular, under Article 30, the international organisation responsible is obligated to cease the unlawful conduct if it is continuing and to offer appropriate assurances and guarantees of non-repetition. The responsible international organisation is also obligated to make 'full reparation for the injury caused by the internationally wrongful act'.[41] Injury includes both material and moral damage.[42] Finally, in accordance with Article 29, if the internationally wrongful act results from the failure to perform an obligation, the existence of other heads of responsibility as evoked here does 'not affect the continued duty of the responsible international organization to perform the obligation breached'.

ACTS ATTRIBUTABLE TO THE INTERNATIONAL ORGANISATION

33.18 The Draft Articles consider which acts may be attributed to the international organisation for the purpose of responsibility under international law. According to Draft Article 6(1), the conduct of an organ or agent of an international organisation in the performance of functions of that organ or agent shall be considered an act of that organisation under international law, whatever position in the organisation the organ or agent holds. The term 'agent' is to be construed broadly. It is 'intended to refer not only to officials but also to other persons acting for the United Nations on the basis of functions conferred by an organ of the organization'.[43]

33.19 In its Advisory Opinion of 1999 on *Difference Relating to Immunity from Legal Process of a Special Rapporteur of the Commission on Human Rights*, the International Court of Justice held that a UN special rapporteur was an agent of the United Nations.[44] The case concerned Dato Param Cumaraswamy, the Special Rapporteur of the erstwhile UN Commission on Human Rights on the independence of judges and lawyers. Mr Cumaraswamy gave an interview in which he commented on litigation in Malaysian courts. As a result of an article published on the basis of the interview, two companies in Malaysia sued him for slander and libel. The UN Secretary-General issued certificates attesting to the Special Rapporteur's immunity, but these were dismissed by the Malaysian courts. The International Court of Justice observed that Special Rapporteurs 'usually are entrusted not only with a research mission but also with the task of monitoring human rights violations and reporting on them'.[45]

33.20 More difficult is to determine whether an organ of a State that implements a decision of an international organisation is acting on its own behalf or on behalf of the

---

[41] Article 31(1), 2011 Draft Articles.
[42] Article 31(2), 2011 Draft Articles.
[43] Commentary para. 3 on Draft Article 6, 2011 Draft Articles.
[44] ICJ, *Difference Relating to Immunity from Legal Process of a Special Rapporteur of the Commission on Human Rights*, Advisory Opinion, 29 April 1999, paras. 51, 52, and 65.
[45] Ibid., para. 43.

The Right to Life and the Responsibility of International Organisations

international organisation (or both). Key to determining attribution – and hence potential responsibility for any internationally wrongful act – is which entity exercises effective control over the conduct in question. As Article 7 of the 2011 Draft Articles clarifies: 'The conduct of an organ of a State or an organ or agent of an international organization that is placed at the disposal of another international organization shall be considered under international law an act of the latter organization if the organization exercises effective control over that conduct.' Unfortunately, the ILC does not define what amounts to 'effective control'. Dapo Akande suggests that an international organisation would only have effective control over military personnel from a troop-contributing country where the organisation 'has operational control of it'.[46]

33.21 In 2007, while the Draft Articles were still in the process of elaboration, the European Court of Human Rights issued its decision on admissibility in the *Behrami and Behrami* case,[47] holding that the conduct of NATO-led peacekeepers in Kosovo was attributable neither to NATO as an international organisation nor to any of its member States, but rather to the UN alone. The presence in the province of a NATO peacekeeping force had been endorsed by the UN Security Council in its Resolution 1244,[48] but its conduct could not be genuinely said to be under the operational control of the United Nations. Indeed, in 2008 (and possibly in response to the decision of the European Court of Human Rights the previous year), the UN Secretary-General stated in a report on the UN Mission in Kosovo (UNMIK): 'The European Union will, over a period of time, gradually assume increasing operational responsibilities in the areas of international policing, justice and customs throughout Kosovo. It is understood that the international responsibility of the United Nations will be limited in the extent of its effective operational control.'[49] The European Court's decision in *Behrami* has been widely criticised, including, indirectly, by the ILC itself. In its commentary on Article 7 of the 2011 Draft Articles, it

---

[46] D. Akande, 'Classification of Armed Conflicts', in B. Saul and D. Akande (eds.), *The Oxford Guide to International Humanitarian Law*, Oxford University Press, Oxford, 2020, p. 49.

[47] European Court of Human Rights, *Behrami and Behrami v. France*, and *Saramati v. France, Germany and Norway*, Decision on Admissibility (Grand Chamber), 2 May 2007.

[48] UN Security Council Resolution 1244, adopted on 10 June 1999 by fourteen votes to none with one abstention (China), operative para. 1 and Annex 2.

[49] Report of the Secretary-General on the United Nations Interim Administration Mission in Kosovo, UN doc. S/2008/354, 12 June 2008, para. 16. Kosovo is not a party to the International Covenant on Civil and Political Rights (ICCPR), though UNMIK submitted a report in 2006 to the Human Rights Committee. Report submitted by the United Nations Interim Administration Mission in Kosovo to the Human Rights Committee on the Human Rights Situation in Kosovo since June 1999: Kosovo (Serbia and Montenegro), UN doc. CCPR/C/UNK/1, 13 March 2006. The report addressed several aspects of the right to life: the death penalty, use of force and firearms by the Kosovo police, environmental pollution, and measures to 'eliminate' epidemics. Ibid., paras. 8–22. At the same time, UNMIK stated: 'It must be remembered throughout that the situation of Kosovo under interim administration by UNMIK is *sui generis*. Accordingly, it has been the consistent position of UNMIK that treaties and agreements, to which the State Union of Serbia and Montenegro is a party, are not automatically binding on UNMIK.' Ibid., para. 124. In its Concluding Observations on the report, the Human Rights Committee noted its concern about 'allegations of excessive use of force by UNMIK, the Kosovo Force (KFOR) and the Kosovo Police Service (KPS) and the reported failure to investigate, prosecute and convict many of those responsible for such acts'. Human Rights Committee, Concluding Observations: Kosovo (Serbia), UN doc. CCPR/C/UNK/CO/1, 14 August 2006, para. 15.

observed: 'Various authors pointed out that the European Court did not apply the criterion of effective control in the way that had been envisaged by the Commission.'[50]

33.22 As the ILC general commentary on attribution observes: 'The articles do not say, but only imply, that conduct of military forces of States or international organizations is not attributable to the United Nations when the Security Council authorizes States or international organizations to take necessary measures outside a chain of command linking those forces to the United Nations.'[51] This notion of a chain of operational command is thus a critical element. In the case of military contingents that a State places at the disposal of the United Nations for a peacekeeping operation, the State retains disciplinary powers and criminal jurisdiction over the members of that contingent.[52] But the chain of command in a UN peacekeeping mission lies ordinarily – at least in theory – with the UN commander (or the Special Representative of the Secretary-General where that individual oversees his or her work). Thus, as the commentary on the 2011 Draft Articles recall: 'The United Nations assumes that in principle it has exclusive control of the deployment of national contingents in a peacekeeping force.'[53]

33.23 In any event, the responsibility of an international organisation may be alternative to, or in addition to, the responsibility of a State for specific conduct. As the 2011 Draft Articles make explicit, 'where an international organization and one or more States or other international organizations are responsible for the same internationally wrongful act, the responsibility of each State or organization may be invoked in relation to that act'.[54] While contested by certain authorities, this is an accurate statement of international law.

33.24 The issue arose with respect to the right to life in the case of the conduct of Dutch peacekeepers at Srebrenica during the armed conflicts in Bosnia and Herzegovina in the 1990s. When ethnic Serb forces overran the town in July 1995, they engaged in genocide against the Bosniak men and boys they deemed to be of fighting age, massacring in cold blood some eight thousand in less than two weeks. Thousands were executed and then pushed into mass graves with bulldozers. Reports suggest some were buried alive and in a number of instances adults were forced to watch their children being killed.[55] The Dutch peacekeepers handed over to the Serb forces under the command of General Ratko Mladic 350 men who had sought refuge in the UN compound.[56] All, it appears, were later killed. The issue arose as to whether, at the salient times, the Dutch military contingent – Dutchbat – was acting as an organ of the Netherlands or the United Nations.

[50] Commentary para. 10 and footnote 115 on Draft Article 7, 2011 Draft Articles. One of the papers cited is the thoughtful piece by Marko Milanovic and Tatjana Papic: 'As Bad as It Gets: The European Court of Human Rights' Behrami and Saramati Decision and General International Law', *International and Comparative Law Quarterly*, vol. 58, no. 2 (April 2009), pp. 267–96.
[51] Commentary para. 5 on Chapter II: Attribution of conduct to an international organization, 2011 Draft Articles.
[52] Commentary para. 1 on Draft Article 7, 2011 Draft Articles.
[53] Commentary para. 6 on Draft Article 7, 2011 Draft Articles.
[54] Art. 48(1), 2011 Draft Articles on the Responsibility of International Organisations.
[55] BBC, 'Srebrenica: Bosnia Marks 25 Years since Massacre', 11 July 2020, at http://bbc.in/32kbN3H.
[56] BBC, 'Srebrenica Massacre: Dutch State "10% Liable" for 350 Deaths', 19 July 2019, at http://bbc.in/35pbpTq.

33.25 In its 2013 judgment in the *Nuhanović* case,[57] the Supreme Court of the Netherlands adjudged Dutchbat to be neither an organ of the UN nor of the Netherlands though it endorsed the concept advocated in the 2011 Draft Articles whereby conduct could be attributed to both.[58] Instead, the Court attributed the battalion's conduct to the Netherlands because it exercised effective control over the specific acts at the heart of the dispute. These centred on the refusal to allow the relatives of the plaintiff, an interpreter for Dutchbat, to stay in the compound protected by Dutchbat. Mr Nuhanović's brother and father were both murdered by Serb forces at Srebrenica after they were expelled from the compound.

33.26 In the later *Mothers of Srebrenica* case,[59] the Supreme Court based its judgment on Article 7 of the 2011 Draft Articles and its analysis of the notion of 'effective control'. It also referred in that regard to the 1986 judgment of the International Court of Justice in the *Nicaragua* case,[60] although that case concerned effective control by a State over an ostensibly non-State armed group, the Contras, not forces ostensibly acting on behalf of an international organisation. The Supreme Court distinguished its earlier judgment in the *Nuhanović* case on the basis that the conduct in question occurred after the enclave had been overrun. But it concluded that 'in the period starting from 23:00 on 11 July 1995, after Srebrenica had been conquered and after it was decided to evacuate the Bosnian Muslims who had fled to the mini safe area, the State did have effective control of Dutchbat's conduct'. It therefore attributed responsibility for this conduct to the State.[61]

33.27 Having attributed the conduct of Dutchbat in question to the Netherlands, the Supreme Court then proceeded to determine the State's responsibility for a failure to protect the right to life under Article 2 of the European Convention on Human Rights.[62] Specifically, the decision to hand over the 350 boys and men seeking refuge in the Dutchbat compound was the basis for an internationally wrongful act: a violation of the right to life. The separation of boys and men deemed to be of military age from the remainder of the Bosnian Muslim population was not held to have violated the right to life. The Court reached this decision in part on the basis of the judgment of the European Court of Human Rights in the *Finogenov* case,[63] wherein it had accorded a margin of

---

[57] Supreme Court of the Netherlands, *Nuhanović v. The Netherlands*, Judgment (Case ECLI:NL:HR:2013: BZ9225), 6 September 2013. An English translation of the judgment is available at http://bit.ly/3bOYgnL.

[58] A. Nollkaemper, 'Dual Attribution: Liability of the Netherlands for Conduct of Dutchbat in Srebrenica', Amsterdam Law School Research Paper No. 2011-29, posted online 26 September 2011; see also International Crimes Database, 'The State of the Netherlands v. Hasan Nuhanović', TMC Asser Institute, The Netherlands, 2013, at http://bit.ly/2GSlheb.

[59] Supreme Court of the Netherlands, *Mothers of Srebrenica Association and others v. The Netherlands*, Judgment (Case No. ECLI:NL:HR:2019:1223), 19 July 2019. An English translation of the judgment is available at http://bit.ly/2FdtSb1.

[60] International Court of Justice, *Military and Paramilitary Activities in and against Nicaragua (Nicaragua v. United States)*, Judgment (Merits), 27 June 1986, para. 115.

[61] Supreme Court of the Netherlands, *Mothers of Srebrenica Association and others v. The Netherlands*, Judgment, para. 5.1.

[62] European Convention for the Protection of Human Rights and Fundamental Freedoms; adopted and opened for signature at Strasbourg, 4 November 1950; entered into force 3 September 1953.

[63] Supreme Court of the Netherlands, *Mothers of Srebrenica Association and others v. The Netherlands*, Judgment, para. 5.21.

appreciation to Russia for its military operation against a group of terrorists who were holding upwards of one thousand people hostage in a theatre in Moscow. The European Court had stated that it would accord such a margin to the State, 'even if now, with hindsight, some of the decisions taken by the authorities may appear open to doubt'.[64]

33.28 Based on its analysis of case-law in the European Court of Human Rights, the Supreme Court of the Netherlands concluded:

> From the matters discussed above regarding the State's obligations under the ECHR, I am of the opinion that it can be concluded that in the event that the State knows or ought to know that there is a real risk, as a result of the conduct of third parties, of death or inhumane treatment of certain individuals or groups of people over whom the State has legal authority or for whom the State has an obligation of care ..., the State has an obligation to take all reasonable measures to avoid that risk to the extent possible. That obligation also exists in situations of armed conflict in which peacekeeping troops have been deployed by the State.[65]

33.29 The Dutch Supreme Court concluded that 'the prospects of the male refugees were very bleak, even if they were to remain in the compound'. The Court assumed that the Bosnian Serbs, after discovering that some 350 male refugees had stayed behind in the compound, 'probably would have done everything within their power to remove the men from the compound or to have them removed'. But the Court could not completely rule out 'that if Dutchbat had been able to withstand the threat of violence, the Bosnian Serbs would not have been willing to risk attacking the compound in order to deport the male refugees'. 'All in all', the Court said, 'it must be ruled that the chance that the male refugees, had they been offered the choice of remaining in the compound, could have escaped the Bosnian Serbs, was indeed small, but not negligible. In view of all of the circumstances, the Supreme Court estimates that chance at 10%'.[66] As a consequence, damages awarded to the plaintiffs were '10% of the damages suffered by the surviving relatives of approximately 350 victims'.[67]

ADHERENCE BY INTERNATIONAL ORGANISATIONS TO TREATIES

33.30 While many international organisations are themselves created by treaty, such organisations may also formally adhere to treaties where the relevant instrument provides

---

[64] European Court of Human Rights, *Finogenov and others v. Russia*, Judgment, 20 December 2011 (as rectified and then rendered final on 4 June 2012), para. 213.
[65] Supreme Court of the Netherlands, *Mothers of Srebrenica Association and others v. The Netherlands*, Judgment, para. 5.24.
[66] Supreme Court of the Netherlands, *Mothers of Srebrenica Association and others v. The Netherlands*, Judgment, para. 4.7.9.
[67] Agence France-Presse, 'Dutch Court Reduces State Liability for Srebrenica Massacre', *The Guardian*, 19 July 2019, at http://bit.ly/3hnVeIl; and see generally on the case, C. Ryngaert and O. Spijkers, 'The End of the Road: State Liability for Acts of UN Peacekeeping Contingents after the Dutch Supreme Court's Judgment in Mothers of Srebrenica', *Netherlands International Law Review*, vol. 66 (2019), pp. 537–53.

for this possibility. Thus, for example, the EU is a party to the 1988 UN Convention against Illicit Traffic in Narcotic Drugs.[68]

Adherence by the European Union to Human Rights Treaties

33.31 With respect to global human rights treaties, the EU is party to the 2006 Convention on the Rights of Persons with Disabilities (CRPD).[69] To date, the EU is the only 'regional integration organization' to have become party to a global human rights treaty. Under Article 10 of the CRPD, 'States Parties reaffirm that every human being has the inherent right to life and shall take all necessary measures to ensure its effective enjoyment by persons with disabilities on an equal basis with others.' In its declaration upon adherence to the Convention, the EU declared: 'The European Community notes that for the purpose of the Convention, the term "State[s] Parties" applies to regional integration organisations within the limits of their competence.'[70]

33.32 In addition, consonant with the 2007 Lisbon Treaty,[71] the Union is obligated to become a party to the European Convention on Human Rights.[72] It has not yet done so. On 15 January 2020, the work of a Steering Committee for Human Rights was tasked to 'finalise as a matter of priority' the legal instruments 'setting out the modalities' of EU accession to the Convention, 'including its participation in the Convention system'.[73]

33.33 Theoretically, it might even be possible for the EU to be bound by a human rights (or other) treaty, even where the possibility of adherence is not foreseen in the treaty itself. A formal declaration that it would comply with a treaty as a matter of law might be deemed a binding unilateral declaration, akin to the International Court of Justice's holding in 1974 in the *Nuclear Tests* case.[74]

EU Military Operations and the Right to Life

33.34 A number of EU operations have the mandate or potential to use force and thus potentially to violate the right to life. Operation Althea is the EU's military contribution to

---

[68] United Nations Convention against Illicit Traffic in Narcotic Drugs and Psychotropic Substances; adopted at Vienna 20 December 1988; entered into force 11 November 1990.
[69] Convention on the Rights of Persons with Disabilities; adopted at New York 13 December 2006; entered into force 3 May 2008. Articles 42–4 of the CRPD govern the adherence to the treaty of a 'regional integration organization'.
[70] Declaration of EU, at http://bit.ly/32cBWkV.
[71] The accession of the European Union to the ECHR is obligated by Article 6(2) of the Treaty of Lisbon: 'The Union shall accede to the European Convention for the Protection of Human Rights and Fundamental Freedoms.' Treaty on the Functioning of the European Union; adopted at Lisbon 13 December 2007; entered into force on 1 December 2009.
[72] The legal basis for the accession of the EU to the ECHR is provided for by Article 59(2) of the 1950 Convention ('the European Union may accede to this Convention'), as amended by Protocol No. 14 to the ECHR, which entered into force on 1 June 2010.
[73] Council of Europe, 'EU Accession to the ECHR', 2020, at http://bit.ly/2HI13kz.
[74] International Court of Justice, *Nuclear Tests* (*Australia v. France*; *New Zealand v. France*), Judgments of 20 December 1974, *ICJ Reports* 1974, pp. 267–8, paras. 43 and 46; and pp. 472–3, paras. 46 and 49.

the 'stabilisation and integration' of Bosnia and Herzegovina into 'the European Family of Nations'. Operation Althea was launched on 2 December 2004, nine years after the war in Bosnia and Herzegovina ended. This followed the decision by NATO to hand over its own peacekeeping mission that had been responsible for the maintenance of security in the region since the end of the armed conflicts in 1995. The EU deployed a 'robust' military force (EUFOR) of almost seven thousand troops to ensure continued compliance with the Dayton Peace Agreement and to contribute to a 'safe and secure environment' in the country.[75] Today, a total of twenty nations, including EU Member States and non-EU Troop Contributing Countries (TCCs), contribute to a far smaller EUFOR.[76]

33.35 At sea, the EU Naval Force Operation Atalanta (EU NAVFOR), the EU's first maritime operation, has operated since 2008 with a view to preventing piracy off the coast of Somalia. EU NAVFOR operates within the framework of the European Common Security and Defence Policy and relevant UN Security Council resolutions.[77] Its operations involve the use of force against suspected pirates: 'the necessary measures, including use of force, in order to deter, prevent and interfere, so that acts of piracy and armed robbery may be ended'.[78]

33.36 Use of force in counterpiracy is governed by the rules of law enforcement. Thus a violation of the right to life would occur should potentially lethal force be used other than where necessary to confront an imminent threat of death or serious injury or a grave but proximate threat to life. Based on maritime law, a failure to save the life of suspected pirates whose skiff was sinking in the high seas could also constitute a violation of the right to life: specifically the duty to protect life.

33.37 On 30 July 2018, the Council of the EU extended the Mandate of Operation Atalanta until December 2020.[79] It was subsequently extended until the end of 2022.

VIOLATIONS OF THE RIGHT TO LIFE CONSTITUTING INTERNATIONALLY WRONGFUL ACTS

33.38 A range of conduct will violate the right to life and thereby constitute an internationally wrongful act. Examples include the most flagrant instances of arbitrary deprivation of life: deliberate extrajudicial executions and other arbitrary killings by agents of an international organisation that often uses force, such as by NATO in its operations, or by UN Police or a UN peacekeeping operation. This is so whether the killings occur in peacetime or during and in connection with a situation of armed conflict.

---

[75] EU, 'About EUFOR', 24 February 2020, at http://bit.ly/2DHktaH.
[76] Albania, Austria, Bulgaria, Chile, Czechia, France, Greece, Hungary, Ireland, Italy, North Macedonia, Poland, Portugal, Romania, Slovakia, Slovenia, Spain, Switzerland, Turkey, and the United Kingdom.
[77] See on this issue E. Papastavridis, 'EUNAVFOR Operation Atalanta Off Somalia: The EU in Unchartered Legal Waters?', *International and Comparative Law Quarterly*, vol. 64, no. 3 (July 2015), pp. 533–68.
[78] 'European Union Naval Force Operation ATALANTA (EU NAVFOR ATALANTA) in the Indian Ocean and the Gulf of Aden', at http://bit.ly/3hb54wX.
[79] EU NAVFOR, 'Operation ATALANTA', 2020, at http://bit.ly/2R77jH1.

33.39 In that regard, a violation of an international humanitarian law rule, such as the principle of distinction and proportionality in attack, will also amount to arbitrary deprivation of life where it results in death (or was likely or intended to do so) and is therefore constitutive of a violation of the right to life. Cases in which UN peacekeepers are a party to an armed conflict are rare, but they do occur – the most obvious example being the Intervention Brigade within the UN Stabilization Mission in the Democratic Republic of the Congo (MONUSCO).[80] The Brigade was tasked by the UN Security Council with 'neutralising' armed groups in the Democratic Republic of Congo,[81] which transformed not only the Brigade but also potentially the entire UN peacekeeping operation, into a party to the non-international armed conflicts between the Congolese State and a number of non-State armed groups.

33.40 As noted previously, the failure to provide adequate food and water to a person detained by an international organisation or to ensure the provision of appropriate medical care where needed may also amount to arbitrary deprivation of life. This is so, either where the detainee perishes or where he or she suffers life-threatening or life-changing conditions as a result of those failures. The negligent transmission of a deadly disease by UN personnel, including UN peacekeepers, is also violative of the right to life. This occurred in Haiti, as Chapter 17 described.

33.41 With respect to the prohibition on enforced disappearance – also a jus cogens norm – the Human Rights Committee has observed that the deprivation of liberty, followed by a refusal to acknowledge that deprivation of liberty or by concealment of the fate of the disappeared person, in effect removes that person from the protection of the law and places his or her life at serious and constant risk. Such conduct 'results in a violation of the right to life as well as other rights recognized in the Covenant',[82] making an enforced disappearance an internationally wrongful act on a number of grounds. This rule binds an international organisation in the same way as it does a State.

33.42 Both in the case of enforced disappearance and more generally, a violation of the procedural element of the right to life – the duty to investigate potentially unlawful death[83] – is also an internationally wrongful act. With respect to an international organisation, however, the duty to investigate would pertain primarily to instances where the involvement of the organisation in the death was suspected or alleged. In a peacekeeping situation, however, where the relevant organisation was tasked with the protection of civilians, an

---

[80] MONUSCO replaced MONUC in 2010.

[81] UN Security Council Resolution 2098 (2013), adopted by unanimous vote on 28 March 2013, operative para. 9. The Brigade was authorised to consist of 'three infantry battalions, one artillery and one Special force and Reconnaissance company with headquarters in Goma, under direct command of the MONUSCO Force Commander'.

[82] Human Rights Committee, General Comment No. 36: Article 6: right to life, UN doc. CCPR/C/GC/36, 3 September 2019, para. 58.

[83] See *Minnesota Protocol on the Investigation of Potentially Unlawful Death* (2016), The Revised United Nations Manual on the Effective Prevention and Investigation of Extra-legal, Arbitrary and Summary Executions, Office of the UN High Commissioner for Human Rights, New York/Geneva, 2017, paras. 2, 8 (c), 9, 15–21.

apparent failure to protect civilians in a situation where the organisation could reasonably have intervened would also demand that a thorough investigation be carried out. Thus, although the Minnesota Protocol on the Investigation of Potentially Unlawful Death (2016) is focused on the obligations of States, the Protocol 'is also relevant to cases where the United Nations ... have a responsibility to respect the right to life and to remedy any abuses they cause or to which they contribute'.[84]

33.43 In late November 2019, protests against MONUSCO's failure to protect civilians from rebel attacks entered a second day in Beni, North Kivu province. At least two people were killed as security forces engaged in running street battles with protesters. In the cities of Butembo and Goma, demonstrators attempted to find their way to a UN base near the airport before being repulsed by government soldiers.[85] On 27 November 2019, the UN announced that it would open an investigation into the death of one of the demonstrators, which may have occurred at the hands of a peacekeeper.[86]

33.44 As the Minnesota Protocol recalls, international law requires that investigations be prompt, effective, thorough, independent, impartial, and transparent.[87] This dictates that the relevant organisation must conduct an investigation as soon as possible and proceed without unreasonable delay.[88]

33.45 To meet the requirements of effectiveness and thoroughness, investigators should, to the extent possible, collect and confirm all testimonial, documentary, and physical evidence. Investigations must be capable of ensuring accountability for unlawful death, leading to the identification and, if justified by the evidence and seriousness of the case, the prosecution and punishment of all those responsible.[89] Investigations must also, at a minimum, take all reasonable steps to identify the victim or victims; recover and preserve all material probative of the cause of death, the identity of the perpetrator(s), and the circumstances surrounding the death; identify possible witnesses and obtain their evidence in relation to the death and the circumstances surrounding the death; and determine the cause, manner, place, and time of death, along with all the surrounding circumstances.[90]

33.46 In determining the manner of death, the investigation should distinguish between natural death, accidental death, suicide, and homicide. It should also seek to determine who was involved in the death and their individual responsibility for the death. An autopsy is, as a general rule, required. In cases of enforced disappearance, an investigation must

---

[84] Ibid., para. 5.
[85] J Tasamba, 'DR Congo: 2 Killed in Protests against UN Peacekeepers. Security Forces Engage in Running Street Battles with Protesters in Second Day of Unrest in Beni', *Anadolu Agency*, 27 November 2019, at http://bit.ly/33MiCbw.
[86] BBC, 'DR Congo Protests: UN to Open Investigation into Demonstrator's Death', 27 November 2019, at http://bbc.in/35VEJhl.
[87] *Minnesota Protocol on the Investigation of Potentially Unlawful Death* (2016), para. 22.
[88] Ibid., para. 23.
[89] Ibid., para. 24.
[90] Ibid., para. 25.

seek to determine the fate of the disappeared and, if applicable, the location of their remains.[91]

33.47 The investigation must further determine whether a violation of the right to life has occurred. Investigations must seek to identify not only direct perpetrators but also all others who were responsible for the death, including officials in the chain of command who were complicit in the death.[92]

33.48 Investigators and investigative mechanisms must be independent of undue influence. They must be independent institutionally and formally, as well as in practice and perception, at all stages. Investigations must be independent of any suspected perpetrators and the units, institutions, or agencies to which they belong. Investigations of law enforcement killings, for example, must be capable of being carried out free from undue influence that may arise from institutional hierarchies and chains of command. Inquiries into serious human rights violations, such as extrajudicial executions and torture, must be conducted under the jurisdiction of ordinary civilian courts.[93] Investigators must be impartial and must act at all times without bias. They must analyse all evidence objectively. They must consider and appropriately pursue exculpatory as well as inculpatory evidence.[94]

33.49 Finally, investigative processes and outcomes must be transparent, including through openness to the scrutiny of the general public and of victims' families.[95] Any limitations on transparency must be strictly necessary for a legitimate purpose: protecting the privacy and safety of affected individuals, ensuring the integrity of ongoing investigations, or securing sensitive information about intelligence sources or military or police operations. In no circumstances may the international organisation in question restrict transparency in a way that would conceal the fate or whereabouts of any victim of an enforced disappearance or unlawful killing or result in impunity for those responsible.[96]

33.50 In fact, the United Nations did not appear to have undertaken a detailed investigation either into the death of the demonstrator (which had reportedly occurred at the hands of a UN peacekeeper) or into its broader failure to protect civilians. It did, however, conduct an 'independent assessment' of 'the high number of attacks against civilians allegedly committed by the Allied Democratic Forces (ADF) in Beni territory, North Kivu Province, and attacks against the Ebola response in Mambasa territory in Ituri Province'. On 9 December 2019, the UN Under-Secretary-General for Peace Operations asked Lieutenant-General Carlos Alberto Dos Santos Cruz to lead an assessment of the circumstances leading to the attacks; the ability of MONUSCO to effectively implement the Mission's mandate to ensure the protection of civilians under threat of physical violence and to neutralise armed groups in the Beni area, as well as provide a secure

---

[91] Ibid.
[92] Ibid., para. 26.
[93] Ibid., para. 28.
[94] Ibid., para. 31.
[95] Ibid., para. 32.
[96] Ibid., para. 33.

environment for the Ebola response; and to make practical recommendations on how to enhance the Force's performance. The scope of the assessment was limited to events between 30 October and 31 December 2019.[97]

33.51 The assessment found that in the months of November and December alone, more than 260 civilians, mainly women and children, were killed by presumed ADF combatants in brutal attacks, mostly at night. The high number of civilian casualties was one of the main triggers of violent demonstrations against MONUSCO in North Kivu, including the destruction and looting of a MONUSCO Office in Beni on 25 November 2019. The attacks against civilians occurred against the backdrop of a major offensive that the Congolese Army launched against the ADF on 30 October 2019.[98]

33.52 The assessment concluded that protecting civilians in Beni territory requires a 'comprehensive response', involving all components of MONUSCO and the UN Country Team, as well as external partners. The team recommended that MONUSCO, UN Headquarters, and troop-contributing countries 'coordinate their actions to improve the mindset, capabilities and mobility of the MONUSCO Force Intervention Brigade to better address the unconventional threat posed by the ADF, in a particularly challenging environment'. The assessment noted that strengthened cooperation between MONUSCO and the DRC Army and Police is critical to sustaining the gains made by the Congolese Army during this latest offensive against the ADF. It further recommended the development of a comprehensive, joint strategy between the government and MONUSCO, including at the political level, to counter the ADF and sustainably address insecurity in the Beni area. The Department of Peace Operations was said to be developing an Action Plan 'to implement the key recommendations of the assessment'.[99]

33.53 In early September 2020, an article in *The Economist* described an interview with one of the individuals who took part in burning down the MONUSCO offices in Beni. 'We have suffered years of massacres', he told the journalist. 'We see UN soldiers all over town, but when the rebels are killing us they never come."[100] Moreover, dozens of women in the east of the country have alleged that they were raped by UN peacekeepers. This demands an independent investigation consonant with the customary law duty to investigate under the prohibition of torture and other forms of cruel, inhuman, or degrading treatment. The article in *The Economist* noted that a report commissioned by the UN Security Council in 2019 had recommended that MONUSCO pack up and leave by 2022, on the basis that it is too expensive and that it has been there for too long.[101]

---

[97] UN, 'Independent Assessment of MONUSCO'S Response to Recent Attacks against Civilians in Béni Area, DRC', MONUSCO, 22 January 2020, at http://bit.ly/33lurYg.
[98] Ibid.
[99] Ibid.
[100] 'All Helmet and No Mettle: The UN's Peacekeepers Are Under Pressure to Quit Congo', *The Economist*, 3 September 2020, at http://econ.st/3bWq4Xy.
[101] Ibid.

34

Corporate Responsibility and the Right to Life

INTRODUCTION

34.01 This chapter addresses the responsibility of certain 'legal persons' under international law for violations of the right to life. It assesses the extent to which a private corporation has obligations under international law to respect, protect, and fulfil the right to life of individuals within its sphere of influence. As is the case with non-State armed groups, obligations may be imposed by treaty or under customary law. State responsibility for the internationally wrongful acts of a corporation that acts as a State agent, on the basis that it is 'acting on the instructions of, or under the direction or control of, that State in carrying out the conduct',[1] was considered in Chapter 32 and will not be addressed further herein. This chapter concerns only the responsibility of a private corporation, acting as such.

34.02 The traditional view holds that, under international law, companies of any size have no legal duty to respect, much less to protect or fulfil human rights, including the right to life. Those duties are, so the argument goes, the exclusive domain of the sovereign, by which is meant the State and its organs.[2] When understood as such, corporations do not violate human rights, they 'abuse' them. This restrictive notion of international human rights law is, however, being challenged in recent decades by the United Nations and by leading publicists, as well as by jurisprudence in an increasing number of States.

34.03 It is generally accepted that bodies corporate are, at the least, partial subjects of international law and enjoy a measure of international legal personality when they are party to an armed conflict, as that notion is understood by international humanitarian law. It is further unquestioned that the members of a private corporation may be held individually responsible under international criminal law for international crimes they have committed in the course of their work. This was made clear in judgments in a series of

---

[1] Art. 8, Draft articles on Responsibility of States for Internationally Wrongful Acts, with commentaries, 2001; Text adopted by the International Law Commission (ILC) at its fifty-third session, in 2001, and submitted to the UN General Assembly as a part of the Commission's report covering the work of that session, in UN doc. A/56/10, at http://bit.ly/32A3ocT (hereinafter, Draft Articles on State Responsibility).

[2] See, e.g., N. S. Rodley, 'Can Armed Opposition Groups Violate Human Rights?', in K. Mahoney and P. Mahoney (eds.), *Human Rights in the Twenty-First Century*, Martinus Nijhoff, Dordrecht, 1993, pp. 297–318.

trials in the 'Trials of War Criminals before the Nuremberg Military Tribunals' that followed the end of the Second World War. The question arises as to whether, and, if so, by what legal means corporations *qua* bodies corporate and their members are also bound directly by international human rights law.

34.04 The chapter continues by defining the various terms 'corporation', 'company', 'legal person', and 'body corporate'. It then discusses in which circumstances such bodies may become subjects of international law as a party to an armed conflict, and later in other circumstances, first under treaty in the realm of European competition law and then under international human rights law. Finally, the chapter considers which obligations within the right to life are binding upon a corporation and therefore which conduct forming part of the right to life may amount to an internationally wrongful act.

Definitions of Key Terms

34.05 A corporation is not the same as a company. In the United States, for instance, a company is a broader term encompassing 'any entity that engages in business', which can be a proprietorship, a partnership, or a corporation.[3] A corporation is a business entity that legally exists separately from its owners. The owners of a corporation are the shareholders; their percentage of ownership in the business is represented by their shares. Shareholders can choose a board of directors to manage business operations, or they can create a shareholders' agreement, which allows them to manage the business directly.[4] Size is a potentially distinguishing factor: corporations tend to be larger, and thus, although companies can also be owned by shareholders, there are generally fewer such individuals.[5]

34.06 Under international treaty law, the term 'legal person' tends to be used to refer to companies and other undertakings. Thus, for example, under the 1992 Chemical Weapons Convention, each State Party is obligated to 'prohibit natural *and legal persons* anywhere on its territory or in any other place under its jurisdiction as recognized by international law from undertaking any activity prohibited to a State Party under this Convention, including enacting penal legislation with respect to such activity'.[6] Accordingly, in its implementing legislation for the Convention (the 1996 Chemical Weapons Act), the United Kingdom stipulates: 'So far as it applies to acts done outside the United Kingdom, section 2 [on prohibited acts] applies to United Kingdom nationals, *Scottish partnerships, and bodies incorporated* under the law of any part of the United Kingdom.'[7]

---

[3] A. Measures, 'The Difference between a Corporation and a Company', *Chron*, last updated 6 February 2019, at http://bit.ly/35fphxI.
[4] Ibid.
[5] P. Taylor, 'What's the Difference between a Corporation and a Company?', Lawpath blog, 30 July 2019, at http://bit.ly/37loIp4. Companies can also be shareholders in other companies, of course.
[6] Art. VII(1)(a), Convention on the Prohibition of the Development, Production, Stockpiling and Use of Chemical Weapons and on their Destruction; adopted at Geneva 3 September 1992; entered into force 29 April 1997 (added emphasis).
[7] S. 2, 1996 Chemical Weapons Act (added emphasis).

34.07 In domestic law, especially among certain common law States, however, the term 'body corporate' is also often used to denote a legal person.[8] Thus, for instance, in its implementing legislation for the 2017 Treaty on the Prohibition of Nuclear Weapons, Ireland provides:

> Where an offence under this Act is committed by a body corporate and it is proved that the offence was committed with the consent or connivance, or was attributable to any wilful neglect, of a person who was a director, manager, secretary or other officer of the body corporate, or a person purporting to act in that capacity, that person shall, as well as the body corporate, be guilty of an offence and may be liable to be proceeded against and punished as if he or she were guilty of the first-mentioned offence.[9]

The legislation determines that while an offence may be committed by a corporation, only in certain circumstances will the individuals running the company, or in a decision-making position related to the offence, be held responsible in criminal law.

34.08 For the purpose of this chapter, the term 'private corporation' will be generally employed henceforward. A State may of course own, wholly or in part, a corporation. When this is the case, the corporation will not be, or is unlikely to be, acting in a private capacity, but rather as an agent of the State. In addition, the term 'private international law' is sometimes used. This nomenclature describes the 'conflict of laws' governing individuals and corporations operating internationally. The descriptor 'private international law' may be considered something of a misnomer, as this body of law does not concern rules on the international plane, but rather the choice of which *domestic* law to apply and which court has jurisdiction, along with the issues of recognition and enforcement of foreign judgments.[10]

ARE PRIVATE CORPORATIONS SUBJECTS OF INTERNATIONAL LAW?

The Application of International Humanitarian and Criminal Law

34.09 In its 2004 decision on jurisdiction in the *Sam Hinga Norman* case, the Appeals Chamber of the Special Court for Sierra Leone held that 'it is well settled that all parties to an armed conflict, whether states or non-state actors, are bound by international humanitarian law, even though only states may become parties to international treaties'.[11] Although non-State armed groups are manifestly the primary focus of this holding,[12]

---

[8] It is also used in a different sense domestically in a number of countries, such as Australia, to denote a legal body that holds properties. See, e.g., C. Irons, 'What Is a Body Corporate?', Haynes Legal, at http://bit.ly/2FMxaCh.
[9] S. 6(1), Prohibition of Nuclear Weapons Act 2019, Act No. 40 of 2019.
[10] H. Swift, 'An Introduction to Legal Research in Private International Law', Private International Law: IALS (Institute for Advanced Legal Studies) Library Guides, July 2019, at http://bit.ly/34jOKHn.
[11] Special Court for Sierra Leone, *Prosecutor v. Sam Hinga Norman*, Decision on Preliminary Motion Based on Lack of Jurisdiction (Appeals Chamber; Case No. SCSL-2004-14-AR72(E)), 31 May 2004, para. 22.
[12] See further Chapter 35 on how it is argued that non-State parties to an armed conflict are bound by international humanitarian law.

a corporation can also similarly be an object of international law and bound by international humanitarian law. While the most obvious case of this would be a private military company, there is no reason why another form of corporation could not also become a party to an armed conflict by virtue of the conduct of a preponderance of its members in the course of their work.

34.10 As its name suggests, the Montreux Document 'On Pertinent International Legal Obligations and Good Practices for States Related to Operations of Private Military and Security Companies during Armed Conflict'[13] addresses the responsibility of States rather than imposing obligations directly upon private military and security companies (PMSCs).[14] In this regard, the Montreux Document, elaborated in 2008, recalls that 'Contracting States' to the Document are obligated to ensure respect for IHL by PMSCs they contract. This includes a duty to 'take measures to suppress violations' of IHL committed by the personnel of PMSCs 'through appropriate means'.[15] That said, the Document also affirms that 'PMSCs are obliged to comply with international humanitarian law'[16] and that PMSC personnel 'are subject to prosecution if they commit conduct recognized as crimes under applicable national or international law'.[17]

34.11 There is thus consequent criminal liability when an official in a private corporation engages in conduct that amounts to a war crime. In the Trials of War Criminals before the Nuremberg Military Tribunals, a number of leading officials within German corporations were put on trial for a range of international crimes, including war crimes. In its 1948 judgment in the I. G. Farben trial, which concerned among other things the production and supply of Zyklon B used by the Nazis in the Holocaust, the Tribunal reiterated earlier jurisprudence whereby 'it can no longer be questioned that the criminal sanctions of international law are applicable to private individuals'.[18] The imposition of such criminal sanctions occurred by virtue of customary law.

---

[13] International Committee of the Red Cross (ICRC), *Montreux Document: On Pertinent International Legal Obligations and Good Practices for States Related to Operations of Private Military and Security Companies during Armed Conflict*, Geneva, 2009, available at http://bit.ly/3m74PpQ.

[14] PMSCs are defined in the Montreux Document as 'private business entities that provide military and/or security services, irrespective of how they describe themselves. Military and security services include, in particular, armed guarding and protection of persons and objects, such as convoys, buildings and other places; maintenance and operation of weapons systems; prisoner detention; and advice to or training of local forces and security personnel'. Ibid., preface, para. 9(a). Under the International Code of Conduct for Private Security Service Providers, the Signatory Companies to the Code endorse the principles of the Montreux Document and the 'Respect, Protect, Remedy' framework as they apply to such providers, thereby committing to the responsible provision of security services 'so as to support the rule of law, respect the human rights of all persons, and protect the interests of their clients'. International Code of Conduct Association, 'The Code: The International Code of Conduct for Private Security Service Providers', at http://bit.ly/3kiOpds. These commitments, while serious in nature, are not obligations contracted on the international legal plane.

[15] Montreux Document, Part One: Pertinent international legal obligations relating to private military and security companies, para. 3(c).

[16] Montreux Document, Part One, para. 22.

[17] Ibid., para. 26(e).

[18] *Law Reports of Trials of War Criminals*, Vol X: The I. G. Farben and Krupp Trials, Published for the United Nations War Crimes Commission, His Majesty's Stationery Office, London, 1949, available at http://bit.ly/348kEpU, p. 47.

34.12 The cases concerned the actions of an I. G. Farben subsidiary, Degesch, which had manufactured Zyklon B.[19] The chemical agent had been widely used as an insecticide long before the war and continued to be so used during the Second World War itself, a fact that the defendants used with a view to evading a finding of criminal culpability. While the Tribunal held that certain charges against the company officials were not proven, it did decide that, with respect to Auschwitz Birkenau, 'Farben had through its officials displayed initiative in the procurement and utilisation of prisoners of war, forced labour and concentration camp inmates, fully aware of the sufferings to which they were exposed.'[20] According to the Court, the evidence established that this and related undertakings 'were wholly private projects operated by Farben, with considerable freedom and opportunity for initiative on the part of Farben. There was no matter of compulsion, although the projects were favoured by the Reich authorities.'[21] Thus the company had acted as a private actor, a status that did not preclude its officials from being held criminally culpable.

The Application of International Obligations by Treaty: The Case of European Competition Law

34.13 Corporations may be bound by treaty law even though they are not party to them. Outside the realm of armed conflict and within the confines of international law governing competition on commercial markets – in which companies are a central concern – private corporations are also directly bound by international treaty law. Under the Treaty on European Union (a revised treaty that was more popularly known as the Maastricht Treaty), it was specified that the Union 'shall establish an internal market. It shall work for the sustainable development of Europe based on ... a highly competitive social market economy.'[22] European competition law, which aims to ensure that competition in the internal market is not 'distorted', is incorporated, in particular, in the Treaty on the Functioning of the European Union (TFEU).[23]

34.14 Two provisions of the TFEU are especially important in this regard. Under Article 101, 'the following shall be prohibited as incompatible with the internal market: all agreements between undertakings[24] ... which have as their object or effect the prevention, restriction or distortion of competition within the internal market, and in particular those which ... directly or indirectly fix purchase or selling prices or any other trading conditions'.[25] This pertains to a cartel – the 'supreme evil of antitrust',[26] in the words of

---

[19] 'Phillips Nuremberg Trials Collection: Trial 6 – I. G. Farben Case', School of Law, University of Georgia, last updated 8 September 2020, at http://bit.ly/3o8H16u.
[20] *Law Reports of Trials of War Criminals*, Vol X: The I. G. Farben and Krupp Trials, p. 27.
[21] Ibid.
[22] Art. 3(3), Treaty on European Union; adopted at Maastricht 12 December 1991; entered into force 1 November 1993.
[23] Treaty on the Functioning of the European Union; adopted at Lisbon 13 December 2007; entered into force 1 December 2009.
[24] An undertaking primarily pertains to companies but also encompasses non-profit entities.
[25] Art. 101(1)(a), TFEU.
[26] In the United States, competition law is known as 'antitrust'. Today the term is also used in Europe.

the US Supreme Court.[27] A cartel is where companies operating in the same horizontal market secretly agree not to compete with each other but to set higher prices than would otherwise be the case as a result of market competition, to the obvious detriment of the consumer.[28] The European Commission has the power to impose fines directly upon a company engaged in a cartel that may attain 10 per cent of annual global turnover.[29]

34.15 The second main violation of European competition law concerns the abuse of a dominant position in the internal market. Under Article 102 of the TFEU, 'any abuse by one or more undertakings of a dominant position within the internal market or in a substantial part of it shall be prohibited as incompatible with the internal market in so far as it may affect trade between Member States'.[30] Again, the European Commission has the power to impose fines directly upon a company engaged in such abusive behaviour that may attain 10 per cent of annual global turnover.[31]

34.16 In both instances, companies are, in effect, bound directly by the rules set out in the TFEU. As Richard Whish and David Bailey explain, 'Articles 101 and 102 are essentially private law provisions, conferring rights and imposing obligations on undertakings; many other articles in the TFEU are primarily of a public law nature, imposing obligations on Member States.'[32] Moreover, private corporations of significant size are directly answerable to the European Commission Directorate-General for Competition for their actions[33] (and to the Court of Justice of the European Union, should they chose to appeal against a decision of the Directorate-General). This international legal regulation does not occur merely by means of the domestic incorporation of the TFEU by a member State of the European Union.[34]

34.17 The language used in Articles 101 and 102 of the TFEU recalls that employed in the 1977 Additional Protocol II to the 1949 Geneva Conventions, whereby 'the following acts against [all persons who do not take a direct part or who have ceased to take part in hostilities] are and shall remain prohibited at any time and in any place whatsoever'.[35] The

---

[27] US Supreme Court, *Verizon Communications* v. *Law Offices of Curtis V. Trinko*, 540 US 398, 408 (2004).
[28] The problem is a long-standing one. In his great work of 1776, *An Inquiry into the Nature and Causes of the Wealth of Nations*, Adam Smith already recognised the problem, observing: 'People of the same trade seldom meet together, even for merriment and diversion, but the conversation ends in a conspiracy against the public, or in some contrivance to raise prices.'
[29] Art. 23(2)(a), Council Regulation (EC) No 1/2003 of 16 December 2002 on the implementation of the rules on competition laid down in Articles 81 and 82 of the Treaty, at http://bit.ly/2H62fSd.
[30] A dominant position is considered to be one where the 'undertaking' has at least 40 per cent of a specific market.
[31] Art. 23(2)(a), Council Regulation (EC) No 1/2003 of 16 December 2002 on the implementation of the rules on competition laid down in Articles 81 and 82 of the Treaty, at http://bit.ly/2H62fSd.
[32] R. Whish and D. Bailey, *Competition Law*, 9th ed., Oxford University Press, Oxford, 2018, p. 223.
[33] European Commission, 'Directorate-General for Competition', last updated 29 July 2020, at http://bit.ly/34l6i5y.
[34] Under Article 131 of the TFEU, 'Each Member State shall ensure that its national legislation ... is compatible with the Treaties.'
[35] Art. 4(2), Protocol additional to the Geneva Conventions of 12 August 1949, and relating to the protection of victims of non-international armed conflicts (Protocol II); adopted at Geneva 8 June 1977; entered into force 7 December 1978.

commentary by the International Committee of the Red Cross (ICRC) declares that 'the parties to the conflict are still subjects of international law in the limited context of humanitarian rights and obligations resting upon them'.[36] The same principles apply to companies operating in the European internal market.

34.18 A further European competition law issue exists with respect to large mergers of companies. Thus, where two companies wish to merge, or one company wishes to take over a second company, and combined the two companies will have a global turnover of at least €5 billion, with a combined turnover of at least €250 million in at least two European Union member States, they must seek prior approval from the Directorate-General for Competition. This obligation is stipulated in the European Community (EC) Merger Regulation,[37] which was adopted by the European Council in January 2004.[38]

34.19 Under the 2004 Regulation, 'concentrations with a Community dimension defined in this Regulation shall be notified to the Commission prior to their implementation and following the conclusion of the agreement, the announcement of the public bid, or the acquisition of a controlling interest'.[39] The power of the Directorate-General, and specifically the EU Commissioner for Competition, is remarkable. In 2001, the then Commissioner, Mario Monti, blocked a proposed merger between two *American* companies, General Electric and Honeywell, on the basis that it would significantly impede competition within the European internal market. The Commissioner's decision was highly controversial, not least because the proposed merger had already been approved by the US Department of Justice.[40] Nonetheless, the planned merger was duly abandoned.

The Application of International Human Rights Law

34.20 It is clear from the above that customary law (at least during and in connection with armed conflict) and treaty law (in peacetime) may impose obligations directly upon private corporations. But does the application of international humanitarian law to private corporations (in certain circumstances) or their regulation under European competition law imply that other bodies of international law, specifically international human rights law, may also apply directly to them? And, if so, how does that occur as a matter of law? There is no consensus on the issue, but there is increasing acceptance that the application of customary international law — or at the very least with respect to customary norms that

---

[36] ICRC, Commentary on the 1977 Additional Protocols, 1987, p. 1372, at http://bit.ly/2IGhscP.
[37] EU Regulations 'always have direct effect'. Art. 288, TFEU specifies that regulations are directly applicable in EU member States. The Court of Justice clarifies in the judgement of *Politi* of 14 December 1971 that this is a 'complete direct effect'. EUR-Lex, 'The Direct Effect of European Law', 14 January 2015, at http://bit.ly/3knSuwM.
[38] Council Regulation (EC) No. 139/2004 of 20 January 2004 on the control of concentrations between undertakings (the EC Merger Regulation).
[39] Art. 4(1), 2004 Merger Regulation.
[40] See, e.g., J. Grant and D. J. Neven, 'The Attempted Merger between General Electric and Honeywell: A Case Study of Transatlantic Conflict', March 2005, at http://bit.ly/3klo4eK.

are of a peremptory nature – is the primary means by which private corporations are bound by human rights norms.

34.21 There is no doubt that corporations can influence the enjoyment of fundamental human rights. As the UN Guiding Principles Reporting Framework explains: 'The actions of business enterprises can affect people's enjoyment of their human rights either positively or negatively. Indeed, experience shows that enterprises can and do infringe human rights where they are not paying sufficient attention to this risk.'[41] With respect to the right to life, the Framework details three ways in which private corporations can do so: the lethal use of force by security forces (State or private) to protect company resources, facilities, or personnel; operations that pose life-threatening safety risks to workers or neighbouring communities through, for example, exposure to toxic chemicals; and the manufacture and sale of products with lethal flaws.[42]

34.22 With respect to the use of weapons, Ralph Steinhardt has observed:

> If it is now reasonable to ask whether corporations bear responsibility under international human rights law for the use of weapons, it is because four foundational principles in four traditionally unrelated bodies of law are softening simultaneously: (1) the categorical principle that has historically separated the international law governing the conduct of hostilities in armed conflict and the international law protecting human rights; (2) the state primacy doctrine in international human rights law (under which governments bear the exclusive obligation to comply with human rights norms); (3) the shareholder primacy doctrine of corporate law (under which companies cannot lawfully take discretionary decisions that fail to maximise shareholders' return on their investment); and (4) the principle of criminal law that only human beings, that is natural persons and not juridical or legal entities, can be subject to criminal responsibility.[43]

34.23 Steinhardt suggests that these principles 'are no longer absolute, that the multinational corporation increasingly does have enforceable obligations under international criminal law and international human rights law', but notes that 'these are clearly not as extensive as the obligations that bind human beings under the former and governments under the latter'.[44] Under a most restrictive approach, which is today the most credible source of international normative regulation, peremptory norms of international law bind all private corporations.

Jus Cogens Norms Binding on All Private Corporations

34.24 Indeed, it is widely asserted that peremptory norms of international law are binding on all entities, groups, and organisations, including private corporations. As the

---

[41] UN Guiding Principles Reporting Framework, 'How Can Businesses Impact Human Rights?', 2015, at http://bit.ly/30cjfGM.
[42] Ibid.
[43] R. Steinhardt, 'Weapons and the Human Rights Responsibilities of Multinational Corporations', chap. 17 in S. Casey-Maslen (ed.), *Weapons under International Human Rights Law*, Cambridge University Press, Cambridge, 2014, p. 509.
[44] Ibid.

Independent International Commission of Inquiry on the Syrian Arab Republic declared in 2012, 'at a minimum, human rights obligations constituting peremptory international law (*ius cogens*) bind States, individuals and non-State collective entities, including armed groups'.[45] There has been support for this notion by States and by case-law in domestic courts. This has included an endorsement of the broader tenet that customary norms may bind private corporations even if they are not peremptory in nature. Whether, as a matter of international law, that more expansive understanding is *lex lata* or *lex ferenda* may be open to question. But a State's domestic law may certainly incorporate or 'adopt' international custom.

34.25 In its judgment of February 2020 in *Nevsun Resources Ltd.* v. *Araya*,[46] the Supreme Court of Canada held that Canadian corporations may be sued in tort for violations of international human rights law that occur abroad.[47] Nevsun Resources is a Canadian company that owns a mine in Eritrea. The plaintiffs suing Nevsun claimed that they had been conscripted by the Eritrean military as 'slaves', forced to work at the mine, where they were subjected to cruel, inhuman, and degrading treatment in violation of customary international law. By five votes to four, the Supreme Court held that claims for violations of international human rights norms abroad may be brought in Canadian courts on the grounds that Canadian common law has 'adopted' custom. It declared that some norms of customary international law 'prohibit conduct regardless of whether the perpetrator is a state'[48] and that there 'is no reason, in principle, why "private actors" excludes corporations'.[49]

34.26 The majority of the Justices concluded that 'it is not "plain and obvious" that corporations today enjoy a blanket exclusion under customary international law from direct liability for violation of "obligatory, definable, and universal norms of international law", or indirect liability for their involvement in ... "complicity offenses"'.[50] 'Ultimately', the Court held, 'for the purposes of this appeal, it is enough to conclude that the breaches of customary international law, or *jus cogens*, relied on by the Eritrean workers may well apply to Nevsun'.[51] By 'universal norm', one might be tempted to suggested peremptory norm as a suitable synonym.

34.27 The situation in law in the United States is similar, albeit more complex. The Alien Tort Statute of 1789[52] stipulates: 'The district courts shall have original jurisdiction of any civil action by an alien for a tort only, committed in violation of the law of nations or a treaty of the

---

[45] Report of the Independent International Commission of Inquiry on the Syrian Arab Republic, UN doc. A/HRC/19/69, 22 February 2012, para. 106.
[46] Supreme Court of Canada, *Nevsun Resources Ltd.* v. *Araya*, 2020 SCC 5, Judgment rendered on 28 February 2020.
[47] See generally W. S. Dodge, 'Supreme Court of Canada Recognizes Corporate Liability for Human Rights Violations', *Just Security*, 26 March 2020, at http://bit.ly/2HkLu5s.
[48] Supreme Court of Canada, *Nevsun Resources Ltd.* v. *Araya*, Judgment, para. 105.
[49] Ibid., para. 111.
[50] Ibid., para. 113.
[51] Ibid., para. 114.
[52] 28 USC 1350.

United States.' In its 2004 judgment in *Sosa*,[53] the US Supreme Court concluded that the Alien Tort Statute allows federal courts to enforce a limited class of international norms that are 'specific, universal, and obligatory'.[54] It left open the question of when corporations would be liable for violations of such norms. That said, as Steinhardt has observed,[55] in *Presbyterian Church v. Talisman*, the Court of Appeal for the Second Circuit (covering the states of Connecticut, New York, and Vermont) assumed 'without deciding, that corporations . . . may be held liable for the violations of customary international law'.[56]

34.28 Successive US administrations have submitted *amicus curiae* briefs to the Court supporting the notion that corporations are liable for violations of certain customary norms. In the *Kiobel* case,[57] the brief filed by the Obama Administration declared that the prohibitions against torture, genocide, and war crimes apply equally to natural persons and to corporations: 'Both natural persons and corporations can violate international-law norms that require state action. And both natural persons and corporations can violate international-law norms that do not require state action.'[58] In the later *Jesner* case,[59] the brief filed by the Trump administration took the same position:

> Both corporations and their agents are capable of committing a 'tort . . . in violation of the law of nations', 28 USC 1350. A tort by either type of actor could thus support a federal common-law cause of action against a corporation under the ATS [Alien Tort Statute]. No principle of international law precludes the existence of a norm for the conduct of private actors that applies to the conduct of corporations.[60]

In its judgment in the case, the US Supreme Court held that the causes of actions under the Alien Tort Statute do not extend to foreign corporations, but did not expressly preclude a case against a US corporation.[61]

[53] The case concerned the kidnapping and rendition of Humberto Álvarez-Machaín in Mexico for the kidnap and murder of a US Drug Enforcement Administration (DEA) special agent by a Mexican drug cartel in 1985. Mr Álvarez-Machaín was found not guilty in a US court for want of sufficient evidence. He then sued one of his kidnappers under the Alien Tort Statute. The US Supreme Court held that this fell outside the activities justiciable under the Statute.

[54] US Supreme Court, *Sosa v. Alvarez-Machain*, 542 US 692, 732 (2004).

[55] Steinhardt, 'Weapons and the Human Rights Responsibilities of Multinational Corporations', p. 537.

[56] US Court of Appeals (for the Second Circuit), *The Presbyterian Church of Sudan and others v. Talisman Energy, Inc.*, 582 F.3d 244 (2009), Judgment, Conclusion 12.

[57] Brought by Nigerian refugees in the United States against the entity which is now Royal Dutch Shell, the lawsuit accused the Dutch/British multinational corporation of aiding and abetting the Nigerian military in the systematic torture and killing of peaceful environmental protesters in the 1990s. Center for Justice and Accountability, 'Kiobel v. Shell', 2020, at http://bit.ly/2Hs3Ykg.

[58] US Supreme Court, *Kiobel and others v. Royal Dutch Petroleum Co. and others*, Amicus Curiae of the United States supporting the Petitioners, December 2011, p. 21.

[59] Several Israeli citizens were killed, injured, or kidnapped by terrorists in attacks outside the United States. The survivors and the families of those who perished in the attacks accused Arab Bank, PLC, a bank corporation headquartered in Jordan, of financing and facilitating various terrorist organisations involved in the attacks.

[60] US Supreme Court, *Joseph Jesner and others v. Arab Bank PLC*, Amicus Curiae of the United States supporting neither party, June 2017, p. 13.

[61] See, e.g., Z. ZhenHe Tan, 'Assessing the Impact of Jesner v. Arab Bank', Lawfare, 20 December 2018, at http://bit.ly/3jeBZBW.

34.29 A separate amicus curiae brief in the *Jesner* case by the Yale Law School Center for Global Legal Challenges declared that extrajudicial killing should also fall within the scope of the Alien Tort Statute and that the norm applies also to corporations.[62] Oona Hathaway, the brief's author, cited the 1984 judgment of the Court of Appeal for the District of Colombia in the case of *Tel-Oren* v. *Libyan Arab Republic*, wherein it was noted that 'at least four acts [are] subject to unequivocal international condemnation: torture, summary execution, genocide and slavery'.[63] She suggested, however, that 'the prohibitory norm against extrajudicial killing resembles the prohibitory norm against torture', and that this would limit the case of extrajudicial killing 'to any actor acting with the acquiescence of the State or under color of law'.[64] As a formulation of the rule under customary law, this is too narrowly cast.

34.30 As of writing, the US Supreme Court was due to hear arguments in *Nestle USA* v. *Doe* (on 1 December 2020), a case alleging that a US corporation aided and abetted child slavery abroad. Issues to be debated are whether an aiding and abetting claim against a domestic corporation brought under the Alien Tort Statute may overcome the extraterritoriality bar where the claim is based on allegations of general corporate activity in the United States and where the plaintiffs cannot trace the alleged harms, which occurred abroad at the hands of unidentified foreign actors, to that activity; and whether the judiciary has the authority under the Alien Tort Statute to impose liability on domestic corporations.[65]

34.31 In May 2020, the Trump administration filed an amicus brief[66] reversing its earlier position and averring that domestic corporations are not subject to suit for human rights violations under the Alien Tort Statute.[67] One of its main arguments was that 'in light of Jesner's holding rejecting foreign corporate liability under the ATS, a contrary rule for domestic corporate liability would facially discriminate against U.S. corporations'.[68] Taken to a fanciful extreme, the logic seems to be that US companies should be allowed to murder and torture because to prevent them from doing so would be discriminatory and even anti-competitive? As William Dodge observes: 'It is not fanciful to think that U.S. corporations might engage in some of these activities. U.S. corporations have been sued under the ATS for torture and war crimes. And, of course, Cargill itself [a case joined with the action against Nestlé] involves allegations that U.S. corporations aided and abetted slavery.'[69]

---

[62] US Supreme Court, *Joseph Jesner and others* v. *Arab Bank PLC*, Brief of Yale Law School Center for Global Legal Challenges as Amicus Curiae in Support of Petitioners, June 2017, p. 24.
[63] US Court of Appeals for the District of Colombia, *Tel-Oren* v. *Libyan Arab Republic*, 726 F.2d 774, 791 note 20 (1984).
[64] US Supreme Court, *Joseph Jesner and others* v. *Arab Bank PLC*, Brief of Yale Law School Center for Global Legal Challenges as Amicus Curiae in Support of Petitioners, June 2017, p. 25.
[65] 'Nestlé USA, Inc. v. Doe I', SCOTUS blog, accessed 21 October 2020 at http://bit.ly/37qAY7v.
[66] US Supreme Court, *Nestle* v. *John Doe I and others*, Amicus Curiae of the United States, May 2020.
[67] W. S. Dodge, 'Trump Administration Reverses Position on Corporate Liability Under Alien Tort Statute', *Just Security*, 1 June 2020, at http://bit.ly/31q7rqE.
[68] US Supreme Court, *Nestle* v. *John Doe I and others*, Amicus Curiae of the United States, May 2020, p. 11.
[69] Dodge, 'Trump Administration Reverses Position on Corporate Liability under Alien Tort Statute'.

VIOLATIONS OF THE RIGHT TO LIFE THAT CONSTITUTE INTERNATIONALLY WRONGFUL ACTS BY A PRIVATE CORPORATION

34.32 A range of conduct will violate the jus cogens elements of respect for the right to life and thereby constitute an internationally wrongful act by a private corporation. The most obvious examples are arbitrary deprivation of life through deliberate extrajudicial executions or other arbitrary killings perpetrated either by staff of a private corporation in connection with the operations and activities of that corporation or by individuals or groups that they employ or direct to this effect. This is so whether the killings occur in peacetime or during, and in connection with, a situation of armed conflict and irrespective of the direct involvement of the State. In this regard, a serious violation, by a private corporation that is party to an armed conflict, of a basic international humanitarian law rule governing the conduct of hostilities, in particular the principle of distinction or of proportionality in attack, will also amount to arbitrary deprivation of life, at the least where it results in death. Such conduct constitutes an internationally wrongful act by the private corporation in question.

34.33 The failure by a private corporation to provide adequate food and water to a detainee or to ensure the provision of appropriate medical care where he or she needs it will also amount to arbitrary deprivation of life, at the least where the detainee perishes. If this occurs during an armed conflict, it may also be a war crime. In either case, an internationally wrongful act has been perpetrated by the private corporation in question.

34.34 With respect to the prohibition on enforced disappearance – another jus cogens norm – the 2006 International Convention for the Protection of All Persons from Enforced Disappearance stipulates simply: 'No one shall be subjected to enforced disappearance.'[70] Thus, as the UN Secretary-General has stated: 'The prohibition of enforced disappearance is absolute.'[71] This renders an enforced disappearance perpetrated by a private corporation also an internationally wrongful act.

---

[70] Art. 1(1), International Convention for the Protection of All Persons from Enforced Disappearance; adopted at New York 20 December 2006; entered into force 23 December 2010.

[71] UN, 'Amid Growing Use of Enforced Disappearances by Non-State Actors, Secretary-General Urges Prompt Action in Message on International Day Commemorating Victims', press release SG/SM/17038-OBV/1508, 28 August 2015, at http://bit.ly/3lPFO30.

35

The Right to Life and the Responsibility of Non-State Armed Groups

INTRODUCTION

35.01 This chapter addresses the responsibility of non-State armed groups under international law for violations of the right to life. The chapter assesses the extent to which a non-State armed group has obligations under international law to respect and protect the right to life of individuals within its sphere of influence and the extent to which a failure to comply with those duties amounts to an internationally wrongful act. The nature and consequences of international legal responsibility pertaining to non-State armed groups are also explored.

35.02 State responsibility for the internationally wrongful acts of an erstwhile non-State armed group that later becomes either the new government of a State or the government of a new State[1] was considered in Chapter 32 and will not be addressed further in this chapter. So too was State responsibility for the actions of an armed group that is 'acting on the instructions of, or under the direction or control of, that State in carrying out the conduct',[2] and which therefore acts as a State agent. This chapter concerns the responsibility of a non-State armed group, acting as such.

35.03 The traditional view holds that non-State armed groups have no legal duty to respect, much less protect or fulfil human rights, including the right to life. Those duties are, so the argument goes, the exclusive domain of the sovereign, by which is meant the State.[3] So understood, non-State armed groups do not violate human rights; they 'abuse' them. This restrictive notion of international human rights law has, however, been fundamentally challenged in recent decades by the United Nations and by leading publicists, as well as by an increasing number of States. Moreover, it is generally accepted that armed groups are at the least partial subjects of international law when they are party to an armed conflict as that notion is understood in accordance with international

---

[1] Art. 10, Draft articles on Responsibility of States for Internationally Wrongful Acts, with commentaries, 2001; Text adopted by the International Law Commission (ILC) at its fifty-third session, in 2001, and submitted to the UN General Assembly as a part of the Commission's report covering the work of that session, in UN doc. A/56/10, at http://bit.ly/32A3ocT.
[2] Art. 8, Draft Articles on State Responsibility.
[3] See, e.g., N. S. Rodley, 'Can Armed Opposition Groups Violate Human Rights?', in K. Mahoney and P. Mahoney (eds.), *Human Rights in the Twenty-First Century*, Martinus Nijhoff, Dordrecht, 1993, pp. 297–318.

humanitarian law. It is further unquestioned that the members of a non-State armed group may be held individually responsible under international criminal law for international crimes they have committed. The question arises of whether and, if so, how armed groups *qua* collective entities are also bound by international human rights law.

35.04 The chapter continues by describing the notions of an internationally wrongful act and responsibility under international law as they pertain to a non-State armed group. It moves on to discuss how armed groups may become subjects of international law, first as a party to an armed conflict and later in other circumstances. Finally, the chapter considers which obligations within the right to life are binding upon a non-State armed group and therefore which conduct forming part of the right to life may amount to an internationally wrongful act.

THE NOTION OF AN INTERNATIONALLY WRONGFUL ACT

35.05 Simply put, an internationally wrongful act by a non-State armed group is its violation of a rule of international law that is binding upon it. Potentially the rule may be demarcated in a treaty or customary in nature, or it may originate in a general principle of law. The rule may be discerned by a competent judicial body. It must, however, be applicable to the group in question. To paraphrase Article 13 of the 2001 International Law Commission (ILC) Draft Articles on State Responsibility, *mutatis mutandis*: an act of a non-State armed group does not constitute a breach of an international obligation unless the group is bound by the obligation in question at the time the act occurs. As is the case with respect to State responsibility, however, the term 'act' should be understood to also potentially encompass an 'omission'.[4]

THE NOTION OF INTERNATIONAL LEGAL RESPONSIBILITY

35.06 Responsibility describes the circumstances and consequences for a non-State armed group that violates a primary rule of international law. The rules governing such responsibility are thus secondary rules that apply once an internationally wrongful act has occurred. Every internationally wrongful act of a non-State armed group entails the international responsibility of that group. There is a consequent obligation to cease wrongful conduct if it is continuing and to offer, as and where appropriate, a guarantee of non-repetition. There is also a duty to make due reparation, which may encompass financial compensation, restitution, and an apology.

35.07 The consequences of certain internationally wrongful acts are primarily, if not exclusively, bilateral – that is, between the group that has perpetrated the internationally wrongful act and the person or persons who have been harmed. But in a number of instances, internationally wrongful acts pertaining to violations of the right to life – in particular, insofar as they amount to arbitrary deprivation of life – are violations of jus

---

[4] Commentary, para. 8, on Draft Article 1, 2001 Draft Articles on State Responsibility.

cogens norms that are therefore obligations erga omnes.[5] In its noted discussion of such obligations erga omnes in its judgment in the *Barcelona Traction* case, the International Court of Justice had included in an indicative list the 'principles and rules concerning the basic rights of the human person'.[6]

ARE NON-STATE ARMED GROUPS SUBJECTS OF INTERNATIONAL LAW?

The Application of International Humanitarian Law

35.08 In its 2004 decision on jurisdiction in the *Sam Hinga Norman* case, the Appeals Chamber of the Special Court for Sierra Leone held that 'it is well settled that all parties to an armed conflict, whether states or non-state actors, are bound by international humanitarian law, even though only states may become parties to international treaties'.[7] Non-State armed groups are therefore objects of international law. Surprisingly, though, the Appeals Chamber did not find that armed groups had sufficient international legal personality to enter into binding relations under international law, a concern to which the discussion later returns.

35.09 A key issue to ascertain first is how non-State armed groups may be bound by IHL given that 'only states may become parties to international treaties'. There is no general agreement, much less consensus, as to how legally this may occur. Even the International Committee of the Red Cross (ICRC), which benefits from a special role under international humanitarian law, is unable to furnish a clear basis on which, as a matter of international law, a non-State armed group deemed to be party to an armed conflict is constrained directly by IHL. In its commentary of 2020 on Article 3 of the 1949 Geneva Convention III,[8] the ICRC observes: 'The exact mechanism [sic] by which common Article 3 becomes binding on an entity that is not a High Contracting Party to the Geneva Conventions is the subject of debate.'[9]

35.10 As the ICRC correctly recalls, however, a number of legal theories have been advanced, particularly by publicists, to explain how international humanitarian law obligations are imposed upon non-State armed groups. They may be summarised as the following four concepts: third-party acceptance, legislative jurisdiction, prescriptive jurisdiction, and customary law.

35.11 The first of these concepts, third-party acceptance, holds that, akin to the fundamental principle of treaty law whereby treaties may only impose obligations on third party

---

[5] Draft Conclusion 17(1) in ILC, *Report of the International Law Commission*, Seventy-first session, UN doc. A/74/10, 2019, chap. V.
[6] ICJ, *Barcelona Traction, Light and Power Company Ltd. (Belgium v. Spain)*, Judgment, 5 February 1970, para. 34.
[7] Special Court for Sierra Leone, *Prosecutor v. Sam Hinga Norman*, Decision on Preliminary Motion Based on Lack of Jurisdiction (Appeals Chamber; Case No SCSL-2004-14-AR72(E)), 31 May 2004, para. 22.
[8] Art. 3, Convention (III) relative to the Treatment of Prisoners of War; adopted at Geneva 12 August 1949; entered into force 21 October 1950.
[9] ICRC Commentary on Article 3, 1949 Geneva Convention III, 2020, at http://bit.ly/2Zc8Q3g, para. 541.

States with their consent,[10] a non-State armed group may similarly consent to the application of international humanitarian law treaty rules. Indeed, this is expressly reflected in the provisions of the 1977 Additional Protocol I to the four Geneva Conventions of 1949. Thereunder, an authority representing a people fighting colonial domination, alien occupation, or a racist regime in the exercise of the right of self-determination against a State Party to the Protocol 'may undertake to apply' the Geneva Conventions and the Protocol in relation to that conflict. This it does by means of a unilateral declaration submitted to the depositary (the Swiss Federal Council).[11]

35.12 In the more than forty years that the 1977 Additional Protocol I has been in force, however, and despite numerous attempts by non-State armed groups, only once has such application been accepted. This was in 2015 when the Polisario Front made a unilateral declaration on behalf of the people of Western Sahara, undertaking to apply the 1949 Geneva Conventions and the 1977 Additional Protocol I to the long-standing conflict between it and Morocco. Morocco had ratified the 1977 Additional Protocol I in 2011 without reservation to the pertinent provisions. The Swiss Federal Council accepted Polisario's declaration and issued a corresponding notification to that effect to the States Parties to the 1977 Additional Protocol I – 173 as of this writing – whereby an international armed conflict existed between Morocco and the Polisario Front as of 23 June 2015.[12]

35.13 This exception, however, serves to prove the general rule. This cannot be the means by which non-State armed groups routinely become bound by international humanitarian law rules. Most are not national liberation movements, as that term is understood in international law,[13] and thus cannot use this mechanism to express their consent to be bound by certain rules. Moreover, the application to non-State armed groups is ordinarily of the rules governing non-international armed conflict, as partially reflected in Article 3 common to the 1949 Geneva Conventions, which is not the case here. No similar mechanism applies with respect to the 1977 Additional Protocol II,[14] which in any event

---

[10] The Latin maxim *pacta tertiis nec nocent nec prosunt* is given voice in the vernacular in the 1969 Vienna Convention on the Law of Treaties. Article 34 stipulates: 'A treaty does not create either obligations or rights for a third State without its consent.' Art. 34, Vienna Convention on the Law of Treaties; adopted at Vienna 23 May 1969; entered into force 27 January 1980.

[11] Arts. 1(4) and 96(3), Protocol Additional to the Geneva Conventions of 12 August 1949, and relating to the Protection of Victims of International Armed Conflicts (Protocol I); adopted at Geneva 8 June 1977; entered into force 7 December 1978.

[12] Swiss Federal Department of Foreign Affairs, 'Notification to the Governments of the States parties to the Geneva Conventions of 12 August 1949 for the Protection of War Victims', Ref. 242.512.0–GEN 4/15, Bern, 2015, at http://bit.ly/31YZwRR.

[13] Under the 1970 UN Declaration on Principles of International Law, 'every State has the duty to refrain from any forcible action which deprives peoples referred to in the elaboration of the principle of equal rights and self-determination of their right to self-determination and freedom and independence'. Principle 1(7) of The Declaration on Principles of International Law concerning Friendly Relations and Co-operation among States, annexed to UN General Assembly Resolution 2625, adopted by the UN General Assembly without a vote on 24 October 1970.

[14] Protocol Additional to the Geneva Conventions of 12 August 1949, and relating to the Protection of Victims of Non-International Armed Conflicts (Protocol II); adopted at Geneva 8 June 1977; entered into force 7 December 1978.

applies to only certain high-intensity armed conflicts (and does not ever apply to non-international armed conflicts between two or more non-State armed groups).

35.14 A second commonly cited theory to explain how non-State armed groups are bound by IHL is known as legislative jurisdiction. This doctrine asserts that international humanitarian law rules bind any private individuals, including armed groups, through the medium of domestic law. This occurs by means of domestic implementation of international legal rules in national legislation or as a result of the direct applicability, in a monist State, of self-executing norms. This explanatory theory is also imperfect, however, since what is questioned is not whether armed groups are subjects of domestic law – which they clearly are – but how their acts are directly regulated by international law.[15]

35.15 A third theory is known as prescriptive jurisdiction. This holds that armed groups are bound because States declare that they are in international humanitarian law treaties. Thus, Common Article 3 explicitly states that the provision binds 'each Party to the conflict', a formulation that is generally understood to encompass non-State actors.[16] This is legally tricky as it appears to contravene the fundamental treaty law principle evoked above whereby treaties may not impose obligations on – or, for that matter, accord rights to – third parties without their consent. But as was indicated with respect to corporations in the previous chapter, a partial subject of international law, one might conceive of the rule as applying only to States and international organisations, but not other (partial) subjects of international law.

35.16 A further flaw with the prescriptive jurisdiction approach is, however, that it implies that where a treaty does not use such express language, as is the case, for instance, in the 1977 Additional Protocol II, it would logically not bind a non-State armed group that otherwise meets the criteria to be party to a non-international armed conflict governed by that instrument.[17] The theory of prescriptive jurisdiction also does not explain how non-treaty international humanitarian law rules come to be binding upon non-State armed groups (although it does perhaps indicate the direction of an approach that will do so).

35.17 Thus, overall, the most persuasive explanation for the direct imposition upon non-State armed groups of international humanitarian law rules is the argument that they are subject to customary international law. With respect to Common Article 3, for instance, the Appeals Chamber of the Special Court for Sierra Leone declared that a 'convincing theory' is that insurgents 'are bound as a matter of customary international law to observe the obligations declared by Common Article 3 which is aimed at the protection of

---

[15] See, e.g., S. Sivakumaran, 'Binding Armed Opposition Groups', *International and Comparative Law Quarterly*, vol. 55 (2006) pp. 369–94, at 381.

[16] The use of a capital 'P' in Party is sometimes cited to discount the application of Common Article 3 to non-State actors, but this is not, or at least no longer, a widely held view.

[17] Indeed, during the negotiation of the 1977 Additional Protocol II a number of participating States clearly believed that insurgent groups would not be bound by the instrument they were elaborating. L. Moir, *The Law of Internal Armed Conflict*, Cambridge University Press, Cambridge, 2002, p. 97.

humanity'.[18] Such an approach ensures that both Geneva Law and Hague Law rules applicable to non-international armed conflict impose on non-State armed groups direct and legally binding obligations under international humanitarian law.

35.18 That said, the theory is also not without its problems. First, it is unclear at what precise point in time the rules expounded in Common Article 3 became binding as a matter of custom. Undoubtedly a controversial innovation at the time of their adoption (in 1949), in 1986 the International Court of Justice strongly implied that they already amounted to customary law by then.[19] If so, and if that explains the direct imposition of those obligations upon non-State armed groups, that of course begs the question: What was the legal situation with respect to such groups before the period at which the rules became custom. Were the groups not previously bound as a matter of law?

35.19 The best explanation is to be found in a combination of the doctrinal theories summarised herein. International humanitarian law rules may be imposed on non-State armed groups by treaty just as the theory of prescriptive jurisdiction argues. The restriction on imposition of treaty rules on third parties without their consent is overcome on the basis that the principle applies to safeguard the sovereignty of States not party but not any non-State actors operating within the jurisdiction of a State Party. The theory of prescriptive jurisdiction also applies to rules of customary international humanitarian law, which are applied to all non-State armed groups that are party to an armed conflict on the basis of State practice and accompanying *opinio juris*. There is no persistent objector status for a non-State armed group under international law. Moreover, and in any event, the core provisions of Common Article 3 that protect life and limb and the Hague Law principles of distinction and proportionality in attack are peremptory norms of international law from which no derogation is possible.

35.20 Thus, as customary international law, both the international humanitarian law rules in Common Article 3 (Geneva Law) and the fundamental rules governing the conduct of hostilities (Hague Law) become applicable without reservation. Violations of these rules entail international responsibility. According to Gérard Cahin, through its 2001 Draft Articles on State Responsibility, the International Law Commission (ILC) 'has clearly accepted the existence of a principle of international responsibility of insurrectional movements, albeit without expressly including it in the text of the Articles'.[20]

---

[18] Special Court for Sierra Leone (SCSL), *Prosecutor v. Morris Kallon and Brima Buzzy Kamara*, Decision on Challenge to Jurisdiction: Lomé Accord Amnesty (Appeals Chamber; Case Nos. SCSL-2004-15-AR72(E) and SCSL-2004-16-AR72(E)), 13 March 2004, paras. 45–7.

[19] 'There is no doubt that, in the event of international armed conflicts, these rules also constitute a minimum yardstick, in addition to the more elaborate rules which are also to apply to international conflicts'. International Court of Justice (ICJ), *Case concerning Military and Paramilitary Activities in and against Nicaragua (Nicaragua v. United States)* Judgment (Merits), 27 June 1986, para. 218.

[20] G. Cahin, 'Responsibility of Other Entities: Armed Bands and Criminal Groups', chap. 23.2 in J. Crawford, A. Pellet, and S. Olleson (eds.), *The Law of International Responsibility*, Oxford Commentaries on International Law, Oxford University Press, Oxford, 2010, p. 339.

35.21 Is it possible to go further and determine that armed groups are a partial subject of international law? As noted previously, the Appeals Chamber had rejected the argument that armed groups could conclude a treaty with a State as is the case for an international organisation.[21] The Appeals Chamber concluded that the 1999 Lomé Agreement between the Revolutionary United Front (RUF) and the government of Sierra Leone 'created neither rights nor obligations capable of being regulated by international law'.[22] Its argumentation was that the RUF had no treaty-making capacity so, as a logical consequence, the Lomé Agreement itself could not, by definition, be a treaty.[23]

35.22 This is, however, a conclusory argument and one that is unpersuasive as a matter of law. Indeed, if one accepts the theory of prescriptive jurisdiction for Common Article 3, States also appear to provide therein for the treaty-making capacity of non-State armed groups. In the fourth paragraph of Common Article 3, it is stipulated that 'the Parties to the conflict should further endeavour to bring into force, by means of special agreements, all or part of the other provisions of the present Convention'. Thus the Convention itself foresees that an agreement between a State and a non-State actor (or even two non-State actors) can agree, in a manner that binds them both, to apply in non-international armed conflict the other provisions of the Convention that are normally only applicable in international armed conflict . This is a matter of international law, not domestic law.

35.23 As the ICRC wrote in 2008, special agreements 'can provide a plain statement of the law applicable in the context – *or of an expanded set of provisions of IHL beyond the law that is already applicable* – and secure a clear commitment from the parties to uphold that law'.[24] This is more than a 'commitment'; this is an acceptance of binding international legal obligations akin to treaty-making.[25] A non-State armed group that is party to a non-international armed conflict is thus a partial subject of international law.

The Application of International Human Rights Law

35.24 But does the application of IHL to non-State armed groups and their associated status as a partial subject of international law imply that other branches of public international law may apply directly to non-State actors? Does that extend, in particular, to international human rights law? And, if so, how does that occur as a matter of law?

35.25 There is increasing acceptance that both prescriptive jurisdiction and the application of customary law can serve to bind entities other than States or international organisations. A third approach is to consider de facto authorities – those that do not

---

[21] See Chapter 33 on this issue.
[22] SCSL, *Prosecutor* v. *Kallon and Kamara*, Decision on Challenge to Jurisdiction: Lomé Accord Amnesty (Appeals Chamber), 13 March 2004, para. 42.
[23] Ibid., paras. 48 and 49.
[24] ICRC, 'Increasing Respect for International Humanitarian Law in Non-International Armed Conflicts', Geneva, February 2008, p. 16 (added emphasis).
[25] The final paragraph of Article 3 stipulates: 'The application of the preceding provisions shall not affect the legal status of the Parties to the conflict.' This reconfirms that a non-State armed group remains just that: not a State.

represent a recognised State but which exercise effective control over a significant populace – as having some of the human rights obligations incumbent on States.

35.26 There is also no doubt as to the extent of the threat posed by non-State armed groups to the enjoyment of fundamental human rights. As the UN Special Rapporteur on extrajudicial, summary or arbitrary executions has remarked, such actors 'have become a pervasive challenge to human rights protection'.[26] But in her 2018 report to the Human Rights Council, she also maintained that such groups are bound by human rights obligations.[27]

35.27 It is clearly insufficient to rely on the application of international humanitarian law for the protection of the right to life. There may not be an armed conflict underway to which international humanitarian law is applicable. Or there may be an ongoing armed conflict to which a particular armed group is not a party, for instance because it does not meet the criterion of 'organisation' or because the extent and level of combat with State armed forces is insufficiently intense. There may also be important duties that apply under human rights law, in particular the right to life, but do not exist as such under international humanitarian law. An obvious example is the duty to investigate potentially unlawful death. Moreover, even when international humanitarian law is applicable the lack of implementing mechanisms it offers compared to human rights law is a serious weakness.[28]

Jus Cogens Norms Binding on All Non-State Armed Groups

35.28 There is support for the notion that peremptory norms of international law are binding on all entities, groups, and organisations, whether State or non-State in character. As the Independent International Commission of Inquiry on the Syrian Arab Republic declared in 2012 that 'at a minimum, human rights obligations constituting peremptory international law (*ius cogens*) bind States, individuals and non-State collective entities, *including armed groups*'.[29] More broadly, the UN Mission in South Sudan (UNMISS) stated in 2014: 'The most basic human rights obligations, *in particular* those emanating from peremptory international law (*ius cogens*) bind both the State and armed opposition groups in times of peace and during armed conflict.'[30]

35.29 A challenge in accepting the widest of these assertions may be the lack of hard evidence that justifies them, in particular the lack of *opinio juris*. It is duly noted that the 1948 Universal Declaration of Human Rights[31] is laid down as 'a common standard of

---

[26] Report of the Special Rapporteur on extrajudicial, summary or arbitrary executions on non-State actors, UN doc. A/HRC/38/44, 5 June 2018, para. 4.
[27] Ibid., para. 8.
[28] The Special Rapporteur on extrajudicial, summary or arbitrary executions also refers to the absence of an IHL duty upon non-State armed groups to make reparation for a violation of international humanitarian law. Ibid., para. 28.
[29] Report of the Independent International Commission of Inquiry on the Syrian Arab Republic, UN doc. A/HRC/19/69, 22 February 2012, para. 106 (added emphasis).
[30] UNMISS, *Conflict in South Sudan: A Human Rights Report*, 8 May 2014, at http://bit.ly/3lpLYqi, para. 18 (added emphasis).
[31] Universal Declaration of Human Rights; adopted at Paris by UN General Assembly Resolution 217, 10 December 1948. Resolution 217 was adopted by forty-eight votes to zero, with eight abstentions

achievement for all peoples and all nations'. The Declaration further exhorts 'that every individual and every organ of society, keeping this Declaration constantly in mind, shall strive by teaching and education to promote respect for these rights and freedoms'.[32] But it is not enough to hang the application of international legal rules on references in the preamble of an international instrument that is, a priori, non-binding (even though it has been widely asserted that many, if not all, of the Declaration's articles are reflective of customary law).[33] Several of the articles, however, codify norms that are considered today to be of a peremptory nature.

35.30 There is greater *opinio juris* in favour of the prohibition of international crimes applying as a matter of international law, not only to individuals by virtue of international criminal law but also to non-State armed groups. The ILC Special Rapporteur on crimes against humanity presented his first report on the issue of a possible treaty providing for the prohibition of such crimes in 2015. He noted that the ILC, commenting in 1991 on the draft provision on crimes against humanity for what would become the 1996 draft code of crimes, 'stated that the draft article does not confine possible perpetrators of the crimes to public officials or representatives alone and that it does not rule out the possibility that private individuals with de facto power or organized in criminal gangs or groups might also commit the kind of systematic or mass violations of human rights covered by the article'.[34] But at the time, as he observes, this claim was not uncontroversial.

35.31 *Opinio juris* has evolved rapidly, however. The definition of crimes against humanity in Article 7 of the Rome Statute of the International Criminal Court (ICC) refers to acts including murder, extermination, or enslavement when committed as part of a widespread or systematic attack directed against any civilian population, with knowledge of the attack.[35] It is further stipulated that the notion of an attack directed against any civilian population means conduct involving multiple commission of such acts pursuant to or in furtherance of a State *or organizational* policy to commit such attack.[36]

35.32 An organisation encompasses an armed group. In 2008, a Pre-Trial Chamber of the International Criminal Court held in the *Katanga* case that the policy 'may be made either by groups of persons who govern a specific territory or by any organization with the capability to commit a widespread or systematic attack against a civilian population'.[37] In

---

(Byelorussian SSR, Czechoslovakia, Poland, Saudi Arabia, South Africa, Soviet Union, Ukrainian SSR, and Yugoslavia). Honduras and Yemen did not take part in the vote.

[32] UDHR, eighth preambular para.

[33] See, e.g., H. Charlesworth, 'Universal Declaration of Human Rights (1948)', *Max Planck Encyclopedia of Public International Law*, February 2008, paras. 13–18, at http://bit.ly/2zKA9nC; and H. Hannum, 'The Status of the Universal Declaration of Human Rights in National and International Law', *Georgia Journal of International and Comparative Law*, vol. 25 (1995–96), pp. 287–397, available at http://bit.ly/2DgGyKw.

[34] First report on crimes against humanity by Sean D. Murphy, Special Rapporteur, UN doc. A/CN.4/680, 17 February 2015, para. 145.

[35] Art. 7(1), Rome Statute of the International Criminal Court; adopted at Rome 17 July 1998; entered into force 1 July 2002 (hereinafter, Rome Statute).

[36] Art. 7(2)(1), Rome Statute (added emphasis).

[37] ICC, *Prosecutor v. Katanga*, Decision on the Confirmation of Charges (Pre-Trial Chamber I; Case No. ICC 01/04 01/07), 30 September 2008, para. 396.

the Elements of Crime pertaining to crimes against humanity it is clarified that a 'policy to commit such attack' requires that the State or organisation in question 'actively promote or encourage such an attack against a civilian population'.[38]

35.33 In 2012, a Pre-Trial Chamber in the *Ruto* case stated that, when determining whether a particular group qualifies as an organisation under Article 7 of the Rome Statute, the Chamber may take into account a number of factors, including whether the group is under a responsible command or has an established hierarchy; whether the group possesses the means to carry out a widespread or systematic attack against a civilian population; whether the group exercises control over part of the territory of a State; whether the group has criminal activities against the civilian population as a primary purpose; and whether the group articulates, explicitly or implicitly, an intention to attack a civilian population.[39]

35.34 The prohibition of crimes against humanity is certainly a jus cogens rule,[40] 'and the punishment of such crimes is obligatory pursuant to the general principles of international law'.[41] Furthermore, crimes against humanity are the 'culmination of violations of fundamental human rights, such as the right to life and the prohibition of torture or other forms of inhuman and degrading treatment'.[42] Crimes against humanity may be committed both in peacetime and in situations of armed conflict. They violate, in the words of the Inter-American Court of Human Rights, 'a series of non-derogable rights recognised in the American Convention'.[43]

Prescriptive Application of Human Rights Law

35.35 In contrast, the 2000 Protocol to the Convention on the Rights of the Child on the involvement of children in armed conflict[44] is sometimes cited as an instance of the prescriptive application of human rights to non-State armed groups. According to Article 4(1) of the Protocol, 'armed groups that are distinct from the armed forces of a State should not, under any circumstances, recruit or use in hostilities persons under the age of 18 years'. While such prescriptive jurisdiction is theoretically possible, this provision is better cast as evidence of State practice towards a customary rule than it is of direct imposition of a treaty

---

[38] Para. 3, Article 7: Crimes against humanity, in *Official Records of the Assembly of States Parties to the Rome Statute of the International Criminal Court, First session, New York, 3–10 September 2002*, Part II(B).

[39] ICC, *Prosecutor v. Ruto*, Decision on the Confirmation of Charges (Pre-Trial Chamber II; Case No. ICC 01/09 01/11), 23 January 2012, para. 185.

[40] Annex, ILC draft conclusions on peremptory norms of general international law (jus cogens), UN doc. A/74/10, Chap. V.

[41] Report of the Independent International Commission of Inquiry on the Syrian Arab Republic, UN doc. A/HRC/21/50, 16 August 2012, Annex II, para. 26, citing Inter-American Court of Human Rights, *Almonacid-Arellano and others v. Chile*, Judgment (Preliminary Objections, Merits, Reparations and Costs), 26 September 2006, para. 99.

[42] Report of the Independent International Commission of Inquiry on the Syrian Arab Republic, UN doc. A/HRC/21/50, 16 August 2012, Annex II, para. 26.

[43] Inter-American Court of Human Rights, *Almonacid-Arellano and others v. Chile*, Judgment, 26 September 2006, para. 111.

[44] Optional Protocol to the Convention on the Rights of the Child on the involvement of children in armed conflict; adopted at New York 25 May 2000; entered into force 12 February 2002.

rule upon non-State armed groups. The onus of legal obligation in the Protocol remains on States (Parties). Thus, Article 4(2) provides that 'States Parties shall take all feasible measures to prevent such recruitment and use, including the adoption of legal measures necessary to prohibit and criminalize such practices.'

35.36 The same conclusion pertains to the 2009 Kampala Convention, adopted within the auspices of the African Union.[45] The Convention stipulates that members of armed groups 'shall be prohibited from' inter alia 'denying internally displaced persons the right to live in satisfactory conditions of dignity, security, sanitation, food, water, health and shelter'.[46] The framing of the provision clearly focuses on the conduct of States rather than directing the conduct of the non-State armed groups themselves.

De Facto Authorities

35.37 There is also some support for the notion that de facto authorities must respect fundamental or customary human rights obligations. In this regard, in its Resolution 1417 (2002), the UN Security Council reiterated that it held the Rassemblement Congolais pour la Démocratie-Goma – a non-State actor but the 'de facto authority' – 'responsible to bring to an end all extrajudicial executions, human rights violations and arbitrary harassment of civilians in Kisangani, and all other areas under [its] control'.[47] The UN Assistance Mission in Afghanistan (UNAMA) states that 'non-State actors, including armed groups, are not precluded from being subject to human rights obligations under customary international law. Non-state actors are increasingly deemed to be bound by certain international human rights obligations, particularly those actors exercising *de facto* control over some areas, such as the Taliban.'[48]

35.38 This formulation is robust. It may not yet be accurate to state that customary international rules bind all de facto authorities, including non-State armed groups, but application is assuredly *de lege ferenda*. The requisite *opinio juris* among a preponderance of States is what is lacking for such crystallisation. Today, only jus cogens norms are directly binding on all non-State actors, including non-State armed groups.

VIOLATIONS OF THE RIGHT TO LIFE THAT CONSTITUTE INTERNATIONALLY WRONGFUL ACTS BY A NON-STATE ARMED GROUP

35.39 A range of conduct will thus violate the jus cogens elements of respect for the right to life and thereby constitute an internationally wrongful act by a non-State armed group. The most obvious examples are arbitrary deprivation of life through deliberate

---

[45] African Union Convention for the Protection and Assistance of Internally Displaced Persons in Africa; adopted at Kampala 23 October 2009; entered into force 6 December 2012.
[46] Art. VII(5)(c), Kampala Convention.
[47] UN Security Council Resolution 1417, adopted by unanimous vote on 14 June 2002, para. 4.
[48] UNAMA, *2019 Annual Report on the Protection of Civilians in Armed Conflict in Afghanistan*, Kabul, February 2020, at http://bit.ly/34GCBg6, p. 81.

extrajudicial executions or other arbitrary killings by members of non-State armed groups. This is so whether the killings occur in peacetime or during, and in connection with, a situation of armed conflict. In this regard, a violation, by a non-State armed group that is party to an armed conflict, of a basic international humanitarian law rule governing the conduct of hostilities, in particular the principle of distinction or of proportionality in attack, will also amount to arbitrary deprivation of life. Where it results in death, such conduct constitutes an internationally wrongful act by the group in question.

35.40 The failure by an armed group to provide adequate food and water to a detainee or to ensure the provision of appropriate medical care where he or she needs it will also amount to arbitrary deprivation of life where the detainee perishes. On a broader scope, preventing food from being accessed by a civilian population in need leading to starvation may amount to a crime against humanity. If this occurs during an armed conflict, it may also be a war crime. In either case, an internationally wrongful act has been perpetrated by the group in question.

35.41 With respect to the prohibition on enforced disappearance – another jus cogens norm – the 2006 International Convention for the Protection of All Persons from Enforced Disappearance stipulates simply: 'No one shall be subjected to enforced disappearance.'[49] Thus, as the UN Secretary-General has stated, 'the prohibition of enforced disappearance is absolute'.[50] This reflects the reality that an enforced disappearance by a non-State armed group is also an internationally wrongful act.

35.42 The execution of the death penalty after an unfair trial – highly likely in the case of a non-State actor – or for any crime that is not 'most serious' (i.e., intentional, unlawful homicide) will further be an internationally wrongful act, as it constitutes arbitrary deprivation of life. So too will be the execution in any circumstance of a pregnant woman or, potentially, of a person who was under eighteen years of age at the time of the commission of a crime, even if he or she has avowedly committed a most serious crime.

35.43 The duty to protect life may not be a norm of jus cogens, at least insofar as it pertains to a non-State armed group. Both in the case of enforced disappearance and more generally, a failure by a non-State armed group to comply with the procedural element of the right to life – the duty to investigate potentially unlawful death[51] – is a clear failure to protect life, but this may not yet amount to an internationally wrongful act by such a group. That said, in its 2009 Fact-Finding Mission on the Gaza conflict – and therefore prior to

[49] Art. 1(1), International Convention for the Protection of All Persons from Enforced Disappearance; adopted at New York 20 December 2006; entered into force 23 December 2010.
[50] UN, 'Amid Growing Use of Enforced Disappearances by Non-State Actors, Secretary-General Urges Prompt Action in Message on International Day Commemorating Victims', press release SG/SM/17038-OBV/1508, 28 August 2015, at http://bit.ly/3lPFO30.
[51] *Minnesota Protocol on the Investigation of Potentially Unlawful Death* (2016), *The Revised United Nations Manual on the Effective Prevention and Investigation of Extra-legal, Arbitrary and Summary Executions*, Office of the UN High Commissioner for Human Rights, New York/Geneva, 2017, esp. para. 5.

the organisation's recognition of Palestine as a State – the UN Mission established by the President of the Human Rights Council to investigate compliance by the parties to that conflict stated: 'The Gaza authorities are responsible for ensuring that effective measures for accountability for violations of IHRL and IHL committed by armed groups acting in or from the Gaza Strip are established. The Mission points out that such responsibility would continue to rest on any authority exercising government-like functions in the Gaza Strip.'[52]

---

[52] Report of the United Nations Fact-Finding Mission on the Gaza Conflict, UN doc. A/HRC/12/48, 25 September 2009, para. 1836.

36

The Right to Life and Non-governmental Organisations

INTRODUCTION

36.01 This chapter addresses the responsibility of non-governmental organisations (NGOs) under international law for violations of the right to life. It assesses the extent to which an NGO has obligations under international law to respect and protect the right to life of individuals within its sphere of influence. As is the case with corporations, obligations may be imposed by treaty or under customary law.

36.02 The traditional view holds that, under international law, NGOs have no legal duty to respect, much less to protect or fulfil human rights, including the right to life. Those duties are, so the argument goes, the exclusive domain of the sovereign, by which is meant the State and its organs.[1] So understood, NGOs could not *violate* human rights, though they might *abuse* them. This restrictive notion of international human rights law is, however, being increasingly challenged, at least with respect to peremptory norms of international law (jus cogens).

36.03 It is generally accepted that certain NGOs are, in the least, addressed by international law during a situation of armed conflict, as that notion is understood by international humanitarian law.[2] It is further unquestioned that employees of an NGO may be held individually responsible under international criminal law for international crimes they have committed in the course of their work. Analogous responsibility for members of bodies corporate was decreed in judgments in a series of trials before the Nuremberg Military Tribunals that followed the end of the Second World War.[3] The question arises as to whether, and, if so, by what legal means NGOs as organisations are also bound directly by international human rights law.

---

[1] See, e.g., N. S. Rodley, 'Can Armed Opposition Groups Violate Human Rights?', in K. Mahoney and P. Mahoney (eds.), *Human Rights in the Twenty-First Century*, Martinus Nijhoff, Dordrecht, 1993, pp. 297–318.

[2] See, generally, C. Barrat, *Status of NGOs in International Humanitarian Law*, Brill, Leiden, 2014.

[3] In its 1948 judgment in the I. G. Farben trial, which concerned among other things the production and supply of Zyklon B used by the Nazis in the Holocaust, the Nuremberg Military Tribunal reiterated earlier jurisprudence whereby 'it can no longer be questioned that the criminal sanctions of international law are applicable to private individuals'. *Law Reports of Trials of War Criminals*, Vol. X: The I. G. Farben and Krupp Trials, Published for the United Nations War Crimes Commission, His Majesty's Stationery Office, London, 1949, available at http://bit.ly/348kEpU, p. 47.

36.04 The chapter continues by defining the term 'non-governmental organisation'. It then discusses in which circumstances the actions of such entities are regulated by international law, both during armed conflicts and in peacetime. Finally, the chapter considers which obligations within the right to life are directly binding upon an NGO.

The Definition of an NGO

36.05 An NGO is not formally defined under international law. An ordinary dictionary definition holds that a non-governmental organisation is 'a non-profit organization that operates independently of any government, typically one whose purpose is to address a social or political issue'.[4] Within the United Nations, the Committee on Non-Governmental Organizations (NGO Committee) was established by an Economic and Social Council (ECOSOC) resolution adopted in 1946.[5] Under the resolution, an *international* NGO is defined in a footnote in broad terms as 'any international organisation which is not established by inter-governmental agreement'.[6] In 1994, The Code of Conduct for the International Red Cross and Red Crescent Movement and Non-Governmental Organisations (NGOs) in Disaster Relief defined NGOs as referring therein to 'organisations, both national and international, which are constituted separately from the government of the country in which they are founded'.[7] A 2019 UK research paper suggested that NGOs were 'non-governmental organisations working for a charitable purpose'.[8]

36.06 In domestic law and practice, an NGO may operate as a corporation, a foundation, or a charitable trust[9] but does not necessarily exist in any of these forms. In France, for example, an NGO is an association which makes no profit and which is registered as an 'Association Loi 1901', a reference to a law adopted in 1901 that reflected a burgeoning 'right of association' in thought prevailing in the late nineteenth century. Other terms are used to describe NGOs, such as 'civil society organisations' (e.g., in Ethiopia)[10] and 'public benefit organisations' (in Kenya).[11] In Tanzania, the applicable law has a detailed definition of an NGO as follows:

a voluntary grouping of individuals or organizations which is autonomous, non-partisan, non-profit making, which is organized locally at grassroots, national or international levels

---

[4] Definition in *Oxford English Dictionary*.
[5] ECOSOC Resolution E/RES/3(II) of 21 June 1946.
[6] Ibid., footnote to Section I: Principles to be Applied in Placing Organizations on the List of Non-Governmental Organizations Eligible for Consultation under Article 71.
[7] The Code of Conduct for the International Red Cross and Red Crescent Movement and Non-Governmental Organisations (NGOs) in Disaster Relief, Prepared jointly by the International Federation of Red Cross and Red Crescent Societies and the ICRC, Geneva, 1994, at http://bit.ly/2UcBnTl, p. 2.
[8] L. Kelly, 'Legislation on Non-governmental Organisations (NGOs) in Tanzania, Kenya, Uganda, Ethiopia, Rwanda and England and Wales', K4D, University of Manchester, 21 August 2019, at http://bit.ly/36mXFrb, p. 2.
[9] In England and Wales, the Charity Commission regulates NGOs with charitable status.
[10] Ethiopia 2019 Organization of Civil Societies Proclamation.
[11] Kenya Public Benefit Organisations (PBO) Act of 2013.

for the purpose of enhancing or promoting economic, environmental, social or cultural development or protecting the environment, lobbying or advocating on issues of public interest of a group of individuals or organizations, and includes a Non-Governmental Organization, established under the auspices of any religious organization or faith propagating organization, trade union, sports club, political party, or Community Based Organization; but does not include a trade, union, a social club or a sports club, a political party, a religious organization or a community based organization.[12]

APPLICATION OF TREATY LAW TO NGOS

36.07 Under international treaty law, the term 'legal person' is used to refer to companies and other undertakings.[13] The notion of an 'undertaking', a term employed in Articles 101 and 102 of the Treaty on the Functioning of the European Union (TFEU),[14] is sufficiently broad to encompass NGOs. The rules set out in the TFEU effectively bind directly all 'undertakings'.[15]

36.08 Also of direct normative effect with respect to NGOs – and closer to our subject matter – is Article VI of the 2009 'Kampala Convention': the African Union Convention for the Protection and Assistance of Internally Displaced Persons in Africa.[16] Therein it is stipulated that 'in providing protection and assistance to Internally Displaced Persons, international organizations and humanitarian agencies shall respect the rights of such persons in accordance with international law'.[17] Further, international organisations and humanitarian agencies 'shall be bound by the principles of humanity, neutrality, impartiality and independence of humanitarian actors, and ensure respect for relevant international standards and codes of conduct'.[18]

The Regulation of NGOs under International Humanitarian Law

36.09 NGOs are addressed by international humanitarian law treaty even though the term is not specifically employed. Indeed, the term 'NGO' is not employed in the Geneva Conventions; instead, reference is made to 'impartial humanitarian body' or 'impartial humanitarian organisation'. By 'impartiality' is meant 'the requirement not to make any

---

[12] Tanzania 2012 Non-Governmental Organizations Act.
[13] See, e.g., Art. VII(1)(a), Convention on the Prohibition of the Development, Production, Stockpiling and Use of Chemical Weapons and on Their Destruction; adopted at Geneva 3 September 1992; entered into force 29 April 1997.
[14] See Arts. 101(1)(a) and 102, Treaty on the Functioning of the European Union; adopted at Lisbon 13 December 2007; entered into force 1 December 2009.
[15] As Richard Whish and David Bailey explain, 'Articles 101 and 102 are essentially private law provisions, conferring rights and imposing obligations on undertakings; many other articles in the TFEU are primarily of a public law nature, imposing obligations on Member States.' R. Whish and D. Bailey, *Competition Law*, 9th ed., Oxford University Press, Oxford, 2018, p. 223.
[16] As of 1 May 2021, thirty-one of fifty-five African States had adhered to the Kampala Convention and a further thirteen were signatories.
[17] Art. VI(2), Kampala Convention.
[18] Art. VI(3), Kampala Convention.

"discrimination as to nationality, race, religious beliefs, class or political opinions" or any other similar criteria'.[19] Thus not every NGO may be considered an impartial humanitarian organisation, but some certainly fall within this category.

36.10 The International Committee of the Red Cross (ICRC), established by private individuals as a private association under Swiss law,[20] is given specific tasks and powers under the Geneva Conventions and its Additional Protocols. In a situation of international armed conflict, for instance, the ICRC may visit prisoners of war to provide assistance. As the 1949 Geneva Convention III specifies: 'The special position of the International Committee of the Red Cross in this field shall be recognized and respected at all times.'[21] Although not formally considered an NGO – especially by itself[22] – the ICRC manifests features common to NGOs, such as independence from governments and a humanitarian mission.[23] Under the Statutes of the International Committee of the Red Cross, however, which were adopted in 2017, it is stipulated that 'the ICRC enjoys a status equivalent to that of an international organization and has international legal personality in carrying out its work'.[24]

36.11 As the 1949 Geneva Convention I (a provision common to the other three Conventions of 1949) stipulates: 'The provisions of the present Convention constitute no obstacle to the humanitarian activities which the International Committee of the Red Cross or any other impartial humanitarian organization may, subject to the consent of the Parties to the conflict concerned, undertake for the protection of wounded and sick, medical personnel and chaplains, and for their relief.'[25] Furthermore, under the 1977 Additional Protocol I:

> The Parties to the conflict shall grant to the International Committee of the Red Cross all facilities within their power so as to enable it to carry out the humanitarian functions assigned to it by the Conventions and this Protocol in order to ensure protection and

[19] ICRC, Commentary on Article 3 of 1949 Geneva Convention III, 2020, para. 831.
[20] E. Debuf, 'Tools To Do the Job: The ICRC's Legal Status, Privileges and Immunities', *International Review of the Red Cross*, vol. 97, nos. 897/898 (2016), pp. 319–44, at http://bit.ly/2GNwywy, at 323.
[21] Art. 125, Convention Relative to the Treatment of Prisoners of War; adopted at Geneva 12 August 1949; entered into force 21 October 1950 (hereinafter, 1949 Geneva Convention III).
[22] The organization itself states that 'the ICRC is a neutral, impartial and independent humanitarian organization. We have a mandate to help and protect people affected by armed conflict and other violence or – as our mission statement puts it "other situations of violence". . . . This mandate was given to us by States through the four Geneva Conventions of 1949, their Additional Protocols of 1977 and 2005 and the Statutes of the International Red Cross and Red Crescent Movement of 1986. . . . Our mandate and legal status sets us apart from both intergovernmental organizations (such as the specialized agencies of the United Nations) and non-governmental organizations. This status allows us to function independently from governments and to serve, with complete impartiality, the people most in need of protection and assistance.' ICRC, 'What Is the ICRC?', undated but accessed 10 November 2020, at http://bit.ly/36mPx9X.
[23] See, e.g., The Code of Conduct for the International Red Cross and Red Crescent Movement and Non-Governmental Organisations (NGOs) in Disaster Relief.
[24] Art. 2(2), Statutes of the International Committee of the Red Cross; adopted at Geneva 21 December 2017; entered into force 1 January 2018, at http://bit.ly/3eKdw6Y. See, on the issue of its international legal personality, Debuf, 'Tools To Do the Job: The ICRC's Legal Status, Privileges and Immunities', p. 324.
[25] Art. 9, Convention (I) for the Amelioration of the Condition of the Wounded and Sick in Armed Forces in the Field; adopted at Geneva 12 August 1949; entered into force 21 October 1950.

assistance to the victims of conflicts; the International Committee of the Red Cross may also carry out any other humanitarian activities in favour of these victims, subject to the consent of the Parties to the conflict concerned.[26]

36.12 In situations of non-international armed conflict, the powers granted to all impartial humanitarian entities are substantially less than is the case in international armed conflict. Thus Article 3 common to the four Geneva Conventions of 1949 stipulates: 'An impartial humanitarian body, such as the International Committee of the Red Cross, may offer its services to the Parties to the conflict.' Under the 1977 Additional Protocol II, which applies in certain non-international armed conflicts: 'Relief societies located in the territory of the High Contracting Party, such as Red Cross (Red Crescent, Red Lion and Sun) organizations, may offer their services for the performance of their traditional functions in relation to the victims of the armed conflict.'[27]

36.13 The ICRC avers:

> Arguably, humanitarian protection and humanitarian assistance activities both have the same objective, i.e. to safeguard the life and dignity of the persons affected by the armed conflict. Therefore, in practice, they should be seen neither as separate, nor as mutually exclusive: assisting the persons affected by an armed conflict also protects them, and vice versa. Thus, activities of 'humanitarian protection' may simultaneously qualify as activities of 'humanitarian relief'.[28]

This implies that a serious breach of the duty to safeguard the lives of those affected by an armed conflict may entail legal responsibility. Where, as is often the case, the ICRC has status agreements in place pertaining to its operations in a particular country (also known as 'headquarters agreements'),[29] there may be no liability under that nation's domestic law, but there may be responsibility under international law.

NGOS AND THE PRINCIPLE OF HUMANITY

36.14 Indeed, as Claudie Barrat argues, with power comes responsibility.[30] A central principle pertaining to all NGOs and the ICRC operating in a situation of armed conflict and providing humanitarian assistance and/or engaging in protection work is also one of the central principles of humanity: the alleviation of suffering. Thus, under the UN Guiding Principles on Humanitarian Action, adopted by the General Assembly in 1991,

---

[26] Art. 81(1), Protocol Additional to the Geneva Conventions of 12 August 1949, and Relating to the Protection of Victims of International Armed Conflicts; adopted at Geneva 8 June 1977; entered into force 7 December 1978 (hereinafter, 1977 Additional Protocol I).
[27] Art. 18(1), Protocol Additional to the Geneva Conventions of 12 August 1949, and Relating to the Protection of Victims of Non-International Armed Conflicts; adopted at Geneva 8 June 1977; entered into force 7 December 1978 (hereinafter, 1977 Additional Protocol II).
[28] ICRC, Commentary on Article 3 of 1949 Geneva Convention III, 2020, para. 847.
[29] See, e.g., ICRC, 'Status Update: The ICRC's Legal Standing Explained', Geneva, 12 March 2019, at http://bit.ly/2IrSXjq.
[30] Barrat, *Status of NGOs in International Humanitarian Law*, §4.4.

it is stipulated that 'humanitarian assistance must be provided in accordance with the principles of humanity, neutrality and impartiality'.[31] The provision dictating similar respect in the 2009 Kampala Convention, applicable to the territory of States Parties in Africa, was cited previously.[32] More recently, The Core Humanitarian Standard on Quality and Accountability (CHS), elaborated by the Humanitarian Accountability Partnership (HAP) International, People in Aid, and the Sphere Project for NGOs worldwide and issued in 2014, described the notion of humanity as meaning that 'human suffering must be addressed wherever it is found. The purpose of humanitarian action is to protect life and health and ensure respect for human beings.'[33]

36.15 In his review of the notion of humanity in 2001, Robin Coupland defined humanity as signifying 'restraining the capacity for armed violence and limiting its effects on security and health' and asserted that 'humanity and international law go hand in hand as universal necessities for human existence'.[34] Indeed, as the Core Humanitarian Standard explains:

> The CHS places communities and people affected by crisis at the centre of humanitarian action and promotes respect for their fundamental human rights. It is underpinned by the right to life with dignity, and the right to protection and security as set forth in international law, including within the International Bill of Human Rights.[35]

Thus it may be argued that a negligent – or at the very least a reckless – failure by an NGO to perform its activities of either assistance or protection, where that failure leads to the death of a civilian or other person *hors de combat* at the hands of a party to an armed conflict, may be considered as complicity in a violation of international humanitarian law. This could further amount to complicity in a violation of the right to life.

36.16 In March 2019, BuzzFeed News reported that the UK branch of the World Wildlife Fund (WWF) might have equipped and worked directly with anti-poaching squads that had been accused of beating, torturing, sexually assaulting, and murdering indigenous people in national parks across six countries in Africa and Asia between 2002 and 2016.[36] On 4 April 2019, the UK Charity Commission opened a formal inquiry into allegations that WWF-UK may have been complicit in violence perpetrated against indigenous people overseas.[37] In April 2019, WWF appointed Navi Pillay, the former UN High Commissioner for Human Rights, to chair its own inquiry into alleged abuses. The panel originally planned to publish its findings by the end of 2019 but failed

---

[31] UN General Assembly Resolution 46/82, adopted without a vote on 19 December 1991, Annex, para. 2.
[32] Art. VI(3), Kampala Convention.
[33] The Core Humanitarian Standard on Quality and Accountability (CHS), Geneva, 2014, at http://bit.ly/35gQu4z, p. 8.
[34] See, e.g., R. Coupland, 'Humanity: What Is It and How Does It Influence International Law?', *International Review of the Red Cross*, vol. 83, no. 844 (December 2001), pp. 969–89, at http://bit.ly/3p8SHHo, at 988 and 989, respectively.
[35] The Core Humanitarian Standard on Quality and Accountability (CHS), p. 2.
[36] K. J. M. Baker and T. Warren, 'WWF Funds Guards Who Have Tortured and Killed People', post, *BuzzFeed News*, 4 March 2019, at http://bit.ly/2UbiOyG.
[37] D. Carolei, 'What Happens When NGOs Are Accused of Violating Human Rights?', *OpenDemocracy*, 16 April 2019, at http://bit.ly/3lvfQ4t.

to do so.[38] The issue was taken up by the US House of Representatives' Natural Resources Committee in 2019.[39]

The Application of International Human Rights Law

36.17 It is clear from the examples provided thus far that international law in connection with armed conflict and in peacetime may impose obligations directly upon NGOs. While there is no consensus on the issue, there is increasing acceptance that the application of customary international law – at the very least with respect to those customary norms that are of a peremptory nature – is the primary means by which organisations are bound by human rights norms.

Jus Cogens Norms Binding on All NGOs

36.18 Indeed, it has been unequivocally asserted that peremptory norms of international law are binding on all entities, groups, and organisations, which would include NGOs. As the Independent International Commission of Inquiry on the Syrian Arab Republic declared in 2012, 'at a minimum, human rights obligations constituting peremptory international law (*ius cogens*) bind States, individuals and non-State collective entities, including armed groups'.[40]

36.19 In its judgment of February 2020 in *Nevsun Resources Ltd. v. Araya*,[41] the Supreme Court of Canada held that Canadian corporations may be sued in tort for violations of international human rights law that occur abroad.[42] By five votes to four, the Supreme Court held that claims for violations of international human rights norms abroad may be brought in Canadian courts on the grounds that Canadian common law has 'adopted' custom. It declared that some norms of customary international law 'prohibit conduct regardless of whether the perpetrator is a state'.[43]

VIOLATIONS OF THE RIGHT TO LIFE THAT CONSTITUTE INTERNATIONALLY WRONGFUL ACTS BY AN NGO

36.20 A range of conduct will violate the jus cogens elements of respect for the right to life and thereby constitute an internationally wrongful act by an NGO. The most obvious

---

[38] K. J. M. Baker and T. Warren, 'WWF Says It Is "Troubled" by an Alleged Human Rights Violation at a Park with a History of Violence', post, *BuzzFeed News*, 31 July 2020, at http://bit.ly/3lgqmMM.
[39] Natural Resources Committee of the House of Representatives, 'Chair Grijalva, Ranking Member Bishop Seek Documents as Investigation of Alleged Human Rights Abuses by Wildlife Advocacy Groups Intensifies', press release, Washington, DC, 1 July 2019, at http://bit.ly/3nehoS4. See further the House hearing on the issue on 24 September 2019, at http://bit.ly/32A9LMp.
[40] Report of the Independent International Commission of Inquiry on the Syrian Arab Republic, UN doc. A/HRC/19/69, 22 February 2012, para. 106.
[41] Supreme Court of Canada, *Nevsun Resources Ltd. v. Araya*, 2020 SCC 5, judgment rendered on 28 February 2020.
[42] See generally W. S. Dodge, 'Supreme Court of Canada Recognizes Corporate Liability for Human Rights Violations', *Just Security*, 26 March 2020, at http://bit.ly/2HkLu5s.
[43] Supreme Court of Canada, *Nevsun Resources Ltd. v. Araya*, Judgment, para. 105.

examples are arbitrary deprivation of life through deliberate extrajudicial executions or other arbitrary killings perpetrated either by staff of an NGO in connection with the operations and activities of that organisation or by individuals or groups that they employ. This is so whether the killings occur in peacetime or during, and in connection with, a situation of armed conflict.

36.21 With respect to the prohibition on enforced disappearance – another jus cogens norm – the 2006 International Convention for the Protection of All Persons from Enforced Disappearance stipulates simply that 'no one shall be subjected to enforced disappearance'.[44] Thus, as the UN Secretary-General has stated, 'The prohibition of enforced disappearance is absolute.'[45] This renders an enforced disappearance perpetrated by an NGO or its personnel or contractors also an internationally wrongful act.

36.22 In sum, therefore, non-governmental organisations have a duty under customary international law to respect the prohibition on arbitrary deprivation of life and to exercise due diligence in their activities to protect those on behalf of whom they are directly working from any such arbitrary deprivation. While their actions are often directed towards broader fulfilment of the right to life, under extant international law this cannot be said to be an international legal obligation.

---

[44] Art. 1(1), International Convention for the Protection of All Persons from Enforced Disappearance; adopted at New York 20 December 2006; entered into force 23 December 2010.
[45] UN, 'Amid Growing Use of Enforced Disappearances by Non-State Actors, Secretary-General Urges Prompt Action in Message on International Day Commemorating Victims', press release SG/SM/17038-OBV/1508, 28 August 2015, at http://bit.ly/3lPFO3o.

37

The Right to Life and the Responsibility of Individuals

INTRODUCTION

37.01 In certain circumstances, individuals can be held directly responsible for violations of the right to life, notably when they act as an agent of a State, an international organization, an armed group, a corporation, or a non-governmental organisation (NGO). As the 1998 Declaration of Human Duties and Responsibilities stipulated: 'No one shall participate, by act or by failure to act where required, in violating human rights and fundamental freedoms.'[1]

37.02 Under international law, individual responsibility exists for violation of jus cogens norms, which include arbitrary deprivation of life.[2] Such arbitrary deprivation of life may result from acts or omissions. Peremptory norms of international law are binding for not only all States, corporations, armed groups, and organisations, but also individuals. As the Independent International Commission of Inquiry on the Syrian Arab Republic declared in 2012, 'at a minimum, human rights obligations constituting peremptory international law (*ius cogens*) bind States, individuals and non-State collective entities, including armed groups'.[3]

37.03 While the most obvious route for realising individual responsibility for a violation of the right to life is through criminal law – domestic or international – there are also civil remedies available in certain States. This is most notably the case in the United States, based on the Alien Tort Statute of 1789 or actions under Section 1983 of the US Code.

INDIVIDUAL CRIMINAL RESPONSIBILITY FOR INTERNATIONAL CRIMES

37.04 There is clear *opinio juris* dating back seventy-five years in favour of international crimes pertaining to the right to life applying directly to individuals by virtue of international criminal law. In his opening statement for the prosecution in the *Einsatzgruppen*[4]

---

[1] Declaration on the Right and Responsibility of Individuals, Groups and Organs of Society to Promote and Protect Universally Recognized Human Rights and Fundamental Freedoms; adopted by UN General Assembly Resolution 53/144, resolution adopted without a vote on 9 December 1998.
[2] On this issue, see Chapter 1.
[3] Report of the Independent International Commission of Inquiry on the Syrian Arab Republic, UN doc. A/HRC/19/69, 22 February 2012, para. 106.
[4] The *Einsatzgruppen* were paramilitary units tasked by the SS with exterminating Jews, Communist functionaries, gypsies, 'Asiatic inferiors', and those with intellectual disabilities in occupied Europe, particular in the East.

trial before the Nuremberg Military Tribunal in 1947, Benjamin Ferencz declared: 'Vengeance is not our goal, nor do we seek merely a just retribution. We ask this Court to affirm by international penal action man's right to live in peace and dignity regardless of his race or creed. The case we present is a plea of humanity to law.'[5] In its judgment, the Tribunal stated the following:

> The books have shown through the ages why man has slaughtered his brother. He has always had an excuse, criminal and ungodly though it may have been. He has killed to take his brother's property, his wife, his throne, his position; he has slain out of jealousy, revenge, passion, lust, and cannibalism. He has murdered as a monarch, a slave owner, a madman, a robber. But it was left to the twentieth century to produce so extraordinary a killing that even a new word had to be created to define it.
>
> One of counsel has characterized this trial as the biggest murder trial in history. Certainly never before have twenty-three men been brought into court to answer to the charge of destroying over one million of their fellow human beings. There have been other trials imputing to administrators and officials responsibility for mass murder, but in this case the defendants are not simply accused of planning or directing wholesale killings through channels. They are not charged with sitting in an office hundreds and thousands of miles away from the slaughter. It is asserted with particularity that these men were in the field actively superintending, controlling, directing, and taking an active part in the bloody harvest.[6]

The Tribunal further observed:

> There is no authority which denies any belligerent nation jurisdiction over individuals in its actual custody charged with violation of international law. And if a single nation may legally take jurisdiction in such instances, with what more reason may a number of nations agree, in the interest of justice, to try alleged violations of the international code of war?[7]

37.05 The prohibition of genocide, war crimes, and crimes against humanity are certainly jus cogens rules,[8] 'and the punishment of such crimes is obligatory pursuant to the general principles of international law'.[9] Crimes against humanity are the 'culmination of violations of fundamental human rights, such as the right to life and the prohibition of torture or other forms of inhuman and degrading treatment'.[10] Crimes against humanity may be committed both in peacetime and in situations of armed conflict. They violate, in the

---

[5] B. B. Ferencz, Opening Statement for the Prosecution in *United States of America v. Otto Ohlendorf and others*, Trial of the Major War Criminals, Vol. IV (1947), Nuremberg, at http://bit.ly/2JUPiLN, p. 30.

[6] Nuremberg Military Tribunal, *United States of America v. Otto Ohlendorf and others*, Judgment, in *Trial of the Major War Criminals*, Vol. IV (1947), p. 412.

[7] Ibid., p. 460.

[8] Annex, International Law Commission (ILC) draft conclusions on peremptory norms of general international law (jus cogens), UN doc. A/74/10, Chap. V.

[9] Report of the Independent International Commission of Inquiry on the Syrian Arab Republic, UN doc. A/HRC/21/50, 16 August 2012, Annex II, para. 26, citing Inter-American Court of Human Rights, *Almonacid-Arellano and others v. Chile*, Judgment (Preliminary Objections, Merits, Reparations and Costs), 26 September 2006, para. 99.

[10] Report of the Independent International Commission of Inquiry on the Syrian Arab Republic, UN doc. A/HRC/21/50, 16 August 2012, Annex II, para. 26.

682   Accountability

words of the Inter-American Court of Human Rights, 'a series of non-derogable rights recognised in the American Convention'.[11] First among these is the right to life. As the Nuremberg Military Tribunal further declared in its judgment of 1947 in the *Einsatzgruppen* case: 'In the main, the defendants in this case are charged with murder. Certainly no one can claim with the slightest pretense at reasoning that there is any taint of *ex post factoism* in the law of murder.'[12]

Command Responsibility for International Crimes

37.06 In addition to the direct perpetrator, international criminal law also provides for command responsibility as a mode of liability with respect to international crimes. In a situation of international armed conflict, the 1977 Additional Protocol I provides:

> The High Contracting Parties and Parties to the conflict shall require any commander who is aware that subordinates or other persons under his control are going to commit or have committed a breach of the Conventions or of this Protocol, to initiate such steps as are necessary to prevent such violations of the Conventions or this Protocol, and, where appropriate, to initiate disciplinary or penal action against violators thereof.[13]

This includes, first and foremost, the wilful killing of civilians or others *hors de combat* or the targeting of civilians in the conduct of hostilities.

37.07 In addition, the 'fact that a breach of the Conventions or of this Protocol was committed by a subordinate does not absolve his superiors from penal or disciplinary responsibility, as the case may be'. This is so, 'if they knew, or had information which should have enabled them to conclude in the circumstances at the time, that he was committing or was going to commit such a breach and if they did not take all feasible measures within their power to prevent or repress the breach'.[14] Indeed, the criminal responsibility of commanders for war crimes committed by their subordinates, 'based on the commanders' failure to take measures to prevent or punish the commission of such crimes', is, as the International Committee of the Red Cross has noted, 'a longstanding rule of customary international law'.[15] It was on that basis that commanders were found guilty of war crimes committed by their subordinates in trials following the Second World War.[16]

37.08 *A fortiori*, where a commander orders the commission of a war crime, he or she is criminally responsible, but in such an instance, liability under international criminal law

---

[11] Inter-American Court of Human Rights, *Almonacid-Arellano and others v. Chile*, Judgment, 26 September 2006, para. 111.
[12] *United States of America v. Otto Ohlendorf and others*, Judgment, in *Trial of the Major War Criminals*, Vol. IV (1947), p. 459.
[13] Art. 87(3), Protocol Additional to the Geneva Conventions of 12 August 1949, and relating to the Protection of Victims of International Armed Conflicts; adopted at Geneva 8 June 1977; entered into force 7 December 1978 (hereinafter, 1977 Additional Protocol I).
[14] Art. 86(2), 1977 Additional Protocol I.
[15] ICRC, Customary IHL Rule 153: 'Command Responsibility for Failure to Prevent, Repress or Report War Crimes', at http://bit.ly/2InKTRn.
[16] Ibid.

is as a co-perpetrator.[17] In contradistinction, in relation to the war crime of denying quarter, a commander may well be the sole perpetrator. Denial of quarter occurs where it is declared or ordered that there shall be no survivors. The war crime is committed by the mere declaration or order 'in order to threaten an adversary or to conduct hostilities on the basis that there shall be no survivors', irrespective of whether the order is carried out. But the perpetrator must have been 'in a position of effective command or control over the subordinate forces to which the declaration or order was directed'.[18] It is thus primarily directed at commanders. In any event, individual criminal responsibility for commanders with respect to war crimes applies regardless of whether the conflict is international or non-international in character.

37.09 But command responsibility is not limited to the commission of war crimes. It pertains also to genocide and crimes against humanity, regardless of whether the constituent acts are committed during a situation of armed conflict or in peacetime.[19] As the Rome Statute of the International Criminal Court decrees:

> A military commander or person effectively acting as a military commander shall be criminally responsible for crimes within the jurisdiction of the Court committed by forces under his or her effective command and control, or effective authority and control as the case may be, as a result of his or her failure to exercise control properly over such forces, where:
> (i) That military commander or person either knew or, owing to the circumstances at the time, should have known that the forces were committing or about to commit such crimes; and
> (ii) That military commander or person failed to take all necessary and reasonable measures within his or her power to prevent or repress their commission or to submit the matter to the competent authorities for investigation and prosecution.[20]

INDIVIDUAL CRIMINAL RESPONSIBILITY IN THE UNITED STATES FOR CIVIL RIGHTS VIOLATIONS

37.10 Decades of police brutality against African Americans, capped by a succession of violations in the summer of 1964, led to riots in Chicago, Jersey City, New York, and Philadelphia.[21] The Civil Rights Act signed into law by US President Lyndon Baines

---

[17] ICRC, Customary IHL Rule 152: 'Command Responsibility for Orders to Commit War Crimes', at http://bit.ly/3eTBtJo.
[18] Elements 2–4, Art. 8(2)(b)(xii) and (e)(x): War crime of denying quarter, Elements of Crimes, reproduced from the *Official Records of the Assembly of States Parties to the Rome Statute of the International Criminal Court*, First Session, New York, 3–10 September 2002, Part II(B) (hereinafter, 2002 Elements of Crimes).
[19] Potentially, the commander of armed forces of a State that commits an act of aggression may also be held individually criminally responsible.
[20] Art. 28(a), Rome Statute of the International Criminal Court; adopted at Rome 17 July 1998; entered into force 1 July 2002 (hereinafter, ICC Statute).
[21] A. Taylor, '1964: Civil Rights Battles', *The Atlantic*, 28 May 2014, at http://bit.ly/3ltndJw.

Johnson in 1964 was a landmark piece of legislation in the United States. Martin Luther King Jr declared that the Act was nothing less than a 'second emancipation'.[22] At the time, the possibility to charge individuals for federal crimes committed against African Americans in the course of law enforcement existed in theory but was, in practice, limited.[23] Section 242 of Title 18 of the US code provides:

> Whoever, under color of any law, statute, ordinance, regulation, or custom, willfully subjects any person in any State, Territory, Commonwealth, Possession, or District to the deprivation of any rights, privileges, or immunities secured or protected by the Constitution or laws of the United States, or to different punishments, pains, or penalties, on account of such person being an alien, or by reason of his color, or race, than are prescribed for the punishment of citizens, shall be fined under this title or imprisoned not more than one year, or both.[24]

It is further stipulated that if death results from the acts committed in violation of Section 242, the perpetrator 'shall be fined under this title, or imprisoned for any term of years or for life, or both, or may be sentenced to death'.[25]

37.11 A Rubicon was crossed once more after the Rodney King case in 1991–3. Four Los Angeles Police Department (LAPD) police officers savagely beat Rodney King after a traffic stop in Los Angeles early in the morning of 3 March 1991, in an incident captured on videotape. Two of the officers inflicted more than fifty baton blows and several kicks on Mr King, and a third officer stomped on his shoulder, causing his head to hit hard against the asphalt. One or more of the baton blows seem to land, contrary to LAPD policy, on Mr King's head.[26] His injuries resulted in skull fractures, broken bones and teeth, and permanent brain damage.[27]

37.12 Despite the graphic video, however, the four officers were acquitted of charges of assault and use of excessive force in a criminal trial held under California state law.[28] The not-guilty verdicts led to the worst civil disturbances in the history of the United States. More than 50 people were killed – 10 of whom were shot and killed by LAPD officers and National Guardsmen – and more than 2,350 others were injured during 5 days of rioting across Los Angeles that caused almost US$1 billion of damage to property. The four officers were subsequently retried under the federal civil rights law laid down in Section

---

[22] 'Civil Rights Act of 1964', *History*, last updated 10 February 2020, at http://bit.ly/32JNewW.
[23] See, e.g., S. Brady Siff, 'Policing the Police: A Civil Rights Story', *Origins*, vol. 9, no. 8 (May 2016), at http://bit.ly/3kunZoh. With respect to the 1871 Civil Rights Act (also known as the Ku Klux Klan Act), see, e.g., A. Y. Cover, 'Reconstructing the Right Against Excessive Force', *Florida Law Review*, vol. 68 (2016), pp. 1773–1837, text available at http://bit.ly/35oBiCq.
[24] 18 US Code §242: 'Deprivation of rights under color of law', text available at Legal Information Institute, Cornell School of Law, Cornell University, at http://bit.ly/3pnIYN7.
[25] Ibid.
[26] Prof. Douglas O. Linder, 'The Trials of Los Angeles Police Officers in Connection with the Beating of Rodney King', *Famous Trials*, at http://bit.ly/3lx1b8H.
[27] A. Sastry and K. Grigsby Bates, 'When LA Erupted in Anger: A Look Back at the Rodney King Riots', *NPR*, 26 April 2017, at http://n.pr/36BVTCw.
[28] S. Mydans, 'Police Beating Trial Opens with Replay of Videotape', *New York Times*, 6 March 1992, at http://nyti.ms/3eYeNXW.

242,[29] at the issue of which two of the officers, Sergeant Stacey C. Koon and Officer Laurence M. Powell, were convicted and each sentenced to two-and-a-half years imprisonment.[30] In his 1992 book prior to the trial, *Presumed Guilty: The Tragedy of the Rodney King Affair*, Mr Koon defended his actions, blaming the riots on the media and community leaders.[31]

INDIVIDUAL CIVIL RESPONSIBILITY FOR INTERNATIONAL CRIMES

37.13 The United States also leads in providing for individual civil responsibility for violations of international law, in particular international crimes. The Alien Tort Statute of 1789[32] stipulates: 'The district courts shall have original jurisdiction of any civil action by an alien for a tort only, committed in violation of the law of nations or a treaty of the United States.' In its 2004 judgment in the *Sosa* case,[33] the US Supreme Court concluded that the Alien Tort Statute allows federal courts to enforce a limited class of international norms that are 'specific, universal, and obligatory'.[34] In the *Kiobel* case,[35] a brief filed by the Obama administration declared that the prohibitions against torture, genocide, and war crimes apply to natural persons, irrespective of whether they act on behalf of a State: 'Both natural persons and corporations can violate international-law norms that require state action. And both natural persons and corporations can violate international-law norms that do not require state action.'[36]

37.14 Two decades earlier, in 1993, Radovan Karadžić, president of the self-styled Republika Srpska, was sued under the Alien Tort Statute for genocide, war crimes, and crimes against humanity against Bosnians during the armed conflicts in Bosnia and Herzegovina in 1992–5. Mr Karadžić appeared in the case until 1997, when he defaulted. In default proceedings, a jury at the District Court for the Southern District of New York awarded US$4.5 billion in damages to his victims on 25 September 2000.[37] None of the award has ever been paid.

---

[29] J. Newton and L. Berger, 'U.S. Files Civil Rights Charges against 4 Officers in King Case: Indictments: Federal Prosecutor Says Beating "Was an Unreasonable Use of Force." If Convicted, Each Man Faces Up to 10 Years in Prison and Fines', *Los Angeles Times*, 6 August 1992, at http://lat.ms/38DDlof.

[30] S. Mydans, 'Sympathetic Judge Gives Officers 2 1/2 Years in Rodney King Beating', *New York Times*, 5 August 1993, at http://nyti.ms/2UlR1vN.

[31] S. C. Koon with R. Deitz, *Presumed Guilty: The Tragedy of the Rodney King Affair*, Regnery, New York, 1992.

[32] 28 USC 1350.

[33] The case concerned the kidnapping and rendition of Humberto Álvarez-Machaín in Mexico for the kidnap and murder of a US Drug Enforcement Administration (DEA) special agent by a Mexican drug cartel in 1985. Mr Álvarez-Machaín was found not guilty in a US court for want of sufficient evidence. He then sued one of his kidnappers under the Alien Tort Statute. The US Supreme Court held that this fell outside the activities justiciable under the Statute.

[34] US Supreme Court, *Sosa v. Alvarez-Machain*, 542 US 692, 732 (2004).

[35] Brought by Nigerian refugees in the United States against the entity which is now Royal Dutch Shell, the lawsuit accused the Dutch/British multinational corporation of aiding and abetting the Nigerian military in the systematic torture and killing of peaceful environmental protesters in the 1990s. Center for Justice and Accountability, 'Kiobel v. Shell', 2020, at http://bit.ly/2Hs3Ykg.

[36] US Supreme Court, *Kiobel and others v. Royal Dutch Petroleum Co. and others*, Amicus Curiae of the United States supporting the Petitioners, December 2011, p. 21.

[37] Center for Constitutional Rights, 'Doe v. Karadzic', at http://bit.ly/3lyAuAI.

37.15 Initially indicted with international crimes in 1995, Mr Karadžić was arrested in Belgrade on 21 July 2008 and transferred to the International Criminal Tribunal for the former Yugoslavia (ICTY) nine days later. An ICTY Trial Chamber delivered its judgment on 24 March 2016, finding him guilty of genocide, crimes against humanity, and war crimes. Mr Karadžić was sentenced to forty years of imprisonment. He appealed against both his conviction and his sentence. On 20 March 2019, the Appeals Chamber rendered its judgment, reversing certain parts of his criminal convictions but affirming those for, among others, genocide, persecution, extermination, and murder as crimes against humanity, as well as for murder and terror as war crimes. His sentence was increased to life imprisonment.[38] In accordance with the Rome Statute, the International Criminal Court 'may make an order directly against a convicted person specifying appropriate reparations to, or in respect of, victims, including restitution, compensation and rehabilitation'.[39] No such order was made in the case of Radovan Karadžić.

INDIVIDUAL CIVIL RESPONSIBILITY FOR VIOLATIONS OF FUNDAMENTAL HUMAN RIGHTS

37.16 Within the United States, most civil actions against police officers for misconduct, which effectively include violations of fundamental human rights even though they are not labelled as such, are filed under Section 1983 of Title 42 of the US Code.[40] This reflects a law originally adopted as the Civil Rights Act in 1871.[41] To prove a violation under Section 1983 for claims of excessive force, the plaintiff must prove both that the law enforcement officer in question deprived the individual of his or her right to be free from unreasonable seizures under the Fourth Amendment or his or her right to life under the Fourteenth Amendment, and that the officer acted 'under color of law'.[42] But the doctrine of qualified immunity often serves to protect law enforcement officials.[43]

---

[38] UN International Residual Mechanism for International Tribunals, 'Karadžić, Radovan (MICT-13-55)', at http://bit.ly/35pg872.

[39] Art. 75(2), ICC Statute.

[40] 'Every person who, under color of any statute, ordinance, regulation, custom, or usage, of any State or Territory or the District of Columbia, subjects, or causes to be subjected, any citizen of the United States or other person within the jurisdiction thereof to the deprivation of any rights, privileges, or immunities secured by the Constitution and laws, shall be liable to the party injured in an action at law, suit in equity, or other proper proceeding for redress, except that in any action brought against a judicial officer for an act or omission taken in such officer's judicial capacity, injunctive relief shall not be granted unless a declaratory decree was violated or declaratory relief was unavailable. For the purposes of this section, any Act of Congress applicable exclusively to the District of Columbia shall be considered to be a statute of the District of Columbia.' 42 USC §1983 (1994).

[41] Civil Rights Act of 1871, chap. 22, §1, 17 Stat. 13.

[42] US Supreme Court, *West v. Atkins*, 487 US 42 (1988), at 48; see 'Police Use of Force: Rules, Remedies, and Reforms', Congressional Research Service, Washington, DC, 30 October 2015, at http://bit.ly/2UqGSOu.

[43] US Commission on Civil Rights, *Racial and Ethnic Tensions in American Communities: Poverty, Inequality, and Discrimination, Volume III: The Chicago Report*, September 1995, p. 139; see USCCR, Revisiting *Who Is Guarding the Guardians?*, A Report on Police Practices and Civil Rights in America, November 2000, chap. 5 ('Remedies and Legal Developments'), at http://bit.ly/35plBuL.

37.17 The US example has not been followed by other States.[44] In the United Kingdom, for instance, the 1998 Human Rights Act does not foresee individual responsibility under civil law for violations of the right protected therein.[45] This is despite the fact that, as Sascha-Dominik Bachmann has observed, in many instances, 'civil remedies against individual perpetrators could be the only feasible way to claim financial damages for human rights atrocities'.[46]

VIOLATIONS OF THE RIGHT TO LIFE BY INDIVIDUALS

37.18 A range of conduct will violate the jus cogens elements of respect for the right to life and thereby engender potential individual responsibility. The most obvious instance is any arbitrary deprivation of life, such as that realised through extrajudicial executions or other arbitrary killings perpetrated by State agents or members of non-State armed groups or other collectives. This is so whether the killings occur in peacetime or during, and in connection with, a situation of armed conflict. In this regard, an intentional violation of a basic IHL rule governing the conduct of hostilities, in particular the principle of distinction or of proportionality in attack, will also amount to arbitrary deprivation of life, at the least where it results in death. Such conduct also constitutes a war crime.

37.19 The failure by a responsible individual to provide adequate food and water to a detainee or to ensure the provision of appropriate medical care where he or she needs it will also amount to arbitrary deprivation of life, most obviously where the detainee perishes. On a broader scope, preventing food from being accessed by a civilian population in need leading to starvation may amount to a crime against humanity. If this occurs during an armed conflict, it may also be a war crime. In either case, responsible individuals have violated the right to life.

37.20 In connection with an armed conflict, the passing of a sentence by a judge, and especially the imposition of the death penalty, after a manifestly unfair trial or for any crime that is not 'most serious' (i.e., intentional, unlawful homicide) will also constitute an arbitrary deprivation of life and render the judge liable to prosecution for a war crime.[47] So too will be the imposition in any circumstance of a death sentence upon a person who was under eighteen years of age at the time of the commission of a crime, even if he or she has avowedly committed a most serious crime. In each case, the individual judge has violated the right to life.

---

[44] S.-D. Bachmann, *Civil Responsibility for Gross Human Rights Violations – The Need for a Global Instrument*, Pretoria University Law Press, Pretoria, 2007, text available at http://bit.ly/38ML6rM, p. 47.
[45] Citizens Advice, 'The Human Rights Act 1998', at http://bit.ly/3lvlwuW.
[46] Bachmann, *Civil Responsibility for Gross Human Rights Violations – The Need for a Global Instrument*, p. 50.
[47] Art. 8(2)(c)(iv), ICC Statute. In the corresponding elements of crime, it is stipulated that 'the court that rendered judgement did not afford all other judicial guarantees generally recognized as indispensable under international law'. Element 4, Art. 8(2)(c)(iv): 'War crime of sentencing or execution without due process', 2002 Elements of Crimes.

37.21 With respect to the prohibition on enforced disappearance – another jus cogens norm – the 2006 International Convention for the Protection of All Persons from Enforced Disappearance stipulates simply: 'No one shall be subjected to enforced disappearance.'[48] Thus, as the UN Secretary-General has stated: 'The prohibition of enforced disappearance is absolute.'[49] This renders an enforced disappearance by an individual acting on behalf of a State, an international organisation, a non-State armed group, a corporation, or an NGO an international crime.

---

[48] Art. 1(1), International Convention for the Protection of All Persons from Enforced Disappearance; adopted at New York 20 December 2006; entered into force 23 December 2010.

[49] UN, 'Amid Growing Use of Enforced Disappearances by Non-State Actors, Secretary-General Urges Prompt Action in Message on International Day Commemorating Victims', press release SG/SM/17038-OBV/1508, 28 August 2015, at http://bit.ly/3lPFO3o.

PART V

Human Rights Machinery Protecting the Right to Life

38

The UN Human Rights Machinery and the Right to Life

INTRODUCTION

38.01 Within the United Nations, a range of human rights procedures and mechanisms explicitly seek to interpret, promote, and protect human rights, including the right to life, while other judicial and quasi-judicial fora may be called upon to do so. The Human Rights Committee and the Special Rapporteur on extrajudicial, summary, or arbitrary executions are most heavily engaged in the promotion of the right to life, but many other treaty bodies and special procedures address the right to life in some form. In a number of instances, this is because the relevant treaty specifically provides for the right to life (the case with respect to children, international migrants, and persons with disabilities). In others, it is because the customary right to life is not respected whether as a result of a form of discrimination (whether racial or gender-based) or because it and related rights are implicitly protected by the treaty in question (enforced disappearance).

38.02 This chapter first discusses the central role within the United Nations of the Human Rights Council. It then details the relevance of the different treaty bodies, followed by a summary of action and positions taken by key special procedures. Their dicta can be considered as soft law – not directly legally binding but with considerable authority and, consonant with their status, as subsidiary means for determining a rule of law. Next are considered the roles in promoting and protecting the right to life of the International Court of Justice and the International Criminal Court, and subsequently the General Assembly and Security Council, respectively. Finally, the limited international mechanisms dedicated to fact-finding with respect to the application and implementation of international humanitarian law are considered.

THE HUMAN RIGHTS COUNCIL

38.03 The UN Human Rights Council is an intergovernmental body that is mandated to promote and protect all human rights around the world. It is a subsidiary organ of the UN General Assembly to which it reports each year. Established in 2005 pursuant to General

Assembly Resolution 60/251,[1] the Human Rights Council replaced the discredited UN Commission on Human Rights within the UN system.[2] The Commission was formally abolished on 16 June 2006 by a resolution of the UN Economic and Social Council (ECOSOC)[3] to which it had reported.

38.04 The Human Rights Council comprises forty-seven UN member States elected onto it by the General Assembly, whereafter they serve for a three-year term (though they may be re-elected).[4] The Council typically holds three regular sessions a year, for a total of at least ten weeks: in March (four weeks), in June (three weeks), and in September (three weeks). If a vote is called for, each resolution is adopted by a simple majority of the members present and voting as long as at least twenty-four members are present.[5] In addition, if one-third of the member States requests, the Council can decide at any time to hold a special session to address human rights violations and emergencies.[6] As of this writing, in the past five years, it had done so with respect to Palestine (in May 2018), Myanmar (in December 2017), South Sudan (in December 2016), Syria (in October 2016), and Burundi (in December 2015).[7]

38.05 The final regular session of the Council of 2020, its forty-fifth in total, was held from 14 September to 7 October. Many of the resolutions adopted by the Council in that session, covering an array of issues, actors, and situations, addressed or concerned the right to life. Thus, for instance, the preamble to an uncontested resolution on enforced or involuntary disappearances reaffirmed the relevant articles of the Universal Declaration of Human Rights[8] and the International Covenant on Civil and Political Rights (ICCPR)[9] that protect the right of life.[10] A separate resolution on human rights and the regulation of civilian acquisition, possession, and use of firearms noted the Council's alarm 'that

---

[1] UN General Assembly Resolution 60/251: 'Human Rights Council', adopted on 15 March 2006 by 170 votes to 4 (Israel, Marshall Islands, Palau, and the United States) with 3 abstentions (Belarus, Iran, and Venezuela). See the procès-verbal of the debate surrounding the adoption of the resolution at http://bit.ly/2IRsoWY.

[2] UN News, 'Replaced by Stronger Body, UN Rights Commission Formally Told to Close Shop', 23 March 2006, at http://bit.ly/3feGHPQ.

[3] ECOSOC Resolution 2006/2: 'Implementation of General Assembly resolution 60/251', adopted without a vote on 23 March 2006, at http://bit.ly/3kQ1muu.

[4] Seats are allocated in accordance with an agreed geographical distribution which corresponds to the regional groupings within the United Nations: thirteen seats for African States, thirteen seats for Asia-Pacific states, eight seats for Latin American and Caribbean (GRULAC) States, seven seats for Western European and Other States (WEOG), and six seats for Eastern European States.

[5] Rules 19 and 20, Rules of Procedure, adopted under Human Rights Council Resolution 5/1: 'Institution-building of the United Nations Human Rights Council', adopted without a vote on 18 June 2007.

[6] OHCHR, 'UN Human Rights Council: Sessions', at http://bit.ly/35NrtOF.

[7] Details of all Special Sessions of the Council are available on the OHCHR website at http://bit.ly/3kHNBOE.

[8] Universal Declaration of Human Rights; adopted at Paris by UN General Assembly Resolution 217, 10 December 1948. Resolution 217 was adopted by forty-eight votes to zero with eight abstentions (Byelorussian SSR, Czechoslovakia, Poland, Saudi Arabia, South Africa, Soviet Union, Ukrainian SSR, and Yugoslavia). Honduras and Yemen did not take part in the vote.

[9] International Covenant on Civil and Political Rights; adopted at New York, 16 December 1966; entered into force 23 March 1976. In addition to the 173 States Parties as of 1 May 2021, a further 6 States were signatories.

[10] Human Rights Council Resolution 45/3: 'Enforced or involuntary disappearances', adopted without a vote on 6 October 2020, second preambular para.

hundreds of thousands of human beings of all ages around the world continue to have their human rights, in particular their right to life and security of person ... negatively affected by the misuse, intentional or unintentional, of firearms'.[11] The Council explicitly recognised that 'civilian firearms-related violence and insecurity pose direct risks to the right to life and to security of person'.[12] In a resolution on the safety of journalists, also adopted without a vote, the Council expressed its concern 'about incidents of the extraterritorial targeting of journalists and media workers, including harassment, surveillance and the arbitrary deprivation of life' and expressed deep concern 'that the work of journalists and media workers often puts them at specific risk of human rights violations and abuses, including killing, torture, [and] enforced disappearance'.[13]

38.06 A resolution on Yemen, subject to a vote, demanded 'the immediate release of all persons arbitrarily detained or forcibly disappeared, including all political prisoners and journalists', and noted 'the additional, potentially life-threatening risks to health created by the COVID-19 pandemic and its potential to exacerbate the already dire situation of detainees'.[14] The Resolution further urged 'all parties in Yemen to end any use of starvation of civilians as a method of warfare' and to 'conduct, in an independent manner, full, prompt, impartial and effective investigations within their jurisdiction into violations of international humanitarian law relating to the use of starvation of civilians as a method of warfare'.[15]

38.07 In a resolution on Burundi, also contested, the Council condemned 'in the strongest terms' all human rights violations and abuses committed in Burundi, including in the context of the recent election process, and including extrajudicial killings [and] enforced disappearances'.[16] The Council urged the government 'to fight the impunity enjoyed by perpetrators of grave crimes, including members of the security forces and the youth league of the ruling party Conseil national pour la défense de la démocratie – Forces pour la défense de la démocratie, known as the Imbonerakure, who have been carrying out extrajudicial killings'.[17]

---

[11] Human Rights Council Resolution 45/13: 'Human rights and the regulation of civilian acquisition, possession and use of firearms', adopted without a vote on 6 October 2020, sixth preambular para.
[12] Ibid., operative para. 3.
[13] Human Rights Council Resolution 45/18: 'The safety of journalists', adopted without a vote on 6 October 2020, nineteenth and eighteenth preambular paras, respectively.
[14] Human Rights Council Resolution 45/15: 'Situation of human rights in Yemen', operative para. 5. The resolution was adopted on 6 October 2020 by twenty-two votes (Argentina, Australia, Austria, Bahamas, Brazil, Bulgaria, Chile, Czechia, Denmark, Fiji, Germany, Italy, Marshall Islands, Mexico, Netherlands, Peru, Poland, Qatar, Republic of Korea, Slovakia, Spain, and Uruguay) to twelve (Afghanistan, Bahrain, Burkina Faso, Eritrea, India, Libya, Mauritania, Pakistan, Philippines, Somalia, Sudan, and Venezuela), with twelve abstentions (Angola, Armenia, Bangladesh, Cameroon, Democratic Republic of Congo, Indonesia, Japan, Namibia, Nepal, Nigeria, Senegal, and Togo).
[15] Human Rights Council Resolution 45/15, operative para. 6.
[16] Human Rights Council Resolution 45/19: 'Situation of human rights in Burundi', operative para. 1. The resolution was adopted on 6 October 2020 by twenty-four votes to six (Cameroon, Pakistan, Philippines, Somalia, Togo, and Venezuela), with 17 abstentions.
[17] Human Rights Council Resolution 45/19: 'Situation of human rights in Burundi', operative para. 4.

38.08 With respect to Venezuela, a member of the Human Rights Council, a resolution deplored the 'continued killings of young men by security forces in marginalized neighbourhoods characterized by high levels of insecurity' and expressed 'profound alarm' that the independent international fact-finding mission on the Bolivarian Republic of Venezuela had found 'reasonable grounds to believe' that murder and enforced disappearance had been committed in Venezuela as crimes against humanity since 2014.[18] In its Resolution 42/25 of 27 September 2019, the Council had established the independent fact-finding mission 'to investigate extrajudicial executions, enforced disappearances, arbitrary detentions and torture and other cruel, inhuman or degrading treatment since 2014 with a view to ensuring full accountability for perpetrators and justice for victims'.[19]

38.09 Fact-finding missions, commissions of inquiry, and groups of experts have become a powerful mechanism of the Council for the in-depth but temporally confined investigation of widespread violations of fundamental human rights, in particular the right to life.[20] Thus, for example, in October 2020, in what was described as 'the first report of its kind by a UN panel', the Commission on Human Rights in South Sudan documented how, between January 2017 and November 2018, government forces intentionally deprived Fertit and Luo communities living under the control of the opposition in Western Bahr el Ghazal state of critical resources, in acts amounting to collective punishment and starvation as a method of warfare.[21] In presenting the report, Commissioner Andrew Clapham stated: 'Sustained attacks were carried out against numerous towns and villages across Western Bahr el Ghazal State over a number of years, which resulted in significant numbers of deaths.' These violations 'formed part of a widespread or systematic attack directed against the civilian population in Western Bahr el Ghazal, and can amount to crimes against humanity'.[22]

38.10 With respect to Yemen, in its Resolution 36/31, adopted in 2017, the Human Rights Council called for a Group of Eminent Experts to carry out a comprehensive examination of all alleged violations and abuses of international human rights and other appropriate and applicable fields of international law committed by all parties to the conflict since September 2014, including the possible gender dimensions of such violations. In its third report to the Council in September 2020, entitled 'A Pandemic of Impunity in a Tortured Land', the Group urged an end to impunity 'in a conflict with no clean hands', referring in

---

[18] Human Rights Council Resolution 45/20: 'Situation of human rights in the Bolivarian Republic of Venezuela', operative paras. 10 and 11. The resolution was adopted on 6 October 2020 by twenty-two votes to three (Eritrea, the Philippines, and Venezuela), with two abstentions.

[19] See Report of the independent international fact-finding mission on the Bolivarian Republic of Venezuela, UN doc. A/HRC/45/33 (Advance Unedited Version), 15 September 2020, esp. paras. 91–95, 111–15, 145–50, 151–53, 161.

[20] OHCHR, 'International Commissions of Inquiry, Commissions on Human Rights, Fact-Finding missions and other Investigations', at http://bit.ly/35OJtZ6. On occasion, they are also mandated by other UN bodies, such as the General Assembly or the Security Council.

[21] 'There is nothing left for us': starvation as a method of warfare in South Sudan, Conference room paper of the Commission on Human Rights in South Sudan, UN doc. A/HRC/45/CRP.3, 5 October 2020.

[22] OHCHR, 'Starvation Being Used as a Method of Warfare in South Sudan – UN Panel', news release, Geneva, 6 October 2020, at http://bit.ly/3fideEr.

detail to many serious violations of international human rights law and IHL. These included airstrikes that did not respect the principles of distinction and proportionality, indiscriminate mortar shelling, and unlawful killings at checkpoints.[23] Pointedly, the Group remarked that notwithstanding its strong recommendations in its previous reports, third States, including Canada, France, Iran, the United Kingdom, and the United States, 'continued their support of parties to the conflict, including through arms transfers, thereby helping to perpetuate the conflict'.[24]

UN TREATY BODIES

The Human Rights Committee

38.11 The Human Rights Committee has a critical role in promoting the right to life within the UN human rights system. As of this writing, of 197 States recognised by the UN Secretary-General, the depositary of the ICCPR, 173 were party to the Covenant.[25] The Human Rights Committee, which is composed of 18 independent experts 'of high moral character and recognized competence in the field of human rights',[26] has issued three General Comments on the right to life, protected in Article 6 of the ICCPR, the most recent of which was concluded and adopted by the Committee in October 2018, expressly replacing the two earlier Comments.[27]

38.12 The Committee's General Comment No. 6, issued in 1982, was its first on the right to life. A mere two pages in length, it nonetheless addressed a considerable range of issues: war (jus ad bellum), the meaning of arbitrary deprivation of life, enforced disappearance, the duty to adopt positive measures to reduce infant mortality and reduce disease, and the application of the death penalty. Perhaps most significantly, the Committee declared that the right to life – the 'supreme' human right – 'should not be interpreted narrowly'.[28]

38.13 Two years later, in its twenty-third session, the Committee again addressed the interpretation and application of Article 6 of the Covenant, in its General Comment No. 14, which this time was only a page in length.[29] Dedicated to the issue of weapons of mass destruction, the Committee concluded the Comment with a rhetorical flourish, asserting: 'The production, testing, possession, deployment and use of nuclear weapons

---

[23] Situation of human rights in Yemen, including violations and abuses since September 2014, Report of the Group of Eminent International and Regional Experts on Yemen, UN doc. A/HRC/45/6, 28 September 2020, paras. 30–1, 32–5, and 41–5.
[24] Ibid., para. 25.
[25] In addition to the 173 States Parties as of 1 May 2021, a further 6 States were signatories.
[26] OHCHR, 'Human Rights Committee: Membership', at http://bit.ly/3fiZitS. Members of the Committee are elected for a term of four years, and may be re-elected.
[27] Human Rights Committee, General Comment No. 36: Article 6: right to life, UN doc. CCPR/C/GC/36, 3 September 2019 (hereinafter, Human Rights Committee, General Comment 36 on the right to life), para. 1.
[28] Human Rights Committee, General Comment No. 6: Article 6 (Right to life), adopted at the Committee's sixteenth session, 1982, para. 1.
[29] Human Rights Committee, General Comment No. 14: Article 6 (Right to life), adopted at its twenty-third session, 1984.

should be prohibited and recognized as crimes against humanity' and calling upon 'all States, whether Parties to the Covenant or not, to take urgent steps, unilaterally and by agreement, to rid the world of this menace'.[30] Amounting to advocacy rather than authoritative legal interpretation, the Committee's call for nuclear disarmament remains largely unheeded to this day.[31]

38.14 In contrast, the Human Rights Committee's General Comment No. 36 is an expansive and detailed exploration of the right to life in many of its aspects. While considerable space in the Comment is allocated to the application of the death penalty, also addressed are issues of suicide, abortion, the use of force in law enforcement and in personal self-defence, the use of force in the conduct of hostilities, terrorism, homicides perpetrated by private individuals, the protection of the especially vulnerable, treatment of detainees, the prevention of disease and accidents, the protection of the environment, non-refoulement, jus ad bellum, weapons, respect for international humanitarian law, and investigations and remedies for violations of the right to life. The interpretation of the term 'arbitrary' is discussed, as is the geographical and jurisdictional reach of the right to life under Article 6. Although this work has questioned a number of the assertions made by the Committee in this General Comment, the overwhelming majority of the interpretations delineated therein are robust.

38.15 The staple of the Committee's work is, however, its review of the periodic reports submitted by States Parties to the Covenants. States must report initially one year after adhering to the Covenant and then whenever the Committee requests, which is usually every four years. The Committee sends a detailed list of issues that it wishes the State Party in question to address in its report, reflecting earlier recommendations and current challenges. The Committee then examines each report, listens to and questions representatives of the State (as well as considering reports by UN agencies and non-governmental organisations) and addresses its concerns and recommendations to the State Party in the form of 'Concluding Observations'.[32] The right to life is systematically considered by the Committee; rare are those States for whom none of the Concluding Observations considers Article 6.

38.16 In its Session in March 2020, for instance, the Committee assessed reports by the Central African Republic, Portugal, Tunisia, and Uzbekistan. In its Concluding Observations on the Central African Republic, the Committee expressed its concern at reports that extrajudicial killings 'have been and continue to be committed against civilians in conflict areas where various armed groups and militias are active and at the fact that these acts are not investigated because they occur in areas that are outside the

---

[30] Ibid., paras. 6 and 7.
[31] As of this writing, despite the entry into force of the Treaty on the Prohibition of Nuclear Weapons, none of the nine nuclear-armed States was either party or signatory. Since 1984, only four nuclear-armed States have disarmed: Belarus, Kazakhstan, and Ukraine (where nuclear weapons were stationed after the collapse of the Soviet Union), and South Africa (which renounced its nuclear weapons programme as apartheid was coming to an end.
[32] OHCHR, 'Human Rights Committee', accessed 1 December 2020 at http://bit.ly/36XYBT4.

control of the State'.[33] The Committee was also concerned about allegations of 'lynchings and killings for acts of witchcraft or charlatanism'.[34]

38.17 With respect to Portugal, the Committee welcomed the adoption of a national Action Plan on preventing and combating violence against women and domestic violence (2018–30), but expressed its concern that domestic violence against women persisted. While noting the explanation proffered by the authorities on the difficulties encountered in investigating cases of domestic violence, 'including when the victim refuses or is unable to cooperate with the inquiries', the Committee reminded Portugal of its obligations 'to take all necessary measures to realize the rights enshrined in the Covenant'.[35] The Committee was further concerned about the high rate of suicide among detainees in Portugal.[36]

38.18 In its Concluding Observations on Tunisia's sixth periodic report, the Committee was concerned about the 'lack of availability and accessibility of abortion services, which continues to lead pregnant women to resort to clandestine abortions in conditions that endanger their life and health'.[37] With respect to the death penalty, the Committee noted the de facto moratorium observed by Tunisia since 1993. It was nonetheless concerned about the 'large number of crimes for which the death penalty continues to apply in legislation and be imposed by the courts, including certain crimes related to terrorism'. Some of these crimes 'do not fall within the category of the most serious crimes under the Covenant', the Committee observed.[38] The Committee further observed that the legislative framework governing the law enforcement did not fully conform to international standards. It expressed its concern that 'excessive force is often used by law enforcement officers, especially during demonstrations, which has resulted in injuries and deaths'.[39]

38.19 With respect to Uzbekistan, the Human Rights Committee reiterated its concern, previously expressed, 'about the lack of a full, independent and effective investigation into the mass killings and injuries by military and security services during the Andijan events in May 2005'. It regretted the assertion by Uzbekistan that those events did not require international investigation and that this matter was considered closed.[40] The Committee was also concerned about 'numerous reports of deaths in custody and about the lack of official statistics and investigations into these cases'.[41] The Committee called on the authorities to take 'all measures necessary to prevent deaths in connection with cotton

---

[33] Human Rights Committee, Concluding Observations on the third periodic report of the Central African Republic, UN doc. CCPR/C/CAF/CO/3, 30 April 2020, para. 19.
[34] Ibid.
[35] Human Rights Committee, Concluding Observations on the fifth periodic report of Portugal, UN doc. CCPR/C/PRT/CO/5, 28 April 2020, para. 22.
[36] Ibid., para. 28.
[37] Human Rights Committee, Concluding Observations on the sixth periodic report of Tunisia, UN doc. CCPR/C/TUN/CO/6, 24 April 2020, para. 25.
[38] Ibid., para. 27.
[39] Ibid., para. 47.
[40] Human Rights Committee, Concluding Observations on the fifth periodic report of Uzbekistan, UN doc. CCPR/C/UZB/CO/5, 1 May 2020, para. 16.
[41] Ibid., para. 32.

harvesting, thoroughly investigating such cases when they occur and providing effective remedies, including adequate compensation, to victims' families'.[42]

38.20 Individual communications may be made by an individual under the jurisdiction of any State Party to the First Optional Protocol to the Covenant, which gives the Committee competence to examine specific complaints about a violation of the ICCPR.[43] A model complaint form is available on the OHCHR website.[44] The Office of the UN High Commissioner for Human Rights publishes regular analysis of the Committee's jurisprudence, categorised by Covenant right.[45] As of this writing, the most recent concerned a series of complaints of violation of the right to life against Algeria, Bosnia and Herzegovina, Kyrgyzstan, and Nepal.[46]

38.21 One of the two complaints against Algeria described in the analysis concerned the detention of Mohammed Belamrania on the night of 13 to 14 July 1995 by army paratroopers of the Algerian People's National Army. Mr Belamrania was taken by a military convoy to an unknown destination. Subsequently, his brother, Youssef Belamrania, was informed that several persons had been executed by paratroopers stationed at the El Milia barracks and that one of the victims might be Mohammed Belamrania. Youssef Belamrania went there and recognised the mutilated, bullet-ridden body of his brother, whose hands were bound with metal wire and who showed unmistakable signs of torture. He had been abandoned by the side of the national highway.[47]

38.22 It was further alleged that in exchange for the return of his body, the authorities demanded that the family pay over a large sum of money and aver in writing that Mohammed Belamrania belonged to a terrorist group. Articles 45 and 46 of Order No. 06-01 on the implementation of the Charter for Peace and National Reconciliation criminalise all complaints about the Algerian defence and security forces, putting the family in fear of reprisals. The Committee found that Algeria had denied Mohammed Belamrania the right to life in violation of Article 6(1) of the Covenant 'in particularly serious circumstances, in view of the fact that he was clearly the victim of a summary execution by members of the State party's regular army'.[48]

38.23 With respect to a communication against Nepal, the Committee recalled that 'in cases of enforced disappearance, the deprivation of liberty followed by a refusal to acknowledge the deprivation of liberty, or by concealment of the fate of the disappeared person, denies the person the protection of the law and places his or her life at serious and constant risk, for which the State is accountable'. In September 2003, the author

---

[42] Ibid., para. 35.
[43] As of 1 May 2021, 116 States were party to the Protocol and a further 3 States were signatories.
[44] At http://bit.ly/3kRJIGP.
[45] At http://bit.ly/2UKrlcr.
[46] Human Rights Committee, 'Consideration by the Human Rights Committee at its 117th, 118th and 119th sessions of communications received under the Optional Protocol to the International Covenant on Civil and Political Rights', UN doc. CCPR/C/119/3, 6 October 2017 (advance unedited version).
[47] Ibid., para. 35.
[48] Ibid., paras. 36–8.

approached two barracks of the Royal Nepalese Army in Kathmandu, as well as the Nepal Police Headquarters in Naxal and a District Police Office in Kathmandu, inquiring as to her husband's whereabouts and fate. The authorities denied that he had been detained on several occasions, a position it maintained before the Supreme Court in responding to a writ of mandamus proceedings instituted by the author.[49]

38.24 In contrast, former detainees at the BhairabNath Barracks indicated that the author's husband was last seen there in the custody of the army between December 2003 and February 2004, that he fell very ill, and that it was believed that he died as a result of torture. The Committee noted that Nepal had produced no evidence to show that it met its obligations to protect the life of Mr Nakarmi, and accordingly it concluded that Nepal had failed in its duty to protect Mr Nakarmi's life.[50]

The Committee on the Rights of the Child

38.25 The Committee on the Rights of the Child operates on a similar basis to the Human Rights Committee. The Committee on the Rights of the Child is the body of 18 Independent experts that monitors the implementation of the Convention on the Rights of the Child[51] by its States Parties. The Convention is the mostly widely ratified human rights treaty in history, with 196 States Parties (only the United States, a signatory, is a State not party). Article 6 of the Convention protects the right to life of every child within the jurisdiction of a State Party. There is no provision for derogation under the Convention. In its General Comment No. 5, the Committee reiterated that 'in all circumstances the State which ratified or acceded to the Convention remains responsible for ensuring the full implementation of the Convention throughout the territories under its jurisdiction'.[52]

38.26 The Committee reviews periodic reports by States Parties (which are to be submitted every five years) and issues General Comments on specific articles of the Convention and on cross-cutting thematic issues. The Committee also monitors the implementation of two Optional Protocols to the Convention, on the involvement of children in armed conflict and on the sale of children, child prostitution, and child pornography. On 19 December 2011, the UN General Assembly approved a third Optional Protocol on a communications procedure, which allows individual children to submit complaints regarding specific violations of their rights under the Convention and its first two optional protocols. The Protocol entered into force in April 2014.[53]

---

[49] Ibid., para. 40.
[50] Ibid.
[51] Convention on the Rights of the Child; adopted at New York, 20 November 1989; entered into force 2 September 1990.
[52] Committee on the Rights of the Child, General Comment No. 5: 'General measures of implementation of the Convention on the Rights of the Child (arts. 4, 42 and 44, para. 6)', UN doc. CRC/GC/2003/5, 27 November 2003, para. 41.
[53] As of 1 May 2021, forty-seven States were party to the Optional Protocol to the Convention on the Rights of the Child on a communications procedure; adopted at New York 19 December 2011; entered into force 14 April 2014. A further seventeen States were signatories.

38.27 Surprisingly, the Committee on the Rights of the Child has not yet issued a General Comment dedicated to the right to life as protected under Article 6 of the Convention. This is long overdue. A number of its General Comments have, though, concerned aspects of the right. Thus, for instance, in its General Comment No. 9 on the rights of children with disabilities, the Committee observed that the inherent right to life is particularly at risk where children with disabilities are concerned.[54] They are more vulnerable to infanticide than other children, since 'some cultures view a child with any form of disability as a bad omen that may "tarnish the family pedigree" and, accordingly, a certain designated individual from the community systematically kills children with disabilities. These crimes often go unpunished or perpetrators receive reduced sentences.'[55]

38.28 In its General Comment on the right of children to enjoy the highest attainable standard of health (protected in Article 24 of the Convention), the Committee observed that a 'significant number of infant deaths occur during the neonatal period, related to the poor health of the mother prior to, and during, the pregnancy and the immediate post-partum period, and to suboptimal breastfeeding practices'.[56] In its General Comment on the right of the child to freedom from all forms of violence, the Committee recognised that 'much of the violence experienced by children, including sexual abuse, takes place within a family context'. The Committee stressed the need to intervene in families to protect children if they are exposed to violence by family members.[57] This may, in certain cases, demand that the child be taken out of the family for his or her own protection and well-being.[58]

38.29 With respect to individual communications to the Committee, thus far those that have concerned the right to life have largely concerned issues of non-refoulement. In W. M. C. v. Denmark,[59] the author of the communication was a Chinese national acting on behalf of her three children, each of whom had been born in Denmark. The author escaped China after the Chinese authorities performed a forced abortion on her. The author and her children were subject to a deportation order to China.[60] She had sought asylum after arriving on an illegal passport but was informed by the Danish Immigration Service that the examination of her application would be conducted in accordance with the procedure for manifestly unfounded applications. In her communication to the Committee, she claimed that their return would constitute a serious risk to the life, survival, and development of her children, and thus would constitute an infringement of Article 6.[61]

---

[54] Committee on the Rights of the Child, 'General Comment No. 9 (2006): The rights of children with disabilities', UN doc. CRC/C/GC/9, 27 February 2007, para. 31.

[55] Ibid.

[56] Committee on the Rights of the Child, 'General Comment No. 15 (2013) on the right of the child to the enjoyment of the highest attainable standard of health', UN doc. CRC/C/GC/15, 17 April 2013, para. 18.

[57] Committee on the Rights of the Child, General Comment No. 13, para. 72(d).

[58] K. Sandberg, 'Children's Right to Protection Under the CRC', chap. 2 in A. Falch-Eriksen and E. Backe-Hansen (eds.), Human Rights in Child Protection: Implications for Professional Practice and Policy, Springer, Switzerland, August 2018, pp. 15–38, at 16, available at http://bit.ly/2QokoxT.

[59] Committee on the Rights of the Child, W. M. C. v. Denmark, Views (adopted on 28 September 2020), UN doc. CRC/C/85/D/31/2017, 3 November 2020.

[60] Ibid., paras. 1.1, 2.1.

[61] Ibid., para. 3.1.

38.30 The Committee noted the author's allegations that, if deported, her children would not be registered in the *hukou* (the family household register), which is required to ensure their access to health, education, and social services, and is the only means to prove their identity in China. In light of this fact, and the reality that children born to unmarried parents face numerous difficulties in being registered in the *hukou*, the Committee considered that the decision of the Danish authorities to deport the author's children would entail a violation of their right to life, survival, and development under Article 6.[62]

The Committee on Migrant Workers

38.31 The Committee on Migrant Workers is the body of independent experts that monitors the implementation of the International Convention on the Protection of the Rights of All Migrant Workers and Members of Their Families by Its States Parties.[63] The Convention has the lowest level of adherence of any global UN human rights treaty.[64] The Committee, which held its first session in March 2004, has not issued a General Comment specifically on the right to life, as protected under Article 9 of the Convention. In a joint Comment with the Committee on the Rights of the Child, however, it was noted that at any point during the migratory process, a migrant child's right to life and survival may be endangered at stake owing to, among others, 'violence as a result of organized crime, violence in camps, push-back or interception operations, excessive use of force of border authorities, refusal of vessels to rescue them, or extreme conditions of travel and limited access to basic services'.[65]

38.32 The Committee will be able to receive individual communications in relation to a State Party once ten States Parties have made the requisite declaration in accordance with Article 77 of the Convention. As of 1 December 2020, only four had done so: Ecuador, El Salvador, Mexico, and Uruguay.

The Committee on the Elimination of Discrimination against Women

38.33 The 1979 Convention on the Elimination of All Forms of Discrimination against Women[66] does not explicitly refer in its substantive provisions to the rights of women to life or even to freedom from violence. In its General Recommendation 12 on violence against

---

[62] Ibid., para. 8.9.
[63] International Convention on the Protection of the Rights of All Migrant Workers and Members of Their Families; adopted at New York 18 December 1990; entered into force 1 July 2003.
[64] As of 1 May 2021, fifty-six States were party to the Convention and a further twelve States were signatories.
[65] Committee on the Rights of the Child and the Committee on the Protection of the Rights of All Migrant Workers and Members of Their Families, Joint General Comment No. 3 (2017) of the Committee on the Protection of the Rights of All Migrant Workers and Members of Their Families and No. 22 (2017) of the Committee on the Rights of the Child on the general principles regarding the human rights of children in the context of international migration, UN doc. CMW/C/GC/3-CRC/C/GC/22, 16 November 2017, para. 40.
[66] Convention on the Elimination of All Forms of Discrimination against Women; adopted at New York 18 December 1979; entered into force 3 September 1981. As of 1 May 2021, 189 States were party to CEDAW and a further 2 (Palau and the United States) were signatories, making it one of the most widely ratified human rights treaties.

women, however, issued in 1989, the Committee on the Elimination of Discrimination against Women[67] affirmed that the Convention requires its States Parties to act to protect women against violence of any kind occurring within the family, at the workplace, or in any other area of social life.[68] In addition, where discrimination against women also constitutes an abuse of other human rights, such as the right to life in, for example, cases of domestic and other forms of violence, States Parties 'are obliged to initiate criminal proceedings, bring the perpetrator(s) to trial and impose appropriate penal sanctions'.[69]

38.34 In accordance with the Optional Protocol to the Convention, the Committee is mandated to receive communications from individuals or groups of individuals alleging violations of rights protected under the Convention, as well as to initiate inquiries into situations of grave or systematic violations of women's rights. On 25 October 2011, the Committee received information from three organisations pursuant to Article 8 of the Optional Protocol, alleging that Mali was committing such grave and systematic violations 'because it has failed to fulfil its duty to protect women and girls in its territory against female genital mutilation and its duty to prosecute and punish those who carry out such mutilation'. The sources asserted that Mali's failure was resulting in serious physical and psychological effects for the victim, including the risk of death and the possibility of complications in childbirth.[70]

38.35 Among findings of fact by the Committee, it was noted that practitioners are aware that their actions can result in death. A practitioner whom the experts met in Bamako acknowledged that two girls had died following the procedure that she performed.[71] In its evaluation, the Committee considered that the violations committed in Mali were grave 'in the light of the numerous and repeated instances of considerable suffering inflicted on women and girls from a very young age'. It noted that the harmful practice of female genital mutilation 'has serious effects on physical and psychological health, including sexual and reproductive health, and affects the victim's development both immediately and throughout her life'. The Committee further noted that female genital mutilation can result in the victim's death.[72] It also affirmed the systematic nature of the violations, which stems from the fact that the practice is extensive and persistent and not a random phenomenon. 'Indeed', the Committee recalled, 'as at 2015, 82.7 per cent of women

---

[67] The Committee consists of twenty-three experts on women's rights from around the world.
[68] Committee on the Elimination of Discrimination against Women, General Recommendation No. 12: Violence against women, 1989, first preambular para. The Committee referred specifically to Articles 2, 5, 11, 12, and 16 of the Convention as underpinning those duties.
[69] Committee on the Elimination of Discrimination against Women, General Recommendation No. 28 on the core obligations of States parties under article 2 of the Convention on the Elimination of All Forms of Discrimination against Women, UN doc. CEDAW/C/GC/28, 16 December 2010, para. 34.
[70] Committee on the Elimination of Discrimination against Women, Inquiry concerning Mali under Article 8 of the Optional Protocol to the Convention on the Elimination of All Forms of Discrimination against Women, UN doc. CEDAW/C/IR/MLI/1, 24 December 2019, para. 3.
[71] Ibid., para. 31.
[72] Ibid., para. 78.

aged from 15 to 49 years and 76.4 per cent of girls aged from 0 to 14 years had undergone female genital mutilation'.[73]

The Committee on the Elimination of Racial Discrimination

38.36 The Committee on the Elimination of Racial Discrimination oversees the implementation of the 1965 International Convention on the Elimination of All Forms of Racial Discrimination.[74] In its General Recommendation XIII on the training of law enforcement officials in the protection of human rights, the Committee stated that compliance by States Parties with their obligations under the Convention to refrain from racial discrimination and to ensure the right to security of person and protection by the State against violence or bodily harm 'very much depends upon national law enforcement officials who exercise police powers'.[75] The Committee called on States Parties to review and improve the training of law enforcement officials so that the standards of the Convention as well as the 1979 UN Code of Conduct 'are fully implemented'.[76]

38.37 The Committee includes in its regular agenda preventive measures which involve early warnings aimed at preventing existing situations escalating into conflicts and urgent procedures to respond to problems requiring immediate attention to prevent or limit the scale or number of serious violations of the Convention.[77] Thus, for example, with respect to the Philippines, in 2018 the Committee issued a decision in which it noted it was

> highly concerned by the court petition of February 2018 filed by the Philippines State Prosecutor seeking to declare the Communist Party of the Philippines and the New People's Army as terrorist organizations, which includes a list of more than 600 individuals alleged to be affiliated with those organisations, many of whom are indigenous leaders and defenders along with other human rights defenders.

It further noted its particular alarm at the inclusion on the list of the UN Special Rapporteur on the Rights of Indigenous Peoples, Ms. Victoria Tauli-Corpuz, as well as two former members of the UN Permanent Forum on Indigenous Issues.[78]

38.38 The Committee recommended that the Philippines 'take effective measures to ensure that Indigenous Peoples and defenders of the rights of Indigenous Peoples, can fully exercise their rights stipulated in the Convention, including the right to

---

[73] Ibid., para. 79.
[74] International Convention on the Elimination of All Forms of Racial Discrimination; adopted at New York 21 December 1965; entered into force 4 January 1969 (hereinafter, CERD). As of 1 May 2021, 182 States were party to CERD.
[75] Committee on the Elimination of Racial Discrimination, 'General Recommendation XIII on the training of law enforcement officials in the protection of human rights', Forty-second session (1993), paras. 1 and 2.
[76] Ibid., para. 3.
[77] OHCHR, 'Committee on the Elimination of Racial Discrimination: Early-Warning Measures and Urgent Procedures', at http://bit.ly/36S0cgg.
[78] Committee on the Elimination of Racial Discrimination, 'Decision 1 (95): Philippines', at http://bit.ly/2IWN9Ps, second and third preambular paras.

security of person and protection against violence or bodily harm'.[79] The Committee further invited the UN High Commissioner for Human Rights 'to draw the attention of the Association of Southeast Asian Nations to the dire human rights situation of Indigenous Peoples and defenders of the rights of Indigenous Peoples in the Philippines'.[80]

SPECIAL PROCEDURES

38.39 The Special Procedures are set up by and report to the Human Rights Council. The Special Rapporteur on extrajudicial, summary, or arbitrary executions serves, in effect, as a special rapporteur on the right to life in many of its aspects. The position was first established by ECOSOC Resolution 1982/35, which established the mandate of the Special Rapporteur on summary or arbitrary executions in 1982, initially for a period of one year.[81] The position has been consistently renewed subsequently. In 1992, the Commission on Human Rights widened the title of the mandate to include 'extrajudicial' as well as summary or arbitrary executions.[82]

38.40 These days, the Special Rapporteur reports annually to both the Human Rights Council and later in the year to the UN General Assembly. Reports of particular importance include the 2010 report to the Human Rights Council on armed drones,[83] the 2014 report to the Human Rights Council on the use of force in law enforcement,[84] and the 2016 report to the General Assembly on the death penalty.[85] The Special Rapporteur's report on the killing of Jamal Khashoggi by the Saudi government was also a significant contribution to understanding accountability for violations of the right to life and the nature of the duty to investigate.[86]

38.41 In certain instances of especial concern, special procedures may jointly issue statements. Thus, for example, in November 2020, the special rapporteurs on freedom from torture and on human rights while countering terrorism joined the Special Rapporteur on extrajudicial, summary, or arbitrary executions in expressing alarm at reports that some fifty prisoners convicted of terrorism-related crimes in Iraq faced impending execution. They urged the Iraqi government 'to immediately halt all mass executions' on the basis of serious concern about the conduct of the trials and the extraction of confessions under torture. They affirmed that 'any death sentence carried

---

[79] Ibid., operative para. 5.
[80] Ibid., operative para. 7.
[81] ECOSOC Resolution 1982/35, adopted on 7 May 1982.
[82] UN Commission on Human Rights Resolution 1992/72, adopted without a vote on 5 March 1992.
[83] Report of the Special Rapporteur on extrajudicial, summary or arbitrary executions, Philip Alston, Addendum: Study on targeted killings, UN doc. A/HRC/14/24/Add.6, 28 May 2010.
[84] Report of the Special Rapporteur on extrajudicial, summary or arbitrary executions, UN doc. A/HRC/26/36, 1 April 2014.
[85] 'Report of the Special Rapporteur on extrajudicial, summary or arbitrary executions', UN doc. A/71/372, 2 September 2016.
[86] 'Annex to the Report of the Special Rapporteur on extrajudicial, summary or arbitrary executions: Investigation into the unlawful death of Mr. Jamal Khashoggi', UN doc. A/HRC/41/CRP.1, 19 June 2019.

out following an unfair trial or on the basis of an ambiguous law, amounts to an arbitrary deprivation of life. ... When carried out on a widespread and systematic basis, arbitrary executions may well amount to crimes against humanity and may entail universal criminal responsibility for any official involved in such acts.'[87]

38.42 Most of the special procedures tackle right-to-life issues to some degree in their work. This is the case for both the country mandates[88] and the thematic mandates.[89] Beyond the Special Rapporteur on extrajudicial, summary or arbitrary executions, thematic mandates that have addressed the right to life include but are not limited to the Rapporteur on extreme poverty and human rights; the Independent Expert on the enjoyment of human rights by persons with albinism; the Special Rapporteur on the rights of persons with disabilities; the Special Rapporteur on the issue of human rights obligations relating to the enjoyment of a safe, clean, healthy and sustainable environment; the Special Rapporteur on the situation of human rights defenders; the Special Rapporteur on the human rights of internally displaced persons; the Special Rapporteur on the rights of indigenous peoples; the Special Rapporteur on the promotion and protection of human rights and fundamental freedoms while countering terrorism; the Special Rapporteur on violence against women, its causes and consequences; and the Independent Expert on protection against violence and discrimination based on sexual orientation and gender identity.

38.43 While generally accurate in their interpretation of international human rights law, special rapporteurs do not always get it right. Thus, for instance, in 2019 the Special Rapporteur on the issue of human rights obligations relating to the enjoyment of a safe, clean, healthy and sustainable environment issued his report to the Human Rights Council,[90] noting that 'air pollution causes 7 million premature deaths annually, including the deaths of more than 600,000 children'.[91] He asserted, without proffering supporting evidence or analysis, that 'these staggering and almost incomprehensible statistics represent an egregious violation of the right to life'.[92] While the figures, if accurate, are undoubtedly shocking, his claim does not faithfully represent international human rights law.

---

[87] OHCHR, 'Iraq: Wave of Mass Executions Must Stop, Trials Are Unfair – UN Experts', press release, Geneva, 20 November 2020, at http://bit.ly/393yVXM. The experts were Nils Melzer, Special Rapporteur on torture and other cruel, inhuman or degrading treatment or punishment; Fionnuala Ní Aoláin, Special Rapporteur on the promotion and protection of human rights while countering terrorism; and Agnes Callamard, Special Rapporteur on extrajudicial, summary or arbitrary executions.

[88] As of 1 December 2020, there were twelve country mandates: Belarus, Cambodia, Central African Republic, Democratic People's Republic of Korea, Eritrea, Iran, Mali, Myanmar, the Palestinian territories occupied since 1967, and Somalia. See Office of the UN High Commissioner for Human Rights (OHCHR), 'Country Mandates', at http://bit.ly/36S54Pl.

[89] For the full list of the (currently) forty-four thematic mandates, see OHCHR, 'Thematic Mandates', at http://bit.ly/2Kqn77T.

[90] Issue of human rights obligations relating to the enjoyment of a safe, clean, healthy and sustainable environment: Report of the Special Rapporteur, UN doc. A/HRC/40/55, 8 January 2019.

[91] Ibid., para. 52.

[92] Ibid.

INTERNATIONAL COURTS AND THE RIGHT TO LIFE

The International Court of Justice

38.44 The International Court of Justice has issued a number of judgments and advisory opinions that concern directly and indirectly the right to life. In its judgment in 1970 in the *Barcelona Traction* case, the Court's noted discussion of rights erga omnes – peremptory norms of international law (jus cogens) giving rise to a duty towards the international community as a whole[93] – the Court included the 'principles and rules concerning the basic rights of the human person'.[94]

38.45 In its 1971 Advisory Opinion in the *Namibia* case, the Court stated that under the UN Charter, member States pledged 'to observe and respect, in a territory having an international status, human rights and fundamental freedoms for all without distinction as to race'.[95] The Court declared: 'To establish instead, and to enforce, distinctions, exclusions, restrictions and limitations exclusively based on grounds of race, colour, descent or national or ethnic origin which constitute a denial of fundamental human rights is a flagrant violation of the purposes and principles of the Charter.' This decision dispelled the notion that human rights obligations referred to in the Charter were somehow not legally binding on States.

38.46 In its 2004 Advisory Opinion on the *Legal Consequences of the Construction of a Wall in the Occupied Palestinian Territory* (the *Wall* case), the Court observed that the *travaux préparatoires* of the Covenant confirm the Human Rights Committee's broad interpretation of Article 2 of the ICCPR. As it stated:

> These show that, in adopting the wording chosen, the drafters of the Covenant did not intend to allow States to escape from their obligations when they exercise jurisdiction outside their national territory. They only intended to prevent persons residing abroad from asserting, vis-à-vis their State of origin, rights that do not fall within the competence of that State, but of that of the State of residence.[96]

Furthermore, in its judgment in the *Armed Activities* case in the Democratic Republic of Congo, the Court explicitly held that the African Charter on Human and Peoples' Rights, including its protection of the right to life, applied extraterritorially to a situation of military occupation.[97]

---

[93] The International Law Commission (ILC) has determined that 'peremptory norms of general international law (jus cogens) give rise to obligations owed to the international community as a whole (obligations *erga omnes*), in which all States have a legal interest'. ILC, *Report of the International Law Commission*, Seventy-first session, UN doc. A/74/10, 2019, chap. V, Conclusion 17(1).

[94] International Court of Justice, *Barcelona Traction, Light and Power Company Ltd. (Belgium v. Spain)*, Judgment, 5 February 1970, para. 34.

[95] International Court of Justice, *Legal Consequences for States of the Continued Presence of South Africa in Namibia (South West Africa) Notwithstanding Security Council Resolution 276 (1970)*, Advisory Opinion, 21 June 1971, para. 131.

[96] International Court of Justice, *Legal Consequences of the Construction of a Wall in the Occupied Palestinian Territory*, Advisory Opinion, 9 July 2004, para. 109.

[97] International Court of Justice, *Case Concerning Armed Activities on the Territory of the Congo (Democratic Republic of the Congo v. Uganda)*, Judgment, 19 December 2005, paras. 217, 219.

38.47 The Court has also confirmed the application of the ICCPR in situations of armed conflict and sought to clarify the relationship between the Covenant and IHL when interpreting the right to life during the conduct of hostilities. Thus, in its 1996 Advisory Opinion on the legality of the use of nuclear weapons, the Court observed that 'the protection of the International Covenant of [sic] Civil and Political Rights does not cease in times of war, except by operation of Article 4 of the Covenant whereby certain provisions may be derogated from in a time of national emergency. Respect for the right to life is not, however, such a provision.'[98] The Court affirmed:

> In principle, the right not arbitrarily to be deprived of one's life applies also in hostilities. The test of what is an arbitrary deprivation of life, however, then falls to be determined by the applicable *lex specialis*, namely, the law applicable in armed conflict which is designed to regulate the conduct of hostilities. Thus, whether a particular loss of life, through the use of a certain weapon in warfare, is to be considered an arbitrary deprivation of life contrary to Article 6 of the Covenant, can only be decided by reference to the law applicable in armed conflict and not deduced from the terms of the Covenant itself.[99]

38.48 The Court has also acted to protect fundamental human rights, even though individuals have no locus standi before it. In its judgment on admissibility in the *Ahmadou Sadio Diallo* case,[100] the Court found that Guinea's application to it was admissible in so far as it concerned the protection of Mr Diallo's rights as an individual.[101] A national of Guinea, Mr Diallo alleged that a range of his human rights had been violated. The Court held that 'owing to the substantive development of international law over recent decades in respect of the rights it accords to individuals, the scope *ratione materiae* of diplomatic protection, originally limited to alleged violations of the minimum standard of treatment of aliens, has subsequently widened to include, *inter alia*, internationally guaranteed human rights'.[102]

The International Criminal Court

38.49 The International Criminal Court is also not a human rights institution but nonetheless acts to protect fundamental human rights including the right to life. When widespread violations of the right to life occur, they may, depending on the circumstances, be subject to the jurisdiction of the Court as war crimes, crimes against humanity, or even acts of genocide. Indeed, the Rome Statute makes it explicit that the interpretation and application of the law 'must be consistent with internationally recognized human rights, and be without any adverse distinction founded on grounds such as gender . . ., age, race,

---

[98] International Court of Justice, *Legality of the Threat or Use of Nuclear Weapons*, Advisory Opinion, 8 July 1996, para. 25.
[99] Ibid.
[100] International Court of Justice, *Ahmadou Sadio Diallo (Guinea v. Democratic Republic of Congo)*, Judgment (Admissibility), 24 May 2007.
[101] Ibid., para. 96.
[102] Ibid., para. 39.

colour, language, religion or belief, political or other opinion, national, ethnic or social origin, wealth, birth or other status'.[103]

38.50 A crime against humanity encompasses acts such as murder or extermination and enforced disappearance when committed as part of and with knowledge of a widespread or systematic attack against a civilian population.[104] The situation in Venezuela led to the involvement of the Court when, on 8 February 2018, the Prosecutor decided to open a preliminary examination into alleged crimes in the context of demonstrations and related political unrest.[105] With respect to genocide, the Statute reaffirms the customary law definition whereby the killing of members of a national, ethnical, racial, or religious group with the intent to destroy that group, in whole or in part, constitutes genocide.[106]

38.51 Consonant with the evolving rule of international law prohibiting the death penalty, the Rome Statute does not allow the death penalty to be imposed on anyone who is convicted by the ICC.[107] Indeed, the imposition of a death sentence at the issue of an unfair trial in connection with a non-international armed conflict is a war crime within the jurisdiction of the Court.[108]

THE UN SECURITY COUNCIL AND THE RIGHT TO LIFE

38.52 Under Article 25(1) of the 1945 Charter of the United Nations[109] (UN Charter), member States confer on the Security Council primary responsibility for the maintenance of international peace and security. Paragraph 2 of the same article dictates that in discharging these duties the Council 'shall act in accordance with the Purposes and Principles of the United Nations'. These purposes explicitly include achieving international cooperation in 'promoting and encouraging respect for human rights and for fundamental freedoms for all without distinction as to race, sex, language, or religion'.[110]

38.53 The focus of the Security Council has traditionally been on ensuring respect for rules of jus ad bellum, but since the end of the last millennium in particular, its interpretation of

---

[103] Art. 21(3), Rome Statute of the International Criminal Court; adopted at Rome 17 July 1998; entered into force 1 July 2002 (hereinafter, Rome Statute).

[104] Art. 7(1), Rome Statute.

[105] Statement of the Prosecutor of the International Criminal Court, Fatou Bensouda, on opening Preliminary Examinations into the situations in the Philippines and in Venezuela, 8 February 2018, at http://bit.ly/2PpEt60.

[106] Art. 6(1), Rome Statute. See also: Art. II, 1948 Genocide Convention; ICTY, *Prosecutor v. Krstić*, Judgment (Case No. IT-98-33-T; Trial Chamber), para. 541.

[107] Art. 77(1), Rome Statute.

[108] Art. 8(2)(c)(iv), Rome Statute. In the corresponding elements of crimes, the Court is asked to consider whether, 'in the light of all relevant circumstances, the cumulative effect of factors with respect to guarantees deprived the person or persons of a fair trial'. Elements of Crimes, *Official Records of the Assembly of States Parties to the Rome Statute of the International Criminal Court, First session, New York, 3–10 September 2002*, p. 34.

[109] Charter of the United Nations; adopted at San Francisco 26 June 1945; entered into force 24 October 1945 (hereinafter, UN Charter). As of 1 May 2021, 193 States were bound directly by the UN Charter.

[110] Art. 1(3), UN Charter.

what amounts to a threat to international peace and security has broadened to encompass the protection of civilians in armed conflict – that is, respect for IHL and fundamental human rights. For in this area, the record of the Council is decidedly mixed, as acknowledged by Andrew Gilmour, the Director of Political, Peacekeeping, Humanitarian, and Human Rights Affairs in the Executive Office of the UN Secretary-General:

> The spring of 2014 saw the twentieth anniversary of one of the two emblematic failures of the United Nations: the genocide in Rwanda in April 1994. Two weeks after the killings began, the Security Council reduced the number of peacekeepers in the country to just a tenth of the mission's original 2,500. Had UN peacekeepers been kept in place and authorized to take action, it might have been possible to save many of the 800,000 people killed over the following twelve weeks.[111]

38.54 At the same time, Gilmour noted the new tendency of the Security Council to include human rights components in all peace operations and 'to authorize peacekeepers to prevent or intervene when civilians face massacre'.[112] Indeed, incorporating a Chapter VII 'protection of civilians' mandate has become standard these days whenever a UN peacekeeping operation is authorised. This is a fundamental change from the traditional peacekeeping by consent.

38.55 With respect to children, in 1999, the first resolution on children and armed conflict adopted by the Council placed the issue of their protection on its agenda. Resolution 1261 condemned grave violations of international law affecting children in situations of armed conflict, asking the Secretary-General to report on the issue.[113] The six grave violations are the following: killing and maiming of children, recruitment or use of children as soldiers, sexual violence against children, abduction of children, attacks against schools or hospitals, and denial of humanitarian access for children. A Monitoring and Reporting Mechanism, commonly known as the MRM, was later created pursuant to Security Council Resolution 1612.[114]

THE UN GENERAL ASSEMBLY AND THE RIGHT TO LIFE

38.56 More active on the promotion of human rights, including the right to life, has been the UN General Assembly. Many of the UN human rights treaties, including the ICCPR, were negotiated under the auspices of the General Assembly and adopted by it. The UN Charter stipulates that the General Assembly 'shall initiate studies and make recommendations for the purpose of … assisting in the realization of human rights and fundamental freedoms for all without distinction as to race, sex, language, or religion'.[115]

---

[111] A. Gilmour, 'The Future of Human Rights: A View from the United Nations', *Ethics & International Affairs*, vol. 28, no. 2 (2014), pp. 239–50, at http://bit.ly/395FPvN, at 239. Mr Gilmour was later UN Assistant Secretary-General for Human Rights until 2019.
[112] Ibid., p. 249.
[113] UN Security Council Resolution 1261, adopted by unanimous vote on 25 August 1999, operative paras. 2, 10, 11, and 16.
[114] UN Security Council Resolution 1612, adopted by unanimous vote on 26 July 2005, operative paras. 2 and 3.
[115] Art. 13(1)(b), UN Charter.

The General Assembly's Third Committee (Social, Humanitarian and Cultural) examines a range of issues, including human rights. The Third Committee also discusses questions relating to the advancement of women, the protection of children, indigenous issues, the treatment of refugees, the promotion of fundamental freedoms through the elimination of racism and racial discrimination, and the right to self-determination.[116]

38.57 Resolutions adopted by the General Assembly concerning human rights issues may constitute *opinio juris* towards the formation or crystallisation of a customary rule. There are also country-specific resolutions where human rights are an especially significant concern. In 2019, this pertained to the Democratic People's Republic of Korea, Iran, Syria, and Crimea, and the city of Sevastopol in Ukraine. The resolution on Syria, for instance, included an operative paragraph that demanded that the Syrian regime, 'in accordance with its obligations under relevant provisions of international human rights law, including the right to life and the right to the enjoyment of the highest attainable standard of physical and mental health, promote non-discriminatory access to health services and respect and protect medical and health personnel from obstruction, threats and physical attacks'.[117]

38.58 A resolution on the protection of human rights defenders expressed grave concern at the situation of human rights defenders around the world, strongly condemning 'the killing of human rights defenders, including women, environmental and indigenous human rights defenders, by State and non-State actors', and stressing that such acts may violate international law.[118]

38.59 The UN General Assembly has also adopted or endorsed instruments that inform the interpretation of the right to life, and particularly the notion of 'arbitrary' deprivation of life, such as the 1979 Code of Conduct for Law Enforcement Officials[119] and the 1990 Basic Principles on the Use of Force and Firearms by Law Enforcement Officials.[120]

THE UN SECRETARY-GENERAL'S MECHANISM

38.60 Of relevance to the protection of the right to life during situations of armed conflict, is the UN Secretary-General's Mechanism (SGM), which allows the Secretary-General to investigate alleged use of biological or chemical weapons. In the late 1980s, following the

---

[116] UN, 'Protect Human Rights', at http://bit.ly/3pTMU8u.
[117] UN General Assembly Resolution 74/169, adopted on 18 December 2019 by 106 votes to 15 with 57 abstentions, operative para. 23.
[118] UN General Assembly Resolution 74/146: 'Implementing the Declaration on the Right and Responsibility of Individuals, Groups and Organs of Society to Promote and Protect Universally Recognized Human Rights and Fundamental Freedoms through providing a safe and enabling environment for human rights defenders and ensuring their protection', adopted without a vote on 18 December 2019, operative para. 1.
[119] Code of Conduct for Law Enforcement Officials; adopted under UN General Assembly Resolution 34/169; resolution adopted without a vote on 17 December 1979.
[120] Basic Principles on the Use of Force and Firearms by Law Enforcement Officials; adopted at Havana by the Eighth UN Congress on the Prevention of Crime and the Treatment of Offenders, 7 September 1990. The Assembly welcomed the Basic Principles and invited governments to respect them. UN General Assembly Resolution 45/166, adopted without a vote on 18 December 1990.

use of chemical weapons by Iraq both against Iran and against the Kurds at Halabja, the Mechanism was set out first in a UN General Assembly Resolution in 1987[121] and then reaffirmed the following year by UN Security Council Resolution 620. It was further endorsed by the Assembly in 1990.[122]

38.61 Under the 1977 Additional Protocol I, a broader fact-finding mechanism was created to study, upon request from the parties to an (international) armed conflict, potential violations of IHL. The International Fact-Finding Commission, consisting of fifteen members 'of high moral standing and acknowledged impartiality'[123] has, however, never been used in international armed conflict and only one used, ad hoc, in non-international armed conflict, in Ukraine in 2017. The Commission's Independent Forensic Investigation (IFI) team presented its report to the Permanent Council of the Organization for Security and Co-opertion in Europe (OSCE) on the incident that occurred on 23 April 2017, when an OSCE armoured vehicle was struck by an explosion, resulting in the death of an OSCE paramedic.[124]

38.62 Renamed the International Humanitarian Fact-finding Commission (IHFFC), its Annual Meeting was held in Geneva on 1–3 April 2019. 'Building upon the momentum reached on the occasion of the successful Eastern Ukraine mission, the 15 Members discussed ways to further capitalise on this significant development.'[125] Most recently, in October 2020, the IHFFC offered its services to the governments of Armenia and Azerbaijan, declaring that it stood ready to assist both nations with regard to the 'situation' in Nagorno-Karabakh.[126]

---

[121] UN General Assembly Resolution 42/37C, adopted without a vote on 30 November 1987.
[122] UN General Assembly Resolution 45/57, adopted without a vote on 4 December 1990. In this resolution, the Assembly endorsed 'the proposals of the group of qualified experts established in pursuance of its resolution 42/37 C of 30 November 1987 concerning technical guidelines and procedures to guide the Secretary-General in the conduct of timely and efficient investigation of the reports of use of chemical and bacteriological (biological) or toxin weapons'. Ibid., para. 3.
[123] Art. 90(1)(a), Protocol Additional to the Geneva Conventions of 12 August 1949, and Relating to the Protection of Victims of International Armed Conflicts; adopted at Geneva 8 June 1977; entered into force 7 December 1978.
[124] IHFFC, 'OSCE Special Monitoring Mission Was Not Targeted, Concludes Independent Forensic Investigation into Tragic Incident of 23 April 2017', 7 September 2017, at http://bit.ly/35Tgpj5.
[125] IHFFC, 'Welcome', at http://bit.ly/3nLZBjX.
[126] IHFFC, 'News from the IHFFC', 23 October 2020, at http://bit.ly/3nLZBjX.

39

Regional Human Rights Machinery and the Right to Life

INTRODUCTION

39.01 As Chapter 1 describes, the right to life is protected by all the main regional human rights instruments. However, the formulation of this right and the extent of the protection that is offered by the regional human rights machinery differ to some extent. By far the most prolific in terms of jurisprudence is the European Court of Human Rights: between its first judgment on the right to life in September 1995 and through late November 2020, 3,875 judgments concerned the right, of which 476 were issued by the Court's Grand Chamber. But the Inter-American Court of Human Rights has also made a significant contribution to our understanding of the scope and legal status of the right to life, while the African Commission on Human and Peoples' Rights brought together learning at the regional and global level in an important General Comment issued in 2015.

39.02 The Arab Charter on Human Rights lacks credible regional machinery to enforce its provisions, including on the right to life, and its articles pertaining thereto also fail to comply with general international law in a number of material aspects. More generally, a major gap in regional human rights protection exists across Asia[1] and the Pacific.[2]

39.03 This chapter summarises, in turn, the regional understandings of the right to life within the auspices of the Council of Europe, the European Union, the Organization of American States (OAS), the African Union, the Arab League, and the Association of South-East Asian Nations (ASEAN). For each case, the machinery that has been created to enforce respect for human rights is summarised, in particular the right to life.

---

[1] Of the twenty-four States not party to the International Covenant on Civil and Political Rights (ICCPR) as at 1 May 2021, nine were from Asia (outside the Pacific): Bhutan, Brunei, China (a signatory), Malaysia, Myanmar, Oman, Saudi Arabia, Singapore, and the United Arab Emirates.

[2] With respect to the situation in the Pacific, see, e.g., K. Hay, 'A Pacific Human Rights Mechanism: Specific Challenges and Requirements', *Victoria University of Wellington Law Review*, vol. 40 (2009), pp. 195–214, at http://bit.ly/3lY7LFw. Of the twenty-four States not party to the ICCPR, eleven are Pacific nations: the Cook Islands, Kiribati, Micronesia, Nauru (a signatory), Niue, Palau (a signatory), Saint Kitts and Nevis, Saint Lucia (a signatory), the Solomon Islands, Tonga, and Tuvalu.

THE EUROPEAN HUMAN RIGHTS SYSTEM AND THE RIGHT TO LIFE

39.04 The European Court of Human Rights has played a leading role not just regionally but also globally in interpreting and applying the right to life. The Court is a permanent institution created by the Convention for the Protection of Human Rights and Fundamental Freedoms in order to enforce its provisions. Adopted by the Council of Europe in 1950,[3] the treaty is better known as the European Convention on Human Rights.[4] As of 1 May 2021, forty-seven States were 'High Contracting Parties' to the Convention.[5] On the European continent, Belarus and the Holy See are the only States not party to the Convention. The European Union is also committed to becoming party to the Convention, but as of this writing has not yet done so.

39.05 For the adjudging of cases, the Court is divided into two types of tribunals: Chambers (of seven judges) and a Grand Chamber (of seventeen judges). The Chambers are organised within five 'Sections' and ordinarily hear cases at first instance that are not ruled out as being inadmissible.[6] The initiation of proceedings before the Grand Chamber occurs on the basis of either referral or relinquishment. After a Chamber judgment has been delivered, the parties may request referral of the case to the Grand Chamber, and such requests are accepted on an exceptional basis. A panel of five judges of the Grand Chamber decides whether a case should be referred to the Grand Chamber for fresh consideration. Cases are also sent to the Grand Chamber when relinquished by a Chamber, although this is also exceptional. The Chamber to which a case is assigned can relinquish it to the Grand Chamber if the case raises a serious question of interpretation of the Convention or if there is a risk of inconsistency with a previous judgment of the Court.[7]

39.06 The judgment of the Court, once it is final, is binding on the respondent State.[8] Since its establishment in 1959, and through the end of 2019, the European Court of Human Rights delivered more than 22,500 judgments. Around 40 per cent of these

---

[3] Art. 19, Convention for the Protection of Human Rights and Fundamental Freedoms; adopted at Rome by the Council of Europe 4 November 1950; entered into force 3 September 1953. The Council of Europe was formed pursuant to the Treaty of London, which was signed by ten States on 5 May 1949.
[4] The United Kingdom was the first State to ratify, on 8 March 1951.
[5] Albania, Andorra, Armenia, Austria, Azerbaijan, Belgium, Bosnia and Herzegovina, Bulgaria, Croatia, Cyprus, Czechia, Denmark, Estonia, Finland, France, Georgia, Germany, Greece, Hungary, Iceland, Ireland, Italy, Latvia, Liechtenstein, Lithuania, Luxembourg, Malta, Moldova, Monaco, Montenegro, the Netherlands, North Macedonia, Norway, Poland, Portugal, Romania, Russian Federation, San Marino, Serbia, Slovak Republic, Slovenia, Spain, Sweden, Switzerland, Turkey, Ukraine, and the United Kingdom. Such States are also referred to by the Court as Contracting States or, more generally in international law, States Parties.
[6] Guidance is given on the European Court's website on how to make a valid application. See http://bit.ly/35U97vb.
[7] European Court of Human Rights, 'The Grand Chamber', FAQ, at http://bit.ly/2IZl3mG.
[8] Art. 46(1), European Convention on Human Rights. The judgment of the Grand Chamber is immediately final. The judgment of a Chamber becomes final either when the parties declare they will not request a referral to the Grand Chamber; or three months after the date of the judgment, if referral has not been requested; or when the panel of the Grand Chamber rejects the request for referral. Art. 44(1) and (2), European Convention on Human Rights.

concerned three member States of the Council of Europe: Turkey (3,645), the Russian Federation (2,699), and Italy (2,410). In 84 per cent of the judgments it has delivered since 1959, the Court has found at least one violation of the Convention by the respondent State.[9] Where a judgment determined that one or more of the articles of the Convention had been violated, the right to life was contravened in 4.5 per cent of cases.[10] As of the end of 2019, a violation of the right to life had been found against Russia in 310 judgments, against Turkey in 141 judgments, against Bulgaria in 15 judgments, and against Ukraine in 12.[11]

39.07 The Court is 'not formally bound to follow any of its previous judgments', although 'it is in the interests of legal certainty, foreseeability and equality before the law that it should not depart, without good reason, from precedents laid down in previous cases'.[12] If the Court finds a violation of the Convention, and if the relevant domestic law 'allows only partial reparation to be made, the Court shall, if necessary, afford just satisfaction to the injured party'.[13]

39.08 Article 2 of the European Convention on Human Rights, which is based on text proposed by the United Kingdom,[14] circumscribes the right to life as follows:

1. Everyone's right to life shall be protected by law. No one shall be deprived of his life intentionally save in the execution of a sentence of a court following his conviction of a crime for which this penalty is provided by law.
2. Deprivation of life shall not be regarded as inflicted in contravention of this Article when it results from the use of force which is no more than absolutely necessary:
    (a) in defence of any person from unlawful violence;
    (b) in order to effect a lawful arrest or to prevent the escape of a person lawfully detained;
    (c) in action lawfully taken for the purpose of quelling a riot or insurrection.

Under Article 15(2) of the Convention, the right to life is non-derogable 'except in respect of deaths resulting from lawful acts of war'.

39.09 The first judgment on the right to life by the European Court of Human Rights was in 1995, in the *McCann* case against the United Kingdom. Its determination that a violation of Article 2 had occurred contrasted with the earlier European Commission on Human Rights' finding that the right to life had not been violated.[15] In its judgment, the

---

[9] European Court of Human Rights, 'Overview 1959–2019: ECHR', Strasbourg, February 2020, at http://bit.ly/3fn2jcT, p. 3.
[10] Ibid., p. 6.
[11] Ibid., pp. 8–9.
[12] European Court of Human Rights, *Herrmann v. Germany*, Judgment (Grand Chamber), 26 June 2012, para. 78.
[13] Art. 41, European Convention of Human Rights.
[14] W. A. Schabas, *European Convention on Human Rights: A Commentary*, Oxford University Press, Oxford, 2017, pp. 120–1.
[15] European Commission on Human Rights, *McCann and others v. United Kingdom*, Report adopted on 4 March 1994, available at http://bit.ly/3flM3J6. The European Convention on Human Rights originally created two organs to ensure compliance with its provisions: the European Commission on Human Rights

Grand Chamber stated that it 'must be guided by the fact that the object and purpose of the Convention as an instrument for the protection of individual human beings requires that its provisions be interpreted and applied so as to make its safeguards practical and effective'.[16] The right 'ranks as one of the most fundamental provisions in the Convention', admitting, in peacetime, of no derogation. Together with Article 3 (prohibiting torture or inhuman or degrading treatment or punishment), it 'also enshrines one of the basic values of the democratic societies making up the Council of Europe'. As such, the Court declared, 'its provisions must be strictly construed'.[17]

39.10 The Grand Chamber read into Article 2 that not only must force be used 'no more than absolutely necessary', as the article expressly stipulates; it must also be 'strictly proportionate' to the achievement of the aims set out in the three subparagraphs of Article 2(2).[18] That said, a use of force which is based 'on an honest belief which is perceived, for good reasons, to be valid at the time but which subsequently turns out to be mistaken' will not violate the right to life.[19] However, the Court also introduced a precautionary principle to Article 2, declaring that it must 'carefully scrutinise' whether an operation 'was planned and controlled by the authorities so as to minimise, to the greatest extent possible, recourse to lethal force'.[20]

39.11 The Court further held that the obligation to protect the right to life under the Convention, read in conjunction with a Contracting State's general duty under Article 1 to secure to everyone within its jurisdiction the rights and freedoms set out in the Convention, demands an effective official investigation when individuals have been killed as a result of the use of force by, inter alia, agents of the State.[21] This 'duty to investigate' is now understood as the procedural aspect of the right to life.

39.12 The principles that the Court espoused in its judgment in the *McCann* case remain those that guide its interpretation of Article 2 to this day. Thus, Rainey et al. have summarised the Court's approach to the right to life as three-pronged: a duty on the State and its agents to refrain from unlawful killing; a duty to investigate suspicious deaths (and, where it is required by the situation, also to prosecute); and 'in certain circumstances', a positive duty

---

and the European Court of Human Rights. Any Contracting State could refer to the Commission an allegation of a violation by another Contracting State while any individual, non-governmental organisation (NGO), or group of individuals claiming to be the victim of a violation could make an application to the Commission if the Contracting State in question had accepted the right of individual petition. In the 1990s, such a right of individual petition came to be considered as inherent to the acceptance of the Convention system. Protocol 11 to the Convention abolished the Commission. B. Rainey, E. Wicks, and C. Ovey, *Jacobs, White & Ovey: The European Convention on Human Rights*, 6th ed., Oxford University Press, Oxford, 2014, pp. 8, 9.

[16] European Court of Human Rights, *McCann and others v. United Kingdom*, Judgment (Grand Chamber), 27 September 1995, para. 146.
[17] Ibid., para. 147.
[18] Ibid., para. 149.
[19] Ibid., para. 194.
[20] Ibid., para. 200.
[21] Ibid., para. 161.

to prevent avoidable loss of life.[22] An unlawful killing will not, however, occur when a State agent makes an honest but reasonable mistake in believing that he or she is entitled to use deadly force in the circumstances prevailing at the time.[23]

39.13 The positive obligation to take preventive operational measures to protect an identified individual from another individual – or, in specific circumstances, from himself or herself – exists where the authorities knew or ought to have known of a real and immediate risk to life from the criminal acts of a third party.[24] A violation will occur when the authorities 'failed to take measures within the scope of their powers which, judged reasonably, might have been expected to avoid that risk'.[25] In its 2017 judgment in the *Tagayeva* case,[26] a chamber of the Court held that Russia had failed to take reasonable measures to prevent a terrorist attack (the Beslan school siege of 2004 in North Ossetia). The authorities had learned of a planned attack on an educational institution in the region but had not stepped up security (indeed it had been reduced); nor had they warned schools, teachers, or pupils of the danger. Russia was not granted leave to appeal the decision to the Grand Chamber.[27]

39.14 By virtue of the duty upon each Contracting State under Article 2 to protect the right to life by law, an effective domestic legislative framework, including under the criminal law, must be in place.[28] The substance of the Convention's safeguarding of the right to life must be protected by domestic law, though the Convention does not oblige its Contracting Parties to incorporate its provisions into national law.[29] Moreover, 'it is not the role of the Convention institutions to examine in abstracto the compatibility of national legislative or constitutional provisions with the requirements of the Convention'.[30]

39.15 That said, Article 2 'implies a primary duty on the State to secure the right to life by putting in place an appropriate legal and administrative framework defining the limited circumstances in which law enforcement officials may use force and firearms, in the light of the relevant international standards'.[31] Furthermore, in line with the principle of strict proportionality 'inherent in Article 2', the Court has held that the 'national legal

---

[22] Rainey, Wicks, and Ovey, *Jacobs, White & Ovey: The European Convention on Human Rights*, 6th ed., p. 143.
[23] European Court of Human Rights, *Armani da Silva v. United Kingdom*, Judgment (Grand Chamber), 30 March 2016, para. 248.
[24] European Court of Human Rights, *Kotilainen and others v. Finland*, Judgment (First Section), 17 September 2020, para. 69.
[25] Ibid.
[26] European Court of Human Rights, *Tagayeva and others v. Russia*, Judgment (First Section), 13 April 2017.
[27] BBC, 'Beslan Siege: Russia "Will Comply" with Critical Ruling', 20 September 2017, at http://bbc.in/2OM9bmr.
[28] European Court of Human Rights, *Tërshana v. Albania*, Judgment (Second Section), 4 August 2020, para. 149.
[29] European Court of Human Rights, *McCann and others v. United Kingdom*, Judgment (Grand Chamber), paras. 152, 153.
[30] Ibid., para. 153.
[31] European Court of Human Rights, *Nachova v. Bulgaria*, Judgment (Grand Chamber), 6 July 2005, para. 96. These standards include the relevant provisions of the UN Basic Principles on the Use of Force and Firearms by Law Enforcement Officials.

framework regulating arrest operations must make recourse to firearms dependent on a careful assessment of the surrounding circumstances, and, in particular, on an evaluation of the nature of the offence committed by the fugitive and of the threat he or she posed'.[32]

39.16 Ordinarily, the Court applies a standard to the assessment of evidence of 'beyond reasonable doubt'[33] in order to find a violation of the substantive aspect of the right to life. This may occur where there coexists 'sufficiently strong, clear and concordant inferences or of similar unrebutted presumptions of fact'.[34] But where a person is killed by State agents, the burden of proof is on the Government to provide a satisfactory and convincing explanation as to how exactly the events in question unfolded.[35] Similarly, 'where the events in issue lie wholly or in large part within the exclusive knowledge of the authorities, as in the case of persons under their control in detention, strong presumptions of fact will arise in respect of injuries and death occurring during that detention'.[36] Indeed, the Court has affirmed, 'the burden of proof may be regarded as resting on the authorities to provide a satisfactory and convincing explanation'.[37]

39.17 Since a Grand Chamber judgment in 2000, it has not been absolutely necessary for the victim to die for a violation of the right to life to occur. In its judgment in the *Ilhan* case, the Court held that 'the degree and type of force used and the unequivocal intention or aim behind the use of force may, among other factors, be relevant in assessing whether in a particular case the State agents' actions in inflicting injury short of death must be regarded as incompatible with the object and purpose of Article 2 of the Convention'.[38]

39.18 Where a killing occurs during and in connection with an armed conflict, the Court has held that Article 2 'must be interpreted in so far as possible in light of the general principles of international law, including the rules of international humanitarian law which play an indispensable and universally accepted role in mitigating the savagery and inhumanity of armed conflict'.[39] The Court cites in this regard – in a rare footnote to a judgment – the four Geneva Conventions of 1949, and the three Additional Protocols thereto.[40]

39.19 Finally, although the death penalty is specifically provided for in Article 2, a Chamber of the Court held In 2010, in its judgment in the *Al-Saadoon* case, that the

---

[32] European Court of Human Rights, *Nachova v. Bulgaria*, Judgment (Grand Chamber), para. 96. In its judgment in this case, the Court found that the domestic legal framework in Bulgaria was 'fundamentally deficient' and that it fell 'well short of the level of protection "by law" of the right to life that is required by the Convention in present-day democratic societies in Europe'. Ibid., para. 100.
[33] European Court of Human Rights, *Shuriyya Zeynalov v. Azerbaijan*, Judgment (Fifth Section), 10 September 2020, para. 51.
[34] European Court of Human Rights, *Tsechoyev v. Russia*, Judgment (First Section), 15 March 2011, para. 128.
[35] European Court of Human Rights, *Shavadze v. Georgia*, Judgment (Fifth Section), 19 November 2020.
[36] European Court of Human Rights, *Shchebetov v. Russia*, Judgment (First Section), 10 April 2012, para. 44.
[37] Ibid.
[38] European Court of Human Rights, *Ilhan v. Turkey*, Judgment (Grand Chamber), 27 June 2000, para. 76.
[39] European Court of Human Rights, *Varnava v. Turkey*, Judgment (Grand Chamber), 18 September 2009, para. 185. See on this issue: Schabas, *European Convention on Human Rights: A Commentary*, pp. 154–6.
[40] Ibid., note 1.

wording of the second sentence of Article 2(1) no longer acted 'as a bar to its interpreting the words "inhuman or degrading treatment or punishment" in Article 3 as including the death penalty'.[41] It may be taken that the imposition and execution of the death penalty are now prohibited to any Contracting Party to the European Convention since that decision.[42] In addition, Article 2 of the Convention 'prohibits the extradition or deportation of an individual to another State where substantial grounds have been shown for believing that he or she would face a real risk of being subjected to the death penalty there'.[43]

THE EUROPEAN UNION CHARTER OF FUNDAMENTAL RIGHTS

39.20 The EU Charter of Fundamental Rights was nominally concluded in 2000 but its text was only formally adopted in 2007 under the Treaty on the Functioning of the European Union (TFEU),[44] also referred to as the Lisbon Treaty. The 'rights, freedoms and principles' delineated in the Charter, whose provisions became legally binding on the EU and its member States in December 2009 with the Lisbon Treaty's entry into force has 'the same legal value' as the core EU Treaties.[45] The Charter's provisions are stated to be 'consistent' with the European Convention on Human Rights. Thus, when the Charter 'contains rights that stem from' the European Convention, 'their meaning and scope are the same'.[46]

39.21 Article 2 of the Charter of Fundamental Rights provides simply as follows:

1. Everyone has the right to life.
2. No one shall be condemned to the death penalty, or executed.

The Court of Justice of the European Union has the power to enforce Article 2, including by annulling EU legal acts where an EU act violates fundamental rights.[47] To date, it has not been called upon to do so. Once the European Union becomes a party to the European Convention on Human Rights, the European Court of Human Rights will be able to determine whether, in specific circumstances, the EU has violated the right to life of any person that comes within the Union's jurisdiction.

THE INTER-AMERICAN SYSTEM OF HUMAN RIGHTS AND THE RIGHT TO LIFE

39.22 Writing in 1979, Dennis Driscoll affirmed that the only regional organisation that 'rivals the Council of Europe in the generality of its human rights program is the

---

[41] European Court of Human Rights, *Al-Saadoon and Mufdhi v. United Kingdom*, Judgment (Fourth Section), 2 March 2010, para. 120.
[42] Schabas, *European Convention on Human Rights: A Commentary*, p. 17.
[43] European Court of Human Rights, *Al Nashiri v. Poland*, Judgment (Fourth Section), 24 July 2014, para. 576.
[44] Treaty on the Functioning of the European Union; adopted at Lisbon 13 December 2007; entered into force 1 December 2009.
[45] Art. 6(1), Consolidated version of the Treaty on European Union.
[46] European Commission, 'Why Do We Need the Charter?', at http://bit.ly/2KucwZv.
[47] European Union, 'Court of Justice of the European Union (CJEU)', at http://bit.ly/3pSTqfX.

Organization of American States'.[48] While that statement is no longer true, as a consequence of the emergence of the African human rights system, the Inter-American system of human rights is nonetheless an impressive edifice, with highly consequential jurisprudence on the right to life and the production of valuable research papers on major issues of concern, such as on terrorism and counterterrorism in 2002[49] and on racially motivated killings among law enforcement personnel in the United States in a 2018 report.[50]

39.23 In fact, the building blocks of the Inter-American system began prior to the conclusion of the European Convention on Human Rights, with the adoption by the OAS of the American Declaration on the Rights and Duties of Man in 1948.[51] The Inter-American Commission on Human Rights was established a decade later in 1959 during a conference of ministers for foreign affairs of OAS member States[52] in order to 'promote the observance and protection of human rights'.[53] The American Convention on Human Rights was concluded in 1969, three years after the adoption of the ICCPR.[54] The Inter-American Court of Human Rights was created pursuant to the Convention.[55]

39.24 As of 1 May 2021, twenty-four OAS member States were party to the American Convention on Human Rights,[56] while the remaining eleven were not.[57] Of the twenty-four States Parties to the Convention, only Grenada and Jamaica do not permit the Inter-American Court of Human Rights to hear allegations by an individual or a non-governmental organisation of a violation of any of the rights the Convention protects.[58] The Court consists of seven judges drawn from the member States of the OAS but elected

---

[48] D. J. Driscoll, 'The Development of Human Rights in International Law', in W. Laqueur and B. Rubin (eds.), *The Human Rights Reader*, Meridien, New York, 1979, p. 51.
[49] Inter-American Commission on Human Rights, *Report on Terrorism and Human Rights*, OAS doc. OEA/Ser. L/V/II.116 Doc. 5 rev. 1 corr., 22 October 2002, at http://bit.ly/318A2RC.
[50] Inter-American Commission on Human Rights, *African Americans, Police Use of Force, and Human Rights in the United States*, report approved by the Commission on 26 November 2018, Washington, DC.
[51] Adopted by the Ninth International Conference of American States, at Bogota, Colombia, 2 May 1948.
[52] The Commission was created by Resolution VIII of the Fifth Meeting of Ministers of Foreign Affairs of OAS member States, held in Santiago.
[53] As Article 106 of the OAS Charter provides: 'There shall be an Inter-American Commission on Human Rights, whose principal function shall be to promote the observance and protection of human rights and to serve as a consultative organ of the Organization in these matters.' Under Article 41 of the American Convention, 'the main function of the Commission shall be to promote respect for and defense of human rights'.
[54] American Convention on Human Rights; adopted at San José 22 November 1969; entered into force 18 July 1978.
[55] Art. 33, American Convention on Human Rights.
[56] States Parties are as follows: Argentina, Barbados, Bolivia, Brazil, Chile, Colombia, Costa Rica, Dominica, Dominican Republic, Ecuador, El Salvador, Grenada, Guatemala, Haiti, Honduras, Jamaica, Mexico, Nicaragua, Panama, Paraguay, Peru, Suriname, Uruguay, and Venezuela. Trinidad and Tobago denounced the Convention in 1998, while Venezuela denounced it in 2012. In 2019, however, Venezuela deposited anew its instrument of ratification. For the updated list of adherence to the Inter-American Convention on Human Rights, see http://bit.ly/2EraKCa.
[57] Antigua and Barbuda, Bahamas, Belize, Canada, Cuba, Guyana, St. Kitts and Nevis, St. Lucia, St. Vincent and Grenadines, Trinidad and Tobago, and the United States (a signatory) are States not party.
[58] Such recognition is done pursuant to Article 62(1).

'in an individual capacity from among jurists of the highest moral authority and of recognized competence in the field of human rights'.[59] They must 'possess the qualifications required for the exercise of the highest judicial functions in conformity with the law of the state of which they are nationals or of the state that proposes them as candidates'.[60]

39.25 The Inter-American system has retained the bifurcated system that has since been abandoned by the European human rights system. Thus the Inter-American Commission on Human Rights examines a case before transmitting it to the Court. If the Court finds a violation of a right or freedom protected by the Convention, it 'shall rule that the injured party be ensured the enjoyment of his right or freedom that was violated'.[61] Where appropriate, it must also rule that the consequences of the measure or situation that constituted the breach be remedied 'and that fair compensation be paid to the injured party'.[62] It has proven adept at adjudicating reparation other than of a financial nature to remedy human rights violations.[63] In a case of 'extreme gravity and urgency, and when necessary to avoid irreparable damage to persons', the Court is required to adopt 'such provisional measures as it deems pertinent in matters it has under consideration'.[64]

39.26 For the eleven States not party to the Convention, the Inter-American Commission is still competent to consider whether fundamental human rights protected under the American Declaration on the Rights and Duties of Man, including the right to life, may have been violated, including through receipt of individual communications.[65] According to Article I of the Declaration: 'Every human being has the right to life, liberty and the security of his person.'

39.27 Article 4 of the American Convention on Human Rights protects the right to life. It stipulates the following:

1. Every person has the right to have his life respected. This right shall be protected by law and, in general, from the moment of conception. No one shall be arbitrarily deprived of his life.
2. In countries that have not abolished the death penalty, it may be imposed only for the most serious crimes and pursuant to a final judgment rendered by a competent court and in accordance with a law establishing such punishment, enacted prior to the commission of the crime. The application of such punishment shall not be extended to crimes to which it does not presently apply.
3. The death penalty shall not be re-established in states that have abolished it.
4. In no case shall capital punishment be inflicted for political offenses or related common crimes.

---

[59] Art. 52(1), American Convention on Human Rights.
[60] Ibid.
[61] Art. 61(1), American Convention on Human Rights.
[62] Ibid.
[63] See, e.g., T. M. Antkowiak, 'Remedial Approaches to Human Rights Violations: The Inter-American Court of Human Rights and Beyond', *Columbia Journal of Transnational Law*, vol. 46 (2008), pp. 351–419.
[64] Art. 61(2), American Convention on Human Rights.
[65] Grenada's compliance with the Convention is monitored by the Inter-American Commission.

5. Capital punishment shall not be imposed upon persons who, at the time the crime was committed, were under 18 years of age or over 70 years of age; nor shall it be applied to pregnant women.
6. Every person condemned to death shall have the right to apply for amnesty, pardon, or commutation of sentence, which may be granted in all cases. Capital punishment shall not be imposed while such a petition is pending decision by the competent authority.

39.28 The drafting of the right is unusual as it specifies that 'in general' the right is to be protected from 'the moment of conception'. This implies that in certain circumstances abortion will amount to a violation of the right to life. That said, Cecilia Medina, a former judge at the Inter-American Court, wrote that 'given a choice between the risk to the life or health of the mother and potential risk to the life of the fetus, the decision should be to terminate the pregnancy'.[66] In its judgment in *Artavia Murillo and others ('In Vitro Fertilization') v. Costa Rica*, the Inter-American Court had already considered under which circumstances an embryo could be considered a person for the purposes of Article 4(1). The Court concluded that 'conception' occurred legally at the moment when the embryo becomes implanted in the uterus and not before.[67] It further held that the words 'in general' in paragraph 1 of the article entailed 'that the protection of the right to life under this provision is not absolute, but rather gradual and incremental according to its development'.[68]

39.29 The first case heard by the Inter-American Court of Human Rights was that of *Velásquez Rodríguez*, which concerned an enforced disappearance by State agents. In its judgment, the Court held that a State Party to the American Convention has a duty of due diligence to prevent violations of all human rights protected therein, including the right to life. 'This duty to prevent includes all those means of a legal, political, administrative and cultural nature that promote the protection of human rights and ensure that any violations are considered and treated as illegal acts, which, as such, may lead to the punishment of those responsible and the obligation to indemnify the victims for damages.'[69]

39.30 The Inter-American Court has perceived of a general duty to investigate alleged or suspected human rights violations – including but not limited to the right to life – as inhering in the general duty to respect rights in Article 1(1) of the American Convention on Human Rights. Where there is a breach of the procedural obligation to investigate a suspicious death along with a violation of the prohibition on arbitrary deprivation of life, the Court has framed it as a violation of the right to life in combination with

---

[66] C. Medina, *The American Convention on Human Rights. Crucial Rights and Their Theory and Practice*, Intersentia, Cambridge, 2014, p. 50, para. 12.
[67] Inter-American Court of Human Rights, *Artavia Murillo and others ('In Vitro Fertilization') v. Costa Rica*, Judgment (preliminary objections, merits, reparations and costs), 28 November 2012, para. 264.
[68] Ibid.
[69] Inter-American Court of Human Rights, *Velásquez Rodríguez v. Honduras*, Judgment (Merits), 29 July 1988, para. 175.

Article 1(1).[70] This differs slightly from the approach taken by the European Court, which, as noted previously, considers the duty to investigate as an autonomous, procedural aspect of the right to life distinct from the general duty to ensure/secure human rights.

39.31 The Inter-American Court took a similar constructed approach with respect to the duty to respect and protect life and not to arbitrarily deprive a person of his or her life. Thus it is the combination of the duty to respect and ensure human rights (in Article 1(1)) and the right to life (in Article 4) that led the Court to hold: 'That duty is to ensure every person subject to its jurisdiction the inviolability of the right to life and the right not to have one's life taken arbitrarily.'[71]

39.32 In situations of law enforcement, if an action that leads to death involves unnecessary or disproportionate force on the part of the law enforcement official, the right to life will be violated. In its judgment in the *Montero-Aranguren* case, the Court stated: 'When excessive force is used, any deprivation of life is arbitrary.'[72] In its later judgment in the *Cruz Sánchez* case, the Court stated that a violation of the right to life would occur when the use of force is 'illegitimate, excessive or disproportionate'.[73] In making the necessary assessment, the Court has applied the UN Basic Principles on the Use of Force or Firearms by Law Enforcement Officials.[74]

39.33 With respect to the precautionary principle identified by the European Court in the *McCann* case, the Inter-American Court has espoused a broadly similar norm, though it has tended to consider the duty of precaution as being subsumed within the principle of proportionality.[75] In the later *Nadege Dorzema* case, it endorsed this approach, holding that proportionality 'is also related to the planning of preventive measures, since it involves an assessment of the reasonableness of the use of force. Thus, it is useful to analyze the facts rigorously to determine ... whether the violations could have been avoided with the implementation of less harmful measures.'[76]

39.34 In situations of armed conflict, the Court has explicitly applied international humanitarian law. Thus, for instance, in 2012, in its judgment in the *Santo Domingo*

---

[70] Ibid., para. 188; see also Inter-American Court of Human Rights, *Godínez Cruz v. Honduras*, Judgment (Merits), 20 January 1989, paras. 175–6, 184, 198.
[71] Inter-American Court of Human Rights, *Velásquez Rodríguez v. Honduras*, Judgment (Merits), para. 188.
[72] Inter-American Court of Human Rights, *Montero-Aranguren and others (Detention Centre of Catia) v. Venezuela*, Judgment (Preliminary Objection, Merits, Reparations, and Costs), 5 July 2006, para. 68.
[73] Inter-American Court of Human Rights, *Cruz Sánchez and others v. Peru*, Judgment (Preliminary Objections, Merits, Reparation, and Costs), 17 April 2015, para. 261.
[74] Ibid., para. 264.
[75] In the *Detention Centre of Catia* case against Venezuela, the Inter-American Court of Human Rights declared that 'use of force by the security forces ... should be planned and proportionally limited by the government authorities'. Inter-American Court of Human Rights, *Montero-Aranguren and others (Detention Centre of Catia) v. Venezuela*, Judgment, para. 67. This official translation is of questionable faith to the original Spanish, which reads: 'El uso de la fuerza por parte de los cuerpos de seguridad estatales ... debe ser planeado y limitado proporcionalmente por las autoridades'. Arguably, a more faithful rendition of the Spanish would be 'must be planned and restricted by the authorities on the basis of proportionality'.
[76] Inter-American Court of Human Rights, *Nadege Dorzema and others v. Dominican Republic*, Judgment (Merits, Reparations, and Costs), 24 October 2012, para. 87.

massacre case, the Court found violations of the right to life (as well as violations of other rights protected by the American Convention) by applying the customary IHL duty to take precautions in attack to the non-international armed conflict between Colombia and the non-State armed group, the Colombian Revolutionary Armed Forces.[77] Previously, in 2006, the Court had accepted the potential for IHL to interpret rights protected under the Convention in its judgment in the *Case of the Ituango Massacres*.[78] In that case, the acts of terrorism were perpetrated by paramilitary groups of which the State was not only aware but also involved the active participation of State agents in a number of instances.[79]

39.35 Article 4 of the Convention guarantees not only the right of every human being not to be arbitrarily deprived of life, but also, the Court affirmed, 'the obligation of the State to take the necessary measures to establish an adequate legal framework to dissuade any threat to the right to life'.[80] The Court stated that the 'negative obligation to not harm life' was violated when the complainant's blood 'was contaminated by a private entity'.[81] The harm to her health, 'owing to the severity of the illness involved and the risks that the victim may face at different moments of her life', constituted a violation of the right to life, 'in view of the danger of death that the victim has faced, and may face in the future, owing to her illness'.[82]

39.36 Thus, akin to the approach taken by the European Court with regard to the survivors of attempted killings (and citing jurisprudence from the European Court in the *Acar* case),[83] in exceptional circumstances, the Inter-American Court will find that the right to life has been violated. Thus, in its judgment in the *Rochela Massacre* case, the Inter-American Court found 'extraordinary circumstances that lay a foundation' for a violation of the right to life under the American Convention with respect to the three survivors of the massacre. The Court reached its decision 'taking into account the force employed, the intent and objective of the use of this force, and the situation in which the victims found themselves'.[84]

39.37 In contrast, in issues such as extreme poverty and the right to a life with a modicum of dignity, the Inter-American Court has led the way. In 2015, in its judgment in *Gonzales Lluy v. Ecuador*,[85] the Court considered poverty as one of the factors that combined to give rise to the discrimination suffered by the victim, who was infected by HIV when she was three years old. For the first time, the Court used the concept of 'intersectionality' in its

---

[77] Inter-American Court of Human Rights, *Santo Domingo massacre v. Colombia*, Judgment (Preliminary Objections, Merits and Reparations), 30 November 2012, esp. paras. 229–30.
[78] Inter-American Court of Human Rights, *Ituango Massacres v. Colombia*, Judgment (Preliminary Objections, Merits, Reparations and Costs), 1 July 2006, para. 179.
[79] Ibid., para. 133.
[80] Ibid., para. 169.
[81] Ibid., para. 190.
[82] Ibid.
[83] European Court of Human Rights, *Acar and others v. Turkey*, Judgment (Fourth Section), 24 May 2005 (as rendered final on 12 October 2005), para. 77.
[84] Inter-American Court of Human Rights, *Rochela Massacre v. Colombia*, Judgment (Merits, Reparations, and Costs), 11 May 2007, paras. 123–5.
[85] Inter-American Court of Human Rights, *Gonzales Lluy and others v. Ecuador*, Judgment (Preliminary Objections, Merits, Reparations and Costs), 1 September 2015.

analysis of discrimination, holding that a confluence of multiple intersecting vulnerability factors and risks of discrimination had associated with her status as a child, a female, a person living in poverty, and someone living with HIV.[86]

39.38 The Court has also held that the right to life also encompasses guarantees ensuring the conditions necessary for a dignified existence. In its judgment in 1999 in the *Street Children* case, the Court affirmed that

> the fundamental right to life includes not only the right of every human being not to be deprived of his life arbitrarily, but also the right that he [or she] will not be prevented from having access to the conditions that guarantee a dignified existence. States have the obligation to guarantee the creation of the conditions required in order that violations of this basic right do not occur.[87]

Thus, the Inter-American Commission has observed, 'it is possible to state that poverty, particularly extreme poverty, may constitute, in certain circumstances, a violation of the right to life, interpreted broadly'.[88]

39.39 This interpretation was 'echoed' in the Inter-American Court's judgments in the *Yakye Axa, Sawhoyamaxa, and Xákmok Kásek indigenous communities* cases, in which it found that Paraguay had not taken the necessary measures to ensure a life with dignity, having failed to guarantee the provision of, among other things, water, food, health, and education to the members of these indigenous communities. In the first of these cases, adjudged in 2005, the Court found that the State had 'abridged' the right to life of the members of the Yakye Axa Community 'for not taking measures regarding the conditions that affected their possibility of having a decent life'. However, in the case of alleged responsibility for the death of sixteen individuals named in the complaint, the Court did not have 'sufficient evidence to establish the causes of [their] deaths' and thus could not hold that their right to life had been specifically violated.[89]

39.40 In its subsequent judgment in 2006 in the *Sawhoyamaxa* case, the Court clarified that it was 'clear' that a State cannot be held responsible 'for all situations in which the right to life is at risk'.[90] 'Taking into account the difficulties involved in the planning and adoption of public policies and the operational choices that have to be made in view of the priorities and the resources available', the Court said, the positive obligations upon the State must be interpreted without imposing upon the authorities 'an impossible or disproportionate burden'.[91] In order for this positive obligation to arise, the Court held,

---

[86] Ibid., para. 290.
[87] Inter-American Court of Human Rights, 'Street Children' (*Villagran-Morales and others*) v. Guatemala, Judgment (Merits) 19 November 1999, para. 144.
[88] Inter-American Commission on Human Rights, 'Report on Poverty and Human Rights in the Americas', 2017, para. 196.
[89] Inter-American Court of Human Rights, *Yakye Axa Indigenous Community* v. Paraguay, Judgment (Merits, Reparations and Costs), 17 June 2005, paras. 176, 177, 178.
[90] Inter-American Court of Human Rights, *Sawhoyamaxa Indigenous Community* v. Paraguay, Judgment (Merits, Reparations and Costs), 29 March 2006, para. 155.
[91] Ibid.

it must be determined that at the moment of the occurrence of the events, the authorities knew or should have known about the existence of a situation posing an immediate and certain risk to the life of an individual or of a group of individuals, and that the necessary measures were not adopted within the scope of their authority which could be reasonably expected to prevent or avoid such risk.[92]

One such risk may emanate from a situation of extreme poverty.[93]

39.41 The Inter-American Court has also played an important role in highlighting the pervasive phenomenon of gender-based violence, and the failure of certain States to tackle it. The so-called *Cotton Field* case was instrumental in this regard, with the judgment embracing 'a gender perspective' with a judgment that is said to represent 'at least symbolic progress toward the protection of women's rights'.[94] The authorities had denied any violations of the right to life had occurred as State agents 'did not take part in any of the three murders'.[95]

39.42 In its judgment in the case, however, the Court noted that despite the denial by Mexico of 'any kind of pattern in the motives for the murders of women in Ciudad Juárez', the State had told the Committee on the Elimination of Discrimination against Women 'that "they are all influenced by a culture of discrimination against women based on the erroneous idea that women are inferior"'.[96] After reviewing the available evidence, the Court concluded that murders in Ciudad Juárez were to be generally considered as '"gender-based murders of women", also known as femicide'.[97] Even when suspects were identified and successfully prosecuted, sentences imposed for the intentional murder of women averaged no more than fifteen years' imprisonment, even though most of the killings had been committed with aggravating circumstances.[98]

39.43 The drafters of the Convention could not agree to outlaw all imposition and execution of the death penalty, despite calls by several of the negotiating States to do so.[99] But the Inter-American Commission on Human Rights has narrowed the permissible circumstances where a death sentence could be imposed or executed. Thus, in its report in 2000 on a series of death row cases in Jamaica, the Commission held the mandatory death penalty to be an arbitrary deprivation of life and therefore a violation of the right to life under the Convention.[100]

---

[92] Ibid.
[93] Ibid., para. 154.
[94] J. I. Acosta López, 'The Cotton Field Case: Gender Perspective and Feminist Theories in the Inter-American Court of Human Rights Jurisprudence', *Revista Colombiana de Derecho Internacional*, vol. 21 (2012), pp. 17–54, at 18, 51.
[95] Inter-American Court of Human Rights, *González and others ('Cotton Field') v. Mexico*, Judgment (Preliminary Objection, Merits, Reparations, and Costs), 16 November 2009, para. 20.
[96] Ibid., para. 132.
[97] Ibid., para. 143.
[98] Ibid., para. 160.
[99] Ibid., p. 40, para. 2.
[100] Inter-American Commission on Human Rights, Report No. 41/00 (Cases 12.023 (Desmond McKenzie), 12.044 (Andrew Downer and Alphonso Tracey), 12.107 (Carl Baker), 12.126 (Dwight Fletcher), and 12.146 (Anthony Rose)), Jamaica, 13 April 2000, para. 196.

39.44 Similarly, in 2018, in its consolidated judgment in the cases of *Jabari Sensimania Nervais v. The Queen* and *Dwayne Omar Severin v. The Queen*,[101] the Caribbean Court of Justice held that a section of the Offences Against the Person Act in Barbados was unconstitutional because it provided for a mandatory sentence of death. The Court stated that 'the principle of a fair trial must be accorded to the sentencing stage too and also includes the right to appeal or apply for review by a higher court prescribed by law. The right to a fair trial as an element of protection of the law is one of the corner stones of a just and democratic society, without which the rule of law and public faith in the justice system would inevitably collapse.'[102]

39.45 A Protocol to the American Convention on Human Rights to Abolish the Death Penalty was adopted in 1990. A total of thirteen States were party to the Protocol as of this writing,[103] which obligates them to 'not apply the death penalty in their territory to any person subject to their jurisdiction'.[104] Akin to the exceptions provided for in both the Second Optional Protocol to the ICCPR and the Protocol 6 to the European Convention on Human Rights, however, when adhering to the Protocol to the Inter-American Convention, States are permitted to continue to apply the death penalty to the most serious crimes committed in wartime.[105] To date, both Brazil and Chile have chosen to do so.[106]

THE AFRICAN HUMAN RIGHTS SYSTEM AND THE RIGHT TO LIFE

39.46 The African human rights system was slow to evolve compared to Europe and the Americas and has been stuttering as of late. The African Charter on Human and Peoples' Rights (also known as the 'Banjul Charter') was adopted only in 1981, by the erstwhile Organization of African Unity (OAU). Its elaboration has been cast as a 'drastic curtailment' of the principle, prevailing in the 1960s and 1970s, of non-interference in OAU member States.[107] Indeed, the 1963 OAU Charter had not even explicitly included human rights as part of its mandate.[108] The African Commission on Human and Peoples' Rights was established in 1987, a year after the entry into force of the Banjul Charter, but it did not become fully functional until June 1989, and 'only in 1994 did it start to make public its decisions on communications brought before it'.[109]

---

[101] Caribbean Court of Justice, *Jabari Sensimania Nervais v. The Queen* and *Dwayne Omar Severin v. The Queen*, Judgment, 27 June 2018 [2018] CCJ 19 (AJ).
[102] Ibid., para. 49.
[103] Argentina, Brazil, Chile, Costa Rica, Dominican Republic, Ecuador, Honduras, Mexico, Nicaragua, Panama, Paraguay, Uruguay, and Venezuela. See http://bit.ly/2Sz5O4S.
[104] Art. 1, Protocol to the American Convention on Human Rights to Abolish the Death Penalty; adopted at Asuncion 8 June 1990; entered into force 28 August 1991.
[105] Ibid., Art. 2.
[106] See the respective declarations at http://bit.ly/2Sz5O4S.
[107] F. Viljoen, *International Human Rights Law in Africa*, 2nd ed., Oxford University Press, Oxford, 2012, p. 158.
[108] Ibid., p. 156.
[109] Ibid., p. 161.

39.47 The African Charter enshrines the right to life for 'every human being' as follows: 'Human beings are inviolable. Every human being shall be entitled to respect for his life and the integrity of his person. No one may be arbitrarily deprived of this right.'[110] In its General Comment on the right, issued in 2015, the African Commission on Human and Peoples' Rights noted that the right to life is 'universally recognised as a foundational human right'.[111]

39.48 Further African treaties have been adopted since 1990 to address specific groups or human rights issues. The first of these was the African Charter on the Rights and Welfare of the Child, again adopted under OAU auspices.[112] An African Children's Rights Committee oversees its implementation. The Protocol on the Rights of Women in Africa (also known as the 'Maputo Protocol'), whose elaboration was initiated by the OAU, was concluded by the African Union (AU), in 2003.[113] An AU Protocol on the Rights of Older Persons in Africa was concluded in 2016 but has not entered into force as of this writing.[114] In stark contrast to the OAU Charter, in the AU Constitutive Act, concluded in 2000, six of sixteen guiding principles[115] refer to human rights either explicitly or implicitly.[116]

39.49 The African Court on Human and Peoples' Rights was created pursuant to a 1998 Protocol which entered into force in 2004.[117] As in the Americas, the African human rights system has a bifurcated institutional set-up, combing the Commission and the Court. In the African Commission on Human and Peoples' Rights, eleven Commissioners, elected by the AU Assembly of Heads of State and Government, serve part-time and in a personal capacity.[118] The Commission's home is in Banjul, the 'slumbering capital' of The Gambia.[119]

---

[110] Art. 4(1), African Charter on Human and Peoples' Rights; adopted at Nairobi 27 June 1981; entered into force 21 October 1986. As of 1 May 2021, every African Union member State apart from Morocco was a party to the Charter.

[111] African Commission on Human and Peoples' Rights, 'General Comment No. 3 on the African Charter on Human and Peoples' Rights: The Right to Life (Article 4)', adopted at Banjul (57th Ordinary Session), November 2015 (hereinafter, African Commission General Comment on the Right to Life), para. 5.

[112] African Charter on the Rights and Welfare of the Child; adopted at Addis Ababa 1 July 1990; entered into force 29 November 1999. As of 1 May 2021, forty-nine of fifty-five African Union member States were party to the Charter. The Democratic Republic of Congo, Sahrawi Arab Democratic Republic, Somalia, South Sudan, and Tunisia were all signatories, while Morocco had not signed the Charter.

[113] Protocol to the African Charter on Human and Peoples' Rights on the Rights of Women in Africa; adopted at Maputo 11 July 2003; entered into force 25 November 2005. As of 1 May 2021, forty-two States were party to the Protocol and another ten States were signatories.

[114] Protocol to the African Charter on Human and Peoples' Rights on the Rights of Older Persons; adopted at Addis Ababa 31 January 2016; not yet in force. Under its Article 26(1), the Protocol will enter into force thirty days after the fifteenth ratification by an African Union member State. As of 1 May 2021, there were two ratifications and fifteen signatories.

[115] Art. 4, Constitutive Act of the African Union; adopted at Addis Ababa 7 November 2000; entered into force 26 May 2001.

[116] Viljoen, *International Human Rights Law in Africa*, 2nd ed., p. 165.

[117] Protocol to the African Charter on Human and Peoples' Rights on the Establishment of an African Court on Human and Peoples' Rights; adopted at Ouagadougou, 10 June 1998; entered into force 25 January 2004.

[118] Viljoen, *International Human Rights Law in Africa*, 2nd ed., pp. 289–90.

[119] Ibid., p. 291.

39.50 Cases can be referred to the Court, established in Arusha, by the Commission. States Parties to the 1998 Protocol can also accept the competence of the Court to allow NGOs and individuals to petition the Court directly.[120] As of 1 May 2021, ten States had done so – Benin, Burkina Faso, Cote d'Ivoire, The Gambia, Ghana, Malawi, Mali, Rwanda, Tanzania, and Tunisia – but Benin, Cote d'Ivoire, Rwanda, and Tanzania had subsequently withdrawn their acceptance.[121] This was a significant body blow to the credibility of the Court, with the African Commission having referred only three cases to it as of late 2019.[122] Indeed, writing in May 2020, Apollin Koagne Zouapet asked – rhetorically, one hopes – whether the epitaph of the African Court on Human and Peoples' Rights should be prepared.[123] Years earlier, he noted, he had expressed concern 'about the perceived lack of rigour in the reasoning' of the Court's judgments.[124]

39.51 More rigorous has been the African Commission's appreciation of the right to life under Article 4 of the Banjul Charter, in particular in its 2015 General Comment on the provision. In particular, it stated that 'any deprivation of life resulting from a violation of the procedural or substantive safeguards in the African Charter, including on the basis of discriminatory grounds or practices, is arbitrary and as a result unlawful'.[125] The Commission also stressed the interrelationship with the other rights recognised in the Charter: 'In order to secure a dignified life for all, the right to life requires the realisation of all human rights recognised in the Charter, including civil, political, economic, social and cultural rights and peoples' rights, particularly the right to peace.'[126]

39.52 In similar terms to the approach taken in the European and Inter-American human rights system, the African Commission on Human and Peoples' Rights has stated:

> Where a State or its agent has attempted unlawfully to kill a person, but that person survives, where it has unlawfully threatened the life of a person, or where it has forcibly caused a person to disappear and that person's fate remains unknown, in addition to the violation of other rights, a violation of the right to life has occurred.[127]

---

[120] Article 34 of the Protocol stipulates that 'at the time of ratification of this Protocol or any time thereafter, the State shall make a declaration accepting the competence of the Court to receive cases under Article 5(3) of this Protocol. The Court shall not receive any petition under article 5(3) involving a State which has not made such a declaration.' Article 5(3) states the following: 'The Court may entitle relevant Non Governmental Organizations (NGOs) with observer status before the Commission, and individuals to institute cases directly before it, in accordance with article 34(6) of this Protocol.'

[121] International Commission of Jurists, 'Withdrawal of States from African Court a Blow to Access to Justice in the Region', 1 May 2020, at http://bit.ly/35WVfk4.

[122] N. De Silva, 'Individual and NGO Access to the African Court on Human and Peoples' Rights: The Latest Blow from Tanzania', EJIL: Talk!, 16 December 2019, at http://bit.ly/3kUaaja.

[123] A. K. Zouapet, '"Victim of Its Commitment ... You, Passerby, a Tear to the Proclaimed Virtue": Should the Epitaph of the African Court on Human and Peoples' Rights Be Prepared?', EJIL: Talk!, May 2020, at http://bit.ly/3m1Pibo.

[124] Cited in ibid.

[125] African Commission on Human and Peoples' Rights, 'General Comment No. 3 on the African Charter on Human and Peoples' Rights: The Right to Life (Article 4)', adopted at Banjul (57th Ordinary Session), November 2015 (hereinafter, African Commission General Comment on the right to life), para. 12.

[126] Ibid., para. 6.

[127] Ibid., para. 8.

Where a person dies in State custody, the Commission has held that there is 'a presumption of State responsibility' with the burden of proof resting upon the State 'to prove otherwise through a prompt, impartial, thorough and transparent investigation carried out by an independent body. This heightened responsibility extends to persons detained in prisons, in other places of detention (official and otherwise), and to persons in other facilities where the State exercises heightened control over their lives.'[128]

39.53 The procedural obligation to carry out an effective investigation under Article 2 of the European Convention has been followed by the African Commission. In its General Comment, it states: 'The failure of the State transparently to take all necessary measures to investigate suspicious deaths and all killings by State agents and to identify and hold accountable individuals or groups responsible for violations of the right to life constitutes in itself a violation by the State of that right.'[129]

39.54 With respect to armed conflict, the Commission has stated: 'The right to life continues to apply during armed conflict. During the conduct of hostilities, the right to life needs to be interpreted with reference to the rules of international humanitarian law. In all other situations the intentional deprivation of life is prohibited unless strictly unavoidable to protect another life or other lives.'[130]

39.55 A Special Rapporteur on Extrajudicial, Summary or Arbitrary Executions in Africa was appointed in 1995 based on a proposal made two years earlier by Amnesty International. Its only mandate holder, Ben Salem, had 'little relevant expertise', and was 'ill-fitted' for the position as he was serving at the time as Tunisian Ambassador to Senegal.[131] He resigned in 2001 and the mandate has not been revived since, despite the expressed intention to appoint a new Special Rapporteur.[132] Instead, the African Commission established the Working Group on the Death Penalty in 2005, which became the Working Group on Death Penalty and Extra-Judicial, Summary or Arbitrary Killings in Africa in 2012.[133]

39.56 In November 2019, in one of its relatively rare judgments, the African Court reaffirmed in its decision in *Ally Rajabu v. Tanzania* that the mandatory death penalty does not uphold the requirements of fairness and due process guaranteed under Article 7(1) of the Charter, thereby rendering the death penalty contrary to Article 4 of the Charter.[134] Earlier, on 25 March 2011, the African Court on Human and Peoples' Rights

---

[128] Ibid., para. 37. See similarly Human Rights Committee, *Sanjeevan v. Sri Lanka*, Views (Communication No. 1436/05), 8 July 2008, para. 6.2.
[129] African Commission General Comment on the right to life, para. 15.
[130] Ibid., para. 13.
[131] Viljoen, *International Human Rights Law in Africa*, 2nd ed., p. 371.
[132] African Commission on Human and Peoples' Rights, 'Background Information on the Mandate of the Special Rapporteur on Extra-Judicial, Summary or Arbitrary Executions of the African Commission on Human and Peoples' Rights', at http://bit.ly/3pRSwQZ, para. 3.
[133] African Commission on Human and Peoples' Rights, 'Mandate of the Working Group on Death Penalty and Extrajudicial, Summary or Arbitrary Killings in Africa', at http://bit.ly/3q4iivl.
[134] African Court on Human and Peoples' Rights, *Ally Rajabu and others v. Tanzania*, Decision (App. No. 007/2015), 28 November 2019, paras. 112–14.

ordered provisional measures against Libya in a case presented by the African Commission. The Commission had alleged that demonstrations in Benghazi and other cities and towns on 19 February 2011 were 'violently suppressed by security forces who opened fire at random on the demonstrators killing and injuring many people'.[135] The provisional measures ordered by the Court demanded that Libya 'immediately refrain from any action that would result in loss of life or violation of physical integrity of persons, which could be a breach of the provisions of the African Charter on Human and Peoples' Rights or of other international human rights instruments to which it is a party'.[136]

THE ARAB CHARTER ON HUMAN RIGHTS

39.57 It is not yet possible to speak of an Arab 'system' of human rights,[137] given the lack of even minimally credible institutional structure that has been created around the 2004 Arab Charter on Human Rights.[138] Indeed, the Charter currently lacks any enforcement mechanism. An Arab Human Rights Committee, established in 2009 to monitor and oversee compliance with the Charter, is little other than a straw man. A Statute of the Arab Court of Human Rights was approved by the Ministerial Council of the League of Arab States on 7 September 2014, but it has remained unratified and its content has been heavily criticised by leading human rights organisations.[139] The International Commission of Jurists, for instance, has stated: 'The deficiencies are manifest, particularly those provisions relating to the Arab Court's jurisdiction; the guarantees of the independence of the Arab Court, including the independence of its judges; the admissibility of cases; and access to the court for victims of human rights violations.'[140]

39.58 Article 5(1) of the Arab Charter on Human Rights[141] specifies that 'every human being has an inherent right to life'. It is further specified that 'this right shall be protected by law. No one shall be arbitrarily deprived of his life'.[142] The Arab Human Rights Committee, established under the 2004 Charter, has not elucidated its understanding of the normative status of the right to life under general international law.

39.59 The Arab Charter on Human Rights does not address the issue of terrorism or counterterrorism.[143] The 1998 Arab Convention on the Suppression of Terrorism had determined that 'all cases of struggle by whatever means, including armed struggle, against

---

[135] African Court of Human and Peoples' Rights, *African Commission on Human and Peoples' Rights v. Libya*, Order for Provisional Measures (App. No. 004/2011), 25 March 2011, para. 2.
[136] Ibid., para. 25.
[137] See, e.g., University of Melbourne, 'Emerging Arab States Human Rights Mechanisms', at http://bit.ly/3fFkHxT.
[138] Arab Charter on Human Rights; adopted at Tunis 22 May 2004; entered into force 15 March 2008.
[139] An unofficial English translation of the Statute is contained on pages 35–43 of the International Commission of Jurists' 2015 report: 'The Arab Court of Human Rights: a Flawed Statute for an Ineffective Court', available at http://bit.ly/3pVvOHo.
[140] Ibid., p. 5.
[141] Arab Charter on Human Rights; adopted at Tunis 22 May 2004; entered into force 15 March 2008.
[142] Art. 5(2), 2004 Arab Charter on Human Rights.
[143] See 2004 Arab Charter on Human Rights.

foreign occupation and aggression for liberation and self-determination, in accordance with the principles of international law, shall not be regarded as an offence'.[144] There is no mention of constraints imposed on the use of force in counterterrorism operations. The Charter also does not address directly enforced disappearance.

39.60 The Arab Charter on Human Rights breaches customary international law on the death penalty in a number of respects, particularly with regard to the possibility it foresees of executing child offenders. Three provisions are dedicated to the death penalty, which are the least progressive of all the regional human rights treaties. Article 6 provides as follows:

> The death penalty shall be inflicted only for the most serious crimes in accordance with the law in force at the time of the commission of the crime. Such a penalty can only be carried out pursuant to a final judgment rendered by a competent court. Anyone sentenced to death shall have the right to seek pardon or commutation of the sentence.

Thus the court need only be competent – the trial does not need to be fair, as international law dictates. Moreover, while Article 8(1) prohibits 'physical or mental torture' and 'cruel, inhuman or degrading treatment or punishment', no provision in the Charter explicitly protects detainees or establishes minimum conditions of detention.

39.61 Article 7(1) of the Charter violates customary international law. It provides that the death penalty 'shall not be inflicted on a person under 18 years of age, unless otherwise provided by the law in force at the time of the commission of the crime'. This ostensibly allows a State to derogate in its national law from the customary prohibition on executing children and potentially also allows the execution of a death sentence once the convicted person has attained the age of eighteen. This is despite the provision directing 'special protection' for children.[145]

39.62 Article 43 of the Arab Charter stipulates that 'nothing in the present Charter shall be interpreted as impairing the rights and freedoms protected by the State Parties' own laws'. This has particular – and potentially ominous – ramifications for human rights defenders.

THE ASEAN DECLARATION ON HUMAN RIGHTS

39.63 The 2012 Association of South-East Asian Nations (ASEAN) Declaration on Human Rights,[146] an instrument that is not legally binding, stipulates in its Article 11 that 'every person has an inherent right to life which shall be protected by law. No person shall be deprived of life save in accordance with law.' The lack of a treaty on human rights for the region is regrettable given that, 'due to the diverse cultures and varying political structures

---

[144] Art. 2(a), Arab Convention on the Suppression of Terrorism; adopted at Cairo 22 April 1998; entered into force 7 May 1999.
[145] Art. 33, 2004 Arab Charter on Human Rights.
[146] ASEAN Declaration on Human Rights, adopted by the Heads of State/Government of ASEAN Member States at Phnom Penh, 18 November 2012.

in Southeast Asia, tackling human rights issues remains a major hurdle'.[147] The issues faced by all ten member States 'tend to overlap each other, ranging from press freedoms, religious freedoms, blasphemy, extrajudicial killings, right up to the issue of gender identity'.[148]

39.64 The Declaration on the Elimination of Violence against Women in the ASEAN Region had been adopted by the ASEAN Ministerial Meeting on 30 June 2004. Under the Declaration, member States pledged to ensure that their domestic laws serve to prevent violence against women and to enhance the protection and recovery of survivors, including through measures to investigate, prosecute, and punish the perpetrators. This is so, whether violence occurs in the home, in the workplace, in the community, or in custody.[149]

39.65 In May 2019, the High Level Dialogue on Human Rights in ASEAN, organised by the Asian Forum for Human Rights and Development (FORUM-ASIA), ASEAN Parliamentarians for Human Rights, and the Centre for Strategic and International Studies, expressed 'grave concern about the ineffectiveness of the ASEAN Intergovernmental Commission on Human Rights (AICHR)[150] to provide protection for the human rights of the peoples in Southeast Asia'.[151] 'Ten years of silence is enough', the organisation declared. 'If the AICHR would like to be relevant to the struggle of the peoples of Southeast Asia and merit to be called a human rights commission, it needs to make major institutional changes, and take genuine steps towards the promise behind its creation.'[152] Indeed, as of this writing, the coup in Myanmar – and especially the widespread and serious violations of human rights associated with it – are posing a major challenge to ASEAN, which is, in the words of one media organization, 'struggling to decide whether to stick to its principle of non-interference in members' internal affairs or not'.[153] Action (or inaction) by ASEAN will shape both its legacy and its future.

---

[147] A. Farhan, 'The Sad Case of Human Rights in ASEAN', *The ASEAN Post*, 21 April 2019, at http://bit.ly/371CATn.
[148] Ibid.
[149] Ibid., operative para. 4.
[150] See https://aichr.org/.
[151] APHR and Forum-Asia, 'Joint Statement: ASEAN Needs a Stronger Human Rights Mechanism', news and press release, 9 May 2019, available at http://bit.ly/3pY5VGY.
[152] Ibid. See also A. Eby Hara, 'The Struggle to Uphold a Regional Human Rights Regime: The Winding Role of ASEAN Intergovernmental Commission on Human Rights (AICHR)', *Revista Brasileira de Política Internacional*, vol. 62 no. 1 (2019), available at http://bit.ly/372txlb.
[153] R. Ebbighausen, 'Myanmar Coup: ASEAN Split Over the Way Forward', Deutsche Welle, 29 March 2021, at http://bit.ly/31CO3GQ.

PART VI

Outlook

40

Customary Rules Pertaining to the Right to Life

INTRODUCTION

40.01 That the right to life in toto and applicable to every human being is a norm of customary international law is beyond dispute. The inherence of the right and the ubiquity of its enunciation by States, their legislatures, international organisations, judicial decision, and publicist attest beyond any reasonable doubt to its customary status. But behind this simplicity lies a web of complexity, interweaving treaty rules with customary rules and a small number of peremptory rules.

40.02 This chapter summarises the customary rules pertaining to the right to life. They bind not only States but also international organisations and, with respect to specific rules in certain circumstances, also non-State actors. The chapter further identifies those rules of general international law that have attained the status of peremptory norms (jus cogens) on the basis of their acceptance and recognition as such by the international community of States as a whole. A peremptory norm 'enjoys a higher rank in the international hierarchy than treaty law and even "ordinary" customary rules'.[1] Such norms bind all actors, whether State or non-State in character. Finally, the chapter delineates those rules that are custom in the making – *de lege ferenda* – but which have not yet crystallised as binding law, for want of *opinio juris* that is both general among States and specific among those States that are 'specially affected' by it.

CUSTOMARY RULES OF INTERNATIONAL LAW PERTAINING TO THE RIGHT TO LIFE

40.03 Every person has the right to life without distinction as to race, colour, sex, gender, sexual preference, language, religion, political or other opinion, national or social origin, property, birth, disability, or other status.

40.04 Every person without distinction has the right to protection of their life. A duty of special protection applies to individuals facing foreseeable threats to life whether they emanate from governmental or private actors.

---

[1] International Criminal Tribunal for the former Yugoslavia (ICTY), *Prosecutor v. Anto Furundžija*, Judgment (Case No. IT-95-17/1-T) (Trial Chamber), 10 December 1998, para. 153.

40.05 No one shall be sentenced to death after an unfair trial.

40.06 No one shall be sentenced to death for any crime that does not involve the direct perpetration of murder.

40.07 The death penalty shall not be imposed for crimes committed by those under eighteen years of age at the time of the commission of an offence.

40.08 The death penalty shall not be executed on pregnant women.

40.09 Law enforcement officials shall not use firearms against persons except, where necessary, in self-defence or defence of others against an imminent threat of death or serious injury or against a grave and temporally proximate threat to life.

40.10 States shall adopt a clear legislative framework for the use of deadly force by law enforcement officials that complies with international standards (principle of legality).

40.11 Any law enforcement operation shall be planned and conducted with a view to minimising the risk of death or serious injury (principle of precaution).

40.12 Any death other than that resulting from natural causes, as determined objectively by an impartial and qualified physician, or from the lawful execution of a sentence of death, shall be effectively and thoroughly investigated. This duty applies in peacetime and during emergencies, including natural disasters and armed conflicts. The nature and extent of the investigation may, however, depend on the prevailing circumstances, taking into account, inter alia, the existence of an armed conflict or other national emergencies.

40.13 It is prohibited to deport or extradite a person against their will to the jurisdiction of another State or any other subject of international law (*non-refoulement*) where they are likely to face death or inhumane treatment.

40.14 Where a pregnancy threatens the life of the mother it shall be terminated where it is not possible for the foetus to be delivered safely and viably.

40.15 Every State shall ensure that activities within its jurisdiction or control do not cause damage to the environment of other States or areas beyond the limits of national jurisdiction, putting at risk human lives.

40.16 A wilful failure to prevent and tackle disease and natural disasters and to prevent and address accidents violates the right to life of those who die as a result.

40.17 In general, the family of a deceased person have the right to dispose of the body in an appropriate manner. Restrictions imposed on that right must be legal, necessary for a legitimate aim, and proportionate in the circumstances.

40.18 During and in connection with an armed conflict, the dead must be disposed of in a respectful manner, and their graves respected and properly maintained.

40.19 Each party to an armed conflict must take all possible measures to prevent the dead from being despoiled. Mutilation of dead bodies is prohibited.

40.20 The explosive testing of nuclear weapons or other nuclear explosive devices is prohibited. The right to life is violated of any person who is killed or seriously injured as a result of an explosive nuclear test.

PEREMPTORY RULES OF INTERNATIONAL LAW (JUS COGENS) PERTAINING TO THE RIGHT TO LIFE

40.21 No one shall be arbitrarily deprived of their life.

40.22 Any act of genocide is prohibited.

40.23 Crimes against humanity are prohibited. Such crimes encompass murder and extermination when committed as part of a widespread or systematic attack directed against any civilian population, with knowledge of the attack.

40.24 Acts of aggression are prohibited.

40.25 No one shall be subject to enforced disappearance.

40.26 The wilful killing of any detainee, including by starvation or through the refusal of medical treatment, is prohibited.

40.27 The wilful killing of any civilian or other person *hors de combat* during and in connection with an armed conflict is prohibited.

40.28 The targeting of civilians in the conduct of hostilities, unless and for such time as they take a direct part in hostilities, is prohibited. Where civilians not participating directly in hostilities are killed or their life seriously endangered as a result, their right to life has been violated.

40.29 Where civilians are killed as a result of an indiscriminate attack during the conduct of hostilities, including as a consequence of the use of an inherently indiscriminate weapon, their right to life has been violated.

40.30 The intentional starvation of the civilian population as a method of warfare is prohibited. The right to life is violated of any person who dies or who is seriously harmed as a result.

40.31 No one shall be executed following the imposition of a sentence of death at the issue of a trial that is manifestly unfair. It is prohibited to execute any persons on the basis of their race or colour. It is prohibited to execute LGBTI persons on the basis of their gender or sexual identity.

40.32 It is prohibited to deport or extradite a refugee against their will to the jurisdiction of another State or any other subject of international law (*non-refoulement*) where they are likely to face death or torture.

40.33 Enslavement of any person is prohibited.

EMERGING CUSTOMARY RULES OF INTERNATIONAL LAW (*de lege ferenda*) PERTAINING TO THE RIGHT TO LIFE

40.34 The death penalty shall not be executed on nursing mothers.

40.35 It is prohibited to execute any person with severe psycho-social or intellectual disabilities.

40.36 Retentionist States should move towards the abolition of the death penalty.

40.37 An act of aggression that causes loss of life is a violation of the right to life of each of the victims.

40.38 A woman or girl who is carrying a pregnancy that has a fatal foetal abnormality has the right to be granted access to an abortion.

40.39 A woman or girl who is carrying a pregnancy that is the result of rape or incest has the right to be granted access to an abortion, should she so wish.

40.40 The use of anti-personnel mines is prohibited. The right to life is violated of any person who is killed or seriously injured by an anti-personnel mine where due diligence obligations were not met.

41

The Future of the Right to Life

41.01 The right to life is at the heart of the protection of all human rights. Its respect and protection are required by manifold treaties and by customary international law. Further, given its inclusion in the Constitution of 158 States, the right to life exists also as a general principle of law that suffuses the law of nations.

41.02 At the heart of the protection of the right to life is, as this work has emphasised, the prohibition on arbitrary deprivation of life. Not only a customary rule, it is also a peremptory norm of international law (jus cogens). This formulation, first incorporated in Article 6 of the International Covenant on Civil and Political Rights (ICCPR),[1] was initially controversial. During the elaboration of the provision, several States suggested that it was overly vague. In fact, its succinct, uncluttered construction has proved to be a masterstroke, permitting the necessary dynamism that characterises and empowers human rights law. Thus the notion of arbitrariness in deprivation of life potentially comprises all violations of international law that cause death. Disarmament law, law of law enforcement, international humanitarian law, disability law, environmental law, public health regulations, and jus ad bellum – all may be the source of a violation of the right to life.

41.03 In the first two decades following the adoption of the ICCPR, the focus of attention on the right to life was on the need to prevent and repress extrajudicial or summary killings and to end the execution of the death penalty, at least following a manifestly unfair trial. The notion of due diligence in protecting life has evolved as a general principle of law. Already in 1982, however, in its first General Comment on the right to life, the Human Rights Committee opened the door to an even more expansive application, noting that the right to life had been 'too often narrowly interpreted'. The expression 'inherent right to life', the Committee declared, 'cannot properly be understood in a restrictive manner, and the protection of this right requires that States adopt positive measures'.

---

[1] International Covenant on Civil and Political Rights; adopted at New York 16 December 1966; entered into force 23 March 1976.

41.04 As examples of such measures, the Committee considered it 'desirable' for States Parties to take 'all possible measures to reduce infant mortality and to increase life expectancy, especially in adopting measures to eliminate malnutrition and epidemics'. These first tentative steps would lead to a reinterpretation of the right to life as demanding action to fulfil the right to life, by, for instance, alleviating poverty and tackling discrimination. And it is not just a bare minimum of survival to which one is entitled, but one with a minimum of dignity. It is not by chance that the very first article in the European Union Charter of Fundamental Rights stipulates: 'Human dignity is inviolable. It must be respected and protected.'[2]

41.05 The duty to protect life by law has come to be widely appreciated as also demanding of effective investigation whenever a suspicious death occurs and whoever is suspected in its involvement. At the least under the ICCPR and regional human rights systems, a person does not need to die for a violation of the right to life to occur. And we know today that it is not only States who violate the jus cogens prohibition on arbitrary deprivation of life: international organisations, corporations, armed groups, and even non-governmental organisations and individuals are also duty-bound to respect the rule.

41.06 The reinterpretation and reinvigoration of the right to life is a process that, as this work has sought to illustrate, is – and will always be – a work in progress. It is always dangerous to predict the future, but a narrow focus on prolonging the lives of human beings may not be sustainable. The dying may come to be entitled to choose the time of their passing (if nature does not intervene beforehand). The dead may also have recognised rights one day, at the least to their remains being disposed of in a dignified manner. This should not be left to their family or relatives, should any survive them.

41.07 And why limit the right to life to *homo sapiens*? Already there are efforts to see international legal recognition of the right to life of certain animals. Less than two hundred years ago, millions of human beings were held as slaves: chattels in the hands of their 'masters'. One day soon, we may see States admit by treaty that animals – also sentient beings, capable of empathy and of course physical suffering – have a right to be free of human exploitation and to recognition that their life is also of inherent value and obligating protection.

41.08 More broadly, we may come to articulate climate change, and the damage that human enterprise and economic development have inflicted on the planet we inhabit. The right to life of the Earth may sound like a fatuous bumper sticker, but its content could, in decades to come, become hard law. We cannot continue to abuse our common environment as we do as a species without, ultimately, killing ever greater numbers of people. For, 'in the final analysis', as President Kennedy famously recalled in June 1963, 'our most basic common link is that we all inhabit this small planet. We all breathe the same air.'[3] In June 2021, proposals were made for a new international crime of 'ecocide'.

---

[2] Art. 1, European Union Charter of Fundamental Rights, incorporated into EU law by Article 6(1) of the Consolidated version of the Treaty on European Union.

[3] Speech of John F. Kennedy at the American University, Washington, DC, 10 June 1963, text available at http://bit.ly/3m13fWF.

The draft text defined ecocide as 'unlawful or wanton acts committed with knowledge that there is a substantial likelihood of severe and widespread or long-term damage to the environment being caused by those acts'.[4]

41.09 The right to life inheres in us all. Its widespread and sometimes systematic violation does not undermine its existence, much less the importance of its perpetuation. The right is a candle of hope, caught often in the force of a hurricane. And, as the great Brazilian author Paulo Coelho wrote at the beginning of the current millennium in *The Devil and Miss Prym*: 'The challenge will not wait. Life does not look back.'[5]

41.10 At the beginning of Coelho's novel, a stranger arrives at a remote village, seeking a reply to the question that is tormenting him: are human beings, in essence, good or evil? The existence of the right to life, understood broadly, is an affirmation that perhaps the choice is not inevitably a binary one.

---

[4] H. Siddique, 'Legal experts worldwide draw up "historic" definition of ecocide', *The Guardian*, 22 June 2021, at https://bit.ly/3wDMWUu.
[5] P. Coelho, *The Devil and Miss Prym*, Harper, New York, 2002.

Index

21-foot rule, 157
9/11 attacks, 185
Abdeslam, Salah, 160
abortion, 39, 254, 459
   criminalisation of, 254, 465
   definition, 256
   right to, 256, 470
   right to regulate, 40
   SDGs, 266
   unsafe, 258
   viable point of foetus in pregnancy, 267
Abortion Act (1967), 267
abuse of a dominant position, 652
accidental death, 59
accidents, 26, 375
   industrial, 44, 45
accountability, 403
accountability challenges, 412
Aceh, 388
active hostilities, 80
acts attributable to an international organisation, 636
acute respiratory failure, 395
Adams, John, 3
Additional Protocol I (1977), 130, 222, 337, 401, 409, 447, 618, 620, 662
   Basic rule (on conduct of hostilities), 338
Additional Protocol II (1977), 64, 107, 202, 222, 238, 409, 421, 447, 652
adequate standard of living, right of child to, 295
Adoo-Kissi-Debrah, Ella, 395
adult
   definition, 454
adultery, 216, 473
adults with disabilities, 270
Afghanistan, 207, 349, 489, 516, 578, 592
African Americans, 151, 504
African Charter on Human and Peoples' Rights (1981), 15, 21, 30, 49, 76, 92, 198, 225, 245, 265, 302, 310, 435, 615
   scope of application, 76

African Charter on the Rights and Welfare of the Child (1990), 266, 310, 463, 468
African Commission on Human and Peoples' Rights, 28, 49
   Peoples' Rights, 15, 17, 19, 20, 25, 28, 38, 51, 54, 57, 76, 92, 143, 152, 198, 205, 217, 245, 248, 265, 302, 323, 370, 375, 390, 402, 535, 549, 573, 712
   death penalty, 226
   Special Rapporteur on Extrajudicial, Summary or Arbitrary Executions in Africa, 729
   Special Rapporteur on Human Rights Defenders, 583
   Working Group on Death Penalty and Extra-Judicial, Summary or Arbitrary Killings in Africa, 729
African Committee of Experts on the Rights and Welfare of the Child, 469
African Court on Human and Peoples' Rights, 323, 727
African human rights system and the right to life, 726
African Union, 129, 463, 529, 633
   Regional Action Plan on Albinism in Africa covering 2017–21, 537
age of majority, 454
agents provocateurs, 324
aggression, 18, 68, 122, 130, 183
   as violation of the right to life, 122
   determination by UN Security Council, 131
aggression, prohibition of, 130
   as jus cogens norm, 125
Ago, Roberto, 613
agrotoxins, 95
Ahmadou Sadio Diallo case, 615, 707
AIDS, 50, 51, 374, 478, 544
air pollution, 394, 478, 492. *See also* pollution
airspace, 66
Alabama, 429
al-Anfal campaign, 494
Albania, 440
albinism, persons with, 536
alcohol, 479

alcohol addiction
    link with suicide, 270
Algeria, 358, 363, 429, 698
al-Ghomgham, Israa, 579
algorithms, 410
alien, 54, 55
Alien Tort Statute (1789), 655, 657, 680
Allain, Jean, 419
Allied Democratic Forces (ADF), 645
al-Qaeda, 180
Al-Saadoon case, 224, 432, 605, 717
Alston, Philip, 381
Alzheimer's disease, 376, 561
American Academy of Family Physicians (AAFP), 480
American Convention on Human Rights (1969), 21, 54, 57, 61, 195, 224, 243, 264, 281, 297, 310, 560
    scope of application, 74
American Declaration of the Rights and Duties of Man (1948), 11, 14, 81
American Psychiatric Association (APA), 376, 529
ammunition, 37, 120. *See also* munition
Amnesty, 218
Amnesty International, 207, 213, 256, 350, 473, 519, 548, 578, 592, 729
Andorra, 260, 263
    Penal Code, 260
Angola, 131
animals, rights of, 5, 740
annexation (of territory), 126
anthrax, 342
anti-aircraft gun, execution by, 232
antibiotics, 343
anticipatory self-defence, 128
Anti-Personnel Mine Ban Convention (1997), 240, 346
anti-personnel mines, 35, 63, 115, 240, 336, 346, 596
apartheid, 68, 496
application of international human rights law to armed groups, 665
apology, 382
apostasy, 216
Arab Charter on Human Rights (2004), 15, 22, 30, 199, 223, 228, 247, 302, 310, 470
    scope of application, 77
Arab Convention on Regulating Status of Refugees in the Arab Countries (1994), 603
Arab Convention on the Suppression of Terrorism (1998), 199
Arab Group, 545
Arab Human Rights Committee, 15
arbitrary
    definition of, 24, 25
    negotiation of term, 24
arbitrary deprivation of life
    definition of, 26
Arctic, 399

Argentina, 97, 132, 267, 311, 456, 533, 534
Argentine Forensic Anthropology Team, 438
armed attack, 131
armed conflict, 28, 32, 34, 35, 36, 39, 63, 82, 87, 103, 104, 122, 199, 221, 237, 270, 328, 337, 360, 411, 472, 496, 510, 549, 566, 594, 596, 673
    definition, 107
    in Chechnya, 200
    targeting of women, 448
armed conflict in Turkey, 511
armed conflict, international
    definition of, 107
armed conflict, non-international
    definition of, 111
armed forces, 617
armed groups
    treaty obligations, 598
armed groups and customary law, 663
armed robbery, 216
Armenia, 138
arms control, 334
    definition, 335
    origin of term, 335
Arms Trade Treaty (2013), 56, 334, 624, 625
    and right to life, 352
arrest, 411
Arthur, Thomas, 230
artificial intelligence, 400
Aryan blood, 506
ASEAN, 445, 530
ASEAN Convention on Counter Terrorism (2007), 199
ASEAN Declaration on Human Rights (2012), 15, 310, 546
ASEAN Declaration on the Elimination of Violence against Women (2004), 445, 732
Asian Centre for Human Rights, 474
asphyxiation, 229, 250
assault rifles, 192
assembly
    definition, 309
assembly, dispersal of, 312
Association Loi 1901, 673
asthma, 47, 395
asylum, claim for, 601
asylum, right of, 602
Atkins v. Virginia, 547
attention deficit hyperactivity disorder (ADHD), 376
Auschwitz, 423
Australia, 271, 311
    High Court, 418
Austria, 4, 441
automatic weapons, 166
autonomous use of force, 36, 400

autonomous weapon
    definition, 403
autonomous weapon systems, 36, 334
    definition, 404
autonomy
    definition, 404
autonomy, right to, 559
autopsy, 120, 192, 250, 319, 438
autopsy, duty to perform, 59
average life expectancy, 555
Avon and Somerset Police, 179
Axworthy, Lloyd, 347
Azerbaijan, 90, 138, 212
Azevedo, Philadelpho, 613

Bachelet, Michelle, 473, 506
Badme, 127
Bahrain, 181, 207
Bailey, David, 652
Bajpai, Asha, 491
ballistics, 89, 319
Baltimore City Police Department, 155
Bangkok, 48, 395
Bangladesh, 207
Banković case, 77, 78, 82
Barcelona Traction case, 311, 617, 635, 661, 706
Barrat, Claudie, 676
Basic Principles on the Use of Force and Firearms by
    Law Enforcement Officials (1990), 33, 115, 133,
    188, 196, 198, 238
    and assemblies, 314
baton, 172
baton strikes, 173
Baxter, Robert, 287
Beazley, Napoleon, 467
Behrami and Behrami case, 632, 637
Belarus, 11, 45, 63, 207, 713
Belgian Act Concerning Euthanasia, 272
Belgian Euthanasia Act (2002), 284
Belgium, 242, 271, 280, 494, 558
Belgrade, 77
Belize, 145
    Court of Appeal, 211
*Bellagio-Harvard Guidelines on the Legal Parameters
    of Slavery*, 419
Benghazi, 323
Bensouda, Fatou, 19
Benzer case, 116, 120, 156, 202, 238, 511
Beslan school siege (2004), 179, 186, 187, 191, 193
beyond a reasonable doubt standard, 92, 216
Bhopal, 384
Bhutan, 12, 145, 267
Biden, Joe, 381
Bihać, 592
Bill of Rights (1689), 3

biological agents, 125, 342
biological weapons, 35, 336, 340
    examples of agents, 342
Biological Weapons Convention (1971), 35, 342
biological weapons, proliferation of, 343
biological weapons, use of
    as war crime, 340
Birmingham (Alabama), 151
Black Lives Matter movement, 52, 504
blastocyst, 456
blinding laser weapons, 339, 340, 341
    as war crime, 340
blockade, 131
BLU-97 submunitions, 350
blunt force trauma, 325
Bolsonaro, Jair, 380
bombardment, 126, 131
bomber, 34
bombing, 81
Bosnia and Herzegovina, 339, 354, 358, 422, 493, 592,
    638, 642
Bosniaks, 493
Botswana, 145, 207, 434, 455
    Children's Act, 455
botulinum toxin, 342
Boyd, David, 47, 391
Brazil, 167, 212, 225, 244, 380, 404, 415, 439, 450, 451,
    484, 540, 571, 582
breach of the peace, 132
Britain, 415
British Colombia
    Supreme Court, 290
Brookings–Bern Project on Internal Displacement,
    46
Brunei Darussalam, 12, 229, 311, 516, 519
Bucharest, 522
Buchenwald, 423
Buck v. Bell, 274
Buck, Carrie, 275
Bulgaria, 145, 300, 509
bullets, metal-jacketed, 97
burden of proof, 33, 38, 90, 148, 236, 241
burden of responsibility, 38
burden of evidence, 241
Burge, Jon, 504
burial, 91
burial, right of, 59
Burke, Edmund, 4
Burkina Faso, 51, 378, 479
Burst mode (of firing), 166
Burundi, 693
burying alive, 31

caesium-137, 45
Cahin, Gérard, 620, 664

Cairo Declaration on Human Rights in Islam
  (1990), 418
Callamard, Agnès, 574, 578
Cambodia, 349
Cameroon, 51
camps for IDPs, 594
Canada, 55, 67, 69, 97, 123, 208, 271, 401, 695
  Supreme Court, 288, 655
Canadian Charter of Rights and Freedoms (1982), 288
cancer, 50, 394
cancers, 376
capital trial. *See also* death penalty
carbon monoxide, 276
cardiac arrest, 175
Caribbean Court of Justice, 211
cartel, 652
Carter, Jimmy, 1
Caruana Galizia, Daphne, 570
Casa de Reposo Guararapes, 540
cause of death, determination of, 438
CBU-105 cluster munition, 406
CCW Amended Protocol II (1996), 347
CCW Protocol II (1980), 346
Center for Reproductive Rights, 259, 267
Centers for Disease Control (CDC), 52, 376
Central African Convention for the Control of Small
  Arms and Light Weapons (2010), 355
Central African Republic, 489, 595, 696
Chad, 207, 342
Charter of the Organization of American States
  (OAS), 81
Chattel slavery, 415
chattel, rights of ownership, 419
Chauvin, Derek, 505
Chechnya, 200, 201, 368, 523, 569
checkpoints, 489
chemical irritant
  risk of death, 178
chemical weapons, 35, 67, 336, 339, 340
  definition, 344
Chemical Weapons Convention (1992), 35, 66, 239,
  343, 648
  universalisation, 344
chemical weapons, use of
  as war crime, 340
chemotherapy, 54
Chernobyl, 352
Chernobyl nuclear power plant, 45, 385
Chicago, 504
Chicago Police Department (CPD), 151, 505
child
  definition, 257
  definition, legal, 454, 456
  right to life of, 454
child detention in adult prison, 242

child labour, 482
child offenders, 213
child recruitment, 488
child soldiers, 423
child, right to special protection, 466, 469
child, survival and development of, 458
children associated with gangs, 483
children in the workplace, 490
children living in the streets, 480, 481
  prevalence of, 482
children with disabilities, 270, 475, 532
children, detention of, 237
children, right to life of, 454
Chile, 97, 212, 225, 267, 401, 516
  Supreme Court, 521
China, 1, 12, 207, 213, 244, 347, 351, 407, 473, 475, 489,
  493, 532, 586, 605
China Constitution, 459
Chlorine (as chemical weapon), 345
cholera, 381, 382
circular error probable, 411
cisnormativity, 515
Citizens' Association for the Decriminalization of
  Therapeutic, Ethical and Eugenic Abortion (El
  Salvador), 265
Ciudad Juárez, 436, 437
civilian, 36, 118
civilian immunity from attack, 338
civilian internees, 64
civilian objects, 56
civilians, 56, 112, 116, 221, 237
civilians with disabilities, 550
civilians, intentional starvation of, 303
Clapham, Andrew, 56, 694
clean air, right to, 392
clemency, 216
  right to seek, 218
climate change, 48, 390, 740
  impact on human rights, 396
cluster munition, 118
  definition, 349
cluster munitions, 35, 336
cluster swarm (of drones), 407
Code of Conduct for law enforcement officials (1979),
  32, 133, 142, 148, 150, 503
Code of Conduct for the International Red Cross and
  Red Crescent Movement and
  Non-Governmental Organisations (NGOs) in
  Disaster Relief (1994), 673
Coelho, Paulo, 741
collective graves, 64
collective punishment, 694
Colombia, 97, 118, 204, 271, 362, 571, 582
colonial (era), 145
colonial domination, 110

Colorado, 209
combatant, 36, 116
combatant's privilege, 113, 221, 446, 563
combatants, 113, 193, 331, 338
command responsibility, 682
Commission for International Justice and Accountability, 425
Committee against Torture, 53, 497
Committee on Economic, Social and Cultural Rights, 98, 292, 294, 295
Committee on Enforced Disappearances, 362, 364, 622
  Guiding Principles for the Search for Disappeared Persons (2019), 365
Committee on Migrant Workers, 590
Committee on Migrant Workers and the right to life, 701
Committee on the Elimination of Discrimination against Women, 260, 261, 430, 433, 434, 437, 450, 452, 557
Committee on the Elimination of Discrimination against Women and the right to life, 702
Committee on the Elimination of Racial Discrimination, 493, 503, 506, 513
Committee on the Elimination of Racial Discrimination and the right to life, 703
Committee on the Rights of Persons with Disabilities, 296
Committee on the Rights of the Child, 73, 296, 395, 458, 460, 475, 476, 482, 485, 487, 490, 590
Committee on the Rights of the Child and the right to life, 699
Committee to Protect Journalists (CPJ), 572
Common Article 3, 111, 222, 447, 550, 563, 620, 676. *See also* Geneva Conventions (1949)
Commonwealth Caribbean, 520
Communicating with Disaster-Affected Communities (CDAC) Network, 388
Comoros, 12, 342
company
  definition, 648
compensation, 58, 75, 139
complicity, 625
Comprehensive Convention on International Terrorism, 181, 183
Comprehensive Nuclear-Test-Ban Treaty (CTBT), 347
computer algorithm, 411
conception, 465
  moment of, 5
  occurrence in law, 264
conduct of hostilities, 32, 34, 36, 82, 104, 106, 114, 134, 165, 184, 198, 239, 330, 335, 337, 496, 498, 594
Conference on Disarmament, 343
Congo, Víctor Rosario, 537
Congress of Vienna, 415

Connecticut, 274
Constitutions, 20
consulate, 79
containment, 327. *See also* Containment; kettling
continuous combat function, 332
  concept of, 331
Convention against Illicit Traffic in Narcotic Drugs (1988), 641
Convention against Torture (1984), 53, 73, 234, 497
Convention of Saint-Germain-en-Laye (1919), 416
Convention on Certain Conventional Weapons (1980), 346, 401
Convention on Cluster Munitions (2008), 349, 406
Convention on Enforced Disappearance (2006), 28
Convention on the Elimination of All Forms of Discrimination against Women (1979), 260, 430, 557
Convention on the Elimination of All Forms of Racial Discrimination (1965), 310
Convention on the Rights of Persons with Disabilities (2006), 22, 228, 256, 295, 417, 641
  and right of peaceful assembly, 311
  in armed conflict, 551
Convention on the Rights of the Child (1989), 22, 74, 213, 295, 310, 395, 429, 454, 527
  status of, 22
Convention on the Transboundary Effects of Industrial Accidents (1992), 45
Convention to Suppress the Slave Trade and Slavery (1926), 416
conventional weapons, 56
  definition, 336
Cook Islands, 12
Core Humanitarian Standard on Quality and Accountability (CHS), 677
coronary artery disease (CAD), 376
coronavirus, 232, 379
coroner, 395
corporate responsibility (for violations of the right to life), 647
corporation
  definition, 648
  violation of the right to life, 658
corporations, 67
  and treaty law, 651
  as subjects of international law, 647
  duty to respect human rights law, 653
corruption, 32
Costa Rica, 264, 517
Cotonou Declaration on strengthening and expanding the protection of all Human Rights Defenders in Africa (2017), 584
Cotton Field case, 430, 437, 438
Council of Europe, 11, 25, 568, 580, 633, 713

Council of Europe Committee of Ministers Recommendation (2014), 560
Council of Europe Convention on the Prevention of Terrorism (2005), 180
counterpiracy, 642
Counterterrorism, 32
counterterrorism operations, 180
Coupland, Robin, 677
COVID-19, 293, 297, 374, 377, 379, 381, 388, 439, 553, 593, 693. *See also* coronavirus
  deaths, 379
COVID-19 and the rights of persons with disabilities, 553
Crăciun, Chețan, 507
Cranston, Maurice, 5
Crawford, James, 17
cremation, 63
Crimea, 137
Crimea, annexation of, 137
crimes against humanity, 18, 56, 97, 139, 326, 352, 448, 493, 496, 668, 681
criminal law (in England and Wales), 262
cruise missiles, 350
Cryer, Robert, 494
Cuba, 12, 429, 539
  age of majority, 456
Cumaraswamy, Dato Param, 636
custody, 80, 82
  definition, 233
customary law, 10, 15, 30, 49, 78, 103, 108, 110, 116, 128, 133, 156, 184, 208, 222, 240, 329, 445, 446, 499, 526, 601, 611, 621, 653, 669, 672
customary law, breach of, 228
customary rule, 50, 53, 59, 64, 113, 118, 124, 143, 162, 188, 215, 227, 256, 310, 337, 342, 345, 360, 371, 411, 415, 422, 445, 458, 459, 471, 546, 597, 601
Customary rules, list of, 735
cyber operations, 125
cyberattacks, 46
Cyprus, 160, 623
Czechia, 60

Dagestan, 194
Danish Refugee Council, 591
Darwin, Charles, 274
  and eugenics, 274
David, Eric, 630
de Albuquerque, Pinto, 383
de Jonge, Hugo, 278
De Jure Belli ac Pacis. *See also* Grotius
de Menezes, Jean-Charles, 163, 192
dead, rights of, 59
deadly force, 87, 89, 156
death
  definition of, 5

natural, 5
unnatural, 5
death by natural causes, 59. *See also* Natural death
death by stoning, 229
death certificate, need for, 358
death in custody, 37
death penalty, 2, 18, 31, 54, 55, 63, 92, 114, 207
  abolition of, 108
  as inhumane punishment, 224
  child offenders, 208
  imposition after unfair trial (status as jus cogens), 19
  imposition on children, 471
  imposition on older persons, 225
  imposition on persons with disabilities, 219
  imposition on women, 215
  in non-international armed conflict, 114
  in wartime, 108
  mandatory, 209
  mothers nursing a baby, 215
  pregnant women, 208
  progressive abolition of, 215
  re-establishment, 213
  retentionist States, 207
  status under international law, 209
  women, 445
death row, 31, 54
death squads, 481, 619
Death with Dignity Act (Oregon), 285
deaths in custody, 233
Declaration of Human Duties and Responsibilities (1998), 680
Declaration of Independence (1776), 3
Declaration of the Rights of Man (1789), 4
Declaration of the Rights of the Child (1924), 257, 454
Declaration of the Rights of the Child (1959), 257, 454, 456
Declaration on Euthanasia and Physician-Assisted Suicide (2019), 271
Declaration on Human Rights Defenders (1998), 577
Declaration on the Elimination of Violence against Women (1993), 431
Declaration on the Granting of Independence to Colonial Countries and Peoples (1960), 129
Declaration on the Rights of Disabled Persons (1975), 527
Declaration on the Rights of Peasants and Other People Working in Rural Areas (2018), 296
Deepwater Horizon, 385
Degesch, 651
degrading (treatment)
  definition, 242
delict, 612
dementia, 47, 555
Democratic People's Republic of Korea, 352. *See also* North Korea

Democratic Republic of Congo, 51, 76, 213, 423, 449, 473, 500, 595, 615
demonstrations as crimes against humanity, 322
demonstrators, duty to protect the life of, 97
Deng, Francis, 596
Denmark, 155, 168, 415
deportation, 52, 53
deprivation of life
    by private individuals, 24
derogate, 19
derogation, 13, 19, 103, 208, 228
despoilation (of dead bodies), 63
detention
    definition, 233
Detention Centre of Catia case, 244
Deutsche Welle, 572
Devandas, Catalina, 536
development, 23, 49
development of children, 458
development, unsustainable, 48
Devon and Cornwall Police, 176
diabetes, 47, 376
Diagnostic and Statistical Manual of Mental Disorders, 376, 529
diarrhoea, 376
Dignitas, 280
dignity, 2, 9, 23, 47, 85, 98, 209, 215, 243, 277, 282, 286, 295, 358, 374, 390, 398, 425, 460, 469, 496, 555, 559
Dinstein, Yoram, 412
diphtheria, 478
direct participation in hostilities, 10, 112
    during assemblies, 328
directed energy weapons, 341
disarmament
    as category of arms control, 335
    definition, 335
disarmament law, 26, 35, 66, 334
disaster
    definition, 46, 386
    natural, 47
disaster management, 46
disasters, 46
discrimination, prohibition of, 9, 17, 26, 40, 47, 51, 85, 150, 218, 310, 311, 431, 535
discrimination, prohibition of, 47
disease, 26, 27, 50, 374, 461
    and children, 477
    definition, 375
diseases, deadliest, 376
dispersal
    effects of, 324
    justification for, 324
    using firearms, 316
dispersal (of assembly), 96
    alternatives to, 314
    as main tactic, 324
    using firearms, 161
    using less-lethal weapons, 316
distinction, principle of, 36
    in the conduct of hostilities, 117
distinction, rule of, 408
Djibouti, 311, 342
DNA evidence, 220, 547
DNA testing, 193
Docherty, Bonnie, 413
dogs (police), 142
domestic law, 25
domestic terrorism, 181
domestic violence
    treatment of, 441
Domínguez, Blanco, 96, 312
Dominican Republic, 10, 94
Dos Santos Cruz, Carlos Alberto, 645
Draft Articles on State Responsibility (2001), 139
Draft Articles on the Protection of Persons in the Event of Disasters (2016), 387
drive-stun mode (TASER), 174
drone, 128
drones, 36, 82, 163
drug dealing, 19
drug trafficking, 155
drug use, 479
due diligence, 236
Dutch Law on the Termination of Life on Request and Assisted Suicide (2002), 278
Dutch peacekeepers at Srebrenica, 638
Duterte, Rodrigo, 578
duty of precaution, 193
duty of protection
    due diligence, 37
duty to assist, 191
duty to cease (unlawful act), 616
duty to ensure, 55
duty to ensure survival (of children), 22
duty to fulfil, 23
duty to investigate, 21, 23, 56, 82, 90, 118, 192
    deaths in custody, 233
    in armed conflict, 251
    racial animus, 496
duty to investigate (as autonomous rule), 57
duty to investigate (deaths in custody), 247
duty to prevent, 361
duty to prevent extreme poverty, 294
duty to prevent terrorism, 186
duty to protect, 21, 23, 39, 93, 141, 178, 233, 236
    due diligence, 37
duty to protect by law, 57
duty to protect children, 86
duty to protect life
    due diligence, 26

duty to protect the natural environment, 390
duty to rescue at sea, 80
duty to resolve disputes peacefully, 127
duty to respect, 21, 23, 37, 48, 55, 67
dying in childbirth
   prevalence of, 452

Earth, right to life of, 740
earthquake, 46
East Timor, 619
Eastern Caribbean Court of Appeal, 210, 211
Ebola, 645
Ebola virus, 388
Ebrahimi, Bijan, 179
eclampsia, 453
Economic Community of West African States (ECOWAS), 633
   Court of Justice, 435
economic, social, and cultural rights, 23, 26, 292
Ecuador, 257, 277, 281, 537
effective control, 77, 119
Egypt, 183, 207, 342, 343, 434, 494
Einsatzgruppen, 680
El Boathi, Brahim, 362–64
El Salvador, 182, 212, 256, 265, 467, 484, 519
   Supreme Court, 264
El Salvador Seguro Plan, 484
elder persons. *See also* older person
   and euthanasia, 278
   and the right to life, 555
electric-shock weapon. *See also* TASER
electric-shock weapons, 174
Eleven Guiding Principles (2019), 403
embargoes, 125
embassies, 66, 79
embryo, 456, 465
enforced disappearance, 56, 68, 70, 86, 94, 97, 98, 357, 626
   as crime against humanity, 360
   as violation of the right to life, 29
   definition, 357
   definition of, 28
   in armed conflict, 371
   prohibition in armed conflict, 360
   status of prohibition, 360
   temporal jurisdiction, 369
enslavement, 655
   as a crime against humanity, 418, 423
   as a war crime, 418
environment, 45, 49
environment, right to healthy, 49
environmental damage, 139
environmental degradation, 48
environmental law, 26
environmental protection, 48

equality (of rights), 85
Equatorial Guinea, 207, 355
erga omnes obligations, 617
Eritrea, 127, 342
Eritrea-Ethiopia Claims Commission, 127
Ero, Ikponwosa, 536
escape from custody, 159, 233
espace juridique, 78
ethical, 334
Ethiopia, 38, 127
   Police University College, 483
EUFOR, 642
eugenics, 274
European Code of Police Ethics (2001), 168
European Commission, 652
European Commission Directorate-General for Competition, 652
European Commission on Human Rights, 88, 160, 353, 512
European Community (EC) Merger Regulation, 653
European Convention on Human Rights (1950), 11, 19, 22, 25, 30, 54, 88, 103, 138, 153, 187, 189, 200, 223, 240, 262, 279, 299, 310, 500
   Status of, 11
European Court of Human Rights, 25, 29, 33, 54, 57, 61, 81, 87, 94, 144, 147, 148, 149, 150, 156, 177, 178, 186, 189, 200, 223, 236, 241, 262, 279, 297, 308, 315, 327, 355, 383, 420, 439, 463, 522, 542, 561, 562, 568
   Grand Chamber, 14, 25, 27, 54, 69, 77, 83, 87, 119, 135, 148, 166, 192, 238, 252, 301, 315, 327, 369, 393, 442, 544, 622
European Court of Human Rights and the right to life, 713
European Disability Forum, 553
European human rights system and the right to life, 713
European Instrument for Democracy and Human Rights (EIDHR), 583
European Union, 380
   duty to become a party to the European Convention on Human Rights, 641
   High Representative for Foreign Affairs and Security Policy, 450
   party to CRPD, 526
European Union (EU), 212, 633
   Charter of Fundamental Rights, 718
Euroregional Center for Public Initiatives (ECPI), 544
euthanasia, 269, 558
   and children, 278
   and older persons, 555
   as murder, 272
   definition, 272
   genuine consent, 269
euthanasia, active
   definition, 272
euthanasia, involuntary, 272

euthanasia, non-voluntary, 272
euthanasia, passive, 272, 273
euthanasia, voluntary, 272
evolutionary theory, 274
excessive use of force, 58, 96
execution
    method of, 31, 229
    public, 31
executions, summary or extrajudicial, 10
exemption for law enforcement
    chemical weapons, 344
exhumation, 96
expanding ammunition, 37, 165
expanding bullets, 339, 340
    as war crime, 340
exploding bullets, 339, 340
extermination, 97
extermination camps, 276
extradition, 52, 53, 54
extrajudicial execution, 205, 626
extrajudicial killings, 19
extraterritorial, 50
extraterritorial application of human rights law, 75
extreme poverty
    definition, 293

Fact-Finding Mission on the Gaza conflict (2009), 670
Factory at Chorzów case, 616
fair trial, 211
fair trial rights, 216
fair trial, right to, 58, 86, 92, 212
    nature of, 92
Falkland Islands/Malvinas
    invasion of, 132
fallopian tubes, cutting of, 275
family planning, 459
famine, 38, 294, 626
FARC (armed group), 118, 203
fatal foetal abnormality, 256
Fauci, Anthony, 381
feasible precautions, 409
Federal Control and Evaluation Commission on
    Euthanasia (FCECE) (Belgium), 285
Federation Internationale de Football Association
    (FIFA), 592
feeblemindedness, 274
female genital mutilation, 702
female infanticide, 432, 475
fentanyl, 191, 480
Ferencz, Benjamin, 681
Ferguson Police Department, 151
Fifth World Water Forum, 318
Finland, 183
Finogenov case, 147, 191, 204, 205, 639
fire extinguisher, 316

firearm, use of, 509
    against escapee, 238
    against escaping prisoner of war, 238
    definition of, 155
    international legal rule, 34
firearms, 27, 34, 37, 115, 142, 154, 188, 313
    and dispersal of assembly, 312
    definition of, 154
Firearms Protocol (2001), 154
firing squad, 229, 230
First World War, 4, 345, 510
Fitzmaurice, Malgosia, 49
flagged vessels, 78, 79
flame-throwers, 193
floods, 387, 396
Floyd, George, 505, 572
foetus, 175, 256, 435, 456, 465
    intentional killing of, 270
    protection of, 256
    with physical or intellectual disabilities, 256
food, duty to provide, 113
food, right to, 86
football matches, 327
forced displacement, prohibition of, 597
Forces armées de la République démocratique du
    Congo (FARDC), 630
Forces Patriotiques pour la Libération du Congo, 423
forensic doctor, 90
France, 4, 122, 184, 213, 254, 311, 401, 415, 460, 489, 508,
    591, 695
Franklin, Benjamin, 3
French Revolution, 4
Fukushima, 352
full-metal-jacket bullets, 165
fully automatic (weapon), 166, 167
fundamental human rights, 9, 14, 23, 26
fundamental right, 88, 308
fundamental right to family life, 61
funeral, 90
Future of Life Institute, 402

G4S, 246
G8 Summit (2001), 315
Galić case, 409
Galton, Francis, 274
gas chambers, 31
Gates Foundation, 50
Gaza, 161
Gaza conflict (2014), 339
Gaza Strip, 74
gender expression, 515
gender identity, 515
gender-based murders, 437
gender-based violence, 431, 439
    and abortion, 260

and discrimination, 433
and poverty, 291
prohibition of, 433
Gene drive, 379
General Act of Brussels (1890), 416
general international law, 92
general principle of international law, 53, 547, 681
general principle of law, 20, 143, 311, 616
Geneva Academy of International Humanitarian Law and Human Rights, 551
Geneva Convention III (1949), 114, 221, 238, 305, 576, 661
Geneva Convention IV (1949), 113, 114, 222, 306, 447, 498, 605
Geneva Conventions (1949), 10, 63, 65, 107, 110, 119, 528
genocide, 18, 56, 123, 130, 139, 352, 354, 448, 449, 494, 496, 681
Genocide case (2007), 625
Genocide Convention (1948), 10, 499
Georgia, 54
Georgia Fact-Finding Mission, 126, 127
Georgian police, 523
Geriatrics and Gerontology International, 556
German Empire, 556
Germany, 4, 60, 123, 168, 401
Gerontological Society of America, 559
Ghana, 51, 283, 378, 401
Giacca, Gilles, 39
Gibraltar, 190
Girl
definition, legal, 429
Giuliani, Carlo, 316
GlaxoSmithKline, 479
Global Compact for Migration, 586
Global Compact on Migration (2018), 590
Global Study on Homicide, 483
Golan heights, 74
Goldblat, Jozef, 335
Gongadze, Georgiy, 569
Grant, Madison, 276
grave threat to life, 158
grave threat to life criterion, 34
Greece, 88, 168, 212
Greenpeace, 384
Grenada, 719
Grenada, invasion of, 75
grenade launcher, 154, 193
GREVIO, 444
Grotius, 59
Guantánamo Bay facility, 72, 73
guarantees of non-repetition, 616
Guatemala, 456, 582
Guerdner, Joseph, 508

Guiding Principles on Internal Displacement (1998), 594
Guinea, 325, 615
Gulf Cooperation Council (GCC), 578
Gulf of Mexico, 385
gunshot wounds, self-inflicted, 270
Guterres, António, 382
Guzman, Paola, 281
Gypsies, 276

Hague Convention III on the Opening of Hostilities (1907), 108
Hague Declaration IV,2 (1899). *See also* chemical weapons
Haiti, 342, 381, 382, 494
Halabja, 343, 494
Hamas, 331
Hamburg, 327
Hammurabi
Code of, 1
King, 1
handicapped, 528
hanging, 230
Hariri, Rafik, 184
Harpy, 406
hate crime, 52
Hayat, Khizar, 549
health and safety laws, 44
health, right to, 390
heart disease, 47, 50
Heller, Kevin Jon, 20
hepatitis, 51
Herrera, Esmeralda, 438
Herrera, Josh, 362
Hess, Rudolf, 276
Heston, Robert, 175
Heyns, Christof, 167
hierarchy of rights, 13
Hillsborough Stadium disaster, 272
Hiroshima, 386
Hiroshima bombing, 45
Hitler, Adolf, 277
HIV, 478
hollow-point bullets, 165
Holocaust, 9, 493, 650
Holy See, 11, 12, 257, 456, 713
Homayounnejad, Maziar, 405, 410
homicide, 32, 37, 52, 59, 114, 216
homosexuality, 216, 376
homosexuality and the death penalty, 519
homosexuals. *See* LGBTI persons
Honduras, 502, 571, 582
honest (but mistaken) belief, 190
honest (but mistaken) belief test, 149, 164
honour killing, 433, 441

hors de combat, 112, 113, 411, 677
hostage taker, 34, 163, 191
Hostage-Taking Convention (1979), 182
hostage-taking, crime of
  definition, 182
hostilities, 109
Human Development Report (2015), 292
Human Dignity Trust, 516
Human Rights Act (1998, UK), 687
Human Rights Committee, 12, 17, 18, 23, 25, 26, 28, 29, 30, 31, 40, 46, 48, 50, 55, 56, 57, 63, 69, 70, 71, 73, 79, 80, 81, 85, 86, 93, 95, 96, 97, 104, 105, 116, 117, 118, 122, 130, 136, 138, 144, 146, 172, 181, 186, 188, 206, 211, 213, 215, 217, 219, 220, 229, 236, 238, 247, 250, 255, 256, 258, 277, 291, 309, 313, 314, 321, 326, 327, 333, 334, 336, 337, 351, 357, 358, 361, 362, 374, 392, 393, 396, 425, 431, 432, 457, 460, 462, 474, 476, 478, 504, 518, 530, 547, 548, 559, 567, 579, 589, 596, 601, 602, 603, 604, 626, 691, 739
  General Comment No. 6 on the right to life, 29, 123
  General Comment No. 14 on the right to life, 337
  General Comment No. 36 on the right to life, 13, 122, 258
  General Comment No. 37 on the right of peaceful assembly, 96
Human Rights Committee and the right to life, 695
Human Rights Council, 171, 315, 391, 481, 516, 517, 552, 567, 574, 691
Human Rights Council and the right to life, 691
Human rights defender
  definition, 577
Human Rights Watch, 201, 261, 350, 371, 401, 406, 408, 413
humane treatment, 237
Humanitarian Accountability Partnership (HAP), 677
humanitarian intervention, 128
humanity, 99
hunger, right to freedom from, 99, 295
hurricanes, 387

I.G. Farben trial, 650
ICCPR. See 1966 International Covenant on Civil and Political Rights (1966)
  jurisdiction of, 70
ICESCR. See International Covenant on Economic, Social and Cultural Rights (1966)
ICRC (International Committee of the Red Cross), 665
  Interpretive Guidance on the notion of direct participation in hostilities, 329
  Legal status of, 675
  Report on the Use of Force (2014), 330
  Study of customary IHL, 118

IDPs
  number of, 595
  vulnerabilities of, 595
ill-treatment, 3, 40, 52, 90, 195, 241, 246, 302. See also Torture
imminent, 128
imminent threat, 34, 157, 312
  definition of, 34, 188
immunity, 382. See also Impunity; Amnesty
impartial humanitarian organisation, 674
imperative military necessity (for displacement), 598
improvised explosive devices (IEDs), 489
incest, 256, 435
Independent International Commission of Inquiry on Syria, 315, 425, 598, 655, 666, 680
Independent International Fact-Finding Mission on Myanmar, 449
Independent International Fact-Finding Mission on the Conflict in Georgia. See Georgia Fact-Finding Commission
Independent Police Complaints Commission, 179
Independent Police Investigative Directorate (South Africa), 543
India, 2, 48, 51, 207, 234, 347, 384, 458, 475, 506, 565, 586
  Supreme Court, 210, 384
Indian Ocean, 387
Indian Ocean Tsunami Warning System, 387
indiscriminate
  weapon, 36, 194, 201, 340
indiscriminate shooting, 98, 313
individual civil responsibility for violations of international law, 685
Individual communications, 698
individual responsibility for violations of the right to life, 680
indivisibility (of rights), 292
indivisibility of human rights, 13
Indonesia, 145, 207, 387
infant mortality, 458, 476
infanticide, 474
  definition, 256
Ingushetia, 187
inherent
  right to life, 17, 21
inherently indiscriminate (weapons), 337, 338
inhuman (treatment)
  definition, 242
inhumane, 31, 55, 61, 63, 256. See also Ill-treatment
inhumane (form of punishment), 229
inhumane treatment, 67, 98, 106, 113, 150
inhumane treatment, prohibition on
  use of weapons, 340
inquest, 395
insecticides, 51, 392

Institut de Formation en Droits de l'Homme du Barreau de Paris, 89
insurrection, 111, 190, 201
insurrectional movements, 619
intentional lethal use of firearms, 34
intentional lethal use of force, 89, 162, 189, 240
  in armed conflict, 115
Inter-Agency Steering Committee (IASC)
  Guidelines on persons with disabilities in humanitarian disasters, 552
  Operational Guidelines on the Protection of Persons in Situations of Natural Disasters, 46
Inter-American Commission on Human Rights, 74, 75, 81, 83, 170, 172, 189, 196, 197, 224, 233, 244, 265, 281, 297, 315, 320, 365, 372, 439, 472, 488, 502, 504, 520, 537, 538, 546, 570, 575, 719
  Office of the Rapporteur on the Situation of Human Rights Defenders, 580
  Special Rapporteur for Freedom of Expression, 320
  Unit for Human Rights Defenders, 580
Inter-American Convention Against Terrorism (2002), 196
Inter-American Convention on Forced Disappearance of Persons (1994), 362, 366
Inter-American Convention on the Elimination of Discrimination against Persons with Disabilities (1999), 535
Inter-American Convention on the Prevention, Punishment, and Eradication of Violence against Women (1994), 430
Inter-American Convention to Prevent, Punish and Eradicate Violence Against Women (1994), 502
Inter-American Court of Human Rights, 14, 18, 27, 29, 57, 61, 75, 89, 91, 118, 133, 141, 146, 153, 156, 159, 189, 196, 197, 203, 244, 251, 292, 297, 361, 365, 366, 436, 465, 467, 502, 521, 540, 560, 571, 618, 668, 712
  Advisory Opinion on the Juridical Condition and Human Rights of the Child, 466
Inter-American Court of Human Rights and the right to life, 721
Inter-American system of human rights and the right to life, 718
Intergovernmental Panel on Climate Change, 399
Internal Displacement Monitoring Centre (IDMC), 595
Internally displaced persons, 594
Internally displaced persons and the right to life, 594
International Law Commission, 667
International Atomic Energy Agency (IAEA), 632
International Campaign to Ban Landmines (ICBL), 348
International Commission on Inquiry on Guinea, 326
International Conference of the Red Cross (1981), 59, 63, 109, 221, 233, 239, 305, 329, 346, 371, 404, 421, 446, 472, 499, 556, 564, 575, 592, 597, 653, 661, 675

International Conference on Population and Development, 266
International Convention on the Suppression and Punishment of Apartheid (1973), 496
International Court of Justice, 10, 12, 14, 24, 39, 67, 68, 70, 72, 74, 76, 81, 104, 106, 115, 116, 124, 129, 134, 136, 206, 311, 351, 354, 450, 495, 612, 613, 615, 617, 625, 635, 661, 664, 691
  Advisory Opinion on the legality of nuclear weapons, 12, 14
  Fisheries judgment, 17
  Nicaragua judgment, 10, 16, 39
  North Sea Continental Shelf judgment, 16
  Statute of, 11, 15
International Court of Justice and the right to life, 706
International Covenant on Civil and Political Rights (1966), 11, 21, 67, 103, 104, 122, 144, 181, 207, 234, 255, 291, 309, 334, 357, 374, 390, 400, 415, 429, 457, 496, 615
  entry into force, 11
  geographical scope of application, 67
  scope of application, 70
  States not party, 12
  status of, 11
International Covenant on Economic, Social and Cultural Rights (1966), 99, 292
international crime, 56, 303, 613
international crimes, 19, 68, 312, 620, 667
International Criminal Court, 10, 19, 39, 68, 69, 97, 110, 165, 216, 223, 304, 322, 340, 360, 422, 423, 490, 499, 500, 564, 667, 683, 686, 691
  Prosecutor of, 19
International Criminal Court and the right to life, 707
international criminal law, 488, 597, 647, 672, 680
International Criminal Tribunal for the former Yugoslavia (ICTY), 110, 305, 409, 422, 686
International Day for the Elimination of Sexual Violence in Conflict, 450
International Day of Victims of Enforced Disappearance, 366
International Disability Alliance, 543
international environmental law, 48, 134, 391, 394
International Fact-Finding Commission, 711
International Federation of Red Cross and Red Crescent Societies (IFRC), 386
International Human Rights Clinic (IHRC) at Harvard Law School, 408
International Humanitarian Fact-finding Commission (IHFFC), 711
international humanitarian law, 10, 26, 28, 36, 65, 81, 87, 104, 105, 106, 107, 109, 116, 134, 138, 200, 201, 203, 204, 205, 208, 237, 328, 331, 336, 371, 409, 410, 413, 446, 469, 471, 488, 495, 498, 510, 511, 556, 576, 594, 596, 605, 620, 631, 661, 666
  and poverty, 303

international humanitarian law (cont.)
  and starvation, 303
  death penalty, 220
  Geneva Law, 106, 112
  Hague Law, 106
  relationship with right to life, 106
  serious violation of, 563
international humanitarian law, violation of
  as violation of the right to life, 112
International Labour Organization (ILO), 490,
  491, 527
international law, 52
  disputes of, 11
  paternalistic, 447
  primary sources of, 11, 15, 20
International Law Commission, 17, 24, 46, 124, 130,
  235, 311, 338, 354, 360, 386, 432, 472, 496, 611,
  629, 660
international law, progressive development of, 458,
  611, 625
international legal rule
  subsidiary means for determination, 17
International Military Tribunal, 423. *See also*
  Nuremberg Military Tribunals
International Military Tribunal for the Far East,
  423
international organisation
  definition, legal, 632
international organisation, consequences of commission of internationally wrongful act, 636
international organisations
  adherence to treaties, 640
  as subjects of international law, 629
  responsibility of, 629
International Organization for Migration (IOM), 586
international peace and security, 123
International Red Cross and Red Crescent
  Movement, 564
International Service for Human Rights, 585
International Strategy Conference: Towards a Global
  Ban on Anti-Personnel Mines, 347
international terrorism
  definition of, 181, 183
internationally wrongful act, 613
  definition, 612, 633
internationally wrongful act, consequences of, 614, 616
intersectionality, 297
iodine-131, 45
Iran, 78, 207, 213, 229, 267, 352, 473, 516, 592, 695
  age of majority, 455
Iran–Iraq War, 494
Iraq, 69, 80, 98, 120, 132, 139, 180, 207, 349, 353, 494,
  510, 516
Ireland, 60, 258, 259, 263, 461, 649
  and euthanasia, 290

Health (Regulation of Termination of Pregnancy)
  Act 2018, 462
  Supreme Court, 264
Ireland Constitution, 259, 264
Irish Republican Army (IRA), 163, 190
iron curtain, 602
Islamic faith, 62
Islamic State, 180, 425, 597, 598
  and slavery, 425
Israel, 71, 72, 104, 161, 168, 311, 342, 343
Israeli Security Forces, 332
Istanbul Convention (2011), 442, 486, 545
  and right to life, 443
Italian *carabiniere*, 315
Italy, 127, 353

Jamaica, 224
Japan, 207, 429, 548
Jasinskis case, 542, 544
Jay Lifton, Robert, 276
Jefferson, Thomas, 3
Jenner Institute, 378, 479
Jews, 276, 493
Jha, Abhas, 387
Jimenez-Damary, Cecilia, 552
Johnson, Lyndon Baines, 684
Jordan, 207
Jost, Adolf, 276
journalists
  protection in armed conflict, 565
  right to life of, 565
Julius, Nathaniel, 542
jurisdiction, 65, 437
  definition, 65
  geographical, 66
  material, 68
  personal, 68
  temporal, 69, 83, 612
jurisdiction, criminal, 66
jus ad bellum, 26, 36, 122
jus cogens, 17, 19, 31, 53, 67, 68, 124, 134, 180, 256, 312,
  338, 360, 366, 415, 432, 457, 468, 472, 481, 495, 518,
  567, 617, 654, 669, 672
  definition and effects of, 17
  right to life as, 18
  status of right to life, 19
jus cogens (human rights norms), 621
jus cogens norms, 635
  and armed groups, 666
  responsibility for serious violations of, 623
Jus cogens rules, list of, 737
jus gentium, 2

kafala, 592
Kälin, Walter, 596

Index

Kampala Convention, 529, 594, 598, 674
Karadžić, Radovan, 685
Katanga, Germain, 499
Kazakhstan, 417
Kenya, 50, 283, 378, 479
Keown, John, 289
kettling, 327
Khashoggi, Jamal, 79, 574
Kiai, Maina, 167
killer robots, 401
Ki-moon, Ban, 382
kinetic impact, 178
kinetic impact projectiles, 176
King, Rodney, 684
Kiobel case, 656, 685
Kiribati, 12, 342, 396, 397, 604
Klare, Michael, 406
Knox, John, 391
Korean peninsula, 348
Kosovo, 596
Kunarac case, 422
Kurdish People's Protection Units (YPG/YPJ), 489
Kurdish Workers' Party (PKK), 120, 202, 372
Kurdistan Democratic Party (KDP), 514
Kurds, 343, 510
Kurt case, 440, 441, 442, 463, 464, 486
Kurt, Üzeyir, 367
Kuwait, 139, 207, 473
    Iraqi invasion of, 132
Kuwaiti Armed Forces, 139
Kyrgyzstan, 250

LA riots, 684
Laki Muhumuza, Duncan, 398
landmines, 595. *See also* Anti-personnel mines
Lao People's Democratic Republic, 349
Laos
    submunitions, 349
law enforcement, 133
    agencies, 618
    definition of, 141
law of armed conflict, 105, 134, 165, 413, 447. *See also* International humanitarian law
law of nations, 59. *See also* International law
law of treaties, 208, 341, 612
Law on Police Use of Force Worldwide website, 314
Lawlor, Mary, 577
Lawyers for Human Rights (Moldova), 583
League of Nations, 4, 416, 454
Lebanon, 349
legal person, 648
legal person and NGOs, 674
legality, principle of, 33, 143
legislative jurisdiction, 663
less-lethal weapons, 240

    comparison with lethal weapons, 321
    definition of, 169
    design and testing, 171
    duty to provide, 170
    in assemblies, 313
    in detention centres, 236
Lethal Autonomous Weapon Systems (LAWS), 402
lethal drugs, 31
leukaemia, 54
lex specialis, 115
LGBTI persons, 218, 270
    enforced disappearance, 365
LGBTI persons and right to life, 515
liberty, deprivation of, 28
liberty, right to, 86, 93
Liechtenstein, 456
life
    arbitrary deprivation of, 12, 13, 19, 21, 22, 24, 58, 79, 133, 188, 256, 312
    arbitrary deprivation in conduct of hostilities, 116
life-threatening, 54, 88, 94, 367
live ammunition, 98, 161, 162, 170
Locke, John, 3
loitering munition, 412
Lomé Agreement (1999), 665
López Soto, Linda Loaiza, 420
Lord's Resistance Army (LRA), 469
Los Angeles Police Department (LAPD), 157, 176, 684
Louisiana, 267
Luanda Guidelines (2014), 246
lung cancer, 47
Luxembourg, 271, 460
Lyon, Beth, 587

Madhya Pradesh, 384
Madison, Vernon, 563
Madrid Declaration (2002), 564
Madrigal-Borloz, Victor, 517
Maduro, Nicolas, 39
Magna Carta, 3
magnesium sulphate, 453
malaria, 50, 51, 374, 479
    cases, 51
    prevalence, 376, 377
    vaccine, 51, 378
Malaria, 50
    cause, 377
Malawi, 283, 378
Malaysia, 12, 207, 283, 636
Maldives, 548
Mali, 51, 378, 479
malnutrition, 396, 477, 478
Malta, 263, 570, 583
manslaughter, 262

margin of appreciation, 191
Marikana, 167
Marshall Islands, 352
Martin Luther King Jr, 684
Mason, George, 3
mass graves, 638
maternal mortality, 450
maternal mortality ratio
   high, 453
Mattar, Mohamed, 584
Mauritania, 129, 415, 516
Mauritius, 10, 448
McCann case, 146, 149, 163, 190, 247
McDonald, Laquan, 151, 505
Mead, David, 328
measles, 478
medical assistance
   denial of, 24
medical care, duty of, 113
medical killing (Nazis), 276
medical treatment, 37
Medina, Cecilia, 465
megatons, 337
Mellet, Amanda, 258
Mental Disability Rights International (MDRI), 539
mental health, 38
mental illness, 147
mercenaries, 131
mercy killings, 270
methane, 392
Metropolitan Police Service (MPS), 163, 192, 327
Mexico, 401, 436, 531, 565, 571, 572, 582, 586
Micronesia, 12, 267, 342
migrant worker
   definition, legal, 586
Migrant Workers Convention (1990), 23, 417
Migrant Workers Convention and right to life, 588
migrants
   deaths of, 590
   number of, 586
military court, 92, 217
military occupation, 83, 109, 110, 126, 183
mine clearance, 347
mine victims, duty to assist, 347
minefields, 592
Mines Advisory Group (MAG), 353
minimum necessary force, 148
Minneapolis, 505, 572
Minnesota Protocol on the Investigation of Potentially Unlawful Death (2016), 5, 38, 58, 178, 248, 249, 365, 627
Minorities Treaty (1919), 4
minority rights, 4

missile attack, 81
missiles, 162
missing, duty to search for, 64
Mississippi, 429
Missouri, 230
Mitrovica, 596
Mixed Migration Centre (MMC), 591
Mladic, Ratko, 638
modern slavery, 415, 420
Modern Slavery Act (2015), 426
modern slavery, notion of, 425
modified air-bombs, 339
Moldova, 77, 241, 354, 583
Molina, Julio César Cano, 539
moment of conception, 456
Montana
   Supreme Court, 286
Montero, Etienne, 284, 558
Montgomery, Lisa, 219
Montreux Document, 650
MONUSCO, 644
Mooney, Erin, 597
Moore, Bobby James, 548
Morocco, 110, 129, 434, 662
moron, 275
morphine, 480
Morris, Hollman, 571
Moscow, 569
Moscow theatre siege (2002), 147, 191
mosquito
   control, 51
   genetically modified, 51
most serious crimes, 32, 108, 208, 211, 216. *See also* death penalty
   definition, 216
Mothers of Srebrenica case, 639
Mousa, Baha, 119, 252
Mozambique, 51, 131
Multidimensional Poverty Index (MPI), 293
murder, 10, 19, 20, 57, 88, 97, 212, 262, 448
Murphy, Daniel, 19
Muscat, Joseph, 570
mustard gas, 345, 494
Mutilation (of dead bodies), 63
Myanmar, 12, 207, 348, 449, 495

Nachova case, 34, 145, 166, 238, 240, 496, 500, 716, 717
Nagasaki bombing, 45
Nagorno-Karabakh, 138
Namibia, 342
Napoleonic Wars, 415
narcotics, limiting access to, 459
Nascimbene, Bruno, 53
National Agency for Disaster Management (Indonesia), 388

national liberation movement, 108, 110, 620
National Right to Life Educational Trust Fund, 278, 558
national security, 328
NATO, 637, 642
natural disasters, 270, 374
natural right, 3, 4
Nature (journal), 399
Navalnyy, Alexei, 148
Nazi Germany, 5, 270, 274, 276, 506, 650
Nebraska, 429
necessity, principle of
  in law enforcement, 32, 147
Nelson Mandela Rules, 58, 235, 238, 246, 249
Nencheva case, 543
Nepal, 358, 381, 698
  age of majority, 455
neurodegenerative diseases, 47
neuro-muscular incapacitation, 174
neutrality, law of, 106
Nevada, 210
New Orleans Police Department, 174
new weapons, duty to review, 401
New York City Police Department (NYPD), 165
New Zealand, 396
  Immigration and Protection Tribunal, 397
  referendum on euthanasia, 290
NGOs bound by jus cogens norms, 678
Nicaragua, 125, 177
Nicaragua case, 639
Nicaragua judgment, 124
Niger, 51
Nigeria, 51, 167, 207, 213, 283, 473, 516, 595
Non-Aligned Movement (NAM), 402
non-governmental organisation
  definition, 673
non-governmental organisations
  treaty obligations, 600
non-governmental organisations (NGOs), responsibility for violations of the right to life, 672
non-refoulement, 53, 54
non-refoulement, principle of, 52
non-refoulement, rule of, 443
non-State armed groups, 331, 661
non-State armed groups bound by jus cogens norms, 669
non-State armed groups' responsibility for violations of the right to life, 659
non-viable pregnancy
  definition, 258
North American Space Agency (NASA), 399
North Atlantic Treaty Organization (NATO), 78, 335, 407, 632

North Caucasus, 61
North Korea, 207, 284, 352. *See also* Democratic People's Republic of Korea
  testing of nuclear weapons, 352
North Ossetia, 179
North Sea, 384
Northern Ireland, 155, 268
Norway, 371
Norwegian Refugee Council, 595
Novichok, 345
Nowak, Manfred, 23, 25, 160, 534
NPT (Treaty on the Non-Proliferation of Nuclear Weapons), 351
Ntaganda case, 423, 499
nuclear disarmament, 334
  duty to negotiate, 351
nuclear reactor, 45
Nuclear Tests case, 641
nuclear weapons, 12, 35, 336, 337
  prohibition of, 350
  testing of, 351
Nuhanović case, 639
Nuremberg Military Tribunals, 648
Nuremberg Tribunal, 681
nursing mother
  death penalty, 446
Nys, Hermann, 284

OAU Refugees Convention (1969), 607
obese, 381
object and purpose, 87, 213, 225, 393
object and purpose (of a treaty), 612
obligations *erga omnes*, 361
Obrador, López, 572
Occupying Power, 113, 114, 115, 307
Ogoniland, 49, 390
older person
  and euthanasia, 558
  and the death penalty, 562
  and the right to life, 555
  definition, 112
  protection in armed conflict, 555
  right to special respect and protection, 564
  with disabilities, 525, 532
Oman, 207
omission, 613
Operation Althea, 641
Operation Atalanta, 642
Operation Peace Spring, 513
opinio juris, 16, 433, 667
Opioids, 480
Optional Protocol to the CRC on the involvement of children in armed conflict (2000), 488
Orakhelashvili, Alexander, 53
Oregon, 271

Organisation for the Prohibition of Chemical Weapons (OPCW), 633
organised armed group. *See also* non-State armed group
Organization for Security and Co-operation in Europe (OSCE), 711
Organization of African Unity, 463
Organization of American States (OAS), 439, 520, 633
Organization of Islamic Cooperation, 182
Ormaniçi, 511
Osman case, 88, 178
Osman test, 440, 464
osteoporosis, 376
Ottawa, 347
Ottawa Process, 347
overall control. *See also* Effective control
overpenetration (of bullet), 166
overriding risk, 352
Overseas Development Institute (ODI), 484
Oxford Poverty and Human Development Initiative, 293
oxycodone, 480

Paget-Lewis, Paul, 88
Paine, Thomas, 4
Pakistan, 109, 183, 207, 208, 209, 213, 347, 473, 516, 548, 549, 592
Palestine, 71, 74, 207, 339
Palestine Liberation Organisation, 131
Palestinians, 603
Paraguay, 95, 96, 97, 136, 312, 392, 539
Paraguayan National Police, 97
paramilitary groups, 203, 619
Paris terror attacks (2015), 160
particulate matter. *See also* PM2.5
Passing of the Great Race, 276
Patten, Pramila, 448
peace and security, 352
peaceful assembly
  and terrorism, 181
  definition, 309
peaceful assembly, right of, 86
  in armed conflict, 328
  in national constitutions, 311
  relationship with the right to life, 96
  status of, 310
peaceful purposes, 343
peacetime, 37, 673
penal law, 65
People In Aid, 677
pepper spray, 142
peremptory norm of international law. *See* jus cogens
Permanent Court of International Justice, 613, 616, 617
persecution, 97
persistent objector, status of. *See also* Customary law

person of colour, 52
person with disabilities and law enforcement, 541
personal protective equipment (PPE), 326
persons living in poverty
  targeting of, 291
persons with disabilities, 311, 525
  and international humanitarian law, 550
  and the death penalty, 546
  as forgotten victims of armed conflict, 549
  definition, legal, 526
  in custodial settings, 533
  right to life, 22
  terminology, 528
  world's largest minority, 525
persons with disabilities and disasters, 552
pertussis, 478
Peru, 97, 367, 372, 575
Peru armed forces, 196
Peruvian Congressional Commission, 197
peshmergas, 514
pesticide, 135, 270, 392
pesticide poisoning, 393
Petrov, Vasil Sashov, 508
Philippines, 19, 703
phosgene, 345
physician-assisted suicide, 558
Piccone, Ted, 412
Pictet, Jean, 307, 621
Pillay, Navanethem (Navi), 382, 677
Pimlott, Andrew, 176
Pinker, Steven, 44, 50
Piper Alpha, 384
piracy, 32, 216
pirate, 80
PKK, 513
placenta, 47, 394, 451
plague, 342
plastic bullet, 317
  inaccuracy of, 317
Plato, 274
Plato's Republic, 275
PM 2.5 dust particles, 47, 396
poison, 339
poisoned weapons, 339
  use as war crime, 340
Poland, 4, 209
police, 617
police (actions attributable to the State), 618
police brutality against African Americans, 683
police custody, 235
police powers, 142
police shooting, 52
policing. *See also* Law enforcement
Polisario Front, 111, 130, 662
political independence, 127

political organisation, 360
Politkovskaya, Anna, 569
pollution, 47, 48, 96, 390, 394, 459
   and children, 491
   right to life of children, 394
polyarthritis, 558
Porajmos, 506
Portillo Cáceres, Ruben, 95
Portugal, 271, 415, 696
potentially unlawful death, 56
poverty, 23, 98, 291, 491
   as violation of the right to life, 298
   definition, 292
   in armed conflict, 303
   link with abortion, 265
   prevalence of, 293
precaution, duty of, 165
precaution, principle of (in law enforcement), 143, 145
precautionary measures, 49
precautionary principle
   in law enforcement, 316
precautions in attack
   duty of, 204
   principle of, 118
precursors, 345
Pre-eclampsia, 453
pregnancy, non-viable, 258
pregnant woman, 47
   death penalty, 431
   execution of, 114
premature death, 47, 54, 394
prescriptive jurisdiction, 663
Press Emblem Campaign (PEC), 565
presumption of State responsibility, 245
Pretty v. United Kingdom case, 279
prison officers, 618
prisoner of war, 64, 113, 119, 221, 237
prisoner-of-war camp, 115
privacy, right to, 86
private and family life, right to, 94
private detention centres, 233
private security companies, 235
procedural component (of the right to life), 56, 57, 69
prohibition on inter-State use of force
   use of chemical agent, 345
proliferation, 336
proliferation (of weapons), 56
property, damage to
   as grounds for use of firearms, 316
property, threat to, 157
prophylactic purposes, 343
proportionality in attack, rule of, 331, 412

proportionality, principle of
   in law enforcement, 33
   in the conduct of hostilities, 117
proportionality, principle of (in law enforcement), 152
Prosecutor (ICC), 97
protect by law, 21, 22, 29, 30, 457
ProtectDefenders.eu, 583
protection by law, 30
protests. *See also* Assemblies
Protocol on the Rights of Older Persons in Africa (2016), 555, 560
Protocol on the Rights of Persons with Disabilities in Africa (2018), 527, 534, 535, 551
Protocol on the Rights of Women in Africa (2003), 266, 430, 434, 470, 529
Protocol to the Convention on the Rights of the Child on the involvement of children in armed conflict (2000), 668
protracted (armed violence), 111
psycho-social disabilities
   link with suicide, 270
public health, 26
public powers, 78
Purposes not prohibited, 344
Putin, Vladimir, 569

Q fever, 342
Qatar, 592
Quebec
   Superior Court, 289
Qur'an, 2, 282

R-11 Zemlya, 339
race
   definition, 494
racial animus, 52, 498
racial discrimination, 18
racist régimes, 110
Radio Televizije Srbije, 77
radioactivity, 45
Rakhine state, 449
rape, 256, 435, 448
real and immediate risk, 179, 236, 369, 440, 464
real and immediate risk to life, 88
real and imminent risk, 88
red-dotting (by TASER), 174
refoulement, 397
refoulement, prohibition of, 601
refugee, 53, 55
   and death penalty, 604
   definition, 601
   definition, legal, 601
   protection under international humanitarian law, 605
refugees and the right to life, 601

refugee law, 52, 495, 497, 631
refugee status, 594
Refugees Convention (1951), 53, 497, 602
refugees in occupied territory, 606
regional human rights machinery and the right to life, 712
rehabilitation, 58
religious tenets, 40
remote use of force, 36
reparation, 23, 58, 138, 249, 614, 616
   duty of, 139
Report on Poverty and Human Rights in the Americas (2017), 297
Reporters without Borders, 565
reprisal, belligerent, 35
respect, protect, fulfil typology, 23, 38
respiratory infections, 394
responsibility, notion of, 635
retarded, 528
Revolutionary United Front (RUF), 665
Rhodesia, 131
Richmond Hill case, 75, 82
Richmond Hill Mental Health Facility, 75
ricin, 342, 345
ricochet, 316
rifles, 165
Right of Peaceful Assembly Worldwide website, 311
right of peoples to self-determination, 18
right to an adequate standard of living, 291
right to development (of children), 86
right to die, 287
right to food, 38, 291
   relationship with right to life, 98
right to life, egregious violation of, 392
right to private and family life, 61
right to survival (of children), 86
right to water, 38
   nature of, 98
   relationship with the right to life, 98
private and family life, 263
Rio de Janeiro, 483
riot, 161, 316
riot-control agent, 178, 344. *See also* Tear gas
riots, 111, 196, 314, 330
risk and right to life, 87
Riyadus-Salikhin Reconnaissance and Sabotage Battalion of Chechen Martyrs, 186, 187
road traffic
   accidents, 383
   death, 375
Robair, Raymond, 173
Robben Island Guidelines, 246
rockets, improvised, 339
Rodley, Nigel, 17, 19, 31, 55, 153
Roe v. Wade case, 267

Rohingya, 449, 450, 495
Roma, 493, 506
Roma, right to special protection, 507
Romania, 83, 94, 108, 243
rubber (coated) bullets, 97, 171, 313
   risk of death, 177
Russia, 29, 45, 137, 147, 179, 186, 195, 200, 261, 346, 347, 351, 368, 407, 442, 541, 582
   Suppression of Terrorism Act, 194
Russian Constitutional Court, 62
Russian Orthodox Church, 261
Russian special forces, 191
Rwanda, 266, 493
   High Court, 266, 470

Saavedra, Hugo Bustíos, 575
Sadaam Hussein, 343
Safe El Salvador Plan, 484
Saharan Arab Democratic Republic, 129
Sahrawi Arab Democratic Republic, 129
Saint Kitts and Nevis, 12, 432
Saint Lucia, 12, 211
Saint Petersburg Declaration (1868), 337
Saint Vincent and the Grenadines, 211
Saker, Salah, 358
Salisbury (attack), 345
Sam Hinga Norman case, 649, 661
San Juan Bautista prison, 196
San Marino, 263, 311
San Salvador Protocol (1988), 49
Sancin, Vasilka, 398
sarin, 345, 494
satisfaction, 58, 138
Sauckel, Fritz, 423
Saudi Arabia, 12, 109, 182, 207, 213, 283, 311, 350, 406, 407, 455, 473, 516, 574, 579
Schabas, William, 136, 424
Scharre, Paul, 407
Schmitt, Michael, 331, 408
Scotland
   age of majority, 455
Scud missile, 339
Scully, Jackie Leach, 376
SDG, 491
Second World War, 9, 118, 307, 349, 493, 506, 564, 602, 648, 651, 672
secondary injuries (from weapon use), 176
secondary rules, 614
security forces, 25, 32, 142
security, right to, 4, 86, 93
   relationship with right to life, 93
Sekaanvand, Zeinab, 473
self-defence (ad bellum), 35
   inherent right of, 136
   right of, 131

self-determination, right of peoples to, 108, 128, 129, 183, 199
self-harm, 37
self-harming, 242, 281
semi-automatic (weapon), 166
Sendai Framework for Disaster Risk Reduction 2015–30, 45
Senegal, 474
Serbia, 567
Serbia and Montenegro, 354
serious injury
    definition of, 157
serious violation of human rights law, 52
serious violation of the right to life, 38
sex characteristics, 515
sexual abuse
    in prison, 246
sexual enslavement, 420, 448
sexual offences, 32, 216
sexual orientation, 515
    definition, 515
sexual slavery
    as a war crime, 423
    as a crime against humanity, 424
sexual violence, 97
Seychelles, 387
Shari'a law, 444
Sharia law, 208, 209
Shaw, Malcolm, 16
Shchiborshch, Kirill, 541
Shelton, Dinah, 1
Shining Path, 366
shooting to kill, 156
shooting to stop, 156
shotguns, 154
shrapnel, 332
Sierra Leone, 665
Simons, Stefan, 572
Singapore, 12, 207, 283, 401, 548
skeet, 406
skiff, 642
Skripal, Sergei, 346
slave
    definition, 419
slavery, 2, 68
    and armed conflict, 421
    as a violation of the right to life, 424
    as an international crime, 422
    as genocide, 425
    definition, 418
    prohibition of, 18, 415
Slovakia, 237
smallpox, 342
smoking, 479
snatch squads, 324

Social Darwinism, 274
sodomy, 473
Soering case, 353
soldiers. *See also* Combatant
Soleimani, Qassem, 128
solitary confinement, 31
Solomon Islands, 12
Somalia, 207, 267, 342, 387, 449, 516, 573, 595
soman, 345
Sotomayor, Sonia, 230
South Africa, 167, 246, 387, 516
    Constitutional Court, 209
South African police, 542
South African Police Service (SAPS), 167
South Asia, 50
South Sudan, 12, 207, 213, 342, 344, 348, 449, 473, 595, 694
sovereign territory, 66, 82
    definition, 66
sovereignty, 126
Soviet Union, 335, 343
Spain, 129
Special Court for Sierra Leone, 661, 663
special measures of protection, 457
Special Tribunal for Lebanon, 184
Sphere Project, 677
spiked batons, 341
Srebrenica, 639
stampede, 178
    from tear gas, 325
staphylococcal toxins, 342
starvation, 98, 596
    as method of warfare, 303, 694
    duty to prevent, 294
    prevention of, 291
    to death of a detainee, as violation of right to life, 300
starve to death, 38
State agents, 24, 27, 28, 34, 37, 57, 61, 75, 87, 88, 94, 143, 149, 190, 235, 393, 437, 512, 518, 523, 565, 611
    definition, 617
State in waiting, 130
State practice. *See* Customary law
State responsibility, 53, 496
    notion of, 614
State responsibility and the right to life, 611
Steinhardt, Ralph, 654
Stewart, Brian, 177
Stockholm Convention on Persistent Organic Pollutants (2001), 136, 393
Stockholm Declaration (1972), 49, 134, 394
Stockholm International Peace Research Institute (SIPRI), 352, 401, 404
Stoicism, 2
Stone, Julius, 4
stoning, 31, 229

Street Children case, 298, 466
strict liability, 37
stroke, 47
Sturgess, Dawn, 346
Sub-Commission on Prevention of Discrimination and Protection of Minorities, 538
submachine guns, 154, 165
submunitions, 406
  effects, 349
sub-Saharan Africa, 50, 51, 293, 377, 477, 478
substance abuse, 482. *See also* drug abuse; narcotics
Sudan, 207, 213, 323, 449, 473, 516, 595
suicide, 5, 24, 26, 37, 59, 233, 269
  and religion, 269
  assisted, 270, 271
  criminalisation of, 269
  definition, 270
  duty to prevent, 277
  methods of, 270
  physician-assisted, 271
  prevalence of, 270
suicide bomber, 34, 163
suicide bombings, 489
suicide note, 237
Sultan Hassanal Bolkiah, 519
summary execution, 112
Sunni Muslims, 510
Supreme Iraqi Criminal Tribunal, 494
supreme right, 13, 17
Suriname, 61
surrender, 411
suspicious death, 241
Sustainable Development Goal (SDG), 266, 378, 452, 476
Sweden, 313, 349, 494
Swiss Federal Council, 110, 130, 662
Switzerland, 60, 168, 271, 280
Syria, 180, 207, 315, 342, 348, 352, 449, 489, 513, 595, 603, 624
  use of chlorine as chemical weapon, 345

Tadić case, 111
Taliban, 109
Tamil Nadu, Indian state of, 475
Tang case, 418
tank, 193
Tanzania, 51, 283, 378, 479, 673
TASER, 141, 151, 153, 172, 174
Tbilisi, 523
tear gas, 35, 97, 141, 171, 178, 239, 313, 318, 344
  canister, 25, 98
  indiscriminate use of, 320
  use to disperse an assembly, 325
tear-gas grenades
  kinetic impact, 319

terra nullius, 129
Terre des Hommes, 481
territorial integrity, 126
territorial sea
  definition, 66
terrorist, 160
terrorist attack, duty to prevent, 179
Terrorist Bombings Convention (1997), 181, 182
Terrorist Financing Convention (1999), 183
terrorists, 146
tetanus, 478
Thailand, 207, 396
The Descent of Man, 274
The Gambia, 182, 214, 283, 450, 495
The Lancet, 387
The Netherlands, 24, 60, 69, 168, 208, 271, 278, 415, 558
  Supreme Court, 639
The Philippines, 93
third party acceptance, 661
Thirlway, Hugh, 16
threat of violence, 143
thyroid cancer, 386
Tladi, Dire, 17
tobacco smoke, second-hand, 394, 491
Tomlinson, Ian, 174
Tomuschat, Christian, 18, 20
Tonga, 12
tort (in international law), 612
tort law, 37
torture, 18, 68, 73, 97, 241, 657
  definition, 497
torture, right to freedom from, 85
  relationship with right to life, 86
toxic agrochemicals, 135, 392
toxic chemical, 191
toxic chemicals, 125, 336, 344
  examples, 345
toxic substances, 50
Trans Murder Monitoring (TMM) project, 516
Transdnistria, 354
transfer (of weapons), 342
transgender people, 515
Transnistria, 77, 243
Transrespect versus Transphobia Worldwide Project, 516
Treaty
  definition of, 11
treaty interpretation, 24
Treaty of Saint-Germain-en-Laye (1919), 4
Treaty of Sevres (1920), 510
Treaty on European Union, 651
Treaty on the Functioning of the European Union (TFEU), 651
Treaty on the Prohibition of Nuclear Weapons (2017), 350, 649

Triepel, Heinrich, 612
Trinidad & Tobago, 14
tropical disease, 51
Trump, Donald, 218, 381, 572
Tsang, FanMan, 388
tsunami, 46, 387
tuberculosis, 50, 51, 374, 376
tularaemia, 342
Tunisia, 131, 168, 460, 696
Tupac Amaru Revolutionary Movement (MRTA), 197, 205
Turkey, 77, 78, 168, 169, 191, 200, 202, 317, 348, 368, 369, 370, 510, 569, 623
Turkish Air Force, 120
Turkish Republic of Northern Cyprus (TRNC), 623
Turkmenistan, 236
Tutsis, 493
Tuvalu, 12, 342

Uganda, 51, 173, 283, 469, 519
    Supreme Court, 212, 230
Ugandan People's Defence Force (UPDF), 469
Uighurs, 493
Ukraine, 45, 137, 241, 348, 385, 569, 582
    Minister of the Interior, 570
ultra vires (actions), 618
unborn child (as person), 262
unborn, right to life of, 259
unexploded ordnance, 63, 595
UNICEF, 461, 483, 486, 487
Union Carbide, 384
Union Carbide Corporation (UCC), 384
United Arab Emirates, 12, 109, 207, 350
United Kingdom, 79, 122, 155, 162, 174, 179, 193, 257, 260, 279, 283, 311, 346, 351, 388, 405, 407, 462, 489, 492, 591, 648, 673, 687, 695
    Charity Commission, 677
    House of Lords, 272, 603
    Ministry of Defence, 405
United Nations, 9
    Action Against Sexual Violence in Conflict, 448
    Assistance Mission in Afghanistan (UNAMA), 621, 669
    Assistance Mission in Iraq (UNAMI), 98
    Charter, 85, 110, 124, 128, 493
    Children's Fund, See UNICEF
    Commission of Inquiry into the protests in Gaza, 331
    Commission on Human Rights, 596
    Committee on Non-Governmental Organizations (NGO Committee), 673
    Compensation Commission (UNCC), 139
    Counter-Terrorism Committee Executive Directorate (CTED), 180
    Definition of Aggression (1974), 127
    Development Programme (UNDP), 293
    duty to investigate suspected unlawful death, 645
    duty to respect customary human rights law, 631
    Economic and Social Council (ECOSOC), 546, 673
    Economic Commission for Europe (UNECE), 45
    Educational, Scientific and Cultural Organization (UNESCO), 566
    Food and Agriculture Organization (FAO), 294
    General Assembly, 11, 28, 46, 64
    General Assembly and the right to life, 709
    Global Counter-Terrorism Strategy, 185
    Guidance on Less-Lethal Weapons in Law Enforcement (2020), 169
    Guiding Principles on Extreme Poverty and Human Rights (2012), 291
    Guiding Principles on Humanitarian Action (1991), 676
    High Commissioner for Human Rights, 323, 473, 481, 495
    Human Rights Council, 36, 310
    Human Rights Guidance on Less-Lethal Weapons (2020), 326
    Independent Expert on human rights and the environment, 391
    Independent Expert on protection against violence and discrimination based on sexual orientation and gender identity, 517
    Independent Expert on the enjoyment of human rights by persons with albinism, 536
    Independent Special Commission of Inquiry for Timor-Leste, 619
    Member States, 9
    Mission in Kosovo (UNMIK), 637
    Mission in South Sudan (UNMISS), 621, 666
    Office for the Coordination of Humanitarian Affairs (OCHA), 594
    Office of Legal Affairs (OLA), 631
    Office of the High Commissioner for Human Rights, 33
    Office of the High Commissioner for Human Rights (OHCHR), 98, 142, 357, 516, 698
    Office of the High Commissioner for Refugees (UNHCR), 52, 53, 591
    Office of the Special Representative of the Secretary-General on Sexual Violence in Conflict, 448
    Office on Drugs and Crime (UNODC), 142, 480
    Organization Mission in the Democratic Republic of the Congo (MONUC), 630
    peacekeeping mission, 381
    Plan of Action on the Safety of Journalists and the Issue of Impunity, 566
    responsibility for its peacekeeping forces, 638
    Secretary-General, 207, 209, 215, 218, 566, 595

United Nations (cont.)
  Secretary-General's Mechanism (SGM), 710
  Security Council, 64, 108, 131, 132, 138, 186, 488, 565, 669
  Security Council and the right to life, 708
  Security Council Counter-Terrorism Committee, 185
  Security Council Resolution 1540 (2004), 336, 343
  Special Rapporteur on extrajudicial, summary or arbitrary executions, 33, 36, 58, 144, 146, 159, 163, 188, 189, 215, 252, 413, 516, 567, 666, 691
  Special Rapporteur on extreme poverty and human rights, 291, 293, 381
  Special Rapporteur on freedom of assembly, 308
  Special Rapporteur on human rights and the environment, 47
  Special Rapporteur on the human rights of internally displaced persons, 552
  Special Rapporteur on the human rights of migrants, 591, 592
  Special Rapporteur on the independence of judges and lawyers, 437
  Special Rapporteur on the issue of human rights obligations relating to the enjoyment of a safe, clean, healthy and sustainable environment, 391
  Special Rapporteur on the right to food, 294
  Special Rapporteur on the Rights of Indigenous Peoples, 703
  Special Rapporteur on the rights of persons with disabilities, 532
  Special Rapporteur on the situation of human rights defenders, 577, 578
  Special Rapporteur on torture and other cruel, inhuman or degrading treatment or punishment, 534
  Special Rapporteur on violence against women, 434
  Special Rapporteur on violence against women, its causes and consequences, 619
  Special Representative of the Secretary-General on Migration, 586
  Study on Violence against Children, 475
  Sustainable Development Goal 3, 51
  Sustainable Development Goals, 45, 283, 293
United Nations human rights machinery and the right to life, 691
United Nations Special Procedures and the right to life, 704
United States, 44, 52, 54, 60, 71, 72, 73, 104, 122, 125, 128, 136, 167, 175, 176, 185, 207, 213, 218, 219, 230, 234, 239, 244, 254, 267, 271, 274, 335, 347, 349, 350, 351, 376, 399, 415, 439, 467, 472, 473, 479, 484, 489, 547, 548, 618, 655, 686, 695
  Bureau of Safety and Environmental Enforcement, 385
  Constitution (Eighth Amendment), 210
  Department of Defense, 336, 400, 404, 409, 413
  Department of Justice, 148, 151, 417, 505, 653
  House of Representatives' Natural Resources Committee, 678
  National Consensus Policy on Use of Force, 168
  Restatement of the Law, Third, Foreign Relations Law, 361
  Supreme Court, 149, 154, 155, 209, 210, 213, 230, 272, 274, 472, 547, 548, 563, 652, 656, 657
United States law enforcement agencies
  number of, 618
Universal Declaration of Human Rights (1948), 9, 10, 11, 21, 85, 93, 255, 417, 602, 666
unnecessary suffering, 36
  prohibition of, 116, 134
  and weapons, 337
unsafe abortions, 431
Upper Silesia, 4
Uribe, Álvaro, 571
Urresti, Daniel, 575
Uruguay, 415, 494, 516
use of force
  against person escaping from custody, 238
  in law enforcement, 32
  justification for, 33
use of force in law enforcement
  definition of, 142
usus. See Customary law; State practice
uterus, 465
Uzbekistan, 696, 697

vaccination, 477
Valencia-Ospina, Eduardo, 46
van Boven, Theo, 13
Van Dyke, Jason, 505
Varnava case, 203, 369, 372, 623
vascular dementia, 563
Velásquez Rodríguez case, 618
Venezuela, 14, 19, 39, 97, 321, 402, 420, 694
Vienna Convention on Consular Relations (1963), 218
Vienna Convention on the Law of Treaties (1969), 11, 17, 24, 124, 208, 258, 342, 369, 612
Vienna Convention on the Law of Treaties between States and International Organizations (1986), 629
Vietnam, 207, 231, 349
Vietnam War, 349
Villagran Morales case, 482
violation of the right to life of survivors, 26, 27, 86
violence, 10
violence (by private individuals), 94
violence against children, 480
violence against women, 432
  definition, legal, 436, 443

violence in educational establishments, 487
violent extremism, 180
Virginia Declaration of Rights (1776), 3
Virginia Eugenical Sterilization Act, 274
Virginia State Colony of Epileptics and Feeble Minded, 275
Vocational Rehabilitation and Employment (Disabled Persons) Convention (1983), 527
Voltaire, 3
VX gas, 345

Wakene, Dagnachew, 311
war
    definition of, 108
war crime, 10, 37, 39, 56, 113, 118, 165, 221, 223, 251, 303, 305, 340, 345, 352, 422, 448, 500, 597, 626, 657, 681, 683
warning shots, 145, 155, 239
    legality of, 167
Washington, Earl, 220
water cannon, 97, 171, 313, 318
water, right to, 86, 294
weapon, 34
weapon of mass destruction, 336
weapons, destruction of, 56, 334, 335
weapons
    transfer of, 56
    use of, international legal regulation, 335
West Bank, 74
Western Sahara, 110, 129, 130, 662
Whish, Richard, 652
WMD
    definition, 336
Wollstonecraft, Mary, 4
women
    and poverty, 296
    definition, legal, 429, 430
    in armed forces, 447
    rights of, 4
    with disabilities, 537
World Bank, 293, 387, 461, 525
World Cup, 592
World Health Organization (WHO), 47, 270, 305, 376, 383, 453, 485, 525, 547, 586
World Medical Association (WMA), 271
World Migration Report 2020, 586
World Report on Violence and Health, 485
World Wildlife Fund (WWF), 677
Wuhan, 379

Yarus, Michael, 382
Yaşa, Haşim, 512
Yazidi, 425
Yellow Vest movement, 184
Yemen, 207, 213, 311, 348, 350, 406, 473, 516, 595, 624, 693, 694
Yildirim, Fatma, 434
Ypres, 345

Zambia, 86, 283
Zimbabwe, 162
zoonotic, 379
zygote, 456
Zyklon B, 650